Lecture Notes in Computer Science 11211

Commenced Publication in 1973
Founding and Former Series Editors:
Gerhard Goos, Juris Hartmanis, and Jan van Leeuwen

More information about this series at http://www.springer.com/series/7412

Vittorio Ferrari · Martial Hebert
Cristian Sminchisescu · Yair Weiss (Eds.)

Computer Vision – ECCV 2018

15th European Conference
Munich, Germany, September 8–14, 2018
Proceedings, Part VII

Editors
Vittorio Ferrari
Google Research
Zurich
Switzerland

Martial Hebert
Carnegie Mellon University
Pittsburgh, PA
USA

Cristian Sminchisescu
Google Research
Zurich
Switzerland

Yair Weiss
Hebrew University of Jerusalem
Jerusalem
Israel

ISSN 0302-9743 ISSN 1611-3349 (electronic)
Lecture Notes in Computer Science
ISBN 978-3-030-01233-5 ISBN 978-3-030-01234-2 (eBook)
https://doi.org/10.1007/978-3-030-01234-2

Library of Congress Control Number: 2018955489

LNCS Sublibrary: SL6 – Image Processing, Computer Vision, Pattern Recognition, and Graphics

This Springer imprint is published by the registered company Springer Nature Switzerland AG
The registered company address is: Gewerbestrasse 11, 6330 Cham, Switzerland

Foreword

It was our great pleasure to host the European Conference on Computer Vision 2018 in Munich, Germany. This constituted by far the largest ECCV event ever. With close to 2,900 registered participants and another 600 on the waiting list one month before the conference, participation more than doubled since the last ECCV in Amsterdam. We believe that this is due to a dramatic growth of the computer vision community combined with the popularity of Munich as a major European hub of culture, science, and industry. The conference took place in the heart of Munich in the concert hall Gasteig with workshops and tutorials held at the downtown campus of the Technical University of Munich.

One of the major innovations for ECCV 2018 was the free perpetual availability of all conference and workshop papers, which is often referred to as open access. We note that this is not precisely the same use of the term as in the Budapest declaration. Since 2013, CVPR and ICCV have had their papers hosted by the Computer Vision Foundation (CVF), in parallel with the IEEE Xplore version. This has proved highly beneficial to the computer vision community.

We are delighted to announce that for ECCV 2018 a very similar arrangement was put in place with the cooperation of Springer. In particular, the author's final version will be freely available in perpetuity on a CVF page, while SpringerLink will continue to host a version with further improvements, such as activating reference links and including video. We believe that this will give readers the best of both worlds; researchers who are focused on the technical content will have a freely available version in an easily accessible place, while subscribers to SpringerLink will continue to have the additional benefits that this provides. We thank Alfred Hofmann from Springer for helping to negotiate this agreement, which we expect will continue for future versions of ECCV.

September 2018

Horst Bischof
Daniel Cremers
Bernt Schiele
Ramin Zabih

Preface

Welcome to the proceedings of the 2018 European Conference on Computer Vision (ECCV 2018) held in Munich, Germany. We are delighted to present this volume reflecting a strong and exciting program, the result of an extensive review process. In total, we received 2,439 valid paper submissions. Of these, 776 were accepted (31.8%): 717 as posters (29.4%) and 59 as oral presentations (2.4%). All oral presentations were presented as posters as well. The program selection process was complicated this year by the large increase in the number of submitted papers, +65% over ECCV 2016, and the use of CMT3 for the first time for a computer vision conference. The program selection process was supported by four program co-chairs (PCs), 126 area chairs (ACs), and 1,199 reviewers with reviews assigned.

We were primarily responsible for the design and execution of the review process. Beyond administrative rejections, we were involved in acceptance decisions only in the very few cases where the ACs were not able to agree on a decision. As PCs, and as is customary in the field, we were not allowed to co-author a submission. General co-chairs and other co-organizers who played no role in the review process were permitted to submit papers, and were treated as any other author is.

Acceptance decisions were made by two independent ACs. The ACs also made a joint recommendation for promoting papers to oral status. We decided on the final selection of oral presentations based on the ACs' recommendations. There were 126 ACs, selected according to their technical expertise, experience, and geographical diversity (63 from European, nine from Asian/Australian, and 54 from North American institutions). Indeed, 126 ACs is a substantial increase in the number of ACs due to the natural increase in the number of papers and to our desire to maintain the number of papers assigned to each AC to a manageable number so as to ensure quality. The ACs were aided by the 1,199 reviewers to whom papers were assigned for reviewing. The Program Committee was selected from committees of previous ECCV, ICCV, and CVPR conferences and was extended on the basis of suggestions from the ACs. Having a large pool of Program Committee members for reviewing allowed us to match expertise while reducing reviewer loads. No more than eight papers were assigned to a reviewer, maintaining the reviewers' load at the same level as ECCV 2016 despite the increase in the number of submitted papers.

Conflicts of interest between ACs, Program Committee members, and papers were identified based on the home institutions, and on previous collaborations of all researchers involved. To find institutional conflicts, all authors, Program Committee members, and ACs were asked to list the Internet domains of their current institutions. We assigned on average approximately 18 papers to each AC. The papers were assigned using the affinity scores from the Toronto Paper Matching System (TPMS) and additional data from the OpenReview system, managed by a UMass group. OpenReview used additional information from ACs' and authors' records to identify collaborations and to generate matches. OpenReview was invaluable in refining conflict definitions and in generating quality matches. The only glitch is that, once the matches were generated, a small percentage of papers were unassigned because of discrepancies between the OpenReview conflicts and the conflicts entered in CMT3. We manually assigned these papers. This glitch is revealing of the challenge of using multiple systems at once (CMT3 and OpenReview in this case), which needs to be addressed in future.

After assignment of papers to ACs, the ACs suggested seven reviewers per paper from the Program Committee pool. The selection and rank ordering were facilitated by the TPMS affinity scores visible to the ACs for each paper/reviewer pair. The final assignment of papers to reviewers was generated again through OpenReview in order to account for refined conflict definitions. This required new features in the OpenReview matching system to accommodate the ECCV workflow, in particular to incorporate selection ranking, and maximum reviewer load. Very few papers received fewer than three reviewers after matching and were handled through manual assignment. Reviewers were then asked to comment on the merit of each paper and to make an initial recommendation ranging from definitely reject to definitely accept, including a borderline rating. The reviewers were also asked to suggest explicit questions they wanted to see answered in the authors' rebuttal. The initial review period was five weeks. Because of the delay in getting all the reviews in, we had to delay the final release of the reviews by four days. However, because of the slack included at the tail end of the schedule, we were able to maintain the decision target date with sufficient time for all the phases. We reassigned over 100 reviews from 40 reviewers during the review period. Unfortunately, the main reason for these reassignments was reviewers declining to review, after having accepted to do so. Other reasons included technical relevance and occasional unidentified conflicts. We express our thanks to the emergency reviewers who generously accepted to perform these reviews under short notice. In addition, a substantial number of manual corrections had to do with reviewers using a different email address than the one that was used at the time of the reviewer invitation. This is revealing of a broader issue with identifying users by email addresses that change frequently enough to cause significant problems during the timespan of the conference process.

The authors were then given the opportunity to rebut the reviews, to identify factual errors, and to address the specific questions raised by the reviewers over a seven-day rebuttal period. The exact format of the rebuttal was the object of considerable debate among the organizers, as well as with prior organizers. At issue is to balance giving the author the opportunity to respond completely and precisely to the reviewers, e.g., by including graphs of experiments, while avoiding requests for completely new material or experimental results not included in the original paper. In the end, we decided on the two-page PDF document in conference format. Following this rebuttal period, reviewers and ACs discussed papers at length, after which reviewers finalized their evaluation and gave a final recommendation to the ACs. A significant percentage of the reviewers did enter their final recommendation if it did not differ from their initial recommendation. Given the tight schedule, we did not wait until all were entered.

After this discussion period, each paper was assigned to a second AC. The AC/paper matching was again run through OpenReview. Again, the OpenReview team worked quickly to implement the features specific to this process, in this case accounting for the existing AC assignment, as well as minimizing the fragmentation across ACs, so that each AC had on average only 5.5 buddy ACs to communicate with. The largest number was 11. Given the complexity of the conflicts, this was a very efficient set of assignments from OpenReview. Each paper was then evaluated by its assigned pair of ACs. For each paper, we required each of the two ACs assigned to certify both the final recommendation and the metareview (aka consolidation report). In all cases, after extensive discussions, the two ACs arrived at a common acceptance decision. We maintained these decisions, with the caveat that we did evaluate, sometimes going back to the ACs, a few papers for which the final acceptance decision substantially deviated from the consensus from the reviewers, amending three decisions in the process.

We want to thank everyone involved in making ECCV 2018 possible. The success of ECCV 2018 depended on the quality of papers submitted by the authors, and on the very hard work of the ACs and the Program Committee members. We are particularly grateful to the OpenReview team (Melisa Bok, Ari Kobren, Andrew McCallum, Michael Spector) for their support, in particular their willingness to implement new features, often on a tight schedule, to Laurent Charlin for the use of the Toronto Paper Matching System, to the CMT3 team, in particular in dealing with all the issues that arise when using a new system, to Friedrich Fraundorfer and Quirin Lohr for maintaining the online version of the program, and to the CMU staff (Keyla Cook, Lynnetta Miller, Ashley Song, Nora Kazour) for assisting with data entry/editing in CMT3. Finally, the preparation of these proceedings would not have been possible without the diligent effort of the publication chairs, Albert Ali Salah and Hamdi Dibeklioğlu, and of Anna Kramer and Alfred Hofmann from Springer.

September 2018

Vittorio Ferrari
Martial Hebert
Cristian Sminchisescu
Yair Weiss

Organization

General Chairs

Horst Bischof	Graz University of Technology, Austria
Daniel Cremers	Technical University of Munich, Germany
Bernt Schiele	Saarland University, Max Planck Institute for Informatics, Germany
Ramin Zabih	CornellNYCTech, USA

Program Committee Co-chairs

Vittorio Ferrari	University of Edinburgh, UK
Martial Hebert	Carnegie Mellon University, USA
Cristian Sminchisescu	Lund University, Sweden
Yair Weiss	Hebrew University, Israel

Local Arrangements Chairs

Björn Menze	Technical University of Munich, Germany
Matthias Niessner	Technical University of Munich, Germany

Workshop Chairs

Stefan Roth	TU Darmstadt, Germany
Laura Leal-Taixé	Technical University of Munich, Germany

Tutorial Chairs

Michael Bronstein	Università della Svizzera Italiana, Switzerland
Laura Leal-Taixé	Technical University of Munich, Germany

Website Chair

Friedrich Fraundorfer	Graz University of Technology, Austria

Demo Chairs

Federico Tombari	Technical University of Munich, Germany
Joerg Stueckler	Technical University of Munich, Germany

Publicity Chair

Giovanni Maria Farinella	University of Catania, Italy

Industrial Liaison Chairs

Florent Perronnin	Naver Labs, France
Yunchao Gong	Snap, USA
Helmut Grabner	Logitech, Switzerland

Finance Chair

Gerard Medioni	Amazon, University of Southern California, USA

Publication Chairs

Albert Ali Salah	Boğaziçi University, Turkey
Hamdi Dibeklioğlu	Bilkent University, Turkey

Area Chairs

Kalle Åström	Lund University, Sweden
Zeynep Akata	University of Amsterdam, The Netherlands
Joao Barreto	University of Coimbra, Portugal
Ronen Basri	Weizmann Institute of Science, Israel
Dhruv Batra	Georgia Tech and Facebook AI Research, USA
Serge Belongie	Cornell University, USA
Rodrigo Benenson	Google, Switzerland
Hakan Bilen	University of Edinburgh, UK
Matthew Blaschko	KU Leuven, Belgium
Edmond Boyer	Inria, France
Gabriel Brostow	University College London, UK
Thomas Brox	University of Freiburg, Germany
Marcus Brubaker	York University, Canada
Barbara Caputo	Politecnico di Torino and the Italian Institute of Technology, Italy
Tim Cootes	University of Manchester, UK
Trevor Darrell	University of California, Berkeley, USA
Larry Davis	University of Maryland at College Park, USA
Andrew Davison	Imperial College London, UK
Fernando de la Torre	Carnegie Mellon University, USA
Irfan Essa	GeorgiaTech, USA
Ali Farhadi	University of Washington, USA
Paolo Favaro	University of Bern, Switzerland
Michael Felsberg	Linköping University, Sweden

Sanja Fidler	University of Toronto, Canada
Andrew Fitzgibbon	Microsoft, Cambridge, UK
David Forsyth	University of Illinois at Urbana-Champaign, USA
Charless Fowlkes	University of California, Irvine, USA
Bill Freeman	MIT, USA
Mario Fritz	MPII, Germany
Jürgen Gall	University of Bonn, Germany
Dariu Gavrila	TU Delft, The Netherlands
Andreas Geiger	MPI-IS and University of Tübingen, Germany
Theo Gevers	University of Amsterdam, The Netherlands
Ross Girshick	Facebook AI Research, USA
Kristen Grauman	Facebook AI Research and UT Austin, USA
Abhinav Gupta	Carnegie Mellon University, USA
Kaiming He	Facebook AI Research, USA
Martial Hebert	Carnegie Mellon University, USA
Anders Heyden	Lund University, Sweden
Timothy Hospedales	University of Edinburgh, UK
Michal Irani	Weizmann Institute of Science, Israel
Phillip Isola	University of California, Berkeley, USA
Hervé Jégou	Facebook AI Research, France
David Jacobs	University of Maryland, College Park, USA
Allan Jepson	University of Toronto, Canada
Jiaya Jia	Chinese University of Hong Kong, SAR China
Fredrik Kahl	Chalmers University, USA
Hedvig Kjellström	KTH Royal Institute of Technology, Sweden
Iasonas Kokkinos	University College London and Facebook, UK
Vladlen Koltun	Intel Labs, USA
Philipp Krähenbühl	UT Austin, USA
M. Pawan Kumar	University of Oxford, UK
Kyros Kutulakos	University of Toronto, Canada
In Kweon	KAIST, South Korea
Ivan Laptev	Inria, France
Svetlana Lazebnik	University of Illinois at Urbana-Champaign, USA
Laura Leal-Taixé	Technical University of Munich, Germany
Erik Learned-Miller	University of Massachusetts, Amherst, USA
Kyoung Mu Lee	Seoul National University, South Korea
Bastian Leibe	RWTH Aachen University, Germany
Aleš Leonardis	University of Birmingham, UK
Vincent Lepetit	University of Bordeaux, France and Graz University of Technology, Austria
Fuxin Li	Oregon State University, USA
Dahua Lin	Chinese University of Hong Kong, SAR China
Jim Little	University of British Columbia, Canada
Ce Liu	Google, USA
Chen Change Loy	Nanyang Technological University, Singapore
Jiri Matas	Czech Technical University in Prague, Czechia

Yasuyuki Matsushita	Osaka University, Japan
Dimitris Metaxas	Rutgers University, USA
Greg Mori	Simon Fraser University, Canada
Vittorio Murino	Istituto Italiano di Tecnologia, Italy
Richard Newcombe	Oculus Research, USA
Minh Hoai Nguyen	Stony Brook University, USA
Sebastian Nowozin	Microsoft Research Cambridge, UK
Aude Oliva	MIT, USA
Bjorn Ommer	Heidelberg University, Germany
Tomas Pajdla	Czech Technical University in Prague, Czechia
Maja Pantic	Imperial College London and Samsung AI Research Centre Cambridge, UK
Caroline Pantofaru	Google, USA
Devi Parikh	Georgia Tech and Facebook AI Research, USA
Sylvain Paris	Adobe Research, USA
Vladimir Pavlovic	Rutgers University, USA
Marcello Pelillo	University of Venice, Italy
Patrick Pérez	Valeo, France
Robert Pless	George Washington University, USA
Thomas Pock	Graz University of Technology, Austria
Jean Ponce	Inria, France
Gerard Pons-Moll	MPII, Saarland Informatics Campus, Germany
Long Quan	Hong Kong University of Science and Technology, SAR China
Stefan Roth	TU Darmstadt, Germany
Carsten Rother	University of Heidelberg, Germany
Bryan Russell	Adobe Research, USA
Kate Saenko	Boston University, USA
Mathieu Salzmann	EPFL, Switzerland
Dimitris Samaras	Stony Brook University, USA
Yoichi Sato	University of Tokyo, Japan
Silvio Savarese	Stanford University, USA
Konrad Schindler	ETH Zurich, Switzerland
Cordelia Schmid	Inria, France and Google, France
Nicu Sebe	University of Trento, Italy
Fei Sha	University of Southern California, USA
Greg Shakhnarovich	TTI Chicago, USA
Jianbo Shi	University of Pennsylvania, USA
Abhinav Shrivastava	UMD and Google, USA
Yan Shuicheng	National University of Singapore, Singapore
Leonid Sigal	University of British Columbia, Canada
Josef Sivic	Czech Technical University in Prague, Czechia
Arnold Smeulders	University of Amsterdam, The Netherlands
Deqing Sun	NVIDIA, USA
Antonio Torralba	MIT, USA
Zhuowen Tu	University of California, San Diego, USA

Tinne Tuytelaars	KU Leuven, Belgium
Jasper Uijlings	Google, Switzerland
Joost van de Weijer	Computer Vision Center, Spain
Nuno Vasconcelos	University of California, San Diego, USA
Andrea Vedaldi	University of Oxford, UK
Olga Veksler	University of Western Ontario, Canada
Jakob Verbeek	Inria, France
Rene Vidal	Johns Hopkins University, USA
Daphna Weinshall	Hebrew University, Israel
Chris Williams	University of Edinburgh, UK
Lior Wolf	Tel Aviv University, Israel
Ming-Hsuan Yang	University of California at Merced, USA
Todd Zickler	Harvard University, USA
Andrew Zisserman	University of Oxford, UK

Technical Program Committee

Hassan Abu Alhaija
Radhakrishna Achanta
Hanno Ackermann
Ehsan Adeli
Lourdes Agapito
Aishwarya Agrawal
Antonio Agudo
Eirikur Agustsson
Karim Ahmed
Byeongjoo Ahn
Unaiza Ahsan
Emre Akbaş
Eren Aksoy
Yağız Aksoy
Alexandre Alahi
Jean-Baptiste Alayrac
Samuel Albanie
Cenek Albl
Saad Ali
Rahaf Aljundi
Jose M. Alvarez
Humam Alwassel
Toshiyuki Amano
Mitsuru Ambai
Mohamed Amer
Senjian An
Cosmin Ancuti
Peter Anderson
Juan Andrade-Cetto
Mykhaylo Andriluka
Anelia Angelova
Michel Antunes
Pablo Arbelaez
Vasileios Argyriou
Chetan Arora
Federica Arrigoni
Vassilis Athitsos
Mathieu Aubry
Shai Avidan
Yannis Avrithis
Samaneh Azadi
Hossein Azizpour
Artem Babenko
Timur Bagautdinov
Andrew Bagdanov
Hessam Bagherinezhad
Yuval Bahat
Min Bai
Qinxun Bai
Song Bai
Xiang Bai
Peter Bajcsy
Amr Bakry
Kavita Bala
Arunava Banerjee
Atsuhiko Banno
Aayush Bansal
Yingze Bao
Md Jawadul Bappy
Pierre Baqué
Dániel Baráth
Adrian Barbu
Kobus Barnard
Nick Barnes
Francisco Barranco
Adrien Bartoli
E. Bayro-Corrochano
Paul Beardlsey
Vasileios Belagiannis
Sean Bell
Ismail Ben
Boulbaba Ben Amor
Gil Ben-Artzi
Ohad Ben-Shahar
Abhijit Bendale
Rodrigo Benenson
Fabian Benitez-Quiroz
Fethallah Benmansour
Ryad Benosman
Filippo Bergamasco
David Bermudez

Jesus Bermudez-Cameo
Leonard Berrada
Gedas Bertasius
Ross Beveridge
Lucas Beyer
Bir Bhanu
S. Bhattacharya
Binod Bhattarai
Arnav Bhavsar
Simone Bianco
Adel Bibi
Pia Bideau
Josef Bigun
Arijit Biswas
Soma Biswas
Marten Bjoerkman
Volker Blanz
Vishnu Boddeti
Piotr Bojanowski
Terrance Boult
Yuri Boykov
Hakan Boyraz
Eric Brachmann
Samarth Brahmbhatt
Mathieu Bredif
Francois Bremond
Michael Brown
Luc Brun
Shyamal Buch
Pradeep Buddharaju
Aurelie Bugeau
Rudy Bunel
Xavier Burgos Artizzu
Darius Burschka
Andrei Bursuc
Zoya Bylinskii
Fabian Caba
Daniel Cabrini Hauagge
Cesar Cadena Lerma
Holger Caesar
Jianfei Cai
Junjie Cai
Zhaowei Cai
Simone Calderara
Neill Campbell
Octavia Camps
Xun Cao
Yanshuai Cao
Joao Carreira
Dan Casas
Daniel Castro
Jan Cech
M. Emre Celebi
Duygu Ceylan
Menglei Chai
Ayan Chakrabarti
Rudrasis Chakraborty
Shayok Chakraborty
Tat-Jen Cham
Antonin Chambolle
Antoni Chan
Sharat Chandran
Hyun Sung Chang
Ju Yong Chang
Xiaojun Chang
Soravit Changpinyo
Wei-Lun Chao
Yu-Wei Chao
Visesh Chari
Rizwan Chaudhry
Siddhartha Chaudhuri
Rama Chellappa
Chao Chen
Chen Chen
Cheng Chen
Chu-Song Chen
Guang Chen
Hsin-I Chen
Hwann-Tzong Chen
Kai Chen
Kan Chen
Kevin Chen
Liang-Chieh Chen
Lin Chen
Qifeng Chen
Ting Chen
Wei Chen
Xi Chen
Xilin Chen
Xinlei Chen
Yingcong Chen
Yixin Chen
Erkang Cheng
Jingchun Cheng
Ming-Ming Cheng
Wen-Huang Cheng
Yuan Cheng
Anoop Cherian
Liang-Tien Chia
Naoki Chiba
Shao-Yi Chien
Han-Pang Chiu
Wei-Chen Chiu
Nam Ik Cho
Sunghyun Cho
TaeEun Choe
Jongmoo Choi
Christopher Choy
Wen-Sheng Chu
Yung-Yu Chuang
Ondrej Chum
Joon Son Chung
Gökberk Cinbis
James Clark
Andrea Cohen
Forrester Cole
Toby Collins
John Collomosse
Camille Couprie
David Crandall
Marco Cristani
Canton Cristian
James Crowley
Yin Cui
Zhaopeng Cui
Bo Dai
Jifeng Dai
Qieyun Dai
Shengyang Dai
Yuchao Dai
Carlo Dal Mutto
Dima Damen
Zachary Daniels
Kostas Daniilidis
Donald Dansereau
Mohamed Daoudi
Abhishek Das
Samyak Datta

Achal Dave
Shalini De Mello
Teofilo deCampos
Joseph DeGol
Koichiro Deguchi
Alessio Del Bue
Stefanie Demirci
Jia Deng
Zhiwei Deng
Joachim Denzler
Konstantinos Derpanis
Aditya Deshpande
Alban Desmaison
Frédéric Devernay
Abhinav Dhall
Michel Dhome
Hamdi Dibeklioğlu
Mert Dikmen
Cosimo Distante
Ajay Divakaran
Mandar Dixit
Carl Doersch
Piotr Dollar
Bo Dong
Chao Dong
Huang Dong
Jian Dong
Jiangxin Dong
Weisheng Dong
Simon Donné
Gianfranco Doretto
Alexey Dosovitskiy
Matthijs Douze
Bruce Draper
Bertram Drost
Liang Du
Shichuan Du
Gregory Dudek
Zoran Duric
Pınar Duygulu
Hazım Ekenel
Tarek El-Gaaly
Ehsan Elhamifar
Mohamed Elhoseiny
Sabu Emmanuel
Ian Endres
Aykut Erdem
Erkut Erdem
Hugo Jair Escalante
Sergio Escalera
Victor Escorcia
Francisco Estrada
Davide Eynard
Bin Fan
Jialue Fan
Quanfu Fan
Chen Fang
Tian Fang
Yi Fang
Hany Farid
Giovanni Farinella
Ryan Farrell
Alireza Fathi
Christoph Feichtenhofer
Wenxin Feng
Martin Fergie
Cornelia Fermuller
Basura Fernando
Michael Firman
Bob Fisher
John Fisher
Mathew Fisher
Boris Flach
Matt Flagg
Francois Fleuret
David Fofi
Ruth Fong
Gian Luca Foresti
Per-Erik Forssén
David Fouhey
Katerina Fragkiadaki
Victor Fragoso
Jan-Michael Frahm
Jean-Sebastien Franco
Ohad Fried
Simone Frintrop
Huazhu Fu
Yun Fu
Olac Fuentes
Christopher Funk
Thomas Funkhouser
Brian Funt
Ryo Furukawa
Yasutaka Furukawa
Andrea Fusiello
Fatma Güney
Raghudeep Gadde
Silvano Galliani
Orazio Gallo
Chuang Gan
Bin-Bin Gao
Jin Gao
Junbin Gao
Ruohan Gao
Shenghua Gao
Animesh Garg
Ravi Garg
Erik Gartner
Simone Gasparin
Jochen Gast
Leon A. Gatys
Stratis Gavves
Liuhao Ge
Timnit Gebru
James Gee
Peter Gehler
Xin Geng
Guido Gerig
David Geronimo
Bernard Ghanem
Michael Gharbi
Golnaz Ghiasi
Spyros Gidaris
Andrew Gilbert
Rohit Girdhar
Ioannis Gkioulekas
Georgia Gkioxari
Guy Godin
Roland Goecke
Michael Goesele
Nuno Goncalves
Boqing Gong
Minglun Gong
Yunchao Gong
Abel Gonzalez-Garcia
Daniel Gordon
Paulo Gotardo
Stephen Gould

Venu Govindu
Helmut Grabner
Petr Gronat
Steve Gu
Josechu Guerrero
Anupam Guha
Jean-Yves Guillemaut
Alp Güler
Erhan Gündoğdu
Guodong Guo
Xinqing Guo
Ankush Gupta
Mohit Gupta
Saurabh Gupta
Tanmay Gupta
Abner Guzman Rivera
Timo Hackel
Sunil Hadap
Christian Haene
Ralf Haeusler
Levente Hajder
David Hall
Peter Hall
Stefan Haller
Ghassan Hamarneh
Fred Hamprecht
Onur Hamsici
Bohyung Han
Junwei Han
Xufeng Han
Yahong Han
Ankur Handa
Albert Haque
Tatsuya Harada
Mehrtash Harandi
Bharath Hariharan
Mahmudul Hasan
Tal Hassner
Kenji Hata
Soren Hauberg
Michal Havlena
Zeeshan Hayder
Junfeng He
Lei He
Varsha Hedau
Felix Heide
Wolfgang Heidrich
Janne Heikkila
Jared Heinly
Mattias Heinrich
Lisa Anne Hendricks
Dan Hendrycks
Stephane Herbin
Alexander Hermans
Luis Herranz
Aaron Hertzmann
Adrian Hilton
Michael Hirsch
Steven Hoi
Seunghoon Hong
Wei Hong
Anthony Hoogs
Radu Horaud
Yedid Hoshen
Omid Hosseini Jafari
Kuang-Jui Hsu
Winston Hsu
Yinlin Hu
Zhe Hu
Gang Hua
Chen Huang
De-An Huang
Dong Huang
Gary Huang
Heng Huang
Jia-Bin Huang
Qixing Huang
Rui Huang
Sheng Huang
Weilin Huang
Xiaolei Huang
Xinyu Huang
Zhiwu Huang
Tak-Wai Hui
Wei-Chih Hung
Junhwa Hur
Mohamed Hussein
Wonjun Hwang
Anders Hyden
Satoshi Ikehata
Nazlı Ikizler-Cinbis
Viorela Ila
Evren Imre
Eldar Insafutdinov
Go Irie
Hossam Isack
Ahmet Işcen
Daisuke Iwai
Hamid Izadinia
Nathan Jacobs
Suyog Jain
Varun Jampani
C. V. Jawahar
Dinesh Jayaraman
Sadeep Jayasumana
Laszlo Jeni
Hueihan Jhuang
Dinghuang Ji
Hui Ji
Qiang Ji
Fan Jia
Kui Jia
Xu Jia
Huaizu Jiang
Jiayan Jiang
Nianjuan Jiang
Tingting Jiang
Xiaoyi Jiang
Yu-Gang Jiang
Long Jin
Suo Jinli
Justin Johnson
Nebojsa Jojic
Michael Jones
Hanbyul Joo
Jungseock Joo
Ajjen Joshi
Amin Jourabloo
Frederic Jurie
Achuta Kadambi
Samuel Kadoury
Ioannis Kakadiaris
Zdenek Kalal
Yannis Kalantidis
Sinan Kalkan
Vicky Kalogeiton
Sunkavalli Kalyan
J.-K. Kamarainen

Martin Kampel
Kenichi Kanatani
Angjoo Kanazawa
Melih Kandemir
Sing Bing Kang
Zhuoliang Kang
Mohan Kankanhalli
Juho Kannala
Abhishek Kar
Amlan Kar
Svebor Karaman
Leonid Karlinsky
Zoltan Kato
Parneet Kaur
Hiroshi Kawasaki
Misha Kazhdan
Margret Keuper
Sameh Khamis
Naeemullah Khan
Salman Khan
Hadi Kiapour
Joe Kileel
Chanho Kim
Gunhee Kim
Hansung Kim
Junmo Kim
Junsik Kim
Kihwan Kim
Minyoung Kim
Tae Hyun Kim
Tae-Kyun Kim
Akisato Kimura
Zsolt Kira
Alexander Kirillov
Kris Kitani
Maria Klodt
Patrick Knöbelreiter
Jan Knopp
Reinhard Koch
Alexander Kolesnikov
Chen Kong
Naejin Kong
Shu Kong
Piotr Koniusz
Simon Korman
Andreas Koschan
Dimitrios Kosmopoulos
Satwik Kottur
Balazs Kovacs
Adarsh Kowdle
Mike Krainin
Gregory Kramida
Ranjay Krishna
Ravi Krishnan
Matej Kristan
Pavel Krsek
Volker Krueger
Alexander Krull
Hilde Kuehne
Andreas Kuhn
Arjan Kuijper
Zuzana Kukelova
Kuldeep Kulkarni
Shiro Kumano
Avinash Kumar
Vijay Kumar
Abhijit Kundu
Sebastian Kurtek
Junseok Kwon
Jan Kybic
Alexander Ladikos
Shang-Hong Lai
Wei-Sheng Lai
Jean-Francois Lalonde
John Lambert
Zhenzhong Lan
Charis Lanaras
Oswald Lanz
Dong Lao
Longin Jan Latecki
Justin Lazarow
Huu Le
Chen-Yu Lee
Gim Hee Lee
Honglak Lee
Hsin-Ying Lee
Joon-Young Lee
Seungyong Lee
Stefan Lee
Yong Jae Lee
Zhen Lei
Ido Leichter
Victor Lempitsky
Spyridon Leonardos
Marius Leordeanu
Matt Leotta
Thomas Leung
Stefan Leutenegger
Gil Levi
Aviad Levis
Jose Lezama
Ang Li
Dingzeyu Li
Dong Li
Haoxiang Li
Hongdong Li
Hongsheng Li
Hongyang Li
Jianguo Li
Kai Li
Ruiyu Li
Wei Li
Wen Li
Xi Li
Xiaoxiao Li
Xin Li
Xirong Li
Xuelong Li
Xueting Li
Yeqing Li
Yijun Li
Yin Li
Yingwei Li
Yining Li
Yongjie Li
Yu-Feng Li
Zechao Li
Zhengqi Li
Zhenyang Li
Zhizhong Li
Xiaodan Liang
Renjie Liao
Zicheng Liao
Bee Lim
Jongwoo Lim
Joseph Lim
Ser-Nam Lim
Chen-Hsuan Lin

Shih-Yao Lin
Tsung-Yi Lin
Weiyao Lin
Yen-Yu Lin
Haibin Ling
Or Litany
Roee Litman
Anan Liu
Changsong Liu
Chen Liu
Ding Liu
Dong Liu
Feng Liu
Guangcan Liu
Luoqi Liu
Miaomiao Liu
Nian Liu
Risheng Liu
Shu Liu
Shuaicheng Liu
Sifei Liu
Tyng-Luh Liu
Wanquan Liu
Weiwei Liu
Xialei Liu
Xiaoming Liu
Yebin Liu
Yiming Liu
Ziwei Liu
Zongyi Liu
Liliana Lo Presti
Edgar Lobaton
Chengjiang Long
Mingsheng Long
Roberto Lopez-Sastre
Amy Loufti
Brian Lovell
Canyi Lu
Cewu Lu
Feng Lu
Huchuan Lu
Jiajun Lu
Jiasen Lu
Jiwen Lu
Yang Lu
Yujuan Lu
Simon Lucey
Jian-Hao Luo
Jiebo Luo
Pablo Márquez-Neila
Matthias Müller
Chao Ma
Chih-Yao Ma
Lin Ma
Shugao Ma
Wei-Chiu Ma
Zhanyu Ma
Oisin Mac Aodha
Will Maddern
Ludovic Magerand
Marcus Magnor
Vijay Mahadevan
Mohammad Mahoor
Michael Maire
Subhransu Maji
Ameesh Makadia
Atsuto Maki
Yasushi Makihara
Mateusz Malinowski
Tomasz Malisiewicz
Arun Mallya
Roberto Manduchi
Junhua Mao
Dmitrii Marin
Joe Marino
Kenneth Marino
Elisabeta Marinoiu
Ricardo Martin
Aleix Martinez
Julieta Martinez
Aaron Maschinot
Jonathan Masci
Bogdan Matei
Diana Mateus
Stefan Mathe
Kevin Matzen
Bruce Maxwell
Steve Maybank
Walterio Mayol-Cuevas
Mason McGill
Stephen Mckenna
Roey Mechrez
Christopher Mei
Heydi Mendez-Vazquez
Deyu Meng
Thomas Mensink
Bjoern Menze
Domingo Mery
Qiguang Miao
Tomer Michaeli
Antoine Miech
Ondrej Miksik
Anton Milan
Gregor Miller
Cai Minjie
Majid Mirmehdi
Ishan Misra
Niloy Mitra
Anurag Mittal
Nirbhay Modhe
Davide Modolo
Pritish Mohapatra
Pascal Monasse
Mathew Monfort
Taesup Moon
Sandino Morales
Vlad Morariu
Philippos Mordohai
Francesc Moreno
Henrique Morimitsu
Yael Moses
Ben-Ezra Moshe
Roozbeh Mottaghi
Yadong Mu
Lopamudra Mukherjee
Mario Munich
Ana Murillo
Damien Muselet
Armin Mustafa
Siva Karthik Mustikovela
Moin Nabi
Sobhan Naderi
Hajime Nagahara
Varun Nagaraja
Tushar Nagarajan
Arsha Nagrani
Nikhil Naik
Atsushi Nakazawa

P. J. Narayanan
Charlie Nash
Lakshmanan Nataraj
Fabian Nater
Lukáš Neumann
Natalia Neverova
Alejandro Newell
Phuc Nguyen
Xiaohan Nie
David Nilsson
Ko Nishino
Zhenxing Niu
Shohei Nobuhara
Klas Nordberg
Mohammed Norouzi
David Novotny
Ifeoma Nwogu
Matthew O'Toole
Guillaume Obozinski
Jean-Marc Odobez
Eyal Ofek
Ferda Ofli
Tae-Hyun Oh
Iason Oikonomidis
Takeshi Oishi
Takahiro Okabe
Takayuki Okatani
Vlad Olaru
Michael Opitz
Jose Oramas
Vicente Ordonez
Ivan Oseledets
Aljosa Osep
Magnus Oskarsson
Martin R. Oswald
Wanli Ouyang
Andrew Owens
Mustafa Özuysal
Jinshan Pan
Xingang Pan
Rameswar Panda
Sharath Pankanti
Julien Pansiot
Nicolas Papadakis
George Papandreou
N. Papanikolopoulos
Hyun Soo Park
In Kyu Park
Jaesik Park
Omkar Parkhi
Alvaro Parra Bustos
C. Alejandro Parraga
Vishal Patel
Deepak Pathak
Ioannis Patras
Viorica Patraucean
Genevieve Patterson
Kim Pedersen
Robert Peharz
Selen Pehlivan
Xi Peng
Bojan Pepik
Talita Perciano
Federico Pernici
Adrian Peter
Stavros Petridis
Vladimir Petrovic
Henning Petzka
Tomas Pfister
Trung Pham
Justus Piater
Massimo Piccardi
Sudeep Pillai
Pedro Pinheiro
Lerrel Pinto
Bernardo Pires
Aleksis Pirinen
Fiora Pirri
Leonid Pischulin
Tobias Ploetz
Bryan Plummer
Yair Poleg
Jean Ponce
Gerard Pons-Moll
Jordi Pont-Tuset
Alin Popa
Fatih Porikli
Horst Possegger
Viraj Prabhu
Andrea Prati
Maria Priisalu
Véronique Prinet
Victor Prisacariu
Jan Prokaj
Nicolas Pugeault
Luis Puig
Ali Punjani
Senthil Purushwalkam
Guido Pusiol
Guo-Jun Qi
Xiaojuan Qi
Hongwei Qin
Shi Qiu
Faisal Qureshi
Matthias Rüther
Petia Radeva
Umer Rafi
Rahul Raguram
Swaminathan Rahul
Varun Ramakrishna
Kandan Ramakrishnan
Ravi Ramamoorthi
Vignesh Ramanathan
Vasili Ramanishka
R. Ramasamy Selvaraju
Rene Ranftl
Carolina Raposo
Nikhil Rasiwasia
Nalini Ratha
Sai Ravela
Avinash Ravichandran
Ramin Raziperchikolaei
Sylvestre-Alvise Rebuffi
Adria Recasens
Joe Redmon
Timo Rehfeld
Michal Reinstein
Konstantinos Rematas
Haibing Ren
Shaoqing Ren
Wenqi Ren
Zhile Ren
Hamid Rezatofighi
Nicholas Rhinehart
Helge Rhodin
Elisa Ricci
Eitan Richardson
Stephan Richter

Gernot Riegler
Hayko Riemenschneider
Tammy Riklin Raviv
Ergys Ristani
Tobias Ritschel
Mariano Rivera
Samuel Rivera
Antonio Robles-Kelly
Ignacio Rocco
Jason Rock
Emanuele Rodola
Mikel Rodriguez
Gregory Rogez
Marcus Rohrbach
Gemma Roig
Javier Romero
Olaf Ronneberger
Amir Rosenfeld
Bodo Rosenhahn
Guy Rosman
Arun Ross
Samuel Rota Bulò
Peter Roth
Constantin Rothkopf
Sebastien Roy
Amit Roy-Chowdhury
Ognjen Rudovic
Adria Ruiz
Javier Ruiz-del-Solar
Christian Rupprecht
Olga Russakovsky
Chris Russell
Alexandre Sablayrolles
Fereshteh Sadeghi
Ryusuke Sagawa
Hideo Saito
Elham Sakhaee
Albert Ali Salah
Conrad Sanderson
Koppal Sanjeev
Aswin Sankaranarayanan
Elham Saraee
Jason Saragih
Sudeep Sarkar
Imari Sato
Shin'ichi Satoh
Torsten Sattler
Bogdan Savchynskyy
Johannes Schönberger
Hanno Scharr
Walter Scheirer
Bernt Schiele
Frank Schmidt
Tanner Schmidt
Dirk Schnieders
Samuel Schulter
William Schwartz
Alexander Schwing
Ozan Sener
Soumyadip Sengupta
Laura Sevilla-Lara
Mubarak Shah
Shishir Shah
Fahad Shahbaz Khan
Amir Shahroudy
Jing Shao
Xiaowei Shao
Roman Shapovalov
Nataliya Shapovalova
Ali Sharif Razavian
Gaurav Sharma
Mohit Sharma
Pramod Sharma
Viktoriia Sharmanska
Eli Shechtman
Mark Sheinin
Evan Shelhamer
Chunhua Shen
Li Shen
Wei Shen
Xiaohui Shen
Xiaoyong Shen
Ziyi Shen
Lu Sheng
Baoguang Shi
Boxin Shi
Kevin Shih
Hyunjung Shim
Ilan Shimshoni
Young Min Shin
Koichi Shinoda
Matthew Shreve
Tianmin Shu
Zhixin Shu
Kaleem Siddiqi
Gunnar Sigurdsson
Nathan Silberman
Tomas Simon
Abhishek Singh
Gautam Singh
Maneesh Singh
Praveer Singh
Richa Singh
Saurabh Singh
Sudipta Sinha
Vladimir Smutny
Noah Snavely
Cees Snoek
Kihyuk Sohn
Eric Sommerlade
Sanghyun Son
Bi Song
Shiyu Song
Shuran Song
Xuan Song
Yale Song
Yang Song
Yibing Song
Lorenzo Sorgi
Humberto Sossa
Pratul Srinivasan
Michael Stark
Bjorn Stenger
Rainer Stiefelhagen
Joerg Stueckler
Jan Stuehmer
Hang Su
Hao Su
Shuochen Su
R. Subramanian
Yusuke Sugano
Akihiro Sugimoto
Baochen Sun
Chen Sun
Jian Sun
Jin Sun
Lin Sun
Min Sun

Qing Sun
Zhaohui Sun
David Suter
Eran Swears
Raza Syed Hussain
T. Syeda-Mahmood
Christian Szegedy
Duy-Nguyen Ta
Tolga Taşdizen
Hemant Tagare
Yuichi Taguchi
Ying Tai
Yu-Wing Tai
Jun Takamatsu
Hugues Talbot
Toru Tamak
Robert Tamburo
Chaowei Tan
Meng Tang
Peng Tang
Siyu Tang
Wei Tang
Junli Tao
Ran Tao
Xin Tao
Makarand Tapaswi
Jean-Philippe Tarel
Maxim Tatarchenko
Bugra Tekin
Demetri Terzopoulos
Christian Theobalt
Diego Thomas
Rajat Thomas
Qi Tian
Xinmei Tian
YingLi Tian
Yonghong Tian
Yonglong Tian
Joseph Tighe
Radu Timofte
Massimo Tistarelli
Sinisa Todorovic
Pavel Tokmakov
Giorgos Tolias
Federico Tombari
Tatiana Tommasi
Chetan Tonde
Xin Tong
Akihiko Torii
Andrea Torsello
Florian Trammer
Du Tran
Quoc-Huy Tran
Rudolph Triebel
Alejandro Troccoli
Leonardo Trujillo
Tomasz Trzcinski
Sam Tsai
Yi-Hsuan Tsai
Hung-Yu Tseng
Vagia Tsiminaki
Aggeliki Tsoli
Wei-Chih Tu
Shubham Tulsiani
Fred Tung
Tony Tung
Matt Turek
Oncel Tuzel
Georgios Tzimiropoulos
Ilkay Ulusoy
Osman Ulusoy
Dmitry Ulyanov
Paul Upchurch
Ben Usman
Evgeniya Ustinova
Himanshu Vajaria
Alexander Vakhitov
Jack Valmadre
Ernest Valveny
Jan van Gemert
Grant Van Horn
Jagannadan Varadarajan
Gul Varol
Sebastiano Vascon
Francisco Vasconcelos
Mayank Vatsa
Javier Vazquez-Corral
Ramakrishna Vedantam
Ashok Veeraraghavan
Andreas Veit
Raviteja Vemulapalli
Jonathan Ventura
Matthias Vestner
Minh Vo
Christoph Vogel
Michele Volpi
Carl Vondrick
Sven Wachsmuth
Toshikazu Wada
Michael Waechter
Catherine Wah
Jacob Walker
Jun Wan
Boyu Wang
Chen Wang
Chunyu Wang
De Wang
Fang Wang
Hongxing Wang
Hua Wang
Jiang Wang
Jingdong Wang
Jinglu Wang
Jue Wang
Le Wang
Lei Wang
Lezi Wang
Liang Wang
Lichao Wang
Lijun Wang
Limin Wang
Liwei Wang
Naiyan Wang
Oliver Wang
Qi Wang
Ruiping Wang
Shenlong Wang
Shu Wang
Song Wang
Tao Wang
Xiaofang Wang
Xiaolong Wang
Xinchao Wang
Xinggang Wang
Xintao Wang
Yang Wang
Yu-Chiang Frank Wang
Yu-Xiong Wang

Zhaowen Wang
Zhe Wang
Anne Wannenwetsch
Simon Warfield
Scott Wehrwein
Donglai Wei
Ping Wei
Shih-En Wei
Xiu-Shen Wei
Yichen Wei
Xie Weidi
Philippe Weinzaepfel
Longyin Wen
Eric Wengrowski
Tomas Werner
Michael Wilber
Rick Wildes
Olivia Wiles
Kyle Wilson
David Wipf
Kwan-Yee Wong
Daniel Worrall
John Wright
Baoyuan Wu
Chao-Yuan Wu
Jiajun Wu
Jianxin Wu
Tianfu Wu
Xiaodong Wu
Xiaohe Wu
Xinxiao Wu
Yang Wu
Yi Wu
Ying Wu
Yuxin Wu
Zheng Wu
Stefanie Wuhrer
Yin Xia
Tao Xiang
Yu Xiang
Lei Xiao
Tong Xiao
Yang Xiao
Cihang Xie
Dan Xie
Jianwen Xie
Jin Xie
Lingxi Xie
Pengtao Xie
Saining Xie
Wenxuan Xie
Yuchen Xie
Bo Xin
Junliang Xing
Peng Xingchao
Bo Xiong
Fei Xiong
Xuehan Xiong
Yuanjun Xiong
Chenliang Xu
Danfei Xu
Huijuan Xu
Jia Xu
Weipeng Xu
Xiangyu Xu
Yan Xu
Yuanlu Xu
Jia Xue
Tianfan Xue
Erdem Yörük
Abhay Yadav
Deshraj Yadav
Payman Yadollahpour
Yasushi Yagi
Toshihiko Yamasaki
Fei Yan
Hang Yan
Junchi Yan
Junjie Yan
Sijie Yan
Keiji Yanai
Bin Yang
Chih-Yuan Yang
Dong Yang
Herb Yang
Jianchao Yang
Jianwei Yang
Jiaolong Yang
Jie Yang
Jimei Yang
Jufeng Yang
Linjie Yang
Michael Ying Yang
Ming Yang
Ruiduo Yang
Ruigang Yang
Shuo Yang
Wei Yang
Xiaodong Yang
Yanchao Yang
Yi Yang
Angela Yao
Bangpeng Yao
Cong Yao
Jian Yao
Ting Yao
Julian Yarkony
Mark Yatskar
Jinwei Ye
Mao Ye
Mei-Chen Yeh
Raymond Yeh
Serena Yeung
Kwang Moo Yi
Shuai Yi
Alper Yılmaz
Lijun Yin
Xi Yin
Zhaozheng Yin
Xianghua Ying
Ryo Yonetani
Donghyun Yoo
Ju Hong Yoon
Kuk-Jin Yoon
Chong You
Shaodi You
Aron Yu
Fisher Yu
Gang Yu
Jingyi Yu
Ke Yu
Licheng Yu
Pei Yu
Qian Yu
Rong Yu
Shoou-I Yu
Stella Yu
Xiang Yu

Yang Yu
Zhiding Yu
Ganzhao Yuan
Jing Yuan
Junsong Yuan
Lu Yuan
Stefanos Zafeiriou
Sergey Zagoruyko
Amir Zamir
K. Zampogiannis
Andrei Zanfir
Mihai Zanfir
Pablo Zegers
Eyasu Zemene
Andy Zeng
Xingyu Zeng
Yun Zeng
De-Chuan Zhan
Cheng Zhang
Dong Zhang
Guofeng Zhang
Han Zhang
Hang Zhang
Hanwang Zhang
Jian Zhang
Jianguo Zhang
Jianming Zhang
Jiawei Zhang
Junping Zhang
Lei Zhang
Linguang Zhang
Ning Zhang
Qing Zhang
Quanshi Zhang
Richard Zhang
Runze Zhang
Shanshan Zhang
Shiliang Zhang
Shu Zhang
Ting Zhang
Xiangyu Zhang
Xiaofan Zhang
Xu Zhang
Yimin Zhang
Yinda Zhang
Yongqiang Zhang
Yuting Zhang
Zhanpeng Zhang
Ziyu Zhang
Bin Zhao
Chen Zhao
Hang Zhao
Hengshuang Zhao
Qijun Zhao
Rui Zhao
Yue Zhao
Enliang Zheng
Liang Zheng
Stephan Zheng
Wei-Shi Zheng
Wenming Zheng
Yin Zheng
Yinqiang Zheng
Yuanjie Zheng
Guangyu Zhong
Bolei Zhou
Guang-Tong Zhou
Huiyu Zhou
Jiahuan Zhou
S. Kevin Zhou
Tinghui Zhou
Wengang Zhou
Xiaowei Zhou
Xingyi Zhou
Yin Zhou
Zihan Zhou
Fan Zhu
Guangming Zhu
Ji Zhu
Jiejie Zhu
Jun-Yan Zhu
Shizhan Zhu
Siyu Zhu
Xiangxin Zhu
Xiatian Zhu
Yan Zhu
Yingying Zhu
Yixin Zhu
Yuke Zhu
Zhenyao Zhu
Liansheng Zhuang
Zeeshan Zia
Karel Zimmermann
Daniel Zoran
Danping Zou
Qi Zou
Silvia Zuffi
Wangmeng Zuo
Xinxin Zuo

Contents – Part VII

Poster Session

Poster Session

CBAM: Convolutional Block Attention Module

Sanghyun Woo[1], Jongchan Park[2], Joon-Young Lee[3], and In So Kweon[1(✉)]

[1] Korea Advanced Institute of Science and Technology, Daejeon, Korea
{shwoo93,iskweon77}@kaist.ac.kr

[2] Lunit Inc., Seoul, Korea
jcpark@lunit.io

[3] Adobe Research, San Jose, CA, USA
jolee@adobe.com

Abstract. We propose Convolutional Block Attention Module (CBAM), a simple yet effective attention module for feed-forward convolutional neural networks. Given an intermediate feature map, our module sequentially infers attention maps along two separate dimensions, channel and spatial, then the attention maps are multiplied to the input feature map for adaptive feature refinement. Because CBAM is a lightweight and general module, it can be integrated into any CNN architectures seamlessly with negligible overheads and is end-to-end trainable along with base CNNs. We validate our CBAM through extensive experiments on ImageNet-1K, MS COCO detection, and VOC 2007 detection datasets. Our experiments show consistent improvements in classification and detection performances with various models, demonstrating the wide applicability of CBAM. The code and models will be publicly available.

Keywords: Object recognition · Attention mechanism
Gated convolution

1 Introduction

Convolutional neural networks (CNNs) have significantly pushed the performance of vision tasks [1–3] based on their rich representation power. To enhance performance of CNNs, recent researches have mainly investigated three important factors of networks: *depth*, *width*, and *cardinality*.

From the LeNet architecture [4] to Residual-style Networks [5–8] so far, the network has become deeper for rich representation. VGGNet [9] shows that stacking blocks with the same shape gives fair results. Following the same spirit, ResNet [5] stacks the same topology of residual blocks along with skip connection to build an extremely deep architecture. GoogLeNet [10] shows that width is another important factor to improve the performance of a model. Zagoruyko and

Sanghyun Woo and Jongchan Park—Both authors have equally contributed.
Jongchan Park—The work was done while the author was at KAIST.

V. Ferrari et al. (Eds.): ECCV 2018, LNCS 11211, pp. 3–19, 2018.
https://doi.org/10.1007/978-3-030-01234-2_1

Komodakis [6] propose to increase the width of a network based on the ResNet architecture. They have shown that a 28-layer ResNet with increased width can outperform an extremely deep ResNet with 1001 layers on the CIFAR benchmarks. Xception [11] and ResNeXt [7] come up with to increase the cardinality of a network. They empirically show that cardinality not only saves the total number of parameters but also results in stronger representation power than the other two factors: depth and width.

Apart from these factors, we investigate a different aspect of the architecture design, *attention*. The significance of attention has been studied extensively in the previous literature [12–17]. Attention not only tells where to focus, it also improves the representation of interests. Our goal is to increase representation power by using attention mechanism: focusing on important features and suppressing unnecessary ones. In this paper, we propose a new network module, named "Convolutional Block Attention Module". Since convolution operations extract informative features by blending cross-channel and spatial information together, we adopt our module to emphasize meaningful features along those two principal dimensions: channel and spatial axes. To achieve this, we sequentially apply channel and spatial attention modules (as shown in Fig. 1), so that each of the branches can learn 'what' and 'where' to attend in the channel and spatial axes respectively. As a result, our module efficiently helps the information flow within the network by learning which information to emphasize or suppress.

In the ImageNet-1K dataset, we obtain accuracy improvement from various baseline networks by plugging our tiny module, revealing the efficacy of CBAM. We visualize trained models using the grad-CAM [18] and observe that CBAM-enhanced networks focus on target objects more properly than their baseline networks. We then conduct user study to quantitatively evaluate improvements in interpretability of models. We show that better performance and better interpretability are possible at the same time by using CBAM. Taking this into account, we conjecture that the performance boost comes from accurate attention and noise reduction of irrelevant clutters. Finally, we validate performance improvement of object detection on the MS COCO and the VOC 2007 datasets, demonstrating a wide applicability of CBAM. Since we have carefully designed our module to be light-weight, the overhead of parameters and computation is negligible in most cases.

Contribution. Our main contribution is three-fold.

1. We propose a simple yet effective attention module (CBAM) that can be widely applied to boost representation power of CNNs.
2. We validate the effectiveness of our attention module through extensive ablation studies.
3. We verify that performance of various networks is greatly improved on the multiple benchmarks (ImageNet-1K, MS COCO, and VOC 2007) by plugging our light-weight module.

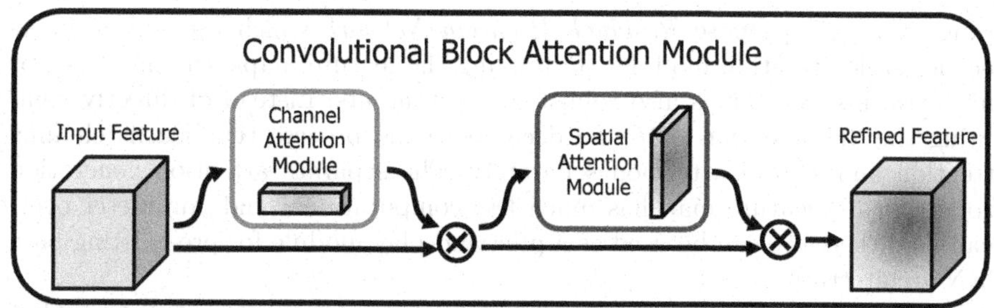

Fig. 1. The overview of CBAM. The module has two sequential sub-modules: *channel* and *spatial*. The intermediate feature map is adaptively refined through our module (CBAM) at every convolutional block of deep networks.

2 Related Work

Network Engineering. "Network engineering" has been one of the most important vision research, because well-designed networks ensure remarkable performance improvement in various applications. A wide range of architectures has been proposed since the successful implementation of a large-scale CNN [19]. An intuitive and simple way of extension is to increase the depth of neural networks [9]. Szegedy *et al.* [10] introduce a deep Inception network using a multi-branch architecture where each branch is customized carefully. While a naive increase in depth comes to saturation due to the difficulty of gradient propagation, ResNet [5] proposes a simple identity skip-connection to ease the optimization issues of deep networks. Based on the ResNet architecture, various models such as WideResNet [6], Inception-ResNet [8], and ResNeXt [7] have been developed. WideResNet [6] proposes a residual network with a larger number of convolutional filters and reduced depth. PyramidNet [20] is a strict generalization of WideResNet where the width of the network gradually increases. ResNeXt [7] suggests to use grouped convolutions and shows that increasing the cardinality leads to better classification accuracy. More recently, Huang *et al.* [21] propose a new architecture, DenseNet. It iteratively concatenates the input features with the output features, enabling each convolution block to receive raw information from all the previous blocks. While most of recent network engineering methods mainly target on three factors *depth* [5,9,10,19], *width* [6,8,10,22], and *cardinality* [7,11], we focus on the other aspect, '*attention*', one of the curious facets of a human visual system.

Attention Mechanism. It is well known that attention plays an important role in human perception [23–25]. One important property of a human visual system is that one does not attempt to process a whole scene at once. Instead, humans exploit a sequence of partial glimpses and selectively focus on salient parts in order to capture visual structure better [26].

Recently, there have been several attempts [27,28] to incorporate attention processing to improve the performance of CNNs in large-scale classification tasks.

Wang *et al.* [27] propose *Residual Attention Network* which uses an encoder-decoder style attention module. By refining the feature maps, the network not only performs well but is also robust to noisy inputs. Instead of directly computing the 3D attention map, we decompose the process that learns channel attention and spatial attention separately. The separate attention generation process for 3D feature map has much less computational and parameter overhead, and therefore can be used as a plug-and-play module for pre-existing base CNN architectures.

More close to our work, Hu *et al.* [28] introduce a compact module to exploit the inter-channel relationship. In their *Squeeze-and-Excitation* module, they use global average-pooled features to compute channel-wise attention. However, we show that those are suboptimal features in order to infer fine channel attention, and we suggest to use max-pooled features as well. They also miss the spatial attention, which plays an important role in deciding 'where' to focus as shown in [29]. In our CBAM, we exploit both spatial and channel-wise attention based on an efficient architecture and empirically verify that exploiting both is superior to using only the channel-wise attention as [28]. Moreover, we empirically show that our module is effective in detection tasks (MS-COCO and VOC). Especially, we achieve state-of-the-art performance just by placing our module on top of the existing one-shot detector [30] in the VOC2007 test set.

Concurrently, *BAM* [31] takes a similar approach, decomposing 3D attention map inference into channel and spatial. They place BAM module at every bottleneck of the network while we plug at every convolutional block.

3 Convolutional Block Attention Module

Given an intermediate feature map $\mathbf{F} \in \mathbb{R}^{C\times H\times W}$ as input, CBAM sequentially infers a 1D channel attention map $\mathbf{M_c} \in \mathbb{R}^{C\times 1\times 1}$ and a 2D spatial attention map $\mathbf{M_s} \in \mathbb{R}^{1\times H\times W}$ as illustrated in Fig. 1. The overall attention process can be summarized as:

$$\begin{aligned} \mathbf{F}' &= \mathbf{M_c}(\mathbf{F}) \otimes \mathbf{F}, \\ \mathbf{F}'' &= \mathbf{M_s}(\mathbf{F}') \otimes \mathbf{F}', \end{aligned} \tag{1}$$

where $\otimes$ denotes element-wise multiplication. During multiplication, the attention values are broadcasted (copied) accordingly: channel attention values are broadcasted along the spatial dimension, and vice versa. $\mathbf{F}''$ is the final refined output. Figure 2 depicts the computation process of each attention map. The following describes the details of each attention module.

Channel Attention Module. We produce a channel attention map by exploiting the inter-channel relationship of features. As each channel of a feature map is considered as a feature detector [32], channel attention focuses on 'what' is meaningful given an input image. To compute the channel attention efficiently, we squeeze the spatial dimension of the input feature map. For aggregating spatial information, average-pooling has been commonly adopted so far. Zhou *et al.* [33]

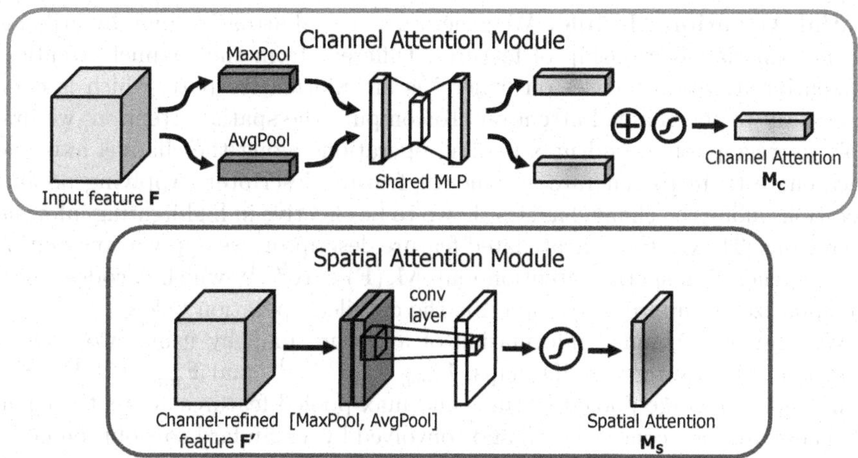

Fig. 2. Diagram of each attention sub-module. As illustrated, the channel sub-module utilizes both max-pooling outputs and average-pooling outputs with a shared network; the spatial sub-module utilizes similar two outputs that are pooled along the channel axis and forward them to a convolution layer.

suggest to use it to learn the extent of the target object effectively and Hu *et al.* [28] adopt it in their attention module to compute spatial statistics. Beyond the previous works, we argue that max-pooling gathers another important clue about distinctive object features to infer finer channel-wise attention. Thus, we use both average-pooled and max-pooled features simultaneously. We empirically confirmed that exploiting both features greatly improves representation power of networks rather than using each independently (see Sect. 4.1), showing the effectiveness of our design choice. We describe the detailed operation below.

We first aggregate spatial information of a feature map by using both average-pooling and max-pooling operations, generating two different spatial context descriptors: $\mathbf{F^c_{avg}}$ and $\mathbf{F^c_{max}}$, which denote average-pooled features and max-pooled features respectively. Both descriptors are then forwarded to a shared network to produce our channel attention map $\mathbf{M_c} \in \mathbb{R}^{C\times1\times1}$. The shared network is composed of multi-layer perceptron (MLP) with one hidden layer. To reduce parameter overhead, the hidden activation size is set to $\mathbb{R}^{C/r\times1\times1}$, where r is the reduction ratio. After the shared network is applied to each descriptor, we merge the output feature vectors using element-wise summation. In short, the channel attention is computed as:

$$\begin{aligned}\mathbf{M_c}(\mathbf{F}) &= \sigma(MLP(AvgPool(\mathbf{F})) + MLP(MaxPool(\mathbf{F}))) \\ &= \sigma(\mathbf{W_1}(\mathbf{W_0}(\mathbf{F^c_{avg}})) + \mathbf{W_1}(\mathbf{W_0}(\mathbf{F^c_{max}}))),\end{aligned} \tag{2}$$

where σ denotes the sigmoid function, $\mathbf{W_0} \in \mathbb{R}^{C/r\times C}$, and $\mathbf{W_1} \in \mathbb{R}^{C\times C/r}$. Note that the MLP weights, $\mathbf{W_0}$ and $\mathbf{W_1}$, are shared for both inputs and the ReLU activation function is followed by $\mathbf{W_0}$.

Spatial Attention Module. We generate a spatial attention map by utilizing the inter-spatial relationship of features. Different from the channel attention, the spatial attention focuses on 'where' is an informative part, which is complementary to the channel attention. To compute the spatial attention, we first apply average-pooling and max-pooling operations along the channel axis and concatenate them to generate an efficient feature descriptor. Applying pooling operations along the channel axis is shown to be effective in highlighting informative regions [34]. On the concatenated feature descriptor, we apply a convolution layer to generate a spatial attention map $\mathbf{M_s}(\mathbf{F}) \in \mathbf{R}^{H\times W}$ which encodes where to emphasize or suppress. We describe the detailed operation below.

We aggregate channel information of a feature map by using two pooling operations, generating two 2D maps: $\mathbf{F^s_{avg}} \in \mathbb{R}^{1\times H\times W}$ and $\mathbf{F^s_{max}} \in \mathbb{R}^{1\times H\times W}$. Each denotes average-pooled features and max-pooled features across the channel. Those are then concatenated and convolved by a standard convolution layer, producing our 2D spatial attention map. In short, the spatial attention is computed as:

$$\begin{aligned} \mathbf{M_s}(\mathbf{F}) &= \sigma(f^{7\times7}([AvgPool(\mathbf{F}); MaxPool(\mathbf{F})])) \\ &= \sigma(f^{7\times7}([\mathbf{F^s_{avg}}; \mathbf{F^s_{max}}])), \end{aligned} \tag{3}$$

where σ denotes the sigmoid function and $f^{7\times7}$ represents a convolution operation with the filter size of 7×7.

Arrangement of Attention Modules. Given an input image, two attention modules, channel and spatial, compute complementary attention, focusing on 'what' and 'where' respectively. Considering this, two modules can be placed in a parallel or sequential manner. We found that the sequential arrangement gives a better result than a parallel arrangement. For the arrangement of the sequential process, our experimental result shows that the channel-first order is slightly better than the spatial-first. We will discuss experimental results on network engineering in Sect. 4.1.

4 Experiments

We evaluate CBAM on the standard benchmarks: ImageNet-1K for image classification; MS COCO and VOC 2007 for object detection. In order to perform better apple-to-apple comparisons, we reproduced all the evaluated networks [5–7,28,35] in the PyTorch framework [36] and report our reproduced results in the whole experiments.

To thoroughly evaluate the effectiveness of our final module, we first perform extensive ablation experiments. Then, we verify that CBAM outperforms all the baselines without bells and whistles, demonstrating the general applicability of CBAM across different architectures as well as different tasks. One can seamlessly integrate CBAM in any CNN architectures and jointly train the combined CBAM-enhanced networks. Figure 3 shows a diagram of CBAM integrated with a ResBlock in ResNet [5] as an example.

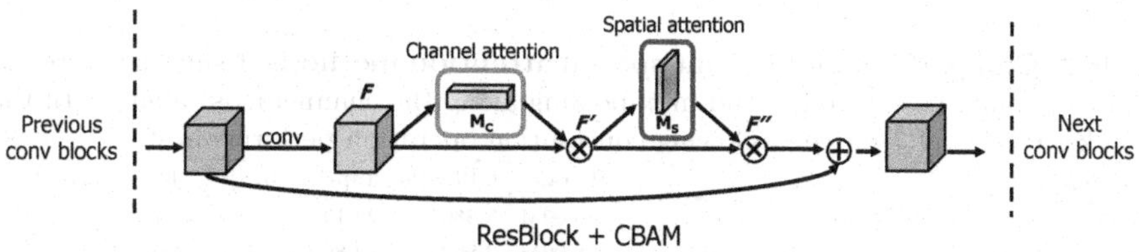

Fig. 3. CBAM integrated with a ResBlock in ResNet [5]. This figure shows the exact position of our module when integrated within a ResBlock. We apply CBAM on the convolution outputs in each block.

4.1 Ablation Studies

In this subsection, we empirically show the effectiveness of our design choice. For this ablation study, we use the ImageNet-1K dataset and adopt ResNet-50 [5] as the base architecture. The ImageNet-1K classification dataset [1] consists of 1.2 million images for training and 50,000 for validation with 1,000 object classes. We adopt the same data augmentation scheme with [5,37] for training and apply a single-crop evaluation with the size of 224×224 at test time. The learning rate starts from 0.1 and drops every 30 epochs. We train the networks for 90 epochs. Following [5,37,38], we report classification errors on the validation set.

Our module design process is split into three parts. We first search for the effective approach to computing the channel attention, then the spatial attention. Finally, we consider how to combine both channel and spatial attention modules. We explain the details of each experiment below.

Channel Attention. We experimentally verify that using both average-pooled and max-pooled features enables finer attention inference. We compare 3 variants of channel attention: average pooling, max pooling, and joint use of both poolings. Note that the channel attention module with an average pooling is the same as the SE [28] module. Also, when using both poolings, we use a shared MLP for attention inference to save parameters, as both of aggregated channel features lie in the same semantic embedding space. We only use channel attention modules in this experiment and we fix the reduction ratio to 16.

Table 1. Comparison of different channel attention methods. We observe that using our proposed method outperforms recently suggested Squeeze and Excitation method [28].

Description	Parameters	GFLOPs	Top-1 error (%)	Top-5 error (%)
ResNet50 (baseline)	25.56M	3.86	24.56	7.50
ResNet50 + AvgPool (SE [28])	25.92M	3.94	23.14	6.70
ResNet50 + MaxPool	25.92M	3.94	23.20	6.83
ResNet50 + AvgPool & MaxPool	25.92M	4.02	**22.80**	**6.52**

Table 2. Comparison of different spatial attention methods. Using the proposed channel-pooling (*i.e.* average- and max-pooling along the channel axis) along with the large kernel size of 7 for the following convolution operation performs best.

Description	Param.	GFLOPs	Top-1 error (%)	Top-5 error (%)
ResNet50 + channel (SE [28])	28.09M	3.860	23.14	6.70
ResNet50 + channel	28.09M	3.860	22.80	6.52
ResNet50 + channel + spatial (1 × 1 conv, k = 3)	28.10M	3.862	22.96	6.64
ResNet50 + channel + spatial (1 × 1 conv, k = 7)	28.10M	3.869	22.90	6.47
ResNet50 + channel + spatial (avg & max, k = 3)	28.09M	3.863	22.68	6.41
ResNet50 + channel + spatial (avg & max, k = 7)	28.09M	3.864	**22.66**	**6.31**

Table 3. Combining methods of channel and spatial attention. Using both attention is critical while the best-combining strategy (*i.e.* sequential, channel-first) further improves the accuracy.

Description	Top-1 error (%)	Top-5 error (%)
ResNet50 + channel (SE [28])	23.14	6.70
ResNet50 + channel + spatial	**22.66**	**6.31**
ResNet50 + spatial + channel	22.78	6.42
ResNet50 + channel & spatial in parallel	22.95	6.59

Experimental results with various pooling methods are shown in Table 1. We observe that max-pooled features are as meaningful as average-pooled features, comparing the accuracy improvement from the baseline. In the work of SE [28], however, they only exploit the average-pooled features, missing the importance of max-pooled features. We argue that max-pooled features which encode the degree of the most salient part can compensate the average-pooled features which encode global statistics softly. Thus, we suggest to use both features simultaneously and apply a shared network to those features. The outputs of a shared network are then merged by element-wise summation. We empirically show that our channel attention method is an effective way to push performance further from SE [28] without additional learnable parameters. As a brief conclusion, we use both average- and max-pooled features in our channel attention module with the reduction ratio of 16 in the following experiments.

Spatial Attention. Given the channel-wise refined features, we explore an effective method to compute the spatial attention. The design philosophy is symmetric with the channel attention branch. To generate a 2D spatial attention map, we first compute a 2D descriptor that encodes channel information at each pixel over all spatial locations. We then apply one convolution layer to the 2D descriptor, obtaining the raw attention map. The final attention map is normalized by the sigmoid function.

We compare two methods of generating the 2D descriptor: *channel pooling* using average- and max-pooling across the channel axis and *standard* 1×1

convolution reducing the channel dimension into 1. In addition, we investigate the effect of a kernel size at the following convolution layer: kernel sizes of 3 and 7. In the experiment, we place the spatial attention module after the previously designed channel attention module, as the final goal is to use both modules together.

Table 2 shows the experimental results. We can observe that the channel pooling produces better accuracy, indicating that explicitly modeled pooling leads to finer attention inference rather than learnable weighted channel pooling (implemented as 1×1 convolution). In the comparison of different convolution kernel sizes, we find that adopting a larger kernel size generates better accuracy in both cases. It implies that a broad view (*i.e.* large receptive field) is needed for deciding spatially important regions. Considering this, we adopt the channel-pooling method and the convolution layer with a large kernel size to compute spatial attention. In a brief conclusion, we use the average- and max-pooled features across the channel axis with a convolution kernel size of 7 as our spatial attention module.

Arrangement of the Channel and Spatial attention. In this experiment, we compare three different ways of arranging the channel and spatial attention submodules: sequential channel-spatial, sequential spatial-channel, and parallel use of both attention modules. As each module has different functions, the order may affect the overall performance. For example, from a spatial viewpoint, the channel attention is globally applied, while the spatial attention works locally. Also, it is natural to think that we may combine two attention outputs to build a 3D attention map. In the case, both attentions can be applied in parallel, then the outputs of the two attention modules are added and normalized with the sigmoid function.

Table 3 summarizes the experimental results on different attention arranging methods. From the results, we can find that generating an attention map sequentially infers a finer attention map than doing in parallel. In addition, the channel-first order performs slightly better than the spatial-first order. Note that all the arranging methods outperform using only the channel attention independently, showing that utilizing both attentions is crucial while the best-arranging strategy further pushes performance.

4.2 Image Classification on ImageNet-1K

We perform ImageNet-1K classification experiments to rigorously evaluate our module. We follow the same protocol as specified in Sect. 4.1 and evaluate our module in various network architectures including ResNet [5], WideResNet [6], and ResNext [7].

Table 4 summarizes the experimental results. The networks with CBAM outperform all the baselines significantly, demonstrating that the CBAM can generalize well on various models in the large-scale dataset. Moreover, the models with CBAM improve the accuracy upon the one of the strongest method – SE [28]

Table 4. Classification results on ImageNet-1K. Single-crop validation errors are reported.

Architecture	Param.	GFLOPs	Top-1 error (%)	Top-5 error (%)
ResNet18 [5]	11.69M	1.814	29.60	10.55
ResNet18 [5] + SE [28]	11.78M	1.814	29.41	10.22
ResNet18 [5] + CBAM	11.78M	1.815	**29.27**	**10.09**
ResNet34 [5]	21.80M	3.664	26.69	8.60
ResNet34 [5] + SE [28]	21.96M	3.664	26.13	8.35
ResNet34 [5] + CBAM	21.96M	3.665	**25.99**	**8.24**
ResNet50 [5]	25.56M	3.858	24.56	7.50
ResNet50 [5] + SE [28]	28.09M	3.860	23.14	6.70
ResNet50 [5] + CBAM	28.09M	3.864	**22.66**	**6.31**
ResNet101 [5]	44.55M	7.570	23.38	6.88
ResNet101 [5] + SE [28]	49.33M	7.575	22.35	6.19
ResNet101 [5] + CBAM	49.33M	7.581	**21.51**	**5.69**
WideResNet18 [6] (widen = 1.5)	25.88M	3.866	26.85	8.88
WideResNet18 [6] (widen = 1.5) + SE [28]	26.07M	3.867	26.21	8.47
WideResNet18 [6] (widen = 1.5) + CBAM	26.08M	3.868	**26.10**	**8.43**
WideResNet18 [6] (widen = 2.0)	45.62M	6.696	25.63	8.20
WideResNet18 [6] (widen = 2.0) + SE [28]	45.97M	6.696	24.93	7.65
WideResNet18 [6] (widen = 2.0) + CBAM	45.97M	6.697	**24.84**	**7.63**
ResNeXt50 [7] (32 × 4d)	25.03M	3.768	22.85	6.48
ResNeXt50 [7] (32 × 4d) + SE [28]	27.56M	3.771	**21.91**	6.04
ResNeXt50 [7] (32 × 4d) + CBAM	27.56M	3.774	21.92	**5.91**
ResNeXt101 [7] (32 × 4d)	44.18M	7.508	21.54	5.75
ResNeXt101 [7] (32 × 4d) + SE [28]	48.96M	7.512	21.17	5.66
ResNeXt101 [7] (32 × 4d) + CBAM	48.96M	7.519	**21.07**	**5.59**

* All results are reproduced in the PyTorch framework.

which is the winning approach of the ILSVRC 2017 classification task. It implies that our proposed approach is powerful, showing the efficacy of *new pooling method* that generates richer descriptor and *spatial attention* that complements the channel attention effectively.

We also find that the overall overhead of CBAM is quite small in terms of both parameters and computation. This motivates us to apply our proposed module CBAM to the light-weight network, MobileNet [35]. Table 5 summarizes the experimental results that we conducted based on the MobileNet architecture. We have placed CBAM to two models, basic and capacity-reduced model (*i.e.* adjusting width multiplier (α) to 0.7). We observe similar phenomenon as shown in Table 4. CBAM not only boosts the accuracy of baselines significantly but also favorably improves the performance of SE [28]. This shows the great potential of CBAM for applications on low-end devices.

Table 5. Classification results on ImageNet-1K using the light-weight network, MobileNet [35]. Single-crop validation errors are reported.

Architecture	Parameters	GFLOPs	Top-1 error (%)	Top-5 error (%)
MobileNet [35] α = 0.7	2.30M	0.283	34.86	13.69
MobileNet [35] α = 0.7 + SE [28]	2.71M	0.283	32.50	12.49
MobileNet [35] α = 0.7 + CBAM	2.71M	0.289	**31.51**	**11.48**
MobileNet [35]	4.23M	0.569	31.39	11.51
MobileNet [35] + SE [28]	5.07M	0.570	29.97	10.63
MobileNet [35] + CBAM	5.07M	0.576	**29.01**	**9.99**

* All results are reproduced in the PyTorch framework.

4.3 Network Visualization with Grad-CAM [18]

For the qualitative analysis, we apply the Grad-CAM [18] to different networks using images from the ImageNet validation set. Grad-CAM is a recently proposed visualization method which uses gradients in order to calculate the importance of the spatial locations in convolutional layers. As the gradients are calculated with respect to a unique class, Grad-CAM result shows attended regions clearly. By observing the regions that network has considered as important for predicting a class, we attempt to look at how this network is making good use of features. We compare the visualization results of CBAM-integrated network (ResNet50 + CBAM) with baseline (ResNet50) and SE-integrated network (ResNet50 + SE). Figure 4 illustrate the visualization results. The softmax scores for a target class are also shown in the figure.

In Fig. 4, we can clearly see that the Grad-CAM masks of the CBAM-integrated network cover the target object regions better than other methods. That is, the CBAM-integrated network learns well to exploit information in target object regions and aggregate features from them. Note that target class scores also increase accordingly.

4.4 Quantitative Evaluation of Improved Interpretability

Following the Sect. 5.1 in Grad-CAM paper, we conduct a user study based on Grad-CAM visualizations. We randomly selected 50 images which are correctly classified with both methods (*i.e.* baseline and CBAM) from ImageNet validation set. The user study is conducted on the Google Forms platform. For each question, randomly shuffled visualizations are shown to the respondents. For the visualizations, regions of the image with Grad-CAM values of 0.6 or greater are shown. In practice, respondents were given full input image, ground-truth label, and two image regions from each methods (see Fig. 5). The comparison criterion is "Given class label, which region seems more class-discriminative?". The respondents can choose that either one is better, or both are similar. There are 50 question sets of images and 25 respondents, resulting in a total of 1250 votes. The results are shown in the Table 6. We can clearly see that CBAM outperforms baseline, showing the improved interpretability.

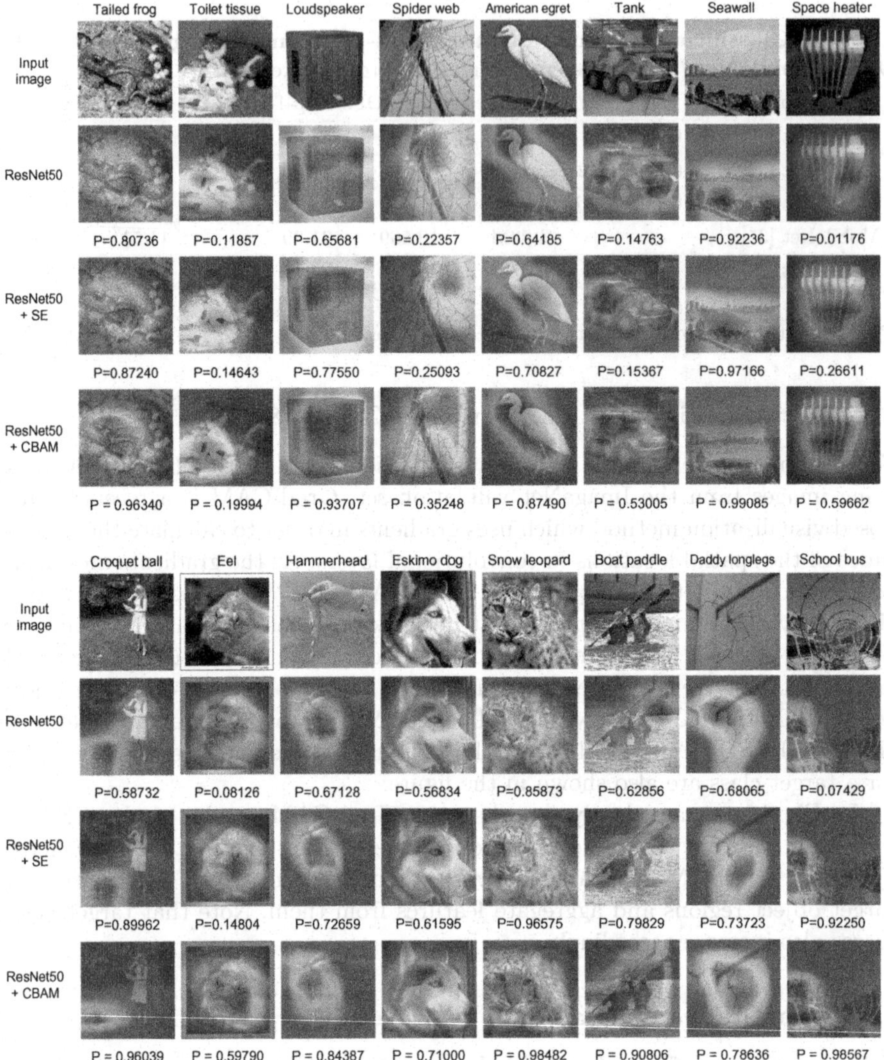

Fig. 4. Grad-CAM [18] visualization results. We compare the visualization results of CBAM-integrated network (ResNet50 + CBAM) with baseline (ResNet50) and SE-integrated network (ResNet50 + SE). The grad-CAM visualization is calculated for the last convolutional outputs. The ground-truth label is shown on the top of each input image and P denotes the softmax score of each network for the ground-truth class.

4.5 MS COCO Object Detection

We conduct object detection on the Microsoft COCO dataset [3]. This dataset involves 80k training images ("2014 train") and 40k validation images ("2014 val"). The average mAP over different IoU thresholds from 0.5 to 0.95 is used

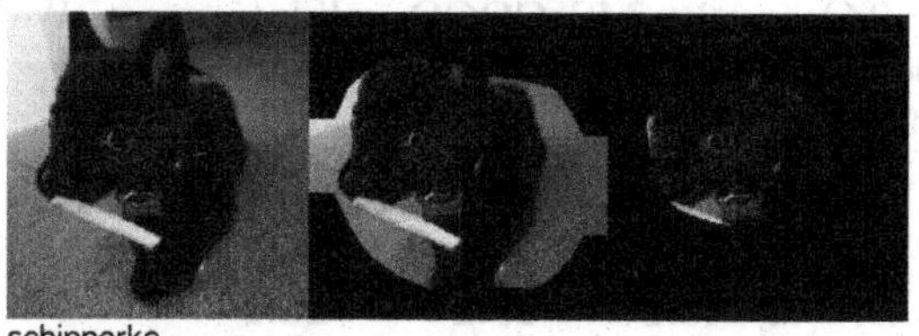

Fig. 5. Example of question image for the user study.

Table 6. Results of user study.

Survey choice	Votes
Seems equal	295
Baseline better	288
CBAM better	**667**

for evaluation. According to [39,40], we trained our model using all the training images as well as a subset of validation images, holding out 5,000 examples for validation. Our training code is based on [41] and we train the network for 490K iterations for fast performance validation. We adopt *Faster-RCNN* [42] as our detection method and ImageNet pre-trained ResNet50 and ResNet101 [5] as our baseline networks. Here we are interested in performance improvement by plugging CBAM to the baseline networks. Since we use the same detection method in all the models, the gains can only be attributed to the enhanced representation power, given by our module CBAM. As shown in the Table 7, we observe significant improvements from the baseline, demonstrating generalization performance of CBAM on other recognition tasks.

4.6 VOC 2007 Object Detection

We further perform experiments on the PASCAL VOC 2007 test set. In this experiment, we apply CBAM to the detectors, while the previous experiments (Table 7) apply our module to the base networks. We adopt the StairNet [30] framework, which is one of the strongest multi-scale method based on the SSD [40]. For the experiment, we reproduce SSD and StairNet in our PyTorch platform in order to estimate performance improvement of CBAM accurately and achieve 77.8% and 78.9% mAP@.5 respectively, which are higher than the original accuracy reported in the original papers. We then place SE [28] and CBAM right before every classifier, refining the final features which are composed of up-sampled global features and corresponding local features before the prediction, enforcing model to adaptively select only the meaningful features. We train all the models on the union set of VOC 2007 trainval and VOC 2012 trainval ("07+12"), and evaluate on the VOC 2007 test set. The total number of training epochs is 250. We use a weight decay of 0.0005 and a momentum of 0.9. In all the experiments, the size of the input image is fixed to 300 for the simplicity.

The experimental results are summarized in Table 8. We can clearly see that CBAM improves the accuracy of all strong baselines with two backbone networks. Note that accuracy improvement of CBAM comes with a negligible parameter overhead, indicating that enhancement is not due to a naive

Table 7. Object detection mAP (%) on the MS COCO validation set. We adopt the Faster R-CNN [42] detection framework and apply our module to the base networks. CBAM boosts mAP@[.5, .95] by 0.9 for both baseline networks.

Backbone	Detector	mAP@.5	mAP@.75	mAP@[.5, .95]
ResNet50 [5]	Faster-RCNN [42]	46.2	28.1	27.0
ResNet50 [5] + CBAM	Faster-RCNN [42]	**48.2**	**29.2**	**28.1**
ResNet101 [5]	Faster-RCNN [42]	48.4	30.7	29.1
ResNet101 [5] + CBAM	Faster-RCNN [42]	**50.5**	**32.6**	**30.8**

* All results are reproduced in the PyTorch framework.

Table 8. Object detection mAP (%) on the VOC 2007 test set. We adopt the StairNet [30] detection framework and apply SE and CBAM to the detectors. CBAM favorably improves all the strong baselines with negligible additional parameters.

Backbone	Detector	mAP@.5	Parameters (M)
VGG16 [9]	SSD [40]	77.8	26.5
VGG16 [9]	StairNet [30]	78.9	32.0
VGG16 [9]	StairNet [30] + SE [28]	79.1	32.1
VGG16 [9]	StairNet [30] + CBAM	**79.3**	32.1
MobileNet [35]	SSD [40]	68.1	5.81
MobileNet [35]	StairNet [30]	70.1	5.98
MobileNet [35]	StairNet [30] + SE [28]	70.0	5.99
MobileNet [35]	StairNet [30] + CBAM	**70.5**	6.00

* All results are reproduced in the PyTorch framework.

capacity-increment but because of our effective feature refinement. In addition, the result using the light-weight backbone network [35] again shows that CBAM can be an interesting method to low-end devices.

5 Conclusion

We have presented the convolutional block attention module (CBAM), a new approach to improve representation power of CNN networks. We apply attention-based feature refinement with two distinctive modules, channel and spatial, and achieve considerable performance improvement while keeping the overhead small. For the channel attention, we suggest to use the max-pooled features along with the average-pooled features, leading to produce finer attention than SE [28]. We further push the performance by exploiting the spatial attention. Our final module (CBAM) learns what and where to emphasize or suppress and refines intermediate features effectively. To verify its efficacy, we conducted extensive experiments with various state-of-the-art models and confirmed that CBAM outperforms all the baselines on three different benchmark datasets: ImageNet-1K, MS COCO, and VOC 2007. In addition, we visualize how the module exactly infers given an input image. Interestingly, we observed that our module induces the network to focus on target object properly. We hope CBAM become an important component of various network architectures.

Acknowledgement. This work was supported by the Technology Innovation Program (No. 10048320), funded by the Ministry of Trade, Industry & Energy (MI, Korea).

References

1. Deng, J., Dong, W., Socher, R., Li, L.J., Li, K., Fei-Fei, L.: ImageNet: a large-scale hierarchical image database. In: Proceedings of the Computer Vision and Pattern Recognition (CVPR) (2009)
2. Krizhevsky, A., Hinton, G.: Learning multiple layers of features from tiny images
3. Lin, T.-Y., et al.: Microsoft COCO: common objects in context. In: Fleet, D., Pajdla, T., Schiele, B., Tuytelaars, T. (eds.) ECCV 2014, Part V. LNCS, vol. 8693, pp. 740–755. Springer, Cham (2014). https://doi.org/10.1007/978-3-319-10602-1_48
4. LeCun, Y., Bottou, L., Bengio, Y., Haffner, P.: Gradient-based learning applied to document recognition. Proc. IEEE **86**(11), 2278–2324 (1998)
5. He, K., Zhang, X., Ren, S., Sun, J.: Deep residual learning for image recognition. In: Proceedings of the Computer Vision and Pattern Recognition (CVPR) (2016)
6. Zagoruyko, S., Komodakis, N.: Wide residual networks. arXiv preprint arXiv:1605.07146 (2016)
7. Xie, S., Girshick, R., Dollár, P., Tu, Z., He, K.: Aggregated residual transformations for deep neural networks. arXiv preprint arXiv:1611.05431 (2016)
8. Szegedy, C., Ioffe, S., Vanhoucke, V., Alemi, A.A.: Inception-v4, inception-ResNet and the impact of residual connections on learning. In: Proceedings of the Association for the Advancement of Artificial Intelligence (AAAI) (2017)
9. Simonyan, K., Zisserman, A.: Very deep convolutional networks for large-scale image recognition. arXiv preprint arXiv:1409.1556 (2014)
10. Szegedy, C., Liu, W., Jia, Y., Sermanet, P., Reed, S., Anguelov, D., Erhan, D., Vanhoucke, V., Rabinovich, A.: Going deeper with convolutions. In: Proceedings of the Computer Vision and Pattern Recognition (CVPR) (2015)
11. Chollet, F.: Xception: Deep learning with depthwise separable convolutions. arXiv preprint arXiv:1610.02357 (2016)
12. Mnih, V., Heess, N., Graves, A., et al.: Recurrent models of visual attention. In: Proceedings of the Neural Information Processing Systems (NIPS). Advances in Neural Information Processing Systems (2014)
13. Ba, J., Mnih, V., Kavukcuoglu, K.: Multiple object recognition with visual attention (2014)
14. Bahdanau, D., Cho, K., Bengio, Y.: Neural machine translation by jointly learning to align and translate (2014)
15. Xu, K., Ba, J., Kiros, R., Cho, K., Courville, A., Salakhudinov, R., Zemel, R., Bengio, Y.: Show, attend and tell: neural image caption generation with visual attention (2015)
16. Gregor, K., Danihelka, I., Graves, A., Rezende, D.J., Wierstra, D.: DRAW: a recurrent neural network for image generation (2015)
17. Jaderberg, M., Simonyan, K., Zisserman, A., et al.: Spatial transformer networks. In: Proceedings of the Neural Information Processing Systems (NIPS) (2015)

18. Selvaraju, R.R., Cogswell, M., Das, A., Vedantam, R., Parikh, D., Batra, D.: Grad-CAM: visual explanations from deep networks via gradient-based localization. In: Proceedings of the IEEE Conference on Computer Vision and Pattern Recognition, pp. 618–626 (2017)
19. Krizhevsky, A., Sutskever, I., Hinton, G.E.: ImageNet classification with deep convolutional neural networks. In: Proceedings of the Neural Information Processing Systems (NIPS) (2012)
20. Han, D., Kim, J., Kim, J.: Deep pyramidal residual networks. In: Proceedings of the Computer Vision and Pattern Recognition (CVPR) (2017)
21. Huang, G., Liu, Z., Weinberger, K.Q., van der Maaten, L.: Densely connected convolutional networks. arXiv preprint arXiv:1608.06993 (2016)
22. Szegedy, C., Vanhoucke, V., Ioffe, S., Shlens, J., Wojna, Z.: Rethinking the inception architecture for computer vision. In: Proceedings of the Computer Vision and Pattern Recognition (CVPR) (2016)
23. Itti, L., Koch, C., Niebur, E.: A model of saliency-based visual attention for rapid scene analysis. In: IEEE Transactions on Pattern Analysis and Machine Intelligence (TPAMI) (1998)
24. Rensink, R.A.: The dynamic representation of scenes. Vis. Cogn. **7**(1–3), 17–42 (2000)
25. Corbetta, M., Shulman, G.L.: Control of goal-directed and stimulus-driven attention in the brain. Nat. Rev. Neurosci. **3**(3), 201–215 (2002)
26. Larochelle, H., Hinton, G.E.: Learning to combine foveal glimpses with a third-order Boltzmann machine. In: Proceedings of the Neural Information Processing Systems (NIPS) (2010)
27. Wang, F., Jiang, M., Qian, C., Yang, S., Li, C., Zhang, H., Wang, X., Tang, X.: Residual attention network for image classification. arXiv preprint arXiv:1704.06904 (2017)
28. Hu, J., Shen, L., Sun, G.: Squeeze-and-excitation networks. arXiv preprint arXiv:1709.01507 (2017)
29. Chen, L., Zhang, H., Xiao, J., Nie, L., Shao, J., Chua, T.S.: SCA-CNN: spatial and channel-wise attention in convolutional networks for image captioning. In: Proceedings of the Computer Vision and Pattern Recognition (CVPR) (2017)
30. Sanghyun, W., Soonmin, H., So, K.I.: StairNet: top-down semantic aggregation for accurate one shot detection. In: Proceedings of the Winter Conference on Applications of Computer Vision (WACV) (2018)
31. Park, J., Woo, S., Lee, J.Y., Kweon, I.S.: BAM: bottleneck attention module. In: Proceedings of the British Machine Vision Conference (BMVC) (2018)
32. Zeiler, M.D., Fergus, R.: Visualizing and understanding convolutional networks. In: Fleet, D., Pajdla, T., Schiele, B., Tuytelaars, T. (eds.) ECCV 2014, Part I. LNCS, vol. 8689, pp. 818–833. Springer, Cham (2014). https://doi.org/10.1007/978-3-319-10590-1_53
33. Zhou, B., Khosla, A., Lapedriza, A., Oliva, A., Torralba, A.: Learning deep features for discriminative localization. In: 2016 IEEE Conference on Computer Vision and Pattern Recognition (CVPR), pp. 2921–2929. IEEE (2016)
34. Zagoruyko, S., Komodakis, N.: Paying more attention to attention: improving the performance of convolutional neural networks via attention transfer. In: ICLR (2017)
35. Howard, A.G., Zhu, M., Chen, B., Kalenichenko, D., Wang, W., Weyand, T., Andreetto, M., Adam, H.: MobileNets: efficient convolutional neural networks for mobile vision applications. arXiv preprint arXiv:1704.04861 (2017)

36. : PyTorch. http://pytorch.org/. Accessed 08 Nov 2017
37. He, K., Zhang, X., Ren, S., Sun, J.: Identity mappings in deep residual networks. In: Leibe, B., Matas, J., Sebe, N., Welling, M. (eds.) ECCV 2016, Part IV. LNCS, vol. 9908, pp. 630–645. Springer, Cham (2016). https://doi.org/10.1007/978-3-319-46493-0_38
38. Huang, G., Sun, Y., Liu, Z., Sedra, D., Weinberger, K.Q.: Deep networks with stochastic depth. In: Leibe, B., Matas, J., Sebe, N., Welling, M. (eds.) ECCV 2016, Part IV. LNCS, vol. 9908, pp. 646–661. Springer, Cham (2016). https://doi.org/10.1007/978-3-319-46493-0_39
39. Bell, S., Lawrence Zitnick, C., Bala, K., Girshick, R.: Inside-outside net: detecting objects in context with skip pooling and recurrent neural networks. In: Proceedings of the Computer Vision and Pattern Recognition (CVPR) (2016)
40. Liu, W., et al.: SSD: single shot multibox detector. In: Leibe, B., Matas, J., Sebe, N., Welling, M. (eds.) ECCV 2016, Part I. LNCS, vol. 9905, pp. 21–37. Springer, Cham (2016). https://doi.org/10.1007/978-3-319-46448-0_2
41. Chen, X., Gupta, A.: An implementation of faster RCNN with study for region sampling. arXiv preprint arXiv:1702.02138 (2017)
42. Ren, S., He, K., Girshick, R., Sun, J.: Faster R-CNN: towards real-time object detection with region proposal networks. In: Proceedings of the Neural Information Processing Systems (NIPS) (2015)

BodyNet: Volumetric Inference of 3D Human Body Shapes

Gül Varol[1(✉)], Duygu Ceylan[3], Bryan Russell[4], Jimei Yang[3], Ersin Yumer[3], Ivan Laptev[1], and Cordelia Schmid[2]

[1] Inria, Paris, France
gul.varol@inria.fr
[2] Inria, Grenoble, France
[3] Adobe Research, San Jose, USA
[4] Adobe Research, San Francisco, USA

Abstract. Human shape estimation is an important task for video editing, animation and fashion industry. Predicting 3D human body shape from natural images, however, is highly challenging due to factors such as variation in human bodies, clothing and viewpoint. Prior methods addressing this problem typically attempt to fit parametric body models with certain priors on pose and shape. In this work we argue for an alternative representation and propose BodyNet, a neural network for direct inference of volumetric body shape from a single image. BodyNet is an end-to-end trainable network that benefits from (i) a volumetric 3D loss, (ii) a multi-view re-projection loss, and (iii) intermediate supervision of 2D pose, 2D body part segmentation, and 3D pose. Each of them results in performance improvement as demonstrated by our experiments. To evaluate the method, we fit the SMPL model to our network output and show state-of-the-art results on the SURREAL and Unite the People datasets, outperforming recent approaches. Besides achieving state-of-the-art performance, our method also enables volumetric body-part segmentation.

1 Introduction

Parsing people in visual data is central to many applications including mixed-reality interfaces, animation, video editing and human action recognition. Towards this goal, human 2D pose estimation has been significantly advanced by

G. Varol and I. Laptev—École normale supérieure, Inria, CNRS, PSL Research University, Paris, France.
C. Schmid—Univ. Grenoble Alpes, Inria, CNRS, INPG, LJK, Grenoble, France.
E. Yumer— Currently at Argo AI, USA. This work was performed while EY was at Adobe.

Electronic supplementary material The online version of this chapter (https://doi.org/10.1007/978-3-030-01234-2_2) contains supplementary material, which is available to authorized users.

V. Ferrari et al. (Eds.): ECCV 2018, LNCS 11211, pp. 20–38, 2018.
https://doi.org/10.1007/978-3-030-01234-2_2

Fig. 1. Our BodyNet predicts a volumetric 3D human body shape and 3D body parts from a single image. We show the input image, the predicted human voxels, and the predicted part voxels.

recent efforts [1–4]. Such methods aim to recover 2D locations of body joints and provide a simplified geometric representation of the human body. There has also been significant progress in 3D human pose estimation [5–8]. Many applications, however, such as virtual clothes try-on, video editing and re-enactment require accurate estimation of both 3D human *pose* and *shape*.

3D human shape estimation has been mostly studied in controlled settings using specific sensors including multi-view capture [9], motion capture markers [10], inertial sensors [11], and 3D scanners [12]. In uncontrolled single-view settings 3D human shape estimation, however, has received little attention so far. The challenges include the lack of large-scale training data, the high dimensionality of the output space, and the choice of suitable representations for 3D human shape. Bogo *et al.* [13] present the first automatic method to fit a deformable body model to an image but rely on accurate 2D pose estimation and introduce hand-designed constraints enforcing elbows and knees to bend naturally. Other recent methods [14–16] employ deformable human body models such as SMPL [17] and regress model parameters with CNNs [18,19]. In this work, we compare to such approaches and show advantages.

The optimal choice of 3D representation for neural networks remains an open problem. Recent work explores voxel [20–23], octree [24–27], point cloud [28–30], and surface [31] representations for modeling generic 3D objects. In the case of human bodies, the common approach has been to regress parameters of predefined human shape models [14–16]. However, the mapping between the 3D shape and parameters of deformable body models is highly nonlinear and is currently difficult to learn. Moreover, regression to a single set of parameters cannot represent multiple hypotheses and can be problematic in ambigous situations. Notably, skeleton regression methods for 2D human pose estimation, e.g., [32], have recently been overtaken by heatmap based methods [1,2] enabling representation of multiple hypotheses.

In this work we propose and investigate a volumetric representation for body shape estimation as illustrated in Fig. 1. Our network, called BodyNet, generates likelihoods on the 3D occupancy grid of a person. To efficiently train our network, we propose to regularize BodyNet with a set of auxiliary losses. Besides the main volumetric 3D loss, BodyNet includes a multi-view re-projection loss and multi-task losses. The multi-view re-projection loss, being efficiently approximated on

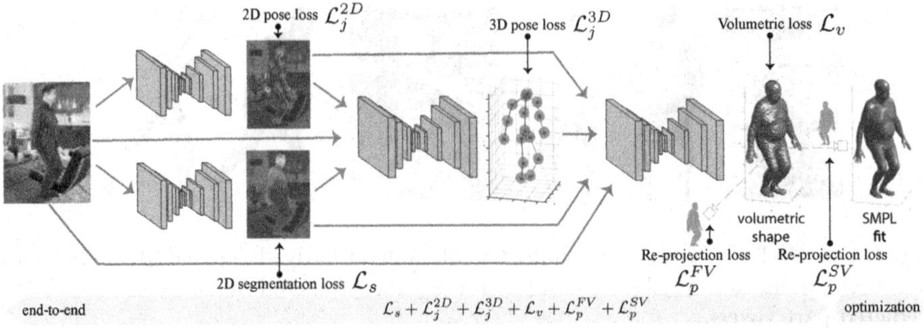

Fig. 2. BodyNet: End-to-end trainable network for 3D human body shape estimation. The input RGB image is first passed through subnetworks for 2D pose estimation and 2D body part segmentation. These predictions, combined with the RGB features, are fed to another network predicting 3D pose. All subnetworks are combined to a final network to infer volumetric shape. The 2D pose, 2D segmentation and 3D pose networks are first pre-trained and then fine-tuned jointly for the task of volumetric shape estimation using multi-view re-projection losses. We fit the SMPL model to volumetric predictions for the purpose of evaluation

voxel space (see Sect. 3.2), increases the importance of the boundary voxels. The multi-task losses are based on the additional intermediate network supervision in terms of 2D pose, 2D body part segmentation, and 3D pose. The overall architecture of BodyNet is illustrated in Fig. 2.

To evaluate our method, we fit the SMPL model [13] to the BodyNet output and measure single-view 3D human shape estimation performance in the recent SURREAL [33] and Unite the People [34] datasets. The proposed BodyNet approach demonstrates state-of-the-art performance and improves accuracy of recent methods. We show significant improvements provided by the end-to-end training and auxiliary losses of BodyNet. Furthermore, our method enables volumetric body-part segmentation. BodyNet is fully-differentiable and could be used as a subnetwork in future application-oriented methods targeting e.g., virtual cloth change or re-enactment.

In summary, this work makes several contributions. First, we address single-view 3D human shape estimation and propose a volumetric representation for this task. Second, we investigate several network architectures and propose an end-to-end trainable network BodyNet combining a multi-view re-projection loss together with intermediate network supervision in terms of 2D pose, 2D body part segmentation, and 3D pose. Third, we outperform previous regression-based methods and demonstrate state-of-the art performance on two datasets for human shape estimation. In addition, our network is fully differentiable and can provide volumetric body-part segmentation.

2 Related Work

3D Human Body Shape. While the problem of localizing 3D body joints has been well-explored in the past [5–8,35–38], 3D human *shape* estimation from a single image has received limited attention and remains a challenging problem. Earlier work [39,40] proposed to optimize pose and shape parameters of the 3D deformable body model SCAPE [41]. More recent methods use the SMPL [17] body model that again represents the 3D shape as a function of pose and shape parameters. Given such a model and an input image, Bogo *et al.* [13] present the optimization method SMPLify estimating model parameters from a fit to 2D joint locations. Lassner *et al.* [34] extend this approach by incorporating silhouette information as additional guidance and improves the optimization performance by densely sampled 2D points. Huang *et al.* [42] extend SMPLify for multi-view video sequences with temporal priors. Similar temporal constraints have been used in [43]. Rhodin *et al.* [44] use a sum-of-Gaussians volumetric representation together with contour-based refinement and successfully demonstrate human shape recovery from multi-view videos with optimization techniques. Even though such methods show compelling results, inherently they are limited by the quality of the 2D detections they use and depend on priors both on pose and shape parameters to regularize the highly complex and costly optimization process.

Deep neural networks provide an alternative approach that can be expected to learn appropriate priors automatically from the data. Dibra *et al.* [45] present one of the first approaches in this direction and train a CNN to estimate the 3D shape parameters from silhouettes, but assume a frontal input view. More recent approaches [14–16] train neural networks to predict the SMPL body parameters from an input image. Tan *et al.* [14] design an encoder-decoder architecture that is trained on silhouette prediction and indirectly regresses model parameters at the bottleneck layer. Tung *et al.* [15] operate on two consecutive video frames and learn parameters by integrating re-projection loss on the optical flow, silhouettes and 2D joints. Similarly, Kanazawa *et al.* [16] predict parameters with re-projection loss on the 2D joints and introduce an adversary whose goal is to distinguish unrealistic human body shapes.

Even though parameters of deformable body models provide a low-dimensional embedding of the 3D shape, predicting such parameters with a network requires learning a highly non-linear mapping. In our work we opt for an alternative volumetric representation that has shown to be effective for generic 3D objects [21] and faces [46]. The approach of [21] operates on low-resolution grayscale images for a few rigid object categories such as chairs and tables. We argue that human bodies are more challenging due to significant non-rigid deformations. To accommodate for such deformation, we use segmentation and 3D pose as proxy to 3D shape in addition to 2D pose [46]. Conditioning our 3D shape estimation on a given 3D pose, the network focuses on the more complicated problem of shape deformation. Furthermore, we regularize our voxel predictions with additional re-projection loss, perform end-to-end multi-task training with intermediate supervision and obtain volumetric body part segmentation.

Others have studied predicting 2.5D projections of human bodies. DenseReg [47] and DensePose [48] estimate image-to-surface correspondences, while [33] outputs quantized depth maps for SMPL bodies. Differently from these methods, our approach generates a full 3D body reconstruction.

Multi-task Neural Networks. Multi-task networks are well-studied. A common approach is to output multiple related tasks at the very end of the neural network architecture. Another, more recently explored alternative is to stack multiple subnetworks and provide guidance with *intermediate supervision*. Here, we only cover related works that employ the latter approach. Guiding CNNs with relevant cues has shown improvements for a number of tasks. For example, 2D facial landmarks have shown useful guidance for 3D face reconstruction [46] and similarly optical flow for action recognition [49]. However, these methods do not perform joint training. Recent work of [50] jointly learns 2D/3D pose together with action recognition. Similarly, [51] trains for 3D pose with intermediate tasks of 2D pose and segmentation. With this motivation, we make use of 2D pose, 2D human body part segmentation, and 3D pose, that provide cues for 3D human *shape* estimation. Unlike [51], 3D pose becomes an auxiliary task for our final 3D shape task. In our experiments, we show that training with a joint loss on all these tasks increases the performance of all our subnetworks (see Appendix C.1).

3 BodyNet

BodyNet predicts 3D human body shape from a single image and is composed of four subnetworks trained first independently, then jointly to predict 2D pose, 2D body part segmentation, 3D pose, and 3D shape (see Fig. 2). Here, we first discuss the details of the volumetric representation for body shape (Sect. 3.1). Then, we describe the multi-view re-projection loss (Sect. 3.2) and the multi-task training with the intermediate representations (Sect. 3.3). Finally, we formulate our model fitting procedure (Sect. 3.4).

3.1 Volumetric Inference for 3D Human Shape

For 3D human body shape, we propose to use a voxel-based representation. Our shape estimation subnetwork outputs the 3D shape represented as an occupancy map defined on a fixed resolution voxel grid. Specifically, given a 3D body, we define a 3D voxel grid roughly centered at the root joint, (i.e., the hip joint) where each voxel inside the body is marked as occupied. We voxelize the ground truth meshes (i.e., SMPL) into a fixed resolution grid using binvox [52,53]. We assume orthographic projection and rescale the volume such that the xy-plane is aligned with the 2D segmentation mask to ensure spatial correspondence with the input image. After scaling, the body is centered on the z-axis and the remaining areas are padded with zeros.

Our network minimizes the binary cross-entropy loss after applying the sigmoid function on the network output similar to [46]:

$$\mathcal{L}_v = \sum_{x=1}^{W}\sum_{y=1}^{H}\sum_{z=1}^{D} V_{xyz} \log \hat{V}_{xyz} + (1 - V_{xyz}) \log(1 - \hat{V}_{xyz}), \tag{1}$$

where V_{xyz} and $\hat{V}_{xyz}$ denote the ground truth value and the predicted sigmoid output for a voxel, respectively. Width (W), height (H) and depth (D) are 128 in our experiments. We observe that this resolution captures sufficient details.

The loss $\mathcal{L}_v$ is used to perform foreground-background segmentation of the voxel grid. We further extend this formulation to perform 3D body part segmentation with a multi-class cross-entropy loss. We define 6 parts (head, torso, left/right leg, left/right arm) and learn 7-class classification including the background. The weights for this network are initialized by the shape network by copying the output layer weights for each class. This simple extension allows the network to directly infer 3D body parts without going through the costly SMPL model fitting.

3.2 Multi-view Re-projection Loss on the Silhouette

Due to the complex articulation of the human body, one major challenge in inferring the volumetric body shape is to ensure high confidence predictions across the whole body. We often observe that the confidences on the limbs away from the body center tend to be lower (see Fig. 5). To address this problem, we employ additional 2D re-projection losses that increase the importance of the boundary voxels. Similar losses have been employed for rigid objects by [54,55] in the absence of 3D labels and by [21] as additional regularization. In our case, we show that the multi-view re-projection term is critical, particularly to obtain good quality reconstruction of body limbs. Assuming orthographic projection, the front view projection, $\hat{S}^{FV}$, is obtained by projecting the volumetric grid to the image with the *max* operator along the z-axis [54]. Similarly, we define $\hat{S}^{SV}$ as the *max* along the x-axis:

$$\hat{S}^{FV}(x, y) = \max_z \hat{V}_{xyz} \quad \text{and} \quad \hat{S}^{SV}(y, z) = \max_x \hat{V}_{xyz}. \tag{2}$$

The true silhouette, S^{FV}, is defined by the ground truth 2D body part segmentation provided by the datasets. We obtain the ground truth side view silhouette from the voxel representation that we computed from the ground truth 3D mesh: $S^{SV}(y, z) = \max_x V_{xyz}$. We note that our voxels remain slightly larger than the original mesh due to the voxelization step that marks every voxel that intersects with a face as occupied. We define a binary cross-entropy loss per view as follows:

$$\mathcal{L}_p^{FV} = \sum_{x=1}^{W}\sum_{y=1}^{H} S(x, y) \log \hat{S}^{FV}(x, y) + (1 - S(x, y)) \log(1 - \hat{S}^{FV}(x, y)), \tag{3}$$

$$\mathcal{L}_p^{SV} = \sum_{y=1}^{H}\sum_{z=1}^{D} S(y, z) \log \hat{S}^{SV}(y, z) + (1 - S(y, z)) \log(1 - \hat{S}^{SV}(y, z)). \tag{4}$$

We train the shape estimation network initially with $\mathcal{L}_v$. Then, we continue training with a combined loss: $\lambda_v \mathcal{L}_v + \lambda_p^{FV} \mathcal{L}_p^{FV} + \lambda_p^{SV} \mathcal{L}_p^{SV}$, Sect. 3.3 gives details on how to set the relative weighting of the losses. Sect. 4.3 demonstrates experimentally the benefits of the multi-view re-projection loss.

3.3 Multi-task Learning with Intermediate Supervision

The input to the 3D shape estimation subnetwork is composed by combining RGB, 2D pose, segmentation, and 3D pose predictions. Here, we present the subnetworks used to predict these intermediate representations and detail our multi-task learning procedure. The architecture for each subnetwork is based on a stacked hourglass network [1], where the output is over a spatial grid and is, thus, convenient for pixel- and voxel-level tasks as in our case.

2D Pose. Following the work of Newell *et al.* [1], we use a heatmap representation of 2D pose. We predict one heatmap for each body joint where a Gaussian with fixed variance is centered at the corresponding image location of the joint. The final joint locations are identified as the pixel indices with the maximum value over each output channel. We use the first two stacks of an hourglass network to map RGB features $3 \times 256 \times 256$ to 2D joint heatmaps $16 \times 64 \times 64$ as in [1] and predict 16 body joints. The mean-squared error between the ground truth and predicted 2D heatmaps is $\mathcal{L}_j^{2D}$.

2D Part Segmentation. Our body part segmentation network is adopted from [33] and is trained on the SMPL [17] anatomic parts defined by [33]. The architecture is similar to the 2D pose network and again the first two stacks are used. The network predicts one heatmap per body part given the input RGB image, which results in an output resolution of $15 \times 64 \times 64$ for 15 body parts. The spatial cross-entropy loss is denoted with $\mathcal{L}_s$.

3D Pose. Estimating the 3D joint locations from a single image is an inherently ambiguous problem. To alleviate some uncertainty, we assume that the camera intrinsics are known and predict the 3D pose in the camera coordinate system. Extending the notion of 2D heatmaps to 3D, we represent 3D joint locations with 3D Gaussians defined on a voxel grid as in [6]. For each joint, the network predicts a fixed-resolution volume with a single 3D Gaussian centered at the joint location. The $xy-$dimensions of this grid are aligned with the image coordinates, and hence the 2D joint locations, while the z dimension represents the depth. We assume this voxel grid is aligned with the 3D body such that the root joint corresponds to the center of the 3D volume. We determine a reasonable depth range in which a human body can fit (roughly 85cm in our experiments) and quantize this range into 19 bins. We define the overall resolution of the 3D grid to be $64 \times 64 \times 19$, i.e., four times smaller in spatial resolution compared to the input image as is the case for the 2D pose and segmentation networks. We define one such grid per body joint and regress with mean-squared error $\mathcal{L}_j^{3D}$.

The 3D pose estimation network consists of another two stacks. Unlike 2D pose and segmentation, the 3D pose network takes multiple modalities as input, all spatially aligned with the output of the network. Specifically, we concatenate RGB channels with the heatmaps corresponding to 2D joints and body parts. We upsample the heatmaps to match the RGB resolution, thus the input resolution becomes $(3 + 16 + 15) \times 256 \times 256$. While 2D pose provides a significant cue for the x, y joint locations, some of the depth information is implicitly contained in body part segmentation since unlike a silhouette, occlusion relations among individual body parts provide strong 3D cues. For example a discontinuity on the torso segment caused by an occluding arm segment implies the arm is in front of the torso. In Appendix C.4, we provide comparisons of 3D pose prediction with and without using this additional information.

Combined Loss and Training Details. The subnetworks are initially trained independently with individual losses, then fine-tuned jointly with a combined loss:

$$\mathcal{L} = \lambda_j^{2D}\mathcal{L}_j^{2D} + \lambda_s\mathcal{L}_s + \lambda_j^{3D}\mathcal{L}_j^{3D} + \lambda_v\mathcal{L}_v + \lambda_p^{FV}\mathcal{L}_p^{FV} + \lambda_p^{SV}\mathcal{L}_p^{SV}. \tag{5}$$

The weighting coefficients are set such that the average gradient of each loss across parameters is at the same scale at the beginning of fine-tuning. With this rule, we set $(\lambda_j^{2D}, \lambda_s, \lambda_j^{3D}, \lambda_v, \lambda_p^{FV}, \lambda_p^{SV}) \propto (10^7, 10^3, 10^6, 10^1, 1, 1)$ and make the sum of the weights equal to one. We set these weights on the SURREAL dataset and use the same values in all experiments. We found it important to apply this balancing so that the network does not forget the intermediate tasks, but improves the performance of all tasks at the same time.

When training our full network, see Fig. 2, we proceed as follows: (i) we train 2D pose and segmentation; (ii) we train 3D pose with fixed 2D pose and segmentation network weights; (iii) we train 3D shape network with all the preceding network weights fixed; (iv) then, we continue training the shape network with additional re-projection losses; (v) finally, we perform end-to-end fine-tuning on all network weights with the combined loss.

Implementation Details. Each of our subnetworks consists of two stacks to keep a reasonable computational cost. We take the first two stacks of the 2D pose network trained on the MPII dataset [56] with 8 stacks [1]. Similarly, the segmentation network is trained on the SURREAL dataset with 8 stacks [33] and the first two stacks are used. Since stacked hourglass networks involve intermediate supervision [1], we can use only part of the network by sacrificing slight performance. The weights for 3D pose and 3D shape networks are randomly initialized and trained on SURREAL with two stacks. Architectural details are given in Appendix B. SURREAL [33], being a large-scale dataset, provides pre-training for the UP dataset [34] where the networks converge relatively faster. Therefore, we fine-tune the segmentation, 3D pose, and 3D shape networks on UP from those pre-trained on SURREAL. We use RMSprop [57] algorithm with mini-batches of size 6 and a fixed learning rate of 10^{-3}. Color jittering augmentation is applied on the RGB data. For all the networks, we assume that the bounding box of the person is given, thus we crop the image to center the person. Code is made publicly available on the project page [58].

3.4 Fitting a Parametric Body Model

While the volumetric output of BodyNet produces good quality results, for some applications, it is important to produce a 3D surface mesh, or even a parametric model that can be manipulated. Furthermore, we use the SMPL model for our evaluation. To this end, we process the network output in two steps: (i) we first extract the isosurface from the predicted occupancy map, (ii) next, we optimize for the parameters of a deformable body model, SMPL model in our experiments, that fits the isosurface as well as the predicted 3D joint locations.

Formally, we define the set of 3D vertices in the isosurface mesh that is extracted [59] from the network output to be $\mathbf{V}^n$. SMPL [17] is a statistical model where the location of each vertex is given by a set $\mathbf{V}^s(\theta, \beta)$ that is formulated as a function of the pose (θ) and shape (β) parameters [17]. Given $\mathbf{V}^n$, our goal is to find $\{\theta^\star, \beta^\star\}$ such that the weighted Chamfer distance, i.e., the distance among the closest point correspondences between $\mathbf{V}^n$ and $\mathbf{V}^s(\theta, \beta)$ is minimized:

$$\{\theta^\star, \beta^\star\} = \underset{\{\theta,\beta\}}{\operatorname{argmin}} \sum_{\mathbf{p}^n \in \mathbf{V}^n} \min_{\mathbf{p}^s \in \mathbf{V}^s(\theta,\beta)} w^n \|\mathbf{p}^n - \mathbf{p}^s\|_2^2 +$$
$$\sum_{\mathbf{p}^s \in \mathbf{V}^s(\theta,\beta)} \min_{\mathbf{p}^n \in \mathbf{V}^n} w^n \|\mathbf{p}^n - \mathbf{p}^s\|_2^2 + \lambda \sum_{i=1}^{J} \|\mathbf{j}_i^n - \mathbf{j}_i^s(\theta, \beta)\|_2^2. \quad (6)$$

We find it effective to weight the closest point distances by the confidence of the corresponding point in the isosurface which depends on the voxel predictions of our network. We denote the weight associated with the point p^n as w^n. We define an additional term to measure the distance between the predicted 3D joint locations, $\{\mathbf{j}_i^n\}_{i=1}^J$, where J denotes the number of joints, and the corresponding joint locations in the SMPL model, denoted by $\{\mathbf{j}_i^s(\theta, \beta)\}_{i=1}^J$. We weight the contribution of the joints' error by a constant λ (empirically set to 5 in our experiments) since J is very small (e.g., 16) compared to the number of vertices (e.g., 6890). In Sect. 4, we show the benefits of fitting to voxel predictions compared to our baseline of fitting to 2D and 3D joints, and to 2D segmentation, i.e., to the inputs of the shape network.

We optimize for Eq. (6) in an iterative manner where we update the correspondences at each iteration. We use Powell's dogleg method [60] and Chumpy [61] similar to [13]. When reconstructing the isosurface, we first apply a thresholding (0.5 in our experiments) to the voxel predictions and apply the marching cubes algorithm [59]. We initialize the SMPL pose parameters to be aligned with our 3D pose predictions and set $\beta = \mathbf{0}$ (where $\mathbf{0}$ denotes a vector of zeros).

4 Experiments

This section presents the evaluation of BodyNet. We first describe evaluation datasets (Sect. 4.1) and other methods used for comparison in this paper (Sect. 4.2). We then evaluate contributions of additional inputs (Sect. 4.3) and losses (Sect. 4.4). Next, we report performance on the UP dataset (Sect. 4.5). Finally, we demonstrate results for 3D body part segmentation (Sect. 4.6).

4.1 Datasets and Evaluation Measures

SURREAL Dataset [33] is a large-scale synthetic dataset for 3D human body shapes with ground truth labels for segmentation, 2D/3D pose, and SMPL body parameters. Given its scale and rich ground truth, we use SURREAL in this work for training and testing. Previous work demonstrating successful use of synthetic images of people for training visual models include [62–64]. Given the SMPL shape and pose parameters, we compute the ground truth 3D mesh. We use the standard train split [33]. For testing, we use the middle frame of the middle clip of each test sequence, which makes a total of 507 images. We observed that testing on the full test set of 12, 528 images yield similar results. To evaluate the quality of our shape predictions for difficult cases, we define two subsets with extreme body shapes, similar to what is done for example in optical flow [65]. We compute the surface distance between the average shape ($\beta = \mathbf{0}$) given the ground truth pose and the true shape. We take the 10th (*s10*) and 20th (*s20*) percentile of this distance distribution that represent the meshes with extreme body shapes.

Unite the People Dataset (UP) [34] is a recent collection of multiple datasets (e.g., MPII [56], LSP [66]) providing additional annotations for each image. The annotations include 2D pose with 91 keypoints, 31 body part segments, and 3D SMPL models. The ground truth is acquired in a semi-automatic way and is therefore imprecise. We evaluate our 3D body shape estimations on this dataset. We report errors on two different subsets of the test set where 2D segmentations as well as pseudo 3D ground truth are available. We use notation T1 for images from the LSP subset [34], and T2 for images used by [14].

3D Shape Evaluation. We evaluate body shape estimation with different measures. Given the ground truth and our predicted volumetric representation, we measure the intersection over union directly on the voxel grid, i.e., voxel IOU. We further assess the quality of the projected silhouette to enable comparison with [14,16,34]. We report the intersection over union (silhouette IOU), F1-score computed for foreground pixels, and global accuracy (ratio of correctly predicted foreground and background pixels). We evaluate the quality of the fitted SMPL model by measuring the average error in millimeters between the corresponding vertices in the fit and ground truth mesh (surface error). We also report the average error between the corresponding 91 landmarks defined for the UP dataset [34]. We assume the depth of the root joint and the focal length to be known to transform the volumetric representation into a metric space.

4.2 Alternative Methods

We demonstrate advantages of BodyNet by comparing it to alternative methods. BodyNet makes use of 2D/3D pose estimation and 2D segmentation. We define alternative methods in terms of the same components combined differently.

SMPLify++. Lassner *et al.* [34] extended SMPLify [13] with an additional term on 2D silhouette. Here, we extend it further to enable a fair comparison with BodyNet. We use the code from [13] and implement a fitting objective with additional terms on 2D silhouette and 3D pose besides 2D pose (see Appendix D). As shown in Table 2, results of SMPLify++ remain inferior to BodyNet despite both of them using 2D/3D pose and segmentation inputs (see Fig. 3).

Shape Parameter Regression. To validate our volumetric representation, we also implement a regression method by replacing the 3D shape estimation network in Fig. 2 by another subnetwork directly regressing the 10-dim. shape parameter vector β using L2 loss. The network architecture corresponds to the encoder part of the hourglass followed by 3 additional fully connected layers (see Appendix B for details). We recover the pose parameters θ from our 3D pose prediction (initial attempts to regress θ together with β gave worse results). Table 2 demonstrates inferior performance of the β regression network that often produces average body shapes (see Fig. 3). In contrast, BodyNet results in better SMPL fitting due to the accurate volumetric representation.

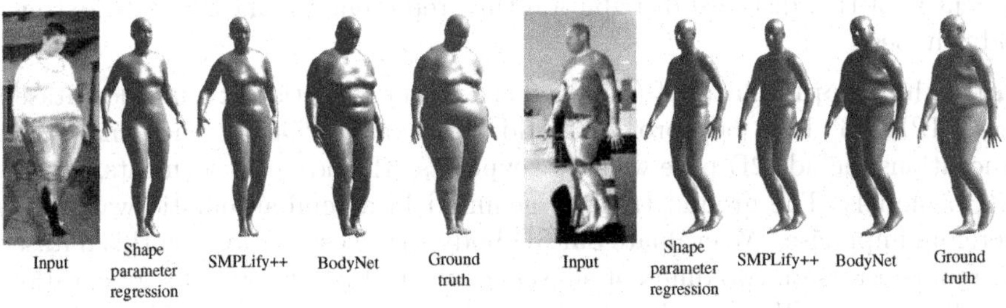

Fig. 3. SMPL fit on BodyNet predictions compared with other methods. While shape parameter regression and the fitting only to BodyNet inputs (SMPLify++) produce shapes close to average, BodyNet learns how the true shape observed in the image deviates from the average deformable shape model. Examples taken from the test subset *s10* of SURREAL dataset with extreme shapes.

Table 1. Performance on the SURREAL dataset using alternative combinations of intermediate representations at the input.

	voxel IOU (%)	SMPL surface error (mm)
2D pose	47.7	80.9
RGB	51.8	79.1
Segm	54.6	79.1
3D pose	56.3	74.5
Segm + 3D pose	56.4	74.0
RGB + 2D pose + Segm + 3D pose	**58.1**	**73.6**

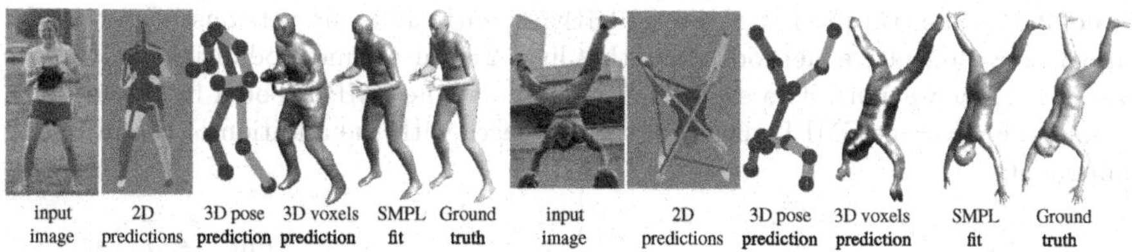

Fig. 4. Our predicted 2D pose, segmentation, 3D pose, 3D volumetric shape, and SMPL model alignments. Our 3D shape predictions are consistent with pose and segmentation, suggesting that the shape network relies on the intermediate representations. When one of the auxiliary tasks fails (2D pose on the right), 3D shape can still be recovered with the help of the other cues.

4.3 Effect of Additional Inputs

We first motivate our proposed architecture by evaluating performance of 3D shape estimation in the SURREAL dataset using alternative inputs (see Table 1). When only using one input, 3D pose network, which is already trained with additional 2D pose and segmentation inputs, performs best. We observe improvements as more cues, specifically 3D cues are added. We also note that intermediate representations in terms of 3D pose and 2D segmentation outperform RGB. Adding RGB to the intermediate representations further improves shape results on SURREAL. Figure 4 illustrates intermediate predictions as well as the final 3D shape output. Based on results in Table 1, we choose to use all intermediate representations as parts of our full network that we call BodyNet.

4.4 Effect of Re-projection Error and End-to-End Multi-task Training

We evaluate contributions provided by additional supervision from Sects. 3.2-3.3.

Effect of Re-projection Losses. Table 2 (lines 4–10) provides results when the shape network is trained with and without re-projection losses (see also Fig. 5). The voxels network without any additional loss already outperforms the baselines described in Sect. 4.2. When trained with re-projection losses, we observe increasing performance both with single-view constraints, i.e., front view (FV), and multi-view, i.e., front and side views (FV+SV). The multi-view re-projection loss puts more importance on the body surface resulting in a better SMPL fit.

Effect of Intermediate Losses. Table 2 (lines 7–10) presents experimental evaluation of the proposed intermediate supervision. Here, we first compare the end-to-end network fine-tuned jointly with auxiliary tasks (lines 9–10) to the networks trained independently from the fixed representations (lines 4–6). Comparison of results on lines 6 and 10 suggests that multi-task training regularizes all subnetworks and provides better performance for 3D shape. We refer to Appendix C.1 for the performance improvements on auxiliary tasks. To assess

Table 2. Volumetric prediction on SURREAL with different versions of our model compared to alternative methods. Note that lines 2–10 use same modalities (i.e., 2D/3D pose, 2D segmentation). The evaluation is made on the SMPL model fit to our voxel outputs. The average SMPL surface error decreases with the addition of the proposed components.

		full	*s20*	*s10*
1.	Tung *et al.* [15] (using GT 2D pose and segmentation)	74.5	-	-
Alternative methods:				
2	SMPLify++ (θ, β optimized)	75.3	79.7	86.1
3.	Shape parameter regression (β regressed, θ fixed)	74.3	82.1	88.7
BodyNet:				
4	Voxels network	73.6	81.1	86.3
5	Voxels network with [FV] silhouette re-projection	69.9	76.3	81.3
6	Voxels network with [FV+SV] silhouette re-projection	68.2	74.4	79.3
7	End-to-end without intermediate tasks [FV]	72.7	78.9	83.2
8	End-to-end without intermediate tasks [FV+SV]	70.5	76.9	81.3
9	End-to-end with intermediate tasks [FV]	67.7	74.7	81.0
10	End-to-end with intermediate tasks [FV+SV]	**65.8**	**72.2**	**76.6**

the contribution of intermediate losses on 2D pose, segmentation, and 3D pose, we implement an additional baseline where we again fine-tune end-to-end, but remove the losses on the intermediate tasks (lines 7–8). Here, we keep only the voxels and the re-projection losses. These networks not only forget the intermediate tasks, but are also outperformed by our base networks without end-to-end refinement (compare lines 8 and 6). On all the test subsets (i.e., full, *s20*, and *s10*) we observe a consistent improvement of the proposed components against baselines. Figure 3 presents qualitative results and illustrates how BodyNet successfully learns the 3D shape in extreme cases.

Comparison to the State of the Art. Table 2 (lines 1,10) demonstrates a significant improvement of BodyNet compared to the recent method of Tung *et al.* [15]. Note that [15] relies on ground truth 2D pose and segmentation on the test set, while our approach is fully automatic. Other works do not report results on the recent SURREAL dataset.

4.5 Comparison to the State of the Art on Unite the People

For the networks trained on the UP dataset, we initialize the weights pre-trained on SURREAL and fine-tune with the complete training set of UP-3D where the 2D segmentations are obtained from the provided 3D SMPL fits [34]. We show results of BodyNet trained end-to-end with multi-view re-projection loss. We provide quantitative evaluation of our method in Table 3 and compare to recent approaches [14,16,34]. We note that some works only report 2D metrics

Table 3. Body shape performance and comparison to the state of the art on the UP dataset. Unlike in SURREAL, the 3D ground truth in this dataset is imprecise.

		2D metrics			*3D metrics (mm)*	
		Acc. (%)	IOU	F1	Landmarks	Surface
T1	3D ground truth [34]	92.17	-	0.88	0	0
	Decision forests [34]	86.60	-	0.80	-	-
	HMR [16]	91.30	-	0.86	-	-
	SMPLify, UP-P91 [34]	90.99	-	0.86	-	-
	SMPLify on DeepCut [13][a]	91.89	-	**0.88**	-	-
	BodyNet *(end-to-end multi-task)*	92.75	**0.73**	0.84	**83.3**	**102.5**
T2	3D ground truth [34][b]	95.00	0.82	-	0	0
	Indirect learning [14]	**95.00**	**0.83**	-	190.0	-
	Direct learning [14]	91.00	0.71	-	105.0	-
	BodyNet *(end-to-end multi-task)*	92.97	0.75	**0.86**	**69.6**	**80.1**

[a] This result is reported in [34].
[b] This result is reported in [14].

measuring how well the 3D shape is aligned with the manually annotated segmentation. The ground truth is a noisy estimate obtained in a semi-automatic way [34], whose projection is mostly accurate but not its depth. While our results are on par with previous approaches on 2D metrics, we note that the provided manual segmentations and the 3D SMPL fits [34] are noisy and affect both the training and the evaluation [48]. Therefore, we also provide a large set of visual results in Appendices A, E to illustrate our competitive 3D estimation quality. On 3D metrics, our method significantly outperforms both direct and indirect learning of [14]. We also provide qualitative results in Fig. 4 where we show both the intermediate outputs and the final 3D shape predicted by our method. We observe that voxel predictions are aligned with the 3D pose predictions and provide a robust SMPL fit. We refer to Appendix E for an analysis on the type of segmentation used as re-projection supervision.

4.6 3D Body Part Segmentation

As described in Sect. 3.1, we extend our method to produce not only the foreground voxels for a human body, but also the 3D part labeling. We report quantitative results on SURREAL in Table 4 where accurate ground truth is available. When the parts are combined, the foreground IOU becomes 58.9 which is comparable to 58.1 reported in Table 1. We provide qualitative results in Fig. 6 on the UP dataset where the parts network is only trained on SURREAL. To the best of our knowledge, we present the first method for 3D body part labeling from a single image with an end-to-end approach. We infer volumetric body parts directly with a network without iterative fitting of a deformable model and obtain successful results. Performance-wise BodyNet can produce foreground and per-limb voxels in 0.28s and 0.58s per image, respectively, using modern GPUs.

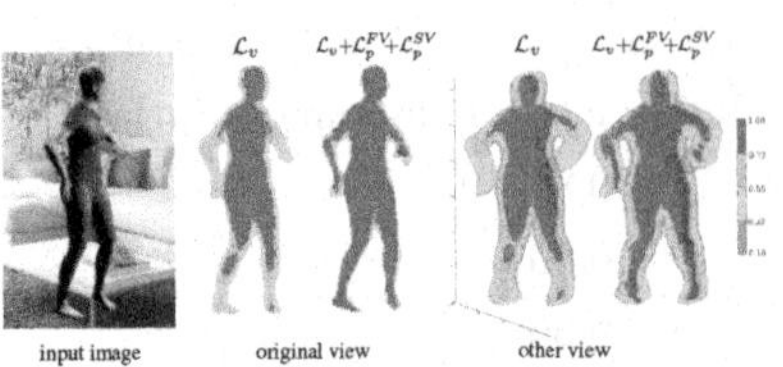

Fig. 5. Voxel predictions color-coded based on the confidence values. Notice that our combined 3D and re-projection loss enables our network to make more confident predictions across the whole body. Example taken from SURREAL.

Fig. 6. BodyNet is able to directly regress volumetric body parts from a single image on examples from UP.

Table 4. 3D body part segmentation performance measured per part on SURREAL. The articulated and small limbs appear more difficult than torso.

	Head	Torso	Left arm	Right arm	Left leg	Right leg	Background	Foreground
Voxel IOU (%)	49.8	67.9	29.6	28.3	46.3	46.3	99.1	58.9

5 Conclusion

We have presented BodyNet, a fully automatic end-to-end multi-task network architecture that predicts the 3D human body shape from a single image. We have shown that joint training with intermediate tasks significantly improves the results. We have also demonstrated that the volumetric regression together with a multi-view re-projection loss is effective for representing human bodies. Moreover, with this flexible representation, our framework allows us to extend our approach to demonstrate impressive results on 3D body part segmentation from a single image. We believe that BodyNet can provide a trainable building block for future methods that make use of 3D body information, such as virtual cloth-change. Furthermore, we believe exploring the limits of using only intermediate representations is an interesting research direction for 3D tasks where acquiring training data is impractical. Another future direction is to study the 3D body shape under clothing. Volumetric representation can potentially capture such additional geometry if training data is provided.

Acknowledgement. This work was supported in part by Adobe Research, ERC grants ACTIVIA and ALLEGRO, the MSR-Inria joint lab, the Alexander von Humbolt Foundation, the Louis Vuitton ENS Chair on Artificial Intelligence, DGA project DRAAF, an Amazon academic research award, and an Intel gift.

References

1. Newell, A., Yang, K., Deng, J.: Stacked hourglass networks for human pose estimation. In: Leibe, B., Matas, J., Sebe, N., Welling, M. (eds.) ECCV 2016. LNCS, vol. 9912, pp. 483–499. Springer, Cham (2016). https://doi.org/10.1007/978-3-319-46484-8_29
2. Wei, S.E., Ramakrishna, V., Kanade, T., Sheikh, Y.: Convolutional pose machines. In: CVPR (2016)
3. Pishchulin, L., et al.: DeepCut: joint subset partition and labeling for multi person pose estimation. In: CVPR (2016)
4. Cao, Z., Simon, T., Wei, S.E., Sheikh, Y.: Realtime multi-person 2D pose estimation using part affinity fields. In: CVPR (2017)
5. Martinez, J., Hossain, R., Romero, J., Little, J.J.: A simple yet effective baseline for 3D human pose estimation. In: ICCV (2017)
6. Pavlakos, G., Zhou, X., Derpanis, K.G., Daniilidis, K.: Coarse-to-fine volumetric prediction for single-image 3D human pose. In: CVPR (2017)
7. Rogez, G., Weinzaepfel, P., Schmid, C.: LCR-Net: localization-classification-regression for human pose. In: CVPR (2017)
8. Zhou, X., Huang, Q., Sun, X., Xue, X., Wei, Y.: Towards 3D human pose estimation in the wild: a weakly-supervised approach. In: ICCV (2017)
9. Leroy, V., Franco, J.S., Boyer, E.: Multi-view dynamic shape refinement using local temporal integration. In: ICCV (2017)
10. Loper, M.M., Mahmood, N., Black, M.J.: MoSh: motion and shape capture from sparse markers. In: SIGGRAPH (2014)
11. von Marcard, T., Rosenhahn, B., Black, M., Pons-Moll, G.: Sparse inertial poser: automatic 3D human pose estimation from sparse IMUs. In: Eurographics (2017)
12. Yang, J., Franco, J.-S., Hétroy-Wheeler, F., Wuhrer, S.: Estimation of human body shape in motion with wide clothing. In: Leibe, B., Matas, J., Sebe, N., Welling, M. (eds.) ECCV 2016. LNCS, vol. 9908, pp. 439–454. Springer, Cham (2016). https://doi.org/10.1007/978-3-319-46493-0_27
13. Bogo, F., Kanazawa, A., Lassner, C., Gehler, P., Romero, J., Black, M.J.: Keep It SMPL: automatic estimation of 3d human pose and shape from a single image. In: Leibe, B., Matas, J., Sebe, N., Welling, M. (eds.) ECCV 2016. LNCS, vol. 9909, pp. 561–578. Springer, Cham (2016). https://doi.org/10.1007/978-3-319-46454-1_34
14. Tan, V., Budvytis, I., Cipolla, R.: Indirect deep structured learning for 3D human body shape and pose prediction. In: BMVC (2017)
15. Tung, H., Tung, H., Yumer, E., Fragkiadaki, K.: Self-supervised learning of motion capture. In: NIPS (2017)
16. Kanazawa, A., Black, M.J., Jacobs, D.W., Malik, J.: End-to-end recovery of human shape and pose. In: CVPR (2018)
17. Loper, M., Mahmood, N., Romero, J., Pons-Moll, G., Black, M.: SMPL: a skinned multi-person linear model. In: SIGGRAPH (2015)
18. Krizhevsky, A., Sutskever, I., Hinton, G.E.: ImageNet classification with deep convolutional neural networks. In: NIPS (2012)
19. LeCun, Y., et al.: Backpropagation applied to handwritten zip code recognition. Neural Comput. **1**(4), 541–551 (1989)
20. Maturana, D., Scherer, S.: VoxNet: a 3D convolutional neural network for real-time object recognition. In: IROS (2015)
21. Yan, X., Yang, J., Yumer, E., Guo, Y., Lee, H.: Perspective transformer nets: learning single-view 3D object reconstruction without 3D supervision. In: NIPS (2016)

22. Yumer, M.E., Mitra, N.J.: Learning semantic deformation flows with 3D convolutional networks. In: Leibe, B., Matas, J., Sebe, N., Welling, M. (eds.) ECCV 2016. LNCS, vol. 9910, pp. 294–311. Springer, Cham (2016). https://doi.org/10.1007/978-3-319-46466-4_18
23. Yumer, M.E., Mitra, N.J.: Learning semantic deformation flows with 3D convolutional networks. In: Leibe, B., Matas, J., Sebe, N., Welling, M. (eds.) ECCV 2016. LNCS, vol. 9910, pp. 294–311. Springer, Cham (2016). https://doi.org/10.1007/978-3-319-46466-4_18
24. Tatarchenko, M., Dosovitskiy, A., Brox, T.: Octree generating networks: Efficient convolutional architectures for high-resolution 3D outputs. In: ICCV (2017)
25. Riegler, G., Ulusoy, A.O., Geiger, A.: OctNet: learning deep 3D representations at high resolutions. In: CVPR (2017)
26. Wang, P.S., Liu, Y., Guo, Y.X., Sun, C.Y., Tong, X.: O-CNN: Octree-based convolutional neural networks for 3D shape analysis. In: SIGGRAPH (2017)
27. Riegler, G., Ulusoy, A.O., Bischof, H., Geiger, A.: OctNetFusion: learning depth fusion from data. In: 3DV (2017)
28. Su, H., Fan, H., Guibas, L.: A point set generation network for 3D object reconstruction from a single image. In: CVPR (2017)
29. Su, H., Qi, C., Mo, K., Guibas, L.: PointNet: deep learning on point sets for 3D classification and segmentation. In: CVPR (2017)
30. Deng, H., Birdal, T., Ilic, S.: PPFNet: global context aware local features for robust 3D point matching. In: CVPR (2018)
31. Groueix, T., Fisher, M., Kim, V.G., Russell, B., Aubry, M.: AtlasNet: a Papier-Mâché approach to learning 3D surface generation. In: CVPR (2018)
32. Toshev, A., Szegedy, C.: DeepPose: human pose estimation via deep neural networks. In: CVPR (2014)
33. Varol, G., et al.: Learning from synthetic humans. In: CVPR (2017)
34. Lassner, C., Romero, J., Kiefel, M., Bogo, F., Black, M.J., Gehler, P.V.: Unite the people: closing the loop between 3D and 2D human representations. In: CVPR (2017)
35. Ionescu, C., Papava, D., Olaru, V., Sminchisescu, C.: Human3.6M: large scale datasets and predictive methods for 3D human sensing in natural environments. PAMI **36**(7), 1325–1339 (2014)
36. Kostrikov, I., Gall, J.: Depth sweep regression forests for estimating 3D human pose from images. In: BMVC (2014)
37. Yasin, H., Iqbal, U., Kruger, B., Weber, A., Gall, J.: A dual-source approach for 3D pose estimation from a single image. In: CVPR (2016)
38. Rogez, G., Schmid, C.: MoCap-guided data augmentation for 3D pose estimation in the wild. In: NIPS (2016)
39. Balan, A., Sigal, L., Black, M.J., Davis, J., Haussecker, H.: Detailed human shape and pose from images. In: CVPR (2007)
40. Guan, P., Weiss, A., O. Balan, A., Black, M.: Estimating human shape and pose from a single image. In: ICCV (2009)
41. Anguelov, D., Srinivasan, P., Koller, D., Thrun, S., Rodgers, J., Davis, J.: SCAPE: shape completion and animation of people. In: SIGGRAPH (2005)
42. Huang, Y., et al.: Towards accurate marker-less human shape and pose estimation over time. In: 3DV (2017)
43. Alldieck, T., Kassubeck, M., Wandt, B., Rosenhahn, B., Magnor, M.: Optical flow-based 3D human motion estimation from monocular video. In: GCPR (2017)

44. Rhodin, H., Robertini, N., Casas, D., Richardt, C., Seidel, H.-P., Theobalt, C.: General automatic human shape and motion capture using volumetric contour cues. In: Leibe, B., Matas, J., Sebe, N., Welling, M. (eds.) ECCV 2016. LNCS, vol. 9909, pp. 509–526. Springer, Cham (2016). https://doi.org/10.1007/978-3-319-46454-1_31
45. Dibra, E., Jain, H., Öztireli, C., Ziegler, R., Gross, M.: HS-Nets: estimating human body shape from silhouettes with convolutional neural networks. In: 3DV (2016)
46. Jackson, A.S., Bulat, A., Argyriou, V., Tzimiropoulos, G.: Large pose 3D face reconstruction from a single image via direct volumetric CNN regression. In: ICCV (2017)
47. Güler, R.A., George, T., Antonakos, E., Snape, P., Zafeiriou, S., Kokkinos, I.: DenseReg: fully convolutional dense shape regression in-the-wild. In: CVPR (2017)
48. Güler, R.A., Neverova, N., Kokkinos, I.: DensePose: dense human pose estimation in the wild. In: CVPR (2018)
49. Simonyan, K., Zisserman, A.: Two-stream convolutional networks for action recognition in videos. In: NIPS (2014)
50. Luvizon, D.C., Picard, D., Tabia, H.: 2D/3D pose estimation and action recognition using multitask deep learning. In: CVPR (2018)
51. Popa, A., Zanfir, M., Sminchisescu, C.: Deep multitask architecture for integrated 2D and 3D human sensing. In: CVPR (2017)
52. Nooruddin, F.S., Turk, G.: Simplification and repair of polygonal models using volumetric techniques. IEEE Trans. Vis. Comput. Graph. **9**(2), 191–205 (2003)
53. Min, P.: binvox. http://www.patrickmin.com/binvox
54. Zhu, R., Kiani, H., Wang, C., Lucey, S.: Rethinking reprojection: closing the loop for pose-aware shape reconstruction from a single image. In: ICCV (2017)
55. Tulsiani, S., Zhou, T., Efros, A.A., Malik, J.: Multi-view supervision for single-view reconstruction via differentiable ray consistency. In: CVPR (2017)
56. Andriluka, M., Pishchulin, L., Gehler, P., Schiele, B.: 2D human pose estimation: new benchmark and state of the art analysis. In: CVPR (2014)
57. Tieleman, T., Hinton, G.: Lecture 6.5—RmsProp: divide the gradient by a running average of its recent magnitude. COURSERA: Neural Networks for Machine Learning (2012)
58. http://www.di.ens.fr/willow/research/bodynet/
59. Lewiner, T., Lopes, H., Vieira, A.W., Tavares, G.: Efficient implementation of marching cubes cases with topological guarantees. J. Graph. Tools **8**(2), 1–15 (2003)
60. Nocedal, J., Wright, S.J.: Numerical Optimization. Springer, New York (2006). https://doi.org/10.1007/978-0-387-40065-5
61. http://chumpy.org
62. Barbosa, I.B., Cristani, M., Caputo, B., Rognhaugen, A., Theoharis, T.: Looking beyond appearances: synthetic training data for deep CNNs in re-identification. CVIU **167**, 50–62 (2018)
63. Ghezelghieh, M.F., Kasturi, R., Sarkar, S.: Learning camera viewpoint using CNN to improve 3D body pose estimation. In: 3DV (2016)
64. Chen, W., et al.: Synthesizing training images for boosting human 3D pose estimation. In: 3DV (2016)

65. Butler, D.J., Wulff, J., Stanley, G.B., Black, M.J.: A naturalistic open source movie for optical flow evaluation. In: Fitzgibbon, A., Lazebnik, S., Perona, P., Sato, Y., Schmid, C. (eds.) ECCV 2012. LNCS, vol. 7577, pp. 611–625. Springer, Heidelberg (2012). https://doi.org/10.1007/978-3-642-33783-3_44
66. Johnson, S., Everingham, M.: Clustered pose and nonlinear appearance models for human pose estimation. In: BMVC (2010)

Learning to Segment via Cut-and-Paste

Tal Remez[1(✉)], Jonathan Huang[2], and Matthew Brown[2]

[1] Google, Tel Aviv, Israel
talremez@google.com
[2] Google, Seattle, USA
jonathanhuang@google.com, mtbr@google.com

Abstract. This paper presents a weakly-supervised approach to object instance segmentation. Starting with known or predicted object bounding boxes, we learn object masks by playing a game of cut-and-paste in an adversarial learning setup. A mask generator takes a detection box and Faster R-CNN features, and constructs a segmentation mask that is used to cut-and-paste the object into a new image location. The discriminator tries to distinguish between real objects, and those cut and pasted via the generator, giving a learning signal that leads to improved object masks. We verify our method experimentally using Cityscapes, COCO, and aerial image datasets, learning to segment objects without ever having seen a mask in training. Our method exceeds the performance of existing weakly supervised methods, without requiring hand-tuned segment proposals, and reaches 90% of supervised performance.

Keywords: Instance segmentation · Weakly-supervised
Deep-learning

1 Introduction

Instance segmentation has seen much progress in recent years, with methods such as Mask R-CNN [1] now able to generate realistic masks, by building on the success of convolutional object detectors [2,3]. Success has come at the cost of a significant labelling effort; the COCO segmentation dataset [4] required around 40 person-years of labelling time for its 80 object categories.

Modern object detection datasets have bounding boxes for up to 30k categories [5]. While still a considerable labelling effort, these bounding boxes can be generated roughly 10 times faster than the per-pixel segmentation masks required for fully supervised instance segmentation training. Moreover, labelling boxes has fixed complexity, whereas pixel-level labelling takes longer for objects with complex boundaries. In the COCO dataset, for example, some complex object classes, such as 'bicycle', are at best approximately labelled (see Fig. 15 in [4]). This motivates the question we address in this paper (Fig. 2): can we learn instance segmentation directly from bounding box data, and without ground truth masks? We will propose a simple idea, which we call the "cut-and-paste prior", to solve this problem (see Fig. 1).

V. Ferrari et al. (Eds.): ECCV 2018, LNCS 11211, pp. 39–54, 2018.
https://doi.org/10.1007/978-3-030-01234-2_3

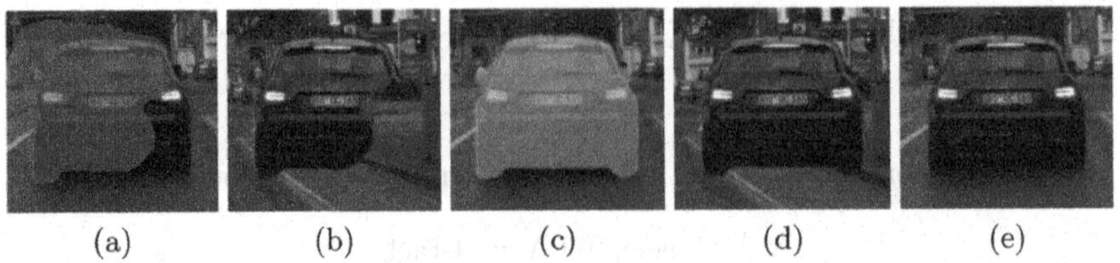

(a) (b) (c) (d) (e)

Fig. 1. Learning to Segment by Cut and Paste. We iterate to learn accurate segmentation masks by trying to generate realistic images. A poor mask estimate (a) generates an unconvincing paste (b), while a good mask (c) results in a convincing one (d). Training a discriminator network to distinguish pasted from real images (e) creates a learning signal that encourages the generator to create better segmentations.

Fig. 2. Our method learns to segment objects without ever seeing ground truth masks and uses only bounding boxes as input.

We are not the first to address the problem of box-supervised instance or semantic segmentation. Dai et al. propose a box-supervised method that uses an unsupervised candidate mask generator to create regression targets for semantic segmentation [6]. The process is then iterated with the learned mask generator. Papandreou et al. [7] propose a similar alternation, but using EM to calculate the pixel labels (E-step), and optimise the segmentation network parameters (M-step). "Simple Does It" by Khoreva et al. [8] also follow Dai et al. in proposing synthetic regression targets. They experiment with using detection boxes alone, as well as Grabcut [9] and MCG [10] proposal generators, and also extend their approach to instance segmentation (using just 1 iteration in this case). Deepcut [11] propose a modification to Grabcut using a CNN+CRF model. All of these approaches involve initialization and iteration between label estimation and generator training stages. Pathak et al. [12] take a different approach, specifying hand-tuned constraints on the output label space (e.g., 75% of pixels taking on the true label). Also related is [13], who grow object segmentation regions by sequentially discovering and erasing discriminative image regions, using classification rather than box supervision.

Our approach is qualitatively different from all these prior approaches. We require no segment proposals, pre-trained boundary detectors, or other hand-tuned initialization/constraints. Neither do we require iteration towards prediction and label consistency. Instead, our priors will be encapsulated in the structure of our generator/discriminator networks, and in our "cut-and-paste" prior for object segmentation. The cut-and-paste prior encapsulates the basic idea that objects can move independently of their background. More precisely, objects may be cut out from one portion of an image, and pasted into another, and still appear realistic (see Fig. 1). With the help of a discriminator network to judge realism, we can use this process to provide a training signal for an instance segmentation network.

We build on the successful approach of Generative Adversarial Networks (GANs) [14], which have proved to be effective in modelling realistic images, e.g., hallucinating faces [15] and translating between image modalities [16]. However, rather than trying to generate images, we aim to generate segmentation masks. This allows us to use objective measures of performance (e.g., IoU against ground truth) for evaluation. Related to our approach is the work of Luc et al. [17], who also use an adversarial network to train a (semantic) segmentation algorithm. However, different to our approach, they use ground truth label maps as input to the discriminator. In our work we assume no such ground truth is available at training time. Also related is the work of Hu et al. [18] who use a partially supervised approach to generate object masks for a very large set of categories. They achieve this by joint learning using a set of fully supervised object classes and a larger set of box-only supervised classes, with a transfer function to map between box estimation and mask segmentation parameters. This seems to be a promising approach. However, in this work we focus on the unsupervised case, with only bounding boxes available for training.

Note that our approach of using cut-and-paste to form a loss function is *not* the same as training data augmentation via cut-and-paste, e.g., [19], which takes existing masks and creates more training data out of it. This and related methods [20,21] do however exploit the same idea that image compositing can be used to create realistic imagery for training. They also note that object placement, lighting etc. are important; we revisit this topic in Sects. 2.1 and 4.3.

1.1 Contributions

The main contributions of this paper can be summarized as follows:

- We propose and formalize a new *cut-and-paste* adversarial training scheme for box-supervised instance segmentation, which captures an intuitive prior, that objects can move independently of their background.
- We discuss the problem of identifying *where* to paste new objects in an image. Even though objects are rarely truly independent of their background (e.g., cars do not typically appear in the middle of blue skies or on top of trees), we show that simple randomized heuristics for selecting pasting locations are surprisingly effective on real data.

- Finally we showcase the success and generality of our approach by demonstrating that our method effectively learns to segment objects on a variety of datasets (street scenes, everyday objects, aerial imagery), without ever having access to masks as supervision. We also show that our training method is stable and yields models that outperform existing weakly supervised methods, reaching 90% of supervised model performance.

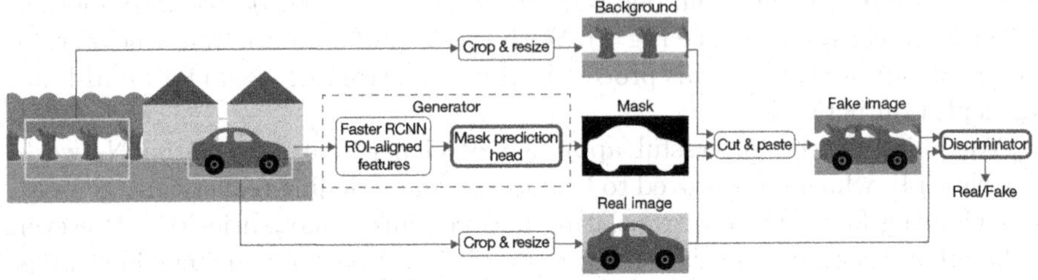

Fig. 3. Learning by cut-and-paste. A generator network receives a bounding box containing a car and predicts its mask. The discriminator alternately sees a cut+pasted car with a new background, or a real car image. Simultaneous training of generator and discriminator leads to improved object masks. Trainable blocks are outlined in **bold**.

2 An Adversarial Formulation of the Cut and Paste Loss

An overview of our learning approach is shown in Fig. 3. We wish to train a model taking the form: $\mathcal{M} = G(X, \mathcal{B})$ that predicts an instance mask $\mathcal{M}$ given an image X and a bounding box $\mathcal{B}$ surrounding the instance of interest. For simplicity we will ignore classes and typically assume that instances are of the same class (e.g., 'person' or 'car'), training an independent model per class. Intuitively, we would like to assign a low loss to a predicted mask if copying the pixels from the mask $\mathcal{M}$ and pasting into a new part of the image X yields a *plausible* image patch and high loss otherwise (see Fig. 1).

In order to measure the notion of "plausibility", we use a GAN, viewing the function G as a *generator*. Given a generated mask $\mathcal{M}$, we synthesize a new image patch F by compositing image $X_{\mathcal{B}}$ from bounding box $\mathcal{B}$ with a new background image $X_{\mathcal{B}'}$ from location $\mathcal{B}'$ (typically in the same image):

$$F = \mathcal{M}X_{\mathcal{B}} + (1 - \mathcal{M})X_{\mathcal{B}'}. \tag{1}$$

The fake image F is fed to a second model, the *discriminator*, whose job is to distinguish whether F is real or synthesized. We now simultaneously train the discriminator to distinguish reals from fakes and the generator to make the discriminator's error rate as high as possible. More formally, we maximize with respect to parameters of the discriminator D and minimize with respect to parameters of the generator G in the following loss function:

$$\mathcal{L}_{CPGAN} = \mathbb{E}\ \log D(X_{\mathcal{B}}) + \log(1 - D(F)). \tag{2}$$

(a) (b)

Fig. 4. Cut-and-paste locations. A few objects have been cut-and-pasted to new locations in the original image. In (a) they were pasted along the same scanline as their original position, making it harder to tell them apart (can you spot them?); In (b) they were pasted at random positions making it much easier.

We refer to this as the *cut-and-paste* loss, since it aims to align real images and their cut-and-pasted counterparts. Note that the fake image F is a function of the generator G via the mask $\mathcal{M} = G(X, \mathcal{B})$, as specified in Eq. 1. The expectations are over $(X, \mathcal{B}) \sim p_{data}$ being the input set of images and bounding boxes, with $\mathcal{B}'$ drawn randomly as described in the Sect. 2.1 below.

Over training iterations, the hope is that the only way that the generator can successfully "fool" the discriminator is by generating correct masks. We now discuss several critical stepping stones to get such a model to train effectively.

2.1 Where to Paste

The choice of where to paste an object to generate a realistic looking result is clearly important for human observers, e.g., see Fig. 4. It is also data dependent. For example, buildings may appear at any (x, y) location in our aerial imagery with equal probability (Fig. 11), but realistic pedestrian placement and scale is highly constrained in street scenes. Whilst sophisticated pasting strategies might be devised, we find that good results can still be obtained using simple ones. In this work we experiment with two main pasting strategies: (1) Uniform pasting: paste anywhere into the same image, taking care not to overlap the same object class, (2) Depth sensitive pasting: we take care to preserve the correct scale when pasting using knowledge of the scene geometry. We discuss this further in the experiments reported in Sect. 4.3 on the Cityscapes, COCO, and aerial imagery datasets.

2.2 Avoiding Degenerate Solutions

Our learning objective is based on realism in the pasted result; this strategy usually leads to good solutions, but there are a few degenerate cases. For example, realistic images can be generated by choosing all of the pixels or none of the pixels in the bounding box (though in the latter case this doesn't contain the object). Also, some objects are modular and part of the object can be pasted and still give a realistic image. We examine each of these cases in turn.

The first case (generator marks all pixels as foreground) can be mitigated by giving the discriminator a larger viewport than the region into which the generator pastes. Giving the discriminator a small band of context around the pasted object (typically 10% of box width) allows for easy identification of this failure mode, as the background will change abruptly at the bounding box borders.[1]

If the generator decides to label none of the pixels as belonging to the object, the resulting fake image will look realistic, but will not contain the object of interest. This case should be automatically solved in our framework, since the discriminator will expect to see the object present. However, we found that adding an explicit classification loss significantly aids stability and improves performance in some cases. To this end we add an additional classification network D_{CLS} which explicitly encourages the model to ensure that the object of interest is really present (see Fig. 10(b)). One way to think about this new loss is that our generator is now trying to fool two discriminators: one that had been trained on a previous classification task (and is frozen), and another that is training and evolving with the generator. This gives an additional classification loss term for the generator:

$$\mathcal{L}_{CLS} = \mathbb{E} \, \log(1 - D_{CLS}(F)). \quad (3)$$

A final failure mode can occur if the generator chooses to paste some subpart of an object that may still be realistic in isolation, e.g., part of a building or other modular structure. This is to some extent addressed by the classification loss $\mathcal{L}_{CLS}$, which favours complete objects being pasted.

2.3 Overall Loss Function

Our overall loss function is the sum of the cut+paste and classification losses:

$$\mathcal{L} = \mathcal{L}_{CPGAN} + w_{cls}\mathcal{L}_{CLS}. \quad (4)$$

In practice, we use a LSGAN [22] formulation, which converts min/max optimization of GAN loss terms of the form $\mathcal{L} = \mathbb{E} \, \log(1-D(X)) + \log(1-D(G(X)))$ into separate optimizations for the discriminator and generator:

$$\min_D \mathbb{E} \, (D(G(X))^2 + (D(X) - 1)^2, \; \min_G \mathbb{E} \, (D(G(X) - 1)^2. \quad (5)$$

3 Architecture

There are three modules in our model: (1) the generator, which predicts a mask, (2) the cut-and-paste module, which produces a "fake patch" given the predicted mask, and (3), the discriminator, which distinguishes between real and fake patches, see Fig. 3. In the following, we describe the architecture for each of these modules that we have used in our experiments.

[1] Note that this strategy will fail in cases where source and destination backgrounds are identical, e.g., pasting an airplane from one blue sky to another, but these cases are rare for most classes.

Table 1. Generator and discriminator architectures. Our generator takes ROI-aligned features from a Faster R-CNN detector and applies a mask prediction head similar to that used in Mask R-CNN [1]. Our discriminator is applied directly on 34 × 34 image patches. After each convolution we use ReLU nonlinearities for the generator and Leaky ReLUs (with $\alpha = 0.2$) for the discriminator.

Generator

Output size	Layer
7x7x2048	Input, ROI-aligned features
7x7x256	Conv, 1x1 × 256, stride 1
7x7x256	Conv, 3x3x256, stride 1
14x14x256	Bilinear upsampling
14x14x256	Conv, 3x3x256, stride 1
28x28x256	Bilinear upsampling
28x28x256	Conv, 3x3x256, stride 1
28x28x1	Conv, 3x3x1, stride 1
28x28x1	Sigmoid

Discriminator

Output size	Layer
34x34x3	Input image patch
32x32x64	Conv, 3x3x64, stride 1, valid
15x15x128	Conv, 3x3x128, stride 2, valid
7x7x256	Conv, 3x3x256, stride 2, valid
3x3x512	Conv, 3x3x512, stride 2, valid
4608	Flatten
2	Fully connected
2	Softmax

Generator: Our generator is similar to that of Mask R-CNN [1]. A ResNet-50 backbone is used to extract ROI-aligned features and a mask prediction head is applied to these features. Our mask prediction head is described in Table 1, and is comprised of a series of convolutions, bilinear upsampling operations, and a Sigmoid nonlinearity resulting in a 28 × 28 mask output. We find that using corner-aligned bilinear upsampling generally provides better results than transposed convolutions and nearest neighbour upsampling layers.

Cut-and-Paste Module: We implement the cut-and-paste operation using standard alpha compositing (Eq. 1). The inferred mask is typically at a lower resolution than the foreground and background images, so we downsample to the mask resolution before compositing. Note that careful sampling in this step is critical, as convolutional networks can easily detect any aliasing or blurring artifacts, which are easy indicators that an image is fake. As explained in Sect. 2.2, we allow the discriminator a larger viewport than the original mask size, therefore our 28 × 28 masks are padded with 3 pixels of zeros on each side.

Discriminator: Our discriminator receives an $N \times N$ image patch as input, and predicts whether the given patch is real or fake. Our discriminator architecture is presented in Table 1, and is comprised of a series of valid convolutions (convolutions without padding) followed by a fully connected layer and a Softmax.

Training Procedure: Our models are implemented in TensorFlow [23] and are trained using a batch size of 4 instances for the generator and 8 instances for the discriminator (4 real and 4 fake). We use the Adam optimizer [24] with learning rate of $5 \cdot 10^{-5}$, $\beta_1 = 0.9$, $\beta_2 = 0.999$, and $\epsilon = 10^{-8}$. We train for 1 million iterations, alternating optimization equally between generator and discriminator. Our supervised model is trained similarly but with a cross-entropy loss on the ground truth masks. The backbone generating the features for our generator was pretrained on the COCO detection challenge data and is held frozen through training. The rest of the generator and discriminator layers are initialized using random Xavier initialization [25]. CityScapes and COCO training data are augmented by adding random horizontal flips.

4 Experiments

In this section we present the results of experiments using street scenes (Cityscapes), common objects (COCO) and aerial image datasets. Overall results (Tables 2 and 3) indicate that our models are competitive or better than other weakly supervised baselines. We also investigate some of the strengths and failure modes of our approach, including analysing dataset specific performance, effect of pasting strategies, settings for loss hyperparameters, and the effect of data scaling.

Table 2. mIOU performance on Cityscapes

Method	Car	Person	Traffic-light	Traffic-sign
Box	0.62	0.49	0.76	0.79
GrabCut [9]	0.62	0.50	0.64	0.65
Simple Does It [8]	**0.68**	0.53	0.60	0.51
Cut&Paste (Ours)	0.67	**0.54**	**0.77**	**0.79**
FullySupervised	0.80	0.61	0.79	0.81

4.1 Evaluation Methodology and Baselines

We compare our proposed approach (which we will refer to in below tables as **Cut&Paste**) to a few baseline methods, all of which take as input (1) an image and (2) a bounding box surrounding the instance to be segmented, and output a segmentation mask. The simplest baseline strategy (which we call **Box**) is to simply declare all pixels within the given ground truth bounding box to be the foreground/object. Since bounding boxes are tight around the objects in the datasets that we use, this is often a reasonable guess, assuming that no additional information is available. Another baseline is the **GrabCut** [9] algorithm. We use 5 iterations of the OpenCV implementation, guiding with a central foreground rectangle 40% of the box size if the initial iterations return a zero-mask.

We also evaluate the performance of the recent **Simple Does It** approach by Khoreva et al. [8] by running their publicly available pretrained instance segmentation model $DeepLab_{BOX}$, which was trained on PASCAL VOC [26] and COCO.

In addition to these baselines, we also train a fully supervised version of our model (called **FullySupervised**), which uses the same architecture as our generator, but is trained using cross entropy loss against ground truth masks. This gives us an idea of the best performance we should expect from our weakly supervised methods.

For methods outputting low-resolution masks (this includes **Cut&Paste**, **FullySupervised**, and **Simple Does It**), we resize their masks using bicubic interpolation back to the original image resolution prior to evaluation.

In contrast to typical generative models of images based on GANs, we can evaluate our method based on objective measures. We present results in this section in terms of the mean intersection-over-union (*mIoU*) measure, a commonly used metric for segmentation. Since our bounding boxes are assumed to be given, we refrain from presenting average precision/recall based measures such as those used by the COCO dataset since they depend on the detected boxes.

4.2 CityScapes

The CityScapes dataset [27] consists of densely annotated imagery of street scenes from cameras mounted on a car. Images are usually wide enough that it is easy to find plausible pasting positions for fake objects, so one would expect our method to perform well on this kind of data.

To prepare the CityScapes data for training our models, we separate the official training set into a training set and a development set (the latter containing the sequences of Aachen, Bremen and Bochum), using the official validation set as a test set for all methods. We extract instance segmentation masks from the fine-grained annotated "left-camera" images for four classes: "car", "person",

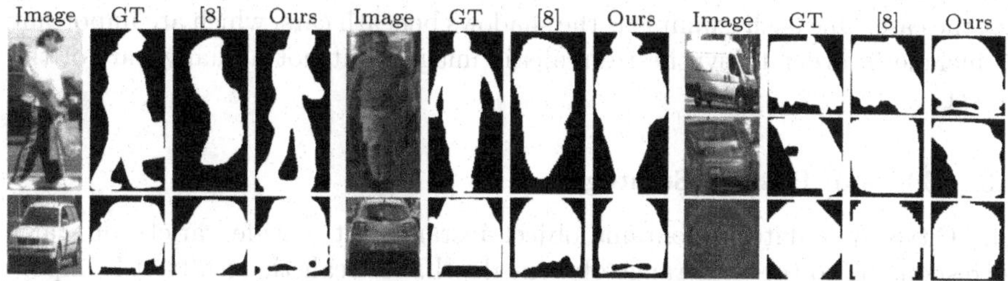

Fig. 5. Cityscapes mask comparison. From left to right: the original image, the ground truth mask (GT), the mask predicted by Simple Does It [8], and our mask.

Fig. 6. Cityscapes examples. Masks produced by our method.

"traffic-light" and "traffic-sign"[2], removing any cars or people smaller than 100 pixels along either axis, and any traffic lights or signs smaller than 25 pixels. Ground truth instance segmentations are used for evaluation, and for training the supervised version of our model. For the box-supervised version, we use a combination of ground truth bounding boxes from the 2,975 annotated images, and additional bounding boxes generated by running a Faster R-CNN object detector[3] on the 89,240 unannotated images in the `leftImg8bit_sequence` set.

Our results, shown in Table 2, demonstrate that across all four classes, we are consistently better than the **Box** and **GrabCut** baselines. Note that **Box** performs suprisingly well on some of these classes, notably signs and traffic lights, for which the ground truth bounding box is typically already a good fit. We also outperform the **Simple Does It** approach and are within 90% of our fully supervised baseline on all but the "Car" class. Figure 5 shows a qualitative comparison between masks generated by our method and those by **Simple Does It**. Typically the masks from both methods are comparable in quality, except in the case of people where our **Cut&Paste** method performs noticeably better, especially in fine details such as arms and legs. Figure 6 presents more examples of our masks. These results used the $\mathcal{L}_{CPGAN}$ loss, with zero weight to the classification loss term ($w_{cls} = 0$). See Sect. 4.6 for discussion and results of loss term weightings. All methods were evaluated on images at 600×1200 resolution.

Figure 7 shows "fake images" created by cut-and-pasting objects using our generated masks. Generally, the task of generating a realistic composite is well aligned with accurate object segmentation, but there are examples where this is not the case. One such example is the shadows beneath cars, which are important to include in order to synthesize realistic images, but not actually part of the object.

4.3 Effect of Pasting Strategy

The CityScapes dataset contains object instances at a wide variety of scales corresponding to the wide range of scene depth. For realistic results, it is important to paste objects at the appropriate scale (see Fig. 4). A simple heuristic to achieve this is to paste the object along the same horizontal scanline. We experiment with this approach, shifting with a mean translation of $2 \times W$ and standard deviation W (disallowing overlaps), where W is the bounding box width. This strategy leads to a 4% absolute increase in per-pixel mask prediction accuracy (from 68% to 72%), when compared to uniformly pasting objects along both the horizontal and vertical axes. As a sanity check, we also tried pasting Cityscape images into random COCO images for training. This reduced the accuracy to 60% on average and the training process was less stable.

---

2 "Traffic-light" and "Traffic-sign" instance segmentation masks are not provided with the dataset, but semantic segmentation masks *are* provided; thus to extract masks, we consider each connected component of these classes as a separate instance.

3 The detector is pretrained on the COCO dataset, the model can be found in TensorFlow Object Detection API model zoo: https://github.com/tensorflow/models/blob/master/research/object_detection/.

4.4 Sampling Issues for the Discriminator Network

Convolutional networks are highly sensitive to low-level image statistics, and unintended subtle cues may allow them to "cheat", rather than solving the intended problem. An example is described in [28], where a convnet used chromatic aberration cues to judge image position. We find a similar effect with sampling artifacts in our approach. In particular, we find that pasting with a mask at lower resolution than the source/destination images leads to a significant drop in performance. In our final implementation we perform compositing at the resolution of the mask. If we instead attempt to composite at 2× this resolution, we observe that the performance decreases from 71% to 66% in terms of per-pixel mask accuracy. We hypothesize that the discriminator picks up on the additional blurring incurred by the lower resolution mask in real vs fake images in this case. This suggests that careful image processing is important when dealing with adversarial networks.

Fig. 7. Examples of Cityscapes images and masks generated by our method. The top row shows the original image, and the middle row is the fake generated by compositing onto a random background with the inferred mask (bottom row).

Table 3. mIoU performance on the 10 most common COCO categories. The final column shows average performance across all 80 categories.

Method	Person	Chair	Car	Cup	Bottle	Book	Bowl	Handbag	Potted plant	Umbrella	All
Box	0.53	0.54	0.64	0.75	0.67	0.58	0.70	0.52	0.58	0.51	0.57
GrabCut [9]	0.57	0.54	0.59	0.70	0.62	0.58	0.69	0.53	0.57	**0.63**	0.61
Simple Does It [8]	**0.60**	**0.56**	0.62	0.72	0.67	0.55	0.72	0.54	0.62	0.61	0.62
Cut&Paste (Ours)	**0.60**	**0.56**	**0.66**	**0.78**	**0.74**	**0.61**	**0.77**	**0.58**	**0.65**	0.61	**0.64**
FullySupervised	0.70	0.63	0.75	0.83	0.79	0.67	0.81	0.63	0.70	0.67	0.70

4.5 COCO

The COCO dataset [4] contains a much wider variety of scene content and geometry than our CityScapes and aerial imagery experiments, and the objects typically occupy a much larger fraction of the image. Whilst these appear to be

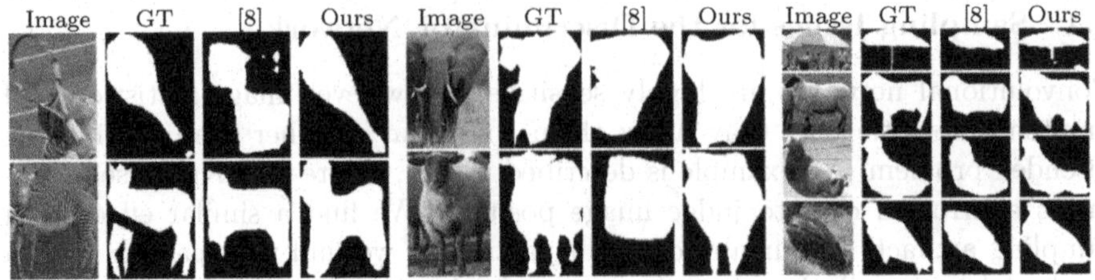

Fig. 8. COCO examples. From left to right: the original image, the ground truth mask (GT), the mask predicted by Simple Does It [8], and our mask.

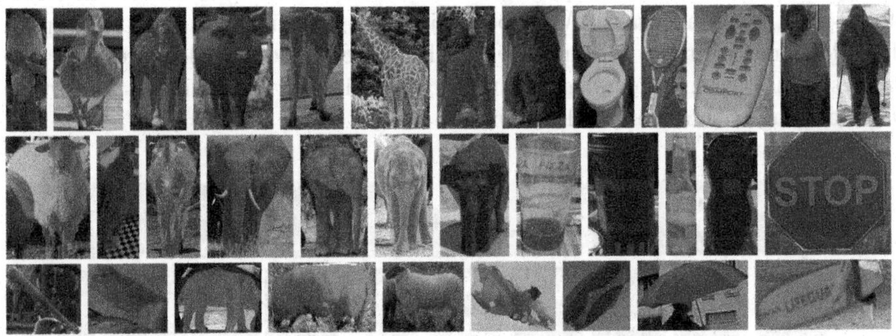

Fig. 9. COCO examples. Examples of the masks produced by our method.

more difficult conditions for our cut+paste approach, we find that our method still works well.

Since our method requires an object to be pastable within the same image at a new position, we remove objects that are more than 30% of image width as well as very small objects (less than 14 pixels). This results in removing 36% of the total number of objects, approximately half of which are too small and half too large. For all instances, we define the ground truth bounding box as the tightest axis-aligned box that encloses the instance mask. We set aside 15% of the official training set as a development set.

Table 3 presents the results for the 10 most common COCO classes, and summary results for all 80 classes. These models were trained using $w_{cls} = 0$. Our method exceeds the performance of **GrabCut** in all cases, and **Simple Does It** [8] in 70% of all COCO classes. We perform particularly well in comparison to [2] on "baseball bat" (0.43 vs 0.32 mIoU) and "skis" (0.27 vs 0.23 mIoU). These objects occupy a small fraction of the bounding box, which is problematic for [8], but fine for our method. We perform less well on "kite" (0.51 vs 0.56 mIoU) and "airplane" (0.48 vs 0.55). This is perhaps due to the uniform backgrounds that are common for these classes, which will reduce the training signal we see from the cut-and-paste operation (the boundary is arbitrary when pasting with identical backgrounds). See Figs. 8 and 9 for examples of masks produced by our method and by **Simple Does It**.

4.6 Aerial Imagery

To demonstrate the effectiveness of our method in a different setting, we experiment with building segmentation using a proprietary dataset of aerial images consisting of 1000×1000 image tiles with annotated building masks. From this dataset, we select a subset of images each of which contain no more than 15 houses (in order to allow space in the same image for pasting), yielding a dataset with 1 million instances. We also similarly generate a validation set containing 2000 instances. The large size of this dataset also allows us to test performance gains as a function dataset size.

For these experiments, we trained a Faster R-CNN Inception Resnet v2 (atrous) house detector using the TensorFlow Object Detection API [3] to be used as a backbone for feature extraction. Since our aerial images are taken at a single scale and orthorectified, we paste objects into images at locations selected uniformly at random in both x and y directions, rejecting pasting locations that overlap with other bounding boxes in the image.

Effect of Dataset Scale. Figure 10(a) shows the effect of data size on the average performance of our models. Increasing data size helps the training process, increasing the number of training instances from 5K to 1M reduces the mask prediction error by about 10%.

Effect of Loss Weightings. Figure 10(b) shows the effect of the classification loss weight w_{cls} on the overall performance of the model. With no classification loss ($w_{cls} = 0$) the performance is poor and the model is unstable, as indicated by the error bars. With increasing classification loss, performance improves and the error bars become tighter showing the training process is much more stable. The optimal weight in this case is in the range of $w_{cls} \in [1, 4]$. When conducting a similar experiment for the Cityscapes dataset we found that the classification weight increases stability but does not improve performance overall. This may be due to the high incidence of occlusion in our aerial image data, e.g., a subsection of a mask often resembles a building occluded by trees. Figure 11 shows

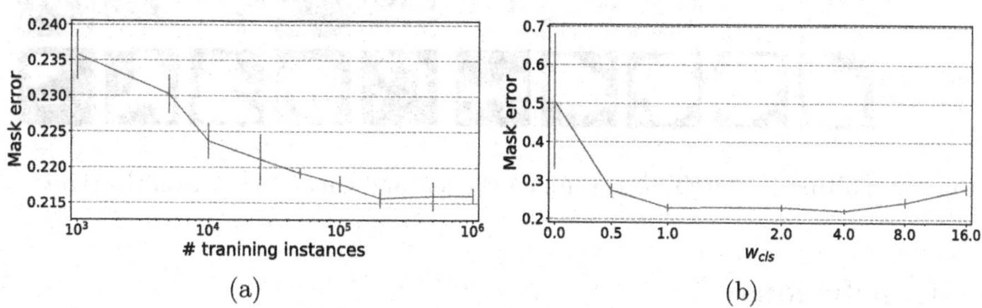

Fig. 10. Effect of classification loss and dataset scale on mask accuracy. (a) demonstrates the effect of scale of the training set on mask accuracy for aerial imagery. (b) demonstrates the effect of classification loss weight w_{cls} on the accuracy of the predicted masks; curves show mean and standard deviation over 4 runs for (a) and 5 models for (b).

Fig. 11. Aerial imagery examples. Examples of masks produced by our method.

a few examples of typical aerial images and the segmentation masks our method produces when trained using $w_{cls} = 1$.

4.7 Failure Cases

A few failure cases of our method are presented in Fig. 12. For the Giraffe and Kite examples, the mask is overestimated, but the non-unique backgrounds lead to convincing fake images. Note that the shadow of the Giraffe is copied in the first case, another common failure mode. Other examples include missing or added parts, such as the missing head and extra "skirt" connecting the legs for the people towards the right of the figure. Next to these is an interesting example with a person carrying a suitcase. The generator decides it would be more realistic to change this to legs in this example, presumably because suitcases are a rare occurrence in the training set. Note that the "fake" images are often still realistic in many of these cases.

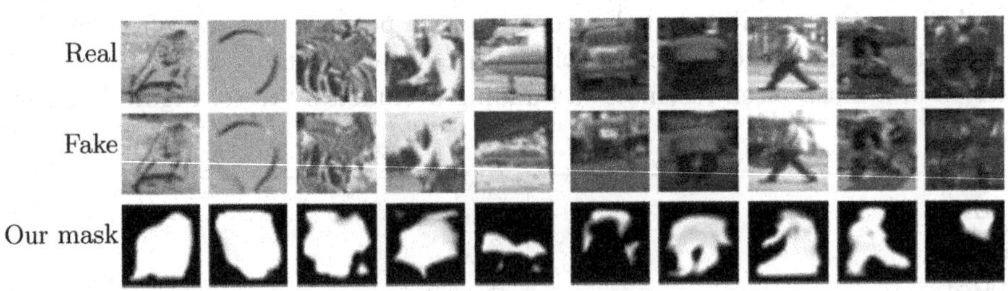

Fig. 12. Failures. COCO images are on the left and Cityscapes are on the right.

5 Conclusions

We have presented a new approach to instance segmentation that uses a simple property of objects, namely that they are "cut-and-pastable", coupled with a generative adversarial network to learn object masks. Our method exceeds the performance of existing box-supervised methods on the CityScapes and COCO datasets, with no mask ground truth and without the need for pre-trained segment or boundary detectors.

We have shown that intelligent object placement in the paste step can significantly improve mask estimation. This suggests an interesting direction for future work, where the compositing step is also data-dependent. For example, object placement, colour and illumination could depend on the destination image. Related work shows this works well for data augmentation [19–21].

More generally, and as in work such as [29], we could envisage a range of settings where vision+graphics imitate photography, with adversarial losses to jointly optimise image understanding and rendering stages. Such methods could open up the possibility of performing detailed visual perception with reduced dependence on large-scale supervised datasets.

References

1. He, K., Gkioxari, G., Dollár, P., Girshick, R.: Mask R-CNN. In: IEEE International Conference on Computer Vision (ICCV), pp. 2980–2988 (2017)
2. Ren, S., He, K., Girshick, R., Sun, J.: Faster R-CNN: towards real-time object detection with region proposal networks. In: Advances in Neural Information Processing Systems, pp. 91–99 (2015)
3. Huang, J., et al.: Speed/accuracy trade-offs for modern convolutional object detectors. In: IEEE CVPR (2017)
4. Lin, T.-Y., et al.: Microsoft COCO: common objects in context. In: Fleet, D., Pajdla, T., Schiele, B., Tuytelaars, T. (eds.) ECCV 2014. LNCS, vol. 8693, pp. 740–755. Springer, Cham (2014). https://doi.org/10.1007/978-3-319-10602-1_48
5. Krishna, R., et al.: Visual genome: connecting language and vision using crowdsourced dense image annotations. Int. J. Comput. Vis. **123**(1), 32–73 (2017)
6. Dai, J., He, K., Sun, J.: BoxSup: exploiting bounding boxes to supervise convolutional networks for semantic segmentation. In: Proceedings of the IEEE International Conference on Computer Vision, pp. 1635–1643 (2015)
7. Papandreou, G., Chen, L.C., Murphy, K.P., Yuille, A.L.: Weakly-and semi-supervised learning of a deep convolutional network for semantic image segmentation. In: Proceedings of the IEEE International Conference on Computer Vision, pp. 1742–1750 (2015)
8. Khoreva, A., Benenson, R., Hosang, J., Hein, M., Schiele, B.: Simple does it: weakly supervised instance and semantic segmentation. In: IEEE International Conference on Computer Vision and Pattern Recognition, pp. 876–885 (2017)
9. Rother, C., Kolmogorov, V., Blake, A.: GrabCut: interactive foreground extraction using iterated graph cuts. ACM Trans. Graph. **23**, 309–314 (2004)
10. Pont-Tuset, J., Arbelaez, P., Barron, J.T., Marques, F., Malik, J.: Multiscale combinatorial grouping for image segmentation and object proposal generation. IEEE Trans. Pattern Anal. Mach. Intell. **39**(1), 128–140 (2017)
11. Rajchl, M., et al.: DeepCut: object segmentation from bounding box annotations using convolutional neural networks. IEEE Trans. Med. Imaging **36**(2), 674–683 (2017)
12. Pathak, D., Krahenbuhl, P., Darrell, T.: Constrained convolutional neural networks for weakly supervised segmentation. In: Proceedings of the IEEE International Conference on Computer Vision, pp. 1796–1804 (2015)

13. Wei, Y., Feng, J., Liang, X., Cheng, M.M., Zhao, Y., Yan, S.: Object region mining with adversarial erasing: a simple classification to semantic segmentation approach. In: IEEE CVPR (2017)
14. Goodfellow, I., et al.: Generative adversarial nets. In: Advances in Neural Information Processing Systems, pp. 2672–2680 (2014)
15. Karras, T., Aila, T., Laine, S., Lehtinen, J.: Progressive growing of GANs for improved quality, stability, and variation. In: International Conference on Learning Representations (ICLR) (2018)
16. Isola, P., Zhu, J.Y., Zhou, T., Efros, A.A.: Image-to-image translation with conditional adversarial networks. In: International Conference on Computer Vision and Pattern Recognition (CVPR), pp. 1125–1134 (2017)
17. Luc, P., Couprie, C., Chintala, S., Verbeek, J.: Semantic Segmentation using adversarial networks. In: NIPS Workshop on Adversarial Training, Barcelona, Spain (December 2016)
18. Hu, R., Dollár, P., He, K., Darrell, T., Girshick, R.: Learning to segment every thing. In: IEEE Conference on Computer Vision and Pattern Recognition (CVPR) (2018)
19. Dwibedi, D., Misra, I., Hebert, M.: Cut, paste and learn: surprisingly easy synthesis for instance detection. In: Proceedings of the IEEE International Conference on Computer Vision, pp. 1301–1310 (2017)
20. Georgakis, G., Mousavian, A., Berg, A.C., Kosecka, J.: Synthesizing training data for object detection in indoor scenes. In: Robotics Science and Systems (RSS) (2017)
21. Abu Alhaija, H., Mustikovela, S.K., Mescheder, L., Geiger, A., Rother, C.: Augmented reality meets computer vision: efficient data generation for urban driving scenes. Int. J. Comput. Vis. **126**, 961–972 (2018)
22. Mao, X., Li, Q., Xie, H., Lau, R.Y., Wang, Z., Smolley, S.P.: Least squares generative adversarial networks. In: 2017 IEEE International Conference on Computer Vision (ICCV), pp. 2813–2821. IEEE (2017)
23. Abadi, M., et al.: TensorFlow: a system for large-scale machine learning. In: OSDI, vol. 16, pp. 265–283 (2016)
24. Kingma, D.P., Ba, J.: Adam: a method for stochastic optimization. In: International Conference on Learning Representations (ICLR) (2015)
25. Glorot, X., Bengio, Y.: Understanding the difficulty of training deep feedforward neural networks. In: Proceedings of the Thirteenth International Conference on Artificial Intelligence and Statistics, pp. 249–256 (2010)
26. Everingham, M., Van Gool, L., Williams, C.K.I., Winn, J., Zisserman, A.: The PASCAL Visual Object Classes Challenge 2012 (VOC2012) Results. http://www.pascal-network.org/challenges/VOC/voc2012/workshop/index.html
27. Cordts, M., et al.: The Cityscapes dataset for semantic urban scene understanding. In: Proceedings of the IEEE Conference on Computer Vision and Pattern Recognition (CVPR) (2016)
28. Doersch, C., Gupta, A., Efros, A.A.: Unsupervised visual representation learning by context prediction. In: Proceedings of the IEEE International Conference on Computer Vision, pp. 1422–1430 (2015)
29. Tung, H.Y.F., Harley, A.W., Seto, W., Fragkiadaki, K.: Adversarial inverse graphics networks: learning 2D-to-3D lifting and image-to-image translation from unpaired supervision. In: The IEEE International Conference on Computer Vision (ICCV), vol. 2 (2017)

Explainable Neural Computation via Stack Neural Module Networks

Ronghang Hu[1(✉)], Jacob Andreas[1], Trevor Darrell[1], and Kate Saenko[2]

[1] University of California, Berkeley, Berkeley, USA
{ronghang,jda,trevor}@eecs.berkeley.edu
[2] Boston University, Boston, USA
saenko@bu.edu

Abstract. In complex inferential tasks like question answering, machine learning models must confront two challenges: the need to implement a compositional *reasoning* process, and, in many applications, the need for this reasoning process to be *interpretable* to assist users in both development and prediction. Existing models designed to produce interpretable traces of their decision-making process typically require these traces to be supervised at training time. In this paper, we present a novel neural modular approach that performs compositional reasoning by automatically inducing a desired sub-task decomposition without relying on strong supervision. Our model allows linking different reasoning tasks though shared modules that handle common routines across tasks. Experiments show that the model is more interpretable to human evaluators compared to other state-of-the-art models: users can better understand the model's underlying reasoning procedure and predict when it will succeed or fail based on observing its intermediate outputs.

Keywords: Neural module networks · Visual question answering
Interpretable reasoning

1 Introduction

Deep neural networks have achieved impressive results on many vision and language tasks. Yet the predictive power of generic deep architectures comes at a cost of lost interpretability, as these architectures are essentially black boxes with respect to human understanding of their predictions. This can impair human users' trust in learning systems and make them harder to refine [8].

These issues have led to recent efforts in explaining neural models, ranging from building in attention layers to post-hoc extraction of implicit model attention, e.g. by gradient propagation [27,28,33,37,40], post-hoc natural language

Electronic supplementary material The online version of this chapter (https://doi.org/10.1007/978-3-030-01234-2_4) contains supplementary material, which is available to authorized users.

V. Ferrari et al. (Eds.): ECCV 2018, LNCS 11211, pp. 55–71, 2018.
https://doi.org/10.1007/978-3-030-01234-2_4

explanations [2,15] and network dissection [7]. Such approaches can highlight the image regions that are most important for predicting a particular label or provide a textual interpretation of the network output. However, explainable models of more complex problems involving multiple sub-tasks, such as Visual Question Answering (VQA) [6] and Referential Expression Grounding (REF) [30], are less studied in comparison. Complex problems may require several reasoning steps to solve. For example in Fig. 1, the question "There is a small gray block; are there any spheres to the left of it?" might require solving the following subtasks: find the "small gray block", look for "spheres to the left of it" and decide whether such object exists in the image. Therefore, a single heat-map highlighting important spatial regions such as [28] may not tell the full story of how a model performs.

In this paper, we present a new model that makes use of an explicit, modular reasoning process, but which allows fully differentiable training with back-propagation and without expert supervision of reasoning steps. Existing modular networks first analyze the question and then predict a sequence of pre-defined modules (each implemented as a neural net) that chain together to predict the answer. However, they need an "expert layout", or supervised module layouts for training the layout policy in order to obtain good accuracy. Our proposed approach, the *Stack Neural Module Network* or *Stack-NMN*, can be trained without layout supervision, and replaces the layout graph of [16] with a stack-based data structure. Instead of making discrete choices on module layout, in this work we make the layout soft and continuous, so that our model can be optimized in a fully differentiable way using gradient descent. We show that this improves both the accuracy and interpretability compared to existing modular approaches. We also show that this model can be extended to handle both Visual Question Answering (VQA) [6] and Referential Expression Grounding (REF) [30] seamlessly in a single model by sharing knowledge across related tasks through common routines as in Fig. 1.

A variety of different model architectures have been proposed for complex reasoning and question answering. Our evaluation in this paper focuses on both the accuracy and interpretability of these models. In particular, we ask: *does explicit modular structure make models more interpretable?* We use the CLEVR dataset [18] as a testbed, as it poses a task of high complexity. State-of-the-art models for this task vary in the degree to which they provide "explanations". Relation Networks [31] and FiLM [26] achieve high performance but do not expose their internal decision process. Other state-of-the-art models on CLEVR use recurrent layers to compute the answer over multiple steps and output different image and/or text attention at each step. These include modular networks [4,5,16,19,21], and non-modular recurrent attention models [17,36]. It has been suggested by the authors that the attention and/or module layouts inferred by these methods can be regarded as explanations of the networks' internal reasoning process. Yet, to the best of our knowledge, their meaningfulness to humans has never been explicitly evaluated; we provide a more rigorous assessment of the interpretability of multi-step attentional VQA models here.

We categorize existing multi-step models in terms of whether they have a discrete library of structured modules for each step (e.g., NMN and related approaches [3–5,16,19,21]), vs. homogeneous subtask computational elements (e.g., multi-hop attention networks [35,36], MAC [17], etc.). We assess these models below and identify tradeoffs between accuracy and interpretability of these existing model classes. We find that our proposed Stack-NMN model has comparable performance to existing modular approaches even without expert supervision, while achieving the greatest interpretability among evaluated models with respect to both subjective and objective measures of human understanding.

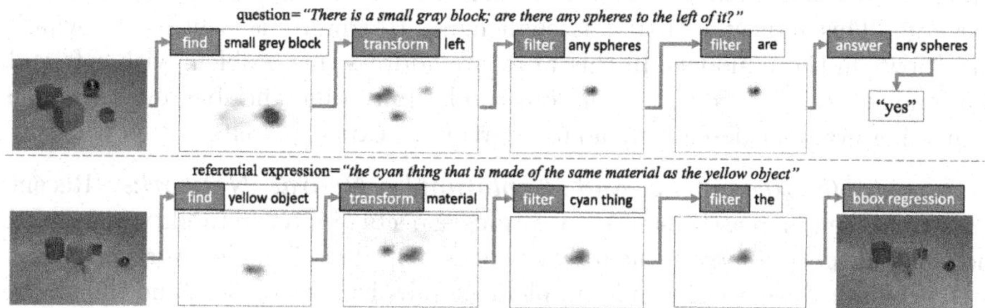

Fig. 1. Our model reveals interpretable subtask structure by inducing a decomposition of the reasoning procedure into several sub-tasks, each addressed by a neural module. It can simultaneously answer visual questions and ground referential expressions.

2 Related Work

Visual Question Answering (VQA). The task of visual question answering is to infer the answer based on the input question and image. Existing methods on VQA can be mainly categorized into holistic approaches (e.g., [1,10,17,26,31,35,36]), and neural module approaches [4,5,16,19,21]. The major difference between these two lines of work is that neural module approaches explicitly decompose the reasoning procedure into a sequence of sub-tasks, and have specialized modules to handle the sub-tasks, while holistic approaches do not have explicit sub-task structure, and different kinds of reasoning routines are all handled homogeneously.

Some holistic models perform sequential interactions between the image and the question. For example, SAN [36] uses multi-hop attention to extract information from the image. FiLM [26] uses multiple conditional batch normalization layers to fuse the image representation and question representation. Among these methods, MAC [17] performs multiple steps of reading and writing operations to extract information from the image and update its memory. Although these models have sequential interactions between the input image and the question, they do not explicitly decompose the reasoning procedure into semantically-typed sub-tasks. In our model, we adopt a similar textual attention mechanism as in [17] in Sect. 3.1, while also predicting module weights from the input text.

Neural Module Networks (NMNs). In NMN [5], N2NMN [16], PG+EE [19] and TbD [21], the inference procedure is performed by analyzing the question and decomposing the reasoning procedure into a sequence of sub-tasks. In [16,19,21], a layout policy is used to turn the question into a module layout. Then the module layout is executed with a neural module network. Here, given an input question, the layout policy learns what sub-tasks to perform, and the neural modules learn how to perform each individual sub-tasks.

However, it is shown in these previous work that "expert layouts" (i.e. human annotations of the desired layout) are needed to pretrain or supervise the layout policy in order to get compositional behavior and good accuracy. Without expert guidance, existing models suffer from significant performance drops or fail to converge. This indicates that it is challenging to simultaneously learn "what" and "how" in these models. In this work, we address this problem with soft and continuous module layout, making our model fully differentiable and trainable with using gradient descent without resorting to expert layouts.

Interpretable Reasoning and Explainable Neural Networks. Recent years have seen increased interest in various aspects of interpretability in learned models [24], particularly in neural networks [23]. This includes work aimed at both explaining the decision rules implemented by learned models, and the mechanisms by which these rules are derived from data [20,32]. In the present work we are primarily interested in the former. One line of research in this direction attempts to generate post-hoc explanations of decisions from generic model architectures, either by finding interpretable local surrogates in the form of linear models [29], logical rules [9,38] or natural language descriptions [2,39], or by visualizing salient features [27,28].

An alternative line of work investigates the extent to which models can be explicitly designed from the outset to provide enhanced interpretability, where main focus of study has been visual attention [22,25]. While the various modular approaches described above are sometimes described as "interpretable" [16], we are not aware of any research evaluating this in practice. In the present work, our goal is to evaluate whether this kind of explicit modular structure, and not just iterated attention, improves interpretability in concrete evaluation scenarios.

Multi-task Learning. Different from existing multi-task approaches such as sharing common features (e.g., [13]), our model simultaneously handles both Visual Question Answering (VQA) [6] and Referential Expression Grounding (REF) [30] by exploiting the intuition that related tasks should have common sub-routines, and addressing them with a common set of neural modules.

3 Approach

In this paper, we analyze and design interpretable neural networks for high-complexity VQA and REF tasks. We evaluate the interpretability of multi-step VQA networks to humans, and in particular compare modular networks to non-modular networks in terms of how well humans can understand the internal computation process. We describe our proposed evaluation strategy and results in Sect. 4.2. We also improve modular networks by proposing a new formulation, which we describe in this section. Specifically, we describe Stack Neural Module Networks (Stack-NMNs) with the following components. (1) A layout controller that decomposes the reasoning task into a sequence of sub-tasks, and translates the input question into a *soft layout*, specified via a soft distribution over module weights $w^{(t)}$ at each timestep t. The controller also supplies each module with a textual parameter c_t at every time-step using textual attention. (2) A set of neural modules M to handle the sub-tasks specified by the controller. Each neural module is a differentiable parameterized function that performs a specific sub-task, and can be executed dynamically on-the-fly according to the soft layout. (3) A differentiable memory stack to store and retrieve intermediate outputs from each module during execution.

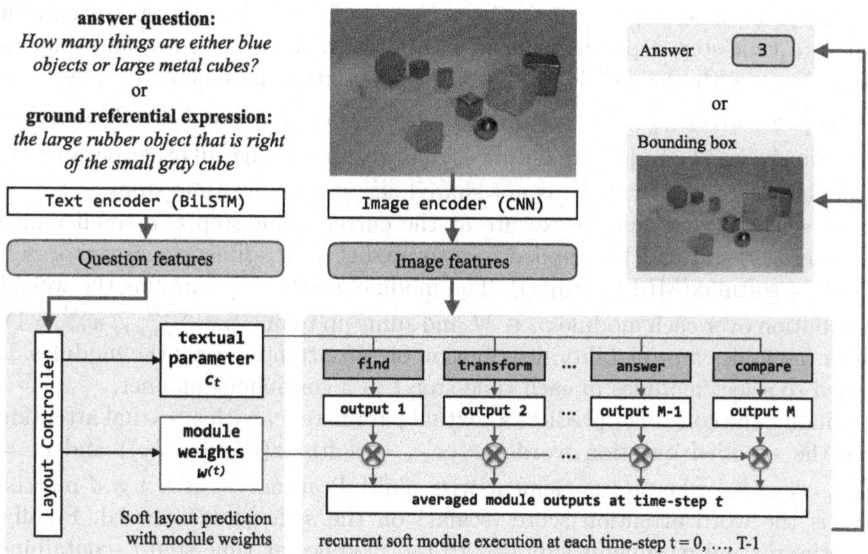

Fig. 2. Overview of our model. Our model predicts a continuous layout via module weights $w^{(t)}$ and executes the modules in a soft manner with a memory stack.

Figure 2 shows an overview of our model. The overall architecture of our model is conceptually similar to N2NMN [16], where layout controller in our model resembles the previous layout policy. The major difference between our model and this prior work lies in whether the layout selection is continuous or discrete. N2NMN makes discrete choices of module layout in a graph structure and can only be end-to-end optimized with reinforcement learning approaches. On the other hand, our model makes soft layout selection with a differentiable stack structure, by giving each module a continuous-valued weight parameter and averaging the outputs of all modules according to their weights. This makes the execution procedure fully differentiable so that our model is trainable with back-propagation like other neural networks.

3.1 Module Layout Controller

The layout controller in our model decides what subtask to perform at each execution time step t by selecting a module m_t for that time step, and also supplying it with a textual parameter c_t to give specific instruction to the module $m_t \in M$. For example, the controller may decide to look for red things at $t = 0$, by running a `Find` module with a textual parameter c_t that contains the information for the word "red".

The structure of our layout controller is similar to the control unit in [17]. Suppose there are S words in the input question. The layout controller first encodes the input question q into a d-dimensional sequence $[h_1, \cdots, h_S]$ of length S using a bi-directional LSTM as $[h_1, \cdots, h_S] = \text{BiLSTM}(q; \theta_{\text{BiLSTM}})$, where each h_s is the concatenation of the forward LSTM output and the backward LSTM output at the s-th input word. Next, the controller runs in a recurrent manner from time-step $t = 0$ to time-step $t = T - 1$. At each time-step t, it applies a time-step dependent linear transform to the question q, and linearly combines it with the previous d-dimensional textual parameter c_{t-1} as $u = W_2 \left[W_1^{(t)} q + b_1; c_{t-1}\right] + b_2$, where $W_1^{(t)}$ and W_2 are $d \times d$ and $d \times 2d$ matrices respectively, and b_1 and b_2 are d-dimensional vectors. Unlike all other parameters in the layout controller, $W_1^{(t)}$ is not shared across different time steps.

To select the module to execute at the current time-step t, a small multi-layer perceptron (MLP) is applied to u to predict a $|M|$-dimensional vector $w^{(t)}$ as $w^{(t)} = \text{softmax}(\text{MLP}(u; \theta_{\text{MLP}}))$. The module weight $w^{(t)}$ contains the weight distribution over each module $m \in M$ and sums up to one (i.e. $\sum_{m \in M}^{M} w_m^{(t)} = 1$), which resembles a probability distribution or soft attention over the modules. It is used to select modules in each time-step t in a continuous manner.

Finally, the controller predicts a textual parameter c_t with a textual attention over the encoded question words as $cv_{t,s} = \text{softmax}(W_3(u \odot h_s))$ and $c_t = \sum_{s=1}^{S} cv_{t,s} \cdot h_s$, where $\odot$ is element-wise multiplication, W_3 is a $1 \times d$ matrix, $cv_{t,s}$ is the word attention score (scalar) on the s-th question word. Finally, c_t is the textual parameter supplied to the modules at time-step t, containing question information needed for a sub-task.

3.2 Neural Modules with a Memory Stack

Module Implementation. Following the terminology in N2NMN, a neural module is a differentiable function with some internal trainable parameters, and can be used to perform a specific sub-task. For example, the question "how many objects are right of the blue object?" can be possibly answered by the layout `Answer['how many'](Transform['right'](Find['blue']()))`, where the modules such as `Transform` are selected with module weight $w^{(t)}$ and the textual information such as 'blue' is contained in the textual parameter c_t.

The module implementation basically follows [16]. We also simplify the implementation in [16] by merging unary answering modules (`Count`, `Exist`, `Describe`) into a single `Answer` module, and pairwise comparison (`More`, `Less`,

Equal, Compare) into a single Compare module. Finally, we introduce a NoOp module that does nothing, which can be used to pad arbitrary module layouts to a maximum length T. Our module implementation is summarized in Table 1.

Table 1. Neural modules used in our model. The modules take image attention maps as inputs, and output either a new image attention a_{out} or a score vector y over all possible answers ($\odot$ is elementwise multiplication; $\sum$ is sum over spatial dimensions).

Module name	Input attention	Output type	Implementation details (x: image feature map, c: textual parameter)
Find	(none)	Attention	$a_{out} = \text{conv}_2\left(\text{conv}_1(x) \odot Wc\right)$
Transform	a	Attention	$a_{out} = \text{conv}_2\left(\text{conv}_1(x) \odot W_1 \sum(a \odot x) \odot W_2 c\right)$
And	a_1, a_2	Attention	$a_{out} = \text{minimum}(a_1, a_2)$
Or	a_1, a_2	Attention	$a_{out} = \text{maximum}(a_1, a_2)$
Filter	a	Attention	$a_{out} = \texttt{And}(a, \texttt{Find}())$, i.e. reusing Find and And
Scene	(none)	Attention	$a_{out} = \text{conv}_1(x)$
Answer	a	Answer	$y = W_1^T \left(W_2 \sum(a \odot x) \odot W_3 c\right)$
Compare	a_1, a_2	Answer	$y = W_1^T \left(W_2 \sum(a_1 \odot x) \odot W_3 \sum(a_2 \odot x) \odot W_4 c\right)$
NoOp	(none)	(none)	(does nothing)

Differentiable Memory Stack. In our model, different modules may take different numbers of input, and the model sometimes needs to take what it currently sees and compare it with what it has previously seen before. This is typical in tree-structured layouts, such as Compare(Find(), Transform(Find())). To handle tree-structured layouts, the model needs to have a memory to remember the outputs from the previous reasoning time-steps. Similar to Memory Networks [34], we provide a differentiable memory pool to store and retrieve the intermediate outputs. However, to encourage compositional behavior, we restrict our memory pool to be a Last-In-First-Out (LIFO) stack similar to [12]. The LIFO behavior encourages the neural modules to work like functions in a computer program, allowing only arguments and returned values to be passed between the modules, without arbitrary memory modification.

Our memory stack can be used to store vectors with fixed dimensions. It consists of a length-L memory array $A = \{A_i\}_{i=1}^{L}$ (where L is the stack length) and a stack-top pointer p, implemented as a L-dimensional one-hot vector. The stack (A, p) implements differentiable push and pop operations as follows. Pushing a new vector z into stack (A, p) is done via pointer increment as $p := \text{1d\_conv}(p, [0, 0, 1])$ followed by value writing as $A_i := A_i \cdot (1 - p_i) + z \cdot p_i$, for each $i = 1, ..., L$. Similarly, popping the current stack-top vector z from stack (A, p) is done via value reading as $z := \sum_{i=1}^{L} A_i \cdot p_i$ followed by pointer decrement as $p := \text{1d\_conv}(p, [1, 0, 0])$. Here A_i is the vector at stack depth i in A. In both push and pop operations, the one-hot stack pointer p is incremented or decremented using 1-d convolution.

In our model, we use the above memory stack to store the $H \times W$ dimensional image attention maps, where H and W are the height and the width of the image feature map. Using the memory stack, each module first pops from the stack to obtain input image attentions, and then pushes its result back to the stack. For example, in tree-like layouts such as `Compare(Find(), Transform(Find()))`, the `Find` module pushes its localization result into the stack, the `Transform` module pops one image attention map from the stack and pushes back the transformed attention, and the `Compare` module pops two image attention maps and uses them to predict the answer.

3.3 Soft Program Execution

Our model performs continuous selection of module layout through the soft module weights $w^{(t)}$. At each time step t, we execute all the modules in our module list M (shown in Table 1), and perform a weighted average of their results with respect to the weights $w^{(t)}$ predicted by the layout controller. Specifically, the resulting memory stacks from the execution of each module are weighted-averaged with respect to $w_m^{(t)}$ to produce a single updated memory stack.

At time step $t=0$, we initialize the memory stack (A, p) with uniform image attention and set stack the pointer p to point at the bottom of the stack (one-hot vector with 1 in the 1st dimension). Then, at each time step t, for every module $m \in M$ we execute it on the current memory stack $(A^{(t)}, p^{(t)})$. During execution, each module m may pop from the stack and push back its results, producing an updated stack $(A_m^{(t)}, p_m^{(t)})$ as $\left(A_m^{(t)}, p_m^{(t)}\right) = \text{run\_module}\left(m, A^{(t)}, p^{(t)}\right)$, for each $m \in M$. We average the resulting new stack from each module according to its weight $w_m^{(t)}$ as $A^{(t+1)} = \sum_{m \in M} A_m^{(t)} \cdot w_m^{(t)}$, and then sharpen the stack pointer with a softmax operation to keep it as a (nearly) one-hot vector as $p^{(t+1)} = \text{softmax}\left(\sum_{m \in M} p_m^{(t)} \cdot w_m^{(t)}\right)$.

Final Output. We apply this model to both the Visual Question Answering (VQA) task and the Referential Expressions Grounding (REF) task. To obtain the answer in the VQA task, we collect the output answer logits (i.e. scores) in all time-steps from those modules that have answer outputs (`Answer` and `Compare` in Table 1), and accumulate them with respect to their module weights as $y = \sum_{t=0}^{T-1} \sum_{m \in M_{\text{ans}}} y_m^{(t)} w_m^{(t)}$ where M_{ans} contains `Answer` and `Compare`.

To output grounding results in the REF task, we take the image-attention map at the top of the final stack at $t = T$, and extract attended image features from this attention map. Then, a linear layer is applied on the attended image feature to predict the bounding box offsets from the feature grid location.

3.4 Training

Unlike previous modular approaches N2NMN [16], PG+EE [19] and TbD [21], our model does not require expert layouts to achieve good performance. When such expert layout supervision is available, our model can also utilize it by supervising the soft module weights $w_{(t)}$ with a cross-entropy loss to match the expert's module choice. But as the entire network is fully differentiable, it can be trained effectively without reinforcement learning, from task supervision alone, in the absence of expert layout supervision.

For VQA, we train with softmax cross entropy loss on the final answer scores y. For REF, we map the center of the ground-truth bounding box to a location on the feature grid. Then we train with a softmax cross entropy loss on the final image attention map to put all the attention on the ground-truth feature grid, and a bounding box regression loss on the bounding box offsets to match the ground-truth box. We train with the Adam optimizer with 10^{-4} learning rate.

Table 2. Validation accuracy on the CLEVR dataset (VQA) and the CLEVR-Ref dataset (REF). Our model simultaneously handles both tasks with high accuracy.

Trained on	Expert layout	VQA accuracy	REF accuracy
VQA	Yes	**96.6**	n/a
REF	Yes	n/a	96.0
VQA+REF	Yes	96.5	**96.2**
VQA	No	93.0	n/a
REF	No	n/a	93.4
VQA+REF	No	**93.9**	**95.4**

4 Experiments

We evaluate our model on the Visual Question Answering (VQA) task on the large-scale CLEVR dataest [18]. The dataset consists of 70000, 15000 and 15000 images for training, validation and test, and each image is associated with 10 questions. The images in the dataset are rendered from a graphics engine, and the questions are synthesized with complex reasoning procedure.

To evaluate our model on the Referential Expression Grounding (REF) task [30], we build a new *CLEVR-Ref* dataset with images and referential expressions in CLEVR style using the code base of [18]. Our new CLEVR-Ref dataset has the same scale as the original CLEVR dataset for VQA, but contains referential expressions instead of questions. Each referential expression refers to a unique object in the image, and the model is required to ground (i.e. localize) the corresponding object with a bounding box. The grounded bounding box is considered correct if it overlaps with the ground-truth bounding box by at least 0.5 intersection-over-union (IoU). Similar to question answering in the CLEVR dataset, the referential expressions also involve complex reasoning and relationship handling. See Fig. 3 for an example of the CLEVR-Ref dataset.

4.1 Model Performance

Our model aims to simultaneously handle both VQA and REF tasks, and to decompose the reasoning procedure into sub-tasks by inducing a suitable module layout on each question or referential expression.

We train our model on the CLEVR dataset for the VQA task, and the CLEVR-Ref dataset for the REF task. We experiment with training only on the VQA task, training only on the REF task, and joint training on both tasks (VQA+REF) using the loss from both tasks. To test whether our model can induce a reasonable sub-task decomposition and module layout, we experiment with both using expert layout supervision (same as in [16]) and training from scratch without expert layout. We use a ResNet-101 convnet [14] pretrained on ImageNet classification to extract visual features from the image.

The results are summarized in Table 2. It can be seen that when training on each individual task, our model achieves over 90% accuracy on both tasks (which is reasonably good performance), whether using expert layout supervision or not.

VQA (expert layout) VQA (from scratch) REF (expert layout) REF (from scratch)

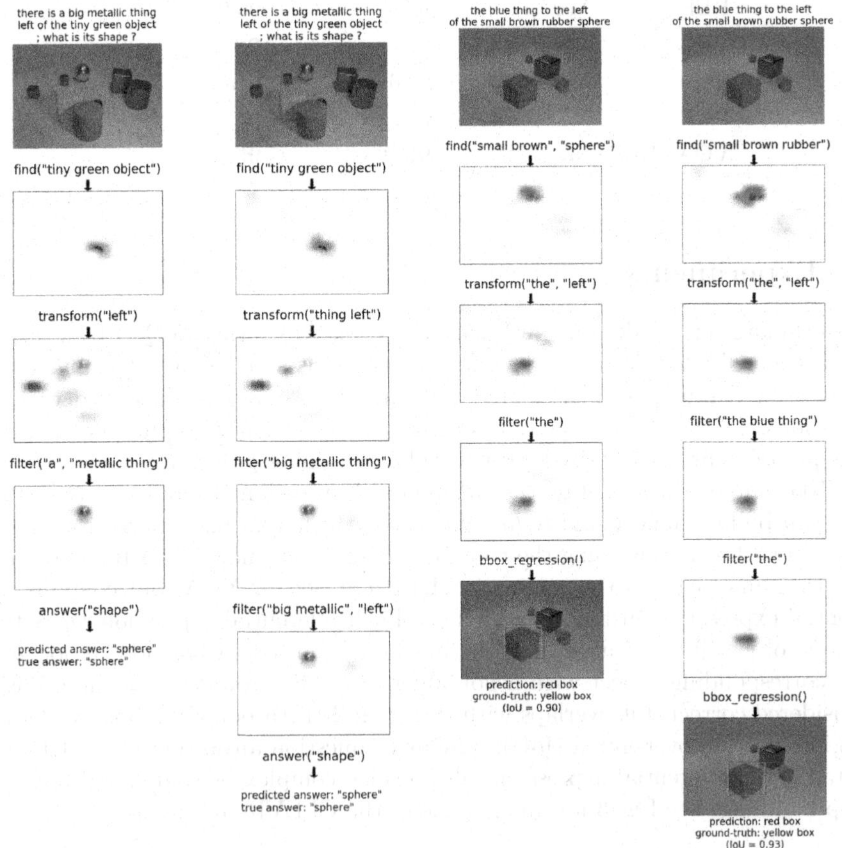

Fig. 3. Examples of our model on VQA (left) and REF (right). At each step, we visualize the module with the highest weight, the words receiving most textual attention ($cv_{t,s}$ in Sect. 3.1) and the module output.

Furthermore, joint training can lead to even higher accuracy on these two tasks (especially when not using expert layout). Our model can simultaneously handle these two tasks by exploiting the common sub-tasks in them, such as finding object and handling relationships.

Sub-task Decomposition and Layout Induction. By comparing the bottom 3 rows (trained without using expert layout) and the top 3 rows (trained with expert layout supervision), it can be seen that although the models trained with expert layout still outperforms training from scratch, the gap between the two scenarios is relatively small. This indicates that our model can still work well without layout supervision, which is something previous modular approaches such as N2NMN [16], PG+EE [19] and TbD [21] could not handle.

We visualize the reasoning procedure our multi-task model on both VQA and REF task, for both with expert layout and without expert layout supervision. Figure 3 shows the module layout, the intermediate reasoning outputs and the most attended words from textual attention ($cv_{t,s}$ in Sect. 3.1). It can be seen that our model can induce a reasonable decomposition of the inference procedure into sub-tasks without expert layout supervision, and it learns to share common sub-tasks such as find (localization) and transform in across the two tasks.

We note that our model learns peaky module weights after convergence. The average entropy of the learned soft module weights (which can be seen as a probability distribution) is 0.082 when trained without layout supervision (corresponds to putting over 98% weights on one module), and 7.5×10^{-5} when trained with layout supervision (corresponds to putting over 99.99% weights on one module). This shows that even without any strong supervision on module layout, our model learns to almost discretely select one module through the soft module weights at test time. Hence, our proposed framework can be regarded as a novel end-to-end differentiable training approach for modular networks.

We further experiment with test-time layout discretization by replacing the soft module weights with a one-hot argmax vector. This results in sightly lower performance on the CLEVR validation set (90.0% when trained without layout supervision and 94.8% with layout supervision). Considering the discrepancy between training and test time, the relatively small accuracy drop (<4%) from test-time layout discretization indicates that our model works similar to previous modular networks at test time, rather than acting as a mixture of experts.

Evaluation of Accuracy. We first compare the accuracy of our model on the CLEVR VQA dataset with the previous modular approaches N2NMN [16], PG+EE [19] and TbD [21]. N2NMN uses a layout policy to predict discrete layouts and a neural module network to answer the question. PG+EE and TbD are also modular approaches similar to N2NMN, where the program generator is similar to the layout policy, and the execution engine is essentially a neural module network. For fair comparison with previous work, we train our model on the CLEVR VQA dataset only (without using CLEVR-Ref for joint training).

The results are shown in Table 3. It can be seen from the top 4 rows that among all the modular approaches (N2NMN, PG+EE, TbD and Ours), when layout supervision is available, our model outperforms N2NMN by a large margin, and achieves comparable performance with PG+EE while underperforms TbD by a small margin. We note that even when using expert layout, our model still uses less supervision than PG+EE or TbD as they both require fine-grained module specification (e.g. finding shape and finding color are different modules in [19,21] while the same module with different textual attention in our model).

The bottom 4 rows show the results without using expert layout supervision, where our model significantly outperform N2NMN. In this case, N2NMN has large performance drop while PG+EE and TbD fails to converge or cannot not be trained without layout supervision. This can be attributed to the fact that N2NMN, PG+EE and TbD all use discrete non-differentiable layout, while our model is fully differentiable and can be trained with back-propagation.

We note that the best non-modular architectures [17] achieve higher performance without using expert layout supervision, and compare those against modular performance on both accuracy and interpretability in Sect. 4.2.

Results on Real-Image VQA Datasets. We also evaluate our method on real-image visual question answering datasets and compare with N2NMN [16]. We run our approach on both VQAv1 and VQAv2 datasets [6,11] following the

Table 3. Comparison of our model and other modular approaches on the CLEVR dataset for VQA. Our model achieves the best accuracy when not relying on expert layout, while N2NMN has significant performance drop in this case. The best non-modular architectures (e.g., [17]) do achieve higher performance; we compare those against modular performance on both accuracy and interpretability in Sect. 4.2.

Method	Expert layout	Accuracy on CLEVR
N2NMN [16]	Yes	83.7
PG+EE [19]	Yes	96.9
TbD [21]	Yes	**99.1**
Ours	Yes	96.5
N2NMN [16]	No	69.0
PG+EE [19]	No	(does not converge)
TbD [21]	No	(not supported)
Ours	No	**93.0**

Table 4. Single-model accuracy of our method and N2NMN [16] on both VQAv1 [6] and VQAv2 [11] datasets, using the same experimental settings (e.g. visual features).

Method	Expert layout	Accuracy on VQAv1	Accuracy on VQAv2
N2NMN [16]	Yes	64.9	63.3
Ours	No	65.5	**64.1**
Ours	Yes	**66.0**	64.0

same settings (e.g. using ResNet-152 image features and single model at test time without ensemble) as in [16], where the results are in Table 4. Although the question answering task in these datasets focuses more on visual recognition than on compositional reasoning, our method still outperforms [16] even without expert layout supervision (the expert layouts are obtained by a syntactic parser).

4.2 Model Interpretability

Evaluation of Interpretability. It is often suggested in existing works [16, 19, 21] that modular networks can be more interpretable to humans compared to holistic models. However, there is a lack of human studies in these works to support this claim. In this section, we evaluate how well the user can understand the internal reasoning process within our model, and compare it with MAC [17]. We compare to MAC because it is a state-of-the-art holistic model that also performs multi-step sequential reasoning and has image and textual attention at each time-step, while other models (e.g., FiLM [26] and Relation Net [31]) have lower performance and do not have any image or textual attention to visualize. MAC is a multi-step recurrent structure with a control unit and a reading-writing unit. Similar to our model, it also attend to text and image in each reasoning step. But unlike our model, there is not explicit modular structure in MAC.

Here, we investigate two distinct, but related questions: does modular structure improve humans' *subjective perceptions* of model interpretability, and does this structure allow users to form *truthful beliefs* about model behavior? To this end, we present two different sets of experiments (subjective understanding and forward prediction) with human evaluators. With respect to the taxonomy of interpretability evaluations presented in [8], these are both "human-grounded" metrics aimed at testing "general notions of the quality of an explanation".

In the **subjective understanding** evaluation, we visualize model's intermediate outputs such as the image attention and textual attention at each step, and we also show the model's final prediction. The visualizations can be seen in Fig. 3. Then the human evaluators are asked to judge how well they can understand the internal reasoning process, or whether it clear to the user what the model is doing at each step. Each example is rated on a 4-point Likert scale (*clear*, *mostly clear*, *somewhat unclear* and *unclear*) corresponding to numerical scores of 4, 3, 2 and 1. The averaged scores and the percentage of each choice are shown in Table 5, where it can be seen that our model has higher subjective understanding scores than MAC [17] and is much more often rated as "clear" in both cases (using or not using expert layout supervision). This shows that the users can more clearly understand the reasoning procedure in our model.

In the **forward prediction** evaluation, we investigate whether humans can predict the model's answer and detect its failure based on these visualizations. We split the test set into half correct and half incorrect model predictions, and the final answer output is not shown, so that human baseline performance should be chance or 50%. Our hypothesis is that if humans can predict whether the model succeed or fail better than chance, they understand something about the model's decision process. In Table 5, we show the human accuracy on this task along with 95% confidence interval. It can be seen that our model allows them to predict whether the model will get the correct answer or fail consistently higher than chance when trained without expert layout supervision. We also notice that when using supervision from expert layout, our model does worse at human prediction of model's failure. We suspect it is because predicting the answer requires human to understand how the model works. When supervising the layout, the model may overfit to the expert layout, at the expense of predictability. It may output an "intuitive" layout by mimicking the training data, but that layout may not actually be how it is solving the problem. On the other hand, the unsupervised model is not being forced to predict any particular layouts to minimize loss, so its layouts may be more directed at minimizing the answer loss.

Finally, we compare our model with MAC on VQA accuracy in Table 5. Our model underperforms the state-of-the-art MAC in terms of VQA accuracy. However, our model is more interpretable to a human user. This is in line with the intuition that there may be an accuracy-explainability tradeoff, e.g., linear models are less accurate but more interpretable than non-linear models. However, our model greatly reduces the accuracy gap with the top performing models, without requiring expert layout supervision at training time.

Table 5. Human evaluation of our model and the state-of-the-art non-modular MAC model [17]. Based on the models' intermediate outputs, the evaluators are asked to (a) judge how clearly they can understand the reasoning steps performed by these models on a 4-point scale (i.e. subjective understanding) and (b) do forward prediction (failure detection) and decide whether the model fails without seeing the final output answer. The results show that our model is more interpretable to human users. However, our model underperforms the non-modular MAC approach in VQA accuracy, which is in line with the intuition that there may be an accuracy-explainability tradeoff.

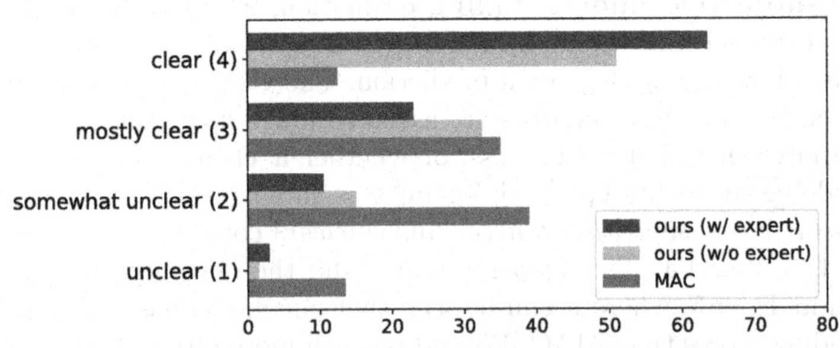

percentage of each choice (*clear*, *mostly clear*, *somewhat unclear* and *unclear*)

Method	expert layout	subjective understanding	forward prediction (failure detection) accuracy ± 95% confidence interval	VQA accuracy
Ours	yes	**3.47**	0.545 ± 0.069	96.5
Ours	no	3.33	**0.625 ± 0.067**	93.0
MAC [17]	n/a	2.46	0.565 ± 0.069	**98.9**

5 Conclusion

In this paper, we have proposed a novel model for visual question answering and referential expression grounding. We demonstrate that our model simultaneously addresses both tasks by exploiting the intuition that related tasks should share common sub-tasks, and sharing a common set of neural modules between tasks. Compared with previous modular approaches, our model induces a decomposition of the inference procedure into sub-tasks while not requiring expert layout supervision. The proposed model can explain its reasoning steps with a sequence of soft module choices, image attentions, and textual attentions. Experimental evaluation found that these explanations produced better understanding in human users with respect to both subjective and objective evaluations, even in the absence of human-provided explanations at training time.

Acknowledgement. This work was partially supported by US DoD and DARPA XAI and D3M, and the Berkeley Artificial Intelligence Research (BAIR) Lab.

References

1. Anderson, P., et al.: Bottom-up and top-down attention for image captioning and VQA. arXiv preprint arXiv:1707.07998 (2017)
2. Andreas, J., Dragan, A., Klein, D.: Translating neuralese. In: ACL (2017)
3. Andreas, J., Klein, D., Levine, S.: Modular multitask reinforcement learning with policy sketches. In: Proceedings of the International Conference on Machine Learning (ICML) (2017)
4. Andreas, J., Rohrbach, M., Darrell, T., Klein, D.: Learning to compose neural networks for question answering. In: Proceedings of the Conference of the North American Chapter of the Association for Computational Linguistics (NAACL) (2016)
5. Andreas, J., Rohrbach, M., Darrell, T., Klein, D.: Neural module networks. In: Proceedings of the IEEE Conference on Computer Vision and Pattern Recognition (CVPR) (2016)
6. Antol, S., et al.: VQA: visual question answering. In: Proceedings of the IEEE International Conference on Computer Vision, pp. 2425–2433 (2015)
7. Bau, D., Zhou, B., Khosla, A., Oliva, A., Torralba, A.: Network dissection: quantifying interpretability of deep visual representations. In: 2017 IEEE Conference on Computer Vision and Pattern Recognition (CVPR), pp. 3319–3327. IEEE (2017)
8. Doshi-Velez, F., Kim, B.: Towards a rigorous science of interpretable machine learning (2017)
9. Duch, W., Adamczak, R., Grabczewski, K.: Extraction of logical rules from neural networks. Neural Process. Lett. **7**(3), 211–219 (1998)
10. Fukui, A., Park, D.H., Yang, D., Rohrbach, A., Darrell, T., Rohrbach, M.: Multimodal compact bilinear pooling for visual question answering and visual grounding. In: Proceedings of the Conference on Empirical Methods in Natural Language Processing (EMNLP) (2016)
11. Goyal, Y., Khot, T., Summers-Stay, D., Batra, D., Parikh, D.: Making the V in VQA matter: elevating the role of image understanding in visual question answering. In: CVPR (2017)

12. Grefenstette, E., Hermann, K.M., Suleyman, M., Blunsom, P.: Learning to transduce with unbounded memory. In: Advances in Neural Information Processing Systems, pp. 1828–1836 (2015)
13. He, K., Gkioxari, G., Dollár, P., Girshick, R.: Mask R-CNN. In: 2017 IEEE International Conference on Computer Vision (ICCV), pp. 2980–2988. IEEE (2017)
14. He, K., Zhang, X., Ren, S., Sun, J.: Deep residual learning for image recognition. In: Proceedings of the IEEE Conference on Computer Vision and Pattern Recognition, pp. 770–778 (2016)
15. Hendricks, L.A., Akata, Z., Rohrbach, M., Donahue, J., Schiele, B., Darrell, T.: Generating visual explanations. In: Leibe, B., Matas, J., Sebe, N., Welling, M. (eds.) ECCV 2016. LNCS, vol. 9908, pp. 3–19. Springer, Cham (2016). https://doi.org/10.1007/978-3-319-46493-0_1
16. Hu, R., Andreas, J., Rohrbach, M., Darrell, T., Saenko, K.: Learning to reason: end-to-end module networks for visual question answering. In: Proceedings of the IEEE International Conference on Computer Vision (ICCV) (2017)
17. Hudson, D.A., Manning, C.D.: Compositional attention networks for machine reasoning. In: Proceedings of the International Conference on Learning Representation (ICLR) (2018)
18. Johnson, J., Hariharan, B., van der Maaten, L., Fei-Fei, L., Zitnick, C.L., Girshick, R.: CLEVR: a diagnostic dataset for compositional language and elementary visual reasoning. In: 2017 IEEE Conference on Computer Vision and Pattern Recognition (CVPR), pp. 1988–1997. IEEE (2017)
19. Johnson, J., et al.: Inferring and executing programs for visual reasoning. In: Proceedings of the IEEE International Conference on Computer Vision (ICCV) (2017)
20. Koh, P.W., Liang, P.: Understanding black-box predictions via influence functions. arXiv preprint arXiv:1703.04730 (2017)
21. Mascharka, D., Tran, P., Soklaski, R., Majumdar, A.: Transparency by design: closing the gap between performance and interpretability in visual reasoning. In: Proceedings of the IEEE Conference on Computer Vision and Pattern Recognition, pp. 4942–4950 (2018)
22. Mnih, V., Heess, N., Graves, A., et al.: Recurrent models of visual attention. In: Advances in Neural Information Processing Systems, pp. 2204–2212 (2014)
23. Olah, C., Satyanarayan, A., Johnson, I., Carter, S., Schubert, L., Ye, K., Mordvintsev, A.: The building blocks of interpretability. Distill **3**(3), e10 (2018)
24. Otte, C.: Safe and interpretable machine learning: a methodological review. In: Moewes, C., Nürnberger, A. (eds.) Computational Intelligence in Intelligent Data Analysis. SCI, vol. 445, pp. 111–122. Springer, Heidelberg (2013). https://doi.org/10.1007/978-3-642-32378-2_8
25. Park, D.H., Hendricks, L.A., Akata, Z., Schiele, B., Darrell, T., Rohrbach, M.: Attentive explanations: justifying decisions and pointing to the evidence. arXiv preprint arXiv:1612.04757 (2016)
26. Perez, E., Strub, F., De Vries, H., Dumoulin, V., Courville, A.: FiLM: visual reasoning with a general conditioning layer. In: AAAI (2018)
27. Ramanishka, V., Das, A., Zhang, J., Saenko, K.: Top-down visual saliency guided by captions. In: Proceedings of the IEEE Conference on Computer Vision and Pattern Recognition (CVPR), vol. 1, p. 7 (2017)
28. Ramprasaath, R., Abhishek, D., Ramakrishna, V., Michael, C., Devi, P., Dhruv, B.: Grad-CAM: why did you say that? Visual explanations from deep networks via gradient-based localization. In: CVPR 2016 (2016)

29. Ribeiro, M.T., Singh, S., Guestrin, C.: Why should I trust you?: explaining the predictions of any classifier. In: Proceedings of the 22nd ACM SIGKDD International Conference on Knowledge Discovery and Data Mining, pp. 1135–1144. ACM (2016)
30. Rohrbach, A., Rohrbach, M., Hu, R., Darrell, T., Schiele, B.: Grounding of textual phrases in images by reconstruction. In: Leibe, B., Matas, J., Sebe, N., Welling, M. (eds.) ECCV 2016. LNCS, vol. 9905, pp. 817–834. Springer, Cham (2016). https://doi.org/10.1007/978-3-319-46448-0_49
31. Santoro, A., et al.: A simple neural network module for relational reasoning. In: Advances in Neural Information Processing Systems, pp. 4974–4983 (2017)
32. Selbst, A.D., Barocas, S.: The intuitive appeal of explainable machines. SSRN (2018)
33. Springenberg, J.T., Dosovitskiy, A., Brox, T., Riedmiller, M.: Striving for simplicity: the all convolutional net. arXiv preprint arXiv:1412.6806 (2014)
34. Sukhbaatar, S., Weston, J., Fergus, R., et al.: End-to-end memory networks. In: Advances in Neural Information Processing Systems, pp. 2440–2448 (2015)
35. Xu, H., Saenko, K.: Ask, attend and answer: exploring question-guided spatial attention for visual question answering. In: Leibe, B., Matas, J., Sebe, N., Welling, M. (eds.) ECCV 2016. LNCS, vol. 9911, pp. 451–466. Springer, Cham (2016). https://doi.org/10.1007/978-3-319-46478-7_28
36. Yang, Z., He, X., Gao, J., Deng, L., Smola, A.: Stacked attention networks for image question answering. In: Proceedings of the IEEE Conference on Computer Vision and Pattern Recognition, pp. 21–29 (2016)
37. Zhang, J., Lin, Z., Brandt, J., Shen, X., Sclaroff, S.: Top-down neural attention by excitation backprop. In: Leibe, B., Matas, J., Sebe, N., Welling, M. (eds.) ECCV 2016. LNCS, vol. 9908, pp. 543–559. Springer, Cham (2016). https://doi.org/10.1007/978-3-319-46493-0_33
38. Zhang, Q., Yang, Y., Wu, Y.N., Zhu, S.C.: Interpreting CNNs via decision trees. arXiv preprint arXiv:1802.00121 (2018)
39. Zhou, B., Bau, D., Oliva, A., Torralba, A.: Interpreting deep visual representations via network dissection. In: 2017 IEEE Conference on Computer Vision and Pattern Recognition (CVPR) (2017)
40. Zhou, B., Khosla, A., Lapedriza, A., Oliva, A., Torralba, A.: Learning deep features for discriminative localization. In: 2016 IEEE Conference on Computer Vision and Pattern Recognition (CVPR), pp. 2921–2929. IEEE (2016)

Learning to Blend Photos

Wei-Chih Hung[1(✉)], Jianming Zhang[2], Xiaohui Shen[3], Zhe Lin[2], Joon-Young Lee[2], and Ming-Hsuan Yang[1,4]

[1] UC Merced, Merced, USA
whung8@ucmerced.edu
[2] Adobe Research, San Jose, USA
[3] Bytedance Lab, Menlo Park, USA
[4] Google Cloud, Menlo Park, USA

Abstract. Photo blending is a common technique to create aesthetically pleasing artworks by combining multiple photos. However, the process of photo blending is usually time-consuming, and care must be taken in the process of blending, filtering, positioning, and masking each of the source photos. To make photo blending accessible to general public, we propose an efficient approach for automatic photo blending via deep learning. Specifically, given a foreground image and a background image, our proposed method automatically generates a set of blending photos with scores that indicate the aesthetics quality with the proposed quality network and policy network. Experimental results show that the proposed approach can effectively generate high quality blending photos with efficiency.

1 Introduction

Photo blending is a common technique in photography to create aesthetically pleasing artworks by superimposing multiple photos together. For example, "Double Exposure" is one of the popular effects in photo blending (see Fig. 1), which can be achieved with skillful camera capture techniques or advanced image editing software. This effect is widely used in posters, magazines, and various print advertisements to produce impressive visual effects and facilitate storytelling. However, the process of photo blending is usually time-consuming even for experts and requires a lot of expertise. To make this process faster, many image editing software products like Photoshop support the use of action scripts to simplify the photo blending operations. But these scripts are predefined and do not consider how to adjust the photos based on the context. Therefore, they may not work out-of-the-box, and it still takes a fairly amount of skill and time to tweak the results to the users' satisfaction.

W.-C. Hung—This work was done during the author's internship at Adobe Research.
X. Shen—This work was done when the author was at Adobe Research.

Electronic supplementary material The online version of this chapter (https://doi.org/10.1007/978-3-030-01234-2_5) contains supplementary material, which is available to authorized users.

V. Ferrari et al. (Eds.): ECCV 2018, LNCS 11211, pp. 72–88, 2018.
https://doi.org/10.1007/978-3-030-01234-2_5

Fig. 1. Sample blending photos. These results are generated by our proposed system to simulate the "Double Exposure" effect with different blending engines. Best viewed in color. (Color figure online)

By observing blending artworks, we identify two critical factors in the making of a satisfactory double exposure effect: **background alignment** and **photometric adjustment**. Since the background photo can contain scene elements of different textures and colors, how to align the background elements with the foreground object is of great importance for appealing blending results. On the other hand, since the blending function is a numerical function of two pixel values from foreground and background, the photometric adjustment of foreground photo, including brightness, contrast, and color modification, can affect the visibility of different regions in the photos, leading to visually different results.

In this work, we propose a fully automatic method to generate appealing double exposure effects by jointly predicting the background alignment region and the photometric adjustment parameters. The first challenge is how to design an evaluation metric to access the aesthetics quality of the blending results. Though many works [18,21,30,31,39] have been proposed for general photo quality assessment, we find that the result rankings of these methods are not consistent with user preference since the models are trained with common photos. Furthermore, these methods usually train a Convolutional Neural Network (CNN) to directly predict the provided fine-level aesthetics score from existing datasets [21,34,39]. However, we find that it is difficult for users to annotate the fine-level scores on these artworks such as photo blending. Therefore, we train a quality network on a newly collected dataset with course level annotation. We also propose to use a combination of ranking loss and binary cross entropy loss for as we find that it improves the training stability.

Given the proposed quality network, the second task is to find a region of interest (ROI) in the given background photo and a set of photometric adjustment parameters for the foreground photo, generating a blending result with the optimal rating according to the quality network. We view this problem as a derivative-free optimization task, which is subject to parameter search range and time constraints. There exist many non-learning based search methods for global function optimization, e.g., grid search, random search, simulated annealing [20], or particle swarm optimization [19]. However, in our experiments, we find that these methods could not find a good optimum within the constrained time since the system has to blend the images for each set of selected parameters and pass it through the quality network. Therefore, we propose to train an agent with deep reinforcement learning (DRL) to search for the best combination of background ROI and foreground adjustment. Specifically, we transform the quality network to a two-stream policy network that outputs both state quality value and action values to make the search process efficient. To evaluate the proposed algorithm, we compare the proposed method with existing search algorithms, e.g., Particle Swarm Optimization [19] and Simulated Annealing [20], showing that the proposed DRL search generates results with higher quality values with the same time constraint. Also, we conduct the user study to compare our method with other baselines as well as human experts. The results show that the quality scores indicated by the proposed quality network are consistent with user preference, and the proposed method effectively generates aesthetically pleasing blending photos within few seconds.

The contributions of this work are as follows. First, to the best of our knowledge, it is the first work to introduce the task of automatic photo blending. Second, we propose a quality network trained with ranking loss and binary cross entropy loss using a newly collected dataset for double exposure. Third, we transform the quality network into a two-stream policy network trained with deep reinforcement learning, performing the automatic photo blending with consideration of user preference, aesthetics quality, image contexts, as well as a tight runtime constraint.

2 Related Work

Learning-Based Photo Editing. Recently, many CNN based methods for image editing tasks have been proposed with impressive results, such as image filtering [22,24,29], enhancement [1,9,14,50], inpainting [38,51], composition [44, 45,49,57], colorization [15,23,54,56], and image translation [3,16,28,58,59]. Most of these approaches consist of a CNN model that directly transforms a single input photo to the desired output. However, since there is no specific constraint on how the CNNs transform the photos, visual artifacts are inevitable in some of the results. Also, the resulting photos' resolution is usually low because of the limited GPU memory. Though Gharbi *et al.* [9] propose to use deep bilateral learning to process high-resolution images, it only works with the effects that can be interpreted as pixel affine transform. In this work, since all the image processing modules are predefined such as pixel blending, photometric adjustment, or predefined filtering, the blending results generated by our method is artifact-free, and there is no limited resolution since most image processing modules operate with CPU. Style transfer methods [6,8,13,17,25–27,32,40] also relate to our task. In style transfer, an input photo is stylized with a reference style

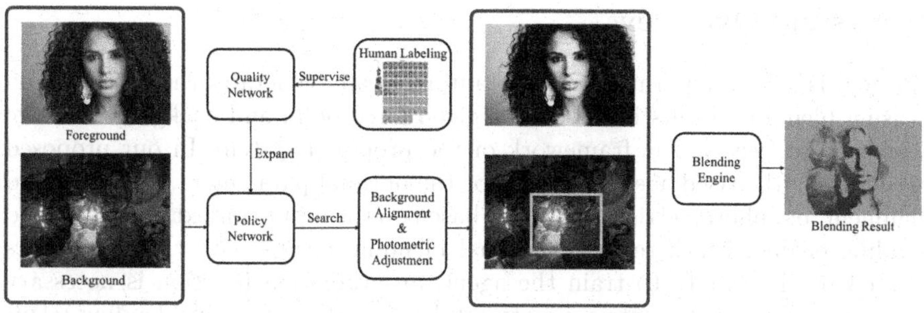

Fig. 2. Overview of the automatic blending framework. The inputs of our method are two photos: foreground and background. We first train a quality network to evaluate the aesthetics quality of blending photos with human preference annotation on random blending photos. Then a deep reinforcement learning based agent is trained to optimize the parameter for the background alignment and photometric adjustment. Using the predicted parameters, the blending engine renders the final blending photo.

image by matching the correlations between deep features while preserving the content with the perceptual loss on higher level features. In our task, content preservation is also important. While style transfer methods preserve the content with perceptual loss [17], we find that the perceptual loss values are not consistent with the blending results, i.e., the loss is not always low when the blending results preserve the content well.

Aesthetics Quality Assessment. The objective of aesthetics quality assessment methods is to rank the photos according to the general aesthetics preference automatically. These methods can be applied to image search, album curation, and composition ranking. Recently, many methods [18,21,30,31,33,39] are proposed based on CNN models. However, when we test these models with the blending photos, we find that the result rankings are not consistent with user preference since the models are trained with common photos.

Deep Reinforcement Learning. Recently, deep reinforcement learning methods [35,36,46,48] have draw much attention due to the great success in computer games [36] and board games [41]. Our approach of learning a quality network from user annotation is closely related to some existing reward learning methods such as inverse RL [7,37], imitation learning [12,43], and human-in-the-loop RL [5], where the reward function is not explicitly available in the environment. In vision community, some works have been proposed to apply DRL for object localization [2], visual tracking [53], and object detection [52]. Similar to our proposed background alignment approach, these methods model the object localization problem as a sequence of actions that move or scale the ROIs. The major difference between our work and these methods is that we are not searching for a single object but a suitable blending position that considers both the foreground and background context, as well as the subjective user preference.

3 System Overview

Our goal is to develop a method that automatically generates the aesthetically pleasing blending results based on the given foreground and background image pairs. Figure 2 shows the framework of the proposed system. In our proposed method, a DRL-based agent searches for the optimal parameters of background alignment and photometric adjustment based on the input context and a selected blending engine, which renders the final blending results with the parameters selected by the agent. To train the agent, an evaluation function is necessary to generate the quality metric, i.e., to tell how good the current blending result is during the optimization process. In typical RL environments, the reward is usually well defined, e.g., the scores (win or lose) in games environment. However, there is no well-defined evaluation function for artworks such as photo blending. Therefore, we propose to learn an evaluation from user annotation. Specifically, we generate blending results with random parameters on the collected foreground and background images. We then invite participants to evaluate the blending results based on their subjective preference. Based on the labels, we train a quality network served as the evaluation function for blending results. Once we have the evaluation function, we train the DRL agent to search in the parameter space effectively with the proposed policy network and existing DRL algorithms.

4 Quality Network

Our objective is to learn a function that assesses a blending photo with a numerical score that indicates the aesthetic quality, and the quality scores should be consistent with the user preferences, i.e., the higher user rating suggests higher quality score, and vice versa. We observe that most people evaluate the blending results by comparing them with the original foreground photos. If one blending photo does not preserve the original image contexts well, the users would often rate it as unacceptable. However, if the blending photo preserves context but fails to have artistic effects, it would still not be rated as a good one. Therefore, we consider the evaluation function conditional on the foreground image and build it with a CNN model that takes both the blending photo and the foreground image as input. We denote the proposed CNN as quality network since it indicates the aesthetic quality of the blending result.

4.1 Network Structure

Figure 3 shows the structure of the proposed quality network. The network is composed of two VGG16 networks [42] pre-trained on ImageNet as feature extractors where the weights are shared as a Siamese network [4]. We remove the last classifier layer of VGG and concatenate the features of both base networks, and add two fully-connected layers with the 512-channel as the middle layer to output a single score. It takes the foreground image and a blended image as input, which both are downsized to 224×224, and outputs a single scalar as the blending reward score.

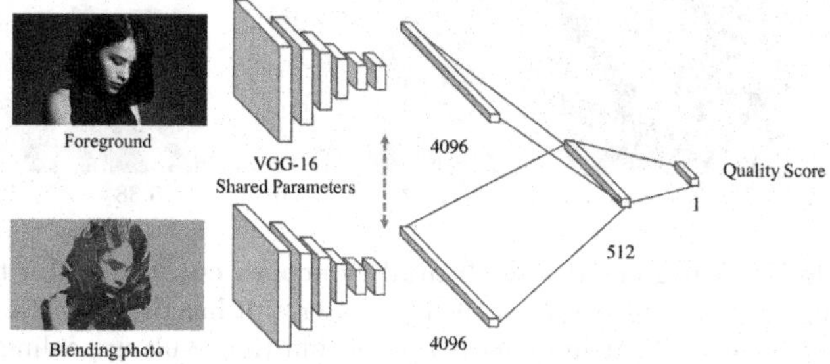

Fig. 3. Network structure of the proposed quality network. The quality network consists of two of VGG16 networks that share the same parameters. The quality network takes the original foreground photo and the blending results as input and outputs a numeric score that indicates the aesthetic quality of the blending result.

4.2 Learning Objective

Given two blending images B_i and B_j as well as their original foreground image F_i and F_j, our objective is to train a mapping function $S(\cdot)$ (quality network) that maps (F_i, B_i) and (F_j, B_j) to two numerical scores, such that if B_i is more visually pleasing than B_j according to user rating then

$$S(F_i, B_i) > S(F_j, B_j), \tag{1}$$

and vice versa. To achieve this, we use the ranking loss $\mathcal{L}_r$ as the training loss function for the quality network. We denote $S_i = S(F_i, B_i)$, and let $y = 1$ if S_i has better user rating than S_j, while $y = -1$ otherwise. We formulate the loss as

$$\mathcal{L}_r(S_i, S_j) = \max\{0, -y(S_i - S_j) + m\}, \tag{2}$$

where m is the margin term.

However, the ranking loss only enforces the property that for a given photo the scores of good examples are higher than the fair/bad ones but lack of a universal threshold of differentiating good ones for every input photo. If the score ranges are consistent with different input sets, one can choose a score threshold to filter out the blending results that are not acceptable by most users. Therefore, we propose to add additional binary cross entropy loss on top of the predicted scores to enforce that all the bad examples have scores that are less than zero. The binary cross entropy loss function can be formulated as

$$\mathcal{L}_{bce}(S_i) = -r\log(\sigma(S_i)) - (1-r)\log(1-\sigma(S_i)), \tag{3}$$

where $r = 1$ if the user labeling is "good/fair", and $r = 0$ if the user labeling is "bad", and $\sigma(\cdot)$ is the sigmoid function. Combining the ranking loss and cross entropy loss, the overall optimization objective then becomes $\mathcal{L} = \mathcal{L}_r + \lambda\mathcal{L}_{bce}$, where both the ranking property and the score offset can be preserved. Please see supplementary materials for implementation details.

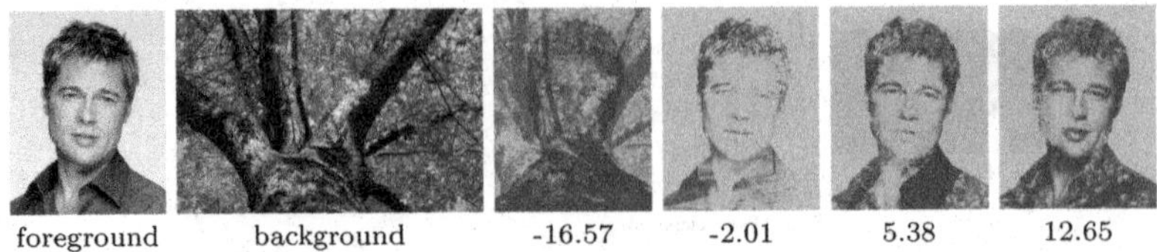

Fig. 4. Sample blending results with quality scores computed by the quality network. A higher score suggests that the blending result has better aesthetics quality, and a lower score suggest that most users do not find the result appealing.

Figure 4 shows some example blending results with their scores indicated by our trained quality network. Among the results of high scores, the background usually has good alignment with foreground, and the brightness/contrast is adequate to control the level of blending.

4.3 Dataset Collection

To generate the blending images, we download 5,000 portrait photos from the internet as foreground images, as well as 8,000 scenic photos as background images. Then we apply the blending engines on random pairs of foreground and background images with random alignment/adjustment parameters. During the labeling process, the users are asked to label each blended image a score according to their preference. In our implementation, the preference score has three levels: "good", "fair", and "bad", where we provide some basic guidelines: "good" denotes the one that one likes, "bad" represents the one would like to discard, and "fair" means the one is acceptable but needs to be further adjusted to make it better.

However, we find that most of the randomly generated blending results are of worse quality, where the original foreground context (face) is often not recognizable and will be annotated as "Bad" for almost all annotators. To increase the labeling efficiency, we first train a quality network as described in Sect. 4 with 5,000 ratings from annotators, who are asked only to consider how well can you recognize the original foreground content. Then we apply the quality network to all the generated blending results and filter out the results that have scores below a designed threshold. As a result, we collect 30,000 ratings on 1,305 image sets with 16 annotators.

5 Deep Reinforcement Search

Given the quality network, we seek to predict a region of interest (ROI) on the background image and the photometric adjustment parameters that could generate the highest score concerning the quality network. We view the problem as a derivative-free optimization task, which is subject to parameter search range and time constraints. There exist many non-learning based search methods for

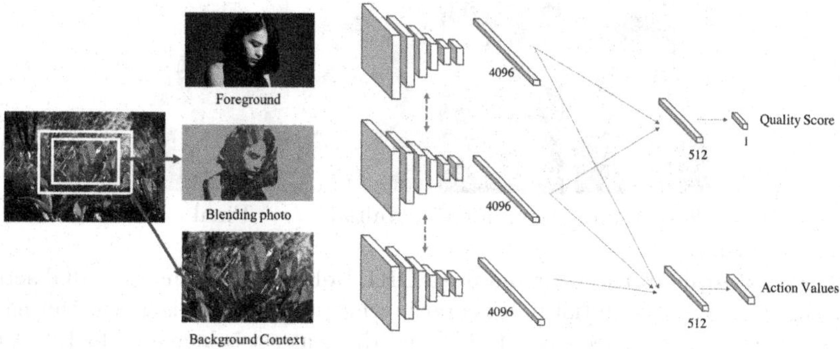

Fig. 5. Network structure of the proposed policy network. We extend the quality network with an additional background context input and action values output. The designed structure enables the agent to jointly predict the quality value as well as search action values, reducing the time complexity during the process of parameter search.

global function optimization, e.g., grid search, random search, simulated annealing [20], or particle swarm optimization [19]. However, in our experiments, we find that these methods could not find a good optimum within the constrained time since the system has to blend the images for each set of selected parameters and pass it through the quality network.

To tackle the above-mentioned problem, we introduce a DRL-based agent to predict actions for searching the parameters efficiently. Given the selected foreground image, background image, and blending engine, the agent takes the state values and pass them through the proposed policy network to get the action values. The agent then performs the action with the highest action value and getting an immediate reward that suggests the blending quality changes. The goal of the agent is to learn a policy for maximizing the expected accumulated future award. In our task, it is equivalent to maximizing the score of the final blending result output by the quality network.

5.1 Search Space and Actions

We define total ten actions for the DRL agent, in which six actions are used to move the current ROI for alignment: (Right, Left, Up, Down, Bigger, Smaller), and the other four actions are for the foreground photometric adjustment: (Brightness+, Brightness−, Contrast+, Contrast−). All the actions are performed relatively. For instance, the action "Right" means moving the ROI right for $\alpha \times w$, where w is the width of current ROI, and α is set to 0.05 in our experiments. It is similar for photometric actions, where "Brightness+" means increasing the pixel values for a ratio β, which is set to 0.1. We provide the detail action operations in the supplementary materials.

Fig. 6. An example of the intermediate DRL behavior. We show the ROI actions with color encoding. The initial ROI is orange while the last ROI is green. During the process, the brightness is decreased to 0.9, and the contrast is increased to 1.2. (Color figure online)

5.2 Network Structure

We show the structure of the policy network in Fig. 5. In deep reinforcement learning, a policy network takes the observation states as input and output the action values which indicates the expected accumulated reward after performing corresponding actions. In the proposed method, we select three state variables: foreground image, the blended image concerning the currently selected region, and the background context. The background context is the enlarged background region that enables the policy network to see what are the potential directions to go for optimizing the expected reward. In our experiments, we choose the context ROI as 1.3 times larger than the blending ROI. Based on the pretrained quality network in Fig. 3, we add an input stream for background context information as well as the action values output. Since the designed structure enables the agent to jointly predict the quality value as well as search action values, we could record the quality score output of policy network during the test time while performing the actions and use the state with the maximum score as the final result.

5.3 Reward Shaping

We set the reward value as the score difference after performing the selected action:

$$R_t = S(F, B_t) - S(F, B_{t-1}), \tag{4}$$

where R_t is the reward value at step t, $S(\cdot)$ is the quality network, F is the foreground image, and B_t is the blending results at step t. That is, if the selected action increases the score, we provide a positive reward to encourage such behavior. Otherwise, we provide a negative reward to discourage it.

5.4 Implementation Details

We train the DRL agent Dueling-DQN [48] as well as A2C [47], which is a synchronous version of A3C [35] that enables GPU training. Training a model requires around 20 h to get stable performance for both methods. The details of the training process and parameters can be found in the supplementary materials. During the training process, the agent randomly picks a foreground image, a background image, and a random initial ROI for simulation. We set the maximum steps as 50 for each episode since there is no terminal signal in our task. When the selected action causes ROI to outside the background image or causing extreme photometric adjustment value, we provide a negative reward of value -1.0 to the agent and maintain the current state. We show an example of the intermediate search steps in Fig. 6. The code and data will be made available at https://github.com/hfslyc/LearnToBlend.

6 Blending Engine

The blending process is deterministic and composed of three major components: pre-processing, pixel blending, and post-processing. Pixel blending is a function that transforms two pixel values from foreground and background respectively to a blended pixel, and it is applied to every pixel pair after background is cropped and aligned with the foreground. The commonly used pixel blending functions are often simple mathematical functions, e.g., Add, Subtract, or Multiply. In this work, we focus on the most widely used blending variant: Double Exposure, in which the blending mode is called "Screen". The blending function can be formulated as:

$$x_i^{blend} = 1 - (1 - x_i^{fg}) \cdot (1 - x_i^{bg}), \tag{5}$$

where x_i^{fg}, x_i^{bg} are two pixels of location i from the foreground and cropped background images, and x_i^{blend} is the "Screen" blended pixel values. We assume the pixel value range $[0, 1]$, and the function is applied to all color channels independently. According to (5), the resulting value would be bright (1.0) if either the foreground pixel or background pixel is close to 1.0. Since in most cases the foreground photos are brighter, the overall effect could be seen as the dark parts of the foreground replaced by the background as shown in Fig. 1.

The pre-processing and post-processing could consist of any filtering, styling, or enhancement modules. For example, one engine can apply the Instagram filters and the background removal algorithms on foreground images either as pre- or post-processing modules. For simplicity, we carry out the experiments with only the foreground removal as pre-processing and one specific color tone adjustment as post-processing. We show more qualitative results with different styles of blending engine in the supplementary materials.

7 Experimental Results

7.1 Evaluation of Quality Network

To show the effectiveness of the proposed quality network, we compare the proposed method with Perceptual Loss [17] and Learned Perceptual Image Patch Similarity (LPIPS) [55] between the foreground image and blending result since a higher perceptual similarity often implies better user rating. We collect a validation set with 3205 user ratings on 100 image sets as stated in Sect. 4.3. Among the ratings that correspond the same foreground image, we sample all possible good-bad and fair-bad pairs to evaluate the mean accuracy, i.e., blending results with better user ratings should have a higher quality score/perceptual similarity and lower perceptual loss. As shown in Table 1, the proposed quality network can align the user preference better than existing methods. We also carry out ablation studies to validate the design choices of the quality network in Table 1. When removing the foreground branch in the quality network (no FG), the accuracy drops by 4.46%, reflecting the fact that the result aesthetics quality often depends on the original foreground. In addition, without the binary cross entropy (no BCE), the accuracy drops 3.52%, showing that the binary cross entropy can effectively regularize the quality network.

Table 1. Evaluation of quality network.

Method	Mean accuracy
Perceptual loss [17]	55.30%
LPIPS [55]	61.78%
Quality network (no FG)	75.23%
Quality network (no BCE)	76.17%
Quality network	**79.69%**

Table 2. Comparisons of random search.

Method	Steps	Mean Q.
Random-10	10	5.69 ± 0.75
Random-50	50	7.08 ± 0.64
Random-100	100	8.07 ± 0.53
Random-500	500	9.47 ± 0.47
Random-1k	1,000	9.99 ± 0.41
Random-5k	5,000	11.51 ± 0.10
Random-10k	10,000	11.76 ± 0.06

Table 3. Comparisons of search methods.

Method	Steps	Mean Q.
Tree Search	150	7.15 ± 0.61
Gaussian Process	100	7.33 ± 0.35
Greedy	100	7.43 ± 0.66
Simulated Annealing	100	8.12 ± 0.63
PSO [19]	100	8.91 ± 0.44
Dueling-DQN	100	9.86 ± 0.30
A2C	100	10.93 ± 0.26

7.2 Evaluation of DRL Search

In Tables 2 and 3, we evaluate the effectiveness of the proposed DRL search. First, we select 20 input pairs as the evaluation set and perform the random search to obtain the upper bound of quality score that we can achieve. During the search, the ROIs and photometric parameters are randomly sampled within the effective range to generate blending results, and the resulting photo is the one with the highest quality score. We report the search time cost in terms of evaluation steps since the forward time of quality network dominates the search process. We note that the forward time of the policy network is similar to the quality network. In our machine, each evaluation step takes 0.07 s with GPU. Note that during the search process, since only low-resolution results are rendered by blending, the overhead is much less than the final blending. As shown in Table 2, it will cost 10,000 evaluation steps, which takes around 11 min in our setup, to achieve the highest mean quality score of 11.76. However, in time-critical applications, complexity is of great importance. Therefore, we set a constraint to the evaluation steps as 100, and we compare the DRL based search with following derivative-free optimization methods:

- **Tree Search.** Use Random-50 as the initial point and search for all possible action sequences with depth 2.
- **Gaussian Process.** Use random 50 initial evaluation points and update the Gaussian approximation with 5 sampled points for 10 iterations. [22] also applies the Gaussian process for estimating the editing parameters.
- **Greedy.** Use Random-50 as the initial point and choose the best action for 5 steps (each cost 10 steps).
- **Simulated Annealing** [20]. (SA) Use Random-50 as the initial point and perform Simulated Annealing for 50 steps.
- **Particle Swarm Optimization** [19]. (PSO) Use 20 particles to perform 5 parallel updates.

All methods except PSO use Random-50 as the initial seed since it is a good trade-off between time cost and performance. We optimize the parameters of SA and PSO for best performance and report them in the supplementary materials. We show the comparisons in Table 3. Among the baselines, tree search performs the worst because it can only perform a depth-2 search within the time limit. Similarly, greedy search also suffers from the evaluation cost and can only perform 5 updates. SA can escape local optimum while performing the local search. But it only outperforms random-100 by a small margin, suggesting that the short schedule of SA does not converge well. Of all non-learning based methods, PSO performs the best with quality score 8.91 because of the joint combination of local and global optimization.

Both Dueling-DQN and A2C perform favorably against other baselines since the agent can perform different policy based on current image contexts for better exploration. A2C performs better than Dueling-DQN by 1.07, and we find that the non-deterministic action sampling (on-policy) of A2C helps to escape the local optimum, while with DQN the random exploration can only be used during training stage with ϵ-greedy.

7.3 User Study

We set up a user study to evaluate the effectiveness of the proposed method. To compare with human experts, we ask an expert to generate the same effect with a predefined Photoshop action script that automatically performs Double

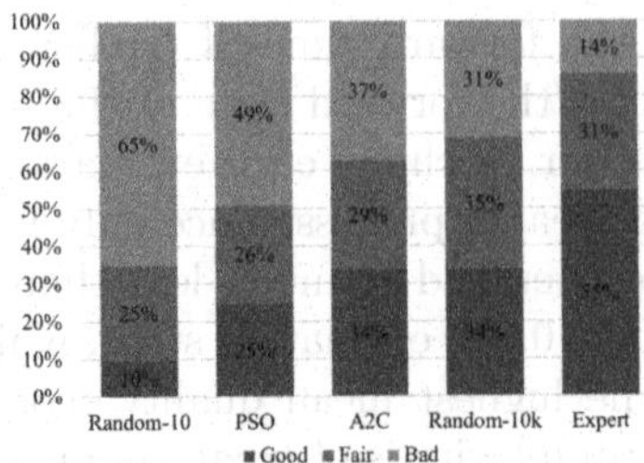

Fig. 7. Qualitative comparisons of selected baseline methods. We show the ratios of user ratings of selected baseline methods.

Exposure. To have a fair comparison with our baselines, the expert can only manipulate the background alignment and photometric adjustment. We record the expert adjusting process, and the average time for complete one blending photo is around 5 min with the help of action script. The user is asked to evaluate a total of 20 set images. During the study, each user sees five blending results for each foreground image that correspond to the following baselines: Random-10, PSO, Ours (A2C), Random-10k, and the human expert results. For each blending result, the user is asked to label each result as "good", "fair", or "bad". As a result, a total of 41 subjects participated in the study with a total of 4,100 votes.

We show the user study results in Fig. 7 and show some qualitative comparisons in Fig. 8. If we perform blending with only 10 random searches, 65% of blending results are considered bad to users, and only 10% of them are considered good. This shows that the task for photo blending is not trivial, as random parameters usually do not result in appealing results. Compared with Random-10, both PSO and Ours (A2C) obtain more aesthetically pleasing results. However, the proposed DRL search performs favorably against PSO with the same time cost (5 s) since it can exploit the current image contexts for better search policy. Random-10k represents the upper bound of the most aesthetically pleasing result that could be generated by the quality network. The performance of Random-10k only outperforms the proposed method by few percentage points but costs 7 more minutes per image, demonstrating that the proposed DRL search is an efficient way for searching in the parameter space.

The blending results of expert have the best aesthetics quality. The major difference is that the expert rarely makes blending results that are not acceptable to the user, resulting only 14% of "bad" ratings while our method has 37%. The fact that the exhaustive search (Random-10k) cannot outperform human expert with higher mean quality score (11.76 v.s. 11.32) suggests that there is still room for improving the proposed method.

Interestingly, we find that our method receives more "good" user ratings than the expert results in 6 sets out of 20 sets of blending results. It shows that our proposed method can, in some cases, produces results with higher quality than the one generated by the expert. However, there is no blending set where the expert result gets more "bad" ratings than other baselines. It suggests that even

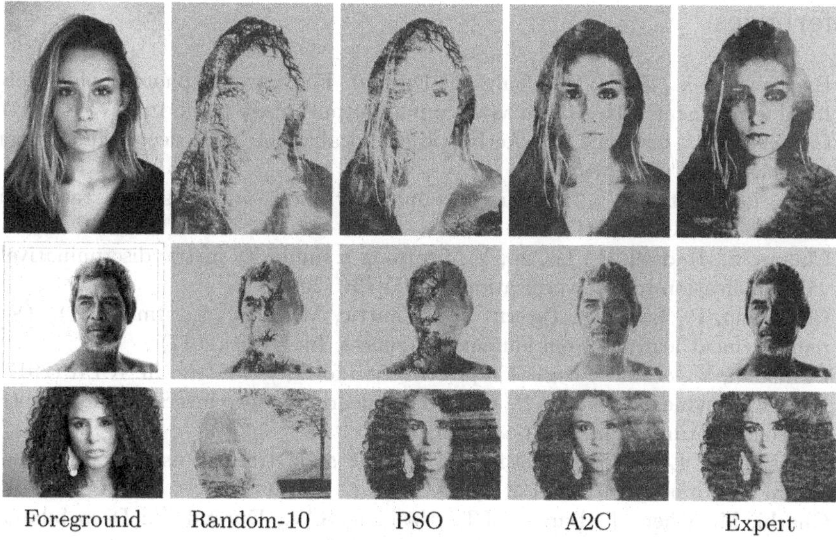

Fig. 8. Qualitative comparisons of different baseline methods. These results are generated with same foreground and background image pairs for each method. All of them are used in the user study.

some people do not see the expert-generated results as the best one, they still do not consider them not acceptable.

The quality differences between the baseline methods are also consistent with the average quality scores indicated by the proposed quality network. The better user rating methods have higher average quality scores, demonstrating that the proposed quality network is effective.

8 Concluding Remarks

In this paper, we propose a method for automatic photo blending. To evaluate the aesthetic quality of blending photos, we collect a new dataset and design a quality network to learn from coarse user preferences with ranking loss and binary cross entropy. We tackle the photo blending problem by designing a deep reinforcement learning based agent to search for background alignment and photometric adjustment parameters that result in the highest score of the quality network. The proposed method can serve as a generic framework for automatic photo art generation.

Acknowledgments. This work is supported in part by the NSF CAREER Grant #1149783, gifts from Adobe and NVIDIA.

References

1. Bychkovsky, V., Paris, S., Chan, E., Durand, F.: Learning photographic global tonal adjustment with a database of input/output image pairs. In: CVPR (2011)
2. Caicedo, J.C., Lazebnik, S.: Active object localization with deep reinforcement learning. In: ICCV (2015)
3. Chen, Q., Koltun, V.: Photographic image synthesis with cascaded refinement networks. In: ICCV (2017)
4. Chopra, S., Hadsell, R., LeCun, Y.: Learning a similarity metric discriminatively, with application to face verification. In: CVPR (2005)
5. Christiano, P., Leike, J., Brown, T.B., Martic, M., Legg, S., Amodei, D.: Deep reinforcement learning from human preferences. In: NIPS (2017)
6. Dumoulin, V., et al.: A learned representation for artistic style. In: ICLR (2017)
7. Finn, C., Levine, S., Abbeel, P.: Guided cost learning: deep inverse optimal control via policy optimization. In: ICML (2016)
8. Gatys, L.A., Ecker, A.S., Bethge, M.: Image style transfer using convolutional neural networks. In: CVPR (2016)
9. Gharbi, M., Chen, J., Barron, J.T., Hasinoff, S.W., Durand, F.: Deep bilateral learning for real-time image enhancement (2017)
10. Girshick, R.: Fast R-CNN. In: ICCV (2015)
11. Guzman-Rivera, A., Batra, D., Kohli, P.: Multiple choice learning: learning to produce multiple structured outputs. In: NIPS (2012)
12. Ho, J., Ermon, S.: Generative adversarial imitation learning. In: NIPS (2016)
13. Huang, X., Belongie, S.: Arbitrary style transfer in real-time with adaptive instance normalization. In: CVPR (2017)
14. Hwang, S.J., Kapoor, A., Kang, S.B.: Context-based automatic local image enhancement. In: Fitzgibbon, A., Lazebnik, S., Perona, P., Sato, Y., Schmid, C. (eds.) ECCV 2012. LNCS, vol. 7572, pp. 569–582. Springer, Heidelberg (2012). https://doi.org/10.1007/978-3-642-33718-5_41
15. Iizuka, S., Simo-Serra, E., Ishikawa, H.: Let there be color!: joint end-to-end learning of global and local image priors for automatic image colorization with simultaneous classification. In: SIGGRAPH (2016)
16. Isola, P., Zhu, J.Y., Zhou, T., Efros, A.A.: Image-to-image translation with conditional adversarial networks. In: CVPR (2017)
17. Johnson, J., Alahi, A., Fei-Fei, L.: Perceptual losses for real-time style transfer and super-resolution. In: Leibe, B., Matas, J., Sebe, N., Welling, M. (eds.) ECCV 2016. LNCS, vol. 9906, pp. 694–711. Springer, Cham (2016). https://doi.org/10.1007/978-3-319-46475-6_43
18. Kang, L., Ye, P., Li, Y., Doermann, D.: Convolutional neural networks for no-reference image quality assessment. In: CVPR (2014)
19. Kennedy, J.: Particle swarm optimization. In: Sammut, C., Webb, G.I. (eds.) Encyclopedia of Machine Learning, pp. 760–766. Springer, Boston (2011). https://doi.org/10.1007/978-0-387-30164-8_630
20. Kirkpatrick, S., Gelatt, C.D., Vecchi, M.P.: Optimization by simulated annealing. Science **220**(4598), 671–680 (1983)
21. Kong, S., Shen, X., Lin, Z., Mech, R., Fowlkes, C.: Photo aesthetics ranking network with attributes and content adaptation. In: Leibe, B., Matas, J., Sebe, N., Welling, M. (eds.) ECCV 2016. LNCS, vol. 9905, pp. 662–679. Springer, Cham (2016). https://doi.org/10.1007/978-3-319-46448-0_40

22. Koyama, Y., Sato, I., Sakamoto, D., Igarashi, T.: Sequential line search for efficient visual design optimization by crowds. ACM TOG **36**(4), article no. 48 (2017). Proceedings of the SIGGRAPH
23. Larsson, G., Maire, M., Shakhnarovich, G.: Learning representations for automatic colorization. In: Leibe, B., Matas, J., Sebe, N., Welling, M. (eds.) ECCV 2016. LNCS, vol. 9908, pp. 577–593. Springer, Cham (2016). https://doi.org/10.1007/978-3-319-46493-0_35
24. Lee, J.Y., Sunkavalli, K., Lin, Z., Shen, X., So Kweon, I.: Automatic content-aware color and tone stylization. In: CVPR (2016)
25. Li, C., Wand, M.: Combining markov random fields and convolutional neural networks for image synthesis. In: CVPR (2016)
26. Li, Y., Fang, C., Yang, J., Wang, Z., Lu, X., Yang, M.H.: Diversified texture synthesis with feed-forward networks. In: CVPR (2017)
27. Li, Y., Fang, C., Yang, J., Wang, Z., Lu, X., Yang, M.H.: Universal style transfer via feature transforms. In: NIPS (2017)
28. Liu, M.Y., Breuel, T., Kautz, J.: Unsupervised image-to-image translation networks. In: NIPS (2017)
29. Liu, S., Pan, J., Yang, M.-H.: Learning recursive filters for low-level vision via a hybrid neural network. In: Leibe, B., Matas, J., Sebe, N., Welling, M. (eds.) ECCV 2016. LNCS, vol. 9908, pp. 560–576. Springer, Cham (2016). https://doi.org/10.1007/978-3-319-46493-0_34
30. Lu, X., Lin, Z., Jin, H., Yang, J., Wang, J.Z.: Rapid: rating pictorial aesthetics using deep learning. In: ACM MM (2014)
31. Lu, X., Lin, Z., Shen, X., Mech, R., Wang, J.Z.: Deep multi-patch aggregation network for image style, aesthetics, and quality estimation. In: ICCV (2015)
32. Luan, F., Paris, S., Shechtman, E., Bala, K.: Deep photo style transfer. In: CVPR (2017)
33. Mai, L., Jin, H., Liu, F.: Composition-preserving deep photo aesthetics assessment. In: CVPR (2016)
34. Marchesotti, L., Perronnin, F., Larlus, D., Csurka, G.: Assessing the aesthetic quality of photographs using generic image descriptors. In: ICCV (2011)
35. Mnih, V., et al.: Asynchronous methods for deep reinforcement learning. In: ICML (2016)
36. Mnih, V., et al.: Human-level control through deep reinforcement learning. Nature **518**, 529–533 (2015)
37. Ng, A.Y., Russell, S.J., et al.: Algorithms for inverse reinforcement learning. In: ICML (2000)
38. Pathak, D., Krahenbuhl, P., Donahue, J., Darrell, T., Efros, A.A.: Context encoders: feature learning by inpainting. In: CVPR (2016)
39. Ren, J., Shen, X., Lin, Z., Mech, R., Foran, D.J.: Personalized image aesthetics. In: ICCV (2017)
40. Shih, Y., Paris, S., Barnes, C., Freeman, W.T., Durand, F.: Style transfer for headshot portraits. In: SIGGRAPH (2014)
41. Silver, D., et al.: Mastering the game of go with deep neural networks and tree search. Nature **529**, 484–489 (2016)
42. Simonyan, K., Zisserman, A.: Very deep convolutional networks for large-scale image recognition. In: ICLR (2015)
43. Stadie, B.C., Abbeel, P., Sutskever, I.: Third-person imitation learning. In: ICLR (2017)
44. Tsai, Y.H., Shen, X., Lin, Z., Sunkavalli, K., Yang, M.H.: Sky is not the limit: semantic-aware sky replacement. In: SIGGRAPH (2016)

45. Tsai, Y.H., Shen, X., Lin, Z., Sunkavalli, K., Lu, X., Yang, M.H.: Deep image harmonization. In: CVPR (2017)
46. Van Hasselt, H., Guez, A., Silver, D.: Deep reinforcement learning with double Q-learning. In: AAAI (2016)
47. Wang, J.X., et al.: Learning to reinforcement learn. arXiv preprint arXiv:1611.05763 (2016)
48. Wang, Z., Schaul, T., Hessel, M., Van Hasselt, H., Lanctot, M., De Freitas, N.: Dueling network architectures for deep reinforcement learning. In: arXiv preprint arXiv:1511.06581 (2015)
49. Wei, Z., et al.: Good view hunting: learning photo composition from dense view pairs. In: CVPR (2018)
50. Yan, Z., Zhang, H., Wang, B., Paris, S., Yu, Y.: Automatic photo adjustment using deep neural networks. ACM TOG **35**(2), article no. 11 (2016). Proc. SIGGRAPH
51. Yeh, R., Chen, C., Lim, T.Y., Hasegawa-Johnson, M., Do, M.N.: Semantic image inpainting with perceptual and contextual losses. In: CVPR (2017)
52. Yoo, D., Park, S., Lee, J.Y., Paek, A.S., So Kweon, I.: AttentionNet: aggregating weak directions for accurate object detection. In: ICCV (2015)
53. Yoo, S.Y.J.C.Y., Yun, K., Choi, J.Y.: Action-decision networks for visual tracking with deep reinforcement learning. In: CVPR (2017)
54. Zhang, R., Isola, P., Efros, A.A.: Colorful image colorization. In: Leibe, B., Matas, J., Sebe, N., Welling, M. (eds.) ECCV 2016. LNCS, vol. 9907, pp. 649–666. Springer, Cham (2016). https://doi.org/10.1007/978-3-319-46487-9_40
55. Zhang, R., Isola, P., Efros, A.A., Shechtman, E., Wang, O.: The unreasonable effectiveness of deep networks as a perceptual metric. In: CVPR (2018)
56. Zhang, R., et al.: Real-time user-guided image colorization with learned deep priors. In: SIGGRAPH (2017)
57. Zhu, J.Y., Krahenbuhl, P., Shechtman, E., Efros, A.A.: Learning a discriminative model for the perception of realism in composite images. In: ICCV (2015)
58. Zhu, J.Y., Park, T., Isola, P., Efros, A.A.: Unpaired image-to-image translation using cycle-consistent adversarial networks. In: ICCV (2017)
59. Zhu, J.Y., et al.: Toward multimodal image-to-image translation. In: NIPS (2017)

Switchable Temporal Propagation Network

Sifei Liu[1(✉)], Guangyu Zhong[1,3], Shalini De Mello[1], Jinwei Gu[1], Varun Jampani[1], Ming-Hsuan Yang[1,2], and Jan Kautz[1]

[1] NVIDIA, Santa Clara, USA
sifeil@nvidia.com
[2] UC Merced, Merced, USA
[3] Dalian University of Technology, Dalian, China

Abstract. Videos contain highly redundant information between frames. Such redundancy has been studied extensively in video compression and encoding, but is less explored for more advanced video processing. In this paper, we propose a learnable unified framework for propagating a variety of visual properties of video images, including but not limited to color, high dynamic range (HDR), and segmentation mask, where the properties are available for only a few key-frames. Our approach is based on a temporal propagation network (TPN), which models the transition-related affinity between a pair of frames in a purely data-driven manner. We theoretically prove two essential properties of TPN: (a) by regularizing the global transformation matrix as orthogonal, the "style energy" of the property can be well preserved during propagation; and (b) such regularization can be achieved by the proposed switchable TPN with bi-directional training on pairs of frames. We apply the switchable TPN to three tasks: colorizing a gray-scale video based on a few colored key-frames, generating an HDR video from a low dynamic range (LDR) video and a few HDR frames, and propagating a segmentation mask from the first frame in videos. Experimental results show that our approach is significantly more accurate and efficient than the state-of-the-art methods.

1 Introduction

Videos contain highly redundant information between frames. Consider a pair of consecutive frames randomly sampled from a video, it is likely that they are similar in terms of appearance, structure and content in most regions. Such redundancy has been extensively studied in video compression to reduce storage and speedup the transmission of videos, but is less explored for more advanced video processing. A number of recent algorithms, such as optical-flow based warping [1], similarity-guided filtering [2,3] and the bilateral CNN model [4], explore

Electronic supplementary material The online version of this chapter (https://doi.org/10.1007/978-3-030-01234-2_6) contains supplementary material, which is available to authorized users.

V. Ferrari et al. (Eds.): ECCV 2018, LNCS 11211, pp. 89–104, 2018.
https://doi.org/10.1007/978-3-030-01234-2_6

the local relationships between frames to propagate information. These methods model the similarity among pixels, regions or frames from either hand-crafted pixel-level features (e.g., pixel intensities and locations) or apparent motion (e.g., optical flow). They have several potential issues: (a) the designed similarity may not faithfully reflect the image structure, and (b) such similarity may not express the high-level pairwise relationships between frames, e.g., for propagating a segmentation mask in the semantic domain.

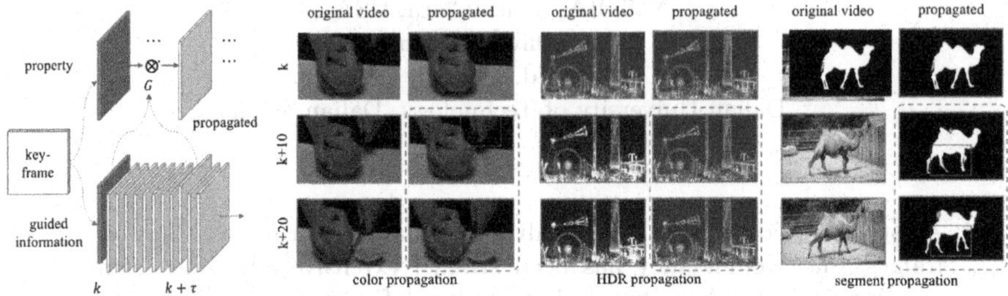

Fig. 1. We propose the TPN model that takes a known property (e.g., color, HDR, segmentation mask) from a key-frame (k), and transform it to a nearby frame ($k + \tau$), denoted by "propagated". The transformation is guided by a learnable matrix G, which is learned from some known information (e.g., lightness, LDR, RGB image). We show three tasks on the right size, where k denotes the key-frame for which the ground-truth property is provided. The orange bounding boxes shows the propagated results of our algorithm, when guided by the information in the left columns. We highlight (red bounding boxes) the regions where the proposed method successfully deals with large transitions or preserves fine details. Zoom-in to see details. (Color figure online)

In this paper, we develop a temporal propagation network (TPN) to explicitly learn pixel-level similarity between a pair of frames (see Fig. 1). It contains a propagation module that transfers a property (e.g., color) of one frame to a nearby frame through a global, linear transformation matrix which is learned with a CNN from any available guidance information (e.g., lightness).

We enforce two principles when learning propagation in the temporal domain: (a) **bi-directionality**, i.e., the propagation between a pair of frames should be invertible, and (b) **consistency**, i.e., the "style energy" (e.g., the global saturation of color) of the target property should be preserved during propagation. We theoretically prove that: enforcing both principles in the TPN is *equivalent* to ensuring that the transformation matrix is orthogonal with respect to each propagation direction. This theoretical result allows us to implement TPN as a novel, special network architecture—the switchable TPN (see Fig. 2)—without explicitly solving for the transformation matrix. It uses bi-directional training for a pair of frames in the propagation module, which is guided by switched output maps from the guidance CNN network. Experiments demonstrate that the proposed architecture is effective in preserving the style energy even between two widely separated frames.

We validate the proposed model for three propagation tasks: (a) video colorization from a few color key-frames and a grayscale video (Sect. 5.2).

With such temporal propagation, the workload of black-and-white video colorization can be largely reduced to only annotating a small number of key-frames. (b) HDR video reconstruction from an LDR video with a few HDR key-frames (Sect. 5.3). This is a new way for HDR video capture, where the whole video can be reconstructed with a few provided HDR frames. (c) video segmentation when only the segmentation mask of the target in the first frame is provided. We show that even without any image-based segmentation model, the proposed method can achieve comparable performance to the state-of-the-art algorithm. All of these tasks reveal that video properties between temporally close frames are highly redundant, and that the relationships between them can be learned from corresponding guidance information. Compared to the existing methods, and aside from the novel architecture, our proposed method also has the following advantages: **(a) High accuracy.** Compared to prior work [4,5], the TPN significantly improves video quality. More importantly, the switchable TPN preserves the style energy significantly better than the network without the switchable structure. **(b) High efficiency.** Our method runs in real-time on a single Titan XP GPU for all the three tasks, which is about 30x to 50x faster than the prior work [4,5] (see Table 1). Moreover, our model does not require sequential processing of video frames, i.e., all video frames can be processed in parallel, which can further improve its efficiency.

2 Related Work and Problem Context

Modeling Affinity for Pixel Propagation. Affinity is a generic measure of closeness between two pixels/entities and is widely used in vision tasks at all levels. Well-modeled affinity reveals how to propagate information from the known pixels to the unknown ones. Most prior methods design affinity measures based on simple, intuitive functions [2,3,6]. Recently, a deep CNN model is proposed to learn task-dependent affinity metric [7] by modeling the propagation of pixels as an image diffusion process.

While [7] is limited to the spatial propagation of pixels for image segmentation, its high-level idea inspires us to learn pixel affinity in other domains via CNNs, e.g., in video sequences as proposed in this work.

Considerably less attention has been paid to develop methods for propagating temporal information across video frames. Jampani et al. [4] propose to propagate video segmentation and color information by embedding pixels into a bilateral space [8] defined based on spatial, temporal and color information. While pixels of the same region from different frames can be closer in this space, it requires several previous frames stacked together to generate a new frame, which results in a high computational cost. Our proposed algorithm is different in that it explicitly *learns* the pixel affinity that describes the task-specific temporal frame transitions, instead of manually defining a similarity measure.

Colorizing Grayscale Videos. Colorization in images and videos is achieved via an interactive procedure in [3], which propagates manually annotated strokes spatially within or across frames, based on a matting Laplacian matrix and with manually defined similarities. Recently, several methods based on CNNs have been developed to colorize pixels in images with fully-automatic or sparsely annotated colors [9,10]. Due to the multinomial nature of color pixels [10], the interactive procedure usually gives better results. While interactive methods can be employed for single images, it is not practical to annotate them for all frames of a monochrome video. In this work, we suggest a more plausible approach by using a few color key-frames to propagate visual information to all frames in between. To this end, colorizing a full video can be easily achieved by annotating at sparse locations in only a few key-frames, as described in Sect. 5.2.

Video Propagation for HDR Imaging. Most consumer-grade digital cameras have limited dynamic range and often capture images with under/over-exposed regions, which not only degrades the quality of the captured photographs and videos, but also impairs the performance of computer vision tasks in numerous applications. A common way to achieve HDR imaging is to capture a stack of LDR images with different exposures and to fuse them together [11,12]. Such an approach assumes static scenes and thus requires deghosting techniques [13–15] to remove artifacts. Capturing HDR videos for dynamic scenes poses a more challenging problem. Prior methods to create HDR videos are mainly based on hardware that either alternate exposures between frames [16,17], or use multiple cameras [18], or specialized image sensors with pixel-wise exposure controls [19,20]. A few recent methods based on deep models have been developed for HDR imaging. Kalantari et al. [21] use a deep neural network to align multiple LDR images into a single HDR image for dynamic scenes. Zhang et al. [22] develop an auto-encoder network to predict a single HDR panorama from a single exposed LDR image for image-based rendering. In addition, Eilertsen et al. [5] propose a similar network for HDR reconstruction from a single LDR input image, which primarily focuses on recovering details in the high intensity saturated regions.

In this paper, we apply the TPN for HDR video reconstruction from a LDR video. Given a few HDR key-frames and an LDR video, the TPN propagates the scene radiance information from the key-frames to the remaining frames. Note that unlike all the existing single LDR-based methods [5,22], which hallucinate the missing HDR details in images, we focus on propagating the HDR information from the input few HDR images to neighboring LDR frames, which provides an alternative solution for efficient, low cost HDR video reconstruction.

3 Proposed Algorithm

We exploit the redundancy in videos, and propose the TPN for learning affinity and propagating target properties between frames. Take the video colorization as an example. Given an old black-and-white movie with a few key-frames colorized by artists, can we automatically colorize the entire movie? This problem can be equivalently reformulated as propagating a target property (i.e., color) based on the affinity of some features (e.g., lightness) between two frames. Intuitively, this is feasible because (1) videos have redundancy over time—nearby frames tend to have similar appearance, and (2) the pixel correlation between two frames in the lightness domain is often consistent with that in the color domain.

In this work, we model the propagation of a target property (e.g., color) between two frames as a *linear transformation*,

$$U_t = GU_k, \tag{1}$$

where $U_k \in \mathcal{R}^{n^2 \times 1}$ and $U_t \in \mathcal{R}^{n^2 \times 1}$ are the vectorized version of the $n \times n$ property maps of a key-frame and a nearby frame, and $G \in \mathcal{R}^{n^2 \times n^2}$ is the transformation matrix to be estimated[1]. Suppose we observe some features of the two frames (e.g., lightness) V_k and V_t, the transformation matrix G is thus a function of V_k and V_t,

$$G = g(\theta, V_k, V_t). \tag{2}$$

The matrix G should be dense in order to model any type of pixel transition in a global scope, but G should also be concise for efficient estimation and propagation. In Sect. 3.1, we propose a solution, called basic TPN, by formulating the linear transformation G as an image diffusion process similar to [7]. Following that, in Sect. 3.2, we introduce the key part of our work, the switchable TPN, which enforces the bi-directionality and the style consistency for temporal propagation. We prove that enforcing these two principles is equivalent to ensuring the transformation matrix G is orthogonal, which in turn can be easily implemented by equipping an ordinary temporal propagation network with a switchable structure.

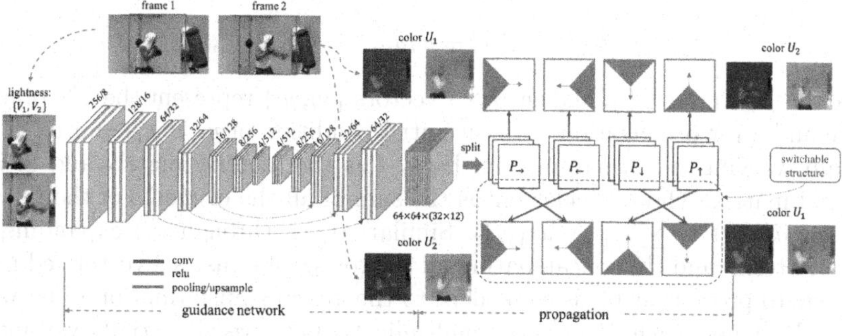

Fig. 2. The architectures of a switchable TPN, which contains two propagation modules for bi-directional training. We specifically use a red-dashed box to denote the switchable structure In the reversed pair, the output channels $\{P\}$ are switched (red) for horizontal and vertical propagation. (Color figure online)

[1] For property maps with multiple channels $n \times n \times c$, we treat each channel separately.

3.1 Learning Pixel Transitions via the Basic TPN

Directly learning the transformation matrix G via a CNN is prohibitive, since G has a huge dimension (e.g., $n^2 \times n^2$). Instead, inspired by the recent work [7], we formulate the transformation as a diffusion process, and implement it efficiently by propagating information along each row and each column in an image linearly. Suppose we keep only $k = 3$ nearest neighbors from a previous column (row) during the propagation, and we perform the propagation in $d = 4$ directions, the total number of parameters to be estimated is significantly reduced from $n^2 \times n^2$ to $n^2 \times k \times d$ (see example of Fig. 2).

Linear Transformation as a Diffusion Process. The diffusion process from frame k to frame t can be expressed with a partial differential equation (PDE) in the discrete form as:

$$\nabla U = U_t - U_k = -LU_k = (A - D)U_k, \tag{3}$$

where $L = D - A$ is the Laplacian matrix, D is the diagonal degree matrix and A is the affinity matrix. In our case, this represents the propagation of the property map U over time. (3) can be re-written as $U_t = (I - D + A)\,U_k = GU_k$, where G is the transformation matrix between the two states, as defined in (1), and I is an identity matrix.

Linear Propagation Network. With a propagation structure, the diffusion between frames can be implemented as a linear propagation along the rows or columns of an image. Here we briefly show their equivalence. Following [7], we take the left-to-right spatial propagation operation as an example:

$$y_i = (I - d_i)\,x_i + w_i y_{i-1}, \quad i \in [2, n], \tag{4}$$

where $x \in U_k$ and $y \in U_t$, and the $n \times 1$ vectors $\{x_i, y_i\}$ represent the ith columns before and after propagation with an initial condition of $y_1 = x_1$, and w_i is the spatially varying $n \times n$ sub-matrix. Here, I is the identity matrix and d_i is a diagonal matrix, whose t^{th} element is the sum of all the elements of the tth row of w_i as $d_i(t,t) = \sum_{j=1, j\neq t}^{n} w_i(j,t)$. Similar to [7], through (a) expanding its recursive term, and (b) concatenating all the rows/columns as a vectorized map, it is easy to prove that (4) is equivalent to the global transformation G between U_k and U_t, where each entry is the multiplication of several spatially variant w_i matrices [7]. Essentially, instead of predicting all the entries in G as independent variables, the propagation structure transfers the problem into learning each sub-matrix w_i in (4), which significantly reduces the output dimensions.

Learning the Sub-matrix $\{w_i\}$. We adopt an independent deep CNN, namely the guidance network, to output all the sub-matrices w_i. Note that the propagation in (1) is carried out for $d = 4$ directions independently, as shown in Fig. 2. For each direction, it takes a pair of images $\{V_k, V_t\}$ as its input, and outputs a feature map P that has the same spatial size as U (see Fig. 2). Each pixel in the feature map $p_{i,j}$ contains all the values of the jth row in w_i, which describes a local relation between the adjacent columns, but results in a global connection in G though the propagation structure. Similar to [7], we keep only $k = 3$ nearest neighbors from the previous column, which results in w_i being a tridiagonal matrix. Thus, a total of $n \times n \times (k \times d)$ parameters are used to implement the transformation matrix G. Such a structure significantly compresses the guidance network while still ensuring that the corresponding G is a dense matrix that can describe global and dense pairwise relationships between a pair of frames.

3.2 Preserving Consistency via Switchable TPN

In this part, we show that there are two unique characteristics of propagation in the temporal domain, which do not exist for propagation in the spatial domain [7]. First, temporal propagation is bi-directional for two frames, i.e., a network capable of transforming a frame U_1 into a frame U_2, should also be able to transform from U_2 to U_1, with a corresponding reversed ordering of inputs to the guidance network. Second, during propagation, the overall "style" of the propagated property across the image should stay constant between frames, e.g., during color propagation, the color saturation of all frames within a short video clip should be similar. We call this feature "consistency property". As shown below, we prove that enforcing the bi-directionality and the consistency is equivalent to ensure the transformation matrix G to be orthogonal, which in turn can be easily implemented by equipping an ordinary temporal propagation network with a switchable structure.

Bi-directionality of TPN. We assume that properties in nearby video frames do not have a causal relationship. This assumption holds for most properties that naturally exist in the real-world, e.g., color and HDR. Hence, temporal propagation of these properties can often be switched in direction without breaking the process. Given a diffusion model G and a pair of frames $\{U_1, U_2\}$, we have a pair of equations:

$$U_2 = G_{1\to 2} U_1, \quad U_1 = G_{2\to 1} U_2, \tag{5}$$

where the arrow denotes the propagation direction. The bi-directionality property implies that reversing the roles of the two frames as inputs by $\{V_1, V_2\} \to \{V_2, V_1\}$, and the corresponding supervision signals to the network corresponds to applying an inverse transformation matrix $G_{2\to 1} = G_{1\to 2}^{-1}$.

Style Preservation in Sequences. Style consistency refers to whether the generated frames can maintain similar chromatic properties or brightness when propagating color or HDR information, which is important for producing high-quality videos without the property vanishing over time. In this work, we ensure such global temporal consistency by minimizing the difference in style loss of the propagated property for the two frames. Style loss has been intensively used in style transfer [23], but has not yet been used for regularizing temporal propagation. In our work, we represent the style by the Gram matrix, which is proportional to the un-centered covariance of the property map. The style loss is the squared Frobenius norm of the difference between the Gram matrices of the key-frame and the succeeding frame:

Theorem 1. *By regularizing the style loss we have the following optimization w.r.t. the guidance network:*

$$\min \frac{1}{N} \parallel U_1^\top U_1 - U_2^\top U_2 \parallel_F^2 \tag{6}$$

$$s.t. \quad U_2 = GU_1. \tag{7}$$

The optimal solution is reached when G is orthogonal.

Proof. Since the function (6) is non-negative, the minimum is reached when $U_1^\top U_1 = U_2^\top U_2$. Combining it with (7) we have $G^\top G = I$.

Given that G is orthogonal, the $G_{2\to1}$ in (5) can be replaced by $G_{1\to2}^\top$, which equals to $G_{1\to2}^{-1}$. Therefore, the bi-directionality propagation can be represented via a pair of transformation matrices that are *transposed* w.r.t each other. In the following part, we show how to enforce this property for the transformation matrix G in the linear propagation network via a special network architecture. Note that in our implementation, even though we use the channel-wise propagation described in Sect. 3.1, where the $U^\top U$ actually reduces to an uncentered variance, the conclusions of Theorem 1 still hold.

A Switchable Propagation Network. The linear transformation matrix G has an important property: since the propagation is directed, the transformation matrix G is a triangular matrix. Consider the two directions along the horizontal axis (i.e., $\rightarrow, \leftarrow$) in Fig. 2. G is an upper triangular matrix for a particular direction (e.g., $\rightarrow$), while it is lower triangular for the opposite one (e.g., $\leftarrow$). Suppose $P_\rightarrow$ and $P_\leftarrow$ are the output maps of the guidance network w.r.t. these two opposite directions. This means that the transformation matrix, which is lower-triangular for propagation in the left-to-right direction, becomes upper-triangular for the opposite direction of propagation. Since the upper-triangular matrix: (a) corresponds to propagating in the right-to-left direction, and (b) contains the same set of weight sub-matrices, *switching the CNN output channels w.r.t. the opposite directions* $P_\rightarrow$ and $P_\leftarrow$ *is equivalent to transposing the transformation matrix G in the TPN.* This fact is exploited as a regularization structure (see the red box in Fig. 2) during training.

To summarize, the switchable structure of the TPN is derived from the two principles (i.e., the bi-directionality and the style consistency) for temporal propagation and the fact that the matrix G is triangular due to the specific form of propagation. Note that [7] did not address the triangulation of the matrix and thus were limited to propagation in the spatial domain only. We show the switchable TPN (STPN) largely improve performance over the basic TPN, with no computational overhead at inference time.

4 Network Implementation

We provide the network implementation details shared by color, HDR and segmentation mask propagation, which are proposed in this work. These settings can be potentially generalized to other properties of videos as well.

The Basic TPN. The basic TPN contains two separate branches: (a) a deep CNN for the guidance network, which takes as input the provided information $\{V_1, V_2\}$ from a pair of frames, and outputs all elements (P) that constitute the state transformation matrix G, and (b) a linear propagation module that takes the property map of one frame U_1 and outputs U_2. It also takes as input $\{P\}$ the propagation coefficients following the formulation of (4), where $\{P\}$ contains kd channels ($k = 3$ connections for each pixel per direction, and $d = 4$ directions in total). $\{V, U, P\}$ have the same spatial size according to (4). We use node-wise max-pooling [7,24] to integrate the hidden layers and to obtain the final propagation result. All submodules are differentiable and jointly trained using stochastic gradient descent (SGD), with the base learning rate of 10^{-5} (Fig. 3).

The Switchable TPN. Figure 2 shows how the switchable structure of the TPN is exploited as an additional regularization loss term during training. For each pair (U_1, U_2) of the training data, the first term in (8) shows the regular supervised loss between the network estimation $\hat{U}_2$ and the groundtruth U_2. In addition, as shown in Fig. 2(b), since we want to enforce the bi-directionality and the style consistency in the switchable TPN, the same network should be able to propagate from U_2 back to U_1 by simply switching the channels of the output of the guidance networks, i.e., switching the channels of $\{P\rightarrow, P\leftarrow\}$ and $\{P\downarrow, P\uparrow\}$ for propagating information in the opposite direction. This will form the second loss term in (8), which serves as a regularization (weighted by λ) during the training. We set $\lambda = 0.1$ for all the experiments in this paper.

$$L(U_1, \hat{U}_1, U_2, \hat{U}_2) = \left\|U_2(i) - \hat{U}_2(i)\right\|^2 + \lambda \left\|U_1(i) - \hat{U}_1(i)\right\|^2. \quad (8)$$

At inference time, the switchable TPN reduces to the basic TPN introduced in Sect. 3.1 and therefore does not have any extra computational expense.

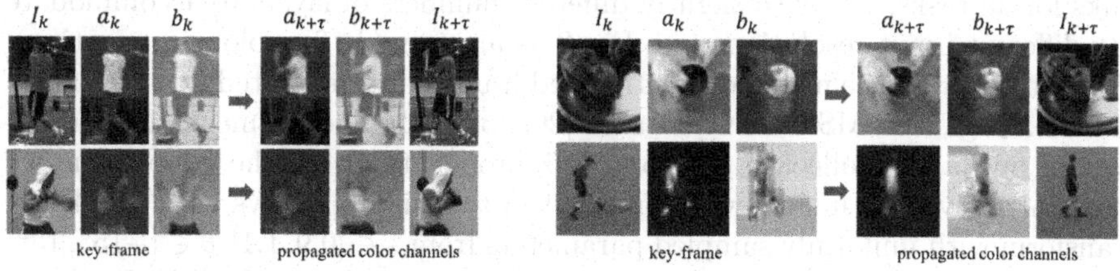

Fig. 3. We show two groups of color transitions output through a basic TPN. For each group, the left side is key-frames with the ground truth color images provided, and the right side is new frames propagated from the left. $\{a_k, b_k\}$ and $\{a_{k+\tau}, b_{k+\tau}\}$ are the inputs and outputs of the TPN. All four examples show obvious appearance transitions caused by movement of objects. Zoom-in to see details.

Table 1. Run-times of different methods. We set $K = 30$ for VPN color propagation [4] to calculate its run-time. The last four columns are our methods.

Method	VPN [4] (color)	VPN [4] (seg)	HDRCNN [5]	Color	HDR	SEG(t)	SEG(t+s)
(ms)	730	750	365	15	25	17	84

5 Experimental Results

In this section, we present our experimental results for propagating color channels, HDR images, and segmentation mask across videos. We note that propagating information across relatively longer temporal intervals may not satisfy the assumptions of a diffusion model, especially when new objects or scenes appear. Hence, for color and HDR propagation, instead of considering such complex scenarios, we set "key-frames" at regular fixed intervals for both tasks. That is, the ground truth color or HDR information is provided for every K frames and propagated to all frames in between them. This is a practical strategy for real-world applications. Note that for video segmentation mask propagation, we still follow the protocol of the DAVIS dataset [25] and only use the mask from the first frame.

5.1 General Network Settings and Run-Times

We use a guidance network and a propagation module similar to [7], with two cascaded propagation units. For computational and memory efficiency, the propagation is implemented with a smaller resolution, where U is downsampled from the original input space to a hidden layer before being fed into the propagation module. The hidden layer is then bi-linearly upsampled to the original size of the image. We adopt a symmetric U-net shaped, light-weight deep CNN with skip links for all tasks, but with slightly different numbers of layers to accommodate the different input resolutions (see Fig. 2 as an example for color propagation). We first pre-train the model on synthesized frame pairs generated from an image dataset. (e.g., the MS-COCO dataset [26] for color and segmentation propagation, and a self-collected one for HDR propagation, see the supplementary material). Given an image, we augment it in two different ways via a similarity transform with uniformly sampled parameters from $s \in [0.9, 1.1], \theta \in [-15°, 15°]$ and $dx \in [-0.1, 0.1] \times b$, where $b = \min(H, W)$. We also apply this data augmentation while training with patches from video sequences. We present the run-times for different methods on an 512×512 image using a single TITAN X (Pascal) NVIDIA GPU (without cuDNN) in Table 1.

5.2 Color Propagation in Videos

We use the ACT dataset [27], which contains 7260 training sequences with about 600K frames in total of various categories of actions. All the sequences are short

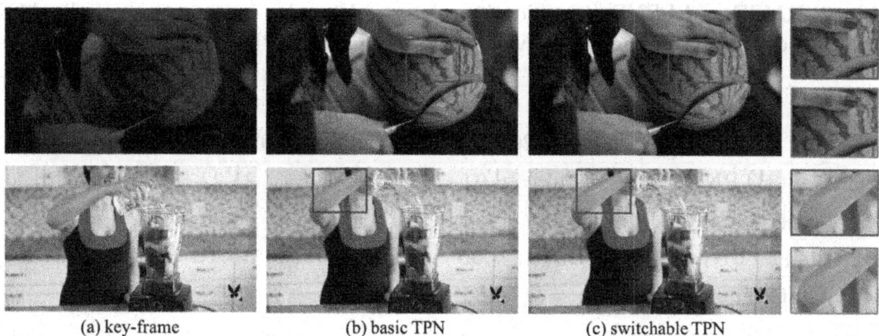

Fig. 4. An example of color propagation from a key-frame (a) to a new frame with considerably large appearance transitions, using either (b) the basic TPN or (c) the switchable TPN. The closeups show the detailed comparison. Zoom-in to see details. (Color figure online)

with small camera or scene transitions, and thus are more suitable for the proposed task. We re-train and evaluate the VPN network on the ACT dataset for a fair comparison. The original testing set contains 3974 sequences with more than 300K frames. For faster processing, we randomly select five videos from every action category in order to maintain the prior distribution of the original ACT dataset. We use one for testing and the remaining four for training.

We perform all computations in the *CIE-Lab* color space. After pretraining on the MS-COCO dataset, we fine-tune the models on the ACT dataset by randomly selecting two frames from a sequence and cropping both frames at the same spatial location as a single training sample. Specifically, our TPN takes as input the concatenated *ab* channels that are randomly cropped to 256×256 from a key-frame. The patches are then transformed to $64 \times 64 \times 32$ via 2 convoluitional layers with $stride = 2$ before being input to the propagation module. After propagation, the output maps are upsampled as a transformed *ab* image map for the frames following the key-frame. The guidance CNN takes as input a pair of lightness images (L) for the two frames. We optimize the Euclidean loss (in the *ab* color space) between the ground truth and the propagated color channels generated by our network. Note that for the switchable TPN, we have two losses with different weights according to (8). During testing, we combine the estimated *ab* channels with the given L channel to generate a color RGB image. All our evaluation metrics are computed in the RGB color space.

We compare the models with three combinations. We refer to the basic and switchable TPN networks as BTPN and STPN, the suffix "im" and "vd" denote pretraining on MS-COCO and finetuning on ACT, respectively. The methods that we compare include: (a) BTPNim+BTPNvd, (b) BTPNim+STPNvd, and (c) STPNim+STPNvd; and evaluate different key-frames intervals, including $K = \{10, 20, 30, 40\}$. The quantitative results for root mean square error (RMSE) and peak signal-to-noise ratio (PSNR) are presented in Table 2. Two trends can be inferred from the results. First, the switchable TPN consistently outperforms the basic TPN and the VPN [4], and using the switchable TPN structure for

Table 2. RMSE and PSNR (in parentheses) for video color propagation on the ACT dataset for different key-frame interval K. We compared VPN with $K = 30$.

Eval	RMSE				PSNR			
Interval	$K = 10$	$K = 20$	$K = 30$	$K = 40$	$K = 10$	$K = 20$	$K = 30$	$K = 40$
BTPNim+BTPNvd	4.43	5.46	6.04	6.44	36.65	35.22	34.46	33.96
BTPNim+STPNvd	4.00	5.00	5.58	6.01	37.63	36.09	35.26	34.70
STPNim+STPNvd	**3.98**	**4.97**	**5.55**	**5.99**	**37.64**	**36.12**	**35.29**	**34.73**
VPN (stage-1) [4]	-	-	6.86	-	-	-	32.86	-

both the pre-training and fine-tuning stages generates the best results. Second, while the errors decrease drastically on reducing time intervals between adjacent key-frames, the colorized video maintains overall high-quality even when K is set close to a common frame rate (e.g., 25 to 30 fps). We also show in Fig. 4(b) and (c) that the switchable structure significantly improves the qualitative results by preserving the saturation of color, especially when there are large transitions between the generated images and their corresponding key-frames. The TPN also maintains good colorization for fairly long video sequences, which is evident from a comparison of the colorized video frames with the ground truth in Fig. 5. Over longer time intervals, the quality of the switchable TPN degrades much more gracefully than that of the basic TPN and the VPN [4].

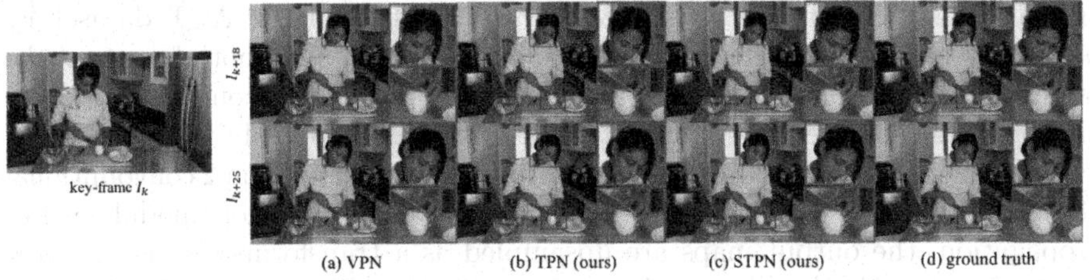

Fig. 5. Results using propagation of color from a key-frame to two proceeding frames (the 18th and the 25th) at different time intervals with the basic/switchable TPN, and the VPN [4] models. Zoom-in to see details. (Color figure online)

5.3 HDR Propagation in Videos

We compare our method against the work of [5], which directly reconstructs the HDR frames given the corresponding LDR frames as inputs. While this is not an apples-to-apples comparison because we also use an HDR key-frame as input, the work [5] is the closest related state-of-the-art method to our approach for HDR reconstruction. To our knowledge, no prior work exists on propagating HDR information in videos using deep learning and ours is the first work to address this problem. We use a similar network architecture as color propagation except that U is transformed to $128 \times 128 \times 16$ via one convolution layer to preserve more image details, and a two-stage training procedure by first pre-training the network with randomly augmented pairs of patches created from a dataset of HDR images, and then fine-tuning on an HDR video dataset. We collect the majority of the publicly available HDR image and video datasets listed in the supplementary material, and utilize all the HDR images and every 10-th frame of the HDR videos for training in the first stage [5]. Except for the four videos (the same as [5]) that we use for testing, we train our TPN with all the collected videos. We evaluate our method on the four videos that [5] used for testing and compare against their method.

To deal with the long-tail, skewed distribution of pixel values in HDR images, similarly to [5], we use the logarithmic space for HDR training with $U = \log(H + \varepsilon)$, where H denotes an HDR image and ε is set to 0.01. Since the image irradiance values recorded in HDR images vary significantly across cameras, naively merging different datasets together often generates domain differences in the training samples. To resolve this issue, before merging the datasets acquired by different cameras, we subtract from each input image the mean value of its corresponding dataset. We use the same data augmentation as in [5] of varying exposure values and camera curves [28] during training. During testing, we follow [5] to blend the inverse HDR image created from the input LDR image with the HDR image predicted by our TPN network to obtain the final output HDR image. More details are presented in the supplementary material.

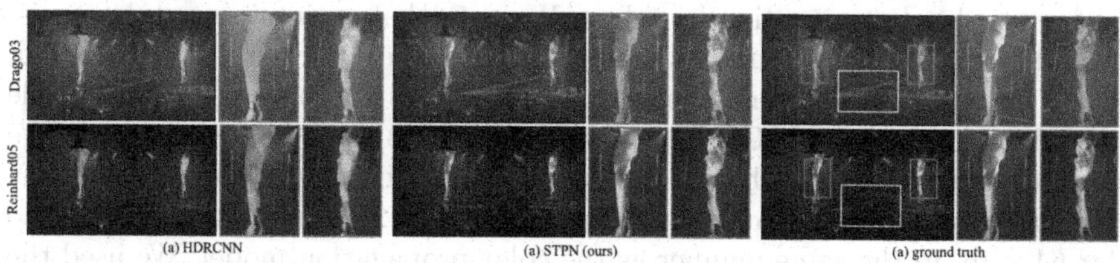

Fig. 6. Results of HDR Video Propagation. We show one HDR frame ($\tau = 19$ frames away from the key frame) reconstructed with our switchable TPN (middle column). The top row shows the ground truth HDR, and the bottom row shows the output of HDRCNN [5]. The HDR images are displayed with two popular tone mapping algorithms, Drago03 [29] and Reinhard05 [30]. The insets show that the switchable TPN can effectively propagate the HDR information to new frames and preserve the dynamic range of scene details. Zoom-in to see details.

We compare the RMSE of the generated HDR frames for different intervals between the key-frames, with or without the blending of LDR information with the HDR image generated by the TPN in Table 3. Our results indicate that the switchable TPN can also significantly improve the results for HDR propagation compared to the basic TPN. We also compare with the frame-wise reconstruction method [5], with and without the blending-based post-processing in Fig. 6. As shown, our TPN recovers HDR images with up to $K = 30$ frames away from each key frame. The reconstructed HDR images preserve the same scene details as the ground truth, under different tone mapping algorithms. More results are

Table 3. RMSE for video HDR propagation for the TPN output, the output with LDR blending, for different intervals for the key-frames K. Reconstruction from single LDR [5] is compared under the same experimental settings.

Settings	HDR with blending				HDR without blending			
Interval	$K = 10$	$K = 20$	$K = 30$	$K = 40$	$K = 10$	$K = 20$	$K = 30$	$K = 40$
BTPNim+BTPNvd	0.031	0.034	0.038	0.042	0.119	0.160	0.216	0.244
BTPNim+BTPNvd	0.028	0.031	0.034	0.038	**0.096**	**0.115**	0.146	**0.156**
BTPNim+BTPNvd	**0.027**	**0.030**	0.034	**0.037**	0.098	0.121	**0.142**	0.159
HDRCNN [5]	0.038				0.480			

presented in the supplementary material. As noted earlier, since we have additional HDR key-frames as input, it is not an apples-to-apples comparison with single-image based HDR methods like [5]. Nevertheless, the results in Fig. 6 show the feasibility of using sparsely-sampled HDR key-frames to reconstruct HDR videos from LDR videos with the proposed TPN approach.

5.4 Segmentation Mask Propagation in Videos

In addition, we conduct video segmentation on the DAVIS dataset [25] with the same settings as VPN [4], to show that the proposed method can also generalized to semantic-level propagation in videos. We note that maintaining style consistency does not apply to semantic segmentation. For each frame to be predicted, we use the segmentation mask of the first frame as the only key-frame, while using the corresponding RGB images as the input to the guidance network. We train two versions of the basic TPN network for this task: (a) A basic TPN with the input/output resolution reduced to 256×256, the U transformed to $64 \times 64 \times 16$, in the same manner as the color propagation model. We used the same guidance network architecture as [7], while removing the last convolution unit to fit the dimensions of the propagation module. This model, denoted as SEG(t) in Table 1, is much more efficient than the majority of the recent video segmentation methods [4,25,31]. (b) A more accurate model with an SPN [7] refinement applied to the output of the basic TPN, denoted as SEG(t+s). This model utilizes the same architecture as [7], except that it replaces the loss with Sigmoid cross entropy for the per-pixel classification task. Similar to color and HDR propagation, We pretrain (a) on the MS-COCO dataset and then finetune it on the DAVIS training set. For the SPN model in (b), we first train it on the VOC image segmentation task as described in [7]. We treat each class in an image as binary mask in order to transfer the original model to a two-class classification model, while replacing the corresponding loss module. We then finetune the SPN on the coarse masks from the DAVIS training set, which are produced by an intermediate model – the pre-trained version of (a) from the MS-COCO dataset. More details are introduced in the supplementary materiel.

We compare our method to VPN [4] and one recent state-of-the-art method [31]. Both VPN and our method rely purely on the propagation module

Table 4. Comparisons for video segmentation on the DAVIS dataset.

J-mean				F-mean			
VPN [4]	OSVOS [31]	SEG(t)	SEG(t+s)	VPN [4]	OSVOS [31]	SEG(t)	SEG(t+s)
70.2	79.8	71.1	76.19	65.5	80.6	75.65	73.53

from the first frame and does not utilize any image segmentation pre-trained modules (in contrast with [31]). Similar to the other two tasks, both models significantly outperform VPN [4] for video segmentation propagation (see Table 4), while all running one order of magnitude faster (see Table 1). The SEG(t+s) model performs comparatively to the OSVOS [31] method, which utilizes the pretrained image segmentation model and requires a much long inference time (7800 ms).

References

1. Gadde, R., Jampani, V., Gehler, P.V.: Semantic video CNNs through representation warping. In: Proceedings of IEEE International Conference on Computer Vision (ICCV) (2017)
2. He, K., Sun, J., Tang, X.: Guided image filtering. IEEE Trans. Pattern Anal. Mach. Intell. (TPAMI) **35**(6), 1397–1409 (2013)
3. Levin, A., Lischinski, D., Weiss, Y.: Colorization using optimization. In: ACM Transactions on Graphics (TOG) (2004)
4. Jampani, V., Gadde, R., Gehler, P.: Video propagation networks. In: Proceedings of IEEE Conference on Computer Vision and Pattern Recognition (CVPR) (2017)
5. Eilertsen, G., Kronander, J., Denes, G., Mantiuk, R., Unger, J.: HDR image reconstruction from a single exposure using deep CNNs. In: ACM Transactions on Graphics (SIGGRAPH Asia) (2017)
6. Levin, A., Lischinski, D., Weiss, Y.: A closed-form solution to natural image matting. IEEE Trans. Pattern Anal. Mach. Intell. (TPAMI) **30**(2), 228–242 (2008)
7. Liu, S., Mello, S.D., Gu, J., Zhong, G., Yang, M., Kautz, J.: Learning affinity via spatial propagation networks. In: Neural Information Processing Systems (NIPS) (2017)
8. Jampani, V., Kiefel, M., Gehler, P.V.: Learning sparse high dimensional filters: image filtering, dense CRFs and bilateral neural networks. In: Proceedings of IEEE Conference on Computer Vision and Pattern Recognition (CVPR) (2016)
9. Zhang, R., Isola, P., Efros, A.A.: Colorful image colorization. In: Leibe, B., Matas, J., Sebe, N., Welling, M. (eds.) ECCV 2016. LNCS, vol. 9907, pp. 649–666. Springer, Cham (2016). https://doi.org/10.1007/978-3-319-46487-9_40
10. Zhang, R., Zhu, J.Y., Isola, P., Geng, X., Lin, A.S., Yu, T., Efros, A.A.: Real-time user-guided image colorization with learned deep priors. In: ACM Transactions on Graphics (SIGGRAPH) (2017)
11. Debevec, P., Malik, J.: Recovering high dynamic range radiance maps from photographs. In: ACM Transactions on Graphics (SIGGRAPH) (1997)
12. Reinhard, E., Heidrich, W., Debevec, P., Pattanaik, S., Ward, G., Myszkowski, K.: High Dynamic Range Imaging: Acquisition, Display, and Image-based Lighting. Morgan Kaufmann, San Francisco (2010)

13. Hu, J., Gallo, O., Pulli, K., Sun, X.: HDR deghosting: how to deal with saturation? In: Proceedings of IEEE Conference on Computer Vision and Pattern Recognition (CVPR) (2013)
14. Oh, T., Lee, J., Tai, Y., Kweon, I.: Robust high dynamic range imaging by rank minimization. IEEE Trans. Pattern Anal. Mach. Intell. (TPAMI) **37**(6), 1219–1232 (2015)
15. Gallo, O., Troccoli, A., Hu, J., Pulli, K., Kautz, J.: Locally non-right registration for mobile HDR photography. In: Proceedings of IEEE Conference on Computer Vision and Pattern Recognition (CVPR) (2015)
16. Kang, S., Uyttendaele, M., Winder, S., Szeliski, R.: High dynamic range video. In: ACM Transactions on Graphics (SIGGRAPH) (2003)
17. Kalantari, N., Shechtman, E., Barnes, C., Darabi, S., Goldman, D., Sen, P.: Patch-based high dynamic range video. In: ACM Transactions on Graphics (SIGGRAPH) (2013)
18. Tocci, M., Kiser, C., Tocci, N., Sen, P.: A versatile HDR video production system. In: ACM Transactions on Graphics (SIGGRAPH) (2011)
19. Nayar, S., Mitsunaga, T.: High dynamic range imaging: Spatially varying pixel exposure. In: Proceedings of IEEE Conference on Computer Vision and Pattern Recognition (CVPR) (2000)
20. Gu, J., Hitomi, Y., Mitsunaga, T., Nayar, S.: Coded rolling shutter photography: flexible space-time sampling. In: Proceedings of IEEE International Conference on Computational Photography (ICCP) (2010)
21. Kalantari, N., Ramamoorthi, R.: Deep high dynamic range imaging of dynamic scenes. In: ACM Transactions on Graphics (SIGGRAPH) (2017)
22. Zhang, J., Lalonde, J.: Learning high dynamic range from outdoor panoramas. In: Proceedings of IEEE International Conference on Computer Vision (ICCV) (2017)
23. Gatys, L.A., Ecker, A.S., Bethge, M.: A neural algorithm of artistic style. CoRR abs/1508.06576 (2015)
24. Liu, S., Pan, J., Yang, M.-H.: Learning recursive filters for low-level vision via a hybrid neural network. In: Leibe, B., Matas, J., Sebe, N., Welling, M. (eds.) ECCV 2016. LNCS, vol. 9908, pp. 560–576. Springer, Cham (2016). https://doi.org/10.1007/978-3-319-46493-0_34
25. Perazzi, F., Pont-Tuset, J., McWilliams, B., Van Gool, L., Gross, M., Sorkine-Hornung, A.: A benchmark dataset and evaluation methodology for video object segmentation. In: Proceedings of IEEE Conference on Computer Vision and Pattern Recognition (CVPR) (2016)
26. Lin, T.-Y., et al.: Microsoft COCO: common objects in context. In: Fleet, D., Pajdla, T., Schiele, B., Tuytelaars, T. (eds.) ECCV 2014. LNCS, vol. 8693, pp. 740–755. Springer, Cham (2014). https://doi.org/10.1007/978-3-319-10602-1_48
27. Wang, X., Farhadi, A., Gupta, A.: Actions ~ transformations. In: Proceedings of IEEE Conference on Computer Vision and Pattern Recognition (CVPR) (2016)
28. Grossberg, M.D., Nayar, S.K.: Modeling the space of camera response functions. IEEE Trans. Pattern Anal. Mach. Intell. (TPAMI) **26**(10), 1272–1282 (2004)
29. Drago, F., Myszkowski, K., Annen, T., Chiba, N.: Adaptive logarithmic mapping for displaying high contrast scenes. Comput. Graph. Forum **22**(3), 419–426 (2003)
30. Reinhard, E., Devlin, K.: Dynamic range reduction inspired by photoreceptor physiology. IEEE Trans. Vis. Comput. Graph. **11**(1), 13–24 (2005)
31. Caelles, S., Maninis, K.K., Pont-Tuset, J., Leal-Taixé, L., Cremers, D., Van Gool, L.: One-shot video object segmentation. In: Proceedings of IEEE Conference on Computer Vision and Pattern Recognition (CVPR) (2017)

Multiresolution Tree Networks for 3D Point Cloud Processing

Matheus Gadelha(✉), Rui Wang, and Subhransu Maji

College of Information and Computer Sciences,
University of Massachusetts - Amherst, Amherst, USA
{mgadelha,ruiwang,smaji}@cs.umass.edu

Abstract. We present multiresolution tree-structured networks to process point clouds for 3D shape understanding and generation tasks. Our network represents a 3D shape as a set of locality-preserving 1D ordered list of points at multiple resolutions. This allows efficient feed-forward processing through 1D convolutions, coarse-to-fine analysis through a multi-grid architecture, and it leads to faster convergence and small memory footprint during training. The proposed tree-structured encoders can be used to classify shapes and outperform existing point-based architectures on shape classification benchmarks, while tree-structured decoders can be used for generating point clouds directly and they outperform existing approaches for image-to-shape inference tasks learned using the ShapeNet dataset. Our model also allows unsupervised learning of point-cloud based shapes by using a variational autoencoder, leading to higher-quality generated shapes.

1 Introduction

One of the challenges in 3D shape processing concerns the question of representation. Shapes are typically represented as triangle meshes or point clouds in computer graphics applications due to their simplicity and light-weight nature. At the same time an increasing number of robotic and remote-sensing applications are deploying sensors that directly collect point-cloud representations of the environment. Hence architectures that efficiently operate on point clouds are becoming increasingly desirable.

On the other hand the vast majority of computer vision techniques rely on grid-based representation of 3D shapes for analyzing and generating them. These include multiview representations that render a shape from a collection of views [31,37,39] or voxel-based representations [4,19,30,43,44] that discretize point occupancy onto a 3D grid. Such representations allow the use of convolution and pooling operations for efficient processing. However, voxel-representations scale poorly with resolution and are inefficient for modeling surface details. Even multiscale or sparse variants [17,25,33] incur relatively high processing cost. Image-based representations, while more efficient, are not effective at modeling shapes with concave or filled interiors due to self occlusions.

V. Ferrari et al. (Eds.): ECCV 2018, LNCS 11211, pp. 105–122, 2018.
https://doi.org/10.1007/978-3-030-01234-2_7

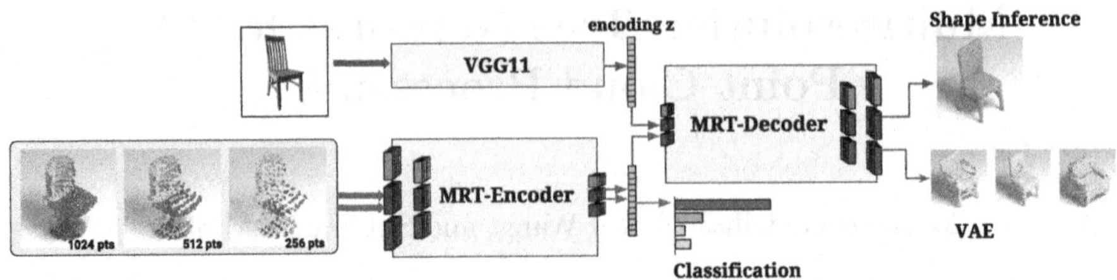

Fig. 1. Overview of MRTNet. On the left, the MRT-Encoder takes as input a 1D ordered list of points and represents it at multiple resolutions. Points are colored by their indices in the list. On the right, the MRT-Decoder directly outputs a point cloud. Our network can be used for several shape processing tasks, including classification (red), image-to-shape inference (blue), and unsupervised shape learning (green). Refer to Fig. 2 for details on the encoder and decoder. (Color figure online)

Moreover, generating shapes as a collection of views requires subsequent reasoning about geometric consistency to infer the 3D shape, which can be challenging.

The main contribution of our work is a multiresolution tree network capable of both recognizing and generating 3D shapes directly as point clouds. An overview of the network and how it can be applied to different applications are shown in Fig. 1. Our approach represents a 3D shape as a set of locality-preserving 1D ordered list of points at multiple resolution levels. We can obtain such a ordering by using space-partitioning trees such as kd-tree or rp-tree. Feed-forward processing on the underlying tree can be implemented as 1D convolutions and pooling on the list. However, as our experiments show, processing the list alone is not sufficient since the 1D ordering distorts the underlying 3D structure of the shape. To ameliorate this problem we employ a multi-grid network architecture [22] where the representation at a particular resolution influences feed-forward processing at adjacent resolutions. This preserves the locality of point in the underlying 3D shape, improves information flow across scales, enables the network to learn a coarse-to-fine representation, and results in faster convergence during training. Our network outperforms existing point-based networks [24,32,40] that operate on position (xyz) information of points. Specifically, it obtains **91.7%** accuracy on the ModelNet40 classification task, while remaining efficient. It also outperforms similar graph networks that do not maintain multiresolution representations.

Our multiresolution decoders can be used for directly generating point clouds. This allows us to incorporate order-invariant loss functions, such as Chamfer distance, over point clouds during training. Moreover it can be plugged in with existing image-based encoders for image-to-shape inference tasks. Our method is able to both preserve the overall shape structure as well as fine details. On the task of single-image shape inference using the ShapeNet dataset, our approach outperforms existing voxel-based [9], view-based [26], and point-based [12] techniques.

Finally, the combined encoder-decoder network can be used for unsupervised learning of shape representations in a variational autoencoder (VAE) framework. The features extracted from the encoder of our VAE (trained on the unlabeled ShapeNet dataset) leads to better shape classification results (**86.4%** accuracy on ModelNet40) compared to those extracted from other unsupervised networks [43].

2 Related Work

A number of approaches have studied 3D shape recognition and generation using uniform 3D voxel grids [4,9,19,30,43,44]. However, uniform grids have poor scalability and require large memory footprint, hence existing networks built upon them often operate on a relatively low-resolution grid. Several recent works address this issue through multiscale and sparse representations [16,17,33,38,41,42] at the expense of additional book keeping. Still, voxel-based methods generally incur high processing cost, and are not well suited for modeling fine surface details. Moreover, it's not clear how to incorporate certain geometric attributes, like surface normals, into voxel representation, since these attributes do not exist in the interior of the shape.

Multiview methods [20,28,31,37,39] represent a 3D shape as images rendered from different viewpoints. These methods use efficient convolutional and pooling operations and leverage deep networks pretrained on large labeled image datasets. However, they are not optimal for general shapes with complex interior structures due to self occlusions. Nonetheless since most models on existing shape repositories are described well by their exterior surface, view-based approaches have been adapted for shape classification and segmentation tasks. Recently they have also been used for generation where a set of depth and normal maps from different viewpoints are inferred using image-based networks, and have been successfully used for image to shape generation tasks [26,28]. However such approaches requires subsequent processing to resolve view inconsistencies and outliers which is a challenging task.

Previous work has also studied extensions of ConvNets to mesh surfaces such as spectral CNNs [5,45], geodesic CNNs [29], or anisotropic CNNs [2]. They have shown success for local correspondence and matching tasks. However, some of these methods are constrained on manifold surfaces, and generally it's unclear how well they perform on shape generation tasks. A recent work in [35] generalized the convolution operator from regular grid to arbitrary graphs while avoiding the spectral domain, allowing graphs of varying size and connectivity.

Another branch of recent works focused on processing shapes represented as point clouds. One example is PointNet [32,40], that directly consumes point clouds as input. The main idea is to first process each point identically and independently, then leverage a symmetric function (max pooling) to aggregate information from all points. The use of max pooling preserves the permutation invariance of a point set, and the approach is quite effective for shape classification and segmentation tasks. Similarly, KD-net [24] operates directly on point cloud shapes. It spatially partitions a point cloud using a kd-tree, and imposes a feed-forward network on top of the tree structure. This approach is scalable, memory efficient, achieves competitive performance on shape recognition tasks. While successful as encoders, it hasn't been shown how these networks can be employed as decoders for shape generation tasks.

Generating shapes as a collection of points without intermediate modeling of view-based depth maps has been relatively unexplored in the literature. The difficulty stems from the lack of scalable approaches for generating sets. Two recent works are in this direction. Fan et al. [12] train a neural network to generate point clouds from a single image by minimizing Earth Mover's Distance (EMD) or Chamfer distance (CD) between the generated points and the model points. These distances are order invariant and hence can operate directly on point sets. This approach uses a two-branched decoder, one branch is built with 2D transposed convolutions and the other one is composed by fully connected layers. On the other hand, our approach uses a simpler and shallower decoder built as a composition of 1D deconvolutions that operate at multiple scales. This representation improves information flow across scales, which leads to higher quality generated shapes. Moreover, we use permutation invariant losses along with regularization of latent variables to build a model similar to a variational autoencoder [23] that can be used to sample shapes from Gaussian noise. Another work in [13] learns a distribution over shape coefficients using a learned basis for a given category using a generative adversarial network [15]. However, in this approach, the underlying generative model assumes a linear shape basis, which produces less detailed surfaces. The improved scalability of our method allows generating shapes with more points and more accurate geometric details in comparison to previous work.

Our tree network builds on the ideas of multiscale [18,27], mutligrid [22] and dilated [46] or atrous filters [8,11] effective for a number of image recognition tasks. They allow larger receptive fields during convolutions with a modest increase in the number of parameters. In particular Ke et al. [22] showed that communication across multiresolutions of an image throughout the network leads to improved convergence and better accuracy on a variety of tasks. Our approach provides an efficient way of building multigrid-like representations for 3D point clouds.

3 Method

Figure 2 shows the complete architecture of our multiresolution tree network (MRTNet) that includes both the encoder and decoder. We represent 3D shapes as a point cloud of a fixed size $N = 2^D$ (e.g. $N = 1K$). We center the point cloud at the origin and normalize its bounding box; then spatially sort it using a space-partitioning tree. The input to the network are thus a 1D list ($N \times 3$ tensor) containing the xyz coordinates of the points. The network leverages 1D convolution and represents each layer at three scales, with a ratio of k between each two. MR-CONV refers to multi-resolution convolution, and MR-CONV-T refers to MR-CONV with transposed convolution. The encoding $\mathbf{z}$ is a 512-D vector. Our network architecture is flexible and can be used for several shape processing

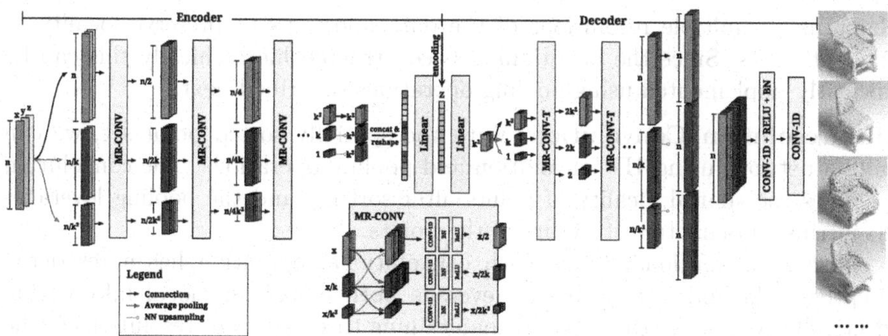

Fig. 2. Our multiresolution tree network (MRTNet) for processing 3D point clouds. We represent a 3D shape as a 1D list of spatially sorted point cloud. The network represents each layer at three scales (indicated by yellow, red, and blue), the scale ratio is k between each two. The last two convolution layers have kernel size 1 and stride 1. MR-CONV refers to multi-resolution convolution (zoom-in to the inset for details); and MR-CONV-T refers to MR-CONV with transposed convolution. Our network is flexible and can be used for several shape processing tasks.

tasks. For shape **classification**, we use only the multiresolution encoder but adding a fully connected layer after the encoding $\mathbf{z}$ to output a 40-D vector representing the ModelNet40 shape classes. For **single-image shape inference**, we employ a pretrained VGG-11 image encoder [36], combined with our multiresolution decoder to directly an output point cloud shape as a $N \times 3$ tensor. For **unsupervised learning of point clouds**, we use both the multiresolution encoder and decoder, forming a variational autoencoder.

Spatial Sorting. As a point cloud is unordered to begin with, we use a space-partitioning tree such as KD-tree to order the points. To start, we sort the entire point set along the x-axis, then split it in half, resulting in equal-sized left and right subsets; we then recursively split each subset, this time along the y-axis; then along z-axis; then back along the x-axis and so on. Basically it's a recursive process to build a full tree where the splitting axes alternate between x, y, z at each level of the tree. The order of leaf nodes naturally becomes the order of the points. There are several variants on the splitting strategy. If at each split we choose an axis among x, y, z with probability proportional to the span of the subset along that axis, it builds a probabilistic KD-tree as described in [24]. If we choose axes from a random set of directions, it builds an RP-tree [10]. Note that after the ordering is obtained, the underlying details of the how the splits were taken are discarded. This is fundamentally different from [24] where the network computations are conditioned on the splitting directions.

The purpose of spatial sorting is to build a hierarchical and locality-preserving order of the points. Thus functions computed based on the local 3D neighborhood at a point can be approximated using convolutions and pooling operations on the 1D structure. However, any ordering of points is distortion inducing and in particular long-range relationships are not preserved well.

Maintaining multiple resolutions of the data allows us to preserve locality at different scales. Since the partitioning is constructed hierarchically this can be efficiently implemented using pooling operations described next.

Multiresolution Convolution. With the spatially sorted point set, we can build a network using 1D convolution and pooling operations. The convolution leverages the spatial locality of points after sorting, and the pooling leverages the intrinsic binary tree structure of the points.

With a conventional CNN, each convolutional operation has a restricted receptive field and is not able to leverage both global and local information effectively. We resolve this issue by maintaining three different resolutions of the same point cloud using a mutligrid architecture [22]. Different resolutions are computed directly through pooling and upsampling operations. Specifically, we use average pooling with kernel size and stride of k, where k is a power of 2. This configuration allows pooling/downsampling the point cloud while preserving its hierarchical tree structure. Figure 1(left) shows an example point cloud at three different resolutions computed by pooling with $k = 2$. For upsampling, we use nearest neighbor (NN) upsampling with a factor of k.

Once we can pool and upsample the point clouds, we are able to combine global and local information in the convolutional operations by using the MR-CONV block in the inset of Fig. 2. The multiresolution block operates in the following way. We maintain the point cloud representations at three resolutions $\mathbf{f}_{(0)}, \mathbf{f}_{(1)}, \mathbf{f}_{(2)}$, where the scale ratio between each two is (as mentioned above) k. The MR-CONV block receives all three as input, and each resolution will be upsampled and/or pooled and concatenated with each other, creating three new representations $\mathbf{f}'_{(0)}, \mathbf{f}'_{(1)}, \mathbf{f}'_{(2)}$:

$$\mathbf{f}'_{(0)} = \mathbf{f}_{(0)} \oplus up(\mathbf{f}_{(1)}); \quad \mathbf{f}'_{(1)} = pool(\mathbf{f}_{(0)}) \oplus \mathbf{f}_{(1)} \oplus up(\mathbf{f}_{(2)}); \quad \mathbf{f}'_{(2)} = pool(\mathbf{f}_{(1)}) \oplus \mathbf{f}_{(2)}.$$

where $\oplus$ is the concatenation operation, *up* and *pool* are the upsampling and average pooling operations. Each new representation $\mathbf{f}'$ then goes through a sequence of operations: 1D convolution (kernel size = 2 and stride = 2), batch normalization and ReLU activation. Note that due to the stride 2, each output is half the size of its associated input. In our generative model and shape inference model we use $k = 4$, while for classification we use $k = 8$.

Shape Classification Model. For classification, we use our multiresolution encoder in Fig. 2, and add a fully connected layer after encoding $\mathbf{z}$ that outputs a 40-D vector representing the ModelNet40 classification. Specifically, we train the network on the ModelNet40 [44] dataset, which contains 12,311 objects covering 40 different categories. It is split into 9,843 shapes for training and 2,468 shapes for testing. For each object, we sample 1K points on the surface using Poisson Disk sampling [3] to evenly disperse the points. Each sampled point cloud is then spatially sorted using the probabilistic kd-tree [24]. Specifically, at each split of the tree we choose a random split axis according to the following PDF:

$$P(\mathbf{n} = \mathbf{e}_i | \mathbf{x}) = \frac{\exp\{span_i(\mathbf{x})\}}{\sum_{j=1}^{d} \exp\{span_j(\mathbf{x})\}}$$

where $\mathbf{x}$ is the subset of points to be split, $\mathbf{n}$ is the split axis chosen from the canonical axes $\mathbf{e}_i$ (i.e. x, y, z in 3D), and $span_i(\mathbf{x})$ returns the span of $\mathbf{x}$ along each axis $\mathbf{e}_i$.

The network parameters are as follows: the first MR-CONV layer has 16 filters and the following layers double the amount of filter of the previous one, unless the previous layer has 1024 filters. In that case, the next layer also has 1024 filters. The network is trained by minimizing a cross-entropy loss using an Adam optimizer with learning rate 10^{-3} and $\beta = 0.9$. The learning rate is decayed by dividing it by 2 every 5 training epochs. We employ scale augmentation at training and test time by applying anisotropic scaling factors drawn from $\mathcal{N}(1, 0.25)$. At test time, for each point cloud we apply the sampled scale factors and build the probabilistic kd-tree 16 times as described above, thus obtaining 16 different versions and orderings of the point set. Our final classification is the mean output of those versions. The test-time average has very little impact on the computation time (a discussion is included in Sect. 4.4).

Single-Image Shape Inference. Our multiresolution decoder can be used to perform image-to-shape inference. Specifically, we use a pretrained VGG-11 image encoder [36] combined with our decoder in Fig. 2. Our decoder is set to generates 4K points. The entire network is trained using the dataset and splits provided by [9], which contains 24 renderings from different views for 43783 shapes from ShapeNet divided in 13 different categories. We sample each ShapeNet mesh at 4K points and use them for supervision. Given a rendered image, the task is to predict the complete point cloud (4K points) representing the object in the image. The decoder in Fig. 2 has the following number of filters per layer: 512-512-256-256-128-64-64-64. As in Fig. 2, the two additional convolutional layers at the end have kernel size 1 and stride 1: the first one has 128 filters and the second one outputs the final 4K point set.

There are many possible choices for the reconstruction loss function. One straightforward choice would be to use the ordering induced by the spatial partitioning and compute the L_2 loss between the output and ground-truth point clouds. However, L_2 loss turns out to work very poorly. We chose to use the Chamfer distance between two point clouds ($\mathbf{x}$ and $\mathbf{y}$), defined as:

$$Ch(\mathbf{x}, \mathbf{y}) = \frac{1}{|\mathbf{x}|} \sum_{x \in \mathbf{x}} \min_{y \in \mathbf{y}} \|x - y\|_2 + \frac{1}{|\mathbf{y}|} \sum_{y \in \mathbf{y}} \min_{x \in \mathbf{x}} \|x - y\|_2$$

The Chamfer distance is invariant to permutations of points, making it suitable to measure dissimilarities between unstructured point clouds. The model is trained using an Adam optimizer with learning rate 10^{-3} and $\beta = 0.9$. Learning rate is divided by two at each two epochs.

Unsupervised Learning of Point Clouds. By combining the multiresolution encoder and decoder together, we can perform unsupervised learning of 3D shapes. The entire network, called MR-VAE, builds upon a variational autoencoder (VAE) [23] framework. The encoder Q receives as an input a point cloud $\mathbf{x}$ and outputs an encoding $\mathbf{z} \in \mathbb{R}^{512}$. The decoder D tries to replicate the point cloud $\mathbf{x}$ from $\mathbf{z}$. Both encoder and decoder are built using a sequence of MR-CONV blocks as in Fig. 2. Similar to above, we use Chamfer distance as the reconstruction loss function. Besides this, we also need a regularization term that forces the distribution of the encoding $\mathbf{z}$ to be as close as possible to the Gaussian $\mathcal{N}(0, I)$. Differently from the original VAE model, we found that we can get more stable training if we try to match the first two moments (mean and variance) of $\mathbf{z}$ to $\mathcal{N}(0, I)$. Mathematically, this regularization term is defined as:

$$\mathcal{L}_{reg} = \|cov(Q(\mathbf{x}) + \delta) - I\|_2 + E[Q(\mathbf{x}) + \delta]$$

where cov is the covariance matrix, Q is the encoder, $\|\cdot\|_2$ is the Frobenius norm and $E[\cdot]$ is the expected value. δ is a random value sampled from $\mathcal{N}(0, cI)$ and $c = 0.01$. Thus, our generative model is trained by minimizing the following loss function:

$$\mathcal{L} = Ch(\mathbf{x}, D(Q(\mathbf{x}))) + \lambda L_{reg}$$

We set $\lambda = 0.1$. The model is trained using an Adam optimizer with learning rate 10^{-4} and $\beta = 0.9$. The encoder follows the classification model and the decoder follows the one used in the shape inference model, both described previously.

Shape Part Segmentation. MRTNet can also be applied for shape part segmentation tasks. For details please refer to the supplemental material.

Table 1. Instance classification accuracy on the ModelNet40 dataset.

Method	Accuracy
View-based methods	
MVCNN [39]	90.1
MVCNN-MultiRes [31]	91.4
Point-based methods (w/o normals)	
KDNet (1K pts) [24]	90.6
PointNet (1K pts) [40]	89.2
PointNet++ (1K pts) [32]	90.7
MRTNet (1K pts)	**91.2**
MRTNet (4K pts)	**91.7**
KDNet (32K pts) [24]	**91.8**
Point-based methods (with normals)	
PointNet++ (5K pts) [32]	91.9
Voxel-based methods	
OctNet [33]	86.5
O-CNN [42]	90.6

(a) **Comparisons with previous work**. Among point-based methods that use xyz data only, ours is the best in the 1K points group; and our 4K result is comparable with KDNet at 32K points.

Method	Accuracy
Full model (MRTNet, 4K pts)	91.7
Filters/4	91.7
Single res.	89.3
Single res., no aug. (kd-tree)	86.2
Single res., no aug. (rp-tree)	87.4

(b) **MRTNet ablation studies**. Filters/4 reduces the number of filters in each layer by 4. The last three rows are the single resolution model.

Method	Accuracy
SPH [21]	68.2
LFD [7]	75.5
T-L Network[14]	74.4
VConv-DAE [34]	75.5
3D-GAN [43]	83.3
MRTNet-VAE (Ours)	**86.4**

(c) **Unsupervised representation learning**. Section 4.3.

4 Experimental Results and Discussions

This section presents experimental results. We implemented MRTNet using PyTorch.

4.1 Shape Classification

To demonstrate the effectiveness of the multiresolution encoder, we trained a baseline model that follows the same classification model but replacing multiresolution convolutions with single-scale 1D convolutions. Also, we apply the same test-time data augmentation and compute the test-time average as described in the Sect. 3.

Classification benchmark results are in Table 1(a). As shown in the table, MRTNet achieves the best results among all **point-based** methods that use xyz data only. In particular, ours is the best in the 1K points group. We also experimented with sampling shapes using 4K points, and the result is comparable with KDNet at 32K points – in this case, KDNet uses 8× more points (hence 8× more memory) than ours, and is only 0.1% better. PointNet++ [32] with 5K points and normals is 0.2% better than ours.

Table 1(b) shows ablation study results with variants of our approach. Particularly, the multiresolution version is more than 2% better than the baseline model (i.e. single resolution), while using the same number of parameters (the Filters/4 version). Besides, MRTNet converges must faster than the baseline model, as we can see in the cross entropy loss decay plots in Fig. 3. This shows that the multiresolution architecture leads to higher quality/accuracy and is memory efficient.

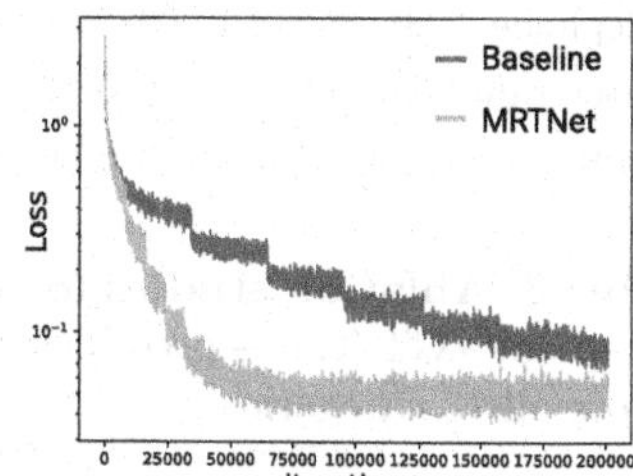

Fig. 3. Cross entropy decay

Our single resolution baseline is akin to KDNet except it doesn't condition the convolutions on the splitting axes. It results in 1.3% less classification accuracy compared to KDNet (1K pts). This suggests that conditioning on the splitting axes during convolutions improves the accuracy. However, this comes at the cost of extra book keeping and at least three times more parameters. MRTNet achieves greater benefits with lesser overhead. Similar to the KDNet, our methods also benefit from data augmentation and can be used with both kd-trees and rp-trees.

4.2 Single-Image Shape Inference

We compare our single-image shape inference results with volumetric [9], view-based [26] and point-based [12] approaches using the evaluation metric by [26]. Given a source point cloud $\mathbf{x}$ and a target point cloud $\mathbf{y}$, we compute the average euclidean distance from each point in $\mathbf{x}$ to its closest in $\mathbf{y}$. We refer to this as pred → GT (prediction to groundtruth) error. It indicates how dissimilar the

Table 2. Single-image shape inference results. The training data consists of 13 categories of shapes provided by [9]. The numbers shown are [pred → GT/GT → pred] errors, scaled by 100. The mean is computed across all 13 categories. Our MRTNet produces 4K points for each shape.

Category	3D-R2N2 [9]			Fan et al. [12] (1 view)	Lin et al. [26] (1 view)	MRTNet (1 view)
	1 view	3 views	5 views			
Airplane	3.207/2.879	2.521/2.468	2.399/2.391	1.301/1.488	1.294/1.541	**0.976/0.920**
Bench	3.350/3.697	2.465/2.746	2.323/2.603	1.814/1.983	1.757/1.487	**1.438/1.326**
Cabinet	1.636/2.817	1.445/2.626	**1.420**/2.619	2.463/2.444	1.814/**1.072**	1.774/1.602
Car	1.808/3.238	1.685/3.151	1.664/3.146	1.800/2.053	1.446/**1.061**	**1.395**/1.303
Chair	2.759/4.207	1.960/3.238	1.854/3.080	1.887/2.355	1.886/2.041	**1.650/1.603**
Display	3.235/4.283	2.262/3.151	2.088/2.953	1.919/2.334	2.142/**1.440**	**1.815**/1.901
Lamp	8.400/9.722	6.001/7.755	5.698/7.331	2.347/2.212	2.635/4.459	**1.944/2.089**
Speaker	2.652/4.335	2.577/4.302	2.487/4.203	3.215/2.788	2.371/**1.706**	**2.165**/2.121
Rifle	4.798/2.996	4.307/2.546	4.193/2.447	1.316/1.358	1.289/1.510	**1.029/1.028**
Sofa	2.725/3.628	2.371/3.252	2.306/3.196	2.592/2.784	1.917/**1.423**	**1.768**/1.756
Table	3.118/4.208	2.268/3.277	2.128/3.134	1.874/2.229	1.689/1.620	**1.570/1.405**
Telephone	2.202/3.314	1.969/2.834	1.874/2.734	1.516/1.989	1.939/**1.198**	**1.346**/1.332
Watercraft	3.592/4.007	3.299/3.698	3.210/3.614	1.715/1.877	1.813/1.550	**1.394/1.490**
Mean	3.345/4.102	2.702/3.465	2.588/3.342	1.982/2.146	1.846/1.701	**1.559/1.529**

Table 3. Ablation studies for the image to shape decoder. The numbers shown are [pred → GT/GT → pred] errors, scaled by 100. The values are the mean computed across all 13 categories.

Fully connected	Single Res.	MRTNet
1.824/2.297	1.708/1.831	**1.559/1.529**

predicted shape is from the ground-truth. The GT → pred error is computed similarly by swapping $\mathbf{x}$ and $\mathbf{y}$, and it measures coverage (i.e. how complete the ground-truth surface was covered by the prediction). For the voxel based model [9], we used the same procedure as [26], where point clouds are formed by creating one point in the center of each surface voxel. Surface voxels are extracted by subtracting the prediction by its eroded version and rescale them such that the tightest 3D bounding boxes of the prediction and the ground-truth CAD models have the same volume.

Table 2 shows our results. Our solution outperforms competing methods in 12 out of 13 categories on the pred → GT error, and in 6 categories on GT → pred error. Note that we are consistently better than the point-based methods such as [12] in both metrics; and we are consistently better than [26] in the pred → GT metric. Furthermore, our method wins by a considerable margin in terms of the mean per category on both metrics. It is important to highlight that the multi-view based method [26] produces tens of thousands of points and many of them

Fig. 4. Shapes generated by (1) the fully connected baseline; (2) the single-resolution baseline; and (3) MRTNet. Colors in the first row indicate the index of a point in the output point list.

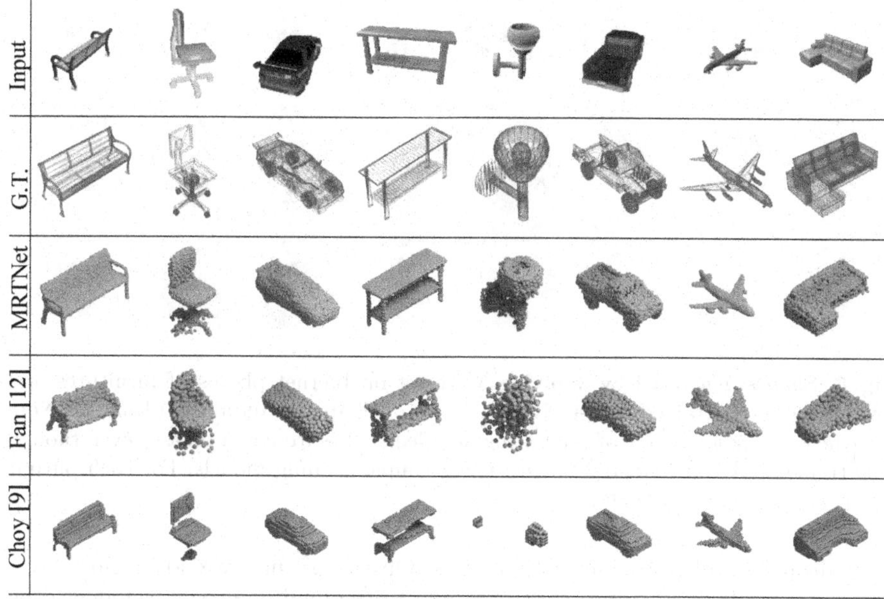

Fig. 5. Qualitative results for single-image shape inference. From top to bottom: input images, ground truth 3D shapes, results of MRTNet, Fan et al. [12], and Choy et al. [9].

are not in the right positions, which penalizes their pred → GT metric, but that helps to improve their GT → pred. Moreover, as mentioned in [26], their method has difficulties capturing thin structures (e.g. lamps) whereas ours is able to capture them relatively well. For example, our GT → pred error for the **lamp** category (which contains many thin geometric structures) is more than two times smaller than the error by [26], indicating that MRTNet is more successful at capturing thin structures in the shapes.

Ablation Studies. In order to quantify the effectiveness of the multiresolution decoder, we compared our method with two different baselines: a fully connected decoder and a single-resolution decoder. The fully connected decoder consists of 3 linear layers with 4096 hidden neurons, each layer followed by batch

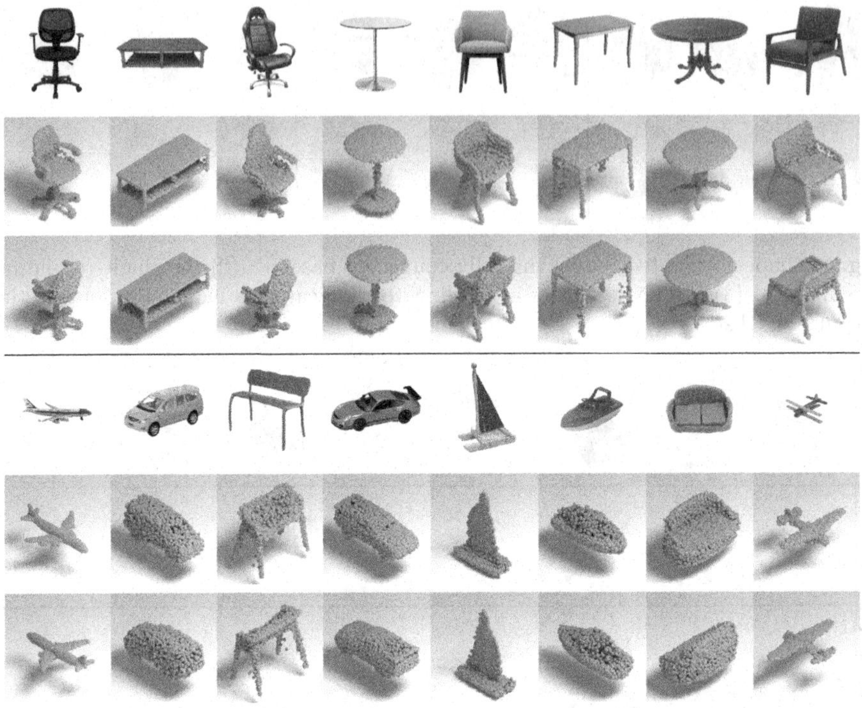

Fig. 6. Shapes generated by applying MRTNet on Inernet photos of furnitures and toys. MRTNet is trained on the 13 categories of ShapeNet database (Table 2). Note how the network is capable of generating detailed shapes from real photos, even though it is trained only on rendered images using simple shading models. For each output shape we show two different views.

normalization and ReLU activation units. On top of that, we add a final layer that outputs 4096×3 values corresponding to the final point cloud, followed by a hyperbolic tangent activation function. The single resolution decoder follows the same architecture of the MRT decoder but replacing multiresolution convolutions with single-scale 1D convolutions. Results are shown in Table 3. Note that both baselines are quite competitive. The single-resolution decoder is comparable to the result of [26], while the fully connected one achieves similar mean errors to [12]. Still, they fall noticeably behind MRTNet.

In Fig. 4 we visualize the structures of the output point clouds generated by the three methods. The point clouds generated by MRTNet present strong spatial coherence: points that are spatially nearby in 3D are also likely to be nearby in the 1D list. This coherence is present to some degree in the single-resolution outputs (note the dark blue points in the chair's arms), but is almost completely absent in the results by the fully connected decoder. This is expected, since fully connected layers do not leverage the spatial correlation of their inputs. Operating at multiple scales enables MRTNet to enforce a stronger spatial coherence,

Fig. 7. Qualitative comparisons of MR-VAE with a single-resolution baseline model. Results are generated by randomly sampling the encoding $\mathbf{z}$. MR-VAE is able to preserve shape details much better than the baseline model, and produces less noisy outputs.

Fig. 8. Test set shapes reconstructed by MR-VAE trained on all categories of ShapeNet (using 80%/20% training/test split). MR-VAE is able to reconstruct high-quality diverse shapes.

allowing it to more efficiently synthesize detailed point clouds with coherent geometric structures.

Qualitative Results. In Fig. 5 we present qualitative results of our method and comparisons to two prior works. The input images have 3 color channels and dimensions 224 × 224. In Fig. 6 we show results of our method applied on photographs downloaded from the Internet. To apply our method, we manually removed the background from the photos using [1], which generally took less than half a minute per photo. As seen from the results, MRTNet is able to capture the structure and interesting geometric details of the objects (e.g. wheels of the office chairs), even though the input images are considerably different from the rendered ones used in training.

4.3 Unsupervised Learning of Point Clouds

For unsupervised learning of point clouds, we train our MR-VAE using the ShapeNet dataset [6]. By default we compute $N = 4K$ points for each shape using Poisson Disk sampling [3] to evenly disperse the points. Each point set is then spatially sorted using a kd-tree. Here we use the vanilla kd-tree where the splitting axes alternate between x, y, z at each level of the tree. The spatially sorted points are used as input to train the MR-VAE network (Sect. 3). Similar to before, we also train a baseline model that follows the same network but replacing multiresolution convolutions with single-scale 1D convolutions in both encoder and decoder. As Fig. 7 shows, the shapes generated by the MR-VAE trained on chairs are of considerably higher quality than those generated by the baseline model.

We also performed multiple-category shape generation by training MR-VAE on 80% of the objects from ShapeNet dataset. The remaining models belong to our test split. Reconstructions of objects in the test split are included in Fig. 8. Even when trained with a greater variety of shapes, the MR-VAE is able to reconstruct high quality shapes from its embedding. This demonstrates that MR-VAE is suitable for various inference tasks such as shape completion or point cloud reconstructions.

Point Ordering in the Generated Shapes. A useful way to analyze shape generation is to see if the generated points have any consistent ordering across different shapes. This is an interesting question because as described previously, our MR-VAE is trained using Chamfer Distance, a metric that's invariant to permutations of points. While the input to the network is all spatially sorted, the output is not restricted to any particular order and can in theory assume any arbitrary order. In practice, similar to the image-to-shape model, we observe that there is a consistent ordering of points in the generated shapes, as shown in Fig. 9. Specifically, we picked three index ranges from one example chair, one at the top, one on the side, and one close to the bottom, then we color coded points in each shape that fall into these three index ranges. In the figure we can see clearly that they fall into approximately corresponding regions on each chair shape.

Fig. 9. Point correspondences among different shapes generated by MR-VAE. We picked three index ranges (indicated by three colors) from one example chair, and then color coded points in every shape that fall into these three ranges. The images clearly show that the network learned to generate shapes with consistent point ordering.

Fig. 10. Shape interpolation results. For each example, we obtain the encodings $\mathbf{z}$ of the starting shape and ending shape, then linearly interpolate the encodings and use the decoder to generate output shapes from the interpolated $\mathbf{z}$. Results show plausible interpolated shapes.

Shape Interpolation. Another common test is shape interpolation: pick two encodings (either randomly sampled, or generated by the encoder for two input shapes), linearly interpolate them and use the decoder to generate the output shape. Figure 10 shows two sets of interpolation results of chairs from the ShapeNet dataset.

Unsupervised Classification. A typical way of assessing the quality of representations learned in a unsupervised setting is to use them as features for classification. To do so, we take the MR-VAE model trained with all ShapeNet objects, and use its features to classify ModelNet40 [44] objects. Our classifier is a single linear layer, where the input is a set of features gathered from the first three layers of the MR-VAE encoder. The features are constructed this way: we apply a pooling operation of size 128, 64 and 32 respectively on these three layers; then at each layer upsample the two smaller resolutions of features to the higher resolution such that all three resolutions have the same size. Finally, we concatenate all those features and pass them through a linear layer to get the final classification. It is important to notice that we did not perform any fine-tuning: the only learned parameters are those from the single linear layer. We used an Adam optimizer with learning rate 10^{-3} and $\beta = 0.9$. The learning rate is decayed by dividing it by 2 every 5 epochs. Using this approach, we obtained an accuracy of 86.34% on the ModelNet40 classification benchmark, as shown in Table 1(c). This result is considerably higher compared to similar features extracted from unsupervised learning in other autoencoders. This shows that the representations learned by our MR-VAE is more effective at capturing and linearizing the latent space of training shapes.

4.4 Discussions

Robustness to Transformations. Kd-trees are naturally invariant to point jittering as long as it's small enough so as to not alter the shape topology. Our approach is invariant to translations and uniform scaling as the models are re-centered at the origin and resized to fit in the unit cube. On the other hand, kd-trees are not invariant to rotations. This can be mitigated by using practices like pooling over different rotations (e.g. MVCNN) or branches that perform pose prediction and transformation (e.g. PointNet). However, we notice that simply having unaligned training data was enough to account for rotations in the classification task, and the ModelNet40 dataset contains plenty of unaligned shapes. Moreover, since the KDNet [24] also employs a kd-tree spatial data structure, the discussions there about transformations also apply to our method.

Computation Time. Building a kd-tree of N points takes $O(N \log N)$ time, where $N = 2^{10}$ for 1K points. While PointNet does not require this step, it's also more than 2.0% worse in the classification task. The time to run a forward pass for classification is as follows: PointNet takes 25.3 ms, while MRTNet takes 8.0 ms on a TITAN GTX1080, both with batch size of 8. Kd-tree building is also much faster than rendering a shape multiple times like in MVCNN [39] or voxelizing it [33]. Using 16 different test-time augmentations does not have significant impact in computational time, as the 16 versions are classified in the same batch. This number of test-time augmentations is comparable to other approaches, e.g. 10 in [24], 80 in [39], and 12 in [42] and [40].

5 Conclusion

In conclusion, we introduced multiresolution tree networks (MRTNet) for point cloud processing. They are flexible and can be used for shape classification, generation, and inference tasks. Our key idea is to represent a shape as a set of locality-preserving 1D ordered list of points at multiple resolutions, allowing efficient 1D convolution and pooling operations. The representation improves information flow across scales, enabling the network to perform coarse-to-fine analysis, leading to faster convergence during training and higher quality for shape generation.

Acknowlegements. We acknowledge support from NSF (IIS-1617917, IIS-1749833, IIS-1423082) and the MassTech Collaborative for funding the UMass GPU cluster.

References

1. https://clippingmagic.com/
2. Boscaini, D., Masci, J., Rodolà, E., Bronstein, M.M.: Learning shape correspondence with anisotropic convolutional neural networks. In: NIPS (2016)
3. Bowers, J., Wang, R., Wei, L.-Y., Maletz, D.: Parallel poisson disk sampling with spectrum analysis on surfaces. ACM Trans. Graph. **29**(6), 166:1–166:10 (2010)
4. Brock, A., Lim, T., Ritchie, J.M., Weston, N.: Generative and discriminative voxel modeling with convolutional neural networks. arXiv preprint arXiv:1608.04236 (2016)
5. Bruna, J., Zaremba, W., Szlam, A., LeCun, Y.: Spectral networks and locally connected networks on graphs. arXiv preprint arXiv:1312.6203 (2013)
6. Chang, A.X., et al.: ShapeNet: an information-rich 3D model repository. arXiv preprint arXiv:1512.03012 (2015)
7. Chen, D.-Y., Tian, X.-P., Shen, Y.-T., Ouhyoung, M.: On visual similarity based 3D model retrieval. Comput. Graph. Forum **22**, 223–232 (2003)
8. Chen, L.-C., Papandreou, G., Kokkinos, I., Murphy, K., Yuille, A.L.: DeepLab: semantic image segmentation with deep convolutional nets, atrous convolution, and fully connected CRFs. arXiv preprint arXiv:1606.00915 (2016)
9. Choy, C.B., Xu, D., Gwak, J.Y., Chen, K., Savarese, S.: 3D-R2N2: a unified approach for single and multi-view 3D object reconstruction. In: Leibe, B., Matas, J., Sebe, N., Welling, M. (eds.) ECCV 2016. LNCS, vol. 9912, pp. 628–644. Springer, Cham (2016). https://doi.org/10.1007/978-3-319-46484-8_38
10. Dasgupta, S., Freund, Y.: Random projection trees and low dimensional manifolds. In: Proceedings of the Fortieth Annual ACM Symposium on Theory of Computing, pp. 537–546 (2008)
11. Dutilleux, P.: An implementation of the "algorithme á trous" to compute the wavelet transform. In: Combes, J.M., Grossmann, A., Tchamitchian, P. (eds.) Wavelets. Inverse Problems and Theoretical Imaging, vol. 222, pp. 298–304. Springer, Heidelberg (1990). https://doi.org/10.1007/978-3-642-97177-8_29

12. Fan, H., Su, H., Guibas, L.: A point set generation network for 3D object reconstruction from a single image. In: CVPR (2017)
13. Gadhela, M., Maji, S., Wang, R.: 3D shape generation using spatially ordered point clouds. In: BMVC (2017)
14. Girdhar, R., Fouhey, D.F., Rodriguez, M., Gupta, A.: Learning a predictable and generative vector representation for objects. In: Leibe, B., Matas, J., Sebe, N., Welling, M. (eds.) ECCV 2016. LNCS, vol. 9910, pp. 484–499. Springer, Cham (2016). https://doi.org/10.1007/978-3-319-46466-4_29
15. Goodfellow, I., Pouget-Abadie, J., Mirza, M., Xu, B., Warde-Farley, D., Ozair, S., Courville, A., Bengio, Y.: Generative adversarial nets. In: Advances in Neural Information Processing Systems (NIPS) (2014)
16. Graham, B., van der Maaten, L.: Submanifold sparse convolutional networks. arXiv preprint arXiv:1706.01307 (2017)
17. Häne, C., Tulsiani, S., Malik, J.: Hierarchical surface prediction for 3D object reconstruction. In: International Conference on 3D Vision (3DV) (2017)
18. He, K., Zhang, X., Ren, S., Sun, J.: Spatial pyramid pooling in deep convolutional networks for visual recognition. In: Fleet, D., Pajdla, T., Schiele, B., Tuytelaars, T. (eds.) ECCV 2014. LNCS, vol. 8691, pp. 346–361. Springer, Cham (2014). https://doi.org/10.1007/978-3-319-10578-9_23
19. Huang, J., You, S.: Point cloud labeling using 3D convolutional neural network. In: ICPR (2016)
20. Kalogerakis, E., Averkiou, M., Maji, S., Chaudhuri, S.: 3D shape segmentation with projective convolutional networks. In: CVPR (2017)
21. Kazhdan, M., Funkhouser, T., Rusinkiewicz, S.: Rotation invariant spherical harmonic representation of 3D shape descriptors. In: Proceedings Eurographics/ACM SIGGRAPH Symposium on Geometry Processing (2003)
22. Ke, T., Maire, M., Yu, S.X.: Multigrid neural architectures. In: CVPR (2017)
23. Kingma, D.P., Welling, M.: Auto-encoding variational bayes. CoRR, abs/1312.6114 (2013)
24. Klokov, R., Lempitsky, V.: Escape from cells: deep Kd-networks for the recognition of 3d point cloud models. In: ICCV (2017)
25. Li, Y., Pirk, S., Su, H., Qi, C.R., Guibas, L.J.: FPNN: field probing neural networks for 3D data. In: NIPS (2016)
26. Lin, C.-H., Kong, C., Lucey, S.: Learning efficient point cloud generation for dense 3D object reconstruction. In: AAAI Conference on Artificial Intelligence (AAAI) (2018)
27. Lin, T.-Y., Dollár, P., Girshick, R., He, K., Hariharan, B., Belongie, S.: Feature pyramid networks for object detection. In: CVPR (2017)
28. Lun, Z., Gadelha, M., Kalogerakis, E., Maji, S., Wang, R.: 3D shape reconstruction from sketches via multi-view convolutional networks. In: International Conference on 3D Vision (3DV) (2017)
29. Masci, J., Boscaini, D., Bronstein, M.M., Vandergheynst, P.: Geodesic convolutional neural networks on Riemannian manifolds. arXiv preprint arXiv:1501.06297 (2015)
30. Maturana, D., Scherer. S.: VoxNet: a 3D convolutional neural network for real-time object recognition. In: IROS (2015)
31. Qi, C.R., Su, H., Nießner, M., Dai, A., Yan, M., Guibas, L.: Volumetric and multi-view CNNs for object classification on 3D data. In: CVPR (2016)
32. Qi, C.R., Yi, L., Su, H., Guibas, L.J.: PointNet++: deep hierarchical feature learning on point sets in a metric space. In: NIPS (2017)

33. Riegler, G., Ulusoy, A.O., Geiger, A.: OctNet: learning deep 3D representations at high resolutions. In: CVPR (2017)
34. Sharma, A., Grau, O., Fritz, M.: VConv-DAE: deep volumetric shape learning without object labels. In: Hua, G., Jégou, H. (eds.) ECCV 2016. LNCS, vol. 9915, pp. 236–250. Springer, Cham (2016). https://doi.org/10.1007/978-3-319-49409-8_20
35. Simonovsky, M., Komodakis, N.: Dynamic edge-conditioned filters in convolutional neural networks on graphs. In: CVPR (2017)
36. Simonyan, K., Zisserman, A.: Very deep convolutional networks for large-scale image recognition. arXiv preprint arXiv:1409.1556 (2014)
37. Soltani, A.A., Huang, H., Wu, J., Kulkarni, T., Tenenbaum, J.: Synthesizing 3D shapes via modeling multi-view depth maps and silhouettes with deep generative networks. In: CVPR (2017)
38. Su, H., Jampani, V., Su, D., Maji, S., Kalogerakis, E., Yang, M.-H., Kautz, J.: SPLATNet: sparse lattice networks for point cloud processing. In: CVPR (2018)
39. Su, H., Maji, S., Kalogerakis, E., Learned-Miller, E.G.: Multi-view convolutional neural networks for 3D shape recognition. In: ICCV (2015)
40. Su, H., Qi, C., Mo, K., Guibas, L.: PointNet: deep learning on point sets for 3D classification and segmentation. In: CVPR (2017)
41. Tatarchenko, M., Dosovitskiy, A., Brox, T.: Octree generating networks: efficient convolutional architectures for high-resolution 3d outputs. In: ICCV (2017)
42. Wang, P.-S., Liu, Y., Guo, Y.-X., Sun, C.-Y., Tong, X.: O-CNN: octree-based convolutional neural networks for 3D shape analysis. ACM Trans. Graph. (SIGGRAPH) **36**(4) (2017)
43. Wu, J., Zhang, C., Xue, T., Freeman, W.T., Tenenbaum, J.B.: Learning a probabilistic latent space of object shapes via 3D generative-adversarial modeling. In: NIPS (2016)
44. Wu, Z., Song, S., Khosla, A., Yu, F., Zhang, L., Tang, X., Xiao, J.: 3D ShapeNets: a deep representation for volumetric shapes. In: CVPR (2015)
45. Yi, L., Su, H., Guo, X., Guibas, L.: SyncSpecCNN: synchronized spectral CNN for 3D shape segmentation. In: CVPR (2017)
46. Yu, F., Koltun, V.: Multi-scale context aggregation by dilated convolutions. arXiv preprint arXiv:1511.07122 (2015)

Propagating LSTM: 3D Pose Estimation Based on Joint Interdependency

Kyoungoh Lee, Inwoong Lee, and Sanghoon Lee(✉)

Department of Electrical Electronic Engineering,
Yonsei University, Seoul, South Korea
{kasinamooth,mayddb100,slee}@yonsei.ac.kr

Abstract. We present a novel 3D pose estimation method based on joint interdependency (JI) for acquiring 3D joints from the human pose of an RGB image. The JI incorporates the body part based structural connectivity of joints to learn the high spatial correlation of human posture on our method. Towards this goal, we propose a new long short-term memory (LSTM)-based deep learning architecture named propagating LSTM networks (p-LSTMs), where each LSTM is connected sequentially to reconstruct 3D depth from the centroid to edge joints through learning the intrinsic JI. In the first LSTM, the seed joints of 3D pose are created and reconstructed into the whole-body joints through the connected LSTMs. Utilizing the p-LSTMs, we achieve the higher accuracy of about 11.2% than state-of-the-art methods on the largest publicly available database. Importantly, we demonstrate that the JI drastically reduces the structural errors at body edges, thereby leads to a significant improvement.

Keywords: 3D human pose estimation · Joint interdependency (JI)
Long short-term memory (LSTM)
Propagating LSTM networks (p-LSTMs)

1 Introduction

Human pose estimation has been extensively studied in computer vision research area [1–6]. In general, human pose estimation can be categorized into 2D and 3D pose estimations. While the former focuses on obtaining human 2D joint positions from an image, the latter aims to acquire human 3D joint positions from an image by additionally inferring human depth information. Since various applications need human depth information including human motion capture, virtual training, augment reality, rehabilitation, and 3D graphic avatar, 3D pose estimation has become more paid attention in this research area [7–12].

Early 3D pose estimation approaches attempted to map 2D image to 3D pose using handcrafted features [13–16]. With a recent development of deep learning technology, many researchers in [17–19] have applied it to their methods to acquire 3D pose directly from an image without the handcrafted features.

V. Ferrari et al. (Eds.): ECCV 2018, LNCS 11211, pp. 123–141, 2018.
https://doi.org/10.1007/978-3-030-01234-2_8

However, these direct approaches limited the input to only 3D pose data captured in laboratory environments [20,21]. Alternatively, the authors in [4,22–30] used 2D poses derived from a generalized environment, so their networks have shown a superior performance to the direct 3D pose estimation approach. Nevertheless, most of these works overlooked the joint dependency of body called structural connectivity, which might lead to a degradation in pose estimation performance.

In [31], the authors applied the structural connectivity at a whole-body level to the cost function of a network. However, the whole-body based structural connectivity makes all the joints be coupled tightly, so it has a difficulty in reflecting actual attributes in regard to joint interdependency. For instance, if a person moves the right wrist, the right elbow and shoulder are triggered to move, but the joints of the left arm may be unaffected. In other words, the joints of the intra-body part are dependently operated while the joints of the inter-body part are quite irrelevant. Based on this observation, we attempt to embed this joint interdependency in conjunction with joint connectivity into our model, which would make it easier to estimate 3D pose more accurately.

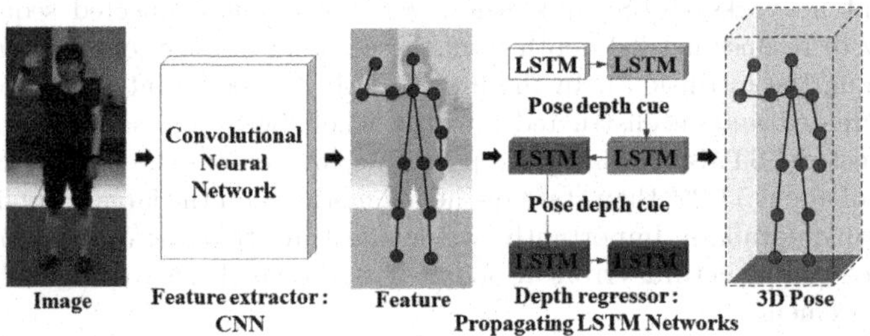

Fig. 1. Concept of the 3D pose estimation method. Convolutional neural network extracts a 2D pose from the input RGB video, which becomes a 3D pose through p-LSTMs via inferring depth cues implicitly.

In this paper, we present a novel 3D pose estimation method reflecting body part based structural connectivity as prior knowledge. Figure 1 gives an overall overview of our model. First, a 2D pose is extracted from the monocular RGB image by employing a 2D pose estimation method [2]. Second, the 3D pose is estimated using a proposed network named propagating long short term memory networks (p-LSTMs), which estimates depth information based on the 2D pose. In order to reflect the prior knowledge into p-LSTMs, we connect several LSTM networks in series. Those connected networks progressively elaborate the 3D pose while transferring the depth information called the pose depth cue. Eventually, the last LSTM network of the p-LSTMs builds the 3D pose of the whole body.

Our contributions are summarized as follows: (1) Unlike traditional approach that did not cover the joint interdependency based on actual human behavior, we develop a new model through utilizing body part based structural connectivity. In particular, to further refine the 3D pose, we adopt a multi-stage architecture in our method. (2) The effectiveness of our method is validated by extensive experiments on the largest 3D pose dataset [21]. It remarkably achieves an estimation accuracy improvement by 11.2% with competitive speed compared to the state-of-the-art methods.

2 Related Work

Estimating depth from an image is one of the most classic and challenging problems in computer vision. Many researchers have tried to reconstruct and analysis the 3D space closer to real world in a variety of areas [10,32–36]. 3D human pose estimation has to be robust against visual characteristics such as appearances, lights and motion. Early methods reconstructed human pose using a variety of invariant features such as silhouette [13], shape [14], SIFT [15], HOG [16]. Since deep learning technology can extract invariant features automatically from images, many researchers have brought this technology into 3D pose estimation [17–19]. Li *et al.* [17] applied a convolutional neural network (CNN) to directly estimate 3D pose from image. Grinciunaite *et al.* [18] exploited a 3D-CNN on sequential frames to obtain 3D pose. Although the 3D-CNN could obtain 3D pose from multiple frames, the estimations of complex 3D poses still do not demonstrate good performance. Pavlakos *et al.* [19] extended the existing 2D pose estimation method [2] to 3D. The authors used a coarse-to-fine strategy to handle the increase in dimensionality of the volumetric representation like 3D heatmap. However, the direct approaches using deep learning have a significant problem with generalization due to the lack of GT 3D pose data.

To efficiently enhance the poor performances, some approaches used 2D pose as a new invariant feature [4,22–27,29,30]. It is easier to convert the 2D pose to a 3D pose with high accuracy compared with conventional features. Moreover, currently, reliable 2D pose can be obtained owing to abundant databases. Many studies have paid attention to lifting dimension of pose from 2D to 3D. Zhou *et al.* [4] formulated an optimization problem in terms of the relationship between 2D pose and sparsity-driven 3D geometric prior, and predicted 3D pose by using an expectation-maximization algorithm. Chen *et al.* [22] and Yasin *et al.* [23] exploited the nearest-neighbor searching method to match the estimated 2D pose to a 3D pose from a large pose library. Tome *et al.* [24] proposed an iterative method which consisted of 2D pose method [1] and probabilistic 3D pose model. However, the systems, which are based on optimization and data retrieval, take a long time to obtain 3D pose and even require normalized input data.

As another attempt, many researchers in [25–27] used deep learning models to learn implicit pose structures from data when estimating 3D pose from 2D pose. Tekin *et al.* [25] extracted the 2D pose from an image by using a CNN and estimated the 3D pose by introducing an auto-encoder for 2D-to-3D estimation. This approach simply utilized an existing 2D pose estimation method by structurally connecting the auto-encoder to the CNN. Lin *et al.* [26] extracted 2D pose from an input image using the method in [1]. In addition, the LSTM was utilized to obtain the corresponding 3D pose from the extracted 2D pose.

Martinez *et al.* [27] proposed a simple model which works fast by using several fully connected networks. The 3D pose estimation performance has been greatly improved since the use of the 2D pose as invariant feature. However, these methods intended to automatically learn the relationship between 2D and 3D poses into the deep learning model without any prior knowledge of 3D human pose.

Some authors manually utilized prior knowledges such as kinematic model, body model, and structural connectivity [5,29–31]. These approaches reinforce our belief that prior knowledges are useful information to effectively train deep learning models when the dimension of pose increases from 2D to 3D. Zhou *et al.* [5] embedded a kinematic model layer into CNN. However, the parameters were hard to set due to the nonlinearity of the model. Furthermore, the method required hard assumptions such as fixed bone length and known scale. Bogo *et al.* [30] proposed an optimization process to fit the estimated 2D pose in [3] into the 3D human body model [37]. Moreno *et al.* [29] converted the input 2D pose from the joint position based vector to the Euclidean distance of joints based N-by-N matrix. Sun *et al.* [31] changed the cost function from per-joint error to per-bone(limb) error, and yet, to the best of our knowledge, the performance of the method [31] is currently highest in terms of pose estimation error.

However, the conventional methods overlooked an important notion from the perspective of interdependency of joints observed from the spatial and temporal behavior of the human body. Namely, the authors in [29,31] have exploited the structural connectivity of whole-body level as prior knowledge. Different to previous works, our novelty lies in embedding the body part based joint connectivity into the deep learning structure to reconstruct 3D pose more accurately.

3 3D Pose Estimation Method

3.1 System Architecture

Figure 2 illustrates the system architecture of our method. The proposed method consists of two deep learning models for 2D and 2D-to-3D pose estimations. The CNN extracts a 2D pose as the feature from the input RGB image in Fig. 2(b). Then, the proposed p-LSTMs, which is composed of 9 p-LSTMs serially, conducts the 2D-to-3D pose estimation stemming from the extracted 2D pose as shown in Fig. 2(d). The first 3D pose is constructed in the fully connected layers (FCs). Finally, the 3D pose is further refined by a multi-stage architecture of the 2D-to-3D pose estimation module as shown in Figs. 2(g) and (h).

3.2 Problem Statement

The main purpose of our method is to estimate the 3D human pose information from a given 2D input image. Towards this, a vast number of images and the corresponding 3D GT pose data are required. In general, the 2D human pose gives a more abstract representation of the human posture than that captured in raw image. Thus, the 2D-to-3D pose estimation by means of 2D pose is effective

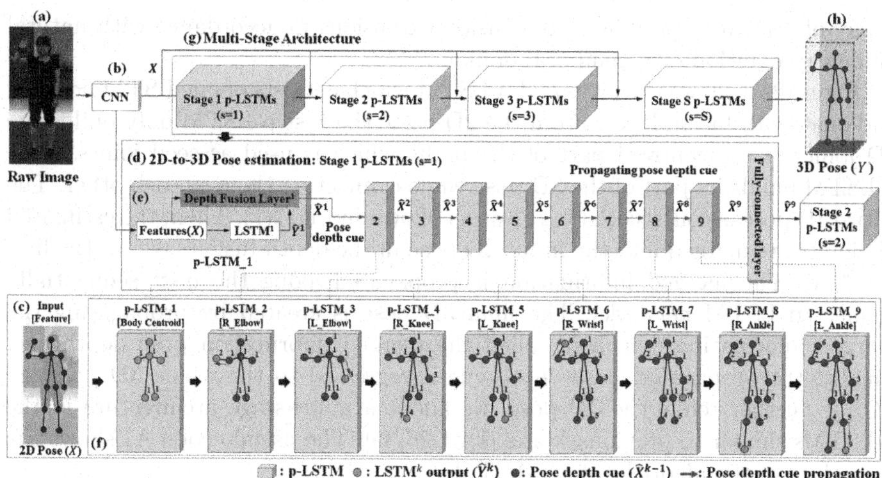

Fig. 2. System architecture of 3D pose estimation. (a) Input RGB image. (b) CNN extracts 2D pose from input data. (c) 2D pose extracted from (b). (d) Proposed p-LSTMs for extracting depth information from (c). (e) A unit of p-LSTM. (f) Procedure of constructing 2D-to-3D pose via p-LSTMs in accordance with the body part based structural connectivity of joints. (g) Multi-stage architecture. (h) Output of 3D pose. (Best seen in color and zoom.)

when estimating 3D pose from image [4,22–27,29–31]. We adopt the 2D pose estimation method in [2] as shown in Fig. 2(b). In this paper, the aim of our method is to learn a mapping function $f^* : \mathbb{R}^{2J} \rightarrow \mathbb{R}^{3J}$ through adding a depth dimension to the 2D pose with J joints. The mapping function uses $2J$ vectors for 2D pose X as input, and $3J$ vectors for 3D pose Y as output where $X = [x_1, \cdots, x_J]$, and $Y = [y_1, \cdots, y_J]$, respectively. The major objective of our method is to design the function f as a depth regressor.

3.3 Propagating LSTM Networks: p-LSTMs

We present a new deep learning model based on LSTM for estimating 3D pose from 2D pose, as shown in Fig. 2(d). In general, there is a limitation to estimate a 3D pose using single-frame 2D image only. If there are self-occluded cases in human pose, it would difficult for even human to answer the pose correctly, which significantly degrades the estimation performance. On the other hand, if multi-frame images are utilized, it should be much easier to handle the self-occluded issue. Hence, LSTM has demonstrated better performance in applications with time-correlated characteristics [26,38]. Lin *et al.* [26] only considered temporal correlation of input frames, but the proposed method includes spatial correlation as well as temporal correlation through the connection of multiple LSTM networks. Namely, in order to learn the spatial correlation of human pose, each LSTM network is sequentially connected to build a human body structure in a way of central-to-peripheral dimension extensions in accordance with natural human recognition over temporal domain.

Figure 2(e) shows the proposed p-LSTM which consists of one LSTM network and one depth fusion layer. From the 2D pose, the first p-LSTM only builds the 3D joints of the centroid part of the body, which is used as seed joints. Each p-LSTM builds its part of the 3D pose while connecting them to each other. The entire 3D pose is constructed in the order shown in Fig. 2(f). Then, the estimated 3D joints are merged into the input 2D pose in the depth fusion layer of the first p-LSTM. The merged information is propagated along the next sequentially connected LSTM networks. The final 3D pose is created by propagating the merged information, which is called the merged information pose depth cue. Finally, the propagated pose depth cue is regressed to the whole 3D pose via FC. To further refine the 3D pose, we adopt a multi-stage architecture in the p-LSTMs similar to previous works [1,24,26,39]. The pseudo code A1 shows the procedure of the algorithm for p-LSTMs.

A1: Algorithm of p-LSTMs

Variables

k: index of the p-LSTM

K: number of the p-LSTM

$\hat{Y}^k$: output of the kth LSTM network

$\hat{X}^k$: output of the kth depth fusion layer

$\mathrm{LSTM^k}$: k^{th} LSTM network

$\mathrm{Depth^k}$: k^{th} depth fusion layer

FC: fully connected layer

Y_{Pred}: output of 3D pose

Input: X (2D pose)

Output: Y (3D pose)

for $k = 1$ to K

  if (k==1)

    $\hat{Y}^k = \mathrm{LSTM^k(X)}$

    $\hat{X}^k = \mathrm{Depth^k(\hat{Y}^k, X)}$

  else

    $\hat{Y}^k = \mathrm{LSTM^k(\hat{X}^{k-1})}$

    $\hat{X}^k = \mathrm{Depth^k(\hat{Y}^k, \hat{X}^{k-1})}$

return $Y_{\mathrm{Pred}} = \mathrm{FC(\hat{X}^K)}$

Propagating Connection: To reflect the joint interdependency (JI) into our method, the body part based structural connectivity is carefully dealt with. The movement of a body part leads to movements of its connected body parts dependently, but the other parts of the body may move independently. For example, a motion of the right elbow triggers the movement of its connected wrists and shoulders, but the other side (left part) may not be affected. In other words, even though the whole body is physically connected to each other, the motion of each body part is independent. Unlike previous studies [29, 31] which simply accounted for prior knowledge of the body, we attempt to embed the body part based structural connectivity into the deep learning structure. Since each body part has different characteristics (range of motion), it is decomposed to several LSTM blocks instead of the whole-body inference. In addition, each p-LSTM is linked to each other according to human body structure to induce dependency because each body part derived from whole-body indirectly influences each other. When the 3D pose to be estimated is based on 14 joints, 9 p-LSTMs are used for representing the human body structure as shown in Fig. 2(f). The first p-LSTM plays a role of populating the 3D joints of the body's centroid part which are utilized as seed joints. After that, the first output is generated from the first p-LSTM, which becomes an input of the next p-LSTM. In the second p-LSTM, the next neighbor parts are constructed according to the human body structure. In this way, the 9 p-LSTMs are connected and each output is propagated to the other parts along the connection.

Pose Depth Cue: From the second p-LSTM to the last p-LSTM, the p-LSTM must rely solely on the output of the preceding p-LSTM because the initial 2D pose information disappears after the first p-LSTM. The spatial correlation of the 2D pose could be useful when estimating a 3D pose. Since human recognizes the structural connectivity (spatial correlation) of pose, human can easily reconstruct 3D pose according to the change of 2D joint position. For example, when the 2D positions of the wrist and elbow joints approach each other, the 3D positions of the two joints move along depth-axis. In fact, the limb connected by the wrist and elbow joints is structurally unchanged in length. To prevent the initial 2D pose from disappearing, each p-LSTM uses the input 2D pose as ancillary data and merges it with its own output in the depth fusion layer. In the proposed method, the depth information is gradually estimated through the newly generated input feature, and the spatial correlation of the human body is learned. Thus, the merged auxiliary and input data are called pose depth cue. In other words, the pose depth cue is created by integrating the 2D with 3D poses in the depth fusion layer, as shown in Fig. 2(e) and lines 4 and 7 of A1.

Different types of the pose depth cues can be created depending on how the 2D and 3D poses are merged. **(1) Elimination and addition method:** it deletes the 2D pose and only uses some of estimated 3D pose (no auxiliary data). **(2) Concatenated method:** it simply concatenates the 2D and 3D poses. **(3) Replacement method:** it replaces some of 2D pose with some of estimated 3D pose. Figure 3 depicts the three pose depth cues in details.

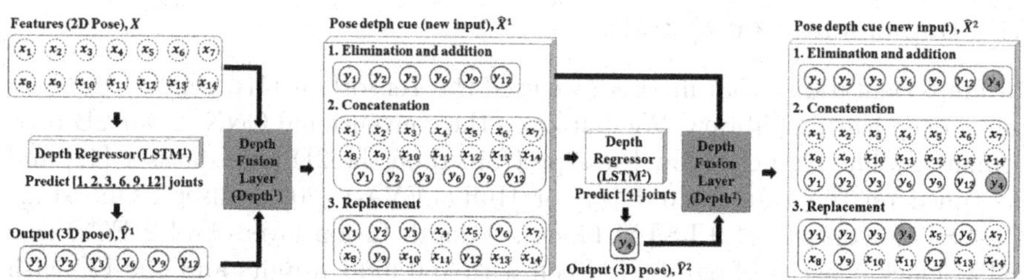

Fig. 3. Different types of the pose depth cues. (Best seen in zoom.)

The proposed 2D-to-3D pose estimation method consists of 9 p-LSTMs as shown in Fig. 2(d), and creates the pose depth cue for each depth fusion layer of the p-LSTMs. Passing through the p-LSTMs, the input pose depth cues change gradually. Figure 2(f) shows the procedure for the final pose depth cue to become the 3D pose. Although the proposed 2D-to-3D pose method is connected to multiple LSTM networks, the learning of the method is simple because it consists of an end-to-end network. To train the proposed p-LSTMs, the basic loss function can be represented by

$$\mathcal{L}_{3D}(Y_{pred}, Y_{GT}) = \frac{1}{|J|} \sum_{j}^{J} (Y_{pred} - Y_{GT})^2, \quad (1)$$

where Y_{pred} and Y_{GT} are predicted and GT 3D poses, respectively.

3.4 Training and Testing

For training, the final loss function of our method for 3D pose estimation is

$$\mathcal{L}_{3D}(Y_{pred}, Y_{GT}) = \sum_{s}^{S} \alpha_s \left[\sum_{t}^{T} \frac{1}{|J|} \sum_{j}^{J} (Y_{pred}^{t,s} - Y_{GT}^{t,s})^2 + \lambda \sum_{k}^{K} (w_k^s)^2 \right], \quad (2)$$

where S is the stage number of the proposed method, T is the length of the input image frames, α_s is the weight for each stage, λ is the regularization parameter, w_k is the weight value of the kth LSTM network, and K is the number of LSTM networks. When S is greater than 2, it means that the method is repeated S times. The final loss function consists of Euclidean distance of the GT 3D joint and the predicted 3D joint, and a regularization term is added for training stability. Our method is learned using an adaptive subgradient method (Adagrad optimizer) [40]. In the testing part, the input image comes in sequentially, and our proposed model processes it to estimate the 3D pose.

4 Experiments

4.1 Implementation Details

For implementation of our method, we used the Tensorflow [41], which is an open source deep learning library. We employed the conventional CNN [2] for 2D pose estimation. The 2D pose model was pretrained on the 2D pose dataset [42] and fine-tuned on the Human3.6M [21] or HumanEVA-I [20] datasets. One stage of p-LSTMs consists of 9 LSTM blocks, 9 depth fusion layers and 2 FCs. One LSTM block consists of one LSTM cell with 100 hidden units and one FC with 150 hidden units. In addition, 2 FCs with 45 hidden units were added after the p-LSTMs. The keeping probability of dropouts was set to 0.9 and 0.6 in the first and second FCs. Finally, in order to estimate the 3D human pose from the RGB image, we unified all of the aforementioned networks into an end-to-end network structure. In the training procedure of the deep learning model, the parameters of the model were initialized to uniform distribution [−0.1, 0.1]. The decay parameter and learning rate were set to 1e−4 and 1e−2, respectively. The stage loss weight α_s was set to 1. The total number of proposed model parameters is 31 million, consisting of 30 million from 2D part and 1 million from p-LSTMs. It took about 2 days to train our method with 10,000 epochs on GeForce TITAN X with 12GB memory. The training batch size was set to 64. The testing time of the proposed method takes about 33.6 ms per image (RGB-to-2D and 2D-to-3D methods take about 33 ms and 0.6 ms per image, respectively).

4.2 Datasets and Evaluation

For performance evaluation, we used two public datasets, namely HumanEva-I [20] and Human3.6M [21], which were the most widely used for performance comparison in the 3D human pose estimation research.

Human3.6M: The Human3.6M dataset consists of 3.6 million images and 3D human poses. In addition, the dataset was recorded from 4 cameras with different views. The 3D human pose data consists of 11 subjects with 15 actions. Previous works [5,18,19,22–24,26–29,31,43,44] performed the evaluation according to several different protocols. In this paper, we followed 2 major protocols for performance comparison. Protocol 1 was used to train 5 subjects (S1, S5, S6, S7, and S8) and to test 2 subjects (S9 and S11). Training and testing were performed independently and all camera views were used. This protocol was used in [5,18,19,22,24,26–29,31,44]. The original videos were down-sampled from 50 fps to 10 fps. Protocol 2 was used to train 6 subjects (S1, S5, S6, S7, S8, and S9) and to test 1 subject (S11). The original videos were down-sampled by keeping every 64th frame. This protocol was used in [22–24,29,31,43]. After the predicted 3D pose and GT 3D pose were aligned with the rigid transformation used in the Procrustes method [45], the error was computed.

HumanEva-I: The HumanEva-I dataset consists of RGB video sequences and 3D human pose. The RGB video sequences were recorded using 3 cameras with different views. The 3D human pose data consists of 3 subjects with 6 actions (walking, jogging, boxing, and so on). We trained the proposed method using the training dataset, and tested the method using the validation dataset in the same protocol as [23,26,27,46–49]. In the experiment, we excluded some results where rigid alignment was performed as post processing.

Evaluation Metric: We used the mean per joint position error (MPJPE) [21] as the evaluation metric, which is the most widely used performance index of 3D human pose estimation. The MPJPE simply calculates from the 3D Euclidean distance between GT and the predicted result. The error in millimeter is measured, and the GT value is obtained using infrared sensors.

4.3 Comparison with State-of-the-art Methods

Performance Comparison on Human3.6M: In Tables 1 and 2, the notations S and T mean the number of stages and the number of input frames, respectively. We compared the performance of the proposed method with state-of-the-art previous works on the Human3.6M dataset. In all the proposed methods of

Table 1. Comparison with the state-of-the-art methods for the Human3.6M under Protocol 1. The marks *, °, and † indicate a method using rigid alignment as post processing, GT 2D pose as input, and multiple frames as input, respectively.

Method (Protocol 1)	Direct.	Discuss	Eating	Greet	Phone	Photo	Pose	Purch.	Sitting	SitD.	Smoke	Wait	Walk	WalkD.	WalkT.	Avg.
Chen, CVPR'17 [22]	89.8	97.5	89.9	107.8	107.3	139.1	93.5	136.0	133.1	240.1	106.6	106.2	87.0	114.0	90.5	114.1
Zhou, ECCV'16 [5]	91.8	102.4	96.9	98.7	113.3	125.2	90.0	93.8	132.1	158.9	106.9	94.4	79.0	126.0	98.9	107.2
Tome, CVPR'17 [24]	64.9	73.4	76.8	86.4	86.2	110.6	68.9	74.7	110.1	173.9	84.9	85.7	71.3	86.2	73.1	88.3
Pavlakos, CVPR'17 [19]	67.3	71.9	66.7	69.0	71.9	76.9	65.0	68.3	83.6	96.5	71.7	65.8	59.1	74.8	63.2	71.9
Martinez, ICCV'17 [27]	51.8	56.2	58.1	59.0	69.5	78.4	55.2	58.1	74.0	94.6	62.3	59.1	49.5	65.1	52.4	62.9
Sun, ICCV'17 [31]	52.8	54.8	54.2	54.3	61.8	**67.2**	53.1	53.6	71.7	86.7	61.5	**53.4**	**47.1**	**61.6**	53.4	59.1
Our p-LSTMs ($S=3$, $T=1$)	**43.8**	**51.7**	**48.8**	**53.1**	**52.2**	74.9	**52.7**	**44.6**	**56.9**	**74.3**	**56.7**	66.4	47.5	68.4	**45.6**	**55.8**
Zhou, ICCV'17 [28]*	54.8	60.7	58.2	71.4	62.0	**65.5**	53.8	55.5	75.2	111.5	64.1	66.0	63.2	**51.4**	55.3	64.9
Martinez, ICCV'17 [27]*	39.5	43.2	46.4	47.0	51.0	56.0	41.4	**40.6**	56.5	69.4	**49.2**	45.0	38.0	**49.5**	43.1	47.7
Our p-LSTMs ($S=3$, $T=1$)*	**38.0**	**39.3**	**46.3**	**44.4**	**49.0**	**55.1**	**40.2**	41.1	**53.2**	**68.9**	51.0	**39.1**	**33.9**	56.4	**38.5**	**46.2**
Moreno, CVPR'17 [29]°	53.5	50.5	65.7	62.4	56.9	80.8	60.6	50.8	55.9	79.6	63.6	61.8	59.4	68.5	62.1	62.1
Martinez, ICCV'17 [27]°	37.7	44.4	40.3	42.1	48.2	54.9	44.4	42.1	54.6	58.0	45.1	46.4	36.4	47.6	40.4	45.5
Our p-LSTMs ($S=3$, $T=1$)°	34.6	39.7	37.2	40.9	45.6	50.5	42.0	39.4	47.3	48.1	39.5	38.0	31.9	41.5	37.2	**40.9**
Grinciunaite, ECCV'16 [18]†	91	89	94	102	105	151	99	112	151	239	109	106	101	141	106	119
Lin, CVPR'17 [26]†	58.0	68.2	63.3	65.8	75.3	93.1	61.2	65.7	98.7	127.7	70.4	68.2	50.6	72.9	57.7	73.1
Hossain, Thesis [44]†	44.2	**46.7**	52.3	**49.3**	59.9	**59.4**	**47.5**	46.2	59.9	**65.6**	55.8	50.4	43.5	**52.3**	45.1	**51.9**
Our p-LSTMs ($S=3$, $T=3$)†	**40.2**	49.2	**47.8**	52.6	**50.1**	75.0	50.2	**43.0**	**55.8**	73.9	**54.1**	55.6	**43.3**	58.2	**43.3**	52.8
Our p-LSTMs ($S=3$, $T=3$)†,°	32.1	36.6	34.3	37.8	44.5	49.9	40.9	36.2	44.1	45.6	35.3	35.9	30.3	37.6	35.5	**38.4**

Table 2. Comparison with the state-of-the-art methods for the Human3.6M under Protocol 2. All methods use rigid alignment as post processing.

Method (Protocol 2)	Direct.	Discuss	Eating	Greet	Phone	Photo	Pose	Purch.	Sitting	SitD.	Smoke	Wait	Walk	WalkD.	WalkT.	Avg.
Yasin, CVPR'16 [23]	88.4	72.5	108.5	110.2	97.1	142.5	81.6	107.2	119.0	170.8	108.2	86.9	92.1	165.7	102.0	110.1
Rogez, NIPS'16 [43]	-	-	-	-	-	-	-	-	-	-	-	-	-	-	-	88.1
Chen, CVPR'17 [22]	71.6	66.6	74.7	79.0	70.0	93.2	67.5	89.3	90.7	195.6	83.4	71.1	55.7	85.8	62.5	82.7
Moreno, CVPR'17 [29]	66.0	61.6	84.5	73.7	65.2	92.5	67.1	60.8	67.2	103.4	74.7	69.5	71.4	78.0	73.2	73.9
Tome, CVPR'17 [24]	-	-	-	-	-	-	-	-	-	-	-	-	-	-	-	70.7
Sun, ICCV'17 [31]	42.1	44.3	45.0	45.4	51.5	**53.0**	43.2	41.3	59.3	73.3	51.0	44.0	38.3	**48.0**	44.8	48.3
Our p-LSTMs ($S=3$, $T=1$)	37.4	38.9	45.6	43.8	48.5	54.6	39.9	39.2	53.0	68.5	51.5	38.4	33.2	55.8	37.8	**45.7**
Our p-LSTMs ($S=3$, $T=3$)	**34.9**	**35.2**	**43.2**	**42.6**	**46.2**	55.0	**37.6**	**38.8**	**50.9**	**67.3**	**48.9**	**35.2**	**31.0**	50.7	**34.6**	**43.4**

Tables 1 and 2, the replacement type of the pose depth cue is used. Tables 1 and 2 show the result of average 3D joint error (mm) w.r.t. the GT 3D joints in Protocol 1 and 2.

For a fair comparisons, Table 1 shows the results separately for the factors affecting performance such as format of input data or usage of post processing. In Table 1, the first sub-table (rows 1 to 7) show performance comparisons for single frame. Our result achieve a performance improvement of about 3.3 mm (5.9%) compared with [31]. Next sub-table is the results obtained by further calibrating the 3D pose using rigid alignment. We obtain a 1.5 mm (3.2%) lower prediction error compared with [27]. Third sub-table show the results when the 2D GT pose is used as input data. In the 3D pose estimation using 2D pose as feature, our method shows a potential performance by eliminating the influence of estimation accuracy of 2D pose methods. We achieve a gain of about 4.6 mm (11.2%) over [27]. Finally, the performances when multiple frames are used as input are shown in rows 14 to 17. The methods using multiple frames can achieve a robust 3D pose against noise such as self-occlusion using temporal correlation. A detailed description of the effects of multiple frames in the proposed method is given in Sect. 4.4. Our performance is slightly less than [44] in terms of accuracy, but the number of parameters is three times fewer than [44], which makes the computation significantly faster. For Protocol 2, our method shows the best performance except for the *photo* and the *walking with dog* scenarios including the case of using single frame. The authors in [24,43] only provided the average joint error. The results are quantitatively compared with [31], which improves the performance about 2.6 mm (5%) to 4.3 mm (9%). The *photo* scenario consists of very complex poses but the performance of our method is competitive. The proposed method outperforms all of state-of-the-art methods on average. The average error of Protocol 2 is lower than that of Protocol 1 because the deep learning based methods are effectively trained on more diverse datasets. From the experiments, it is demonstrated that the learning JI is effective from the regularization point of view.

Table 3. Comparison with the state-of-the-art methods for the HumanEva-I.

Method (HumanEVA-I)	Walking				Jogging				Boxing			
	S1	S2	S3	Avg.	S1	S2	S3	Avg.	S1	S2	S3	Avg.
Radwan, CVPR'13 [46]	75.1	99.8	93.8	89.6	79.2	89.8	99.4	89.5	-	-	-	-
Simo-Serra, CVPR'13 [47]	65.1	48.6	73.5	62.4	74.2	46.6	32.2	56.7	-	-	-	-
Kostrikov, BMVC'14 [48]	44.0	30.9	41.7	38.9	57.2	35.0	33.3	40.3	-	-	-	-
Tekin, CVPR'16 [49]	37.5	25.1	49.2	37.3	-	-	-	-	50.5	61.7	57.5	56.6
Yasin, CVPR'16 [23]	35.8	32.4	41.6	36.6	46.6	41.4	35.4	38.9	-	-	-	-
Lin, CVPR'17 [26]	26.5	20.7	38.0	28.4	41.0	29.7	29.1	33.2	**39.4**	57.8	61.2	52.8
Martinez, CVPR'17 [27]	19.7	**17.4**	46.8	28.0	26.9	18.2	18.6	21.2	-	-	-	-
Our p-LSTMs (S = 3, T = 1)	**18.6**	19.9	**30.5**	**<u>23.0</u>**	**25.7**	**16.8**	**17.7**	**<u>20.1</u>**	42.8	**48.1**	**53.4**	**<u>48.1</u>**

Performance Comparison on HumanEva-I: This dataset is also widely used for performance comparisons due to simple actions and fewer sequences compared to Human3.6M. For a fair comparison with previous works, we only learned and evaluated data recorded with camera 1. The number of hidden units in each LSTM network was 80. The results are summarized in Table 3. Some results of previous works were excluded because there were no results for the *jogging* and *boxing* scenarios. Our result shows the best performance for all the actions, and improves from 1.1 mm (5%) to 5 mm (17.8%) over the state-of-the-art methods. The average joint error of the *boxing* scenario higher than that of the others due to self-occlusion action. For the *jogging* scenario, a margin of performance improvement is the least.

4.4 Ablative Study (Effect of the p-LSTMs)

Tables 4 and 5 show the effect of the p-LSTMs via ablation test. Our baseline consists of one LSTM and 2 FCs and the number of hidden units in LSTM and each FC are 80 and 45, respectively.

Multi-stage Architecture: In order to improve the performance of the proposed method, a multi-stage architecture is used, which consists of concatenated multiple of p-LSTMs. Furthermore, the input of next stage consists of concatenating the initial input 2D pose and the predicted 3D pose from the current stage. Experimental results according to the multi-stage architecture are shown from the rows 1 to 7 of Table 4. The multi-stage parameter S is set to 2, which means that the structure of p-LSTMs are repeated twice. In this experiment, the more stages were configured, the longer the training took, but the better

Table 4. Results of the baseline and variants on Human3.6M under Protocol 1.

Method (Protocol 1)	Direct.	Discuss	Eating	Greet	Phone	Photo	Pose	Purch.	Sitting	SitD.	Smoke	Wait	Walk	WalkD.	WalkT.	Avg.
Single LSTM (S=1, T=1)	97.2	109.8	96.5	95.6	98.4	134.2	93.6	94.8	134.6	145.2	96.7	106.5	117.1	106.9	100.6	108.5
Single LSTM (S=3, T=1)	90.4	98.9	94.8	91.2	95.2	133.9	90.4	91.1	132.6	142.1	95.9	98.9	104.4	105.5	99.1	104.3
Single LSTM (S=1, T=3)	91.1	96.2	93.5	92.4	95.6	133.5	84.8	88.9	131.2	139.4	94.0	100.3	98.4	99.6	90.4	102.0
Single LSTM (S=3, T=3)	86.5	93.4	90.9	88.7	92.1	129.8	80.1	86.2	127.8	135.6	92.1	88.1	92.5	93.2	86.8	97.6
p-LSTMs (S=1, T=1)	45.0	54.3	50.6	57.1	55.8	77.6	56.5	47.0	58.5	77.3	58.0	69.2	50.4	70.6	48.4	58.4
p-LSTMs (S=2, T=1)	44.4	53.1	49.7	54.6	53.8	76.8	54.9	45.1	57.3	76.0	57.6	68.0	48.2	68.9	45.7	56.9
p-LSTMs (S=3, T=1)	**43.8**	**51.7**	**48.8**	**53.1**	**52.2**	**74.9**	**52.7**	**44.6**	**56.9**	**74.3**	**56.7**	**66.4**	**47.5**	**68.4**	**45.6**	**55.8**
p-LSTMs (S=3, T=3)	**40.2**	**49.2**	**47.8**	**52.6**	**50.1**	**75.0**	**50.2**	**43.0**	**55.8**	**73.9**	**54.1**	**55.6**	43.3	**58.2**	**43.3**	**52.8**
p-LSTMs (S=3, T=5)	41.7	59.0	60.2	60.8	58.8	83.5	58.4	54.4	59.4	86.2	60.4	69.9	**39.6**	66.5	44.8	60.2
p-LSTMs (S=3, T=10)	42.5	67.6	65.3	69.2	76.3	90.4	63.8	62.5	79.6	93.9	64.1	76.3	43.2	73.5	61.9	68.8

Table 5. Joints error on Human3.6M. D, o, and i are the type of the pose depth cue, the propagation to outward direction, and the propagation to inward direction, respectively. The p-LSTMs consist of 3 stages and 1 input frame.

Method (Protocol 1)	Head	Neck	R_shld	R_elbow	R_wrist	L_shld	L_elbow	L_wrist	R_hip	R_knee	R_ankle	L_hip	L_knee	L_ankle	Avg.
Single LSTM (baseline)	79.1	39.1	88.9	103.5	130.3	90.0	105.4	140.6	79.5	98.5	197.8	75.7	90.1	200.4	108.5
p-LSTMs (D=1, o)	65.1	33.4	83.5	100.4	110.1	87.6	97.4	108.1	74.5	80.0	117.1	74.3	80.5	116.2	87.6
p-LSTMs (D=2, o)	63.6	28.6	81.5	95.9	103.8	80.4	87.3	102.6	66.1	74.3	99.6	64.1	73.0	97.7	79.8
p-LSTMs (D=3, o)	**52.4**	**16.2**	**34.6**	**56.6**	**74.3**	**34.1**	**58.9**	**74.9**	**44.2**	**63.5**	**83.1**	**48.4**	**58.6**	**81.4**	**55.8**
p-LSTMs (D=3, i)	69.6	35.4	85.1	85.5	96.3	86.6	84.9	97.5	76.8	81.7	105.8	76.9	83.1	105.3	83.6

the performance, which was improved by up to 2.6 mm (4.4%). The multi-stage architecture refined the 3D pose, which was initially estimated, and was repeated as the structure of the same method was repeated.

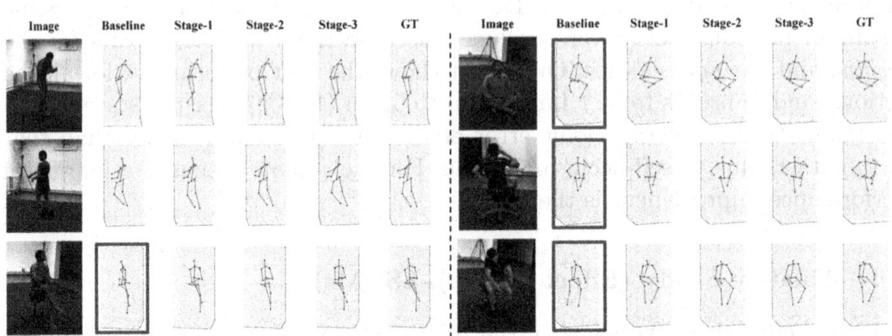

Fig. 4. Qualitative comparisons of the baseline and variants on the Human3.6M dataset. The 3D human poses are represented by the baseline, stage-1, stage-2, stage-3 of our method ($S = 3, T = 1$) and ground-truth, respectively.

Figures 4 and 5 show the qualitative results of the estimated 3D pose. In Fig. 4, the left and right figures w.r.t. the center dotted line, the reconstructed 3D pose show the effect of the multi-stage architecture. As the number of stages increases, the estimated 3D pose becomes closer to the ground truth. This multi-stage structure is very quantitatively and qualitatively effective in the 3D pose estimation. In Fig. 5, the estimated 3D pose of real-world image using the proposed model trained with Human3.6M shows qualitatively satisfactory results.

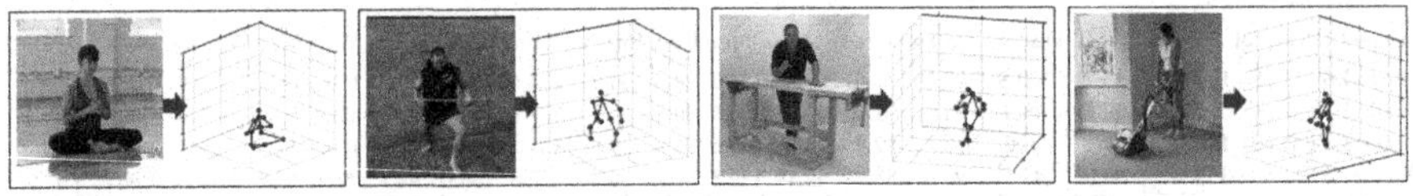

Fig. 5. Qualitative results of real-world image. (Best seen in zoom.)

Effect of Temporal Correlation in Pose Estimation: Estimating 3D pose using single frame 2D image or pose only has a limitation. If there are self-occluded cases in human pose, it would be difficult for even human to guess the pose correctly, which significantly degrades the estimation performance. On the other hand, if multiple frame images or poses are utilized, it should be much easier to handle the self-occluded issue. To reduce these errors, some authors in [18,26,44] used sequential frames as inputs to their methods to learn temporal correlation. Inspired by [26], we used sequential frames as inputs to the proposed method. In Table 4, rows 8 to 10 provide the performance according to the number of input frames. The result on row 9 is the best performance with

3 input frames. The overall performance is worst when 10 frames are used as inputs, and the best performance is shown only in the walking scenario when 5 frames are used as inputs. The performance in the walking scenario consisting of simple repetitive actions can be improved by using more frames. The results show that using a proper quantity of frames contributes to improving the performance, but using excessive frames degrades it.

How to Make the Pose Depth Cue: In the pose depth cue of Sect. 3.2, we have described the type of the pose depth cue. In Table 5, rows 2 to 4 show the performance of each joint according to the type of the pose depth cue. The elimination and addition method ($D = 1$) implies the pure connected p-LSTMs which do not use auxiliary data. The second type is created using the concatenation method, and the last type is created using the replacement method. The results show that the third type has the best performance and the first type has the worst performance. For the third type of the pose depth cue, when some 2D human pose is replaced by some expected 3D human pose, the vector of input pose depth cues will have a constant size even though they pass through p-LSTMs. This type also includes a 2D pose remaining as ancillary data. On the other hand, the first type of the pose depth cue does not use auxiliary data. This result shows the performance of p-LSTMs in a purely connected structure. This ablation study shows that the auxiliary data brings approximately 36.3% performance improvement to the proposed method. The pose depth cue of the third type is very effective in learning the spatial correlation of human poses.

How to Set the Propagating Direction: The pose depth cue is created through a depth fusion layer of a p-LSTM. The created pose depth cue is propagated sequentially to a number of connected p-LSTMs. From the propagation point of view, directions are determined after the initial seed joints are generated. Thus, the direction of the propagating pose depth cue can be divided into outward and inward directions. The outward direction is to propagate the pose depth cue from the centroid part to the edge of the body outward. On the contrary, the inward direction is a method of propagating the pose depth cue from the edge to the centroid part of the body inward. The results of the experiment are explained by the fourth and fifth row results in Table 5. The method of the outward direction is superior in performance. Since the pose depth cue is made up of a combination of some estimated 3D and 2D poses, the 3D pose estimated at the body center delivers more stable pose depth cues.

5 Conclusion

In this study, we have proposed a novel 3D pose estimation method, the p-LSTMs, where 9 LSTM networks are sequentially connected, in order to reflect the spatial information about the JI and the temporal information about the input image frames. In addition, we have defined a depth cue for the pose, and propagated this information across multiple LSTM networks. Through an ablative study, we have proved the validity of the proposed techniques such as propagating direction, pose depth cue, and multi-stage architecture. The proposed method have achieved significant improvement compared with the state-of-the-art methods on two public datasets.

In the future, we plan to investigate failure cases for further improvement. A possible direction will be to weight a frame with a reliability factor when using multiple input frames. Another direction is to adjust the parameters of the proposed method to obtain more accurate poses. Finally, we hope that our approach can provide insight for other research on 3D multiple-human, 3D object and 3D hand pose estimations.

Acknowledgement. This work was supported by Institute for Information & communications Technology Promotion(IITP) grant funded by the Korea government (MSIT) (No. 2016-0-00406, SIAT CCTV Cloud Platform).

References

1. Wei, S.E., Ramakrishna, V., Kanade, T., Sheikh, Y.: Convolutional pose machines. In: Proceedings of the IEEE Conference on Computer Vision and Pattern Recognition, pp. 4724–4732 (2016)
2. Newell, A., Yang, K., Deng, J.: Stacked hourglass networks for human pose estimation. In: Leibe, B., Matas, J., Sebe, N., Welling, M. (eds.) ECCV 2016. LNCS, vol. 9912, pp. 483–499. Springer, Cham (2016). https://doi.org/10.1007/978-3-319-46484-8_29
3. Pishchulin, L., et al.: DeepCut: joint subset partition and labeling for multi person pose estimation. In: Proceedings of the IEEE Conference on Computer Vision and Pattern Recognition, pp. 4929–4937 (2016)
4. Zhou, X., Zhu, M., Leonardos, S., Derpanis, K.G., Daniilidis, K.: Sparseness meets deepness: 3D human pose estimation from monocular video. In: Proceedings of the IEEE Conference on Computer Vision and Pattern Recognition, pp. 4966–4975 (2016)
5. Zhou, X., Sun, X., Zhang, W., Liang, S., Wei, Y.: Deep kinematic pose regression. In: Hua, G., Jégou, H. (eds.) ECCV 2016. LNCS, vol. 9915, pp. 186–201. Springer, Cham (2016). https://doi.org/10.1007/978-3-319-49409-8_17
6. Popa, A.I., Zanfir, M., Sminchisescu, C.: Deep multitask architecture for integrated 2D and 3D human sensing. In: Conference on Computer Vision and Pattern Recognition, vol. 1, p. 5 (2017)
7. Kim, J., Lee, I., Kim, J., Lee, S.: Implementation of an omnidirectional human motion capture system using multiple kinect sensors. IEICE Trans. Fundam. Electron. Commun. Comput. Sci. **98**(9), 2004–2008 (2015)
8. Kwon, B., et al.: Implementation of human action recognition system using multiple kinect sensors. In: Ho, Y.-S., Sang, J., Ro, Y.M., Kim, J., Wu, F. (eds.) PCM 2015. LNCS, vol. 9314, pp. 334–343. Springer, Cham (2015). https://doi.org/10.1007/978-3-319-24075-6_32
9. Kwon, B., Kim, J., Lee, K., Lee, Y.K., Park, S., Lee, S.: Implementation of a virtual training simulator based on 360 multi-view human action recognition. IEEE Access **5**, 12496–12511 (2017)
10. Meng, M., et al.: Kinect for interactive AR anatomy learning. In: 2013 IEEE International Symposium on Mixed and Augmented Reality (ISMAR), pp. 277–278. IEEE (2013)

11. González-Ortega, D., Díaz-Pernas, F., Martínez-Zarzuela, M., Antón-Rodríguez, M.: A kinect-based system for cognitive rehabilitation exercises monitoring. Comput. Methods Programs Biomed. **113**(2), 620–631 (2014)
12. Tong, J., Zhou, J., Liu, L., Pan, Z., Yan, H.: Scanning 3D full human bodies using kinects. IEEE Trans. Vis. Comput. Graph. **18**(4), 643–650 (2012)
13. Agarwal, A., Triggs, B.: 3D human pose from silhouettes by relevance vector regression. In: Proceedings of the 2004 IEEE Computer Society Conference on Computer Vision and Pattern Recognition, CVPR 2004, vol. 2, p. II. IEEE (2004)
14. Mori, G., Malik, J.: Recovering 3D human body configurations using shape contexts. IEEE Trans. Pattern Anal. Mach. Intell. **28**(7), 1052–1062 (2006)
15. Bo, L., Sminchisescu, C., Kanaujia, A., Metaxas, D.: Fast algorithms for large scale conditional 3D prediction. In: IEEE Conference on Computer Vision and Pattern Recognition, CVPR 2008, pp. 1–8. IEEE (2008)
16. Rogez, G., Rihan, J., Ramalingam, S., Orrite, C., Torr, P.H.: Randomized trees for human pose detection. In: IEEE Conference on Computer Vision and Pattern Recognition, CVPR 2008, pp. 1–8. IEEE (2008)
17. Li, S., Chan, A.B.: 3D human pose estimation from monocular images with deep convolutional neural network. In: Cremers, D., Reid, I., Saito, H., Yang, M.-H. (eds.) ACCV 2014. LNCS, vol. 9004, pp. 332–347. Springer, Cham (2015). https://doi.org/10.1007/978-3-319-16808-1_23
18. Grinciunaite, A., Gudi, A., Tasli, E., den Uyl, M.: Human pose estimation in space and time using 3D CNN. In: Hua, G., Jégou, H. (eds.) ECCV 2016. LNCS, vol. 9915, pp. 32–39. Springer, Cham (2016). https://doi.org/10.1007/978-3-319-49409-8_5
19. Pavlakos, G., Zhou, X., Derpanis, K.G., Daniilidis, K.: Coarse-to-fine volumetric prediction for single-image 3D human pose. In: Computer Vision and Pattern Recognition (CVPR) (2017)
20. Sigal, L., Balan, A.O., Black, M.J.: HumanEva: synchronized video and motion capture dataset and baseline algorithm for evaluation of articulated human motion. Int. J. Comput. Vis. **87**(1), 4–27 (2010)
21. Ionescu, C., Papava, D., Olaru, V., Sminchisescu, C.: Human3. 6M: large scale datasets and predictive methods for 3D human sensing in natural environments. IEEE Trans. Pattern Anal. Mach. Intell. **36**(7), 1325–1339 (2014)
22. Chen, C.H., Ramanan, D.: 3D human pose estimation = 2D pose estimation + matching. In: CVPR, vol. 2, p. 6 (2017)
23. Yasin, H., Iqbal, U., Kruger, B., Weber, A., Gall, J.: A dual-source approach for 3D pose estimation from a single image. In: Proceedings of the IEEE Conference on Computer Vision and Pattern Recognition, pp. 4948–4956 (2016)
24. Tome, D., Russell, C., Agapito, L.: Lifting from the deep: convolutional 3D pose estimation from a single image. In: The IEEE Conference on Computer Vision and Pattern Recognition (CVPR), July 2017
25. Tekin, B., Katircioglu, I., Salzmann, M., Lepetit, V., Fua, P.: Structured prediction of 3D human pose with deep neural networks. In: Richard, C. Wilson, E.R.H., Smith, W.A.P. (eds.) Proceedings of the British Machine Vision Conference (BMVC), pp. 130.1–130.11. BMVA Press, September 2016)
26. Lin, M., Lin, L., Liang, X., Wang, K., Chen, H.: Recurrent 3D pose sequence machines. In: CVPR (2017)
27. Martinez, J., Hossain, R., Romero, J., Little, J.J.: A simple yet effective baseline for 3D human pose estimation. In: IEEE International Conference on Computer Vision, vol. 206, p. 3 (2017)

28. Zhou, X., Huang, Q., Sun, X., Xue, X., Wei, Y.: Towards 3D human pose estimation in the wild: a weakly-supervised approach. In: IEEE International Conference on Computer Vision (2017)
29. Moreno-Noguer, F.: 3D human pose estimation from a single image via distance matrix regression. In: 2017 IEEE Conference on Computer Vision and Pattern Recognition (CVPR), pp. 1561–1570. IEEE (2017)
30. Bogo, F., Kanazawa, A., Lassner, C., Gehler, P., Romero, J., Black, M.J.: Keep it SMPL: automatic estimation of 3D human pose and shape from a single image. In: Leibe, B., Matas, J., Sebe, N., Welling, M. (eds.) ECCV 2016. LNCS, vol. 9909, pp. 561–578. Springer, Cham (2016). https://doi.org/10.1007/978-3-319-46454-1_34
31. Sun, X., Shang, J., Liang, S., Wei, Y.: Compositional human pose regression. In: The IEEE International Conference on Computer Vision (ICCV), vol. 2 (2017)
32. Westoby, M., Brasington, J., Glasser, N., Hambrey, M., Reynolds, J.: Structure-from-motionphotogrammetry: a low-cost, effective tool for geoscience applications. Geomorphology **179**, 300–314 (2012)
33. Lee, S.H., Kang, J., Lee, S.: Enhanced particle-filtering framework for vessel segmentation and tracking. Comput. Methods Programs Biomed. **148**, 99–112 (2017)
34. Oh, H., Kim, J., Kim, J., Kim, T., Lee, S., Bovik, A.C.: Enhancement of visual comfort and sense of presence on stereoscopic 3D images. IEEE Trans. Image Process. **26**(8), 3789–3801 (2017)
35. Lee, K., Lee, S.: A new framework for measuring 2D and 3D visual information in terms of entropy. IEEE Trans. Circuits Syst. Video Technol. **26**(11), 2015–2027 (2016)
36. Oh, H., Lee, S., Bovik, A.C.: Stereoscopic 3D visual discomfort prediction: a dynamic accommodation and vergence interaction model. IEEE Trans. Image Process. **25**(2), 615–629 (2016)
37. Loper, M., Mahmood, N., Romero, J., Pons-Moll, G., Black, M.J.: SMPL: a skinned multi-person linear model. ACM Trans. Graph. (TOG) **34**(6), 248 (2015)
38. Lee, I., Kim, D., Kang, S., Lee, S.: Ensemble deep learning for skeleton-based action recognition using temporal sliding LSTM networks. In: 2017 IEEE International Conference on Computer Vision (ICCV), pp. 1012–1020. IEEE (2017)
39. Toshev, A., Szegedy, C.: DeepPose: human pose estimation via deep neural networks. In: Proceedings of the IEEE Conference on Computer Vision and Pattern Recognition, pp. 1653–1660 (2014)
40. Duchi, J., Hazan, E., Singer, Y.: Adaptive subgradient methods for online learning and stochastic optimization. J. Mach. Learn. Res. **12**, 2121–2159 (2011)
41. Abadi, M., et al.: TensorFlow: a system for large-scale machine learning. OSDI **16**, 265–283 (2016)
42. Andriluka, M., Pishchulin, L., Gehler, P., Schiele, B.: 2D human pose estimation: new benchmark and state of the art analysis. In: Proceedings of the IEEE Conference on computer Vision and Pattern Recognition, pp. 3686–3693 (2014)
43. Rogez, G., Schmid, C.: Mocap-guided data augmentation for 3D pose estimation in the wild. In: Advances in Neural Information Processing Systems, pp. 3108–3116 (2016)
44. Hossain, M.R.I.: Understanding the sources of error for 3D human pose estimation from monocular images and videos. Ph.D. thesis, University of British Columbia (2017)
45. Gower, J.C.: Generalized procrustes analysis. Psychometrika **40**(1), 33–51 (1975)
46. Radwan, I., Dhall, A., Goecke, R.: Monocular image 3D human pose estimation under self-occlusion. In: Proceedings of the IEEE International Conference on Computer Vision, pp. 1888–1895 (2013)

47. Simo-Serra, E., Quattoni, A., Torras, C., Moreno-Noguer, F.: A joint model for 2D and 3D pose estimation from a single image. In: Proceedings of the IEEE Conference on Computer Vision and Pattern Recognition, pp. 3634–3641 (2013)
48. Kostrikov, I., Gall, J.: Depth sweep regression forests for estimating 3D human pose from images. In: BMVC, vol. 1, p. 5 (2014)
49. Tekin, B., Rozantsev, A., Lepetit, V., Fua, P.: Direct prediction of 3D body poses from motion compensated sequences. In: Proceedings of the IEEE Conference on Computer Vision and Pattern Recognition, pp. 991–1000 (2016)

Deformable Pose Traversal Convolution for 3D Action and Gesture Recognition

Junwu Weng[1(✉)], Mengyuan Liu[1], Xudong Jiang[1], and Junsong Yuan[2]

[1] School of EEE, Nanyang Technological University, Singapore, Singapore
we0001wu@e.ntu.edu.sg, {liumengyuan,exdjiang}@ntu.edu.sg

[2] Department of CSE, The State University of New York, Buffalo, USA
jsyuan@buffalo.edu

Abstract. The representation of 3D pose plays a critical role for 3D action and gesture recognition. Rather than representing a 3D pose directly by its joint locations, in this paper, we propose a Deformable Pose Traversal Convolution Network that applies one-dimensional convolution to traverse the 3D pose for its representation. Instead of fixing the receptive field when performing traversal convolution, it optimizes the convolution kernel for each joint, by considering contextual joints with various weights. This deformable convolution better utilizes the contextual joints for action and gesture recognition and is more robust to noisy joints. Moreover, by feeding the learned pose feature to a LSTM, we perform end-to-end training that jointly optimizes 3D pose representation and temporal sequence recognition. Experiments on three benchmark datasets validate the competitive performance of our proposed method, as well as its efficiency and robustness to handle noisy joints of pose.

Keywords: Pose Traversal · Pose Convolution
Deformable Convolution · 3D action and gesture recognition

1 Introduction

With the success of pose estimation methods [1–3] using depth sensor, 3D action and hand gesture recognition have drawn considerable attention. To recognize 3D action and gestures, each 3D pose is often characterized by its joints with 3D locations.

However, previous work [4–6] show that not every spatial joint is of equal importance to the recognition of actions, and human body movements exhibit spatial patterns among pose joints [7]. It is thus of great importance to identify those motion patterns and avoid the non-informative joints, via identifying the key combinations of joints that matter for the recognition. For instance, to recognize hand gesture "Okay", the "approaching of index fingertip and thumb tip" as well as the "stretching of other three fingers apart from the palm" should be observed. The coordination of these five key fingertips is important to the recognition of gesture "Okay".

V. Ferrari et al. (Eds.): ECCV 2018, LNCS 11211, pp. 142–157, 2018.
https://doi.org/10.1007/978-3-030-01234-2_9

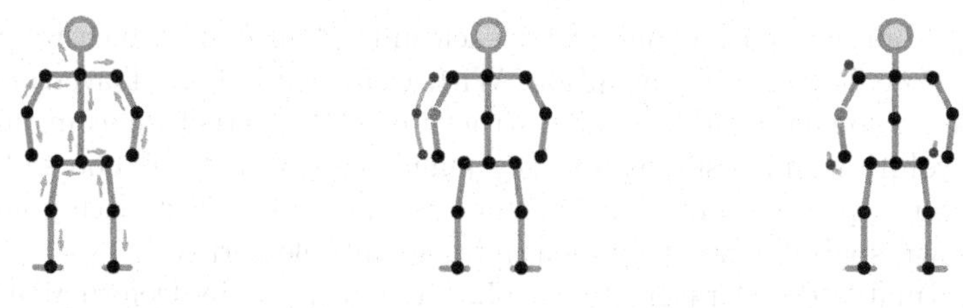

(a) Pose Traversal (b) Pose Traversal Conv (c) D-Pose Traversal Conv

Fig. 1. Illustration of the Pose Traversal Representation, the Pose Traversal Convolution and the Deformable Pose Traversal Convolution. (a) Pose Traversal. The traversal starts from the red torso joint, and follows the guidance of orange arrows. (b) Pose Traversal Convolution. The red dots connected with the orange line indicate a 3×1 pose convolution kernel. The green dot indicates the convolution anchor (c) Deformable Pose Traversal Convolution. The kernel in (b) is deformed to involve two hands and the right shoulder in a convolution. (Color figure online)

To identify the joint patterns for 3D action and gesture recognition, deep-learning-based methods have been popularly utilized recently [4,6,8–11]. For example, [4,6] apply the attention mechanism to 3D action recognition by assigning weights to joints and use the key joints to represent 3D poses. However, each joint is considered individually in these works, and the discriminative cues in the spatial configuration of pose is not fully utilized. Part-based models [12,13] apply recurrent neural network (RNN) to explore the relationship among body parts. Liu *et al.* [14] and Wang *et al.* [15] feed one 3D pose joint into a RNN at each step to model the spatial dependency of joints, and show such spatial dependency modeling can improve the recognition performance. However, considering in each step the current available spatial context is only the hidden state from the previous steps, the spatial dependency of joints is not fully utilized by the sequential way of these two models.

In this work, we propose to identify joint patterns via traditional convolution. In image recognition, Convolution Neural Network (CNN) operates weighted summation in each local window of input image, which involves the local spatial relation of pixels. Meanwhile, each convolution is independent, and CNN is suitable to model the spatial dependency of pixels in parallel rather than sequentially. Similar to the appearance similarity measure among neighboring pixels via convolution, given the coordinates of joints, we can use convolution to obtain the spatial configuration among them. We follow the tree traversal rule in [14] to preserve the spatial neighboring relation of joints, as shown in Fig. 1a. Then we apply one-dimensional convolution to traverse the pose to extract spatial representation.

We use Fig. 1b to illustrate this Pose Traversal Convolution. The kernel anchored at right elbow operates convolution on the right arm, and it continues to slide along the pose joints to obtain pose information following the traversal guides in Fig. 1a. Meanwhile, the Pose Traversal Convolution can be optimized to search appropriate spatial context for each individual joint, which we call it Deformable Pose Traversal Convolution. With Deformable Pose Traversal Convolution, we no longer fix the regular structure of the kernel for convolution, and the convolution can easily involve key joints that are not neighbors of each other, thus can capture essential dependency among joints. Also, each joint will identify its own spatial context by identifying a suitable kernel.

Our Deformable Pose Traversal Convolution is inspired by Deformable Convolution Neural Network [16] that introduces the attention mechanism into convolution. As illustrated in Fig. 1c, the convolution kernel anchored on the right elbow is deformed so that the left and right hands as well as the right shoulder are also included in one convolution operation. We consider, due to the complexity of actions and gestures, the key combination of joints varies during the action performing. Therefore, the deformation offsets for the convolution kernel are predicted by a one-layer ConvLSTM [17] based on the previously observed pose data. The final extracted pose feature will be further fed into a LSTM network [18]. The whole network utilizes Deformable Pose Traversal Convolution to learn the spatial dependency among joints and use LSTM to model the long-term evolution of the pose sequence. This network is trained end-to-end. The performance on benchmark action and gesture datasets, as well as the comparison with the state of the arts, demonstrates the effectiveness of the proposed Deformable Pose Traversal Convolution for 3D action and gesture recognition.

Our contributions can be summarized as follows:

- We introduce a one-dimensional convolution neural network, Deformable Pose Traversal Convolution, to represent 3D pose. It can extract pose feature by identifying key combinations of joints, which is interpretable for action and gesture understanding.
- We apply the ConvLSTM [17] to learn the deformation offsets of convolution kernel. It models the temporal dynamics of key combinations of joints.

2 Related Work

3D Action and Gesture Recognition
3D action and gesture recognition task attracts a lot of attention in these years. The recently proposed methods can be categorized into traditional model [5,7,19–29] and deep-learning-based model [4,6,9–12,14,15,30–33]. Due to the tremendous amount of these works, we limit the review to spatial pose modeling in deep learning.

Part-based models consider 3D actions as the interaction between body parts. In HBRNN [12], a 3D pose is decomposed into five parts, and multiples bi-RNNs are stacked hierarchically to model the relationship between these parts. In [6,14,15], the pose graph is flattened by the tree traversal rule, and the joints are fed into LSTM sequentially to model the spatial dependency among them. In 2D CNN-based methods [30,32–34], a pose sequence is first visualized as images.

Each pixel of the image is related to a joint. Then a two-dimensional CNN is applied on the generated images to extract sequence-level CNN feature, by which the spatio-temporal dependency of joints is implicitly learned. Compared with the 2D CNN methods, we apply one-dimensional convolution on pose traversal data to extract frame-level pose feature, which is more flexible especially for tasks requiring frame-level feature.

Attention Mechanism in 3D Action and Gesture
In 3D action and gesture recognition, not every spatial joint is of equal importance to the recognition task. Hence it is essentially important to identify the key joints that matter for recognition. In STA-LSTM [14], two sub-LSTMs are trained to predict spatial and temporal weights for the discovery of key joints and frames. In ST-NBNN [5], support tensor machine is introduced to assign spatial and temporal weights on nearest-neighbor distance matrices for action classification. In Orderlet [7], actions are described by a few key comparisons of joints' primitive features, and only a subset of joints is involved. The key combinations of joints are fixed during testing. In contrast, the proposed method allows the optimal spatial context of each joint changes during the action performing since we use a RNN structure to model the temporal dynamics of key joint combinations.

3 Proposed Method

In this section, we introduce how the proposed Deformable Pose Traversal Convolution processes the pose data in each frame and recognizes the 3D actions and gestures. The feature maps and the convolution kernels are two-dimensional in our model. One dimension for the spatial domain and the other for the channel domain. The deformable pose convolution operates on the spatial domain, and the deformation of kernel remains the same across the channel dimension. For notation clarity, we describe the module on spatial dimension, omitting the index of the channel dimension.

Each 3D action/gesture is represented as a sequence of 3D poses. Assuming that each pose consists of J joints, a single pose can be represented as $\boldsymbol{X} \in \mathbb{R}^{J \times C}$, where C is the number of channel. A 3D pose has six channels if the coordinates and velocities of the joints are both involved, as shown in Fig. 3. We define $\boldsymbol{x} \in \mathbb{R}^{J}$ as the one-channel version of $\boldsymbol{X}$. Then a 3D action/gesture sequence can be described by a set of poses, $V = \{\boldsymbol{x}^t\}_{t=1}^{T}$, where T is the length of a sequence sample. Given a 3D pose sequence, our goal is to predict the corresponding label $k \in \{1, 2, ..., K\}$, where K is the number of categories. The problem can be formulated following the maximum a posteriori (MAP) rule,

$$k^* = \arg\max_k p(k|V) \tag{1}$$

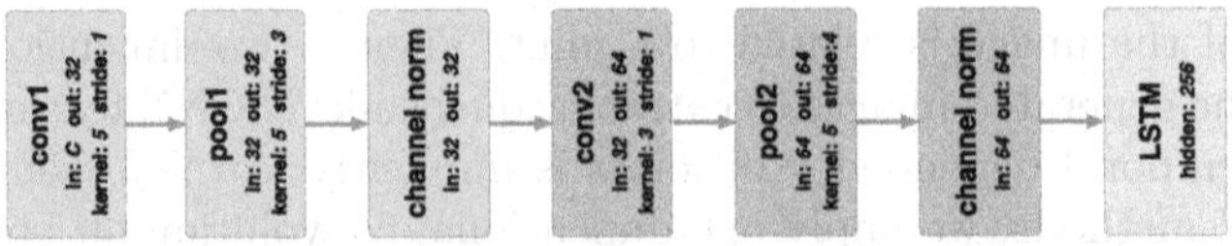

(a) Structure of Pose Traversal Convolution Network

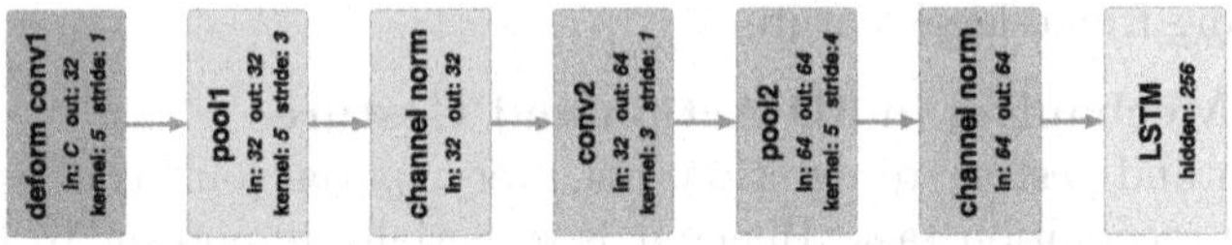

(b) Structure of Deformable Pose Traversal Convolution Network

Fig. 2. Structures of the Pose Traversal Convolution Network and the Deformable Pose Traversal Convolution Network. Each block in the structure represents an operation of the network. The "in" and "out" of each block indicate the number of input channel and output channel, respectively. The "kernel" indicates the kernel size, and the "stride" indicates the stride of convolution operation. The size of the LSTM hidden neuron is indicated by "hidden".

3.1 Pose Traversal Convolution

To fully utilize the spatial kinematic dependency of joints in a single pose, we follow the tree traversal rule in [14] to represent the pose data in our method, as illustrated in Fig. 1a. By this manner, the length of the pose data is extended from J to J_e, and the arrangement of joints becomes a loop. We name it the pose traversal data.

In our method, we apply the modified Temporal Convolution Network [35] (TCN) on the pose traversal data to perform spatial pose convolution, which is named as Pose Traversal Convolution. Each layer of the TCN is composed of one-dimensional convolution, one-dimensional pooling, and channel-wise normalization operations. After each convolution operation, there is a Rectified Linear Unit (ReLU) included to involve nonlinearity. The TCN is an encoder-decoder structure designed to solve temporal segmentation task. In this work, we only use the encoder part of TCN and modify it to a two-layer one-dimensional convolution neural network. The structure of the neural network with Pose Traversal Convolution is shown in Fig. 2a. The two-layer convolution structure extracts pose feature from each single frame, and the pose feature is then further fed into the main LSTM network to model the long-term temporal dynamics of the input pose sequence.

There are two steps for a regular one-dimensional convolution: (1) sampling using a regular set $\mathbf{G}$ on the input pose data; (2) summation of sampled joints' value weighted by $\boldsymbol{w}$. The sampling set $\mathbf{G}$ defines the receptive field size and dilation. For a $N \times 1$ regular convolution kernel with dilation 1, where $N = 2 * M + 1$ and $M \in \mathbb{N}^{+}$, the regular sampling set can be defined as:

$$\mathbf{G} = \{-M, ..., -1, 0, 1, ..., M\} \tag{2}$$

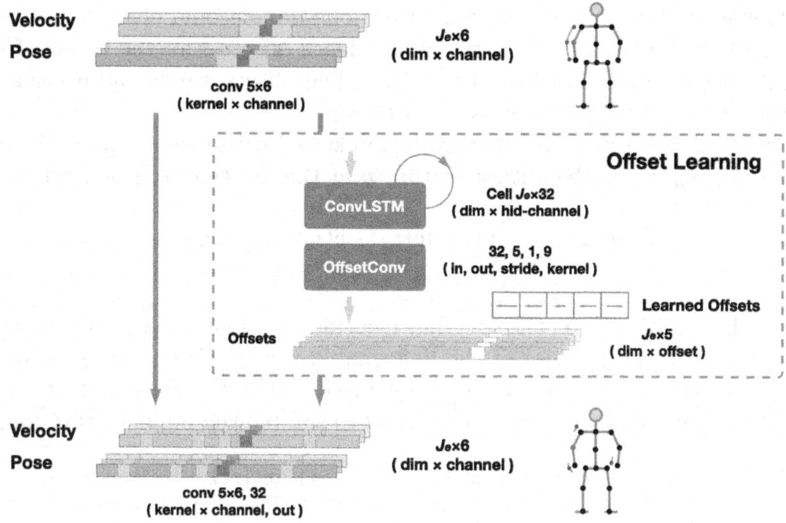

Fig. 3. Illustration of the Deformable Pose Traversal Convolution. A pose is represented by the pose feature and the velocity feature. The gray rectangles represent the convolution kernels and the dark gray rectangles inside of them indicate the convolution anchor. The pose traversal data is fed into the Offset Learning module, which consists of a ConvLSTM and an Offset Convolution. The "in" and "out" in the figure indicate the numbers of the input and output channels, respectively. The orange rectangles are the learned offsets to deform the convolution kernel at each anchor. The Deformable Pose Traversal Convolution is operated at the bottom of the figure based on the learned offsets.

For the location i_0 of the output feature map $\boldsymbol{y}$, we have

$$\boldsymbol{y}(i_0) = \sum_{i_n \in \mathbf{G}} \boldsymbol{w}(i_n) \cdot \boldsymbol{x}(i_0 + i_n) \tag{3}$$

where i_n enumerates the elements in $\mathbf{G}$.

3.2 Deformable Pose Traversal Convolution

Regular pose convolution focuses on the spatial neighboring joints. This traditional operation may involve non-informative joints and cannot well construct the relationship of key joints far away from each other. We consider that the optimal spatial context of a joint does not always come from its neighbors. It is of great importance to break the limitation of regular convolution kernel to learn the optimal spatial context. Inspired by the Deformable Convolution Network [16], which is designed for image recognition, we propose a deformable version of the Pose Traversal Convolution and apply it on pose data to discover better combinations of joints. More specifically, we replace the first layer of the

Pose Traversal Convolution network with a one-dimensional deformable convolution, and a ConvLSTM [17] is involved to learn offsets δ for the kernel of each convolution anchor, as illustrated in Fig. 3. The offsets are the adjustments of convolution sampling locations on feature map.

By using a $N \times 1$ deformable convolution kernel with new irregular sampling set $\tilde{\mathbf{G}} = \{(i_n, \delta_n)\}_{n=1}^{N}$, the output feature $\boldsymbol{y}$ at the location i_0 is defined as,

$$\boldsymbol{y}(i_0) = \sum_{(i_n,\delta_n)\in\tilde{\mathbf{G}}} \boldsymbol{w}(i_n) \cdot \boldsymbol{x}(i_0 + i_n + \delta_n) \tag{4}$$

Now, the sampling is on the irregular locations $i_0+i_n+\delta_n$. The Pose Traversal Convolution is a special case of the deformable version. When $\{\delta_n\}_{n=1}^{N}$ are all set to zeros, the set $\tilde{\mathbf{G}}$ becomes $\mathbf{G}$. Considering that the learned δ_n could be none-integer, bi-linear interpolation is used to sample the input feature map,

$$\boldsymbol{x}(i) = \alpha \cdot \boldsymbol{x}(\lfloor i \rfloor) + (1-\alpha) \cdot \boldsymbol{x}(\lceil i \rceil) \tag{5}$$

where $i = i_0+i_n+\delta_n$ denotes the fractional location (sub-joint), and $\alpha = \lceil i \rceil - i$.

Offset Learning

We involve a sub-path network to learn the offsets δ. Considering that to decide which joints to pay attention to should be inferred from the previously observed action/gesture, the sub-path network is constructed based on a RNN structure, ConvLSTM [17]. With the involved RNN model, the sub-path is able to learn the offsets δ on a temporal progress. ConvLSTM is first proposed for image sequences. Each convolution in ConvLSTM is two dimensional. Here in our proposed method, we modify it to one-dimensional version so that it can be well applied on the pose traversal data. With the pose traversal representation, ConvLSTM takes the spatial neighboring relationship of joints into consideration in each convolution operation.

In each time step, the input of offset learning module is the pose traversal data with C channels, and the corresponding output is the offset with N channels for the kernel on each anchor location. The hidden and memory cell tensor inside ConvLSTM store significant information of an action/gesture. An Offset Convolution is located at the output end of ConvLSTM which transfers the hidden tensor to the offsets at each time step. The illustration of offset learning is shown in Fig. 3, and the key equations of ConvLSTM are detailed in Eq. 6.

$$\begin{aligned}
\boldsymbol{g}_i^t &= \sigma(\boldsymbol{w}_{xi} * \boldsymbol{x}^t + \boldsymbol{w}_{hi} * \boldsymbol{h}^{t-1} + \boldsymbol{b}_i) \\
\boldsymbol{g}_f^t &= \sigma(\boldsymbol{w}_{xf} * \boldsymbol{x}^t + \boldsymbol{w}_{hf} * \boldsymbol{h}^{t-1} + \boldsymbol{b}_f) \\
\boldsymbol{m}^t &= \boldsymbol{g}_f^t \circ \boldsymbol{h}^{t-1} + \boldsymbol{g}_i^t \circ tanh(\boldsymbol{w}_{xm} * \boldsymbol{x}^t + \boldsymbol{w}_{hm} * \boldsymbol{h}^{t-1} + \boldsymbol{b}_m) \\
\boldsymbol{g}_o^t &= \sigma(\boldsymbol{w}_{xo} * \boldsymbol{x}^t + \boldsymbol{w}_{ho} * \boldsymbol{x}^t + \boldsymbol{b}_o) \\
\boldsymbol{h}^t &= \boldsymbol{g}_o^t \circ tanh(\boldsymbol{m}^t)
\end{aligned} \tag{6}$$

where the input, forget and output gates, $\boldsymbol{g}_i^t$, $\boldsymbol{g}_f^t$ and $\boldsymbol{g}_o^t$, of ConvLSTM are vectors. $\boldsymbol{m}^t$ and $\boldsymbol{h}^t$ are memory cell tensor and hidden state tensor respectively.

$\sigma(\cdot)$ is the sigma function. $\boldsymbol{w}$ and $\boldsymbol{b}$ are the corresponding weights and bias in each operation. $*$ is a symbol for one-dimensional convolution, and $\circ$ denotes the element-wise product.

If the size of the convolution kernel is 1, the learned offset is defined as,

$$\boldsymbol{o}^t = \boldsymbol{w}_{of} * \boldsymbol{h}^t + \boldsymbol{b}_{of} \tag{7}$$

where $\boldsymbol{o}^t \in \mathbb{R}^{J_e}$ is the learned offset tensor. If the size of convolution kernel is N, the output offset is a matrix $\boldsymbol{O}^t \in \mathbb{R}^{J_e \times N}$. Each column of $\boldsymbol{O}^t$ corresponds to an offset set $\{\delta_n\}_{n=1}^N$ on a convolution anchor.

3.3 Learning and Classification

After passing through the Deformable Pose Traversal Convolution network, the pose traversal data is transferred to an abstract pose feature. The feature is then fed into the main LSTM to model the long-term temporal evolution of the input action or gesture. We use the hidden state $\boldsymbol{h}_m^T$ from the last time step to predict the label. The hidden state $\boldsymbol{h}_m^T$ is passed into a fully-connected layer and a softmax layer to generate $\hat{\boldsymbol{z}} \in \mathbb{R}^K$ for action and gesture classification. The k-th element of $\hat{\boldsymbol{z}}$ is the estimated probability of the input sequence V belonging to class k, namely $\hat{z}_k = p(k|V)$. The objective function is to minimize the cross-entropy loss, which can be optimized via back-propagation through time(BPTT) [36] in an end-to-end manner.

4 Experiments

In this section, we evaluate and analyze the proposed method on three 3D action and gesture datasets. The implementation details are introduced in Sect. 4.1. Comparison results on the Dynamic Hand Gesture 14/28 dataset (DHG) [29], the NTU-RGB+D dataset (NTU) [13], and the Berkeley Multi-modal Human Action dataset (MHAD) [37] are provided and discussed in Sect. 4.3. Experiment results show that the proposed Deformable Pose Traversal Convolution effectively search the optimal joint combinations on-line and achieves the state-of-the-arts performance for both 3D action and gesture recognition.

4.1 Implementation

Representation. The three datasets include single actions, two-person interactions, and hand gestures. All the body actions and hand gestures are represented as 3D poses. To ensure location and view invariance of the representation, each joint of the pose is centralized by subtracting the temporal average pose-center, and each pose is pre-rotated. For single-person actions and hand gestures, the pose-centers are defined as the hip-joint and palm-joint respectively. For two-person interaction, the pose-center is the average hip-joint of the two involved persons in each frame. The two-person interaction is represented by the absolute difference of corresponding joints in two persons.

Table 1. Comparison of results on hand gesture dataset - DHG (%)

Method	Fine	Coarse	Both-14	Both-28
Skeletal quads [38]	70.6	92.2	84.5	79.4
SoCJ+HoHD+HoWR [29]	73.6	88.3	83.1	80.0
Pose Chain Conv	76.2	90.4	80.4	75.7
Pose Traversal Conv	77.1	91.8	81.1	76.6
D-Pose Traversal Conv	**81.9**	**95.2**	**85.8**	**80.2**

Network. The convolution networks for pose feature extraction in all the experiments share the same network parameters. We modify the Temporal Convolution Network [35] to extract pose feature of each frame. The main parameters of the network are shown in Fig. 2. In our experiments, we use one-layer ConvLSTM for offset learning. The numbers of the main LSTM layer are two, three, and two for DHG, NTU, and MHAD respectively.

Training. Our neural network is implemented by PyTorch. The stochastic optimization method Adam [39] is adapted to train the network. We use gradient clipping similar to [40] to avoid the exploding gradient problem. The initial learning rate of the training is set to 0.001. The batch size for the DHG, NTU, and MHAD dataset are 64, 64, and 32 respectively. For efficient learning, we train the Pose Traversal Convolution network first and use the learned parameters to initialize the deformable network.

4.2 Datasets

Dynamic Hand Gesture 14/28. The Dynamic Hand Gesture 14/28 dataset is collected with Intel Real Sense Depth Camera. It includes 14 hand gesture categories, which are performed in two ways, using one finger and the whole hand. Following the protocol introduced in [29], the evaluation experiment is conducted under four settings, Fine, Coarse, Both-14, and Both-28. In each experiment setting, we use leave-one-subject-out cross-validation strategy.

NTU-RGB+D. The NTU-RGB+D dataset is collected with Kinect V2 depth camera. There are 60 different action classes. We follow the protocol described in [13] to conduct the experiments. There are two standard evaluation settings, the cross-subject (CS) and the cross-view (CV) evaluation. In CS setting, half of the subjects are used for training and the remaining are for testing. In CV setting, two of the three views are used for training and the remaining one is for testing.

Berkeley MHAD. The action sequences in Berkeley MHAD dataset are captured by a motion capture system. There are 11 action categories in this dataset. We follow the experimental protocol introduced in [37] to evaluate the proposed method. The sequences performed by the first seven subjects are for training while the ones performed by the rest subjects are for testing.

Table 2. Comparison on NTU (%)

Method	CS	CV
ST-LSTM [14]	69.2	77.7
Two streams [35]	71.3	79.5
GCA-LSTM [6]	74.4	82.8
RNN tree [10]	74.6	83.2
CNN+MTLN [32]	79.6	84.8
Li *et al.* [41]	**83.2**	**89.3**
Pose Chain Conv	75.2	83.4
Pose Traversal Conv	76.1	84.3
D-Pose Traversal Conv	76.8	84.9

Table 3. Comparison on MHAD (%)

Method	Accuracy
SMIJ [25]	95.4
Meta-Cognitive [42]	97.6
Dynemes and Forward [43]	98.2
HBRNN [12]	**100.0**
ST-LSTM [14]	**100.0**
ST-NBNN [5]	**100.0**
Pose Chain Conv	96.4
Pose Traversal Conv	98.6
D-Pose Traversal Conv	**100.0**

4.3 Results and Analysis

Comparison with Baselines

We compare the proposed method with two baselines on three datasets, DHG, NTU and MHAD. The two baseline methods are the Pose Convolution with single chain representation (Pose Chain Conv), which simply flatten the pose graph without considering the neighboring relation of joints, and the Pose Convolution with Pose Traversal representation (Pose Traversal Conv). The comparison results are shown in Tables 1, 2 and 3 respectively. From the tables we can see that Pose Traversal Convolution achieves better performance than the Pose Chain Convolution, which verifies the effectiveness of the involvement of traversal representation in pose convolution. In these three datasets, we can also witness that the Deformable Pose Traversal Convolution (D-Pose Traversal Conv) performs better than the Pose Traversal Convolution. The Deformable Pose Traversal Convolution is able to find good combinations of key joints in each convolution operation and to avoid non-informative or noisy joints, which can effectively help improve the recognition accuracy. Moreover, the performance improvement is significantly great on dynamic hand gestures which involve coordination of more pose parts than body actions.

Figure 4a shows the comparison of confusion matrices between Pose Traversal Convolution and Deformable Pose Traversal Convolution on DHG-14 dataset, under the Both-14 setting. As can be seen from this figure, compared with the Pose Traversal Convolution, the confusion matrix of the Deformable Pose Traversal Convolution is clearer, which means that the confusion between gestures is reduced by using Deformable Pose Traversal Convolution. We can also see that there is great confusion between the gesture "Grab" and gesture "Pinch". These two gestures both belong to the "Fine" category, and they are very similar to each other. The Deformable Pose Traversal Convolution can greatly reduce the number of "Pinch" testing samples wrongly classified as "Grab", as shown in Fig. 4b. The recognition accuracy of the "Pinch" gesture is greatly improved from 49% to 71.5%.

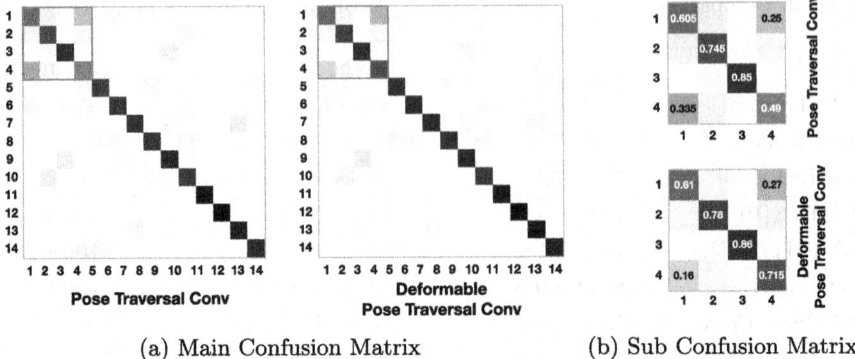

(a) Main Confusion Matrix (b) Sub Confusion Matrix

Fig. 4. (a) Comparison of confusion matrices between Pose Traversal Convolution and Deformable Pose Traversal Convolution on DHG-14. The red rectangle marks the sub part of the matrix, which includes the two similar gestures "Grab" and "Pinch". The gestures in DHG-14 are 1. Grab, 2. Tap, 3. Expand, 4. Pinch, 5. Rotation CW, 6. Rotation CCW, 7. Swipe Right, 8. Swipe Left, 9. Swipe Up, 10. Swipe Down, 11. Swipe X, 12. Swipe V, 13. Swipe +, 14. Shake. (b) Comparison of Sub Confusion Matrices between Pose Traversal Convolution and Deformable Pose Traversal Convolution. (Color figure online)

Comparison with the State-of-the-Arts

In this section, the proposed method is compared with the existing methods on three benchmark datasets, DHG-14/28, NTU-RGBD+D, and Berkeley MHAD. As can be seen from Tables 1, 2 and 3, our method achieves comparable performance with the state-of-the-arts on NTU-RGB+D dataset and Berkeley MHAD dataset. On the Dynamic Hand Gesture dataset, the proposed method performs significantly better than the existing methods. It is worth noting that the proposed method, Deformable Pose Traversal Convolution network, performs better than the ST-LSTM [14] and Two Streams network [15] which use Long-Short-Term-Memory network (LSTM) to model the spatial context of joints.

Robustness Analysis

(1) Rotation. As 2D pose estimation methods [44,45] reach a new level recently, we consider whether the proposed method is able to handle 2D pose data well. We conduct an experiment to compare the performance of the Pose Traversal Convolution (PTC) and the Deformable Pose Traversal Convolution (DPTC) on both 2D and 3D data of DHG dataset. The results are shown in Table 4. As can be seen, the accuracies of the proposed methods on 2D data are comparable with the ones on 3D data under different settings. The reason is that the DHG dataset is collected for human-computer interaction, and all the recorded gestures are performed with the palm facing to the camera. Although there is one dimension missing, the proposed method still achieves the performance that is similar to the one on 3D data. The results verify the effectiveness of DPTC over PTC.

We further evaluate the performance of our method under different data rotation to see its robustness to rotation. We rotate the 3D hand pose along the y-axis with $-90°$, $-60°$, $-30°$, $30°$, $60°$, as well as $90°$, and record the recognition accuracies under these settings. The results are shown in Fig. 5. As can be seen, though with different rotations, the proposed methods can still maintain the performance on 3D data, while on 2D data, the performance changes as along the increase of the rotation degree. Under the 2D data setting, the Deformable Pose Traversal Convolution still finds the optimal joint combinations and performs better than the Pose Traversal Convolution. Considering the rotation of the users' hand is just around $\pm 30°$ in human-computer interaction, our method is able to handle the daily situation well.

(2) Noise. Although pose estimation methods achieve good performance recently, the pose noise caused by the estimation errors and occlusion still cannot be ignored in 3D action and gesture recognition. In this section, we conduct experiments to show the tolerance of the proposed method to the pose noise on Berkeley MHAD dataset. We randomly select 10%, 20%, 30%, 40% and 50% of the pose joints and add severe random noise with maximum amplitude up to 50 on the selected joints. We evaluate the performance of Pose Traversal Convolution and Deformable Pose Traversal Convolution with different percentages of noisy joint. The results are shown in Fig. 6. As can be seen from the figure, thought the accuracy of PTC drops a lot due to the impact of noise, DPTC still can avoid the noisy joints and achieve good performance. Under the setting of 50% noisy joints, the accuracy improvement from PTC to DPTC is 7.64%. Here the noise we use is severe one with amplitude up to 50, and the proposed DPTC can still perform well. Under the setting of 50% noisy joints, we also evaluate PTC and DPTC by using small noise with amplitude up to only 5. The accuracy of PTC and DPTC are 96.36% and 98.18% respectively. We can see that Pose Traversal Convolution is able to well handle small noise by using the neighboring spatial context of joints.

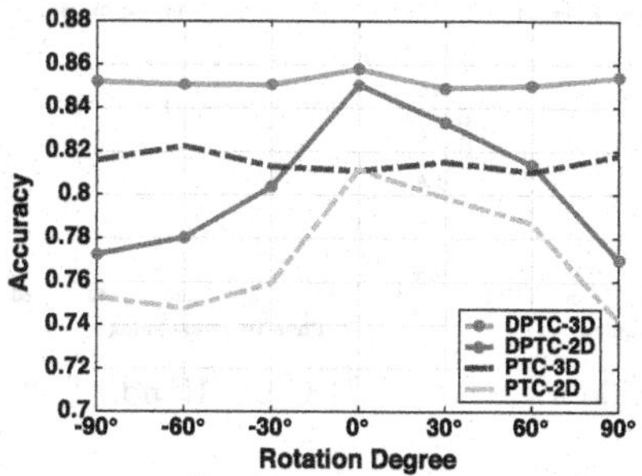

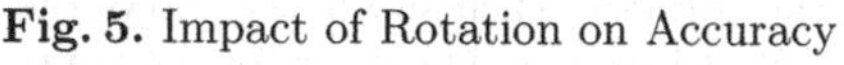

Fig. 5. Impact of Rotation on Accuracy

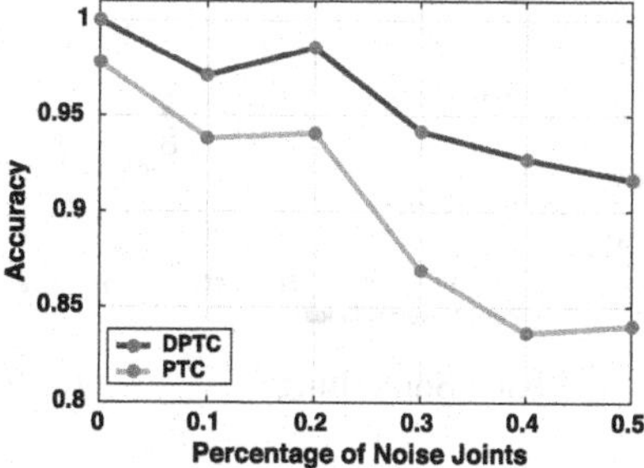

Fig. 6. Impact of Noise on Accuracy

Table 4. Comparison between 2D and 3D Data on DHG (%)

Method	Fine	Coarse	Both-14	Both-28
Pose Traversal Conv-2D	74.6	90.1	81.2	77.1
Pose Traversal Conv-3D	77.1	91.8	81.1	76.6
D-Pose Traversal Conv-2D	81.9	94.9	85.1	80.4
D-Pose Traversal Conv-3D	81.9	95.2	85.8	80.2

Visualization

In this section, we visualize the learned offsets of a single frame from the offset learning module in Fig. 7. The experiment is conducted on the cross-view setting of the NTU dataset. To simplify the visualization of the experiment, we set the size of the convolution kernel to one. Under this setting, the learned offsets re-arrange the sampling points of the convolution and shift these sampling points to key joint locations that matter to the action. For the action "Throw" in Fig. 7a, the high response offsets are located around the right hand, marked by colored points. The sketch part at the corner of the sub-figure is the right hand. As can be seen, the kernels on the both side of the index finger are moving toward it,

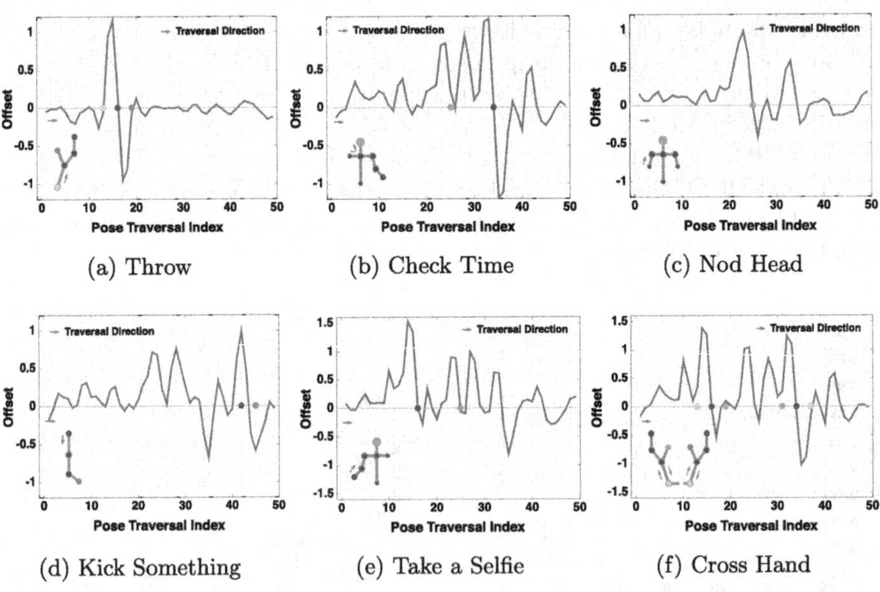

Fig. 7. Visualization of the Learned Offsets. The blue curve shows the offset for convolution kernel on each anchor. The sketch on the corner of each sub-figure shows the part of the pose that has high offset response in offset learning. The colors of the joints in the sketch correspond to the colored marker on the x-axis of the figures. The red arrows in the sketch guide the direction of the traversal. (Color figure online)

which indicates that for the action "Throw" the key joints are near the right index finger, and the model shifts its kernels to obtain better information. For the action "Kick Something" in Fig. 7d, the high response offsets are located in the left foot part, which guide the kernels to move toward the location between the left knee and the left ankle, not the left tiptoe. The reason is that the pose estimation of feet is not always stable in the NTU-RGB+D dataset especially under the cross-view setting, and hence the offset module chooses the point between the knee and the ankle to represent the "Kick" action. The action "Cross Hand" is performed by two hands, and as can be seen from Fig. 7f, there are high responses on the both hand parts.

5 Conclusions

In this work, we introduce a deformable one-dimensional convolution neural network to traverse 3D pose for pose representation. The convolution kernel is guided by ConvLSTM to deform for discovering optimal convolution context. Due to the recurrent property of ConvLSTM, it can model the temporal dynamics of kernel deformation. The proposed Deformable Pose Traversal Convolution is able to discover the optimal key joint combinations, as well as avoid non-informative joints, and hence achieves better recognition accuracy. Experiments validate the proposed contribution and verify the effectiveness and robustness of the proposed Deformable Pose Traversal Convolution.

Acknowledgement. This research is supported by the BeingTogether Centre, a collaboration between NTU Singapore and UNC at Chapel Hill, and the ROSE Lab of NTU. The BeingTogether Centre is supported by the National Research Foundation, Prime Ministers Office, Singapore under its International Research Centres in Singapore Funding Initiative. The ROSE Lab is supported by the National Research Foundation, Prime Ministers Office, Singapore. This work is also supported by the start-up grants of University at Buffalo, Computer Science and Engineering Department.

References

1. Shotton, J., et al.: Real-time human pose recognition in parts from single depth images. In: CVPR, pp. 1297–1304. IEEE (2011)
2. Ge, L., Cai, Y., Weng, J., Yuan, J.: Hand PointNet: 3D hand pose estimation using point sets. In: CVPR, vol. 1, p. 5 (2018)
3. Ge, L., Ren, Z., Yuan, J.: Point-to-point regression PointNet for 3D hand pose estimation. In: Ferrari, V., Hebert, M., Sminchisescu, C., Weiss, Y. (eds.) ECCV 2018, Part XIII. LNCS, vol. 11217, pp. 489–505. Springer, Cham (2018)
4. Song, S., Lan, C., Xing, J., Zeng, W., Liu, J.: An end-to-end spatio-temporal attention model for human action recognition from skeleton data. In: AAAI, vol. 1, p. 7 (2017)
5. Weng, J., Weng, C., Yuan, J.: Spatio-temporal Naive-Bayes Nearest-Neighbor (ST-NBNN) for skeleton-based action recognition. In: CVPR, pp. 4171–4180 (2017)

6. Liu, J., Wang, G., Hu, P., Duan, L.Y., Kot, A.C.: Global context-aware attention LSTM networks for 3D action recognition. In: CVPR, July 2017
7. Yu, G., Liu, Z., Yuan, J.: Discriminative orderlet mining for real-time recognition of human-object interaction. In: Cremers, D., Reid, I., Saito, H., Yang, M.-H. (eds.) ACCV 2014. LNCS, vol. 9007, pp. 50–65. Springer, Cham (2015). https://doi.org/10.1007/978-3-319-16814-2_4
8. Veeriah, V., Zhuang, N., Qi, G.J.: Differential recurrent neural networks for action recognition. In: ICCV, pp. 4041–4049. IEEE (2015)
9. Zhu, W., et al.: Co-occurrence feature learning for skeleton based action recognition using regularized deep LSTM networks. In: AAAI, vol. 2, p. 8 (2016)
10. Li, W., Wen, L., Chang, M.C., Nam Lim, S., Lyu, S.: Adaptive RNN tree for large-scale human action recognition. In: ICCV, October 2017
11. Lee, I., Kim, D., Kang, S., Lee, S.: Ensemble deep learning for skeleton-based action recognition using temporal sliding LSTM networks. In: ICCV, October 2017
12. Du, Y., Wang, W., Wang, L.: Hierarchical recurrent neural network for skeleton based action recognition. In: CVPR, pp. 1110–1118 (2015)
13. Shahroudy, A., Liu, J., Ng, T.T., Wang, G.: NTU RGB+D: a large scale dataset for 3D human activity analysis. In: CVPR, June 2016
14. Liu, J., Shahroudy, A., Xu, D., Wang, G.: Spatio-temporal LSTM with trust gates for 3D human action recognition. In: Leibe, B., Matas, J., Sebe, N., Welling, M. (eds.) ECCV 2016. LNCS, vol. 9907, pp. 816–833. Springer, Cham (2016). https://doi.org/10.1007/978-3-319-46487-9_50
15. Wang, H., Wang, L.: Modeling temporal dynamics and spatial configurations of actions using two-stream recurrent neural networks. In: CVPR, July 2017
16. Dai, J., et al.: Deformable convolutional networks. In: ICCV, October 2017
17. Xingjian, S., Chen, Z., Wang, H., Yeung, D.Y., Wong, W.K., Woo, W.C.: Convolutional LSTM network: a machine learning approach for precipitation nowcasting. In: NIPS, pp. 802–810 (2015)
18. Hochreiter, S., Schmidhuber, J.: Long short-term memory. Neural Comput. **9**(8), 1735–1780 (1997)
19. Ren, Z., Yuan, J., Zhang, Z.: Robust hand gesture recognition based on finger-earth mover's distance with a commodity depth camera. In: ACM MM, pp. 1093–1096 (2011)
20. Wang, J., Liu, Z., Wu, Y., Yuan, J.: Mining actionlet ensemble for action recognition with depth cameras. In: CVPR, pp. 1290–1297. IEEE (2012)
21. Wang, J., Liu, Z., Wu, Y., Yuan, J.: Learning actionlet ensemble for 3D human action recognition. T-PAMI **36**(5), 914–927 (2014)
22. Liang, H., Yuan, J., Thalmann, D., Thalmann, N.M.: AR in hand: egocentric palm pose tracking and gesture recognition for augmented reality applications. In: ACM MM, pp. 743–744. ACM (2015)
23. Ren, Z., Yuan, J., Meng, J., Zhang, Z.: Robust part-based hand gesture recognition using Kinect sensor. T-MM **15**(5), 1110–1120 (2016)
24. Weng, J., Weng, C., Yuan, J., Liu, Z.: Discriminative spatio-tempoal pattern discovery for 3D action recognition. T-CSVT, **PP**, 1 (2018)
25. Ofli, F., Chaudhry, R., Kurillo, G., Vidal, R., Bajcsy, R.: Sequence of the most informative joints (SMIJ): a new representation for human skeletal action recognition. JVCI **25**(1), 24–38 (2014)
26. Vemulapalli, R., Chellapa, R.: Rolling rotations for recognizing human actions from 3D skeletal data. In: CVPR, pp. 4471–4479 (2016)

27. Garcia-Hernando, G., Kim, T.K.: Transition forests: learning discriminative temporal transitions for action recognition and detection. In: CVPR, pp. 432–440 (2017)
28. Wang, P., Yuan, C., Hu, W., Li, B., Zhang, Y.: Graph based skeleton motion representation and similarity measurement for action recognition. In: Leibe, B., Matas, J., Sebe, N., Welling, M. (eds.) ECCV 2016. LNCS, vol. 9911, pp. 370–385. Springer, Cham (2016). https://doi.org/10.1007/978-3-319-46478-7_23
29. De Smedt, Q., Wannous, H., Vandeborre, J.P.: Skeleton-based dynamic hand gesture recognition. In: CVPRW, pp. 1–9 (2016)
30. Liu, M., Yuan, J.: Recognizing human actions as the evolution of pose estimation maps. In: CVPR, June 2018
31. Li, Y., Lan, C., Xing, J., Zeng, W., Yuan, C., Liu, J.: Online human action detection using joint classification-regression recurrent neural networks. In: Leibe, B., Matas, J., Sebe, N., Welling, M. (eds.) ECCV 2016. LNCS, vol. 9911, pp. 203–220. Springer, Cham (2016). https://doi.org/10.1007/978-3-319-46478-7_13
32. Ke, Q., Bennamoun, M., An, S., Sohel, F., Boussaid, F.: A new representation of skeleton sequences for 3D action recognition. In: CVPR, July 2017
33. Wang, P., Li, Z., Hou, Y., Li, W.: Action recognition based on joint trajectory maps using convolutional neural networks. In: ACM MM, pp. 102–106. ACM (2016)
34. Liu, M., Liu, H., Chen, C.: Enhanced skeleton visualization for view invariant human action recognition. Pattern Recogn. **68**, 346–362 (2017)
35. Lea, C., Flynn, M.D., Vidal, R., Reiter, A., Hager, G.D.: Temporal convolutional networks for action segmentation and detection. In: CVPR, July 2017
36. Graves, A.: Supervised sequence labelling. In: Graves, A. (eds.) Supervised Sequence Labelling with Recurrent Neural Networks, pp. 5–13. Springer, Heidelberg (2012). https://doi.org/10.1007/978-3-642-24797-2_2
37. Ofli, F., Chaudhry, R., Kurillo, G., Vidal, R., Bajcsy, R.: Berkeley MHAD: a comprehensive multimodal human action database. In: WACV, pp. 53–60. IEEE (2013)
38. Evangelidis, G., Singh, G., Horaud, R.: Skeletal quads: human action recognition using joint quadruples. In: ICPR, pp. 4513–4518. IEEE (2014)
39. Kingma, D.P., Ba, J.L.: Adam: a method for stochastic optimization (2015)
40. Sutskever, I., Vinyals, O., Le, Q.V.: Sequence to sequence learning with neural networks. In: NIPS, pp. 3104–3112 (2014)
41. Li, C., Zhong, Q., Xie, D., Pu, S.: Skeleton-based action recognition with convolutional neural networks. In: ICMEW, pp. 597–600. IEEE (1997)
42. Vantigodi, S., Radhakrishnan, V.B.: Action recognition from motion capture data using meta-cognitive RBF network classifier. In: ISSNIP, pp. 1–6. IEEE (2014)
43. Kapsouras, I., Nikolaidis, N.: Action recognition on motion capture data using a dynemes and forward differences representation. JVCI **25**(6), 1432–1445 (2014)
44. Cao, Z., Simon, T., Wei, S.E., Sheikh, Y.: Realtime multi-person 2D pose estimation using part affinity fields. In: CVPR, vol. 1, p. 7 (2017)
45. Cai, Y., Ge, L., Cai, J., Yuan, J.: Weakly-supervised 3D hand pose estimation from monocular RGB images. In: Ferrari, V., Hebert, M., Sminchisescu, C., Weiss, Y. (eds.) ECCV 2018, Part VI. LNCS, vol. 11210, pp. 678–694. Springer, Cham (2018)

HybridNet: Classification and Reconstruction Cooperation for Semi-supervised Learning

Thomas Robert[1(✉)], Nicolas Thome[2], and Matthieu Cord[1]

[1] Sorbonne Université, CNRS, LIP6, 75005 Paris, France
{thomas.robert,matthieu.cord}@lip6.fr
[2] CEDRIC - Conservatoire National des Arts et Métiers, 75003 Paris, France
nicolas.thome@cnam.fr

Abstract. In this paper, we introduce a new model for leveraging unlabeled data to improve generalization performances of image classifiers: a two-branch encoder-decoder architecture called HybridNet. The first branch receives supervision signal and is dedicated to the extraction of invariant class-related representations. The second branch is fully unsupervised and dedicated to model information discarded by the first branch to reconstruct input data. To further support the expected behavior of our model, we propose an original training objective. It favors stability in the discriminative branch and complementarity between the learned representations in the two branches. HybridNet is able to outperform state-of-the-art results on CIFAR-10, SVHN and STL-10 in various semi-supervised settings. In addition, visualizations and ablation studies validate our contributions and the behavior of the model on both CIFAR-10 and STL-10 datasets.

Keywords: Deep learning · Semi-supervised learning
Regularization · Reconstruction · Invariance and stability
Encoder-decoder

1 Introduction

Deep learning and Convolutional Neural Networks (ConvNets) have shown impressive state-of-the-art results in the last years on various visual recognition tasks, *e.g.* image classification [1–3], object localization [4–6], image segmentation [7] and even multimodal embedding [8–10]. Some key elements are the use of very deep models with a huge number of parameters and the availability of large-scale datasets such as ImageNet. When dealing with smaller datasets, however, the need for proper regularization methods becomes more crucial to

Electronic supplementary material The online version of this chapter (https://doi.org/10.1007/978-3-030-01234-2_10) contains supplementary material, which is available to authorized users.

V. Ferrari et al. (Eds.): ECCV 2018, LNCS 11211, pp. 158–175, 2018.
https://doi.org/10.1007/978-3-030-01234-2_10

control overfitting [11–14]. An appealing direction to tackle this issue is to take advantage of the huge number of unlabeled data by developing semi-supervised learning techniques.

Many approaches attempt at designing semi-supervised techniques where the unsupervised cost produces encoders that have high data-likelihood or small reconstruction error [15]. This strategy has been followed by historical deep learning approaches [16], but also in some promising recent results with modern ConvNets [17,18]. However, the unsupervised term in reconstruction-based approaches arguably conflicts with the supervised loss, which requires intra-class invariant representations. This is the motivation for designing auto-encoders that are able to discard information, such as the Ladder Networks [19].

Another interesting regularization criterion relies on stability. Prediction functions which are stable under small input variations are likely to generalize well, especially when training with small amounts of data. Theoretical works have shown the stability properties of some deep models, *e.g.* by using harmonic analysis for scattering transforms [20,21] or for Convolution Kernel Machines [22]. In addition, recent semi-supervised models incorporate a stability-based regularizer on the prediction [23–25].

In this paper, we propose a new approach for regularizing ConvNets using unlabeled data. The behavior of our model, called HybridNet, is illustrated in Fig. 1. It consists in a "hybrid" auto-encoder with the feature extraction path decomposed into two branches.

The top branch encoder, of parameters W_c, is connected to a classification layer that produces class predictions while the decoder from this branch is used to partly reconstruct the input image from the discriminative features, leading to $\hat{\mathbf{x}}_c$. Since those features are expected to extract invariant class-specific patterns, information is lost and exact reconstruction is not possible. To complement it, a

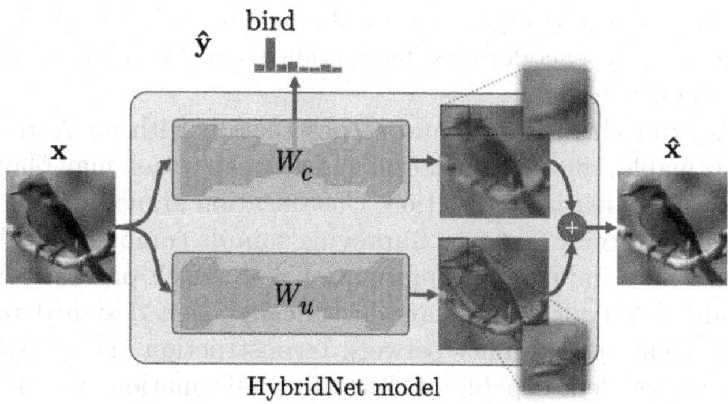

Fig. 1. Illustration of HybridNet behavior: the input image is processed by two network paths of weights W_c and W_u; each path produces a partial reconstruction, and both are summed to produce the final reconstruction, while only one path is used to produce a classification prediction. Thanks to a joint training of both tasks, the weights W_c and W_u influence each other to cooperate

second encoder-decoder branch of parameters W_u is added to produce a complementary reconstruction $\hat{\mathbf{x}}_u$ such that the sum $\hat{\mathbf{x}} = \hat{\mathbf{x}}_c + \hat{\mathbf{x}}_u$ is the final complete reconstruction.

During training, the supervised classification cost impact W_c while an unsupervised reconstruction cost is applied to both W_c and W_u to properly reconstruct the input image. The main assumption behind HybridNet is that the two-path architecture helps in making classification and reconstruction cooperate. To encourage this, we use additional costs and training techniques, namely a stability regularization in the discriminative branch and a branch complementarity training method.

2 Related Work

Training deep models with relatively small annotated datasets is a crucial issue nowadays. To this end, the design of proper regularization techniques plays a central role. In this paper, we address the problem of taking advantage of unlabeled data for improving generalization performances of deep ConvNets with semi-supervised learning [26].

One standard goal followed when training deep models with unlabeled data consists in designing models which fit input data well. Reconstruction error is the standard criterion used in (possibly denoising) Auto-Encoders [15,27–29], while maximum likelihood is used with generative models, *e.g.* Restricted Boltzmann Machines, Deep Belief Networks or Deep Generative Models [16,30–32]. This unsupervised training framework was generally used as a pre-training before supervised learning with back-propagation [33], potentially with an intermediate step [34]. The currently very popular Generative Adversarial Networks [35] also falls into this category. With modern ConvNets, regularization with unlabeled data is generally formulated as a multi-task learning problem, where reconstruction and classification objectives are combined during training [17,18,36]. In these architectures, the encoder used for classification is regularized by a decoder dedicated to reconstruction.

This strategy of classification and reconstruction with an Auto-Encoder is however questionable, since classification and reconstruction may play contradictory roles in terms of feature extraction. Classification arguably aims at extracting invariant class-specific features, improving sample complexity of the learned model [37], therefore inducing an information loss which prevents exact reconstruction. Ladder Networks [19] have historically been designed to overcome the previously mentioned conflict between reconstruction and classification, by designing Auto-Encoders capable of discarding information. Reconstruction is produced using higher-layer representation and a noisy version of the reconstruction target. However, it is not obvious that providing a noisy version of the target and training the network to remove the noise allows the encoder to lose some information since it must be able to correct low-level errors that require details.

Another interesting regularization criterion relies on stability or smoothness of the prediction function, which is at the basis of interesting unsupervised training methods, *e.g.* Slow Feature Analysis [38]. Adding stability to the prediction function was studied in Adversarial Training [39] for supervised learning and further extended to semi-supervised learning in the Virtual Adversarial Training method [40]. Other recent semi-supervised models incorporate a stability-based regularizer on the prediction. The idea was first introduced by [23] and proposes to make the prediction vector stable toward data augmentation (translation, rotation, shearing, noise, *etc.*) and model stochasticity (dropout) for a given input. Following work [24,25] slightly improves upon it by proposing variants on the way to compute stability targets to increase their consistency and better adapt to the model's evolution over training.

When using large modern ConvNets, the problem of designing decoders able to invert the encoding still is an open question [41]. The usual solution is to mirror the architecture of the encoder by using transposed convolutions [42]. This problem is exacerbated with irreversible pooling operations such as max-pooling that must be reversed by an upsampling operation. In [17,18], they use unpooling operations to bring back spatial information from the encoder to the decoder, reusing pooling switches locations for upsampling. Another interesting option is to explicitly create models which are reversible by design. This is the option followed by recent works such as RevNet [43] and i-RevNet [44], being inspired by second generation of bi-orthogonal multi-resolution analysis and wavelets [45] from the signal processing literature.

To sum up, using reconstruction as a regularization cost added to classification is an appealing idea but the best way to efficiently use it as a regularizer is still an open question. As we have seen, when applied to an auto-encoding architecture [17,18], reconstruction and classification would compete. To overcome the aforementioned issues, we propose HybridNet, a new framework for semi-supervised learning. Presented on Fig. 2, this framework can be seen as an extension of the popular auto-encoding architecture. In HybridNet, the usual auto-encoder that does both classification and reconstruction is assisted by an additional auto-encoder so that the first one is allowed to discard information in order to produce intra-class invariant features while the second one retains the lost information. The combination of both branches then produces the reconstruction. This way, our architecture prevents the conflict between classification and reconstruction and allows the two branches to cooperate and accomplish both classification and reconstruction tasks.

Compared to Ladder Networks [19], our two-branch approach without direct skip connection allows for a finer and learned information separation and is thus expected to have a more favorable impact in terms of discriminative encoder regularization. Our HybridNet model also has conceptual connections with wavelet decomposition [46]: the first branch can be seen as extracting discriminative low-pass features from input images, and the second branch acting as a high-pass filter to restore the lost information. HybridNet also differs from reversible models [43,44] by the explicit decomposition between supervised and unsupervised

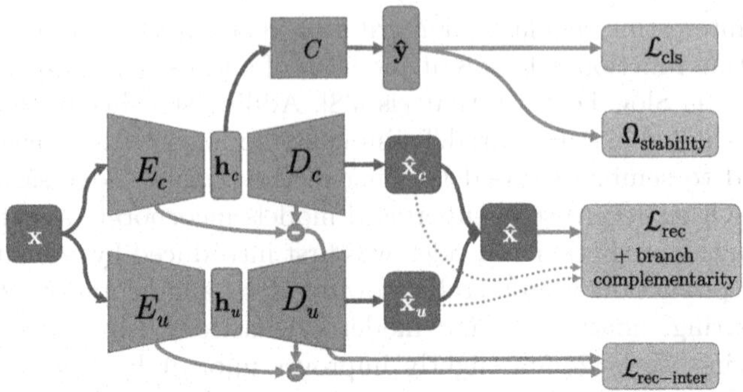

Fig. 2. General description of the HybridNet framework. E_c and C correspond to a classifier, E_c and D_c form an autoencoder that we call *discriminative path*, and E_u and D_u form a second autoencoder called *unsupervised path*. The various loss functions used to train HybridNet are also represented in yellow (Color figure online)

signals, enabling the discriminative encoder to have fewer parameters and better sample complexity.

In this paper, our contributions with the HybridNet framework are twofold: first, in Sect. 3.1, we propose an architecture designed to efficiently allow both reconstruction and classification losses to cooperate; second, in Sect. 3.2, we design a training loss adapted to it that includes reconstruction, stability in the discriminative branch and a branch complementarity technique. In Sect. 4, we perform experiments to show that HybridNet is able to outperform state-of-the-art results in various semi-supervised settings on CIFAR-10, SVHN and STL-10. We also provide ablation studies validating the favorable impact of our contributions. Finally, we show several visualizations on CIFAR-10 and STL-10 datasets analogous to Fig. 1 to validate the behavior of both branches, with a discriminative branch that loses information that is restored by the second branch.

3 HybridNet: A Semi-supervised Learning Framework

In this section, we detail the proposed HybridNet model: the chosen architecture to mix supervised and unsupervised information efficiently in Sect. 3.1, and the semi-supervised training method adapted to this particular architecture in Sect. 3.2.

3.1 Designing the HybridNet Architecture

General Architecture. As we have seen, classification requires intra-class invariant features while reconstruction needs to retain all the information. To circumvent this issue, HybridNet is composed of two auto-encoding paths, the *discriminative path* (E_c and D_c) and the *unsupervised path* (E_u and D_u).

Both encoders E_c and E_u take an input image $\mathbf{x}$ and produce representations $\mathbf{h}_c$ and $\mathbf{h}_u$, while decoders D_c and D_u take respectively $\mathbf{h}_c$ and $\mathbf{h}_u$ as input to produce two partial reconstructions $\hat{\mathbf{x}}_c$ and $\hat{\mathbf{x}}_u$. Finally, a classifier C produces a class prediction using discriminative features only: $\hat{\mathbf{y}} = C(\mathbf{h}_c)$. Even if the two paths can have similar architectures, they should play different and complementary roles. The discriminative path must extract discriminative features $\mathbf{h}_c$ that should eventually be well crafted to perform a classification task effectively, and produce a purposely partial reconstruction $\hat{\mathbf{x}}_c$ that should not be perfect since preserving all the information is not a behavior we want to encourage. Consequently, the role of the unsupervised path is to be complementary to the discriminative branch by retaining in $\mathbf{h}_u$ the information lost in $\mathbf{h}_c$. This way, it can produce a complementary reconstruction $\hat{\mathbf{x}}_u$ so that, when merging $\hat{\mathbf{x}}_u$ and $\hat{\mathbf{x}}_c$, the final reconstruction $\hat{\mathbf{x}}$ is close to $\mathbf{x}$. The HybridNet architecture, visible on Fig. 2, can be described by the following equations:

$$\begin{aligned} \mathbf{h}_c &= E_c(\mathbf{x}) \quad & \hat{\mathbf{x}}_c &= D_c(\mathbf{h}_c) \quad & \hat{\mathbf{y}} &= C(\mathbf{h}_c) \\ \mathbf{h}_u &= E_u(\mathbf{x}) \quad & \hat{\mathbf{x}}_u &= D_u(\mathbf{h}_u) \quad & \hat{\mathbf{x}} &= \hat{\mathbf{x}}_c + \hat{\mathbf{x}}_u \end{aligned} \tag{1}$$

Note that the end-role of reconstruction is just to act as a regularizer for the discriminative encoder. The main challenge and contribution of this paper is to find a way to ensure that the two paths will in fact behave in this desired way. The two main issues that we tackle are the fact that we want the discriminative branch to focus on discriminative features, and that we want both branches to cooperate and contribute to the reconstruction. Indeed, with such an architecture, we could end up with two paths that work independently: a classification path $\hat{\mathbf{y}} = C(E_c(\mathbf{x}))$ and a reconstruction path $\hat{\mathbf{x}} = \hat{\mathbf{x}}_u = D_u(E_u(\mathbf{x}))$ and $\hat{\mathbf{x}}_c = 0$. We address both those issues through the design of the architecture of the encoders and decoders as well as an appropriate loss and training procedure.

Branches Design. To design the HybridNet architecture, we start with a convolutional architecture adapted to the targeted dataset, for example a state-of-the-art ResNet architecture for CIFAR-10. This architecture is split into two modules: the discriminative encoder E_c and the classifier C. On top of this model, we add the discriminative decoder D_c. The location of the splitting point in the original network is free, but C will not be directly affected by the reconstruction loss. In our experiments, we choose $\mathbf{h}_c$ (E_c's output) to be the last intermediate representation before the final pooling that aggregates all the spatial information, leaving in C a global average pooling followed by one or more fully-connected layers. The decoder D_c is designed to be a "mirror" of the encoder's architecture, as commonly done in the literature, *e.g.* [17,19,47].

After constructing the discriminative branch, we add an unsupervised complementary branch. To ensure that both branches are "balanced" and behave in a similar way, the internal architecture of E_u and D_u is mostly the same as for E_c and D_c. The only difference remains in the mirroring of pooling layers, that can be reversed either by upsampling or unpooling. An upsampling will increase the spatial size of a feature map without any additional information while an unpooling, used in [17,18], will use spatial information (*pooling switches*) from the corresponding max-pooling layer to do the upsampling. In our architecture, we propose to use upsampling in the discriminative branch because we want to encourage spatial invariance, and use unpooling in the unsupervised branch to compensate this information loss and favor the learning of spatial-dependent low-level information. An example of HybridNet architecture is presented in Fig. 3.

As mentioned previously, one key problem to tackle is to ensure that this model will behave as expected, *i.e.* by learning discriminative features in the discriminative encoder and non-discriminative features in the unsupervised one. This is encouraged in different ways by the design of the architecture. First, the fact that only $\mathbf{h}_c$ is used for classification means that E_c will be pushed by the classification loss to produce discriminative features. Thus, the unsupervised branch will naturally focus on information lost by E_c. Using upsampling in D_c and unpooling in D_u also encourages the unsupervised branch to focus on low-level information. In addition to this, the design of an adapted loss and training protocol is a major contribution to the efficient training of HybridNet.

3.2 Training HybridNet

The HybridNet architecture has two information paths with only one producing a class prediction and both producing partial reconstructions that should be combined. In this section, we will address the question of training this architecture efficiently. The complete loss is composed of various terms as illustrated on Fig. 2. It comprises terms for classification with $\mathcal{L}_{\text{cls}}$; final reconstruction with $\mathcal{L}_{\text{rec}}$; intermediate reconstructions with $\mathcal{L}_{\text{rec-inter}b,l}$ (for layer l and branch b); and stability with $\Omega_{\text{stability}}$. It is also accompanied by a branch complementarity training method. Each term is weighted by a corresponding parameter λ:

$$\mathcal{L} = \lambda_{\text{c}}\mathcal{L}_{\text{cls}} + \lambda_{\text{r}}\mathcal{L}_{\text{rec}} + \textstyle\sum_{b\in\{c,u\},l} \lambda_{\text{r}b,l}\mathcal{L}_{\text{rec-inter}b,l} + \lambda_{\text{s}}\Omega_{\text{stability}} \,. \tag{2}$$

HybridNet can be trained on a partially labeled dataset, *i.e.* that is composed of labeled pairs $\mathcal{D}_{\text{sup}} = \{(x^{(k)}, y^{(k)})\}_{k=1..N_{\text{s}}}$ and unlabeled images $\mathcal{D}_{\text{unsup}} = \{x^{(k)}\}_{k=1..N_{\text{u}}}$. Each batch is composed of n samples, divided into n_{s} image-label pairs from $\mathcal{D}_{\text{sup}}$ and n_{u} unlabeled images from $\mathcal{D}_{\text{unsup}}$.

Classification. The classification term is a regular cross-entropy term, that is applied only on the n_s labeled samples of the batch and averaged over them:

$$\ell_{\text{cls}} = \ell_{\text{CE}}(\hat{\mathbf{y}}, \mathbf{y}) = -\sum_i \mathbf{y}_i \log \hat{\mathbf{y}}_i, \qquad \mathcal{L}_{\text{cls}} = \frac{1}{n_s}\sum_k \ell_{\text{cls}}(\hat{\mathbf{y}}^{(k)}, \mathbf{y}^{(k)}). \tag{3}$$

Reconstruction Losses. In HybridNet, we chose to keep discriminative and unsupervised paths separate so that they produce two complementary reconstructions $(\hat{\mathbf{x}}_u, \hat{\mathbf{x}}_c)$ that we combine with an addition into $\hat{\mathbf{x}} = \hat{\mathbf{x}}_u + \hat{\mathbf{x}}_c$. Keeping the two paths independent until the reconstruction in pixel space, as well as the merge-by-addition strategy allows us to apply different treatments to them and influence their behavior efficiently. The merge by addition in pixel space is also analogous to wavelet decomposition where the signal is decomposed into low- and high-pass branches that are then decoded and summed in pixel space. The reconstruction loss that we use is a simple mean-squared error between the input and the sum of the partial reconstructions:

$$\ell_{\text{rec}} = ||\hat{\mathbf{x}} - \mathbf{x}||_2^2 = ||\hat{\mathbf{x}}_u + \hat{\mathbf{x}}_c - \mathbf{x}||_2^2, \qquad \mathcal{L}_{\text{rec}} = \frac{1}{n}\sum_k \ell_{\text{rec}}(\hat{\mathbf{x}}^{(k)}, \mathbf{x}^{(k)}). \quad (4)$$

In addition to the final reconstruction loss, we also add reconstruction costs between intermediate representations in the encoders and the decoders which is possible since encoders and decoders have mirrored structure. We apply these costs to the representations $\mathbf{h}_{b,l}$ (for branch b and layer l) produced just after pooling layers in the encoders and reconstructions $\hat{\mathbf{h}}_{b,l}$ produced just before the corresponding upsampling or unpooling layers in the decoders. This is common in the literature [17–19] but is particularly important in our case: in addition to guiding the model to produce the right final reconstruction, it pushes the discriminative branch to produce a reconstruction and avoid the undesired situation where only the unsupervised branch would contribute to the final reconstruction. This is applied in both branches ($b \in \{c, u\}$):

$$\mathcal{L}_{\text{rec-inter}b,l} = \frac{1}{n}\sum_k ||\hat{\mathbf{h}}_{b,l}^{(k)} - \mathbf{h}_{b,l}^{(k)}||_2^2. \quad (5)$$

Branch Cooperation. As described previously, we want to ensure that both branches contribute to the final reconstruction, otherwise this would mean that the reconstruction is not helping to regularize E_c, which is our end-goal. Having both branches produce a partial reconstruction and using intermediate reconstructions already help with this goal. In addition, to balance their training even more, we propose a training technique such that the reconstruction loss is only backpropagated to the branch that contributes less to the final reconstruction of each sample. This is done by comparing $||\hat{\mathbf{x}}_c - \mathbf{x}||_2^2$ and $||\hat{\mathbf{x}}_u - \mathbf{x}||_2^2$ and only applying the final reconstruction loss to the branch with the higher error.

This can be implemented either in the gradient descent or simply by preventing gradient propagation in one branch or the other using features like `tf.stop_gradient` in Tensorflow or `.detach()` in PyTorch:

$$\ell_{\text{rec-balanced}} = \begin{cases} ||\hat{\mathbf{x}}_u + \text{stopgrad}(\hat{\mathbf{x}}_c) - \mathbf{x}||_2^2 & \text{if } ||\hat{\mathbf{x}}_u - \mathbf{x}||_2^2 \geq ||\hat{\mathbf{x}}_c - \mathbf{x}||_2^2 \\ ||\text{stopgrad}(\hat{\mathbf{x}}_u) + \hat{\mathbf{x}}_c - \mathbf{x}||_2^2 & \text{otherwise} \end{cases}. \quad (6)$$

Encouraging Invariance in the Discriminative Branch. We have seen that an important issue that needs to be addressed when training this model is to ensure that the discriminative branch will filter out information and learn

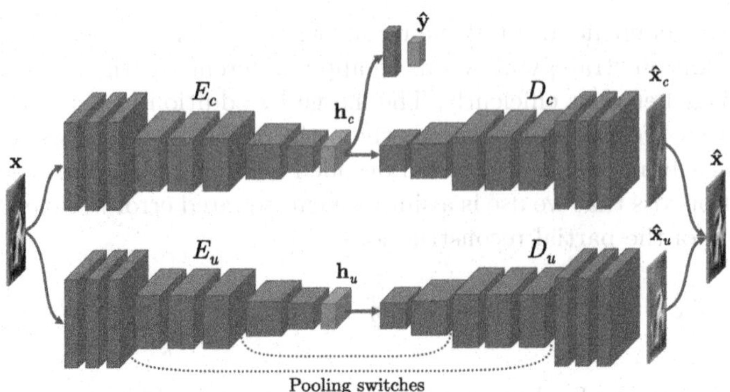

Fig. 3. Example of HybridNet architecture where an original classifier (ConvLarge) constitutes E_c and has been mirrored to create D_c and duplicated for E_u and D_u, with the addition of unpooling in the discriminative branch

invariant features. For now, the only signal that pushes the model to do so is the classification loss. However, in a semi-supervised context, when only a small portion of our dataset is labeled, this signal can be fairly weak and might not be sufficient to make the discriminative encoder focus on invariant features.

In order to further encourage this behavior, we propose to use a *stability regularizer.* Such a regularizer is currently at the core of the models that give state-of-the-art results in semi-supervised setting on the most common datasets [23–25]. The principle is to encourage the classifier's output prediction $\hat{\mathbf{y}}^{(k)}$ for sample k to be invariant to different sources of randomness applied on the input (translation, horizontal flip, random noise, *etc.*) and in the network (*e.g.* dropout). This is done by minimizing the squared euclidean distance between the output $\hat{\mathbf{y}}^{(k)}$ and a "stability" target $\mathbf{z}^{(k)}$. Multiple methods have been proposed to compute such a target [23–25], for example by using a second pass of the sample in the network with a different draw of random factors that will therefore produce a different output. We have:

$$\Omega_{\text{stability}} = \frac{1}{n} \sum_{k} ||\hat{\mathbf{y}}^{(k)} - \mathbf{z}^{(k)}||_2^2 . \tag{7}$$

By applying this loss on $\hat{\mathbf{y}}$, we encourage E_c to find invariant patterns in the data, patterns that have more chances of being discriminative and useful for classification. Furthermore, this loss has the advantage of being applicable to both labeled and unlabeled images.

In the experiments, we tried both Temporal Ensembling [24] and Mean Teacher [25] methods and did not see a major difference. In Temporal Ensembling, the target $\mathbf{z}^{(k)}$ is a moving average of the $\hat{\mathbf{y}}^{(k)}$ over the previous pass of $\mathbf{x}^{(k)}$ in the network during training; while in Mean Teacher, $\mathbf{z}^{(k)}$ is the output of a secondary model where weights are a moving average of the weights of the model being trained.

4 Experiments

In this section, we will study and validate the behavior of our novel framework. We first perform ablation studies to validate the architecture and loss terms of the model. We also propose visualizations of the behavior of the model in various configurations, before demonstrating the capability of HybridNet to obtain state-of-the-art results.

In these experiments, we use three image datasets: SVHN [48], CIFAR-10 [49] and STL-10 [50]. Both SVHN and CIFAR-10 are 10-classes datasets of 32×32 pixels images. SVHN has 73,257 images for training, 26,032 for testing and 531,131 extra images used only as unlabeled data. CIFAR-10 has 50,000 training images and 10,000 testing images. For our semi-supervised experiments, we only keep N labeled training samples (with $N/10$ samples per class) while the rest of the data is kept unlabeled, as is commonly done. STL-10 have the same 10 classes as CIFAR-10 with 96×96 pixels images. It is designed for semi-supervised learning since it contains 10 folds of 1,000 labeled training images, 100,000 unlabeled training images and 8,000 test images with labels.

4.1 HybridNet Framework Validation

First, we propose a thorough analysis of the behavior of our model at two different levels: first by comparing it to baselines that we obtain when disabling parts of the architecture, and second by analyzing the contribution of the different terms of the training loss of HybridNet both quantitatively and through visualizations.

This study was mainly performed using the ConvLarge architecture [19] on CIFAR-10 since it's a very common setup used in recent semi-supervised experiments [23–25]. The design of the HybridNet version of this architecture follows Sect. 3 (illustrated in Fig. 3) and uses Temporal Ensembling to produce stability targets $\mathbf{z}$. Additional results are provided using an adapted version of ConvLarge for STL-10 with added blocks of convolutions and pooling.

Models are trained with Adam with a learning rate of 0.003 for 600 epochs with batches of 20 labeled images and 80 unlabeled ones. The various loss-weighting terms λ of the general loss (Eq. (2)) could have been optimized on a validation set but for these experiments they were simply set so that the different loss terms have values of the same order of magnitude. Thus, all λ were set to either 0 or 1 if activated or not, except λ_s set to 0 or 100. All the details of the experiments – exact architecture, hyperparameters, optimization, *etc.* – are provided in the supplementary material.

Ablation Study of the Architecture. We start this analysis by validating our architecture with an ablation study on CIFAR-10 with various number of labeled samples. By disabling parts of the model and training terms, we compare HybridNet to different baselines and validate the importance of combining both contributions of the paper: the architecture and the training method.

Results are presented in Table 1. The classification and auto-encoder results are obtained with the same code and hyperparameters by simply disabling different losses and parts of the model: the classifier only use E_c and C; and the auto-encoder (similar to [17]) only E_c, D_c and C. For both, we can add the stability loss. The HybridNet architecture only uses the classification and reconstructions loss terms while the second result uses the full training loss.

Table 1. Ablation study performed on CIFAR-10 with ConvLarge architecture

Model	Labeled samples		
	1000	2000	4000
Classification	63.4	71.5	79.0
Classification and stability	65.6	74.6	81.3
Auto-encoder	65.0	73.6	79.8
Auto-encoder and stability	71.8	80.4	84.9
HybridNet architecture	63.2	74.0	80.3
HybridNet architecture and full training loss	**74.1**	**81.6**	**86.6**

First, we can see that the HybridNet architecture alone already yields an improvement over the baseline and the auto-encoder, except at 1000 labels. This could be explained by the fact that with very few labels, the model fails to correctly separate the information between the two branches because of the faint classification signal, and the additional loss terms that control the training of HybridNet are even more necessary. Overall, the architecture alone does not provide an important gain since it is not guided to efficiently take advantage of the two branches, indeed, we see that the addition of the complete HybridNet loss allows the model to provide much stronger results, with an improvement of 6–7 pts over the architecture alone, around 5–6 pts better than the stability or auto-encoding baseline, and 7–10 pts more than the supervised baseline. The most challenging baseline is the stabilized auto-encoder that manages to take advantage of the stability loss but from which we still improve by 1.2–2.8 pts.

This ablation study demonstrates the capability of the HybridNet framework to surpass the different architectural baselines, and shows the importance of the complementarity between the two-branch architecture and the complete training loss.

Importance of the Various Loss Terms. We now propose a more fine-grain study to look at the importance of each loss term of the HybridNet training described in Sect. 3.2, both through classification results and visualizations.

First, in Table 2a we show classification accuracy on CIFAR-10 with 2000 labels and STL-10 with 1000 labels for numerous combinations of loss terms. These results demonstrates that each loss term has it's importance and that all

Table 2. Detailed ablation studies when activating different terms and techniques of the HybridNet learning. These results are obtained with ConvLarge on CIFAR-10 with 2000 labeled samples and ConvLarge-like on STL-10 with 1000 labeled samples

(a) Test accuracy (%)

	$\mathcal{L}_{\text{classif}}$	$\Omega_{\text{stability}}$	$\mathcal{L}_{\text{rec}}$ (hybrid)	$\mathcal{L}_{\text{rec-inter}}$	$\mathcal{L}_{\text{rec-balanced}}$	CIFAR-10	STL-10
a	✓					71.5	65.6
b	✓	✓				74.6	69.8
c	✓		✓			72.4	67.8
d	✓		✓	✓		74.0	–
e	✓		✓	✓	✓	75.2	–
f	✓	✓	✓			77.7	71.5
g	✓	✓	✓		✓	77.4	–
h	✓	✓	✓	✓		80.8	72.2
i	✓	✓	✓	✓	✓	**81.6**	**74.1**

(b) Visualization of partial and combined reconstructions

	$\mathcal{L}_{\text{rec}}$ (hybrid)	$\mathcal{L}_{\text{rec-inter}}$	$\mathcal{L}_{\text{rec-balanced}}$	$\Omega_{\text{stability}}$	$\mathbf{x}$	$\hat{\mathbf{x}}_c$	$\hat{\mathbf{x}}_u$	$\hat{\mathbf{x}}$	$\mathbf{x}$	$\hat{\mathbf{x}}_c$	$\hat{\mathbf{x}}_u$	$\hat{\mathbf{x}}$	$\mathbf{x}$	$\hat{\mathbf{x}}_c$	$\hat{\mathbf{x}}_u$	$\hat{\mathbf{x}}$
c	✓															
d	✓	✓														
e	✓	✓	✓													
i	✓	✓	✓	✓												
c	✓															
d	✓	✓														
e	✓	✓	✓													
i	✓	✓	✓	✓												

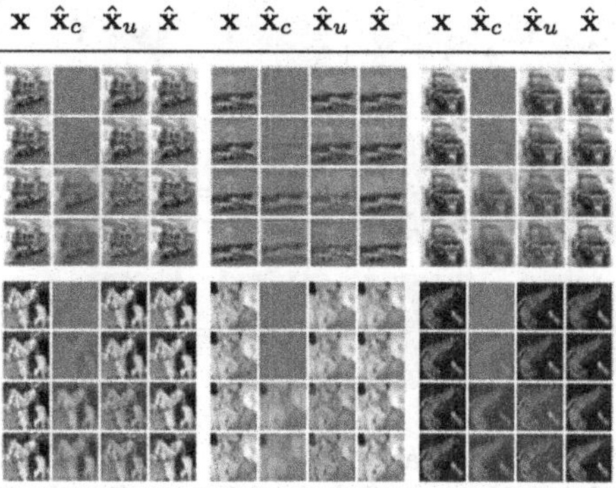

of them cooperate in order to reach the final best result of the full HybridNet model. In particular the stability loss is an important element of the training but is not sufficient as shown by lines *b* and *f*-*h*, while the other terms bring an equivalent gain as shown by lines *c*-*e*. Both those ∼5 pts gains can be combined to work in concert and reach the final score line *i* of a ∼10 pts gain.

Second, to interpret how the branches behave we propose to visualizing the different reconstructions $\hat{\mathbf{x}}_c$, $\hat{\mathbf{x}}_u$ and $\hat{\mathbf{x}}$ for different combinations of loss terms in Table 2b. With only the final reconstruction term (lines *c*), the discriminative branch does not contribute to the reconstruction and is thus barely regularized by the reconstruction loss, showing little gain over the classification baseline. The addition of the intermediate reconstruction terms helps the discriminative branch to produce a weak reconstruction (lines *d*) and is complemented by the branch balancing technique (lines *e*) to produce balanced reconstructions in both branch. The stability loss (lines *i*) adds little visual impact on $\hat{\mathbf{x}}_c$, it has probably more impact on the quality of the latent representation $\mathbf{h}_c$ and seems to help in making the discriminative features and classifier more robust with a large improvement of the accuracy.

Visualization of Information Separation on CIFAR-10 and STL-10. Overall, we can see in Table 2b lines *i* that thanks to the full HybridNet training loss, the information is correctly separated between $\hat{\mathbf{x}}_c$ and $\hat{\mathbf{x}}_u$ than both contribute somewhat equally while specializing on different type of information. For example, for the blue car, $\hat{\mathbf{x}}_c$ produces a blurry car with approximate

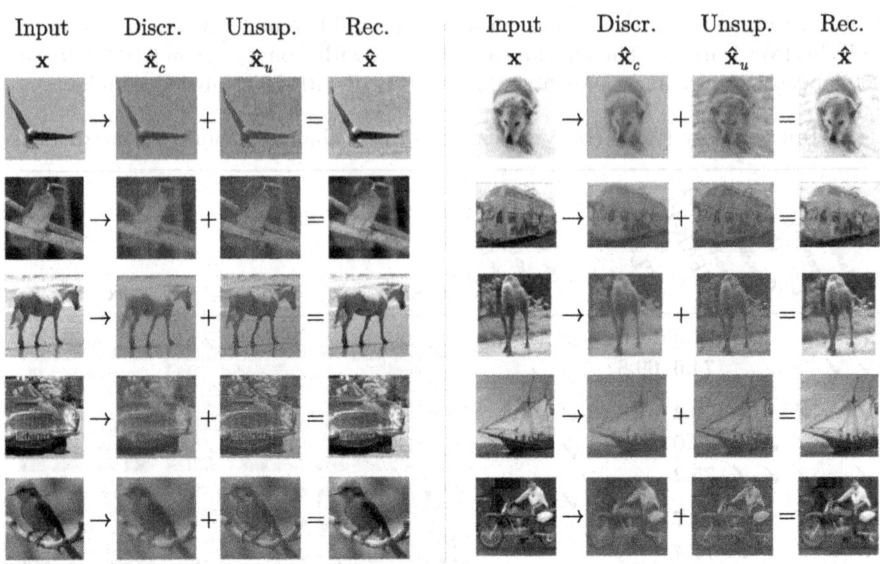

Fig. 4. Visualizations of input, partial and final reconstructions of STL-10 images using a HybridNet model derived from a ConvLarge-like architecture

colors, while $\hat{\mathbf{x}}_u$ provides both shape details and exact color information. For nicer visualizations, we also show reconstructions of the full HybridNet model trained on STL-10 which has larger images in Fig. 4. These confirm the observations on CIFAR-10 with a very good final reconstruction composed of a rough reconstruction that lacks texture and color details from the discriminative branch, completed by low-level details of shape, texture, writings, color correction and background information from the unsupervised branch.

4.2 State-of-the-Art Comparison

After studying the behavior of this novel architecture, we propose to demonstrate its effectiveness and capability to produce state-of-the-art results for semi-supervised learning on three datasets: SVHN, CIFAR-10 and STL-10.

We use ResNet architectures to constitute the supervised encoder E_c and classifier C; and augment them with a mirror decoder D_c and an unsupervised second branch containing an encoder E_u and a decoder D_u using the same architecture. For SVHN and CIFAR-10, we use the small ResNet from [51], which is used in Mean Teacher [25] and currently achieves state-of-the-art results on CIFAR-10. For STL-10, we upscale the images to 224×224 px and use a regular ResNet-50 pretrained on the Places dataset.

We trained HybridNet with the training method described in Sect. 3.2, including Mean Teacher to produce stability targets $\mathbf{z}^{(k)}$. The training protocol follow exactly the protocol of Mean Teacher [25] for CIFAR-10 and a similar one for

Table 3. Results on CIFAR-10, STL-10 and SVHN using a ResNet-based HybridNet. "Mean Teacher ResNet" is our classification & stability baseline; results marked with * are not reported in the original paper and were obtained ourselves

Dataset	CIFAR-10			SVHN		STL-10
Nb. labeled images	1000	2000	4000	500	1000	1000
SWWAE [17]					23.56	25.67
Ladder Network [19]			20.40			
Improved GAN [53]	21.83	19.61	18.63	18.44	8.11	
CatGAN [52]			19.58			
Stability regularization [23]			11.29	6.03		
Temporal Ensembling [24]			12.16	5.12	4.42	
Mean Teacher ConvLarge [25]	21.55	15.73	12.31	4.18	3.95	
Mean Teacher ResNet [25]	10.10		6.28	*2.33	*2.05	*16.8
ResNet baseline [51]	45.2	24.3	15.45	12.27	9.56	18.0
HybridNet [ours]	**8.81**	**7.87**	**6.09**	**1.85**	**1.80**	**15.9**

SVHN and STL-10 for which [25] does not report results with ResNet. The hyper-parameters added in HybridNet, *i.e.* the weights of the reconstruction terms (final and intermediate), were coarsely adjusted on a validation set (we tried values 0.25, 0.5 and 1.0 for both of them). Details are in the supplementary.

The results of these experiments are presented in Table 3. We can see the huge performance boost obtained by HybridNet compared to the ResNet baselines, in particular with CIFAR-10 with 1000 labels where the error rate goes from 45.2% to 8.81%, which demonstrates the large benefit of our regularizer. HybridNet also improves over the strong Mean Teacher baseline [25], with an improvement of 1.29 pt with 1000 labeled samples on CIFAR-10, and 0.9 pt on STL-10. We also significantly improve over other stability-based approaches [23,24], and over the Ladder Networks [19] and GAN-based techniques [52,53].

These results demonstrate the capability of HybridNet to apply to large residual architecture – that are very common nowadays – and to improve over baselines that already provided very good performance.

5 Conclusion

In this paper, we described a novel semi-supervised framework called HybridNet that proposes an auto-encoder-based architecture with two distinct paths that separate the discriminative information useful for classification from the remaining information that is only useful for reconstruction. This architecture is accompanied by a loss and training technique that allows the architecture to behave in the desired way. In the experiments, we validate the significant performance boost brought by HybridNet in comparison with several other common architectures that use reconstruction losses and stability. We also show that HybridNet is able to produce state-of-the-art results on multiple datasets.

With two latent representations that explicitly encode classification information on one side and the remaining information on the other side, our model may be seen as a competitor to the fully reversible RevNets models recently proposed, that implicitly encode both types of information. We plan to further explore the relationships between these approaches.

Acknowledgements. This work was funded by grant DeepVision (ANR-15-CE23-0029-02, STPGP-479356-15), a joint French/Canadian call by ANR & NSERC.

References

1. Krizhevsky, A., Sutskever, I., Hinton, G.E.: ImageNet classification with deep convolutional neural networks. In: Advances in Neural Information Processing Systems (NIPS) (2012)
2. He, K., Zhang, X., Ren, S., Sun, J.: Deep residual learning for image recognition. In: IEEE Conference on Computer Vision and Pattern Recognition (CVPR) (2016)
3. Durand, T., Mordan, T., Thome, N., Cord, M.: WILDCAT: weakly supervised learning of deep ConvNets for image classification, pointwise localization and segmentation. In: IEEE Conference on Computer Vision and Pattern Recognition (CVPR) (2017)
4. Dai, J., Li, Y., He, K., Sun, J.: R-FCN: object detection via region-based fully convolutional networks. In: Advances in Neural Information Processing Systems (NIPS) (2016)
5. Redmon, J., Divvala, S., Girshick, R., Farhadi, A.: You only look once: unified, real-time object detection. In: IEEE Conference on Computer Vision and Pattern Recognition (CVPR) (2016)
6. Mordan, T., Thome, N., Cord, M., Henaff, G.: Deformable part-based fully convolutional network for object detection. In: British Machine Vision Conference (BMVC) (2017)
7. Chen, L.C., Papandreou, G., Kokkinos, I., Murphy, K., Yuille, A.L.: DeepLab: semantic image segmentation with deep convolutional nets, atrous convolution, and fully connected CRFs. IEEE Trans. Pattern Anal. Mach. Intell. (TPAMI) (2018)
8. Engilberge, M., Chevallier, L., Pérez, P., Cord, M.: Finding beans in burgers: deep semantic-visual embedding with localization. In: IEEE Conference on Computer Vision and Pattern Recognition (CVPR) (2018)
9. Carvalho, M., Cadène, R., Picard, D., Soulier, L., Thome, N., Cord, M.: Cross-modal retrieval in the cooking context: learning semantic text-image embeddings. Special Interest Group on Information Retrieval (SIGIR) (2018)
10. Ben-Younes, H., Cadène, R., Thome, N., Cord, M.: MUTAN: multimodal tucker fusion for visual question answering. In: IEEE International Conference on Computer Vision (ICCV) (2017)
11. Krogh, A., Hertz, J.A.: A simple weight decay can improve generalization. In: Advances in Neural Information Processing Systems (NIPS) (1992)
12. Ioffe, S., Szegedy, C.: Batch normalization: accelerating deep network training by reducing internal covariate shift. In: Proceedings of the 32nd International Conference on Machine Learning, vol. 37, pp. 448–456 (2015)

13. Srivastava, N., Hinton, G., Krizhevsky, A., Sutskever, I., Salakhutdinov, R.: Dropout: a simple way to prevent neural networks from overfitting. J. Mach. Learn. Res. (JMLR), **15**, 1929–1958 (2014)
14. Blot, M., Robert, T., Thome, N., Cord, M.: SHADE: information-based regularization for deep learning. In: IEEE International Conference on Image Processing (ICIP) (2018)
15. Bengio, Y., Lamblin, P., Popovici, D., Larochelle, H.: Greedy layer-wise training of deep networks. In: Advances in Neural Information Processing Systems (NIPS) (2007)
16. Hinton, G.E., Salakhutdinov, R.R.: Reducing the dimensionality of data with neural networks. Science **313**, 504–507 (2006)
17. Zhao, J., Mathieu, M., Goroshin, R., LeCun, Y.: Stacked what-where autoencoders. In: International Conference on Learning Representations Workshop (ICLR-W) (2016)
18. Zhang, Y., Lee, K., Lee, H.: Augmenting supervised neural networks with unsupervised objectives for large-scale image classification. In: International Conference on Machine Learning (ICML) (2016)
19. Rasmus, A., Berglund, M., Honkala, M., Valpola, H., Raiko, T.: Semi-supervised learning with ladder networks. In: Advances in Neural Information Processing Systems (NIPS) (2015)
20. Mallat, S.: Group invariant scattering. In: Communications on Pure and Applied Mathematics (CPAM) (2012)
21. Bruna, J., Mallat, S.: Invariant scattering convolution networks. IEEE Trans. Pattern Anal. Mach. Intell. (TPAMI), **35**(8), 1872–1886 (2013)
22. Bietti, A., Mairal, J.: Group invariance, stability to deformations, and complexity of deep convolutional representations. In: Advances in Neural Information Processing Systems (NIPS) (2017)
23. Sajjadi, M., Javanmardi, M., Tasdizen, T.: Regularization with stochastic transformations and perturbations for deep semi-supervised learning. In: Advances in Neural Information Processing Systems (NIPS) (2016)
24. Laine, S., Aila, T.: Temporal ensembling for semi-supervised learning. In: International Conference on Learning Representations (ICLR) (2017)
25. Tarvainen, A., Valpola, H.: Mean teachers are better role models: weight-averaged consistency targets improve semi-supervised deep learning results. In: Advances in Neural Information Processing Systems (NIPS) (2017)
26. Zhu, X.: Semi-supervised learning literature survey. Technical report 1530, Computer Sciences, University of Wisconsin-Madison (2005)
27. Ranzato, M., Szummer, M.: Semi-supervised learning of compact document representations with deep networks. In: International Conference on Machine Learning (ICML) (2008)
28. Ranzato, M., Huang, F.J., Boureau, Y.L., LeCun, Y.: Unsupervised learning of invariant feature hierarchies with applications to object recognition. In: IEEE Conference on Computer Vision and Pattern Recognition (CVPR), June 2007
29. Vincent, P., Larochelle, H., Bengio, Y., Manzagol, P.A.: Extracting and composing robust features with denoising autoencoders. In: International Conference on Machine Learning (ICML) (2008)
30. Ranzato, M., Poultney, C., Chopra, S., Lecun, Y.: Efficient learning of sparse representations with an energy-based model. In: Advances in Neural Information Processing Systems (NIPS) (2007)
31. Larochelle, H., Bengio, Y.: Classification using discriminative restricted Boltzmann machines. In: International Conference on Machine Learning (ICML) (2008)

32. Kingma, D.P., Mohamed, S., Rezende, D.J., Welling, M.: Semi-supervised learning with deep generative models. In: Advances in Neural Information Processing Systems (NIPS) (2014)
33. Erhan, D., Bengio, Y., Courville, A., Manzagol, P.A., Vincent, P., Bengio, S.: Why does unsupervised pre-training help deep learning? J. Mach. Learning Research (JMLR), **11**, 625–660 (2010)
34. Goh, H., Thome, N., Cord, M., Lim, J.H.: Top-down regularization of deep belief networks. In: Advances in Neural Information Processing Systems (NIPS) (2013)
35. Goodfellow, I., et al.: Generative adversarial nets. In: Advances in Neural Information Processing Systems (NIPS) (2014)
36. Makhzani, A., Shlens, J., Jaitly, N., Goodfellow, I.: Adversarial autoencoders. In: International Conference on Learning Representations (ICLR) (2016)
37. Hastie, T., Tibshirani, R., Friedman, J.: The Elements of Statistical Learning. Springer, New York (2009). https://doi.org/10.1007/978-0-387-84858-7
38. Thériault, C., Thome, N., Cord, M.: Dynamic scene classification: learning motion descriptors with slow features analysis. In: IEEE Conference on Computer Vision and Pattern Recognition (CVPR) (2013)
39. Goodfellow, I.J., Shlens, J., Szegedy, C.: Explaining and harnessing adversarial examples. In: International Conference on Learning Representations (ICLR) (2015)
40. Miyato, T., Maeda, S.i., Koyama, M., Nakae, K., Ishii, S.: Distributional smoothing with virtual adversarial training. In: International Conference on Learning Representations (ICLR) (2016)
41. Wojna, Z., et al.: The devil is in the decoder. In: British Machine Vision Conference (BMVC) (2017)
42. Dumoulin, V., Visin, F.: A guide to convolution arithmetic for deep learning. Technical report (2016)
43. Gomez, A.N., Ren, M., Urtasun, R., Grosse, R.B.: The reversible residual network: backpropagation without storing activations. In: Advances in Neural Information Processing Systems (NIPS) (2017)
44. Jacobsen, J.H., Smeulders, A., Oyallon, E.: i-RevNet: deep invertible networks. In: International Conference on Learning Representations (ICLR) (2018)
45. Sweldens, W.: The lifting scheme: a new philosophy in biorthogonal wavelet constructions. In: Wavelet Applications in Signal and Image Processing III (1995)
46. Mallat, S.G., Peyré, G.: A Wavelet Tour Of Signal Processing: The Sparse Way. Academic Press (2009)
47. Zeiler, M.D., Fergus, R.: Visualizing and understanding convolutional networks. In: Fleet, D., Pajdla, T., Schiele, B., Tuytelaars, T. (eds.) ECCV 2014. LNCS, vol. 8689, pp. 818–833. Springer, Cham (2014). https://doi.org/10.1007/978-3-319-10590-1_53
48. Netzer, Y., Wang, T., Coates, A., Bissacco, A., Wu, B., Ng, A.Y.: Reading digits in natural images with unsupervised feature learning. In: NIPS Workshop on Deep Learning and Unsupervised Feature Learning (2011)
49. Krizhevsky, A., Hinton, G.: Learning multiple layers of features from tiny images. Technical report (2009)
50. Coates, A., Ng, A., Lee, H.: An analysis of single-layer networks in unsupervised feature learning. In: International Conference on Artificial Intelligence and Statistics (AISTATS) (2011)
51. Gastaldi, X.: Shake-shake regularization of 3-branch residual networks. In: International Conference on Learning Representations Workshop (ICLR-W) (2017)

52. Springenberg, J.T.: Unsupervised and semi-supervised learning with categorical generative adversarial networks. In: International Conference on Learning Representations (ICLR) (2016)
53. Salimans, T., et al.: Improved techniques for training GANs. In Lee, D.D., Sugiyama, M., Luxburg, U.V., Guyon, I., Garnett, R. (eds.) Advances in Neural Information Processing Systems (NIPS). Curran Associates, Inc. (2016)

Robust Anchor Embedding for Unsupervised Video Person re-IDentification in the Wild

Mang Ye, Xiangyuan Lan, and Pong C. Yuen(✉)

Department of Computer Science, Hong Kong Baptist University, Kowloon Tong, Hong Kong
{mangye,pcyuen}@comp.hkbu.edu.hk, xiangyuanlan@life.hkbu.edu.hk

Abstract. This paper addresses the scalability and robustness issues of estimating labels from imbalanced unlabeled data for unsupervised video-based person re-identification (re-ID). To achieve it, we propose a novel Robust AnChor Embedding (RACE) framework via deep feature representation learning for large-scale unsupervised video re-ID. Within this framework, anchor sequences representing different persons are firstly selected to formulate an anchor graph which also initializes the CNN model to get discriminative feature representations for later label estimation. To accurately estimate labels from unlabeled sequences with noisy frames, robust anchor embedding is introduced based on the regularized affine hull. Efficiency is ensured with kNN anchors embedding instead of the whole anchor set under manifold assumptions. After that, a robust and efficient top-k counts label prediction strategy is proposed to predict the labels of unlabeled image sequences. With the newly estimated labeled sequences, the unified anchor embedding framework enables the feature learning process to be further facilitated. Extensive experimental results on the large-scale dataset show that the proposed method outperforms existing unsupervised video re-ID methods.

Keywords: Unsupervised person re-id · Robust anchor embedding

1 Introduction

Person re-identification (re-ID) addresses the problem of searching specific persons across disjoint camera views [54,55]. Video-based re-ID has gained increasing attention in recent years due to its practicality [53], where the video sequences can be trivially obtained by effective pedestrian detection and tracking algorithms in practical applications [17,18]. Impressive progress has been reported with advanced deep learning methods [22,34,51]. However, the annotation difficulty limits the applicability of supervised methods in large-scale camera network, which motivates us to investigate an unsupervised solution with deep neural networks for video re-ID.

V. Ferrari et al. (Eds.): ECCV 2018, LNCS 11211, pp. 176–193, 2018.
https://doi.org/10.1007/978-3-030-01234-2_11

Fig. 1. Practical imbalanced unlabeled data in re-ID task for unsupervised training.

We follow the cross-camera label estimation approach to mine labels from the unlabeled image sequences [27,29,47], where existing supervised methods can be subsequently used to learn discriminative re-ID models. Thus this approach owns good flexibility and applicability [47]. However, most previous unsupervised learning methods adopt the same training set as in supervised methods, where all persons appear in both cameras [16,27,29]. In practical unsupervised settings, only a small portion of persons appear in both cameras due to the imbalanced unlabeled data, *i.e.*, most persons only appear in one camera as illustrated in Fig. 1. As a result, large amount of false positives would be introduced and significant performance drop is inevitable. Therefore, their performances are somewhat over-estimated for practical wild settings. Moreover, most of these methods suffer from the scalability issues, thus cannot be applied to large-scale applications [9,43,53]. In this paper, we propose a scalable solution with deep neural networks for unsupervised video re-ID under wild settings.

The proposed method is designed on top of the *application-specific characteristics* existing in video re-ID. Specifically, we assume that several training video sequences representing different persons could be collected as *anchor sequences* for initialization. It's reasonable since persons appear in different non-overlapping cameras at the same time interval could be treated as different persons [27,28]. Thus the anchor sequences could be easily collected without manually label efforts in practical applications. In addition, the image frames within each video sequence could be roughly assumed to represent the same person identity, which provides abundant weakly labeled images by treating each sequence as a class (person identity). Therefore, the easily collected anchor sequences provide abundant training samples to initialize the CNN model to obtain discriminative feature representations, which ensures the later label estimation performance from unlabeled sequences. With the learnt feature representations, we propose a novel Robust AnChor Embedding (RACE) framework to estimate labels from unlabelled sequences for large-scale unsupervised video re-ID.

RACE measures the underlying relationship between unlabelled sequences and anchor sequences with embedding process. To address the scalability and efficiency problem, we propose to perform anchors embedding with k-nearest neighbor instead of the whole anchor set under manifold assumptions. To handle the noisy frames within sequences and achieve a more robust label estimation under unsupervised settings, a novel constraint based on regularized affine full is incorporated to suppress the negative effects of noisy frames. With the learnt embedding weights, a robust and efficient top-k counts label prediction strategy is subsequently proposed to predict labels of the unlabeled image sequences. It does not require compulsory label assignment and reduces the false positives, guaranteeing the robustness under wild settings. The main idea is that if two video sequences share the same label, they should be very similar under different measure dimensions. With the newly estimated labeled sequences, the feature learning process is further facilitated. Compared to existing unsupervised re-ID methods, the proposed method is robust and efficient for large-scale video re-ID in the wild. The main contributions are summarized as follows:

- We propose an unsupervised deep feature representation learning framework for large-scale video re-ID under wild settings. It is built on the *application-specific characteristics* existing in video re-ID task.
- We present a novel robust anchor embedding method to measure the underlying similarity relationship between the unlabelled sequences and anchors for better label estimation. The outlier-insensitive affine hull regularization is integrated to handle noisy frames in sequences to enhance the robustness.
- We introduce a robust and efficient top-k counts label prediction strategy to reduce false positives. It considers both visual and intrinsic similarity, achieving higher label estimation accuracy and slightly better efficiency.

2 Related Work

Unsupervised Re-ID. Several unsupervised re-ID methods have been developed in recent years. Unsupervised transfer learning approach learns re-ID models on the unlabelled target dataset with labelled source dataset [28,32]. Salience learning has also been investigated in early years [36,52]. Besides that, other attempts adopted dictionary learning with graph regularization constraints to learn shared feature representations [16,32]. Additionally, Yu *et al.* [49] introduced a cross-view asymmetric metric learning method to learn the distance measures. Meanwhile, Ye *et al.* [47] and Liu *et al.* [27] solved unsupervised video re-ID problem by estimating labels with hand-craft feature representations, and then adopted existing supervised learning methods to learn the re-ID models. Most of previous methods suffer from scalability issues, and it is hard for them to be applied to the large-scale applications [13,15,21].

Unsupervised Deep Learning. Unsupervised deep learning has been widely investigated in general image recognition tasks [3,20,50]. Some approaches attempt to design a self-supervision signal [50], but they do not explicitly aim to learn discriminative features, which are unsuitable for re-ID task due to large intra-class variations. Some other methods adopt ranking [19] or retrieval [4] based label assignment strategies, but they are easy to suffer from the collapsing problem that most unlabeled samples might be assigned to the same class [3]. Additionally, several clustering based unsupervised deep learning methods are introduced for re-ID [9]. However, they are hard to be applied on large-scale person re-ID applications due to time-consuming clustering procedure. Other approaches utilize the graph theory to exploit the relationship among different samples [3,20]. However, large cross-camera variations in person re-ID may introduce lots of false positives which depresses the effectiveness of these methods.

Deep Learning for Re-ID. Existing deep learning re-ID methods can be roughly categorized into three categories according to the learning objectives: triplet loss [5,11,48], contrastive/verification loss [6,35,45] and classification/identity loss [33,56]. Moreover, some works combine them together to improve the performance [42,48]. In addition, some CNN-RNN related network structures are also designed for video re-ID task [26,30,44]. All these methods can be configured in our framework to learn discriminative re-ID models.

Semi-supervised Learning. The proposed method is also related to the anchor graph based semi-supervised learning approaches [25,37,38] since we randomly select the sequences for anchor initialization. Similarly, they also contain the anchor embedding process to measure the relationship between the anchors and unlabelled samples. Different from previous methods, they utilize the graph regularization to estimated labels while we introduce a novel top-k counts strategy to estimate labels, which is more robust and efficient. In addition, we modify the anchor embedding procedure by considering the characteristics of video re-ID tasks under practical wild scenarios.

3 Proposed Method

3.1 Overview

Our goal is to accurately estimate labels with large amount of unlabeled tracking sequences collected from different cameras, where discriminative re-ID models can be subsequently learnt. The proposed framework contains three main steps as shown in Fig. 2: (1) *Anchor Initialization*, several anchor sequences are randomly selected for CNN initialization to get discriminative feature representations for better label estimation (Sect. 3.2). Meanwhile, the selected anchor sequences are consequently used for later label estimation of unlabelled image sequences. (2) *Label Estimation*, with the learnt representation, label estimation of unlabeled sequences via robust anchor embedding and top-k counts label prediction is introduced (Sect. 3.3). Specifically, a robust anchor embedding is introduced to reconstruct any unlabelled sequences with their nearest anchor sequences to ensure efficiency. Meanwhile, each image sequence is represented by its regularized affine hull to reduce the impact of outlier frames. After that, the top-k counts label prediction strategy with the learnt embedding weights is conducted to predict the labels of unlabelled sequences. (3) *Model Updating*, with the newly estimated sequences and anchor sequences, we update the deep feature representation learning with more training samples (Sect. 3.4).

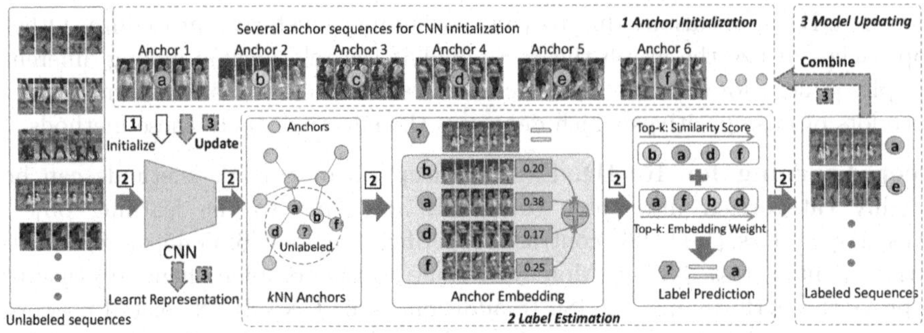

Fig. 2. The proposed RACE framework. It contains three main steps: (1) *Anchor Initialization*, several anchor sequences representing different persons are selected for CNN initialization; (2) *Label Estimation*, label estimation of unlabeled sequences via robust anchor embedding and top-k counts label prediction; (3) *Model Updating*, the deep feature representation is updated with newly labeled sequences and anchor sequences.

3.2 Anchor Initialization

It is well recognized that good model initialization is essential for deep feature representation learning systems. In this paper, we design an effective model initialization strategy according to the characteristics of video re-ID task. We firstly randomly select m anchor sequences ($\mathcal{A}$) to fine-tune the pre-trained ImageNet model [10], where the m anchor sequences are assumed to represent different persons[1]. The assumption is reasonable since the same person cannot be presented at the same instant under different non-overlapping cameras [27,28]. Under this assumption, the anchor sequences can be trivially obtained without human label annotation efforts in real applications. Accordingly, image frames within each sequence are assumed to belong to the same person identity, which could be ensured with effective tracking algorithms [7]. In this manner, the video sequence provides abundant training samples for each person by treating different person identities as different classes. Therefore, these selected anchor sequences could be adopted to initialize the deep neural network to learn discriminative feature representations for label estimation. In this paper, we adopt classification loss (IDE [54]) as the baseline structures, since it is effective for training and has shown good convergency [53]. Correspondingly, an anchor set $\mathcal{A}$ is constructed for these initialized anchor sequences. Denoted by

$$\mathcal{A} = \{A_l \mid l = 1, 2, \cdots, m\} \tag{1}$$

Each node A_l represents a set of frame-level feature vectors from the lth anchor sequence. l denotes the corresponding *initialized pseudo-label* assigned to anchor A_l. Then these anchors are utilized for label estimation from unlabeled sequences.

[1] Anchors are assumed to represent different identities, but somehow it's unrestricted to this assumption (two anchors may belong to the same person) as shown in Fig. 6.

3.3 Label Estimation

Robust Anchor Embedding. With the initialized CNN representation, we could extract the feature representations of the unlabelled sequences $\mathcal{X} = \{X_i \mid i = 1, 2, \cdots, n\}$ and anchor sequences $\mathcal{A}$ for label estimation. In video re-ID, each sequence contains several different frame-level feature vectors, typical way to represent the sequence is adopting mean-pooling or max-pooling to transform multiple frame vectors into single feature vector [30,53]. However, it may deteriorate the label estimation performance by introducing the noisy frames within sequences, which are usually caused by tracking or detection errors (Fig. 3). Indeed, there are some methods trying to learn a better video sequence representation [6,44], but they do not explicitly consider the outlier frames existing within sequences or the efficiency issues. Thus, we adopt the efficient regularized affine hull (RAH) [58] to reduce the impact of outlier frames when measure the sequence to sequence similarity. It can handle arbitrary sequence length thus owns good flexibility. For sequence X_i, its RAH is denoted by

$$\mathbf{x}_i^{\mathcal{H}} = \{\sum \alpha_j \mathbf{x}_{i,j} \Big| \sum \alpha_j = 1, \|\alpha\|_{l_p} \leq \delta\} \tag{2}$$

where $\|\cdot\|_{l_p}$ (e.g, l_2 norm) could make the representation robust to outlier frames by suppressing unnecessary components for the final video sequence representation. The RAH transforms the original set of frame-level feature vectors of each sequence to a single feature vector with the learnt coefficients [58]. For simplification, the RAH of an image sequence i is represented by a d-dimensional feature vector hereinafter, termed as $\mathbf{x}_i^{\mathcal{H}}$ with a superscript $^{\mathcal{H}}$.

For the unlabeled sequences label prediction, we firstly aim at learning an embedding vector $\mathbf{w}_i$ that measure the underlying relationship between the unlabelled sequence $\mathbf{x}_i^{\mathcal{H}}$ and anchor set $\mathcal{A}^{\mathcal{H}}$ represented with RAHs. To ensure the efficiency, we learn the embedding weights of the unlabelled sequence i with its nearest (k) anchors instead of all anchors. It is reasonable that distant sequences are very likely to have different labels and contiguous sequences may have similar labels under the manifold assumptions [25,40,41]. This strategy greatly reduces the unnecessary computational cost since $k \ll m$. Therefore, an unlabeled sequence $\mathbf{x}_i^{\mathcal{H}} \in \mathbb{R}^{d \times 1}$ is formulated as a convex combination of its k nearest anchors ($\mathcal{A}_{\langle i \rangle}^{\mathcal{H}} \in \mathbb{R}^{d \times k}$). We formulate the coefficient learning problem as Robust AnChor Embedding (RACE) represented by:

$$\begin{aligned} &\min_{\mathbf{w}_i \in \mathbb{R}^k} f(\mathbf{w}_i) = \left\| \mathbf{x}_i^{\mathcal{H}} - \mathcal{A}_{\langle i \rangle}^{\mathcal{H}} \mathbf{w}_i \right\|^2 + \lambda \left\| d_{\langle i \rangle} \odot \mathbf{w}_i \right\|^2 \\ &s.t. \quad \mathbf{1}^T \mathbf{w}_i = 1, \mathbf{w}_i \geq 0 \end{aligned} \tag{3}$$

where the k entries of the vector $\mathbf{w}_i$ represent the corresponding embedding weights of unlabeled sequence $\mathbf{x}_i^{\mathcal{H}}$ to its k closest anchors $\mathcal{A}_{\langle i \rangle}^{\mathcal{H}}$. $d_{\langle i \rangle}$ is a vector that represents the visual similarity between the unlabeled sequence $\mathbf{x}_i^{\mathcal{H}}$ and the anchors $\mathcal{A}_{\langle i \rangle}^{\mathcal{H}}$. $\odot$ denotes the element-wise multiplication. λ is a trade-off factor to balance two terms. RACE contains two separate terms, the first *embedding term* aims at reconstructing the unlabelled sequence with its nearest neighbor anchors. The second *smoothing term* constrains the learnt coefficients such that larger weights should be assigned to the anchors with smaller distance. RACE transforms the high-dimensional CNN representation into low-dimensional embedding weight vector to reduce the computational cost.

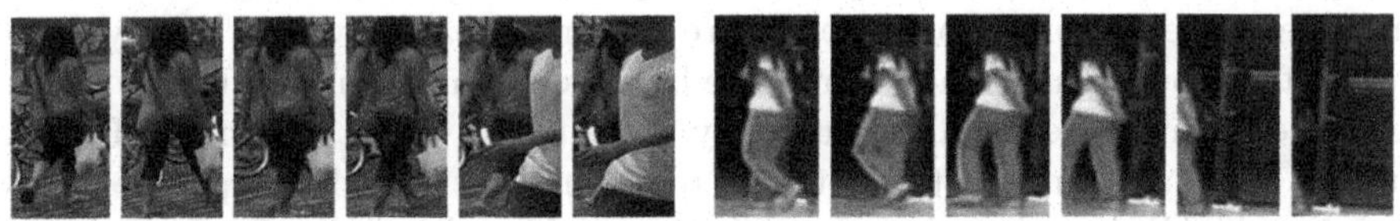

Fig. 3. Noisy frames within the image sequence on MARS dataset.

Smoothing Term. Since the original LAE in [25] does not have any constraint between the embedding weights and sequence to anchor distance. From the manifold assumption perspective, it is reasonable that nearby sequences tend to have similar labels. That is, nearby anchors should have larger reconstruction weights while the distant anchors should be assigned with smaller weights. Correspondingly, we define $d_{\langle i \rangle}$ by

$$d_{\langle i \rangle}(k) = exp(\frac{\|\mathbf{x}_i^{\mathcal{H}} - \mathcal{A}_{\langle i \rangle}^{\mathcal{H}}(k)\|^2}{\sigma}) \tag{4}$$

where σ is a balancing parameter, and is usually defined by the average distance of $\mathbf{x}_i^{\mathcal{H}}$ to its nearest anchors $\mathcal{A}_{\langle i \rangle}^{\mathcal{H}}$.

Optimization. After transforming the multiple frame-level feature vectors in each sequence to RAH with an approximate solution in [58], the optimization problem in Eq. 3 becomes the standard quadratic programming problem. To accelerate the optimization and ensure the sparsity of the learnt weights, we adopt the projected gradient method [8,25] to optimize Eq. 3. The updating rule is expressed by

$$\begin{aligned} \mathbf{w}_i^{(t+1)} &= \mathcal{P}_{\mathbb{S}}(\mathbf{w}_i^{(t)} - \eta_t \nabla f(\mathbf{w}_i^{(t)})) \\ \mathcal{P}_{\mathbb{S}}(\mathbf{w}) &= arg \min_{\mathbf{w}_i \in \mathbb{S}} \|\mathbf{w}' - \mathbf{w}\| \end{aligned} \tag{5}$$

where t denotes the iteration step, $\mathcal{P}_{\mathbb{S}}$ is a simplex projection to ensure the nonnegative normalization constraints in Eq. 3. η_t is a positive step size, $\nabla f(\mathbf{w})$ denotes the gradient of f at $\mathbf{w}$. Details can be found in [8,58]. The embedding weights measure the intrinsic similarity between the unlabeled sequences and anchors, which are subsequently used for label estimation.

Label Prediction with Top-*k* Counts. A straightforward solution for label estimation is to design the graph Laplacian and conduct graph regularization as done in many anchor-graph based semi-supervised learning methods [25,31,37]. However, it is unsuitable for our scenario due to the following reasons:

- Under semi-supervised settings, they usually assume that every unlabeled sample must be assigned with a label according the anchor labels. However, for video re-ID, the identities of the anchor set are usually only a subset of all possible identities. Compulsory label assignment may produce large amount of false positives especially for wild settings, which would deteriorate the later feature representation learning.
- To the best of our knowledge, most graph based learning methods suffer from high computational complexities. Specifically, the graph Laplacian step is $O(m^2n)$, and the graph regularization process is $O(m^2n + n^3)$. In large-scale camera network applications, both m and n might be extremely large, which makes these methods incapable.

To address above robustness and efficiency issues, we design a simple but effective top-k counts strategy for the label prediction. The main idea is that if two image sequences belong to the same person identity, they should be very close to each other under different measure dimensions [14]. Specifically, if unlabeled sequence $\mathbf{x}_i$ is assigned with label l of $\mathcal{A}_l$, it should satisfy two principles: (1) $\mathcal{A}_l$ should be within the nearest ($k' \leq k$) anchors of $\mathbf{x}_i$, denoted by $\mathcal{N}_{\langle i,k' \rangle}$. It means that the sequence $\mathbf{x}_i$ should be extremely visual similar to anchor $\mathcal{A}_l$. This principle guarantees that only visual similar samples could share the same label, it measures the visual similarity. (2) The embedding weight of $\mathbf{w}_{i,l}$ should be large enough since embedding process measures the intrinsic underlying relationship between the unlabelled sequences and anchors, it acts as the intrinsic similarity. Mathematically, we formulate the label prediction as

$$\hat{y}_i = \begin{cases} 0, & if\ \mathcal{A}^{\mathcal{H}}_{\langle i,k' \rangle} \cap \mathcal{N}_{\langle i,k' \rangle} = \emptyset \\ \arg \max\limits_{l \in \mathcal{A}^{\mathcal{H}}_{\langle i,k' \rangle}} \frac{\mathbf{w}_{i,l}}{\mathcal{R}(A_l)}, & others \end{cases} \tag{6}$$

where $\mathcal{R}(A_l)$ represents the ranking order of A_l in $\mathcal{N}_{\langle i,k' \rangle}$ according to the visual similarity, which jointly considers the embedding weights and visual similarity scores. Our label prediction strategy has two main advantages: (1) we could avoid the compulsory label assignment of uncertain sequences, thus could reduce large amount of false positives under wild settings. Smaller k' means stricter constraints. (2) it is quite efficient. The first criteria could be efficiently done with and-or operation, and the second label prediction step only needs to compute less than k' ($k' \leq k \leq m$) times for each unlabelled sequence. The computational complexity of the label prediction stage is $O(kn + k' \lg k'n)$ (intersection operation + ranking operation), which is much lower than the graph models [25,37] with $O(m^2n+n^3)$. Experiments show that the proposed method produces higher label estimation performance with slightly better efficiency for video re-ID.

3.4 Model Updating

With the newly estimated sequences together with the anchor sequences, we could adopt existing supervised methods (e.g. IDE [53], QAN [26], ASTPN [44]) to update the deep feature representation learning. The learnt feature representation is improved with more training samples. Additionally, self-training strategy could also be adopted to refine the label estimation process and feature representation learning. Moreover, with the newly estimated labels by RACE together with anchor set, we could learn an improved similarity measurement. Therefore, the anchor embedding could be updated to get more accurate label prediction results and training samples. With iterative updating, better label estimation performance and feature representation would be achieved.

4 Experimental Results

4.1 Experimental Settings

Datasets. Three publicly available video re-ID datasets are selected for evaluation: two small-scale datasets, PRID-2011 dataset [12], iLIDS-VID dataset [39] and one large-scale MARS dataset [53]. The PRID-2011 dataset is collected from two disjoint surveillance cameras with significant color inconsistency. It contains 385 person video sequences in camera view A and 749 person sequences in camera view B. Among all persons, 200 persons are recorded in both camera views. The iLIDS-VID dataset is captured by two non-overlapping cameras located in an airport arrival hall, 300 person video sequences are sampled in each camera. The MARS dataset is a large-scale dataset, it contains 1,261 different persons whom are captured by at least 2 cameras, totally 20,715 image sequences which are automatically achieved by DPM detector and GMCCP tracker.

Evaluation Protocol. Different from previous unsupervised settings on PRID-2011 and iLIDS-VID datasets [27,47], they adopt the same training set as in supervised methods, which is impractical for real applications. We modify the training settings for *wild evaluation*. For the PRID-2011 dataset, there are totally 600 person sequences from two cameras (300 sequences in each camera) for training, only 100 persons appear in both cameras. For anchor initialization, 300 image sequences representing different persons are randomly selected from two cameras. For the iLIDS-VID dataset, there are totally 300 person sequences from two cameras (100 sequences in each camera) for training, only 50 persons appear in both cameras. For anchor initialization, 100 image sequences representing different persons are randomly selected from two cameras. For the MARS dataset, 625 sequences from 625 persons are randomly selected as anchors for initialization. The anchors are assumed to represent different persons, but somehow it's unrestricted to this assumption (*two anchors may belong to the same person*) as illustrated in Fig. 6. In testing procedure, the Euclidean distance of two sequences is adopted. Rank-k matching rates and mAP values are both reported in the testing phase.

Implementation Details. We use ResNet-50 [10] pre-trained on ImageNet as our basic CNN model. Specifically, we insert a fully connected layer with 512 units after the pooling-5 layer, followed by batch normalization, ReLU and Dropout [33]. The dropout probability is set to 0.5 for all datasets. All images are resized to 128 × 256. Standard data augmentation methods are adopted. Batch size is set to 256 for MARS dataset, and 64 for both PRID-2011 and iLIDS-VID datasets. We use stochastic gradient descent to optimize the neural networks. We adopt the default Normal function of MxNet for the variables initialization. The initial learning rate is set to 0.003 for MARS dataset and 0.01 for both PRID-2011 and iLIDS-VID datasets, it is decreased by 0.1 after 20 epochs. The total training epochs are set to 30 for all datasets unless otherwise specified. The kNN graph construction k in Eq. 3 is set to 15, and the label prediction k' is set to 1. The smoothing parameter λ is set to 0.1. RAH is optimized with [58]. The default experimental results are with 1-round label estimation.

Table 1. Evaluation of label estimation performance (%) on MARS dataset. The label estimation time for DGM [47] is about 2 h, and RACE is only 183 s.

Methods	Recall	Precision	F-Score
1NN	41.76	41.76	41.76
AGR [25]	43.30	43.30	43.30
DGM [47]	42.40	59.64	49.57
RACE	40.87	66.22	**50.54**

Table 2. Evaluation of different components in the proposed RACE. Label estimation performance (%) on MARS dataset.

Settings	Recall	Precision	F-Score
w/o Top-k	47.84	47.84	47.84
w/o RAH	37.20	68.18	48.14
w/o Smooth	42.75	59.22	49.65
RACE	40.87	66.22	**50.54**

4.2 Detailed Analysis

Evaluation of Label Estimation. We adopt the general precision, recall and F-score as the evaluation criteria of label estimation performance. The results on the MARS dataset are shown in Table 1. (1) **Effectiveness**. Results illustrate that the proposed method can improve the precision and F-score by a large margin compared with 1NN (nearest neighbor) and AGR [25] baselines. Specifically, we could achieve 66.22% label estimation accuracy on the large-scale MARS dataset, and the F-score is about 50.54%. (2) **Efficiency**. Compared to the state-of-the-art DGM method in ICCV17 on the large-scale MARS dataset, the proposed method is much more efficient than DGM in terms of the label estimation time (Ours: ∼183 s, DGM [47]: ∼2 h). Meanwhile, better label estimation performance is also achieved. Compared to AGR [25] with 185 s, the proposed RACE is also more efficient in terms of the label estimation process. Furthermore, considering that both methods contain the embedding process with about 157 s, the advantage of our top-k counts label prediction is more obvious.

Evaluation of Each Component. We evaluate each component of the proposed method by removing the corresponding component. The experimental results shown in Table 2 could verify the effectiveness of each component. "w/o Top-k" means that we directly conduct the label estimation according to the maximum embedding weights without top-k counts label prediction. It shows that the top-k counts label prediction improves the label estimation precision from 48% to 66%. Additionally, RAH mainly benefits the recall criterion, since RAH is more robust to outlier frames within sequences than the simply pooling method. Moreover, smoothing term also improves the label estimation performance further with the smoothing similarity constraint in the embedding process. Overall, the F-score is increased by integrating three main components.

Parameters Analysis. Three important parameters: (1) k, the number of nearest anchors selected for RACE, (2) k', the parameter of top-k counts label prediction in Eq. 6, (3) λ, the trade-off parameter balances the embedding and smoothing term in Eq. 3, are evaluated in Fig. 4. (1) For the kNN anchor graph construction, larger k usually could bring better performance as shown in Fig. 4(a). However, it also increases the computational time in later steps. Moreover, we could see that the performance becomes stable when k is up to 15. Therefore, we choose $k = 15$ in our experiments. (2) In terms of k', smaller k' means stricter constraints between the visual similarity and the intrinsic similarity, it also may result in smaller recall values. Since larger recall values means more noisy labels would be encountered for the feature representation learning procedure, we prefer a better label precision performance, so k' is set to 1 in our experiments. (3) Sensitivity to λ, it could also illustrate the improvement of the smoothing term. Besides, larger λ means stricter constraints for the similarity scores between two embedded anchors. Obviously, if λ is large enough, the proposed RACE would

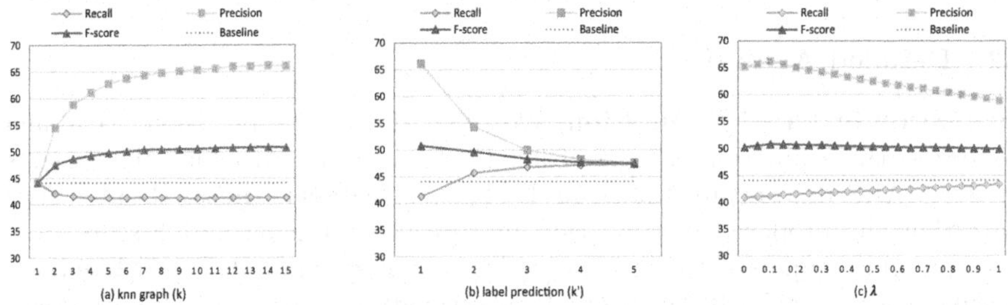

Fig. 4. Parameters Analysis on MARS dataset. (a) The number of nearest anchors (k) selected for RACE; (b) The parameter k' of label prediction in Eq. 6; (c) λ, the trade-off parameter in Eq. 3. '*Baseline*' provide a lower bound of 1NN with RAH representation.

Table 3. Comparison to baseline systems (IDE [53] + Resnet50 [10]). Person reidentification performance (%) at rank-1, 5, 10, 20 and mAP on three datasets. "Baseline" means the performance of initialized feature representation.

Datasets	PRID-2011				iLIDS-VID				MARS				
Rank at r	1	5	10	20	1	5	10	20	1	5	10	20	mAP
Supervised	64.7	91.2	94.6	98.7	45.6	69.9	78.4	87.5	69.3	85.8	89.4	92.8	49.8
Baseline	45.3	72.5	86.6	90.4	13.6	33.7	44.3	58.1	33.2	47.7	54.7	62.0	15.5
RACE	50.6	79.4	88.6	91.8	19.3	39.3	53.3	68.7	41.0	55.6	62.2	67.2	22.3

be degenerated to nearest neighbor method. Overall, a proper choice of λ would improve the overall performance as illustrated in Fig. 4(c).

Evaluation of Re-identification. We evaluate the re-ID performance with the estimated labels on three datasets as shown in Table 3. Note that our evaluation protocols simulate the wild settings, which are slightly different from the standard supervised settings on PRID-2011 and iLIDS-VID datasets. Table 3 illustrates that the proposed RACE improves the baseline feature representation learning method consistently on all three datasets with one-round label estimation and feature learning. Specifically, we improve the rank-1 matching rates from 45.32% to 50.64% on the PRID-2011 dataset, 13.6% to 19.33% on the iLDIS-VID dataset and 33.2% to 41.0% on the MARS dataset. We suppose that the performance would be further boosted with iterative updating. Note that the performance of feature learning process might be improved with other advanced deep learning [26,44] or re-ranking methods [1,2,46,57].

Table 4. Comparison with state-of-the-art unsupervised methods on *small-scale* PRID-2011 and iLIDS-VID datasets *under wild settings*. Rank-k matching rates (%).

Datasets	PRID-2011				iLIDS-VID				Ref.
Rank at r	1	5	10	20	1	5	10	20	
Salience [52]	25.8	43.6	52.6	62.0	10.2	24.8	35.5	52.9	CVPR13
LOMO [23]	40.6	66.7	79.4	92.3	9.2	20.0	27.9	46.9	CVPR15
STFV3D [24]	42.1	71.9	84.4	91.6	**37.0**	**64.3**	**77.0**	**86.9**	ICCV15
GRDL [16]	41.6	76.4	84.6	89.9	21.7	42.9	56.2	71.6	ECCV16
SMP [27]	38.7	68.1	79.6	90.0	16.0	31.8	43.8	56.8	ICCV17
DGM [47]	48.2	78.3	83.9	**92.4**	23.1	46.7	58.3	71.2	ICCV17
RACE (Round1)	**50.6**	**79.4**	**84.8**	91.8	19.3	39.3	53.3	68.7	-

Table 5. Comparison with state-of-the-art unsupervised methods on the *large-scale* MARS dataset. Rank-k matching rates (%) and mAP (%).

Rank at r	1	5	10	20	mAP	Ref.
LOMO [23]	14.9	27.4	33.7	40.8	5.5	ICCV15
GRDL [16]	19.3	33.2	41.6	46.5	9.6	ECCV16
SMP [27]	41.2	55.6	-	66.8	19.7	ICCV17
DGM [47]	36.8	54.0	61.6	**68.5**	21.3	ICCV17
RACE (Round1)	41.0	55.6	61.9	67.2	22.3	-
RACE (Round2)	**43.2**	**57.1**	**62.1**	67.6	**24.5**	-

4.3 Comparison with State-of-the-Arts

This subsection demonstrates the comparison with other state-of-the-art unsupervised re-ID methods, including Salience [52], LOMO [23], STFV3D [24], GRDL [16], DGM [47] and SMP[2] [27]. Note that our evaluation settings on PRID-2011 and iLIDS-VID datatsets are different from the original DGM [47] and SMP [27], where they assume that all persons appear in both cameras. The comparisons on three datasets are shown in Tables 4 and 5.

Results illustrate that we could achieve the best performance under wild settings on PRID-2011 dataset and the large-scale MARS dataset. Specifically, the rank-1 accuracy is about 50.6% on the PRID-2011 dataset as shown in Table 4 under wild settings. For the large-scale MARS dataset, 625 persons randomly appear in 6 cameras, thus it is more related to the practical multi-camera networks. Correspondingly, we could achieve the state-of-the-art performance, the rank-1 matching rate is 43.2% and mAP is 24.5% with 2-round training as shown in Table 5. However, Table 4 shows that our results on iLIDS-VID dataset are lower than the state-of-the-art unsupervised methods, it can be attributed to the limited training data for deep feature representation learning. We suppose that the proposed method can be applied to practical applications where a large amount of unlabeled tracking sequences could be collected for unsupervised deep feature representation initialization and learning.

We also observe that the performance can be further improved with further label estimation/refinement as shown in Table 5. Specifically, it is around 2% improvement for both rank-1 accuracy (41.0% to 43.2%) and mAP values (22.3% to 24.5%) on the large-scale MARS dataset in round 2. With iterative updating scheme, the performance can be further improved by scarifying the efficiency.

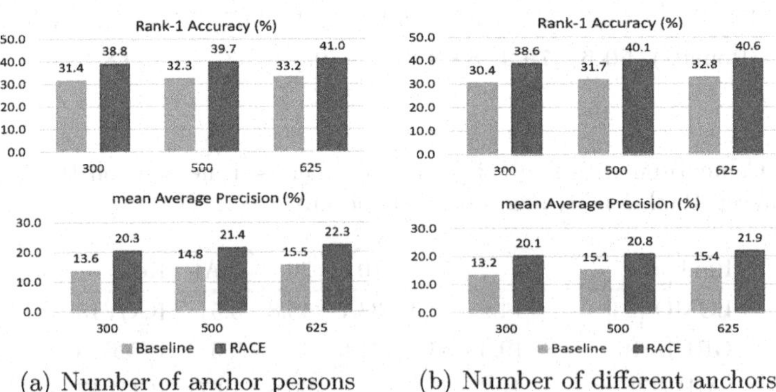

Fig. 5. Sensitivity to anchor selection on the MARS dataset. (a) Number of anchor persons. All these anchors represent different persons. (b) Number of different anchors. Anchors are randomly selected, two anchors may belong to the same person.

[2] GRDL, DGM and SMP are implemented with the released code.

4.4 Robustness in the Wild

In this section, we evaluate RACE under more challenging settings, which are (1) *Sensitivity to anchor selection*, different anchor initialization strategies. (2) *Sensitivity to imbalance ratios*, different imbalance ratios of the training set.

Sensitivity to Anchor Selection. The anchor initialization is very important in our proposed method, especially for the number of selected anchors. Two sets of different anchor selection experiments are evaluated as shown in Fig. 5. (1) *it's hard to know the specific number of person identities in an open environment.* Therefore, we randomly select different number of initialized anchor sequences to test the performance variations on the large-scale MARS dataset as shown in Fig. 5(a). The results illustrate that the proposed method can improve the baseline feature representations consistently with different number of initialized anchors. Specifically, the overall performances are slightly decreased compared to 625 sequences initialization, but they are still competitive to the current state-of-the-art unsupervised methods. (2) *it's hard to ensure the selected anchors truly represent different persons.* Therefore, we relax the assumption, where anchors are randomly selected, thus two anchors may belong to the same person. Figure 5(b) shows that the proposed method still achieves satisfactory performance with slight decrease even without the assumption.

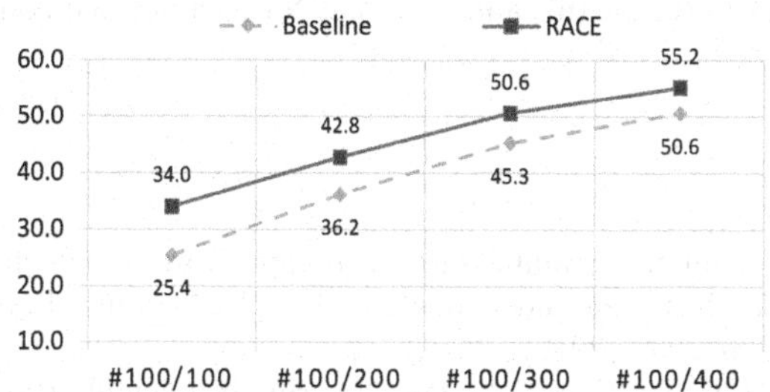

Fig. 6. Rank-1 matching rates (%) of different imbalance ratios on the PRID-2011 dataset. "#m/n" means that m persons out of n different person sequences appear in both cameras.

Sensitivity to Imbalance Ratios. We adopt the additional 734 person sequences together with 200 person training sequence pairs in PRID-2011 dataset to simulate different imbalance ratios as shown in Fig. 6. "#100/400" means that only 100 persons appear in both cameras while each camera contains 400 different person sequences. Specifically, the additional person sequences are simply treated as different persons to initialize the deep feature representation learning. Figure 6 demonstrates that RACE improves the deep feature representation learning performance consistently under different wild settings. Moreover, since deep feature representation learning could benefit from more training data, RACE achieves even better performance with more anchor sequences on

PRID-2011 dataset even with lower positive ratio. Compared with DGM [47], RACE is more robust to lower positive ratios, while DGM drops quickly with low positive ratios. Overall, RACE is superior in the following aspects: (1) it is scalable for large-scale scenarios, which learns discriminative deep feature representations without any manually labeled information. (2) it is efficient in terms of the label estimation procedure. (3) it is robust under wild settings, thus could be applied to real applications with highly imbalanced unlabeled training data.

5 Conclusion

This paper proposes an efficient and scalable unsupervised deep feature representation learning framework for video re-ID under wild settings. To accurately estimate labels from unlabelled sequences, a robust anchor embedding method is designed for this task, regularized affine hull together with a manifold smoothing term is integrated into the embedding process. A novel top-k counts label prediction strategy is then introduced to reduce false positives. Deep feature representation learning could be updated with newly estimated unlabeled sequences. Experimental results on large-scale datasets under wild settings demonstrate the superiority of the proposed method.

Acknowledgments. This work is partially supported by Hong Kong RGC General Research Fund HKBU (12254316), and National Natural Science Foundation of China (61562048).

References

1. Bai, S., Bai, X., Tian, Q.: Scalable person re-identification on supervised smoothed manifold. In: IEEE Conference on Computer Vision and Pattern Recognition (CVPR), pp. 2530–2539 (2017)
2. Bai, S., Sun, S., Bai, X., Zhang, Z., Tian, Q.: Smooth neighborhood structure mining on multiple affinity graphs with applications to context-sensitive similarity. In: Leibe, B., Matas, J., Sebe, N., Welling, M. (eds.) ECCV 2016. LNCS, vol. 9906, pp. 592–608. Springer, Cham (2016). https://doi.org/10.1007/978-3-319-46475-6_37
3. Bojanowski, P., Joulin, A.: Unsupervised learning by predicting noise. In: ICML (2017)
4. Bojanowski, P., et al.: Weakly supervised action labeling in videos under ordering constraints. In: Fleet, D., Pajdla, T., Schiele, B., Tuytelaars, T. (eds.) ECCV 2014. LNCS, vol. 8693, pp. 628–643. Springer, Cham (2014). https://doi.org/10.1007/978-3-319-10602-1_41
5. Cheng, D., Gong, Y., Zhou, S., Wang, J., Zheng, N.: Person re-identification by multi-channel parts-based cnn with improved triplet loss function. In: CVPR (2016)
6. Chung, D., Tahboub, K., Delp, E.J.: A two stream siamese convolutional neural network for person re-identification. In: ICCV (2017)
7. Danelljan, M., Bhat, G., Khan, F.S., Felsberg, M.: Eco: efficient convolution operators for tracking. In: IEEE Conference on Computer Vision and Pattern Recognition (CVPR), pp. 21–26 (2017)

8. Duchi, J., Shalev-Shwartz, S., Singer, Y., Chandra, T.: Efficient projections onto the ℓ_1-ball for learning in high dimensions. In: ICML (2008)
9. Fan, H., Zheng, L., Yang, Y.: Unsupervised person re-identification: clustering and fine-tuning. arXiv preprint arXiv:1705.10444 (2017)
10. He, K., Zhang, X., Ren, S., Sun, J.: Deep residual learning for image recognition. In: CVPR (2016)
11. Hermans, A., Beyer, L., Leibe, B.: In defense of the triplet loss for person re-identification. In: ICCV (2017)
12. Hirzer, M., Beleznai, C., Roth, P.M., Bischof, H.: Person re-identification by descriptive and discriminative classification. In: Heyden, A., Kahl, F. (eds.) SCIA 2011. LNCS, vol. 6688, pp. 91–102. Springer, Heidelberg (2011). https://doi.org/10.1007/978-3-642-21227-7_9
13. Jianming, L., Weihang, C., Qing, L., Can, Y.: Unsupervised cross-dataset person re-identification by transfer learning of spatial-temporal patterns. In: IEEE Conference on Computer Vision and Pattern Recognition (CVPR) (2018)
14. Jin, S., Su, H., Stauffer, C., Learned-Miller, E.: End-to-end face detection and cast grouping in movies using erdos-rényi clustering. In: International Conference on Computer Vision (ICCV), vol. 2, p. 8 (2017)
15. Jingya, W., Xiatian, Z., Shaogang, G., Wei, L.: Transferable joint attribute-identity deep learning for unsupervised person re-identification. In: IEEE Conference on Computer Vision and Pattern Recognition (CVPR) (2018)
16. Kodirov, E., Xiang, T., Fu, Z., Gong, S.: Person re-identification by unsupervised ℓ_1 graph learning. In: Leibe, B., Matas, J., Sebe, N., Welling, M. (eds.) ECCV 2016. LNCS, vol. 9905, pp. 178–195. Springer, Cham (2016). https://doi.org/10.1007/978-3-319-46448-0_11
17. Lan, X., Ma, A.J., Yuen, P.C., Chellappa, R.: Joint sparse representation and robust feature-level fusion for multi-cue visual tracking. IEEE Trans. Image Process. (TIP) **24**(12), 5826–5841 (2015)
18. Lan, X., Zhang, S., Yuen, P.C., Chellappa, R.: Learning common and feature-specific patterns: a novel multiple-sparse-representation-based tracker. IEEE Trans. Image Process. **27**(4), 2022–2037 (2018)
19. Lee, H.Y., Huang, J.B., Singh, M., Yang, M.H.: Unsupervised representation learning by sorting sequences. In: IEEE International Conference on Computer Vision (ICCV), pp. 667–676 (2017)
20. Li, D., Hung, W.-C., Huang, J.-B., Wang, S., Ahuja, N., Yang, M.-H.: Unsupervised visual representation learning by graph-based consistent constraints. In: Leibe, B., Matas, J., Sebe, N., Welling, M. (eds.) ECCV 2016. LNCS, vol. 9908, pp. 678–694. Springer, Cham (2016). https://doi.org/10.1007/978-3-319-46493-0_41
21. Li, J., Ma, A.J., Yuen, P.C.: Semi-supervised region metric learning for person re-identification. Int. J. Comput. Vis. 1–20 (2018)
22. Li, S., Bak, S., Carr, P., Wang, X.: Diversity regularized spatiotemporal attention for video-based person re-identification. In: IEEE Conference on Computer Vision and Pattern Recognition (CVPR), June 2018
23. Liao, S., Hu, Y., Zhu, X., Li, S.Z.: Person re-identification by local maximal occurrence representation and metric learning. In: IEEE Conference on Computer Vision and Pattern Recognition (CVPR), pp. 2197–2206 (2015)
24. Liu, K., Ma, B., Zhang, W., Huang, R.: A spatio-temporal appearance representation for video-based pedestrian re-identification. In: IEEE International Conference on Computer Vision (ICCV), pp. 3810–3818 (2015)
25. Liu, W., He, J., Chang, S.F.: Large graph construction for scalable semi-supervised learning. In: ICML (2010)

26. Liu, Y., Yan, J., Ouyang, W.: Quality aware network for set to set recognition. In: CVPR (2017)
27. Liu, Z., Wang, D., Lu, H.: Stepwise metric promotion for unsupervised video person re-identification. In: IEEE International Conference on Computer Vision (ICCV), pp. 2429–2438 (2017)
28. Ma, A.J., Li, J., Yuen, P.C., Li, P.: Cross-domain person reidentification using domain adaptation ranking svms. IEEE Trans. Image Process. (TIP) **24**(5), 1599–1613 (2015)
29. Ma, X., et al.: Person re-identification by unsupervised video matching. Pattern Recognit. (PR) **65**, 197–210 (2017)
30. McLaughlin, N., Martinez del Rincon, J., Miller, P.: Recurrent convolutional network for video-based person re-identification. In: IEEE Conference on Computer Vision and Pattern Recognition (CVPR), pp. 1325–1334 (2016)
31. Nie, F., Zhu, W., Li, X.: Unsupervised large graph embedding. In: AAAI (2017)
32. Peng, P., Xiang, T., Wang, Y., et al.: Unsupervised cross-dataset transfer learning for person re-identification. In: IEEE Conference on Computer Vision and Pattern Recognition (CVPR), pp. 1306–1315 (2016)
33. Sun, Y., Zheng, L., Deng, W., Wang, S.: SVDNet for pedestrian retrieval. In: ICCV (2017)
34. Sun, Y., Zheng, L., Yang, Y., Tian, Q., Wang, S.: Beyond part models: person retrieval with refined part pooling. arXiv preprint arXiv:1711.09349 (2017)
35. Varior, R.R., Haloi, M., Wang, G.: Gated siamese convolutional neural network architecture for human re-identification. In: Leibe, B., Matas, J., Sebe, N., Welling, M. (eds.) ECCV 2016. LNCS, vol. 9912, pp. 791–808. Springer, Cham (2016). https://doi.org/10.1007/978-3-319-46484-8_48
36. Wang, H., Gong, S., Xiang, T.: Unsupervised learning of generative topic saliency for person re-identification. In: BMVC (2014)
37. Wang, M., Fu, W., Hao, S., Tao, D., Wu, X.: Scalable semi-supervised learning by efficient anchor graph regularization. IEEE TKDE **28**(7), 1864–1877 (2016)
38. Wang, Q., Yuen, P.C., Feng, G.: Semi-supervised metric learning via topology preserving multiple semi-supervised assumptions. Pattern Recognit. **46**(9), 2576–2587 (2013)
39. Wang, T., Gong, S., Zhu, X., Wang, S.: Person re-identification by video ranking. In: Fleet, D., Pajdla, T., Schiele, B., Tuytelaars, T. (eds.) ECCV 2014. LNCS, vol. 8692, pp. 688–703. Springer, Cham (2014). https://doi.org/10.1007/978-3-319-10593-2_45
40. Wang, Z., et al.: Person reidentification via discrepancy matrix and matrix metric. IEEE Trans. Cybern. (2017)
41. Wang, Z., Hu, R., Liang, C., et al.: Zero-shot person re-identification via cross-view consistency. IEEE Trans. Multimed. (TMM) **18**(12), 2553–2566 (2016)
42. Wang, Z., Ye, M., Yang, F., Bai, X., Satoh, S.: Cascaded SR-GAN for scale-adaptive low resolution person re-identification. In: IJCAI, pp. 3891–3897 (2018)
43. Wu, Y., Lin, Y., Dong, X., Yan, Y., Ouyang, W., Yang, Y.: Exploit the unknown gradually: one-shot video-based person re-identification by stepwise learning. In: IEEE Conference on Computer Vision and Pattern Recognition (CVPR), June 2018
44. Xu, S., Cheng, Y., Gu, K., Yang, Y., Chang, S., Zhou, P.: Jointly attentive spatial-temporal pooling networks for video-based person re-identification. In: ICCV (2017)

45. Ye, M., Lan, X., Li, J., Yuen, P.C.: Hierarchical discriminative learning for visible thermal person re-identification. In: Thirty-Second AAAI Conference on Artificial Intelligence (AAAI) (2018)
46. Ye, M., et al.: Person reidentification via ranking aggregation of similarity pulling and dissimilarity pushing. IEEE Trans. Multimed. **18**(12), 2553–2566 (2016)
47. Ye, M., Ma, A.J., Zheng, L., Li, J., Yuen, P.C.: Dynamic label graph matching for unsupervised video re-identification. In: IEEE International Conference on Computer Vision (ICCV), pp. 5142–5150 (2017)
48. Ye, M., Wang, Z., Lan, X., Yuen, P.C.: Visible thermal person re-identification via dual-constrained top-ranking. In: IJCAI, pp. 1092–1099 (2018)
49. Yu, H.X., Wu, A., Zheng, W.S.: Cross-view asymmetric metric learning for unsupervised person re-identification. In: ICCV (2017)
50. Zhang, R., Isola, P., Efros, A.A.: Split-brain autoencoders: unsupervised learning by cross-channel prediction. In: CVPR (2017)
51. Zhao, J., Xiong, L., Cheng, Y., Cheng, Y., et al.: 3D-aided deep pose-invariant face recognition. In: IJCAI (2018)
52. Zhao, R., Ouyang, W., Wang, X.: Unsupervised salience learning for person re-identification. In: IEEE Conference on Computer Vision and Pattern Recognition (CVPR), pp. 3586–3593 (2013)
53. Zheng, L., Bie, Z., Sun, Y., Wang, J., Su, C., Wang, S., Tian, Q.: MARS: a video benchmark for large-scale person re-identification. In: Leibe, B., Matas, J., Sebe, N., Welling, M. (eds.) ECCV 2016. LNCS, vol. 9910, pp. 868–884. Springer, Cham (2016). https://doi.org/10.1007/978-3-319-46466-4_52
54. Zheng, L., Yang, Y., Hauptmann, A.G.: Person re-identification: past, present and future. arXiv (2016)
55. Zheng, L., Yang, Y., Tian, Q.: Sift meets CNN: a decade survey of instance retrieval. IEEE Trans. Pattern Anal. Mach. Intell. (TPAMI) **40**(5), 1224–1244 (2018)
56. Zheng, Z., Zheng, L., Yang, Y.: Unlabeled samples generated by GAN improve the person re-identification baseline in vitro. In: ICCV (2017)
57. Zhong, Z., Zheng, L., Cao, D., Li, S.: Re-ranking person re-identification with k-reciprocal encoding. In: IEEE Conference on Computer Vision and Pattern Recognition (CVPR), pp. 3652–3661 (2017)
58. Zhu, P., Zhang, L., Zuo, W., Zhang, D.: From point to set: extend the learning of distance metrics. In: ICCV (2013)

Holistic 3D Scene Parsing and Reconstruction from a Single RGB Image

Siyuan Huang[1,2(✉)], Siyuan Qi[1,2], Yixin Zhu[1,2], Yinxue Xiao[1], Yuanlu Xu[1,2], and Song-Chun Zhu[1,2]

[1] University of California, Los Angeles, Los Angeles, USA
huangsiyuan@ucla.edu
[2] International Center for AI and Robot Autonomy (CARA), Los Angeles, USA

Abstract. We propose a computational framework to jointly parse a single RGB image and reconstruct a holistic 3D configuration composed by a set of CAD models using a stochastic grammar model. Specifically, we introduce a Holistic Scene Grammar (HSG) to represent the 3D scene structure, which characterizes a joint distribution over the functional and geometric space of indoor scenes. The proposed HSG captures three essential and often latent dimensions of the indoor scenes: (i) latent human context, describing the affordance and the functionality of a room arrangement, (ii) geometric constraints over the scene configurations, and (iii) physical constraints that guarantee physically plausible parsing and reconstruction. We solve this joint parsing and reconstruction problem in an analysis-by-synthesis fashion, seeking to minimize the differences between the input image and the rendered images generated by our 3D representation, over the space of depth, surface normal, and object segmentation map. The optimal configuration, represented by a parse graph, is inferred using Markov chain Monte Carlo (MCMC), which efficiently traverses through the non-differentiable solution space, jointly optimizing object localization, 3D layout, and hidden human context. Experimental results demonstrate that the proposed algorithm improves the generalization ability and significantly outperforms prior methods on 3D layout estimation, 3D object detection, and holistic scene understanding.

Keywords: 3D scene parsing and reconstruction · Analysis-by-synthesis · Holistic Scene Grammar · Markov chain Monte Carlo

---

Electronic supplementary material The online version of this chapter (https://doi.org/10.1007/978-3-030-01234-2_12) contains supplementary material, which is available to authorized users.

V. Ferrari et al. (Eds.): ECCV 2018, LNCS 11211, pp. 194–211, 2018.
https://doi.org/10.1007/978-3-030-01234-2_12

1 Introduction

The complexity and richness of human vision are not only reflected by the ability to recognize visible objects, but also to reason about the latent actionable information [1], including inferring latent human context as the functionality of a scene [2,3], reconstructing 3D hierarchical geometric structure [4,5], and complying with the physical constraints that guarantee the physically plausible scene configurations [6]. Such rich understandings of an indoor scene are the essence for building an intelligent computational system, which transcends the prevailing appearance- and geometry-based recognition tasks to account also for the deeper reasoning of observed images or patterns.

One promising direction is *analysis-by-synthesis* [7] or "vision as inverse graphics" [8,9]. In this paradigm, computer vision is treated as an inverse problem as opposed to computer graphics, of which the goal is to reverse-engineer hidden factors occurred in the physical process that produces observed images.

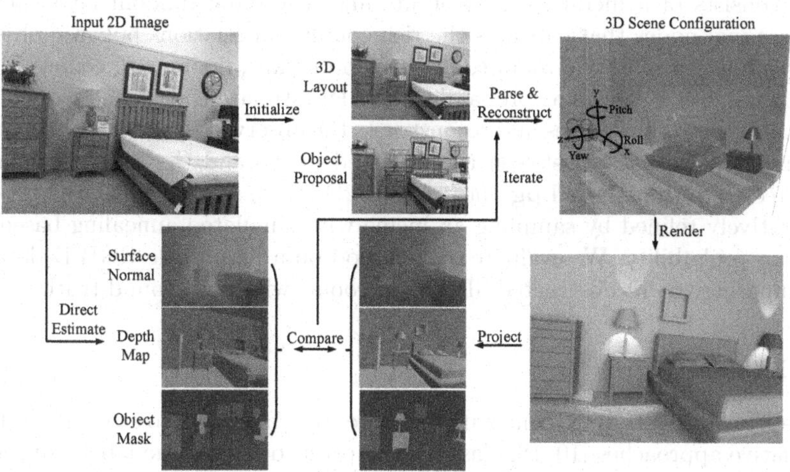

Fig. 1. Illustration of the proposed holistic 3D indoor scene parsing and reconstruction in an analysis-by synthesis fashion. A 3D representation is initialized by individual vision modules (*e.g.*, object detection, 2D layout estimation). A joint inference algorithm compares the differences between the rendered normal, depth, and segmentation map with the ones estimated directly from the input RGB image, and adjust the 3D structure iteratively.

In this paper, we embrace the concept of vision as inverse graphics, and propose a holistic 3D indoor scene parsing and reconstruction algorithm that simultaneously reconstructs the functional hierarchy and the 3D geometric structure of an indoor scene from a single RGB image. Figure 1 schematically illustrates the analysis-by-synthesis inference process. The joint inference algorithm takes proposals from various vision modules and infers the 3D structure by comparing various projections (*i.e.*, depth, normal, and segmentation) rendered from the recovered 3D structure with the ones directly estimated from an input image.

Specifically, we introduce a Holistic Scene Grammar (HSG) to represent the hierarchical structure of a scene. As illustrated in Fig. 2, our HSG decomposes a scene into latent groups in the *functional space* (*i.e.*, hierarchical structure including activity groups) and object instances in the *geometric space* (*i.e.*, CAD models). For the functional space, in contrast to the conventional method that only models the object-object relations, we propose a novel method to model human-object relations by imagining latent human in activity groups to further help explain and parse the observed image. For the geometric space, the geometric attributes (*e.g.*, size, position, orientation) of individual objects are taken into considerations, as well as the geometric relations (*e.g.*, supporting relation) among them. In addition, physical constraints (*e.g.*, collision among the objects, violations of the layout) are incorporated to generate a physically plausible 3D parsing and reconstruction of the observed image.

Here, an indoor scene is represented by a parse graph (**pg**) of a grammar, which consists of a hierarchical structure and a Markov random field (MRF) over terminal nodes that captures the rich contextual relations between objects and room layout (*i.e.*, the room configuration of walls, floors, and ceilings).

A maximum a posteriori probability (MAP) estimate is designed to find the optimal solution that parses and reconstructs the observed image. The likelihood measures the similarity between the observed image and the rendered images projected from the inferred **pg** onto various 2D image spaces. Thus, the **pg** can be iteratively refined by sampling an mcmc with simulated annealing based on posterior probability. We evaluate our method on a large-scale RGB-D dataset by comparing the reconstructed 3D indoor rooms with the ground-truth.

1.1 Related Work

Scene Parsing: Existing scene parsing approaches fall into two streams. (i) Discriminative approaches [10–16] classify each pixel to a semantic label. Although prior work has achieved high accuracy in labeling the pixels, these methods lack a general representation of visual vocabulary and a principle approach to exploring the semantic structure of a general scene. (ii) Generative approaches [17–24] can distill scene structure, making it closer to human-interpretable structure of a scene, enabling potential applications in robotics, VQA, *etc.* In this paper, we combine those two streams in an analysis-by-synthesis framework to infer the hidden factors that generate the image.

Scene Reconstruction from a Single Image: Previous approaches [25–27] of indoor scene reconstruction from a single RGB image can be categorized into three streams. (i) 2D or 3D room layout prediction by extracting geometric features and ranking the 3D cuboids proposals [28–35]. (ii) By representing objects via geometric primitives or CAD models, previous approaches [36–44] utilize 3D object recognition or pose estimation to align object proposals to a RGB or depth image. (iii) Joint estimation of the room layout and 3D objects with contexts [18,19,22–24,33,45,46]. In particular, Izadinia *et al.* [33] show promising results in inferring the layout and objects without the contextual relations and physical constraints. In contrast, our method jointly models the hierarchical scene structure, hidden human context and physical constraints, providing a semantic representation for holistic scene understanding. Furthermore, the proposed method presents a joint inference algorithm using MCMC, which in theory can achieve a global optimal.

Scene Grammar: Scene grammar models have been used to infer the 3D structure and functionality from a RGB image [3,17,18,47]. Our HSG differs from [17,18] in two aspects: (i) Our model represents the 3D objects with CAD models rather than geometric primitives, capable of modeling detail contextual relations (*e.g.*, supporting relation), which provides better realization of parsing and reconstruction. (ii) We infer hidden human and activity groups in the HSG, which helps the explanation and parsing. Compared to [3,47], we model and parse the 3D structure of objects and layouts from a single RGB image, rather than the labelled point-clouds using RGB-D images.

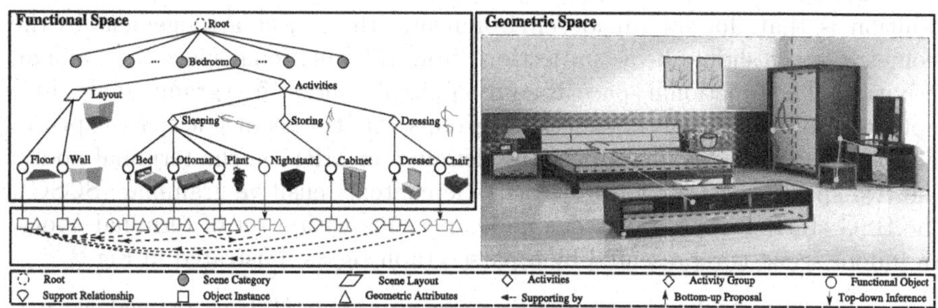

Fig. 2. An indoor scene represented by a parse graph (***pg***) of the HSG that spans across the functional space and the geometric space. The functional space characterizes the hierarchical structure and the geometric space encodes the spatial entities with contextual relations.

1.2 Contributions

This paper makes five major contributions:

1. We integrate geometry and physics to interpret and reconstruct indoor scenes with *CAD models*. We jointly optimize 3D room layouts and object configurations, largely improving the performance of scene parsing and reconstruction on SUN RGB-D dataset [45].
2. We incorporate hidden human context (*i.e.*, functionality) into our grammar, enabling to imagine *latent human pose* in each activity group by grouping and sampling. In this way, we can optimize the joint distribution of both visible and invisible [48] components of the scene.

3. We propose a complete computational framework to combine generative model (*i.e.*, a stochastic grammar), discriminative models (*i.e.*, direct estimations of depth, normal, and segmentation maps), and graphics engines (*i.e.*, rendered images) in scene parsing and reconstruction.
4. To the best of our knowledge, ours is the first work to use the inferred depth, surface normal and object segmentation map to assist parsing and reconstructing 3D scenes (both room layout and multiple objects). Note that [49] uses similar intermediate representation for a single object.
5. By learning the supporting relations among objects, the proposed method eliminates the widely adopted assumption in previous work that all objects must stand on the ground. Such flexibility of the model yields better parsing and reconstruction of the real-world scenes with complex object relations.

2 Holistic Scene Grammar

We represent the hierarchical structure of indoor scenes by a Holistic Scene Grammar (HSG). An HSG consists of a latent hierarchical structure in the functional space $\mathbb{F}$ and terminal object entities in the geometric space $\mathbb{G}$. The intuition is that, for man-made environments, the object arrangement in the geometric space should be a "projection" from the functional space (*i.e.*, human activities). The functional space as a probabilistic context free grammar (PCFG) captures the hierarchy of the functional groups, and the geometric space captures the spatial contexts among objects by defining an MRF on the terminal nodes. The two spaces together form a stochastic context-sensitive grammar (SCSG). The HSG starts from a root scene node and ends with a set of terminal nodes. An indoor scene is represented by a parse graph **pg** as illustrated in Fig. 2.

Definition: The stochastic context-sensitive grammar HSG is defined as a 5-tuple $\langle S, V, R, E, P \rangle$. S denotes the root node of the indoor scene. V is the vertex set that includes both non-terminal nodes $V_f \in \mathbb{F}$ and terminal nodes $V_g \in \mathbb{G}$. R denotes the production rule, and E the contextual relations among the terminal nodes, which are represented by the horizontal links in the **pg**. P is the probability model defined on the **pg**.

Functional Space $\mathbb{F}$*:* The non-terminal nodes $V_f = \{V_f^c, V_f^a, V_f^o, V_f^l\} \in \mathbb{F}$ consist of the scene category nodes V_f^c, activity group nodes V_f^a, objects nodes V_f^o, and layout nodes V_f^l.

Geometric Space $\mathbb{G}$*:* The terminal nodes $V_g = \{V_g^o, V_g^l\} \in \mathbb{G}$ are the CAD models of object entities and room layouts. Each object $v \in V_g^o$ is represented as a CAD model, and the object appearance is parameterized by its 3D size, location, and orientation. The room layout $v \in V_g^l$ is represented as a cuboid which is further decomposed into five planar surfaces of the room (left wall, right wall, middle wall, floor, and ceiling with respect to the camera coordinate).

Production Rule R: The following production rules are defined for HSG:

- $S \rightarrow V_f^c$: scene $\rightarrow$ category 1 | category 2 | ... (*e.g.*, scene $\rightarrow$ office | kitchen)

- $V_f^c \to V_f^a \cdot V_f^l$: category → activity groups · layout (*e.g.*, office → (walking, reading) · layout)
- $V_f^a \to V_f^o$: activity group → functional objects (*e.g.*, sitting → (desk, chair))

where · denotes the deterministic decomposition, | alternative explanations, and () combination. Contextual relations E capture relations among objects, including their relative positions, relative orientations, grouping relations, and supporting relations. The objects could be supported by either other objects or the room layout; *e.g.*, a lamp could be supported by a night stand or the floor.

Finally, a scene configuration is represented by a **pg**, whose terminals are room layouts and objects with their attributes and relations. As shown in Fig. 2, a **pg** can be decomposed as $\mathbf{pg} = (pg_f, pg_g)$, where pg_f and pg_g denote the functional part and geometric part of the **pg**, respectively. $E \in pg_g$ denotes the contextual relations in the terminal layer.

3 Probabilistic Formulation

The objective of the holistic scene parsing is to find an optimal **pg** that represents all the contents and relations observed in the scene. Given an input RGB image I, the optimal **pg** could be derived by an MAP estimator,

$$p(\mathbf{pg}|I) \propto p(\mathbf{pg}) \cdot p(I|\mathbf{pg}) \tag{1}$$

$$\propto p(pg_f) \cdot p(pg_g|pg_f) \cdot p(I|pg_g) \tag{2}$$

$$= \frac{1}{Z} \exp\left\{-\mathcal{E}(pg_f) - \mathcal{E}(pg_g|pg_f) - \mathcal{E}(I|pg_g)\right\}, \tag{3}$$

where the prior probability $p(\mathbf{pg})$ is decomposed into $p(pg_f)p(pg_g|pg_f)$, and $p(I|\mathbf{pg}) = p(I|pg_g)$ since the image space is independent of the functional space given the geometric space. We model the joint distribution with a Gibbs distribution; $\mathcal{E}(pg_f)$, $\mathcal{E}(pg_g|pg_f)$ and $\mathcal{E}(I|pg_g)$ are the corresponding energy terms.

Functional Prior $\mathcal{E}(pg_f)$ characterizes the prior of the functional aspect in a **pg**, which models the hierarchical structure and production rules in the functional space. For production rules of alternative explanations | and combination (), each rule selects child nodes and the probability of the selections is modeled with a multinomial distribution. The production rule · is deterministically expanded with probability 1. Given the production rules R, the energy can be written as $\mathcal{E}(pg_f) = \sum_{r_i \in R} - \log p(r_i)$.

Geometric Prior $\mathcal{E}(pg_g|pg_f)$ is the prior of the geometric aspect in a **pg**. Besides modeling the size, position and orientation distribution of each object, we also consider two types of contextual relations $E = \{E_s, E_a\}$ among the objects: (i) relations E_s between supported objects and their supporting objects; (ii) relations E_a between imagined human and objects in an activity group.

We define different potential functions for each type of contextual relations, constructing an MRF in the geometric space including four terms:

$$\mathcal{E}(pg_g|pg_f) = \mathcal{E}_{sc}(pg_g|pg_f) + \mathcal{E}_{spt}(pg_g|pg_f) + \mathcal{E}_{grp}(pg_g|pg_f) + \mathcal{E}_{phy}(pg_g). \tag{4}$$

- *Size Consistency* $\mathcal{E}_{sc}$ constrains the size of an object. $\mathcal{E}_{sc}(pg_g|pg_f) = \sum_{v_i \in V_g^o} -\log p(s_i|V_f^o)$, where s_i denotes the size of object v_i. We model the distribution of object scale in a non-parametric way, *i.e.*, kernel density estimation (KDE).
- *Supporting Constraint* $\mathcal{E}_{spt}$ characterizes the contextual relations between supported objects and supporting objects (including floors, walls and ceilings). We model the distribution with their relative heights and overlapping areas:

$$\mathcal{E}_{spt}(pg_g|pg_f) = \sum_{(v_i,v_j)\in E_s} \mathcal{K}_o(v_i, v_j) + \mathcal{K}_h(v_i, v_j) - \lambda_s \log p\left(v_i, v_j \mid V_f^l, V_f^o\right), \tag{5}$$

where $\mathcal{K}_o(v_i, v_j) = 1 - area(v_i \cup v_j)/area(v_i)$ defines the overlapping ratio in xy-plane, and $\mathcal{K}_h(v_i, v_j)$ defines the relative height between the lower surface of v_i and the upper surface of v_j. $\mathcal{K}_o(\cdot)$ and $\mathcal{K}_h(\cdot)$ is 0 if supporting object is floor and wall, respectively. $p(v_i, v_j|V_f^l, V_f^o)$ is the prior frequency of the supporting relation modeled by multinoulli distributions. λ_s is a balancing constant.
- *Human-Centric Grouping Constraint* $\mathcal{E}_{grp}$. For each activity group, we imagine the invisible and latent human poses to help parse and understand the scene. The intuition is that the indoor scenes are designed to serve human daily activities, thus the indoor images should be jointly interpreted by the observed entities and the unobservable human activities. This is known as the *Dark Matter* [48] in computer vision that drives the visible components in the scene. Prior methods on scene parsing often merely model the object-object relations. In this paper, we go beyond passive observations to model the latent human-object relations, thereby proposing a human-centric grouping relationship and a joint inference algorithm over both the visible scene and the invisible latent human context. Specifically, for each activity group $v \in V_f^a$, we define correspondent imagined human with a six tuple $< y, \mu, t, r, s, \tilde{\mu} >$, where y is the activity type, $\mu \in \mathbb{R}^{25\times 3}$ is the mean human pose (represented by 25 joints) of activity type y, t denotes the translation, r denotes the rotation, s denotes the scale, and $\tilde{\mu}$ is the imagined human skeleton: $\tilde{\mu} = \mu \cdot r \cdot s + t$. The energy among the imagined human and objects is defined as:

$$\begin{aligned} \mathcal{E}_{grp}(pg_g|pg_f) &= \sum_{v_i \in V_f^a} \mathcal{E}_{grp}(\tilde{\mu}_i|v_i) \\ &= \sum_{v_i \in V_f^a} \sum_{v_j \in ch(v_i)} \mathcal{D}_d(\tilde{\mu}_i, \nu_j; \bar{d}) + \mathcal{D}_h(\tilde{\mu}_i, \nu_j; \bar{h}) + \mathcal{D}_o(\tilde{\mu}_i, \nu_j; \bar{o}), \end{aligned} \tag{6}$$

where $ch(v_i)$ denotes the set of child nodes of v_i, ν_j denotes the 3D position of v_j. $\mathcal{D}_d(\cdot)$, $\mathcal{D}_h(\cdot)$ and $\mathcal{D}_o(\cdot)$ denote geometric distances, heights and orientation differences, respectively, calculated by the center of the imagined human pose to the object center subtracted by their mean (*i.e.*, $\bar{d}$, $\bar{h}$ and $\bar{o}$).
- *Physical Constraints:* Additionally, in order to avoid violating the physical laws during parsing, we define the physical constraints $\mathcal{E}_{phy}(pg_g)$ to penalize

physical violations. Exceeding the room cuboid or overlapping among the objects are defined as violations. This term is formulated as:

$$\mathcal{E}_{phy}(pg_g) = \sum\nolimits_{v_i \in V_g^o} (\sum\nolimits_{v_j \in V_g^o \setminus v_i} \mathcal{O}_o(v_i, v_j) + \sum\nolimits_{v_j \in V_g^l} \mathcal{O}_l(v_i, v_j)), \quad (7)$$

where $\mathcal{O}_o(\cdot)$ denotes the overlapping area between objects, and $\mathcal{O}_l(\cdot)$ denotes the area of objects exceeding the layout.

Likelihood $\mathcal{E}(I|pg_g)$ characterizes the similarity between the observed image and the rendered image generated by the parsing results. Due to various lighting conditions, textures, and material properties, there will be an inevitable difference between the rendered RGB images and the observed scenes. Here, instead of using RGB images, we solve this problem in an *analysis-by-synthesis* fashion by comparing the depth, surface normal, and object segmentation map.

By combining generative models and discriminative models, the proposed approach tries to reverse-engineer the hidden factors that generate the observed image. Specifically, we first use discriminative methods to project the observed image I to various feature spaces. In this paper, we directly estimate three intermediate images—depth map $\Phi_d(I)$, surface normal map $\Phi_n(I)$ and object segmentation map $\Phi_m(I)$, as the feature representation of the observed image I.

Meanwhile, a **pg** inferred by our method represents the 3D structure of the observed image, which is used to reconstruct image I' to recover the corresponding depth map $\Phi_d(I')$, surface normal map $\Phi_n(I')$, and object segmentation map $\Phi_m(I')$ through a forward graphics rendering.

Finally, we compute the likelihood term by comparing these rendered results from the generative model with the directly estimated results calculated by the discriminative models. Specifically, the likelihood is computed by the pixel-wise differences between the two sets of maps,

$$\mathcal{E}(I|pg_g) = \mathcal{D}_p(\Phi_d(I), \Phi_d(I')) + \mathcal{D}_p(\Phi_n(I), \Phi_n(I')) + \mathcal{D}_p(\Phi_m(I), \Phi_m(I')), \quad (8)$$

where $\mathcal{D}_p(\cdot)$ is the sum of pixel-wise Euclidean distances between two maps. Note a weight is associated with each energy term, which is learned by cross-validation or set empirically.

4 Inference

Given a single RGB image as the input, the goal of inference is to find the optimal **pg** that best explains the hidden factors that generate the observed image while recovering the 3D scene structure. The inference includes three major steps:

- *Room geometry estimation:* estimate the room geometry by predicting the 2D room layout and the camera parameter, and by projecting the estimated 2D layout to 3D. Details are provided in Subsect. 4.1.
- *Objects initialization:* detect objects and retrieve CAD models correspondingly with the most similar appearance, then roughly estimate their 3D poses, positions, sizes, and initialize the support relations. See Subsect. 4.2.

- *Joint inference:* optimize the objects, layout and hidden human context in the 3D scene in an analysis-by-synthesis fashion by maximizing the posterior probability of the **pg**. Details are provided in Subsect. 4.3.

4.1 Room Geometry Estimation

Although recent approaches [33–35] are capable of generating a relatively robust prediction of the 2D room layout using CNN features, 3D room layout estimations are still inaccurate due to its sensitivity to camera parameter estimation in clusttered scenes. To address the inconsistency between the 2D layout estimation and camera parameter estimation, we design a deep neural network to estimate the 2D layout, and use the layout heatmap to estimate the camera parameter.

2D Layout Estimation: Similar to [34], we represent the 2D layout with its room layout type and keypoint positions. The network structure is provided in the *supplementary material*. The network optimizes the Euclidean loss for layout heatmap regression and the cross-entropy loss for room type estimation.

Camera Parameter: Traditional geometry-based method [28] computes the camera parameter by estimating the vanishing points from the observed image, which is sensitive and unstable in cluttered indoor scenes with heavy occlusions. Inspired by [43], we propose a learning-based method that uses the keypoints heatmaps to predict the camera parameters, *i.e.*, focal length, together with the yaw, pitch, and roll angles of the camera. Since the yaw angle has already been incorporated into the evaluation of room layout, we estimate the remaining three variables (focal length, pitch and roll) by stacking four FC layers (1024-128-16-3) on the keypoint heatmaps.

3D Layout Initialization: Using the estimated 2D layout and camera parameters, we project the corners of the 2D layout to 3D in order to obtain a 3D room cuboid. We assume the cameras and the ceilings are $1.2m$ and $3.0m$ high, respectively. For simplicity, we translate and rotate the 3D rooms so that one of the visible room corners is at the origin of the world coordinate system.

4.2 Objects Initialization

We fine-tune the Deformable Convolutional Networks [50] using Soft-NMS [51] to detect 2D bounding boxes. To initialize the 3D objects, we retrieve the most similar CAD models and initialize their 3D poses, sizes, and positions.

Model Retrieval: We consider all the models in the ShapeNetSem repository [52,53] and render each model from 48 viewpoints consisting of uniformly sampled 16 azimuth and 3 elevation angles. We extract 7×7 features from the ROI-pooling layer of the fine-tuned detector of images in the detected bounding boxes and candidate rendered images. By ranking the cosine distance between each detected object feature and rendered image feature in the same object category, we obtain the top-10 CAD models with corresponding poses.

Geometric Attributes Estimation: The geometric attributes of an object are represented by a 9D vector of 3D pose, position, and size, where 3D poses are initialized from the retrieval procedure. Prior work roughly projected 2D points to 3D, and recovered the 3D position and size by assuming that all the objects are on the floor. Such approach shows limitations in complex scenarios.

Without making the above assumption, we estimate the depth of each object by computing the average depth value of the pixels that are in both the detection bounding box and the segmentation map. We then compute its 3D position using the depth value. Empirically, this approach is more robust since per-pixel depth estimation error is small even in cluttered scenes. To avoid the alignment problem of the 2D bounding boxes, we initialize the object size by sampling object sizes from a learned distribution and choose the one with the largest probability.

Supporting Relation Estimation: For each object $v_i \in V_f^o$, we find its supporting object v_j^* of minimal supporting energy from objects or layout:

$$v_j^* = \arg\min_{v_j} \mathcal{K}_o(v_i, v_j) + \mathcal{K}_h(v_i, v_j) - \lambda_s \log p(v_i, v_j | V_f^l, V_f^o), \quad v_j \in (V_f^l, V_f^o). \quad (9)$$

4.3 Joint Inference

Given an image I, we first estimate the room geometry, object attributes and relations as described in the above two subsections. As summarized in Algorithm 1, the joint inference includes: (1) optimize the objects and layout (Fig. 3); (2) group objects, assign activity label and imagine human pose in each activity group; and (3) optimize the objects, layout and human pose iteratively.

In each step, we use distinct MCMC processes. Specifically, to traverse non-differentiable solution spaces, we design Markov chain dynamics $\{q_1^o, q_2^o, q_3^o\}$ for objects, $\{q_1^l, q_2^l\}$ for layout, and $\{q_1^h, q_2^h, q_3^h\}$ for human pose. Specifically,

- *Object Dynamics:* Dynamics q_1^o adjusts the position of a random object, which translates the object center in one of the three Cartesian coordinate axes. Instead of translating the object center and changing the object size

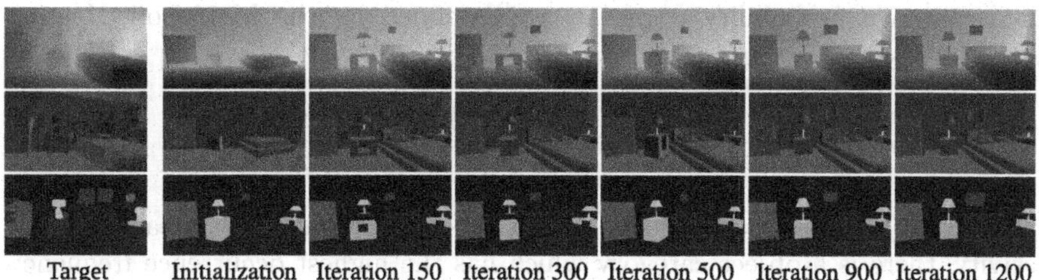

Fig. 3. The process of joint inference of objects and layout by MCMC with simulated annealing. **Top:** depth maps. **Middle:** normal maps. **Bottom:** object segmentation maps. Objects and layout are optimized iteratively.

Algorithm 1. Joint inference algorithm

Given Image I, initialized parse graph $\mathbf{pg}_{\text{init}}$
procedure STEP1(V_g^o, V_g^l) ▷ Inference without hidden human context
  for different temperatures **do** ▷ Different temperatures are adopted in simulated annealing
    for γ_1 iterations **do**
      randomly choose layout, apply layout dynamics to optimize layout V_g^l
    for each object $v_i \in V_g^o$ **do**
      for γ_2 iterations **do**
        randomly apply object dynamics to optimize object v_i
procedure STEP2($V_f^a, \{\tilde{\mu}\}$) ▷ Inference of hidden human context
  group objects and assign activity labels (see last paragraph in subsection 4.3)
  for each activity group $v_i \in V_f^a$ **do**
    repeat
      randomly apply human pose dynamics to optimize $\tilde{\mu}_i$
    until $\mathcal{E}(\tilde{\mu}_i|v_i)$ converges ▷ Maximizing grouping energy in Equation 11
procedure STEP3($V_g^o, V_g^l, \{\tilde{\mu}\}$) ▷ Iterative inference of whole parse graph
  for different temperatures **do**
    for γ_3 iterations **do**
      randomly choose layout, objects or human pose
      apply random dynamics to minimize $P(\mathbf{pg}|I)$
Return $\mathbf{pg}_{\text{optimized}}$

directly, Dynamics q_2^o translates one of the six faces of the cuboid to generate a smoother diffusion. Dynamics q_3^o proposes rotation of the object with a specified angle. Each dynamic can diffuse in two directions, *e.g.*, each object can translate in direction of '$+x$' and '$-x$', or rotate in direction of clockwise and counterclockwise. By computing the local gradient of $P(\mathbf{pg}|I)$, the dynamics propose to move following the direction of the gradient with a proposal probability of 0.8, or the inverse direction of the gradient with proposal probability of 0.2.

- *Layout Dynamics:* Dynamics q_1^l translates the faces of the layout, which also optimizes the camera height when translating the floor. Dynamics q_2^l rotates the layout.
- *Human pose Dynamics:* q_1^h, q_2^h and q_3^h are designed to translate, rotate and scale the human pose, respectively.

Given the current $\mathbf{pg}$, each dynamic will propose a new $\mathbf{pg}'$ according to a proposal probability $p(\mathbf{pg}'|\mathbf{pg}, I)$. The proposal is accepted according to an acceptance probability $\alpha(\mathbf{pg} \rightarrow \mathbf{pg}')$ defined by the Metropolis-Hasting algorithm [54]:

$$\alpha(\mathbf{pg} \rightarrow \mathbf{pg}') = \min\left(1, \frac{p(\mathbf{pg}|\mathbf{pg}', I)p(\mathbf{pg}'|I)}{p(\mathbf{pg}'|\mathbf{pg}, I)p(\mathbf{pg}|I)}\right). \tag{10}$$

In step (2), we group objects and assign activity labels. For each type of activity, there is a object category which has the highest occurrence frequency (*i.e.*, chair in activity 'reading'). Intuitively, the correspondence between objects and activities should be n-to-n but not n-to-one, which means each object can belong to several activity groups. In order to find out all possible activity groups, for each type of activity, we define an activity group around each major object

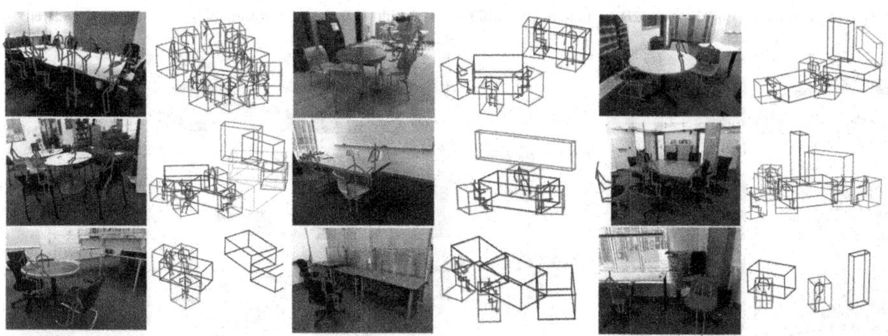

Fig. 4. Sampled human poses in various indoor scenes. Objects in multiple activity groups have multiple poses. We visualize the pose with the highest likelihood.

and incorporate nearby objects (within a distance threshold) with prior larger than 0. For each activity group $v_i \in V_f^a$, the pose of the imagined human is estimated by maximizing the likelihood $p(v_i|\tilde{\mu}_i)$, which is equivalent to minimize the grouping energy $\mathcal{E}_{grp}(\tilde{\mu}_i|v_i)$ defined in Eq. 6,

$$y_i^*, m_i^*, t_i^*, r_i^*, s_i^* = \underset{y_i, m_i, t_i, r_i, s_i}{\arg\min} \; \mathcal{E}_{grp}(\tilde{\mu}_i|v_i), \tag{11}$$

Figure 4 shows the results of sampled human poses in various indoor scenes.

5 Experiments

We use the SUN RGB-D dataset [45] to evaluate our approach on 3D scene parsing, 3D reconstruction, as well as other 3D scene understanding tasks. The dataset has 5050 testing images and 10,355 images in total. Although it provides RGB-D data, we only use the RGB images as the input for training and testing. Figure 5 shows some qualitative parsing results (top 20%).

We evaluate our method on three tasks: (i) 3D layout estimation, (ii) 3D object detection, and (iii) holistic scene understanding with all the 5050 testing images of SUN RGB-D across all scene categories. The capability of generalization to all the scene categories is difficult for most of the conventional methods due to the inaccuracy of camera parameter estimation and severe sensitivity to the occlusions in cluttered scenes. In this paper, we alleviate it by using the proposed learning-based camera parameter estimation and a novel method to initialize the geometric attributes. In addition, we also achieve the state-of-the-art results in 2D layout estimation on LSUN dataset [55] and Hedau dataset [28]. The implementation details, and additional results of camera parameter estimation and 2D layout estimation are summarized in the *supplementary material.*

3D Layout Estimation: The 3D room layout is optimized using the proposed joint inference. We compare the estimation by our method (with and without joint inference) with 3DGP [19]. Following the evaluation protocol defined

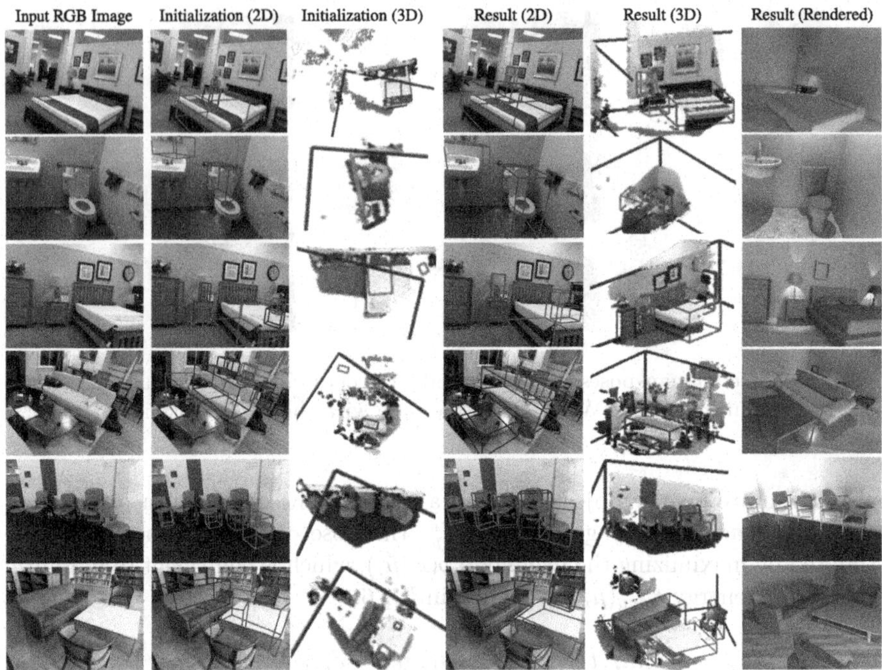

Fig. 5. Qualitative results of the proposed method on SUN RGB-D dataset. The joint inference significantly improves the performance over individual modules.

in [45], we calculate the average Intersection over Union (IoU) between the free space from the ground truth and the free space estimated by our method. Table 1 shows our method outperforms 3DGP by a large margin. We also improve the performance by 8.2% after jointly inferring the objects and layout, demonstrating the usefulness of integrating the joint inference process.

Table 1. 3D scene parsing and reconstruction results on SUN RGB-D dataset

Method	# of image	3D layout estimation	Holistic scene understanding			
		IoU	P_g	R_g	R_r	IoU
3DGP [19]	5050	19.2	2.1	0.7	0.6	13.9
Ours (init.)	5050	46.7	25.9	15.5	12.2	36.6
Ours (joint.)	5050	**54.9**	**37.7**	**23.0**	**18.3**	**40.7**
3DGP [19]	749	33.4	5.3	2.7	2.1	34.2
IM2CAD [33]	484	62.6	-	-	-	49.0
Ours (init.)	749	61.2	29.7	17.3	14.4	47.1
Ours (joint.)	749	**66.4**	**40.5**	**26.8**	**21.7**	**52.1**

Since IM2CAD [33] manually selected 484 images from living rooms and bedrooms without releasing the image list, we compare our method with them on the entire set of living rooms and bedrooms. Table 1 shows our method surpasses IM2CAD, especially after incorporating the joint inference process.

Table 2. Comparisons of 3D object detection on SUN RGB-D dataset

Method	Bed	Chair	Sofa	Table	Desk	Toilet	Fridge	Sink	Bathtub	Bookshelf	Counter	Door	Dresser	Lamp	TV	mAP
[19]	5.62	2.31	3.24	1.23	-	-	-	-	-	-	-	-	-	-	-	-
Ours (init.)	45.55	5.91	23.64	4.20	2.50	1.91	14.00	2.12	0.55	2.16	0.34	0.01	5.69	1.12	0.62	7.35
Ours (joint.)	**58.29**	**13.56**	**28.37**	**12.12**	**4.79**	**16.50**	**15.18**	**2.18**	**2.84**	**7.04**	**1.6**	**1.56**	**13.71**	**2.41**	**1.04**	**12.07**

3D Object Detection: We evaluate our 3D object detection results using the metrics defined in [45]. We compute the mean average precision (mAP) using the 3D IoU between the predicted and ground truth 3D bounding boxes. In the absence of depth, we adjust threshold IoU from 0.25 (evaluation setting with depth as the input) to 0.15 and report our results in Table 2. 15 out of 30 object categories are reported here due to the limited space; full table is reported in the *supplementary material*. The results indicate our method not only exceeds the detection score by a significant margin but also makes it possible to evaluate the entire object categories. Note that although IM2CAD also evaluates the detection, they use the metric related to a specified distance threshold. Here, we also compare with IM2CAD on the subset with this special metric rather than IoU threshold. We are able to obtain an mAP of 80.2%, higher than an mAP of 74.6% reported in the IM2CAD.

Holistic Scene Understanding: We estimate the detailed 3D scene including both objects and room layout. Using the metrics proposed in [45], we evaluate the geometric precision P_g, geometric recall R_g, and semantic recall R_r with the IoU threshold set to 0.15. We also evaluate the IoU of the free space (3D voxels inside the room polygon but outside any object bounding box) between the ground truth and the estimation. Table 1 shows that the proposed method demonstrates a significant improvement. Moreover, we improve the initialization result by 12.2% on geometric precision, 7.5% on geometric recall, 6.1% on semantic recall, and 4.1% on free space estimation. The improvement of total scene understanding indicates that the joint inference can largely improve the performance of each task. Using the same setting with 3D layout estimation, we compare with IM2CAD [33] and improve the free space IoU by 3.1%.

Ablative Analysis: The proposed HSG incorporates several key components including supporting relations, physics constraints and latent human contextual relations. To analyze how each component would influence the final results, as well as how much the joint inference process would benefit each task, we conduct the ablative analysis on holistic scene understanding under different settings,

Table 3. Ablative analysis of our method on SUN RGB-D dataset. We evaluate on holistic scene understanding under different settings. We denote support relation as C_1, physical constraint as C_2 and human imagination as C_3. Similarly, we denote the setting of only optimizing the layout during inference as S_4, only optimizing the objects during inference as S_5

Setting	w/o C_1	w/o C_2	w/o C_3	w/o (C_1, C_2, C_3)	S_4	S_5	All
IoU	42.3	41.3	43.8	38.4	39.4	36.3	**44.7**
P_g	29.3	23.5	32.1	19.4	14.9	28.4	**34.4**
R_g	17.4	15.6	20.4	12.4	11.2	19.7	**24.1**
R_r	14.1	10.5	16.5	8.7	8.6	13.3	**19.2**

through turning on and off certain components or skipping certain steps during joint inference. The experiments are tested on the subset of offices where we incorporate the latent human context. Table 3 summarizes the results. Among all the energy terms we incorporate, physical constraints influence the performance the most, which demonstrates the importance of the physical common sense during inference. It also reflects the efficiency of joint inference as the performances would drop by a large margin without the iterative joint inference.

6 Conclusion

We present an analysis-by-synthesis framework to recover the 3D structure of an indoor scene from a single RGB image using a stochastic grammar model integrated with latent human context, geometry and physics. We demonstrate the effectiveness of our algorithm from three perspectives: (i) the joint inference algorithm significantly improves results in various individual tasks and (ii) outperforms other methods; (iii) ablative analysis shows each of module plays an important role in the whole framework. In general, we believe this will be a step towards a unifying framework for the holistic 3D scene understanding.

Acknowledgments. We thank Professor Ying Nian Wu from UCLA Statistics Department for helpful discussions. This work is supported by DARPA XAI N66001-17-2-4029, MURI ONR N00014-16-1-2007, SPAWAR N66001-17-2-3602, and ARO W911NF-18-1-0296.

References

1. Soatto, S.: Actionable information in vision. In: Cipolla, R., Battiato, S., Farinella, G. (eds.) Machine Learning for Computer Vision. SCI, vol. 411. Springer, Heidelberg (2013). https://doi.org/10.1007/978-3-642-28661-2_2
2. Qi, S., Zhu, Y., Huang, S., Jiang, C., Zhu, S.C.: Human-centric indoor scene synthesis using stochastic grammar. In: CVPR (2018)
3. Jiang, Y., Koppula, H., Saxena, A.: Hallucinated humans as the hidden context for labeling 3D scenes. In: CVPR (2013)

4. Gupta, A., Efros, A.A., Hebert, M.: Blocks world revisited: image understanding using qualitative geometry and mechanics. In: Daniilidis, K., Maragos, P., Paragios, N. (eds.) ECCV 2010. LNCS, vol. 6314, pp. 482–496. Springer, Heidelberg (2010). https://doi.org/10.1007/978-3-642-15561-1_35
5. Liu, X., Zhao, Y., Zhu, S.C.: Single-view 3D scene parsing by attributed grammar. In: CVPR (2014)
6. Zheng, B., Zhao, Y., Joey, C.Y., Ikeuchi, K., Zhu, S.C.: Detecting potential falling objects by inferring human action and natural disturbance. In: IEEE International Conference on Robotics and Automation (ICRA) (2014)
7. Yuille, A., Kersten, D.: Vision as Bayesian inference: analysis by synthesis? Trends Cogn. Sci. **10**, 301–308 (2006)
8. Grenander, U.: Lectures in Pattern Theory I, II and III: Pattern Analysis, Pattern Synthesis and Regular Structures. Springer, New York (1976)
9. Loper, M.M., Black, M.J.: OpenDR: an approximate differentiable renderer. In: Fleet, D., Pajdla, T., Schiele, B., Tuytelaars, T. (eds.) ECCV 2014. LNCS, vol. 8695, pp. 154–169. Springer, Cham (2014). https://doi.org/10.1007/978-3-319-10584-0_11
10. Dai, J., He, K., Sun, J.: BoxSup: exploiting bounding boxes to supervise convolutional networks for semantic segmentation. In: ICCV (2015)
11. Zheng, S., et al.: Conditional random fields as recurrent neural networks. In: ICCV (2015)
12. Noh, H., Hong, S., Han, B.: Learning deconvolution network for semantic segmentation. In: ICCV (2015)
13. Chen, L.C., Papandreou, G., Kokkinos, I., Murphy, K., Yuille, A.L.: Deeplab: semantic image segmentation with deep convolutional nets, atrous convolution, and fully connected CRFs. IEEE Trans. Pattern Anal. Mach. Intell. (TPAMI) **40**, 834–848 (2017)
14. Long, J., Shelhamer, E., Darrell, T.: Fully convolutional networks for semantic segmentation. In: CVPR (2015)
15. Lin, G., Milan, A., Shen, C., Reid, I.: RefineNet: multi-path refinement networks for high-resolution semantic segmentation. In: CVPR (2017)
16. Zhao, H., Shi, J., Qi, X., Wang, X., Jia, J.: Pyramid scene parsing network. In: CVPR (2017)
17. Zhao, Y., Zhu, S.C.: Image parsing with stochastic scene grammar. In: Conference on Neural Information Processing Systems (NIPS) (2011)
18. Zhao, Y., Zhu, S.C.: Scene parsing by integrating function, geometry and appearance models. In: CVPR (2013)
19. Choi, W., Chao, Y.W., Pantofaru, C., Savarese, S.: Understanding indoor scenes using 3D geometric phrases. In: CVPR (2013)
20. Lin, D., Fidler, S., Urtasun, R.: Holistic scene understanding for 3D object detection with RGBD cameras. In: ICCV (2013)
21. Guo, R., Hoiem, D.: Support surface prediction in indoor scenes. In: ICCV (2013)
22. Zhang, Y., Song, S., Tan, P., Xiao, J.: PanoContext: a whole-room 3D context model for panoramic scene understanding. In: Fleet, D., Pajdla, T., Schiele, B., Tuytelaars, T. (eds.) ECCV 2014. LNCS, vol. 8694, pp. 668–686. Springer, Cham (2014). https://doi.org/10.1007/978-3-319-10599-4_43
23. Zhang, Y., et al.: Physically-based rendering for indoor scene understanding using convolutional neural networks. In: CVPR (2017)
24. Zou, C., Li, Z., Hoiem, D.: Complete 3D scene parsing from single RGBD image. arXiv preprint arXiv:1710.09490 (2017)

25. Hoiem, D., Efros, A.A., Hebert, M.: Automatic photo pop-up. ACM Trans. Graph. (TOG) **24**, 577–584 (2005)
26. Han, F., Zhu, S.C.: Bottom-up/top-down image parsing by attribute graph grammar. In: ICCV (2005)
27. Saxena, A., Chung, S.H., Ng, A.Y.: Learning depth from single monocular images. In: Conference on Neural Information Processing Systems (NIPS) (2006)
28. Hedau, V., Hoiem, D., Forsyth, D.: Recovering the spatial layout of cluttered rooms. In: CVPR (2009)
29. Lee, D.C., Hebert, M., Kanade, T.: Geometric reasoning for single image structure recovery. In: CVPR (2009)
30. Mallya, A., Lazebnik, S.: Learning informative edge maps for indoor scene layout prediction. In: ICCV (2015)
31. Dasgupta, S., Fang, K., Chen, K., Savarese, S.: Delay: robust spatial layout estimation for cluttered indoor scenes. In: CVPR (2016)
32. Ren, Y., Li, S., Chen, C., Kuo, C.-C.J.: A coarse-to-fine indoor layout estimation (CFILE) method. In: Lai, S.-H., Lepetit, V., Nishino, K., Sato, Y. (eds.) ACCV 2016. LNCS, vol. 10115, pp. 36–51. Springer, Cham (2017). https://doi.org/10.1007/978-3-319-54193-8_3
33. Izadinia, H., Shan, Q., Seitz, S.M.: IM2CAD. In: CVPR (2017)
34. Lee, C.Y., Badrinarayanan, V., Malisiewicz, T., Rabinovich, A.: RoomNet: end-to-end room layout estimation. In: ICCV (2017)
35. Zhao, H., Lu, M., Yao, A., Guo, Y., Chen, Y., Zhang, L.: Physics inspired optimization on semantic transfer features: an alternative method for room layout estimation. In: CVPR (2017)
36. Salas-Moreno, R.F., Newcombe, R.A., Strasdat, H., Kelly, P.H., Davison, A.J.: SLAM++: simultaneous localisation and mapping at the level of objects. In: CVPR (2013)
37. Aubry, M., Maturana, D., Efros, A.A., Russell, B.C., Sivic, J.: Seeing 3D chairs: exemplar part-based 2D–3D alignment using a large dataset of cad models. In: CVPR (2014)
38. Lim, J.J., Khosla, A., Torralba, A.: FPM: fine pose parts-based model with 3D CAD models. In: Fleet, D., Pajdla, T., Schiele, B., Tuytelaars, T. (eds.) ECCV 2014. LNCS, vol. 8694, pp. 478–493. Springer, Cham (2014). https://doi.org/10.1007/978-3-319-10599-4_31
39. Song, S., Xiao, J.: Sliding shapes for 3D object detection in depth images. In: Fleet, D., Pajdla, T., Schiele, B., Tuytelaars, T. (eds.) ECCV 2014. LNCS, vol. 8694, pp. 634–651. Springer, Cham (2014). https://doi.org/10.1007/978-3-319-10599-4_41
40. Tulsiani, S., Malik, J.: Viewpoints and keypoints. In: CVPR (2015)
41. Bansal, A., Russell, B., Gupta, A.: Marr revisited: 2D–3D alignment via surface normal prediction. In: CVPR (2016)
42. Song, S., Xiao, J.: Deep sliding shapes for Amodal 3D object detection in RGB-D images. In: CVPR (2016)
43. J, W., et al.: Single image 3D interpreter network. In: Leibe, B., Matas, J., Sebe, N., Welling, M. (eds.) ECCV 2016. LNCS, vol. 9910, pp. 365–382. Springer, Cham (2016). https://doi.org/10.1007/978-3-319-46466-4_22
44. Deng, Z., Latecki, L.J.: Amodal detection of 3D objects: inferring 3D bounding boxes from 2D ones in RGB-depth images. In: CVPR (2017)
45. Song, S., Lichtenberg, S.P., Xiao, J.: Sun RGB-D: a RGB-D scene understanding benchmark suite. In: CVPR (2015)
46. Song, S., Yu, F., Zeng, A., Chang, A.X., Savva, M., Funkhouser, T.: Semantic scene completion from a single depth image. In: CVPR (2017)

47. Jiang, Y., Saxena, A.: Modeling high-dimensional humans for activity anticipation using Gaussian process latent CRFs. In: Robotics: Science and Systems (RSS) (2014)
48. Xie, D., Todorovic, S., Zhu, S.C.: Inferring "dark matter" and "dark energy" from videos. In: ICCV (2013)
49. Wu, J., Wang, Y., Xue, T., Sun, X., Freeman, W.T., Tenenbaum, J.B.: MarrNet: 3D shape reconstruction via 2.5D sketches. In: Conference on Neural Information Processing Systems (NIPS) (2017)
50. Dai, J., Qi, H., Xiong, Y., Li, Y., Zhang, G., Hu, H., Wei, Y.: Deformable convolutional networks. In: ICCV (2017)
51. Bodla, N., Singh, B., Chellappa, R., Davis, L.S.: Soft-NMS - improving object detection with one line of code. In: ICCV (2017)
52. Chang, A.X., et al.: ShapeNet: an information-rich 3D model repository. arXiv preprint arXiv:1512.03012 (2015)
53. Savva, M., Chang, A.X., Hanrahan, P.: Semantically-enriched 3D models for common-sense knowledge. In: CVPR Workshop (2015)
54. Hastings, W.K.: Monte Carlo sampling methods using Markov chains and their applications. Biometrika **57**, 97–109 (1970)
55. Zhang, Y., Yu, F., Song, S., Xu, P., Seff, A., Xiao, J.: Large-scale scene understanding challenge: room layout estimation. In: CVPR Workshop (2015)

Escaping from Collapsing Modes in a Constrained Space

Chia-Che Chang[1], Chieh Hubert Lin[1], Che-Rung Lee[1], Da-Cheng Juan[2], Wei Wei[2], and Hwann-Tzong Chen[1(✉)]

[1] Department of Computer Science, National Tsing Hua University, Hsinchu, Taiwan
chang810249@gmail.com, hubert052702@gmail.com, cherung@gmail.com, htchen@cs.nthu.edu.tw

[2] Google AI, Mountain View, CA, USA
dacheng@google.com, wewei@google.com

Abstract. Generative adversarial networks (GANs) often suffer from unpredictable mode-collapsing during training. We study the issue of mode collapse of Boundary Equilibrium Generative Adversarial Network (BEGAN), which is one of the state-of-the-art generative models. Despite its potential of generating high-quality images, we find that BEGAN tends to collapse at some modes after a period of training. We propose a new model, called *BEGAN with a Constrained Space* (BEGAN-CS), which includes a latent-space constraint in the loss function. We show that BEGAN-CS can significantly improve training stability and suppress mode collapse without either increasing the model complexity or degrading the image quality. Further, we visualize the distribution of latent vectors to elucidate the effect of latent-space constraint. The experimental results show that our method has additional advantages of being able to train on small datasets and to generate images similar to a given real image yet with variations of designated attributes on-the-fly.

1 Introduction

The main goal of this paper is to provide new insights into the problem of mode collapse in training Generative Adversarial Networks (GANs) [9]. GANs have shown great potential in generating new data based on real samples and have been applied to various vision tasks [4,6,10,19,20,26,27,29]. Our study points out a simple but effective approach that can be used to improve the stability of training GANs for generating high-quality images with respect to disentangled representations.

GANs comprise two core components: generator G and discriminator D. The two components are optimized with respect to two spaces. One is the latent

C.-C. Chang and C.H. Lin—Equal contribution.

Electronic supplementary material The online version of this chapter (https://doi.org/10.1007/978-3-030-01234-2_13) contains supplementary material, which is available to authorized users.

V. Ferrari et al. (Eds.): ECCV 2018, LNCS 11211, pp. 212–227, 2018.
https://doi.org/10.1007/978-3-030-01234-2_13

space Z for the generator, and the other is the data space X associated with a real data distribution $p_{\text{real}}(x)$ for training data $x \in X$. The objective of the generator is to find a mapping $G : Z \rightarrow X$ that maximizes the probability of the discriminator mistakenly accepting a generated image $G(z), z \in Z$ as from $p_{\text{real}}(x)$. On the contrary, the discriminator's objective is to distinguish whether any given $x \in X$ belongs to $p_{\text{real}}(x)$. During training, the generator only learns from the information provided by the discriminator, and aims to estimate a good mapping such that $p_{\text{model}}(G(z))$ is similar to $p_{\text{real}}(x)$.

Compared with auto-encoders [13], GANs can generate sharper images owing to the adversarial loss. However, a downside of adopting the adversarial loss is that it makes the training of GANs unstable. The performance is strongly dependent on hyper-parameters selection, and the generated images tend to have weaker structural coherence.

Boundary Equilibrium Generative Adversarial Network (BEGAN) [3] introduced by Berthelot *et al.* suggests several modifications on the architecture and loss designs, which significantly improve the quality of generated images and the training stability. Another contribution of BEGAN is providing an approximation of convergence for the class of energy-based GANs.

Despite the promising improvements of BEGAN, we empirically observe that BEGAN still unavoidably runs into mode collapses after certain epochs of training. In the meanwhile, neither the approximation of convergence nor the loss functions of BEGAN is able to detect the sudden mode collapses. In our experiments, the exact time when mode collapsing happens is highly related to target image resolution and dataset size. In addition to the typical drawbacks of mode collapsing, this unpredictable behavior also makes BEGAN's intended contribution to providing "global measure of convergence" incomplete.

1.1 Contributions

We propose a new constraint loss toward addressing the mode collapsing problem. We find that the mode-collapsing problem is suppressed after adding the constraint loss. This new loss term does not increase model complexity and is computationally low-cost. Furthermore, it does not introduce any trade-off regarding image quality and diversity. The proposed model is called *BEGAN with a Constrained Space* (BEGAN-CS).

We visualize the latent vectors produced in training phase using Principal Component Analysis (PCA) [1]. In Sect. 3.1, we analyze the effect of the constraint loss and explain why this loss term makes training process stable.

Since BEGAN-CS is more stable during training, it performs consistently well even when the size of training dataset is ten-times smaller than the normal setting, in which BEGAN fails to obtain acceptable results. In Sect. 4.3, our experiment shows that the proposed BEGAN-CS can eventually converge to a better state, while BEGAN ends up at mode collapsing in an early stage.

We further discover that BEGAN is able to learn strong and high-quality disentangled representations in an unsupervised setting. The learned disentangled representations could be used to modify the underlying attributes of generated images. In the meanwhile, owing to the constraint loss, BEGAN-CS can accomplish approximation $Enc(x^*) \simeq z^*$ on-the-fly for any given real image x^*, where $G(z^*)$ is an approximate image to x^* under the fixed generator weights. By leveraging the z^* approximation and the disentangled representations, BEGAN-CS can generate on the fly a set of images conditioning on a real image x^*. The generated images are visually similar to the given real image and are able to exhibit the adjustable disentangled attributes.

2 Related Work

Deep Convolutional Generative Adversarial Network (DCGAN) [24] improves the original GAN [9] by employing a convolutional architecture to achieve better stability of training and enhanced quality of generated images. Salimans *et al.* further present several practical techniques for training GANs [25]. Nevertheless, avoiding mode collapsing while keeping the quality of generated images is still a challenging issue in practice.

Energy-Based Generative Adversarial Network (EBGAN) [30] introduces another perspective for formulating GANs. EBGAN implements the discriminator as an auto-encoder with per-pixel error. Boundary Equilibrium Generative Adversarial Network (BEGAN) [3] shares the same discriminator setting as EBGAN and makes several improvements on the designs of architecture and loss function. One of BEGAN's core contributions is introducing the equilibrium concept, which balances the power between the generator and the discriminator. With these improvements, BEGAN provides fast and stable training convergence, and is capable of generating high visual-quality images. Another contribution of BEGAN is providing an approximate measure of convergence. The earlier class of GANs lacks convergence measurement. Not until later, a new class of GANs exemplified by Wasserstein Generative Adversarial Network (WGAN) [2] introduces a new loss metric, which correlates with the generator's convergence. To our knowledge, BEGAN yields an alternative class of GANs that also has a loss correlated with convergence measurement.

Apart from the class of energy-based GANs, Progressive Growing of Generative Adversarial Networks (PGGANs) [14] is another approach to generating high-quality images. By changing the training procedure without modifying the original GAN loss, PGGANs are able to increase training stability and to produce diverse yet high-resolution (up to 1024 × 1024 pixels) images.

The z^* approximation property of BEGAN-CS is similar to another class of bijective GANs, which constructs a bijection between the latent space Z and the data space X. This class of models includes ALI [8], BiGAN [7], VEEGAN [28] and [15]. These four methods share a similar characteristic, requiring additional effort to optimize an extended network. VEEGAN introduces an extra reconstructor network F_θ, which maps real data distribution $p(x)$ to a Gaussian. ALI/BiGAN both introduce an additional encoder network in the generator, and try to build up a bijection function. For [15], the loss term L_s (Eq. (9) in [15]) has a pre-requirement that the generator must include the real images in its latent space. They introduce an extra encoder network in generator to fulfill this requirement.

In comparison, BEGAN-CS introduces a light-weight loss that utilizes the built-in mechanism of BEGAN without a need of extra networks. This makes the latent space inverting function jointly optimizable with the discriminator. Also, the constraint loss is a very strong indicator, detecting and protecting the model from mode collapsing. We also include further experimental comparisons with the class of bijective GANs in Sect. 4.6.

3 Methods

Mode collapse is a phenomenon that the generated images get stuck in or oscillate between a few modes. This phenomenon under BEGAN's setting has a unique characteristic. Since every sample shares the same encoder in the discriminator of BEGAN, the generated images that collapse at the same mode will share similar latent vectors as encoded by the encoder.

By leveraging this property, we propose the *latent-space constraint loss* ($\mathcal{L}_c$), or the *constraint loss* for short. It constrains the norm of the difference between the latent vector z and the internal state of encoder $Enc(G(z))$, where Enc is the encoder within the discriminator. During the training process, the constraint loss is only optimized with respect to the discriminator. Although the mode-collapsing problem happens on the generator side, adding the constraint loss directly to the generator would expose too much information to the generator about how to exploit the discriminator, and thus turns out accelerating the occurrence of mode collapse. The constraint loss can also be viewed as a regularizer, which guides the function $Enc(G(\cdot))$ to be an identity function, and forces the encoder of the discriminator to retain the diversity and uniformity of randomly sampled $z \in Z$.

Figure 1 is an overview of the full-architecture of BEGAN-CS. The objective function of BEGAN-CS is mostly similar to BEGAN, except the additional constraint loss. The full objective of BEGAN-CS includes

$$\mathcal{L}_G = \mathcal{L}(G(z_G; \theta_G); \theta_D), \quad \text{for } \theta_G \tag{1}$$

and

$$\mathcal{L}_D = \mathcal{L}(x_{\text{real}}; \theta_D) - k_t \cdot \mathcal{L}(G(z_D; \theta_G); \theta_D) + \alpha \cdot \mathcal{L}_c, \quad \text{for } \theta_D \tag{2}$$

with

$$\begin{cases} \mathcal{L}_c = \|z_D - Enc(G(z_D))\|, & \text{(the constraint loss)} \\ k_{t+1} = k_t + \lambda(\gamma \mathcal{L}(x; \theta_D) - \mathcal{L}(G(z_G; \theta_G); \theta_D)), & \text{for each epoch.} \end{cases} \tag{3}$$

The total loss $\mathcal{L}_G$ of the generator and the total loss $\mathcal{L}_D$ of the discriminator are optimized to solve for the parameters θ_G and θ_D, respectively. The function

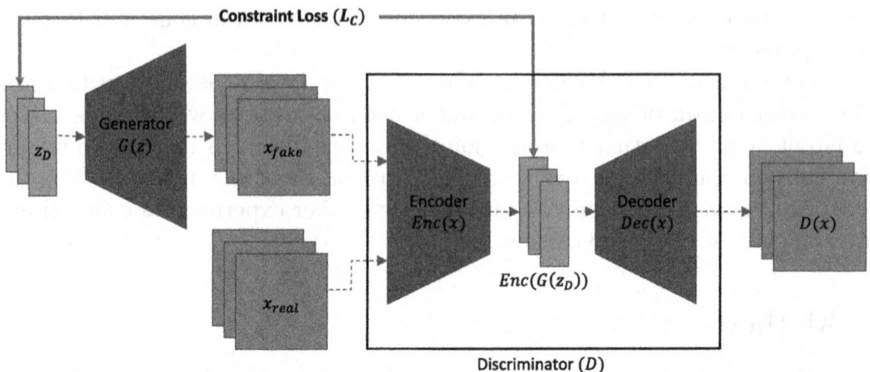

Fig. 1. An overview of BEGAN-CS.

$\mathcal{L}(x;\theta_D) = \|x - D(x)\|$ associated with θ_D computes the norm of the difference between any given image x and its reconstructed image $D(x)$ by the decoder of the discriminator. The latent vectors z_D and z_G are randomly sampled from Z. The variable $k_t \in [0,1]$ controls how much emphasis to put on $\mathcal{L}(G(z_D;\theta_G);\theta_D)$. The hyper-parameter $\gamma \in [0,1]$ balances between the real-image reconstruction loss $\mathcal{L}(x;\theta_D)$ and the generated-image discrimination loss $\mathcal{L}(G(z_G;\theta_G);\theta_D)$. The hyper-parameter α is a weighting factor for constraint loss. The constraint loss $\mathcal{L}_c$ is to enforce $Enc(G(\cdot))$ to be an identity function for z_D.

3.1 Latent Space Analysis

For further illustrating the effectiveness of our method and analyzing the root cause of mode collapsing, we visualize the latent space through time with and without the constraint loss. We take PCA as our choice of dimensionality reduction method, and project the latent vectors onto two-dimensional space. Another common choice of dimensionality reduction for visualization is t-Distributed Stochastic Neighbor Embedding (t-SNE) [22]. For the latent space, we are more interested in the density and distribution of the points rather than the relative nearness between points or clusters. As a result, PCA is more suitable for our analysis.

Figure 2 shows a preliminary analysis of BEGAN and BEGAN-CS. We train both models on the CelebA dataset [21]. The 64-dimensional latent vectors of generated images ($Enc(G(z))$) and real images ($Enc(x)$) are projected onto two-dimensional space via PCA.

In this experiment, BEGAN gets into mode collapse at epoch 23. In addition to the obvious change in the shape of distribution after BEGAN mode-collapsing, our empirical analysis also shows two strong patterns. First, in comparison with BEGAN, the latent-vector distribution (in red) of images generated by BEGAN-CS can better fit the real images' latent-vector distribution (in blue). The latent vectors of BEGAN-CS scatter more uniformly across all epochs.

Second, for BEGAN without adding the constraint loss, both the variance of real images' latent vectors (Var(real)) and the variance of generated images' latent vectors (Var(gen)) grow rapidly as the number of epochs increases. Our hypothesis is that the latent spaces of real images and generated images both expand too rapidly and non-uniformly. Since the number of training data is fixed, as the latent space of real images expands, the density of real images decreases. In the end, the generator of BEGAN reaches a low-density area in the latent space where there is only a few latent vectors of real images nearby. The generator of BEGAN then gets stuck in that area. In contrast, BEGAN-CS has the latent-space constraint as a regularizer, which restricts the latent spaces of real images and generated images expand incautiously. In other words, the constraint loss limits the distribution of $Enc(G(z))$ to be similar to uniform distribution.

3.2 Obtaining Optimal z^* in One-Shot

Given an image x^*, finding an optimal latent vector z^* such that $\|G(z^*) - x^*\| < \epsilon$ for some small ϵ is a challenging problem for GANs. Traditionally, z^* can be obtained by back-propagation for solving the optimization $\min_{z^*}(\|G(z^*) - x^*\|)$. We name this optimization process as z^*-search. However, z^*-search is time-consuming and needs to run for each inference individually, and thus is impractical for real-world applications.

In the case of BEGAN-CS, the constraint loss works as a regularizer, guiding the composite function $Enc(G(z)) \simeq z$ to be similar to an identity function. Consider the definition of z^*, where $G(z^*) = x^*$. We know that $Enc(G(z^*))$ should be close to z^* due to the identity property. This implies that we may take x^* and obtain $Enc(x^*)$ as an approximation to z^* after a single pass through the encoder $Enc(x^*)$.

3.3 Disentangled Representation Learning and Application

We find that BEGAN is able to learn strong and high-quality disentangled representations in an unsupervised setting. The direction of any vector within latent space Z has a universally meaningful semantic, such as mixture of gender, age, smile and hair-style. These learned representations can be combined with vector arithmetic operations to generate images with multiple designated representations.

However, these disentangled representations are only effective for latent vectors, which is a strong restriction that forbids many GAN models to use the disentangled representation for practical applications, since obtaining the latent vectors via z^*-search is computation-demanding. In the meanwhile, as we have shown in Sect. 3.2, BEGAN-CS is able to produce the approximation of z^* on-the-fly. By adding multiple selected representation vectors to the approximated z^* with respect to any given real image x^*, we can generate images that are visually similar to x^* and comprise the selected representations at the same time. We demonstrate this idea with a real example produced by BEGAN-CS in Fig. 3.

In this example, the generated image of Fig. 3d acquires both hair-styles shown Fig. 3b and c. For BEGAN, which lacks the ability of estimating z^* directly, the same effect may be forcibly achieved through time-consuming z^*-search to obtain suitable z^*. Unfortunately, z^*-search causes the major bottleneck at inference time and is therefore hard to use in real-world scenarios.

Similar applications can also be achieved using Variational Auto-Encoder (VAE) based models [12,17,18] or other task-specific GAN models, such as InfoGAN [5]. However, the images generated by VAE-based models tend to be blurry, while InfoGAN cannot generate high-quality results as BEGAN does. In comparison, our results are more promising in terms of stability and quality.

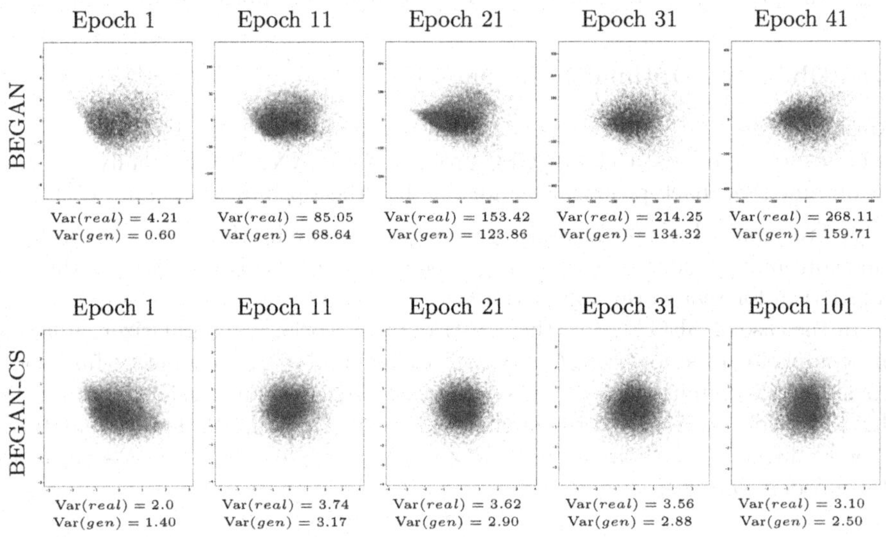

Fig. 2. We visualize the distributions of latent vectors of BEGAN and BEGAN-CS over epochs. Both BEGAN and BEGAN-CS are trained on CelebA dataset under 64×64 resolution and batch size 64. Each graph consists of 6,400 random real images' latent vectors, *i.e.* $Enc(x)$, and 6,400 generated images' latent vectors, *i.e.* $Enc(G(z))$. The upper five graphs are generated by BEGAN, while the bottom five graphs are produced by BEGAN-CS. PCA is performed separately at each epoch based on the latent vectors of the real images. Each blue point represents a latent vector of a real image after applying PCA, and the red points correspond to the latent vectors of the generated images. The text under each graph lists the variance of real images' latent vectors (Var(real)) and the variance of generated images' latent vectors (Var(gen)). During the training of BEGAN, the variances of the distributions of latent vectors keep growing. Note that most of the graphs are created with a fixed interval of 10 epochs, except the bottom-right graph directly skips to the 101st epoch to highlight the effectiveness of BEGAN-CS. BEGAN has already collapsed before the 41st epoch. (Color figure online)

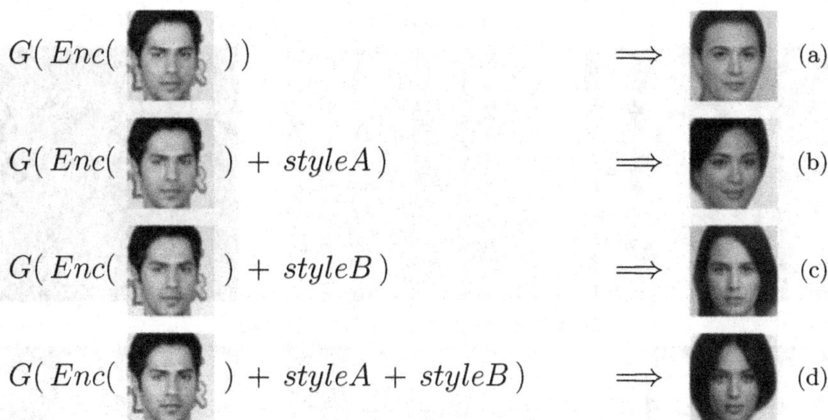

Fig. 3. An example of disentangled representations. The "*styleA*" and "*styleB*" are two learned disentangled representations. Note that these representations are universal and can be applied to any latent vector z for generating images $G(z + style)$ with designated attributes. (a) Approximate z^* by $G(Enc(x^*))$ in one-shot. (b) & (c) The learned disentangled representations can be combined with $G(Enc(x^*))$. (d) Vector arithmetic with multiple disentangled representations. In this case, the generated image has both hair-styles shown in *styleA* and *styleB*.

4 Experiments

We train BEGAN-CS using the CelebA dataset for all the experiments presented in this paper. BEGAN-CS does not adopt the learning rate decay technique described in BEGAN's original paper, since the training process of BEGAN-CS is already very stable. The hyper-parameter α that controls the importance of the constraint loss is set to 0.1 as the default value. We use L2-norm in

$$\mathcal{L}(x; \theta_D) = \|x - D(x)\|$$

throughout the experiments, while in practice, L1-norm can also be used. For any hyper-parameter that is not mentioned, we choose the same value as in BEGAN's original setting.

4.1 Effectiveness of the Constraint Loss

In Fig. 4, we validate the effectiveness of the constraint loss. We show the generated images at specific epochs during the training of BEGAN and BEGAN-CS on the CelebA dataset. The image resolution is 64×64 and the batch size is 64. BEGAN-CS can continuously be trained up to 100 epochs without any evidence of mode collapsing, loss of diversity, or reduction in quality. In contrast, BEGAN encounters mode collapse at the 25th epoch (*i.e.*, the time-step B in Fig. 4). In addition to the advantage of preventing from mode collapse, the proposed BEGAN-CS model also maintains a very good performance in generating high-quality images.

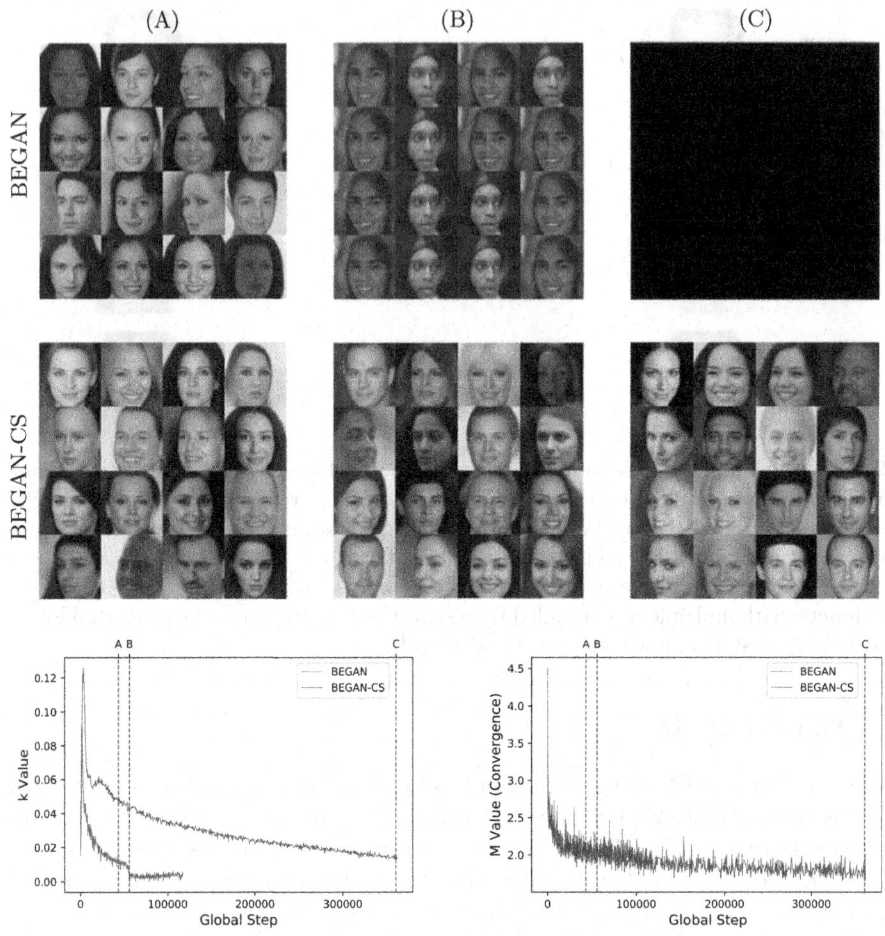

Fig. 4. We validate the effectiveness of the constraint loss by showing the generated images at specific epochs during the training of BEGAN and BEGAN-CS on the CelebA dataset. The image resolution is 64×64 and the batch size is 64. Note that BEGAN fails to reach epoch C since it already collapses at epoch B. In contrast, BEGAN-CS survives after epoch C. Furthermore, BEGAN-CS maintains a very good performance in generating high-quality images.

4.2 Observing the Sudden Mode Collapsing

An interesting finding during our experiments is the timing of mode collapsing.

As is mentioned in [3], the global measure of convergence can be used by BEGAN to determine whether the network has reached the final state or if the model has collapsed. However, in practice we are not able to observe significant evidence of mode collapsing directly from the value of the convergence measure. Instead, the evidence of mode collapse are more often to be observed from the k value. The k value in BEGAN controls how much attention is paid on $\mathcal{L}(G(z))$.

According to our observation, every time the k value suddenly drops, BEGAN is going to collapse shortly.

4.3 Better Convergence on Small Datasets

The dataset size is also an important factor for the timing of mode collapse. Under a setting of reducing the training dataset CelebA to 1/10 of its original size, BEGAN collapses earlier than training on full dataset. The early occurrence of mode collapse keeps BEGAN from converging to an optimal state. The time-step A in Fig. 6 is the best state that BEGAN can achieve during its training on the down-sized CelebA dataset. On the other hand, BEGAN-CS has a more stable training process. In Fig. 6, BEGAN-CS can continuously optimize on the 1/10 down-sized CelebA dataset without encountering mode collapse, and eventually converges to a better state than BEGAN.

4.4 FID Score Curve Comparison

For the quantitative comparison to demonstrate the effectiveness of the proposed constraint loss, we accordingly report "Fréchet Inception Distance" (FID) [11] score through time of BEGAN and BEGAN-CS in Fig. 5. The experiments are conducted at 64 × 64 resolution. It can be seen in Fig. 5 that, during training, the FID of BEGAN-CS does not increase drastically as BEGAN.

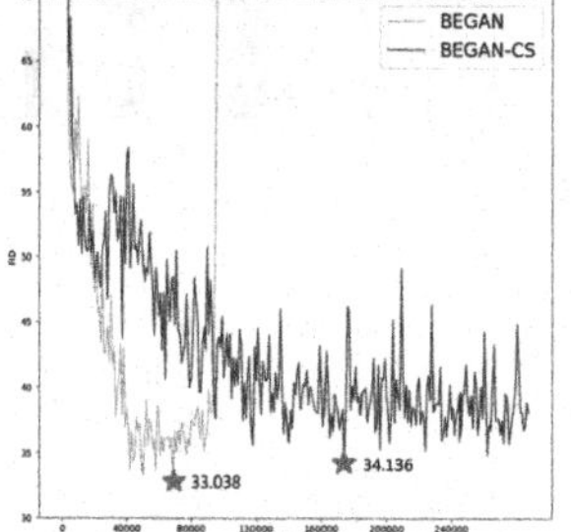

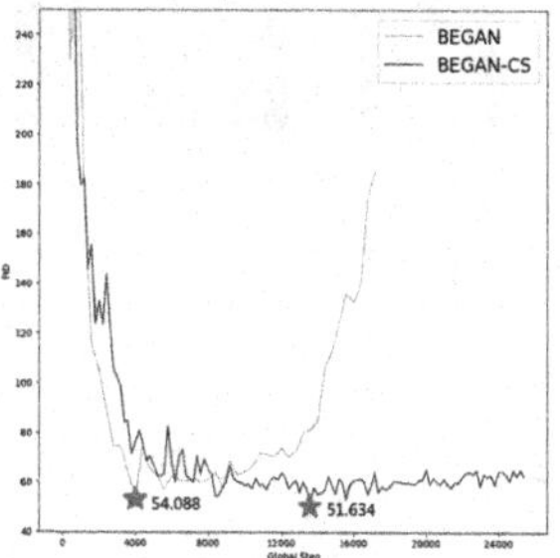

Fig. 5. FID through time. (Left) Full CelebA. (Right) 1/10 CelebA.

4.5 Obtaining Optimal z^* in One-Shot

In Sect. 3.2, we have shown that BEGAN-CS can approximate optimal z^* with $Enc(x^*)$. Appendix A shows the experimental results of interpolation with obtained z^* from z^*-search using different GAN architectures. The experiments may serve as proofs of concept for comparing the well-known GANs architectures, including FisherGAN [23], PGGAN [14], and BEGAN. The experimental results show that the obtained $G(Enc(x^*))$ of BEGAN-CS is visually similar to x^*. In contrast, the original BEGAN and other state-of-the-art GANs require time-consuming z^*-search for 10,000 iterations to obtain competitive results. It would take 340 s to 3,970 s depending on the network architecture. However, the quality of the z^*-search result is still unstable and the searched image frequently looks quite different to the given real image, such as wrong gender or incorrect head pose. More examples on z^*-search with different GAN models and different numbers of optimization iterations are shown in Appendix B.

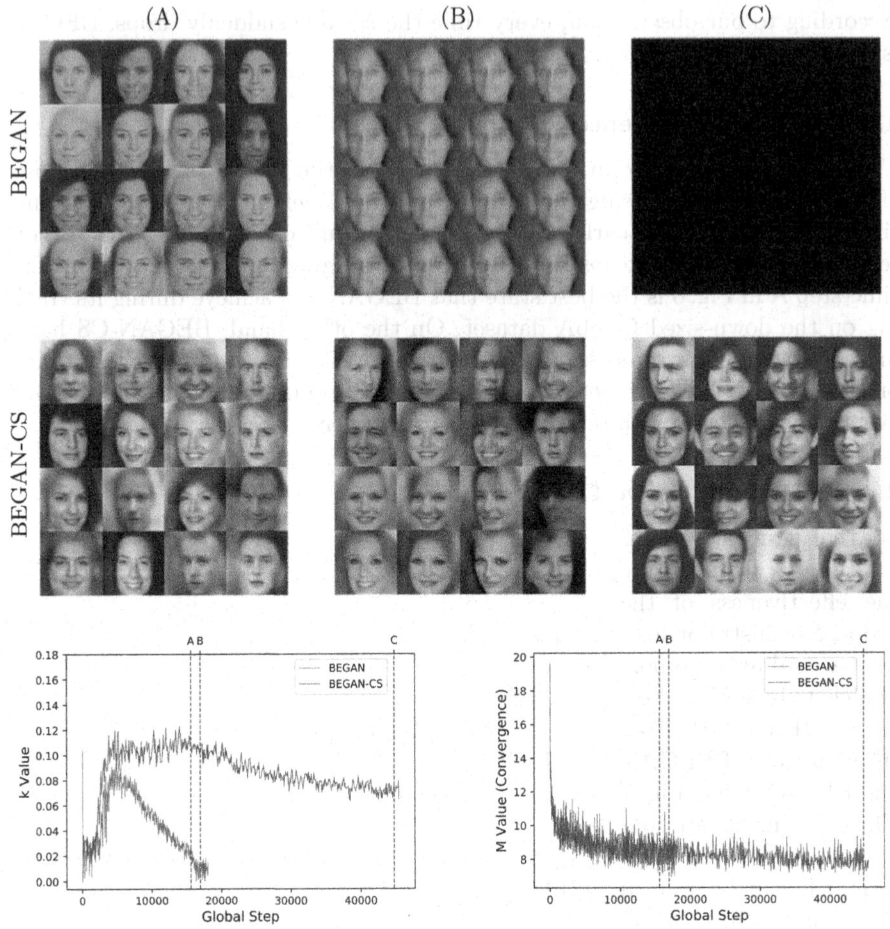

Fig. 6. Better convergence of BEGAN-CS on small datasets. We show the generated images at selected epochs during training BEGAN and BEGAN-CS on a 1/10 sized subset of CelebA. Training images are of 128×128 resolution and the batch size is 24. BEGAN-CS is stable and converges to a particularly better state than BEGAN. The best state of BEGAN is at time-step A with degraded quality, while BEGAN-CS can generate higher-quality results at time-step C.

4.6 Comparison with Bijective Models

VEEGAN runs experiments on a synthetic toy dataset which consists of 25 independent Gaussian distributions, and observes better stable and higher diversity than other GANs. We accordingly run the similar experiment and provide comparisons in Fig. 7 for VEEGAN, ALI, BEGAN, and BEGAN-CS. We find that the vanilla BEGAN can already fit most of the modes of the real data distribution, though it requires extensive hyper-parameters tuning. Furthermore, BEGAN-CS can stabilize the training and converge to a final state of higher quality. Although VEEGAN can fit to all modes, the distribution is relatively blurry and less similar to the real data distribution. Lastly, ALI fails to fit to the real data distribution.

The hyper-parameters we used for BEGAN and BEGAN-CS on the toy dataset are $\alpha = 0.1$, $\gamma = 25$, $\lambda = 1\text{e}-4$. We use Adam [16] optimizer with $lr_d = 1\text{e}-4$, $lr_g = 5\text{e}-4$, $\beta_1 = 0.5$ and $\beta_2 = 0.999$. The latent dimension of Z is set to 32. Both the generator and discriminator are consist of 2 layers of feed-forward network with 128 nodes and ReLU activation. We also set the weight initialization function to be a uniform-random sampler in range $[-\sqrt{9/n}, \sqrt{9/n}]$, which n is the number of layer input.

We also present qualitative comparisons on image reconstruction with BEGAN-CS and ALI in Fig. 8. We find that the loss functions used by all three methods, ALI, BiGAN, and BEGAN-CS, do not guarantee that the reconstruction results are identical to the real images. BEGAN-CS is better at retaining some of the important features, such as hair color, skin color, gaze, and head pose.

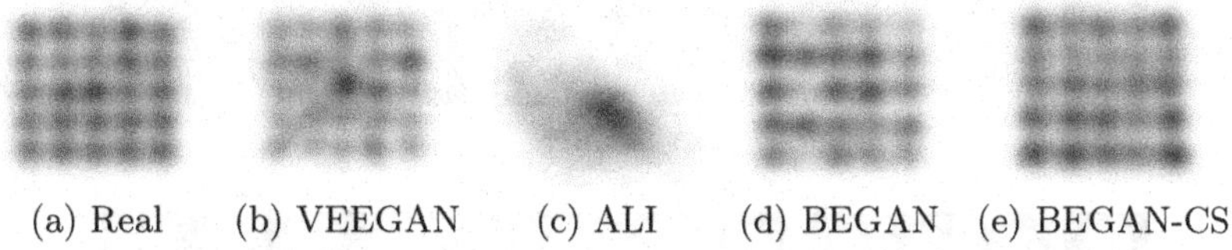

(a) Real (b) VEEGAN (c) ALI (d) BEGAN (e) BEGAN-CS

Fig. 7. Experimental results on the synthetic dataset introduced by VEEGAN.

(a) Real images (b) ALI (c) BEGAN-CS

Fig. 8. Image reconstruction results.

4.7 On-the-Fly Representation Manipulation

In Sect. 3.3, we demonstrate a new application of BEGAN-CS with the disentangled representations. By obtaining the approximation of z^* with $Enc(x^*)$ and applying the selected disentangled representations, BEGAN-CS can generate images that are visually similar to x^* and exhibit the selected representations at the same time. As a proof of concept, we visualize the process of adding single representation in Fig. 9 and multiple representations in Fig. 10.

In Fig. 9, we first obtain the approximation of z^* from $Enc(x^*)$. Then for each dimension i, we linearly interpolate and replace the value of latent vector z^* at its ith dimension by a grid value in $[-5, 5]$ with step size 1, and thus can generate a series of images based on the modified latent vectors. The images show that each dimension of the latent space Z represents a universal disentangled representation. We can perform similar visual transformations to any $z \in Z$. Figure 9 shows some of the interesting disentangled representations. The full visualization across the 64 dimensions is displayed in Appendix C.

The learned disentangled representations can also be used to perform multiple vector arithmetic operations on latent vectors. This property enables us to control multiple attributes of a fixed image at the same time by adjusting

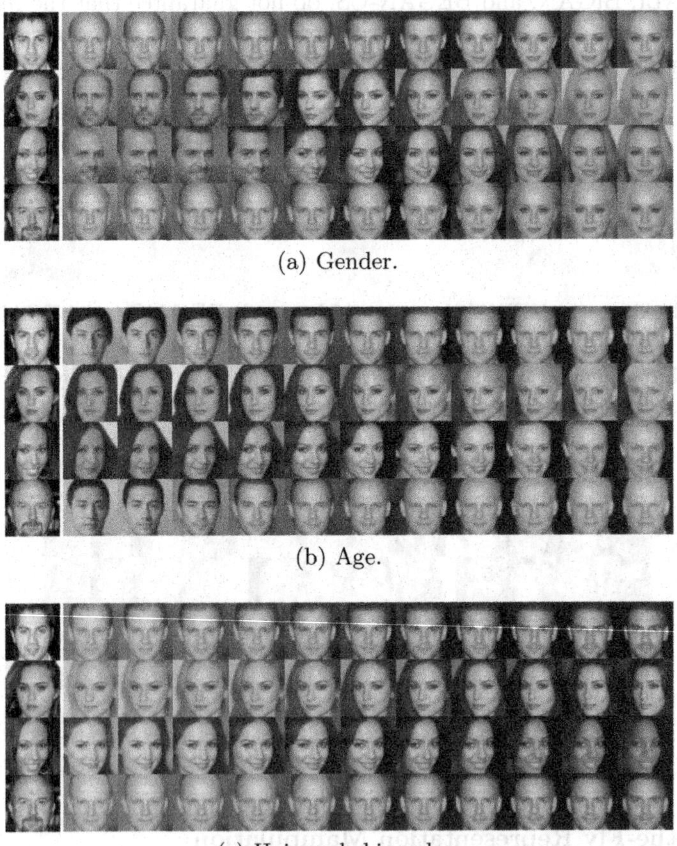

(a) Gender.

(b) Age.

(c) Hair and skin color.

Fig. 9. Selected disentangled representations produced by BEGAN-CS at 64×64 resolution. For each series of images, the left-most image is the fixed real image x^*. In each sub-figure, we first obtain approximation of z^* using $Enc(x^*)$. For each dimension i, we linearly interpolate and replace the ith dimension of z^* by a value in $[-5, 5]$ with step size 1, and then generate the image set $\{G(z_i^*)\}$.

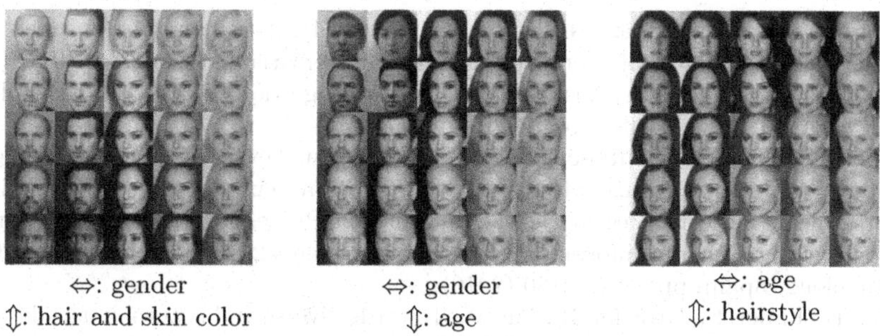

Fig. 10. Two-dimensional combinations of disentangled representations.

multiple dimension values on the corresponding latent vector. We visualize the results of combining two different representations in Fig. 10.

5 Conclusion

We identify that BEGAN suffers from the unpredictable mode-collapsing problem. The precise time when mode collapsing happens is non-deterministic, highly related to the resolution of generated images and the size of training dataset. We propose *BEGAN with a Constrained Space* (BEGAN-CS) toward addressing the mode-collapsing problem and visualize the effect of constraint loss in the latent space. We experimentally show that the model-collapsing problem is suppressed after adding the constraint loss. BEGAN-CS performs particularly better than BEGAN when the size of training dataset is ten-times smaller than the normal setting. These advantages enable the class of energy-based GANs to move on to the next challenge of generating even higher resolution images.

We also discover that BEGAN can learn salient and high-quality disentangled representations in an unsupervised setting. Combined with the particular property that BEGAN-CS is able to approximate z^* on-the-fly, BEGAN-CS can generate images that are visually similar to the given real image and able to exhibit the adjustable disentangled properties. "Obtaining z^* in one-shot" and "adjustable image attributes" are two interesting properties that have various potential applications, such as style manipulation and attribute-based editing.

References

1. Wold, S., Esbensen, K., Geladi, P.: Principal component analysis. Chemom. Intell. Lab. Syst. **2**(1), 37–52 (1987)
2. Arjovsky, M., Chintala, S., Bottou, L.: Wasserstein GAN. CoRR abs/1701.07875 (2017)
3. Berthelot, D., Schumm, T., Metz, L.: BEGAN: boundary equilibrium generative adversarial networks. CoRR abs/1703.10717 (2017)

4. Bousmalis, K., Silberman, N., Dohan, D., Erhan, D., Krishnan, D.: Unsupervised pixel-level domain adaptation with generative adversarial networks. In: 2017 IEEE Conference on Computer Vision and Pattern Recognition, CVPR 2017, Honolulu, HI, USA, 21–26 July 2017, pp. 95–104 (2017)
5. Chen, X., Duan, Y., Houthooft, R., Schulman, J., Sutskever, I., Abbeel, P.: Infogan: interpretable representation learning by information maximizing generative adversarial nets. In: Advances in Neural Information Processing Systems 29: Annual Conference on Neural Information Processing Systems 2016, 5–10 December 2016, Barcelona, Spain, pp. 2172–2180 (2016)
6. Dai, B., Fidler, S., Urtasun, R., Lin, D.: Towards diverse and natural image descriptions via a conditional GAN. In: IEEE International Conference on Computer Vision, ICCV 2017, Venice, Italy, 22–29 October 2017, pp. 2989–2998 (2017)
7. Donahue, J., Krähenbühl, P., Darrell, T.: Adversarial feature learning. CoRR abs/1605.09782 (2016)
8. Dumoulin, V., et al.: Adversarially learned inference. CoRR abs/1606.00704 (2016)
9. Goodfellow, I.J., et al.: Generative adversarial nets. In: Advances in Neural Information Processing Systems 27: Annual Conference on Neural Information Processing Systems 2014, 8–13 December 2014, Montreal, Quebec, Canada, pp. 2672–2680 (2014)
10. Gwak, J., Choy, C.B., Garg, A., Chandraker, M., Savarese, S.: Weakly supervised generative adversarial networks for 3D reconstruction. CoRR abs/1705.10904 (2017)
11. Heusel, M., Ramsauer, H., Unterthiner, T., Nessler, B., Hochreiter, S.: GANs trained by a two time-scale update rule converge to a Local Nash Equilibrium. In: Advances in Neural Information Processing Systems 30: Annual Conference on Neural Information Processing Systems 2017, 4–9 December 2017, Long Beach, CA, USA, pp. 6629–6640 (2017)
12. Higgins, I., et al.: beta-VAE: Learning basic visual concepts with a constrained variational framework (2016)
13. Hinton, G.E., Salakhutdinov, R.R.: Reducing the dimensionality of data with neural networks. Science **313**(5786), 504–507 (2006)
14. Karras, T., Aila, T., Laine, S., Lehtinen, J.: Progressive growing of GANs for improved quality, stability, and variation. CoRR abs/1710.10196 (2017)
15. Khan, S.H., Hayat, M., Barnes, N.: Adversarial training of variational auto-encoders for high fidelity image generation. In: 2018 IEEE Winter Conference on Applications of Computer Vision, WACV 2018, Lake Tahoe, NV, USA, 12–15 March 2018, pp. 1312–1320 (2018)
16. Kingma, D.P., Ba, J.: Adam: a method for stochastic optimization. CoRR abs/1412.6980 (2014)
17. Kingma, D.P., Welling, M.: Auto-encoding variational bayes. CoRR abs/1312.6114 (2013)
18. Larsen, A.B.L., Sønderby, S.K., Larochelle, H., Winther, O.: Autoencoding beyond pixels using a learned similarity metric. In: Proceedings of the 33nd International Conference on Machine Learning, ICML 2016, New York City, NY, USA, pp. 1558–1566, 19–24 June 2016
19. Ledig, C., et al.: Photo-realistic single image super-resolution using a generative adversarial network. In: 2017 IEEE Conference on Computer Vision and Pattern Recognition, CVPR 2017, Honolulu, HI, USA, 21–26 July 2017, pp. 105–114 (2017)
20. Li, Y., Liu, S., Yang, J., Yang, M.: Generative face completion. In: 2017 IEEE Conference on Computer Vision and Pattern Recognition, CVPR 2017, Honolulu, HI, USA, 21–26 July 2017, pp. 5892–5900 (2017)

21. Liu, Z., Luo, P., Wang, X., Tang, X.: Deep learning face attributes in the wild. In: Proceedings of International Conference on Computer Vision (ICCV) (2015)
22. van der Maaten, L., Hinton, G.: Visualizing data using t-SNE. J. Mach. Learn. Res. **9**, 2579–2605 (2008)
23. Mroueh, Y., Sercu, T.: Fisher GAN. In: Advances in Neural Information Processing Systems 30: Annual Conference on Neural Information Processing Systems 2017, 4–9 December 2017, Long Beach, CA, USA, pp. 2510–2520 (2017)
24. Radford, A., Metz, L., Chintala, S.: Unsupervised representation learning with deep convolutional generative adversarial networks. CoRR abs/1511.06434 (2015)
25. Salimans, T., Goodfellow, I.J., Zaremba, W., Cheung, V., Radford, A., Chen, X.: Improved techniques for training GANs. In: Advances in Neural Information Processing Systems 29: Annual Conference on Neural Information Processing Systems 2016, 5–10 December 2016, Barcelona, Spain, pp. 2226–2234 (2016)
26. Shrivastava, A., Pfister, T., Tuzel, O., Susskind, J., Wang, W., Webb, R.: Learning from simulated and unsupervised images through adversarial training. In: 2017 IEEE Conference on Computer Vision and Pattern Recognition, CVPR 2017, Honolulu, HI, USA, 21–26 July 2017, pp. 2242–2251 (2017)
27. Souly, N., Spampinato, C., Shah, M.: Semi supervised semantic segmentation using generative adversarial network. In: IEEE International Conference on Computer Vision, ICCV 2017, Venice, Italy, 22–29 October 2017, pp. 5689–5697 (2017)
28. Srivastava, A., Valkov, L., Russell, C., Gutmann, M.U., Sutton, C.A.: VEEGAN: reducing mode collapse in GANs using implicit variational learning. In: Advances in Neural Information Processing Systems 30: Annual Conference on Neural Information Processing Systems 2017, 4–9 December 2017, Long Beach, CA, USA, pp. 3310–3320 (2017)
29. Tzeng, E., Hoffman, J., Saenko, K., Darrell, T.: Adversarial discriminative domain adaptation. In: 2017 IEEE Conference on Computer Vision and Pattern Recognition, CVPR 2017, Honolulu, HI, USA, 21–26 July 2017, pp. 2962–2971 (2017)
30. Zhao, J.J., Mathieu, M., LeCun, Y.: Energy-based generative adversarial network. CoRR abs/1609.03126 (2016)

Leveraging Motion Priors in Videos for Improving Human Segmentation

Yu-Ting Chen[1(✉)], Wen-Yen Chang[1(✉)], Hai-Lun Lu[1(✉)], Tingfan Wu[2(✉)], and Min Sun[1(✉)]

[1] National Tsing Hua University, Taiwan, China
yuting2401@gmail.com, s0936100879@gmail.com, oscar.lu1007@gmail.com, sunmin@ee.nthu.edu.tw

[2] Umbo Computer Vision, Taiwan, China
tingfan.wu@umbocv.com

Abstract. Despite many advances in deep-learning based semantic segmentation, performance drop due to distribution mismatch is often encountered in the real world. Recently, a few domain adaptation and active learning approaches have been proposed to mitigate the performance drop. However, very little attention has been made toward leveraging information in videos which are naturally captured in most camera systems. In this work, we propose to leverage "motion prior" in videos for improving human segmentation in a weakly-supervised active learning setting. By extracting motion information using optical flow in videos, we can extract candidate foreground motion segments (referred to as motion prior) potentially corresponding to human segments. We propose to learn a memory-network-based policy model to select *strong* candidate segments (referred to as *strong* motion prior) through reinforcement learning. The selected segments have high precision and are directly used to finetune the model. In a newly collected surveillance camera dataset and a publicly available UrbanStreet dataset, our proposed method improves the performance of human segmentation across multiple scenes and modalities (i.e., RGB to Infrared (IR)). Last but not least, our method is empirically complementary to existing domain adaptation approaches such that additional performance gain is achieved by combining our weakly-supervised active learning approach with domain adaptation approaches.

Keywords: Active learning · Domain adaptation
Human segmentation

1 Introduction

Intelligent camera systems with the capability to recognize objects often encounter issues caused by data distribution mismatch in the real world. For instance, surveillance cameras encounter various weather conditions, view angles, lighting conditions, and sensor modalities (e.g., RGB, infrared or even thermal).

V. Ferrari et al. (Eds.): ECCV 2018, LNCS 11211, pp. 228–244, 2018.
https://doi.org/10.1007/978-3-030-01234-2_14

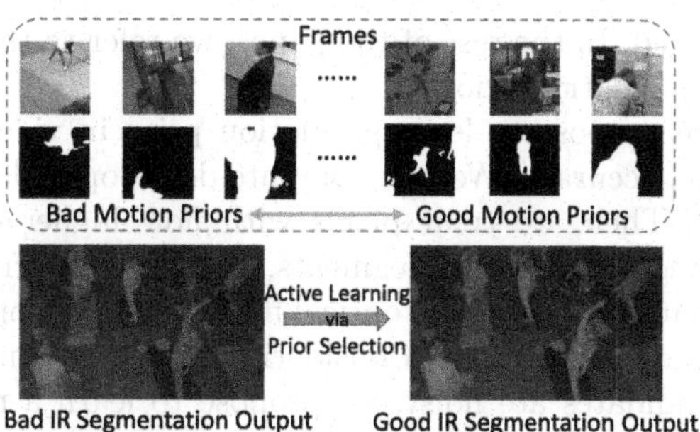

Fig. 1. (top): RGB patches and their corresponding patch-based motion priors extracted from videos. The priors can be classified into "good" and "bad" ones. (bottom): Our proposed active learning strategy can select good motion priors to improve performance in a cross-modality (RGB to IR) segmentation scenario.

A standard solution is to collect more labeled images from various distributions to train a more robust model. However, collecting high-quality labels is very expensive and time-consuming, especially for segmentation and detection tasks. These considerations raise two critical questions: (1) "how to select data points for training such that the accuracy improved as much as possible?" and (2) "how to obtain the label of the selected data points with cost as low as possible?"

Active learning is one of the common paradigms to address the "how to select" question since it is defined as learning to select data points to label, from a pool of unlabeled data points, in order to maximize the accuracy. There exist many heuristics [1] which have been proven to be effective when applied to classical machine learning models. However, Sener and Savarese [2] have shown that these heuristics are less effective when applied to CNN. To overcome the limitation, Sener and Savarese [2] propose a new active learning method specifically designed for Convolutional Neural Networks (CNNs). Despite recent advances, Most active learning methods require human to label the selected data points. For segmentation and detection tasks, the cost of labeling a small set of selected data points can still be relatively expensive and time-consuming.

On the other hand, instead of collecting independent images, it is generally easy to collect a sequence of images (i.e., a video) from always-on camera systems. Sequences of images have two main properties: (1) images close in time are similar/redundant, and (2) difference in two consecutive images reveals motion information potentially corresponding to moving objects. Very little attention, however, has been made toward exploiting these properties in a video to automatically provide supervision to boost recognition performance and mitigate the performance drop caused by distribution mismatch. This is related to the "how to obtain labels" question. If we can obtain labels automatically from videos, it will be immensely beneficial for intelligent camera systems. In fact, researchers have proposed to extract motion information from a sequence of images. For instance, given two consecutive frames, dense optical flow can be extracted for each pixel. Given a longer sequence of frames, sparse long-term trajectories of pixels can be extracted. In the rest of the paper, we refer to these motion information in a video as "motion prior".

In this work, we propose to leverage motion prior in videos for improving human segmentation accuracy. We first compute dense optical flow between two consecutive frames. Then, we treat pixels with flow higher than a threshold as candidates of foreground motion segments, which are referred to as "motion prior". Due to the nature of imperfect optical flow, a majority of the segments are quite noisy (see examples in Fig. 1). Considering that only some candidates are good and many candidates are noisy, we propose to learn a memory-network-based policy model to select good candidate segments through reinforcement learning. The selected good segments are then used as additional ground truth to finetune the human segmenter. In this way, we can achieve active learning without additional human annotation.

Our policy is trained on a hold-out dataset with unlabeled videos and a set of labeled images. The training of the policy is formulated as a reinforcement learning problem where the reward is the accuracy of the labeled images and the action is whether to select each motion segment. Once the policy is trained, we can apply the policy to select motion segments in challenging cross-modality (RGB to IR) or cross-scene settings. We refer our setting as weakly-supervised active learning since the policy needs to be trained on an additional hold-out dataset.

In a newly collected surveillance camera dataset and a publicly available UrbanStreet dataset, our proposed method improves the performance of human segmentation across multiple scenes and modalities (i.e., RGB to Infrared (IR)). Last but not least, our method is empirically complementary to existing domain adaptation approaches such that additional performance gain is achieved by combining our weakly-supervised active learning approach with domain adaptation approaches.

In the following sections, we first describe the related works in Sect. 2. Then, we introduce our new surveillance cameras dataset in Sect. 3. Our main technical contribution—policy-based weakly-supervised active learning for strong motion prior selection—is introduced in Sect. 4. Finally, we report our experimental results in Sect. 5.

2 Related Works

We discuss the related work in the fields of motion segmentation, human segmentation, active learning and domain adaptation.

2.1 Motion Segmentation

Motion segmentation aims to decompose a video into foreground objects and background using motion information. Feature-based motion segmentation methods assume that segmentation of different motions is equivalent to segment the extracted feature trajectories into different clusters. These methods can be classified into two types: affinity-based methods [3,4] and subspace-based method [5,6]. Some of the works utilize properties of trajectory data. For example, Yan and Pollefeys [7] use geometric constraint and locality to solve the problem. Recently, [8,9] propose to jointly tackle the motion segmentation and optical flow tasks. Nirkin et al. [10] use motion as a prior and propose a man in the loop for producing segmentation labels. In our work, we simply obtain candidate moving object segments via high-quality optical flow. Most importantly, none of the work aforementioned leverage motion segmentation for weakly-supervised active learning.

2.2 Human Segmentation

Human segmentation has a wide range of applications. For instance, human segmentation in a high-density scene (crowded or occluded) acquired from a stationary camera has been discussed in early works [11,12]. Spina et al. [13] demonstrate applications in pose estimation and behavior study. On the other hand, in many applications, real-time performance is critical. Song et al. [14] achieve 1000 fps using a CNN-based architecture which outperforms traditional methods in both speed and accuracy. Some works use motion information for helping human segmentation, for instance, Guo et al. [15] base on local color distribution and shape priors through optical flow, and Lu et al. [16] describe a hierarchical MRF model to bridge low-level video fragments with high-level human motion and appearance.

In recent years, thermal and infrared systems have gained popularity for night vision. Hence, human segmentation on infrared images has become an important topic. For example, Tan et al. [17] propose a background subtraction based method for human segmentation on thermal infrared images. He et al. [18] further utilize predicted human segments on infrared images to guide robots search. To demonstrate severe domain shift, we evaluate our method mainly on cross-modality (RGB to IR) domain adaptation for human segmentation.

2.3 Active Learning

An active learning algorithm can explore informative instances, querying desired output form users or other sources. Uncertainty-based approaches are widely used. These works consider uncertainty as the selection strategies. They find hard examples by dropout MC sampling [19], using heuristics like highest entropy [20], or geometric distance to decision boundaries [21,22]. Other approaches consider the diversity of selected samples, using k-means algorithms [2,23] or sparse representation for subset selection [24]. Still other important concepts also help the performance, such as selecting instances which will maximize the variance of output [25,26], or introducing the relationships between data points in structured data [27,28].

Recently, some works model the active learning process as a sequence of querying actions, using deep reinforcement learning. Fang et al. [29] demonstrates on cross-lingual setting and Bachman et al. [30] models the learning algorithm via meta-learning. Our approach is similar to these methods using learnable strategy rather than predefined heuristic. Above methods show their goal to reduce human label cost. However, we use active learning for unsupervised finetuning since our method selects automatically computed motion priors, requiring ZERO human label cost once the policy has learned.

2.4 Domain Adaptation

Domain adaptation leverages information from one or more source domains to improve the performance on target domain. Recent methods focus on learning deep representations to be robust to domain shift [31]. Several other works propose to align source and target domains in feature space based on Maximum Mean Discrepancy (MMD) [32] or Central Moment Discrepancy (CMD) [33].

On the other hand, adversarial training [34] has been applied for domain adaptation as well [35–37]. Liu et al. [35] propose Coupled GAN which generates a joint distribution of two domains for classification. Ganin et al. [36] applies adversarial training for achieving maximal confusion between the two domains. Other works such as Domain Separation Networks (DSN) [38] split the feature into shared representations and private ones, in order to improve the ability to extract domain-invariant features. Most of the works mentioned above focus on classification. Hoffman et al. [39], Chen et al. [40] and more recent works [41,42] extend to segmentation which is closer to our human segmentation task. In this work, we show that our proposed weakly-supervised active learning approach is complementary to state-of-the-art domain adaptation approaches.

3 Surveillance Datasets

In order to create challenging scenarios in videos, we have collected a new surveillance camera dataset consisting of large distribution mismatch due to cross-domains scenarios: cross-modalities (i.e., RGB to InfraRed (IR)) and across-scenes. It is surprisingly difficult to find existing segmentation annotated cross-domains video dataset. Due to the high cost of labeling, most public annotated video dataset are usually very small, not to mention about crossing multiple domains. In our dataset; we highlight cross-modalities for its high appearance mismatch and practical value. For surveillance application, good human segmentations across multiple sensor modality and scenes is essential. This dataset directly validates the proposed method in real-world surveillance scenarios.

We collect four datasets: Gym-RGB, Gym-IR, Store-RGB, and Multi-Scene-IR. There are two different sensor modes on typical surveillance cameras, color and infrared, which we denote as "RGB" and"IR", respectively. To simulate real-world usage, we let the camera ambient light sensor to automatically switch between the two modes. Typically, when there is sufficient lighting, the cameras operate in RGB mode; on the other hand, when it gets dark, the IR mode is activated to improve sensitivity. All datasets are videos collected by stationary cameras, we label a subset of frame sparsely sampled from each video.

3.1 Cross-Domains Settings

We divide our data into source $\mathcal{S}$ and target $\mathcal{T}$ domains. In this dataset, we treat all RGB data as source domain and all IR data as target domain in order to test challenging cross-modalities settings. In both domains, we further define training T and evaluation E sets. All evaluation set contains labeled images. In the source domain, training T consists of a few labeled images $\mathcal{I}_T^{\mathcal{S}}$ and unlabeled video frames $\mathcal{V}_T^{\mathcal{S}}$. The labeled training images $\mathcal{I}_T^{\mathcal{S}}$ are used to pre-train our segmenter. The unlabeled video frames $\mathcal{V}_T^{\mathcal{S}}$ are used to extract motion prior information (Sect. 4.1). Both the unlabeled video frames $\mathcal{V}_T^{\mathcal{S}}$ and the evaluation set $\mathcal{I}_E^{\mathcal{S}}$ in the source domain are used to train our motion prior selector using reinforcement learning (Sect. 4.2). In the target domain, training T consists of only unlabeled video frames $\mathcal{V}_T^{\mathcal{T}}$ which are used to extract motion prior information. Finally, we report the cross-domains performance on the evaluation set $\mathcal{I}_E^{\mathcal{T}}$ in the target domain. The statistics about a number of videos and labeled images in each set of the source and target domain are shown in Tables 1 and 2, respectively.

Table 1. Source domain datasets. "Images" refers to the number of images that are labeled. "Videos" refers to the number of videos that contain unlabeled frames.

Gym-RGB			Store-RGB		
Train		Test	Train		Test
Images	Videos	Images	Images	Videos	Images
749	406	237	985	985	255

Table 2. Target domain datasets. "Images" refers to the number of labeled images. "Videos" refers to the number of videos consist of unlabeled frames. Note that there are no labeled training images in the target domain.

Gym-IR		Multi-Scene-IR	
Train	Test	Train	Test
Videos	Images	Videos	Images
929	492	253	89

3.2 Data Collection Details

For the Store-RGB dataset, we have only color (RGB) images since there is sufficient fluorescent lighting in the stores all day. On the other hand, we collect infrared data (Multi-Scene-IR) from multiple scenes, such as house, office, walkway, park, playground, etc. For Gym scene, the data comes in both RGB and IR modalities due to natural day-and-night lighting transitions. For all videos, there are about 6 to 15 frames in one video with 1080×1920 resolution.

4 Our Method

We describe how to obtain motion prior from optical flow (Sect. 4.1) and select a set of *strong* motion prior. Before that, we first define some common notations below.

Notation. We use i, n, and k to index pixel, patch and the order of input data, respectively. $\mathbf{m}$ indicates motion prior, and m_i denotes the motion prior of the ith pixel.

4.1 Motion Priors from Video Frames

Our goal is to obtain a set of motion prior $\mathbf{m}$ (i.e., candidate foreground mask) from video frames. Although many sophisticated motion segmentation methods can be used, we simply apply a state-of-the-art optical flow method [43]. Then, we obtain $\mathbf{m}$ as the binarized flow map such that $m_i = 1$ if its flow magnitude is larger than a threshold τ. Since surveillance cameras in our dataset are typically stationary, we may assume that most background and foreground pixels corresponding to small and large flow magnitude, respectively. For non-stationary cameras, other motion segmentation methods (e.g., [44]) can be used to handle camera motion.

These automatically obtained motion priors inevitably will be noisy and contain outliers. Hence, we propose a memory-network-based policy model to select more accurate ones instead of directly finetuning the segmenter with all noisy labels. The usage of motion priors is illustrated in Fig. 3.

4.2 Motion Priors Selection

We train a policy model π which learns to select a set of *strong* motion priors. Further, these *strong* motion priors are treated as ground truth to directly fine-tune our model using cross-entropy loss. Instead of manually labeling *strong* motion priors and training the policy in a supervised fashion, we train the policy using reinforcement learning, which rewards from directly improving the human segmentation accuracy on a hold-out evaluation set in source domain. The training procedure of our policy model is illustrated in Fig. 2.

Policy model. We define the policy π as the following probability function:

$$\pi(a|I, \mathbf{m}(I); \phi), \tag{1}$$

where I is an image, $\mathbf{m}(I)$ is its corresponding motion prior, $a \in \{0, 1\}$ is the binary action to select ($a = 1$) or not ($a = 0$), and ϕ is the model parameters.

4.2.1 Network Architecture

Inspired by the ideal using Memory Network [45] in Deep Q-Network (DQN) proposed by Oh at el. [46], we use an memory-network-based policy model which

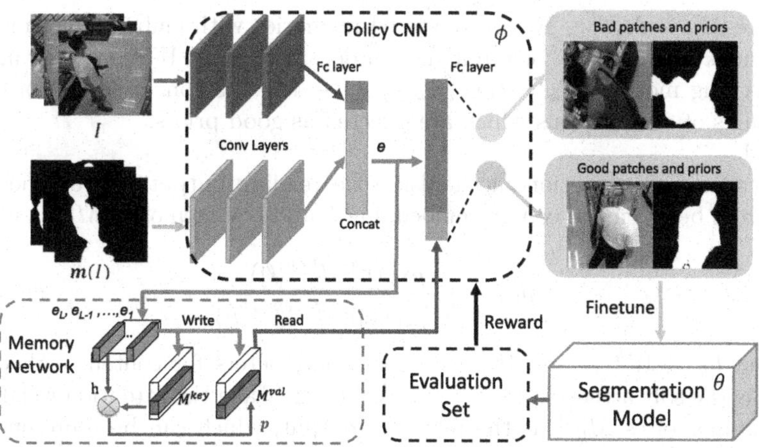

Fig. 2. Training Procedure of Policy Model via reinforcement learning. The policy model ϕ (consist of policy CNN and memory network) takes both the image I and the motion prior $\mathbf{m}(I)$ as inputs and predicts an action, selecting $\mathbf{m}(I)$ as a good prior or not. The selected priors are further used to improve segmenter θ, and then the improvement shown on a hold-out evaluation set will become a reward to update the policy model ϕ.

consists of three components: (1) a feature encoder for extracting features from images and motion priors, (2) a memory retaining a recent history of observations, and (3) an action decision layers taking both content features and retrieved memory state to decide the action.

Feature Encoder. We propose a two-stream CNN to firstly encode image appearance I and motion prior $\mathbf{m}(I)$ separately. To fuse them, we concatenate the embedded features from two streams. Then, we apply a linear transformation on the concatenated feature to mix the features. Not that it is essential to make our policy network robust to domain shift since it is trained only in source domain but applied in the target domain. We found motion priors are more invariant (relative to RGB images) across domains. Hence, we propose late-fusion and increase the number of features for motion priors.

Memory Network. There are two operations, "write" and"read", in memory network, which is similar to the architecture proposed in [46].

- Write.
  The encoded features of last L observations are stored into the memory by linear transformation. Two types of memories are represented as *key* and *value*, which are defined as follows,

$$M_k^{key} = W^{key} E_k \tag{2}$$
$$M_k^{val} = W^{val} E_k, \tag{3}$$

where M_k^{key}, $M_k^{val} \in \mathbb{R}^{d \times L}$ are stored memories with embedding dimension d, and k is the index of input data order. W^{key} and W^{val} are parameters of writing module. $E_k = \{e_{k-i}\}_{i=1,2,...,L} \in \mathbb{R}^{e \times L}$ is concatenation of last L features of observations which are selected as good priors.

- Read.
  Based on soft attention mechanism, the reading output will be the inner product between the content embedding h and key memories M_k^{key}.

$$p_{k,\ell} = \frac{\exp(h_k^\intercal M_k^{key}[\ell])}{\sum_{j=1}^{L} \exp(h_k^\intercal M_k^{key}[j])}, \tag{4}$$

  where $h_k = W^h e_k$, and W^h are model parameters for content embedding. $p_{k,\ell}$ is the soft attention for ℓ^{th} memory block. Take the attention weights on *value* memories M_k^{val} as the retrieved output, which can be represented as below,

$$o_k = M_k^{val} p_k, \tag{5}$$

  where $o_k \in \mathbb{R}^d$ is retrieved memory output.

The memory network is expected to handle the problem of data redundancy, or the policy may tend to select very similar candidates. We concatenate the memory output o_k with current content feature e_k as last features for taking action (select or not).

4.2.2 Reward

We use the improved segmentation accuracy on a hold-out set in the source domain as the reward r as follows,

$$r = \text{IoU}(\mathcal{I}_E^S; \theta) - \text{IoU}(\mathcal{I}_E^S; \theta^0), \tag{6}$$

where IoU is the Intersection over Union (IoU) metric which is standard for semantic segmentation, θ^0 is the initial parameters of the human segmentor, θ is the current parameters of the human segmentor, and $\mathcal{I}_E^S$ is the set of images in the hold-out set in the source domain.

After few earlier episodes, $\text{IoU}(\mathcal{I}_E^S; \theta^0)$ is replaced with other estimated baseline value such as averaged reward in near episodes, in order to maintain learning efficiency.

4.2.3 Policy Gradient

According to above reward function, we compute the policy gradient to update the model parameters ϕ, represented as below,

$$\nabla_\phi \frac{1}{K} \sum_{k=1}^{K} r \cdot \log \pi(a_k \mid I_k, \mathbf{m}(I_k); \phi) \ ; I_k \in \mathcal{V}_T^S, \tag{7}$$

where k is the image index, $K = \mid \mathcal{V}_T^S \mid$, and $\mathcal{V}_T^S$ is the set of unlabelled training video frames in source domain.

4.2.4 Training Procedure

We conduct the following steps iteratively until the reward and policy loss converge.

- Given ϕ, we use the policy network to select a set of image (i.e., $\mathcal{K} = \{k; a_k = 1\}$) with motion priors.
- Given $\mathcal{K}$, we use $(I_k, \mathbf{m}(I_k))_{k \in \mathcal{K}}$ as additional pairs of image and ground truth segmentation to finetune the human segmentation parameters θ.
- Given the new θ, we compute the reward r in Eq. 6.
- Given r, we compute policy gradient in Eq. 7 and update the policy parameters ϕ using Gradient Decent (GD).
- A budget of used data for training the segmenter θ is defined as b, i.e. an episode early stops at step s as $\sum_{k=1}^{s} a_k = b$. Last, we reset the parameters of the segmentor $\theta = \theta^0$ when an episode finishes.

We further extend the procedure above from image-based to patch-based selection. We propose to select motion priors at patch-level since there are very few motion priors which are accurate throughout the entire image. In contrast, there are many patch-based motion priors which are almost completely accurate throughout the entire patch. Next, we define the patch-based selection process.

4.2.5 Patch-Based Selection

Define the nth patch in an image corresponding to a set of pixels R_n, we can write patch-based motion prior as,

$$\mathbf{m}_n = \{m_i; i \in R_n\}. \tag{8}$$

The image-based policy gradient in Eq. 7 is modified to,

$$\nabla_\phi \frac{1}{KN} \sum_{k=1}^{K} \sum_{n=1}^{N} r \cdot \log \pi(a_{k,n} \mid I_{k,n}, \mathbf{m}(I_k)_n; \phi), \tag{9}$$

where $I_{k,n}$ denotes the appearance of the nth patch on the kth image, N is the number of patches in an image. In order to focus on foreground patches and reduce search space, we also automatically filter out patches with all background motion prior (i.e., $m_i = 0$ for all $i \in R(n)$).

4.2.6 Inference on Target Domain

We apply the trained policy π to select a set of image patches $\mathcal{K}_\mathcal{T}$ along with strong motion prior from the unlabeled training frames in the target domain $\mathcal{V}_T^\mathcal{T}$. They are referred to as patch-wise *strong* motion prior as below,

$$\mathcal{K}_\mathcal{T} = \{(k, n); a_{k,n} = 1\}. \tag{10}$$

Given $\mathcal{K}_\mathcal{T}$, we use $(I_{k,n}, \mathbf{m}(I_k)_n)_{k \in \mathcal{K}_\mathcal{T}}$ as additional pairs of image and ground truth human segmentation and introduce cross-entropy loss for fine-tuning in the target domain. See Fig. 3.

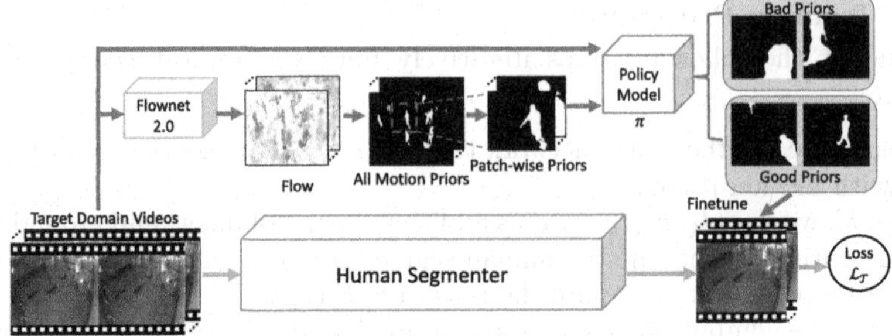

Fig. 3. The figure illustrates the extraction and usage of motion prior. Top-half shows the path to generate motion priors from videos, followed by policy model-based selection. Bottom-half shows selected priors for fine-tuning segmenter on target domain.

5 Experiments

We conduct experiments to validate the proposed weakly-supervised active learning method in cross-modalities and cross-scenes settings. Firstly, the result shows that the proposed policy-based active learning method can select informative samples on a new target domain in Sect. 5.2. Moreover, we show the proposed active learning method is complementary to recent adversarial-based domain adaptation frameworks [38,40]. The performance gains of our method integrated with domain adaptation methods are shown in Sect. 5.3.

We demonstrate the weakly-supervised active learning with the cross-domains setting via our collected source datasets *Gym* and *Store* in camera modality-RGB, along with multiple target datasets, including our remaining datasets in camera modality-IR, and one public available pedestrian dataset, *UrbanStreet* [47], which contains 18 stereo sequences of pedestrians taken from a stereo rig mounted on a car driving in the streets of Philadelphia.

5.1 Implementation Details

In all experiments, we use U-Net structure [48] as our baseline segmentation model for comparison. The code and models are evaluated in the Pytorch framework. For fair comparisons, we use the Intersection over Union (IoU) [49] as evaluation metrics for all experiments, where IoU $= \frac{TP}{TP+TF+FP}$. The quantitative results in Tables 3 and 4 show the IoU scores of foreground class. For training our policy model, we use initial learning rate of 1×10^{-4} with Adam optimizer [50]. The discount factor for policy gradient is set to 1. We train about 5000 episodes. In the training procedure, an initialized segmenter pre-trained on MSCOCO [51] is further fine-tuned with the policy model.

5.2 Weakly-Supervised Active Learning with Cross-Domain Setting

We compare our Policy-based Active Learning method (referred to as *PAL*) with two methods: *Random* and *Human Selection* in Table 3. The number of used

Table 3. Cross-domain human segmentation performance (IoU) comparison of the proposed weakly-supervised active learning method "PAL" with other strategies. U- and Seg- denote the model architectures: U-Net and SegNet, respectively. First row "Source Only" is direct application of pre-trained model on target domain data. To best of our knowledge, none of the existing active learning algorithm use only prior instead of true label for fine-tuning on target domain.

Source		Gym-RGB	Gym-RGB	Gym-RGB	Store-RGB	Store-RGB	Store-RGB
Target		Gym-IR	Multi-Scene-IR	UrbanStreet(-RGB)	Gym-IR	UrbanStreet(-RGB)	Multi-Scene-IR
Source Only	(U-)	48.6%	16.8%	48.5%	26.7%	61.7%	29.2%
	(Seg-)	51.1%	23.6%	52.3%	23.6%	63.5%	35.8%
PAL	(U-)	55.6%	30.5%	51.2%	**32.3%**	64.8%	34.3%
	(Seg-)	**57.0%**	**38.4%**	**56.6%**	26.9%	**65.3%**	**39.0%**
Random	(U-)	52.5%	26.5%	49.3%	29.3%	62.4%	30.2%
	(Seg-)	56.7%	37.2%	55.3%	24.8%	63.4%	33.2%
Human-	(U-)	57.5%	34.6%	55.8%	32.5%	68.5%	41.0%
Selection	(Seg-)	57.5%	42.3%	59.7%	32.7%	65.9%	46.5%

motion-prior patches is pre-defined in all settings as a budget $b = 60$. Note that all methods share the same motion prior candidates (cropped patches).

Random. Randomly select a set of motion priors from a data pool. And we report the average results over ten selected sets.

Human Selection. We manually select a set of motion priors whose motion priors are closer to true annotations while also considering data divergence. The results can be viewed as an upper bound for our method.

We conduct three kinds of cross-domains applications: (1) cross-modalities, (2) cross-scenes, and (3) cross-modalities & -scenes. The experimental results are summarized in Table 3. We choose two baseline segmentation models, U-Net and SegNet, to demonstrate generalization of the method. We also provide qualitative results in Fig. 5.

Cross-modalities in same scene. In our experiment, we change data in Gym from RGB images to infrared images. In Table 3, the first column (Gym-RGB to Gym-IR) shows our method "PAL" has +3.1% IoU performance related to random selection and improves +7% IoU from "Source Only" (not using information on target domain).

Cross-Scenes in Same Modality. We also validate our proposed method on public available datasets. However, it's hard to find a public dataset with IR videos with segmentation annotations. We replace with a public dataset *UrbanStreet* as the target domain whose appearance is very different from our surveillance camera dataset but captured in same modality (RGB). Our method still works under the condition of great appearance change. We conduct two experiments: Gym-RGB → UrbanStreet and Store-RGB → UrbanStreet showed in Table 3. The results show +2.7% and +3.1% relative IoU form source model, respectively. Note that UrbanStreet contains many moving vehicles. Our method still can distinguish human motion segments form another moving segments, which may come from cars or slight camera motions. This result demonstrates the robustness of our weakly-supervised active learning approach.

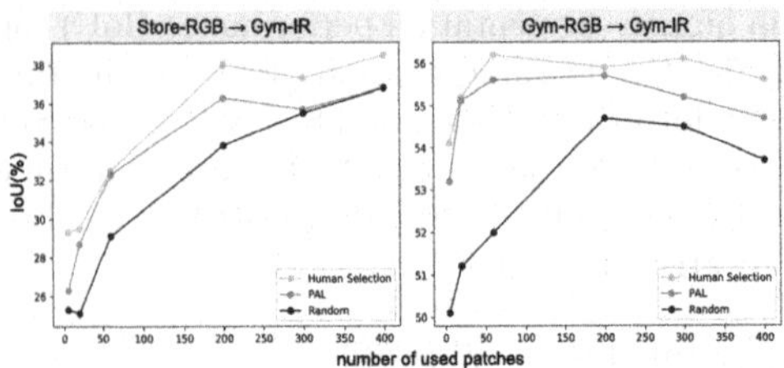

Fig. 4. The performance of human segmentations on target domain using our *PAL* method, where the policy-based active learning is trained on Gym-RGB and Store-RGB (Source), respectively, and is applied to Gym-IR (Target). Note that only motion prior (ZERO label) is used for target domain.

Table 4. Cross-domain human segmentation performance (IoU) comparison of the proposed method (**bold**) with other baselines in 6 diverse source-target domain pairs. The last two rows show the combined methods outperform each of sub-method, implying the active learning approach is complementary to original domain adaptation framework.

Source Target	Gym-RGB	Gym-RGB	Gym-RGB	Store-RGB	Store-RGB	Store-RGB
	Gym-IR	Multi-Scene-IR	UrbanStreet(-RGB)	Gym-IR	UrbanStreet(-RGB)	Multi-Scene-IR
Source only	48.6%	16.8%	48.5%	26.7%	61.7%	29.2%
PAL	55.6%	30.5%	51.2%	32.3%	64.8%	34.3%
DSN [38]	54.3%	25.9%	52.6%	31.8%	62.3%	34.4%
NMD [40]	52.1%	26.1%	52.1%	31.7%	63.1%	34.5%
PAL+DSN	**55.8%**	35.8%	**54.5%**	**36.4%**	**66.2%**	**39.0%**
PAL+NMD	55.6%	**36.7%**	**54.5%**	34.0%	64.6%	36.3%

Cross-Scenes and -Modalities. This is the most general situation to deal with for applications of surveillance cameras. We show the results of Gym → Multi-scene, Store → Gym and Store → Multi-Scene in Table 3. Note that all settings are from RGB to IR. In all settings, the result shows that PAL offers significant improvement from "Source Only" and better than "Random". In the case of Store-RGB → Gym-IR, the result of our method is very close to the upper bound "Human Selection" with only a 0.2% gap.

The performance curves by exploring incrementally more amounts of priors are shown in Fig. 4. We show the effectiveness of PAL comparing with Random and Human selection results. Interestingly, the curve in Store-RGB → Gym-IR implies that the mIoU can increase by adding more strong priors. Since we can obtain motion priors from unlabeled videos with ZERO label cost, our method can be efficient practical to improve performance by simply collecting more unlabeled videos.

5.3 Combined with Adversarial Domain Adaptation

In this part, we integrate the proposed weakly-supervised active learning with other existing unsupervised domain adaptation (DA) methods for two reasons. Firstly, unsupervised DA shares the same goal of ZERO label cost on target

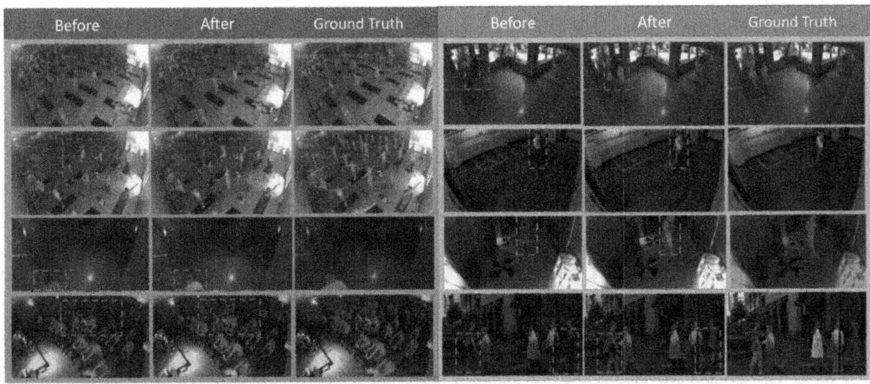

Fig. 5. Qualitative results of improving human segmentation on target domain of the following five source-target settings: Store-RGB → Gym-IR (top-left 6 images), Gym-RGB → Multi-Scene-IR (top-right 6 images), and Store-RGB → Multi-Scene-IR (the third row). The last row shows Gym-RGB → Gym-IR and Gym-RGB→UrbanStreet, respectively. The columns "After" denotes improved segmentations by **PAL+NMD**. Bounding-boxes in dash-line highlight the significant change.

domain. Secondly, intuitively our method should be complementary to unsupervised DA. Most of the unsupervised DA methods only have fine-tuning loss on source domain, since the label is not available on target domain. However, our weakly-supervised active learning policy enables fine-tuning on target domain using the policy-selected strong motion priors.

On the concern of performance and complexity, we combine proposed PAL with two of existing methods, DSN [38] and NMD [40]. Demonstrating in same cross-domains settings as the previous section, we do the comparison between proposed PAL with these unsupervised domain adaptation baselines, and show these two types approaches (PAL vs. UDA) are complementary with each other since the combined method reach the greatest improvement on target domain. See results in Table 4. For instance, in the setting Gym-RGB → Multi-Scene IR (second column), the combined method "PAL+NMD" achieve about 6.2% IoU improvements from each sub-approach.

6 Conclusion

We propose to leverage "motion prior" in videos to improve human segmentation with cross-domain setting. We propose a memory-network-based policy model to select "strong" motion prior through reinforcement learning. The selected segments have high precision and are used to fine-tune the model on target domain. Moreover, the active learning strategy is shown to be complementary to adversarial-based domain adaptation methods. In a newly collected surveillance camera datasets, we show that our proposed method significantly improves the performance of human segmentation across multiple scenes and modalities.

Acknowledgment. We thank Umbo CV, MediaTek, MOST 107-2634-F-007-007 for their support.

References

1. Settles, B.: Active learning literature survey (2010)
2. Sener, O., Savarese, S.: Active learning for convolutional neural networks: a core-set approach. In: ICLR (2018)
3. Dragon, R., Rosenhahn, B., Ostermann, J.: Multi-scale clustering of frame-to-frame correspondences for motion segmentation. In: Fitzgibbon, A., Lazebnik, S., Perona, P., Sato, Y., Schmid, C. (eds.) ECCV 2012. LNCS, pp. 445–458. Springer, Heidelberg (2012). https://doi.org/10.1007/978-3-642-33709-3_32
4. Ochs, P., Malik, J., Brox, T.: Segmentation of moving objects by long term video analysis. IEEE Trans. Pattern Anal. Mach. Intell. **36**(6), 1187–1200 (2014)
5. Elhamifar, E., Vidal, R.: Sparse subspace clustering. In: CVPR. IEEE (2009)
6. Yang, M.Y., Ackermann, H., Lin, W., Feng, S., Rosenhahn, B.: Motion segmentation via global and local sparse subspace optimization. arXiv preprint arXiv:1701.06944 (2017)
7. Yan, J., Pollefeys, M.: A general framework for motion segmentation: independent, articulated, rigid, non-rigid, degenerate and non-degenerate. In: Leonardis, A., Bischof, H., Pinz, A. (eds.) ECCV 2006. LNCS, vol. 3954, pp. 94–106. Springer, Heidelberg (2006). https://doi.org/10.1007/11744085_8
8. Tsai, Y.H., Yang, M.H., Black, M.J.: Video segmentation via object flow. In: CVPR (2016)
9. Cheng, J., Tsai, Y.H., Wang, S., Yang, M.H.: SegFlow: joint learning for video object segmentation and optical flow. In: ICCV (2017)
10. Nirkin, Y., Masi, I., Tuan, A.T., Hassner, T., Medioni, G.: On face segmentation, face swapping, and face perception. In: Automatic Face & Gesture Recognition IEEE International Conference (2018)
11. Zhao, T., Nevatia, R.: Stochastic human segmentation from a static camera. In: Motion and Video Computing, Workshop (2002)
12. Zhao, T., Nevatia, R.: Bayesian human segmentation in crowded situations. In: CVPR (2003)
13. Spina, T.V., et al.: Video human segmentation using fuzzy object models and its application to body pose estimation of toddlers for behavior studies. arXiv preprint arXiv:1305.6918 (2013)
14. Song, C., Huang, Y., Wang, Z., Wang, L.: 1000 fps human segmentation with deep convolutional neural networks. In: ACPR. IEEE (2015)
15. Guo, L.J., Cheng, T.T., Xiao, B., Zhang, R., Zhao, J.Y.: Video human segmentation based on multiple-cue integration. Signal Process. Image Commun. **30**, 166–177 (2015)
16. Lu, J., Corso, J.J., et al.: Human action segmentation with hierarchical supervoxel consistency. In: CVPR (2015)
17. Tan, Y., Guo, Y., Gao, C.: Background subtraction based level sets for human segmentation in thermal infrared surveillance systems. Infrared Phys. Technol. **61**, 230–240 (2013)
18. He, F., Guo, Y., Gao, C.: Human segmentation of infrared image for mobile robot search. Multimedia Tools and Applications, pp. 1–14 (2017)
19. Yarin Gal, R.I., Ghahramani, Z.: Deep Bayesian active learning with image data. In: ICML (2017)

20. Colwell, S.R., Joshi, A.W.: Multi-item scale development for measuring institutional pressures in the context of corporate environmental action. In: IABS (2009)
21. Brinker, K.: Incorporating diversity in active learning with support vector machines. In: ICML (2003)
22. Ducoffe, M., Precioso, F.: Adversarial active learning for deep networks: a margin based approach. arXiv preprint arXiv:1802.09841 (2018)
23. Li, X., Guo, R., Cheng, J.: Incorporating incremental and active learning for scene classification. In: ICMLA (2012)
24. Elhamifar, E., Sapiro, G., Yang, A., Sasrty, S.S.: A convex optimization framework for active learning. In: ICCV (2013)
25. Yang, Y., Loog, M.: A variance maximization criterion for active learning. arXiv preprint arXiv:1706.07642 (2017)
26. Kading, C., Freytag, A., Rodner, E., Perino, A., Denzler, J.: Large-scale active learning with approximations of expected model output changes. In: GCPR (2016)
27. Kuwadekar, A., Neville, J.: Relational active learning for joint collective classification models. In: ICML (2011)
28. Paul, S., Bappy, J.H., Roy-Chowdhury, A.K.: Non-uniform subset selection for active learning in structured data. In: CVPR (2017)
29. Fang, M., Li, Y., Cohn, T.: Learning how to active learn: a deep reinforcement learning approach. In: EMNLP (2017)
30. Philip Bachman, A.S., Trischler, A.: Learning algorithms for active learning. In: ICML (2017)
31. Tzeng, E., Hoffman, J., Darrell, T., Saenko, K.: Simultaneous deep transfer across domains and tasks. In: ICCV (2015)
32. Long, M., Cao, Y., Wang, J., Jordan, M.: Learning transferable features with deep adaptation networks. In: ICML (2015)
33. Zellinger, W., Grubinger, T., Lughofer, E., Natschläger, T., Saminger-Platz, S.: Central moment discrepancy (CMD) for domain-invariant representation learning. In: ICLR (2017)
34. Goodfellow, I., et al.: Generative adversarial nets. In: NIPS (2014)
35. Liu, M.Y., Tuzel, O.: Coupled generative adversarial networks. In: NIPS (2016)
36. Ganin, Y., Lempitsky, V.: Unsupervised domain adaptation by backpropagation. In: ICML (2015)
37. Tzeng, E., Hoffman, J., Saenko, K., Darrell, T.: Adversarial discriminative domain adaptation. arXiv preprint arXiv:1702.05464 (2017)
38. Bousmalis, K., Trigeorgis, G., Silberman, N., Krishnan, D., Erhan, D.: Domain separation networks. In: NIPS (2016)
39. Hoffman, J., Wang, D., Yu, F., Darrell, T.: FCNs in the wild: pixel-level adversarial and constraint-based adaptation. arXiv preprint arXiv:1612.02649 (2016)
40. Chen, Y.H., Chen, W.Y., Chen, Y.T., Tsai, B.C., Wang, Y.C.F., Sun, M.: No more discrimination: cross city adaptation of road scene segmenters. In: ICCV (2017)
41. Zhang, Y., David, P., Gong, B.: Curriculum domain adaptation for semantic segmentation of urban scenes. In: ICCV (2017)
42. Sankaranarayanan, S., Balaji, Y., Jain, A., Lim, S.N., Chellappa, R.: Unsupervised domain adaptation for semantic segmentation with GANs. arXiv preprint arXiv:1711.06969 (2017)
43. Ilg, E., Mayer, N., Saikia, T., Keuper, M., Dosovitskiy, A., Brox, T.: FlowNet 2.0: evolution of optical flow estimation with deep networks. arXiv preprint arXiv:1612.01925 (2016)
44. Brox, T., Malik, J.: Large displacement optical flow: descriptor matching in variational motion estimation. TPAMI **33**(3), 500–513 (2011)

45. Weston, J., Chopra, S., Bordes, A.: Memory networks. In: ICLR (2015)
46. Oh, J., Chockalingam, V., Singh, S., Lee, H.: Control of memory, active perception, and action in minecraft. In: ICML (2016)
47. Fragkiadaki, K., Zhang, W., Zhang, G., Shi, J.: Two-granularity tracking: mediating trajectory and detection graphs for tracking under occlusions. In: Fitzgibbon, A., Lazebnik, S., Perona, P., Sato, Y., Schmid, C. (eds.) ECCV 2012. LNCS, vol. 7576, pp. 552–565. Springer, Heidelberg (2012). https://doi.org/10.1007/978-3-642-33715-4_40
48. Ronneberger, O., Fischer, P., Brox, T.: U-Net: convolutional networks for biomedical image segmentation. In: Navab, N., Hornegger, J., Wells, W.M., Frangi, A.F. (eds.) MICCAI 2015. LNCS, vol. 9351, pp. 234–241. Springer, Cham (2015). https://doi.org/10.1007/978-3-319-24574-4_28
49. Everingham, M., Eslami, S.A., Van Gool, L., Williams, C.K., Winn, J., Zisserman, A.: The pascal visual object classes challenge: a retrospective. IJCV **111**(1), 98–136 (2015)
50. Kingma, D., Ba, J.: Adam: a method for stochastic optimization. In: ICLR (2015)
51. Lin, T.-Y., et al.: Microsoft COCO: common objects in context. In: Fleet, D., Pajdla, T., Schiele, B., Tuytelaars, T. (eds.) ECCV 2014. LNCS, vol. 8693, pp. 740–755. Springer, Cham (2014). https://doi.org/10.1007/978-3-319-10602-1_48

Analyzing Clothing Layer Deformation Statistics of 3D Human Motions

Jinlong Yang[1(✉)], Jean-Sébastien Franco[1], Franck Hétroy-Wheeler[2], and Stefanie Wuhrer[1]

[1] Univ. Grenoble Alpes, Inria, CNRS, Grenoble INP(Institute of Engineering Univ. Grenoble Alpes), LJK, 38000 Grenoble, France
{jinlong.yang,jean-sebastien.franco,stefanie.wuhrer}@inria.fr

[2] ICube, University of Strasbourg, Strasbourg, France
hetroywheeler@unistra.fr

Abstract. Recent capture technologies and methods allow not only to retrieve 3D model sequence of moving people in clothing, but also to separate and extract the underlying body geometry, motion component and the clothing as a geometric layer. So far this clothing layer has only been used as raw offsets for individual applications such as retargeting a different body capture sequence with the clothing layer of another sequence, with limited scope, *e.g.* using identical or similar motions. The structured, semantics and motion-correlated nature of the information contained in this layer has yet to be fully understood and exploited. To this purpose we propose a comprehensive analysis of the statistics of this layer with a simple two-component model, based on PCA subspace reduction of the layer information on one hand, and a generic parameter regression model using neural networks on the other hand, designed to regress from any semantic parameter whose variation is observed in a training set, to the layer parameterization space. We show that this model not only allows to reproduce previous retargeting works, but generalizes the data generation capabilities to other semantic parameters such as clothing variation and size, or physical material parameters with synthetically generated training sequence, paving the way for many kinds of capture data-driven creation and augmentation applications.

Keywords: Clothing motion analysis · 3D garment capture
Capture data augmentation and retargeting

1 Introduction

Sequences showing the dense 3D geometry of dressed humans in motion are used in many 3D content creation applications. Two main approaches may be used

Electronic supplementary material The online version of this chapter (https://doi.org/10.1007/978-3-030-01234-2_15) contains supplementary material, which is available to authorized users.

V. Ferrari et al. (Eds.): ECCV 2018, LNCS 11211, pp. 245–261, 2018.
https://doi.org/10.1007/978-3-030-01234-2_15

to generate them, namely through physical simulation and by dense 3D motion capture. Physical simulators allow to generate realistic motions and cloth folding patterns based on given 3D models of the actor and the clothing, along with actor motion and cloth material parameters [7,9,17]. Dense 3D motion capture of human models has recently become possible at high spatial and temporal resolution, e.g. using multi-camera systems [4,10,23]. While the captured data is unstructured, recent processing algorithms allow to track the captured geometry over time and to separate the actor's body from the clothing [21,38,40].

While these works allow for the generation of accurate dense 3D motion sequences of human models with clothing, the content creation is expensive. Motion capture of the dense 3D geometry requires calibrated acquisition setups and the processing of the captured geometry requires heavy computation. Physical simulation requires artist generated models of actor and clothing and is typically computationally expensive.

In this work, we propose to leverage existing 3D motion sequences of dressed humans by performing a statistical analysis of the dynamically deforming clothing layer in order to allow for efficient synthesis of 3D motion. Performing statistical analysis on the clothing deformation is challenging for two main reasons. First, the motion of the clothing is influenced by numerous factors including the body shape and the motion of the underlying human as well as the cloth material. To allow for controlled synthesis of these effects, they must be explicitly modeled. Second, the geometry of the person with clothing may be significantly different from that of the underlying human body, e.g. in case of a dress, and the clothing may slide w.r.t. the human skin. Hence, computing assignments between the clothing layer and the body is complicated, especially across different subjects who wear the same type of clothing (e.g. shorts and T-shirt).

Two existing lines of work analyze the clothing layer to allow for synthesis. The first one analyzes multiple subjects wearing the same type of clothing based on simulated cloth deformations as training data [15,37]. While these works allow for efficient synthesis, they can only be applied to simulated clothing, where the geometry is free of noise and explicit geometric correspondence information is available across all training data. Hence, the realism of the resulting cloth synthesis is limited by the quality of the cloth simulator used during training. The second line of work addresses this problem by analyzing the deformation of the clothing layer based on dense 3D motion capture data [21]. This work can handle noisy and unstructured data and the resulting model allows to change the body shape and motion under the clothing. However, the model can only be trained on one specific actor wearing a fixed outfit, and can hence not be used to synthesize changes in the clothing itself (e.g. changes of fit or materials).

This work combines the advantages of both methods by enabling to train from various motion data that can either be simulated or captured. To this end, we perform statistical analysis to model the geometric variability of the clothing layer. Our main contribution is that the proposed analysis is versatile in the sense that it can be used to train and regress on semantic parameters, thereby allowing to control e.g. clothing fit or material parameters of the synthesized sequences. Our statistical analysis models the deformation of the clothing layer w.r.t. the deformation behaviour of the underlying human actor represented using a statistical model of 3D body shape. For the analysis, we consider two fairly straightforward models. First, we model the layer variations with a linear subspace. Second, we model the variation of the clothing layer using a statistical regression model, in order to capture some of the underlying causal dynamics in relatively simple form. Our experiments show the validity of the representation with qualitative and quantitative captured sequence reconstruction experiments based on these parameterizations. We further qualitatively demonstrate the value of our approach for three applications. First, following [21], we train from multiple sequences of the same actor in the same clothing acquired using dense 3D motion capture and use this to exchange body shape and motion. Second, following [15], we train from multiple simulated sequences showing the same actor in clothing of different materials and use this to change the material of the clothing. Third, to demonstrate the novelty of our approach, we train from multiple sequences of different actors in the same type of clothing acquired using dense 3D motion capture and use this to change the fit of the clothing.

2 Related Work

This section reviews work on modeling the clothing layer. Furthermore, in case of captured 3D data, the models need to be processed to establish temporal coherence and to extract the clothing layer, and we provide a brief review of related literature.

Simulation-Based Modeling of Clothing Layer. To model the deformation of the clothing layer, a possible solution is direct physics-based simulation, for example with mass-spring systems [7,9], continuum mechanics [34], or individual yarn structures [17]. The physical simulation models are complex and rely on numerous control parameters. Those parameters can be tuned manually, estimated from captures [32] or learned from perceptual experiments [30]. One line of works trains models on physics-based simulations using machine learning techniques, which subsequently allow for more efficient synthesis of novel 3D motion sequences of dressed humans [2,15,37]. In particular, these methods learn a regression from the clothing deformation to low-dimensional parameters representing body motion. These methods allow to modify the body shape, motion, and to alter the clothing. But the main disadvantage is that the methods are limited by the quality of the simulated synthetic training data. Since the simulation of complex clothing with multiple layers remains a challenging problem, this limitation restricts the model to relatively simple clothing. Our work addresses this problem by allowing to train from both simulated and captured sequences.

Capture-Based Modeling of Clothing Layer. Thanks to laser scanners, depth cameras, and multi-camera system, it is now possible to capture and reconstruct 3D human motion sequences as raw mesh sequences [4,10,23], and recent processing algorithms (reviewed in the following) allow to extract semantic information from the raw data. A recent line of work leverages this rich source of data by using captured sequences to learn the deformation of the clothing layer [22,25]. Neophytou and Hilton [22] propose a method that trains from a single subject in fixed clothing and allows to change the body shape and motion after training. Pons-Moll *et al.* [25] extract the body shape and individual pieces of clothing from a raw capture sequence and use this information to transfer the captured clothing to new body shapes. These methods allow to learn from complex deformations without requiring a physical model of the observations. The main disadvantage is that the model does not allow the modification of the clothing itself, such as the fit of the clothing and the cloth material. Our work addresses this problem by exploiting self-redundancies of the deformation to build a regression model from semantic sizing or material parameters to the clothing layer.

Processing Raw Dense 3D Motion Captures for Human Modeling. When captured 3D human motion sequences are used as input to our method, they first need to be processed to compute alignments and estimate the body under clothing. Recently, many solutions have been proposed for these challenging problems.

First approaches to process raw dense 3D motion captures of humans aimed to track human pose by fitting a 3D generic kinematic body-part model to captured 2D [28,29,31] or 3D data of the person [41]. To handle variation in body shape, some of these models adapt the size of rigid components of the skeleton or, taking this one step further, estimate shape parameters based on a human statistical shape space [5,20,21]. This accounts for the morphology of the captured human, for a closer data fit and a more accurate body estimate. Apart from such model fitting methods, other methods try to estimate the body shape by using convolutional neural networks [11–13]. Since all of these approaches assume tight clothing, they typically lead to inflation of the body estimate in the presence of wider clothing. To address this problem, recent methods propose to explicitly include wider clothing in the modeling. Instead of fitting a body shape as close as possible to the observation, the human body shape under clothing is captured by fitting the human model within the observed clothing contour from images [6,8,26] or the 3D clothing surfaces [16,36,38,40]. These methods extract both the underlying body shape morphology and pose, as well as an explicit relative mesh representation of the clothing layer.

Aligning the clothing layer of a moving human is challenging because of the high deformation variability due to both the human pose and the non-rigidity of the cloth. To solve this problem some works combine reconstruction and tracking by deforming a detailed 3D model, typically obtained from a laser scan, to fit the capture data [3,14,18,33]. These methods are usually applied to scenarios where captures are not dense enough to create a high-quality reconstruction, such as multi-camera systems with only few cameras. To prevent vertex drifting along the surface, some works exploit surface features to guide the template deformation [39]. Another line of works uses the estimated underlying body shape to align the clothed surface [25,27,40]. Our work leverages these recent processing methods for captured data to extract body shape estimations and alignments of the surface of the dressed person from given raw captured sequences.

3 Methodology

We propose a general framework to study the deformation of the clothing layer. First, we estimate the human body shape and extract the offset clothing layer in a way that is robust to situations where the geometry of the dressed person differs significantly from the geometry of the human body, as in the case of a dress. A fuzzy vertex association from the clothing surface to the body surface is established, so that we can represent the clothing deformation as an offset mesh based on the body surface. Second, we use statistical analysis to analyze the geometric variability of the clothing layer to greatly reduce self-redundancies. Third, we show how to capture some of the underlying causal dynamics in relatively simple form, by modeling the variation of this clothing layer as a function of body motion as well as semantic variables using a statistical regression model.

The input to our method is a set of 3D sequences showing the dense geometry of a human in clothing performing a motion. These sequences may have been generated using physical simulation or motion capture set-ups. Before further processing, we require for each sequence an estimate of the underlying body shape and motion and an alignment of the clothing layer. Note that the clothing layer may optionally include the geometry of the body itself, i.e. show the body with clothing. If the sequences were generated using physical simulation, this information is typically readily available. For captured data, any of the previously reviewed methods may be used to compute this information. In this work, we estimate the underlying body shape using a recent method that explicitly takes wide clothing into account [38] and compute alignments of the complete deforming surface (i.e. the human in clothing) using an embedded deformation model based on Li *et al.* [18] without refining the deformation graph.

In the following, we denote the aligned sequences of the clothing layer by $\boldsymbol{C}_1, \ldots, \boldsymbol{C}_n$ and the corresponding sequences of underlying body shape estimates by $\boldsymbol{B}_1, \ldots, \boldsymbol{B}_n$. Furthermore, let $\boldsymbol{C}_{i,k}$ and $\boldsymbol{B}_{i,k}$ denote the k-th frames of $\boldsymbol{C}_i$ and $\boldsymbol{B}_i$, respectively. Thanks to the alignment, $\boldsymbol{C}_{i,k}$ has the same number of corresponding vertices as $\boldsymbol{C}_{j,l}$. Similarly, $\boldsymbol{B}_{i,k}$ has the same number of corresponding vertices as $\boldsymbol{B}_{j,l}$. While sequences $\boldsymbol{C}_i$ and $\boldsymbol{C}_j$ (and similarly $\boldsymbol{B}_i$ and $\boldsymbol{B}_j$) may consist of different numbers of frames, $\boldsymbol{C}_i$ and $\boldsymbol{B}_i$ contain corresponding clothing layer and body estimate and therefore consist of the same number of frames.

The body estimates in sequence $\boldsymbol{B}_i$ can be expressed using a generative statistical body model that decouples the influence of identity and posture variation [20,21,24]. This allows to represent $\boldsymbol{B}_i$ using one vector $\boldsymbol{\beta}_i$ for identity information and a vector $\boldsymbol{\theta}_{i,k}$ per frame for pose information. These generative models allow for two important modifications. First, the body shape of the actor can be changed while keeping the same motion by modifying $\boldsymbol{\beta}_i$. Second, the body motion can be changed by modifying $\boldsymbol{\theta}_{i,k}$ for each frame.

In this work, we use S-SCAPE as generative model [24], which uses the A-pose as standard pose $\boldsymbol{\theta}_0$. S-SCAPE combines a linear space learned using principal component analysis (PCA) to represent variations due to identity with a linear blend skinning (LBS) model to represent variations in pose. Consider the j-th vertex $\boldsymbol{v}^{\boldsymbol{B}}_{i,k,j}$ of frame $\boldsymbol{B}_{i,k}$. This vertex is generated by transforming the j-th vertex $\boldsymbol{\mu}_j^B$ of the mean body shape in standard pose $\boldsymbol{\theta}_0$ as $\boldsymbol{v}_{i,k,j}^B = \boldsymbol{T}_j(\boldsymbol{\theta}_{i,k})\boldsymbol{T}_j(\boldsymbol{\beta}_i)\boldsymbol{\mu}_j^B$, where $\boldsymbol{T}_j(\boldsymbol{\theta}_{i,k})$ and $\boldsymbol{T}_j(\boldsymbol{\beta}_i)$ are (homogeneous) transformation matrices applying the transformations modeled by LBS and learned by PCA. We can hence use S-SCAPE to define an operation called *unposing* in the following. This operation changes the pose of $\boldsymbol{B}_{i,k}$ to the standard pose $\boldsymbol{\theta}_0$ while maintaining body shape by replacing vertex $\boldsymbol{v}_{i,k,j}^B$ for all j by

$$\tilde{\boldsymbol{v}}_{i,k,j}^B = \left(\boldsymbol{T}_j(\boldsymbol{\theta}_{i,k})\right)^{-1} \boldsymbol{v}_{i,k,j}^B. \tag{1}$$

3.1 Offset Clothing Layer Extraction

We model the clothing layer as an offset from the body. To this end, we need to find corresponding vertices on the body mesh for each clothing vertex. Because $\boldsymbol{C}_1, \dots, \boldsymbol{C}_n$ and $\boldsymbol{B}_1, \dots, \boldsymbol{B}_n$ are temporally coherent, respectively, we can establish this correspondence on a single pair of frames $(\boldsymbol{C}_{i,k}, \boldsymbol{B}_{i,k})$ and propagate this information to all sequences. In practice, a pair of frames with few concavities is preferred because it enhances the robustness of the sparse association when created using a ray shooting method (see next paragraph). However to prove the generality of our approach, in our experiments, the association is simply estimated on the first frame of the first sequence. Since the following description is limited to a single pair of frames $(\boldsymbol{C}_{1,1}, \boldsymbol{B}_{1,1})$, for simplicity, we will drop frame and sequence index in this subsection.

$\boldsymbol{C}$ and $\boldsymbol{B}$ usually consist of a different number of vertices and have possibly significantly different geometry. Hence, a bijective association is in general not achievable. As our final goal is to model the deformation of the clothing layer using the body layer, our main interest is to find one or more corresponding vertices on $\boldsymbol{B}$ for each vertex on $\boldsymbol{C}$. We achieve this by computing a sparse correspondence that is subsequently propagated to each vertex on $\boldsymbol{C}$ using a probabilistic geodesic diffusion method. Note that unlike Pons-Moll *et al.* [25], our method works for difficult geometries such as skirts without manual intervention.

Sparse Association. For each vertex $\boldsymbol{v}_j^B$ on $\boldsymbol{B}$ we shoot a ray along the surface normal outwards the body. If there is an intersection $\boldsymbol{p}_j^C$ with $\boldsymbol{C}$ and the distance between $\boldsymbol{v}_j^B$ and $\boldsymbol{p}_j^C$ is within a threshold of 15 cm, we search for the vertex $\boldsymbol{v}_i^C$ on $\boldsymbol{C}$ closest to $\boldsymbol{p}_j^C$. Such pairs $\left(\boldsymbol{v}_i^C, \boldsymbol{v}_j^B\right)$ are considered to be associated. If multiple body vertices are associated with the same clothing vertex, we only keep one pair per clothing vertex to put the same weight to each sparsely associated $\boldsymbol{v}_i^C$. The pairs $\left(\boldsymbol{v}_i^C, \boldsymbol{v}_j^B\right)$ are defined as *sparse association.*

Fuzzy Dense Association. We now propagate the sparse association to every clothing vertex. Intuitively, if a clothing vertex $\boldsymbol{v}_i^C$ is associated to a body vertex $\boldsymbol{v}_j^B$ then there is a high probability that the neighboring vertices of $\boldsymbol{v}_i^C$ should be associated to the neighboring vertices of $\boldsymbol{v}_j^B$. Based on this idea, for any pair $\left(\boldsymbol{v}_k^C, \boldsymbol{v}_l^B\right) \in \boldsymbol{C} \times \boldsymbol{B}$ we initialize the association probability $P\left(\boldsymbol{v}_k^C, \boldsymbol{v}_l^B\right)$ to be 0. Then we loop on all the sparse association pairs $\left(\boldsymbol{v}_i^C, \boldsymbol{v}_j^B\right)$ and update the association probability of any vertex pair $\left(\boldsymbol{v}_k^C, \boldsymbol{v}_l^B\right)$ according to:

$$P\left(\boldsymbol{v}_k^C, \boldsymbol{v}_l^B\right) = P\left(\boldsymbol{v}_k^C, \boldsymbol{v}_l^B\right) + exp\left(-\left(r\left(\boldsymbol{v}_k^C, \boldsymbol{v}_i^C\right) + r\left(\boldsymbol{v}_l^B, \boldsymbol{v}_j^B\right)\right)/\sigma^2\right), \quad (2)$$

where $r(,)$ computes the squared geodesic distance between two vertices. In our implementation we set σ to 1 cm. To simplify the computation we only consider vertices $\boldsymbol{v}_k^C$ and $\boldsymbol{v}_l^B$ that lie within 3 cm geodesic distance from $\boldsymbol{v}_i^C$ and $\boldsymbol{v}_j^B$. For the dense association, for each vertex on $\boldsymbol{C}$ we choose a constant number n_f of vertices on S that have the highest association probability values as associated vertices. We normalize the association probability to form fuzzy association weights, and store the indices of the n_f associations in a list I. This step does not only compute body vertex matches for previously unassociated clothing vertices but can also correct wrong matches from the sparse association and make the association more meaningful in situations where $\boldsymbol{C}$ and $\boldsymbol{B}$ differ significantly. This is illustrated in the case of a skirt on the right of Fig. 1 (see also Sect. 4.1 for a discussion).

Offset Representation of Clothing Layer. Since we have established correspondence between $\boldsymbol{C}$ and $\boldsymbol{B}$, we can now get the offset clothing layer by subtracting $\boldsymbol{B}$ from $\boldsymbol{C}$. However, this Euclidean offset depends on the human pose and the global rotation. To account for this, we first unpose both $\boldsymbol{B}$ and $\boldsymbol{C}$. The body estimate $\boldsymbol{B}$ is unposed using Eq. 1, and the clothing layer $\boldsymbol{C}$ is unposed with the help of the fuzzy dense association by replacing vertex $\boldsymbol{v}_j^C$ for all j by

$$\tilde{\boldsymbol{v}}_j^C = \left(\sum_{i=1}^{n_f} \omega_i \boldsymbol{T}_{I_j[i]}(\boldsymbol{\theta})\right)^{-1} \boldsymbol{v}_j^C, \quad (3)$$

where ω_i are the fuzzy association weights and $I_j[i]$ denotes the i-th entry of the index list I associated with vertex $\boldsymbol{v}_j^C$. The offset of each clothing vertex is then obtained as:

$$\boldsymbol{d}_{i,j} = \tilde{\boldsymbol{v}}_i^C - \tilde{\boldsymbol{v}}_j^B, \quad \boldsymbol{d}_{i,j} \in \mathbb{R}^3, \quad (4)$$

where $\left(\tilde{\boldsymbol{v}}_i^C, \tilde{\boldsymbol{v}}_j^B\right)$ form a fuzzily associated pair. We stack all the $\boldsymbol{d}_{i,j}$ from one frame pair $(\boldsymbol{C}, \boldsymbol{B})$ to form a single vector denoted by $\boldsymbol{d} \in \mathbb{R}^{3 \times n_f \times n_v}$, where n_v is the number of vertices in $\boldsymbol{C}$.

3.2 Clothing Layer Deformation Space Reduction

The deformation of the offset clothing layer is now encoded in $\boldsymbol{d}$. To reduce the self-redundancies in $\boldsymbol{d}$, we perform PCA on $\boldsymbol{d}$ from all frame pairs $(\boldsymbol{C}_{i,k}, \boldsymbol{B}_{i,k})$. This allows for the clothing deformation to be represented by PCA coefficients $\boldsymbol{\alpha}_k$. Note we do not assume $\boldsymbol{d}_k$ to form a Gaussian distribution. The purpose of PCA is only to reduce the dimensionality of the space, not to sample from it.

We would like to learn a mapping from semantic parameters of interest, denoted by $\boldsymbol{\gamma}$,to the clothing layer deformation. After obtaining a low dimensional representation, this is equivalent to finding a mapping from $\boldsymbol{\gamma}$ to $\boldsymbol{\alpha}$.

The PCA representation of the offsets successfully gets rid of self-redundancies in clothing layer. Furthermore, in PCA space, we can choose the number of principal components to use in order to balance the speed, storage, and quality.

3.3 Neural Network for Regression

To allow control of the offset clothing layer deformation, we study the relationship between its variation and semantic parameters γ, where γ can be body motion, clothing style, clothing material and so on. We treat this as a regression problem that learns the mapping from γ to $\boldsymbol{\alpha}$. Due to the nonlinearity of the problem itself and the potentially large sample size, we choose a fully connected two-hidden-layer neural network to train the regression, with the size of input layer equal to the dimensionality of the semantic parameters and the size of output layer equal to the number of principal component used. The sizes of the first and second hidden layers are 60 and 80, respectively. In our implementation, the neural network is implemented with OpenNN [1]. For each experiment, we set 20% of the frames from training data as validation frames. We choose mean square error as loss function, quasi-Newton method as optimization strategy, and stop the training once validation error starts to increase.

4 Method Validation

To validate each step of our method, we train on small training sets consisting of a single sequence each ($n = 1$) using ten existing sequences of the Adobe [33] and Inria [38] datasets showing fast, large-scale motion in ample clothing as this is especially challenging to model. In all following experiments, body motion is parameterized by global speed, joint angles and joint angular speed. For offset clothing layer extraction, we show that we can extract the entire clothing layer regardless of the clothing geometry. Then we validate our PCA step to show that it greatly reduces the deformation space with acceptable reconstruction error. Finally, we validate the neural network regression by showing that both training error and testing error are satisfying.

4.1 Offset Clothing Layer Extraction

We model the offset by first constructing a sparse correspondence between clothing and body, and then propagating the correspondence to each clothing vertex. Figure 1 (left) shows an example of the sparse and fuzzy association. Note that if we only use sparse association to store the information about clothing deformation, the information of the lower part of the dress is not recorded sufficiently.

The geometry of the clothing layer and the underlying human body differs significantly in the case of a skirt. Hence, $n_f = 1$ may not be meaningful and robust enough as having a single associated vertex is prone to form a seam in the middle of the front and the back faces of the skirt as some vertices around those areas are associated to the left thigh while neighboring ones are associated

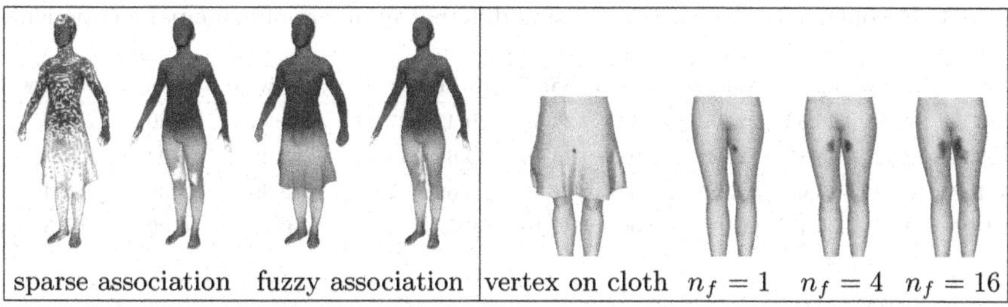

Fig. 1. Left: associations of clothing and body layer ($n_f = 1$), where color indicates the association. Right: a blue vertex on the skirt is associated to body vertices with different n_f. The intensity of the blue color is proportional to the association weight. (Color figure online)

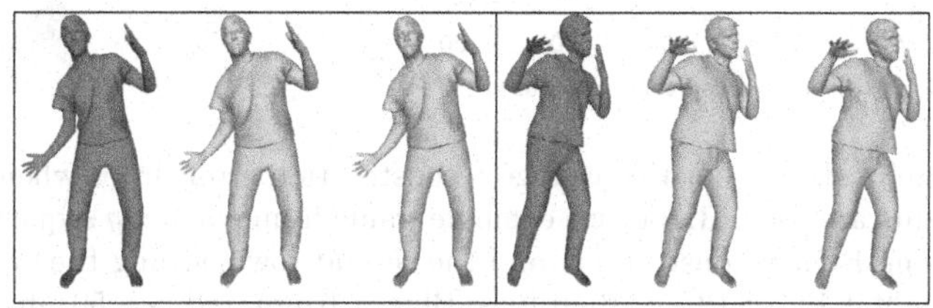

Fig. 2. Comparison to [25]. From left to right: original acquisition, transferred clothing layer with our method, and with [25]. Both methods produce very similar results.

to the right thigh. Using higher n_f, such a skirt vertex is associated to both legs, therefore preventing seams. This is illustrated in Fig. 1 (right).

We use our fuzzy association to directly transfer the offset clothing layer on data from Pons-Moll *et al.* [25]. Compared with their work, our method achieves similar results, shown in Fig. 2, without the need for manual intervention.

4.2 PCA Deformation Space Reduction

In our experiments, the dimension of the offset clothing layer vector generally varies from 20,000 to 80,000. To reduce this dimensionality, we perform PCA on the extracted offset of the clothing layer. To analyze how many PCs to keep, we reconstruct the sequence with different numbers of PCs. We compare the reconstruction against the original sequence by computing the average vertex position error. Table 1 gives errors per sequence for different numbers of principal components. Figure 3 visualizes the effect of increasing the number of PCs for one example. Such an analysis allows to choose the number of PCs to satisfy requirements on accuracy, speed or memory usage. In all following experiments, when training on a single subject with fixed clothing, we use 40 PCs, and when training on multiple subjects or multiple clothings, we use 100PCs as we found these datasets to contain more variation

Table 1. Reconstruction error (mm) using different numbers of principal components.

Seq	Bounc.	Crane	Mar. 1	Squat 1	Samba	Swing	s1 m. w.	s1 w. w.	s6 m. w.	s6 w. w.
1 PC	32.48	26.53	22.95	46.33	24.05	30.42	27.24	23.92	28.20	26.38
5 PC	22.52	14.87	13.94	18.94	14.75	19.68	13.73	13.28	12.94	12.25
40 PC	6.49	3.08	2.68	2.67	2.40	3.62	2.17	2.30	1.38	1.94
All PC	0.10	0.11	0.11	0.09	0.10	0.09	0.13	0.12	0.09	0.13

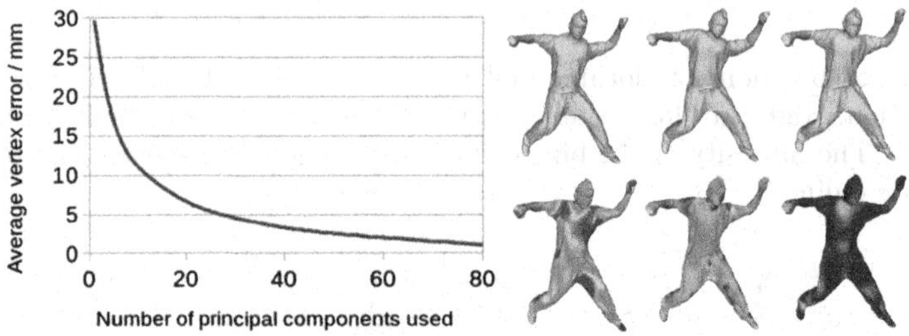

Fig. 3. Left: curve shows that the average reconstruction error drops when more principal components are used. Right: one example frame from *bouncing* sequence with the first row showing PCA reconstruction and the second row showing the error in color. From left to right 1 PC, 5 PCs and 40 PCs. Blue = 0 mm, red >= 50 mm.

4.3 Neural Network Regression

We validate our neural network by regressing 40 PCA coefficients to human body motion. Each sequence consists of 95–275 frames. We choose 20% of the frames from each sequence as testing data and the remaining 80% to be the training data. After training, we feed the motion parameters for all frames to the network and get 40 PCA coefficients for each frame to reconstruct the sequence. This reconstruction is then compared against the ground truth. Table 2 shows the quantitative error of the regression. The training error and the prediction error are generally low and close to the reconstruction error when using 40 principal components, which means our neural network regression is accurate and does not overfit the training data. Figure 4 shows the visual result of some examples of the regression error. Both training and prediction error are almost always low.

Table 2. Reconstruction error based on regression for each sequence.

Seq	Bounc.	Crane	Mar. 1	Squat 1	Samba	Swing	s1 m. w.	s1 w. w.	s6 m. w.	s6 w. w.
E_{train}	9.95	4.71	3.54	6.57	4.27	7.72	10.87	9.09	7.71	5.97
E_{pred}	10.27	4.28	3.93	4.31	7.44	5.95	8.57	9.21	8.19	4.82

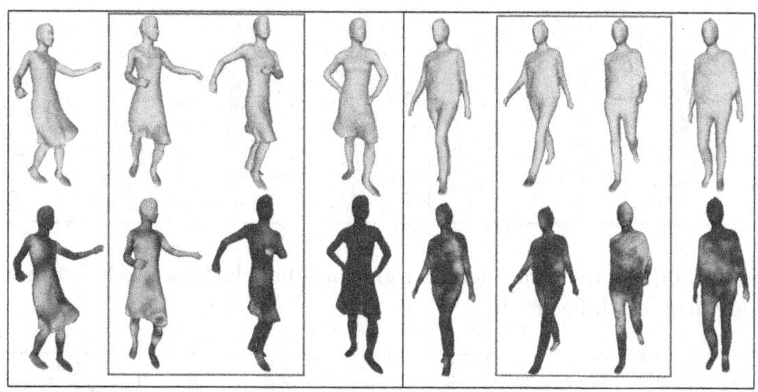

Fig. 4. Regression on two sequences. First row shows reconstruction. Second row shows vertex error on ground truth meshes. The two columns in the red box are predictions from testing frames; others are from training frames. Blue = 0 mm, red >= 50 mm. (Color figure online)

5 Applications

This section shows the virtue of the proposed method by applying it to three scenarios. The first trains from multiple sequences of the same actor in the same clothing and uses this to synthesize similar clothing on new body shapes and under new motions. The second trains from multiple simulated sequences showing the same actor in clothing of different materials and uses this to change the material of the clothing. The third application trains from multiple sequences of different actors in the same type of clothing and uses this to change the fit of the clothing. This entirely new way of synthesizing clothing is possible thanks to our regression to semantic parameters. For better visualizations of the results, refer to the supplemental material.

5.1 Clothing Dynamics Modeling

Change body shape After extracting the offset of the clothing layer, we can add this offset to any body shape under normalized pose and update the pose of the body with clothing using the relations of Eqs. 3 and 4. Figure 5 shows two examples of changing the body shape of a given motion sequence.

Change Clothing Dynamics. In this part, we trained our regression model from multiple sequences of the same actor in the same clothing acquired using dense 3D motion capture. We use the regression model to learn the mapping from the body motion parameters to the PCA coefficients of the offset vectors. To synthesize new sequences, we feed new motion parameters to the model. Figure 6 shows examples of the resulting changes in the clothing dynamics. Note that realistic wrinkling effects are synthesized.

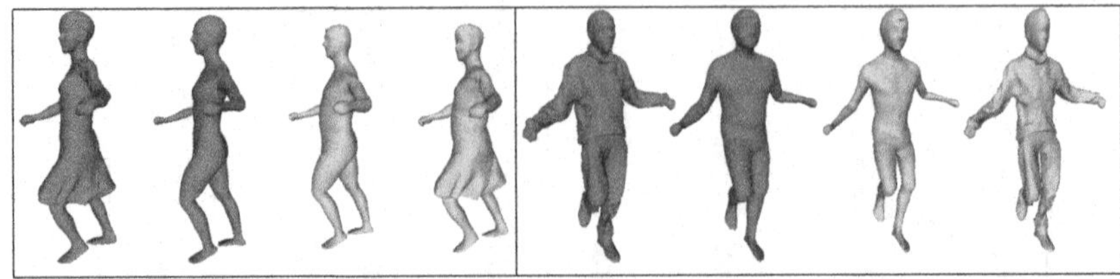

Fig. 5. Change body shape. From left to right: original clothing mesh, estimated body, changed body, new clothing mesh.

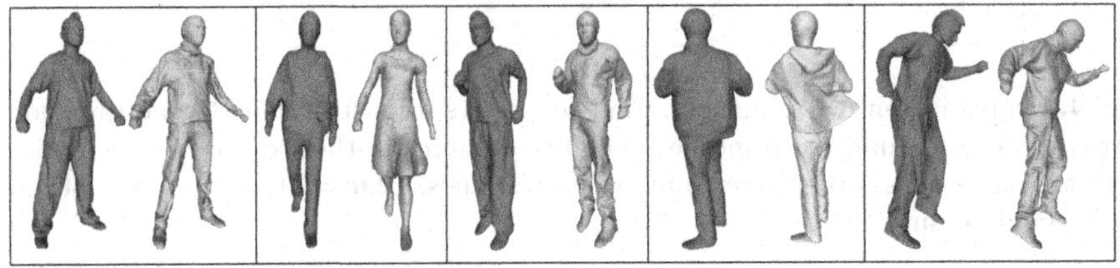

Fig. 6. Examples of changing clothing dynamics. The brighter gray meshes are not in the training data but generated by feeding the motion parameters of the darker gray meshes to the neural network trained on sequences containing the brighter gray clothes.

5.2 Clothing Material Modeling

This section shows how to model material parameters using our method. As material parameters are not readily available for captured data, we train from synthetic data generated using a state-of-art physical simulator [19]. For training, we simulate 8 sequences of the same garment pattern, worn by the same actor in a fixed motion, with varying materials. We choose a detailed garment pattern with garment-to-garment interaction during motion as this generates rich wrinkles that are challenging to model. The materials were generated using 39 parameters [35], and to allow for easier control of the parameters, we reduced their dimensionality to 4 using PCA before regressing from material parameter space to offset space. We used 7 materials to train our regression model, and left 1 material for testing. To avoid over-fitting to these 7 material points, we added a Gaussian random noise to the material parameters for all frames when training the regression. After training, we predicted the clothing layer from the motion parameters and new material parameters. Since for simulated data, segmented and aligned clothing and body meshes are available for each frame, our method uses this information. That is, we use the clothing layer directly and fit the S-SCAPE model to the mesh of the undressed body model used for simulation.

Figure 7 shows the comparison between our prediction and the ground truth for the test sequence. Note that a globally correct deformation is predicted even though the cloth deformation is far from the body shape. In spite of the globally correct deformation, our prediction lacks some detailed wrinkles. We suspect this detailed loss is due to dimension reduction on both material space and deformation space, as well as the limitation of the training data size. For qualitative validation, we randomly sampled material parameters in the PCA subspace and used them to synthesize new sequences. Figure 8 shows some examples. Note that visually plausible sequences are synthesized.

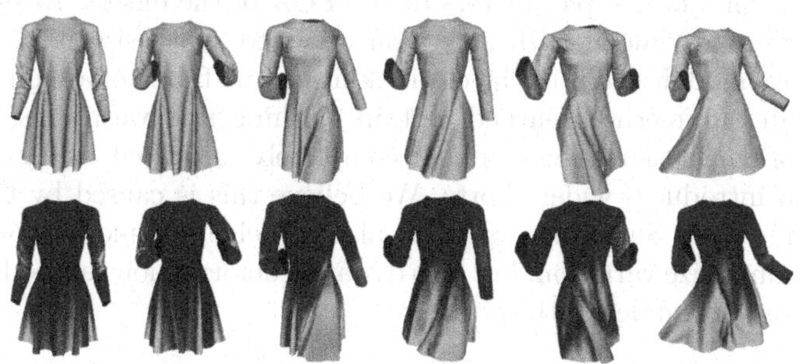

Fig. 7. Comparison to ground truth. First row: our predicted clothing deformation. Second row: ground truth colored with per-vertex error. Blue = 0 cm, red = 10 cm. (Color figure online)

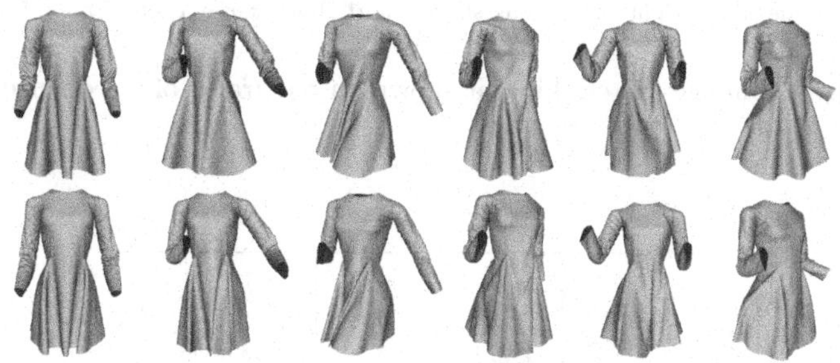

Fig. 8. Two synthesized sequences with new material parameters.

5.3 Clothing Fit Modeling

The proposed analysis is versatile in terms of the parameters of interest we wish to regress to. This allows for entirely new applications if sufficient training data is available. We demonstrate this by explicitly modeling the clothing size variation from acquisition data, which has not been done to be best of our knowledge. For training, we use 8 sequences of an extended version of the Inria dataset [38] of different subjects (4 male and 4 female) wearing different shorts and T-shirts while walking. These sequences are tracked with a common mesh topology. For each sequence, we manually assign a three dimensional vector to describe the size of the clothing, containing the width and length of the shorts and the size of the T-shirt. To model relative fit rather than absolute size, the sizes are expressed as ratio to corresponding measurements on the body. During training, to avoid over-fitting to these 8 sizing points, we add a Gaussian random noise to each size measurement. The regression learns a mapping from the body motion and size parameters to the PCA of the offsets. After training, new size parameters along with a motion allow to synthesize new sequences. Figure 9 shows modifications of the clothing fit on one frame of a sequence. Note that although our method learned certain clothing size variations, the three dimensions of our measurements are not completely separated, as e.g. the "large T-shirt" also introduces wider shorts. We believe this is caused by the limited size of training data. Since the regression also models body motion, our method not only captures size variation, but also dynamic deformation caused by motion. Figure 10 shows examples of this.

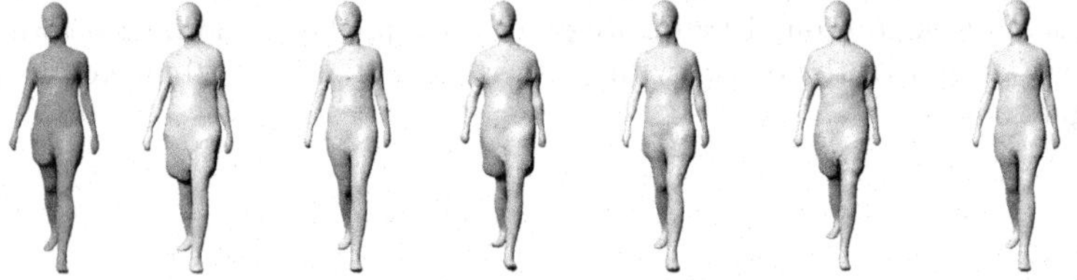

Fig. 9. Change the clothing fit shown on one frame of a sequence.

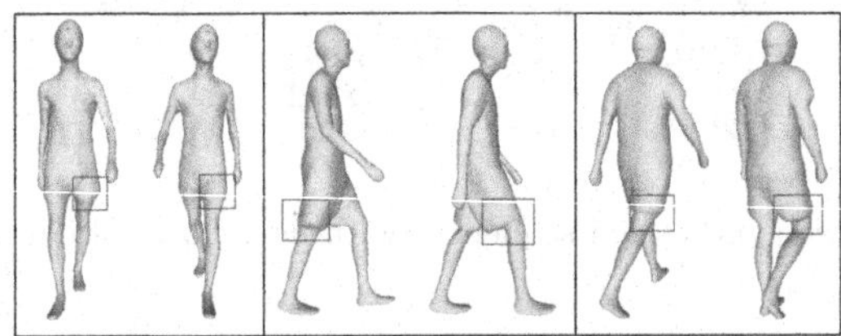

Fig. 10. Our approach captures dynamics caused by both clothing fit and body motion.

6 Conclusion

In this paper we have presented a statistical analysis and modeling of the clothing layer from sets of dense 3D sequences of human motion. Our analysis shows PCA to be a suitable tool to compress the geometric variability information contained in the clothing layer. The regression component of our model is shown to properly capture the relation between layer variations and semantic parameters as well as the underlying motion of the captured body. This allows predictions of the clothing layer under previously unobserved motions, with previously unobserved clothing materials or clothing fits. Our model opens a large number of future possibilities. First, it can be extended to include more variability under different clothing worn by a large number of subjects. Second, more elaborate regression and clothing layer motion subspace models could be devised. Third, several semantic regression groups could be simultaneously considered.

Acknowledgement. Funded by France National Research grant ANR-14-CE24-0030 ACHMOV. We thank G. Pons-Moll for providing ClothCap [25] data, Kinovis platform(https://kinovis.inria.fr/) for acquiring the extended Inria dataset, and F. Bertails-Descoubes and A. H. Rasheed for providing the cloth simulator and generating synthetic data.

References

1. Opennn library. http://www.opennn.net/
2. de Aguiar, E., Sigal, L., Treuille, A., Hodgins, J.K.: Stable spaces for real-time clothing. ACM Trans. Graph. **29**(4), 1–9 (2010)
3. de Aguiar, E., Stoll, C., Theobalt, C., Ahmed, N., Seidel, H.P., Thrun, S.: Performance capture from sparse multi-view video. ACM Trans. Graph. **27**(3), 98 (2008)
4. Allain, B., Franco, J.S., Boyer, E.: An efficient volumetric framework for shape tracking. In: Conference on Computer Vision and Pattern Recognition (2015)
5. Anguelov, D., Srinivasan, P., Koller, D., Thrun, S., Rodgers, J., Davis, J.: SCAPE: shape completion and animation of people. ACM Trans. Graph. **24**(3), 408–416 (2005)
6. Bălan, A., Black, M.: The naked truth: estimating body shape under clothing. In: European Conference on Computer Vision (2008)
7. Baraff, D., Witkin, A.: Large steps in cloth simulation. In: Conference on Computer Graphics and Interactive Techniques (1998)
8. Bogo, F., Kanazawa, A., Lassner, C., Gehler, P., Romero, J., Black, M.J.: Keep it SMPL: automatic estimation of 3D human pose and shape from a single image. In: European Conference on Computer Vision (2016)
9. Bridson, R., Marino, S., Fedkiw, R.: Simulation of clothing with folds and wrinkles. In: Symposium on Computer Animation (2003)
10. Collet, A., et al.: High-quality streamable free-viewpoint video. ACM Trans. Graph. **34**(4), 69 (2015)
11. Dibra, E., Jain, H., Öztireli, A.C., Ziegler, R., Gross, M.H.: HS-Nets: estimating human body shape from silhouettes with convolutional neural networks. In: International Conference on 3D Vision (2016)
12. Dibra, E., Jain, H., Öztireli, A.C., Ziegler, R., Gross, M.H.: Human shape from silhouettes using generative HKS descriptors and cross-modal neural networks. In: Conference on Computer Vision and Pattern Recognition (2017)
13. Dibra, E., Öztireli, A.C., Ziegler, R., Gross, M.H.: Shape from selfies: human body shape estimation using CCA regression forests. In: European Conference of Computer Vision (2016)

14. Gall, J., Stoll, C., De Aguiar, E., Theobalt, C., Rosenhahn, B., Seidel, H.P.: Motion capture using joint skeleton tracking and surface estimation. In: Conference on Computer Vision and Pattern Recognition (2009)
15. Guan, P., Reiss, L., Hirshberg, D.A., Weiss, A., Black, M.J.: Drape: Dressing any person. ACM Trans. Graph. **31**(4), 35-1 (2012)
16. Hasler, N., Stoll, C., Rosenhahn, B., Thormählen, T., Seidel, H.P.: Estimating body shape of dressed humans. Comput. Graph. **33**(3), 211–216 (2009)
17. Kaldor, J.M., James, D.L., Marschner, S.: Efficient yarn-based cloth with adaptive contact linearization. ACM Trans. Graph. **29**(4), 105 (2010)
18. Li, H., Adams, B., Guibas, L., Pauly, M.: Robust single-view geometry and motion reconstruction. ACM Trans. Graph. **28**(5), 175 (2009)
19. Li, J., et al.: An implicit frictional contact solver for adaptive cloth simulation. ACM Trans. Graph. **37**(4), 52 (2018)
20. Loper, M., Mahmood, N., Romero, J., Pons-Moll, G., Black, M.: SMPL: a skinned multi-person linear model. ACM Trans. Graph. **34**(6), 248 (2015)
21. Neophytou, A., Hilton, A.: Shape and pose space deformation for subject specific animation. In: International Conference on 3D Vision (2013)
22. Neophytou, A., Hilton, A.: A layered model of human body and garment deformation. In: International Conference on 3D Vision (2014)
23. Newcombe, R.A., Fox, D., Seitz, S.M.: DynamicFusion: reconstruction and tracking of non-rigid scenes in real-time. In: Conference on Computer Vision and Pattern Recognition (2015)
24. Pishchulin, L., Wuhrer, S., Helten, T., Theobalt, C., Schiele, B.: Building statistical shape spaces for 3D human modeling. Pattern Recogn. **67**, 276–286 (2017)
25. Pons-Moll, G., Pujades, S., Hu, S., Black, M.: ClothCap: seamless 4D clothing capture and retargeting. ACM Trans. Graph. **36**(4), 73 (2017)
26. Rhodin, H., Robertini, N., Casas, D., Richardt, C., Seidel, H.P., Theobalt, C.: General automatic human shape and motion capture using volumetric contour cues. In: European Conference on Computer Vision (2016)
27. Shehu, A., Yang, J., Franco, J.S., Hétroy-Wheeler, F., Wuhrer, S.: Computing temporal alignments of human motion sequences in wide clothing using geodesic patches. In: International Conference on 3D Vision (2016)
28. Sidenbladh, H., Black, M.J., Fleet, D.J.: Stochastic tracking of 3d human figures using 2d image motion. In: European Conference on Computer Vision (2000)
29. Sigal, L., Balan, A.O., Black, M.J.: HumanEva: synchronized video and motion capture dataset and baseline algorithm for evaluation of articulated human motion. Int. J. Comput. Vis. **87**(4), 4 (2010)
30. Sigal, L.: A perceptual control space for garment simulation. ACM Trans. Graph. **34**(4), 117 (2015)
31. Sminchisescu, C., Triggs, B.: Estimating articulated human motion with covariance scaled sampling. Int. J. Robot. Res. **22**(6), 371–391 (2003)
32. Stoll, C., Gall, J., De Aguiar, E., Thrun, S., Theobalt, C.: Video-based reconstruction of animatable human characters. ACM Trans. Graph. **29**(6), 139 (2010)
33. Vlasic, D., Baran, I., Matusik, W., Popović, J.: Articulated mesh animation from multi-view silhouettes. ACM Trans. Graph. **27**(3), 97 (2008)
34. Volino, P., Magnenat-Thalmann, N., Faure, F.: A simple approach to nonlinear tensile stiffness for accurate cloth simulation. ACM Trans. Graph. **28**(4) (2009)
35. Wang, H., O'Brien, J.F., Ramamoorthi, R.: Data-driven elastic models for cloth: modeling and measurement. ACM Trans. Graph. **30**(4), 71 (2011)

36. Wuhrer, S., Pishchulin, L., Brunton, A., Shu, C., Lang, J.: Estimation of human body shape and posture under clothing. Comput. Vis. Image Underst. **127**, 31–42 (2014)
37. Xu, W., Umentani, N., Chao, Q., Mao, J., Jin, X., Tong, X.: Sensitivity-optimized rigging for example-based real-time clothing synthesis. ACM Trans. Graph. **33**(4), 107 (2014)
38. Yang, J., Franco, J.S., Hétroy-Wheeler, F., Wuhrer, S.: Estimation of human body shape in motion with wide clothing. In: European Conference on Computer Vision (2016)
39. Zaharescu, A., Boyer, E., Varanasi, K., Horaud, R.: Surface feature detection and description with applications to mesh matching. In: Conference on Computer Vision and Pattern Recognition (2009)
40. Zhang, C., Pujades, S., Black, M., Pons-Moll, G.: Detailed, accurate, human shape estimation from clothed 3d scan sequences. In: Conference on Computer Vision and Pattern Recognition (2017)
41. Zuffi, S., Black, M.J.: The stitched puppet: a graphical model of 3D human shape and pose. In: Conference on Computer Vision and Pattern Recognition (2015)

Recurrent Squeeze-and-Excitation Context Aggregation Net for Single Image Deraining

Xia Li[1,2,3], Jianlong Wu[2,3], Zhouchen Lin[2,3], Hong Liu[1(✉)], and Hongbin Zha[2,3]

[1] Key Laboratory of Machine Perception, Shenzhen Graduate School, Peking University, Beijing, China
{ethanlee,hongliu}@pku.edu.cn

[2] Key Laboratory of Machine Perception (MOE), School of EECS, Peking University, Beijing, China
{jlwu1992,zlin}@pku.edu.cn, zha@cis.pku.edu.cn

[3] Cooperative Medianet Innovation Center, Shanghai Jiao Tong University, Shanghai, China

Abstract. Rain streaks can severely degrade the visibility, which causes many current computer vision algorithms fail to work. So it is necessary to remove the rain from images. We propose a novel deep network architecture based on deep convolutional and recurrent neural networks for single image deraining. As contextual information is very important for rain removal, we first adopt the dilated convolutional neural network to acquire large receptive field. To better fit the rain removal task, we also modify the network. In heavy rain, rain streaks have various directions and shapes, which can be regarded as the accumulation of multiple rain streak layers. We assign different alpha-values to various rain streak layers according to the intensity and transparency by incorporating the squeeze-and-excitation block. Since rain streak layers overlap with each other, it is not easy to remove the rain in one stage. So we further decompose the rain removal into multiple stages. Recurrent neural network is incorporated to preserve the useful information in previous stages and benefit the rain removal in later stages. We conduct extensive experiments on both synthetic and real-world datasets. Our proposed method outperforms the state-of-the-art approaches under all evaluation metrics. Codes and supplementary material are available at our project webpage: https://xialipku.github.io/RESCAN.

Keywords: Recurrent neural network · Squeeze and excitation block Image deraining

X. Li and J. Wu—Equal contributions.

Electronic supplementary material The online version of this chapter (https://doi.org/10.1007/978-3-030-01234-2_16) contains supplementary material, which is available to authorized users.

V. Ferrari et al. (Eds.): ECCV 2018, LNCS 11211, pp. 262–277, 2018.
https://doi.org/10.1007/978-3-030-01234-2_16

1 Introduction

Rain is a very common weather in actual life. However, it can affect the visibility. Especially in heavy rain, rain streaks from various directions accumulate and make the background scene misty, which will seriously influence the accuracy of many computer vision systems, including video surveillance, object detection and tracking in autonomous driving, etc. Therefore, it is an important task to remove the rain and recover the background from rain images.

Image deraining has attracted much attention in the past decade. Many methods have been proposed to solve this problem. Existing methods can be divided into two categories, including video based approaches and single image based approaches. As video based methods can utilize the relationship between frames, it is relatively easy to remove rain from videos [1–4]. However, single image deraining is more challenging, and we focus on this task in this paper. For single image deraining, traditional methods, such as discriminative sparse coding [5], low rank representation [6], and the Gaussian mixture model [7], have been applied to this task and they work quite well. Recently, deep learning based deraining methods [8,9] receive extensive attention due to its powerful ability of feature representation. All these related approaches achieve good performance, but there is still much space to improve.

There are mainly two limitations of existing approaches. On the one hand, according to [10–12], spatial contextual information is very useful for deraining. However, many current methods remove rain streaks based on image patches, which neglect the contextual information in large regions. On the other hand, as rain steaks in heavy rain have various directions and shapes, they blur the scene in different ways. It is a common way [9,13] to decompose the overall rain removal problem into multiple stages, so that we can remove rain streaks iteratively. Since these different stages work together to remove rain streaks, the information of deraining in previous stages is useful to guide and benefit the rain removal in later stages. However, existing methods treat these rain streak removal stages independently and do not consider their correlations.

Motivated by addressing the above two issues, we propose a novel deep network for single image deraining. The pipeline of our proposed network is shown in Fig. 2. We remove rain streaks stage by stage. At each stage, we use the context aggregation network with multiple full-convolutional layers to remove rain streaks. As rain streaks have various directions and shapes, each channel in our network corresponds to one kind of rain streak. Squeeze-and-Excitation (SE) blocks are used to assign different alpha-values to various channels according to their interdependencies in each convolution layer. Benefited from the exponentially increasing convolution dilations, our network has a large reception field with low depth, which can help us to acquire more contextual information. To better utilize the useful information for rain removal in previous stages, we further incorporate the Recurrent Neural Network (RNN) architecture with three kinds of recurrent units to guide the deraining in later stages. We name the proposed deep network as **RE**current **SE** **C**ontext **A**ggregation **N**et (RESCAN).

Main contributions of this paper are listed as follows:

1. We propose a novel unified deep network for single image deraining, by which we remove the rain stage by stage. Specifically, at each stage, we use the contextual dilated network to remove the rain. SE blocks are used to assign different alpha-values to various rain streak layers according to their properties.
2. To the best of our knowledge, this is the first paper to consider the correlations between different stages of rain removal. By incorporating RNN architecture with three kinds of recurrent units, the useful information for rain removal in previous stages can be incorporated to guide the deraining in later stages. Our network is suitable for recovering rain images with complex rain streaks, especially in heavy rain.
3. Our deep network achieves superior performance compared with the state-of-the-art methods on various datasets.

2 Related Works

During the past decade, many methods have been proposed to separate rain streaks and background scene from rain images. We briefly review these related methods as follows.

Video Based Methods. As video based methods can leverage the temporal information by analyzing the difference between adjacent frames, it is relatively easy to remove the rain from videos [3,14]. Garg and Nayar [2,15,16] propose an appearance model to describe rain streaks based on photometric properties and temporal dynamics. Meanwhile, Zhang et al. [1] exploit temporal and chromatic properties of rain in videos. Bossu et al. [17] detect the rain based on the histogram of orientation of rain streaks. In [4], Tripathi et al. provide a review of video-based deraining methods proposed in recent years.

Single Image Based Methods. Compared with video deraining, single image deraining is much more challenging, since there is no temporal information in images. For this task, traditional methods, including dictionary learning [18], Gaussian mixture models (GMMs) [19], and low-rank representation [20], have been widely applied. Based on dictionary learning, Kang et al. [21] decompose high frequency parts of rain images into rain and nonrain components. Wang et al. [22] define a 3-layer hierarchical scheme. Luo et al. [5] propose a discriminative sparse coding framework based on image patches. Gu et al. [23] integrate analysis sparse representation (ASR) and synthesis sparse representation (SSR) to solve a variety of image decomposition problems. In [7], GMM works as a prior to decompose a rain image into background and rain streaks layer. Chang et al. [6] leverage the low-rank property of rain streaks to separate two layers. Zhu et al. [24] combine three different kinds of image priors.

Recently, several deep learning based deraining methods achieve promising performance. Fu et al. [8,25] first introduce deep learning methods to the deraining problem. Similar to [21], they also decompose rain images into low- and high-frequency parts, and then map high-frequency part to the rain streaks layer using a deep residual network. Yang et al. [9,26] design a deep recurrent dilated network to jointly detect and remove rain streaks. Zhang et al. [27] use the generative adversarial network (GAN) to prevent the degeneration of background image when it is extracted from rain image, and utilize the perceptual loss to further ensure better visual quality. Li et al. [13] design a novel multi-stage convolutional neural network that consists of several parallel sub-networks, each of which is made aware of different scales of rain streaks.

3 Rain Models

It is a commonly used rain model to decompose the observed rain image $\mathbf{O}$ into the linear combination of the rain-free background scene $\mathbf{B}$ and the rain streak layer $\mathbf{R}$:

$$\mathbf{O} = \mathbf{B} + \mathbf{R}. \tag{1}$$

By removing the rain streaks layer $\mathbf{R}$ from the observed image $\mathbf{O}$, we can obtain the rain-free scene $\mathbf{B}$.

Based on the rain model in Eq. (1), many rain removal algorithms assume that rain steaks should be sparse and have similar characters in falling directions and shapes. However, in reality, raindrops in the air have various appearances, and occur in different distances from the camera, which leads to an irregular distribution of rain streaks. In this case, a single rain streak layer $\mathbf{R}$ is not enough to well simulate this complex situation.

To reduce the complexity, we regard rain streaks with similar shape or depth as one layer. Then we can divide the captured rainy scene into the combination of several rain streak layers and an unpolluted background. Based on this, the rain model can be reformulated as follows:

$$\mathbf{O} = \mathbf{B} + \sum_{i=1}^{n} \mathbf{R}^i, \tag{2}$$

where $\mathbf{R}^i$ represents the i-th rain streak layer that consists of one kind of rain streaks and n is the total number of different rain streak layers.

According to [28], things in reality might be even worse, especially in the heavy rain situation. Accumulation of multiple rain streaks in the air may cause attenuation and scattering, which further increases the diversity of rain streaks' brightness. For camera or eye visualization, the scattering causes haze or frog effects. This further pollutes the observed image $\mathbf{O}$. For camera imaging, due to the limitation of pixel number, far away rain streaks cannot occupy full pixels. When mixed with other things, the image will be blurry. To handle the issues above, we further take the global atmospheric light into consideration and assign different alpha-values to various rain streak layers according to their intensities transparencies. We further generalize the rain model to:

$$\mathbf{O} = \left(1 - \sum_{i=0}^{n} \alpha_i\right) \mathbf{B} + \alpha_0 \mathbf{A} + \sum_{i=1}^{n} \alpha_i \mathbf{R}^i, \ s.t. \ \alpha_i \geq 0, \ \sum_{i=0}^{n} \alpha_i \leq 1, \tag{3}$$

where $\mathbf{A}$ is the global atmospheric light, α_0 is the scene transmission, α_i $(i = 1, \cdots, n)$ indicates the brightness of a rain streak layer or a haze layer.

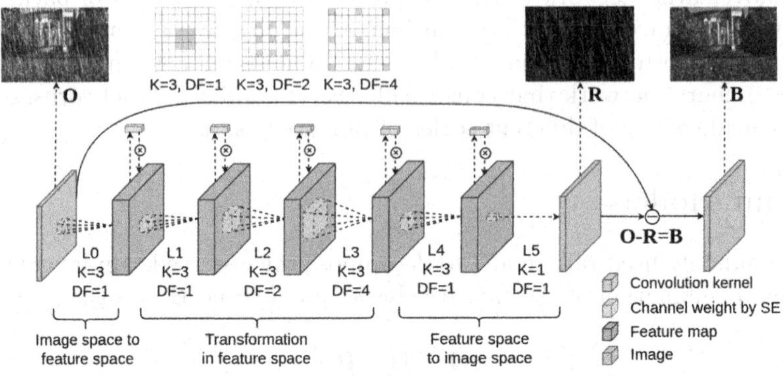

Fig. 1. The architecture of **SE C**ontext **A**ggregation **N**etwork (SCAN).

4 Deraining Method

Instead of using decomposition methods with artificial priors to solve the problem in Eq. (3), we intend to learn a function f that directly maps observed rain image $\mathbf{O}$ to rain streak layer $\mathbf{R}$, since $\mathbf{R}$ is sparser than $\mathbf{B}$ and has simpler texture. Then we can subtract $\mathbf{R}$ from $\mathbf{O}$ to get the rain-free scene $\mathbf{B}$. The function f above can be represented as a deep neural network and be learned by optimizing the loss function $\|f(\mathbf{O}) - \mathbf{R}\|_F^2$.

Based on the motivation above, we propose the **RE**current **SE C**ontext **A**ggregation **N**et (RESCAN) for image deraining. The framework of our network is presented in Fig. 2. We remove rain streaks stage by stage. At each stage, we use the context aggregation network with SE blocks to remove rain streaks. Our network can deal with rain streaks of various directions and shapes, and each feature map in the network corresponds to one kind of rain streak. Dilated convolution used in our network can help us have a large reception field and acquire more contextual information. By using SE blocks, we can assign different alpha-values to various feature maps according to their interdependencies in each convolution layer. As we remove the rain in multiple stages, useful information for rain removal in previous stages can guide the learning in later stages. So we incorporate the RNN architecture with memory unit to make full use of the useful information in previous stages.

In the following, we first describe the baseline model, and then define the recurrent structure, which lifts the model's capacity by iteratively decomposing rain streaks with different characteristics.

4.1 SE Context Aggregation Net

The base model of RESCAN is a forward network without recurrence. We implement it by extending **C**ontext **A**ggregation **N**et (CAN) [11,12] with Squeeze-and-Excitation (SE) blocks [29], and name it as **SE** **C**ontext **A**ggregation **N**et (SCAN).

Table 1. The detailed architecture of SCAN. d is the depth of network.

Layer	0	1	2	...	$d-3$	$d-2$	$d-1$
Convolution	3×3	3×3	3×3	...	3×3	3×3	1×1
Dilation	1	1	2	...	2^{d-4}	1	1
NonLinear	Yes	Yes	Yes	Yes	Yes	Yes	No
SE block	Yes	Yes	Yes	Yes	Yes	Yes	No
Receptive field	3×3	5×5	9×9		$(2^{d-2}+1)^2$	$(2^{d-2}+3)^2$	$(2^{d-2}+3)^2$

Here we provide an illustration and a further specialization of SCAN. We schematically illustrate SCAN in Fig. 1, which is a full-convolution network. In Fig. 1, we set the depth $d = 6$. Since a large receptive field is very helpful to acquire much contextual information, dilation is adopted in our network. For layers L_1 to L_3, the dilation increases from 1 to 4 exponentially, which leads to the exponential growth in receptive field of every elements. As we treat the first layer as an encoder to transform an image to feature maps, and the last two layers as a decoder to map reversely, we do not apply dilation for layers L_0, L_4 and L_5. Moreover, we use 3×3 convolution for all layers before L_5. To recover RGB channels of a color image, or gray channel for a gray scale image, we adopt the 1×1 convolution for the last layer L_5. Every convolution operation except the last one is followed by a nonlinear operation. The detailed architecture of SCAN is summarized in Table 1. Generally, for a SCAN with depth d, the receptive field of elements in the output image equals to $(2^{d-2}+3)^2$.

For feature maps, we regard each channel of them as the embedding of a rain streak layer $\mathbf{R}^i$. Recall in Eq. (3), we assign different alpha-values α_i to different rain steak layers $\mathbf{R}^i$. Instead of setting fixed alpha-values α_i for each rain layer, we update the alpha-values for embeddings of rain streak layers in each network layer. Although the convolution operation implicitly introduces weights for every channel, these implicit weights are not specialized for every image. To explicitly import weight on each network layer for each image, we extend each basic convolution layer with Squeeze-and-Excitation (SE) block [29], which computes normalized alpha-value for every channel of each item. By multiplying alpha-values learned by SE block, feature maps computed by convolution are re-weighted explicitly.

An obvious difference between SCAN and former models [8,27] is that SCAN has no batch normalization (BN) [30] layers. BN is widely used in training deep neural network, as it can reduce internal covariate shift of feature maps. By applying BN, each scalar feature is normalized and has zero mean and unit variance. These features are independent with each other and have the same distribution. However, in Eq. (2) rain streaks in different layers have different distributions in directions, colors and shapes, which is also true for each scalar feature of different rain streak layers. Therefore, BN contradicts with the characteristics of our proposed rain model. Thus, we remove BN from our model. Experimental results in Sect. 5 show that this simple modification can substantially improve the performance. Furthermore, since BN layers keep a normalized copy of feature maps in GPU, removing it can greatly reduce the demand on GPU memory. For SCAN, we can save approximately 40% of memory usage during training without BN. Consequently, we can build a larger model with larger capacity, or increase the mini-batch size to stabilize the training process.

4.2 Recurrent SE Context Aggregation Net

As there are many different rain streak layers and they overlap with each other, it is not easy to remove all rain streaks in one stage. So we incorporate the recurrent structure to decompose the rain removal into multiple stages. This process can be formulated as:

$$\mathbf{O}_1 = \mathbf{O}, \tag{4}$$

$$\mathbf{R}_s = f_{CNN}\left(\mathbf{O}_s\right), 1 \leq s \leq S, \tag{5}$$

$$\mathbf{O}_{s+1} = \mathbf{O}_s - \mathbf{R}_s, 1 \leq s \leq S, \tag{6}$$

$$\mathbf{R} = \sum_{s=1}^{S} \mathbf{R}_s, \tag{7}$$

where S is the number of stages, $\mathbf{R}_s$ is the output of the s-th stage, and $\mathbf{O}_{s+1}$ is the intermediate rain-free image after the s-th stage.

The above model for deraining has been used in [9,13]. However, recurrent structure used in their methods [9,13] can only be regarded as the simple cascade of the same network. They just use the output images of last stage as the input of current stage and do not consider feature connection among these stages. As these different stages work together to remove the rain, input images of different stages $\{\mathbf{O}_1, \mathbf{O}_2, \cdots, \mathbf{O}_S\}$ can be regarded as a temporal sequence of rain images with decreasing levels of rain streaks interference. It is more meaningful to investigate the recurrent connections between features of different stages rather than only using the recurrent structure. So we incorporate recurrent neural network (RNN) [31] with memory unit to better make use of information in previous stages and guide feature learning in later stages.

In our framework, Eq. (5) can be further reformulated as:

$$\mathbf{R}_s = \sum_{i=1}^{n} \alpha_i \bar{\mathbf{R}}_s^i = f_{CNN+RNN}\left(\mathbf{O}_s, x_{s-1}\right), 1 \leq s \leq S, \tag{8}$$

where $\bar{\mathbf{R}}_s^i$ is the decomposed i-th rain streak layer of the s-th stage and x_{s-1} is the hidden state of the $(s-1)$-th stage. Consistent with the rain model in Eq. (3), $\mathbf{R}_s$ is computed by summing $\bar{\mathbf{R}}_s^i$ with different alpha-values.

For the deraining task, we further explore three different recurrent unit variants, including ConvRNN, ConvGRU [32], and ConvLSTM [33]. Due to the space limitation, we only present the details of ConvGRU [32] in the following. For other two kinds of recurrent units, please refer to the supplement materials on our webpage.

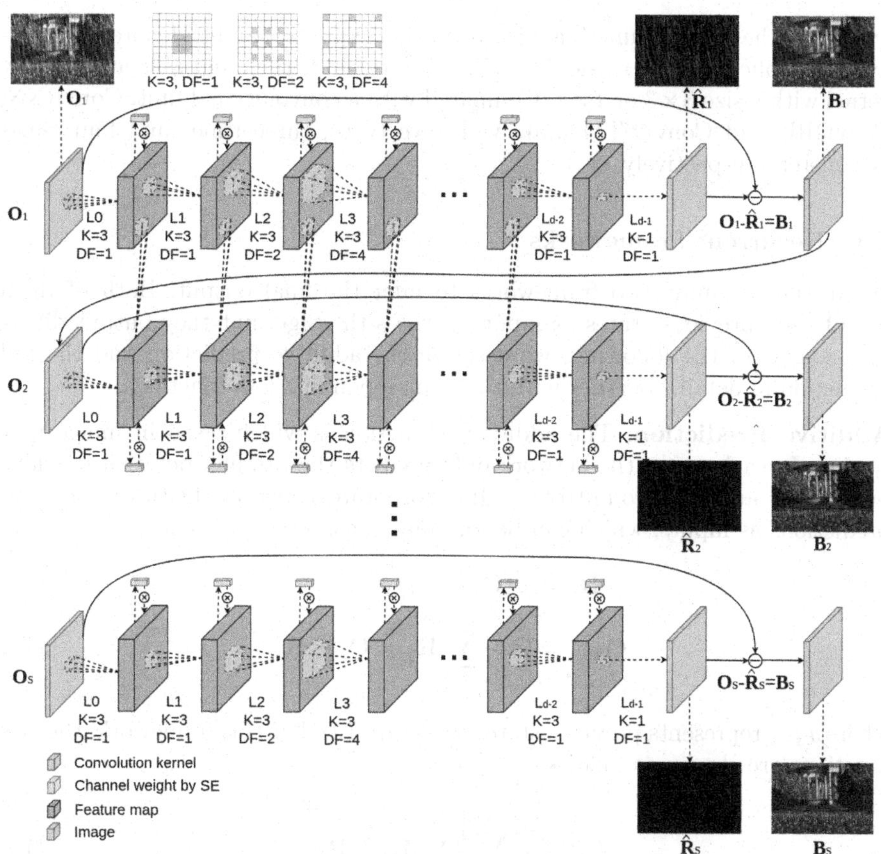

Fig. 2. The unfolded architecture of RESCAN. K is the convolution kernel size, DF indicates the dilation factor, and S represents the number of stages.

ConvGRU. Gated Recurrent Units (GRU) [32] is a very popular recurrent unit in sequential models. Its convolutional version ConvGRU is adopted in our model. Denote x_s^j as the feature map of the j-th layer in the s-th stage, and it can be computed based on the x_{s-1}^{j} (feature map in the same layer of the previous stage) and x_{s}^{j-1} (feature map in the previous layer of the same stage):

$$z_s^j = \sigma\left(W_z^j \circledast x_s^{j-1} + U_z^j \circledast x_{s-1}^j + b_z^j\right), \tag{9}$$

$$r_s^j = \sigma\left(W_r^j \circledast x_s^{j-1} + U_r^j \circledast x_{s-1}^j + b_r^j\right), \tag{10}$$

$$n_s^j = \tanh\left(W_n^j \circledast x_s^{j-1} + U_n^j \circledast \left(r_s^j \odot x_{s-1}^j\right) + b_n^j\right), \tag{11}$$

$$x_s^j = \left(1 - z_s^j\right) \odot x_{s-1}^j + z_s^j \odot n_s^j, \tag{12}$$

where σ is the sigmoid function $\sigma(x) = 1/(1+\exp(-x))$ and $\odot$ denotes element-wise multiplication. W is the dilated convolutional kernel, and U is an ordinary kernel with a size 3×3 or 1×1. Compared with a convolutional unit, ConvRNN, ConvGRU and ConvLSTM units will have twice, three times and four times parameters, respectively.

4.3 Recurrent Frameworks

We further examine two frameworks to infer the final output. Both of them use $\mathbf{O}_s$ and previous states as input for the s-th stage, but they output different images. In the following, we describe the additive prediction and the full prediction in detail, together with their corresponding loss functions.

Additive Prediction. The additive prediction is widely used in image processing. In each stage, the network only predicts the residual between previous predictions and the ground truth. It incorporates previous feature maps and predictions as inputs, which can be formulated as:

$$\mathbf{R}_s = f\left(\mathbf{O}_s, x_{s-1}\right), \tag{13}$$

$$\mathbf{O}_{s+1} = \mathbf{O} - \sum_{j=1}^{s} \mathbf{R}_j = \mathbf{O}_s - \mathbf{R}_s, \tag{14}$$

where x_{s-1} represents previous states as in Eq. (12). For this framework, the loss functions are chosen as follows:

$$L(\mathbf{\Theta}) = \sum_{s=1}^{S} \left\| \sum_{j=1}^{s} \mathbf{R}_j - \mathbf{R} \right\|_F^2, \tag{15}$$

where $\mathbf{\Theta}$ represents the network's parameters.

Full Prediction. The full prediction means that in each stage, we predict the whole rain streaks $\mathbf{R}$. This approach can be formulated as:

$$\hat{\mathbf{R}}_s = f\left(\hat{\mathbf{O}}_s, x_{s-1}\right), \tag{16}$$

$$\hat{\mathbf{O}}_{s+1} = \mathbf{O} - \hat{\mathbf{R}}_s, \tag{17}$$

where $\hat{\mathbf{R}}_s$ represents the predicted full rain streaks in the s-th stage, and $\hat{\mathbf{O}}_{s+1}$ equals to $\mathbf{B}$ plus remaining rain streaks. The corresponding loss function is:

$$L(\Theta) = \sum_{s=1}^{S} \left\| \hat{\mathbf{R}}_s - \mathbf{R} \right\|_F^2, \tag{18}$$

5 Experiments

In this section, we present details of experimental settings and quality measures used to evaluate the proposed SCAN and RESCAN models. We compare the performance of our proposed methods with the state-of-the-art methods on both synthetic and real-world datasets.

5.1 Experiment Settings

Synthetic Dataset. Since it is hard to obtain a large dataset of clean/rainy image pairs from real-world data, we first use synthesized rainy datasets to train the network. Zhang et al. [27] synthesize 800 rain images (Rain800) from randomly selected outdoor images, and split them into testing set of 100 images and training set of 700 images. Yang et al. [9] collect and synthesize 3 datasets, Rain12, Rain100L and Rain100H. We select the most difficult one, Rain100H, to test our model. It is synthesized with the combination of five streak directions, which makes it hard to effectively remove all rain streaks. There are 1, 800 synthetic image pairs in Rain100H, and 100 pairs are selected as the testing set.

Real-World Dataset. Zhang et al. [27] and Yang et al. [9] also provide many real-world rain images. These images are diverse in terms of content as well as intensity and orientation of rain streaks. We use these datasets for objective evaluation.

Training Settings. In the training process, we randomly generate 100 patch pairs with a size of 64×64 from every training image pairs. The entire network is trained on an Nvidia 1080Ti GPU based on Pytorch. We use a batch size of 64 and set the depth of SCAN as $d = 7$ with the receptive field size 35×35. For the nonlinear operation, we use leaky ReLU [34] with $\alpha = 0.2$. For optimization, the ADAM algorithm [35] is adopted with a start learning rate 5×10^{-3}. During training, the learning rate is divided by 10 at 15, 000 and 17, 500 iterations.

Quality Measures. To evaluate the performance on synthetic image pairs, we adopt two commonly used metrics, including peak signal to noise ratio (PSNR) [36] and structure similarity index (SSIM) [37]. Since there are no ground truth rain-free images for real-world images, the performance on the real-world dataset can only be evaluated visually. We compare our proposed approach with five state-of-the-art methods, including image decomposition (ID) [21], discriminative sparse coding (DSC) [5], layer priors (LP) [7], DetailsNet [8], and joint rain detection and removal (JORDER) [9].

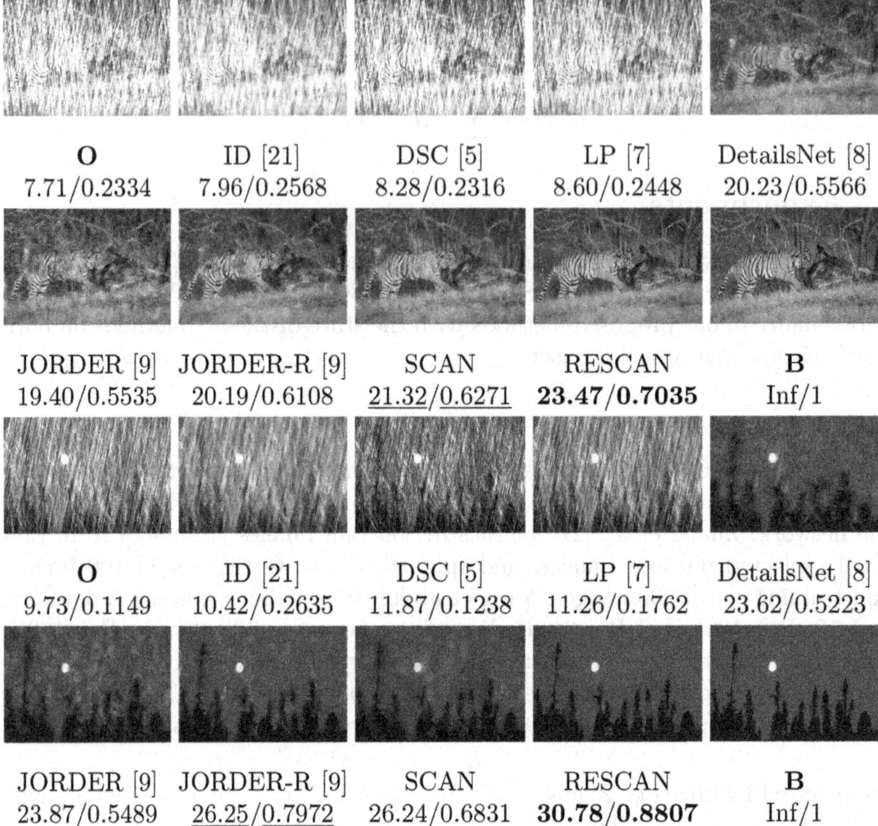

Fig. 3. Results of various methods on synthetic images. **Best viewed at screen!**

5.2 Results on Synthetic Data

Table 2 shows results of different methods on the Rain800 and the Rain100H datasets. We can see that our RESCAN considerably outperforms other methods in terms of both PSNR and SSIM on these two datasets. It is also worth noting that our non-recurrent network SCAN can even outperform JORDER and DetailsNet, and is slightly superior to JORDER-R, the recurrent version of JORDER. This shows the high capacity behind SCAN's shallow structure. Moreover, by using RNN to gradually recover the full rain streak layer $\mathbf{R}$, RESCAN further improves the performance.

To visually demonstrate the improvements obtained by the proposed methods, we present results on several difficult sample images in Fig. 3. Please note that we select difficult sample images to show that our method can outperform others especially in difficult conditions, as we design it to deal with complex conditions. According to Fig. 3, these state-of-the-art methods cannot remove all rain steaks and may blur the image, while our method can remove the majority of rain steaks as well as maintain details of background scene.

Table 2. Quantitative experiments evaluated on two synthetic datasets. Best results are marked in bold and the second best results are underlined.

Dataset	Rain800		Rain100H	
Measure	PSNR	SSIM	PSNR	SSIM
ID [21]	18.88	0.5832	14.02	0.5239
DSC [5]	18.56	0.5996	15.66	0.4225
LP [7]	20.46	0.7297	14.26	0.5444
DetailsNet [8]	21.16	0.7320	22.26	0.6928
JORDER [9]	22.24	0.7763	22.15	0.6736
JORDER-R [9]	22.29	0.7922	23.45	<u>0.7490</u>
SCAN	<u>23.45</u>	<u>0.8112</u>	<u>23.56</u>	0.7456
RESCAN	**24.09**	**0.8410**	**26.45**	**0.8458**

Table 3. Quantitative comparison between SCAN and base model candidates.

Dataset	Meassure	Plain	ResNet	EncDec	CAN+BN	CAN	SCAN+BN	SCAN
Rain800	PSNR	22.10	22.10	22.14	22.27	22.45	<u>23.11</u>	**23.45**
	SSIM	0.7816	0.7856	0.7809	0.7871	<u>0.7960</u>	0.7657	**0.8112**
Rain100H	PSNR	21.46	21.51	21.28	22.63	22.93	<u>23.09</u>	**23.56**
	SSIM	0.6921	0.6940	0.6886	0.7256	0.7333	<u>0.7389</u>	**0.7456**

5.3 Results on Real-World Dataset

To test the practicability of deraining methods, we also evaluate the performance on real-world rainy test images. The predictions for all related methods on four real-world sample rain images are shown in Fig. 4. As observed, LP [7] cannot remove rain steaks efficiently, and DetailsNet [8] tends to add artifacts on derained outputs. We can see that the proposed method can remove most of rain streaks and maintain much texture of background images. To further validate the performance on real-world dataset, we also make a user study. For details, please refer to the supplement material.

5.4 Analysis on SCAN

To show that SCAN is the best choice as a base model for deraining task, we conduct experiments on two datasets to compare the performance of SCAN and its related network architectures, including Plain (dilation=1 for all convolutions), ResNet used in DetailsNet [8] and Encoder-Decoder used in ID-CGAN [27]. For all networks, we set the same depth $d = 7$ and width (24 channels), so we can keep their numbers of parameters and computations at the same order of magnitude. More specifically, we keep layers L_0, L_{d-5} and L_{d-6} of them with the same structure, so they only differ in layers L_1 to L_4. The results are shown in Table 3.

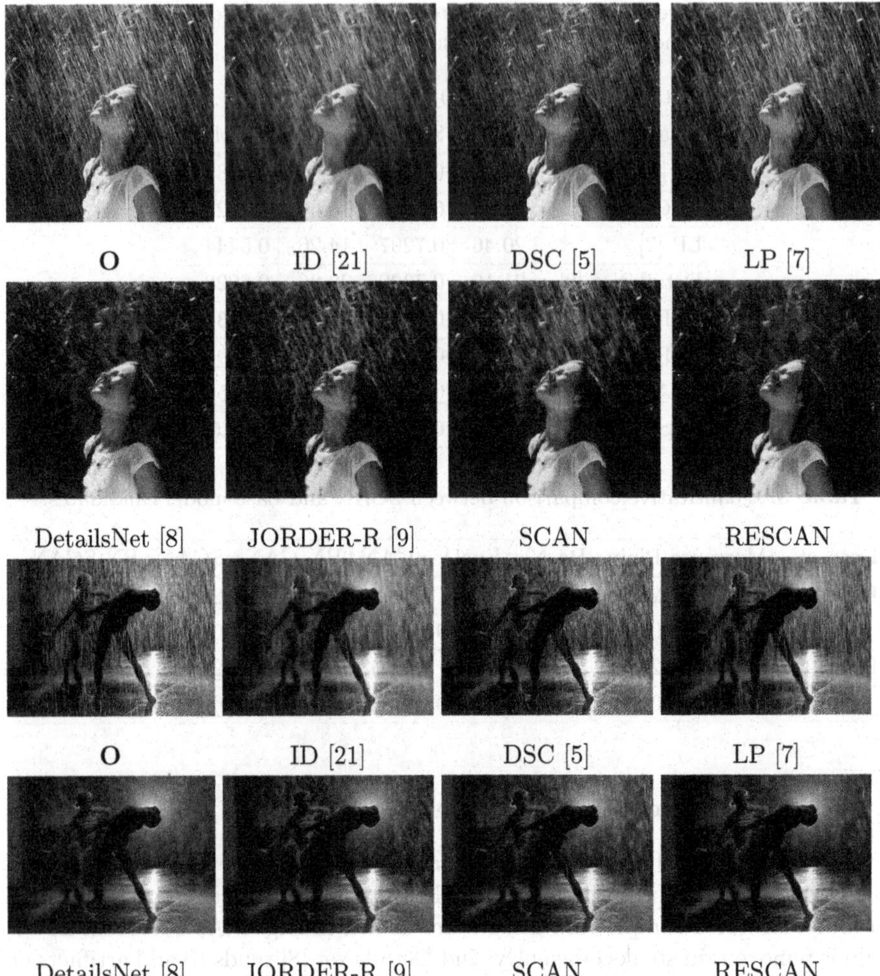

Fig. 4. Results of various methods on real-world images. **Best viewed at screen!**

SCAN and CAN achieve the best performance in both datasets, which can be attributed to the fact that receptive fields of these two methods exponentially increase with the growing of depth, while receptive fields of other methods only have linear relationship with depth.

Moreover, the comparison between results of SCAN and CAN indicates that the SE block contributes a lot to the base model, as it can explicitly learn alpha-value for every independent rain streak layer. We also examine the SCAN model with BN. The results clearly verify that removing BN is a good choice in the deraining task, as rain steak layers are independent on each other.

5.5 Analysis on RESCAN

As we list three recurrent units and two recurrent frameworks in Sect. 4.2, we conduct experiments to compare these different settings, consisting of {ConvRNN, ConvLSTM, ConvGRU} × {Additive Prediction (Add), Full Prediction (Full)}. To compare with the recurrent framework in [9,13], we also implement the settings in Eq. (5) (Iter), in which previous states are not reserved. In Table 4, we report the results.

Table 4. Quantitative comparison between different settings of RESCAN. *Iter* represents the framework that leaves out states of previous stages as [9,13]. *Add* and *Full* represent the additive prediction framework and the full prediction framework, respectively.

Dataset	Rain800		Rain100H	
Meassure	PSNR	SSIM	PSNR	SSIM
SCAN	23.45	0.8112	23.56	0.7456
Iter+Add	23.36	0.8169	22.81	0.7630
ConvRNN+Add	24.09	0.8410	23.34	0.7765
ConvRNN+Full	23.52	0.8269	23.44	0.7643
ConvGRU+Add	23.31	**0.8444**	24.00	0.7993
ConvGRU+Full	<u>24.18</u>	<u>0.8394</u>	**26.45**	**0.8458**
ConvLSTM+Add	22.93	0.8385	25.13	0.8211
ConvLSTM+Full	**24.37**	0.8384	<u>25.64</u>	<u>0.8334</u>

It is obvious that Iter cannot compete with all RNN structures, and is not better than SCAN, as it leaves out information of previous stages. Moreover, ConvGRU and ConvLSTM outperform ConvRNN, as they maintain more parameters and require more computation. However, it is difficult to pick the best unit between ConvLSTM and ConvGRU as they perform similarly in experiments. For recurrent frameworks, results indicate that Full Prediction is better.

6 Conclusions

We propose the RESCAN for single image deraining in this paper. We divide the rain removal into multiple stages. In each stage, the context aggregation network is adopted to remove rain streaks. We also modify CAN to better match the rain removal task, including the exponentially increasing dilation and removal of the BN layer. To better characterize intensities of different rain streak layers, we adopt the squeeze-and-excitation block to assign different alpha-values according to their properties. Moreover, RNN is incorporated to better utilize the useful information for rain removal in previous stages and guide the learning in later stages. We also test the performance of different network architectures and recurrent units. Experiments on both synthetic and real-world datasets show that RESCAN outperforms the state-of-the-art methods under all evaluation metrics.

Acknowledgment. Zhouchen Lin is supported by National Basic Research Program of China (973 Program) (Grant no. 2015CB352502), National Natural Science Foundation (NSF) of China (Grant nos. 61625301 and 61731018), Qualcomm, and Microsoft Research Asia. Hong Liu is supported by National Natural Science Foundation of China (Grant nos. U1613209 and 61673030). Hongbin Zha is supported by Beijing Municipal Natural Science Foundation (Grant no. 4152006).

References

1. Zhang, X., Li, H., Qi, Y., Leow, W.K., Ng, T.K.: Rain removal in video by combining temporal and chromatic properties. In: IEEE ICME, pp. 461–464 (2006)
2. Garg, K., Nayar, S.K.: Vision and rain. Int. J. Comput. Vis. **75**(1), 3–27 (2007)
3. Santhaseelan, V., Asari, V.K.: Utilizing local phase information to remove rain from video. Int. J. Comput. Vis. **112**(1), 71–89 (2015)
4. Tripathi, A.K., Mukhopadhyay, S.: Removal of rain from videos: a review. Signal Image Video Process. **8**(8), 1421–1430 (2014)
5. Luo, Y., Xu, Y., Ji, H.: Removing rain from a single image via discriminative sparse coding. In: IEEE ICCV, pp. 3397–3405 (2015)
6. Chang, Y., Yan, L., Zhong, S.: Transformed low-rank model for line pattern noise removal. In: IEEE ICCV, pp. 1726–1734 (2017)
7. Li, Y., Tan, R.T., Guo, X., Lu, J., Brown, M.S.: Rain streak removal using layer priors. In: IEEE CVPR, pp. 2736–2744 (2016)
8. Fu, X., Huang, J., Zeng, D., Huang, Y., Ding, X., Paisley, J.: Removing rain from single images via a deep detail network. In: IEEE CVPR, pp. 1715–1723 (2017)
9. Yang, W., Tan, R.T., Feng, J., Liu, J., Guo, Z., Yan, S.: Deep joint rain detection and removal from a single image. In: IEEE CVPR, pp. 1357–1366 (2017)
10. Huang, D.A., Kang, L.W., Yang, M.C., Lin, C.W., Wang, Y.C.F.: Context-aware single image rain removal. In: IEEE ICME, pp. 164–169 (2012)
11. Yu, F., Koltun, V.: Multi-scale context aggregation by dilated convolutions. arXiv preprint arXiv:1511.07122 (2015)
12. Chen, Q., Xu, J., Koltun, V.: Fast image processing with fully-convolutional networks. In: IEEE ICCV, pp. 2516–2525 (2017)
13. Li, R., Cheong, L.F., Tan, R.T.: Single image deraining using scale-aware multi-stage recurrent network. arXiv preprint arXiv:1712.06830 (2017)
14. Barnum, P.C., Narasimhan, S., Kanade, T.: Analysis of rain and snow in frequency space. Int. J. Comput. Vis. **86**(2–3), 256 (2010)
15. Garg, K., Nayar, S.K.: Detection and removal of rain from videos. In: IEEE CVPR, vol. 1, pp. 528–535 (2004)
16. Garg, K., Nayar, S.K.: When does a camera see rain? In: IEEE ICCV, vol. 2, pp. 1067–1074 (2005)
17. Bossu, J., Hautière, N., Tarel, J.P.: Rain or snow detection in image sequences through use of a histogram of orientation of streaks. Int. J. Comput. Vis. **93**(3), 348–367 (2011)
18. Mairal, J., Bach, F., Ponce, J., Sapiro, G.: Online dictionary learning for sparse coding. In: ICML, pp. 689–696 (2009)

19. Reynolds, D.A., Quatieri, T.F., Dunn, R.B.: Speaker verification using adapted Gaussian mixture models. Digit. Signal Process. **10**(1–3), 19–41 (2000)
20. Liu, G., Lin, Z., Yan, S., Sun, J., Yu, Y., Ma, Y.: Robust recovery of subspace structures by low-rank representation. IEEE Trans. Pattern Anal. Mach. Intell. **35**(1), 171–184 (2013)
21. Kang, L.W., Lin, C.W., Fu, Y.H.: Automatic single-image-based rain streaks removal via image decomposition. IEEE Trans. Image Process. **21**(4), 1742–1755 (2012)
22. Wang, Y., Liu, S., Chen, C., Zeng, B.: A hierarchical approach for rain or snow removing in a single color image. IEEE Trans. Image Process. **26**(8), 3936–3950 (2017)
23. Gu, S., Meng, D., Zuo, W., Zhang, L.: Joint convolutional analysis and synthesis sparse representation for single image layer separation. In: IEEE ICCV, pp. 1717–1725 (2017)
24. Zhu, L., Fu, C.W., Lischinski, D., Heng, P.A.: Joint bi-layer optimization for single-image rain streak removal. In: IEEE CVPR, pp. 2526–2534 (2017)
25. Fu, X., Huang, J., Ding, X., Liao, Y., Paisley, J.: Clearing the skies: a deep network architecture for single-image rain removal. IEEE Trans. Image Process. **26**(6), 2944–2956 (2017)
26. Yang, W., Tan, R.T., Feng, J., Liu, J., Guo, Z., Yan, S.: Joint rain detection and removal via iterative region dependent multi-task learning. CoRR, abs/1609.07769 (2016)
27. Zhang, H., Sindagi, V., Patel, V.M.: Image de-raining using a conditional generative adversarial network. arXiv preprint arXiv:1701.05957 (2017)
28. Kaushal, H., Jain, V., Kar, S.: Free-space optical channel models. In: Kaushal, H., Jain, V.K., Kar, S. (eds.) Free Space Optical Communication, pp. 41–89. Springer, New Delhi (2017). https://doi.org/10.1007/978-81-322-3691-7_2
29. Hu, J., Shen, L., Sun, G.: Squeeze-and-excitation networks. arXiv preprint arXiv:1709.01507 (2017)
30. Ioffe, S., Szegedy, C.: Batch normalization: accelerating deep network training by reducing internal covariate shift. In: ICML, pp. 448–456 (2015)
31. Mandic, D.P., Chambers, J.A., et al.: Recurrent Neural Networks for Prediction: Learning Algorithms, Architectures and Stability. Wiley Online Library (2001)
32. Cho, K., et al.: Learning phrase representations using RNN encoder-decoder for statistical machine translation. arXiv preprint arXiv:1406.1078 (2014)
33. Zaremba, W., Sutskever, I., Vinyals, O.: Recurrent neural network regularization. arXiv preprint arXiv:1409.2329 (2014)
34. Maas, A.L., Hannun, A.Y., Ng, A.Y.: Rectifier nonlinearities improve neural network acoustic models. In: ICML, vol. 30, p. 3 (2013)
35. Kingma, D.P., Ba, J.: Adam: a method for stochastic optimization. arXiv preprint arXiv:1412.6980 (2014)
36. Huynh-Thu, Q., Ghanbari, M.: Scope of validity of PSNR in image/video quality assessment. IET Electron. Lett. **44**(13), 800–801 (2008)
37. Wang, Z., Bovik, A.C., Sheikh, H.R., Simoncelli, E.P.: Image quality assessment: from error visibility to structural similarity. IEEE Trans. Image Process. **13**(4), 600–612 (2004)

Iterative Crowd Counting

Viresh Ranjan(✉), Hieu Le, and Minh Hoai

Department of Computer Science, Stony Brook University, Stony Brook, USA
{vranjan,hle,minhhoai}@cs.stonybrook.edu

Abstract. In this work, we tackle the problem of crowd counting in images. We present a Convolutional Neural Network (CNN) based density estimation approach to solve this problem. Predicting a high resolution density map in one go is a challenging task. Hence, we present a two branch CNN architecture for generating high resolution density maps, where the first branch generates a low resolution density map, and the second branch incorporates the low resolution prediction and feature maps from the first branch to generate a high resolution density map. We also propose a multi-stage extension of our approach where each stage in the pipeline utilizes the predictions from all the previous stages. Empirical comparison with the previous state-of-the-art crowd counting methods shows that our method achieves the lowest mean absolute error on three challenging crowd counting benchmarks: Shanghaitech, World-Expo'10, and UCF datasets.

Keywords: Crowd counting · Density estimation · Multi-stage CNN

1 Introduction

Gathering of large crowds is commonplace nowadays, and estimating the size of a crowd is an important problem for different purposes ranging from journalism to public safety. Without turnstiles to provide a precise count, the media and crowd safety specialists must estimate the size of the crowd based on images and videos of the crowd. Manual visual estimation, however, is difficult and laborious for humans. Humans are good at subitizing, i.e., predicting fast and accurate counts for small number of items, but the accuracy with which humans count deteriorates as the number of items increase [7]. Furthermore, the addition of each new item beyond a few adds an extra processing time of around 250 to 300 milliseconds [17]. As a result, any crowd monitoring system that relies on humans for counting people in crowded scenes will be slow and unreliable. There is a need for an automatic computer vision algorithm that can accurately count the number of people in crowded scenes based on images and videos of the crowds.

There exist a number of computer vision algorithms for crowd counting, and the current state-of-the-art methods are based on *density estimation* rather than *detection-then-counting*. Density-estimation methods use Convolutional Neural

V. Ferrari et al. (Eds.): ECCV 2018, LNCS 11211, pp. 278–293, 2018.
https://doi.org/10.1007/978-3-030-01234-2_17

Fig. 1. Crowd counting can be posed as a CNN-based density estimation problem, but this problem can be challenging for a single CNN due to the huge variation of density values across pixels of different images. This figure shows two images from the Shanghaitech dataset that have very different crowd densities. As can be seen, crowd count could vary from a few to a few thousand.

Networks (CNNs) [8,9] to output a map of density values, one for each pixel of the input image. The final count estimate can be obtained by summing over the predicted density map. Unlike the detection-then-counting approach (e.g., [5]), the output of the density estimation approach at each pixel is not necessarily binary. Density estimation has been proved to be more robust than the detection-then-counting approach because the former does not have to commit to binarized decisions at an early stage.

Estimating the crowd density per pixel is a challenging task due to the large variation of the crowd density values. As shown in Fig. 1, some images contain hundreds of people, while others have only a few. It is difficult for a single CNN to handle the entire spectrum of crowd densities. Earlier works [15,20] have tackled this challenge by using a multi-column or a switching CNN architecture. These CNN architectures consist of three parallel CNN branches with different receptive field sizes. In such architectures, a branch with smaller receptive fields could handle the high density images well, while a branch with larger receptive fields could handle the low density images. More recently, a five-branch CNN architecture was proposed [16] where three of the branches resembled the previous multi-column CNN [20], while the remaining two branches acted as global and local context estimators. These context estimator branches were trained beforehand on the related task of classifying the image into different density categories. Some of the key takeaways from these previous approaches are: (1) using a multi-column CNN model with varying kernel sizes improves the performance of crowd density estimation; and (2) augmenting the feature set with the ones learned from a task related to density estimation, such as count range classification, improves the performance of the density estimation task.

In this work, we propose iterative counting Convolutional Neural Networks (ic-CNN), a CNN-based iterative approach for crowd counting. Unlike previous approaches, where three [15,20] or more [16] columns are needed to achieve good performance, our ic-CNN approach has a simpler architecture comprising of two columns/branches. The first branch predicts a density map at

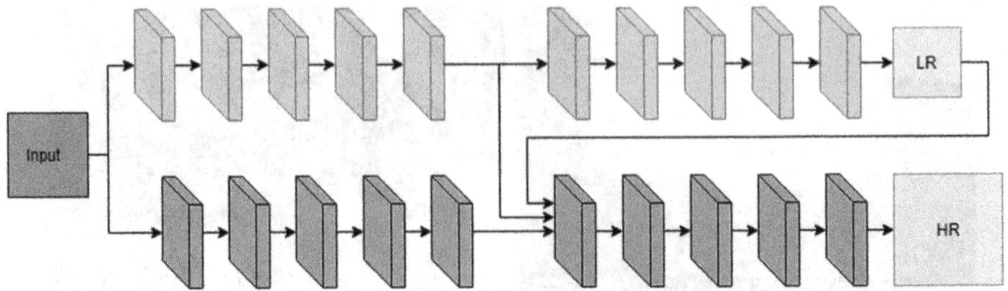

Fig. 2. Figure shows the ic-CNN architecture which consists of two columns/branches. On the top is the Low Resolution CNN branch (LR-CNN) and at the bottom is the High Resolution CNN branch (HR-CNN). LR-CNN predicts a density map at a lower resolution (LR). It passes the predicted density map and the convolutional feature maps to HR-CNN. HR-CNN fuses its feature maps with the feature maps and predicted density map from LR-CNN, and predicts a high resolution density map (HR) at the size of the original image. LR and HR are low and high resolution prediction maps respectively.

a lower resolution of $\frac{1}{4}$ the size of the original image, and passes the predicted map and a set of convolutional features to the second branch. The second branch predicts a high resolution density map at the size of the original image. Density maps contain information about the spatial distribution of crowd in an image. Hence, the first stage map serves as an important feature for the high resolution density map prediction task. We also propose a multi-stage extension of ic-CNN where we combine multiple ic-CNNs sequentially to further improve the quality of the predicted density map. Each ic-CNN in the multi-stage pipeline provides both the low and high resolution density predictions to all subsequent stages. Figure 2 illustrates the schematic architecture for ic-CNN. ic-CNN has two branches: Low Resolution CNN (LR-CNN) and High Resolution CNN (HR-CNN). LR-CNN predicts the density map at a low resolution while HR-CNN predicts the density map at the original image resolution. The key highlights of our work are:

1. We propose ic-CNN, a two-stage CNN framework for crowd density estimation and counting.
2. ic-CNN achieves state of the art results on multiple crowd counting datasets. On Shanghaitech Part B dataset, ic-CNN yields 48.3% improvement in terms of mean absolute error over the previously published results [16].
3. We also propose a multi-stage extension of ic-CNN, which can combine predictions from multiple ic-CNN models.

2 Related Work

Crowd counting is an important research problem and a number of approaches have been proposed by the computer vision community. Earlier work tackled crowd counting as an object detection problem [11,12]. Lin *et al.* [12] extracted

Haar features for head like contours and used an SVM classifier to classify these features as the contour of a head or not. Li *et al.* [11] proposed a detection based approach where the input image was first segmented into foreground-background regions and a HOG feature based head-shoulder detector was used to detect each person in the crowd. These detection based methods often fail to accurately count people in extremely dense scenes. To handle images of dense crowds, some methods [2,3] proposed to use a regression approach to avoid the harder detection problem. They instead extracted local patch level features and learned a regression function to directly estimate the total count for an input image patch. These regression approaches, however, do not fully utilize the available annotation associated with training data; they ignore the spatial density and distribution of people in training images. Several researchers [10,14] proposed to use a density estimation approach to take advantage of the provided crowd density annotation maps of training images. Lempitsky and Zisserman [10] learned a linear mapping between the crowd images and the corresponding ground truth density maps. Pham *et al.* [14] learned a more robust mapping by using a random decision forest to estimate the crowd density map. These density-based methods solve some of the challenges faced by the earlier detection and regression based approaches, by avoiding the harder detection problem and also utilizing the spatial annotation and correlation. All aforementioned methods predated the deep-learning era, and they used hand crafted features for crowd counting.

More recent methods [4,13,15,16,18,20] used CNNs to tackle crowd counting. Wang *et al.* [18] posed crowd counting as a regression problem, and used a CNN model to map the input crowd image to its corresponding count. Instead of predicting the overall count, Fu *et al.* [4] classified an image into five broad crowd density categories and used a cascade of two CNNs in a boosting like strategy where the second CNN was trained on the images misclassified by the first CNN. These methods also overlooked the benefits provided by the crowd density annotation maps.

The methods that are most related to our work are [15,16,20]. Zhang *et al.* [20] proposed a CNN-based method to predict crowd density maps. To handle the large variation in crowd densities and sizes across different images, Zhang *et al.* [20] proposed a multi-column CNN architecture (MCNN) with filters and receptive fields of various sizes. The CNN column with smaller receptive field and filter sizes were responsible for the denser crowd images, while the CNN columns with larger receptive fields and filter sizes were meant for the less dense crowd images. The features from the three columns were concatenated and processed by a 1×1 convolution layer to predict the final density map. To handle the variations in density and size within an image, the authors divided each image into non-overlapping patches, and trained the MCNN architecture on these patches. Given that the number of training samples in annotated crowd counting datasets is much smaller in comparison to the datasets pertaining to image classification and segmentation tasks, training a CNN from scratch on full images might lead to overfitting. Hence, patch-based training of MCNN was essential in preventing overfitting and also improving the overall performance by serving as a data augmentation strategy. One issue with MCNN was that it fused the features form three CNN columns for predicting the density map. For a given patch, it is expected that the counting performance can be made more accurate by choosing the right CNN column that specializes in analyzing images of similar density values. Sam *et al.* [15] built on this idea and decoupled the three columns into separate CNNs, each focused on a subset of the training patches. To decide which CNN to assign a patch to, the authors trained a CNN-based switch classifier. However, since the ground truth label needed to train the switch classifier was unavailable, the authors resorted to a multi-stage training strategy: (1) training the three density predicting CNNs on the entire set of training patches, (2) training the switch classifier using the count from the previous stage to decide the switch labels, and (3) retraining the three CNNs using the patches assigned by the switch classifier. In a more recent work, Sindagi *et al.* [16] further modified the MCNN architecture by adding two more branches for estimating global and local context maps. The global/local context prediction branches were trained beforehand for the related task of classifying an image/patch into five different count categories. The classification scores were used to create a feature map of the same size as the image/patch, which served as the global/local context map. These context maps were fused with the convolutional feature maps obtained using a three branch multi-column CNN, and the resulting features were further processed by convolutional layers and a 1×1 convolution layer to obtain the final density map.

3 Proposed Approach

In this section, we describe the architecture of ic-CNN, its multi-stage extension and the training strategy. ic-CNN is discussed in Sect. 3.1. The multi stage extension of ic-CNN is discussed in Sect. 3.2, and the training details are discussed in Sect. 3.3.

3.1 Iterative Counting CNN

Let $\mathcal{D} = \{(X_1, Y_1, Z_1), \ldots, (X_n, Y_n, Z_n)\}$ be the training set of n (image, high resolution density map, low resolution density map) triplets, where X_i is the ith image, Y_i is the corresponding crowd density map at the same resolution as the image X_i, and Z_i is a low resolution version of the crowd density map. Y_i and Z_i have the same overall count. Let f_l and f_h be the mapping functions which transform the image into the low resolution and high resolution density maps, respectively. Let the parameters of the low resolution branch (LR-CNN) and high resolution branch (HR-CNN) be θ_l and θ_h respectively. Note that f_l depends on only θ_l, while f_h depends on both θ_l and θ_h. Given an input image X_i, the low resolution density map $\hat{Z}_i$ can be obtained by a doing a forward pass through the LR-CNN branch:

$$\hat{Z}_i = f_l(X_i; \theta_l). \tag{1}$$

The inputs to the high resolution branch HR-CNN are: the image X_i, the features computed by the low resolution branch LR-CNN, and the low resolution prediction $\hat{Z}_i$. HR-CNN predicts a high resolution density map of the same size as the original image:

$$\hat{Y}_i = f_h(X_i, \hat{Z}_i; \theta_l, \theta_h). \tag{2}$$

The low resolution prediction $\hat{Z}_i$ contains information about the spatial distribution of the crowd in the image X_i. It serves as an important feature map for the high resolution prediction task. We can learn the parameters θ_l and θ_h by minimizing the loss function $\mathcal{L}(\theta_l, \theta_h)$:

$$\mathcal{L}(\theta_l, \theta_h) = \frac{1}{n}\sum_{i=1}^{n}(\lambda_l L(f_l(X_i; \theta_l), Z_i) + \lambda_h L(f_h(X_i, \hat{Z}_i; \theta_l, \theta_h), Y_i)), \tag{3}$$

where $L(\cdot, \cdot)$ denotes the loss function, and a reasonable choice is to use the squared error between the estimated and ground truth values. λ_l and λ_h are scalar hyperparameters which can be used to give more importance to one of the loss terms. Using Eqs. (1) and (2), the right hand side can be further simplified as:

$$\mathcal{L}(\theta_l, \theta_h) = \frac{1}{n}\sum_{i=1}^{n}(\lambda_l L(\hat{Z}_i, Z_i) + \lambda_h L(\hat{Y}_i, Y_i)). \tag{4}$$

At test time, given an image X_i, we first obtain the low resolution output $\hat{Z}_i$ by doing a forward pass through LR-CNN and then pass the convolutional features and the low resolution map $\hat{Z}_i$ to HR-CNN, which will predict the high resolution map $\hat{Y}_i$. We use the high resolution output predicted by HR-CNN as the final output of ic-CNN. The overall crowd count is obtained by summing over all the pixels in the density map $\hat{Y}_i$.
Below we provide the architecture details for the LR-CNN and HR-CNN branches.

LR-CNN. The LR-CNN branch takes as input an image, and predicts a density map at $\frac{1}{4}$ the size of the original image. LR-CNN has the following architecture: Conv3-64, Conv3-64, MaxPool, Conv3-128, Conv3-128, MaxPool, Conv3-256, Conv3-256, Conv3-256, Conv7-196, Conv5-96, Conv3-32, Conv1-1. Here, ConvX-Y implies a convolution layer having Y filters with $X \times X$ kernel size. MaxPool is the max pooling layer. We use a ReLU nonlinearity after each convolutional layer.

HR-CNN. The HR-CNN branch predicts the high resolution density map at the same size as the input image. HR-CNN has the following architecture: Conv7-16, MaxPool, Conv5-24, MaxPool, Conv3-48, Conv3-48, Conv3-24, Conv7-196, Conv5-96, Upsampling-2, Conv3-32, Upsampling-2, Conv1-1. Here, Upsampling-2 is a bilinear interpolation layer which upsamples the input to twice its size.

3.2 Multi-stage Crowd Counting

A multi-stage ic-CNN is a network that combines multiple building blocks of ic-CNN described in the previous section. Each ic-CNN block inputs the low and high resolution prediction maps from all the previous blocks. Given an input image X_i, the low resolution branch of the kth block, represented by the function f_l^k, outputs the low resolution prediction:

$$\hat{Z}_i^k = f_l^k(X_i, \hat{Z}_i^{1:k-1}, \hat{Y}_i^{1:k-1}, \theta_l^k), \tag{5}$$

where θ_l^k represents the parameters of LR-CNN, $\hat{Z}_i^{1:k-1}$ and $\hat{Y}_i^{1:k-1}$ represent the set of low and high level predictions from the first $k-1$ blocks for the input X_i. The high resolution branch of the kth block, represented by the function f_h^k, takes as input the image X_i, the feature maps computed by the low resolution branch f_l^k, the low resolution prediction $\hat{Z}_i^k$, and the entire set of low and high resolution prediction maps from the first $k-1$ blocks. Hence, the output of the kth HR-CNN can be computed using:

$$\hat{Y}_i^k = f_h^k(X_i, \hat{Z}_i^{1:k}, \hat{Y}_i^{1:k-1}, \theta_l^k, \theta_h^k). \tag{6}$$

Note that f_l^k and f_h^k do not depend on the parameters for the first $k-1$ blocks, and $\hat{Z}_i^{1:k-1}$ and $\hat{Y}_i^{1:k-1}$ are treated as fixed inputs (i.e., the parameters of the corresponding network blocks are frozen). We can learn the parameters θ_l^k and θ_h^k by minimizing the loss function $\mathcal{L}(\theta_l^k, \theta_h^k)$:

$$\begin{aligned} \mathcal{L}(\theta_l^k, \theta_h^k) =& \frac{\lambda_l}{n} \sum_{i=1}^{n} L(f_l^k(X_i, \hat{Z}_i^{1:k-1}, \hat{Y}_i^{1:k-1}, \theta_l^k), Z_i) \\ &+ \frac{\lambda_h}{n} \sum_{i=1}^{n} L(f_h^k(X_i, \hat{Z}_i^{1:k}, \hat{Y}_i^{1:k-1}, \theta_l^k, \theta_h^k), Y_i). \end{aligned} \tag{7}$$

3.3 Training Details

An ic-CNN is trained by minimizing the loss function $\mathcal{L}(\theta_l, \theta_h)$ from Eq. (3). We use the Stochastic Gradient Descent algorithm with the following hyper parameters (unless specified otherwise): learning rate 10^{-4}, momentum 0.9, batch size 1. We give more importance to the high resolution loss term in Eq. (3) and set λ_l and λ_h to 10^{-2} and 10^2, respectively.

We train a multi-stage ic-CNN in multiple stages. In the kth stage, we train the kth ic-CNN block by minimizing the loss function given in Eq. (7), using the Stochastic Gradient Descent algorithm with the same hyper parameters as above. Once the training for the kth stage has converged, we freeze the parameters for the kth stage and proceed to the next stage.

The training data consists of crowd images and corresponding ground truth annotation files. A ground truth annotation for an image specifies the location of each person in the image with a single dot on the person. We convert this annotation into a binary map consisting of 0's at all locations, except for the annotated points which are assigned the value of 1. We convolve this binary map with a Gaussian filter of standard deviation 5. We use the resulting density map for training the networks.

Table 1. Count errors of different methods on the Shanghaitech dataset. This dataset has two parts: A and B. We compare ic-CNN with the previous state-of-the-art approaches, using two metrics: Mean Absolute Error (MAE) and Root Mean Squared Error (RMSE). ic-CNN (one stage) is the single stage ic-CNN with two branches HR-CNN and LR-CNN. ic-CNN (two stages) is the two-stage variant of ic-CNN. Both ic-CNN networks outperform the previous approaches in 3 out of 4 cases. On the Shanghaitech Part B dataset, using the one-stage ic-CNN, which has a simpler architecture than CP-CNN [16], we improve on the previously reported state of the art results by 48.3% using the MAE metric and 46.8% using the RMSE metric

	Part A		Part B	
	MAE	RMSE	MAE	RMSE
Crowd CNN [19]	181.8	277.7	32.0	49.8
MCNN [20]	110.2	173.2	26.4	41.3
Switching CNN [15]	90.4	135.0	21.6	33.4
CP-CNN [16]	73.6	**106.4**	20.1	30.1
ic-CNN (one stage)	69.8	117.3	**10.4**	16.7
ic-CNN (two stages)	**68.5**	116.2	**10.7**	**16.0**

4 Experiments

We conduct experiments on three challenging datasets: Shanghaitech [20], WorldExpo'10 [19], and UCF Crowd Counting Dataset [6].

4.1 Evaluation Metrics

Following previous works for crowd counting, we use the Mean Absolute Error (MAE) and Root Mean Squared Error (RMSE) to evaluate the performance of our proposed method. If the predicted count for image i is $\hat{C}_i$ and the ground truth count is C_i, the MAE and RMSE can be computed as:

$$MAE = \frac{1}{n}\sum_{i=1}^{n}|C_i - \hat{C}_i|, \quad RMSE = \sqrt{\frac{1}{n}\sum_{i=1}^{n}(C_i - \hat{C}_i)^2} \tag{8}$$

where n is the number of test images.

4.2 Experiments on the Shanghaitech Dataset

The Shanghaitech dataset [20] consists of 1198 annotated crowd images. The dataset is divided into two parts, Part-A containing 482 images and Part-B containing 716 images. Part-A is split into train and test subsets consisting of 300 and 182 images, respectively. Part-B is split into train and test subsets consisting of 400 and 316 images. Each person in a crowd image is annotated with one point close to the center of the head. In total, the dataset consists of 330,165 annotated people. Images from Part-A were collected from the Internet, while images from Part-B were collected on the busy streets of Shanghai. To avoid the risk of overfitting to the small number of training images, we trained ic-CNNs on random crops of size $\frac{H}{3} \times \frac{W}{3}$, where H and W are the height and width of a training image. In Table 1, we compare ic-CNNs with the previous state-of-the-art approaches. ic-CNNs outperform the previous approaches in three out of four cases by a large margin. On Part-B of the Shanghaitech dataset, using the one-stage ic-CNN which has a simpler architecture than the five-branch CP-CNN [16], we improve on the previously reported state of the art results by 48.3% for MAE metric and 46.8% for the RMSE metric. On Part A of the Shanghaitech dataset, we achieve a 5.1 absolute improvement in MAE over CP-CNN. Furthermore, for Part A data, the two-stage ic-CNN results in an improvement of 1.3 MAE over the one-stage ic-CNN. We also trained a three-stage ic-CNN on Part A data, which resulted in MAE = 69.4 and RMSE = 116.0. Since adding the 3rd stage did not yield a significant performance gain, we did not experiment with more than three stages.

In Table 2, we analyze the effects of varying the resolution of the intermediate prediction on the overall performance. Using any resolution other than $\frac{1}{4}$ leads to a drop in the performance.

In Table 3, we analyze the effects of varying the hyperparameter λ_h on performance of ic-CNN. We use Shanghaitech Part-A dataset for this experiment. We show the MAE of the high and low resolution branches as the scalar weight λ_h is varied. λ_l is kept fixed at 10^{-2}. We can see that the LR-CNN branch performs

Table 2. MAE and RMSE on Shanghaitech Part-A dataset as we vary the resolution being used for the low resolution branch LR-CNN of ic-CNN. The resolution of HR-CNN is fixed at 1, the size of the input image.

LR-Resolution	HR-Resolution	MAE	RMSE
1/8	1	74.9	131.6
1/4	1	**69.8**	**117.3**
1/2	1	73.3	124.4
1	1	74.4	128.3

Table 3. Effect of varying hyper parameter λ_h: Mean absolute error on Shanghaitech Part A dataset. λ_l is kept fixed at 10^{-2}.

λ_h	LR-CNN	HR-CNN
10^{-4}	73.7	78.8
10^{-2}	73.0	73.6
1	75.1	73.3
10^{2}	79.9	69.8
10^{4}	432.6	74.4

better when λ_l is comparable with λ_h, and its performance degrades when λ_h is too large. The performance of HR-CNN improves as λ_h is varied from 10^{-4} to 10^2. In the extreme case when λ_h is set to 10^4, there is a large degradation in the performance of the LR-CNN branch, which affects the performance of the HR-CNN branch. When λ_h is 10^4, the low resolution prediction task is possibly ignored, and the network solely focuses on solving the high resolution task. In such a scenario, the low resolution prediction does not contain any useful information, which affects the performance of the high resolution branch HR-CNN. We obtain the best results for the HR-CNN branch when λ_h is set to 10^2. In this case, the high resolution loss does not force the network to completely ignore the low resolution task.

In Table 4, we show the training time and the number of parameters of ic-CNN, MCNN, Switching CNN, and CP-CNN. An ic-CNN takes 10 h to train, while a Switching CNN takes around 22 h. An ic-CNN has significantly fewer parameters than a CP-CNN and a Switching CNN. We contacted the authors of MCNN and CP-CNN, but we did not get a response for the training time of these networks.

In Table 5, we analyze the importance of each of the components of our proposed ic-CNN model. We see that both the feature sharing and the feedback

Table 4. Training time, number of parameters, and MAE on Part A of the Shanghaitech dataset. ic-CNN was trained on a single GPU machine (Nvidia GTX 1080 TI).

Model	Training time	Number of parameters	MAE
MCNN [20]	Unknown	1.27×10^5	110.2
Switching CNN [15]	22 h	1.2×10^7	90.4
CP-CNN [16]	unknown	6.3×10^7	73.6
ic-CNN (proposed)	10 hrs	7.9×10^6	69.8

Table 5. Ablation study on Shanghaitech Part A data. HR-CNN is the high resolution branch, LR-CNN is the low resolution branch. LR-CNN alone and HR-CNN alone refer to a counting network that contains either LR-CNN or HR-CNN only. ic-CNN is our proposed approach, where both the features and the low resolution prediction map from LR-CNN are shared with HR-CNN. We also compared with two variants where either the low resolution map or the convolutional feature maps from LR-CNN is not shared with the HR-CNN.

Method	MAE	RMSE
LR-CNN alone	78.5	133.2
HR-CNN alone	136.2	204.0
HR-CNN + LR-CNN features (no low-res prediction)	75.1	129.0
HR-CNN + LR-CNN low-res prediction (no features)	77.4	130.4
ic-CNN (proposed)	**69.8**	**117.3**

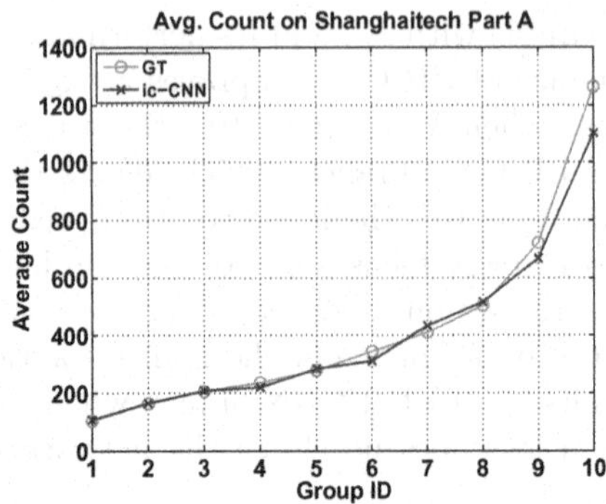

Fig. 3. Performance across different crowd density: We divide the 182 test images from Shanghaitech Part A into 10 groups on the basis of the crowd count. Each group except the last has 18 test images. We average the crowd count across a group to obtain the average count. GT is the ground truth, ic-CNN is prediction from the high resolution branch. For majority of the count groups, the difference between the average counts for ic-CNN and GT is small.

of the low resolution prediction are important for ic-CNN. Removing any of these two components leads to significant drop in performance.

In Fig. 3, we analyze the performance of ic-CNN across different groups of images with varying crowd counts.

4.3 Experiments on the WorldExpo'10 Dataset

The WorldExpo'10 dataset consists of 1132 annotated video sequences captured by 108 surveillance cameras. Annotated frames from 103 cameras are used for training and the annotated frames from the remaining 5 cameras are used for testing. We trained ic-CNN networks using random crops of sizes $\frac{H}{2} \times \frac{W}{2}$. We used the networks trained on Shanghaitech Part A for initializing the models for the experiments on the WorldExpo dataset. In Table 6, we compare ic-CNN with other state of art approaches. ic-CNN outperforms these previous approaches on three out of five cases.

4.4 Experiments on the UCF Dataset

The UCF Crowd Counting dataset [6] consists of 50 crowd images collected from the web. Each person in the dataset is annotated with a single dot annotation. The numbers of people in the images vary from 94 to 4545 with an average of 1280 people per image. The average count for the UCF dataset is much larger than the previous two datasets. Following previous works using this dataset, we perform five-fold cross validation and report the MAE and RMSE values. We trained ic-CNN networks using random crops of sizes $\frac{H}{3} \times \frac{W}{3}$. We compare ic-CNN with previous approaches and show the results in Table 7. Since the dataset is small, adding multiple stages to ic-CNN could lead to overfitting. Hence we

Table 6. Performance of different methods on the WorldExpo'10 dataset. Switch CNN(with perspective) refers to the case when perspective maps are used to obtain the crowd density map, while Switch CNN(sans perspective) refers to the case when the perspective map isn't used. ic-CNN is our proposed two branch approach. We outperform other approaches on 3 of 6 cases.

Method	S1	S2	S3	S4	S5	Avg
Crowd CNN [19]	9.8	14.1	14.3	22.2	**3.7**	12.9
MCNN [20]	3.4	20.6	12.9	13.0	8.1	11.6
Switching CNN (sans perspective) [15]	4.4	15.7	10.0	11.0	5.9	9.4
Switching CNN (with perspective) [15]	4.2	14.9	14.2	18.7	4.3	11.2
CP-CNN [16]	**2.9**	14.7	10.5	10.4	5.8	**8.8**
ic-CNN (proposed)	17.0	**12.3**	**9.2**	**8.1**	4.7	10.3

Table 7. Performance of various methods on the UCF Crowd Counting dataset. The proposed method ic-CNN achieves the best MAE.

Method	MAE	RMSE
Lempitsky and Zisserman [10]	493.4	487.1
Idrees et al. [6]	419.5	487.1
Crowd CNN [19]	467.0	498.5
Crowdnet [1]	452.5	-
MCNN [20]	377.6	509.1
Hydra2s [13]	333.7	425.6
Switch CNN [15]	318.1	439.2
CP-CNN [16]	295.8	**320.9**
ic-CNN (proposed)	**260.9**	365.5

only use one-stage ic-CNN on the UCF dataset. ic-CNN achieves the best MAE on this dataset, outperforming CP-CNN by a large margin.

4.5 Qualitative Results

In Fig. 4, we show some qualitative results on images from the Shanghaitech Part-A dataset obtained using ic-CNN. The first three are success cases for ic-CNN, while the last two are failure cases. In the failure cases, we see that ic-CNN sometimes misclassify tree leaves as tiny people in a crowd. In Fig. 5, we show some qualitative results on images from Shanghaitech Part-B dataset.

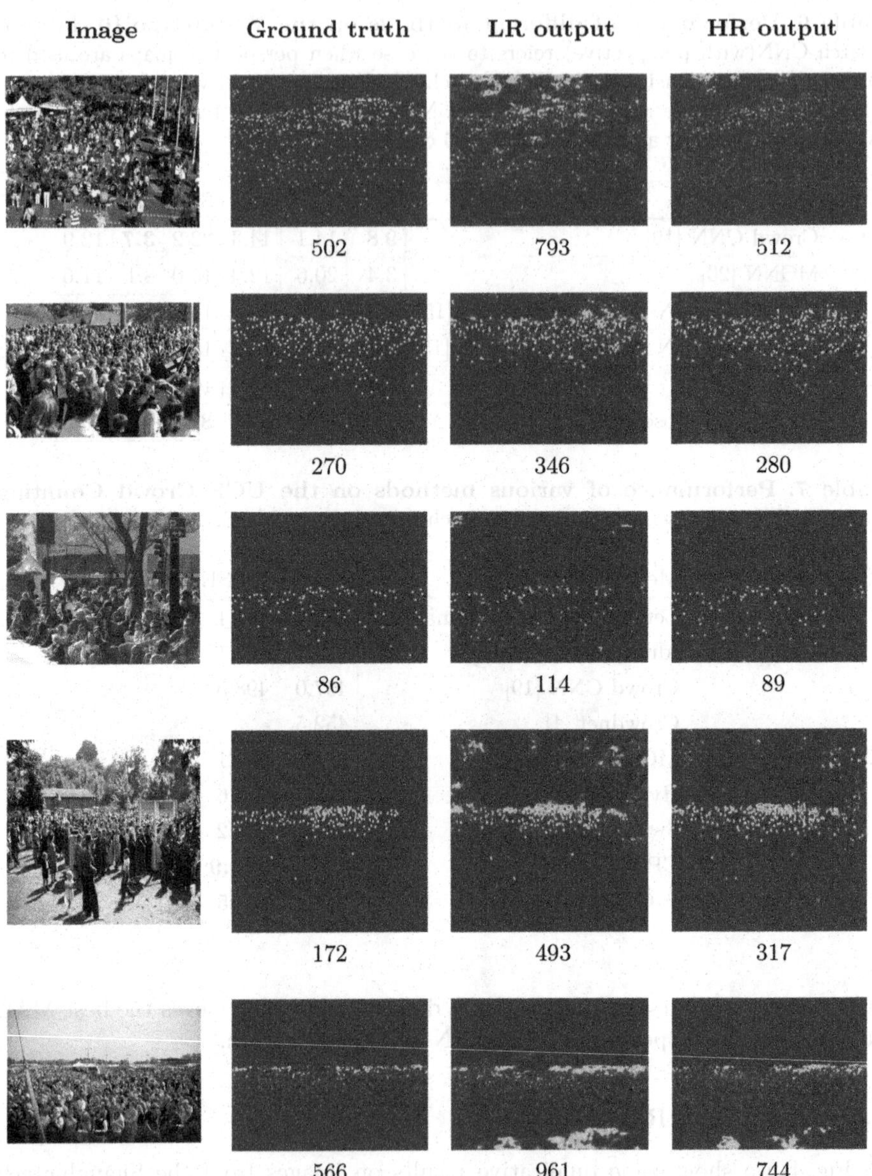

Fig. 4. Qualitative results, some success and failure cases. The four columns show the input image, ground truth annotation map, the low resolution prediction (LR output), and the high resolution prediction map (HR output). The total counts are shown below each density map. The first three rows are success cases for ic-CNN, while the last two are failure cases. ic-CNN sometimes misclassifies tree leaves as people.

Fig. 5. Qualitative results on the Shanghaitech Part B dataset. The four columns show the input image, the ground truth annotation map, the low resolution prediction (LR output), and the high resolution prediction map (HR output). Underneath each density map is the total count, rounded to the nearest integer.

5 Conclusions

In this paper, we have proposed ic-CNN, a two-branch architecture for crowd counting via crowd density estimation based. We have also proposed a multi-stage pipeline comprising of multiple ic-CNNs, where each stage takes into account the predictions of all the previous stages. We performed experiments on three challenging crowd counting benchmark datasets and observed the effectiveness of our iterative approach.

Acknowledgement. This work was supported by SUNY2020 Infrastructure Transportation Security Center. The authors would like to thank Boyu Wang for participating on the discussions and experiments related to an earlier version of the proposed technique. The authors would like to thank NVIDIA for their GPU donation.

References

1. Boominathan, L., Kruthiventi, S.S., Babu, R.V.: CrowdNet: a deep convolutional network for dense crowd counting. In: Proceedings of the ACM Multimedia Conference (2016)
2. Chan, A.B., Vasconcelos, N.: Bayesian Poisson regression for crowd counting. In: Proceedings of the International Conference on Computer Vision (2009)
3. Chen, K., Loy, C.C., Gong, S., Xiang, T.: Feature mining for localised crowd counting. In: Proceedings of the British Machine Vision Conference (2012)
4. Fu, M., Xu, P., Li, X., Liu, Q., Ye, M., Zhu, C.: Fast crowd density estimation with convolutional neural networks. Eng. Appl. Artif. Intell. **43**, 81–88 (2015)
5. Hoai, M., Zisserman, A.: Talking heads: detecting humans and recognizing their interactions. In: Proceedings of the IEEE Conference on Computer Vision and Pattern Recognition (2014)
6. Idrees, H., Saleemi, I., Seibert, C., Shah, M.: Multi-source multi-scale counting in extremely dense crowd images. In: Proceedings of the IEEE Conference on Computer Vision and Pattern Recognition (2013)
7. Kaufman, E.L., Lord, M.W., Reese, T.W., Volkmann, J.: The discrimination of visual number. Am. J. Psychol. **62**(4), 498–525 (1949)
8. Krizhevsky, A., Sutskever, I., Hinton, G.: ImageNet classification with deep convolutional neural networks. In: Advances in Neural Information Processing Systems (2012)
9. LeCun, Y., Boser, B., Denker, J.S., Henderson, D.: Backpropagation applied to handwritten zip code recognition. Neural Comput. **1**(4), 541–551 (1989)
10. Lempitsky, V., Zisserman, A.: Learning to count objects in images. In: Advances in Neural Information Processing Systems (2010)
11. Li, M., Zhang, Z., Huang, K., Tan, T.: Estimating the number of people in crowded scenes by mid based foreground segmentation and head-shoulder detection. In: Proceedings of the International Conference on Pattern Recognition (2008)
12. Lin, S.F., Chen, J.Y., Chao, H.X.: Estimation of number of people in crowded scenes using perspective transformation. IEEE Trans. Syst. Man Cybern. Part A Syst. Hum. **31**(6), 645–654 (2001)
13. Onoro-Rubio, D., López-Sastre, R.J.: Towards perspective-free object counting with deep learning. In: Proceedings of the European Conference on Computer Vision (2016)
14. Pham, V.Q., Kozakaya, T., Yamaguchi, O., Okada, R.: Count forest: Co-voting uncertain number of targets using random forest for crowd density estimation. In: Proceedings of the International Conference on Computer Vision (2015)

15. Sam, D.B., Surya, S., Babu, R.V.: Switching convolutional neural network for crowd counting. In: Proceedings of the IEEE Conference on Computer Vision and Pattern Recognition (2017)
16. Sindagi, V.A., Patel, V.M.: Generating high-quality crowd density maps using contextual pyramid CNNs. In: Proceedings of the International Conference on Computer Vision (2017)
17. Trick, L.M., Pylyshyn, Z.W.: Why are small and large numbers enumerated differently? A limited-capacity preattentive stage in vision. Psychol. Rev. **101**(1), 80 (1994)
18. Wang, C., Zhang, H., Yang, L., Liu, S., Cao, X.: Deep people counting in extremely dense crowds. In: Proceedings of the ACM Multimedia Conference (2015)
19. Zhang, C., Li, H., Wang, X., Yang, X.: Cross-scene crowd counting via deep convolutional neural networks. In: Proceedings of the IEEE Conference on Computer Vision and Pattern Recognition (2015)
20. Zhang, Y., Zhou, D., Chen, S., Gao, S., Ma, Y.: Single-image crowd counting via multi-column convolutional neural network. In: Proceedings of the IEEE Conference on Computer Vision and Pattern Recognition (2016)

Image Super-Resolution Using Very Deep Residual Channel Attention Networks

Yulun Zhang[1(✉)], Kunpeng Li[1], Kai Li[1], Lichen Wang[1], Bineng Zhong[1], and Yun Fu[1,2]

[1] Department of ECE, Northeastern University, Boston, USA
yulun100@gmail.com, li.kai.gml@gmail.com, wanglichenxj@gmail.com, bnzhong@hqu.edu.cn, {kunpengli,yunfu}@ece.neu.edu
[2] College of Computer and Information Science, Northeastern University, Boston, USA

Abstract. Convolutional neural network (CNN) depth is of crucial importance for image super-resolution (SR). However, we observe that deeper networks for image SR are more difficult to train. The low-resolution inputs and features contain abundant low-frequency information, which is treated equally across channels, hence hindering the representational ability of CNNs. To solve these problems, we propose the very deep residual channel attention networks (RCAN). Specifically, we propose a residual in residual (RIR) structure to form very deep network, which consists of several residual groups with long skip connections. Each residual group contains some residual blocks with short skip connections. Meanwhile, RIR allows abundant low-frequency information to be bypassed through multiple skip connections, making the main network focus on learning high-frequency information. Furthermore, we propose a channel attention mechanism to adaptively rescale channel-wise features by considering interdependencies among channels. Extensive experiments show that our RCAN achieves better accuracy and visual improvements against state-of-the-art methods.

Keywords: Super-resolution · Residual in residual · Channel attention

1 Introduction

We address the problem of reconstructing an accurate high-resolution (HR) image given its low-resolution (LR) counterpart, usually referred as single image super-resolution (SR) [8]. Image SR is used in various computer vision applications, ranging from security and surveillance imaging [45], medical imaging [33] to object recognition [31]. However, image SR is an ill-posed problem, since there exists multiple solutions for any LR input. To tackle such an inverse problem, numerous learning based methods have been proposed to learn mappings between LR and HR image pairs.

Electronic supplementary material The online version of this chapter (https://doi.org/10.1007/978-3-030-01234-2_18) contains supplementary material, which is available to authorized users.

V. Ferrari et al. (Eds.): ECCV 2018, LNCS 11211, pp. 294–310, 2018.
https://doi.org/10.1007/978-3-030-01234-2_18

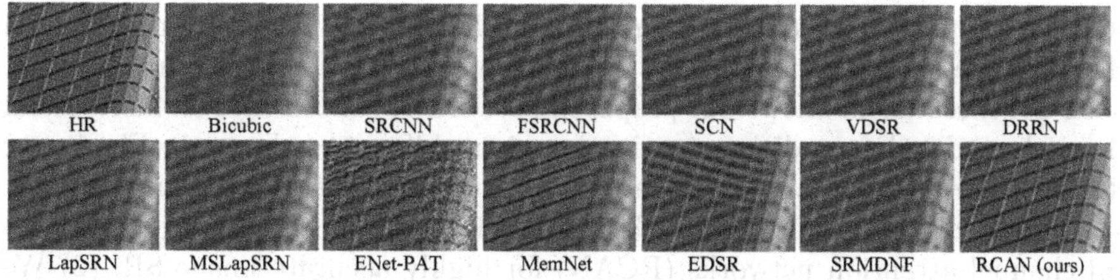

Fig. 1. Visual results with Bicubic (BI) degradation (4×) on "img_074" from Urban100. SRCNN [5], FSRCNN [6], SCN [39], VDSR [16], DRRN [34], LapSRN [19], MSLapSRN [20], ENet-PAT [31], MemNet [35], EDSR [23], and SRMDNF [43]

Recently, deep convolutional neural network (CNN) based methods [5,6,10,16,19,20,23,31,34,35,39,42–44] have achieved significant improvements over conventional SR methods. Among them, Dong et al. [4] proposed SRCNN by firstly introducing a three-layer CNN for image SR. Kim et al. increased the network depth to 20 in VDSR [16] and DRCN [17], achieving notable improvements over SRCNN. Network depth was demonstrated to be of central importance for many visual recognition tasks, especially when He at al. [11] proposed residual net (ResNet). Such effective residual learning strategy was then introduced in many other CNN-based image SR methods [21,23,31,34,35]. Lim et al. [23] built a very wide network EDSR and a very deep one MDSR by using simplified residual blocks. The great improvements on performance of EDSR and MDSR indicate that the depth of representation is of crucial importance for image SR. However, to the best of our knowledge, simply stacking residual blocks to construct deeper networks can hardly obtain better improvements. Whether deeper networks can further contribute to image SR and how to construct very deep trainable networks remains to be explored.

On the other hand, most recent CNN-based methods [5,6,16,19,20,23,31,34,35,39,43] treat channel-wise features equally, which lacks flexibility in dealing with different types of information. Image SR can be viewed as a process, where we try to recover as more high-frequency information as possible. The LR images contain most low-frequency information, which can directly forwarded to the final HR outputs. While, the leading CNN-based methods would treat each channel-wise feature equally, lacking discriminative learning ability across feature channels, and hindering the representational power of deep networks.

To practically resolve these problems, we propose a residual channel attention network (RCAN) to obtain very deep trainable network and adaptively learn more useful channel-wise features simultaneously. To ease the training of very deep networks (e.g., over 400 layers), we propose residual in residual (RIR) structure, where the residual group (RG) serves as the basic module and long skip connection (LSC) allows residual learning in a coarse level. In each RG module, we stack several simplified residual block [23] with short skip connection (SSC). The long and short skip connection as well as the short-cut in residual block allow abundant low-frequency information to be bypassed through these identity-based skip connections, which can ease the flow of information. To make a further step, we propose channel attention (CA) mechanism to adaptively rescale each channel-wise feature by modeling the interdependencies across feature channels. Such CA mechanism allows our proposed network to concentrate on more useful channels and enhance discriminative learning ability. As shown in Fig. 1, our RCAN achieves better visual SR result compared with state-of-the-art methods.

Overall, our contributions are three-fold: (1) We propose the very deep residual channel attention networks (RCAN) for highly accurate image SR. (2) We propose residual in residual (RIR) structure to construct very deep trainable networks. (3) We propose channel attention (CA) mechanism to adaptively rescale features by considering interdependencies among feature channels.

2 Related Work

Numerous image SR methods have been studied in the computer vision community [5,6,13,16,19,20,23,31,34,35,39,43]. Attention mechanism is popular in high-level vision tasks, but is seldom investigated in low-level vision applications [12]. Due to space limitation, here we focus on works related to CNN-based methods and attention mechanism.

Deep CNN for SR. The pioneer work was done by Dong et al. [4], who proposed SRCNN for image SR and achieved superior performance against previous works. SRCNN was further improved in VDSR [16] and DRCN [17]. These methods firstly interpolate the LR inputs to the desired size, which inevitably loses some details and increases computation greatly. Extracting features from the original LR inputs and upscaling spatial resolution at the network tail then became the main choice for deep architecture. A faster network structure FSRCNN [6] was proposed to accelerate the training and testing of SRCNN. Ledig et al. [21] introduced ResNet [11] to construct a deeper network with perceptual losses [15] and generative adversarial network (GAN) [9] for photo-realistic SR. However, most of these methods have limited network depth, which has demonstrated to be very important in visual recognition tasks [11]. Furthermore, most of these methods treat the channel-wise features equally, hindering better discriminative ability for different features.

Attention Mechanism. Generally, attention can be viewed as a guidance to bias the allocation of available processing resources towards the most informative components of an input [12]. Recently, tentative works have been proposed to apply attention into deep neural networks [12,22,38], ranging from localization and understanding in images [3,14] to sequence-based networks [2,26]. It's usually combined with a gating function (e.g., sigmoid) to rescale the feature maps. Wang et al. [38] proposed residual attention network for image classification with a trunk-and-mask attention mechanism. Hu et al. [12] proposed squeeze-and-excitation (SE) block to model channel-wise relationships to obtain significant performance improvement for image classification. However, few works have been proposed to investigate the effect of attention for low-level vision tasks (e.g., image SR).

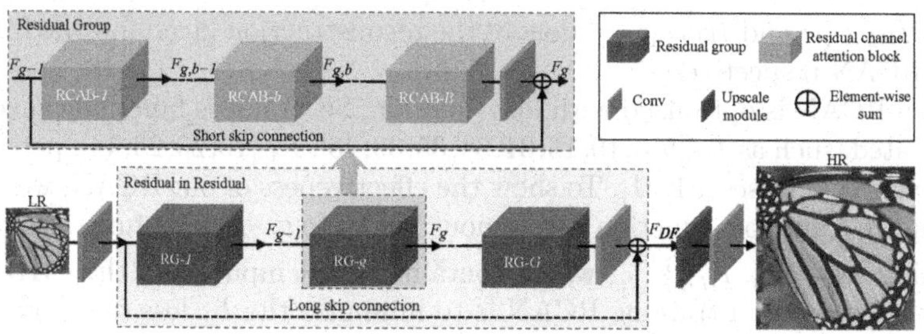

Fig. 2. Network architecture of our residual channel attention network (RCAN)

3 Residual Channel Attention Network (RCAN)

3.1 Network Architecture

As shown in Fig. 2, our RCAN mainly consists four parts: shallow feature extraction, residual in residual (RIR) deep feature extraction, upscale module, and reconstruction part. Let's denote I_{LR} and I_{SR} as the input and output of RCAN. As investigated in [21,23], we use only one convolutional layer (Conv) to extract the shallow feature F_0 from the LR input

$$F_0 = H_{SF}(I_{LR}), \tag{1}$$

where $H_{SF}(\cdot)$ denotes convolution operation. F_0 is then used for deep feature extraction with RIR module. So we can further have

$$F_{DF} = H_{RIR}(F_0), \tag{2}$$

where $H_{RIR}(\cdot)$ denotes our proposed very deep residual in residual structure, which contains G residual groups (RG). To the best of our knowledge, our proposed RIR achieves the largest depth so far and provides very large receptive field size. So we treat its output as deep feature, which is then upscaled via a upscale module

$$F_{UP} = H_{UP}(F_{DF}), \tag{3}$$

where $H_{UP}(\cdot)$ and F_{UP} denote a upscale module and upscaled feature respectively.

There're several choices to serve as upscale modules, such as deconvolution layer (also known as transposed convolution) [6], nearest-neighbor upsampling + convolution [7], and ESPCN [32]. Such post-upscaling strategy has been demonstrated to be more efficient for both computation complexity and achieve higher performance than pre-upscaling SR methods (e.g., DRRN [34] and MemNet [35]). The upscaled feature is then reconstructed via one Conv layer

$$I_{SR} = H_{REC}(F_{UP}) = H_{RCAN}(I_{LR}), \tag{4}$$

where $H_{REC}(\cdot)$ and $H_{RCAN}(\cdot)$ denote the reconstruction layer and the function of our RCAN respectively.

Then RCAN is optimized with loss function. Several loss functions have been investigated, such as L_2 [5,6,10,16,31,34,35,39,43], L_1 [19,20,23,44], perceptual and adversarial losses [21,31]. To show the effectiveness of our RCAN, we choose to optimize same loss function as previous works (e.g., L_1 loss function). Given a training set $\left\{I_{LR}^i, I_{HR}^i\right\}_{i=1}^N$, which contains N LR inputs and their HR counterparts. The goal of training RCAN is to minimize the L_1 loss function

$$L(\Theta) = \frac{1}{N}\sum_{i=1}^{N}\left\|H_{RCAN}\left(I_{LR}^i\right) - I_{HR}^i\right\|_1, \tag{5}$$

where Θ denotes the parameter set of our network. The loss function is optimized by using stochastic gradient descent. More details of training would be shown in Sect. 4.1. As we choose the shallow feature extraction $H_{SF}(\cdot)$, upscaling module $H_{UP}(\cdot)$, and reconstruction part $H_{UP}(\cdot)$ as similar as previous works (e.g., EDSR [23] and RDN [44]), we pay more attention to our proposed RIR, CA, and the basic module RCAB.

3.2 Residual in Residual (RIR)

We now give more details about our proposed RIR structure (see Fig. 2), which contains G residual groups (RG) and long skip connection (LSC). Each RG further contains B residual channel attention blocks (RCAB) with short skip connection (SSC). Such residual in residual structure allows to train very deep CNN (over 400 layers) for image SR with high performance.

It has been demonstrated that stacked residual blocks and LSC can be used to construct deep CNN in [23]. In visual recognition, residual blocks [11] can be stacked to achieve more than 1,000-layer trainable networks. However, in image SR, very deep network built in such way would suffer from training difficulty and can hardly achieve more performance gain. Inspired by previous works in SRRestNet [21] and EDSR [23], we proposed residual group (RG) as the basic module for deeper networks. A RG in the g-th group is formulated as

$$F_g = H_g\left(F_{g-1}\right) = H_g\left(H_{g-1}\left(\cdots H_1\left(F_0\right)\cdots\right)\right), \tag{6}$$

where H_g denotes the function of g-th RG. F_{g-1} and F_g are the input and output for g-th RG. We observe that simply stacking many RGs would fail to achieve better performance. To solve the problem, the long skip connection (LSC) is further introduced in RIR to stabilize the training of very deep network. LSC also makes better performance possible with residual learning via

$$F_{DF} = F_0 + W_{LSC}F_G = F_0 + W_{LSC}H_g\left(H_{g-1}\left(\cdots H_1\left(F_0\right)\cdots\right)\right), \tag{7}$$

where W_{LSC} is the weight set to the Conv layer at the tail of RIR. The bias term is omitted for simplicity. LSC can not only ease the flow of information

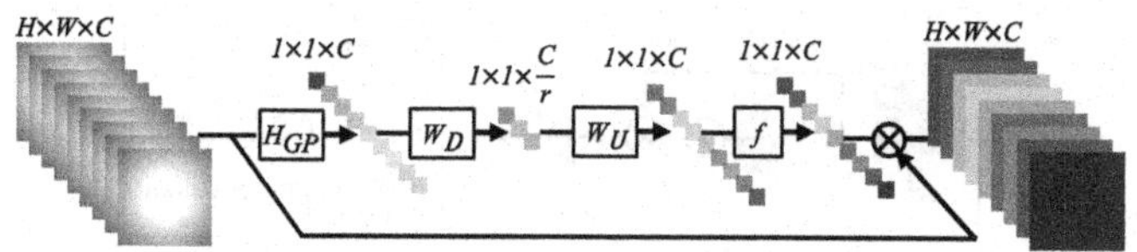

Fig. 3. Channel attention (CA). ⊗ denotes element-wise product

across RGs, but only make it possible for RIR to learning residual information in a coarse level.

As discussed in Sect. 1, there are lots of abundant information in the LR inputs and features and the goal of SR network is to recover more useful information. The abundant low-frequency information can be bypassed through identity-based skip connection. To make a further step towards residual learning, we stack B residual channel attention blocks in each RG. The b-th residual channel attention block (RCAB) in g-th RG can be formulated as

$$F_{g,b} = H_{g,b}\left(F_{g,b-1}\right) = H_{g,b}\left(H_{g,b-1}\left(\cdots H_{g,1}\left(F_{g-1}\right)\cdots\right)\right), \tag{8}$$

where $F_{g,b-1}$ and $F_{g,b}$ are the input and output of the b-th RCAB in g-th RG. The corresponding function is denoted with $H_{g,b}$. To make the main network pay more attention to more informative features, a short skip connection (SSC) is introduced to obtain the block output via

$$F_g = F_{g-1} + W_g F_{g,B} = F_{g-1} + W_g H_{g,B}\left(H_{g,B-1}\left(\cdots H_{g,1}\left(F_{g-1}\right)\cdots\right)\right), \tag{9}$$

where W_g is the weight set to the Conv layer at the tail of g-th RG. The SSC further allows the main parts of network to learn residual information. With LSC and SSC, more abundant low-frequency information is easier bypassed in the training process. To make a further step towards more discriminative learning, we pay more attention to channel-wise feature rescaling with channel attention.

3.3 Channel Attention (CA)

Previous CNN-based SR methods treat LR channel-wise features equally, which is not flexible for the real cases. In order to make the network focus on more informative features, we exploit the interdependencies among feature channels, resulting in a channel attention (CA) mechanism (see Fig. 3).

How to generate different attention for each channel-wise feature is a key step. Here we mainly have two concerns: First, information in the LR space has abundant low-frequency and valuable high-frequency components. The low-frequency parts seem to be more complanate. The high-frequency components would usually be regions, being full of edges, texture, and other details. On the other hand, each filter in Conv layer operates with a local receptive field. Consequently, the output after convolution is unable to exploit contextual information outside of the local region.

Based on these analyses, we take the channel-wise global spatial information into a channel descriptor by using global average pooling. As shown in Fig. 3,

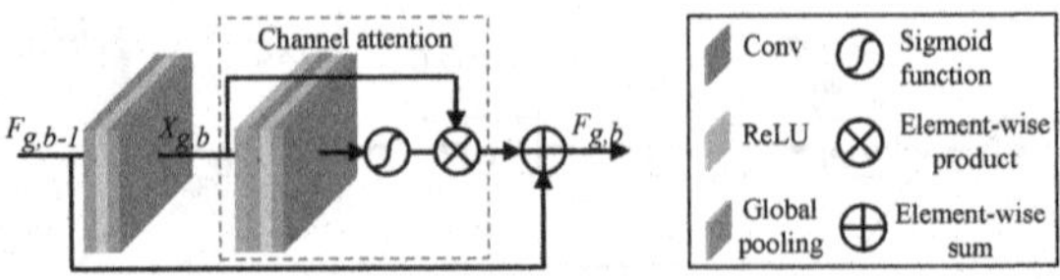

Fig. 4. Residual channel attention block (RCAB)

let $X = [x_1, \cdots, x_c, \cdots, x_C]$ be an input, which has C feature maps with size of $H \times W$. The channel-wise statistic $z \in \mathbb{R}^C$ can be obtained by shrinking X through spatial dimensions $H \times W$. Then the c-th element of z is determined by

$$z_c = H_{GP}(x_c) = \frac{1}{H \times W} \sum_{i=1}^{H} \sum_{j=1}^{W} x_c(i, j), \tag{10}$$

where $x_c(i, j)$ is the value at position (i, j) of c-th feature x_c. $H_{GP}(\cdot)$ denotes the global pooling function. Such channel statistic can be viewed as a collection of the local descriptors, whose statistics contribute to express the whole image [12]. Except for global average pooling, more sophisticated aggregation techniques could also be introduced here.

To fully capture channel-wise dependencies from the aggregated information by global average pooling, we introduce a gating mechanism. As discussed in [12], the gating mechanism should meet two criteria: First, it must be able to learn nonlinear interactions between channels. Second, as multiple channel-wise features can be emphasized opposed to one-hot activation, it must learn a non-mututually-exclusive relationship. Here, we opt to exploit simple gating mechanism with sigmoid function

$$s = f(W_U \delta(W_D z)), \tag{11}$$

where $f(\cdot)$ and $\delta(\cdot)$ denote the sigmoid gating and ReLU [27] function, respectively. W_D is the weight set of a Conv layer, which acts as channel-downscaling with reduction ratio r. After being activated by ReLU, the low-dimension signal is then increased with ratio r by a channel-upscaling layer, whose weight set is W_U. Then we obtain the final channel statistics s, which is used to rescale the input x_c

$$\widehat{x}_c = s_c \cdot x_c, \tag{12}$$

where s_c and x_c are the scaling factor and feature map in the c-th channel. With channel attention, the residual component in the RCAB is adaptively rescaled.

3.4 Residual Channel Attention Block (RCAB)

As discussed above, residual groups and long skip connection allow the main parts of network to focus on more informative components of the LR features. Channel attention extracts the channel statistic among channels to further enhance the discriminative ability of the network.

Table 1. Investigations of RIR (including LSC and SSC) and CA. We observe the best PSNR (dB) values on Set5 (2×) in 5×10^4 iterations

Residual in Residual (RIR)	LSC	✗	✓	✗	✓	✗	✓	✗	✓
	SSC	✗	✗	✓	✓	✗	✗	✓	✓
Channel attention (CA)		✗	✗	✗	✗	✓	✓	✓	✓
PSNR on Set5 (2×)		37.45	37.77	37.81	37.87	37.52	37.85	37.86	37.90

At the same time, inspired by the success of residual blocks (RB) in [23], we integrate CA into RB and propose residual channel attention block (RCAB) (see Fig. 4). For the b-th RB in g-th RG, we have

$$F_{g,b} = F_{g,b-1} + R_{g,b}\left(X_{g,b}\right) \cdot X_{g,b}, \tag{13}$$

where $R_{g,b}$ denotes the function of channel attention. $F_{g,b}$ and $F_{g,b-1}$ are the input and output of RCAB, which learns the residual $X_{g,b}$ from the input. The residual component is mainly obtained by two stacked Conv layers

$$X_{g,b} = W_{g,b}^{2} \delta\left(W_{g,b}^{1} F_{g,b-1}\right), \tag{14}$$

where $W_{g,b}^{1}$ and $W_{g,b}^{2}$ are weight sets the two stacked Conv layers in RCAB.

We further show the relationships between our proposed RCAB and residual block (RB) in [23]. We find that the RBs used in MDSR and EDSR [23] can be viewed as special cases of our RCAB. For RB in MDSR, there is no rescaling operation. It is the same as RCAB, where we set $R_{g,b}(\cdot)$ as constant 1. For RB with constant rescaling (e.g., 0.1) in EDSR, it is the same as RCAB with $R_{g,b}(\cdot)$ set to be 0.1. Although the channel-wise feature rescaling is introduced to train a very wide network, the interdependencies among channels are not considered in EDSR. In these cases, the CA is not considered.

Based on residual channel attention block (RCAB) and RIR structure, we construct a very deep RCAN for highly accurate image SR and achieve notable performance improvements over previous leading methods. More discussions about the effects of each proposed component are shown in Sect. 4.2.

4 Experiments

4.1 Settings

Following [23,36,43,44], we use 800 training images from DIV2K dataset [36] as training set. For testing, we use five standard benchmark datasets: Set5 [1], Set14 [41], B100 [24], Urban100 [13], and Manga109 [25]. We conduct experiments with Bicubic (BI) and blur-downscale (BD) degradation models [42–44]. The SR results are evaluated with PSNR and SSIM [40] on Y channel (i.e., luminance) of transformed YCbCr space. Data augmentation is performed on the 800 training images, which are randomly rotated by 90°, 180°, 270° and flipped horizontally. In each training batch, 16 LR color patches with the size of

48×48 are extracted as inputs. Our model is trained by ADAM optimizor [18] with $\beta_1 = 0.9$, $\beta_2 = 0.999$, and $\epsilon = 10^{-8}$. The initial leaning rate is set to 10^{-4} and then decreases to half every 2×10^5 iterations of back-propagation. We use PyTorch [28] to implement our models with a Titan Xp GPU.[1]

We set RG number as G=10 in the RIR structure. In each RG, we set RCAB number as 20. We set 3×3 as the size of all Conv layers except for that in the channel-downscaling and channel-upscaling, whose kernel size is 1×1. Conv layers in shallow feature extraction and RIR structure have C=64 filters, except for that in the channel-downscaling. Conv layer in channel-downscaling has $\frac{C}{r}$=4 filters, where the reduction ratio r is set as 16. For upscaling module $H_{UP}(\cdot)$, we use ESPCNN [32] to upscale the coarse resolution features to fine ones.

4.2 Effects of RIR and CA

We study the effects of residual in residual (RIR) and channel attention (CA).

Residual in Residual (RIR). To demonstrate the effect of our proposed residual in residual structure, we remove long skip connection (LSC) or/and short skip connection (SSC) from very deep networks. Specifically, we set the number of residual block as 200. In Table 1, when both LSC and SSC are removed, the PSNR value on Set5 (×2) is relatively low, no matter channel attention (CA) is used or not. This indicates that simply stacking residual blocks is not applicable to achieve very deep and powerful networks for image SR. These comparisons show that LSC and SSC are essential for very deep networks. They also demonstrate the effectiveness of our proposed residual in residual (RIR) structure for very deep networks.

Channel Attention (CA). We further show the effect of channel attention (CA) based on the observations and discussions above. When we compare the results of first 4 columns and last 4 columns, we find that networks with CA would perform better than those without CA. Benefitting from very large network depth, the very deep trainable networks can achieve a very high performance. It's hard to obtain further improvements from such deep networks, but we obtain improvements with CA. Even without RIR, CA can improve the performance from 37.45 dB to 37.52 dB. These comparisons firmly demonstrate the effectiveness of CA and indicate adaptive attentions to channel-wise features really improves the performance.

4.3 Results with Bicubic (BI) Degradation Model

We compare our method with 11 state-of-the-art methods: SRCNN [5], FSRCNN [6], SCN [39], VDSR [16], LapSRN [19], MemNet [35], EDSR [23], SRMDNF [43], D-DBPN [10], and RDN [44]. Similar to [23,37,44], we also introduce self-ensemble strategy to further improve our RCAN and denote the self-ensembled one as RCAN+. More comparisons are provided in supplementary material.

[1] The RCAN source code is available at https://github.com/yulunzhang/RCAN.

Table 2. Quantitative results with BI degradation model. Best and second best results are **highlighted** and underlined

Method	Scale	Set5		Set14		B100		Urban100		Manga109	
		PSNR	SSIM	PSNR	SSIM	PSNR	SSIM	PSNR	SSIM	PSNR	SSIM
Bicubic	×2	33.66	0.9299	30.24	0.8688	29.56	0.8431	26.88	0.8403	30.80	0.9339
SRCNN [5]	×2	36.66	0.9542	32.45	0.9067	31.36	0.8879	29.50	0.8946	35.60	0.9663
FSRCNN [6]	×2	37.05	0.9560	32.66	0.9090	31.53	0.8920	29.88	0.9020	36.67	0.9710
VDSR [16]	×2	37.53	0.9590	33.05	0.9130	31.90	0.8960	30.77	0.9140	37.22	0.9750
LapSRN [19]	×2	37.52	0.9591	33.08	0.9130	31.08	0.8950	30.41	0.9101	37.27	0.9740
MemNet [35]	×2	37.78	0.9597	33.28	0.9142	32.08	0.8978	31.31	0.9195	37.72	0.9740
EDSR [23]	×2	38.11	0.9602	33.92	0.9195	32.32	0.9013	32.93	0.9351	39.10	0.9773
SRMDNF [43]	×2	37.79	0.9601	33.32	0.9159	32.05	0.8985	31.33	0.9204	38.07	0.9761
D-DBPN [10]	×2	38.09	0.9600	33.85	0.9190	32.27	0.9000	32.55	0.9324	38.89	0.9775
RDN [44]	×2	38.24	0.9614	34.01	0.9212	32.34	0.9017	32.89	0.9353	39.18	0.9780
RCAN (ours)	×2	38.27	0.9614	34.12	0.9216	32.41	0.9027	33.34	0.9384	39.44	0.9786
RCAN+ (ours)	×2	**38.33**	**0.9617**	**34.23**	**0.9225**	**32.46**	**0.9031**	**33.54**	**0.9399**	**39.61**	**0.9788**
Bicubic	×3	30.39	0.8682	27.55	0.7742	27.21	0.7385	24.46	0.7349	26.95	0.8556
SRCNN [5]	×3	32.75	0.9090	29.30	0.8215	28.41	0.7863	26.24	0.7989	30.48	0.9117
FSRCNN [6]	×3	33.18	0.9140	29.37	0.8240	28.53	0.7910	26.43	0.8080	31.10	0.9210
VDSR [16]	×3	33.67	0.9210	29.78	0.8320	28.83	0.7990	27.14	0.8290	32.01	0.9340
LapSRN [19]	×3	33.82	0.9227	29.87	0.8320	28.82	0.7980	27.07	0.8280	32.21	0.9350
MemNet [35]	×3	34.09	0.9248	30.00	0.8350	28.96	0.8001	27.56	0.8376	32.51	0.9369
EDSR [23]	×3	34.65	0.9280	30.52	0.8462	29.25	0.8093	28.80	0.8653	34.17	0.9476
SRMDNF [43]	×3	34.12	0.9254	30.04	0.8382	28.97	0.8025	27.57	0.8398	33.00	0.9403
RDN [44]	×3	34.71	0.9296	30.57	0.8468	29.26	0.8093	28.80	0.8653	34.13	0.9484
RCAN (ours)	×3	34.74	0.9299	30.65	0.8482	29.32	0.8111	29.09	0.8702	34.44	0.9499
RCAN+ (ours)	×3	**34.85**	**0.9305**	**30.76**	**0.8494**	**29.39**	**0.8122**	**29.31**	**0.8736**	**34.76**	**0.9513**
Bicubic	×4	28.42	0.8104	26.00	0.7027	25.96	0.6675	23.14	0.6577	24.89	0.7866
SRCNN [5]	×4	30.48	0.8628	27.50	0.7513	26.90	0.7101	24.52	0.7221	27.58	0.8555
FSRCNN [6]	×4	30.72	0.8660	27.61	0.7550	26.98	0.7150	24.62	0.7280	27.90	0.8610
VDSR [16]	×4	31.35	0.8830	28.02	0.7680	27.29	0.0726	25.18	0.7540	28.83	0.8870
LapSRN [19]	×4	31.54	0.8850	28.19	0.7720	27.32	0.7270	25.21	0.7560	29.09	0.8900
MemNet [35]	×4	31.74	0.8893	28.26	0.7723	27.40	0.7281	25.50	0.7630	29.42	0.8942
EDSR [23]	×4	32.46	0.8968	28.80	0.7876	27.71	0.7420	26.64	0.8033	31.02	0.9148
SRMDNF [43]	×4	31.96	0.8925	28.35	0.7787	27.49	0.7337	25.68	0.7731	30.09	0.9024
D-DBPN [10]	×4	32.47	0.8980	28.82	0.7860	27.72	0.7400	26.38	0.7946	30.91	0.9137
RDN [44]	×4	32.47	0.8990	28.81	0.7871	27.72	0.7419	26.61	0.8028	31.00	0.9151
RCAN (ours)	×4	32.63	0.9002	28.87	0.7889	27.77	0.7436	26.82	0.8087	31.22	0.9173
RCAN+ (ours)	×4	**32.73**	**0.9013**	**28.98**	**0.7910**	**27.85**	**0.7455**	**27.10**	**0.8142**	**31.65**	**0.9208**
Bicubic	×8	24.40	0.6580	23.10	0.5660	23.67	0.5480	20.74	0.5160	21.47	0.6500
SRCNN [5]	×8	25.33	0.6900	23.76	0.5910	24.13	0.5660	21.29	0.5440	22.46	0.6950
FSRCNN [6]	×8	20.13	0.5520	19.75	0.4820	24.21	0.5680	21.32	0.5380	22.39	0.6730
SCN [39]	×8	25.59	0.7071	24.02	0.6028	24.30	0.5698	21.52	0.5571	22.68	0.6963
VDSR [16]	×8	25.93	0.7240	24.26	0.6140	24.49	0.5830	21.70	0.5710	23.16	0.7250
LapSRN [19]	×8	26.15	0.7380	24.35	0.6200	24.54	0.5860	21.81	0.5810	23.39	0.7350
MemNet [35]	×8	26.16	0.7414	24.38	0.6199	24.58	0.5842	21.89	0.5825	23.56	0.7387
MSLapSRN [20]	×8	26.34	0.7558	24.57	0.6273	24.65	0.5895	22.06	0.5963	23.90	0.7564
EDSR [23]	×8	26.96	0.7762	24.91	0.6420	24.81	0.5985	22.51	0.6221	24.69	0.7841
D-DBPN [10]	×8	27.21	0.7840	25.13	0.6480	24.88	0.6010	22.73	0.6312	25.14	0.7987
RCAN (ours)	×8	27.31	0.7878	25.23	0.6511	24.98	0.6058	23.00	0.6452	25.24	0.8029
RCAN+ (ours)	×8	**27.47**	**0.7913**	**25.40**	**0.6553**	**25.05**	**0.6077**	**23.22**	**0.6524**	**25.58**	**0.8092**

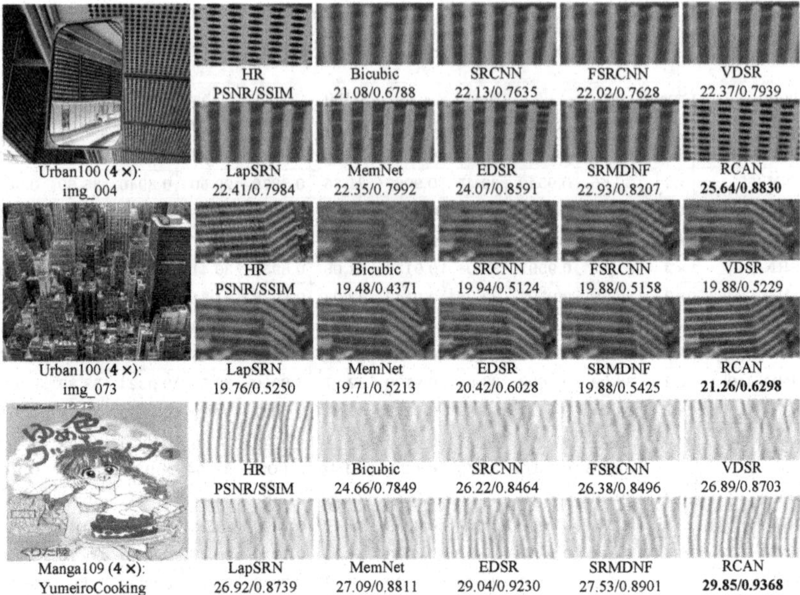

Fig. 5. Visual comparison for 4× SR with BI model on Urban100 and Manga109 datasets. The best results are **highlighted**

Quantitative results by PSNR/SSIM. Table 2 shows quantitative comparisons for ×2, ×3, ×4, and ×8 SR. The results of D-DBPN [10] are cited from their paper. When compared with all previous methods, our RCAN+ performs the best on all the datasets with all scaling factors. Even without self-ensemble, our RCAN also outperforms other compared methods. On the other hand, when the scaling factor become larger (e.g., 8), the gains of our RCAN over EDSR also becomes larger. EDSR has much larger number of parameters (43 M) than ours (16 M), but our RCAN obtains much better performance. CA allows our network to further focus on more informative features. This observation indicates that very large network depth and CA improve the performance.

Visual results. In Fig. 5, we show visual comparisons on scale ×4. For image "img_004", we observe that most of the compared methods cannot recover the lattices and would suffer from blurring artifacts. In contrast, our RCAN can alleviate the blurring artifacts better and recover more details. Similar observations are shown in images "img_073" and "YumeiroCooking". Such obvious comparisons demonstrate that networks with more powerful representational ability can extract more sophisticated features from the LR space. To further illustrate the analyses above, we show visual comparisons for 8× SR in Fig. 6. For image "img_040", due to very large scaling factor, the result by Bicubic would lose the structures and produce different structures. This wrong pre-scaling result would also lead some state-of-the-art methods (e.g., SRCNN, VDSR, and MemNet) to generate totally wrong structures. Even starting from the original LR

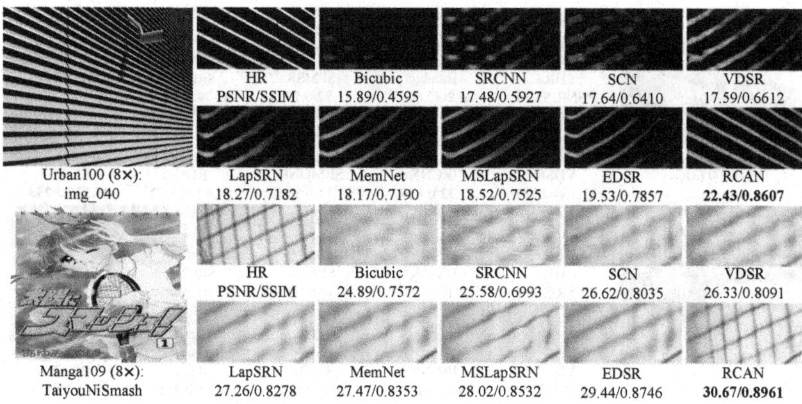

Fig. 6. Visual comparison for 8× SR with BI model on Urban100 and Manga109 datasets. The best results are **highlighted**

input, other methods cannot recover the right structure either. While, our RCAN can recover them correctly. Similar observations are shown in image "TaiyouNiSmash". Our proposed RCAN makes the main network learn residual information and enhance the representational ability.

Table 3. Quantitative results with BD degradation model. Best and second best results are **highlighted** and underlined

Method	Scale	Set5		Set14		B100		Urban100		Manga109	
		PSNR	SSIM	PSNR	SSIM	PSNR	SSIM	PSNR	SSIM	PSNR	SSIM
Bicubic	×3	28.78	0.8308	26.38	0.7271	26.33	0.6918	23.52	0.6862	25.46	0.8149
SPMSR [29]	×3	32.21	0.9001	28.89	0.8105	28.13	0.7740	25.84	0.7856	29.64	0.9003
SRCNN [5]	×3	32.05	0.8944	28.80	0.8074	28.13	0.7736	25.70	0.7770	29.47	0.8924
FSRCNN [6]	×3	26.23	0.8124	24.44	0.7106	24.86	0.6832	22.04	0.6745	23.04	0.7927
VDSR [16]	×3	33.25	0.9150	29.46	0.8244	28.57	0.7893	26.61	0.8136	31.06	0.9234
IRCNN [42]	×3	33.38	0.9182	29.63	0.8281	28.65	0.7922	26.77	0.8154	31.15	0.9245
SRMDNF [43]	×3	34.01	0.9242	30.11	0.8364	28.98	0.8009	27.50	0.8370	32.97	0.9391
RDN [44]	×3	34.58	0.9280	30.53	0.8447	29.23	0.8079	28.46	0.8582	33.97	0.9465
RCAN (ours)	×3	34.70	0.9288	30.63	0.8462	29.32	0.8093	28.81	0.8647	34.38	0.9483
RCAN+ (ours)	×3	**34.83**	**0.9296**	**30.76**	**0.8479**	**29.39**	**0.8106**	**29.04**	**0.8682**	**34.76**	**0.9502**

4.4 Results with Blur-Downscale (BD) Degradation Model

We further apply our method to super-resolve images with blur-down (BD) degradation model, which is also commonly used recently [42–44].

Quantitative results by PSNR/SSIM. Here, we compare 3× SR results with 7 state-of-the-art methods: SPMSR [29], SRCNN [5], FSRCNN [6], VDSR [16],

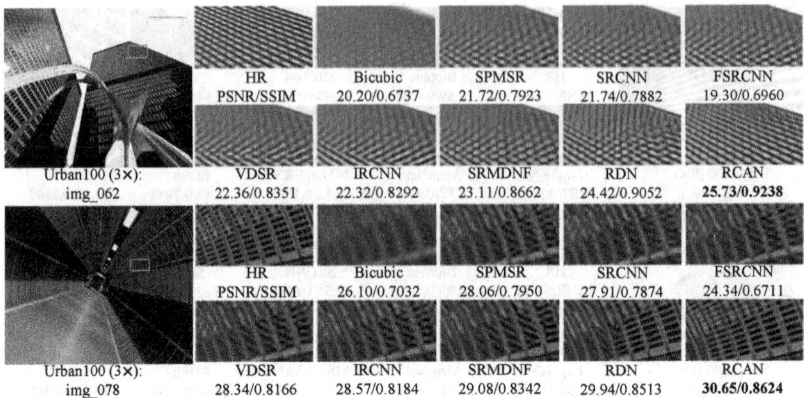

Fig. 7. Visual comparison for 3× SR with BD model on Urban100 dataset. The best results are **highlighted**

IRCNN [42], SRMDNF [43], and RDN [44]. As shown in Table 3, RDN has achieved very high performance on each dataset. While, our RCAN can obtain notable gains over RDN. Using self-ensemble, RCAN+ achieves even better results. Compared with fully using hierarchical features in RDN, a much deeper network with channel attention in RCAN achieves better performance. This comparison also indicates that there has promising potential to investigate much deeper networks for image SR.

Visual Results. We also show visual comparisons in Fig. 7. For challenging details in images "img_062" and "img_078", most methods suffer from heavy blurring artifacts. RDN alleviates it to some degree and can recover more details. In contrast, our RCAN obtains much better results by recovering more informative components. These comparisons indicate that very deep channel attention guided network would alleviate the blurring artifacts. It also demonstrates the strong ability of RCAN for BD degradation model.

Table 4. ResNet object recognition performance. The best results are **highlighted**

Evaluation	Bicubic	DRCN [17]	FSRCNN [6]	PSyCo [30]	ENet-E [31]	RCAN	Baseline
Top-1 error	0.506	0.477	0.437	0.454	0.449	**0.393**	0.260
Top-5 error	0.266	0.242	0.196	0.224	0.214	**0.167**	0.072

4.5 Object Recognition Performance

Image SR also serves as pre-processing step for high-level visual tasks (e.g., object recognition). We evaluate the object recognition performance to further demonstrate the effectiveness of our RCAN. Here we use the same settings as ENet [31]. We use ResNet-50 [11] as the evaluation model and use the first 1,000

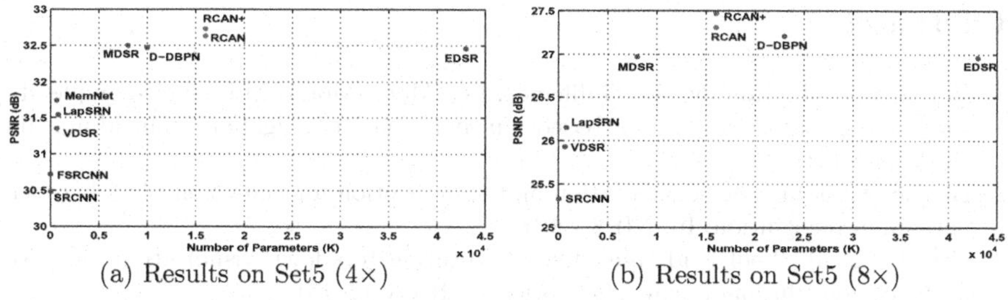

(a) Results on Set5 (4×) (b) Results on Set5 (8×)

Fig. 8. Performance and number of parameters. Results are evaluated on Set5

images from ImageNet CLS-LOC validation dataset for evaluation. The original cropped 224×224 images are used for baseline and downscaled to 56×56 for SR methods. We use 4 stat-of-the-art methods (e.g., DRCN [17], FSRCNN [6], PSyCo [30], and ENet-E [31]) to upscale the LR images and then calculate their accuracies. As shown in Table 4, our RCAN achieves the lowest top-1 and top-5 errors. These comparisons further demonstrate the highly powerful representational ability of our RCAN.

4.6 Model Size Analyses

We show comparisons about model size and performance in Fig. 8. Although our RCAN is the deepest network, it has less parameter number than that of EDSR and RDN. Our RCAN and RCAN+ achieve higher performance, having a better tradeoff between model size and performance. It also indicates that deeper networks may be easier to achieve better performance than wider networks.

5 Conclusions

We propose very deep residual channel attention networks (RCAN) for highly accurate image SR. Specifically, the residual in residual (RIR) structure allows RCAN to reach very large depth with LSC and SSC. Meanwhile, RIR allows abundant low-frequency information to be bypassed through multiple skip connections, making the main network focus on learning high-frequency information. Furthermore, to improve ability of the network, we propose channel attention (CA) mechanism to adaptively rescale channel-wise features by considering interdependencies among channels. Extensive experiments on SR with BI and BD models demonstrate the effectiveness of our proposed RCAN. RCAN also shows promising results for object recognition.

Acknowledgements. This research is supported in part by the NSF IIS award 1651902, ONR Young Investigator Award N00014-14-1-0484, and U.S. Army Research Office Award W911NF-17-1-0367.

References

1. Bevilacqua, M., Roumy, A., Guillemot, C., Alberi-Morel, M.L.: Low-complexity single-image super-resolution based on nonnegative neighbor embedding. In: BMVC (2012)
2. Bluche, T.: Joint line segmentation and transcription for end-to-end handwritten paragraph recognition. In: NIPS (2016)
3. Cao, C., et al.: Look and think twice: capturing top-down visual attention with feedback convolutional neural networks. In: ICCV (2015)
4. Dong, C., Loy, C.C., He, K., Tang, X.: Learning a deep convolutional network for image super-resolution. In: Fleet, D., Pajdla, T., Schiele, B., Tuytelaars, T. (eds.) ECCV 2014. LNCS, vol. 8692, pp. 184–199. Springer, Cham (2014). https://doi.org/10.1007/978-3-319-10593-2_13
5. Dong, C., Loy, C.C., He, K., Tang, X.: Image super-resolution using deep convolutional networks. TPAMI **38**(2), 295–307 (2016)
6. Dong, C., Loy, C.C., Tang, X.: Accelerating the super-resolution convolutional neural network. In: Leibe, B., Matas, J., Sebe, N., Welling, M. (eds.) ECCV 2016. LNCS, vol. 9906, pp. 391–407. Springer, Cham (2016). https://doi.org/10.1007/978-3-319-46475-6_25
7. Dumoulin, V., Shlens, J., Kudlur, M.: A learned representation for artistic style. In: ICLR (2017)
8. Freeman, W.T., Pasztor, E.C., Carmichael, O.T.: Learning low-level vision. IJCV **40**(1), 25–47 (2000)
9. Goodfellow, I., et al.: Generative adversarial nets. In: NIPS (2014)
10. Haris, M., Shakhnarovich, G., Ukita, N.: Deep back-projection networks for super-resolution. In: CVPR (2018)
11. He, K., Zhang, X., Ren, S., Sun, J.: Deep residual learning for image recognition. In: CVPR (2016)
12. Hu, J., Shen, L., Sun, G.: Squeeze-and-excitation networks. arXiv preprint arXiv:1709.01507 (2017)
13. Huang, J.B., Singh, A., Ahuja, N.: Single image super-resolution from transformed self-exemplars. In: CVPR (2015)
14. Jaderberg, M., Simonyan, K., Zisserman, A., Kavukcuoglu, K.: Spatial transformer networks. In: NIPS (2015)
15. Johnson, J., Alahi, A., Fei-Fei, L.: Perceptual losses for real-time style transfer and super-resolution. In: Leibe, B., Matas, J., Sebe, N., Welling, M. (eds.) ECCV 2016. LNCS, vol. 9906, pp. 694–711. Springer, Cham (2016). https://doi.org/10.1007/978-3-319-46475-6_43
16. Kim, J., Kwon Lee, J., Mu Lee, K.: Accurate image super-resolution using very deep convolutional networks. In: CVPR (2016)
17. Kim, J., Kwon Lee, J., Mu Lee, K.: Deeply-recursive convolutional network for image super-resolution. In: CVPR (2016)
18. Kingma, D., Ba, J.: Adam: A method for stochastic optimization. In: ICLR (2014)
19. Lai, W.S., Huang, J.B., Ahuja, N., Yang, M.H.: Deep laplacian pyramid networks for fast and accurate super-resolution. In: CVPR (2017)
20. Lai, W.S., Huang, J.B., Ahuja, N., Yang, M.H.: Fast and accurate image super-resolution with deep laplacian pyramid networks. arXiv:1710.01992 (2017)
21. Ledig, C., et al.: Photo-realistic single image super-resolution using a generative adversarial network. In: CVPR (2017)

22. Li, K., Wu, Z., Peng, K.C., Ernst, J., Fu, Y.: Tell me where to look: Guided attention inference network. In: CVPR (2018)
23. Lim, B., Son, S., Kim, H., Nah, S., Lee, K.M.: Enhanced deep residual networks for single image super-resolution. In: CVPRW (2017)
24. Martin, D., Fowlkes, C., Tal, D., Malik, J.: A database of human segmented natural images and its application to evaluating segmentation algorithms and measuring ecological statistics. In: ICCV (2001)
25. Matsui, Y., Ito, K., Aramaki, Y., Fujimoto, A., Ogawa, T., Yamasaki, T., Aizawa, K.: Sketch-based manga retrieval using manga109 dataset. Multimedia Tools Appl. **76**(20), 21811–21838 (2017)
26. Miech, A., Laptev, I., Sivic, J.: Learnable pooling with context gating for video classification. arXiv preprint arXiv:1706.06905 (2017)
27. Nair, V., Hinton, G.E.: Rectified linear units improve restricted Boltzmann machines. In: ICML (2010)
28. Paszke, A., et al.: Automatic differentiation in pytorch (2017)
29. Peleg, T., Elad, M.: A statistical prediction model based on sparse representations for single image super-resolution. TIP **23**(6), 2569–2582 (2014)
30. Pérez-Pellitero, E., Salvador, J., Ruiz-Hidalgo, J., Rosenhahn, B.: PSyCo: manifold span reduction for super resolution. In: CVPR (2016)
31. Sajjadi, M.S., Schölkopf, B., Hirsch, M.: EnhanceNet: single image super-resolution through automated texture synthesis. In: ICCV (2017)
32. Shi, W., et al.: Real-time single image and video super-resolution using an efficient sub-pixel convolutional neural network. In: CVPR (2016)
33. Shi, W., et al.: Cardiac image super-resolution with global correspondence using multi-atlas patchmatch. In: Mori, K., Sakuma, I., Sato, Y., Barillot, C., Navab, N. (eds.) MICCAI 2013. LNCS, vol. 8151, pp. 9–16. Springer, Heidelberg (2013). https://doi.org/10.1007/978-3-642-40760-4_2
34. Tai, Y., Yang, J., Liu, X.: Image super-resolution via deep recursive residual network. In: CVPR (2017)
35. Tai, Y., Yang, J., Liu, X., Xu, C.: MemNet: a persistent memory network for image restoration. In: ICCV (2017)
36. Timofte, R., et al.: Ntire 2017 challenge on single image super-resolution: Methods and results. In: CVPRW (2017)
37. Timofte, R., Rothe, R., Van Gool, L.: Seven ways to improve example-based single image super resolution. In: CVPR (2016)
38. Wang, F., et al.: Residual attention network for image classification. In: CVPR (2017)
39. Wang, Z., Liu, D., Yang, J., Han, W., Huang, T.: Deep networks for image super-resolution with sparse prior. In: ICCV (2015)
40. Wang, Z., Bovik, A.C., Sheikh, H.R., Simoncelli, E.P.: Image quality assessment: from error visibility to structural similarity. TIP **13**(4), 600–612 (2004)
41. Zeyde, R., Elad, M., Protter, M.: On single image scale-up using sparse-representations. In: Proceedings of 7th International Conference Curves Surfaces (2010)
42. Zhang, K., Zuo, W., Gu, S., Zhang, L.: Learning deep CNN denoiser prior for image restoration. In: CVPR (2017)

43. Zhang, K., Zuo, W., Zhang, L.: Learning a single convolutional super-resolution network for multiple degradations. In: CVPR (2018)
44. Zhang, Y., Tian, Y., Kong, Y., Zhong, B., Fu, Y.: Residual dense network for image super-resolution. In: CVPR (2018)
45. Zou, W.W., Yuen, P.C.: Very low resolution face recognition problem. TIP **21**(1), 327–340 (2012)

Layer-Structured 3D Scene Inference via View Synthesis

Shubham Tulsiani[1(✉)], Richard Tucker[2], and Noah Snavely[2]

[1] University of California, Berkeley, Berkeley, USA
shubhtuls@cs.berkeley.edu
[2] Google, Menlo Park, USA

Abstract. We present an approach to infer a layer-structured 3D representation of a scene from a single input image. This allows us to infer not only the depth of the visible pixels, but also to capture the texture and depth for content in the scene that is not directly visible. We overcome the challenge posed by the lack of direct supervision by instead leveraging a more naturally available multi-view supervisory signal. Our insight is to use view synthesis as a proxy task: we enforce that our representation (inferred from a single image), when rendered from a novel perspective, matches the true observed image. We present a learning framework that operationalizes this insight using a new, differentiable novel view renderer. We provide qualitative and quantitative validation of our approach in two different settings, and demonstrate that we can learn to capture the hidden aspects of a scene. The project website can be found at https://shubhtuls.github.io/lsi/.

1 Introduction

Humans have the ability to perceive beyond what they see, and to imagine the structure of the world even when it is not directly visible. Consider the image in Fig. 1. While we can clearly see a street scene with objects such as cars and trees, we can also reason about the shape and appearance of aspects of the scene hidden from view, such as the continuation of the buildings behind the trees, or the ground underneath the car.

While we humans can perceive the full 3D structure of a scene from a single image, scene representations commonly used in computer vision are often restricted to modeling the visible aspects, and can be characterized as *2.5D representations* [17]. 2.5D representations such as depth maps are straightforward to use and learn because there is a one-to-one mapping between the pixels of an input image and the output representation. For the same reason, they also fail

S. Tulsiani—The majority of the work was done while interning at Google.

Electronic supplementary material The online version of this chapter (https://doi.org/10.1007/978-3-030-01234-2_19) contains supplementary material, which is available to authorized users.

V. Ferrari et al. (Eds.): ECCV 2018, LNCS 11211, pp. 311–327, 2018.
https://doi.org/10.1007/978-3-030-01234-2_19

Fig. 1. Perception beyond the visible. On the left is an image of a street scene. While some parts of the scene are occluded, such as the building behind the tree highlighted by the red box, humans have no trouble reasoning about the shape and appearance of such hidden parts. In this work we go beyond 2.5D shape representations and learn to predict *layered* scene representations from single images that capture more complete scenes, including hidden objects. On the right, we show our method's predicted 2-layer texture and shape for the highlighted area: (a, b) show the predicted textures for the foreground and background layers respectively, and (c, d) show the corresponding predicted inverse depth. Note how both predict structures behind the tree, such as the continuation of the building. (Color figure online)

to allow for any extrapolation beyond what is immediately visible. In contrast, a robot or other agent might wish to predict the appearance of a scene from a different viewpoint, or reason about which parts of the scene are navigable. Such tasks are beyond what can be achieved in 2.5D.

In this work, we take a step towards reasoning about the 3D structure of scenes by learning to predict a *layer-based* representation from a single image. We use a representation known as a *layered depth image* (LDI), originally developed in the computer graphics community [22]. Unlike a depth map, which stores a single depth value per pixel, an LDI represents multiple ordered depths per pixel, along with an associated color for each depth, representing the multiple intersections of a ray with scene geometry (foreground objects, background behind those objects, etc.) In graphics, LDIs are an attractive representation for image-based rendering applications. For our purposes, they are also appealing as a 3D scene representation as they maintain the direct relationship between input pixels and output layers, while allowing for much more flexible and general modeling of scenes.

A key challenge towards learning to predict such layered representations is the lack of available training data. Our approach, depicted in Fig. 2, builds on the insight that multiple images of the same scene, but from different views, can provide us with indirect supervision for learning about the underlying 3D structure. In particular, given two views of a scene, there will often be parts of the scene that are hidden from one view but visible from the second. We therefore use view synthesis as a proxy task: given a single input image, we predict an LDI representation and enforce that the novel views rendered using the prediction correspond to the observed reality.

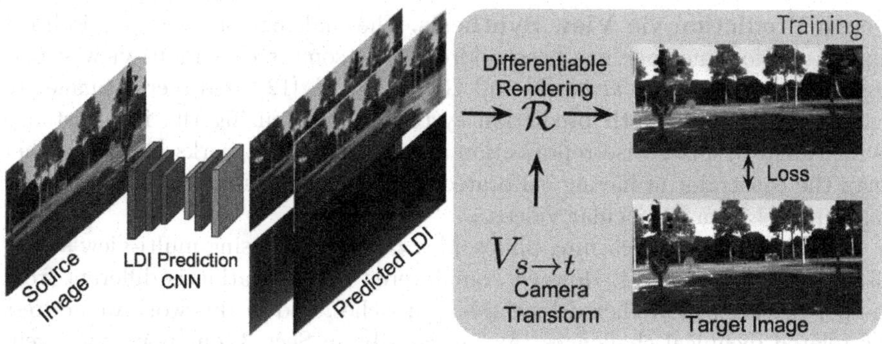

Fig. 2. Approach overview. We learn a CNN that can predict, from a single input image, a layered representation of the scene (an LDI). During training, we leverage multi-view supervision using view synthesis as a proxy task, thereby allowing us to overcome the lack of direct supervision. While training our prediction CNN, we enforce that the predicted representation, when (differentiably) rendered from a novel view, matches the available target image.

In Sect. 3, we present our learning setup that builds on this insight, and describe a training objective that enforces the desired prediction structure. To operationalize this learning procedure, we introduce an LDI rendering mechanism based on a new differentiable forward splatting layer. This layer may also be useful for other tasks at the intersection of graphics and learning. We then provide qualitative and quantitative validation of our approach in Sect. 4 using two settings: (a) analysis using synthetic data with known ground truth 3D, and (b) a real outdoor driving dataset.

2 Related Work

Single-View Depth/Surface Normal Prediction. Estimating pixel-wise depth and/or surface orientation has been a long-standing task in computer vision. Initial attempts treated geometric inference as a part of the inverse vision problem, leveraging primarily learning-free optimization methods for inference [4,23]. Over the years, the use of supervised learning has enabled more robust approaches [14,21], most recently with CNN-based methods [3,7,28], yielding impressive results.

We also adopt a learning-based approach, but go beyond commonly used 2.5D representations that only infer shape for the *visible* pixels. Some recent methods, with a similar goal, predict volumetric 3D from a depth image [24], or infer amodal aspects of a scene [6]. However, these methods require direct 3D supervision and are thus restricted to synthetically generated data. In contrast, our approach leverages indirect multi-view supervision that is more naturally obtainable, as well as ecologically plausible.

Depth Prediction via View Synthesis. The challenge of leveraging indirect supervision for inference has been addressed by some recent multi-view supervised approaches. Garg *et al.* [9] and Godard *et al.* [12] used stereo images to learn a single-view depth prediction system by minimizing the inconsistency as measured by pixel-wise reprojection error. Subsequent works [26,33] further relax the constraint of having calibrated stereo images, and learn a single-view depth model from monocular videos.

We adopt a similar learning philosophy, *i.e.* learning using multi-view supervision via view synthesis. However, our layered representation is different from the per-pixel depth predicted by these approaches, and in this work we address the related technical challenges. As we describe in Sect. 3, our novel view rendering process is very different from the techniques used by these approaches.

Multi-view Supervised 3D Object Reconstruction. Learning-based approaches for single-view 3D object reconstruction have seen a similar shift in the forms of supervision required. Initial CNN-based methods [5,11] predicted voxel occupancy representations from a single input image but required full 3D supervision during training. Recent approaches have advocated alternate forms of supervision, *e.g.* multi-view foreground masks [19,25,32] or depth [25].

While these methods go beyond 2.5D predictions and infer full 3D structure, they use volumetric-occupancy-based representations that do not naturally extend to general scenes. The layered representations we use are instead closer to depth-based representations often used for scenes. Similarly, these methods commonly rely on cues like foreground masks from multiple views, which are more applicable to isolated objects than to complex scenes. In our scenario, we therefore rely only on multiple RGB images as supervision.

Layered Scene Representations. Various layer-based scene representations are popular in the computer vision and graphics communities for reasons of parsimony, efficiency and descriptive power. Single-view based [14,15,20] or optical flow methods [29] often infer a parsimonious representation of the scene or flow by grouping the visible content into layers. While these methods do not reason about occlusion, Adelson [1] proposed using a planar layer-based representation to capture hidden surfaces and demonstrated that these can be inferred using motion [27]. Similarly, Baker *et al.* [2] proposed a stereo method that represents scenes as planar layers. Our work is most directly inspired by Shade *et al.* [22], who introduced the layered depth image (LDI) representation to capture the structure of general 3D scenes for use in image-based rendering.

We aim for a similar representation. However, in contrast to classical approaches that require multiple images for inference, we use machine learning to predict this representation from a single image at test time. Further, unlike previous single-view based methods, our predicted representation also reasons about occluded aspects of the scene.

3 Learning LDI Prediction

Our aim is to predict a 3D representation of a scene that includes not only the geometry of what we see, but also aspects of the scene not directly visible. A standard approach to geometric inference is to predict a depth map, which answers, for each pixel the question: *'how far from the camera is the point imaged at this pixel?'*. In this work, we propose to predict a Layered Depth Image (LDI) [22] representation that, in addition to the question above, also answers: *'what lies behind the visible content at this pixel?'*.

As we do not have access to a dataset of paired examples of images with their corresponding LDI representations, we therefore exploit *indirect* forms of supervision to learn LDI prediction. We note that since an LDI representation of a scene captures both visible and amodal aspects of a scene, it can allow us to geometrically synthesize novel views of the same scene, including aspects that are hidden to the input view. Our insight is that we can leverage *view synthesis as a proxy target task*. We first formally describe our training setup and representation, then present our approach based on this insight. We also introduce a differentiable mechanism for rendering an LDI representation from novel views via a novel 'soft z-buffering'-based forward splatting layer.

3.1 Overview

Training Data. We leverage multi-view supervision to learn LDI prediction. Our training dataset is comprised of multiple scenes, with images from a few views available per scene. We assume a known camera transformation between the different images of the same scene. This form of supervision can easily be obtained using a calibrated camera rig, or by any natural agent which has access to its egomotion. Equivalently, we can consider the training data to consist of numerous source and target image pairs, where the two images in each pair are from the same scene and are related by a known transformation.

Concretely, we denote our training dataset of N image pairs with associated cameras as $\{(I_s^n, I_t^n, \mathbf{K}_s^n, \mathbf{K}_t^n, \mathbf{R}^n, \mathbf{t}^n)\}_{n=1}^N$. Here I_s^n, I_t^n represent two (source and target) images of the same scene, with camera intrinsics denoted as $\mathbf{K}_s^n, \mathbf{K}_t^n$ respectively. The relative camera transformation between the two image frames is captured by a rotation $\mathbf{R}^n$ and translation $\mathbf{t}^n$. We note that the training data leveraged does not assume any direct supervision for the scene's 3D structure.

Predicted LDI Representation. A Layered Depth Image (LDI) representation (see Fig. 3 for an illustration) represents the 3D structure of a scene using layers of depth and color images. An LDI representation with L layers is of the form $\{(I^l, D^l)\}_{l=1}^L$. Here (I^l, D^l) represent the texture (*i.e.*, color) image I and disparity (inverse depth) image D corresponding to layer l. An important property of the LDI representation is that the structure captured in the layers is increasing in depth *i.e.* for any pixel p, if $l_1 < l_2$, then $D^{l_1}(p) \geq D^{l_2}(p)$ (disparity is monotonically decreasing over layers, or, equivalently, depth is increasing). Therefore, the initial layer $l = 1$ represents the visible content from the camera viewpoint (layers in an LDI do not have an alpha channel or mask). In fact, a standard depth map representation can be considered as an LDI with a single layer, with I^1 being the observed image.

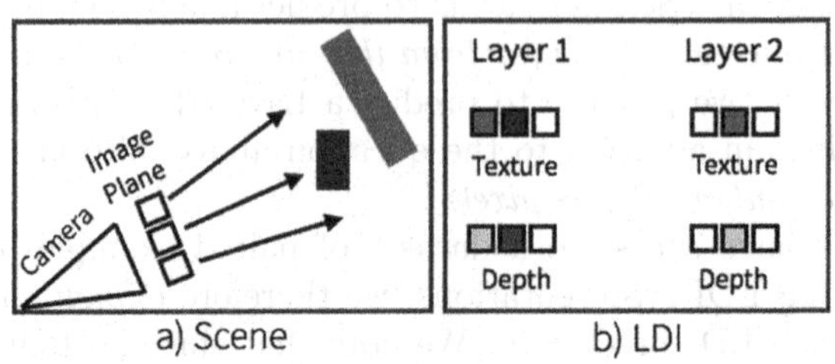

Fig. 3. Layered Depth Images (LDIs). Illustration of a layered depth image (LDI) for a simple scene. The first layer captures the depth (darker indicates closer) and texture of the visible points, and the second layer describes the occluded structure.

In our work, we aim to learn an LDI prediction function f, parametrized as a CNN f_θ, which, given a single input image I, can infer the corresponding LDI representation $\{(I^l, D^l)\}_{l=1}^L$. Intuitively, the first layer corresponds to the aspects of the scene visible from the camera viewpoint, and the subsequent layers capture aspects occluded in the current view. Although in this work we restrict ourselves to inferring two layers, the learning procedure presented is equally applicable for the more general scenario.

View Synthesis as Supervision. Given a source image I_s, we predict the corresponding LDI representation $f_\theta(I_s) = \{(I_s^l, D_s^l)\}_{l=1}^L$. During training, we also have access to an image I_t of the same scene as I_s, but from a different viewpoint. We write $V_{s \to t} \equiv (\mathbf{K}_s, \mathbf{K}_t, \mathbf{R}, \mathbf{t})$ to denote the camera transform between the source frame and the target frame, including intrinsic and extrinsic camera parameters. With this transform and our predicted LDI representation, we can render a predicted image from the target viewpoint. In particular, using a geometrically defined rendering function $\mathcal{R}$, we can express the novel target view rendered from the source image as $\mathcal{R}(f_\theta(I_s); V_{s \to t})$.

We can thus obtain a learning signal for our LDI predictor f_θ by enforcing similarity between the predicted target view $\mathcal{R}(f_\theta(I_s); V_{s \to t})$ and the observed target image I_t. There are two aspects of this learning setup that allow us to learn meaningful prediction: (a) the novel view I_t may contain new scene content compared to I_s, *e.g.* disoccluded regions, therefore the LDI $f_\theta(I_s)$ must capture more than the visible structure; and (b) the LDI $f_\theta(I_s)$ is predicted *independently* of the target view/image I_t which may be sampled arbitrarily, and hence the predicted LDI should be able to explain content from many possible novel views.

The Need for Forward-Rendering. As noted by Shade *et al.* when introducing the LDI representation [22], the rendering process for synthesizing a novel view given a source LDI requires forward-splatting-based rendering. This requirement leads to a subtle but important difference in our training procedure compared to prior multi-view supervised depth prediction methods [9,12,33]: while prior approaches rely on inverse warping for rendering, our representation necessitates the use of forward rendering.

Concretely, prior approaches, given a source image I_s, predict a per-pixel depth map. Then, given a novel view image, I_t, they reconstruct the source image by 'looking up' pixels from I_t via the predicted depth and camera transform. Therefore, the 'rendered view' is the same as the input view for which the geometry is inferred, *i.e.* these methods do not render a novel view, but instead re-render the source view. This procedure only enforces that correct geometry is learned for pixels visible to both views.

However, in our scenario, since we explicitly want to predict beyond the visible structure, we cannot adopt this approach. Instead, we synthesize novel views using our layered representation, thereby allowing us to learn about both the visible and the occluded scene structure. This necessitates forward rendering, *i.e.* constructing a target view given the source view texture and geometry, as opposed to inverse warping, *i.e.* reconstructing a source view by using source geometry and target frame texture.

3.2 Differentiable Rendering of an LDI

Given a predicted LDI representation $\{(I_s^l, D_s^l)\}$ in a source image frame, we want to render a novel viewpoint related by a transform $V_{s \to t}$. We do so by treating the LDI as a textured point cloud, with each pixel in each layer corresponding to a point. We first forward-project each source point onto the target frame, then handle occlusions by proposing a 'soft z-buffer', and finally render the target image by a weighted average of the colors of projected points.

Forward Projection. Denoting by p_s^l the pixel $p_s \equiv (x_s, y_s)$ in layer l, we can compute its projected position and inverse depth in the target frame coordinates using the (predicted) inverse depth $d_s^l \equiv D_s^l(p_s)$ and the camera parameters.

$$\begin{bmatrix} \bar{x}_t(p_s^l) \\ \bar{y}_t(p_s^l) \\ 1 \\ \bar{d}_t(p_s^l) \end{bmatrix} \sim \begin{bmatrix} \mathbf{K}_t & \hat{0} \\ \hat{0} & 1 \end{bmatrix} \begin{bmatrix} \mathbf{R} & \hat{\mathbf{t}} \\ \hat{0} & 1 \end{bmatrix} \begin{bmatrix} \mathbf{K}_s^{-1} & \hat{0} \\ \hat{0} & 1 \end{bmatrix} \begin{bmatrix} x_s \\ y_s \\ 1 \\ d_s^l \end{bmatrix} \tag{1}$$

Splatting with soft z-buffering. Using the above transformation, we can *forward splat* this point cloud to the target frame. Intuitively, we consider the target frame image as an empty canvas. Then, each source point p_s^l adds paint onto the canvas, but only at the pixels immediately around its projection. Via this process, many source points may contribute to the same target image pixel, and we want the closer ones to occlude the further ones. In traditional rendering, this can be achieved using a z-buffer, with only the closest point contributing to the rendering of a pixel.

However, this process results in a discontinuous and non-differentiable rendering function that is unsuitable for our framework. Instead, we propose a *soft* z-buffer using a weight $w(p_t, p_s^l)$ that specifies the contribution of p_s^l to the target image pixel p_t. Defining $\mathcal{B}(x_0, x_1) \equiv \max\ (0, 1 - |x_0 - x_1|)$, we compute the weights as:

$$w(p_t, p_s^l) = \exp\left(\frac{\bar{d}_t(p_s^l)}{\tau}\right)\ \mathcal{B}(\bar{x}_t(p_s^l), x_t)\ \mathcal{B}(\bar{y}_t(p_s^l), y_t) \tag{2}$$

The initial exponential factor, modulated by the temperature τ, enforces higher precedence for points closer to the camera. A large value of τ results in 'softer' z-buffering, whereas a small value yields a rendering process analogous to standard z-buffering. The latter terms simply represent bilinear interpolation weights and ensure that each source point only contributes non-zero weight to target pixels in the immediate neighborhood.

Rendering. Finally, we compute the rendered texture $\bar{I}_t(p_t)$ at each target pixel p_t as a weighted average of the contributions of points that splat to that pixel:

$$\bar{I}_t(p_t) = \frac{\sum_{p_s^l} I_s^l\ w(p_t, p_s^l)\ \ +\ \ \epsilon}{\sum_{p_s^l} w(p_t, p_s^l)\ \ +\ \ \epsilon} \tag{3}$$

The small ϵ in the denominator ensures numerical stability for target pixels that correspond to no source point. A similar term in the numerator biases the color for such pixels towards white. All operations involved in rendering the novel target view are differentiable, including the forward projection, depth-dependent weight computation, and final color computation. Hence, we can use this *rendering via forward splatting* process as the differentiable $\mathcal{R}(f_\theta(I_s); V_{s\to t})$ required in our learning framework.

3.3 Network Architecture

We adopt the DispNet [18] architecture for our LDI prediction CNN shown in Fig. 4. Given the input color image, a convolutional encoder processes it to compute spatial features at various resolutions. We then decode these via upconvolutions to get back to the image resolution. Each layer in the decoder also receives the features from the corresponding encoder layer via skip connections. While we use a single CNN to predict disparities and textures for all LDI layers, we find it critical to have disjoint prediction branches to infer each LDI layer. We hypothesize that this occurs because the foreground layer gets more learning signal, and sharing all the prediction weights makes it difficult for the learning signals for the background layer to compete. Therefore, the last three decoding blocks and final prediction blocks are independent for each LDI layer.

3.4 Training Objective

To train our CNN f_θ, we use view synthesis as a proxy task: given a source image I_s, we predict a corresponding LDI and render it from a novel viewpoint. As a training objective, we enforce that this rendered image should be similar

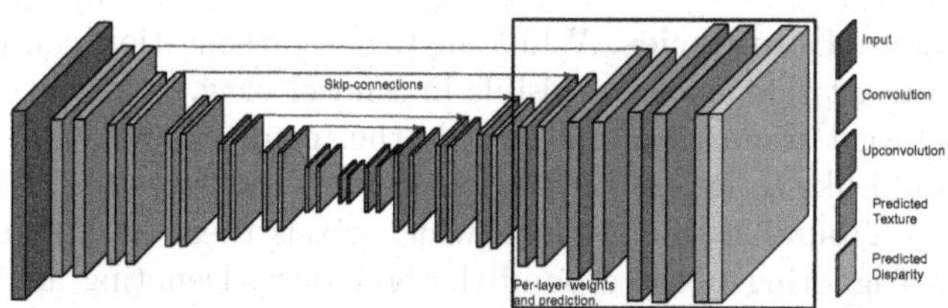

Fig. 4. Overview of our CNN architecture. We take as input an image and predict per-layer texture and inverse depth. Our CNN architecture consists of a convolutional encoder and decoder with skip-connections. We use disjoint prediction branches for inferring the texture and depth for each LDI layer.

to the observed image from that viewpoint. However, there are some additional nuances that we need to consider when formulating our training objective.

Depth Monotonicity. The layers in our LDI representation are supposed to capture content at increasing depths. We therefore enforce that the inverse depth across layers at any pixel is non-increasing:

$$L_{\text{inc}}(I_s) = \sum_{p_s,l} \max(0, D_s^{l+1}(p_s) - D_s^l(p_s)). \quad (4)$$

Consistency with Source. The typical LDI representation enforces that the first layer's texture corresponds to the observed source. We additionally enforce a similar constraint even for background layers when the predicted geometry is close to the foreground layer. We compute a normalized weight for the layers at each pixel, denoted as $w(p_s, l) \propto \exp \frac{D_s^l(p_s)}{\tau}$, and define a weighted penalty for deviation from the observed image:

$$L_{\text{sc}}(I_s) = \sum_{p_s,l} w(p_s, l) \| I_s(p_s) - I_s^l(p_s) \|_1. \quad (5)$$

This loss encourages the predicted texture at each layer to match the source texture, while allowing significant deviations in case of occlusions, *i.e.* where the background layer is much further than the foreground. In conjunction with L_{inc}, this loss enforces that the predicted representation adheres to the constraints of being an LDI.

Allowing Content Magnification. The forward-splatting rendering method described in Sect. 3.2 computes a novel view image by splatting each source pixel onto the target frame. This may result in 'cracks' [13]—target pixels that are empty because no source pixels splat onto them. For example, if the target image contains a close-up view of an object that is faraway in the source image, too few source points will splat into that large target region to cover it completely. To overcome this, we simply render the target frame at half the input resolution, *i.e.* the output image from the rendering function described in Sect. 3.2 is half the size of the input LDI.

Ignoring Image Boundaries. While an LDI representation can explain the disoccluded content that becomes visible in a novel view, it cannot capture the pixels in the target frame that are outside the image boundary in the source frame. We would like to ignore such pixels in the view synthesis loss. However, we do not have ground-truth to tell us which pixels these are. Instead, we use the heuristic of ignoring pixels around the boundary. Denoting as M a binary mask that is zero around the image edges, we define our view synthesis loss as:

$$L_{\text{vs}}(I_s, I_t, V_{s\to t}) = \|M \odot I_t - M \odot \bar{I}_t\|_1 \quad \text{where } \bar{I}_t = \mathcal{R}(f_\theta(I_s); V_{s\to t}). \tag{6}$$

As described above, the rendered image $\bar{I}_t$ and the target image I_t are spatially smaller than I_s.

Overcoming Depth Precedence. Consider synthesizing pixel p_t as described in Eq. 3. While the weighted averaging across layers resembles z-buffer-based rendering, it has the disadvantage of making it harder to learn a layer if there is another preceding (and possibly incorrectly predicted) layer in front of it. To overcome this, and therefore to speed up the learning of layers independent of other layers, we add an additional loss term. Denoting as $\bar{I}_t^l$ a target image rendered using *only layer* l, we add an additional 'min-view synthesis' loss measuring the minimum pixel-wise error across per-layer synthesized views:

$$L_{\text{m-vs}}(I_s, I_t, V_{s\to t}) = \sum_{p_t} \min_l M(p_t)\|I_t(p_t) - \bar{I}_t^l(p_t)\|_1 \tag{7}$$

In contrast to the loss in Eq. 6, which combines the effects of all layers when measuring the reconstruction error at p_t, this loss term simply enforces that at least one layer should correctly explain the observed $I_t(p_t)$. Therefore, a background layer can still get a meaningful learning signal even if there is a foreground layer incorrectly occluding it. Empirically, we found that this term is crucial to allow for learning the background layer.

Smoothness. We use a depth smoothness prior L_{sm} which minimizes the L_1 norm of the second-order spatial derivatives of the predicted inverse depths D_s^l.

Our final learning objective, combining the various loss terms defined above (with different weights) is:

$$L_{\text{final}} = L_{\text{vs}} + L_{\text{m-vs}} + L_{\text{sc}} + L_{\text{inc}} + L_{\text{sm}} \tag{8}$$

Using this learning objective, we can train our LDI prediction CNN f_θ using a dataset comprised only of paired source and target images of the same scene.

4 Experiments

We consider two different scenarios to learn single-view inference of a layer-structured scene representation. We first study our approach in a synthetic, but nevertheless challenging, setting using procedurally generated data. We then use our method to learn from stereo pairs in an outdoor setting.

4.1 Analysis Using Synthetic Data

In order to examine our method in a controlled setting with full knowledge of the underlying 3D scene structure, we create a dataset of procedurally generated scenes. We first describe the details of the generation process, and then discuss the training details and our results.

Dataset. We generate our synthetic data to have a room-like layout with two side 'walls', one back 'wall', a 'ceiling' and a 'floor'. We additionally place one to three upright segmented objects on the floor. The 'room' box is always at a fixed location in the world frame, and is of a fixed size. The segmented foreground objects are randomly placed, from left to right, at increasing depths and lie on a front-facing planar surface. To obtain the foreground objects, we randomly sample from the unoccluded and untruncated object instances in the PASCAL VOC dataset [8]. The textures on the room walls are obtained using random images from the SUN 2012 dataset [30].

To sample the source and target views for training our LDI prediction, we randomly assign one of them to correspond to the canonical front-facing world view. The other view corresponds to a random camera translation with a random rotation. We ensure that the transformation can be large enough such that the novel views can often image the content behind the foreground object(s) in the source view. We show some sample source and target pairs in Fig. 5.

Note that while the geometry of the scene layout is relatively simple, the foreground objects can have differing shapes due their respective segmentation. Further, the surface textures are drawn from diverse real images and significantly

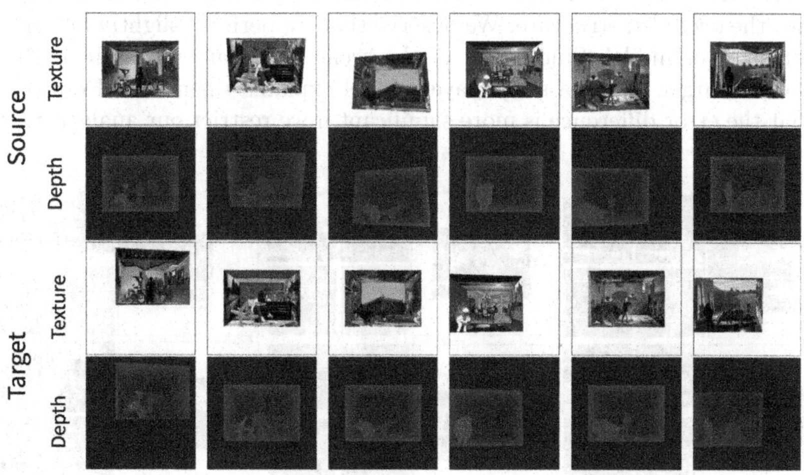

Fig. 5. Procedurally generated synthetic data. We show 6 random training samples (top: source image and corresponding inverse depth, bottom: target image with corresponding inverse depth). Note that only the color images are used for learning. (Color figure online)

add to the complexity, particularly as our aim is to infer both the geometry and the texture for the scene layers.

Training Details. We split the PASCAL VOC objects and the SUN 2012 images into random subsets corresponding to a train/validation/test split of 70% – 15% – 15%. We use the corresponding images and objects to generate training samples to train our LDI prediction CNN f_θ. We train our CNN for 600k iterations using the ADAM optimizer [16]. Based on the dataset statistics, we restrict the maximum inverse depth predicted to correspond to 1 m.

Results. We visualize the predictions of our learned LDI prediction CNN in Fig. 6. We observe that it is able to predict the correct geometry for the foreground layer *i.e.* per-pixel depth. More interestingly, it can leverage the background layer to successfully infer the geometry of the occluded scene content and hallucinate plausible corresponding textures. We observe some interesting error modes in the prediction, *e.g.* incorrect background layer predictions at the base of wide objects, or spurious details in the background layer at pixels outside the 'room'. Both these occur because we do not use any direct supervision for learning, but instead rely on a view synthesis loss. The first error mode occurs because we never fully 'see behind' the base of wide objects even in novel views. Similarly, the spurious details are only present in regions which are consistently occluded by the foreground layer and therefore ignored for view synthesis.

We analyze our learned representation by evaluating how well we can synthesize novel views using it. We report in Table 1 the mean ℓ_1 error for view synthesis and compare our 2 layer model vs a single layer model also trained for the view synthesis task, using the same architecture and hyper-parameters. Note that the single layer model can only hope to capture the visible aspects, but not the occluded structure. We observe that we perform slightly better than the single layer model. Since most of the scene pixels are visible in both, the source and target views, a single layer model explains them well. However, we see that the error difference is more significant if we restrict our analysis to only

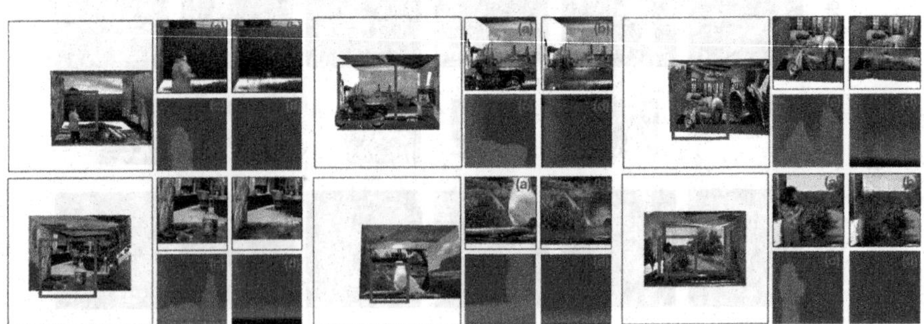

Fig. 6. Sample LDI prediction results on synthetic data. For each input image on the left, we show our method's predicted 2-layer texture and geometry for the highlighted area: (a, b) show the predicted textures for the foreground and background layers respectively, and (c, d) depict the corresponding predicted disparity.

Fig. 7. Sample LDI prediction results on the KITTI dataset. For each input image on the left, we show our method's predicted 2-layer texture and geometry for the highlighted area: (a, b) show the predicted textures for the foreground and background layers respectively, and (c, d) depict the corresponding predicted disparity.

Table 1. View synthesis error on synthetic data. We compare our 2 layer LDI prediction CNN against a single layer model that can only capture the visible aspects. We report the mean pixel-wise ℓ_1 error between the ground-truth novel view and the corresponding view rendered using the predicted representations.

View synthesis error	All pixels	Dis-occluded pixels
1 layer model	0.0398	0.1439
2 layer model	0.0392	0.1301

the dis-occluded pixels *i.e.* pixels in the target image which are not visible in the source view. This supports the claim that our predicted LDI representation does indeed capture more than the directly visible structure.

We also report in Table 2 the error in the predicted inverse depth(s) against the known ground-truth. We restrict the error computation for the background layer to pixels where the depth differs from the foreground layer. Since the one layer model only captures the foreground, and does not predict the background depths, we measure its error for the background layer using the foreground layer predictions. While this is an obviously harsh comparison, as the one layer model, by design, cannot capture the hidden depth, the fact that our predicted background layer is 'closer' serves to empirically show that our learned model infers meaningful geometry for the background layer.

4.2 Experiments on KITTI

We demonstrate the applicability of our framework in a more realistic setting: outdoor scenes with images collected using a calibrated stereo camera setup. We note that previous methods applied to this setting have been restricted to

Table 2. Geometry prediction error on synthetic data. We measure mean pixel-wise error in the predicted inverse depth(s) against the ground-truth. (*) As the single layer model does not infer background, we evaluate its error for the background layer using the foreground depth predictions. This serves to provide an instructive upper bound for the error of the LDI model.

Inverse depth error	Foreground layer (All pixels)	Background layer (Hidden pixels)
1 layer model	0.0092	0.1307 (*)
2 layer model	0.0102	0.0152

inferring the depth of the visible pixels, and that it is encouraging that we can go beyond this representation.

Dataset. We use the 'raw' sequences from the KITTI dataset [10], restricting our data to the 30 sequences from the *city* category as these more often contain interesting occluders *e.g.* people or traffic lights. The multi-view supervision we use corresponds to images from calibrated stereo cameras that are 0.5 m apart. We use both the left and the right camera images as source images, and treat the other as the target view for which the view synthesis loss is minimized. Due to the camera setup, the view sampling corresponds to a lateral motion of 0.5 m and is more restrictive compared to the synthetic data.

Training Details. We randomly choose 22 among the 30 *city* sequences for training, and use 4 each for validation and testing. This results in a training set of about 6,000 stereo pairs. We use similar hyper-parameters and optimization algorithm to the synthetic data scenario, but alter the closest possible depth to correspond to 2 m.

Table 3. View synthesis error on KITTI. We compare our 2 layer LDI prediction CNN against a single layer model that can only capture the visible aspects. We report the mean pixel-wise view synthesis error when rendering novel views using the predicted representations.

View synthesis error	All pixels	Dis-occluded pixels
1 layer model	0.0583	0.0813
2 layer model	0.0581	0.0800

Results. We visualize sample predictions of our learned LDI prediction CNN in Fig. 7. We observe that it is able to predict the correct geometry for the foreground layer *i.e.* per-pixel depth. Similar to the synthetic data scenario, we observe that it can leverage the background layer to hallucinate plausible geometry and texture of the occluded scene content, although to a lesser extent. We hypothesize that the reduction in usage of the background layer is because the view transformation between the source and target views is small compared to the scene scale, and we therefore only infer background layer mostly corresponding to (a) thin scene structures smaller than the stereo baseline, or (b) around the boundaries of larger objects/structures *e.g.* cars.

We do not have the full 3D structure of the scenes to compare our predicted LDI against, but we can evaluate the ability of this representation to infer the available novel views, and we report these evaluations in Table 3. As we do not have the ground-truth for the dis-occluded pixels, we instead use the unmatched pixels from an off-the-shelf stereo matching algorithm [31]. This algorithm, in addition to computing disparity, attempts to identify pixels with no correspondence in the other view, thus providing (approximate) dis-occlusion labels (see supplementary material for visualizations). Measuring the pixel-wise reconstruction error, we again observe that our two-layer LDI model performs slightly better than a single layer model which only models the foreground. Additionally, the difference is a bit more prominent for the dis-occluded pixels.

While the above evaluation indicates our ability to capture occluded structure, it is also worth examining the accuracy of the predicted depth. To this end, we compared results on our test set against the publicly available model from Zhou *et al.* [33], since we use a similar CNN architecture facilitating a more apples-to-apples comparison. We perform comparably, achieving an Absolute Relative error of 0.1856, compared to an error of 0.2079 by [33]. While other monocular depth estimation approaches can further achieve improved results using stronger supervision, better architectures or cycle consistency [12], we note that achieving state-of-the-art depth prediction is not our central goal. However, we find it encouraging that our proposed LDI prediction approach does yield somewhat competitive depth prediction results.

5 Discussion

We have presented a learning-based method to infer a layer-structured representation of scenes that can go beyond common 2.5D representations and allow for reasoning about occluded structures. There are, however, a number of challenges yet to be addressed. As we only rely on multi-view supervision, the learned geometry is restricted by the extent of available motion across training views. Additionally, it would be interesting to extend our layered representation to include a notion of grouping, incorporate semantics and semantic priors (*e.g.* 'roads are flat'). Finally, we are still far from full 3D understanding of scenes. However, our work represents a step beyond 2.5D prediction and towards full 3D.

Acknowledgments. We would like to thank Tinghui Zhou and John Flynn for helpful discussions and comments. This work was done while ST was an intern at Google.

References

1. Adelson, E.H.: Layered representations for image coding. Technical report (1991)
2. Baker, S., Szeliski, R., Anandan, P., Szeliski, R.: A layered approach to stereo reconstruction. In: CVPR (1998)
3. Bansal, A., Russell, B., Gupta, A.: Marr revisited: 2D-3D alignment via surface normal prediction. In: CVPR (2016)
4. Barron, J.T., Malik, J.: Shape, illumination, and reflectance from shading. TPAMI **37**(8), 1670–1687 (2015)
5. Choy, C.B., Xu, D., Gwak, J.Y., Chen, K., Savarese, S.: 3D-R2N2: a unified approach for single and multi-view 3D object reconstruction. In: Leibe, B., Matas, J., Sebe, N., Welling, M. (eds.) ECCV 2016. LNCS, vol. 9912, pp. 628–644. Springer, Cham (2016). https://doi.org/10.1007/978-3-319-46484-8_38
6. Ehsani, K., Mottaghi, R., Farhadi, A.: SeGAN: segmenting and generating the invisible. CoRR abs/1703.10239 (2017)
7. Eigen, D., Fergus, R.: Predicting depth, surface normals and semantic labels with a common multi-scale convolutional architecture. In: ICCV (2015)
8. Everingham, M., Van Gool, L., Williams, C.K.I., Winn, J., Zisserman, A.: The PASCAL Visual Object Classes Challenge 2012 (VOC2012) Results. http://www.pascal-network.org/challenges/VOC/voc2012/workshop/index.html
9. Garg, R., Vijay Kumar, B.G., Carneiro, G., Reid, I.: Unsupervised CNN for single view depth estimation: geometry to the rescue. In: Leibe, B., Matas, J., Sebe, N., Welling, M. (eds.) ECCV 2016. LNCS, vol. 9912, pp. 740–756. Springer, Cham (2016). https://doi.org/10.1007/978-3-319-46484-8_45
10. Geiger, A., Lenz, P., Stiller, C., Urtasun, R.: Vision meets robotics: the KITTI Dataset. IJRR **32**(11), 1231–1237 (2013)
11. Girdhar, R., Fouhey, D.F., Rodriguez, M., Gupta, A.: Learning a predictable and generative vector representation for objects. In: Leibe, B., Matas, J., Sebe, N., Welling, M. (eds.) ECCV 2016. LNCS, vol. 9910, pp. 484–499. Springer, Cham (2016). https://doi.org/10.1007/978-3-319-46466-4_29
12. Godard, C., Mac Aodha, O., Brostow, G.J.: Unsupervised monocular depth estimation with left-right consistency. In: CVPR (2017)
13. Grossman, J.P., Dally, W.J.: Point sample rendering. In: Drettakis, G., Max, N. (eds.) Rendering Techniques 1998. Eurographics, pp. 181–192. Springer, Vienna (1998). https://doi.org/10.1007/978-3-7091-6453-2_17
14. Hoiem, D., Efros, A.A., Hebert, M.: Automatic photo pop-up. In: SIGGRAPH (2005)
15. Isola, P., Liu, C.: Scene collaging: analysis and synthesis of natural images with semantic layers. In: ICCV (2013)
16. Kingma, D., Ba, J.: Adam: a method for stochastic optimization. arXiv preprint arXiv:1412.6980 (2014)
17. Marr, D.: Vision: a computational investigation into the human representation and processing of visual information (1982)
18. Mayer, N., et al.: A large dataset to train convolutional networks for disparity, optical flow, and scene flow estimation. In: CVPR (2016)
19. Rezende, D.J., Eslami, S.A., Mohamed, S., Battaglia, P., Jaderberg, M., Heess, N.: Unsupervised learning of 3D structure from images. In: NIPS (2016)
20. Russell, B., Efros, A., Sivic, J., Freeman, B., Zisserman, A.: Segmenting scenes by matching image composites. In: NIPS (2009)

21. Saxena, A., Sun, M., Ng, A.Y.: Make3D: learning 3D scene structure from a single still image. TPAMI **31**(5), 824–840 (2009)
22. Shade, J., Gortler, S., He, L.w., Szeliski, R.: Layered depth images. In: SIGGRAPH (1998)
23. Sinha, P., Adelson, E.: Recovering reflectance and illumination in a world of painted polyhedra. In: ICCV (1993)
24. Song, S., Yu, F., Zeng, A., Chang, A.X., Savva, M., Funkhouser, T.: Semantic scene completion from a single depth image. In: CVPR (2017)
25. Tulsiani, S., Zhou, T., Efros, A.A., Malik, J.: Multi-view supervision for single-view reconstruction via differentiable ray consistency. In: CVPR (2017)
26. Vijayanarasimhan, S., Ricco, S., Schmid, C., Sukthankar, R., Fragkiadaki, K.: SfM-Net: learning of structure and motion from video. arXiv preprint arXiv:1704.07804 (2017)
27. Wang, J.Y., Adelson, E.H.: Layered representation for motion analysis. In: CVPR (1993)
28. Wang, X., Fouhey, D., Gupta, A.: Designing deep networks for surface normal estimation. In: CVPR (2015)
29. Wulff, J., Sevilla-Lara, L., Black, M.J.: Optical flow in mostly rigid scenes. arXiv preprint arXiv:1705.01352 (2017)
30. Xiao, J., Hays, J., Ehinger, K.A., Oliva, A., Torralba, A.: SUN database: large-scale scene recognition from abbey to zoo. In: CVPR (2010)
31. Yamaguchi, K., McAllester, D., Urtasun, R.: Efficient joint segmentation, occlusion labeling, stereo and flow estimation. In: Fleet, D., Pajdla, T., Schiele, B., Tuytelaars, T. (eds.) ECCV 2014. LNCS, vol. 8693, pp. 756–771. Springer, Cham (2014). https://doi.org/10.1007/978-3-319-10602-1_49
32. Yan, X., Yang, J., Yumer, E., Guo, Y., Lee, H.: Perspective transformer nets: learning single-view 3D object reconstruction without 3D supervision. In: NIPS (2016)
33. Zhou, T., Brown, M., Snavely, N., Lowe, D.: Unsupervised learning of depth and ego-motion from video. In: CVPR (2017)

Real-Time 'Actor-Critic' Tracking

Boyu Chen[1], Dong Wang[1(✉)], Peixia Li[1], Shuang Wang[2], and Huchuan Lu[1]

[1] School of Information and Communication Engineering, Dalian University of Technology, Dalian, China
{bychen,pxli}@mail.dlut.edu.cn, {wdice,lhchuan}@dlut.edu.cn
[2] Alibaba Group, Hangzhou, China
uu.ws@alibaba-inc.com

Abstract. In this work, we propose a novel tracking algorithm with real-time performance based on the 'Actor-Critic' framework. This framework consists of two major components: 'Actor' and 'Critic'. The 'Actor' model aims to infer the optimal choice in a continuous action space, which directly makes the tracker move the bounding box to the object's location in the current frame. For offline training, the 'Critic' model is introduced to form a 'Actor-Critic' framework with reinforcement learning and outputs a Q-value to guide the learning process of both 'Actor' and 'Critic' deep networks. Then, we modify the original deep deterministic policy gradient algorithm to effectively train our 'Actor-Critic' model for the tracking task. For online tracking, the 'Actor' model provides a dynamic search strategy to locate the tracked object efficiently and the 'Critic' model acts as a verification module to make our tracker more robust. To the best of our knowledge, this work is the first attempt to exploit the continuous action and 'Actor-Critic' framework for visual tracking. Extensive experimental results on popular benchmarks demonstrate that the proposed tracker performs favorably against many state-of-the-art methods, with real-time performance.

Keywords: Visual tracking · Real-time tracking
Reinforcement learning

1 Introduction

Visual tracking aims to locate the target specified in the initial frame, which has many realistic applications such as video surveillance, augment reality and behavior analysis. In spite of many efforts having been done [1–3], it is still a challenge task due to many factors such as deformation, illumination change, rotation, occlusion, to name a few.

Deep-learning-based tracking algorithms have significantly improved the tracking performance in recent years [4–7]. The pre-trained convolutional neural networks (e.g., AlexNet, VGG-16 and VGG-M) are usually adopted to obtain rich feature representation for robust tracking. Among these methods,

V. Ferrari et al. (Eds.): ECCV 2018, LNCS 11211, pp. 328–345, 2018.
https://doi.org/10.1007/978-3-030-01234-2_20

the MDNet tracker [5] achieves top-ranked performance in popular benchmarks (such as OTB-100 [8] and VOT2015 [9]). This method embeds the offline trained VGG-M network into the particle filter framework, where 256 candidate samples are randomly generated and each sample is verified using a CNN-based observation model in each frame. However, it is very slow due to the random sampling search strategy. To address this issue, Yun *et al.* [10] propose a reinforcement-learning-based tracker with an action-decision network (ADNet). This method takes a series of discrete actions to iteratively search the tracked object in each frame. Experimental results show that the ADNet tracker achieves slightly worse but three times faster performance than the MDNet method. The search strategies of MDNet and ADNet methods are illustrated in Fig. 1(a) and (b), respectively. We note that the learned iterative strategy in [10] is also far from the real-time requirement since it requires many iterative steps in every frame.

Fig. 1. The search strategies of different trackers. (a) MDNet [5]: search with random sampling; (b) ADNet [10]: iterative search with a series of discrete actions; and (c) our tracker: fast search with only one continuous action.

In this work, we develop a learning-based search strategy with continuous actions based on the 'Actor-Critic' framework. The core idea of this work is to predict only one continuous action using the 'Actor' model to locate the tracked object in each frame (see Fig. 1(c)). The reinforcement learning is exploited to offline train a good policy for determining the optimal action. In addition, the 'Critic' network acts as a verification scheme for both offline training and online tracking. The experimental results demonstrate that our 'Actor-Critic' tracker achieves better performance than other competing methods with real-time performance.

The contributions of this work can be summarized as follows.

(1) Our work is the first attempt to exploit the continuous actions for visual tracking. Visual tracking is treated as a dynamic search process where only one

action output by the 'Actor' model is taken to locate the tracked object in each frame.

(2) Our work is also the first attempt to develop the 'Actor-Critic' tracking framework. The 'Actor-Critic' model is not only used to offline train the 'Actor' model based on reinforcement learning but also adopted to improve the robustness of our tracker during the tracking process. In addition, we improve the deep deterministic policy gradient algorithm to effectively train our 'Actor-Critic' model with supervised learning and probability expert decision guidance.

(3) The proposed tracker is compared with some state-of-the-art trackers using the popular benchmarks, and the experimental results show that our tracker achieves good results with real-time performance.

2 Related Work

Visual Tracking. From the perspective of object localization, visual tracking can be treated as a dynamic search process to accurately locate the target in the current frame based on previous observations. Usually, this dynamic search process can be achieved with the sampling-verification framework. In each frame, a set of candidate states are randomly or densely sampled to describe possible object locations [11–13]. Then, an observation model is exploited to verify each candidate and determine the optimal state of the tracked object. However, the tracker with a robust observation model will be very slow since it requires calculating verification scores for a large number of sampled candidates, for both traditional methods [14–17] and deep visual trackers [5,18,19]. The correlation filter (CF) technique [20] could speed up verifying the densely sampled candidates with circulant matrix structures, resulting in many real-time trackers with good performance. Many attempts have been done to improve the original CF model in terms of feature combination [21,22], scale estimation [23,24], part-based extension [25,26], multi-task learning [27,28], bound effect [29,30], to name a few. However, this speed merit of CF significantly whittled away when we combine it with deep features to pursuit higher accuracies (like HCFT [4], C-COT [31], ECO [7], LSART [32], DRT [33]).

Besides, the iterative search process can be adopted to conduct visual tracking, such as Meanshift [34], Lucas-Kanade [35] and their variants [36–39]. These methods are very efficient since they merely require a relative small of iterative steps (rather than a large number of sampled candidates) for locating the tracked object in each frame. However, their tracking accuracies are not satisfactory due to the following two reasons. First, the adopted low-level hand-crafted features limit their performance. Second, their search strategies are derived based on image or histogram gradients, without considering the high-level semantic information. Thus, the study of learning-based search strategies with deep neural networks may facilitate the trackers' taking a better trade-off between robustness and efficiency. Yun *et al.* [10] develop an ADNet tracking algorithm based on reinforcement learning, in which a series of iterative steps (corresponding to motion actions) are determined by the offline trained action-decision network.

It speeds up the relevant MDNet method [5] more than three times without losing much accuracy. However, the learned iterative strategy in [10] is also far from the real-time requirement since it requires many iterative steps in each frame. In this work, we attempt to develop a learning-based search strategy with only one continuous action in each frame, which will significantly speed up the tracking method.

Reinforcement Learning. Reinforcement learning (RL) is a sequence learning method benefiting from trail and error, aiming to generate an agent for maximizing the cumulative future rewards. Due to the strong ability of deep neural networks, the RL technique has been applied on many computer vision tasks [40–42]. Recently, there exist some attempts to exploit the RL technique for visual tracking. In [10], Yun *et al.* propose an action-decision network based on RL, which learns a good policy to select a series of actions from the action pool (including eleven candidate actions for translation moves, scale changes, and stop). Then, the tracker decides sequential actions to search the optimal position of the tracked object in the current frame, and then goes to deal with the next frame. In [43], Huang *et al.* exploit RL to learn an early decision policy for adaptively selecting efficient features during the tracking process. Based on the learned policy, eight discrete actions are taken to decide whether the tracker locates the tracked object on an early layer or continues processing subsequence layers. This method could effectively speed up the deep tracker without losing accuracy since it encourages the tracker to handle easy frames with cheap features while still to deal with difficult frames with expensive deep features. In [44], the tracker is modeled as an active agent to make online decisions whether the agent is still to 'track' or requires to 'reinitialize' and whether the current observation should be 'update' or 'ignored'. In [45], the RL method is utilized to construct a template selection strategy, encouraging the tracker choose the best template from finite candidate templates in every frame. Different from abovementioned methods, we propose a novel 'Actor-Critic' tracking framework, which can effectively learn a good policy to determine one optimal action based on reinforcement learning.

3 Tracking via the 'Actor-Critic' Network

3.1 Overview

Visual tracking aims to infer the location of an arbitrary object in each subsequent frame given its initial position in the first frame. In this work, we attempt to conduct tracking within a novel 'Actor-Critic' framework, the overall pipeline of which is illustrated in Fig. 2. The 'Actor' model aims to give one continuous action to directly make the tracker move the bounding box to the object location in the current frame. It can be effectively offline trained with a 'Critic' network based on deep reinforcement learning. During the tracking process, the 'Critic' model combines the action produced by 'Actor' to determine the quality of the action and facilitates improving the tracking performance. The details of our tracking framework are presented as follows.

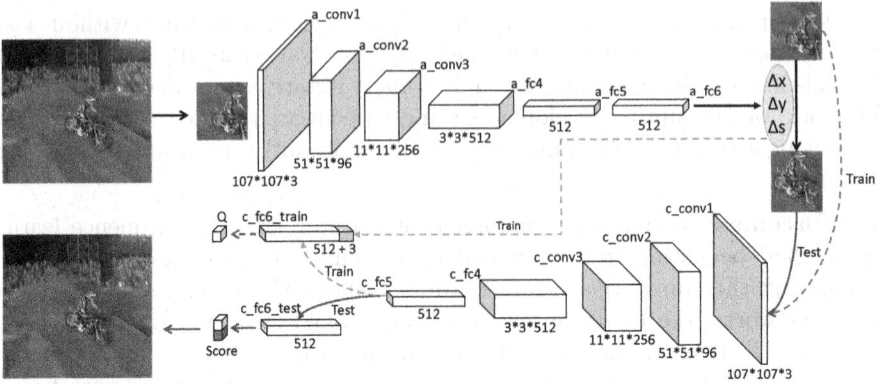

Fig. 2. The pipeline of the proposed tracking algorithm. 'a' means 'Actor' and 'c' means 'Critic'.

3.2 Problem Settings

Considering tracking as a sequential decision problem, our algorithm follows Markov Decision Process (MDP). The basic components of MDP include states $s \in S$, actions $a \in A$, the state transition function $s^{'} = f(s, a)$, and the reward $r(s, a)$. In our MDP framework, the tracker is treated as an agent to infer the accurate bounding box of the tracked object in each frame. This agent is interacted with an environment through a sequence of observations $s_1, s_2, ..., s_t$, actions $a_1, a_2, ..., a_t$ and rewards $r_1, r_2, ..., r_t$. In the t-th frame, the agent gives the continuous action a_t according to the current state s_t and obtains the tracking result as $s_t^{'}$. In this work, the action a_t is defined as the relative motion of the tracked object indicating how its bounding box should move directly in frame t. Different with ADNet [10], our tracker takes only one continuous action to locate the tracked object, which makes our tracker more efficient. The detailed settings of s, a, $f(s, a)$ and r are presented as follows (we drop the frame index t for clarity in this subsection).

State. In this work, we define the state s as the observation image patch within the bounding box $b = [x, y, h, w]$, where (x, y) is the center position and h and w stand for the height and width respectively. To be specific, we define a perprocessing function $s = \phi(b, F)$ to crop the image patch within the bounding box b in a given frame F and resize it to fit the input size of the deep network.

Action and State Transition. To conduct continuous control, the action space is assumed to be continuous, indicating how the bounding box should move directly. Here, we use the action $a = [\Delta x, \Delta y, \Delta s]$ to depict the relative motion of the tracked object, where Δx and Δy denote the relative horizontal and vertical translations and Δs stands for the relative scale change. Considering the temporal continuity in the tracking problem, we introduce some constraints to restrict the range of the action a: $-1 \leq \Delta x \leq 1$, $-1 \leq \Delta y \leq 1$ and $-0.05 \leq$

$\Delta s \leq 0.05$. By applying the action a to the original bounding box b, the new bounding box $b^{'} = \left[x^{'}, y^{'}, h^{'}, w^{'}\right]$ can be obtained as

$$\begin{cases} x^{'} = x + \Delta x \times h \\ y^{'} = y + \Delta y \times w \\ h^{'} = h + \Delta s \times h \\ w^{'} = w + \Delta s \times w \end{cases}. \tag{1}$$

Then, the state transition process $s^{'} = f(s, a)$ can be implicitly achieved by applying the per-processing function $\phi\left(b^{'}, F\right)$.

In this work, we attempt to directly infer the optimal action a based on the state s using an 'Actor' model, i.e., $a = \mu(s|\theta^{\mu})$. $\mu(.)$ denotes the deep network for our 'Actor' model with the parameter θ^{μ}. The 'Actor' model is trained offline with the proposed training strategy in Sect. 3.3, and then applied for online tracking. In practice, we exploit a double bounding box scheme to build the 'Actor' model (i.e., two bounding boxes of the target size and twice target size with the same center location).

Reward. The reward function $r(s, a)$ describes the localization accuracy improvement when transferring state s into state $s^{'}$ with a given action a. Thus, it can be defined based on the overlap ratio of the new bounding box $b^{'}$ and the ground truth G,

$$r(s, a) = \begin{cases} 1 & \text{if } \mathrm{IoU}(b^{'}, G) > 0.7 \\ -1 & \text{else} \end{cases}, \tag{2}$$

where IoU denotes the Intersection-over-Union criterion (i.e., $\mathrm{IoU}(u, v) = u \cap v / u \cup v$ for bounding boxes u and v). With every action, the reward will be generated and then be used to update the deep networks in offline learning.

3.3 Offline Training

Network Structure. Inspired by the recent successful trackers with lightweight deep networks, we use the pre-trained VGG-M model to initialize our 'Actor' and 'Critic' networks. As illustrated in Fig. 2, there are three convolutional layers in both two networks, which are consistent with the first three convolutional layers of the VGG-M network. For the 'Actor' network, the next two fully connected layers with 512 output nodes are combined with the ReLU operation, and the last fully connected layer generates a three-dimensional output. For offline training, the 'Critic' model has similar structures with 'Actor' expect the last fully connected layer as it requires concatenating the three-dimensional action vector to obtain a Q-value for action evaluation according to the current state.

Training via DDPG. In this work, we train our 'Actor-Critic' network using the DDPG approach [46], the core idea of which is to iteratively update the 'Critic' and 'Actor' models with training sample pairs collected based on the RL rule. Given N pairs of $(s_i, a_i, r_i, s_i^{'})$, the 'Critic' model $Q(s, a)$ can be learned using the Bellman equation as in Q-learning. With the utilization of the target networks $\mu^{'}$ and $Q^{'}$, the learning process can be achieved by minimizing the following loss,

$$L = \frac{1}{N}\sum_i (y_i - Q(s_i, a_i|\theta^Q))^2, \tag{3}$$

where $y_i = r_i + \gamma Q^{'}(s_i^{'}, \mu^{'}(s_i^{'}|\theta^{\mu^{'}})|\theta^{Q^{'}})$.

Then, the 'Actor' model can be updated by applying the chain rule to the expected return from the start distribution J with respect to the model parameters:

$$\nabla_{\theta^\mu} J \approx \frac{1}{N}\sum_i \nabla_a Q(s, a|\theta^Q)\big|_{s=s_i, a=\mu(s_i)} \nabla_{\theta^\mu}\mu(s|\theta^\mu)|_{s=s_i}. \tag{4}$$

During the training iteration, we randomly select a piece of training sequences $[F_k, F_{k+1}, \ldots, F_{k+T}]$ with their ground truth $[G_k, G_{k+1}, \ldots, G_{k+T}]$ from the training data (k is the start frame number and T is the frame length). After that, we apply our tracker in the selected sequence to obtain a training pair $(s_t, a_t, r_t, s_t^{'})$ at frame t.

Training Process Improvement. It is not feasible to directly apply the original DDPG framework to train our model, since the action space is very huge in our tracking problem. Thus, we attempt to improve the training process from two following aspects.

(1) Due to the huge action space, it is difficult to obtain a positive reward when an agent follows a random exploration strategy for a given video clip. This will make the DDPG method less effective in training our model. To solve this problem, we utilize the supervised information from the first frame to initialize the 'Actor' model for adapting the current environment. That is, the 'Actor' model is fine-tuned through the adaptive moment estimation method to minimize the following L_2 loss function,

$$\min \frac{1}{M}\sum_{m=1}^{M} \left[\mu\left(s_m|\theta^\mu\right) - a_m\right]^2, \tag{6}$$

where M is the number of training samples and $\mu\left(.|\theta^\mu\right)$ denotes the 'Actor' network with parameter θ^μ. s_m is the m-th sampled state and a_m denotes its ground truth action.

(2) The initialization scheme above cannot fully solve the imbalance problem of positive and negative samples as there are many unpredicted challenges causing tracking drifts. Thus, we exploit expert decisions to guide the learning process. The original DDPG algorithm introduces an exploration policy $\mu^{'}$ by adding noise sampled from a noise process $\mathcal{N}$ to the actor policy $\mu(s_t) = \mu(s_t|\theta_t^\mu) + \mathcal{N}$. However, this similar exploration mechanism is not suitable for our tracking task due to the huge action space. Therefore, we adopt a probabilistic expert decision guidance to supersede exploration mechanism in reinforcement learning. In

Algorithm 1. Offline training the 'Actor' network

Input: Training sequences [F] and their corresponding ground truths [G]
Output: Trained weights for the 'Actor' network

Initialize 'Critic' $Q(s,a)$ and 'Actor' $\mu(s|\theta^{\mu})$ with weights θ^{Q} and θ^{μ}.
Initialize the target network $Q^{'}$ and $\mu^{'}$ with weights $\theta^{Q^{'}} \leftarrow \theta^{Q}, \theta^{\mu^{'}} \leftarrow \theta^{\mu}$
Initialize the replay buffer R
repeat
  Randomly select a piece of frames $[F_k, F_{k+1}, \ldots, F_{k+T}]$ with their ground truth $[G_k, G_{k+1}, \ldots, G_{k+T}]$
  Receive initial observation state s_k according to F_k and G_k
  Train the 'Actor' network for an iteration utilizing s_1
  for each $t = 2, T+1$ **do**
    1. Obtain state s_t according to state s_{t-1} and F_{k-1+t}
    2. Select action $a_t = \mu(s_t|\theta^{\mu})$ according to the current policy and exploration probability ϵ;
    3. Execute action a_t according to the transition in Eq. 1, observe reward r_t as Eq. 2 and the next state $s_t^{'}$
    4. Store transition $(s_t, a_t, r_t, s_t^{'})$ in R
  end for
  Sample a random mini-batch of N transitions $(s_i, a_i, r_i, s_i^{'})$ from R
  Update 'Critic' $Q(s,a)$ by minimizing the loss following Eq. 3
  Update 'Actor' $\mu(s|\theta^{\mu})$ using the sampled policy gradient following Eq. 4
  Update the target networks:

$$\begin{aligned} \theta^{Q^{'}} &\leftarrow \tau\theta^{Q} + (1-\tau)\theta^{Q^{'}} \\ \theta^{\mu^{'}} &\leftarrow \tau\theta^{\mu} + (1-\tau)\theta^{\mu^{'}} \end{aligned} \tag{5}$$

until Reward become stable

a video sequence, with a certain probability ϵ, an expert decision guidance is applied to replace the action output by the 'Actor' network. The probability ϵ gradually decreases during the training process.

Our 'Actor' network can be effectively trained offline by the DDPG method with two improvements above. The overall training process is summarized in Algorithm 1.

3.4 Online Tracking

Network Initialization. To make our tracker further suitable for the current sequence, we initialize both 'Actor' and 'Critic' models with the ground truth in the first frame.

For 'Actor', we first sample M candidate bounding boxes $b_m|_{m=1}^{M}$ around the ground truth and calculate their corresponding accurate actions $a_m|_{m=1}^{M}$. Then, we extract the image observation s_m for the candidate location b_m using per-processing function $s_m = \phi(b_m, F)$ (defined in Sect. 3.2). Thus, the 'Actor' network can be fine-tuned using the Adam method to minimize the L2 loss $\frac{1}{M}\sum_{m=1}^{M}\left[\mu\left(s_m|\theta^{\mu}\right)-a_m\right]^2$.

For online tracking, the 'Critic' model $v\left(s|\theta^{\nu}\right)$ is a classification network. To initialize it, we assign a binary label l_m to the m-th candidate using the following rule,

$$l_m=\begin{cases}1 & \text{if IoU}(b_m,G)>0.7\\ 0 & \text{else}\end{cases}, \tag{7}$$

where G denotes the ground truth bounding box. With the collected image-label pairs $\{s_m,l_m\}|_{m=1}^{M}$, the 'Critic' network is initialized using the Adam method to minimize the following loss function,

$$\arg\min_{\theta^{\nu}} -\sum\nolimits_{s\in S_+} p_+(s|\nu;\theta^{\nu})-\sum\nolimits_{s\in S_-} p_-(s|\nu;\theta^{\nu}), \tag{8}$$

where S_+ and S_- denote positive and negative training sets respectively. The 'Critic' network outputs the foreground and background probabilities $p_+(s|\nu;\theta^{\nu})$ and $p_-(s|\nu;\theta^{\nu})$ for a given state (or observation patch) s.

Tracking via 'Actor-Critic'. For online tracking, we exploit both 'Actor' and 'Critic' networks within a tracking-and-verification scheme. In the t-th frame, we first calculate the state s_t using the preprocessing function $\phi\left(b_{t-1}^{'},F_t\right)$ ($b_{t-1}^{'}$ denotes the optimal object location in the $t-1$ frame and F is the image frame). Second, we put the state s_t into the the 'Actor' network resulting in the action a_t, i.e., $a_t=\mu\left(s_t|\theta^{\mu}\right)$. With the action a_t and location $b_{t-1}^{'}$, we can obtain the new location $b_t^{'}$ and its corresponding state $s_t^{'}$ in the current frame. Then, we utilize the 'Critic' network to verify the observation $s_t^{'}$, i.e., $v\left(s_t^{'}|\theta^{\nu}\right)$. If the score given by the 'Critic' network is large than 0, we treat the action a_t being reliable and adopt the location $b_t^{'}$ as the optimal location in the t-th frame. Otherwise, we exploit a re-detection technique using the 'Critic' network to evaluate a series of sampled candidates $b_t^m|_{m=1}^{M}$ around $b_{t-1}^{'}$ (same as the sampling strategy in Network Initialization). After that, the optimal location $b_t^{'}$ is obtained as the candidate with the highest score outputed by 'Critic'.

Network Update. An effective updating strategy helps our tracker take a good trade-off between robustness and efficiency. The 'Actor' model has a stable performance during the tracking process due to our offline training, thus, we merely update the 'Critic' network when needed. If the verification score given by 'Critic' is less than 0, we think it does not fit well with the appearance change in the current environment and use positive and negative samples collected in previous 10 frames to update the network based on Eq. 8.

3.5 Implementation Details

Samples Generation. To train the networks in both offline and online tracking stages, we sample $X_t^i=\left(x_t^i,y_t^i,z_t^i\right), i=1,\ldots,N$ (x and y are horizontal and vertical translations; z denotes the scale) from a Gaussian distribution centered by the object location in frame $t-1$. The covariance is a diagonal matrix $diag\left(0.09d^2, 0.09d^2, 0.25\right)$, where d is the mean of the width and height of the tracked object.

Offline Training. To train our 'Actor' network offline, we use 768 video sequences from the ImageNet Video [47] trainval set. We randomly choose continuous twenty to forty frames in a video for each iteration. For initializing the 'Actor' network in the first frame, we collect 32 samples whose IoU scores with ground truth are larger than 0.7. The learning rate is set to 1e−4 in the initialization stage.

The possibility of adopting the expert decision ϵ is set to 0.5 at first and reduced by 5% after every ten thousand iterations. We update the target networks every ten thousand iterations. τ in the target networks updating is set to 0.001. The learning rates of the 'Actor' and 'Critic' networks are set to 1e−6 and 1e−5, respectively. In addition, we use a replay buffer size of 10^4. We finish the training of the 'Actor' network after two hundred and fifty thousand iterations.

Online Tracking. For online tracking, we collect 500 positive samples and 5000 negative samples with ground truth in the first frame. Only positive samples are used for training the 'Actor' network. We initialize the 'Actor' network with learning rates 1e−4 until the loss is less than 1e−4 and initialize the 'Critic' network with learning rates 1e−4 for 30 iterations. The batch sizes for the 'Actor' and 'Critic' models are 64 and 128, respectively. When the predicted target location of the highest foreground score of all candidates are less than 0, we consider it as the tracking failure, and the re-detection is conducted to capture the missed target. We draw 256 samples for the re-detection scheme. Simultaneously, the 'Critic' model is online updated with collected samples from 10 recent successful tracking frames. We collect 50 positive samples and 150 negative samples from each successful tracking frame.

4 Experiment

Our tracker is implemented in Python with the Pytorch framework, which runs at 30 fps on a PC with a 3.4 GHz CPU with 32G memory and a TITAN GPU with 12G memory. The website of our ACT method is available on https://github.com/bychen515/ACT. Our tracker based on the 'Actor-Critic' network is denoted as ACT for clarity. We compare our tracker with many state-of-the-art trackers using standard tracking benchmarks such as Online Tracking Benchmark (OTB) [8,48] and Visual Object Tracking challenge 2016 (VOT2016) [49]. Some representative visual results are shown in Fig. 3.

4.1 Evaluation on OTB

In this subsection, we evaluate our tracker using both OTB-2013 [48] and OTB-2015 [8] datasets. The proposed tracker is compared with ten state-of-the-art trackers with real-time performance including PTAV [50], CFNet [51],

Fig. 3. Qualitative results of our ACT method and other trackers on some challenging sequences (ClifBar, Girl2, Matrix, MotorRolling, Skiing, Walking2).

ACFN [52], SiameFC [6], ECO-HC [7], LCT [53], LMCF [54], Staple [22], DSST [55] and KCF [20]. The first four algorithms employ the feature descriptors from CNNs while the rest of the methods are based on the traditional hand-crafted features.

In this work, we adopt both precision and success plots to evaluate different trackers. The precision plot illustrates the percentage of frames where the center location error between the object location and ground truth is smaller than a per-defined threshold. Whereas the success plot demonstrates the percentage of frames the Intersection Over Union (IOU) of the predicted and the ground truth bounding boxes is higher than a given ratio. The trackers can be ranked the accuracy at 20 pixel threshold in the precision plot and the Area Under Curve (AUC) score in the success plot.

OTB-2013. We first evaluate our tracker in comparison with ten competing methods using the OTB-2013 dataset [48]. This dataset is one of the most popular benchmark including 50 fully-annotated video sequences with 11 various challenging factors such as fast motion, occlusion, illumination change, motion blur, and background clutter. These attributes could facilitate understanding the characteristics of our tracker.

Figure 4(a) illustrates the precision and success plots over 50 sequences in OTB-2013. From this figure, we can see that our ACT method achieves best performance in terms of precision and the second best result in terms of success. These outstanding results are partly attributed to the strength of CNN features, which makes our tracker effectively depict the appearance of the tracked object compared with low-level hand-crafted features. In comparison with CFNet, SiameFC and ACFN methods using deep networks, our ACT algorithm still achieves better performance due to the proposed learning scheme for determining the accurate action. Table 1 summarizes the average precision scores of different trackers for 11 challenging attributes in OTB-2013. It can be seen from this

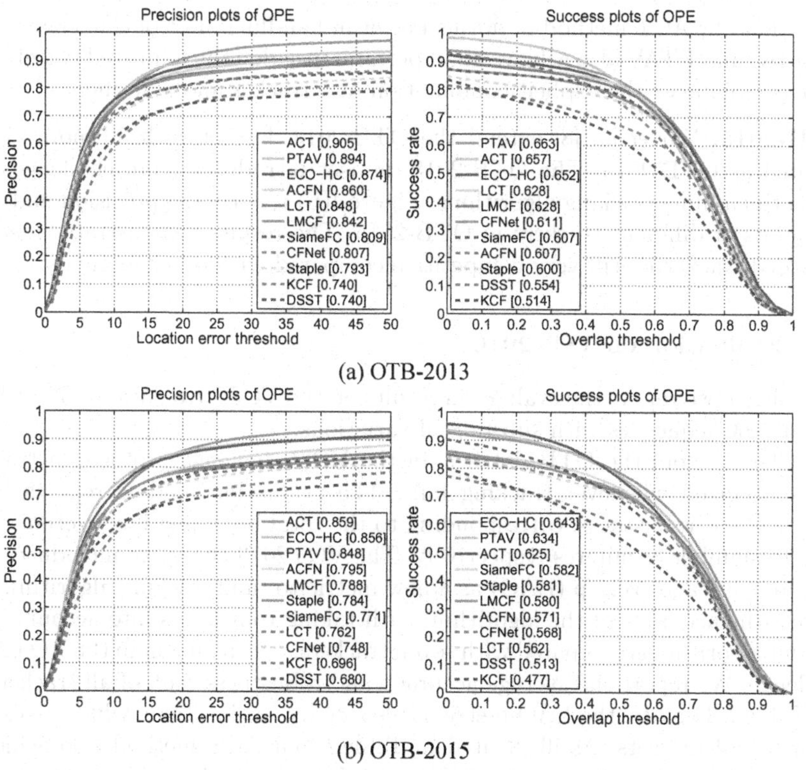

Fig. 4. The precision and success plots of different trackers on the OTB-2013 (a) and OTB-2015 (b) datasets. We can see that our ACT method performs better than other competing trackers

Table 1. Average precision scores on different attributes: illumination variation (IV), out-of-plane rotation (OPR), scale variation (SV), occlusion (OCC), deformation (DEF), motion blur (MB), fast motion (FM), in-plane rotation (IPR), out-of-view(OV), background cluttered (BC) and low resolution (LR).

	IV	SV	OCC	DEF	MB	FM	IPR	OPR	OV	BC	LR	AV
ACT(Ours)	0.855	0.910	0.871	0.882	0.806	0.805	0.867	0.889	0.788	0.915	0.873	0.905
PTAV [50]	0.848	0.837	0.902	0.892	0.815	0.805	0.853	0.894	0.853	0.880	0.615	0.894
ECO-HC[7]	0.793	0.838	0.913	0.863	0.777	0.797	0.801	0.862	0.883	0.816	0.666	0.874
ACFN[52]	0.793	0.813	0.856	0.902	0.709	0.719	0.814	0.870	0.788	0.783	0.429	0.860
LCT[53]	0.792	0.758	0.845	0.873	0.664	0.665	0.802	0.850	0.728	0.796	0.352	0.848
LMCF[54]	0.783	0.775	0.844	0.869	0.714	0.730	0.779	0.826	0.695	0.848	0.555	0.842
SiameFC[6]	0.709	0.796	0.802	0.743	0.698	0.723	0.743	0.788	0.780	0.732	0.659	0.809
CFNet [51]	0.728	0.799	0.758	0.759	0.705	0.691	0.762	0.785	0.500	0.806	0.619	0.807
Staple[22]	0.741	0.733	0.787	0.812	0.688	0.643	0.773	0.773	0.679	0.753	0.550	0.793
DSST[55]	0.730	0.738	0.706	0.658	0.544	0.531	0.768	0.736	0.511	0.694	0.479	0.740
KCF[20]	0.728	0.679	0.749	0.740	0.650	0.602	0.725	0.729	0.650	0.753	0.381	0.740

table that our ACT method performs better in handling most of challenges. The ECO-HC and PTAV also achieve good performance due the improved correlation filter technique or the explicit combination of a tracker and a verifier.

OTB-2015. Wu *et al.* [8] extend the OTB-2013 dataset with 50 more video, denoted as OTB-2015. The OTB-2015 dataset introduces more challenges for evaluating online tracking algorithms. Figure 4(b) reports the precision and success plots of different trackers in OTB-2015. The results demonstrate that the proposed tracker is still very competitive compared with other methods.

4.2 Evaluation on VOT2016

In addition, we report the evaluation results on the VOT2016 dataset [49], which contains 60 sequences with substantial variations.

Different from the OTB dataset, in the VOT challenge protocol, a tracker is re-initialized whenever tracking fails. The evaluation module reports both accuracy and robustness, corresponding to the total bounding box overlap ratio and the number of failures respectively. The VOT2016 challenge introduces the expected average overlap (EAO) as a new metric to rank tracking algorithms. It reflects the accuracy of the algorithm, with taking robustness into account.

Our algorithm is compared with seven trackers, which all join in the VOT2016 challenge. We report the average accuracy and robustness rank of all trackers in the Table 2. Besides, the EAO metric is also shown in this Table which gives the orders of all trackers. As illustrated in Table 2, our ACT method also achieves very competitive results. The C-COT and MLDF methods perform better than our ACT method, however, they merely run less than 2 fps.

Table 2. The overall ranking score of accuracy (A), robustness (R) and expected overlap (EAO) in VOT2016.

Tracker	C-COT[31]	MLDF	ACT (ours)	MDNet-N	SiamAN	SO-DLT[56]	KCF	DSST
Accuracy	1.87	2.77	2.25	1.63	2.37	2.23	2.98	2.60
Robustness	2.08	1.95	3.47	2.55	3.43	3.98	3.87	4.45
EAO	0.3310	0.3106	0.2746	0.2572	0.2352	0.2213	0.1924	0.1814

4.3 Analysis

Self-comparison. To verify the contribution of each component in our algorithm, we implement several variations of our approach and evaluate them using OTB-2013. These versions include: (1) 'ACT-vgg': the ACT method is not pertrained and simple adopts initial parameters of the VGG-M model to initialize the 'Actor' network; (2) 'ACT-rl': the ACT method without the reinforcement learning process; (3) 'ACT-init': the ACT method without using the initialization in the first frame among the training video sequence; (4) 'ACT-ex': the ACT method replacing the expert decision guidance by normal exploration in tradition DDPG methods. The performance of all variations and our final ACT is reported in Fig. 5, from which we can see that all components facilitates improving the tracking performance. For examples, the comparison of the 'ACT-rl' and final ACT methods demonstrates the reinforcement learning process could effectively learn a good policy for action decision. The 'ACT-rl' method cannot learn the action policy from the training data. We note that the 'ACT-vgg' method without offline training runs at only 2 fps with not good performance, which means the 'Actor' model without pre-trained cannot output the accurate action and the 'Critic' verification scheme requires to be invoked more frequently.

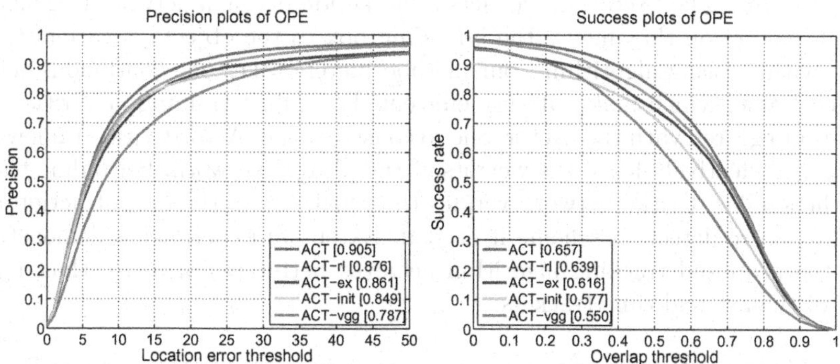

Fig. 5. Precision and success plots on OTB50 for different variations of our algorithm.

Compared with ADNet [10] **and MDNet** [5]**.** We note that the most relevant trackers of our ACT method are ADNet [10] and MDNet [5] since they adopt the

VGG-M model as the basic network structure but with different search strategies. The detailed comparisons are reported in Table 3. The MDNet method performs the best in terms of accuracy but runs very slow due to the random sampling search strategy. The ADNet tracker exploits the iterative search strategy with few discrete actions in each frame, the fast version of which could achieve 15 fps with losing about 3% accuracy compared with MDNet. Our ACT method performs slightly worse than the ADNet tracker and achieves comparable accuracies with the ADNet-fast one. However, our tracker runs at 30 fps, twice than ADNet-fast and more than ten times than the original ADNet. This can be mainly attributed to the adopted continuous action, which locates the tracked object using merely one action in each frame.

Table 3. The comparisons of our ACT tracker with ADNet [10] and MDNet [5] methods in OTB.

Method	ACT (ours)	ADNet [10]	ADNet-fast [10]	MDNet [5]
Prec. (20 px) on OTB-2013	0.905	0.903	0.898	0.948
IOU (AUC) on OTB-2013	0.657	0.659	0.670	0.708
Prec. (20 px) on OTB-2015	0.859	0.880	0.851	0.909
IOU (AUC) on OTB-2015	0.625	0.646	0.635	0.678
FPS	30	3	15	1

5 Conclusions

This work presents a novel 'Actor-Critic' tracking method based on reinforcement learning. The 'Actor' model acts as an action decision network to generate an optimal action that moves the bounding box to the object's location. Compared with existing algorithms, our method merely takes one continuous action in each frame, which makes it very efficient. For offline training, a 'Critic' network is integrated with the 'Actor' one to construct the 'Actor-Critic' framework, which can effectively learn the weights of the 'Actor' network. For online tracking, the similar 'Critic' network verifies the reliability of the output action and invokes the re-detection scheme if needed. Extensive experiments demonstrate that the proposed tracking algorithm achieves better performance than many state-of-the-art real-time trackers.

Acknowledgment. This paper was supported in part by the Natural Science Foundation of China #61751212, #61502070, #61725202, #61771088, #61472060, #61632006, #91538201, and in part by the Fundamental Research Funds for the Central Universities under Grant #DUT18JC30. This work was also supported by Alibaba Group through Alibaba Innovative Research (AIR) program.

References

1. Yilmaz, A., Javed, O., Shah, M.: Object tracking: a survey. ACM Comput. Surv. **38**(4), 13 (2006)
2. Li, X., Hu, W., Shen, C., Zhang, Z., Dick, A.R., van den Hengel, A.: A survey of appearance models in visual object tracking. ACM Trans. Intell. Syst. Technol. **4**(4), 58:1–58:48 (2013)
3. Li, P., Wang, D., Wang, L., Lu, H.: Deep visual tracking: review and experimental comparison. Pattern Recognit. **76**, 323–338 (2018)
4. Ma, C., Huang, J.B., Yang, X., Yang, M.H.: Hierarchical convolutional features for visual tracking. In: ICCV (2015)
5. Nam, H., Han, B.: Learning multi-domain convolutional neural networks for visual tracking. In: CVPR (2016)
6. Bertinetto, L., Valmadre, J., Henriques, J.F., Vedaldi, A., Torr, P.H.S.: Fully-convolutional siamese networks for object tracking. In: Hua, G., Jégou, H. (eds.) ECCV 2016. LNCS, vol. 9914, pp. 850–865. Springer, Cham (2016). https://doi.org/10.1007/978-3-319-48881-3_56
7. Danelljan, M., Bhat, G., Khan, F.S., Felsberg, M.: ECO: efficient convolution operators for tracking. In: CVPR (2017)
8. Wu, Y., Lim, J., Yang, M.: Object tracking benchmark. IEEE Trans. Pattern Anal. Mach. Intell. **37**(9), 1834–1848 (2015)
9. Kristan, M., et al.: The visual object tracking VOT2015 challenge results. In: ICCV (2015)
10. Yun, S., Choi, J., Yoo, Y., Yun, K., Choi, J.Y.: Action-decision networks for visual tracking with deep reinforcement learning. In: CVPR (2017)
11. Grabner, H., Bischof, H.: On-line boosting and vision. In: CVPR (2006)
12. Ross, D.A., Lim, J., Lin, R., Yang, M.: Incremental learning for robust visual tracking. Int. J. Comput. Vis. **77**(1–3), 125–141 (2008)
13. Babenko, B., Yang, M., Belongie, S.J.: Robust object tracking with online multiple instance learning. IEEE Trans. Pattern Anal. Mach. Intell. **33**(8), 1619–1632 (2011)
14. Jia, X., Lu, H., Yang, M.: Visual tracking via adaptive structural local sparse appearance model. In: CVPR (2012)
15. Zhong, W., Lu, H., Yang, M.: Robust object tracking via sparse collaborative appearance model. IEEE Trans. Image Process. **23**(5), 2356–2368 (2014)
16. Hare, S., et al.: Struck: structured output tracking with kernels. IEEE Trans. Pattern Anal. Mach. Intell. **38**(10), 2096–2109 (2016)
17. Li, Z., Zhang, J., Zhang, K., Li, Z.: Visual tracking with weighted adaptive local sparse appearance model via spatio-temporal context learning. IEEE Trans. Image Process. **27**(9), 4478–4489 (2018)
18. Wang, N., Yeung, D.: Learning a deep compact image representation for visual tracking. In: NIPS (2013)
19. Li, H., Li, Y., Porikli, F.: DeepTrack: learning discriminative feature representations by convolutional neural networks for visual tracking. In: BMVC (2014)
20. Henriques, J.F., Rui, C., Martins, P., Batista, J.: High-speed tracking with kernelized correlation filters. IEEE Trans. Pattern Anal. Mach. Intell. **37**(3), 583–596 (2015)
21. Zhu, G., Wang, J., Wu, Y., Zhang, X., Lu, H.: MC-HOG correlation tracking with saliency proposal. In: AAAI (2016)
22. Bertinetto, L., Valmadre, J., Golodetz, S., Miksik, O., Torr, P.H.S.: Staple: complementary learners for real-time tracking. In: CVPR (2016)

23. Li, Y., Zhu, J.: A scale adaptive kernel correlation filter tracker with feature integration. In: Agapito, L., Bronstein, M.M., Rother, C. (eds.) ECCV 2014. LNCS, vol. 8926, pp. 254–265. Springer, Cham (2015). https://doi.org/10.1007/978-3-319-16181-5_18
24. Danelljan, M., Häger, G., Khan, F.S., Felsberg, M.: Discriminative scale space tracking. IEEE Trans. Pattern Anal. Mach. Intell. **39**(8), 1561–1575 (2017)
25. Li, Y., Zhu, J., Hoi, S.C.H.: Reliable patch trackers: robust visual tracking by exploiting reliable patches. In: CVPR (2015)
26. Liu, T., Wang, G., Yang, Q.: Real-time part-based visual tracking via adaptive correlation filters. In: CVPR (2015)
27. Tang, M., Feng, J.: Multi-kernel correlation filter for visual tracking. In: ICCV (2015)
28. Zhang, T., Xu, C., Yang, M.: Multi-task correlation particle filter for robust object tracking. In: CVPR (2017)
29. Danelljan, M., Hager, G., Khan, F.S., Felsberg, M.: Learning spatially regularized correlation filters for visual tracking. In: ICCV (2015)
30. Galoogahi, H.K., Fagg, A., Lucey, S.: Learning background-aware correlation filters for visual tracking. In: ICCV (2017)
31. Danelljan, M., Robinson, A., Shahbaz Khan, F., Felsberg, M.: Beyond correlation filters: learning continuous convolution operators for visual tracking. In: Leibe, B., Matas, J., Sebe, N., Welling, M. (eds.) ECCV 2016. LNCS, vol. 9909, pp. 472–488. Springer, Cham (2016). https://doi.org/10.1007/978-3-319-46454-1_29
32. Sun, C., Wang, D., Lu, H., Yang, M.H.: Learning spatial-aware regressions for visual tracking. In: CVPR (2018)
33. Sun, C., Wang, D., Lu, H., Yang, M.H.: Correlation tracking via joint discrimination and reliability learning. In: CVPR (2018)
34. Comaniciu, D., Ramesh, V., Meer, P.: Kernel-based object tracking. IEEE Trans. Pattern Anal. Mach. Intell. **25**(5), 564–575 (2003)
35. Baker, S., Matthews, I.A.: Lucas-kanade 20 years on: a unifying framework. Int. J. Comput. Vis. **56**(3), 221–255 (2004)
36. Jiang, N., Liu, W., Wu, Y.: Learning adaptive metric for robust visual tracking. IEEE Trans. Image Process. **20**(8), 2288–2300 (2011)
37. Li, P., Wang, Q.: Robust registration-based tracking by sparse representation with model update. In: Lee, K.M., Matsushita, Y., Rehg, J.M., Hu, Z. (eds.) ACCV 2012. LNCS, vol. 7726, pp. 205–216. Springer, Heidelberg (2013). https://doi.org/10.1007/978-3-642-37431-9_16
38. Ning, J., Zhang, L., Zhang, D., Wu, C.: Robust mean-shift tracking with corrected background-weighted histogram. IET Comput. Vis. **6**(1), 62–69 (2012)
39. Oron, S., Bar-Hille, A., Avidan, S.: Extended Lucas-Kanade tracking. In: Fleet, D., Pajdla, T., Schiele, B., Tuytelaars, T. (eds.) ECCV 2014. LNCS, vol. 8693, pp. 142–156. Springer, Cham (2014). https://doi.org/10.1007/978-3-319-10602-1_10
40. Caicedo, J.C., Lazebnik, S.: Active object localization with deep reinforcement learning. In: ICCV (2015)
41. Bellver, M., Giro-i Nieto, X., Marques, F., Torres, J.: Hierarchical object detection with deep reinforcement learning. In: NIPS (2016)
42. Jayaraman, D., Grauman, K.: Look-ahead before you leap: end-to-end active recognition by forecasting the effect of motion. In: Leibe, B., Matas, J., Sebe, N., Welling, M. (eds.) ECCV 2016. LNCS, vol. 9909, pp. 489–505. Springer, Cham (2016). https://doi.org/10.1007/978-3-319-46454-1_30
43. Huang, C., Lucey, S., Ramanan, D.: Learning policies for adaptive tracking with deep feature cascades. In: ICCV (2017)

44. Supancic III, J.S., Ramanan, D.: Tracking as online decision-making: learning a policy from streaming videos with reinforcement learning. In: ICCV (2017)
45. Choi, J., Kwon, J., Lee, K.M.: Visual tracking by reinforced decision making. CoRR abs/1702.06291 (2017)
46. Lillicrap, T.P., et al.: Continuous control with deep reinforcement learning. CoRR abs/1509.02971 (2015)
47. Russakovsky, O., et al.: ImageNet large scale visual recognition challenge. Int. J. Comput. Vis. **115**(3), 211–252 (2015)
48. Wu, Y., Lim, J., Yang, M.H.: Online object tracking: a benchmark. In: CVPR (2013)
49. Kristan, M., et al.: The visual object tracking VOT2016 challenge results. In: Hua, G., Jégou, H. (eds.) ECCV 2016. LNCS, vol. 9914, pp. 777–823. Springer, Cham (2016). https://doi.org/10.1007/978-3-319-48881-3_54
50. Fan, H., Ling, H.: Parallel tracking and verifying: a framework for real-time and high accuracy visual tracking. In: ICCV (2017)
51. Valmadre, J., Bertinetto, L., Henriques, J.F., Vedaldi, A., Torr, P.H.S.: End-to-end representation learning for correlation filter based tracking. In: CVPR (2017)
52. Choi, J., Chang, H.J., Yun, S., Fischer, T., Demiris, Y., Choi, J.Y.: Attentional correlation filter network for adaptive visual tracking. In: CVPR (2017)
53. Ma, C., Yang, X., Zhang, C., Yang, M.: Long-term correlation tracking. In: CVPR (2015)
54. Wang, M., Liu, Y., Huang, Z.: Large margin object tracking with circulant feature maps. In: CVPR (2017)
55. Danelljan, M., Häger, G., Khan, F.S., Felsberg, M.: Accurate scale estimation for robust visual tracking. In: BMVC (2014)
56. Wang, N., Li, S., Gupta, A., Yeung, D.: Transferring rich feature hierarchies for robust visual tracking. CoRR abs/1501.04587 (2015)

Deep Bilinear Learning for RGB-D Action Recognition

Jian-Fang Hu[1], Wei-Shi Zheng[1,3,4](✉), Jiahui Pan[1], Jianhuang Lai[1], and Jianguo Zhang[2]

[1] Sun Yat-sen University, Guangzhou, China
{hujf5,zhwshi,stsljh}@mail.sysu.edu.cn, panjh7@mail2.sysu.edu.cn
[2] University of Dundee, Dundee, UK
j.n.zhang@dundee.ac.uk
[3] Key Laboratory of Machine Intelligence and Advanced Computing, MOE, Guangzhou, China
[4] Inception Institute of Artificial Intelligence, Abu Dhabi, United Arab Emirates

Abstract. In this paper, we focus on exploring modality-temporal mutual information for RGB-D action recognition. In order to learn time-varying information and multi-modal features jointly, we propose a novel deep bilinear learning framework. In the framework, we propose bilinear blocks that consist of two linear pooling layers for pooling the input cube features from both modality and temporal directions, separately. To capture rich modality-temporal information and facilitate our deep bilinear learning, a new action feature called modality-temporal cube is presented in a tensor structure for characterizing RGB-D actions from a comprehensive perspective. Our method is extensively tested on two public datasets with four different evaluation settings, and the results show that the proposed method outperforms the state-of-the-art approaches.

Keywords: Deep bilinear · RGB-D action · Feature learning · Cube

1 Introduction

Recognizing human actions based on low-cost depth camera has attracted increasing attention recently. Compared to RGB cameras, the Kinect, as one widely used depth camera, has many advantages. Firstly, it can capture depth maps, which was shown useful for geometric modeling [32]. Secondly, it can output 3D human poses (skeletons) in real-time, which also benefits action recognition [30].

Recent works have shown that the RGB, depth, and skeleton data captured by depth cameras can complement to each other for describing human actions; integrating them together can largely improve the system performance [12,37,39]. Specifically, in [37], the features extracted from different modalities and body parts are combined by a multi-kernel learning model. In [12,28], features from various modalities are pooled together by explicitly mining the shared-specific

V. Ferrari et al. (Eds.): ECCV 2018, LNCS 11211, pp. 346–362, 2018.
https://doi.org/10.1007/978-3-030-01234-2_21

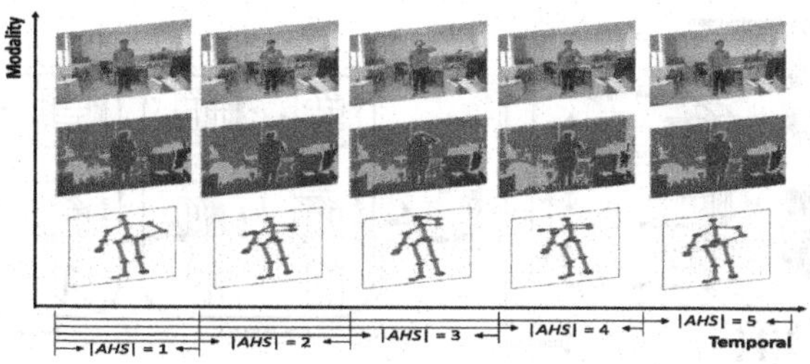

Fig. 1. Action snapshots with multi-modalities, showing actions can be recognized from sequences of different modalities and of different progress levels (the length of action history sequence (AHS, which will be discussed in detail in Sect. 3.1.))

components. However, the systems in these works only consider features from different modalities, all extracted from *full* action sequence. Relatively few works have explored the action context at different temporal levels, i.e, the time-varying information of sequences involving partial action executions.

Indeed, partial action executions in multi-modal sequences could contain informative action contexts from recognition perspective. Taking the action presented in Fig. 1 for example, we can recognize that the person is drinking by observing any of the RGB, depth, or skeleton sequences. Meanwhile, the action can also be recognized by only observing the first 80% of the full sequence (i.e., $|AHS| = 4$), which means that sequences with partial action executions and of various modalities can be exploited in recognition. The use of time-varying information for action recognition could be traced back to the early work of motion history images (MHI) [2], where the history of motion is encoded in a single *static* image. Each MHI corresponds to one sequence at a certain progress level. However, few work has yet considered to deeply encode and learn the time-varying information together with the modalities. In this paper, we present a novel tensor-structured cube feature, and propose to learn time-varying information from multi-modal action history sequences for RGB-D action recognition.

The multi-modal sequences with temporal information can be regarded as a tensor, structured with two different dimensions (temporal and modality). Learning and pooling the tensor is a rather challenging task, due to the complexity of the arriving sequences, which are of varied progress levels and modalities. For the sequences at a certain progress level, since different modalities depict action from different perspectives, the features of varied modalities can complement to each other for describing actions context. While for a certain modality, sequences of various progress levels encode the temporal dynamics. And the time-varying information depicted in the sequences varies for different modalities. The time-varying information together with multi-modal features can give a comprehensive picture of the action, but how to learn the modality-temporal mutual information from highly structured sequence (tensor) remains a challenge.

In this paper, we address this challenge by proposing a novel deep bilinear framework, where a bilinear block consisting of two linear pooling layers

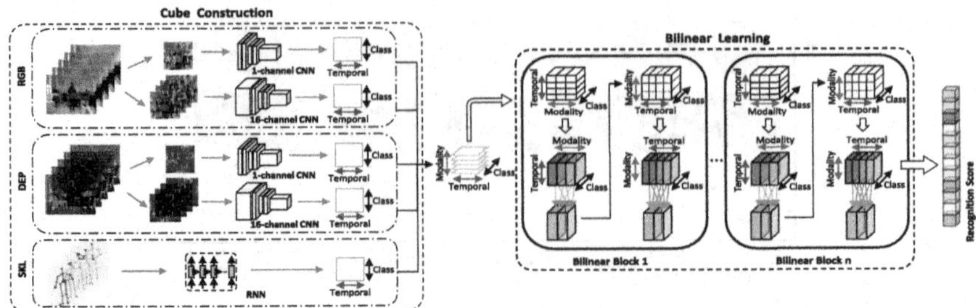

Fig. 2. Graphic illustration of our recognition system. Our system consists of two parts: cube feature construction and deep bilinear learning. The cube construction part is to extract multiple temporal feature maps for representing RGB-D actions. And the deep bilinear learning part is used to mine informative action representation for recognition.

(modality pooling layer and temporal pooling layer) is defined to pool the input tensor along the modality and temporal directions, separately. In this way, the structures along the temporal and modal dimensions are both preserved. By stacking the proposed bilinear blocks and other network layers (e.g., Relu and softmax), we develop our deep bilinear model to jointly learn the action history and modality information in videos. Results have shown that learning modality-temporal mutual information is beneficial for the recognition of RGB-D actions.

Note that the use of bilinear pooling has also been explored in [9,10] for pooling pair of features. However, their bilinear layer is defined as the outer product of two input features, which aims at pooling two vectors to a higher dimensional feature representation. These approaches are developed for pooling 1D vectors. In contrast, our objective is to integrate the input modality-temporal tensors from different dimensions, in order to preserve the tensor structures of the input. Our bilinear block is constructed based on the bilinear map, which learns the time-varying dynamics and multi-modal information in the sequences iteratively, and thus is more suitable for learning RGB-D sequences with complex tensor structures in the temporal and modality directions.

To encode rich modality-temporal information in the sequences and facilitate our deep bilinear learning, we further present a novel action descriptor called modality-temporal cube to characterize RGB-D actions from a comprehensive perspective. Our cube includes five feature maps, each of which is extracted from the sequences of various progress levels within a certain modality and describes actions from a certain perspective. Our experiments show that the proposed modality-temporal features fit the proposed deep bilinear model and can complement well to each other.

In summary, our contributions are: (1) a novel deep bilinear framework for learning multiple modality-temporal features; (2) a modality-temporal cube descriptor for characterizing RGB-D actions. Extensive experimental analysis and evaluations on two public benchmark RGB-D action sets, with four different evaluation settings, showing our method achieves state-of-the-art performances. A graphical illustration of our *system* is presented in Fig. 2.

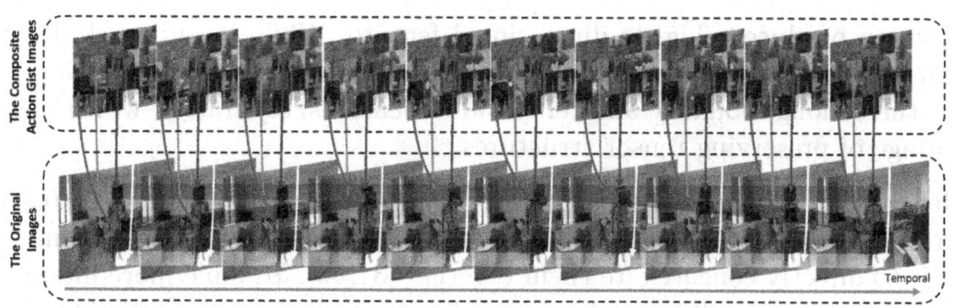

Fig. 3. Illustration of generating composite action GIST frames from original sequences.

2 Related Work

In the following, we briefly review the approaches (depth or skeleton based and RGB-D based) for action recognition with Kinect, which are closely related to our work. We also outline the bilinear pooling techniques and the methods that learn multi-modal features and time-varying information for action recognition.

Depth or Skeleton Based Action Recognition. The geometric information depicted in depth sequences can be used to characterize action [18,24,26,36,42]. For instance, the histograms of oriented normal within each spatio-temporal depth cube was used to describe actions in [26,42]. These methods mainly develop their systems based on the observed depth sequences. On the other hand, human action can also be characterized by the dynamics of human poses (or skeletons). The temporal dynamics of each skeleton joint [5,15,33,40] and joint pairs [20,25,29,41,43] are explored for mining the structure motions depicted in the skeleton sequences. However, each of the modalities has its own insufficiency for characterizing complex actions involving objects and interactions. In comparison, our method explores the collaboration among different modalities, and thus the weakness of losing contextual information by only using depth or skeleton features can be overcome by working colloborately with RGB features.

RGB-D Based Action Recognition. Recent works show that combining RGB, depth, and skeleton together can improve the system performance [12,19,28,37,39]. For instance, [13] proposed a joint learning framework to mine the structures shared and specified by different modal features. A deep shared-specific structure learning method is explored in [28]. Different from these works that choose to combine multi-modal features extracted from full sequences, in this paper, we formulate a deep learning approach to learn features from various modalities and progress levels. Thus the modality-temporal mutual structures are explored.

Bilinear Pooling. Bilinear pooling has been introduced to combine features extracted by two CNN models [9,10,21]. In [9], for example, a deep architecture with bilinear pooling is developed for improving question answering. However in these works, bilinear pooling is defined as the outer product of two features in order to produce a higher dimensional feature. While in our work, bilinear is defined as an operation block consisting of two linear operators pooling tensor features along modality and temporal dimensions, separately, which has the advantage of preserving tensor structures.

Multi-modal Action Recognition. Integrating multi-modal features can improve the recognition performance. A straightforward way to combine features is to directly concatenate them together [31,46]. To mine more interactive information among multi-modal features, lots of methods are proposed to explicitly learn shared-specific structures among features [11,13,28]. However, these works do not explore the time-varying information among the multiple modal features extracted from sequences of different progress levels.

Time-Varying Information for Action Recognition. Studies show that explicitly capturing time-varying information in sequences is beneficial. Intuitively, the time-varying information can be captured by a non-parametric model like mean or max pooling [16] and Fourier transform [13] etc. Learning time-varying information by data-driven approaches [7,8,35] can generalize better to unseen sequences. For example, [7] used a ranking machine to encode the dynamics among the sequential features. Note that the TSN [38] also intends to learn time-varying information within sequences of varies modalities. However, they modeled the time-varying and modality-varying information isolately. The time-varying information mined from each modality is empirically summarized, which makes their method less applicable for modelling temporal-modality mutual information. In contrast, we develop a flexible learning framework for learning the dynamics among sequences of various modalities and temporal lengths jointly.

3 Approach

We aim to explore the time-varying and modality-varying information for RGB-D action recognition by proposing a novel deep bilinear framework, which aims to integrate modality-temporal cubes in the modality and temporal directions. We also present a cube descriptor for characterizing RGB-D actions.

3.1 Modality-Temporal Cube Construction

Here, we describe how to construct our modality-temporal cube for representing RGB-D actions. Our cube includes temporal feature maps extracted from the sequences of various progress levels within a certain modality (skeleton, RGB or depth), each of which characterizes actions from a certain perspective.

Action History Sequence. For extracting temporal features, we uniformly divide each sequence into D segments and consider the sequence including the first d segments as an *action history sequence* (AHS) with length d ($|AHS| = d$). Therefore, we have a total of D AHSs, whose lengths range from 1 to D. Then, for each sequence of skeleton, RGB, or depth, we extract temporal features from the corresponding AHSs, which forms the base to capture time-varying information.

Skeleton Temporal Feature Map. We employ a sequence-sequence RNN to extract temporal features from each skeleton sequence, where the AHSs are encoded by the dynamic skeleton descriptor (DS) [13]. Thus, the dependencies among the DS features of consecutive AHSs are modeled. Then, we use the outputs of RNN as our feature map, which can capture some dynamic skeleton information depicted in each sequence.

RGB and Depth Temporal Feature Maps. Inspired by [13], where the visual features extracted from local image patches around each skeleton joint are used to represent human action, we also consider extracting our temporal feature maps in a similar way. Here, for each RGB/D image frame, we collect the local image patches around each skeleton joint, and tile them to compose a new image, which we termed as action *gist* image, a compact representation of the action frame as illustrated in Fig. 3. Therefore, an action gist sequence are formed by pooling its GIST frames sequentially. Noted that local patches corresponding to the same (tracked) skeleton joint are tiled at the same spatial location in the frame, but across time, forming a trajectory-based patch sequence in the temporal dimension. There are two merits of using such a composition: (1) it enables efficient training of trajectory-based CNN as we don't need to train a CNN for each trajectory-based patch sequence; and (2) it captures the dynamics of patch appearances along each trajectory. In Fig. 3, we have presented some examples about the composite action GIST frames. As can be seen, the gist image frames condense most of the action context and automatically remove the irrelated information, such as background. Patches at the same spatial location correspond to a long-term trajectory of a joint. In this end, our work could be among the family of trajectory-based action recognition [34].

Then, we construct our RGB and depth temporal feature maps by extracting K-channel CNN[1] descriptors from all the composite action gist AHSs, respectively. To train K-channel CNN, we selected K ordered action GIST frames for each training sequence. Specifically, the temporal location of the u-th selected frame is given by $max(1, 1 + (u-1)\frac{ls}{K} + \delta)$, where ls indicates the length of sequence and perturbation δ is a random integer obeying uniform distribution $U(-\frac{ls}{2K}, \frac{ls}{2K})$. In our experiments, two different settings ($K = 1$ and $K = 16$) are used. The feature map extracted from $K = 1$ can capture static appearance information, while the map from $K = 16$ characterizes dynamic appearance.

Feature Cube Construction. Finally, we concatenate all the feature maps along the modality dimension to construct the modality-temporal cube, whose size is modality number×AHS number×feature dimension. In total, our cube descriptor contains five temporal feature maps, with two from RGB AHSs (1-channel CNN and 16-channel CNN), two from depth AHSs ((1-channel CNN and 16-channel CNN), and one from the skeleton AHSs (RNN), each of which

[1] The input of K-channel CNN is K gray images concatenated along the channel dimension. Thus, it is a CNN whose input size is $224 \times 224 \times K$.

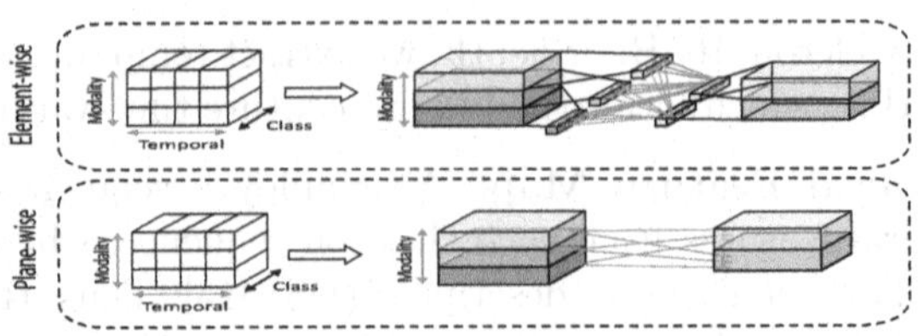

Fig. 4. Pooling by element-wise fully connected vs. plane-wise fully connected layer.

characterizes actions at different AHS lengths from a specific modality. The combination of them can form a comprehensive action representation.

Note that for constructing the temporal feature for the AHS of a specific modality and temporal length, we use the output of the final layer of CNN (or RNN for skeleton AHSs), whose size is the same as the number of action classes. Those features can be considered as soft classification scores (i.e., before the use of softmax operator). Thus, the third dimension of our cube encodes the classification information, and the elements along this dimension are highly related with each other. We call this feature dimension as the *class* dimension.

3.2 Deep Bilinear Learning

Our cube descriptor includes multiple temporal features extracted from RGB-D AHSs, making most of the existing multi-modal feature learning methods not applicable to learn an informative action representation. As each element in the (cube) class dimension corresponds to the confidence of assigning the given sample to a certain action class, pooling the confidences of different classes does not make much sense. Moreover, our experimental results in Table 5 confirm that merging elements of different classes is not the best for our framework. In the following, we introduce a novel deep learning framework to pool the modality and temporal information, while keeping the class dimension unchanged. We call our framework *deep bilinear* as it is inspired by the formulation of bilinear map.

Bilinear Map Revisited. In mathematics, a bilinear map is a function combining elements of two vector spaces to yield an element of a third vector space. The formulation of a widely used bilinear function in the community is

$$f(\boldsymbol{x}, \boldsymbol{y}) = \boldsymbol{x}^T \boldsymbol{A} \boldsymbol{y} \tag{1}$$

where $\boldsymbol{A} \in R^{m \times n}$, $\boldsymbol{x} \in R^m$, and $\boldsymbol{y} \in R^n$. As can be seen, $f(\boldsymbol{x}, \boldsymbol{y})$ is linear with respect to each of the variables $\boldsymbol{x}$ and $\boldsymbol{y}$.

It is straightforward to extend the above formulation in the matrix form as

$$f(\boldsymbol{X}, \boldsymbol{Y}) = \boldsymbol{X}^T \boldsymbol{A} \boldsymbol{Y} \tag{2}$$

where $\boldsymbol{A} \in R^{m \times n}$, $\boldsymbol{X} \in R^{m \times p}$, and $\boldsymbol{Y} \in R^{n \times q}$. This formula can be considered as a combination of two linear operators. The first operator $\boldsymbol{L} = \boldsymbol{X}^T \boldsymbol{A}$ is to combine the rows of $\boldsymbol{A}$ using the weights indicated by the columns of $\boldsymbol{X}$. It pools the rows of the input matrix, while holding the column dimension constant. We call it *row-pooling operator*. And the second operator $\boldsymbol{LY}$ (named *column-pooling operator*) is to calculate the weighted summation of all the columns in the latent matrix $\boldsymbol{L}$, where the combining weights are indicated by the rows of $\boldsymbol{Y}$. It is used to pool the columns of $\boldsymbol{L}$. The combination of the row-pooling and column-pooling transforms the $m \times n$-sized $\boldsymbol{A}$ to a matrix of $p \times q$.

Bilinear Block. Given a modality-temporal cube, here we would define a block, named *bilinear block*, to pool it in the modality and temporal dimensions, separately, based on the bilinear map (2). Therefore, the tensor structures along the modality and temporal dimensions are preserved during feature pooling. Note that the block would keep the *class* dimension constant. Our bilinear block is consisted of two neural layers (i.e., temporal pooling layer and modality pooling layer), each of which corresponds to one operator in the bilinear function.

Modality Pooling Layer. This layer is defined to pool the input cube in the modality dimension. We formulate it as a plane-wise linear combination problem:

$$\boldsymbol{L}(:,:,c) = \boldsymbol{X}^T \boldsymbol{A}(:,:,c), c = 1, 2, ..., C \tag{3}$$

where $\boldsymbol{X} \in R^{M_A \times M_L}$ is the model parameter to be learned, where M_A and M_L are the modality dimension of cube $\boldsymbol{A}$ and $\boldsymbol{L}$. Specially, M_L is a parameter to be specified by the user. $\boldsymbol{A} \in R^{M_A \times T \times C}$ is the input cube and $\boldsymbol{L}$ is the output cube, whose size is $M_L \times T \times C$. The layer defined by Eq. (3) pools the modality dimension from M_A to M_L. Let's denote the layer as f_M for simplification.

It is worth noting that the modality pooling layer (3) can be rewritten as

$$\boldsymbol{L}(m_L,:,:) = \sum_{m_A=1,2,...,M_A} \boldsymbol{X}(m_A, m_L)\boldsymbol{A}(m_A,:,:), m_L = 1, 2, ..., M_L \tag{4}$$

which means that elements corresponding to the same modality are weighted by the same parameter. That is, the cube is pooled in a plane-wise manner. An alternative way is to pool it in an element-wise manner, where each element is weighted by a specific parameter, as illustrated in Fig. 4. However, this would introduce a large number of learnable parameters, making the model easily fall into over-fitting. We will demonstrate it in the experiment Sect. 5.

Temporal Pooling Layer. The temporal pooling layer is defined to pool the input 3D cube in the temporal dimension. Specifically, it can be formulated as

$$\boldsymbol{Z}(:,:,c) = \boldsymbol{L}(:,:,c)\boldsymbol{Y}, c = 1, 2, ..., C \tag{5}$$

here, $\boldsymbol{Z}$ and $\boldsymbol{Y}$ indicate the output cube and the pooling parameters, respectively.

We would like to point out that the temporal pooling layer can be equivalently calculated using the modality pooling layer if we permute the temporal dimension and modality dimension of the input cubes. In the following, we use f_T to indicate the temporal pooling layer. To improve the generalization capability, we additionally constrain the model parameters $\boldsymbol{X}$ ($\boldsymbol{Y}$), corresponding to each layer in the block, by L_2-norm and L_1-norm constraint. The L_1-norm is

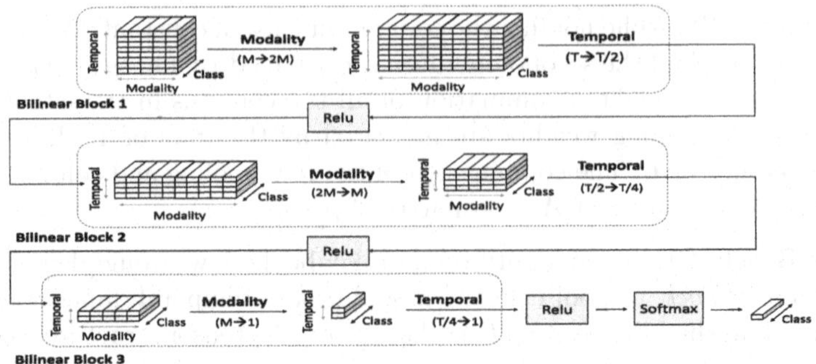

Fig. 5. Graphic illustration of the employed deep architecture.

employed to penalize non-zero elements in $\boldsymbol{X}$ ($\boldsymbol{Y}$), which could result in a sparse solution. The L_2-norm serves as a decay term.

Then the bilinear block can be defined by $b = f_T \circ f_M(\boldsymbol{A})$. Here, we construct our bilinear block based on the modality pooling and temporal pooling layers, pooling the cube from one dimension to another, separately.

Deep Bilinear Architecture. Given a set of $M \times T \times C$-sized modality-temporal cubes, our goal is to learn an underlying mapping f, which merges all the cube elements into a robust representation $\boldsymbol{y} \in R^C$. In other word, the objective is to find a mapping that pools the modality dimension and temporal dimension of the input cube to 1. In this paper, we define the mapping f as a stack of bilinear blocks, Relu, and softmax operators, i.e., $f = g_1 \circ g_2 \circ ... g_n ...(\bullet)$, where g_n refers to one of the above operators or bilinear block.

The form of our deep bilinear architecture is flexible. Experiments in this paper involve a deep architecture with three bilinear blocks, three Relu layers and a softmax layer, while more layers are possible. In the architecture, each bilinear block is followed by a Relu layer to map the outputs of the block non-linearly. A graphic illustration for the employed deep architecture can be found in Fig. 5. Please refer to the experiment section for more details.

Optimization. We optimize our deep bilinear by stochastic gradient descent (SGD) with momentum, where the gradients are determined by back propagation algorithm. We use the logistic loss as our loss function. For the gradient of L_1-norm of $\boldsymbol{X}$ ($\boldsymbol{Y}$), we use the generalized gradient $\boldsymbol{X}./|\boldsymbol{X}|$ ($\boldsymbol{Y}./|\boldsymbol{Y}|$) for simplicity.

4 Experiment

We evaluated our methods on two public benchmark 3D action datasets: NTU RGB+D Dataset [22] and SYSU 3D HOI dataset [14], with two different evaluation protocols employed in each set. In the following, we will briefly introduce the implementation details and then describe our experimental results.

4.1 Implementation Details

Following the observation in [13], we extract the 64 × 64 patches around the skeleton joints to form our composite action GIST frames[2]. For extracting temporal feature maps from RGB and Depth videos on the NTU RGB+D set, we trained a set of K-channel VGG-16 networks without pre-training on other auxiliary datasets[3], where we set the momentum factor and dropout rate as 0.9 and 0.7, respectively. While for the SYSU 3D HOI dataset, since we do not have enough data to train CNN, we chose to finetune the models trained on the NTU RGB+D set. For the training of RNN on both sets, we used the back propagation through time (BPTT) algorithm with momentum for optimization, where the momentum rate was set as 0.9. The neuron number in the hidden layer of RNN was set as 256. To speed up the optimization of RNN, we used PCA to reduce the dimension of the extracted DS features, where 98% of variance is retained.

Table 1. Recognition results (accuracies) on the NTU RGB+D set. '—' indicates that the performance is not reported in the literature.

Method	Data used	Cross-subject	Cross-view
Skeletal quads [6]	SKL	38.6%	41.4%
Dynamic skeletons [12]	SKL	60.2%	65.2%
Part-aware LSTM [27]	SKL	62.9%	70.3%
ST-LSTM [22]	SKL	69.2%	77.7%
GCA-LSTM network [23]	SKL	74.4%	82.8%
Deep multi modal [28]	RGB+DEP+SKL	74.9%	—
MTLN [17]	SKL	79.6%	84.8%
View-adaption LSTM [44]	SKL	79.4%	87.6%
Pose-attention [1]	RGB+SKL	82.5%	88.6%
Deep Bilinear	RGB+DEP	79.2%	81.1%
	RGB+SKL	83.0%	87.1%
	DEP+SKL	83.3%	89.5%
	RGB+DEP+SKL	**85.4%**	**90.7%**

In the following experiments, our deep bilinear learning model is defined as a stack of three bilinear blocks, three Relu layers and one softmax layer, unless stated otherwise. The detailed architecture is modality pooling layer M⟶2M, temporal pooling layer T⟶T/2, modality pooling layer 2M⟶M, temporal pooling layer T/2⟶T/4, Relu, modality pooling layer M⟶1, temporal pooling layer T/4⟶1, Relu, softmax, which is illustrated in Fig. 5. Here modality

[2] The gist images are linearly resized to 224 × 224.

[3] Indeed, we do not observe a significant improvement in the recognition performance by pre-training the network on the imageNet set.

pooling layer 2M⟶M means the layer pools the cube in the modality dimension from 2M to M. T, C, M indicate the temporal length, class number, and modality number, respectively. We empirically found that upscaling the modality dimension can produce better recognition results in our experiments. It might be because that features of different modalities have large variations and upscaling modality dimension can produce meta-modal features with better expressive power, which is in line with the basic idea of developing kernel tricks. The model parameters are initialized by an altered xavier algorithm, where the random weights are produced by an uniformly distribution rather than a Gaussian distribution. We experimentally find that initializing the network in this way can significantly reduce the time of training. Temporal feature maps extracted from AHSs containing 70%–100% of the full sequence (i.e., $|AHS| = 7, 8, 9, 10$) are used to construct the cube descriptor in most of the experiments. The learning rate is initialized as 10^{-3} and it would drop to 10^{-4} after several iterations.

Table 2. Recognition results (accuracies) on the SYSU 3D HOI set. '—' indicates that the performance is not reported in the literature.

Method	Data Used	setting-1	setting-2
HON4D [13,26]	DEP	73.4%	79.2%
HFM [4,13]	RGB+DEP+SKL	75%	76.7%
ST-LSTM [22]	SKL	76.5%	—
View-adaption LSTM [44]	SKL	76.9%	77.5%
MPCCA [3,13]	RGB+DEP+SKL	76.3%	80.7%
MTDA [13,45]	RGB+DEP+SKL	79.2%	84.2%
JOULE [13]	RGB+DEP+SKL	79.6%	84.9%
Deep Bilinear	RGB+DEP	77.2%	83.1%
	RGB+SKL	81.5%	86.2%
	DEP+SKL	82.6%	84.8%
	RGB+DEP+SKL	**84.8%**	**88.9%**

4.2 NTU RGB+D Dataset

The NTU RGB+D dataset was specifically collected for the researches of large scale RGB-D human action recognition. For collecting this set, 40 subjects were asked to perform 60 different actions and the complete action executions were captured from three different views using a Kinect v2. In total, it contains more than 56 K action samples for both training and testing. Compared to most of the existing dataset, this set is very challenging and larger in terms of the number of action classes, views, and samples with large intra-class variations [13,37]. For experiment, we follow exactly the same evaluation settings specified in [22], where two different training-testing splits (i.e. cross-subject and cross-view) are used to evaluate the recognition performances. In the cross-subject setting, the sequences performed by 20 subjects are used to train, and the rest to test. While in the cross-view setting, samples for two views (camera 2 and camera 3) are used as training set, and the other samples form the testing set.

The comparison results are presented in Table 1. As shown, our approach with deep bilinear learning obtains the best results on this set and outperforms the state-of-the-art approaches, such as MTLN [17] and View-adaption LSTM model [44], by a large margin (e.g., $\geq 6\%$ for the cross subject setting). In detail, our method obtains an accuracy of 85.4% and 90.7% for the cross-subject and cross-view setting, respectively. We can observe that even for the cross-view setting, our model can still perform better than all the other competitors, and in particular outperforms the view adaption model [44] by 3.1%, which was specifically designed for recognizing actions across different views. It is interesting to note that our bilinear framework performs better than the model developed in [28] (85.4% vs. 74.9%), which also learns features extracted from RGB, depth, and skeleton by a deep model, however only using full sequences. This demonstrates the efficacy of our bilinear framework, which aims at exploring AHS with partial action executions and of different modalities for action recognition.

We can also observe that even using the temporal feature maps extracted from two of the RGB, depth, and skeleton data, we can still obtain a good performance, which is comparable to the state-of-the-art models, e.g., Pose-attention network. This means that explicitly mining some informative modality-temporal structures with our deep bilinear model is beneficial for recognition. As expected, the performance is largely improved when we fuse all the features together using the proposed deep bilinear learning algorithm. This also indicates that the temporal feature maps extracted from different modality sequences can complement well to each other for obtaining a comprehensive action representation.

4.3 SYSU 3D HOI Set

The SYSU 3D HOI set was collected for studying complex actions with human-object interactions. This set contains 480 samples from 6 pairs of interaction actions including *playing with a cell-phone* and *calling with a cell-phone*, *mopping* and *sweeping* etc. This set is challenging because each pair of the considered interactions contains similar object contexts and interactive motions. For experiments, we employ the two evaluation criterions defined in [14] to test. In the first setting (named setting-1), for each action class, half of the samples are used for training and the rest for testing. The second setting (named setting-2) is a cross-subject setting, where sequences performed by half of the subjects are used to train the model parameters and the rest to test. For each setting, the mean accuracies obtained by 30 random training-testing splits are reported.

We report the results in Table 2. As can be seen, in both settings, our deep bilinear model outperforms the state-of-the-art model JOULE [13], which aims to learn action representation from the full sequences of different modalities. Especially for the setting-1, our method has a performance gain of 4.8%. This indicates that explicitly exploring time-varying information depicted in multiple modality sequences is beneficial for RGB-D action recognition. The same as that on NTU RGB+D set, fusing the multiple modality-temporal cube descriptors can obtain much better performances, which illustrates that the our deep bilinear model can learn a comprehensive action representation from the cubes for characterizing human actions. We can also observe that the RGB-D based models (JOULE [13] and our deep bilinear model) obtain better results than the single modality based methods (e.g. View-adaption LSTM [44], ST-LSTM [22], and HON4D [26]). This is as expected as only using depth or skeleton data is intrinsically limited in overcoming the ambiguity caused by appearance changes, occlusion, cluttered background, etc.

5 Analysis in Depth

Here, we provide more discussions and analysis on the proposed deep bilinear learning method. All the following conclusions are obtained based on the experiments on NTU RGB+D dataset with the challenging cross-subject setting.

Evaluations on the Temporal Modelling. Our deep bilinear model learns dynamics from modality-temporal cubes. Here, we study the influence of the temporal dimension by only using the features corresponding to full sequences. The detailed results are presented in Table 3. As shown, with temporal dynamic modelling, we can see a valuable improvement (about 1.5–3% in the term of accuracy), which demonstrates the efficacy of learning time-varying information among AHSs of varied lengths for action recognition.

Here, we further study the influence of the lengths of the AHSs. We test on the AHSs whose lengths are larger than or equal to $1, 3, 5, 7, 9$, respectively. The results are presented in Table 4. We can observe that our system obtains the best result when the length is larger than or equal to 7. The accuracy would drop when the length goes smaller. This is because the AHSs with small length do not contain enough action context for characterizing actions. Introducing short AHSs could add more noise to the learning.

Comparison with Other Fusion and Bilinear Schemes. Here, we compare our bilinear learning framework with other fusion and bilinear schemes. Specifically, we test different settings in which cube are pooled by max pooling (max),

Table 3. Evaluations on with vs. without temporal modelling.

	RGB	DEP	Skeleton	RGB+DEP+SKL
Without	72.5%	73.1%	69.8%	83.5%
With	75.3%	75.9%	72.5%	85.4%

Table 4. Evaluations on the lengths of AHSs.

AHS lengths	≥1	≥3	≥5	≥7	≥9
Accuracy	84.1%	84.1%	84.3%	85.4%	84.3%

Table 5. Comparison with other fusion schemes, which used our feature netowrks.

Method	max	mean	Linear SVM	FCN	MCB [9]	MKL	Ours
Parameter No.	0	0	72K	6.7M	16K	$\approx$ 72K	115
Accuracy	77.5%	83.0%	83.5%	76.3%	84%	84.1%	85.4%

Table 6. Evaluations on the number of bilinear blocks used in deep bilinear model.

Block number	1	2	3	4	5
Accuracy	83.8%	84.4%	85.4%	85.1%	84.9%

mean pooling (mean), linear SVM, and multi-modal compact bilinear (MCB [9]) models. We also replace the plane-wise connected pooling in our bilinear block (denoted by Ours in Table 5) by the element-wise FCN (see Fig. 4 for details) and compare their performances. The comparison results are presented in Table 5. As can be seen, our model offers distinct advantages over the hard-coded non-learning fusion methods (e.g., max and mean). This is because each layer of block in our model is specifically driven by either modality or temporal variate. Thus our bilinear model offers learning capability towards better fusion. While these hard-coded methods lack this key point. By examining the results obtained by the data-driven fusion schemes (e.g., FCN, linear-SVM, MCB and multi-kernel learning (MKL)), we can see that data-driven fusion can achieve better results than the hard-coded ones. The best result among them is achieved by MKL, with an accuracy of 84.3%, which outperforms all other methods in the table except ours. It is also noted that if we use element-wise FCN to pool cube descriptor instead of the plane-wise one, the performance decreases. This is as expected, as FCN has a large number of parameters to be learned, which makes the model easily fall into over-fitting. And the more parameters the model has, the worse performance is observed. Our method also outperforms the MCB [9] by 1.4%, which pools the features by an out-product bilinear operator without exactly considering the tensor structures in different dimensions. This demonstrates that learning temporal-modality mutual information in an iterative manner with our bilinear model can help to enhance recognition performance.

Effect of Bilinear Depth and Pooling Order. Our deep bilinear is constructed by stacking a set of bilinear blocks and other network layers. Here, we evaluate the influence of the number of bilinear blocks (depth). The results are listed in Table 6. It could be observed that when the number of blocks is small, increasing the depth will increase the performance (e.g., 85.4% vs. 83.8%); when the number gets larger (e.g., larger than 3), performance tends to saturate, being insensitive to the increase of depth. Our method is also not sensitive to the order of fusion. For example, if we fuse the temporal dimension first and then fuse over modality in each bilinear block, the recognition accuracy drops slightly (85.0% vs. 85.4%).

6 Conclusion

We present a novel deep bilinear learning framework to learn modality-temporal information (i.e., time-varying information across varies modalities) for RGB-D action recognition. In the framework, a bilinear block consisting of two linear pooling layers is constructed to extract the mutual information from modality and temporal directions, respectively. Furthermore, we present a new action feature representation to encode the action context in a tensor structure, named modality-temporal cube. Extensive experiments have been reported to demonstrate the efficacy of the proposed framework.

Acknowledgment. This work was supported by the NSFC (U1611461) and NSFC (61702567, 61522115, 61661130157, 61628212). This work was also partially supported by the National Key Research and Development Program of China (2018YFB1004903). The corresponding author for this paper is Wei-Shi Zheng.

References

1. Baradel, F., Wolf, C., Mille, J.: Human action recognition: pose-based attention draws focus to hands. In: International Conference on Computer Vision Workshop (2017)
2. Bobick, A.F., Davis, J.W.: The recognition of human movement using temporal templates. IEEE Trans. Pattern Anal. Mach. Intell. **23**(3), 257–267 (2001)
3. Cai, Z., Wang, L., Peng, X., Qiao, Y.: Multi-view super vector for action recognition. In: International Conference on Computer Vision and Pattern Recognition, pp. 596–603 (2014)
4. Cao, L., Luo, J., Liang, F., Huang, T.S.: Heterogeneous feature machines for visual recognition. In: International Conference on Computer Vision, pp. 1095–1102 (2009)
5. Du, Y., Wang, W., Wang, L.: Hierarchical recurrent neural network for skeleton based action recognition. In: International Conference on Computer Vision and Pattern Recognition, pp. 1110–1118 (2015)
6. Evangelidis, G., Singh, G., Horaud, R.: Skeletal quads: human action recognition using joint quadruples. In: International Conference on Pattern Recognition, pp. 4513–4518 (2014)
7. Fernando, B., Gavves, E., Oramas, J., Ghodrati, A., Tuytelaars, T.: Rank pooling for action recognition. IEEE Trans. Pattern Anal. Mach. Intell. **39**(4), 773–787 (2017)
8. Fernando, B., Gould, S.: Learning end-to-end video classification with rank-pooling. In: International Conference on Machine Learning, pp. 1187–1196 (2016)
9. Fukui, A., Park, D.H., Yang, D., Rohrbach, A., Darrell, T., Rohrbach, M.: Multimodal compact bilinear pooling for visual question answering and visual grounding. arXiv preprint arXiv:1606.01847 (2016)
10. Gao, Y., Beijbom, O., Zhang, N., Darrell, T.: Compact bilinear pooling. In: International Conference on Computer Vision and Pattern Recognition, pp. 317–326 (2016)
11. Gu, Q., Zhou, J.: Learning the shared subspace for multi-task clustering and transductive transfer classification. In: International Conference on Data Mining, pp. 159–168 (2009)

12. Hu, J.F., Zheng, W.S., Lai, J., Zhang, J.: Jointly learning heterogeneous features for RGB-D activity recognition. In: International Conference on Computer Vision and Pattern Recognition, pp. 5344–5352 (2015)
13. Hu, J.F., Zheng, W.S., Lai, J., Zhang, J.: Jointly learning heterogeneous features for RGB-D activity recognition. IEEE Trans. Pattern Anal. Mach. Intell. **39**(11), 2186–2200 (2017)
14. Hu, J.F., Zheng, W.S., Ma, L., Wang, G., Lai, J.: Real-time RGB-D activity prediction by soft regression. In: European Conference on Computer Vision, pp. 280–296 (2016)
15. Hussein, M.E., Torki, M., Gowayyed, M.A., El-Saban, M.: Human action recognition using a temporal hierarchy of covariance descriptors on 3D joint locations. In: International Joint Conferences on Artificial Intelligence, vol. 13, pp. 2466–2472 (2013)
16. Karpathy, A., Toderici, G., Shetty, S., Leung, T., Sukthankar, R., Fei-Fei, L.: Large-scale video classification with convolutional neural networks. In: International Conference on Computer Vision and Pattern Recognition, pp. 1725–1732 (2014)
17. Ke, Q., Bennamoun, M., An, S., Sohel, F., Boussaid, F.: A new representation of skeleton sequences for 3D action recognition. arXiv preprint arXiv:1703.03492 (2017)
18. Klaser, A., Marszałek, M., Schmid, C.: A spatio-temporal descriptor based on 3D-gradients. In: British Machine Vision Conference, p. 275 (2008)
19. Koppula, H.S., Gupta, R., Saxena, A.: Learning human activities and object affordances from RGB-D videos. Int. J. Robot. Res. **32**(8), 951–970 (2013)
20. Lillo, I., Soto, A., Niebles, J.C.: Discriminative hierarchical modeling of spatio-temporally composable human activities. In: International Conference on Computer Vision and Pattern Recognition. pp. 812–819 (2014)
21. Lin, T.Y., RoyChowdhury, A., Maji, S.: Bilinear CNN models for fine-grained visual recognition. In: IEEE International Conference on Computer Vision, pp. 1449–1457 (2015)
22. Liu, J., Shahroudy, A., Xu, D., Wang, G.: Spatio-temporal LSTM with trust gates for 3D human action recognition. In: European Conference on Computer Vision, pp. 816–833 (2016)
23. Liu, J., Wang, G., Hu, P., Duan, L.Y., Kot, A.C.: Global context-aware attention LSTM networks for 3D action recognition. In: International Conference on Computer Vision and Pattern Recognition, pp. 1647–1656 (2017)
24. Lu, C., Jia, J., Tang, C.K.: Range-sample depth feature for action recognition. In: International Conference on Computer Vision and Pattern Recognition, pp. 772–779 (2014)
25. Ofli, F., Chaudhry, R., Kurillo, G., Vidal, R., Bajcsy, R.: Sequence of the most informative joints (SMIJ): a new representation for human skeletal action recognition. J. Vis. Commun. Image Represent. **25**(1), 24–38 (2014)
26. Oreifej, O., Liu, Z.: HON4D: histogram of oriented 4D normals for activity recognition from depth sequences. In: International Conference on Computer Vision and Pattern Recognition, pp. 716–723 (2013)
27. Shahroudy, A., Liu, J., Ng, T.T., Wang, G.: NTU RGB+D: a large scale dataset for 3D human activity analysis. arXiv preprint arXiv:1604.02808 (2016)
28. Shahroudy, A., Ng, T.T., Gong, Y., Wang, G.: Deep multimodal feature analysis for action recognition in RGB+D videos. IEEE Trans. Pattern Anal. Mach. Intell. **27**(3), 305–317 (2017)

29. Shahroudy, A., Ng, T.T., Yang, Q., Wang, G.: Multimodal multipart learning for action recognition in depth videos. IEEE Trans. Pattern Anal. Mach. Intell. **38**(10), 2123–2129 (2016)
30. Shotton, J., Sharp, T., Kipman, A., Fitzgibbon, A., Finocchio, M., Blake, A., Cook, M., Moore, R.: Real-time human pose recognition in parts from single depth images. Commun. ACM **56**(1), 116–124 (2013)
31. Simonyan, K., Zisserman, A.: Two-stream convolutional networks for action recognition in videos. In: Advances in Neural Information Processing Systems, pp. 568–576 (2014)
32. Smisek, J., Jancosek, M., Pajdla, T.: 3D with Kinect. In: Fossati, A., Gall, J., Grabner, H., Ren, X., Konolige, K. (eds.) Consumer Depth Cameras for Computer Vision, pp. 3–25. Springer, Heidelberg (2013). https://doi.org/10.1007/978-1-4471-4640-7_1
33. Vemulapalli, R., Arrate, F., Chellappa, R.: Human action recognition by representing 3D skeletons as points in a lie group. In: Proceedings of the IEEE Conference on Computer Vision and Pattern Recognition, pp. 588–595 (2014)
34. Wang, H., Kläser, A., Schmid, C., Liu, C.L.: Dense trajectories and motion boundary descriptors for action recognition. Int. J. Comput. Vis. **103**(1), 60–79 (2013)
35. Wang, H., Wang, L.: Modeling temporal dynamics and spatial configurations of actions using two-stream recurrent neural networks. arXiv preprint arXiv:1704.02581 (2017)
36. Wang, J., Liu, Z., Chorowski, J., Chen, Z., Wu, Y.: Robust 3D action recognition with random occupancy patterns. In: European Conference on Computer Vision, pp. 872–885 (2012)
37. Wang, J., Liu, Z., Wu, Y., Yuan, J.: Learning actionlet ensemble for 3D human action recognition. IEEE Trans. Pattern Anal. Mach. Intell. **20**(11), 379–385 (2013)
38. Wang, L., et al.: Temporal segment networks: towards good practices for deep action recognition. In: European Conference on Computer Vision (2016)
39. Wei, P., Zhao, Y., Zheng, N., Zhu, S.C.: Modeling 4D human-object interactions for event and object recognition. In: International Conference on Computer Vision, pp. 3272–3279 (2013)
40. Xia, L., Chen, C.C., Aggarwal, J.: View invariant human action recognition using histograms of 3D joints. In: International Conference on Computer Vision and Pattern Recognition, pp. 20–27 (2012)
41. Yang, X., Tian, Y.: EigenJoints-based action recognition using Naive-Bayes-nearest-neighbor. In: International Conference on Computer Vision and Pattern Recognition, pp. 14–19 (2012)
42. Yang, X., Tian, Y.: Super normal vector for activity recognition using depth sequences. In: International Conference on Computer Vision and Pattern Recognition, pp. 804–811 (2014)
43. Zanfir, M., Leordeanu, M., Sminchisescu, C.: The moving pose: an efficient 3D kinematics descriptor for low-latency action recognition and detection. In: International Conference on Computer Vision, pp. 2752–2759 (2013)
44. Zhang, P., Lan, C., Xing, J., Zeng, W., Xue, J., Zheng, N.: View adaptive recurrent neural networks for high performance human action recognition from skeleton data. arXiv preprint arXiv:1703.08274 (2017)
45. Zhang, Y., Yeung, D.Y.: Multi-task learning in heterogeneous feature spaces. In: Conference on Artificial Intelligence (2011)
46. Zhu, Y., Chen, W., Guo, G.: Fusing spatiotemporal features and joints for 3D action recognition. In: International Conference on Computer Vision and Pattern Recognition, pp. 486–491 (2013)

Superpixel Sampling Networks

Varun Jampani[1(✉)], Deqing Sun[1], Ming-Yu Liu[1], Ming-Hsuan Yang[1,2], and Jan Kautz[1]

[1] NVIDIA, Westford, USA
{vjampani,deqings,mingyul,jkautz}@nvidia.com
[2] UC Merced, Merced, USA
mhyang@ucmerced.edu

Abstract. Superpixels provide an efficient low/mid-level representation of image data, which greatly reduces the number of image primitives for subsequent vision tasks. Existing superpixel algorithms are not differentiable, making them difficult to integrate into otherwise end-to-end trainable deep neural networks. We develop a new differentiable model for superpixel sampling that leverages deep networks for learning superpixel segmentation. The resulting *Superpixel Sampling Network* (SSN) is end-to-end trainable, which allows learning task-specific superpixels with flexible loss functions and has fast runtime. Extensive experimental analysis indicates that SSNs not only outperform existing superpixel algorithms on traditional segmentation benchmarks, but can also learn superpixels for other tasks. In addition, SSNs can be easily integrated into downstream deep networks resulting in performance improvements.

Keywords: Superpixels · Deep learning · Clustering

1 Introduction

Superpixels are an over-segmentation of an image that is formed by grouping image pixels [33] based on low-level image properties. They provide a perceptually meaningful tessellation of image content, thereby reducing the number of image primitives for subsequent image processing. Owing to their representational and computational efficiency, superpixels have become an established low/mid-level image representation and are widely-used in computer vision algorithms such as object detection [35,42], semantic segmentation [13,15,34], saliency estimation [18,30,43,46], optical flow estimation [20,28,37,41], depth estimation [6], tracking [44] to name a few. Superpixels are especially widely-used in traditional energy minimization frameworks, where a low number of image primitives greatly reduce the optimization complexity.

The recent years have witnessed a dramatic increase in the adoption of deep learning for a wide range of computer vision problems. With the exception of a

Electronic supplementary material The online version of this chapter (https://doi.org/10.1007/978-3-030-01234-2_22) contains supplementary material, which is available to authorized users.

V. Ferrari et al. (Eds.): ECCV 2018, LNCS 11211, pp. 363–380, 2018.
https://doi.org/10.1007/978-3-030-01234-2_22

few methods (e.g., [13,18,34]), superpixels are scarcely used in conjunction with modern deep networks. There are two main reasons for this. First, the standard convolution operation, which forms the basis of most deep architectures, is usually defined over regular grid lattices and becomes inefficient when operating over irregular superpixel lattices. Second, existing superpixel algorithms are non-differentiable and thus using superpixels in deep networks introduces non-differentiable modules in otherwise end-to-end trainable network architectures.

In this work, we alleviate the second issue by proposing a new deep differentiable algorithm for superpixel segmentation. We start by revisiting the widely-used *Simple Linear Iterative Clustering* (SLIC) superpixel algorithm [1] and turn it into a differentiable algorithm by relaxing the nearest neighbor constraints present in SLIC. This new differentiable algorithm allows for end-to-end training and enables us to leverage powerful deep networks for learning superpixels instead of using traditional hand-crafted features. This combination of a deep network with differentiable SLIC forms our end-to-end trainable superpixel algorithm which we call *Superpixel Sampling Network* (SSN). Figure 1 shows an overview of the proposed SSN. A given input image is first passed through a deep network producing features at each pixel. These deep features are then passed onto the differentiable SLIC, which performs iterative clustering, resulting in the desired superpixels. The entire network is end-to-end trainable. The differentiable nature of SSN allows the use of flexible loss functions for learning task-specific superpixels. Figure 1 shows some sample SSN generated superpixels.

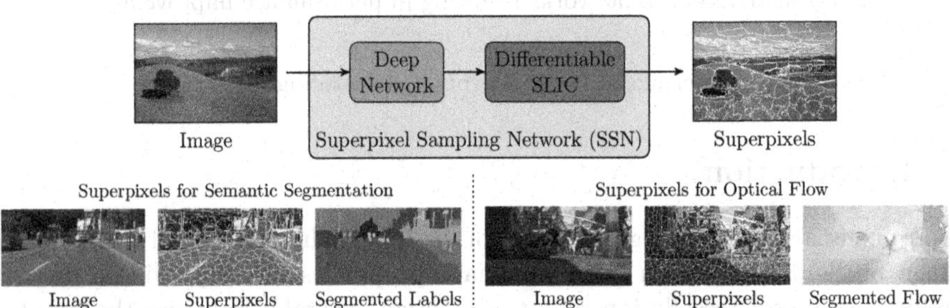

Fig. 1. Overview of Superpixel Sampling Networks. A given image is first passed onto a deep network that extracts features at each pixel, which are then used by differentiable SLIC to generate the superpixels. Shown here are a couple of example SSN generated task-specific superpixels for semantic segmentation and optical flow.

Experimental results on 3 different segmentation benchmark datasets including BSDS500 [4], Cityscapes [10] and PascalVOC [11] indicate that the proposed superpixel sampling network (SSN) performs favourably against existing prominent superpixel algorithms, while also being faster. We also demonstrate that by simply integrating our SSN framework into an existing semantic segmentation network [13] that uses superpixels, performance improvements are achieved. In addition, we demonstrate the flexibility of SSN in learning superpixels for other vision tasks. Specifically, in a proof-of-concept experiment on the Sintel optical flow dataset [7], we demonstrate how we can learn superpixels that better align with optical flow boundaries rather than standard object boundaries. The proposed SSN has the following favorable properties in comparison to existing superpixel algorithms:

- **End-to-end trainable:** SSNs are end-to-end trainable and can be easily integrated into other deep network architectures.
  To the best of our knowledge, this is the first end-to-end trainable superpixel algorithm.
- **Flexible and task-specific:** SSN allows for learning with flexible loss functions resulting in the learning of task-specific superpixels.
- **State-of-the-art performance:** Experiments on a wide range of benchmark datasets show that SSN outperforms existing superpixel algorithms.
- **Favorable runtime:** SSN also performs favorably against prominent superpixel algorithms in terms of runtime, making it amenable to learn on large datasets and also effective for practical applications.

2 Related Work

Superpixel Algorithms. Traditional superpixel algorithms can be broadly classified into graph-based and clustering-based approaches. Graph-based approaches formulate the superpixel segmentation as a graph-partitioning problem where graph nodes are represented by pixels and the edges denote the strength of connectivity between adjacent pixels. Usually, the graph partitioning is performed by solving a discrete optimization problem. Some widely-used algorithms in this category include the normalized-cuts [33], Felzenszwalb and Huttenlocher (FH) [12], and the entropy rate superpixels (ERS) [26]. As discrete optimization involves discrete variables, the optimization objectives are usually non-differentiable making it difficult to leverage deep networks in graph-based approaches.

Clustering-based approaches, on the other hand, leverage traditional clustering techniques such as k-means for superpixel segmentation. Widely-used algorithms in this category include SLIC [1], LSC [25], and Manifold-SLIC [27]. These methods mainly do k-means clustering but differ in their feature representation. While the SLIC [1] represents each pixel as a 5-dimensional positional and *Lab* color features (*XYLab* features), LSC [25] method projects these 5-dimensional features on to a 10-dimensional space and performs clustering in the projected space. Manifold-SLIC [27], on the other hand, uses a 2-dimensional manifold feature space for superpixel clustering. While these clustering algorithms require iterative updates, a non-iterative clustering scheme for superpixel segmentation is proposed in the SNIC method [2]. The proposed approach is also a clustering-based approach. However, unlike existing techniques, we leverage deep networks to learn features for superpixel clustering via an end-to-end training framework.

As detailed in a recent survey paper [36], other techniques are used for superpixel segmentation, including watershed transform [29], geometric flows [24], graph-cuts [39], mean-shift [9], and hill-climbing [5]. However, these methods all rely on hand-crafted features and it is non-trivial to incorporate deep networks into these techniques. A very recent technique of SEAL [38] proposed a way to learn deep features for superpixel segmentation by bypassing the gradients through non-differentiable superpixel algorithms. Unlike our SSN framework, SEAL is not end-to-end differentiable.

Deep Clustering. Inspired by the success of deep learning for supervised tasks, several methods investigate the use of deep networks for unsupervised data clustering. Recently, Greff *et al.* [17] propose the neural expectation maximization framework where they model the posterior distribution of cluster labels using deep networks and unroll the iterative steps in the EM procedure for end-to-end training. In another work [16], the Ladder network [31] is used to model a hierarchical latent variable model for clustering. Hershey *et al.* [19] propose a deep learning-based clustering framework for separating and segmenting audio signals. Xie *et al.* [40] propose a deep embedded clustering framework, for simultaneously learning feature representations and cluster assignments. In a recent survey paper, Aljalbout *et al.* [3] give a taxonomy of deep learning based clustering methods. In this paper, we also propose a deep learning-based clustering algorithm. Different from the prior work, our algorithm is tailored for the superpixel segmentation task where we use image-specific constraints. Moreover, our framework can easily incorporate other vision objective functions for learning task-specific superpixel representations.

3 Preliminaries

At the core of SSN is a differentiable clustering technique that is inspired by the SLIC [1] superpixel algorithm. Here, we briefly review the SLIC before describing our SSN technique in the next section. SLIC is one of the simplest and also one of the most widely-used superpixel algorithms. It is easy to implement, has fast runtime and also produces compact and uniform superpixels.

Although there are several different variants [25,27] of SLIC algorithm, in the original form, SLIC is a k-means clustering performed on image pixels in a five dimensional position and color space (usually scaled $XYLab$ space). Formally, given an image $I \in \mathbb{R}^{n \times 5}$, with 5-dimensional $XYLab$ features at n pixels, the task of superpixel computation is to assign each pixel to one of the m superpixels i.e., to compute the pixel-superpixel association map $H \in \{0, 1, \cdots, m-1\}^{n \times 1}$. The SLIC algorithm operates as follows. First, we sample initial cluster (superpixel) centers $S^0 \in \mathbb{R}^{m \times 5}$ in the 5-dimensional space. This sampling is usually done uniformly across the pixel grid with some local perturbations based on image gradients. Given these initial superpixel centers S^0, the SLIC algorithm proceeds in an iterative manner with the following two steps in each iteration t:

1. *Pixel-Superpixel association*: Associate each pixel to the nearest superpixel center in the five-dimensional space, i.e., compute the new superpixel assignment at each pixel p,

$$H_p^t = \underset{i \in \{0,\dots,m-1\}}{\arg\min} D(I_p, S_i^{t-1}), \tag{1}$$

where D denotes the distance computation $D(\mathbf{a}, \mathbf{b}) = ||\mathbf{a} - \mathbf{b}||^2$.

2. *Superpixel center update*: Average pixel features ($XYLab$) inside each superpixel cluster to obtain new superpixel cluster centers S^t. For each superpixel i, we compute the centroid of that cluster,

$$S_i^t = \frac{1}{Z_i^t} \sum_{p|H_p^t=i} I_p, \tag{2}$$

where Z_i^t denotes the number of pixels in the superpixel cluster i.

These two steps form the core of the SLIC algorithm and are repeated until either convergence or for a fixed number of iterations. Since computing the distance D in Eq. 1 between all the pixels and superpixels is time-consuming, this computation is usually constrained to a fixed neighborhood around each superpixel center. At the end, depending on the application, there is an optional step of enforcing spatial connectivity across pixels in each superpixel cluster. More details regarding the SLIC algorithm can be found in Achanta *et al.* [1]. In the next section, we elucidate how we modify the SLIC algorithm to develop SSN.

4 Superpixel Sampling Networks

As illustrated in Fig. 1, SSN is composed of two parts: A deep network that generates pixel features, which are then passed on to differentiable SLIC. Here, we first describe the differentiable SLIC followed by the SSN architecture.

4.1 Differentiable SLIC

Why is SLIC not differentiable? A closer look at all the computations in SLIC shows that the non-differentiability arises because of the computation of pixel-superpixel associations, which involves a non-differentiable nearest neighbor operation. This nearest neighbor computation also forms the core of the SLIC superpixel clustering and thus we cannot avoid this operation.

A key to our approach is to convert the nearest-neighbor operation into a differentiable one. Instead of computing hard pixel-superpixel associations $H \in \{0, 1, \cdots, m-1\}^{n \times 1}$ (in Eq. 1), we propose to compute soft-associations $Q \in \mathbb{R}^{n \times m}$ between pixels and superpixels. Specifically, for a pixel p and superpixel i at iteration t, we replace the nearest-neighbor computation (Eq. 1) in SLIC with the following pixel-superpixel association.

$$Q_{pi}^t = e^{-D(I_p, S_i^{t-1})} = e^{-||I_p - S_i^{t-1}||^2} \tag{3}$$

Correspondingly, the computation of new superpixels cluster centers (Eq. 2) is modified as the weighted sum of pixel features,

$$S_i^t = \frac{1}{Z_i^t} \sum_{p=1}^{n} Q_{pi}^t I_p, \tag{4}$$

where $Z_i^t = \sum_p Q_{pi}^t$ is the normalization constant. For convenience, we refer to the column normalized Q^t as $\hat{Q}^t$ and thus we can write the above superpixel center update as $S^t = \hat{Q}^{t\top} I$. The size of Q is $n \times m$ and even for a small number of superpixels m, it is prohibitively expensive to compute Q_{pi} between all the pixels and superpixels. Therefore, we constrain the distance computations from each pixel to only 9 surrounding superpixels as illustrated using the red and green boxes in Fig. 2. For each pixel in the green box, only the surrounding superpixels in the red box are considered for computing the association. This brings down the size of Q from $n \times m$ to $n \times 9$, making it efficient in terms of both computation and memory. This approximation in the Q computation is similar in spirit to the approximate nearest-neighbor search in SLIC.

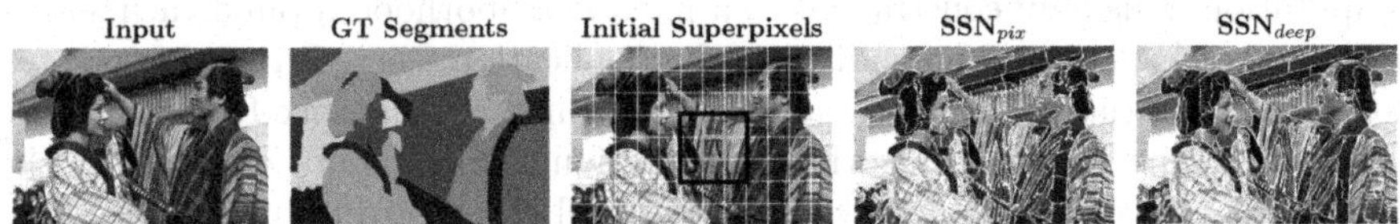

Fig. 2. From initial grid to learned superpixels. An example visual result from BSDS500 dataset showing the initial superpixel grid and the superpixels obtained with SSN$_{pix}$ and SSN$_{deep}$. To compute the pixel-superpixel associations for every pixel in the green box, only the surrounding superpixels in the red box are considered.

Now, both the computations in each SLIC iteration are completely differentiable and we refer to this modified algorithm as *differentiable SLIC*. Empirically, we observe that replacing the hard pixel-superpixel associations in SLIC with the soft ones in differentiable SLIC does not result in any performance degradations. Since this new superpixel algorithm is differentiable, it can be easily integrated into any deep network architecture. Instead of using manually designed pixel

Algorithm 1. Superpixel Sampling Network (SSN)

Input: Image $\underset{n\times 5}{I}$. ▷ *XYLab* features

Output: Pixel-Superpixel association $\underset{n\times m}{Q}$.

Pixel features using a CNN, $\underset{n\times k}{F} = \mathcal{F}(I)$.

Initial superpixel centers with average features in regular grid cells, $\underset{m\times k}{S^0} = \mathcal{J}(F)$.

for each iteration t in 1 to v **do**

  Compute association between each pixel p and the surrounding superpixel i, $Q_{pi}^t = e^{-||F_p - S_i^{t-1}||^2}$.

  Compute new superpixel centers, $S_i^t = \frac{1}{Z_i^t}\sum_{p=1}^n Q_{pi}^t F_p$; $Z_i^t = \sum_p Q_{pi}^t$.

end for

(*Optional*) Compute hard-associations $\underset{n\times 1}{H^v}$; $H_p^v = \underset{i\in\{0,\ldots,m-1\}}{\arg\max}\ Q_{pi}^v$.

(*Optional*) Enforce spatial connectivity.

features I_p, we can leverage deep feature extractors and train the whole network end-to-end. In other words, we replace the image features I_p in the above computations (Eqs. 3 and 4) with k dimensional pixel features $F_p \in \mathbb{R}^{n \times k}$ computed using a deep network. We refer to this coupling of deep networks with the differentiable SLIC as *Superpixel Sampling Network* (SSN).

Algorithm 1 outlines all the computation steps in SSN. The algorithm starts with deep image feature extraction using a CNN (line 1). We initialize the superpixel cluster centers (line 2) with the average pixels features in an initial regular superpixel grid (Fig. 2). Then, for v iterations, we iteratively update pixel-superpixel associations and superpixel centers, using the above-mentioned computations (lines 3–6). Although one could directly use soft pixel-superpixel associations Q for several downstream tasks, there is an optional step of converting soft associations to hard ones (line 7), depending on the application needs. In addition, like in the original SLIC algorithm, we can optionally enforce spatial connectivity across pixels inside each superpixel cluster. This is accomplished by merging the superpixels, smaller than certain threshold, with the surrounding ones and then assigning a unique cluster ID for each spatially-connected component. Note that these two optional steps (lines 7, 8) are not differentiable.

Mapping between pixel and superpixel representations. For some downstream applications that use superpixels, pixel representations are mapped onto superpixel representations and vice versa. With the traditional superpixel algorithms, which provide hard clusters, this mapping from pixel to superpixel representations is done via averaging inside each cluster (Eq. 2). The inverse mapping from superpixel to pixel representations is done by assigning the same superpixel feature to all the pixels belonging to that superpixel. We can use the same pixel-superpixel mappings with SSN superpixels as well, using the hard clusters (line 7 in Algorithm 1) obtained from SSN. However, since this computation of hard-associations is not differentiable, it may not be desirable to use hard clusters when integrating into an end-to-end trainable system. It is worth noting that the soft pixel-superpixel associations generated by SSN can also be easily used for mapping between pixel and superpixel representations. Equation 4 already describes the mapping from a pixel to superpixel representation which is a simple matrix multiplication with the transpose of column-normalized Q matrix: $S = \hat{Q}^\top F$, where F and S denote pixel and superpixel representations respectively. The inverse mapping from superpixel to pixel representation is done by multiplying the row-normalized Q, denoted as $\tilde{Q}$, with the superpixel representations, $F = \tilde{Q}S$. Thus the pixel-superpixel feature mappings are given as simple matrix multiplications with the association matrix and are differentiable. Later, we will make use of these mappings in designing the loss functions to train SSN.

4.2 Network Architecture

Figure 3 shows the SSN network architecture. The CNN for feature extraction is composed of a series of convolution layers interleaved with batch normalization [21] (BN) and ReLU activations. We use max-pooling, which downsamples

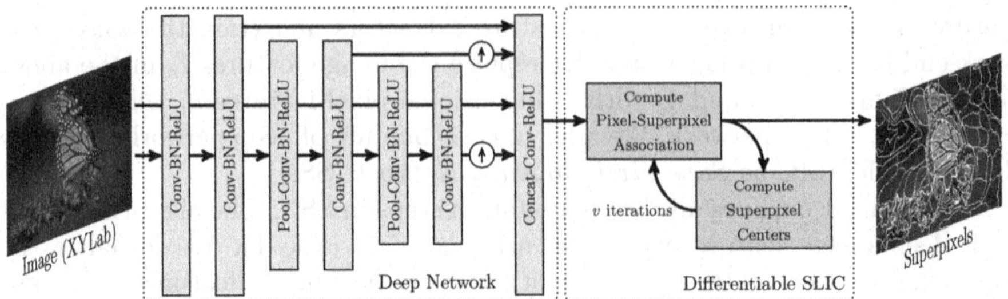

Fig. 3. Computation flow of SSN. Our network is composed of a series of convolution layers interleaved with Batch Norm (BN) and ReLU nonlinearities. $\uparrow$ denotes bilinear upsampling to the original image resolution. The features from CNNs are then passed onto iterative updates in the differentiable SLIC to generate superpixels.

the input by a factor of 2, after the 2nd and 4th convolution layers to increase the receptive field. We bilinearly upsample the 4th and 6th convolution layer outputs and then concatenate with the 2nd convolution layer output to pass onto the final convolution layer. We use 3×3 convolution filters with the number of output channels set to 64 in each layer, except the last CNN layer which outputs $k - 5$ channels. We concatenate this $k - 5$ channel output with the $XYLab$ of the given image resulting in k-dimensional pixel features. We choose this CNN architecture for its simplicity and efficiency. Other network architectures are conceivable. The resulting k dimensional features are passed onto the two modules of differentiable SLIC that iteratively updates pixel-superpixel associations and superpixel centers for v iterations. The entire network is end-to-end trainable.

4.3 Learning Task-Specific Superpixels

One of the main advantages of end-to-end trainable SSN is the flexibility in terms of loss functions, which we can use to learn task-specific superpixels. Like in any CNN, we can couple SSN with any task-specific loss function resulting in the learning of superpixels that are optimized for downstream computer vision tasks. In this work, we focus on optimizing the representational efficiency of superpixels i.e., learning superpixels that can efficiently represent a scene characteristic such as semantic labels, optical flow, depth etc. As an example, if we want to learn superpixels that are going to be used for downstream semantic segmentation task, it is desirable to produce superpixels that adhere to semantic boundaries. To optimize for representational efficiency, we find that the combination of a task-specific reconstruction loss and a compactness loss performs well.

Task-Specific Reconstruction Loss. We denote the pixel properties that we want to represent efficiently with superpixels as $R \in \mathbb{R}^{n \times l}$. For instance, R can be semantic label (as one-hot encoding) or optical flow maps. It is important to note that we do not have access to R during the test time, i.e., SSN predicts superpixels only using image data. We only use R during training so that SSN can learn to predict superpixels suitable to represent R. As mentioned previously in Sect. 4.1, we can map the pixel properties onto superpixels using the column-normalized association matrix $\hat{Q}$, $\breve{R} = \hat{Q}^\top R$, where $\breve{R} \in \mathbb{R}^{m \times l}$. The resulting superpixel representation $\breve{R}$ is then mapped back onto pixel representation R^* using row-normalized association matrix $\tilde{Q}$, $R^* = \tilde{Q}S$, where $R^* \in \mathbb{R}^{n \times l}$. Then the reconstruction loss is given as

$$L_{recon} = \mathcal{L}(R, R^*) = \mathcal{L}(R, \tilde{Q}\hat{Q}^\top R) \tag{5}$$

where $\mathcal{L}(.,.)$ denotes a task-specific loss-function. In this work, for segmentation tasks, we used cross-entropy loss for $\mathcal{L}$ and used L1-norm for learning superpixels for optical flow. Here Q denotes the association matrix Q^v after the final iteration of differentiable SLIC. We omit v for convenience.

Compactness Loss. In addition to the above loss, we also use a compactness loss to encourage superpixels to be spatially compact i.e., to have lower spatial variance inside each superpixel cluster. Let I^{xy} denote positional pixel features. We first map these positional features into our superpixel representation, $S^{xy} = \hat{Q}^\top I^{xy}$. Then, we do the inverse mapping onto the pixel representation using the hard associations H, instead of soft associations Q, by assigning the same superpixel positional feature to all the pixels belonging to that superpixel, $\bar{I}^{xy}_p = S^{xy}_i | H_p = i$. The compactness loss is defined as the following L2 norm:

$$L_{compact} = ||I^{xy} - \bar{I}^{xy}||_2. \tag{6}$$

This loss encourages superpixels to have lower spatial variance. The flexibility of SSN allows using many other loss functions, which makes for interesting future research. The overall loss we use in this work is a combination of these two loss functions, $L = L_{recon} + \lambda L_{compact}$, where we set λ to 10^{-5} in all our experiments.

4.4 Implementation and Experiment Protocols

We implement the differentiable SLIC as neural network layers using CUDA in the Caffe neural network framework [22]. All the experiments are performed using Caffe with the Python interface. We use scaled *XYLab* features as input to the SSN, with position and color feature scales represented as γ_{pos} and γ_{color} respectively. The value of γ_{color} is independent of the number of superpixels and is set to 0.26 with color values ranging between 0 and 255. The value of γ_{pos} depends on the number of superpixels, $\gamma_{pos} = \eta \max(m_w/n_w, m_h/n_h)$, where m_w, n_w and m_h, n_h denotes the number of superpixels and pixels along the image width and height respectively. In practice, we observe that $\eta = 2.5$ performs well.

For training, we use image patches of size 201×201 and 100 superpixels. In terms of data augmentation, we use left-right flips and for the small BSDS500 dataset [4], we use an additional data augmentation of random scaling of image patches. For all the experiments, we use Adam stochastic optimization [23] with a batch size of 8 and a learning rate of 0.0001. Unless otherwise mentioned, we trained the models for 500 K iterations and choose the final trained models based on validation accuracy. For the ablation studies, we trained models with varying parameters for 200 K iterations. It is important to note that we use a single trained SSN model for estimating varying number of superpixels by scaling the input positional features as described above. We use 5 iterations ($v = 5$) of differentiable SLIC for training and used 10 iterations while testing as we observed only marginal performance gains with more iterations. Refer to https://varunjampani.github.io/ssn/ for the code and trained models.

5 Experiments

We conduct experiments on 4 different benchmark datasets. We first demonstrate the use of learned superpixels with experiments on the prominent superpixel benchmark BSDS500 [4] (Sect. 5.1). We then demonstrate the use of task-specific superpixels on the Cityscapes [10] and PascalVOC [11] datasets for semantic segmentation (Sect. 5.2), and on MPI-Sintel [7] dataset for optical flow (Sect. 5.3). In addition, we demonstrate the use of SSN superpixels in a downstream semantic segmentation network that uses superpixels (Sect. 5.2).

5.1 Learned Superpixels

We perform ablation studies and evaluate against other superpixel techniques on the BSDS500 benchmark dataset [4]. BSDS500 consists of 200 train, 100 validation, and 200 test images. Each image is annotated with ground-truth (GT) segments from multiple annotators. We treat each annotation as a separate sample resulting in 1633 training/validation pairs and 1063 testing pairs.

In order to learn superpixels that adhere to GT segments, we use GT segment labels in the reconstruction loss (Eq. 5). Specifically, we represent GT segments in each image as one-hot encoding vectors and use that as pixel properties R in the reconstruction loss. We use the cross-entropy loss for $\mathcal{L}$ in Eq. 5. Note that, unlike in the semantic segmentation task where the GT labels have meaning, GT segments in this dataset do not carry any semantic meaning. This does not pose any issue to our learning setup as both the SSN and reconstruction loss are agnostic to the meaning of pixel properties R. The reconstruction loss generates a loss value using the given input signal R and its reconstructed version R^* and does not consider whether the meaning of R is preserved across images.

Evaluation Metrics. Superpixels are useful in a wide range of vision tasks and several metrics exist for evaluating superpixels. In this work, we consider Achievable Segmentation Accuracy (ASA) as our primary metric while also reporting boundary metrics such as Boundary Recall (BR) and Boundary Precision (BP) metrics. ASA score represents the upper bound on the accuracy achievable by any segmentation step performed on the superpixels. Boundary precision and recall on the other hand measures how well the superpixel boundaries align with the GT boundaries. We explain these metrics in more detail in the supplementary material. The higher these scores, the better is the segmentation result. We report the average ASA and boundary metrics by varying the average number of generated superpixels. A fair evaluation of boundary precision and recall expects superpixels to be spatially connected. Thus, for the sake of unbiased comparisons, we follow the optional post-processing of computing hard clusters and enforcing spatial connectivity (lines 7–8 in Algorithm 1) on SSN superpixels.

Ablation Studies. We refer to our main model illustrated in Fig. 3, with 7 convolution layers in deep network, as SSN_{deep}. As a baseline model, we evaluate the superpixels generated with differentiable SLIC that takes pixel $XYLab$ features as input. This is similar to standard SLIC algorithm, which we refer to as SSN_{pix} and has no trainable parameters. As an another baseline model, we replaced the deep network with a single convolution layer that learns to linearly transform input $XYLab$ features, which we refer to as SSN_{linear}.

Figure 4 shows the average ASA and BR scores for these different models with varying feature dimensionality k and the number of iterations v in differentiable SLIC. The ASA and BR of SSN_{linear} is already reliably higher than the baseline SSN_{pix} showing the importance of our loss functions and back-propagating the loss signal through the superpixel algorithm. SSN_{deep} further improves ASA and BR scores by a large margin. We observe slightly better scores with higher feature dimensionality k and also more iterations v. For computational reasons, we choose $k = 20$ and $v = 10$ and from here on refer to this model as SSN_{deep}.

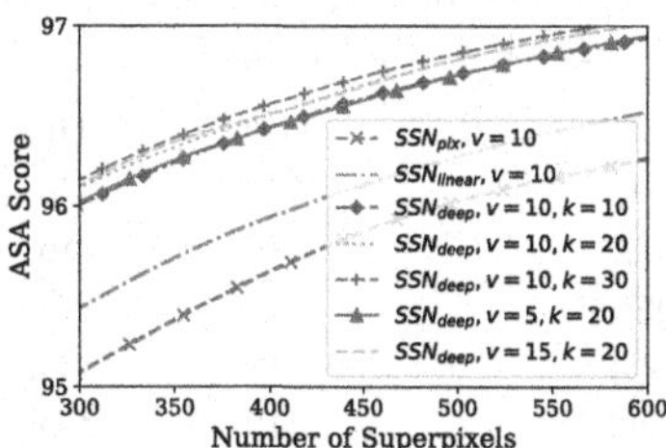

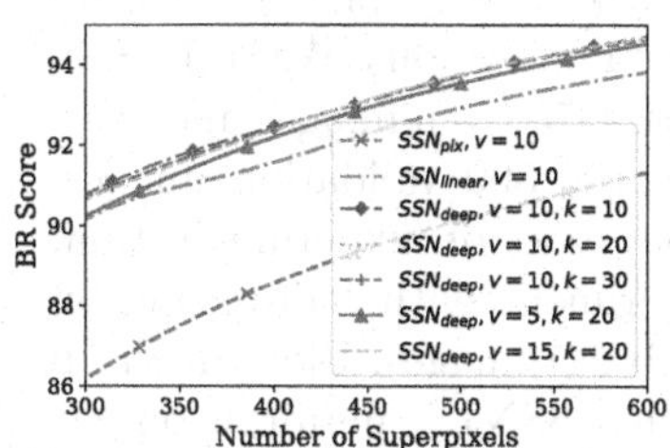

Fig. 4. Ablation studies on BSDS500. Results on the test set show that both the ASA and BR scores considerably improve with deep network, and marginally improve with higher number of feature dimensions k and differentiable SLIC iterations v.

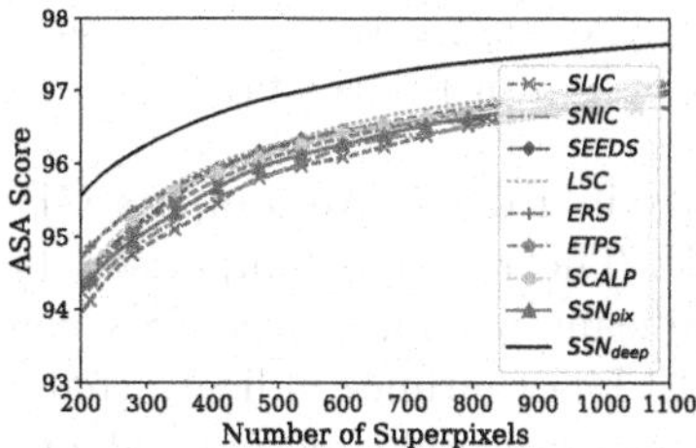

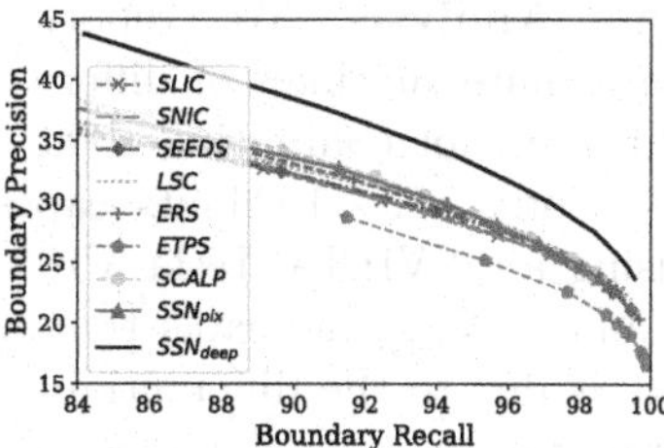

Fig. 5. Results on BSDS500 test. SSN performs favourably against other techniques in terms of both ASA score and boundary precision-recall.

Comparison with the state-of-the-arts. Fig. 5 shows the ASA and precision-recall comparison of SSN with state-of-the-art superpixel algorithms.

We compare with the following prominent algorithms: SLIC [1], SNIC [2], SEEDS [5], LSC [25], ERS [26], ETPS [45] and SCALP [14]. Plots indicate that SSN_{pix} performs similarly to SLIC superpixels, showing that the performance of SLIC does not drop when relaxing the nearest neighbor constraints. Comparison with other techniques indicate that SSN performs considerably better in terms of both ASA score and precision-recall. Figure 2 shows a visual result comparing SSN_{pix} and SSN_{deep} and, Fig. 7 shows visual results comparing SSN_{deep} with state-of-the-arts. Notice that SSN_{deep} superpixels smoothly follow object boundaries and are also more concentrated near the object boundaries.

5.2 Superpixels for Semantic Segmentation

In this section, we present results on the semantic segmentation benchmarks of Cityscapes [10] and PascalVOC [11]. The experimental settings are quite similar to that of the previous section with the only difference being the use of semantic labels as the pixel properties R in the reconstruction loss. Thus, we encourage SSN to learn superpixels that adhere to semantic segments.

Cityscapes. Cityscapes is a large scale urban scene understanding benchmark with pixel accurate semantic annotations. We train SSN with the 2975 train images and evaluate on the 500 validation images. For the ease of experimentation, we experiment with half-resolution (512 × 1024) images. Plots in Fig. 6 shows that SSN_{deep} performs on par with SEAL [38] superpixels in terms of ASA while being better in terms of precision-recall. We show a visual result in Fig. 7 with more in the supplementary.

Table 1. Runtime Analysis. Average runtime (in ms) of different superpixel techniques, for computing 1000 superpixels on a 512 × 1024 cityscapes image.

Model	GPU/CPU	Time (ms)
SLIC [1]	CPU	350
SNIC [2]	CPU	810
SEEDS [5]	CPU	160
LSC [25]	CPU	1240
ERS [26]	CPU	4600
SEAL-ERS [38]	GPU-CPU	4610
GSLICR [32]	GPU	10
SSN models		
SSN_{pix}, v = 10	GPU	58
SSN_{deep}, v = 5, k = 10	GPU	71
SSN_{deep}, v = 10, k = 10	GPU	90
SSN_{deep}, v = 5, k = 20	GPU	80
SSN_{deep}, v = 10, k = 20	GPU	101

Runtime Analysis. We report the approximate runtimes of different techniques, for computing 1000 superpixels on a 512 × 1024 cityscapes image in Table 1. We compute GPU runtimes using an NVIDIA Tesla V100 GPU. The runtime comparison between SSN_{pix} and SSN_{deep} indicates that a significant portion of the SSN computation time is due to the differentiable SLIC. The runtimes indicate that SSN is considerably faster than the implementations of several superpixel algorithms.

PascalVOC. PascalVOC2012 [11] is another widely-used semantic segmentation benchmark, where we train SSN with 1464 train images and validate on 1449 validation images. Figure 8(a) shows the ASA scores for different techniques. We do not analyze boundary scores on this dataset as the GT semantic boundaries are dilated with an ignore label. The ASA scores indicate that SSN_{deep}

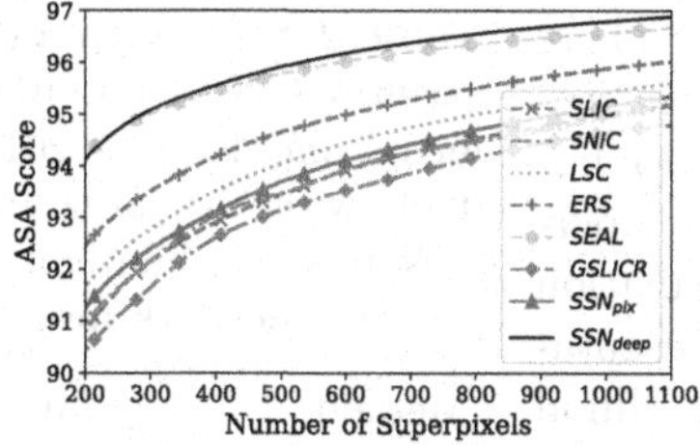

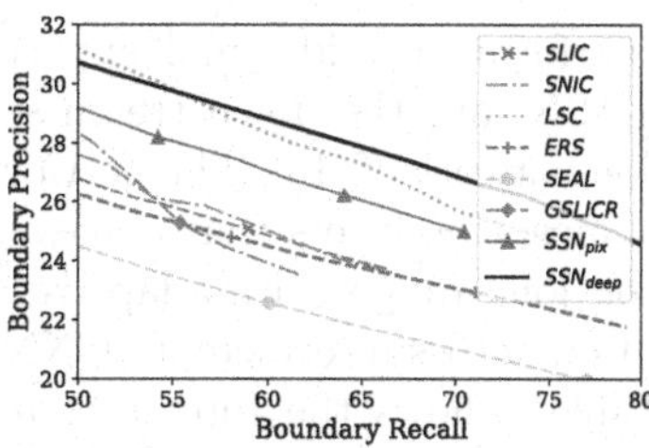

Fig. 6. Results on Cityscapes validation. ASA and boundary precision-recall shows that SSN performs favourably against other techniques.

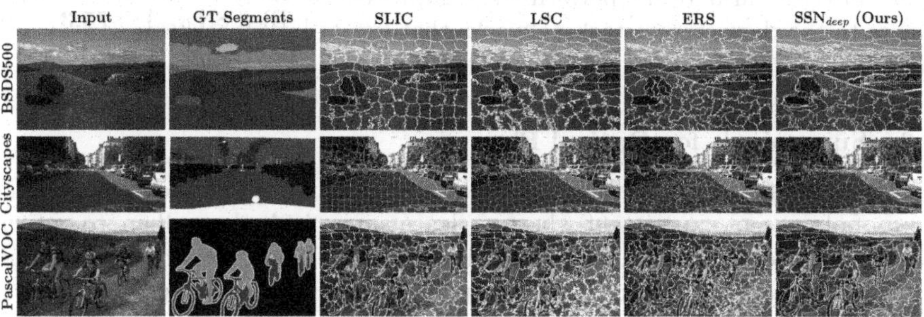

Fig. 7. Example visual results on different segmentation benchmarks. Notice the segregation of SSN_{deep} superpixels around object boundaries.

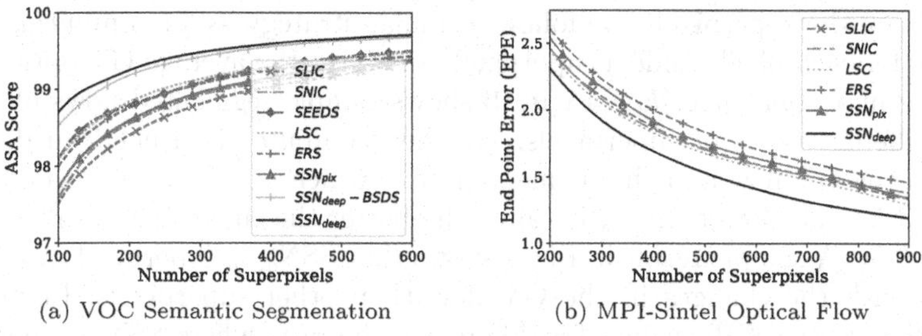

Fig. 8. Learning task-specific superpixels. (a) ASA scores on PascalVOC2012 validation dataset and (b) EPE scores on Sintel optical flow validation dataset showing the robustness of SSN across different tasks and datasets.

outperforms other techniques. We also evaluated the BSDS-trained model on this dataset and observed only a marginal drop in accuracy ('SSN_{deep}-BSDS' in Fig. 8(a)). This shows the generalization and robustness of SSN to different datasets. An example visual result is shown in Fig. 7 with more in the supplementary.

We perform an additional experiment where we plug SSN into the downstream semantic segmentation network of [13], The network in [13] has bilateral inception layers that makes use of superpixels for long-range data-adaptive information propagation across intermediate CNN representations. Table 2 shows the Intersection over Union (IoU) score for this joint model evaluated on the test data. The improvements in IoU with respect to original SLIC superpixels used in [13] shows that SSN can also bring performance improvements to the downstream task networks that use superpixels.

Table 2. SSN with a downstream CNN. IoU improvements, on the VOC2012 test data, with the integration of SSN into the bilateral inception (BI) network from [13].

Method	IoU
DeepLab [8]	68.9
+ CRF [8]	72.7
+ BI (SLIC) [13]	74.1
+ BI (SSN_{deep})	**75.3**

5.3 Superpixels for Optical Flow

To demonstrate the applicability of SSN for regression tasks as well, we conduct a proof-of-concept experiment where we learn superpixels that adhere to optical flow boundaries. To this end, we experiment on the MPI-Sintel dataset [7] and use SSN to predict superpixels given a pair of input frames. We use GT optical flow as pixel properties R in the reconstruction loss (Eq. 5) and use L1 loss for $\mathcal{L}$, encouraging SSN to generate superpixels that can effectively represent flow.

The MPI-Sintel dataset consists of 23 video sequences, which we split into disjoint sets of 18 (836 frames) training and 5 (205 frames) validation sequences. To evaluate the superpixels, we follow a similar strategy as for computing ASA. That is, for each pixel inside a superpixel, we assign the average GT optical flow resulting in a *segmented flow*. Figure 9 shows sample segmented flows obtained using different types of superpixels. We then compute the Euclidean distance between the GT flow and the segmented flow, which is referred to as end-point error (EPE). The lower the EPE value, the better the superpixels are for representing flow. A sample result in Fig. 9 shows that SSN_{deep} superpixels are better aligned with the changes in the GT flow than other superpixels. Figure 8(b) shows the average EPE values for different techniques where SSN_{deep} performs favourably against existing superpixel techniques. This shows the usefulness of SSN in learning task-specific superpixels.

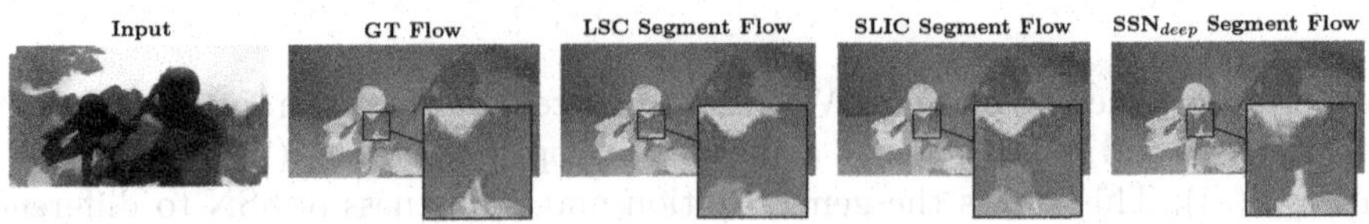

Fig. 9. Sample visual result on Sintel optical flow. Segmented flow visuals obtained with different types of superpixels indicate that SSN_{deep} superpixels can better represent GT optical flow compared to other techniques.

6 Conclusion

We propose a novel superpixel sampling network (SSN) that leverages deep features learned via end-to-end training for estimating task-specific superpixels. To our knowledge, this is the first deep superpixel prediction technique that is end-to-end trainable. Experiments several benchmarks show that SSN consistently performs favorably against state-of-the-art superpixel techniques, while also being faster. Integration of SSN into a semantic segmentation network [13] also results in performance improvements showing the usefulness of SSN in downstream computer vision tasks. SSN is fast, easy to implement, can be easily integrated into other deep networks and has good empirical performance.

SSN has addressed one of the main hurdles for incorporating superpixels into deep networks which is the non-differentiable nature of existing superpixel algorithms. The use of superpixels inside deep networks can have several advantages. Superpixels can reduce the computational complexity, especially when processing high-resolution images. Superpixels can also be used to enforce piece-wise constant assumptions and also help in long-range information propagation [13]. We believe this work opens up new avenues in leveraging superpixels inside deep networks and also inspires new deep learning techniques that use superpixels.

Acknowledgments. We thank Wei-Chih Tu for providing evaluation scripts. We thank Ben Eckart for his help in the supplementary video.

References

1. Achanta, R., Shaji, A., Smith, K., Lucchi, A., Fua, P., Süsstrunk, S.: SLIC superpixels compared to state-of-the-art superpixel methods. IEEE Trans. Pattern Anal. Mach. Intell. (TPAMI) **34**(11), 2274–2282 (2012)
2. Achanta, R., Susstrunk, S.: Superpixels and polygons using simple non-iterative clustering. In: IEEE Conference on Computer Vision and Pattern Recognition (CVPR) (2017)
3. Aljalbout, E., Golkov, V., Siddiqui, Y., Cremers, D.: Clustering with deep learning: taxonomy and new methods. arXiv preprint arXiv:1801.07648 (2018)
4. Arbelaez, P., Maire, M., Fowlkes, C., Malik, J.: Contour detection and hierarchical image segmentation. IEEE Trans. Pattern Anal. Mach. Intell. (TPAMI) **33**(5), 898–916 (2011)
5. Van den Bergh, M., Boix, X., Roig, G., Van Gool, L.: SEEDS: superpixels extracted via energy-driven sampling. Int. J. Comput. Vis. (IJCV) **111**(3), 298–314 (2015)
6. Van den Bergh, M., Carton, D., Van Gool, L.: Depth SEEDS: recovering incomplete depth data using superpixels. In: IEEE Workshop on Applications of Computer Vision (WACV), pp. 363–368 (2013)
7. Butler, D.J., Wulff, J., Stanley, G.B., Black, M.J.: A naturalistic open source movie for optical flow evaluation. In: Fitzgibbon, A., Lazebnik, S., Perona, P., Sato, Y., Schmid, C. (eds.) ECCV 2012. LNCS, vol. 7577, pp. 611–625. Springer, Heidelberg (2012). https://doi.org/10.1007/978-3-642-33783-3_44
8. Chen, L.C., Papandreou, G., Kokkinos, I., Murphy, K., Yuille, A.L.: Semantic image segmentation with deep convolutional nets and fully connected CRFs. In: International Conference on Learning Representations (ICLR) (2015)

9. Comaniciu, D., Meer, P.: Mean shift: a robust approach toward feature space analysis. IEEE Trans. Pattern Anal. Mach. Intell. (TPAMI) **24**(5), 603–619 (2002)
10. Cordts, M., et al.: The cityscapes dataset for semantic urban scene understanding. In: IEEE Conference on Computer Vision and Pattern Recognition (CVPR) (2016)
11. Everingham, M., Eslami, S.A., Van Gool, L., Williams, C.K., Winn, J., Zisserman, A.: The Pascal visual object classes challenge: a retrospective. Int. J. Comput. Vis. (IJCV) **111**(1), 98–136 (2015)
12. Felzenszwalb, P.F., Huttenlocher, D.P.: Efficient graph-based image segmentation. International J. Comput. Vis. (IJCV) **59**, 167–181 (2004)
13. Gadde, R., Jampani, V., Kiefel, M., Kappler, D., Gehler, P.V.: Superpixel convolutional networks using bilateral inceptions. In: Leibe, B., Matas, J., Sebe, N., Welling, M. (eds.) ECCV 2016. LNCS, vol. 9905, pp. 597–613. Springer, Cham (2016). https://doi.org/10.1007/978-3-319-46448-0_36
14. Giraud, R., Ta, V.T., Papadakis, N.: SCALP: superpixels with contour adherence using linear path. In: International Conference on Pattern Recognition (ICPR) (2016)
15. Gould, S., Rodgers, J., Cohen, D., Elidan, G., Koller, D.: Multi-class segmentation with relative location prior. Int. J. Comput. Vis. **80**(3), 300–316 (2008)
16. Greff, K., Rasmus, A., Berglund, M., Hao, T., Valpola, H., Schmidhuber, J.: Tagger: deep unsupervised perceptual grouping. In: Advances in Neural Information Processing Systems (NIPS) (2016)
17. Greff, K., van Steenkiste, S., Schmidhuber, J.: Neural expectation maximization. In: Advances in Neural Information Processing Systems (NIPS) (2017)
18. He, S., Lau, R.W., Liu, W., Huang, Z., Yang, Q.: SuperCNN: a superpixelwise convolutional neural network for salient object detection. Int. J. Comput. Vis. (IJCV) **115**(3), 330–344 (2015)
19. Hershey, J.R., Chen, Z., Le Roux, J., Watanabe, S.: Deep clustering: discriminative embeddings for segmentation and separation. In: IEEE International Conference on Acoustics, Speech and Signal Processing (ICASSP) (2016)
20. Hu, Y., Song, R., Li, Y., Rao, P., Wang, Y.: Highly accurate optical flow estimation on superpixel tree. Image Vis. Comput. **52**, 167–177 (2016)
21. Ioffe, S., Szegedy, C.: Batch normalization: accelerating deep network training by reducing internal covariate shift. In: International Conference on Machine Learning (ICML), pp. 448–456 (2015)
22. Jia, Y., et al.: Caffe: convolutional architecture for fast feature embedding. In: ACM Multimedia (MM), pp. 675–678 (2014)
23. Kingma, D.P., Ba, J.: Adam: a method for stochastic optimization. In: International Conference on Learning Representations (ICLR) (2015)
24. Levinshtein, A., Stere, A., Kutulakos, K.N., Fleet, D.J., Dickinson, S.J., Siddiqi, K.: TurboPixels: fast superpixels using geometric flows. IEEE Trans. Pattern Anal. Mach. Intell. (TPAMI) **31**(12), 2290–2297 (2009)
25. Li, Z., Chen, J.: Superpixel segmentation using linear spectral clustering. In: IEEE Conference on Computer Vision and Pattern Recognition (CVPR) (2015)
26. Liu, M.Y., Tuzel, O., Ramalingam, S., Chellappa, R.: Entropy rate superpixel segmentation. In: IEEE Conference on Computer Vision and Pattern Recognition (CVPR) (2011)
27. Liu, Y.J., Yu, C.C., Yu, M.J., He, Y.: Manifold SLIC: a fast method to compute content-sensitive superpixels. In: IEEE Conference on Computer Vision and Pattern Recognition (CVPR) (2016)

28. Lu, J., Yang, H., Min, D., Do, M.N.: Patch match filter: efficient edge-aware filtering meets randomized search for fast correspondence field estimation. In: IEEE Conference on Computer Vision and Pattern Recognition (CVPR), pp. 1854–1861 (2013)
29. Machairas, V., Faessel, M., Cárdenas-Peña, D., Chabardes, T., Walter, T., Decencière, E.: Waterpixels. IEEE Trans. Image Process. (TIP) **24**(11), 3707–3716 (2015)
30. Perazzi, F., Krähenbühl, P., Pritch, Y., Hornung, A.: Saliency filters: contrast based filtering for salient region detection. In: IEEE Conference on Computer Vision and Pattern Recognition (CVPR), pp. 733–740 (2012)
31. Rasmus, A., Berglund, M., Honkala, M., Valpola, H., Raiko, T.: Semi-supervised learning with ladder networks. In: Advances in Neural Information Processing Systems (NIPS) (2015)
32. Ren, C.Y., Prisacariu, V.A., Reid, I.D.: gSLICr: SLIC superpixels at over 250hz. arXiv preprint arXiv:1509.04232 (2015)
33. Ren, X., Malik, J.: Learning a classification model for segmentation. In: IEEE Conference on Computer Vision and Pattern Recognition (CVPR) (2003)
34. Sharma, A., Tuzel, O., Liu, M.Y.: Recursive context propagation network for semantic scene labeling. In: Advances in Neural Information Processing Systems (NIPS) (2014)
35. Shu, G., Dehghan, A., Shah, M.: Improving an object detector and extracting regions using superpixels. In: IEEE Conference on Computer Vision and Pattern Recognition (CVPR), pp. 3721–3727 (2013)
36. Stutz, D., Hermans, A., Leibe, B.: Superpixels: an evaluation of the state-of-the-art. Comput. Vis. Image Underst. **166**(C), 1–27 (2018)
37. Sun, D., Liu, C., Pfister, H.: Local layering for joint motion estimation and occlusion detection. In: Proceedings of the IEEE Conference on Computer Vision and Pattern Recognition, pp. 1098–1105 (2014)
38. Tu, W.C., et al.: Learning superpixels with segmentation-aware affinity loss. In: IEEE Conference on Computer Vision and Pattern Recognition (CVPR) (2018)
39. Veksler, O., Boykov, Y., Mehrani, P.: Superpixels and supervoxels in an energy optimization framework. In: Daniilidis, K., Maragos, P., Paragios, N. (eds.) ECCV 2010. LNCS, vol. 6315, pp. 211–224. Springer, Heidelberg (2010). https://doi.org/10.1007/978-3-642-15555-0_16
40. Xie, J., Girshick, R., Farhadi, A.: Unsupervised deep embedding for clustering analysis. In: International conference on machine learning (ICML) (2016)
41. Yamaguchi, K., McAllester, D., Urtasun, R.: Robust monocular epipolar flow estimation. In: IEEE Conference on Computer Vision and Pattern Recognition (CVPR), pp. 1862–1869 (2013)
42. Yan, J., Yu, Y., Zhu, X., Lei, Z., Li, S.Z.: Object detection by labeling superpixels. In: IEEE Conference on Computer Vision and Pattern Recognition (CVPR), pp. 5107–5116 (2015)
43. Yang, C., Zhang, L., Lu, H., Ruan, X., Yang, M.H.: Saliency detection via graph-based manifold ranking. In: IEEE Conference on Computer Vision and Pattern Recognition (CVPR) (2013)
44. Yang, F., Lu, H., Yang, M.H.: Robust superpixel tracking. IEEE Trans. Image Process. **23**(4), 1639–1651 (2014)

45. Yao, J., Boben, M., Fidler, S., Urtasun, R.: Real-time coarse-to-fine topologically preserving segmentation. In: IEEE Conference on Computer Vision and Pattern Recognition (CVPR) (2015)
46. Zhu, W., Liang, S., Wei, Y., Sun, J.: Saliency optimization from robust background detection. In: IEEE Conference on Computer Vision and Pattern Recognition (CVPR) (2014)

Towards Robust Neural Networks via Random Self-ensemble

Xuanqing Liu[1(✉)], Minhao Cheng[1], Huan Zhang[1], and Cho-Jui Hsieh[1,2]

[1] Electrical and Computer Science, UC Davis, Davis, CA 95616, USA
{xqliu,mhcheng,ecezhang,chohsieh}@ucdavis.edu
[2] Department of Statistics, UC Davis, Davis, CA 95616, USA

Abstract. Recent studies have revealed the vulnerability of deep neural networks: A small adversarial perturbation that is imperceptible to human can easily make a well-trained deep neural network misclassify. This makes it unsafe to apply neural networks in security-critical applications. In this paper, we propose a new defense algorithm called Random Self-Ensemble (RSE) by combining two important concepts: **randomness** and **ensemble**. To protect a targeted model, RSE adds random noise layers to the neural network to prevent the strong gradient-based attacks, and ensembles the prediction over random noises to stabilize the performance. We show that our algorithm is equivalent to ensemble an infinite number of noisy models f_ϵ without any additional memory overhead, and the proposed training procedure based on noisy stochastic gradient descent can ensure the ensemble model has a good predictive capability. Our algorithm significantly outperforms previous defense techniques on real data sets. For instance, on CIFAR-10 with VGG network (which has 92% accuracy without any attack), under the strong C&W attack within a certain distortion tolerance, the accuracy of unprotected model drops to less than 10%, the best previous defense technique has 48% accuracy, while our method still has 86% prediction accuracy under the same level of attack. Finally, our method is simple and easy to integrate into any neural network.

1 Introduction

Deep neural networks have demonstrated their success in many machine learning and computer vision applications, including image classification [7,9,14,34,35], object recognition [30] and image captioning [38]. Despite having near-perfect prediction performance, recent studies have revealed the vulnerability of deep neural networks to adversarial examples—given a correctly classified image, a carefully designed perturbation to the image can make a well-trained neural network misclassify. Algorithms crafting these adversarial images, called attack algorithms, are designed to minimize the perturbation, thus making adversarial

Electronic supplementary material The online version of this chapter (https://doi.org/10.1007/978-3-030-01234-2_23) contains supplementary material, which is available to authorized users.

V. Ferrari et al. (Eds.): ECCV 2018, LNCS 11211, pp. 381–397, 2018.
https://doi.org/10.1007/978-3-030-01234-2_23

images hard to be distinguished from natural images. This leads to security concerns, especially when applying deep neural networks to security-sensitive systems such as self-driving cars and medical imaging.

To make deep neural networks more robust to adversarial attacks, several defense algorithms have been proposed recently [16,17,23,39,40]. However, recent studies showed that these defense algorithms can only marginally improve the accuracy under the adversarial attacks [4,5].

In this paper, we propose a new defense algorithm: Random Self-Ensemble (RSE). More specifically, we introduce the new "noise layer" that fuses input vector with randomly generated noise, and then we insert this layer before each convolution layer of a deep network. In the training phase, the gradient is still computed by back-propagation but it will be perturbed by random noise when passing through the noise layer. In the inference phase, we perform several forward propagations, each time with different prediction scores due to the noise layers, and then ensemble the results. We show that RSE makes the network more resistant to adversarial attacks, by virtue of the proposed training and testing scheme. Meanwhile, it will only slightly affect test accuracy when no attack is performed on natural images. The algorithm is trivial to implement and can be applied to any deep neural networks for the enhancement.

Intuitively, RSE works well because of two important concepts: **ensemble** and **randomness**. It is known that ensemble of several trained models can improve the robustness [29], but will also increase the model size by k folds. In contrast, without any additional memory overhead, RSE can construct infinite number of models f_ϵ, where ϵ is generated randomly, and then ensemble the results to improve robustness. But how to guarantee that the ensemble of these models can achieve good accuracy? After all, if we train the original model without noise, yet only add noise layers at the inference stage, the algorithm is going to perform poorly. This suggests that adding random noise to an pre-trained network will only degrade the performance. Instead, we show that if the noise layers are taken into account in the training phase, then the training procedure can be considered as minimizing the upper bound of the loss of model ensemble, and thus our algorithm can achieve good prediction accuracy.

The contributions of our paper can be summarized below:

- We propose the Random Self-Ensemble (RSE) approach for improving the robustness of deep neural networks. The main idea is to add a "noise layer" before each convolution layer in both training and prediction phases. The algorithm is equivalent to ensemble an infinite number of random models to defense against the attackers.
- We explain why RSE can significantly improve the robustness toward adversarial attacks and show that adding noise layers is equivalent to training the original network with an extra regularization of Lipschitz constant.
- RSE significantly outperforms existing defense algorithms in all our experiments. For example, on CIFAR-10 data and VGG network (which has 92% accuracy without any attack), under C&W attack the accuracy of unprotected model drops to less than 10%; the best previous defense technique has

48% accuracy; while RSE still has 86.1% prediction accuracy under the same strength of attacks. Moreover, RSE is easy to implement and can be combined with any neural network.

2 Related Work

Security of deep neural networks has been studied recently. Let us denote the neural network as $f(w, x)$ where w is the model parameters and x is the input image. Given a correctly classified image x_0 ($f(w, x_0) = y_0$), an attacking algorithm seeks to find a slightly perturbed image x' such that: (1) the neural network will misclassify this perturbed image; and (2) the distortion $\|x' - x_0\|$ is small so that the perturbation is hard to be noticed by human. A defense algorithm is designed to improve the robustness of neural networks against attackers, usually by slightly changing the loss function or training procedure. In the following, we summarize some recent works along this line.

2.1 White-Box Attack

In the white-box setting, attackers have all information about the targeted neural network, including network structure and network weights (denoted by w). Using this information, attackers can compute gradient with respect to input data $\nabla_x f(w, x)$ by back-propagation. Note that gradient is very informative for attackers since it characterizes the sensitivity of the prediction with respect to the input image.

To craft an adversarial example, [11] proposed a fast gradient sign method (FGSM), where the adversarial example is constructed by

$$x' = x_0 - \epsilon \cdot \text{sign}(\nabla_x f(w, x_0)) \tag{1}$$

with a small $\epsilon > 0$. Based on that, several followup works were made to improve the efficiency and availability, such as Rand-FGSM [32] and I-FGSM [17]. Recently, Carlini and Wagner [5] showed that constructing an adversarial example can be formulated as solving the following optimization problem:

$$x' = \min_{x \in [0,1]^d} c \cdot g(x) + \|x - x_0\|_2^2, \tag{2}$$

where the first term is the loss function that characterizes the success of the attack and the second term is to enforce a small distortion. The parameter $c > 0$ is used to balance these two requirements. Several variants were proposed recently [6,20], but most of them can be categorized in the similar framework. The C&W attack has been recognized as a strong attacking algorithm to test defense methods.

For untargeted attack, where the goal is to find an adversarial example that is close to the original example but yields different class prediction, the loss function in (2) can be defined as

$$g(x) = \max\{\max_{i \neq t}(Z(x')_i) - Z(x')_t, -\kappa\}, \tag{3}$$

where t is the correct label, $Z(x)$ is the network's output before softmax layer (logits).

For targeted attack, the loss function can be designed to force the classifier to return the target label. For attackers, targeted attack is strictly harder than untargeted attack (since once the targeted attack succeeds, the same adversarial image can be used to perform untargeted attack without any modification). On the contrary, for defenders, untargeted attacks are strictly harder to defense than targeted attack. Therefore, we focus on defending the untargeted attacks in our experiments.

2.2 Defense Algorithms

Because of the vulnerability of adversarial examples [31], several methods have been proposed to improve the network's robustness against adversarial examples. [24] proposed *defensive distillation*, which uses a modified softmax layer controlled by temperature to train the "teacher" network, and then use the prediction probability (soft-labels) of teacher network to train the student network (it has the same structure as the teacher network). However, as stated in [5], this method does not work properly when dealing with the C&W attack. Moreover, [40] showed that by using a modified ReLU activation layer (called BReLU) and adding noise into origin images to augment the training dataset, the learned model will gain some stability to adversarial images. Another popular defense approach is *adversarial training* [16,17]. It generates and appends adversarial examples found by an attack algorithm to the training set, which helps the network to learn how to distinguish adversarial examples. Through combining adversarial training with enlarged model capacity, [20] is able to create an MNIST model that is robust to the first order attacks, but this approach does not work very well on more difficult datasets such as CIFAR-10.

It is worth mentioning that there are many defense algorithms (*r.f.* [3,8, 13,19,25,27,36]) against white box attacks in literature. Unfortunately, as [1,2] pointed out, these algorithms are not truly effective to white box attacks. Recall the "white box" means that the attackers know *everything* concerning how models make decisions, these include the potential defense mechanisms. In this condition, the white box attacks can walk around all defense algorithms listed above and the accuracy under attack can still be nearly zero. In addition to changing the network structure, there are other methods [10,12,21,39] "detecting" the adversarial examples, which are beyond the scope of our paper.

There is another highly correlated work (*r.f.* [18]) which also adopts very similar idea, except that they view this problem from the angle of differential privacy, while we believe that the adversarial robustness is more correlated with regularization and ensemble learning. Furthermore, our work is public available earlier than this similar work on Arxiv.

3 Proposed Algorithm: Random Self-Ensemble

In this section, we propose our self-ensemble algorithm to improve the robustness of neural networks. We will first motivate and introduce our algorithm and then discuss several theoretical reasons behind it.

It is known that ensemble of several different models can improve the robustness. However, an ensemble of finite k models is not very practical because it will increase the model size by k folds. For example, AlexNet model on ImageNet requires 240 MB storage, and storing 100 of them will require 24 GB memory. Moreover, it is hard to find many heterogeneous models with similar accuracy. To improve the robustness of practical systems, we propose the following self-ensemble algorithm that can generate an infinite number of models on-the-fly without any additional memory cost.

Our main idea is to add randomness into the network structure. More specifically, we introduce a new "noise layer" that fuses input vector with a randomly generated noise, i.e. $x \to x+\epsilon$ when passing through the noise layer. Then we add this layer before each convolution layer as shown in Fig. 1. Since most attacks require computing or estimating gradient, the noise level in our model will control the success rate of those attacking algorithms. In fact, we can integrate this layer into any other neural network.

If we denote the original neural network as $f(w, x)$ where $w \in \mathbb{R}^{d_w}$ is the weights and $x \in \mathbb{R}^{d_x}$ is the input image, then considering the random noise layer, the network can be denoted as $f_\epsilon(w, x)$ with random $\epsilon \in \mathbb{R}^{d_e}$. Therefore we have an infinite number of models in the pocket (with different ϵ) without

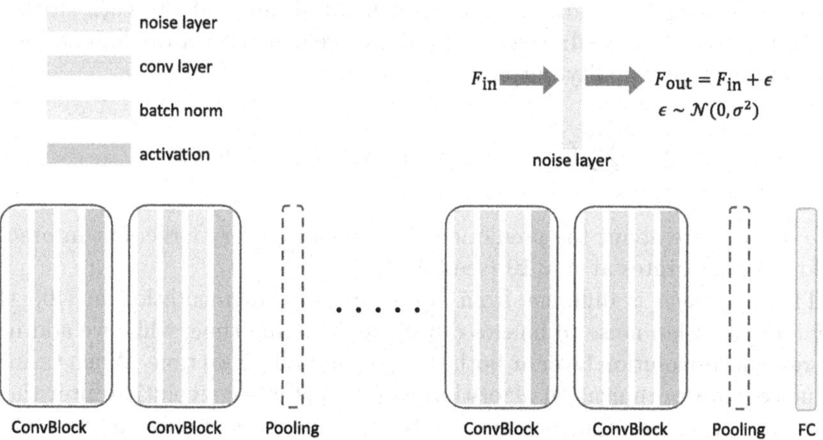

Fig. 1. Our proposed noisy VGG style network, we add a noise layer before each convolution layer. For simplicity, we call the noise layer before the first convolution layer the "init-noise", and all other noise layer"inner-noise". For these two kinds of layers we adopt different variances of Gaussian noise. Note that similar design can be transplanted to other architectures such as ResNet.

Algorithm 1. Training and Testing of Random Self-Ensemble (RSE)

Training phase:
for iter $= 1, 2, \ldots$ **do**
  Randomly sample (x_i, y_i) in dataset
  Randomly generate $\epsilon \sim \mathcal{N}(0, \sigma^2)$ for each noise layer.
  Compute $\Delta w = \nabla_w \ell(f_\epsilon(w, x_i), y_i)$ (Noisy gradient)
  Update weights: $w \leftarrow w - \Delta w$.
end for
Testing phase:
Given testing image x, initialize $p = (0, 0, \ldots, 0)$
for $j = 1, 2, \ldots, \#\text{Ensemble}$ **do**
  Randomly generate $\epsilon \sim \mathcal{N}(0, \sigma^2)$ for each noise layer.
  Forward propagation to calculate probability output

$$p^j = f_\epsilon(w, x)$$

  Update p: $p \leftarrow p + p^j$.
end for
Predict the class with maximum score $\hat{y} = \arg\max_k p_k$

having any memory overhead. However, adding randomness will also affect the prediction accuracy of the model. How can we make sure that the ensemble of these random models have enough accuracy?

A critical observation is that we need to add this random layer in both training and testing phases. The training and testing algorithms are listed in Algorithm 1. In the training phase, gradient is computed as $\nabla_w f_\epsilon(w, x_i)$ which includes the noise layer, and the noise is generated randomly for each stochastic gradient descent update. In the testing phase, we construct n random noises and ensemble their probability outputs by

$$p = \sum_{j=1}^{n} f_{\epsilon_j}(w, x), \text{ and predict } \hat{y} = \arg\max_k p_k. \tag{4}$$

If we do not care about the prediction time, n can be very large, but in practice we found it saturates at $n \approx 10$ (see Fig. 4).

This approach is different from Gaussian data augmentation in [40]: they only add Gaussian noise to images during the training time, while we add noise before each convolution layer at both training and inference time. When training, the noise helps optimization algorithm to find a stable convolution filter that is robust to perturbed input, while when testing, the roles of noise are two-folded: one is to perturb the gradient to fool gradient-based attacks. The other is it gives different outputs by doing multiple forward operations and a simple ensemble method can improve the testing accuracy.

3.1 Mathematical Explanations

Training and testing of RSE. Here we explain our training and testing procedure. In the training phase, our algorithm is solving the following optimization problem:

$$w^* = \arg\min_w \frac{1}{|\mathcal{D}_{\text{train}}|} \sum_{(x_i,y_i)\in\mathcal{D}_{\text{train}}} \mathop{\mathbb{E}}_{\epsilon\sim\mathcal{N}(0,\sigma^2)} \ell\big(f_\epsilon(w,x_i),y_i\big), \tag{5}$$

where $\ell(\cdot,\cdot)$ is the loss function and $\mathcal{D}_{\text{train}}$ is the training dataset. Note that for simplicity we assume ϵ follows a zero-mean Gaussian, but in general our algorithm can work for a large variety of noise distribution such as Bernoulli-Gaussian: $\epsilon_i = b_i e_i$, where $e_i \overset{\text{iid}}{\sim} \mathcal{N}(0,\sigma^2)$ and $b_i \overset{\text{iid}}{\sim} \mathcal{B}(1,p)$.

At testing time, we ensemble the outputs through several forward propagation, specifically:

$$\hat{y}_i = \arg\max \mathbb{E}_{\epsilon\sim\mathcal{N}(0,\sigma^2)} f_\epsilon(w,x_i). \tag{6}$$

Here arg max means the index of maximum element in a vector. The reason that our RSE algorithm achieves the similar prediction accuracy with original network is because (5) is minimizing an upper bound of the loss of (6) – Similar to the idea of [22], if we choose negative log-likelihood loss, then $\forall w \in \mathbb{R}^{d_w}$:

$$\begin{aligned}
&\frac{1}{|\mathcal{D}_{\text{train}}|} \sum_{(x_i,y_i)\in\mathcal{D}_{\text{train}}} \mathbb{E}_{\epsilon\sim\mathcal{N}(0,\sigma^2)} \ell\big(f_\epsilon(w,x_i),y_i\big) \\
&\overset{(a)}{\approx} \mathbb{E}_{(x_i,y_i)\sim\mathcal{P}_{\text{data}}}\Big\{-\mathbb{E}_{\epsilon\sim\mathcal{N}(0,\sigma^2)} \log f_\epsilon(w,x_i)[y_i]\Big\} \\
&\overset{(b)}{\geq} \mathbb{E}_{(x_i,y_i)\sim\mathcal{P}_{\text{data}}}\Big\{-\log \mathbb{E}_{\epsilon\sim\mathcal{N}(0,\sigma^2)} f_\epsilon(w,x_i)[y_i]\Big\} \\
&\overset{(c)}{\geq} \mathbb{E}_{(x_i,y_i)\sim\mathcal{P}_{\text{data}}}\Big\{-\log \mathbb{E}_{\epsilon\sim\mathcal{N}(0,\sigma^2)} f_\epsilon(w,x_i)[\hat{y}_i]\Big\} \\
&\overset{(a)}{\approx} \frac{1}{|\mathcal{D}_{\text{test}}|} \sum_{x_i\in\mathcal{D}_{\text{test}}} -\log \mathbb{E}_{\epsilon\sim\mathcal{N}(0,\sigma^2)} f_\epsilon(w,x_i)[\hat{y}_i].
\end{aligned} \tag{7}$$

where $\mathcal{P}_{\text{data}}$ is the data distribution, $\mathcal{D}_{\text{train/test}}$ is the training set and test set, respectively. And (a) follows from generalization bound (see [28] or appendix for details), (b) comes from Jensen's inequality and (c) is by the inference rule (6). So by minimizing (5) we are actually minimizing the upper bound of inference confidence $-\log f_\epsilon(w,x_i)[\hat{y}_i]$, this validates our ensemble inference procedure.

RSE is Equivalent to Lipschitz Regularization. Another point of view is that perturbed training is equivalent to Lipschitz regularization, which further helps defensing gradient based attack. If we fix the output label y then the loss function $\ell(f_\epsilon(w,x),y)$ can be simply denoted as $\ell \circ f_\epsilon$. Lipchitz of the function $\ell \circ f_\epsilon$ is a constant $L_{\ell\circ f_\epsilon}$ such that

$$|\ell(f_\epsilon(w,x),y) - \ell(f_\epsilon(w,\tilde{x}),y)| \leq L_{\ell\circ f_\epsilon}\|x-\tilde{x}\| \tag{8}$$

for all $x, \tilde{x}$. In fact, it has been proved recently that Lipschitz constant can be used to measure the robustness of machine learning model [15,33]. If $L_{\ell \circ f_\epsilon}$ is large enough, even a tiny change of input $x - \tilde{x}$ can significantly change the loss and eventually get an incorrect prediction. On the contrary, by controlling $L_{\ell \circ f}$ to be small, we will have a more robust network.

Next we show that our noisy network indeed controls the Lipschitz constant. Following the notation of (5), we can see that

$$\begin{aligned}\mathbb{E}_{\epsilon\sim\mathcal{N}(0,\sigma^2)}\ell\big(f_\epsilon(w,x_i),y_i\big) &\overset{(a)}{\approx} \mathbb{E}_{\epsilon\sim\mathcal{N}(0,\sigma^2)}\Big[\ell\big(f_0(w,x_i),y_i\big) + \epsilon^\intercal\nabla_\epsilon\ell\big(f_0(w,x_i),y_i\big) \\ &\quad + \frac{1}{2}\epsilon^\intercal\nabla_\epsilon^2\ell\big(f_0(w,x_i),y_i\big)\epsilon\Big] \\ &\overset{(b)}{=} \ell\big(f_0(w,x_i),y_i\big) + \frac{\sigma^2}{2}\mathrm{Tr}\Big\{\nabla_\epsilon^2\ell\big(f_0(w,x_i),y_i\big)\Big\}.\end{aligned} \tag{9}$$

For (a), we do Taylor expansion at $\epsilon = 0$. Since we set the variance of noise σ^2 very small, we only keep the second order term. For (b), we notice that the Gaussian vector ϵ is i.i.d. with zero mean. So the linear term of ϵ has zero expectation, and the quadratic term is directly dependent on variance of noise and the trace of Hessian. As a convex relaxation, if we assume $\ell \circ f_0$ is convex, then we have that $d \cdot \|A\|_{\max} \geq \mathrm{Tr}(A) \geq \|A\|_{\max}$ for $A \in \mathbb{S}_+^{d\times d}$, we can rewrite (9) as

$$\mathrm{Loss}(f_\epsilon, \{x_i\}, \{y_i\}) \simeq \mathrm{Loss}(f_0, \{x_i\}, \{y_i\}) + \frac{\sigma^2}{2} L_{\ell \circ f_0}, \tag{10}$$

which means the training of noisy networks is equivalent to training the original model with an extra regularization of Lipschitz constant, and by controlling the variance of noise we can balance the robustness of network with training loss.

3.2 Discussions

Here we show both *randomness* and *ensemble* are important in our algorithm. Indeed, if we remove any component, the performance will significantly drop.

First, as mentioned before, the main idea of our model is to have infinite number of models f_ϵ, each with a different ϵ value, and then ensemble the result. A naive way to achieve this goal is to fix a pre-trained model f_0 and then generate many f_ϵ in the testing phase by adding different small noise to f_0. However, Fig. 2 shows this approach (denoted as Test noise only) will result in much worse performance (20% without any attack). Therefore it is non-trivial to guarantee the model to be good after adding small random noise. In our random self-ensemble algorithm, in addition to adding noise in the testing phase, we also **add noise layer in the training phase**, and this is important for getting good performance.

Second, we found adding noise in the testing phase and then ensemble the predictions is important. In Fig. 2, we compare the performance of RSE with the version that only adds the noise layer in the training phase but not in the testing phase (so the prediction is $f_\epsilon(w, x)$ instead of $\mathbb{E}_\epsilon f_\epsilon(w, x)$). The results clearly

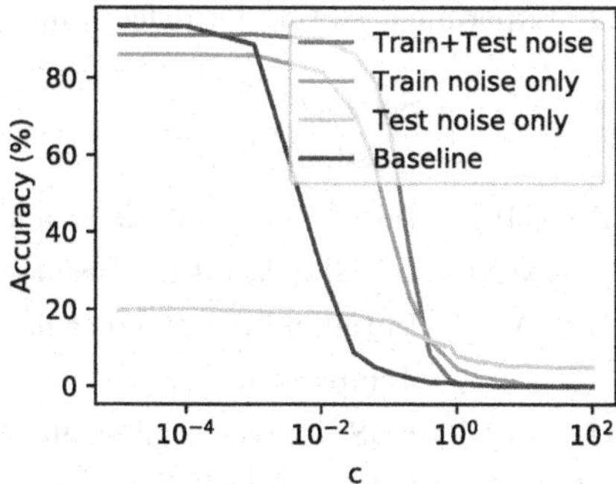

Fig. 2. We test three models on CIFAR10 and VGG16 network: In the first model noise is added both at training and testing time, in the second model noise is added only at training time, in the last model we only add noise at testing time. As a comparison we also plot baseline model which is trained conventionally. For all models that are noisy at testing time, we automatically enable self-ensemble.

show that the performance drop under smaller attacks. This proves **ensemble in the testing phase is crucial.**

4 Experiments

Datasets and Network Structure. We test our method on two datasets—CIFAR10 and STL10. We do not compare the results on MNIST since it is a much easier dataset and existing defense methods such as [16,17,23,40] can effectively increase image distortion under adversarial attacks. On CIFAR10 data, we evaluate the performance on both VGG-16 [26] and ResNeXt [37]; on STL10 data we copy and slightly modify a simple model[1] which we name it as "Model A".

Defense Algorithms. We include the following defense algorithms into comparison (their parameter settings can be found in Table 1):

- Random Self-Ensemble (RSE): our proposed method.
- Defensive distillation [24]: first train a teacher network at temperature T, then use the teacher network to train a student network of the same architecture and same temperature. The student network is called the distilled network.
- Robust optimization combined with BReLU activation [40]: first we replace all ReLU activation with BReLU activation. And then at the training phase, we randomly perturb training data by Gaussian noise with $\sigma = 0.05$ as suggested.
- Adversarial retraining by FGSM attacks [16,17]: we first pre-train a neural network without adversarial retraining. After that, we either select an original data batch or an adversarial data batch with probability 1/2. We continue training it until convergence.

[1] Publicly available at https://github.com/aaron-xichen/pytorch-playground.

Table 1. Experiment setting for defense methods

Methods	Settings
No defense	Baseline model
RSE(for CIFAR10 + VGG16)	Initial noise: 0.2, inner noise: 0.1, 50-ensemble
RSE(for CIFAR10 + ResNeXt)	Initial noise: 0.1, inner noise 0.1, 50-ensemble
RSE(for STL10 + Model A)	Initial noise: 0.2, inner noise: 0.1, 50-ensemble
Defensive distill	Temperature = 40
Adversarial training (I)	FGSM adversarial examples, $\epsilon \sim \mathcal{U}(0.1, 0.3)$
Adversarial training (II)	Following [20], PGD adversary with $\epsilon_\infty = \frac{8.0}{256}$
Robust Opt. + BReLU	Following [40]

Attack Models. We consider the white-box setting and choose the state-of-the-art C&W attack [5] to evaluate the above-mentioned defense methods. Moreover, we test our algorithm under untargeted attack, since untargeted attack is strictly harder to defense than targeted attack. In fact, C&W untargeted attack is the most challenging attack for a defense algorithm.

Moreover, we assume C&W attack knows the randomization procedure of RSE, so the C&W objective function will change accordingly (as proposed in [1] for attacking an ensemble model). The details can be found in the appendix.

Measure. Unlike attacking models that only need to operate on correctly classified images, a competitive defense model not only protects the model when attackers exist, but also keeps a good performance on clean datasets. Based on this thought, we compare the accuracy of guarded models under different strengths of C&W attack, the strength can be measured by L_2-norm of image distortion and further controlled by parameter c in (2). Note that an adversarial image is correctly predicted under C&W attack if and only if the original image is correctly classified and C&W attack cannot find an adversarial example within a certain distortion level.

4.1 The Effect of Noise Level

We first test the performance of RSE under different noise levels. We use Gaussian noise for all the noise layers in our network and the standard deviation σ of Gaussian controls the noise level. Note that we call the noise layer before the first convolution layer the "init-noise", and all other noise layers the "inner-noise".

In this experiment, we apply different noise levels in both training and testing phases to see how different variances change the robustness as well as generalization ability of networks. As an example, we choose

$$(\sigma_{\text{init}}, \sigma_{\text{inner}}) = \{(0, 0), (0.05, 0.02), (0.1, 0.05), (0.2, 0.1)\} \tag{11}$$

on VGG16+CIFAR10. The result is shown in Fig. 3 (*left*).

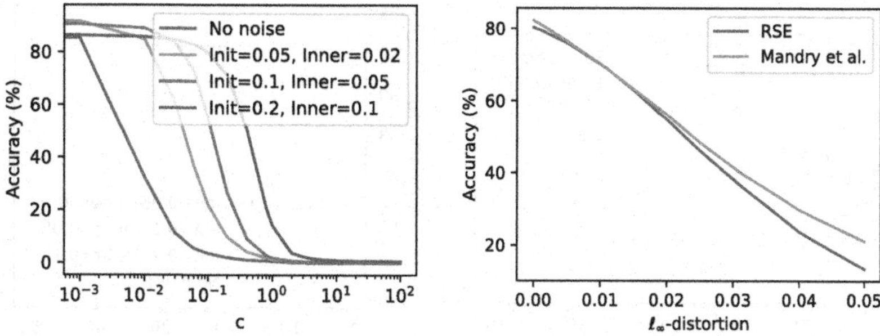

Fig. 3. *Left*: the effect of noise level on robustness and generalization ability. Clearly random noise can improve the robustness of the model. *Right*: comparing RSE with adversarial defense method [20].

As we can see, both "init-noise" and"inner-noise" are beneficial to the robustness of neural network, but at the same time, one can see higher noise reduces the accuracy for weak attacks ($c \lesssim 0.01$). From Fig. 3, we observe that if the input image is normalized to $[0, 1]$, then choosing $\sigma_{\text{init}} = 0.2$ and $\sigma_{\text{inner}} = 0.1$ is good. Thus we fix this parameter for all the experiments.

4.2 Self-ensemble

Next we show self-ensemble helps to improve the test accuracy of our noisy mode. As an example, we choose VGG16+CIFAR10 combination and the standard deviation of initial noise layer is $\sigma = 0.2$, other noise layers is $\sigma = 0.1$. We compare 50-ensemble with 1-ensemble (i.e. single model), and the result can be found in Fig. 4.

We find the 50-ensemble method outperform the 1-ensemble method by $\sim$8% accuracy when $c < 0.4$. This is because when the attack is weak enough, the majority choice of networks has lower variance and higher accuracy. On the other hand, we can see if $c > 1.0$ or equivalently the average distortion greater than 0.93, the ensemble model is worse. We conjecture that this is because when the attack is strong enough then the majority of random sub-models make wrong prediction, but when looking at any individual model, the random effect might be superior than group decision. In this situation, self-ensemble may have a negative effect on accuracy.

Practically, if running time is the primary concern, it is not necessary to calculate many ensemble models. In fact, we find the accuracy saturates rapidly with respect to number of models, moreover, if we inject smaller noise then ensemble benefit would be weaker and the accuracy gets saturated earlier. Therefore, we find 10-ensemble is good enough for testing accuracy, see Fig. 4.

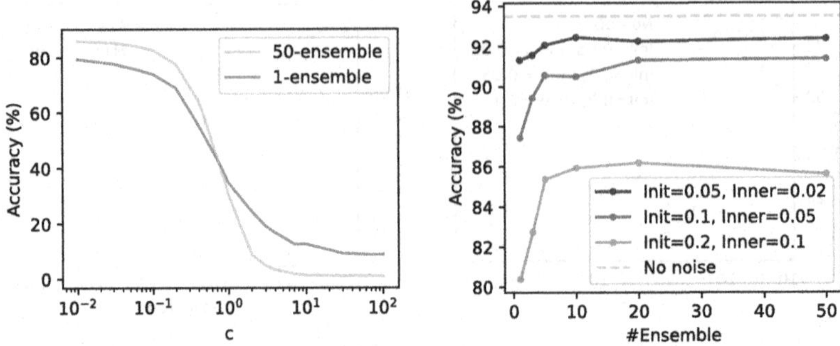

Fig. 4. *Left*: Comparing the accuracy under different levels of attack, here we choose VGG16+CIFAR10 combination. We can see that the ensemble model achieves better accuracy under weak attacks. *Right*: Testing accuracy (without attack) of different n (number of random models used for ensemble).

4.3 Comparing Defense Methods

Finally, we compare our RSE method with other existing defense algorithms. Note that we test all of them using C&W untargeted attack, which is the most difficult setting for defenders.

The comparison across different datasets and networks can be found in Table 2 and Fig. 5. As we can see, previous defense methods have little effect on C&W attacks. For example, Robust Opt+BReLU [40] is useful for CIFAR10+ResNeXt, but the accuracy is even worse than no defense model for STL10+Model A. In contrast, our RSE method acts as a good defence across all cases. Specifically, RSE method enforces the attacker to find much more distorted adversarial images in order to start a successful attack. As showed in Fig. 5, when we allow an average distortion of 0.21 on CIFAR10+VGG16, C&W attack is able to conduct untargeted attacks with success rate > 99%. On the contrary, by defending the networks via RSE, C&W attack only yields a success rate of ~20%. Recently, another version of adversarial training is proposed [20].

Table 2. Prediction accuracy of defense methods under C&W attack with different c. We can clearly observe that RSE is the most robust model. Our accuracy level remains at above 75% when other methods are below 30%.

	$c = 0.01$	$c = 0.03$	$c = 0.06$	$c = 0.1$	$c = 0.2$
RSE (ours)	**90.00%**	**86.06%**	**79.44%**	**67.19%**	**34.75%**
Adv retraining	27.00%	9.81%	4.13%	3.69%	1.44%
Robust Opt+BReLU	75.06%	47.93%	30.94%	20.69%	13.50%
Distill	49.88%	17.69%	4.56%	3.13%	1.44%
No defense	30.38%	8.93%	5.06%	3.56%	2.19%

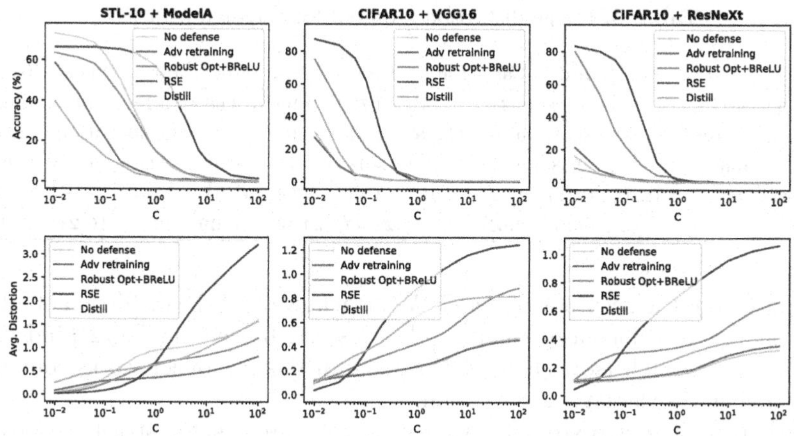

Fig. 5. Comparing the accuracy of CIFAR10+{VGG16, ResNeXt} and STL10+Model A. We show both the change of accuracy and average distortion w.r.t. attacking strength parameter c (the parameter in the C&W attack). Our model (RSE) clearly outperforms all the existing methods under strong attacks in both accuracy and average distortion.

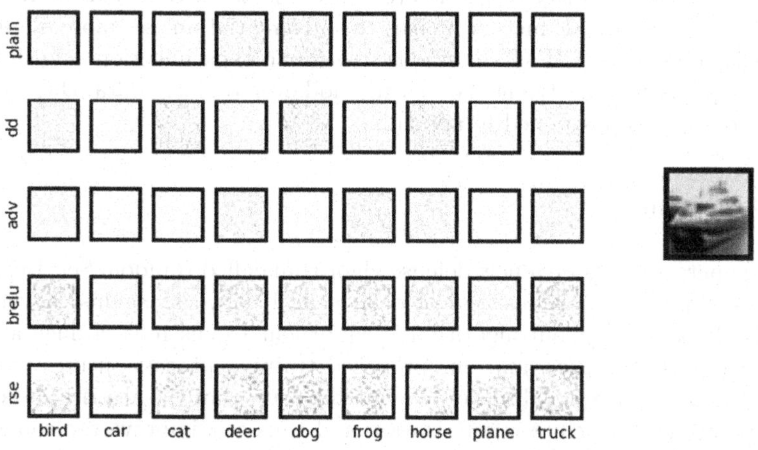

Fig. 6. Targeted adversarial image distortion, each column indicates a defense algorithm and each row is the adversarial target (the original image is in "ship" class, shown in the right side). Here we choose $c = 1$ for targeted C&W attack. Visually, color spot means the distortion of images, thus a successful defending method should lead to more spots.

Different from "Adversarial training (I)" shown in Table 1, it trains the network with adversaries generated by multiple steps of gradient descent (therefore we call it "Adversarial training (II)" in Table 1). Compared with our method, the major weakness is that it takes ~10 times longer to train a robust network despite that the result is only slightly better than our RSE, see Fig. 3 (*right*).

Table 3. Image distortion required for targeted attacks.

	Bird	Car	Cat	Deer	Dog	Frog	Horse	Plane	Truck
No defense	1.94	0.31	0.74	4.72	7.99	3.66	9.22	0.75	1.32
Defensive distill	6.55	0.70	**13.78**	2.54	13.90	2.56	**11.36**	0.66	3.54
Adv. retraining	2.58	0.31	0.75	6.08	0.75	9.01	6.06	0.31	4.08
Robust Opt. + BReLU	**17.11**	1.02	4.07	13.50	7.09	15.34	7.15	2.08	17.57
RSE(ours)	12.87	**2.61**	12.47	**21.47**	**31.90**	**19.09**	9.45	**10.21**	**22.15**

Apart from the accuracy under C&W attack, we find the distortion of adversarial images also increases significantly, this can be seen in Fig. 2 (2nd row), as c is large enough (so that all defense algorithms no longer works) our RSE method achieves the largest distortion.

Although all above experiments are concerning untargeted attack, it does not mean targeted attack is not covered, as we said, targeted attack is harder for attacking methods and easier to defense. As an example, we test all the defense algorithms on CIFAR-10 dataset under targeted attacks. We randomly pick an image from CIFAR10 and plot the perturbation $x_{\text{adv}} - x$ in Fig. 6 (the exact number is in Table 3), to make it easier to print out, we subtract RGB channels from 255 (so the majority of pixels are white and distortions can be noticed). One can easily find RSE method makes the adversarial images more distorted.

Lastly, apart from CIFAR-10, we also design an experiment on a much larger data to support the effectiveness of our method even on large data. Due to space limit, the result is postponed to appendix.

5 Conclusion

In this paper, we propose a new defense algorithm called Random Self-Ensemble (RSE) to improve the robustness of deep neural networks against adversarial attacks. We show that our algorithm is equivalent to ensemble a huge amount of noisy models together, and our proposed training process ensures that the ensemble model can generalize well. We further show that the algorithm is equivalent to adding a Lipchitz regularization and thus can improve the robustness of neural networks. Experimental results demonstrate that our method is very robust against strong white-box attacks. Moreover, our method is simple, easy to implement, and can be easily embedded into an existing network.

Acknowledgement. The authors acknowledge the support of NSF via IIS-1719097 and the computing resources provided by Google cloud and Nvidia.

References

1. Athalye, A., Carlini, N.: On the robustness of the CVPR 2018 white-box adversarial example defenses. arXiv preprint arXiv:1804.03286 (2018)
2. Athalye, A., Carlini, N., Wagner, D.: Obfuscated gradients give a false sense of security: Circumventing defenses to adversarial examples. In: 35th International Conference on Machine Learning (ICML) (2018)
3. Buckman, J., Roy, A., Raffel, C., Goodfellow, I.: Thermometer encoding: one hot way to resist adversarial examples. In: International Conference on Learning Representations (2018). https://openreview.net/forum?id=S18Su-CW
4. Carlini, N., Wagner, D.: Adversarial examples are not easily detected: bypassing ten detection methods. In: Proceedings of the 10th ACM Workshop on Artificial Intelligence and Security, AISec 2017, pp. 3–14. ACM, New York (2017). https://doi.org/10.1145/3128572.3140444, http://doi.acm.org/10.1145/3128572.3140444
5. Carlini, N., Wagner, D.: Towards evaluating the robustness of neural networks. In: 2017 IEEE Symposium on Security and Privacy (SP), pp. 39–57. IEEE (2017)
6. Chen, P.Y., Sharma, Y., Zhang, H., Yi, J., Hsieh, C.J.: EAD: elastic-net attacks to deep neural networks via adversarial examples. In: Proceedings of the Thirty-Second AAAI Conference on Artificial Intelligence (2018)
7. Dean, J., et al.: Large scale distributed deep networks. In: Advances in Neural Information Processing Systems, pp. 1223–1231 (2012)
8. Dhillon, G.S., et al.: Stochastic activation pruning for robust adversarial defense. In: International Conference on Learning Representations (2018). https://openreview.net/forum?id=H1uR4GZRZ
9. Eykholt, K., et al.: Robust physical-world attacks on deep learning visual classification. In: Proceedings of the IEEE Conference on Computer Vision and Pattern Recognition, pp. 1625–1634 (2018)
10. Feinman, R., Curtin, R.R., Shintre, S., Gardner, A.B.: Detecting adversarial samples from artifacts. arXiv preprint arXiv:1703.00410 (2017)
11. Goodfellow, I., Shlens, J., Szegedy, C.: Explaining and harnessing adversarial examples. In: International Conference on Learning Representations (2015). http://arxiv.org/abs/1412.6572
12. Grosse, K., Manoharan, P., Papernot, N., Backes, M., McDaniel, P.: On the (statistical) detection of adversarial examples. arXiv preprint arXiv:1702.06280 (2017)
13. Guo, C., Rana, M., Cisse, M., van der Maaten, L.: Countering adversarial images using input transformations. In: International Conference on Learning Representations (2018). https://openreview.net/forum?id=SyJ7ClWCb
14. He, K., Zhang, X., Ren, S., Sun, J.: Deep residual learning for image recognition. In: Proceedings of the IEEE Conference on Computer Vision and Pattern Recognition, pp. 770–778 (2016)
15. Hein, M., Andriushchenko, M.: Formal guarantees on the robustness of a classifier against adversarial manipulation. In: Advances in Neural Information Processing Systems 30: Annual Conference on Neural Information Processing Systems 2017, 4–9 December 2017, Long Beach, CA, USA, pp. 2263–2273 (2017)
16. Huang, R., Xu, B., Schuurmans, D., Szepesvári, C.: Learning with a strong adversary. arXiv preprint arXiv:1511.03034 (2015)
17. Kurakin, A., Goodfellow, I., Bengio, S.: Adversarial machine learning at scale. In: International Conference on Learning Representations (ICLR) (2017)
18. Lecuyer, M., Atlidakis, V., Geambasu, R., Hsu, D., Jana, S.: Certified Robustness to Adversarial Examples with Differential Privacy. ArXiv e-prints, February 2018

19. Ma, X., et al.: Characterizing adversarial subspaces using local intrinsic dimensionality. In: International Conference on Learning Representations (2018). https://openreview.net/forum?id=B1gJ1L2aW
20. Madry, A., Makelov, A., Schmidt, L., Tsipras, D., Vladu, A.: Towards deep learning models resistant to adversarial attacks. In: 6-th International Conference on Learning Representations (ICLR) (2018)
21. Meng, D., Chen, H.: MagNet: a two-pronged defense against adversarial examples. In: Proceedings of the 2017 ACM SIGSAC Conference on Computer and Communications Security, CCS 2017, pp. 135–147. ACM, New York (2017). https://doi.org/10.1145/3133956.3134057, http://doi.acm.org/10.1145/3133956.3134057
22. Noh, H., You, T., Mun, J., Han, B.: Regularizing deep neural networks by noise: its interpretation and optimization. In: Advances in Neural Information Processing Systems, pp. 5115–5124 (2017)
23. Papernot, N., McDaniel, P., Goodfellow, I., Jha, S., Celik, Z.B., Swami, A.: Practical black-box attacks against deep learning systems using adversarial examples. arXiv preprint arXiv:1602.02697 (2016)
24. Papernot, N., McDaniel, P., Wu, X., Jha, S., Swami, A.: Distillation as a defense to adversarial perturbations against deep neural networks. In: 2016 IEEE Symposium on Security and Privacy (SP), pp. 582–597. IEEE (2016)
25. Samangouei, P., Kabkab, M., Chellappa, R.: Defense-GAN: protecting classifiers against adversarial attacks using generative models. In: International Conference on Learning Representations (2018). https://openreview.net/forum?id=BkJ3ibb0-
26. Simonyan, K., Zisserman, A.: Very deep convolutional networks for large-scale image recognition. In: International Conference on Learning Representation (2015)
27. Song, Y., Kim, T., Nowozin, S., Ermon, S., Kushman, N.: PixelDefend: leveraging generative models to understand and defend against adversarial examples. In: International Conference on Learning Representations (2018). https://openreview.net/forum?id=rJUYGxbCW
28. Steinhardt, J., Koh, P.W.W., Liang, P.S.: Certified defenses for data poisoning attacks. In: Advances in Neural Information Processing Systems, pp. 3520–3532 (2017)
29. Strauss, T., Hanselmann, M., Junginger, A., Ulmer, H.: Ensemble methods as a defense to adversarial perturbations against deep neural networks. arXiv:1709.03423 (2017)
30. Szegedy, C., et al.: Going deeper with convolutions. In: Proceedings of the IEEE Conference on Computer Vision And Pattern Recognition, pp. 1–9 (2015)
31. Szegedy, C., et al.: Intriguing properties of neural networks. In: International Conference on Learning Representation (2014)
32. Tramér, F., Kurakin, A., Papernot, N., Boneh, D., McDaniel, P.: Ensemble adversarial training: attacks and defenses. arXiv preprint arXiv:1705.07204 (2017)
33. Weng, T.W., et al.: Evaluating the robustness of neural networks: an extreme value theory approach. In: 6-th International Conference on Learning Representations (ICLR) (2018)
34. Xiao, C., Li, B., Zhu, J.Y., He, W., Liu, M., Song, D.: Generating adversarial examples with adversarial networks. In: Proceedings of the Twenty-Seventh International Joint Conference on Artificial Intelligence, IJCAI-2018, pp. 3905–3911. International Joint Conferences on Artificial Intelligence Organization, July 2018. https://doi.org/10.24963/ijcai.2018/543
35. Xiao, C., Zhu, J.Y., Li, B., He, W., Liu, M., Song, D.: Spatially transformed adversarial examples. arXiv preprint arXiv:1801.02612 (2018)

36. Xie, C., Wang, J., Zhang, Z., Ren, Z., Yuille, A.: Mitigating adversarial effects through randomization. In: International Conference on Learning Representations (2018). https://openreview.net/forum?id=Sk9yuql0Z
37. Xie, S., Girshick, R., Dollár, P., Tu, Z., He, K.: Aggregated residual transformations for deep neural networks. In: 2017 IEEE Conference on Computer Vision and Pattern Recognition (CVPR), pp. 5987–5995. IEEE (2017)
38. Xu, K., et al.: Show, attend and tell: Neural image caption generation with visual attention. In: International Conference on Machine Learning, pp. 2048–2057 (2015)
39. Xu, W., Evans, D., Qi, Y.: Feature squeezing: detecting adversarial examples in deep neural networks. In: Network and Distributed System Security Symposium (2018)
40. Zantedeschi, V., Nicolae, M.I., Rawat, A.: Efficient defenses against adversarial attacks. In: Proceedings of the 10th ACM Workshop on Artificial Intelligence and Security, pp. 39–49. ACM (2017)

EC-Net: An Edge-Aware Point Set Consolidation Network

Lequan Yu[1,3](✉), Xianzhi Li[1], Chi-Wing Fu[1,3], Daniel Cohen-Or[2], and Pheng-Ann Heng[1,3]

[1] The Chinese University of Hong Kong, Shatin, Hong Kong
{lqyu,xzli,cwfu,pheng}@cse.cuhk.edu.hk
[2] Tel Aviv University, Tel Aviv, Israel
dcor@mail.tau.ac.il
[3] Shenzhen Key Laboratory of Virtual Reality and Human Interaction Technology, Shenzhen Institutes of Advanced Technology, Chinese Academy of Sciences, Shenzhen, China

Abstract. Point clouds obtained from 3D scans are typically sparse, irregular, and noisy, and required to be consolidated. In this paper, we present the first deep learning based *edge-aware* technique to facilitate the consolidation of point clouds. We design our network to process points grouped in local patches, and train it to learn and help consolidate points, deliberately for edges. To achieve this, we formulate a regression component to simultaneously recover 3D point coordinates and point-to-edge distances from upsampled features, and an edge-aware joint loss function to directly minimize distances from output points to 3D meshes and to edges. Compared with previous neural network based works, our consolidation is *edge-aware*. During the synthesis, our network can attend to the detected sharp edges and enable more accurate 3D reconstructions. Also, we trained our network on virtual scanned point clouds, demonstrated the performance of our method on both synthetic and real point clouds, presented various surface reconstruction results, and showed how our method outperforms the state-of-the-arts.

Keywords: Point cloud · Learning · Neural network · Edge-aware

1 Introduction

Point cloud consolidation is *a process of "massaging" a point set into a surface* [1], for enhancing the surface reconstruction quality. In the past two decades, a wide range of techniques have been developed to address this problem, including denoising, completion, resampling, and many more. However, these techniques are mostly based on *priors*, such as piecewise smoothness. Priors are

L. Yu and X. Li—Equal contributions.

Electronic supplementary material The online version of this chapter (https://doi.org/10.1007/978-3-030-01234-2_24) contains supplementary material, which is available to authorized users.

V. Ferrari et al. (Eds.): ECCV 2018, LNCS 11211, pp. 398–414, 2018.
https://doi.org/10.1007/978-3-030-01234-2_24

typically over-simplified models of the actual geometry behavior, thus the prior-based techniques tend to work well for specific class of models rather than being general.

To implicitly model and characterize the geometry behavior, one common way is to take a data-driven approach and model the complex behavior using explicit examples. Data-driven surface reconstruction techniques [2–5] are based on matching local portions (often denoted as patches) to a set of examples. Particularly, the emergence of neural networks and their startling performance provide a new means for 3D reconstruction from point sets by data-driven learning [6–8]. One of the main limitations of these neural network based methods is that they are oblivious to sharp features on 3D objects, where undersampling problems are typically more severe, making it challenging for an accurate object reconstruction.

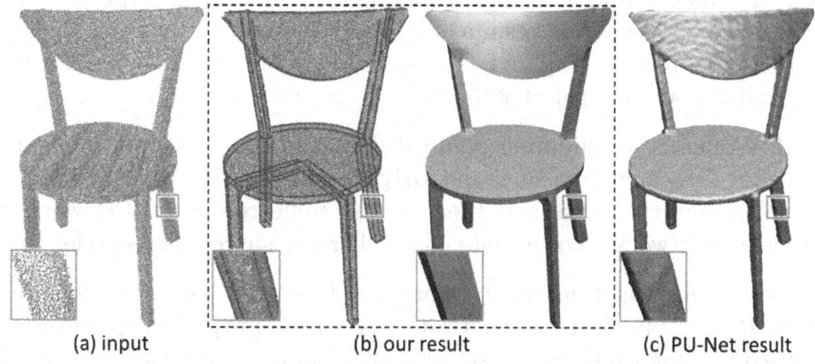

Fig. 1. Given a point cloud (a) with noisy samples in inhomogeneous distribution, our method consolidates it and reconstructs a plausible surface (b). Compared with PU-Net (c), our method is edge-aware and can preserve sharp features

In this paper, we present the first *edge-aware consolidation network*, namely EC-Net, for point cloud consolidation. The network is designed and trained, such that the output points admit to the surface characteristic of the 3D objects in the training set. More importantly, our method is *edge-aware*, in the sense that the network learns the geometry of edges from the training set, and during the test time, it identifies edge points and generates more points along the edges (and over the surface) to facilitate a 3D reconstruction that preserves sharp features.

Generally speaking, scanned point sets are irregular and non-uniform, and thus, do not lend themselves to be learned by common convolutional neural networks (CNN). Inspired by PointNet [9], we directly process 3D points by converting their coordinates into deep features and producing more points by feature expansion [7]. Then, for efficient learning of the edges, we design our network to process points grouped as local patches in the point cloud. To do so, we develop a patch extraction scheme that solely works on points, so that we can extract patches of points for use consistently in both training and testing phases.

In addition, to train the network to be edge-aware, we associate edge and mesh triangle information with the training patches, and train the network to learn features from the patches by regressing point-to-edge distances and then the point coordinates. More importantly, we design a novel edge-ware joint loss function that can be efficiently computed for directly comparison between the output points and ground truth 3D meshes. Our loss function encourages the output points to be located close to the underlying surface and to the edges, as well as distributed more evenly on surface. Then in the inference phase, the network can generate and find output points close to the edges. Since it is difficult to annotate edges directly in real scanned point clouds, we train our network on synthesized virtual scanned point clouds, and show the performance of our method on both real and virtual scanned point clouds. By using our trained network, we show through various experiments that we can improve not only the point cloud consolidation results (see Figs. 1(b) and (c)), but also the surface reconstruction quality, compared to various state-of-the-art methods. All the code is available at the project webpage[1].

Related Works. Consolidating scanned data and imperfect point clouds has been an active research area since the early 90's [10–12]. We briefly review some traditional geometric works and then discuss some recent related works that employ neural networks. For a more comprehensive survey, please refer to [13].

Point Cloud Consolidation. Early works in this area assumed smooth surface [1,14,15]. In [14], the parameterization-free local projection operator (LOP) was devised to enhance the point set quality. However, these methods are oblivious to sharp edges and corners. To consolidate a point set in an edge-aware manner, some methods detected/sensed the sharp edges and arranged points deliberatively along edges to preserve their sharpness [16–19]. Huang *et al.* [20] developed the edge-aware resampling (EAR) algorithm; it computes reliable normals away from edges and then progressively upsamples points towards the surface singularities. Despite its promising results, EAR depends on the accuracy of the given/estimated normal. Preiner *et al.* [21] developed CLOP, a continuous version of the LOP, for fast surface construction using the Gaussian mixture model to describe the point cloud density. To sum up, these geometric approaches either assume strong priors or rely on extra geometric attributes for upsampling point sets.

Neural Networks for Mesh and Point Cloud Processing. Motivated by the promising results that deep learning methods have achieved for image and video problems, there has been increasing effort to leverage neural networks for geometry and 3D shape problems. To do so, early works extracted low-level geometric features as inputs to CNNs [22,23]. Other works converted the input triangular meshes or point clouds to regular voxel grids [24–29] for CNN to process.

[1] https://yulequan.github.io/ec-net/index.html.

However, pre-extracting low-level features may bring bias, while a volume representation demands a high computational cost and is constrained by its resolution.

Recently, point clouds have drawn more attention, and there are some works to utilize neural networks to directly process point clouds. Qi *et al.* [9] firstly developed the PointNet, a network that takes a set of unordered points in 3D as inputs and learns features for object classification and segmentation. Later, they proposed the PointNet++ to enhance the network with a hierarchical feature learning technique [30]. Subsequently, many other networks have been proposed for high-level analysis problems with point clouds [31–40]. However, they all focus on analyzing global or mid-level attributes of point clouds. In some other aspects, Guerrero *et al.* [6] proposed a network to estimate the local shape properties in point clouds, including normal and curvature. 3D reconstruction from 2D images has also been widely studied [8,41,42]. Our work is most related to PU-Net [7], which presented a network to upsample a point set. However, our method is edge-aware, and we extract local patches and train the network to learn edges in patches with a novel edge-aware joint loss function.

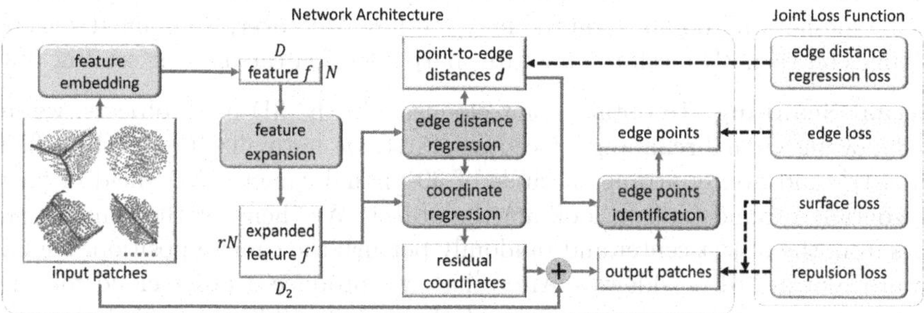

Fig. 2. The pipeline of EC-Net. For each point in an input patch, we first encode its local geometry into a feature vector f (size: $N \times D$) using PointNet++, and expand f into f' (size: $rN \times D_2$) using a feature expansion mechanism. Then, we regress the residual point coordinates and also the point-to-edge distances (d) from the expanded features, and form the output point coordinates by adding the original point coordinates to the residual. Finally, the network identifies points on edges and yields output points. The network was trained with an edge-aware joint loss function that has four terms; see the yellow boxes on the right (Color figure online)

2 Method

In this section, we first present the training data preparation (Sect. 2.1) and the EC-Net architecture (Sect. 2.2). Then, we present the edge-aware joint loss function (Sect. 2.3) and the implementation details (Sect. 2.4). Figure 2 shows the pipeline of EC-Net; see the supplemental material for the detailed architecture.

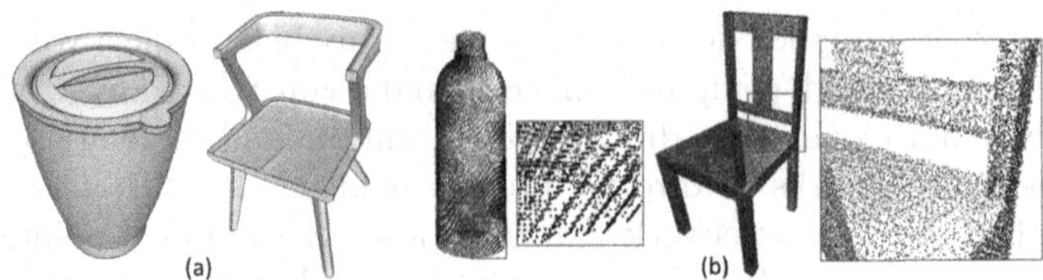

Fig. 3. Example annotated edges (in red) on some of our collected 3D meshes (a). Example point clouds produced from our virtual 3D scans (b). The point density varies and the zoom-in windows also reveal the synthetic noise (Color figure online)

2.1 Training Data Preparation

We train our network using point clouds synthesized from 3D objects, so that we can have ground truth surface and edge information. To start, we collect 3D meshes from ShapeNet [43] and other online repositories, including simple 3D shapes, mechanical parts, and everyday objects such as chairs. Since we train the network with patches as inputs, we prepare a large amount of patches on the 3D meshes and do not require many meshes. Moreover, we manually sketch polylines on each 3D mesh to annotate sharp edges on the meshes; see Fig. 3(a).

Virtual Scanning. To obtain point clouds from the 3D mesh objects, we use the following virtual scanning procedure. First, we normalize the mesh to fit in $[-1,+1]^3$, and evenly arrange a circle of 30 virtual cameras (50° field of view) horizontally around (and to look at) the object. We then put the cameras two units from the object center and randomly perturb the camera positions slightly upward, downward or sideway. After that, we produce a point cloud for each camera by rendering a depth image of the object, adding quantization noise (see Sect. 3) to the depth values and pixel locations, and backprojecting each foreground pixel to obtain a 3D point sample. Then, we can compose the 3D point clouds from different cameras to obtain a virtual scanned data. Such sampling procedure mimics a real scanner with surface regions closer to the virtual camera receiving more point samples; see Fig. 3(b) for two example results.

Patch Extraction. From a point cloud (see Fig. 4(c)), we aim to extract local groups of points (patches), such that the points in a patch are *geodesically* close to one another over the underlying surface. This is very important, since using Euclidean distances to select points could lead to points on opposite sides of a thin surface, e.g., see the thin plates in the chair shown in Fig. 3(b). Compared with [7], our patch extraction procedure directly operates on point clouds, *not* meshes, so we need a *consistent* extraction procedure for *both* network training and inference, where ground truth meshes are not available during the inference.

To this end, we first construct a weighted graph by considering each point as a node and creating an edge from each point to its k-nearest neighboring (k-nn) points, where k = 10; see Fig. 4(d). The edge weight is set as the Euclidean distance between the two points. Then, we randomly select $m = 100$ points as the patch centroids; from each selected point, we use the Dijkstra algorithm to

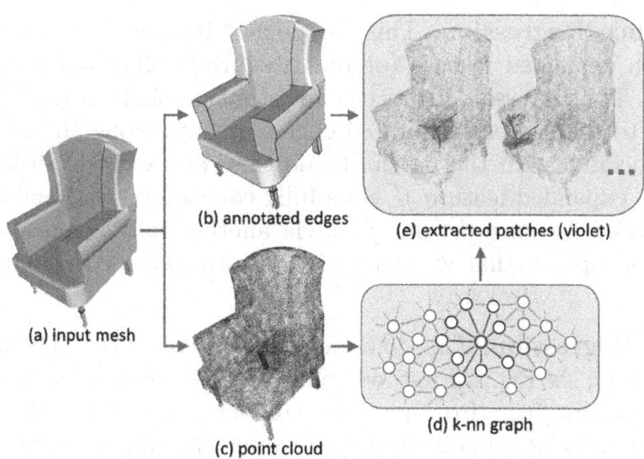

Fig. 4. Procedure to extract patches (a local group of points) from a point cloud; note that (a) and (b) are available only in the training (but not inference) phase

find the 2048 nearest points in terms of shortest path distances in the graph. Hence, we can find points that are approximately within a geodesic radius from the centroid. Further, we randomly select $\hat{N} = 1024$ points out of the 2048 points to introduce randomness into the point distribution, and normalize the 3D coordinates of the points to have zero mean inside a unit ball. For patches used for training, we also find the associated mesh triangles and annotated edge segments near the patches as the ground truth information for training the network; see Fig. 4(e).

2.2 Edge-Aware Point Set Consolidation Network

In this subsection, we present the major components of EC-Net; see Fig. 2.

Feature Embedding and Expansion. This component first maps the neighboring information (raw 3D coordinates of nearby points) around each point into a feature vector using PointNet++ [30] to account for the fact that the input points are irregular and unordered. The output is a D-dimensional multi-scale feature vector for each input point, where D is 256 in our experiments. In this step, we make the following adaptation for our problem. By design, PointNet++ processes a full point cloud of an object, while EC-Net processes local patches. Since patches have open boundary, points near the boundary have neighbors mostly on one of its side only, so we found that the extracted features of these points are less accurate. Hence, out of the $\hat{N}$ feature vectors, we retain the $N = \frac{\hat{N}}{2}$ feature vectors (denoted as f) corresponding to points closer to the patch centroid. Next, the component synthesizes points by expanding features directly in feature space using the feature expansion module in [7], since points and features should be interchangeable. After this module, feature f (dimension: $N \times D$) are expanded to be f' (dimension: $rN \times D_2$), where r is the upsampling rate and D_2 is the new feature dimension, which is set as 128; see again Fig. 2.

Edge Distance Regression. This component regresses a point-to-edge distance for each expanded feature (or point, equivalently) later for edge points identification. The regressed distance is an estimated shortest distance from the output point to the nearest annotated edge segment among all annotated edge segments associated with the patch. To do this, we extract a distance feature f_{dist} from the expanded feature f' via a fully connected layer, and then regress the point-to-edge distance d from f_{dist} via another fully connected layer. We do this in two steps, so that we can feed f_{dist} also to the coordinate regression component.

Coordinate Regression. This component reconstructs the 3D coordinates of the output points; see Fig. 2. First, we concatenate the expanded feature f' with the distance feature f_{dist} (from previous component) to form another feature, since f_{dist} contains certain point-to-edge distance information. Then, we regress the point coordinates from the concatenated feature by applying two fully connected layers. Note that we only regress the residual 3D coordinates, and the network output 3D coordinates of the output points by adding the original 3D coordinates of the input points to the regressed residual 3D coordinates.

Edge Points Identification. Denoting d_i as the regressed point-to-edge distance of output point x_i, we next find a subset of output points, namely *edge points* (denoted as $\mathcal{S}_{\Delta_d}$ with threshold Δ_d) that are near the edges: $\mathcal{S}_{\Delta_d} = \{x_i\}_{d_i < \Delta_d}$. Note that this component is performed in both training and inference phases.

2.3 Edge-Aware Joint Loss Function

The loss function should encourage the output points to be (i) located close to the underlying object surface, (ii) edge-aware (located close to the annotated edges), and (iii) more evenly distributed on the object surface. To this end, we guide the network's behavior by designing an *edge-aware joint loss function* with the following four loss terms (see also the rightmost part of Fig. 2):

Surface loss encourages the output points to be located close to the underlying surface. When extracting each training patch from the input point clouds, we find triangles and edge segments associated with the patch; see Fig. 4. Hence, we can define surface loss using the minimum shortest distance from each output point x_i to all the mesh triangles T associated with the patch: $d_T(x_i, T) = \min_{t \in T} \; d_t(x_i, t)$, where $d_t(x_i, t)$ is the shortest distance from x_i to triangle $t \in T$. It is worth noting that to compute d_t in 3D, we need to consider seven cases, since the point on t that is the closest to x_i may be located at triangle vertices, along triangle edges, or within the triangle face. Experimentally, we found that the algorithm [44] for calculating d_t can be implemented using TensorFlow to automatically calculate the gradients when training the network.

With d_T computed for all the output points, we can sum them up to compute the surface loss:

$$L_{surf} = \frac{1}{\tilde{N}} \sum_{1 \le i \le \tilde{N}} d_T^2(x_i, T), \tag{1}$$

where $\tilde{N} = rN$ is the number of output points in each patch.

Edge loss encourages the output points to be edge-aware, i.e., located close to the edges. Denoting E as the set of annotated edge segments associated with a patch, we define edge loss using the minimum shortest distance from each *edge point* to all the edge segments in the patch: $d_E(x_i, E) = \min_{e \in E} d_e(x_i, e)$, where $d_e(x_i, e)$ is the shortest distance from edge point x_i to any point on edge segment $e \in E$. Again, we implement the algorithm in [45] to calculate d_e for different shortest distance cases using TensorFlow to automatically calculate the gradients. Then, we sum up d_E for all the edge points and obtain the edge loss:

$$L_{edge} = \frac{\sum_{x_i \in \mathcal{S}_{\Delta_d}} d_E^2(x_i, E)}{|\mathcal{S}_{\Delta_d}|}, \quad \text{where } \mathcal{S}_{\Delta_d} \text{ is the edge point set.} \tag{2}$$

Repulsion loss encourages the output points to be more evenly distributed over the underlying surface. Given a set of output points $x_i, i = 1...\tilde{N}$, it is defined as

$$L_{repl} = \frac{1}{\tilde{N} \cdot K} \sum_{1 \le i \le \tilde{N}} \sum_{i' \in \mathcal{K}(i)} \eta(||x_{i'} - x_i||), \tag{3}$$

where $\mathcal{K}(i)$ is the set of indices for the K-nearest neighborhood of x_i (we set $K = 4$), $|| \cdot ||$ is the L2-norm, and $\eta(r) = max(0, h^2 - r^2)$ is a function to penalize x_i if it is too close to some other nearby points, where h is empirically set as 0.03 (which is the mean separation distance between points estimated from the number of points and bounding box diagonal length according to [20]). It is worth noting that we only want to penalize x_i when it is too close to some neighborhood points, so we only consider a few nearest neighboring points around x_i; moreover, we remove the repulsion effect when the point-to-point distance is above h.

Edge distance regression loss aims to guide the network to regress the point-to-edge distances d for the rN output points; see Fig. 2. Considering that it is difficult for the network to regress d, since not all output points are actually close to the annotated edges. Hence, we design a truncated regression loss:

$$L_{regr} = \frac{1}{\tilde{N}} \sum_{1 \le i \le \tilde{N}} \left[\mathcal{T}_b(d_E(x_i, E)) - \mathcal{T}_b(d_i)\right]^2, \tag{4}$$

where $\mathcal{T}_b(x) = max(0, min(x, b))$ is a piecewise linear function with parameter b. Empirically, we found the network training not sensitive to b, and set it as 0.5.

End-to-End Training. When training the network, we minimize the combined edge-aware joint loss function below with balancing weights α and β:

$$\mathcal{L} = L_{surf} + L_{repl} + \alpha L_{edge} + \beta L_{regr}. \quad (5)$$

In our implementation, we set α and β as 0.1 and 0.01, respectively.

2.4 Implementation Details

Network Training. Before the training, each input patch is normalized to fit in $[-1, 1]^3$. Then, we augment each patch on-the-fly in the network via a series of operators: a random rotation, a random translation in all dimensions by -0.2 to 0.2, a random scaling by 0.8 to 1.2, adding Gaussian noise to the patch points with σ set as 0.5% of the patch bounding box size, and randomly shuffling the ordering of points in the patch. We implement our method using TensorFlow, and train the network for 200 epochs using the Adam [46] optimizer with a minibatch size of 12 and a learning rate of 0.001. In our experiments, the default upsampling rate r is set as 4. For threshold Δ_d, we empirically set it as 0.15, since it is not sensitive to slight variation in our experiments. Overall, it took around 5 hrs to train the network on an NVidia TITAN Xp GPU.

Network Inference. We apply a trained network to process point clouds also in a patch-wise manner. To do so, we first find a subset of points in a test point cloud, and take them as centroids to extract patches of points using the procedure in Sect. 2.1. For the patches to distribute more evenly over the point cloud (say with N_{pt} points), we use farthest point sampling to randomly find $M = \beta \frac{N_{pt}}{N}$ points in the test point cloud with parameter β, which is empirically set as three. Hence, each point in the point cloud should appear roughly in β different patches on average. After extracting the patches, we feed them into the network and apply the network to produce 3D coordinates and point-to-edge distances, as well as to identify edge points (see Sect. 2.3). Unlike the training phase, we set a smaller Δ_d, which is 0.05. We use a larger Δ_d in the training because training is an optimization process, where we want the network to consider more points to learn to identify the points near the edges.

Surface Reconstruction. First, we build a k-nn graph for the output points from network. Then, we filter edge points by fitting line segments using RANSAC, and filter surface points (not near edges points) by finding small groups of nearby points in the k-nn graph in an edge-stopping manner and fitting planes using PCA. Edge stopping means we stop the breath-first growth at edge points; this avoids including irrelevant points beyond the edges. These steps are iterated several times. Lastly, we fill the tiny gap between edge and surface points by including some original points in the gap, and by applying dart throwing to add new points. To further reconstruct the surface, we follow the procedure in EAR [20] to downsample the point set and compute normals, use ball pivoting [47] or screened Poisson surface reconstruction [48] to reconstruct the surface, and use a bilateral normal filtering [49] to clean the resulting mesh.

3 Experiments

Dataset Overview. Since most models in [7] are manifolds without sharp edges, we collected 24 CAD models and 12 everyday objects as our training data set, and manually annotate sharp edges on them; see supplemental material. Then, we randomly crop 2,400 patches from the models (see Fig. 2) to train our network; see the procedure in Sect. 2.1. To perform the experiments presented in this section, we do not reuse the models in the training data set but download additional 3D models from ShapeNet [43]. For each testing model, we also use the procedure in Sect. 2.1 to generate the virtual scanned point clouds as input.

Surface Reconstruction Results. We demonstrate the quality of our method by applying it to consolidate point sets and reconstruct surfaces. Figure 5(a) shows the input point clouds generated from the testing models shown in Fig. 5(f), while Fig. 5(b) and (c) show our results (see supplemental material for additional reconstruction results). To reconstruct the surfaces, we follow the procedure in Sect. 2.4 and employ the ball pivoting algorithm (BPA) [47] to reconstruct the surfaces. To show the effect of our network, we apply the same procedure with BPA to reconstruct surfaces directly from (i) the input point clouds (see Fig. 5(d)), and from (ii) the input point clouds with PCA plane fitting for denoising (see Fig. 5(e)), without using our network to process the point clouds.

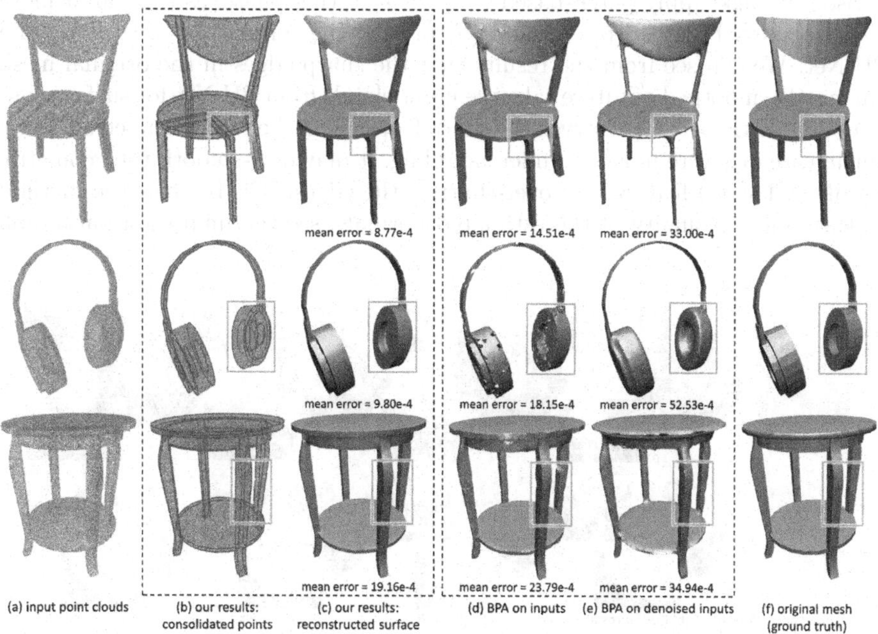

Fig. 5. Our method produces consolidated point clouds (b) that lead to higher quality surface reconstruction results (c). Predicted edge points are shown in red

Comparing the resulting reconstructed surfaces with the ground truth meshes shown in Fig. 5(f), we can see that our method achieves the best visual quality, particularly on preserving the edges. In addition, we compute the mean Hausdorff distance between the reconstructed surfaces and their corresponding ground truth surfaces; see the mean errors shown in Fig. 5(c), (d) and (e); our method consistently has the lowest mean errors among all the testing models. These quantitative results, together with the visual comparison, give evidence that our method produces consolidated point sets and improves the surface reconstruction quality. Note that without the knowledge of edges learnt and recognized by the network, using PCA alone to denoise point clouds is not edge-aware; the sharp edges would be wiped away, if we directly apply PCA to the raw point cloud, leading to the inferior surface reconstructions shown in Fig. 5(e). To sum up, our consolidation facilitates high-quality reconstruction not only on sharp objects but also on usual smooth objects. It is worth to note that with our consolidation, the overall reconstruction quality also improves over the state-of-the-art surface reconstruction methods on the benchmark models in [50]; due to page limit, please see the supplemental material for more details.

Comparing with Other Methods. In the experiment, we compare our method with state-of-the-art methods, EAR [20], CLOP [21], GPF [51], and PU-Net [7], by applying them to process and consolidate point clouds before the screened Poisson surface reconstruction [48]. As for PU-Net, we train a new model using our training objects and code released by the author. For better comparison, we also apply patch-based manner in testing phase, as this can achieve better results. Figures 6(b), (c) and (d) present the comparison with EAR and PU-Net. We can see from the results that the sharp edges in the original mesh are mostly smoothed out if we take the point clouds from PU-Net for surface construction. EAR better preserves the sharp features on the reconstructed surfaces, but in case of severe noise or under-sampling, it may over-smooth the geometric details and sharp features, or over-sharpen the edges. It is because the method depends on the quality of the estimated normals; see the limitation paragraph

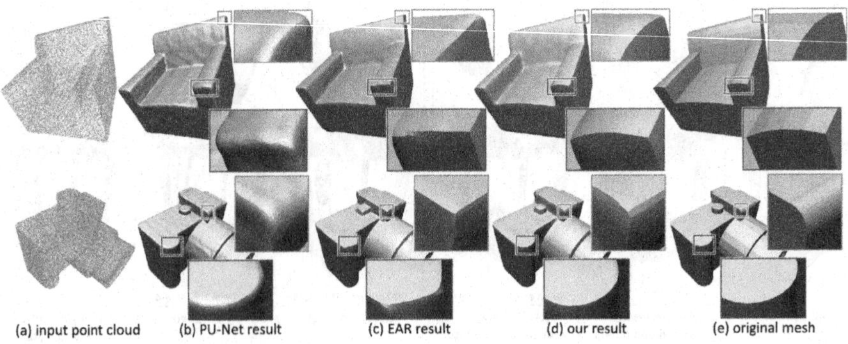

Fig. 6. Comparing surface reconstruction results produced by using PU-Net (b), EAR (c), and our method (d) to consolidate points with the original meshes (e)

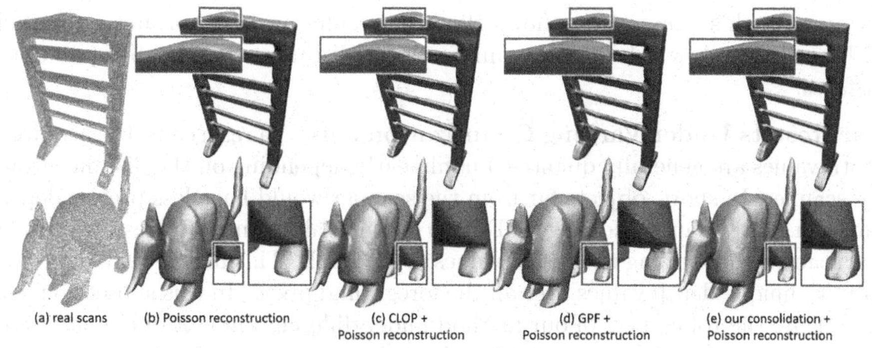

Fig. 7. Comparing reconstruction results on real scans produced by direct reconstruction (b) and with consolidation: CLOP, GPF, and our method (c-e)

in [20]. Our method, which is based on an edge-aware neural network model, is able to learn and capture edge information with high learning generalization, our point cloud consolidation results can lead to surface reconstructions that are closer to the original meshes. Figure 7 also demonstrates that our method helps enhance the Poisson reconstruction quality on real scans in terms of preserving sharp edges compared with CLOP [21] and GPF [51].

Table 1. Quantitative comparison: our method, PU-Net, and EAR

Model	Mean (10^{-3})			RMS (10^{-3})		
	Our	PU-Net	EAR	Our	PU-Net	EAR
Camera	**1.31**	1.91	2.43	**1.99**	2.74	3.75
Sofa	1.72	3.20	**1.56**	**2.40**	4.68	2.87
Chair	**0.88**	1.70	1.93	**1.27**	2.50	3.54
Fandisk	**1.09**	2.86	2.33	**1.77**	4.50	5.63
Switch-pot	**1.36**	2.00	1.76	**1.83**	3.07	2.44
Headphone	**0.81**	1.83	3.71	**1.19**	2.89	6.93
Table	**1.15**	2.14	2.74	**1.62**	3.12	5.34
Monitor	**0.61**	2.01	2.58	**0.97**	2.71	5.73

We also quantitatively compare with EAR and PU-Net by calculating the minimum distances from output points to the associated original mesh (as ground truth) in the test dataset. Table 1 lists the mean and root mean square (RMS) values of different methods on the test models; see supplemental material for visual comparison. We can see from the table that points generated from our method are closer to the original meshes compared to others. The PU-Net uses the EMD loss to encourage output points to be located on the underlying surfaces, so this comparison shows that the results are sub-optimal compared with our method, which directly minimizes the distances from output points to surfaces.

Our Results Under Varying Quantization noise. In real scans, the acquired depth values are generally quantized nonlinearly depending on the distance from the scanner. In short, objects far from the scanner would have less precise depth values in fewer quantization levels. During the virtual scanning process, we mimic real scans by quantizing the depth values in N_q levels. This means that there are only N_q unique depth values over all the foreground pixels. In this subsection, we investigate the robustness of our method under different amount of quantization noise by producing three sets of point cloud data using virtual scan on a testing model with $N_q = 120$ (low noise), $N_q = 80$ (medium noise), and $N_q = 50$ (high noise) and then applying our method to consolidate the resulting point clouds.

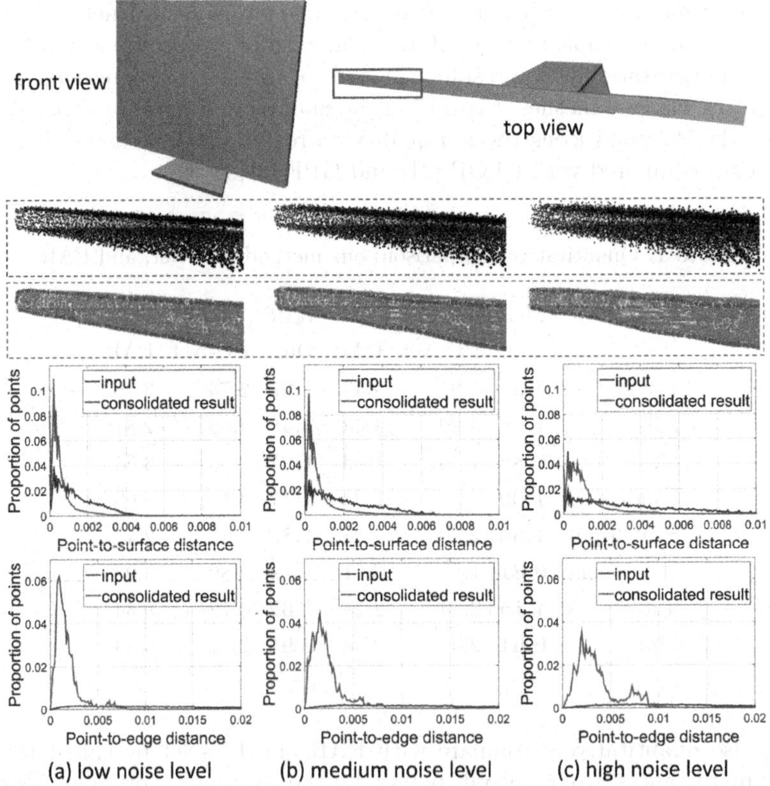

Fig. 8. Results of using our method to consolidate point clouds with different amount of quantization noise. Top row: the testing Monitor model; 2nd and 3rd rows: blown-up views of the input point clouds with different noise level (low to high) and our consolidated results, respectively; 4th and 5th rows: statistics of point-to-surface and point-to-edge distances, respectively (Color figure online)

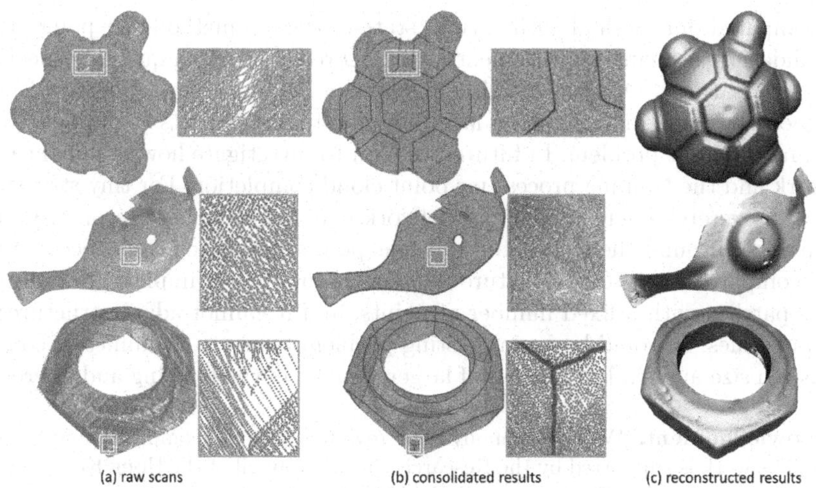

Fig. 9. Three results from real scans (a). Note the diversity of the geometry, the sparseness of the inputs (a), and how well the network locates the edges (in red); see (b). The reconstruction results (c) are yet imperfect due to tiny regions that are severely undersampled (see the blown-up views in (a)) (Color figure online)

Figure 8 presents the results, where the left, middle and right columns correspond to low, medium and high noise levels, respectively. From the blown-up views, we can see more points above the object surface for the point cloud with high noise. The statistics about the point-to-surface distances also reveal the noise level; see the blue plots in the 4th row. After the consolidation, the points are steered to the left (see the red plots in 4th row), meaning that the points are now all closer to the ground truth surface under different noise levels. Similar pattern can also be observed from the statistical results for the point-to-edge distances.

Results on Real Scans. We also apply our method to point clouds produced from real scans downloaded from Aim@Shape and obtained from the EAR project [20]. Figure 7 has shown some results on real scans, and Fig. 9 shows more consolidation and reconstruction results. As we can see, real scan point clouds are often noisy and have inhomogeneous point distribution. Comparing with the input point clouds, our method is still able to generate more points near the edges and on the surface, while better preserving the sharp features.

4 Discussion and Future Works

We presented EC-Net, the first edge-aware network for consolidating point clouds. The network was trained on synthetic data and tested on both virtual and real data. To be edge-aware, we design a joint loss function to identify points along edges, and to encourage points to be located close to the underlying surface and edges, as well as being more evenly distributed over surface.

We compared our method with various state-of-the-art methods for point cloud consolidation, showing improvement in the 3D reconstruction quality, especially at sharp features. Our method has a number of limitations. First, it is not designed for completion, so filling large holes and missing parts would be a separate and different problem. In future, we plan to investigate how to enhance the network and the training process for point cloud completion. For tiny structures that are severely undersampled, our network may not be able to reconstruct the sharp edges around them. With insufficient points, the patch could become too large compared to the tiny structure. Moreover, our current implementation considers patches with a fixed number of points, and it cannot adapt structures of varying scales. It would be an interesting problem to try to dynamically control the patch size and explore the use of larger context in the training and inference.

Acknowledgement. We thank anonymous reviewers for the comments and suggestions. The work is supported by the Research Grants Council of the Hong Kong Special Administrative Region (Project no. GRF 14225616), the Shenzhen Science and Technology Program (No. JCYJ20170413162617606 and No. JCYJ20160429190300857), and the CUHK strategic recruitment fund.

References

1. Alexa, M., Behr, J., Cohen-Or, D., Fleishman, S., Levin, D., Silva, C.T.: Computing and rendering point set surfaces. IEEE Trans. Vis. Comput. Graph. **9**(1), 3–15 (2003)
2. Gal, R., Shamir, A., Hassner, T., Pauly, M., Cohen-Or, D.: Surface reconstruction using local shape priors. In: Symposium on Geometry Processing. Number EPFL-CONF-149318, pp. 253–262 (2007)
3. Sung, M., Kim, V.G., Angst, R., Guibas, L.J.: Data-driven structural priors for shape completion. ACM Trans. Graph. (SIGGRAPH Asia) **34**(6), 175:1–175:11 (2015)
4. Xu, K., Kim, V.G., Huang, Q., Kalogerakis, E.: Data-driven shape analysis and processing. Comput. Graph. Forum **36**(1), 101–132 (2017)
5. Remil, O., Xie, Q., Xie, X., Xu, K., Wang, J.: Surface reconstruction with data-driven exemplar priors. Comput. Aided Des. **88**, 31–41 (2017)
6. Guerrero, P., Kleiman, Y., Ovsjanikov, M., Mitra, N.J.: PCPNet: learning local shape properties from raw point clouds. arXiv preprint arXiv:1710.04954 (2017)
7. Yu, L., Li, X., Fu, C.W., Cohen-Or, D., Heng, P.A.: PU-Net: point cloud upsampling network. arXiv preprint arXiv:1801.06761 (2018)
8. Groueix, T., Fisher, M., Kim, V.G., Russell, B.C., Aubry, M.: AtlasNet: a Papier-Mâché approach to learning 3D surface generation. In: IEEE CVPR, pp. 216–224 (2018)
9. Qi, C.R., Su, H., Mo, K., Guibas, L.J.: PointNet: deep learning on point sets for 3D classification and segmentation. In: IEEE CVPR, pp. 77–85 (2017)
10. Hoppe, H., DeRose, T., Duchamp, T., McDonald, J., Stuetzle, W.: Surface reconstruction from unorganized points. In: Proceedings of SIGGRAPH, pp. 71–78 (1992)
11. Turk, G., Levoy, M.: Zippered polygon meshes from range images. In: Proceedings of SIGGRAPH, pp. 311–318 (1994)

12. Amenta, N., Bern, M., Kamvysselis, M.: A new Voronoi-based surface reconstruction algorithm. In: Proceedings of SIGGRAPH, pp. 415–422 (1998)
13. Berger, M., et al.: A survey of surface reconstruction from point clouds. In: Computer Graphics Forum, vol. 36, pp. 301–329. Wiley Online Library (2017)
14. Lipman, Y., Cohen-Or, D., Levin, D., Tal-Ezer, H.: Parameterization-free projection for geometry reconstruction. ACM Trans. Graph. (SIGGRAPH) **26**(3), 22:1–22:5 (2007)
15. Huang, H., Li, D., Zhang, H.R., Ascher, U., Cohen-Or, D.: Consolidation of unorganized point clouds for surface reconstruction. ACM Trans. Graph. (SIGGRAPH Asia) **28**(5), 176:1–176:8 (2009)
16. Pauly, M., Keiser, R., Kobbelt, L.P., Gross, M.: Shape modeling with point-sampled geometry. ACM Trans. Graph. (SIGGRAPH) **22**(3), 641–650 (2003)
17. Guennebaud, G., Barthe, L., Paulin, M.: Real-time point cloud refinement. In: Symposium on Point Based Graphics, pp. 41–48 (2004)
18. Fleishman, S., Cohen-Or, D., Silva, C.T.: Robust moving least-squares fitting with sharp features. ACM Trans. Graph. (SIGGRAPH) **24**(3), 544–552 (2005)
19. Öztireli, A.C., Guennebaud, G., Gross, M.: Feature preserving point set surfaces based on non-linear kernel regression. Comput. Graph. Forum (Eurographics) **28**(2), 493–501 (2009)
20. Huang, H., Wu, S., Gong, M., Cohen-Or, D., Ascher, U., Zhang, H.R.: Edge-aware point set resampling. ACM Trans. Graph. **32**(1), 9:1–9:12 (2013)
21. Preiner, R., Mattausch, O., Arikan, M., Pajarola, R., Wimmer, M.: Continuous projection for fast L1 reconstruction. ACM Trans. Graph. (SIGGRAPH) **33**(4), 47:1–47:13 (2014)
22. Guo, K., Zou, D., Chen, X.: 3D mesh labeling via deep convolutional neural networks. ACM Trans. Graph. **35**(1), 3:1–3:12 (2015)
23. Boulch, A., Marlet, R.: Deep learning for robust normal estimation in unstructured point clouds. Comput. Graph. Forum (SGP) **35**(5), 281–290 (2016)
24. Qi, C.R., Su, H., Niessner, M., Dai, A., Yan, M., Guibas, L.J.: Volumetric and multi-view CNNs for object classification on 3D data. In: IEEE CVPR, pp. 5648–5656 (2016)
25. Dai, A., Qi, C.R., Nießner, M.: Shape completion using 3D-encoder-predictor CNNs and shape synthesis. In: IEEE CVPR, pp. 5868–5877 (2017)
26. Han, X., Li, Z., Huang, H., Kalogerakis, E., Yu, Y.: High-resolution shape completion using deep neural networks for global structure and local geometry inference. In: IEEE ICCV, pp. 85–93 (2017)
27. Wang, P., Liu, Y., Guo, Y., Sun, C., Tong, X.: O-CNN: Octree-based convolutional neural networks for 3D shape analysis. ACM Trans. Graph. **36**(4), 1–11 (2017)
28. Riegler, G., Ulusoy, A.O., Geiger, A.: OctNet: learning deep 3D representations at high resolutions. In: IEEE CVPR, pp. 6620–6629 (2017)
29. Liu, F., et al.: 3DCNN-DQN-RNN: a deep reinforcement learning framework for semantic parsing of large-scale 3D point clouds. In: IEEE ICCV, pp. 5678–5687 (2017)
30. Qi, C.R., Yi, L., Su, H., Guibas, L.J.: PointNet++: deep hierarchical feature learning on point sets in a metric space. In: Advances in Neural Information Processing Systems, vol. 30, pp. 5105–5114 (2017)
31. Hua, B.-S., Tran, M.-K., Yeung, S.-K.: Pointwise convolutional neural networks. In: Proceedings of the IEEE Conference on Computer Vision and Pattern Recognition (2018)
32. Klokov, R., Lempitsky, V.: Escape from cells: deep Kd-Networks for the recognition of 3D point cloud models. In: IEEE ICCV, pp. 863–872 (2017)

33. Landrieu, L., Simonovsky, M.: Large-scale point cloud semantic segmentation with superpoint graphs. arXiv preprint arXiv:1711.09869 (2017)
34. Xu, D., Anguelov, D., Jain, A.: PointFusion: Deep sensor fusion for 3D bounding box estimation. arXiv preprint arXiv:1711.10871 (2017)
35. Wang, W., Yu, R., Huang, Q., Neumann, U.: SGPN: similarity group proposal network for 3D point cloud instance segmentation. arXiv preprint arXiv:1711.08588 (2017)
36. Yang, Y., Feng, C., Shen, Y., Tian, D.: FoldingNet: interpretable unsupervised learning on 3D point clouds. In: IEEE CVPR, pp. 206–215 (2018)
37. Qi, C.R., Liu, W., Wu, C., Su, H., Guibas, L.J.: Frustum PointNets for 3D object detection from RGB-D data. arXiv preprint arXiv:1711.08488 (2017)
38. Li, Y., Bu, R., Sun, M., Chen, B.: PointCNN. arXiv preprint arXiv:1801.07791 (2018)
39. Wang, Y., Sun, Y., Liu, Z., Sarma, S.E., Bronstein, M.M., Solomon, J.M.: Dynamic graph CNN for learning on point clouds. arXiv preprint arXiv:1801.07829 (2018)
40. Su, H., et al.: SPLATNet: sparse lattice networks for point cloud processing. In: IEEE CVPR, pp. 2530–2539 (2018)
41. Fan, H., Su, H., Guibas, L.J.: A point set generation network for 3D object reconstruction from a single image. In: IEEE CVPR, pp. 2463–2471 (2017)
42. Lin, C.H., Kong, C., Lucey, S.: Learning efficient point cloud generation for dense 3D object reconstruction. In: AAAI (2018, to appear)
43. Chang, A.X., et al.: ShapeNet: an information-rich 3D model repository. arXiv preprint arXiv:1512.03012 (2015)
44. Eberly, D.: Distance between point and triangle in 3D (1999). https://www.geometrictools.com/Documentation/DistancePoint3Triangle3.pdf
45. Eberly, D.: Distance between point and line, ray, or line segment (1999). https://www.geometrictools.com/Documentation/DistancePointLine.pdf
46. Kingma, D., Ba, J.: Adam: a method for stochastic optimization. arXiv preprint arXiv:1412.6980 (2014)
47. Bernardini, F., Mittleman, J., Rushmeier, H., Silva, C., Taubin, G.: The ball-pivoting algorithm for surface reconstruction. IEEE Trans. Vis. Comput. Graph. **5**(4), 349–359 (1999)
48. Kazhdan, M., Hoppe, H.: Screened poisson surface reconstruction. ACM Trans. Graph. **32**(3), 29:1–29:13 (2013)
49. Zheng, Y., Fu, H., Au, O.K.C., Tai, C.L.: Bilateral normal filtering for mesh denoising. IEEE Trans. Vis. Comput. Graph. **17**(10), 1521–1530 (2011)
50. Berger, M., Levine, J.A., Nonato, L.G.: A benchmark for surface reconstruction. ACM Trans. Graph. **32**(2), 20 (2013)
51. Lu, X., Wu, S., Chen, H., Yeung, S.K., Chen, W., Zwicker, M.: GPF: GMM-inspired feature-preserving point set filtering. IEEE Trans. Vis. Comput. Graph. **24**(8), 2315–2326 (2018)

3D Recurrent Neural Networks with Context Fusion for Point Cloud Semantic Segmentation

Xiaoqing Ye[1,2], Jiamao Li[1(✉)], Hexiao Huang[3], Liang Du[1,2], and Xiaolin Zhang[1]

[1] Shanghai Institute of Microsystem and Information Technology, Chinese Academy of Sciences, Shanghai, China
{qingye,jmli}@mail.sim.ac.cn

[2] University of Chinese Academy of Sciences, Beijing, China

[3] School of Science and Technology, Shanghai Open University, Shanghai, China

Abstract. Semantic segmentation of 3D unstructured point clouds remains an open research problem. Recent works predict semantic labels of 3D points by virtue of neural networks but take limited context knowledge into consideration. In this paper, a novel end-to-end approach for unstructured point cloud semantic segmentation, named 3P-RNN, is proposed to exploit the inherent contextual features. First the efficient pointwise pyramid pooling module is investigated to capture local structures at various densities by taking multi-scale neighborhood into account. Then the two-direction hierarchical recurrent neural networks (RNNs) are utilized to explore long-range spatial dependencies. Each recurrent layer takes as input the local features derived from unrolled cells and sweeps the 3D space along two directions successively to integrate structure knowledge. On challenging indoor and outdoor 3D datasets, the proposed framework demonstrates robust performance superior to state-of-the-arts.

Keywords: 3D semantic segmentation · Unstructured point cloud
Recurrent neural networks · Pointwise pyramid pooling

1 Introduction

Scene understanding has been extensively studied due to its critical role in autonomous driving, robot navigation, augmented reality and 3D reconstruction. Despite of the tremendous progress made in the field of semantic segmentation with the help of deep learning strategies, most approaches cope with 2D images [1–3], whereas 3D semantic segmentation of unstructured point clouds remains a challenging problem due to its large-scale point data, irregular shape and non-uniform densities.

V. Ferrari et al. (Eds.): ECCV 2018, LNCS 11211, pp. 415–430, 2018.
https://doi.org/10.1007/978-3-030-01234-2_25

Previous learning-based attempts mainly focus on regularizing input point cloud shapes, so as to draw on the experience of 2D semantic segmentation networks. For example, points are first voxelized by volumetric occupancy grid representation and 3D Convolutional Neural Networks (CNN) are employed to learn voxel-level semantics. Due to the sparsity of point clouds, the voxelization is inefficient and fine-details are missed to avoid high computation cost. Besides, the accuracy is limited because all points within the same voxel are assigned with the same semantic label. To make use of 2D frameworks, snapshots of 2D images taken at multi-views of 3D space are also learned, however, the reprojection back to 3D space is also a nontrivial problem.

The first pioneer work PointNet that directly operates on 3D point cloud is recently proposed [4]. Without the transformation to voxels, the architecture preserves inherent information within the raw points to predict point-level semantics. PointNet takes advantage of Multilayer Perceptron (MLP) to learn high-dimensional local features for each point individually. Then the local features are aggregated by symmetric max pooling to yield global feature, which is invariant against the permutations of points. However, the architecture has two limitations that restrict its performance to larger and more complicated point clouds. For one thing, only the pointwise features along with the pooled global features are integrated, failing to capture local structures represented by neighboring points. For another, a point cloud is first subdivided into small volumetric blocks and each block is predicted independently without any connection. In consequence, the overall accuracy of PointNet is limited in complicated scenes.

To tackle the first problem, we adopt the one-stride pyramid pooling to aggregate multi-scale neighboring knowledge due to its nonparametric feature and efficiency in enlarging receptive field. Instead of replicating the global pooled features for all points as PointNet does, we perform pointwise pooling and each point is represented by particular pyramid local features. Note that we employ one-stride multi-window pooling rather than multi-stride fixed-window pooling units, in view of preserving fine-grained details. With regard to the second problem, we further integrate long-distance context by means of a two-step hierarchical RNN model. Specifically, the point cloud is first subdivided into partially overlapped blocks along the two horizontal directions, namely, x and y, respectively. The first set of RNNs are applied to the blocks along the x-direction, which updates the state and output according to the long-dependency neighboring blocks. Next, the features derived from the first RNN set are further fed into another set of RNNs along y-direction to integrate relevant context across the horizonal dimensions. This is because adjacent objects or large objects indicate some inherent contextual connection, which helps to solve the ambiguity. For example, chairs are often near the table, and windows are generally inside the wall. Experimental results on the challenging point cloud datasets reveal that our strategy largely improves the accuracy for 3D semantic segmentation.

To sum up, the main contributions of our work are as follows:

- We propose a novel end-to-end framework for unstructured point cloud semantic segmentation, incorporating local spatial structures as well as long-dependency context. The pointwise pyramid pooling (3P) module increases the overall accuracy at negligible extra overhead.
- We introduce a two-direction hierarchical RNN model to learn long-range spatial context and inherent connection for pointy cloud semantic segmentation. To the best of our knowledge, this is the first time that a two-direction tactic RNN model is investigated to perform 3D semantic segmentation task.
- Our framework presents new state-of-the-art performance on indoor and outdoor 3D semantic datasets.

2 Related Work

Traditional point cloud semantic segmentation algorithms largely rely on handcrafted features and well-designed optimization approaches, sometimes preprocessing and post-processing strategies are required to achieve better performance. In this work we mainly focus on the review of deep learning strategies that are more related to our work.

Motivated by the large collections of 3D scene datasets such as indoor datasets NYU V2 [5], S3DIS [6], ScanNet [7] and outdoor datasets Semantic.3D [8], KITTI [9], vKITTI [10], great progress of point cloud processing has been made in recent years. However, due to the irregularity and inconsistent point densities of 3D geometric data, classic CNNs are unable to directly deal with point cloud data inputs. As a result, some alternatives have been tailored to the problem.

Voxel-Based 3D CNNs: In order to represent 3D geometric shape, a point cloud is first converted into regular volumetric occupancy grids and then trained by 3D CNNs to yield voxel-level predictions [7,11,12]. However, uniform 3D arrangement is inefficient because of the sparsity of 3D data. Besides, due to the expensive computation of 3D convolutions than 2d ones, the voxel size is constrained to a relatively small size and accordingly, it is challenging for such architectures to be extended to large-scale point clouds. Unbalanced octrees were exploited to tackle the sparsity problem, which allowed to train 3D CNNs at higher resolutions [13]. SEGCloud subsampled large cloud into voxels and post-processed by trilinear interpolation and conditional random field [14]. However, all the voxel-based methods fail to achieve point-level accuracy.

Multi-view CNNs: An alternative is to project the 3D point cloud into 2D image rendering of multiple views and apply well-engineered 2D CNNs [2,15–17] to jointly classify them. Multi-view CNN (MVCNN) [18] was designed on top of image-based classification networks, which integrated the views taken around a 3D meshed object through view pooling. Multi-resolution filtering in 3D space was introduced to further improve the performance of multi-view CNNs [19]. SnapNet [20] generated snapshots around the 3D scene in the form of RGB and

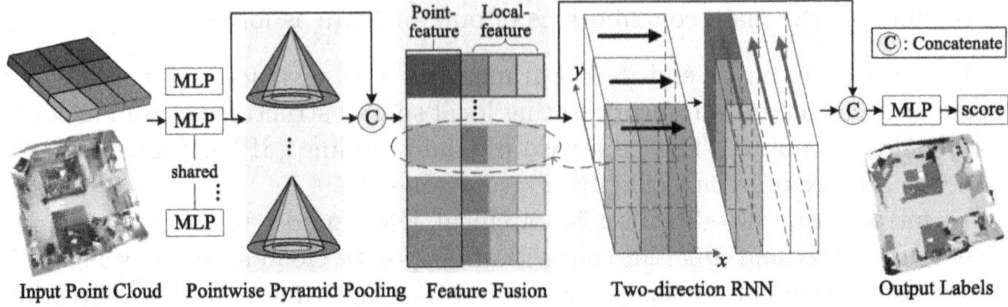

Fig. 1. Overview of the proposed approach. The architecture takes as input the unstructured point cloud and outputs pointwise semantic labels. Point-features and local cell features are concatenated and passed through the two-direction RNN module along x and y. The output of the first RNNs (black arrowed) are reorganized and fed to the next RNNs (red). For details of pointwise pyramid pooling, see Fig. 2 (Color figure online).

depth image pairs and applied 2D neural networks to process them separately. SnapNet-R [21] improved the baseline work SnapNet by directly processing RGB-D snapshots in numerous views for dense 3D point labeling. However, 2D snapshots break the inherent relationship within 3D data and thus fails to exploit the full power of 3D spatial context. Besides, it is not direct enough and requires extra 2D to 3D re-mapping.

Deep Learning on Unordered Point Sets: PointNet [4] was the first architecture that directly worked on raw point sets to produce per-point classes. Pointwise features and the aggregated global feature were concatenated to make pointwise predictions. However, the absence of neighboring context structure limited the segmentation performance on complicated scenes. To overcome this drawback, the hierarchical approach PointNet++ [22] was designed to better capture local structures as well as generalize to variable densities. Also inspired by the recent PointNet work, multi-scale windows or neighboring cell positions were exploited to incorporate neighborhood knowledge [23]. Due to the efficiency in extracting point-features, the PointNet framework was further extended to learn local shape properties [24] as well as predict 3D Object Detection from RGB-D Data [25]. Graph neural networks (GNNs) were undertaken to spread contextual information on top of 3D points [26]. Nevertheless, each node in the k-nearest neighbor graph requires additional 2D appearance features for initialization. A very recent GNN work captured the structure of point clouds by superpoint graph, which partitioned various objects into simple shapes and assigned segmentation labels to each part as a whole [27]. The GNNs iteratively updated the node state by message propagation over neighboring nodes. In terms of realization, the dynamic models can be implemented as Recurrent Neural Network.

3 3D Recurrent Neural Networks with Context Fusion

The proposed framework takes inspiration from PointNet [4], which is briefly reviewed in the following part. The baseline is extended with two distinctive improvements to learn local and long-dependency spatial context for better performance. For one thing, a pointwise pyramid pooling module is proposed to learn multi-scale neighboring context. Though simple, it is more efficient than multi-scale input context aggregation in [22,23] because of the non-parametric pooling units. For another, long-range context is exploited by the two-direction RNN model, which enables the network to learn spatial context in large-scale point clouds. An overview of our approach is presented in Fig. 1.

3.1 Review of PointNet

In the vanilla PointNet work, given a set of unstructured 3D points $\{p_1, p_2, ..., p_N\}$ with $p_i \in R^d$, they are first divided into small overlapped 3D blocks and each block is handled independently. Multi-layer perceptron (MLP) is exploited to learn high-dimensional spatial encoding of each point, i.e., the pointwise features. The block feature is obtained by aggregating pointwise features by a single max pooling within the same block, i.e., the global feature. The global feature is then duplicated for N tiles and concatenated with the corresponding pointwise features to yield the final prediction score. The operation of PointNet can be represented by

$$F(p_1, p_2, ..., p_N) = \underset{i=1,...,N}{MLP}\left(C\{maxpool\{\underset{i=1,...,N}{MLP}(p_i)\}, \underset{i=1,...,N}{MLP}(p_i)\}\right) \quad (1)$$

where C denotes the concatenation operation, indices of points' index from 1 to N below MLP denotes the MLP operation is pointwise. Nevertheless, the semantic segmentation performance is limited by a lack of neighboring structure and long-range context.

3.2 Pointwise Pyramid Pooling

In this work, we propose a simple but efficient strategy to capture local neighboring context robust to densities. Owing to the brutal global max pooling in PointNet, it is prone to missing fine details and causing ambiguity. Multi-scale grouping and multi-resolution grouping of points within a radius to the certain point are leveraged to learn the structure information in [22]. Alternatively, multi-scale and multi-grid input context are employed to compute block-features in [23]. Both of these strategies capture multi-scale local structures at the expense of indirected and complex fusion strategy, as well as extra computation.

Different from classic 2D pooling unit that employs various strides, we adopt a pointwise pyramid pooling (3P) module with multi-size pooling windows inspired by [28]. This is because pooling module with stride larger than one could bring about a loss of resolution and hampers the accuracy of dense prediction.

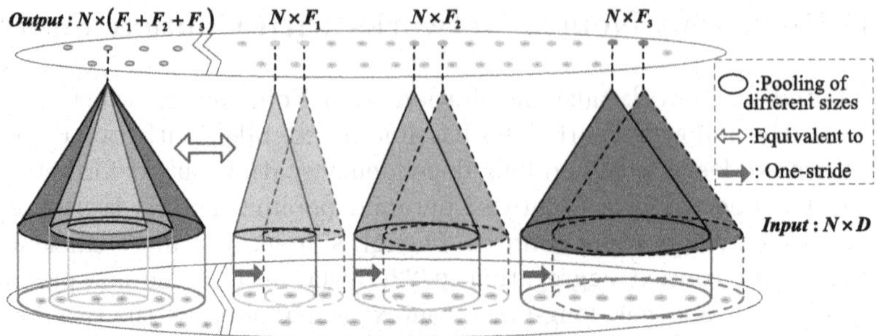

Fig. 2. Pointwise pyramid pooling. Given $N \times D$ input features, each pooling outputs features with the same number of input points (one-stride) and is then concatenated.

In specific, given a set of unordered points, we first divide the whole 3D space into blocks of 1.5 m × 1.5 m along the ground plane. Each block is extended to cover the whole room height. Pyramid pooling is done at neighborhoods with different number of points. Rather than searching k-nearest neighbors for each point, instead we adopt an approximate but more efficient way leveraging multiple scales of cuboids. In other words, we further subdivide each block into smaller cuboids at different scales. At each scale, one-stride max pooling module with corresponding pooling window size is employed. For example, if window size is N, we randomly select N points within the corresponding cuboid for max pooling. The 3P pooling can be denoted as

$$P(p_1, p_2, ...p_N) = \left[\underset{p=p_1,...,p_N}{maxpool}(f, k_1), ..., \underset{p=p_1,...,p_N}{maxpool}(f, k_m) \right] \tag{2}$$

where k_i denotes one-stride pooling window size. f represents high-level features learned by MLP. Notably compared to Eq. 1, we move the representation of point set range $\{p = p_1, p_2, ..., p_N\}$ from inside the max-pooling operation to outside, since Eq. 1 attains a single output for all points within the block, whereas ours in Eq. 2 yields the same size of output features as input vectors, namely, pointwise. In our architecture, the adopted window size are N, $N/8$ and $N/64$, respectively.

The attained coarse-to-fine pooled features are then integrated by a single convolution layer for the subsequent RNN stage. The sketch map of our one-stride 3P module is depicted in Fig. 2. Thanks to its nonparametric feature and efficiency in enlarging the receptive field, it is able to achieve an optimized trade-off between accuracy and cost.

3.3 Recurrent Neural Networks for Context Ensemble

Impelled by the successful application of RNN models in 2D semantic segmentation [29–32], we introduce our two-direction hierarchical RNN model for 3D point cloud labeling to make use of the long-range spatial dependency. The whole 3D space is split into uniformly-spaced blocks along x and y direction on the ground plane, i.e., $L_x \times L_y$, respectively. The space along up-right axis is kept undivided due to its high sparsity and coherency in vertical direction. The detailed pipeline is depicted in Fig. 3.

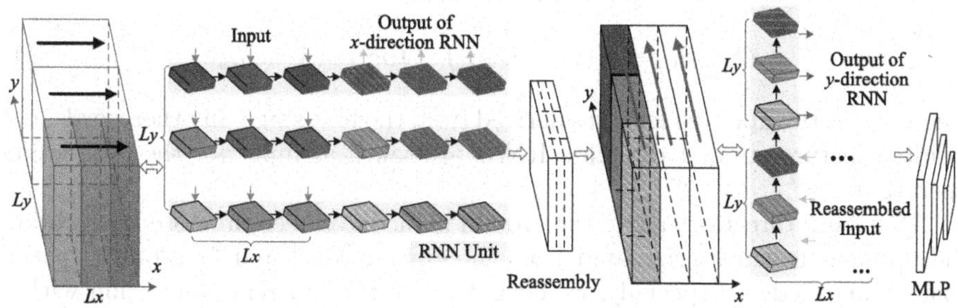

Fig. 3. The pipeline of our two-direction hierarchical RNN module. Output of the first x-direction RNN is reassembled for the input of the second y-direction RNN.

The original input point-features and the output of the pyramid pooling module are first concatenated to be taken as input of the RNN model. In essence, the extra concatenation layer can be omitted if we add a pooling unit with window size equaling to one in the previous pointwise pyramid pooling module. In Fig. 1, we still present the concatenation operation for clear depiction.

The pipeline involves two stages. In the first stage (arrowed in black in Fig. 3), we only consider spatial connection along x direction by coupling L_x small blocks within the same y index as a whole. Note that the operation of each recurrent group is independent and can be realized in parallel. The features derived from point features concatenated with pooled features within each block are unrolled to form a sequence of the corresponding RNN cells. At each time step (corresponding to each small block along the same y index), every RNN takes the concatenated block features as input and based on the previous state from its preceding neighboring blocks to update the new state as follows:

$$O_{i,j}, S_{i,j} = f\left(x_{i,j}, S_{i-1,j}\right) \quad for\ i = 1, ..., L_x \tag{3}$$

where $x_{i,j}, S_{i-1,j}$ denote the current input and the previous state of a certain block, and $O_{i,j}, S_{i,j}$ represent the output and the updated state, respectively. Since the recurrent layers are operated in a many-to-many mode, it is indicated that the complete output will be returned only after the entire input sequence has been passed through the recurrent layer, which is capable of learning long-range dependencies along the x direction. In specific, each one-dimensional recurrent layer can be simply implemented as multi-LSTMs [33] or GRUs [34], in our work multi-LSTM is adopted.

After all the points are swept over the x dimension, the attained brand-new features for each small block are served as input of the following stage. In the second stage, we recompose the features to consider spatial relevance along y

direction. Specifically, for each recurrent layer along y-dimension, block features of the same x index are unrolled and composed to form a new sequence. In other words, there are L_x RNN layers with each consisting of L_y timestamps in the second stage. Analogously, at each time step, we proceed reading one element and update the state asynchronously as follows:

$$O_{i,j}, S_{i,j} = f\left(\tilde{x}_{i,j}, S_{i,j-1}\right) \quad for\ j = 1, ..., L_y \tag{4}$$

where $\tilde{x}_{i,j}$ is the updated features derived from the first stage. In other words, the resulted features from x-direction RNNs are taken as input for the y-direction operation.

After both directions along the ground plane have been processed, we obtain the updated features originated from integrating local and long-range spatial context knowledge. Especially, we do not break the inherent connection within each block. Instead, our model learns to share long-range knowledge by propagating neighboring features along the two directions hierarchically. Note that one can also stack more recurrent layers for processing additional directions, we only choose the mentioned two directions in view of memory and speed. The output features of the RNN-based model are then concatenated with the original input features, including the pointwise features and local pooled features, to predict the final label for each point.

4 Experimental Results

4.1 Dataset and Evaluation Criteria

In this section, evaluations are mainly carried out on the following challenging datasets: Stanford Large-Scale 3D Indoor Spaces (S3DIS) [6], ScanNet [7], as well as outdoor vKITTI [10], KITTI Raw [9] and 3DRMS Challenge [35].

S3DIS dataset is an indoor 3D point cloud dataset that includes six large-scale indoor areas that originate from three different buildings, totally covering over 6,000 m^2 and involving thirteen semantic classes.

ScanNet dataset contains over 1500 scanned 3D indoor scenes and 21 semantic classes. Experiment settings are borrowed from [7] to split the dataset into 4:1 for training and testing, respectively.

vKITTI dataset is a synthetic large-scale outdoor dataset imitating the real-world KITTI dataset, with 13 semantic classes in urban scenes. The annotated point clouds are obtained by projecting 2D semantic labels into 3D space.

KITTI Raw dataset contains sparse Velodyne LiDAR point clouds without color information. Due to a lack of semantic ground truth labels, it can not be employed for supervised training. However, the density is comparable to vKITTI and we leverage it for generalization validation.

For evaluation, we report quantitative and qualitative results on indoor and outdoor datasets. The evaluation metric used in our experiments are: mean intersection over union over all classes (mIoU), per-class IoU, mean per-class accuracy (mAcc) and overall accuracy (OA). In specific, IoU can be computed as

$$IoU = \frac{TP}{(T + P - TP)} \tag{5}$$

where TP is the number of true positives, T is the number of ground truth positive samples, P is the number of predicted positives belonging to that class.

4.2 Implementation Details

For S3DIS dataset, unlike PointNet that adopts 9-dim representation, each point in our model is only represented by 6-dim vector in order to reduce computation cost, namely, normalized XYZ and RGB. The follow-up experimental results also validate that 6-dim input in our model already performs better than the original 9-dim vector in PointNet. During training, each room is split into overlapped blocks of size 1.5 m × 1.5 m along horizontal directions without height constraint, each containing 6400 points. No overlapping is performed during test. The parameters of the proposed pointwise pyramid pooling module are set as follows: 4 pooling layers with the corresponding window kernel size 1, $N/64$, $N/8$, N. With regard to the two-direction hierarchical RNN model, we set time steps to 6 for each direction. The hidden unit size for each RNN cell is 128. For ScanNet [7] we carry out experiments utilizing only the geometry information by removing RGB features. Besides, weighted cross entropy loss is harnessed to tackle with the challenge of imbalanced samples between different classes. To keep fair comparison with PointNet++ [22], we also perform random input dropout for all approaches in the ScanNet experiment. And for vKITTI dataset [10], experiments with XYZ-RGB and with XYZ-only inputs are both conducted. For all experiments, the model is optimized by Adam optimizer [36] with initial learning rate 0.001 and batch size 24.

4.3 Results on Indoor Datasets

S3DIS: Similar to [4,23,27] which adopted 6-fold cross validation strategy for train and test, we trained six models separately and for each one, five areas are used for training and the remaining one for testing. Note that SEGCloud [14] trained their model on two of the three buildings and tested on the other building, since they argued that areas from the same building in training and testing set can result in an increased performance and fail to evaluate the generalizability. For fair comparison, we also retrain our model on the first two buildings and test on the building not present in the other folds, namely, Area 5 (A5). The comparison results are presented in Table 1.

As is depicted in Table 1, our architecture outperforms other approaches on average. The proposed method outperforms baseline work PointNet by 8.7% mIoU, 7.4% mAcc and 8.4% in overall accuracy and even shows higher accuracy than [23,27], which exploit multi-scale context consolidation and superpoint graph, respectively. Besides, our architecture is able to resolve small semantic

Table 1. Comparison results on the S3DIS dataset with XYZ-RGB inputs. IoU data of the referenced works are from [23,27]. The upper results are averaged over the 6 folds and the lower are trained on two buildings and tested on the Area 5 fold. Intersection over union of each class are given.

Method	OA	mAcc	mIoU	Ceiling	Floor	Wall	Beam	Column	Window	Door	Table	Chair	Sofa	Bookca.	Board	Clutter
A5 PointNet [4]	-	49.0	41.1	88.8	97.3	69.8	0.05	3.92	49.3	10.76	58.9	52.6	5.8	40.3	26.3	33.22
A5 SEGCloud [14]	-	57.4	48.9	90.1	96.0	69.9	0	**18.4**	38.3	23.1	70.4	75.9	**40.9**	58.4	13.0	41.6
A5 SPG [27]	85.1	61.7	**54.7**	91.5	97.9	75.9	0	14.2	51.3	**52.3**	77.4	**86.4**	40.4	**65.5**	7.23	50.7
A5 Ours	**85.7**	**71.3**	53.4	**95.2**	**98.6**	**77.4**	**0.80**	9.83	**52.7**	27.9	**78.3**	76.8	27.4	58.6	**39.1**	**51.0**
PointNet [4]	78.5	66.2	47.6	88.0	88.7	69.3	42.4	23.1	47.5	51.6	54.1	42.0	9.6	38.2	29.4	35.2
MS+CU [23]	79.2	59.7	47.8	88.6	**95.8**	67.3	36.9	24.9	48.6	52.3	51.9	45.1	10.6	36.8	24.7	37.5
G+RCU [23]	81.1	66.4	49.7	90.3	92.1	67.9	**44.7**	24.2	**52.3**	51.2	58.1	47.4	6.9	39.0	30.0	41.9
SPG [27]	82.9	64.4	54.1	92.2	95.0	71.9	33.5	15.0	46.5	**60.9**	**69.4**	65.0	**38.2**	56.8	6.86	51.3
Ours	**86.9**	**73.6**	**56.3**	**92.9**	93.8	**73.1**	42.5	**25.9**	47.6	59.2	60.4	**66.7**	24.8	**57.0**	**36.7**	**51.6**

classes such as beam, column and board. With regard to the generalizability evaluation on Area 5, the model trained on two buildings and tested on another diverse building also behaves well, leading the performance of overall accuracy and mAcc and yielding comparable IoU with [27].

Next, we present the qualitative results of the semantic segmentation by our architecture in Fig. 4. As can be seen from Fig. 4, thanks to the pyramid pooling module as well as the two-direction hierarchical RNN model, our architecture is capable of correcting erroneously labelled classes in [4,23] and achieves more accurate segmentation results. Besides, the proposed framework largely retrieves fine-grained details that are missed by other methods. For example, the chair legs are preserved to a great extent (colored in red) and much less noise in semantic segmentation is observed compared to the remaining approaches.

In the previous experiment (S3DIS), geometry as well as color information is utilized to predict semantic labels for each room, since color plays a critical role in feature representation. We wonder whether the proposed architecture works when color is unavailable. Accordingly, a further experiment is conducted on large scanned indoor dataset ScanNet [7] with color information discarded. ScanNet presented a voxel-based coarse prediction framework leveraging 3D fully convolutional networks. Instead, we yield per-point labels and make comparison with PointNet [4] and Pointnet++ [22]. The performance is reported in Table 2, which demonstrates the efficiency of our framework when only geometry information is available. Note that the result is a bit different from that in [22], since the accuracy in our experiment is evaluated by per-point rather than per-voxel.

Table 2. Per-point accuracy on ScanNet [7] with only XYZ information, no RGB.

Method	PointNet [4]	G+RCU [23]	PointNet++ [22]	Ours
OverAll accuracy	0.526	0.634	0.743	**0.765**

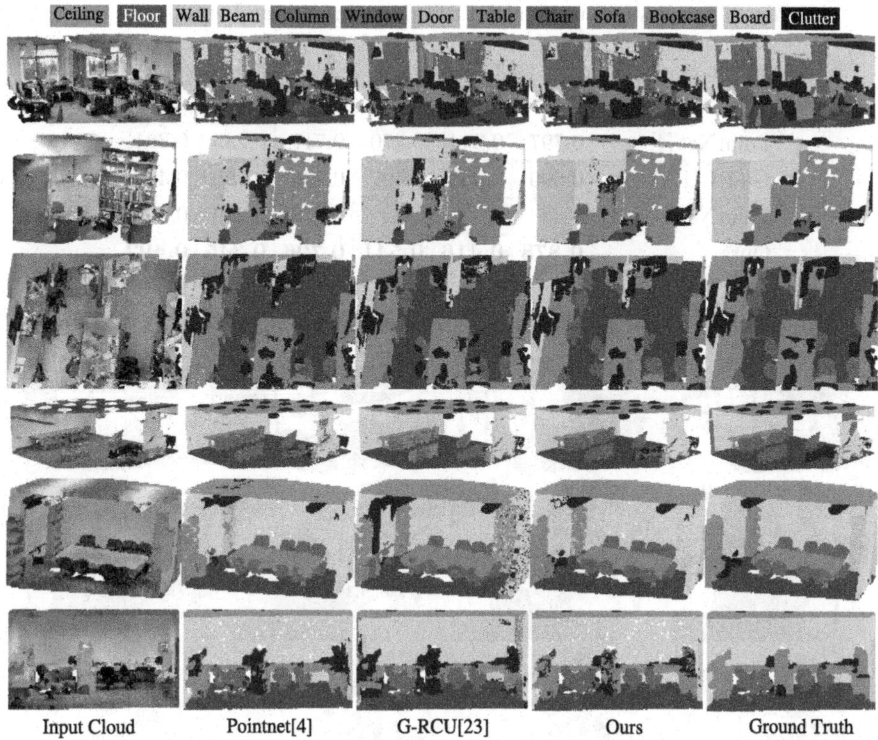

Fig. 4. Qualitative results on indoor S3DIS dataset. Our results demonstrate superior performance over the state-of-the-art methods with more accurate predictions (Color figure online).

4.4 Results on Outdoor Datasets

We also evaluate the performance of the proposed model on outdoor datasets. For fair comparison, we choose vKITTI dataset [10] as [23] does and split the five different urban video sequences into six non-overlapping folds. During training and testing, the six-fold cross validation strategy is adopted as PointNet suggests. Furthermore, we conduct two separate experiments with respect to different input features, i.e., XYZ-RGB and XYZ-only. As is presented in Table 3, our framework successfully predicts the semantic labels of outdoor scenes no matter which input feature strategy is adopted. With color information, our architecture can improve the semantic segmentation performance to a great extent. Even without color clue, our algorithm is able to achieve improvements compared to other state-of-the-art approaches. Notably we obtain slightly higher averaged performance of [4,23] reported in [23] using the same dataset, which is probably due to our data normalization. Besides, we also show qualitative results of vKITTI compared to other recently proposed state-of-the-art algorithms in

Table 3. Results on outdoor vKITTI dataset: with and without RGB.

Method	XYZRGB			XYZ-only		
	OA	mIoU	mAcc	OA	mIoU	mAcc
PointNet [4]	0.797	0.344	0.470	0.717	0.239	0.381
G+RCU [23]	0.806	0.362	0.497	0.739	0.298	0.467
PointNet++ [22]	-	-	-	0.770	0.299	0.400
Ours	**0.878**	**0.416**	**0.541**	**0.796**	**0.345**	**0.492**

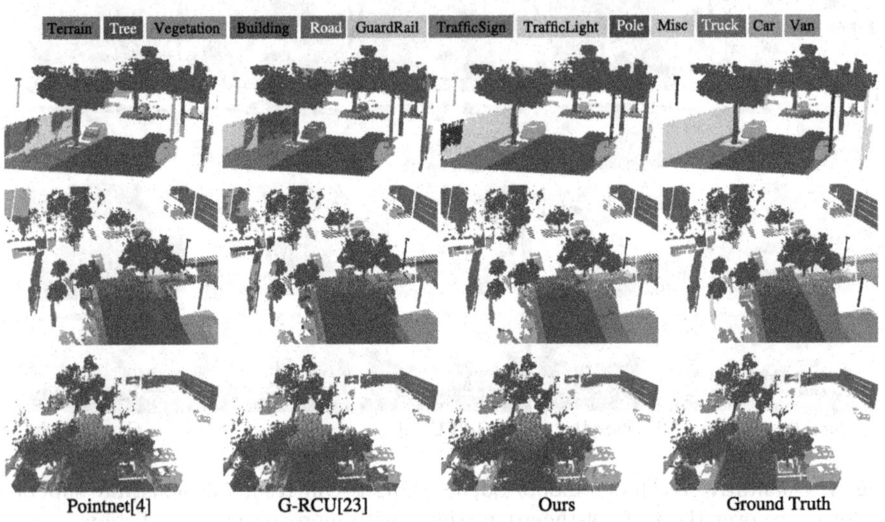

Fig. 5. Semantic segmentation results on outdoor vKITTI dataset. From left to right: PointNet [4], G+RCU [23], our results, the ground truth. The input features are geometry with color for all algorithms.

Fig. 5. As is demonstrated in Fig. 5, our framework retrieves the scene more consistently with less erroneous labels.

To further validate the effectiveness and generalization ability of our model, we apply the model trained on vKITTI to two untrained real-world outdoor datasets, KITTI Raw [9] and 3DRMS [35] laser data. The KITTI Raw point clouds obtained by LiDAR scans only contain XYZ information without ground truth semantic labels, thus we apply geometry-only model of vKITTI to it. With regard to the latter 3DRMS laser data with color information, the geometry-color model of vKITTI is employed, despite of different class labels for these two datasets. The qualitative results are presented in Fig. 6. Without any training, our model still produces reasonable semantic results in both datasets. Note that only some common or similar classes make sense, such as road, tree, terrain, car and building.

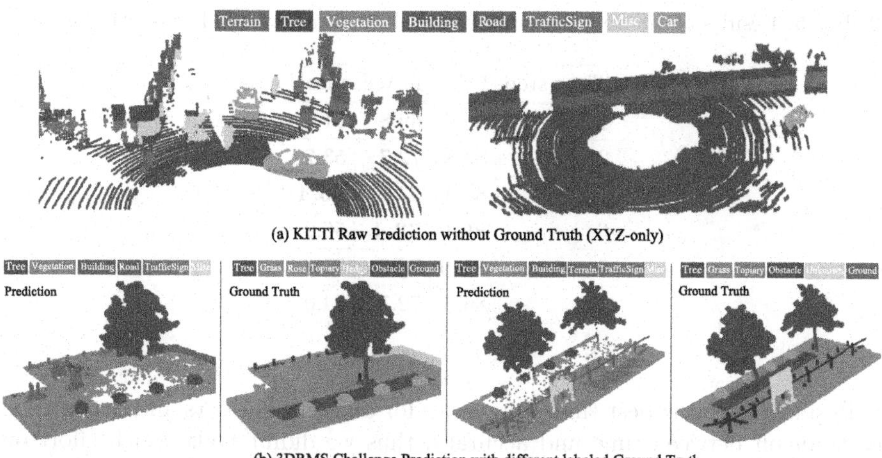

(a) KITTI Raw Prediction without Ground Truth (XYZ-only)

(b) 3DRMS Challenge Prediction with different labeled Ground Truth

Fig. 6. Qualitative prediction results on the untrained KITTI Raw [9] (upper row) and 3DRMS [35] (below row). Our XYZ-only model trained on vKITTI is applied to real KITTI laser scans. Only some shared classes like car, building and road make sense. The XYZ-RGB model trained on vKITTI is employed for 3DRMS scans. Although some classes differ from the annotated labels, reasonable results are still observed.

4.5 Ablation Study

For ablation study, further experiments are carried out to explore the contribution of two key components in our approach. For all experiments here, we compare the performance of different settings with geometry and color features taken as input on S3DIS dataset. As is revealed in Table 4, though being simple, the pyramid pooling module makes significant contribution to the improvement of the overall accuracy, and our two-direction RNN model further reduces errors in small classes and thus improves the mIoU and mAcc. Although the results of 1D RNN are inferior to that with pointwise pyramid pooling, the hierarchical two-direction RNN architecture reveals an improved performance. Finally, the combination of the two components achieves overwhelming results by integrating neighboring local context with long-distance spatial information.

Table 4. Comparison of different variants. Best results are shown in bold.

Method	OA	mAcc	mIoU
Baseline PointNet [4]	78.5	66.2	47.6
Add with Pointwise Pyramid Pooling	82.8	68.3	50.8
Add with one-direction RNNs	80.6	67.9	49.9
Add with two-direction RNNs	82.3	70.0	51.4
Our Full Approach	**86.9**	**73.6**	**56.3**

Table 5. Results of different time steps on S3DIS dataset (6-fold cross validation).

Time step	OA	mAcc	mIoU
1	80.7	69.8	51.3
2	83.8	72.7	53.7
4	85.3	73.2	**56.4**
6	**86.9**	**73.4**	56.2
8	**86.9**	73.3	55.6
10	86.5	72.1	54.0

Besides, since the best time step varies for different datasets and depends on the trade-off between time and accuracy, thus we didn't make much effort on finetuning the best one. However, we conducted experiments concerning different time steps. Results shown in Table 5 reveal that small time steps degrade the performance whereas too large time step also hinders the IoU, generally, a time step between 4 and 8 is feasible.

5 Conclusions

We present an end-to-end approach for efficient 3D semantic segmentation by means of integrating convolution neural networks with recurrent neural networks. The framework consists of two indispensable components, the pointwise pyramid pooling module with no strides to integrate multi-scale local context and the two-direction hierarchical RNNs to learn long-range spatial dependency. Our architecture successfully improves the accuracy of 3D semantic segmentation on indoor and outdoor datasets. With regard to some similar semantic classes, our model also has limited capability to distinguish them, such as door and wall. For future work, we plan to investigate on the problem and extend our method to more applications on unstructured point clouds.

References

1. Chen, L., Papandreou, G., Kokkinos, I., Murphy, K., Yuille, A.L.: DeepLab: semantic image segmentation with deep convolutional nets, atrous convolution, and fully connected CRFs. In: CVPR, p. 1 (2017)
2. Long, J., Shelhamer, E., Darrell, T.: Fully convolutional networks for semantic segmentation. In: CVPR, pp. 3431–3440 (2015)
3. Garcia-Garcia, A., Orts-Escolano, S., Oprea, S., Villena-Martinez, V., Rodríguez, J.G.: A review on deep learning techniques applied to semantic segmentation. CoRR abs/1704.06857 (2017)
4. Qi, C.R., Su, H., Mo, K., Guibas, L.J.: PointNet: deep learning on point sets for 3D classification and segmentation. In: CVPR, pp. 652–660 (2017)

5. Silberman, N., Hoiem, D., Kohli, P., Fergus, R.: Indoor segmentation and support inference from RGBD images. In: Fitzgibbon, A., Lazebnik, S., Perona, P., Sato, Y., Schmid, C. (eds.) ECCV 2012. LNCS, vol. 7576, pp. 746–760. Springer, Heidelberg (2012). https://doi.org/10.1007/978-3-642-33715-4_54
6. Armeni, I., et al.: 3D semantic parsing of large-scale indoor spaces. In: CVPR, pp. 1534–1543 (2016)
7. Dai, A., Chang, A.X., Savva, M., Halber, M., Funkhouser, T., Nießner, M.: ScanNet: richly-annotated 3D reconstructions of indoor scenes. In: CVPR (2017)
8. Hackel, T., Savinov, N., Ladicky, L., Wegner, J.D., Schindler, K., Pollefeys, M.: Semantic3D.net: a new large-scale point cloud classification benchmark. In: ISPRS, vol. IV-1-W 1, pp. 91–98 (2017)
9. Geiger, A., Lenz, P., Stiller, C., Urtasun, R.: Vision meets robotics: the KITTI dataset. Int. J. Robot. Res. **32**(11), 1231–1237 (2013)
10. Gaidon, A., Wang, Q., Cabon, Y., Vig, E.: Virtual worlds as proxy for multi-object tracking analysis. In: CVPR, pp. 4340–4349 (2016)
11. Huang, J., Suya, Y.: Point cloud labeling using 3D convolutional neural network. In: ICPR (2016)
12. Maturana, D., Scherer, S.: VoxNet: a 3D convolutional neural network for real-time object recognition. In: IROS, pp. 922–928 (2015)
13. Riegler, G., Ulusoy, A.O., Geiger, A.: OctNet: learning deep 3D representations at high resolutions. In: CVPR, pp. 3577–3586 (2016)
14. Tchapmi, L.P., Choy, C.B., Armeni, I., Gwak, J., Savarese, S.: SEGCloud: semantic segmentation of 3D point clouds. CoRR abs/1710.07563 (2017)
15. Zhao, H., Shi, J., Qi, X., Wang, X., Jia, J.: Pyramid scene parsing network. CoRR abs/1612.01105 (2016)
16. Li, Z., Gan, Y., Liang, X., Yu, Y., Cheng, H., Lin, L.: LSTM-CF: unifying context modeling and fusion with LSTMs for RGB-D scene labeling. In: Leibe, B., Matas, J., Sebe, N., Welling, M. (eds.) ECCV 2016. LNCS, vol. 9906, pp. 541–557. Springer, Cham (2016). https://doi.org/10.1007/978-3-319-46475-6_34
17. Chen, L., Papandreou, G., Kokkinos, I., Murphy, K., Yuille, A.L.: Semantic image segmentation with deep convolutional nets and fully connected CRFs. In: International Conference on Learning Representations (2015)
18. Su, H., Maji, S., Kalogerakis, E., Learnedmiller, E.G.: Multi-view convolutional neural networks for 3D shape recognition. In: International Conference on Computer Vision, pp. 945–953 (2015)
19. Qi, C.R., Su, H., Niebner, M., Dai, A., Yan, M., Guibas, L.J.: Volumetric and multi-view CNNs for object classification on 3D data. In: CVPR, pp. 5648–5656 (2016)
20. Boulch, A., Saux, B.L., Audebert, N.: Unstructured point cloud semantic labeling using deep segmentation networks. In: Eurographics Workshop on 3D Object Retrieval (2017)
21. Guerry, J., Boulch, A., Le Saux, B., Moras, J., Plyer, A., Filliat, D.: SnapNet-R: consistent 3D multi-view semantic labeling for robotics. In: ICCV (2017)
22. Qi, C.R., Yi, L., Su, H., Guibas, L.J.: Pointnet++: deep hierarchical feature learning on point sets in a metric space. In: NIPS, pp. 5099–5108 (2017)
23. Engelmann, F., Kontogianni, T., Hermans, A., Leibe, B.: Exploring spatial context for 3D semantic segmentation of point clouds. In: ICCV (2017)
24. Guerrero, P., Kleiman, Y., Ovsjanikov, M., Mitra, N.J.: PCPNET: learning local shape properties from raw point clouds. CoRR abs/1710.04954 (2017)
25. Qi, C.R., Liu, W., Wu, C., Su, H., Guibas, L.J.: Frustum pointnets for 3D object detection from RGB-D data. CoRR abs/1711.08488 (2017)

26. Qi, X., Liao, R., Jia, J., Fidler, S., Urtasun, R.: 3D graph neural networks for RGBD semantic segmentation. In: ICCV (2017)
27. Landrieu, L., Simonovsky, M.: Large-scale point cloud semantic segmentation with superpoint graphs. CoRR abs/1711.09869 (2017)
28. Park, H., Lee, K.M.: Look wider to match image patches with convolutional neural networks. IEEE Sig. Process. Lett. **24**(12), 1788–1792 (2017)
29. Byeon, W., Breuel, T.M., Raue, F., Liwicki, M.: Scene labeling with LSTM recurrent neural networks. In: CVPR), pp. 3547–3555 (2015)
30. Stollenga, M.F., Byeon, W., Liwicki, M., Schmidhuber, J.: Parallel multi-dimensional LSTM, with application to fast biomedical volumetric image segmentation. In: NIPS, pp. 2998–3006 (2015)
31. Pinheiro, P.H.O., Collobert, R.: Recurrent convolutional neural networks for scene labeling. In: ICML, pp. 82–90 (2014)
32. Visin, F., et al.: ReSeg: a recurrent neural network-based model for semantic segmentation. In: CVPR, pp. 426–433 (2016)
33. Hochreiter, S., Schmidhuber, J.: Long short-term memory. Neural Comput. **9**(8), 1735–1780 (1997)
34. Cho, K., et al.: Learning phrase representations using RNN encoder-decoder for statistical machine translation. In: Empirical Methods in Natural Language Processing, pp. 1724–1734 (2014)
35. Torsten, S., Thomas, B., Marc, P., Robert, F., Radim, T.: 3D reconstruction meets semantics - reconstruction challenge. In: ICCV Workshops (2017). http://trimbot2020.webhosting.rug.nl/events/3drms/challenge/
36. Kingma, D.P., Ba, J.L.: Adam: a method for stochastic optimization. In: ICLR (2015)

Learning to Capture Light Fields Through a Coded Aperture Camera

Yasutaka Inagaki[1(✉)], Yuto Kobayashi[1], Keita Takahashi[1], Toshiaki Fujii[1], and Hajime Nagahara[2]

[1] Graduate School of Engineering, Nagoya University, Nagoya, Japan
{inagaki,kobayashi,takahasi,fujii}@fujii.nuee.nagoya-u.ac.jp
[2] Institute for Datability Science, Osaka University, Suita, Japan
nagahara@ids.osaka-u.ac.jp

Abstract. We propose a learning-based framework for acquiring a light field through a coded aperture camera. Acquiring a light field is a challenging task due to the amount of data. To make the acquisition process efficient, coded aperture cameras were successfully adopted; using these cameras, a light field is computationally reconstructed from several images that are acquirToshiakied with different aperture patterns. However, it is still difficult to reconstruct a high-quality light field from only a few acquired images. To tackle this limitation, we formulated the entire pipeline of light field acquisition from the perspective of an auto-encoder. This auto-encoder was implemented as a stack of fully convolutional layers and was trained end-to-end by using a collection of training samples. We experimentally show that our method can successfully learn good image-acquisition and reconstruction strategies. With our method, light fields consisting of 5×5 or 8×8 images can be successfully reconstructed only from a few acquired images. Moreover, our method achieved superior performance over several state-of-the-art methods. We also applied our method to a real prototype camera to show that it is capable of capturing a real 3-D scene.

Keywords: Light field · CNN · Coded aperture

1 Introduction

The notion of a light field, which describes all light-rays traveling in 3-D free space [1–3], has been utilized in various applications, such as view synthesis [4–6], depth estimation [7–9], synthetic refocusing [10,11], super resolution [7,12], 3D displays [13–16], and object recognition [17,18]. Several researchers have published light field datasets [19–22] for accelerating research in this field. A light field dataset is usually represented as a set of multi-view images that are aligned densely with tiny viewpoint intervals.

Electronic supplementary material The online version of this chapter (https://doi.org/10.1007/978-3-030-01234-2_26) contains supplementary material, which is available to authorized users.

V. Ferrari et al. (Eds.): ECCV 2018, LNCS 11211, pp. 431–448, 2018.
https://doi.org/10.1007/978-3-030-01234-2_26

Acquiring a light field is a challenging task due to the amount of data because a light field typically consists of dozens of images. Several researchers have employed direct approaches such as using a moving camera gantry [2] or multiple cameras [23–25] to capture a target from different viewpoints. These approaches are costly in terms of the hardware or the time required to capture the entire light field. Meanwhile, lens-array based cameras [11,26–28] and coded aperture/mask cameras [29–35] have also been utilized to achieve more efficient acquisition. In the case of lens-array based cameras, an entire light field can be captured with a single acquired image, but the spatial resolution of each image is in a trade-off relationship with the number of viewpoints. In contrast, coded aperture/mask cameras can capture a light field with the same spatial resolution as that of an image sensor, but the quality of the light field is in a trade-off relationship with the number of acquired images[1]. Other researchers used view synthesis techniques [6,7,36,37] to generate a dense light field from a few images that were acquired with sparser intervals or even from one image. However, view synthesis involves added difficulty in terms of accurately estimating depth/disparity from the given images and reproducing view-dependent phenomena such as non-Lambertian reflections and occlusions.

This paper is focused on the problem of efficiently acquiring a light field by using a coded aperture camera. Using this camera, a light field is computationally reconstructed from several images that are acquired with different aperture patterns. Earlier methods [30–32] could not drastically reduce the number of images required to reconstruct a light field. However, with recent methods [33,35], the number of acquired images has been reduced to only a few for a light field consisting of 5×5 viewpoints. We want to further improve the trade-off relationship between the number of acquired images and the quality of the reconstructed light field. The key to achieving this goal is to find good aperture patterns and a corresponding good reconstruction algorithm.

It is important to understand the principles behind reducing the number of acquired images. In previous works, this problem has been tackled from the perspective of compressive sensing [38–40]. Compressive sensing is a framework for reconstructing a signal from a reduced number of samples, where inherent structures in a target signal are exploited to seek the optimal sampling and reconstruction strategies. Along this theme, light-field acquisition has been formalized from the perspective of sparse representation using a learned dictionary [33] and approximation using the most significant basis vectors [35]. These methods can successfully reconstruct a light field from only a few acquired images. However, they often fail to reconstruct the details of the light field due to the limited representation capability of the dictionary and basis. Moreover, sparse reconstruction requires significant computational time due to the inherent complexity of the iterative algorithms that are used.

In contrast, we view the problem of acquiring a light field from the perspective of an auto-encoder [41,42]. An auto-encoder employs a simple structure, in which

[1] Dappled photography [29] is categorized as a coded mask method, but there is a trade-off between the maximum spatial and angular frequencies.

an encoder network is connected to a decoder network, and it is trained to best approximate the identity mapping between the input and output. In our method, an encoder and decoder correspond to the image acquisition and reconstruction processes, respectively, because the original light field is once reduced (encoded) to only a few images through the physical imaging process of the coded aperture camera, and these images are then combined to reconstruct (decode) a light field with the same size as the original one. We implemented this auto-encoder as a fully convolutional neural network (CNN) and trained it end-to-end by using a collection of training samples. The parameters of the trained network correspond to the aperture patterns and reconstruction algorithm that are jointly optimized over the training dataset. In short, our method can learn to capture and reconstruct a light field through a coded aperture camera by utilizing the powerful framework of a deep neural network (DNN).

We implemented our method by using Chainer [43] and trained it by using samples taken from 51 light-field datasets. We experimentally show that our method can successfully learn good image-acquisition and reconstruction strategies. By using our method, light fields consisting of 5×5 or 8×8 images can be reconstructed with high quality from only a few acquired images. Moreover, our method achieved superior performance over several state-of-the-art methods [6,33,35,36] including both compressive-sensing based and view-synthesis based approaches. We also applied our method to a real prototype camera to show that it is capable of capturing a real 3-D scene.

We briefly review the related works on the usage of DNNs for similar applications. DNNs have been utilized to optimize the imaging pipelines including camera designs for color image acquisition [44], depth estimation [45], and high-speed video acquisition [46]. A learning based approach was also used for temporal interpolation of light field video [47]. As the most similar work to ours, compressively sampled light fields were successfully reconstructed using DNNs in [48]. However, in contrast to our method, the compression process (camera design) in [48] was not optimized in the training stage but determined beforehand. To the best of our knowledge, we are the first to use a DNN for designing the entire pipeline of a computational camera for light-field acquisition. Moreover, the difference between the network architectures resulted in significant difference in the reconstruction time: 6.7 min for [48] and only 1 s for ours.

2 Proposed Method

2.1 Light Field Capturing Through Coded Aperture Camera

A schematic diagram of a coded aperture camera is illustrated in Fig. 1. An architecture that is equivalent to this diagram can be implemented by using relay optics and an LCoS (liquid crystal on silicon) device [31,33,49]. Here, we present a mathematical formulation for acquiring a light field through a coded aperture camera.

All incoming light rays that will be recorded by this camera are parameterized with four variables (s, t, u, v), where (s, t) and (u, v) denote the intersections with

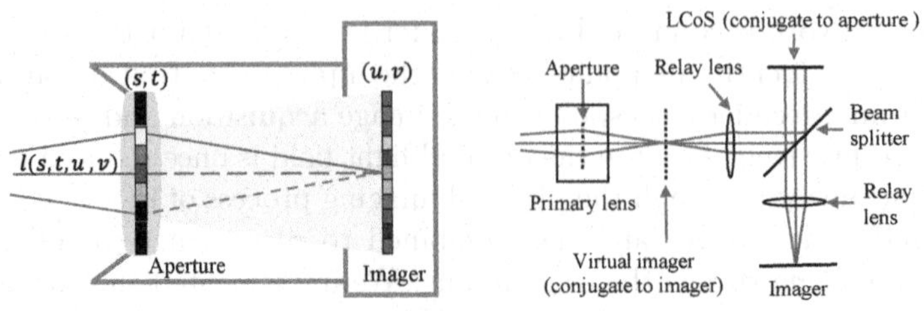

Fig. 1. Schematic diagram and implementation of coded aperture camera

the aperture and imaging planes, respectively. Therefore, the light field is defined over 4-D space (s, t, u, v), with which the light intensity is described as $l(s, t, u, v)$. The light field is equivalently described as a set of rectified multi-view images called "sub-aperture images", $\{x_{s,t}(u, v) = l(s, t, u, v)\}$, where (s, t) corresponds to the viewpoint defined on the aperture plane.

We consider a coded aperture design where the transmittance of the aperture can be controlled for each position and for each acquisition. Let $a_n(s, t)$ be the transmittance at position (s, t) for the n-th acquisition $(n = 1, \ldots, N)$. The observed image $y_n(u, v)$ is formed as

$$y_n(u,v) = \iint a_n(s,t) l(s,t,u,v) ds dt = \iint a_n(s,t) x_{s,t}(u,v) ds dt. \tag{1}$$

When the aperture plane is quantized into a finite number of square blocks, they can be numbered by an integer m $(m = 1, \ldots, M)$. Equation (1) is rewritten as

$$y_n(u,v) = \sum_{m=1}^{M} a_{n,m} x_m(u,v), \tag{2}$$

where M is the total number of blocks, and $a_{n,m}$ [equivalent to $a_n(s, t)$] is the transmittance of the aperture at position m for the n-th acquisition.

Reconstructing the light field is equivalent to estimating M sub-aperture images $x_m(u, v)$ from the N given observations $y_n(u, v)$. In particular, we are interested in the case of $N \ll M$, where the entire light field could be reconstructed from only a few observed images. To this end, we need to find good transmittance patterns $a_{n,m}$ and a corresponding reconstruction method.

In the remainder of this paper, we assume that each image has only a single channel for simplicity, and this applies to both $x_m(u, v)$ and $y_n(u, v)$. When dealing with a color image, we simply divide it into three independent single-channel images and apply the same procedure to them.

2.2 Formulation as Convolutional Neural Network

The observation (image acquisition) process of a coded aperture camera, which is given by Eq. (2), can be written in a form of a mapping as

$$f : \mathcal{X} \rightarrow \mathcal{Y} \tag{3}$$

where $\mathcal{X}$ represents a vector that contains all the pixels of $x_m(u,v)$ for all $m \in \{1,...,M\}$. When each image has $U \times V$ pixels, the length of the vector is UVM. Similarly, $\mathcal{Y}$ represents a vector that contains all the pixels of $y_n(u,v)$ for all $n \in \{1,...,N\}$. The reconstruction is also written as

$$g : \mathcal{Y} \rightarrow \hat{\mathcal{X}} \tag{4}$$

where $\hat{\mathcal{X}}$ corresponds to an estimate of $\mathcal{X}$. The composite mapping $h = g \circ f$ should be as close to the identity as possible, under the condition that $N \ll M$. This problem can be regarded as that of an auto-encoder, where the encoder and decoder correspond to f and g, respectively. The goal of optimization is formulated with the squared error loss as

$$\arg\min_{f,g} |\mathcal{X} - \hat{\mathcal{X}}|^2 = \arg\min_{f,g} \sum_m \sum_{u,v} |x_m(u,v) - \hat{x}_m(u,v)|^2 \tag{5}$$

where an estimate of $x_m(u,v)$ is written as $\hat{x}_m(u,v)$.

On top of this formulation, we implemented composite mapping $h = g \circ f$ as a stack of 2-D convolutional layers. The entire network can be trained end-to-end by using a collection of training samples. The learned parameters in f and g correspond to the aperture patterns $a_{n,m}$ and the reconstruction algorithm, respectively, both of which are jointly optimized over the training dataset. In short, our method can learn to capture a light field through a coded aperture camera by utilizing the powerful framework of a DNN. This network can easily be applied to a physical coded-aperture camera. The mapping f is conducted by the physical imaging process of the camera, the aperture patterns of which are configured in accordance to the learned parameters in f. Then, the images acquired by the cameras are inputted to the network corresponding to g, by which we can computationally reconstruct a target light field.

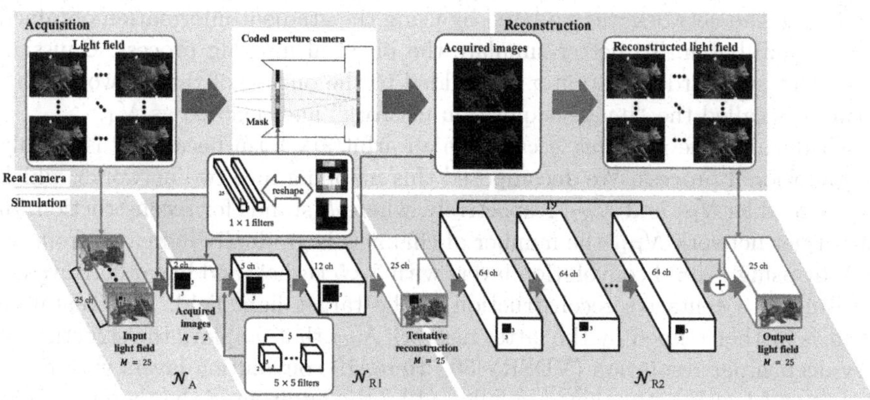

Fig. 2. Modeling light-field acquisition using CNN

An example with $M = 25$ and $N = 2$ is illustrated in Fig. 2. The architecture of our network is summarized below. Note that this is only an example we have found through trial and error, and one may find other architectures that are essentially equivalent in spirit but can perform better than ours.

In a 2-D convolutional network, data are represented as 2-D images with multiple channels. For the l-th convolution layer, the relationship between the input $x_c^l(u, v)$ and output $x_{c'}^{l+1}(u, v)$, where c and c' denote channels, is represented as

$$x_{c'}^{l+1}(u, v) = \sum_c k_{c,c'}(u, v) * x_c^l(u, v) + b_{c'} \tag{6}$$

which is optionally followed by an activation function. The 2-D convolution kernels represented by $k_{c,c'}(u, v)$ and the bias terms $b_{c'}$ are optimized through the training stage. We used one-pixel stride and an appropriate zero padding to keep the image size unchanged before and after the convolution. Meanwhile, the number of channels (the range for c and c') can arbitrarily be changed between the input and output. Therefore, the image size (height and width) is kept constant throughout the network, but only the number of channels is changed as the data proceed in the network. To apply this data structure to our purpose, we treated the indices n and m as the channels. Therefore, the viewpoint m corresponds to the channels in the input and output data, and the index for the acquired images n corresponds to the channel of the intermediate data between f and g.

The mapping f has a few restrictions because it corresponds to the physical imaging process described by Eq. (2); the transmittance $a_{n,m}$ should be limited within $[0, 1]$, each pixel (u, v) cannot be mixed with other neighbors, and the number of channels should be reduced from M to N. We implemented this using a single 2-D convolution layer with 1×1 convolution kernels, where the weights are limited within the range $[0, 1]$, and $b_{c'} = 0$ for all c'. In this case, $k_{c,c'}$ is equivalent to $a_{c',c}$, and Eq. (6) corresponds to Eq. (2). To keep the range limitation during the training stage, we clipped the weights within $[0, 1]$ each time when the network was updated by using the gradient information obtained from a mini-batch. To better simulate the physical imaging process, Gaussian noise with standard deviation σ was added to the output of this network. This network is called the "image acquisition network" and denoted as $\mathcal{N}_A$.

Meanwhile, the mapping g can take an arbitrary form because it is a truly computational process. We decomposed this mapping into two networks, which are denoted as $\mathcal{N}_{R1}$ and $\mathcal{N}_{R2}$, respectively, where R stands for reconstruction. In the former network $\mathcal{N}_{R1}$, the number of channels is gradually increased from M to N by using several convolution layers with 5×5 kernels and linear activations, resulting in a tentative reconstruction of the target light field. This tentative result is further refined by the latter network $\mathcal{N}_{R2}$ that employs the structure of very deep super resolution (VDSR) [50]. Here, 19 convolution layers with 3×3 kernels and ReLU activations are followed by the addition of the tentative light field itself, which forces the network to learn only the residual (difference between the tentative result and ground truth). The former and latter networks are also called the "tentative reconstruction and refinement networks," respectively.

2.3 Implementation and Training Details

We considered several network configurations for different values of M and N, as summarized in Table 1. The number of viewpoints in the target light field (M) was set to 25 (5×5) or 64 (8×8). The number of acquired images (N) was set to 1, 2, or 4. We employed different network architectures for $\mathcal{N}_{R1}$ for different numbers of N. The numbers connected by arrows in the table indicate the transition in the number of channels. The design principle here is to increase the number of channels gradually from N to M. Meanwhile, $\mathcal{N}_{R2}$ was only subject to M, and the number of channels for the intermediate layers was set to 64 for both $M = 25$ and $M = 64$. All of these architectures were found through trial and error, and there might be room for improvement.

Table 1. Network architecture for reconstruction

M	N	Tentative reconstruction	Refinement
25 (5×5)	1	$1 \to 2 \to 5 \to 12 \to 25$	$25 \to 64 \to 64, ..., 64 \to 25$
	2	$2 \to 5 \to 12 \to 25$	
	4	$4 \to 7 \to 13 \to 25$	
64 (8×8)	1	$1 \to 2 \to 4 \to 8 \to 16 \to 32 \to 64$	$64 \to 64 \to 64, ..., 64 \to 64$
	2	$2 \to 4 \to 8 \to 16 \to 32 \to 64$	
	4	$4 \to 8 \to 16 \to 32 \to 64$	

In the training stage, each training sample is a set of 2-D image blocks with 64×64 pixels that are extracted from the same positions in the multi-view images. As mentioned earlier, a viewpoint is considered to be a channel, and thus, each sample is represented as an M channel image that has 64×64 pixels. The training samples were collected from several light field datasets provided at [19–22], the details of which are summarized in Table 2. Three color channels of each dataset were used as three individual datasets. Moreover, we extracted many training samples from each dataset by changing the position of the 2-D blocks; we took blocks every 32 pixels both in the horizontal and vertical directions. We also augmented the data by changing the intensity levels of each sample uniformly; we multiplied 1.0, 0.9, 0.8, 0.7, 0.6 and 0.5 with the original samples. Samples that were too smooth, i.e., those in which the intensity was almost uniform across 64×64 pixels, were removed from the training samples. Finally, we collected 295,200 and 166,680 samples for $M = 25$ and $M = 64$, respectively. Similar to the case with VDSR [50], our network can be trained with a small training dataset because it consists of only convolutional layers with small kernels, and thus, the number of parameters does not increase too much. In the testing stage, the entire light field can be handled at once because fully convolutional networks can accept images with arbitrary size.

Our method was implemented by using Chainer [43] version 3.2.0, a Python based framework for neural networks. The batch size for training was set to 15.

Table 2. Datasets used for training and testing

M	Stage	Datasets
25 (5×5)	Training	Chess, Lego Bulldozer, Lego Truck, Eucalyptus Flowers, Amethyst, Bracelet, The Stanford Bunny, Jelly Beans, Lego Knights, Tarot Cards and Crystal Ball (small angular extent), Treasure Chest (Stanford [20]), Red Dragon, Happy Buddha, Messerschmitt, Dice, Green Dragon, Mini Cooper, Butterfly, Lucy (MIT [19]), Bedroom, Bicycle, Herbs, Origami, Boxes, Cotton, Sideboard, Antinous, Boardgames, Dishes, Greek, Museum, Pens, Pillows, Platonic, Rosemary, Table, Tomb, Town, Vinyl (New HCI [21]), Buddha, Buddha 2, StillLife, Papillon, MonaRoom, Medieval, Horse, Couple, Cube, Maria, Pyramide, Statue (Old HCI [22])
	Testing	Dragon and Bunnies, Fish (MIT [19]), Dino, Kitchen, Medieval2, Tower (New HCI [21])
64 (8×8)	Training	Chess, Lego Bulldozer, Lego Truck, Eucalyptus Flowers, Amethyst, Bracelet, The Stanford Bunny, Jelly Beans, Lego Knights, Tarot Cards and Crystal Ball (small angular extent), Treasure Chest Bedroom (Stanford [20]), Bicycle, Herbs, Origami, Boxes, Cotton, Sideboard, Antinous, Boardgames, Dishes, Greek, Museum, Pens, Pillows, Platonic, Rosemary, Table, Tomb, Town, Vinyl (New HCI [21])
	Testing	Dino, Kitchen, Medieval2, Tower (New HCI [21])

We used a built-in Adam optimizer [51]. The number of epochs was fixed to 20 for all experiments. The training with $M = 25$ and $N = 2$ took approximately 4 h on a PC equipped with an NVIDIA Geforce GTX 1080 Ti. In the testing stage, it took about 0.5 s to reconstruct the entire light field with 840×593 pixels and 25 viewpoints. Our software will be made public soon [52].

3 Experiments

3.1 Network Design and Performance

One of the key factors of our network is the noise that is added to the acquired images. Ideally, the noise level assumed in the training stage should be close to that in real situations. However, it is impractical to train different networks for all possible noise levels. It is more likely that a network trained with a certain noise level will be applied to different noise levels. To see the effect of the discrepancy in noise levels, we used different noise levels in the training and testing stages. Here, the noise level σ was defined with respect to the image intensity range $[0, 1]$ for acquired images $y_n(u, v)$. The results obtained with the Dragon and

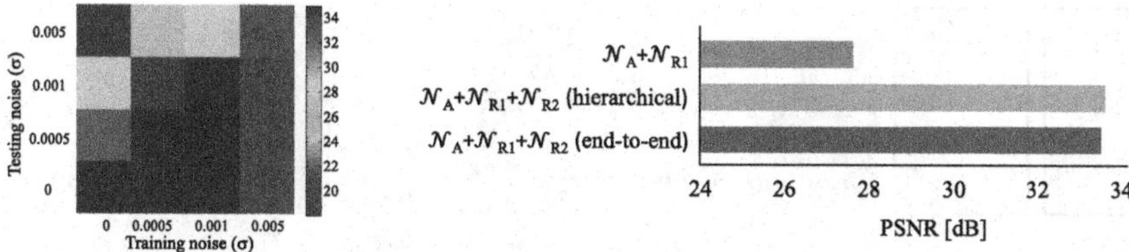

Fig. 3. Performance analysis of our method with different noise levels (left) and different network architectures and training schemes (right)

Bunnies dataset and $N = 2$ are summarized in Fig. 3 (left) [2]. When noise in the testing stage was larger than that in the training stage, the reconstruction quality was largely degraded. Meanwhile, in the opposite case, the degradation was moderate. Therefore, we concluded that assuming a high noise level in the training stage is a safe strategy. We use $\sigma = 0.005$ in the training stage in the remainder of this paper.

We next compared different network architectures and training schemes. We tested three cases: (a) $\mathcal{N}_A + \mathcal{N}_{R1}$, (b) $\mathcal{N}_A + \mathcal{N}_{R1} + \mathcal{N}_{R2}$, where $\mathcal{N}_A + \mathcal{N}_{R1}$ and $\mathcal{N}_{R2}$ were trained individually and then concatenated and fine-tuned, and (c) $\mathcal{N}_A + \mathcal{N}_{R1} + \mathcal{N}_{R2}$, where the entire network was trained end-to-end from scratch. As shown in Fig. 3 (right), the importance of the refinement network $\mathcal{N}_{R2}$ is clear. Meanwhile, the difference between (b) and (c) was negligible despite the fact that (b) required additional complexity for the training stage. Therefore, we adopted training strategy (c) for the remainder of this paper.

We then evaluated the performance of our method over several datasets. The number of viewpoints M was set to 25 (5×5) and 64 (8×8), and the number of acquired images N was set to 1, 2, and 4. The noise level for testing was set to 0.005. The obtained aperture patterns and quantitative scores in PSNR are summarized in Fig. 4. Several reconstructed images are presented in Fig. 5. From these results, we can see that the reconstruction quality improved as the number of acquired images increased. With $N = 1$, our method could not correctly reproduce the disparities among the viewpoints. However, by changing

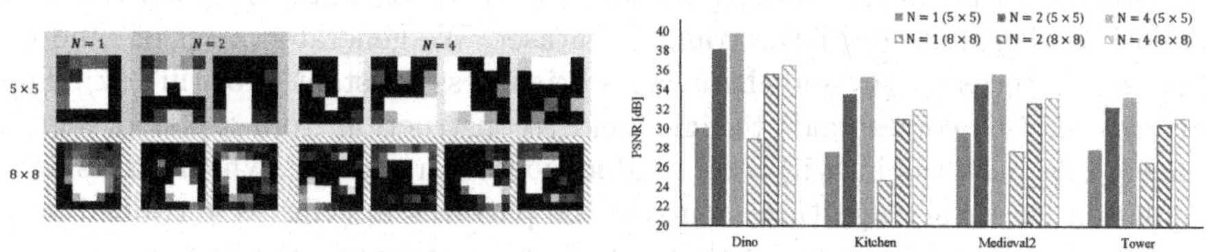

Fig. 4. Obtained aperture patterns (left) and PSNR (right)

[2] The PSNR values were obtained from the mean-squared errors over all viewpoints, pixels, and color channels. These values correspond to a logarithmic representation of the loss function given by Eq. (5).

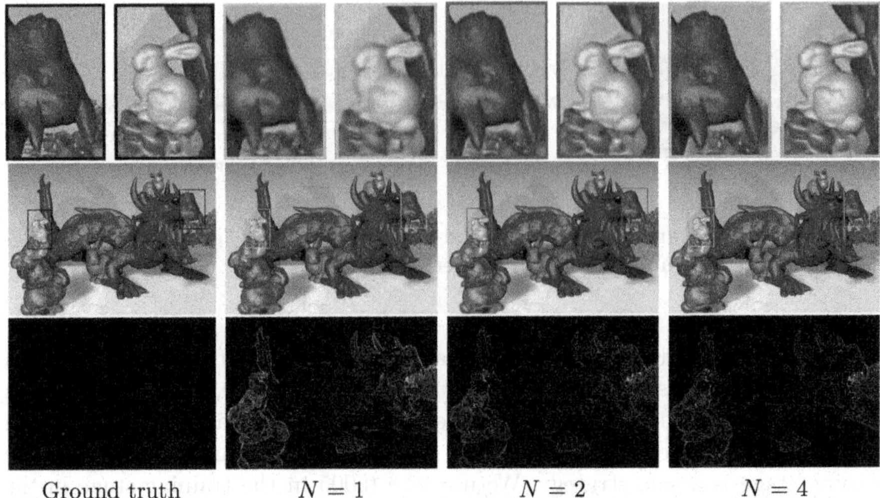

Fig. 5. Central views reconstructed by our method. Differences from ground truth (magnified by 5) are also presented

N from 1 to 2, the reconstruction quality improved significantly; fine details (see the close-ups) were successfully produced, and the correct amount of disparities was observed among the viewpoints. Meanwhile, the quality improvement from $N = 2$ to $N = 4$ was moderate. We observed the same tendency both with $M = 25$ and 64, though $M = 64$ was more challenging than 25 due to the increased number of viewpoints and less number of training samples.

3.2 Analysis on Aperture Patterns

To analyze the effect of aperture patterns, we conducted another experiment. We used several aperture patterns with $M = 25$ and $N = 2$, as summarized in Fig. 6(a). For (i), we used a set of aperture patterns that was trained normally, which is denoted as "ours (normal)" or simply"ours". For (ii)–(vii), we fixed the aperture patterns during the training stage; in this case, only the reconstruction network was optimized for the training dataset. We generated a set of random aperture patterns for (ii) and changed its brightness constantly for (iii)–(v). The patterns for (vi) corresponds to light field reconstruction from a pair of stereo images. The patterns in (vii) took randomized binary values, which serves as a simulation for binary apertures. Finally, the patterns in (viii) were trained over the dataset under the constraint that the second pattern was the first one rotated 90°. This was easily implemented by using the same convolution kernels for the first and second image acquisition but tweaking the order of channels in the input data. This pattern set may have a practical value because it can be implemented by using a static aperture pattern (such as a printed one, instead of an expensive

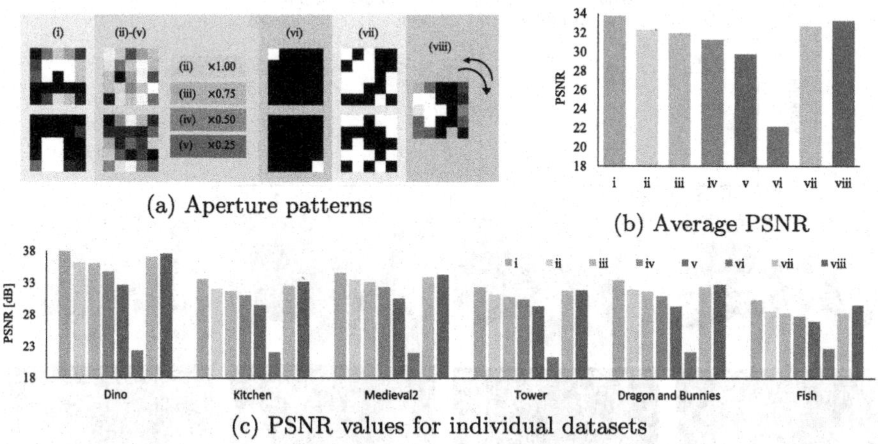

(a) Aperture patterns

(b) Average PSNR

(c) PSNR values for individual datasets

Fig. 6. Analysis on aperture patterns with $M = 25$ and $N = 2$

electronic device such as an LCoS) with a simple rotation mechanism. This is denoted as "ours (rotated)." We set the noise level for testing to 0.005.

3.3 Comparison with State-of-the-Art Methods

Several interesting indications are found from the results shown in Fig. 6(b), (c). First, a good reconstruction quality was attained even with non-optimized aperture patterns such as (ii) and (vii), probably because the reconstruction network is capable of adapting to different aperture patterns. Second, the brightness of the apertures (the total amount of light) is important for the quality. The quality degradation observed in (iii)–(vi) can be attributed to the bad signal-to-noise ratio of the acquired images. Finally, the rotated patterns in (viii) achieved quality close to that of normally trained patterns (i), suggesting the possibility of developing a camera with a rotatable static aperture in the future.

We compared our method against four state-of-the-art methods [6,33,35,36], for which we used the software provided by the respective authors. To make the comparison fair, the configurations for the methods were kept unchanged from the original implementations as much as possible. To see the results more closely, please refer to the supplementary video.

We first present a comparison with two compressive-sensing based methods: Marwah's method [33] using a sparse dictionary and Yagi's method [35] using the most significant basis vectors selected by PCA or NMF. The number of viewpoints M was set to 25 (5×5) in accordance with the original implementations. The noise level was set to $\sigma = 0$ and $\sigma = 0.005$. The results are summarized in Fig. 7. As shown in the graphs of the figure, our method performed clearly better than Yagi's method. Marwah's method achieved slightly better scores than ours with $N = 1$, but with $N = 2$ and $N = 4$, it was inferior to our method with significant margins. Moreover, the main drawback of Marwah's method is

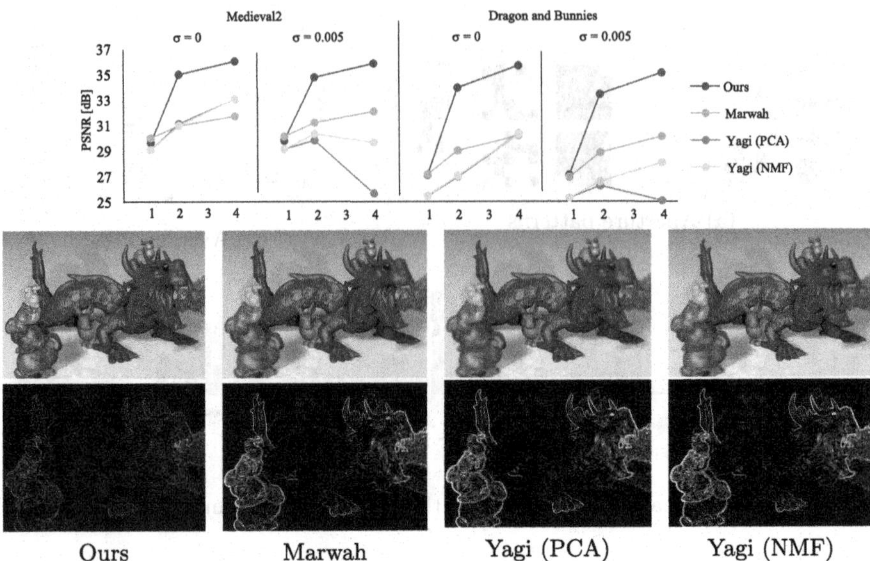

Fig. 7. Comparison with compressive-sensing based methods [33,35]. (Top) quantitative reconstruction quality. (Bottom) reconstructed images and difference from the ground truth (magnified by 5)

the computational complexity; it took 11–90 h to reconstruct a single light field on our desktop computer. Shown in the bottom are reconstructed central views and the differences from the ground truth obtained with Dragon and Bunnies, $N = 2$, and $\sigma = 0.005$. We can see that a better visual quality was achieved by our method over the others.

We next show another comparison with two view-synthesis based methods. Kalantari's method [6] can reconstruct a light field with 8×8 viewpoints given the four corner images. It was reported that this method performed better than several state-of-the-art view synthesis methods. Meanwhile, Srinivasan's method [36] can reconstruct a light field with 8×8 viewpoints only from one image corresponding to the central viewpoint (actually, it is located at the bottom-right nearest neighbor to the center). No noise was applied for these two methods. As for our method, the number of viewpoints M was set to 64 (8×8) as well, but noise with $\sigma = 0.005$ was applied. The results are summarized in Fig. 8. Srinivasan's method produced natural-looking images with around 30–60 s computation time, but it failed to reproduce correct disparities among the viewpoints. Kalantari's method achieved better quality than Srinivasan's method, but it required four images as the input and took about 30 min without GPU boost. Our method achieved overall better reconstruction quality than the other two with much less computation time (about 1 s).

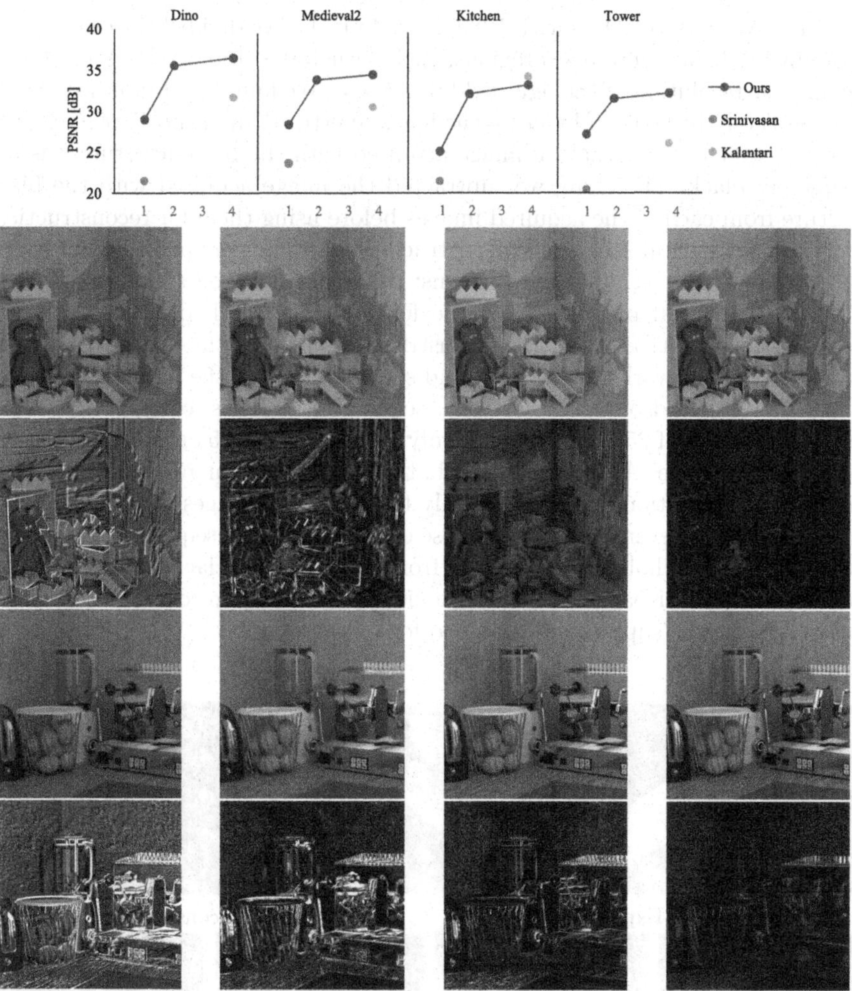

Srinivasan (top-left) Ours (top-left, N=1) Kalantari (central) Ours (central, N=4)

Fig. 8. Comparison with view-synthesis based methods [6,36]. (Top) quantitative reconstruction quality. (Bottom) reconstructed images and difference from ground truth (magnified by 5) obtained with Dino and Kitchen

3.4 Experiment Using Real Camera

Finally, we conducted an experiment using a real coded-aperture camera. We adopted the same hardware design as the ones reported in [31,33,49]. The resolution of the camera (FLIR GRAS-14S5C-C) was 1384 × 1036 pixels, which corresponds to the spatial resolution of the light field acquired with it. The exposure time was set to 40 ms. We used a Nikon Rayfact lens (25 mm F1.4 SF2514MC). The aperture was implemented as an LCoS display (Forth Dimension Displays, SXGA-3DM) with 1280 × 1024 pixels. We divided the central area of the LCoS display into 5 × 5 regions, each with 150 × 150 pixels. Accordingly, the angular resolution of the light field was 5 × 5. We found that light rays could not completely be shut off by using the black aperture (all of the 25 regions were set to 0), which means that an image acquired with the black aperture was not completely black. Therefore, we subtracted the image acquired with the black aperture from each of the acquired images before using them for reconstruction.

The experimental setup and reconstructed light fields are presented in Fig. 9. We used four sets of aperture patterns: ours (normal), ours (rotated), NMF [35], and sequential pinholes.[3] For the former three methods, the number of acquired images was set to 2. The reconstruction was performed with the trained reconstruction networks for the first and second ones and the method presented in [35] for the third one. The last one, sequential pinholes, corresponds to the direct acquisition of 25 images, where only 1 region out of 25 on the aperture was opened in sequence. As shown in the bottom of Fig. 9, our method achieved a striking reconstruction quality with only two acquired images. The results with our methods were even better than those obtained with 25 sequentially acquired images because pinhole patterns suffer from noise due to a lack of light. We also observed natural disparities among the viewpoints in the reconstructed results. Please refer to the supplementary video for more detail.

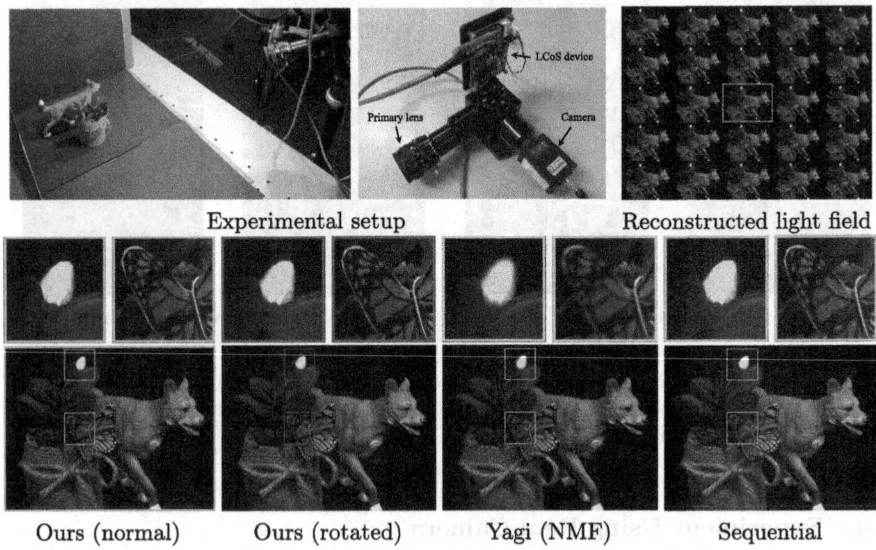

Fig. 9. Experiment using real coded-aperture camera

[3] We did not test Marwah's method [33] with our real camera because this method was designed for an optical configuration different from our camera, and the reconstruction with this method would require prohibitively expensive computation.

4 Conclusion

We proposed a learning-based framework for acquiring a light field through a coded aperture camera to reduce the required number of acquired images to only a few. This framework was formulated from the perspective of an auto-encoder. This auto-encoder was implemented as a stack of fully convolutional layers and was trained end-to-end by using a collection of training samples. We experimentally showed that our method can successfully learn good image-acquisition and reconstruction strategies. Using our method, light fields consisting of 5×5 or 8×8 images can be reconstructed with high quality from only a few acquired images. Moreover, our method achieved superior performance over several state-of-the-art methods. We also applied our method to a real prototype camera to show that it is capable of capturing a real 3-D scene.

Our future work includes several directions. The performance of our method could be improved by tweaking the architecture of the reconstruction network or increasing the number of training samples. The squared loss used in our method could be replaced with or supplemented by other loss functions that are closer to the perceptual image quality such as VGG loss and the framework of a generative adversarial network (GAN) [53]. The development of a camera with a rotatable static aperture pattern would also be an interesting direction.

References

1. Adelson, E.H., Bergen, J.R.: The plenoptic function and the elements of early vision. In: Computational Models of Visual Processing, pp. 3–20 (1991)
2. Levoy, M., Hanrahan, P.: Light field rendering. In: Proceedings of the 23rd Annual Conference on Computer Graphics and Interactive Techniques, pp. 31–42. ACM (1996)
3. Gortler, S.J., Grzeszczuk, R., Szeliski, R., Cohen, M.F.: The lumigraph. In: Proceedings of the 23rd Annual Conference on Computer Graphics and Interactive Techniques, pp. 43–54 (1996)
4. Tanimoto, M., Tehrani, M.P., Fujii, T., Yendo, T.: Free-viewpoint T.V. IEEE Signal Process. Mag. **28**(1), 67–76 (2011)
5. Shi, L., Hassanieh, H., Davis, A., Katabi, D., Durand, F.: Light field reconstruction using sparsity in the continuous Fourier domain. ACM Trans. Graph. (TOG) **34**(1), 12 (2014)
6. Kalantari, N.K., Wang, T.C., Ramamoorthi, R.: Learning-based view synthesis for light field cameras. In: ACM Transactions on Graphics (Proceedings of SIGGRAPH Asia 2016), vol. 35(6) (2016)
7. Wanner, S., Goldluecke, B.: Variational light field analysis for disparity estimation and super-resolution. IEEE Trans. Pattern Anal. Mach. Intell. **36**(3), 606–619 (2014)
8. Wang, T.C., Efros, A.A., Ramamoorthi, R.: Depth estimation with occlusion modeling using light-field cameras. IEEE Trans. Pattern Anal. Mach. Intell. **38**(11), 2170–2181 (2016)
9. Williem, W., Park, I.K., Lee, K.M.: Robust light field depth estimation using occlusion-noise aware data costs. IEEE Trans. Pattern Anal. Mach. Intell. **PP**(99), 1 (2017)

10. Isaksen, A., McMillan, L., Gortler, S.J.: Dynamically reparameterized light fields. In: Proceedings of the 27th Annual Conference on Computer Graphics and Interactive Techniques, pp. 297–306 (2000)
11. Ng, R., Levoy, M., Brédif, M., Duval, G., Horowitz, M., Hanrahan, P.: Light field photography with a hand-held plenoptic camera. Comput. Sci. Tech. Rep. CSTR **2**(11), 1–11 (2005)
12. Bishop, T.E., Zanetti, S., Favaro, P.: Light field superresolution. In: 2009 IEEE International Conference on Computational Photography (ICCP), pp. 1–9. IEEE (2009)
13. Wetzstein, G., Lanman, D., Hirsch, M., Raskar, R.: Tensor displays: compressive light field synthesis using multilayer displays with directional backlighting. ACM Trans. Graph. (Proc. SIGGRAPH), **31**(4), 1–11 (2012)
14. Huang, F.C., Chen, K., Wetzstein, G.: The light field stereoscope: immersive computer graphics via factored near-eye light field displays with focus cues. ACM Trans. Graph. (TOG), **34**(4), 60 (2015)
15. Lee, S., Jang, C., Moon, S., Cho, J., Lee, B.: Additive light field displays: realization of augmented reality with holographic optical elements. ACM Trans. Graph. (TOG), **35**(4), 60 (2016)
16. Saito, T., Kobayashi, Y., Takahashi, K., Fujii, T.: Displaying real-world light fields with stacked multiplicative layers: requirement and data conversion for input multiview images. J. Display Technol. **12**(11), 1290–1300 (2016)
17. Maeno, K., Nagahara, H., Shimada, A., Taniguchi, R.I.: Light field distortion feature for transparent object recognition. In: IEEE Conference on Computer Vision and Pattern Recognition, pp. 2786–2793 (2013)
18. Wang, T.-C., Zhu, J.-Y., Hiroaki, E., Chandraker, M., Efros, A.A., Ramamoorthi, R.: A 4D light-field dataset and CNN architectures for material recognition. In: Leibe, B., Matas, J., Sebe, N., Welling, M. (eds.) ECCV 2016. LNCS, vol. 9907, pp. 121–138. Springer, Cham (2016). https://doi.org/10.1007/978-3-319-46487-9_8
19. MIT Media Lab's Camera Culture Group: Compressive light field camera. http://cameraculture.media.mit.edu/projects/compressive-light-field-camera/
20. Computer Graphics Laboratory, Stanford University: The (new) stanford light field archive (2018). http://lightfield.stanford.edu
21. Heidelberg Collaboratory for Image Processing: 4D light field dataset (2018). http://hci-lightfield.iwr.uni-heidelberg.de/
22. Heidelberg Collaboratory for Image Processing: Datasets and benchmarks for densely sampled 4D light fields (2016). http://lightfieldgroup.iwr.uni-heidelberg.de/?page_id=713
23. Wilburn, B., et al.: High performance imaging using large camera arrays. ACM Trans. Graph. (TOG) **24**(3), 765–776 (2005)
24. Fujii, T., Mori, K., Takeda, K., Mase, K., Tanimoto, M., Suenaga, Y.: Multipoint measuring system for video and sound-100-camera and microphone system. In: 2006 IEEE International Conference on Multimedia and Expo, pp. 437–440. IEEE (2006)
25. Taguchi, Y., Koike, T., Takahashi, K., Naemura, T.: TransCAIP: a live 3D TV system using a camera array and an integral photography display with interactive control of viewing parameters. IEEE Trans. Vis. Comput. Graph. **15**(5), 841–852 (2009)
26. Adelson, E.H., Wang, J.Y.: Single lens stereo with a plenoptic camera. IEEE Trans. Pattern Anal. Mach. Intell. **14**(2), 99–106 (1992)

27. Arai, J., Okano, F., Hoshino, H., Yuyama, I.: Gradient-index lens-array method based on real-time integral photography for three-dimensional images. Appl. Optics **37**(11), 2034–2045 (1998)
28. Ng, R.: Digital light field photography. Ph.D. thesis, Stanford University (2006)
29. Veeraraghavan, A., Raskar, R., Agrawal, A., Mohan, A., Tumblin, J.: Dappled photography: Mask enhanced cameras for heterodyned light fields and coded aperture refocusing. ACM Trans. Graph. (TOG) **26**(3), 69 (2007)
30. Liang, C.K., Lin, T.H., Wong, B.Y., Liu, C., Chen, H.H.: Programmable aperture photography: multiplexed light field acquisition. ACM Trans. Graph. (TOG) **27**(3), 55 (2008)
31. Nagahara, H., Zhou, C., Watanabe, T., Ishiguro, H., Nayar, S.K.: Programmable aperture camera using LCoS. In: Daniilidis, K., Maragos, P., Paragios, N. (eds.) ECCV 2010. LNCS, vol. 6316, pp. 337–350. Springer, Heidelberg (2010). https://doi.org/10.1007/978-3-642-15567-3_25
32. Babacan, S.D., Ansorge, R., Luessi, M., Mataran, P.R., Molina, R., Katsaggelos, A.K.: Compressive light field sensing. IEEE Trans. Image Process. **21**(12), 4746–4757 (2012)
33. Marwah, K., Wetzstein, G., Bando, Y., Raskar, R.: Compressive light field photography using over complete dictionaries and optimized projections. ACM Trans. Graph. (TOG) **32**(4), 46 (2013)
34. Tambe, S., Veeraraghavan, A., Agrawal, A.: Towards motion aware light field video for dynamic scenes. In: Proceedings of the IEEE International Conference on Computer Vision, pp. 1009–1016 (2013)
35. Yagi, Y., Takahashi, K., Fujii, T., Sonoda, T., Nagahara, H.: PCA-coded aperture for light field photography. In: IEEE International Conference on Image Processing (ICIP) (2017)
36. Srinivasan, P.P., Wang, T., Sreelal, A., Ramamoorthi, R., Ng, R.: Learning to synthesize a 4D RGBD light field from a single image. In: IEEE International Conference on Computer Vision, pp. 2262–2270 (2017)
37. Yoon, Y., Jeon, H.G., Yoo, D., Lee, J.Y., Kweon, I.S.: Learning a deep convolutional network for light-field image super-resolution. In: 2015 IEEE International Conference on Computer Vision Workshop (ICCVW), pp. 57–65 (2015)
38. Donoho, D.L.: Compressed sensing. IEEE Trans. Inf. Theory **52**(4), 1289–1306 (2006)
39. Candès, E.J., Wakin, M.B.: An introduction to compressive sampling. IEEE Signal Process. Mag. **25**(2), 21–30 (2008)
40. Candes, E.J., Eldar, Y.C., Needell, D., Randall, P.: Compressed sensing with coherent and redundant dictionaries. Appl. Comput. Harmon. Anal. **31**(1), 59–73 (2011)
41. Hinton, G.E., Salakhutdinov, R.R.: Reducing the dimensionality of data with neural networks. Science **313**(5786), 504–507 (2006)
42. Vincent, P., Larochelle, H., Bengio, Y., Manzagol, P.A.: Extracting and composing robust features with denoising autoencoders. In: Proceedings of the 25th International Conference on Machine Learning, ICML 2008, pp. 1096–1103 (2008)
43. Tokui, S., Oono, K., Hido, S., Clayton, J.: Chainer: a next-generation open source framework for deep learning. In: Workshop on Machine Learning Systems (LearningSys) in the Twenty-ninth Annual Conference on Neural Information Processing Systems (NIPS) (2015)
44. Chakrabarti, A.: Learning sensor multiplexing design through back-propagation. In: Proceedings of the 30th International Conference on Neural Information Processing Systems, pp. 3089–3097 (2016)

45. Shedligeri, P.A., Mohan, S., Mitra, K.: Data driven coded aperture design for depth recovery. In: 2017 IEEE International Conference on Image Processing (ICIP), pp. 56–60 (2017)
46. Iliadis, M., Spinoulas, L., Katsaggelos, A.K.: Deep fully-connected networks for video compressive sensing. arXiv, http://arxiv.org/abs/1603.04930 (2016)
47. Wang, T.C., Zhu, J.Y., Kalantari, N.K., Efros, A.A., Ramamoorthi, R.: Light field video capture using a learning-based hybrid imaging system. ACM Trans. Graph. **36**(4), 133:1–133:13 (2017)
48. Gupta, M., Jauhari, A., Kulkarni, K., Jayasuriya, S., Molnar, A., Turaga, P.: Compressive light field reconstructions using deep learning. In: 2017 IEEE Conference on Computer Vision and Pattern Recognition Workshops (CVPRW), pp. 1277–1286 (2017)
49. Sonoda, T., Nagahara, H., Taniguchi, R.: Motion-invariant coding using a programmable aperture camera. IPSJ Trans. Comput. Vis. Appl. **6**, 25–33 (2014)
50. Kim, J., Kwon Lee, J., Mu Lee, K.: Accurate image super-resolution using very deep convolutional networks. In: IEEE Computer Society Conference on Computer Vision and Pattern Recognition, pp. 1646–1654 (2016)
51. Kingma, D., Ba, J.: Adam: a method for stochastic optimization. In: The International Conference on Learning Representations (ICLR) (2015)
52. Keita Takahashi: Computational camera project. http://www.fujii.nuee.nagoya-u.ac.jp/%7Etakahasi/Research/CompCam/index.html
53. Goodfellow, I., et al.: Generative adversarial nets. Adv. Neural Inf. Process. Syst. **27**, 2672–2680 (2014)

End-to-End Learning of Driving Models with Surround-View Cameras and Route Planners

Simon Hecker[1(✉)], Dengxin Dai[1], and Luc Van Gool[1,2]

[1] ETH Zurich, Zurich, Switzerland
{heckers,dai,vangool}@vision.ee.ethz.ch
[2] KU Leuven, Leuven, Belgium

Abstract. For human drivers, having rear and side-view mirrors is vital for safe driving. They deliver a more complete view of what is happening around the car. Human drivers also heavily exploit their mental map for navigation. Nonetheless, several methods have been published that learn driving models with only a front-facing camera and without a route planner. This lack of information renders the self-driving task quite intractable. We investigate the problem in a more realistic setting, which consists of a surround-view camera system with eight cameras, a route planner, and a CAN bus reader. In particular, we develop a sensor setup that provides data for a 360-degree view of the area surrounding the vehicle, the driving route to the destination, and low-level driving maneuvers (e.g. steering angle and speed) by human drivers. With such a sensor setup we collect a new driving dataset, covering diverse driving scenarios and varying weather/illumination conditions. Finally, we learn a novel driving model by integrating information from the surround-view cameras and the route planner. Two route planners are exploited: (1) by representing the planned routes on OpenStreetMap as a stack of GPS coordinates, and (2) by rendering the planned routes on TomTom Go Mobile and recording the progression into a video. Our experiments show that: (1) 360-degree surround-view cameras help avoid failures made with a single front-view camera, in particular for city driving and intersection scenarios; and (2) route planners help the driving task significantly, especially for steering angle prediction. Code, data and more visual results will be made available at http://www.vision.ee.ethz.ch/~heckers/Drive360.

Keywords: Autonomous driving · End-to-end learning of driving
Route planning for driving · Surround-view cameras · Driving dataset

---

Electronic supplementary material The online version of this chapter (https://doi.org/10.1007/978-3-030-01234-2_27) contains supplementary material, which is available to authorized users.

V. Ferrari et al. (Eds.): ECCV 2018, LNCS 11211, pp. 449–468, 2018.
https://doi.org/10.1007/978-3-030-01234-2_27

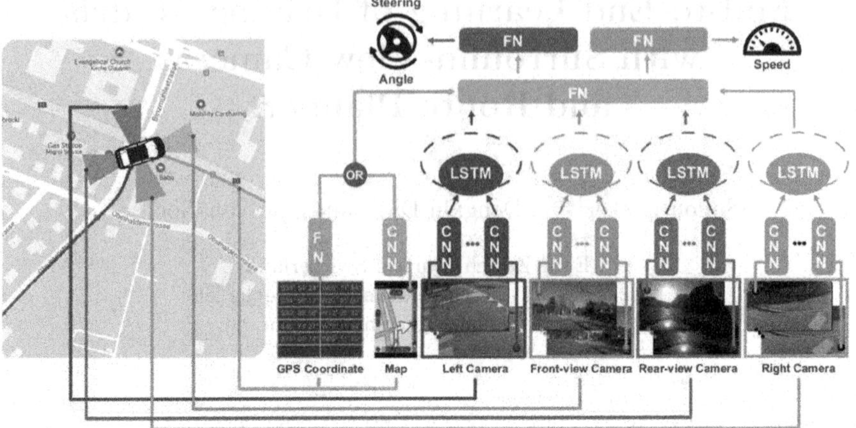

Fig. 1. An illustration of our driving system. Cameras provide a 360-degree view of the area surrounding the vehicle. The driving maps or GPS coordinates generated by the route planner and the videos from our cameras are synchronized. They are used as inputs to train the driving model. The driving model consists of CNN networks for feature encoding, LSTM networks to integrate the outputs of the CNNs over time; and fully-connected networks (FN) to integrate information from multiple sensors to predict the driving maneuvers

1 Introduction

Autonomous driving has seen dramatic advances in recent years, for instance for road scene parsing [1–4], lane following [5–7], path planning [8–11], and end-to-end driving models [12–15]. By now, autonomous vehicles have driven many thousands of miles and companies aspire to sell such vehicles in a few years. Yet, significant technical obstacles, such as the necessary robustness of driving models to adverse weather/illumination conditions [2–4] or the capability to anticipate potential risks in advance [16,17], must be overcome before assisted driving can be turned into full-fletched automated driving. At the same time, research on the next steps towards 'complete' driving systems is becoming less and less accessible to the academic community. We argue that this is mainly due to the lack of large, shared driving datasets delivering more *complete* sensor inputs.

Surround-View Cameras and Route Planners. Driving is inarguably a highly visual and intellectual task. Information from all around the vehicle needs to be gathered and integrated to make safe decisions. As a virtual extension to the limited field of view of our eyes, side-view mirrors and a rear-view mirror are used since 1906 [18] and in the meantime have become obligatory. Human drivers also use their internal maps [19,20] or a digital map to select a route to their destination. Similarly, for automated vehicles, a decision-making system must select a route through the road network from its current position to the requested destination [21–23].

As said, a single front-view camera is inadequate to learn a safe driving model. It has already been observed in [24] that upon reaching a fork - and without a clearcut idea of where to head for - the model may output multiple widely discrepant travel directions, one for each choice. This would result in unsafe driving decisions, like oscillations in the selected travel direction. Nevertheless, current research often focuses on this setting because it still allows to look into plenty of challenges [6,12,25]. This is partly due to the simplicity of training models with a single camera, both in terms of available datasets and the complexity an effective model needs to have. Our work includes a surround-view camera system, a route planner, and a data reader for the vehicle's CAN bus. The setting provides a 360-degree view of the area surrounding the vehicle, a planned driving route, and the 'ground-truth' maneuvers by human drivers. Hence, we obtain a learning task similar to that of a human apprentice, where a (cognitive/digital) map gives an overall sense of direction, and the actual steering and speed controls need to be set based on the observation of the local road situation.

Driving Models. In order to keep the task tractable, we chose to learn the driving model in an end-to-end manner, i.e. to map inputs from our surround-view cameras and the route planner directly to low-level maneuvers of the car. The incorporation of detection and tracking modules for traffic agents (e.g. cars and pedestrians) and traffic control devices (e.g. traffic lights and signs) is future work. We designed a specialized deep network architecture which integrates all information from our surround-view cameras and the route planner, and then maps these sensor inputs directly to low-level car maneuvers. See Fig. 1 and the supplemental material for the network's architecture. The route planner is exploited in two ways: (1) by representing planned routes as a stack of GPS coordinates, and (2) by rendering the planned routes on a map and recording the progression as a video.

Our main contributions are twofold: (1) a new driving dataset of 60 h, featuring videos from eight surround-view cameras, two forms of data representation for a route planner, low-level driving maneuvers, and GPS-IMU data of the vehicle's odometry; (2) a learning algorithm to integrate information from the surround-view cameras and planned routes to predict future driving maneuvers. Our experiments show that: (a) 360-degree views help avoid failures made with a single front-view camera; and (b) a route planner also improves the driving significantly.

2 Related Work

Our work is relevant for (1) driving models, (2) assistive features for vehicles with surround view cameras, (3) navigation and maps, and (4) driving scene understanding.

2.1 Driving Models for Automated Cars

Significant progress has been made in autonomous driving, especially due to the deployment of deep neural networks. Driving models can be clustered into two groups [7]: mediated perception approaches and end-to-end mapping approaches, with some exceptions like [7]. Mediated perception approaches require the recognition of all driving-relevant objects, such as lanes, traffic signs, traffic lights, cars, pedestrians, etc. [1,26,27]. Excellent work [28] has been done to integrate such results. This kind of systems developed by the automotive industry represent the current state-of-the-art for autonomous driving. Most use diverse sensors, such as cameras, laser scanners, radar, and GPS and high-definition maps [29]. End-to-end mapping methods construct a direct mapping from the sensory input to the maneuvers. The idea can be traced back to the 1980s, when a neural network was used to learn a direct mapping from images to steering angles [24]. Other end-to-end examples are [5,12,14,15,25]. In [12], the authors trained a neural network to map camera inputs directly to the vehicle's egomotion. Methods have also been developed to explain how the end-to-end networks work for the driving task [30] and to predict when they fail [17]. Most end-to-end work has been demonstrated with a front-facing camera only. To the best of our knowledge, we present the first end-to-end method that exploits more realistic input. Please note that our data can also be used for mediated perception approaches. Recently, reinforcement learning for driving has received increasing attention [31–33]. The trend is especially fueled by the release of excellent driving simulators [34,35].

2.2 Assistive Features of Vehicle with Surround View Cameras

Over the last decades, more and more assistive technologies have been deployed to vehicles, that increase driving safety. Technologies such as lane keeping, blind spot checking, forward collision avoidance, adaptive cruise control, driver behavior prediction etc., alert drivers about potential dangers [36–39]. Research in this vein recently has shifted focus to surround-view cameras, as a panoramic view around the vehicle is needed for many such applications. Notable examples include object detection, object tracking, lane detection, maneuver estimation, and parking guidance. For instance, a bird's eye view has been used to monitor the surrounding of the vehicle in [40]. Trajectories and maneuvers of surrounding vehicles are estimated with surround view camera arrays [41,42]. Datasets, methods and evaluation metrics of object detection and tracking with multiple overlapping cameras are studied in [43,44]. Lane detection with surround-view cameras is investigated in [45] and the parking problem in [46]. Advanced driver assistance systems often use a 3-D surround view, which informs drivers about the environment and eliminates blind spots [47]. Our work adds autonomous driving to this list. Our dataset can also be used for all aforementioned problems; and it provides a platform to study the usefulness of route planners.

2.3 Navigation and Maps

In-car navigation systems have been widely used to show the vehicle's current location on a map and to inform drivers on how to get from the current position to the destination. Increasing the accuracy and robustness of systems for positioning, navigation and digital maps has been another research focus for many years. Several methods for high-definition mapping have been proposed [48,49], some specifically for autonomous driving [50,51]. Route planning has been extensively studied as well [52–56], mainly to compute the fastest, most fuel-efficient, or a customized trajectory to the destination through a road network. Yet, thus far their usage is mostly restricted to help human drivers. Their accessibility as an aid to learn autonomous driving models has been limited. This work reports on two ways of using two kinds of maps: a s-o-t-a commercial map TomTom Maps[1] and the excellent collaborative project OpenStreetMaps [57].

While considerable progress has been made both in computer vision and in route planning, their integration for learning driving models has not received due attention in the academic community. A trending topic is to combine digital maps and street-view images for accurate vehicle localization [58–61].

2.4 Driving Scene Understanding

Road scene understanding is a crucial enabler for assisted or autonomous driving. Typical examples include the detection of roads [62], traffic lights [63], cars and pedestrians [1,2,64,65], and the tracking of such objects [66–68]. We refer the reader to these comprehensive surveys [69,70]. Integrating recognition results like these of the aforementioned algorithms may well be necessary but is beyond the scope of this paper.

3 The Driving Dataset

We first present our sensor setup, then describe our data collection, and finally compare our dataset to other driving datasets.

3.1 Sensors

Three kinds of sensors are used for data collection in this work: cameras, a route planner (with a map), and a USB reader for data from the vehicle's CAN bus.

Cameras. We use eight cameras and mount them on the roof of the car using a specially designed rig with 3D printed camera mounts. The cameras are mounted under the following angles: 0°, 45°, 90°, 135°, 180°, 225°, 270° and 315° relative to the vehicle's heading direction. We installed GoPro Hero 5 Black cameras, due to their ease of use, their good image quality when moving, and their weather-resistance. All videos are recorded at 60 frames per second (fps) in 1080p. As a

[1] https://www.tomtom.com/en_us/drive/maps-services/maps/.

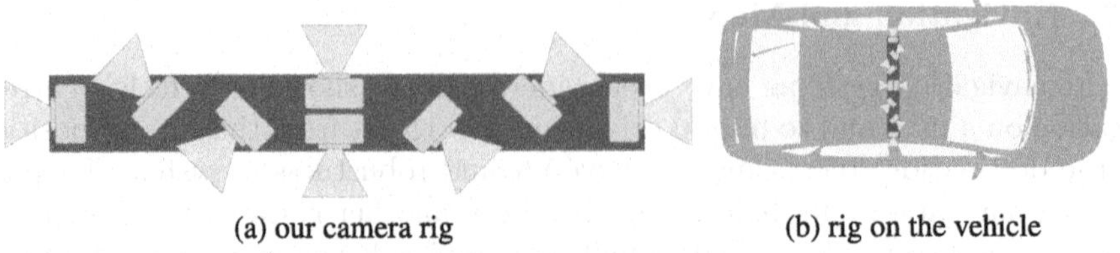

(a) our camera rig (b) rig on the vehicle

Fig. 2. The configuration of our cameras. The rig is 1.6 m wide so that the side-view cameras can have a good view of road surface without the obstruction by the roof of the vehicle. The cameras are evenly distributed laterally and angularly

matter of fact, a full 360-degree view can be covered by four cameras already. Please see Fig. 2 for our camera configuration.

Route Planners. Route planners have been a research focus over many years [53,54]. While considerable progress has been made both in computer vision and in route planning, their integration for learning to drive has not received due attention in the academic community. Routing has become ubiquitous with commercial maps such as Google Maps, HERE Maps, and TomTom Maps, and on-board navigation devices are virtually in every new car. Albeit available in a technical sense, their routing algorithms and the underlying road networks are not yet accessible to the public. In this work, we exploited two route planners: one based on TomTom Map and the other on OpenStreetMap.

TomTom Map represents one of the s-o-t-a commercial maps for driving applications. Similar to all other commercial counterparts, it does not provide open APIs to access their 'raw' data. We thus exploit the visual information provided by their TomTom GO Mobile App [71], and recorded their rendered map views using the native screen recording software supplied by the smart phone, an iPhone 7. Since map rendering comes with rather slow updates, we capture the screen at 30 fps. The video resolution was set to 1280×720 pixels.

Apart from the commercial maps, OpenStreetMaps (OSM) [57] has gained a great attention for supporting routing services. The OSM geodata includes detailed spacial and semantic information about roads, such as name of roads, type of roads (e.g. highway or footpath), speed limits, addresses of buildings, etc. The effectiveness of OSM for Robot Navigation has been demonstrated by Hentschel and Wagner [72]. We thus, in this work, use the real-time routing method developed by Luxen and Vetter for OSM data [73] as our second route planner. The past driving trajectories (a stack of GPS coordinates) are provided to the routing algorithm to localize the vehicle to the road network, and the GPS tags of the planned road for the next 300 m ahead are taken as the representation of the planned route for the 'current' position. Because the GPS tags of the road networks of OSM are not distributed evenly according to distance, we fitted a cubic smoothing spline to the obtained GPS tags and then sampled 300 data points from the fitted spline with a stride of 1 m. Thus, for the OSM route planner, we have a 300×2 matrix (300 GPS coordinates) as the representation of the planned route for every 'current' position.

Human Driving Maneuvers. We record low level driving maneuvers, i.e. the steering wheel angle and vehicle speed, registered on the CAN bus of the car at 50 Hz. The CAN protocol is a simple ID and data payload broadcasting protocol that is used for low level information broadcasting in a vehicle. As such, we read out the specific CAN IDs and their corresponding payload for steering wheel angle and vehicle speed via a CAN-to-USB device and record them on a computer connected to the bus.

Vehicle's Odometry. We use the GoPro cameras' built-in GPS and IMU module to record GPS data at 18 Hz and IMU measurements at 200 Hz while driving. This data is then extracted and parsed from the meta-track of the GoPro created video.

3.2 Data Collection

Synchronization. The correct synchronization amongst all data streams is of utmost importance. For this we devised an automatic procedure that allows for synchronization to GPS for fast dataset generation. During all recording, the internal clocks of all sensors are synchronized to the GPS clock. The resulting synchronization error for the video frames is up to 8.3 ms, i.e. half the frame rate. If the vehicle is at a speed of 100 km/h, the error due to the synchronization for vehicle's longitudinal position is about 23 cm. We acknowledge that a camera which can be triggered by accurate trigger signals are preferable with respect to synchronization error. Our cameras, however, provide good photometric image quality and high frame rates, at the price of moderate synchronization error. The synchronization error of the maps to our video frame is up to 0.5 s. This is acceptable, as the planned route (regardless of its representation) is only needed to provide a global view for navigation. The synchronization error of the CAN bus signal to our video frames is up to 10 ms. This is also tolerable as human drivers issue driving actions at a relative low rate. For instance, the mean reaction times for unexpected and expected human drivers are 1.3 and 0.7 s [74].

***Drive360* Dataset.** With the sensors described, we collect a new dataset *Drive360*. *Drive360* is recorded by driving in (around) multiple cities in Switzerland. We focus on delivering realistic dataset for training driving models. Inspired by how a driving instructor teaches a human apprentice to drive, we chose the routes and the driving time with the aim to maximize the opportunity of exposing to all typical driving scenarios. This reduces the chance of generating a biased dataset with many 'repetitive' scenarios, and thus allowing for an accurate judgment of the performance of the driving models. *Drive360* contains 60 h of driving data.

The drivers always obeyed Swiss driving rules, such as respecting the driving speed carefully, driving on the right lane when not overtaking a vehicle, leaving the required amount of distance to the vehicle in front etc. We have a second person accompanying the drivers to help (remind) the driver to always follow the route planned by our route planner. We have used a manual setup procedure to make sure that the two route planners generate the 'same' planned route, up to the difference between their own representations of the road networks. After choosing the starting point and the destination, we first generate a driving route with the OSM route planner. For TomTom route planner, we obtain the same driving route by using the same starting point and destination, and by adding a consecutive sequence of waypoints (intermediate places) on the route. We manually verified every part of the route before each driving to make sure that the two planned routes are in deed the same. After this synchronization, TomTom Go Mobile is used to guide our human drivers due to its high-quality visual information. The data for our OSM route planner is obtained by using the routing algorithm proposed in [73]. In particular, for each 'current' location, the 'past' driving trajectory is provided to localize the vehicle on the originally planned route in OSM. Then the GPS tags of the route for the next 300 m ahead are retrieved.

3.3 Comparison to Other Datasets

In comparison to other datasets, see Table 1, ours has some unique characteristics.

Planned Routes. Since our dataset is aimed at understanding and improving the fallacies of current end-to-end driving models, we supply map data for navigation and offer the only real-world dataset to do so. It is noteworthy that planned routes cannot be obtained by post-processing the GPS coordinates recorded by the vehicle, because planned routes and actual driving trajectories intrinsically differ. The differences between the two are resulted by the actual driving (e.g. changing lanes in road construction zones and overtaking a stopped bus), and are indeed the objectives meant to be learned by the driving models.

Surround Views and Low-Level Driving Maneuvers. Equally important, our dataset is the only dataset working with real data and offering surround-view videos with low-level driving maneuvers (e.g. steering angle and speed control). This is particularly valuable for end-to-end driving as it allows the model to learn

Table 1. Comparison of our dataset to others compiled for driving tasks (cam = camera)

Datasets	Driving time (h)	# cams	fps	Maneuvers, e.g. steering	Route planner	GPS IMU	Control of cam pose	Data type	Lidar
Drive360	60	8,	60	✓	✓	✓	✓	Real	✗
KITTI [26]	1	2,	10	✗	✗	✓	✓	Real	✓
Cityscapes [1]	<100	2,	16	✗	✗	✓	✓	Real	✗
Comma.ai	7.3	1,	20	✓	✗	✓	N.A.	Real	✗
Oxford [75]	214	4,	16	✗	✗	✓	✓	Real	✓
BDDV [12]	10k	1,	30	✗	✗	✓	✗	Real	✗
Udacity [76]	1.1	3,	30	✓	✗	✓	N.A.	Real	✗
GTA	N.A.	1	✓	✓	✗	N.A.	Rendered	Synthetic	✗

correct steering for lane changes, requiring 'mirrors' when carried out by human drivers, or correct driving actions for making turns at intersections. Compared with BDDV [12] and Oxford dataset [75], we offer low level driving maneuvers of the vehicle via the CAN bus, whereas they only supply the cars ego motion via GPS devices. This allows us to predict input control of the vehicle which is one step closer to a fully autonomous end-to-end trained driving model. Udacity [76] also offers low-level driving maneuvers via the CAN bus. It, however, lacks of route planners and contains only a few hours of driving data.

Dataset Focus. As shown in Table 1, there are multiple datasets compiled for tasks relevant to autonomous driving. These datasets, however, all have their own focuses. KITTI, Cityscapes and GTA focus more on semantic and geometric understanding of the driving scenes. Oxford dataset focus on capturing the temporal (seasonal) changes of driving scenes, and thus limited the driving to a 'single' driving route. BDDV [12] is a very large dataset, collected from many cities in a crowd-sourced manner. It, however, only features a front-facing dashboard camera.

4 Approach

The goal of our driving model is to map directly from the planned route, the historical vehicle states and the current road situations, to the desired driving actions.

4.1 Our Driving Model

Let us denote by I the surround-view video, P the planned route, L the vehicle's location, and S and V the vehicle's steering angle and speed. We assume that the driving model works with discrete time and makes driving decisions every $1/f$ seconds. The inputs are all synchronized and sampled at sampling rate f. Unless stated otherwise, our inputs and outputs all are represented in this discretized form.

We use subscript t to indicate the time stamp. For instance, the current video frame is I_t, the current vehicle's speed is V_t, the kth previous video frame is I_{t-k}, and the kth previous steering angle is S_{t-k}, etc. Then, the k recent samples can be denoted by $\mathbf{V}_{[t-k+1,t]} \equiv \langle V_{t-k+1}, ..., V_t \rangle$, $\mathbf{S}_{[t-k+1,t]} \equiv \langle S_{t-k+1}, ..., S_t \rangle$ and $\mathbf{V}_{[t-k+1,t]} \equiv \langle V_{t-k+1}, ..., V_t \rangle$, respectively. Our goal is to train a deep network that predicts desired driving actions from the vehicle's historical states, historical and current visual observations, and the planned route. The learning task can be defined as:

$$F : (\mathcal{S}_{[t-k+1,t]}, \mathcal{V}_{[t-k+1,t]}, \mathcal{L}_{[t-k+1,t]}, \mathcal{I}_{[t-k+1,t]}, P_t) \rightarrow \mathcal{S}_{t+1} \times \mathcal{V}_{t+1} \quad (1)$$

where $\mathcal{S}_{t+1}$ represents the steering angle space and $\mathcal{V}_{t+1}$ the speed space for future time $t+1$. $\mathcal{S}$ and $\mathcal{V}$ can be defined at several levels of granularity. We consider the continuous values directly recorded from the car's CAN bus, where

$\mathcal{V} = \{V | 0 \leq V \leq 180\}$ for speed and $\mathcal{S} = \{S | -720 \leq S \leq 720\}$ for steering angle. Here, kilometer per hour (km/h) is the unit of V, and degree (°) the unit of S. Since there is not much to learn from the historical values of P, only P_t is used for the learning. P_t is either a video frame from our TomTom route planner or a 300×2 matrix from our OSM route planner.

Given N training samples collected during real drives, learning to predict the driving actions for the future time $t+1$ is based on minimizing the following cost:

$$L(\theta) = \sum_{n=1}^{N} \Big(l(S_{t+1}^n, F_s(\mathbf{S}_{[t-k+1,t]}^n, \mathbf{V}_{[t-k+1,t]}^n, \mathbf{L}_{[t-k+1,t]}^n, \mathbf{I}_{[t-k+1,t]}^n, P_t)) \\ + \lambda l(V_{t+1}^n, F_v(\mathbf{S}_{[t-k+1,t]}^n, \mathbf{V}_{[t-k+1,t]}^n, \mathbf{L}_{[t-k+1,t]}^n, \mathbf{I}_{[t-k+1,t]}^n, P_t)) \Big), \tag{2}$$

where λ is a parameter balancing the two losses, one for steering angle and the other for speed. We use $\lambda = 1$ in this work. F is the learned function for the driving model. For the continuous regression task, $l(.)$ is the $L2$ loss function. Finding a better way to balance the two loss functions constitutes our future work. Our model learns from multiple previous frames in order to better understand traffic dynamics.

4.2 Implementation

Our driving system is trained with four cameras (front, left, right, and rear view), which provide a full panoramic view already. We recorded the data with all eight cameras in order to keep future flexibility.

This work develops a customized network architecture for our learning problem defined in Sect. 4.1, which consists of deep hierarchical sub-networks. It comes with multiple CNNs as feature encoders, four LSTMs as temporal encoders for information from the four surround-view cameras, a fully-connected network (FN) to fuse information from all cameras and the map, and finally two FNs to output future speed and steering angle of the car. The illustrative architecture is show in Fig. 1.

During training, videos are all resized to 256×256 and we augment our data by using 227×227 crops, without mirroring. For the CNN feature encoder, we take ResNet34 [77] model pre-trained on the ImageNet [78] dataset. Our network architecture is inspired by the Long-term Recurrent Convolutional Network developed in [79]. A more detailed description about the network architecture is provided in the supplementary material.

5 Experiments

We train our models on 80% of our dataset, corresponding to 48 h of driving time and around 1.7 million unique synchronized sequence samples. Our driving routes are normally 2 h long. We have selected 24 out of the 30 driving routes for training, and the other 6 for testing. This way, the network would not overfit

Table 2. MSE of speed prediction and steering angle prediction when a single front-facing camera is used (previous driving states are given)

	CAN-only	[25]	[12]	Ours
Steering	0.869	1.312	0.161	**0.134**
Speed	0.0147	0.6533	0.0066	**0.0030**

to any type of specific road or weather. Synchronized video frames are extracted at a rate of 10 fps, as 60 fps will generate a very large dataset. A synchronized sample contains four frames at a resolution of 256×256 for the corresponding front, left, right and rear facing cameras, a rendered image at 256×256 pixels for TomTom route planner or a 300×2 matrix for OSM route planner, CAN bus data and the GPS data of the 'past'.

We train our models using the Adam Optimizer with an initial learning rate of 10^{-4} and a batch size of 16 for 5 epochs, resulting in a training time of around 3 days. For the four surround-view cameras, we have used four frames to train the network: 0.9 s in the past, 0.6 s in the past, 0.3 s in the past, and the current frame. This leads to a sampling rate of $f = 3.33$. A higher value can be used at the price of computational cost. This leads to $4 \times 4 = 16$ CNNs for capturing street-view visual scene.

We structure our evaluation into two parts: evaluating our method against existing methods, and evaluating the benefits of using a route planner and/or a surround-view camera system.

5.1 Comparison to Other Single-Camera Methods

We compare our method to the method of [12] and [25]. Since BDDV dataset does not provide data for driving actions (e.g. steering angle) [12], we train their networks on our dataset and compare with our method directly. For a fair comparison, we follow their settings, by only using a single front-facing camera and predicting the driving actions for the future time at 0.3 s.

We use the mean squared error (MSE) for evaluation. The results for speed prediction and steering angle prediction are shown in Table 2. We include a baseline reference of only training on CAN bus information (no image information given). The table shows that our method outperforms [25] significantly and is slightly better than [12]. [25] does not use a pre-trained CNN; this probably explains why their performance is a lot worse. The comparison to these two methods is to verify that our frontal-view driving model represents the state of the art so that the extension is made to a sensible basis to include multiple-view cameras and to include route planners.

We note that the baseline reference performs quite well, suggesting that due to the inertia of driving maneuvers, the network can already predict speed and steering angle of 0.3 s further into the future quite well, solely based on the supplied ground truth maneuver of the past. For instance, if one steers the wheels to the right at time t, then at $t + 0.3$ s the wheels are very likely to be at

Table 3. MSE (smaller = better) of speed and steering angle prediction by our method, when different settings are used. Predictions on full evaluation set and the subset with human driving maneuver ≤30 km/h

Cameras	Route planner	Full dataset		Subset: GT ≤ 30 km/h	
		Steering	Speed	Steering	Speed
Front-view	None	0.967	0.197	4.053	0.167
	TomTom	0.808	**0.176**	3.357	0.268
	OSM	0.981	0.212	4.087	0.165
Surround-view	None	0.927	0.257	3.870	**0.114**
	TomTom	**0.799**	0.200	**3.214**	0.142
	OSM	0.940	0.228	3.917	0.125

a similar angle to the right. In a true autonomous vehicle the past driving states might not be always correct. Therefore, we argue that the policy employed by some existing methods by relying on the past 'ground-truth' states of the vehicle should be used with caution. For the real autonomous cars, the errors will be exaggerated via a feedback loop. Based on this finding, we remove $\mathcal{S}_{[t-k+1,t]}$ and $\mathcal{V}_{[t-k+1,t]}$, i.e. without using the previous human driving maneuvers, and learn the desired speed and steering angle only based on the planned route, and the visual observations of the local road situation. This new setting 'forces' the network to learn knowledge from route planners and road situations.

5.2 Benefits of Route Planners

We evaluate the benefit of a route planner by designing two networks using either our visual TomTom, or our numerical OSM guidance systems, and compare these against our network that does not incorporate a route planner. The results of each networks speed and steering angle prediction are summarized in Table 3. The evaluation shows that our visual TomTom route planner significantly improves prediction performance, while the OSM approach does not yield a clear improvement. Since, the prediction of speed is easier than the prediction of steering angle, using a route planner will have a more noticeable benefit on the prediction of steering angles.

Why the Visual TomTom Planner Is Better? It is easy to think that GPS coordinates contain more accurate information than the rendered videos do, and thus provide a better representation for planned routes. This is, however, not case if the GPS coordinates are used directly without further, careful, processing. The visualization of a planned route on navigation devices such as TomTom Mobile Go makes use of accurate vehicle localization based on vehicle's moving trajectories to provide accurate procedural knowledge of the routes along the driving direction. The localization based on vehicle's moving trajectories is tackled under the name *map-matching*, and this, in itself, is a long-standing research problem [80–82]. For our TomTom route planner, this is done with TomTom's excellent underlying *map-matching* method, which is unknown to the public though. This rendering process converts the 'raw' GPS coordinates into a more structural representation. Our implemented OSM route planner, however, encodes more of a global spatial information at a map level, making the integration of navigation information and street-view videos more challenging. Readers are referred to Fig. 3 for exemplar representations of the two route planners.

In addition to *map-matching*, we provide further possible explanations: **(1)** raw GPS coordinates are accurate for locations, but fall short of other high-level and contextual information (road layouts, road attributes, etc.) which is 'visible' in the visual route planner. For example, raw GPS coordinates do not distinguish 'highway exit' from 'slight right bend' and do not reveal other alternative roads in an intersection, while the visual route planner does. It seems that those semantic features optimized in navigation devices to assist human driving are useful for machine driving as well. Feature designing/extraction for the navigation task of autonomous driving is an interesting future topic. **(2)** The quality of underlying road networks are different from TomTom to OSM. OSM is crowdsourced, so the quality/accuracy of its road networks is not always guaranteed. It is hard to make a direct comparison though, as TomTom's road networks are inaccessible to the public.

5.3 Benefits of Surround-View Cameras

Surround-view cameras offer a modest improvement for predicting steering angle on the full evaluation set. They, however, appear to reduce the overall performance for speed prediction. Further investigation has shown that surround-view cameras are especially useful for situations where the ego-car is required to give the right of way to other (potential) road users by controlling driving speed. Notable examples include (1) busy city streets and residential areas where the human drives at low velocity; and (2) intersections, especially those without traffic lights and stop signs. For instance, the speed at an intersection is determined by whether the ego-car has a clear path for the planned route. Surround-view cameras can see if other cars are coming from any side, whereas a front camera only is blind to many directions. In order to examine this, we have explicitly selected two specific types of scenes across our evaluation dataset for a more fine-grained evaluation of front-view vs. surround-view: (1) low-speed (city) driving according to the speed of human driving; and (2) intersection scenarios by human annotation. The evaluation results are shown in Tables 3 and 4, respectively. The better-performing TomTom route planner models are used for the experiments in Table 4. Surround-view cameras significantly improve the performance of speed control in these two very important driving situations. For 'high-speed' driving on highway or countryside road, surround-view cameras do not show clear advantages, in line with human driving – human drivers also consult non-frontal views less frequently for high-speed driving.

Table 4. MSE (smaller = better) of speed prediction by our Front-view+TomTom and Surround-view+TomTom driving models. Evaluated on manually annotated intersection scenarios over a 2-h subset of our evaluation dataset. Surround-view significantly outperforms front-view in intersection situations

Cameras	≤10 km/h	≤20 km/h	≤30 km/h	≤40 km/h	≤50 km/h
Front-view	0.118	0.150	0.158	0.157	0.148
Surround-view	**0.080**	**0.127**	**0.145**	**0.146**	**0.143**

As a human driver, we consult our navigation system mostly when it comes to multiple choices of road, namely at road intersections. To evaluate whether route planning improves performance specifically in these scenarios, we select a subset of our test set for examples with a low speed by human, and report the results in this subset also in Table 3. Results in Table 3 supports our claim that route planning is beneficial to a driving model, and improves the driving performance especially for situations where a turning maneuver is performed. In future work, we plan to select other interesting situations for more detailed evaluation.

Qualitative Evaluation. While standard evaluation techniques for neural networks such as mean squared error, do offer global insight into the performance of models, they are less intuitive in evaluating where, at a local scale, using surround view cameras or route planning improves prediction accuracy. To this end, we use our visualization tool to inspect and evaluate the model performances for different 'situations'.

Figure 3 shows examples of three model comparisons (TomTom, Surround, Surround+TomTom) row-wise, wherein the model with additional information is directly compared to our front-camera-only model, shown by the speed and steering wheel angle gauges. The steering wheel angle gauge is a direct map of the steering wheel angle to degrees, whereas the speed gauge is from 0 km/h to 130 km/h. Additional information a model might receive is 'image framed' by the respective color. Gauges should be used for relative model comparison, with the front-camera-only model prediction in orange, model with additional information in red and human maneuver in blue. Thus, for our purposes, we define a well performing model when the magnitude of a model gauge is identical (or similar) to the human gauge. Column-wise we show examples where: (a) both models perform well, (b) model with additional information outperforms, (c) both models fail.

Our qualitative results, in Fig. 3(1, b) and (3, b), support our hypothesis that a route planner is indeed useful at intersections where there is an ambiguity with regards to the correct direction of travel. Both models with route planning information are able to predict the correct direction at the intersection, whereas the model without this information predicts the opposite. While this 'wrong' prediction may be a valid driving maneuver in terms of safety, it nonetheless is not correct in terms of arriving at the correct destination. Our map model on

Fig. 3. Qualitative results for future driving action prediction, to compare three cases to the front camera-only-model: (1) learning with TomTom route planner, (2) learning with surround-view cameras (3) learning with TomTom route planner and surround-view cameras. TomTom route planer and surround-view images shown in red box, while OSM route planner in black box. Better seen on screen (Color figure online)

the other hand is able to overcome this. Figure 3(2, b) shows that surround-view cameras are beneficial at predicting the correct speed. The frontal view supplied could suggest that one is on a country road where the speed limit is significantly higher than in the city, as such, our front-camera-only model predicts a speed much greater than the human maneuver. However, our surround-view system can pick up on the pedestrians on the right of the car, thus adjusts the speed accordingly. The surround-view model thus has a more precise understanding of its surroundings.

Visualization Tool. To obtain further insights into where current driving models perform well or fail, we have developed a visual evaluation tool that lets users select scenes in the evaluation set by clicking on a map, and then rendering the corresponding 4 camera views, the ground truth and predicted vehicle maneuver (steering angle and speed) along with the map at that point in time. These evaluation tools along with the dataset will be released to the public. In particular, visual evaluation is extremely helpful to understand where and why a driving model predicted a certain maneuver, as sometimes, while not coinciding with the human action, the network may still predict a safe driving maneuver.

6 Conclusion

In this work, we have extended learning end-to-end driving models to a more realistic setting from only using a single front-view camera. We have presented a novel task of learning end-to-end driving models with surround-view cameras and rendered maps, enabling the car to 'look' to side, rearward, and to 'check' the driving direction. We have presented two main contributions: (1) a new driving dataset, featuring 60 h of driving videos with eight surround-view cameras, low-level driving maneuvers recorded via car's CAN bus, two representations of planned routes by two route planners, and GPS-IMU data for the vehicle's odometry; (2) a novel deep network to map directly from the sensor inputs to future driving maneuvers. Our data features high temporary resolution and 360° view coverage, frame-wise synchronization, and diverse road conditions, making it ideal for learning end-to-end driving models. Our experiments have shown that an end-to-end learning method can effectively use surround-view cameras and route planners. The rendered videos outperforms a stack of raw GPS coordinates for representing planned routes.

Acknowledgements. This work is funded by Toyota Motor Europe via the research project TRACE-Zürich. One Titan X used for this research was donated by NVIDIA.

References

1. Cordts, M., et al.: The Cityscapes dataset for semantic urban scene understanding. In: Proceedings of the IEEE Conference on Computer Vision and Pattern Recognition (CVPR) (2016)
2. Sakaridis, C., Dai, D., Van Gool, L.: Semantic foggy scene understanding with synthetic data. Int. J. Comput. Vis. (2018)
3. Yu, F., et al.: BDD100K: a diverse driving video database with scalable annotation tooling. CoRR (2018)
4. Dai, D., Van Gool, L.: Progressive model adaptation and knowledge transfer from daytime to nighttime for semantic road scene understanding. In: IEEE International Conference on Intelligent Transportation Systems (2018)
5. LeCun, Y., Muller, U., Ben, J., Cosatto, E., Flepp, B.: Off-road obstacle avoidance through end-to-end learning. In: NIPS (2005)
6. Huval, B., et al.: An empirical evaluation of deep learning on highway driving. CoRR abs/1504.01716 (2015)
7. Chen, C., Seff, A., Kornhauser, A., Xiao, J.: DeepDriving: learning affordance for direct perception in autonomous driving. In: Proceedings of the IEEE International Conference on Computer Vision, pp. 2722–2730 (2015)
8. Caltagirone, L., Bellone, M., Svensson, L., Wahde, M.: Simultaneous perception and path generation using fully convolutional neural networks. arXiv preprint arXiv:1703.08987 (2017)
9. Chen, S., Zhang, S., Shang, J., Chen, B., Zheng, N.: Brain inspired cognitive model with attention for self-driving cars. arXiv preprint arXiv:1702.05596 (2017)
10. Paxton, C., Raman, V., Hager, G.D., Kobilarov, M.: Combining neural networks and tree search for task and motion planning in challenging environments. In: IROS (2017)

11. Pendleton, S.D., et al.: Perception, planning, control, and coordination for autonomous vehicles. Machines **5**(1), 6 (2017)
12. Xu, H., Gao, Y., Yu, F., Darrell, T.: End-to-end learning of driving models from large-scale video datasets. In: Computer Vision and Pattern Recognition (CVPR) (2017)
13. Codevilla, F., Müller, M., López, A., Koltun, V., Dosovitskiy, A.: End-to-end driving via conditional imitation learning (2018)
14. Chen, Y., et al.: LiDAR-video driving dataset: learning driving policies effectively. In: The IEEE Conference on Computer Vision and Pattern Recognition (CVPR), June 2018
15. Maqueda, A.I., Loquercio, A., Gallego, G., Garca, N., Scaramuzza, D.: Event-based vision meets deep learning on steering prediction for self-driving cars. In: The IEEE Conference on Computer Vision and Pattern Recognition (CVPR), June 2018
16. McAllister, R., et al.: Concrete problems for autonomous vehicle safety: advantages of Bayesian deep learning. In: International Joint Conference on Artificial Intelligence (2017)
17. Hecker, S., Dai, D., Van Gool, L.: Failure prediction for autonomous driving models. In: IEEE Intelligent Vehicles Symposium (IV) (2018)
18. The Automobile (weekly), Thursday, 27 December 1906
19. Tolman, E.C.: Cognitive maps in rats and men. Psychol. Rev. **55**, 189–208 (1948)
20. Maguire, E.A., Burgess, N., Donnett, J.G., Frackowiak, R.S.J., Frith, C.D., O'Keefe, J.: Knowing where and getting there: a human navigation network. Science **280**(5365), 921–924 (1998)
21. Urmson, C., et al.: Autonomous driving in urban environments: Boss and the urban challenge. J. Field Robot. Spec. Issue 2007 DARPA Urban Chall. Part I **25**(8), 425–466 (2008)
22. Levinson, J., et al.: Towards fully autonomous driving: systems and algorithms. In: IEEE Intelligent Vehicles Symposium (IV) (2011)
23. Luettel, T., Himmelsbach, M., Wuensche, H.J.: Autonomous ground vehicles—concepts and a path to the future. Proc. IEEE **100**, 1831–1839 (2012)
24. Pomerleau, D.A.: NIPS (1989)
25. Bojarski, M., et al.: End to end learning for self-driving cars. arXiv preprint arXiv:1604.07316 (2016)
26. Geiger, A., Lenz, P., Stiller, C., Urtasun, R.: Vision meets robotics: the KITTI dataset. Int. J. Robot. Res. **32**(11), 1231–1237 (2013)
27. Chen, X., Ma, H., Wan, J., Li, B., Xia, T.: Multi-view 3D object detection network for autonomous driving. In: CVPR (2017)
28. Geiger, A., Lauer, M., Wojek, C., Stiller, C., Urtasun, R.: 3D traffic scene understanding from movable platforms. IEEE Trans. Pattern Anal. Mach. Intell. **36**(5), 1012–1025 (2014)
29. Anderson, J.M., Nidhi, K., Stanley, K.D., Sorensen, P., Samaras, C., Oluwatola, T.A.: Autonomous Vehicle Technology: A Guide for Policymakers. RAND Corporation, Santa Monica (2016)
30. Bojarski, M., et al.: Explaining how a deep neural network trained with end-to-end learning steers a car. CoRR (2017)
31. Mnih, V., et al.: Human-level control through deep reinforcement learning. Nature **518**(7540), 529–533 (2015)
32. Shalev-Shwartz, S., Shammah, S., Shashua, A.: Safe, multi-agent, reinforcement learning for autonomous driving. arXiv preprint arXiv:1610.03295 (2016)
33. Sallab, A.E., Abdou, M., Perot, E., Yogamani, S.: Deep reinforcement learning framework for autonomous driving. Electron. Imaging **2017**(19), 70–76 (2017)

34. Shah, S., Dey, D., Lovett, C., Kapoor, A.: AirSim: high-fidelity visual and physical simulation for autonomous vehicles. In: Hutter, M., Siegwart, R. (eds.) Field and Service Robotics. SPAR, vol. 5, pp. 621–635. Springer, Cham (2018). https://doi.org/10.1007/978-3-319-67361-5_40
35. Dosovitskiy, A., Ros, G., Codevilla, F., Lopez, A., Koltun, V.: CARLA: an open urban driving simulator. In: Proceedings of the 1st Annual Conference on Robot Learning, pp. 1–16 (2017)
36. Carvalho, A., Lefévre, S., Schildbach, G., Kong, J., Borrelli, F.: Automated driving: the role of forecasts and uncertainty—a control perspective. Eur. J. Control. **24**, 14–32 (2015)
37. Shia, V.A., et al.: Semiautonomous vehicular control using driver modeling. IEEE Trans. Intell. Transp. **15**(6), 2696–2709 (2014)
38. Kasper, D., et al.: Object-oriented Bayesian networks for detection of lane change maneuvers. IEEE Intell. Transp. Syst. Mag. **4**(3), 19–31 (2012)
39. Jain, A., Koppula, H.S., Raghavan, B., Soh, S., Saxena, A.: Car that knows before you do: anticipating maneuvers via learning temporal driving models. In: Proceedings of the IEEE International Conference on Computer Vision, pp. 3182–3190 (2015)
40. Liu, Y.-C., Lin, K.-Y., Chen, Y.-S.: Bird's-eye view vision system for vehicle surrounding monitoring. In: Sommer, G., Klette, R. (eds.) RobVis 2008. LNCS, vol. 4931, pp. 207–218. Springer, Heidelberg (2008). https://doi.org/10.1007/978-3-540-78157-8_16
41. Dueholm, J.V., Kristoffersen, M.S., Satzoda, R.K., Moeslund, T.B., Trivedi, M.M.: Trajectories and maneuvers of surrounding vehicles with panoramic camera arrays. IEEE Trans. Intell. Veh. **1**(2), 203–214 (2016)
42. Khosroshahi, A., Ohn-Bar, E., Trivedi, M.M.: Surround vehicles trajectory analysis with recurrent neural networks. In: International Conference on Intelligent Transportation Systems (ITSC), pp. 2267–2272 (2016)
43. Bertozzi, M., Castangia, L., Cattani, S., Prioletti, A., Versari, P.: 360° detection and tracking algorithm of both pedestrian and vehicle using fisheye images. In: IEEE Intelligent Vehicles Symposium (IV), pp. 132–137 (2015)
44. Dueholm, J.V., Kristoffersen, M.S., Satzoda, R.K., Ohn-Bar, E., Moeslund, T.B., Trivedi, M.M.: Multi-perspective vehicle detection and tracking: challenges, dataset, and metrics. In: International Conference on Intelligent Transportation Systems (ITSC) (2016)
45. Kum, C.H., Cho, D.C., Ra, M.S., Kim, W.Y.: Lane detection system with around view monitoring for intelligent vehicle. In: International SoC Design Conference (ISOCC), pp. 215–218 (2013)
46. Yu, M., Ma, G.: A visual parking guidance for surround view monitoring system. In: IEEE Intelligent Vehicles Symposium (IV) (2015)
47. Gao, Y., Lin, C., Zhao, Y., Wang, X., Wei, S., Huang, Q.: 3-D surround view for advanced driver assistance systems. IEEE Trans. Intell. Transp. Syst. **19**(1), 320–328 (2018)
48. Chen, A., Ramanandan, A., Farrell, J.A.: High-precision lane-level road map building for vehicle navigation. In: IEEE/ION Position, Location and Navigation Symposium (2010)
49. Schindler, A., Maier, G., Janda, F.: Generation of high precision digital maps using circular arc splines. In: IEEE Intelligent Vehicles Symposium (2012)
50. Rizaldi, A., Althoff, M.: Formalising traffic rules for accountability of autonomous vehicles. In: International Conference on Intelligent Transportation Systems (2015)

51. Bender, P., Ziegler, J., Stiller, C.: Lanelets: efficient map representation for autonomous driving. In: IEEE Intelligent Vehicles Symposium (2014)
52. Yuan, J., Zheng, Y., Xie, X., Sun, G.: Driving with knowledge from the physical world. In: ACM SIGKDD International Conference on Knowledge Discovery and Data Mining, pp. 316–324 (2011)
53. Bast, H., et al.: Route planning in transportation networks. In: Kliemann, L., Sanders, P. (eds.) Algorithm Engineering. LNCS, vol. 9220, pp. 19–80. Springer, Cham (2016). https://doi.org/10.1007/978-3-319-49487-6_2
54. Zheng, Y.T., et al.: GPSView: a scenic driving route planner. ACM Trans. Multimed. Comput. Commun. Appl. **9**(1), 3:1–3:18 (2013)
55. Chen, C., Zhang, D., Guo, B., Ma, X., Pan, G., Wu, Z.: TripPlanner: personalized trip planning leveraging heterogeneous crowdsourced digital footprints. IEEE Trans. Intell. **16**(3), 1259–1273 (2015)
56. Yang, B., Guo, C., Ma, Y., Jensen, C.S.: Toward personalized, context-aware routing. VLDB J. **24**(2), 297–318 (2015)
57. Haklay, M., Weber, P.: OpenStreetMap: user-generated street maps. IEEE Pervasive Comput. **7**(4), 12–18 (2008)
58. Mattern, N., Schubert, R., Wanielik, G.: High-accurate vehicle localization using digital maps and coherency images. In: IEEE Intelligent Vehicles Symposium (2010)
59. Tao, Z., Bonnifait, P., Frémont, V., Ibañez-Guzman, J.: Mapping and localization using GPS, lane markings and proprioceptive sensors. In: IEEE/RSJ International Conference on Intelligent Robots and Systems (2013)
60. Nedevschi, S., Popescu, V., Danescu, R., Marita, T., Oniga, F.: Accurate ego-vehicle global localization at intersections through alignment of visual data with digital map. IEEE Trans. Intell. Transp. Syst. **14**(2), 673–687 (2013)
61. Brahmbhatt, S., Gu, J., Kim, K., Hays, J., Kautz, J.: MapNet: geometry-aware learning of maps for camera localization. CoRR abs/1712.03342 (2017)
62. Bar Hillel, A., Lerner, R., Levi, D., Raz, G.: Recent progress in road and lane detection: a survey. Mach. Vis. Appl. **25**(3), 727–745 (2014)
63. Jensen, M.B., Philipsen, M.P., Møgelmose, A., Moeslund, T.B., Trivedi, M.M.: Vision for looking at traffic lights: issues, survey, and perspectives. IEEE Trans. Intell. Transp. Syst. **17**(7), 1800–1815 (2016)
64. Ren, S., He, K., Girshick, R., Sun, J.: Faster R-CNN: towards real-time object detection with region proposal networks. In: Advances in Neural Information Processing Systems (NIPS) (2015)
65. Chen, Y., Li, W., Sakaridis, C., Dai, D., Van Gool, L.: Domain adaptive faster R-CNN for object detection in the wild. In: Conference on Computer Vision and Pattern Recognition (CVPR) (2018)
66. Sivaraman, S., Trivedi, M.M.: Looking at vehicles on the road: a survey of vision-based vehicle detection, tracking, and behavior analysis. IEEE Trans. Intell. Transp. Syst. **14**(4), 1773–1795 (2013)
67. Kroeger, T., Timofte, R., Dai, D., Van Gool, L.: Fast optical flow using dense inverse search. In: Leibe, B., Matas, J., Sebe, N., Welling, M. (eds.) ECCV 2016. LNCS, vol. 9908, pp. 471–488. Springer, Cham (2016). https://doi.org/10.1007/978-3-319-46493-0_29
68. Manen, S., Gygli, M., Dai, D., Van Gool, L.: PathTrack: fast trajectory annotation with path supervision. In: International Conference on Computer Vision (ICCV) (2017)
69. Janai, J., Güney, F., Behl, A., Geiger, A.: Computer vision for autonomous vehicles: problems, datasets and state-of-the-art. arXiv preprint arXiv:1704.05519 (2017)

70. Ohn-Bar, E., Trivedi, M.M.: Looking at humans in the age of self-driving and highly automated vehicles. IEEE Trans. Intell. Veh. **1**(1), 90–104 (2016)
71. TomTom GO Mobile App. https://itunes.apple.com/us/app/tomtom-go-mobile/id884963367?mt=8. Accessed from Oct 2017 to Mar 2018
72. Hentschel, M., Wagner, B.: Autonomous robot navigation based on OpenStreetMap geodata. In: IEEE Conference on Intelligent Transportation Systems (2010)
73. Luxen, D., Vetter, C.: Real-time routing with OpenStreetMap data. In: ACM SIGSPATIAL International Conference on Advances in Geographic Information Systems (2011)
74. Ma, X., Andréasson, I.: Estimation of driver reaction time from car-following data: application in evaluation of general motor-type model. Transp. Res. Rec. J. Transp. Res. Board **1965**, 130–141 (2006)
75. Maddern, W., Pascoe, G., Linegar, C., Newman, P.: 1 year, 1000 km: the oxford robotcar dataset. Int. J. Robot. Res. **36**(1), 3–15 (2017)
76. Udacity: Public driving dataset (2017). https://www.udacity.com/self-driving-car
77. He, K., Zhang, X., Ren, S., Sun, J.: Deep residual learning for image recognition. In: 2016 IEEE Conference on Computer Vision and Pattern Recognition (CVPR) (2016)
78. Deng, J., Dong, W., Socher, R., Li, L.J., Li, K., Fei-Fei, L.: ImageNet: a large-scale hierarchical image database. In: CVPR (2009)
79. Donahue, J., et al.: Long-term recurrent convolutional networks for visual recognition and description. In: CVPR (2015)
80. Lou, Y., Zhang, C., Zheng, Y., Xie, X., Wang, W., Huang, Y.: Map-matching for low-sampling-rate GPS trajectories. In: ACM SIGSPATIAL International Conference on Advances in Geographic Information Systems, pp. 352–361 (2009)
81. Yuan, J., Zheng, Y., Zhang, C., Xie, X., Sun, G.Z.: An interactive-voting based map matching algorithm. In: International Conference on Mobile Data Management (2010)
82. Chen, B.Y., Yuan, H., Li, Q., Lam, W.H.K., Shaw, S.L., Yan, K.: Map-matching algorithm for large-scale low-frequency floating car data. Int. J. Geogr. Inf. Sci. **28**(1), 22–38 (2014)

Coreset-Based Neural Network Compression

Abhimanyu Dubey[1(✉)], Moitreya Chatterjee[2], and Narendra Ahuja[2]

[1] Massachusetts Institute of Technology, Cambridge, MA 02139, USA
dubeya@mit.edu

[2] University of Illinois at Urbana-Champaign, Champaign, IL 61820, USA
metro.smiles@gmail.com, n-ahuja@illinois.edu

Abstract. We propose a novel Convolutional Neural Network (CNN) compression algorithm based on coreset representations of filters. We exploit the redundancies extant in the space of CNN weights and neuronal activations (across samples) in order to obtain compression. Our method requires no retraining, is easy to implement, and obtains state-of-the-art compression performance across a wide variety of CNN architectures. Coupled with quantization and Huffman coding, we create networks that provide AlexNet-like accuracy, with a memory footprint that is 832× smaller than the original AlexNet, while also introducing significant reductions in inference time as well. Additionally these compressed networks when fine-tuned, successfully generalize to other domains as well.

1 Introduction

Convolutional neural networks, while immensely powerful, often are resource-intensive [24,26,35,50,54]. Popular CNN models such as AlexNet [35] and VGG-16 [50], for instance, have 61 and 138 million parameters and consume in excess of 200 MB and 500 MB of memory space respectively. This characteristic of deep CNN architectures reduces their portability, and poses a severe bottleneck for implementation in resource constrained environments [17]. Additionally, design choices for CNN architectures, such as network depth, filter sizes, and number of filters seem arbitrary and motivated purely by empirical performance at a particular task, permitting little room for interpretability. Moreover, the architecture design is not necessarily fully optimized for the network to be yielding a certain level of precision, making these models highly resource-inefficient.

Several prior approaches have thus sought to reduce the computational complexity of these models. Work aimed at designing efficient CNN architectures, such as Residual Networks (ResNets) [25] and DenseNets [28] have shown

A. Dubey and M. Chatterjee—Equal Contribution.

Electronic supplementary material The online version of this chapter (https://doi.org/10.1007/978-3-030-01234-2_28) contains supplementary material, which is available to authorized users.

V. Ferrari et al. (Eds.): ECCV 2018, LNCS 11211, pp. 469–486, 2018.
https://doi.org/10.1007/978-3-030-01234-2_28

promise at alleviating the challenge of model complexity. These CNNs provide higher performance on classification at only a fraction of the number of parameters of their more resource intensive counterparts. However, despite being more compact, redundancies remain in such networks, leaving room for further compression.

In this work, we propose a novel method that exploits inter-filter dependencies extant in the convolutional filter banks of CNNs to compress pre-trained computationally intensive neural networks. Additionally we leverage neuronal activation patterns across samples to prune out irrelevant filters. Our compression pipeline consists of finely pruning the filters of every layer of the CNN based on sample activation patterns, followed by the construction of efficient filter *coreset* representations to exploit the inter-filter dependencies. Our method *does not require retraining*, is applicable *to both fully-connected and convolution layers*, and maintains classification performance similar to the uncompressed network. We display state-of-the-art compression rates on several popular CNN models, including multiple ResNets, which show increases from 9.2× to 16.2× in compression rate over prior state-of-the-art techniques. Coupled with *Deep Compression*, we are additionally able to compress other popular CNN models such as VGGNet-16 [50] and AlexNet [35] by 238× and 55× respectively. Moreover, we demonstrate the presence of filter redundancies even in highly efficient models such as SqueezeNet [29], by reducing their parameters by 50% with almost no loss in classification performance, giving us AlexNet-level precision but with *832*× smaller model size, compared to the original AlexNet model. Finally, we empirically validate the generalizability of these compressed CNNs to newer domains.

In the next section, we discuss relevant prior work in this area. In Sect. 3, we present the details of our algorithm. This is followed by Sect. 4, where a discussion on the empirical evaluation of our method vis-à-vis other competing compression techniques is presented. We finally conclude in Sect. 5, laying out some avenues for future research in this area.

2 Related Work

Network Compression: Compressing neural networks has been a topic of active research interest lately. Prior work in this area can be grouped into three distinct categories. The first category of methods direct their attention to the construction of parameter-efficient neural network architectures. For instance, Iandola *et al.* [29] propose SqueezeNets, a neural architecture class containing the parameter efficient, fully convolutional, 'fire' modules. Other examples of such architectures include Residual Networks (ResNets) [25], and Densely Connected Neural Networks (DenseNets) [28], which provide higher classification performance with models much smaller than the previous state-of-the-art, using 'skip-connections' between layers of the network. More recent approaches have sought to adapt CNN architectures so as to make them robust to common transformations (e.g. rotation) within the data, by modifying the filter banks of a

CNN [10,61] or by enforcing sparsity while training [2]. While these approaches seem to hold promise but they fail to fully exploit the inter-filter dependencies, allowing room for further compression of such networks. Meta-learning approaches attempt to decipher the optimum CNN architecture by searching over the space of a gigantic number of possible candidates. However, these techniques are prohibitively resource intensive, (needing well in excess of 400 GPUs to run), and often yield only a locally optimum architecture [46].

A second broad category of compression methods attempt to prune the unimportant network parameters. Han *et al.* [20] demonstrate an efficient pruning-retraining method, based on pruning weights by their ℓ^p norms. Srinivas and Babu [53] remove individual neurons instead of weights, with impressive results. The importance of ordering filters for the purpose of pruning has also been highlighted in Yu *et al.*, He *et al.*, and Molchanov *et al.* [27,42,60]. These approaches have been modified in the works of Polyak *et al.* [45] and Luo *et al.* [41], that focus on removing weights grouped by characteristics of filters (such as norm of filter weights, etc.). Li *et al.* [40] extend the ideas of filter pruning by removing filters from a network following an 'importance' criterion. However, the re-training step in these algorithms is time intensive.

Finally, the third theme of compression techniques is to employ weight-approximation and information-theoretic principles for the compression of neural network parameters. An early example of such work is the approach by Denton *et al.* [9] that uses low-rank approximations to compress fully-connected layers of neural networks. However, this technique doesn't apply to the convolution layers. Lebdev *et al.* fixes this problem and employs a low-rank decomposition approach to the full CNN to construct more efficient representations but their technique's principal bottleneck is re-training, which we avoid [36]. Rosenfield *et al.* consider an efficient utilization of CNN filters by representing them as a linear combination of a bases set [48]. However, our algorithm, different from this line of work, is additionally also capable of introducing structure, such as sparsity, in the approximated weights resulting from the decomposition, which further aids compression. Han *et al.* [20] introduce *Deep Compression*, that uses several steps such as weight-pruning, weight-sharing, and Huffman coding to reduce neural network size. However, their algorithm requires special hardware for inference in the compressed state, making it hard to deploy the compressed networks across platforms.

Our method aims at handling the shortcomings in each of these individual themes of CNN compression. Contrary to the first category of architecture search, our method is applicable to a wide variety of models, is less resource intensive, and does not require any retraining. While we do prune filters inspired by the work of Polyak *et al.* [45] (following the second theme of compression), our criterion for filter pruning, however, is motivated by the accurate reconstruction of sample activations, instead of the magnitude of filter weights. Finally, our compression technique does not require special hardware for running inference unlike Han *et al.* [19] and scales to both fully-connected and convolutional layers, unlike the low-rank (SVD) approach by Denton *et al.* [9].

Coresets for Point Selection: Coresets have been widely studied in computational geometry. They were introduced first by Agarwal *et al.* [1] for approximating a set of points with a smaller set, while preserving some desired criteria, on k-means and k-median problems. Badoiu *et al.* [5] propose a coreset formulation to cluster points using a subset of the total set of points to generate the optimal solution. Har-Peled and Mazumdar [22] give an alternate solution for coresets that include points not in the original set. Feldman *et al.* [13] demonstrate that weak coreset representations can be generated with the number of points independent of the underlying data distribution. These formulations have recently been applied to several problems within computer vision and machine learning [12,14,15], and are primarily used to approximate a set of n points in d dimensions, originating from a domain $\mathbf{S}$, with a smaller set of $\tilde{n} \ll n$ points, while preserving some criterion such as similar pairwise distances. However, coresets have remained unexplored in the context of CNN compression, which constitutes a major novelty of our work.

3 Method

We begin with a fully-trained CNN and compress it without retraining, first by pruning out unimportant filters, followed by extraction of efficient coreset representation of these filters. Some of the major advantages of our method include: (i) Lack of retraining, therefore a major reduction in processing time, (ii) Capacity of our algorithm to significantly compress both convolutional and fully connected layers, and (iii) Ability of the compressed CNN to generalize to newer tasks.

3.1 Background and Notation

An n-layered neural network can be described as a union of the parameter tensors of every layer, $\mathcal{W} = \cup_{k=1}^{n} \boldsymbol{\mathsf{W}}_k$. The parameters $\boldsymbol{\mathsf{W}}_k$ of layer k have the shape $N_k \times C_k \times h_k \times w_k$, where N_k denotes the number of filters, C_k denotes the number of input channels of the filter (since this is typically equal to the number of filters in the previous layer, $C_k = N_{k-1}$), and h_k and w_k denote the height and width of a filter. We can rewrite the parameter tensor $\boldsymbol{\mathsf{W}}_k$ as a 2D matrix $\boldsymbol{W}_k$ of the shape $N_k \times (C_k h_k w_k)$. Next, we append the biases of the filters to $\boldsymbol{W}_k$, to make it a matrix of dimensions $N_k \times (C_k h_k w_k + 1)$. It is well known that using this representation of the weights and biases of a layer, $\boldsymbol{W}_k$, we can represent the output activation of any fully connected layer as a matrix product of $\boldsymbol{W}_k$ with the incoming activation tensor $\boldsymbol{\mathsf{A}}_{k-1}$. This notion can be extended to convolution layers by re-casting the matrices in an appropriate Toeplitz form [56].

The goal of compression is to obtain a compressed representation of the parameters for each layer $\hat{\mathcal{W}} = \cup_{k=1}^{n} \hat{\boldsymbol{\mathsf{W}}}_k$ such that it is smaller and computationally efficient, and preserves the final classification accuracy. Our approach is to construct compressed filter 'coresets' $\hat{\boldsymbol{W}}_k \in \mathbb{R}^{\hat{N}_k \times (C_k h_k w_k + 1)}$ of the parameters of each layer (where $\hat{N}_k < N_k$), such that the output activations (obtained after the Toeplitz matrix multiplication), are well approximated. Ensuring that the output activations remain largely the same at every layer, post compression, ensures that the final classification performance remains largely unchanged. Since the elements of these coresets are typically linear functions of the original parameters, we will additionally require a decompression matrix $\boldsymbol{D}_k \in \mathbb{R}^{\hat{N}_k \times N_k}$ to obtain an approximation to the initial set of parameters, starting with the coreset representation.

Coresets are an effective technique of approximating a large set of points with a smaller set, which need not necessarily be a part the original set, while preserving some desirable property such as mean pairwise distances, diameter of the point set, etc. We seek to obtain a reduced matrix (coreset) $\hat{\boldsymbol{W}}_k$ representation of the original filter weights $\boldsymbol{W}_k$ of every layer, which we do via 3 different approaches, as described below.

3.2 k-Means Coresets

A first approach to constructing such a coreset would be to obtain a reduced representation of the parameter matrix that approximates the sum of distances in the space of neuronal activations of an arbitrary sample between each of the filters. Feldman *et al.* [14] demonstrate that this problem is equivalent to finding a low-rank approximation of the filter matrix. This is representable as follows:

$$\min_{\boldsymbol{U}'_k, \boldsymbol{\Sigma}'_k, \boldsymbol{V}'_k} \|\boldsymbol{W}_k - \boldsymbol{U}'_k \boldsymbol{\Sigma}'_k \boldsymbol{V}_k'^T\|_F^2 \tag{1}$$

Their formulation for constructing a compact set of $\hat{N}_k \ll N$ points using the sum of distances criterion leads to the *k-Means Coresets*, where the coreset representation is given by the solution to the above optimization problem:

$$\hat{\boldsymbol{W}}_k = \boldsymbol{U}'_k \boldsymbol{\Sigma}'_k, \text{ with decompression matrix: } \boldsymbol{D}_k = \boldsymbol{V}_k'^T \tag{2}$$

Here, the matrices $\boldsymbol{U}'_k$, $\boldsymbol{\Sigma}'_k$ and $\boldsymbol{V}_k'^T$ are the $\hat{N}_k$-truncated versions of the matrices $\boldsymbol{U}_k$, $\boldsymbol{\Sigma}_k$ and $\boldsymbol{V}_k^T$, which satisfy the property:

$$\boldsymbol{W}_k = \boldsymbol{U}_k \boldsymbol{\Sigma}_k \boldsymbol{V}_k^T \approx \hat{\boldsymbol{W}}_k = \boldsymbol{U}'_k \boldsymbol{\Sigma}'_k \boldsymbol{V}_k'^T \tag{3}$$

$\boldsymbol{U}_k, \boldsymbol{V}_k$ are unitary matrices, while $\boldsymbol{\Sigma}_k$ is a diagonal matrix. Such a decomposition can be obtained using Singular Value Decomposition (SVD), where the extent of truncation is specified as an input to the algorithm. The truncation determines the amount of compression we get.

Intuitively a significant truncation, while yielding greater compression, leads to a weaker approximation of the filter weights. This also results in a weaker approximation of the output activations, manifesting itself as a drop in classification accuracy. We seek the optimum compression, across all layers, such that the classification accuracy does not deviate by more than 0.5%.

SVD for compressing neural network weights has been investigated previously in [9], however, with two key differences - (i) the naive SVD approach has been applied only to fully-connected layers of neural networks, with limited success, whereas our coreset-based formulation scales to both convolution and fully connected layers, and (ii) our method for selecting the number of components to be retained $\hat{N}_k$ is data-dependent, based on training error obtained on random subsets of the training data, instead of an arbitrary initialization followed by retraining. However, since this decomposition does not explicitly encode any structure on the approximated weights, such as sparsity or considers the impact of activations, we build upon this formulation to create stronger coreset representations. This sets us apart from prior work, which employ simple low-rank decomposition for constructing efficient CNNs [36] (Fig. 1).

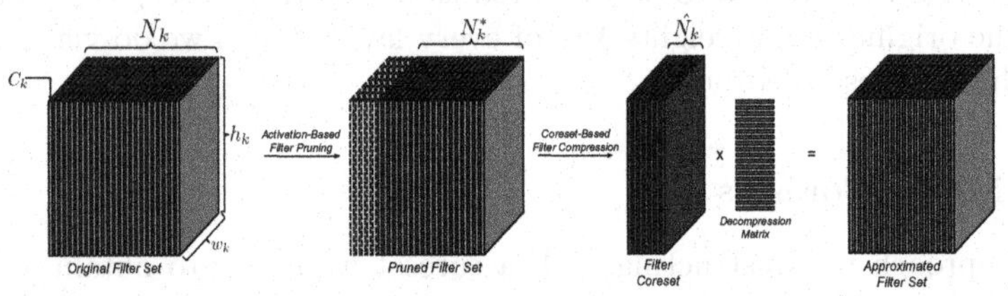

Fig. 1. Visual representation of compression pipeline for layer k of a neural network. Our algorithm proceeds in two steps - (i) filter pruning, and (ii) filter compression, as illustrated

3.3 Structured Sparse Coresets

If we consider the previous coreset decomposition, the optimization problem can be rewritten as (subject to constraints on each of the variables $\boldsymbol{U}'_k$, $\boldsymbol{\Sigma}'_k$ and $\boldsymbol{V}'_k$):

$$\min_{\boldsymbol{U}'_k, \boldsymbol{\Sigma}'_k, \boldsymbol{V}'_k} \|\boldsymbol{W}_k - \boldsymbol{U}'_k \boldsymbol{\Sigma}'_k \boldsymbol{V}'^T_k\|_F^2 \tag{4}$$

To induce sparsity in the obtained decomposition, Jenatton *et al.* [30] introduce a technique known as *Structured Sparse PCA*, which optimizes the following:

$$\begin{aligned} \min_{\boldsymbol{U}'_k, \boldsymbol{\Sigma}'_k, \boldsymbol{V}'_k} \|\boldsymbol{W}_k - \boldsymbol{U}'_k \boldsymbol{\Sigma}'_k \boldsymbol{V}'^T_k\|_F^2 + \lambda \cdot \|V'_k\|_1, \\ \text{subject to} \quad \|(\boldsymbol{U}'_k \cdot \Sigma'_k)_m\|_2 = 1 \ \forall \ m \in [1, \hat{N}_k] \end{aligned} \tag{5}$$

This problem can be solved by a cyclic optimization of two convex problems [30], and provides us with a decomposition that possesses structured sparsity. The motivation behind using such a formulation is to obtain a decomposition that is sparse in the number of components used, while minimizing reconstruction error. While techniques such as SPCA [32] or NMF [39] also construct representations that are sparse in the projected space, this formulation returns a decomposition that makes the approximation in the original space sparse as well, hence, *both* $\hat{\boldsymbol{W}}_k$ and $\boldsymbol{D}_k$ are sparse. Moreover, this formulation allows us to discard those filters for which the corresponding column vector in $\boldsymbol{D}_k$ is a null vector, leading to further compression.

The hyper-parameters $\hat{N}_k$ and λ are chosen jointly so as to obtain the maximum compression while restricting the deviation in classification performance to within 0.5% of the uncompressed network, post the compression of all layers. We observe that this technique provides much more compression than k-Means Coreset, however, this does not take into account the relative importance of the filters during reconstruction, which leads us to our final coreset formulation.

3.4 Activation-Weighted Coresets

Our final coreset formulation is obtained by introducing a relative importance score to every filter (based on their activation magnitudes over the training set), while inducing sparsity. However, if we attempt to directly learn a coreset representation by minimizing the reconstruction error over all the training set activations, the resulting optimization problem will be difficult to solve, owing to the large size of the activation matrix and its degenerate nature. We thus employ an alternate formulation: for each filter f in a layer, we compute its 'importance' $i_k^{(f)}$ as the mean value of its activation over all training set points, normalized over all filters, in the kth layer. This is given by the following:

$$i_k^{(f)} = \frac{\bar{\boldsymbol{A}}_k^{(f)}}{\sum_{p=1}^{N_k} \bar{\boldsymbol{A}}_k^{(p)}}; \qquad \text{where} \quad \bar{\boldsymbol{A}}_k^{(f)} = \frac{1}{T}\sum_{j=1}^{T} \|\boldsymbol{A}_k^{(f)}(j)\|_F \tag{6}$$

Here, $\boldsymbol{A}_k^{(f)}(j)$ is the activation of the fth filter of layer k, for training sample j, and T denotes the total number of training samples. We then construct the *Importance Matrix* $\boldsymbol{I}_k$ for the layer k by tiling the column vectors $(i_k^{(f)})_{f=1}^{N_k}$, for $(C_k \times h_k \times w_k + 1)$ times, creating an *Importance Matrix* $\in \mathbb{R}^{N_k \times (C_k h_k w_k + 1)}$, where each row denotes the 'importance' of each filter, normalized over all filters of the current layer.

We create this form of the importance matrix with every element of a row containing identical values, since we do not want to weigh each component of a particular filter differently. Note, additionally, that we can compute this matrix in only one forward pass of the entire training set. This leads us to the following optimization problem:

$$\min_{\boldsymbol{U}'_k, \boldsymbol{\Sigma}'_k, \boldsymbol{V}'_k} \|\boldsymbol{I}_k \odot (\boldsymbol{W}_k - \boldsymbol{U}'_k \boldsymbol{\Sigma}'_k \boldsymbol{V}'^T_k)\|_F^2 \tag{7}$$

Here $\odot$ denotes the Hadamard (elementwise) product. This problem is essentially, a weighted low-rank decomposition, studied previously by Srerbo and Jaakkola [52] and Delchambre [8] and is solved using an efficient Expectation-Maximization (EM) algorithm [52].

The intuition behind this weighted formulation is to ascribe a relative importance to the filters that contribute most to the activations in the training set (on average in the Frobenius norm sense), instead of attempting to reconstruct all activations with equal priority. Molchanov *et al.* [42] also use the notion of an importance criteria for compression but rather than using it as a weighting scheme in the optimization objective, like we do, they directly use it to prune the 'less important' filters. In this case as well, we compute the optimum number of components to be kept by selecting the least number of components that can be selected such that the classification accuracy is bounded within 0.5% of the original network, once the entire network has been compressed.

3.5 Activation-Based Filter Pruning

In related work, Li*et al.* observe that not all filters are equally important in the context of classification [40]. This motivates us to perform a pre-processing step before coreset compression, to first eliminate unimportant filters pre-emptively, based on the mean of their activation norms over the training set. This step is essential to remove unimportant weights, since pruning out a filter in a layer can completely remove the weights corresponding to that filter, in the next layer as well, inducing greater sparsity. Using the notation from earlier we can write the size of filters $\hat{\boldsymbol{W}}_k$ as:

$$\text{size}(\hat{\boldsymbol{W}}_k) = \hat{N}_k \times (C_k h_k w_k + 1) + N_k \hat{N}_k$$

Setting $C_k = N_{k-1}$ (since number of outgoing activations in the previous layer is equal to the number of input channels in the next layer), and using $N_{k-1} h_k w_k \gg N_k$, we get:

$$\text{size}(\hat{\boldsymbol{W}}_k) \propto \hat{N}_k \cdot N_{k-1}$$

By layer-wise pruning of complete filters, we can hence set the number of post-pruning filters at layer $k-1$ to be $N^*_{k-1} < N_{k-1}$, permitting further compression. In networks with skip-connections (e.g. ResNets), $C_k \neq N_{k-1}$, but it is a positive linear combination of the number of filters of the "source" layers of the (skip) connections, hence the proportionality still holds.

Starting from the first layer in the network, we proceed to evaluate the activation values for the entire training set, layer-by-layer. Inspired by standard "Max-Pool" sub-sampling techniques prevalent in modern CNNs [35,50], we approximate the response from each filter in the convolution layers (a 2D matrix) with its maximum value (a scalar). Once we have this set of pooled filter-wise activations for all samples, we compute the mean squared norm of each filter over all the training samples, and sort the filters by this value. This technique of ordering filters differentiates us from prior pruning-based techniques. We maximize the number of pruned filters, ensuring that the divergence in classification accuracy is only 0.5%, after the pruning has been carried out across all layers. Once we obtain a reduced set of filters with the crucial filters preserved, we compress this set of filters using coresets, as discussed earlier.

3.6 Compression Pipeline and Computational Complexity Analysis

The entire pipeline for compression can be summarized in two stages - (i) activation-based pruning, followed by (ii) coreset-based compression. The pruning procedure can be summarized in the following steps:

1. Sort the layers of the network in order of descending parameter size.
2. For each layer of the sorted network, repeat the following steps:
   (a) Compute activations for every input in the training set, and store the maximum value for each filter activation (max-pool over spatial dimensions).
   (b) Sort the filters in descending order of the mean value of the max-pooled activations, over the entire training set.
   (c) Find the smallest number of filters N_k^* that can be retained while performance deviation, post the compression of all layers, is within 0.5% of original performance - using binary search.

We can see that the complexity of the individual steps are $\mathcal{O}(n \log n)$ for the first sorting step, and $\mathcal{O}(n \cdot (A + N_k \log N_k + A \log N_k))$ for layer-wise activation computation, filter sorting, and binary-search. A denotes the complexity to do one feed-forward operation on the entire training set. Since $A \gg N_k \gg 1$, the total complexity of the filter pruning is $\mathcal{O}(n \cdot A \cdot \log \max_k N_k)$, requiring a maximum of $n \log \max_k N_k$ epochs of feed-forward operations, which, for most neural network architectures, we find to be much smaller than the complexity of fine-tuning.

After filter pruning, we proceed to the coreset-based compression stage. This procedure for compression can be summarized in the following steps:

For each layer in the network, starting from the shallowest, do:

1. Compute the complete decomposition according to the coreset formulation used.
2. Find the minimum number of coreset filters $\hat{N}_k$ that can be retained while performance is within 0.5% of the network prior to coreset compression, post the compression of all layers - by searching over a random subset of the training data using binary search.

The complexity for the coreset construction set is $\mathcal{O}(n \cdot (B + sA \log N_k^*))$, where B is the complexity for the matrix decomposition, and $0 \leq s \leq 1$ is the fraction of random training points used. For our experiments, we set $s = 0.005$. We find that for most networks, $sA \log N_k^* > B$, and hence the total complexity of the compression pipeline is $\mathcal{O}(n \cdot A \cdot \log N_k \cdot (1 + s))$. Note that post the cascading of activation-based pruning with coreset compression across all layers, the total deviation allowed in classification performance is 1% (0.5% for pruning and 0.5% for coreset compression).

4 Experimental Evaluation

We implement our method in PyTorch [44] and Caffe [31], and evaluate on a cluster of NVIDIA TITAN Xp and Tesla GPUs. All of our implementation and other details are available here [1]. For all experiments, we evaluate all 3 coreset construction techniques, as well as the impact of activation-based pruning

[1] https://sites.google.com/site/metrosmiles/research/research-projects/compress_cnn.

coupled with each, and report all results together with the baseline and comparable recent work. The Activation-Based Pruning pipeline is reported as AP, while the coreset techniques are reported as - (1) k-Means Coreset (Coreset-K), (2) Structured Sparse Coreset (Coreset-S) and (3) Activation-Weighted Coreset (Coreset-A). We compare our compression performance with recent compression benchmarks, such as Fast-Food [59], SVD [9], Weight-Based Pruning [21], Deep Compression [20], memory-bounded CNNs [6], Compression Aware Training [2], etc. on a wide array of CNN architectures, including the highly efficient SqueezeNet [29].

4.1 LeNet-5 on MNIST

The first architecture we evaluate is the LeNet-5 network [38] on the MNIST dataset [37]. This is a popular benchmark for network compression, and high values of compression are reported by various recent work, which makes it a very competitive setup. The results for this experiment are summarized in Table 2. We can see that the coreset-based methods outperform the recent work comfortably, with a relative improvement of 18% over the existing state-of-the-art.

Table 1. Compression (Comp.) results for both AlexNet [35] and VGGNet-16 [50] trained on the ImageNet dataset, along with variation in performance with Deep Compression

Method	AlexNet [35]				VGGNet-16 [50]		
	Acc. (%)	#Params	Comp.	#Epochs	Acc. (%)	#Params	Comp.
Baseline	57.22	61M	1×	-	68.88	138M	1×
Fastfood-32-AD [59]	58.07	30M	2×	-	-	-	-
Fastfood-16-AD [59]	57.10	17M	3.7×	-	-	-	-
Collins and Kohli [6]	55.60	15.3M	4×	-	-	-	-
Compression-Aware [2]	-	-	-	-	67.6	64.17M	2.2×
SVD [9]	55.98	12.2M	5×	540	68.85	27M	5.1×
Pruning [20]	57.23	6.8M	9×	960	68.15	15M	9.1×
Dynamic Net Surgery [18]	56.91	3.47M	17.7×	140	-	-	-
Coreset-K	56.97	9.15M	6.7×	17	68.69	15.6M	9.2×
Coreset-S	56.78	5.76M	10.5×	21	68.65	9.9M	13.9×
Coreset-A	56.82	4.97M	12.3×	23	68.01	9.2M	15.1×
AP+Coreset-K	56.51	4.02M	15.2×	26	68.56	9.81M	14×
AP+Coreset-S	56.38	**3.20M**	**19.1** ×	28	67.90	**8.1M**	**17**×
AP+Coreset-A	56.48	3.68M	16.5×	27	68.16	8.7M	15.8×
With deep compression (comparison of model size)							
Baseline	57.22	6.9 MB	35×	-	68.70	10.77 MB	49×
Coreset-K	56.80	4.17 MB	49×	-	68.51	2.52 MB	210×
Coreset-S	56.87	3.92 MB	52×	-	68.25	2.35 MB	225×
Coreset-A	57.19	4.01 MB	51×	-	68.43	2.41 MB	220×
AP+ Coreset-K	56.85	4.01 MB	51×	-	68.02	2.28 MB	232×
AP+ Coreset-S	56.70	3.85 MB	53×	-	68.16	2.26 MB	233×
AP+ Coreset-A	57.08	**3.74 MB**	**55** ×	-	68.14	**2.21 MB**	**238**×

4.2 Large-Scale ImageNet Models

The next set of experiments we perform are on the large-scale ImageNet-trained models - the very deep networks such as Residual Networks [24], AlexNet [35] and VGGNet-16 [50]. These architectures are ubiquitous for countless applied computer vision tasks [7,23], and several recent compression techniques demonstrate remarkable compression on these models which makes them an appropriate benchmark for evaluating compression performance. For these networks, we also demonstrate the impact of coupling *Deep Compression* (which involves quantization, pruning, re-training iteratively) with our method.

Table 3 summarizes the empirical evaluation on Residual Networks. We find state-of-the-art performance achieved by all three coreset methods, and a substantial increase from previous baselines as well. Even in 101-layer deep networks such as ResNet-101, we are able to obtain consistent compression, similar to the shallower ResNets. Note that this improvement is entirely on convolutional layers, which typically have very few redundancies when compared to fully-connected layers. We additionally observe that activation-based pruning buys us significant compression, providing in essence a cascading additive effect.

Table 1 summarizes the empirical evaluation on AlexNet and VGGNet-16 networks, the two of the largest image classification networks in use today. We demonstrate substantial improvements over the state-of-the-art, by compressing AlexNet by **19**×, and VGGNet-16 by **17**× from their baseline sizes. When combined with Deep Compression, these ratios increase, up to 55× and 238× respectively, yielding models with a memory footprint of less than 4 MB. The results additionally highlight the improvement that the activation-based pruning (AP) provides, which is most prominent in the Coreset-K and Coreset-S models.

Table 2. Compression (Comp.) results on LeNet-5

Method	Top-1	Comp.
Baseline	0.97	1×
Wang *et al.* [58]	0.93	16×
Han *et al.* [20]	0.74	39×
Guo *et al.* [18]	0.91	108×
SVD [9]	0.92	118×
Ullric *et al.* [55]	0.97	164×
AP+Coreset-K	0.966	165×
AP+Coreset-S	0.96	192×
AP+Coreset-A	0.96	**193**×

Table 3. Compression results on Residual Networks. Columns Acc. and Comp. represent the Top-1 accuracy and compression factor respectively

Method	Residual network					
	Res-18		Res-50		Res-101	
	Acc.	Comp.	Acc.	Comp.	Acc.	Comp.
Baseline [25]	0.69	1×	0.75	1×	0.76	1×
SVD [9]	0.69	8×	0.74	9.1×	0.75	9.2×
Pruning [21]	0.68	5.2×	0.74	6.2×	0.76	6.4×
N2N [4]	0.67	9.0×	0.73	8.7×	0.74	8.5×
ThiNet [41]	-	-	0.71	2.06×	-	-
ThiNet [41]	-	-	0.68	2.95×	-	-
AP+Coreset-K	0.69	13.3×	0.74	14.7×	0.75	15.1×
AP+Coreset-S	0.68	**15**×	0.74	**15.8**×	0.75	**16.2**×
AP+Coreset-A	0.69	14.2×	0.74	15.6×	0.75	15.8×

4.3 SqueezeNet

We evaluate our method on the highly parameter-efficient SqueezeNet architecture to evaluate if further redundancies still persist after such a compression in the architecture space and if those can be eliminated via efficient filter bank representations. We find that despite beginning with 50× less parameters than AlexNet (while providing the same performance), SqueezeNet can be compressed further (results in Table 4). Using our method, we are able to compress SqueezeNet to half its parameters, providing accuracy similar to AlexNet at 100× compression. By coupling with Deep Compression, we obtain a net compression in model size to the tune of 16.64× over the original model (or **832**× from AlexNet) while maintaining classification performance.

4.4 Additional Observations

Further, we observe that Coreset-S and Coreset-A formulations consistently outperform Coreset-K. We surmise that large extant model redundancies tend to benefit Coreset-A and S formulations where sparsity is explicitly enforced in the objective. Moreover, we observe that for deeper models Coreset-S tends to achieve the most compression. Table 5 shows the superior layer-wise compression achieved by our algorithm vis-á-vis state-of-the-art compression techniques on LeNet-5. The results clearly bring out the efficacy of using our compression

Table 4. Comparison with SqueezeNet [29] trained on the ImageNet dataset. We can compress SqueezeNet to create a model that is **832**× smaller than AlexNet [35] with the same performance.

Method	Acc. (%)	Num. of params	Ratio	Rel. to AlexNet
Baseline	57.01	1.24M	1×	50×
Coreset-K	56.83	0.73M	1.7×	85×
Coreset-S	56.92	0.65M	1.9×	95×
Coreset-A	56.94	0.61M	2×	102×
AP+ Coreset-K	56.52	0.65M	1.9×	95×
AP+ Coreset-S	56.44	0.59M	**2.1**×	**109**×
AP+ Coreset-A	56.80	0.60M	2×	103×
With deep compression (comparing model size)				
Baseline	56.04	0.47 MB	10.14×	507×
Coreset-K	56.08	0.29 MB	16.1×	805×
Coreset-S	56.05	0.28 MB	16.34×	817×
Coreset-A	56.03	0.29 MB	16.23×	812×
AP+ Coreset-K	56.31	0.27 MB	16.50×	825×
AP+ Coreset-S	56.15	0.26 MB	**16.64**×	**832**×
AP+ Coreset-A	56.18	0.27 MB	16.56×	828×

Table 5. LeNet-5 layer-wise compression of our method (denoted by identifiers) vis-á-vis prior work. The entries represent the fraction of parameters retained post compression

Layer	Han *et al.* [21]	Guo *et al.* [18]	K	S	A	AP+K	AP+S	AP+A
conv1	0.66	0.14	0.06	0.03	0.03	0.02	**0.02**	0.02
conv2	0.12	0.03	0.04	0.03	0.03	0.02	**0.02**	0.02
fc1	0.08	**0.01**	0.04	0.03	0.03	0.02	**0.01**	0.02
fc2	0.19	0.04	0.02	0.01	0.02	0.01	**0.01**	0.01

technique, especially for convolution layers. For layer-wise compression results on other CNNs, please refer to the supplementary.

Runtime Analysis: We also perform a study of runtime analysis in both training and inference performance. Since we do not undertake retraining, our method is considerably faster - on our hardware, one forward pass and backward pass of AlexNet (batch size 256) takes 16 ms naively, which corresponds to a total epoch training time (on ImageNet) of 2.5 min. We use this as a base measurement to compare the **total** training time (inclusive of the coreset operations). Table 1 describes the comparison of training times across methods. The previous state of the art method, Dynamic Net Surgery [18], requires 140 epochs (in time units) whereas our method takes *at most* 28 epochs (in time units), a significant reduction of 80%. During inference, we observe a reduction in inference time as well, which can be optimized by using efficient tensor multiplication [51]. On ResNet-50, VGGNet-16 and AlexNet, the naive (uncompressed) runtimes per epoch are: 36 ms, 45 ms and 8 ms respectively. Our best runtimes for these networks (with Coreset-S) are 19 ms, 21 ms and 3.5 ms on average, which is an average improvement of around 50% (Fig. 4).

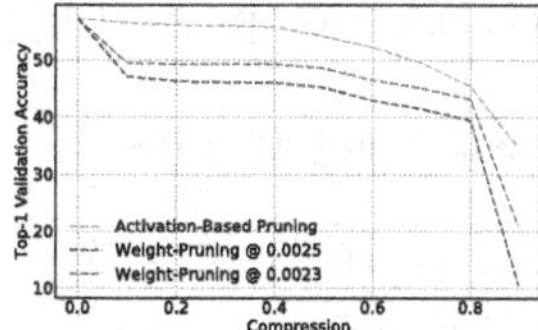

Fig. 2. The comparison of Activation-Based Pruning (AP) with weight-based filter pruning (without retraining), on AlexNet

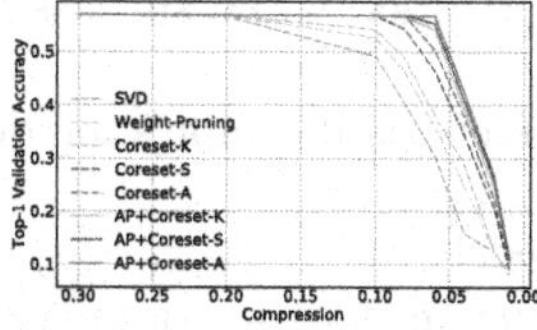

Fig. 3. Variation of classification performance with compression for all coreset compression techniques evaluated on AlexNet [35]

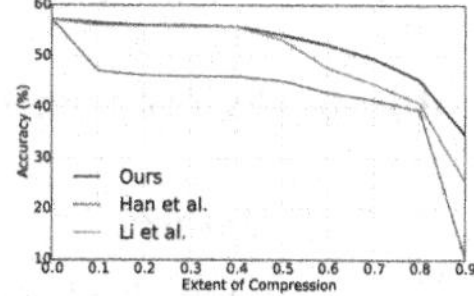

Fig. 4. The comparison of Activation-Based Pruning (AP) with the pruning techniques of Han *et al.* and Li *et al.* [21,40], on AlexNet

4.5 Ablation Analysis

To demonstrate the effect of individual components in our method, we perform some ablation studies as well. We first compare the effect of activation-based pruning (AP) on all coreset compression techniques on three models - AlexNet [35], VGGNet-16 [50] and SqueezeNet [29], and observe that pruning benefits all methods of coreset compression, as described in Tables 1 and 4.

Next, we compare activation-based pruning with weight-based pruning, without re-training, and the pruning technique of Li *et al.* [40] for AlexNet. The results of these comparisons are summarized in Fig. 2. We obtain consistently better performance at all compression ratios, substantiating the merit of data-dependent filter pruning approaches over those based on the magnitudes of filter weights.

Finally, we analyze the variation of performance with compression factor for all coreset compression techniques on the AlexNet classification model, described in Fig. 3. We observe that Coreset-K (with and without AP), while stronger than SVD and Pruning approaches, worsens much more rapidly in comparison to other corresponding coreset techniques. This observation is consistent across all models. For additional results, more layer-wise compression analysis, and filter visualizations we refer the reader to the supplementary material.

4.6 Domain Adaptibility

To measure the generalizability of our compressed models to newer tasks, we evaluate compressed models on domain adaptation benchmarks, following the experimental pipeline proposed in [41]. We evaluate the performance of the compressed CNN model VGGNet-16 [50] on target domain adaptation datasets - CUB-2011 [57] and Stanford-Dogs [34], two popular datasets for fine-grained image classification. These results are summarized in Table 6. We observe that our compressed coreset models are able to provide classification performance close to the uncompressed networks, while surpassing networks compressed by

Table 6. Performance of coreset-based compression on domain-adaptation tasks.

Dataset	Model	#Params	Top-1
CUB-2011	VGG-16 Finetune (FT)	138M	72.30%
	Train from Scratch	138M	44.27%
	SVD [9] + FT	27M	53.65%
	Pruning [21] + FT	15M	57.45%
	AP+Coreset-S + FT	8.1M	**70.66%**
Stanford-Dogs	VGG-16 Finetune (FT)	138M	61.92%
	Train from Scratch	138M	27.16%
	SVD [9] + FT	27M	40.84%
	Pruning [21] + FT	15M	43.28%
	AP+Coreset-S + FT	8.1M	**55.91%**

other techniques. This exhibits the versatility of coreset-compressed models to domain adaptation tasks, as well.

5 Conclusions and Future Work

In this paper we introduce a novel technique that exploits redundancies in the space of convolutional filter weights and sample activations to reduce neural network size, using the long-existing concepts of coresets, coupled with an activation-based pooling technique. The lack of a re-training step in our algorithmic pipeline makes the implementation simple. Empirical evaluation reveals that our algorithm outperforms all other competing methods at compressing a wide array of popular CNN architectures. Our findings uncover the existence of redundancies even in the most compressed CNNs, such as SqueezeNets, which can be further exploited to improve efficiency.

Our method does not require any retraining, scales to both convolution and fully connected layers, and is extensively generalizable to different neural network models without being computationally intensive. Thus, we hope that our algorithm will serve as a valuable tool to obtain leaner and more efficient CNNs. As future work, we hope to apply our algorithm to compress other types of deep neural networks, such as Recurrent Neural Networks (RNNs) which are applicable to time-varying sequential inputs.

Acknowledgments. We are grateful to Prof. Ramesh Raskar for his insightful comments. MC additionally acknowledges Po-han Huang for helpful discussions and NVIDIA for providing the GPUs used for this research.

References

1. Agarwal, P.K., Har-Peled, S., Varadarajan, K.R.: Geometric approximation via coresets. Comb. Comput. Geom. **52**, 1–30 (2005)
2. Alvarez, J.M., Salzmann, M.: Compression-aware training of deep networks. In: Advances in Neural Information Processing Systems, pp. 856–867 (2017)
3. Antol, S., et al.: VQA: visual question answering. In: Proceedings of the IEEE International Conference on Computer Vision, pp. 2425–2433 (2015)
4. Ashok, A., Rhinehart, N., Beainy, F., Kitani, K.M.: N2N learning: network to network compression via policy gradient reinforcement learning. arXiv preprint arXiv:1709.06030 (2017)
5. Bădoiu, M., Har-Peled, S., Indyk, P.: Approximate clustering via core-sets. In: Proceedings of the Thiry-Fourth Annual ACM Symposium on Theory of Computing, pp. 250–257. ACM (2002)
6. Collins, M.D., Kohli, P.: Memory bounded deep convolutional networks. arXiv preprint arXiv:1412.1442 (2014)
7. Dai, J., et al.: Deformable convolutional networks. CoRR, abs/1703.06211 1(2), 3 (2017)
8. Delchambre, L.: Weighted principal component analysis: a weighted covariance eigendecomposition approach. Mon. Not. R. Astron. Soc. **446**(4), 3545–3555 (2014)

9. Denton, E.L., et al.: Exploiting linear structure within convolutional networks for efficient evaluation. In: Advances in NIPS 2014, pp. 1269–1277 (2014)
10. Dieleman, S., De Fauw, J., Kavukcuoglu, K.: Exploiting cyclic symmetry in convolutional neural networks. arXiv preprint arXiv:1602.02660 (2016)
11. Dosovitskiy, A., Springenberg, J.T., Riedmiller, M., Brox, T.: Discriminative unsupervised feature learning with convolutional neural networks. In: Advances in Neural Information Processing Systems, pp. 766–774 (2014)
12. Dubey, A., Naik, N., Raviv, D., Sukthankar, R., Raskar, R.: Coreset-based adaptive tracking. arXiv preprint arXiv:1511.06147 (2015)
13. Feldman, D., Monemizadeh, M., Sohler, C.: A PTAS for k-means clustering based on weak coresets. In: Proceedings of the Twenty-Third Annual Symposium on Computational Geometry, pp. 11–18. ACM (2007)
14. Feldman, D., Schmidt, M., Sohler, C.: Turning big data into tiny data: Constant-size coresets for k-means, PCA and projective clustering. In: Proceedings of the Twenty-Fourth Annual ACM-SIAM Symposium on Discrete Algorithms, pp. 1434–1453. SIAM (2013)
15. Feldman, D., Volkov, M., Rus, D.: Dimensionality reduction of massive sparse datasets using coresets. arXiv preprint arXiv:1503.01663 (2015)
16. Girshick, R.: Fast R-CNN. In: Proceedings of the IEEE International Conference on Computer Vision, pp. 1440–1448 (2015)
17. Gokhale, V., Jin, J., Dundar, A., Martini, B., Culurciello, E.: A 240 G-ops/s mobile coprocessor for deep neural networks. In: Proceedings of the IEEE Conference on Computer Vision and Pattern Recognition Workshops, pp. 682–687 (2014)
18. Guo, Y., Yao, A., Chen, Y.: Dynamic network surgery for efficient DNNs. In: Advances In Neural Information Processing Systems, pp. 1379–1387 (2016)
19. Han, S., et al.: EIE: efficient inference engine on compressed deep neural network. In: Proceedings of the 43rd International Symposium on Computer Architecture, pp. 243–254. IEEE Press (2016)
20. Han, S., Mao, H., Dally, W.J.: Deep compression: Compressing deep neural network with pruning, trained quantization and Huffman coding (2015)
21. Han, S., Pool, J., Tran, J., Dally, W.: Learning both weights and connections for efficient neural network. In: Advances in Neural Information Processing Systems, pp. 1135–1143 (2015)
22. Har-Peled, S., Mazumdar, S.: On coresets for k-means and k-median clustering. In: ACM Symposium on Theory of Computing (2004)
23. He, K., Gkioxari, G., Dollár, P., Girshick, R.: Mask R-CNN. In: 2017 IEEE International Conference on Computer Vision (ICCV), pp. 2980–2988. IEEE (2017)
24. He, K., Zhang, X., Ren, S., Sun, J.: Deep residual learning for image recognition. arXiv preprint arXiv:1512.03385 (2015)
25. He, K., Zhang, X., Ren, S., Sun, J.: Deep residual learning for image recognition. In: Proceedings of the IEEE Conference on Computer Vision and Pattern Recognition, pp. 770–778 (2016)
26. He, K., Zhang, X., Ren, S., Sun, J.: Identity mappings in deep residual networks. arXiv preprint arXiv:1603.05027 (2016)
27. He, Y., et al.: Channel pruning for accelerating very deep NNS. In: ICCV 2017 (2017)
28. Huang, G., Liu, Z., Weinberger, K.Q., van der Maaten, L.: Densely connected convolutional networks. arXiv preprint arXiv:1608.06993 (2016)
29. Iandola, F.N., Moskewicz, M.W., Ashraf, K., Han, S., Dally, W.J., Keutzer, K.: SqueezeNet: AlexNet-level accuracy with 50x fewer parameters and <1mb model size. arXiv preprint arXiv:1602.07360 (2016)

30. Jenatton, R., Obozinski, G., Bach, F.: Structured sparse principal component analysis. In: Proceedings of the Thirteenth International Conference on Artificial Intelligence and Statistics, pp. 366–373 (2010)
31. Jia, Y., et al.: Caffe: convolutional architecture for fast feature embedding. In: Proceedings of the 22nd ACM International Conference on Multimedia, pp. 675–678. ACM (2014)
32. Jolliffe, I.T., Trendafilov, N.T., Uddin, M.: A modified principal component technique based on the LASSO. J. Comput. Graph. Stat. **12**(3), 531–547 (2003)
33. Karpathy, A., Fei-Fei, L.: Deep visual-semantic alignments for generating image descriptions. In: Proceedings of the IEEE Conference on Computer Vision and Pattern Recognition, pp. 3128–3137 (2015)
34. Khosla, A., Jayadevaprakash, N., Yao, B., Li, F.F.: Novel dataset for fine-grained image categorization: Stanford dogs
35. Krizhevsky, A., Sutskever, I., Hinton, G.E.: ImageNet classification with deep convolutional neural networks. In: Advances in Neural Information Processing Systems, pp. 1097–1105 (2012)
36. Lebedev, V., Ganin, Y., Rakhuba, M., Oseledets, I., Lempitsky, V.: Speeding-up convolutional neural networks using fine-tuned cp-decomposition. arXiv preprint arXiv:1412.6553 (2014)
37. LeCun, Y.: The MNIST database of handwritten digits (1998). http://yann.lecun.com/exdb/mnist/
38. LeCun, Y., Bottou, L., Bengio, Y., Haffner, P.: Gradient-based learning applied to document recognition. Proc. IEEE **86**(11), 2278–2324 (1998)
39. Lee, D.D., Seung, H.S.: Learning the parts of objects by non-negative matrix factorization. Nature **401**(6755), 788–791 (1999)
40. Li, H., et al.: Pruning filters for efficient ConvNets. In: ICLR 2017 (2017)
41. Luo, J.H., Wu, J., Lin, W.: ThiNet: a filter level pruning method for deep neural network compression. arXiv preprint arXiv:1707.06342 (2017)
42. Molchanov, P., et al.: Pruning convolutional neural networks for resource efficient transfer learning. In: ICLR 2017 (2017)
43. Nam, H., Han, B.: Learning multi-domain convolutional neural networks for visual tracking. In: Proceedings of the IEEE Conference on Computer Vision and Pattern Recognition, pp. 4293–4302 (2016)
44. Paszke, A., Gross, S., Chintala, S.: PyTorch (2017)
45. Polyak, A., Wolf, L.: Channel-level acceleration of deep face representations. IEEE Access **3**, 2163–2175 (2015)
46. Real, E., et al.: Large-scale evolution of image classifiers. arXiv preprint arXiv:1703.01041 (2017)
47. Ren, S., He, K., Girshick, R., Sun, J.: Faster R-CNN: towards real-time object detection with region proposal networks. In: Advances in Neural Information Processing Systems, pp. 91–99 (2015)
48. Rosenfeld, A., Tsotsos, J.K.: Incremental learning through deep adaptation. arXiv preprint arXiv:1705.04228 (2017)
49. Shin, H.C., et al.: Deep convolutional neural networks for computer-aided detection: CNN architectures, dataset characteristics and transfer learning. IEEE Trans. Med. Imaging **35**(5), 1285–1298 (2016)
50. Simonyan, K., Zisserman, A.: Very deep convolutional networks for large-scale image recognition. arXiv preprint arXiv:1409.1556 (2014)
51. Solomonik, E.: Provably efficient algorithms for numerical tensor algebra. University of California, Berkeley (2014)

52. Srebro, N., Jaakkola, T.: Weighted low-rank approximations. In: Proceedings of the 20th International Conference on Machine Learning (ICML 2003), pp. 720–727 (2003)
53. Srinivas, S., Babu, R.V.: Data-free parameter pruning for deep neural networks. arXiv preprint arXiv:1507.06149 (2015)
54. Szegedy, C., et al.: Going deeper with convolutions. In: Proceedings of the IEEE Conference on Computer Vision and Pattern Recognition, pp. 1–9 (2015)
55. Ullrich, K., Meeds, E., Welling, M.: Soft weight-sharing for neural network compression. arXiv preprint arXiv:1702.04008 (2017)
56. Vasudevan, A., Anderson, A., Gregg, D.: Parallel multi channel convolution using general matrix multiplication. arXiv preprint arXiv:1704.04428 (2017)
57. Wah, C., Branson, S., Welinder, P., Perona, P., Belongie, S.: The Caltech-UCSD birds-200-2011 dataset (2011)
58. Wang, S., Cai, H., Bilmes, J., Noble, W.: Training compressed fully-connected networks with a density-diversity penalty (2016)
59. Yang, Z., et al.: Deep fried ConvNets. In: Proceedings of the IEEE International Conference on Computer Vision, pp. 1476–1483 (2015)
60. Yu, R., et al.: NISP: pruning networks using neuron importance score propagation. arXiv preprint arXiv:1711.05908 (2017)
61. Zhai, S., Cheng, Y., Zhang, Z.M., Lu, W.: Doubly convolutional neural networks. In: Advances in Neural Information Processing Systems, pp. 1082–1090 (2016)

A Joint Sequence Fusion Model for Video Question Answering and Retrieval

Youngjae Yu, Jongseok Kim, and Gunhee Kim(✉)

Department of Computer Science and Engineering,
Seoul National University, Seoul, Korea
{yj.yu,js.kim}@vision.snu.ac.kr, gunhee@snu.ac.kr
http://vision.snu.ac.kr/projects/jsfusion/

Abstract. We present an approach named JSFusion (Joint Sequence Fusion) that can measure semantic similarity between any pairs of multimodal sequence data (*e.g.* a video clip and a language sentence). Our multimodal matching network consists of two key components. First, the *Joint Semantic Tensor* composes a dense pairwise representation of two sequence data into a 3D tensor. Then, the *Convolutional Hierarchical Decoder* computes their similarity score by discovering hidden hierarchical matches between the two sequence modalities. Both modules leverage hierarchical attention mechanisms that learn to promote well-matched representation patterns while prune out misaligned ones in a bottom-up manner. Although the JSFusion is a universal model to be applicable to any multimodal sequence data, this work focuses on video-language tasks including multimodal retrieval and video QA. We evaluate the JSFusion model in three retrieval and VQA tasks in LSMDC, for which our model achieves the best performance reported so far. We also perform multiple-choice and movie retrieval tasks for the MSR-VTT dataset, on which our approach outperforms many state-of-the-art methods.

Keywords: Multimodal retrieval · Video question and answering

1 Introduction

Recently, various video-language tasks have drawn a lot of interests in computer vision research [1–3], including video captioning [4–9], video question answering (QA) [10,11], and video retrieval for a natural language query [8,12,13]. To solve such challenging tasks, it is important to learn a hidden join representation between word and frame sequences, for correctly measuring their semantic similarity. Video classification [14–18] can be a candidate solution, but tagging only a few labels to a video may be insufficient to fully relate multiple latent events in the video to a language description. Thanks to recent advance of deep representation learning, many methods for multimodal semantic embedding (*e.g.* [19–21]) have been proposed. However, most of existing methods embed each of visual and language information into a single vector, which is often insufficient especially for a video and a natural sentence. With single vectors for the two sequence

V. Ferrari et al. (Eds.): ECCV 2018, LNCS 11211, pp. 487–503, 2018.
https://doi.org/10.1007/978-3-030-01234-2_29

modalities, it is hard to directly compare multiple relations between subsets of sequence data (*i.e.* matchings between subevents in a video and short phrases in a sentence), for which hierarchical matching is more adequate. There have been some attempts to learn representation of hierarchical structure of natural sentences and visual scenes (*e.g.* [22,23] using recursive neural networks), but they require groundtruth parse trees or segmentation labels (Fig. 1).

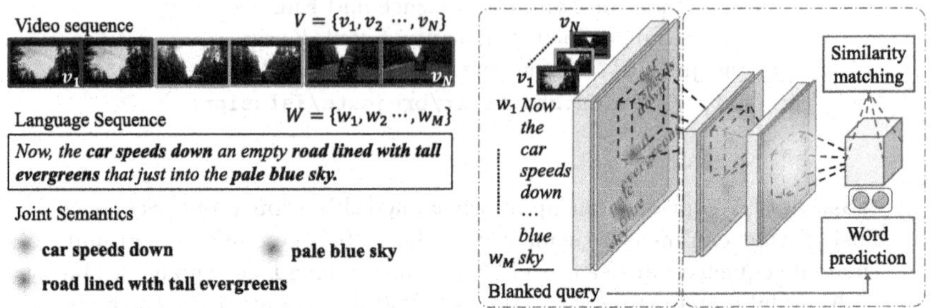

Fig. 1. The intuition of the Joint Sequence Fusion (JSFusion) model. Given a pair of a video clip and a language query, Joint Semantic Tensor (in purple) encodes a pairwise joint embedding between the two sequence data, and Convolutional Hierarchical Decoder (in blue) discovers hierarchical matching relations from JST. Our model is easily adaptable to many video QA and retrieval tasks. (Color figure online)

In this paper, we propose an approach that can measure semantic similarity between any pairs of multimodal sequence data, by learning bottom-up recursive matches via attention mechanisms. We apply our method to tackle several video question answering and retrieval tasks. Our approach, named as Joint Sequence Fusion (JSFusion) model, consists of two key components. First, the Joint Semantic Tensor (JST) performs dense Hadamard products between frames and words and encodes all pairwise embeddings between the two sequence data into a 3D tensor. JST further takes advantage of learned attentions to refine the 3D matching tensor. Second, the Convolutional Hierarchical Decoder (CHD) discovers local alignments on the tensor, by using a series of attention-based decoding modules, consisting of convolutional layers and gates. These two attention mechanisms promote well-matched representation patterns and prune out misaligned ones in a bottom-up manner. Finally, CHD obtains hierarchical composible representations of the two modalities, and computes a semantic matching score of the sequence pair.

We evaluate the performance of our JSFusion model on multiple video question answering and retrieval tasks on LSMDC [1] and MSR-VTT [2] datasets. First, we participate in three challenges of LSMDC: multiple-choice test, movie retrieval, and fill-in-the-blank, which require the model to correctly measure a semantic matching score between a descriptive sentence and a video clip, or to predict the most suitable word for a blank in a sentence for a query video. Our JSFusion model achieves the best accuracies reported so far with significant margins for the lsmdc tasks. Second, we newly create multiple-choice and movie retrieval annotations for the MSR-VTT dataset, on which our approach also outperforms many state-of-the-art methods in diverse video topics (*e.g. TV shows*, *web videos*, and *cartoons*).

We summarize the contributions of this work as follows.

1. We propose the Joint Sequence Fusion (JSFusion) model, consisting of two key components: JST and CHD. To the best of our knowledge, it is a first attempt to leverage recursively learnable attention modules for measuring semantic matching scores between multimodal sequence data. Specifically, we propose two different attention models, including soft attention in JST and Conv-layers and Conv-gates in CHD.
2. To validate the applicability of our JSFusion model, especially on video question answering and retrieval, we participate in three tasks of LSMDC [1], and achieve the best performance reported so far. We newly create video retrieval and QA benchmarks based on MSR-VTT [2] dataset, on which our JSFusion outperforms many state-of-the-art VQA models. Our source code and benchmark annotations are publicly available in our project page.

2 Related Work

Our work can be uniquely positioned in the context of two recent research directions: video retrieval and video question answering.

Video Retrieval with Natural Language Sentences. Visual information retrieval with natural language queries has long been tackled via joint visual-language embedding models [12,19,24–28]. In the video domain, it is more difficult to learn latent relations between a sequence of frames and a sequence of descriptive words, given that a video is not simply a multiple of images. Recently, there has been much progress in this line of research. Several deep video-language embedding methods [8,12,13] has been developed by extending image-language embeddings [20,21]. Other recent successful methods benefit from incorporating concept words as semantic priors [9,29], or relying on strong representation of videos like RNN-FV [30]. Another dominant approach may be leveraging RNNs or their variants like LSTM to encode the whole multimodal sequences (*e.g.* [9,12,29,30]).

Compared to these existing methods, our model first finds dense pairwise embeddings between the two sequences, and then composes higher-level similarity matches from fine-grained ones in a bottom-up manner, leveraging hierarchical attention mechanisms. This idea improves our model's robustness especially for local subset matching (*e.g.* at the activity-phrase level), which places our work in a unique position with respect to previous works.

Video Question Answering. VQA is a relatively new problem at the intersection of computer vision and natural language research [31–33]. Video-based VQA is often recognized as a more difficult challenge than image-based one, because video VQA models must learn spatio-temporal reasoning to answer problems, which requires large-scale annotated data. Fortunately, large-scale video

QA datasets have been recently emerged from the community using crowdsourcing on various sources of data (*e.g.* movies for MovieQA [10] and animated GIFs for TGIF-QA [11]). Rohrbach *et al.* [1] extend the LSMDC movie description dataset to the VQA domain, introducing several new tasks such as multiple-choice [12] and fill-in-the-blank [34].

The multiple-choice problem is, given a video query and five descriptive sentences, to choose a single best answer in the candidates. To tackle this problem, ranking losses on deep representation [9,11,12] or nearest neighbor search on the joint space [30] are exploited. Torabi *et al.* [12] use the temporal attention on the joint representation between the query videos and answer choice sentences. Yu *et al.* [9] use LSTMs to sequentially feed the query and the answer embedding conditioned on detected concept words. The fill-in-the-blank task is, given a video and a sentence with a single blank, to select a suitable word for the blank. To encode the sentential query sentence on the video context, MergingLSTMs [35] and LR/RL LSTMs [36] are proposed. Yu *et al.* [9,29] attempt to detect semantic concept words from videos and integrate them with Bidirectional LSTM that encodes the language query. However, most previous approaches tend to focus too much on the sentence information and easily ignore visual cues. On the other hand, our model focuses on learning multi-level semantic similarity between videos and sentences, and consequently achieves the best results reported so far in these two QA tasks, as will be presented in section 4.

3 The Joint Sequence Fusion Model

We first explain the preprocessing steps for describing videos and sentences in Sect. 3.1, and then discuss the two key components of our JSFusion model in Sects. 3.2–3.4, respectively. We present the training procedure of our model in Sect. 3.5, and its applications to three video-language tasks in Sect. 3.6.

3.1 Preprocessing

Sentence Representation. We encode each sentence in a word level. We first define a vocabulary dictionary $\mathcal{V}$ by collecting the words that occur more than three times in the dataset. (*e.g.* the dictionary size is $|\mathcal{V}| = 16,824$ for LSMDC). We ignore the words that are not in the dictionary. Next we use the pretrained glove.42B.300d [37] to obtain the word embedding matrix $\mathbf{E} \in \mathcal{R}^{d \times |\mathcal{V}|}$ where $d = 300$ is the word embedding dimension. We denote the description of each sentence by $\{\mathbf{w}_m\}_{m=1}^{M}$ where M is the number of words in the sentence. We limit the maximum number of words per sentence to be $M_{max} = 40$. If a sentence is too long, we discard the remaining excess words, because only 0.07% of training sentences excess this limit, and no performance gain is observed for larger M_{max}. Throughout this paper, we use m for denoting the word index.

Video Representation. We sample a video at five fps, to reduce the frame redundancy while minimizing information loss. We employ CNNs to encode both visual and audial information in videos. For visual description, we extract the

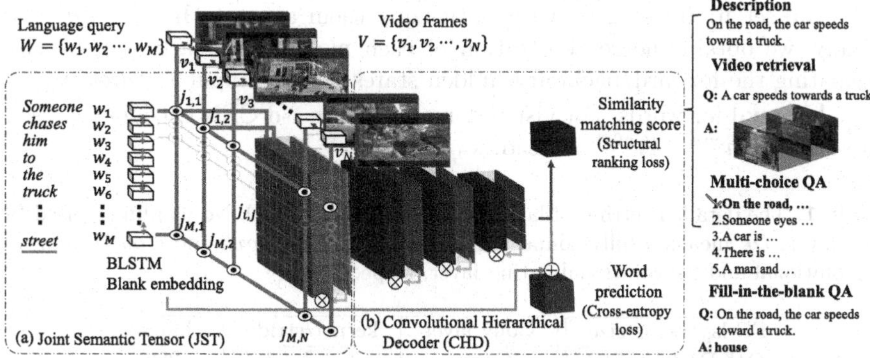

Fig. 2. The architecture of Joint Sequence Fusion (JSFusion) model. **Blue paths** indicate the information flows for multimodal similarity matching tasks, while green paths for the fill-in-the-blank task. (a) JST composes pairwise joint representation of language and video sequences into a 3D tensor, using a soft-attention mechanism. (b) CHD learns hierarchical relation patterns between the sequences, using a series of convolutional decoding module which shares parameters for each stage. $\odot$ is Hadamard product, $\oplus$ is addition, and $\otimes$ is multiplication between representation and attentions described in Eqs. (2)–(4). We omit some fully-connected layers for visualization purpose. (Color figure online)

feature map of each frame from the pool5 layer ($\mathbb{R}^{2,048}$) of ResNet-152 [38] pretrained on ImageNet. For audial information, we extract the feature map using the VGGish [39] followed by PCA for dimensionality reduction ($\mathbb{R}^{128}$). We then concatenate both features as the video descriptor $\{\mathbf{v}_n\}_{n=1}^{N} \in \mathbb{R}^{2,156\times N}$ where N is the number of frames in the video. We limit the maximum number of frames to be $N_{max} = 40$. If a video is too long, we select N_{max} equidistant frames. We observe no performance gain for larger N_{max}. We use n for denoting the video frame index.

3.2 The Joint Semantic Tensor

The Joint Semantic Tensor (JST) first composes pairwise representations between two multimodal sequences into a 3D tensor. Next, JST applies a self-gating mechanism to the 3D tensor to refine it as an attention map that discovers fine-grained matching between all pairwise embeddings of the two sequences while pruning out unmatched joint representations

Sequence Encoders. Give a pair of multimodal sequences, we first represent them using encoders. We use *bidirectional LSTM networks* (BLSTM) encoder [40,41] for word sequence and CNN encoder for video frames. It is often advantageous to consider both future and past contexts to represent each element in a sequence, which motivates the use of BLSTM encoders. $\{\mathbf{h}_t^f\}_{t=1}^T$ and $\{\mathbf{h}_t^b\}_{t=1}^T$ are the forward and backward hidden states of the BLSTM, respectively:

$$\mathbf{h}_t^f = \text{LSTM}(\mathbf{x}_t, \mathbf{h}_{t-1}^f), \quad \mathbf{h}_t^b = \text{LSTM}(\mathbf{x}_t, \mathbf{h}_{t+1}^b), \tag{1}$$

where we set $\mathbf{h}_t^b, \mathbf{h}_t^f \in \mathbb{R}^{512}$, with initializing them as zeros: $\mathbf{h}_{T+1}^b = \mathbf{h}_0^f = \mathbf{0}$. Finally, we obtain the representation of each modality at each step by concatenating the forward/backward hidden states and the input features: $\mathbf{x}_{w,t} = [\mathbf{h}_{w,t}^f, \mathbf{h}_{w,t}^b, \mathbf{w}_t]$ for words. For visual domain, we use 1-d CNN encoder representation for v_t, $h^{cnn} \in \mathbb{R}^{2,048}$ instead, $\mathbf{x}_{v,t} = [\mathbf{h}_{v,t}^{cnn}, \mathbf{v}_t]$.

Table 1. The detailed setting of layers in the JSFusion model. No padding is used for each layer. *Dk* means a fully-connected dense layer, and *Convk* and *ConGk* indicate convolutional and convolutional-gating layer, respectively.

FC layers	size
D1^v,D1^w	512
D2	512
D3, D4	512
D5	256
D6	256
D7	128
D8	1

Conv layer	kernel/stride	channel
Conv1	3 × 3 / 1	256
ConvG1	3 × 3 / 1	1
Conv2	3 × 3 / 1	256
ConvG2	3 × 3 / 1	1
Conv3	3 × 3 / 2	256
ConvG3	3 × 3 / 2	1
MeanPool	17 × 17 / 17	256

Attention-Based Joint Embedding. We then feed the output of the sequence encoder into fully-connected (dense) layer [$D1$] for each modality separately, which results in $D1^v(\mathbf{x}_v), D1^w(\mathbf{x}_w) \in \mathbb{R}^{d_{D1}}$, where d_{D1} is a hidden dimension of [$D1$]. We summarize the details of all the layers in our JSFusion model in Table 1. Throughout the paper, we denote fully-connected layers as *Dk* and convolutional layers as *Convk*.

Next, we compute attention weights $\boldsymbol{\alpha}$ and representation $\boldsymbol{\gamma}$, from which we obtain the JST as a joint embedding between every pair of sequential features:

$$\mathbf{j}_{nm} = \alpha_{nm}\gamma_{nm}, \text{ where } \alpha_{nm} = \sigma(\mathbf{w}^T D2(\mathbf{t}_{nm})), \ \gamma_{nm} = D4(D3(\mathbf{t}_{nm})), \tag{2}$$

$$\mathbf{t}_{nm} = D1^v(\mathbf{x}_{v,n}) \odot D1^w(\mathbf{x}_{w,m}). \tag{3}$$

$\odot$ is a hadamard product, σ is a sigmoid function, and $\mathbf{w} \in \mathbb{R}^{d_{D2}}$ is a learnable parameter. Since the output of the sequence encoder represents each frame conditioned on the neighboring video (or each word conditioned on the whole sentence), the attention α is expected to figure out which pairs should be more weighted for the joint embedding among all possible pairs. For example of Fig. 2, expectedly, $\alpha_{3,6}(v_3, w_6) > \alpha_{8,6}(v_8, w_6)$, if w_6 is *truck*, and the third video frame contains the *truck* while the eighth frame does not.

From Eqs. (2)–(3), we obtain JST in a form of 3D tensor: $\mathbf{J} = [\mathbf{j}_{n,m}]_{m=1:M_{max}}^{n=1:N_{max}}$ and $\mathbf{J} \in \mathbb{R}^{N_{max} \times M_{max} \times d_{D4}}$.

3.3 The Convolutional Hierarchical Decoder

The Convolutional Hierarchical Decoder (CHD) computes a compatibility score for a pair of multimodal sequences by exploiting the compositionality in the joint

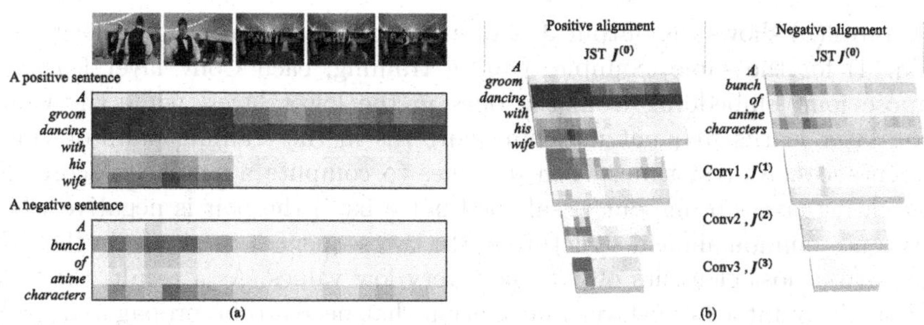

Fig. 3. Attention examples for (a) Joint Semantic Tensor (JST) and (b) Convolutional Hierarchical Decoder (CHD). Higher values are shown in darker. (a) JST assigns high weights on positively aligned joint semantics in the two sequence data. Attentions are highlighted darker where words coincide well with frames. (b) Each layer in CHD assigns high weights to where structure patterns are well matched between the two sequence data. For a wrong pair of sequences, a series of Conv-gating (*ConvG*2) prune out misaligned patterns with low weights.

vector space of JST. We pass the JST tensor through a series of a convolutional (Conv) layer and a Conv-gating block, whose learnable kernels progressively find matched embeddings from those of each previous layer. That is, starting from the JST tensor, the CHD recursively activates the weights of positively aligned pairs than negatively aligned ones.

Specifically, we apply three sets of Conv layer and Conv-gating to the JST:

$$\mathbf{J}^{(k)} = Convk(\mathbf{J}^{(k-1)}) \cdot \sigma(ConvGk(\mathbf{J}^{(k-1)})) \tag{4}$$

for $k = 1, 2, 3$. We initialize $\mathbf{J}^{(0)} = \mathbf{J}$ from the JST, and $[Convk]$ is the k-th Conv layer for joint representation, $[ConvGk]$ is the k-th Conv-gating layer for matching filters, whose details are summarized in Table 1.

We apply mean pooling to $\mathbf{J}^{(3)}$ to obtain a single video-sentence vector representation $\mathbf{J}_{out}$ ($e.g.\, \mathbb{R}^{17\times17\times256} \rightarrow \mathbb{R}^{1\times1\times256}$). Finally, we compute similarity matching score by feeding $\mathbf{J}_{out}$ into four dense layers $[D5, D6, D7, D8]$:

$$\begin{aligned} \text{score} =& \mathbf{W}_{D8}(D7(D6(D5(\mathbf{J}_{out})))) + \mathbf{b}_{D8} \\ \text{where } & Dk(\mathbf{x}) = \tanh(\mathbf{W}_{Dk}\mathbf{x} + \mathbf{b}_{Dk}), \quad k = 5, 6, 7. \end{aligned} \tag{5}$$

We use the tanh activation for all dense layers except $[D8]$.

3.4 An Illustrative Example of How the JSFusion Model Works

Figure 3 illustrates with actual examples how the attentions of JST and CHD work.

Figure 3(a) visualizes the learned attention weights α_{nm} in Eq. (2) of all pairs between frames in a video and words in a positive and a negative sentence. The attentions are highlighted with higher values (shown in darker) when the words coincide better with the content in the frames, dominantly in a positive pair.

Figure 3(b) shows the output $\mathbf{J}^{(k)}$ of each Conv layer and Conv-gating block in Eq. (4) for the same example. During training, each Conv layer learns to compose joint embedding from the ones in the lower layer, while the Conv-gating layer learns frequent matching patterns in the training pairs of videos and sentences. At test time, when it comes to compute a similarity score, the Conv-gating layers prune out misaligned patterns; if the pair is negative where there is no common aligned structure in the two sequences, as shown in the right of Fig. 3(b), most elements of $\mathbf{J}^{(k)}$ have very low values. As a result, the CHD can selectively filter lower-layer information that needs to be propagated to the final-layer representation, and the final layer of CHD assigns a high score only if the jointly aligned patterns are significant between the sequence data.

The motivation behind the JSFusion model is that long sequence data like videos and sentences are too complicated to compare them in a single vector space, although most previous approaches depend on single LSTM embedding such as neural visual semantic embedding [19] and previous LSMDC winners [9,30]. Instead, in our approach, JST first composes a dense pairwise 3D tensor representation between multimodal sequence data, from which CHD then exploits convolutional gated layers to learn multi-stage similarity matching. Therefore, our JST model can be more robust for detecting partial matching between short phrases and subhots.

3.5 Training

We train our JSFusion model using the ranking loss. Each training batch consists of L video-sentence pairs, including a single positive pair and $L-1$ randomly sampled negative pairs. We use batch shuffling in every training epoch. Finally, we train the model using a max-margin structured loss objective as follows:

$$\mathcal{L} = \sum_{k}\sum_{l=1}^{L} \max(0, S_{k,l} - S_{k,l^*} + \Delta) + \lambda||\theta||^2 \tag{6}$$

where l^* is the answer pair among L candidates, λ is a hyperparameter and θ denotes weight parameters. This objective encourages a positive video-sentence pair to have a higher score than a misaligned negative pair by a margin Δ. We use $\lambda = 0.0005, \Delta = 10$ in our experiments. We train all of our models using the Adam optimizer [42], with an initial learning rate in the range of 10^{-4}. For regularization, we apply batch normalization [43] to every dense layer.

3.6 Implementation of Video-Language Models

We below discuss how the JSFusion model is implemented for three video-language tasks, video retrieval, multiple-choice test, and fill-in-the-blank. We apply the same JSFusion model to both video retrieval and multiple-choice test with slightly different hyperparameter settings. For the fill-in-the-blank, we make a minor modification in our model to predict a word for a blank in the middle of the sentence.

For Retrieval. The retrieval model takes a query sentence and ranks 1,000 test videos according to the relevance between the query and videos. For training, we set $L = 10$ as the size of each training batch. At test, for each query sentence k, we compute scores $\{S_{k,l}\}_l$ for all videos l in the test set. From the score matrix, we can rank the videos for the query. As will be presented in Sects. 4.3 and 4.4, our method successfully finds hierarchical matching patterns between complex natural language query and video frames with sounds.

For Multiple-Choice Test. The multiple-choice model takes a video and five choice sentences among which only one is the correct answer. Since our model can calculate the compatibility score between the query video and each sentence choice, we use the same model as the retrieval task. We simply select the choice with the highest score as an answer. For training, we set $L = 10$ so that each training batch contains 10 pairs of videos and sentences, which include only a single correct sentence, four wrong choices, and 5 randomly selected sentences from other training data.

For Fill-in-the-Blank. The fill-in-the-blank model takes a video and a sentence with one blank, and predict a correct word for the blank. Since this task requires more difficult inference (*i.e.* selecting a word out of vocabulary $\mathcal{V}$, instead of computing a similarity score), we make two modifications as follows. First, we use deeper dimensions for layers: $d_{D1} = d_{D5} = d_{D6} = d_{D7} = 1,024$, $d_{D2} = d_{D3} = d_{D4} = 2,048$, $d_{D8} = |\mathcal{V}|$, $d_{Conv1\_1} = d_{Conv2\_1} = d_{Conv3\_1} = 1,024$, instead of the numbers in Table 1.

Second, we add a skip-connection part to our model, which is illustrated as the green paths of Fig. 2. Letting b as the blank position in the query sentence, we use the BLSTM output from the blank word token BLANK as a sentential context of the blank position: $\mathbf{t}_b = \text{D1}^w(\mathbf{w}_b)$. We make a summation between the output of [D7] $\in \mathbb{R}^{1,024}$ and the sentential context $\mathbf{t}_b \in \mathbb{R}^{1,024}$, and then feed it into [D8] to predict a word.

For training, we set the batch size as $L = 32$. We use the different objective, the cross-entropy loss, because this task is classification rather than ranking:

$$\mathcal{L} = -\log p(\mathbf{y}) + \lambda ||\theta||^2 \tag{7}$$

where θ denotes weight parameters and $\lambda = 0.0005$. We use dropout with a rate of 0.2.

4 Experiments

We report the experimental results of JSFusion models for the three tasks of LSMDC [1] and two tasks of MSR-VTT [2].

4.1 LSMDC Dataset and Tasks

The LSMDC 2017 consists of four video-language tasks for movie understanding and captioning, among which we focus on the three tasks in our experiments:

Table 2. Performance comparison for the movie retrieval task using Recall@k (R@k, higher is better) and Median Rank (MedR, lower is better). We report the results on the two datasets of LSMDC [1] (L) and MSR-VTT [2] (M).

Tasks	Movie retrieval							
Metrics	R@1		R@5		R@10		MedR	
Dataset	L	M	L	M	L	M	L	M
LSTM-fusion	3.0	3.0	8.9	9.6	15.9	17.1	95	67
SA-G+SA-FC7 [12]	3.0	3.1	8.8	9.0	13.2	13.4	114	91
LSTM+SA-FC7 [12]	3.3	3.2	10.2	11.1	15.6	15.7	88	69
C+LSTM+SA-FC7 [12]	4.3	4.2	12.6	12.9	18.9	19.9	98	55
VSE-LSTM [19]	3.1	3.8	10.4	12.7	16.5	17.1	79	66
EITanque [30]	4.7	4.7	15.9	16.6	23.4	24.1	64	41
SNUVL [29]	3.6	3.5	14.7	15.9	23.9	23.8	50	44
CT-SAN [9]	4.5	4.4	14.1	16.6	20.9	22.3	67	35
Miech *et al.* [44]	7.3	–	19.2	–	27.1	–	52	–
JSTfc	4.7	5.1	17.2	21.1	25.2	29.1	52	30
JSTlstm	7.6	9.2	19.2	28.2	27.1	41.1	36	18
JSTmax	6.7	8.8	18.0	29.8	27.2	41.0	39	17
JSTmean	7.5	9.0	20.9	27.2	28.2	40.9	36	18
JSFusion-noattention	6.4	8.7	18.4	27.4	28.4	39.5	41	19
JSFusion-noaudio	9.0	9.2	20.9	28.3	32.1	41.3	39	17
JSFusion	**9.1**	**10.2**	**21.2**	**31.2**	**34.1**	**43.2**	**36**	**13**

movie retrieval, multiple-choice test, and fill-in-the-blank. The challenge provides a subset of the LSMDC dataset, which contains a parallel corpus of 118,114 sentences and 118,081 video clips of about 4–5 s long sampled from 202 movies. We strictly follow the evaluation protocols of the challenge. We defer more details of the dataset and challenge rules to [1] and the homepage[1].

Multiple-Choice Test. Given a video query and five candidate captions, the goal is to find the correct one for the query out of five possible choices. The correct answer is the groundtruth (GT) caption and four other distractors are randomly chosen from other captions that have different activity-phrase labels from the correct answer. The evaluation metric is the percentage of correctly answered test questions out of 10,053 public-test data.

Movie Retrieval. The test set consists of 1,000 video/activity phrase pairs sampled from the LSMDC17 public-test data. Then, the objective is, given a short query activity-phrase (*e.g. answering phone*), to find its corresponding video out of 1,000 test videos. The evaluation metrics include Recall@1, Recall@5, Recall@10, and Median Rank (MedR). The Recall@k means the percentage of

[1] https://sites.google.com/site/describingmovies/lsmdc-2017.

Table 3. Left: Performance comparison for the multiple-choice test using the accuracy in percentage. We report the results on the two datasets of LSMDC (L) and MSR-VTT (M). **Right**: Accuracy comparison (in percentage) for the movie fill-in-the-blank task.

Multiple-Choice	Accuracy	
Dataset	L	M
LSTM-fusion	52.8	38.3
SA-G+SA-FC7 [12]	55.1	55.8
LSTM+SA-FC7 [12]	56.3	59.1
C+LSTM+SA-FC7 [12]	58.1	60.2
VSE-LSTM [19]	63.0	67.3
SNUVL [29]	63.1	65.4
ST-VQA-Sp.Tp [11]	63.5	66.1
EITanque [30]	63.7	65.5
CT-SAN [9]	63.8	66.4
MLB [45]	69.0	76.1
JSTfc	64.7	68.7
JSTlstm	72.1	79.7
JSTmax	68.3	74.4
JSTmean	70.2	80.0
JSFusion-noattention	69.4	79.2
JSFusion-VGG-noaudio	68.7	75.6
JSFusion-noaudio	72.5	82.9
JSFusion	**73.5**	**83.4**

Fill-in-the-Blank	Accuracy
Text-only BLSTM [34]	32.0
Text-only Human [34]	30.2
GoogleNet-2D + C3D [34]	35.7
Ask Your Neurons [46]	33.2
Merging-LSTM [35]	34.2
SNUVL [29]	38.0
CT-SAN [9]	41.9
LR/RL LSTMs [36]	40.9
LR/RL LSTMs (Ensemble) [36]	43.5
MLB [45]	41.6
JSTfc	42.9
JSTlstm	43.7
JSTmax	41.3
JSTmean	44.2
JSFusion-noattention	44.5
JSFusion-VGG-noaudio	44.2
JSFusion-noaudio	45.26
JSFusion	**45.52**
Human [34]	68.7

GT videos in the first k retrieved videos, and the MedR indicates the median rank of GT videos. The challenge winner is determined by the metric of Recall@10.

Movie Fill-in-the-Blank. This track is related to visual question answering. The task is, given a video clip and a sentence with a blank in it, to predict a single correct word for the blank. The test set includes 30,000 examples from 10,000 clips (*i.e.* about 3 blanks per sentence). The evaluation metric is the prediction accuracy (*i.e.* the percentage of predicted words that match with GTs).

4.2 MSR-VTT-(RET/MC) Dataset and Tasks

The MSR-VTT [2] is a large-scale video description dataset. It collects 118 videos per query of 257 popular queries, and filters manually to 7,180 videos. From the videos, it selects 10 K video clips with 41.2 h and 200 K clip-sentence pairs.

Based on the MSR-VTT dataset, we newly create two video-text matching tasks: (i) multiple-choice test and (ii) video retrieval. The task objectives for these tasks are identical to those of corresponding tasks in the LSMDC benchmark. To collect annotations for the two tasks, we exactly follow the protocols that are used in the LSMDC dataset, as described in [12].

Multiple-Choice Test: We generate 2,990 questions in total for the multiple-choice test, using all the test video clips of MSR-VTT. For each test video, we use the associated GT caption for the correct answer, while randomly sampled descriptions from other test data for four negative choices.

Video Retrieval: For retrieval, we first sample 1,000 pairs of video clips and description queries from the test set of MSR-VTT We use 1,000 as the size of the test set, following the LSMDC benchmark. As a result, the retrieval task is to find out the video that corresponds to the query caption out of 1000 candidates.

4.3 Quantitative Results

Tables 2 and 3 summarize the results of our experiments for the three video-language tasks. For LSMDC experiments, we report the results in the published papers and the official leaderboard of LSMDC 2017[2]. For MSR-VTT experiments, we run some participants of LSMDC, including SNUVL, EITanque, VSE-LSTM, ST-VQA-Sp.Tp and CT-SAN, using the source codes provided by the original authors. We implement the other baselines by ourselves, only except Miech *et al.* that require an additional person tracker, which is unavailable to use. Other variants of our method will be discussed in details below in the ablation study.

Tables 2 and 3 clearly show that our JSFusion achieves the best performance with significant margins from all the baselines over the three tasks on both datasets. That is, the two components of our approach, JST and CHD, indeed helps measure better the semantic similarity between multimodal sequences than a wide range of state-of-the-art models, such as a multimodal embedding method (VSE-LSTM), a spatio-temporal attention-based QA model (ST-VQA-Sp.Tp), and a language model based QA inference (Text-only BLSTM). Encouragingly, the JSFusion single model outperforms even the ensemble method of runner-up (LR/RL LSTMs) in the fill-in-the-blank task.

Among baselines, multimodal low-rank bilinear attention network (MLB) [45] is competitive. The main differences of our model from (MLB) are two-fold. First, JSFusion embeds both a video and a sentence to feature sequences, whereas (MLB) represents the sentence as a single feature. Second, JSFusion uses the self-gating to generate fine-grained matching between all pairwise embeddings of the two sequences, while (MLB) uses the attention to find a position in the visual feature space that best fits for the sentence vector. Moreover, JSFusion consistently shows better performance than (MLB) in all experiments.

Ablation Study. We conduct ablation experiments on different variants of our JSFusion model and present the results in Tables 2 and 3. As one naive variant of our model, we test a simple LSTM baseline (LSTM-fusion) that only carries out the Hadamard product on a pair of final states of video and language LSTM encoders. That is, (LSTM-fusion) is our JSFusion model that has neither JST nor CHD, which are the two main contributions of our model. We train (LSTM-fusion) in the same way as done for the JSFusion model in Sect. 3.5.

[2] FIB: https://competitions.codalab.org/competitions/11691#results.
Multichoice: https://competitions.codalab.org/competitions/11491#results.

As easily expected, the performance of (LSTM-fusion) is significantly worse than our JSFusion in all the tasks.

To further validate the contribution of each component, we remove or replace key components of our model with simpler ones. To understand the effectiveness of BLSTM encoding, we test two baselines: (JSTfc) that replaces BLSTM with fully-connected layers and (JSTlstm) that replaces BLSTM with LSTM. (JSTmax) and (JSTmean) denote our variants that use max pooling and mean pooling, instead of the *Convk* convolutional layers in CHD. That is, they use fixed max/mean pooling operations instead of convolutions with learnable kernels. These comparisons reveal that the proposed CHD is critical to improve the performance of JSFusion nontrivially on all the tasks on both datasets. We also compare our model with (JSFusion-noattention) that discards Conv-gating operations of CHD. (JSFusion-noattention) shows nontrivial performance drops as MC (acc): $4.1\%p, 4.2\%p$, RET (R@10): $5.7\%p, 3.7\%p$ for LSMDC and MSR-VTT, respectively. Finally, we test our model with using no audio information denoted by (JSFusion-noaudio), which is also much better than other baselines but only slightly worse than our original model.

4.4 Qualitative Results

Figure 4 illustrates qualitative results of our JSFusion algorithm with correct (left) and near-miss (right) examples for each task. In each set, we show natural language query and sampled frames of a video. We present both groundtruth (GT), our prediction (Ours).

Movie Retrieval. Figure 4(a) is an example that our model can understand human behaviors like *gaze*. Figure 4(b) shows the model's failure to distinguish a small motion (*e.g.* facial expression), and simply retrieve the videos containing the face of a *woman*. Figure 4(c) shows that our model successfully catches the features of *horses* in both web videos and 3D animation, and correctly select the highest ranking video by focusing on the word *stall*. In Fig. 4(d), although the model can retrieve relevant videos of *cooking with bowl*, it fails to find out the answer video that contains the query description of *baking mix*.

Movie Multiple-Choice Test. Figure 4(e) delivers an evidence that our model uses the whole sentence for computing matching scores, because the model successfully chooses ⑤ instead of ① that shares the same phrases (*e.g. shakes his head*). Figure 4(f) is an example of focusing on a wrong video subsequence, where our model chooses the word *club* by looking at a subsequence with crowded people, but the answer is related to another subsequence with *grandmother*. Figure 4(g) is an example that the model learns words in a phrase. Choice ④ can be very tempting, since it contains the word *kids*, *tv* and *show*. But our model successfully choose the right answer by identifying that *kids tv show* and *kids in tv show* mean differently. Figure 4(h) shows that our model fails to distinguish the details.

Movie Fill-in-the-Blank. In Fig. 4(i), the model successfully finds the answer by using both structural information of a sentence and a video (*e.g. door* is a

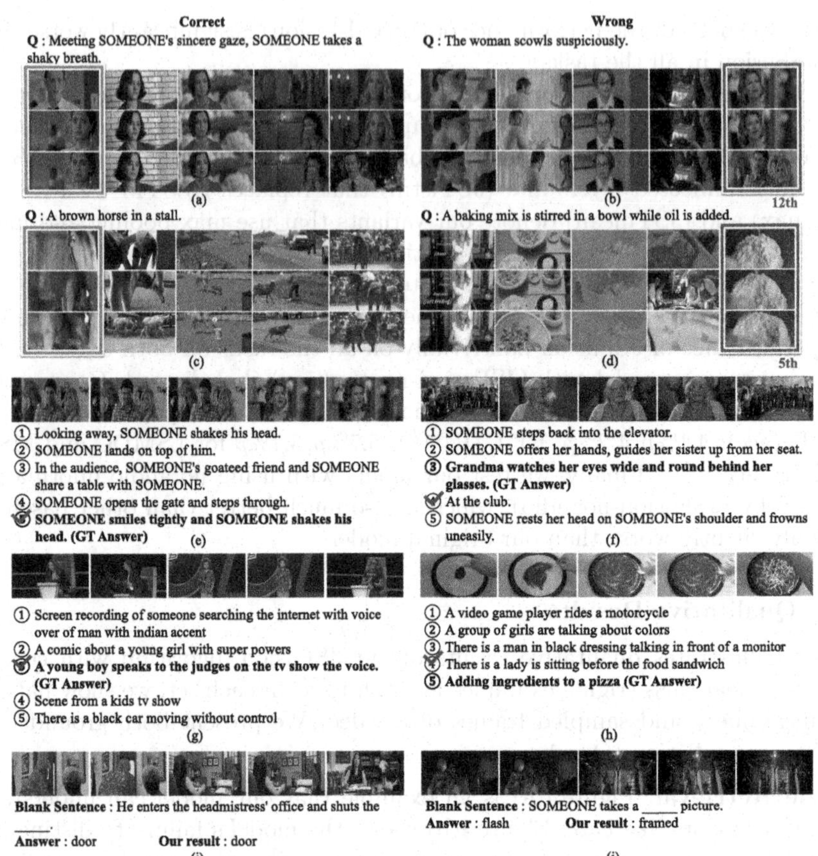

Fig. 4. Qualitative examples of the three video-language tasks: movie retrieval on LSMDC (a)–(b) and MSR-VTT-RET (c)–(d), multiple-choice on LSMDC (e)–(f) and MSR-VTT-MC (g)–(h), and (i)–(j) fill-in-the-blank on LSMDC. The left column shows correct examples, while the right column shows near-miss examples. In (b),(d), we show our retrieval ranks of the GT clips (in the red box). (Color figure online)

likely word after *shuts the*). Figure 4(j) is an example that the model focuses too much on the word *picture* that follows the blank, instead of visual information, and thus choose a wrong answer *framed picture* rather than *flash picture.*

5 Conclusion

We proposed the Joint Sequence Fusion (JSFusion) model for measuring hierarchical semantic similarity between two multimodal sequence data. The two key components of the model, Joint Semantic Tensor (JST) and Convolutional Hierarchical Decoder (CHD), are easily adaptable in many video-and-language tasks, including multimodal matching or video question answering. We demonstrated that our method significantly improved the performance of video understanding through natural language description. Our method achieved the best performance in challenge tracks of LSMDC, and outperformed many state-of-the-art models for VQA and retrieval tasks on the MSR-VTT dataset.

Moving forward, we plan to expand the applicability of JSFusion; since our model is usable to any multimodal sequence data, we can explore other retrieval tasks of different modalities, such as videos-to-voices or text-to-human motions.

Acknowledgements.. We thank Jisung Kim and Antoine Miech for helpful comments about the model. This research was supported by Brain Research Program by National Research Foundation of Korea (NRF) (2017M3C7A1047860).

References

1. Rohrbach, A., et al.: Movie Description. arXiv:1605.03705 (2016)
2. Xu, J., Mei, T., Yao, T., Rui, Y.: MSR-VTT: a large video description dataset for bridging video and language. In: CVPR (2016)
3. Chen, D.L., Dolan, W.B.: Collecting highly parallel data for paraphrase evaluation. In: ACL (2011)
4. Donahue, J., et al.: Long-term Recurrent Convolutional Networks for Visual Recognition and Description. In: CVPR (2015)
5. Guadarrama, S., et al.: YouTube2Text: recognizing and describing arbitrary activities using semantic hierarchies and zero-shot recognition. In: ICCV (2013)
6. Rohrbach, A., Rohrbach, M., Schiele, B.: The long-short story of movie description. In: GCPR (2015)
7. Venugopalan, S., Marcus, R., Jeffrey, D., Raymond, M., Trevor, D., Kate, S.: Sequence to sequence - video to text. In: ICCV (2015)
8. Xu, R., Xiong, C., Chen, W., Corso, J.J.: Jointly modeling deep video and compositional text to bridge vision and language in a unified framework. In: AAAI (2015)
9. Yu, Y., Ko, H., Choi, J., Kim, G.: End-to-end concept word detection for video captioning, retrieval, and question answering. In: CVPR (2017)
10. Tapaswi, M., Zhu, Y., Stiefelhagen, R., Torralba, A., Urtasun, R., Fidler, S.: MovieQA: understanding stories in movies through question-answering. In: CVPR (2016)
11. Jang, Y., Song, Y., Yu, Y., Kim, Y., Kim, G.: TGIF-QA: toward spatio-temporal reasoning in visual question answering. In: CVPR (2017)
12. Torabi, A., Tandon, N., Sigal, L.: Learning language-visual embedding for movie understanding with natural-language. arXiv:1609.08124 (2016)
13. Otani, M., Nakashima, Y., Rahtu, E., Heikkilä, J., Yokoya, N.: Learning joint representations of videos and sentences with web image search. arXiv:1608.02367 (2016)
14. Laptev, I., Lindeberg, T.: Space-time Interest Points. In: ICCV (2003)
15. Laptev, I., Marszalek, M., Schmid, C., Rozenfeld, B.: Learning realistic human actions from movies. In: CVPR (2008)
16. Soomro, K., Zamir, A.R., Shah, M.: UCF101: A Dataset of 101 Human Actions Classes from Videos in the Wild (2012)
17. Karpathy, A., Toderici, G., Shetty, S., Leung, T., Sukthankar, R., Fei-Fei, L.: Large-scale video classification with convolutional neural networks. In: CVPR (2014)

18. Caba Heilbron, F., Escorcia, V., Ghanem, B., Carlos Niebles, J.: ActivityNet: a large-scale video benchmark for human activity understanding. In: CVPR (2015)
19. Kiros, R., Salakhutdinov, R., Zemel, R.S.: Unifying visual-semantic embeddings with multimodal neural language models. In: TACL (2014)
20. Frome, A., et al.: DeViSE: a deep visual-semantic embedding model. In: NIPS (2013)
21. Socher, R., Karpathy, A., Le, Q.V., Manning, C.D., Ng, A.Y.: Grounded compositional semantics for finding and describing images with sentences. TACL (2014)
22. Socher, R., Lin, C.C., Manning, C., Ng, A.Y.: Parsing natural scenes and natural language with recursive neural networks. In: ICML (2011)
23. Socher, R., Bauer, J., Manning, C.D., et al.: Parsing with compositional vector grammars. In: ACL (2013)
24. Hodosh, M., Young, P., Hockenmaier, J.: Framing image description as a ranking task: data, models and evaluation metrics. JAIR **47**, 853–899 (2013)
25. Lin, D., Fidler, S., Kong, C., Urtasun, R.: Visual semantic search: retrieving videos via complex textual queries. In: CVPR (2014)
26. Vendrov, I., Kiros, R., Fidler, S., Urtasun, R.: Order-embeddings of images and language. arXiv:1511.06361 (2015)
27. Hu, R., Xu, H., Rohrbach, M., Feng, J., Saenko, K., Darrell, T.: Natural language object retrieval. In: CVPR (2016)
28. Mao, J., Huang, J., Toshev, A., Camburu, O., Yuille, A.L., Murphy, K.: Generation and comprehension of unambiguous object descriptions. In: CVPR (2016)
29. Yu, Y., Ko, H., Choi, J., Kim, G.: Video captioning and retrieval models with semantic attention. arXiv preprint arXiv:1610.02947 (2016)
30. Kaufman, D., Levi, G., Hassner, T., Wolf, L.: Temporal tessellation for video annotation and summarization. In: ICCV (2017)
31. Malinowski, M., Fritz, M.: A multi-world approach to question answering about real-world scenes based on uncertain input. In: NIPS (2014)
32. Antol, S., et al.: VQA: visual question answering. In: ICCV (2015)
33. Goyal, Y., Khot, T., Summers-Stay, D., Batra, D., Parikh, D.: Making the V in VQA matter: elevating the role of image understanding in visual question answering. In: CVPR (2017)
34. Maharaj, T., Ballas, N., Courville, A.C., Pal, C.J.: A dataset and exploration of models for understanding video data through fill-in-the-blank question-answering. arXiv:1611.07810
35. Mazaheri, A., Zhang, D., Shah, M.: Video fill in the blank with merging LSTMs. arXiv:1610.04062 (2016)
36. Mazaheri, A., Zhang, D., Shah, M.: Video fill in the blank using LR/RL LSTMs with spatial-temporal attentions. In: ICCV (2017)
37. Pennington, J., Socher, R., Manning, C.D.: GloVe: global vectors for word representation. In: EMNLP (2014)
38. He, K., Zhang, X., Ren, S., Sun, J.: Deep residual learning for image recognition. In: CVPR (2016)
39. Hershey, S., et al.: CNN architectures for large-scale audio classification. In: ICASSP (2017)
40. Schuster, M., Paliwal, K.K.: Bidirectional recurrent neural networks. In: IEEE TSP (1997)
41. Hochreiter, S., Schmidhuber, J.: Long short-term memory. In: IEEE (1997)
42. Kingma, D., Ba, J.: Adam: a method for stochastic optimization. In: ICLR (2015)
43. Ioffe, S., Szegedy, C.: Batch normalization: accelerating deep network training by reducing internal covariate shift. In: ICML (2015)

44. Miech, A., Alayrac, J.B., Bojanowski, P., Laptev, I., Sivic, J.: Learning from video and text via large-scale discriminative clustering. In: ICCV (2017)
45. Kim, J.H., On, K.W., Lim, W., Kim, J., Ha, J.W., Zhang, B.T.: Hadamard product for low-rank bilinear pooling. In: ICLR (2017)
46. Tzeng, E., Hoffman, J., Darrell, T., Saenko, K.: Simultaneous deep transfer across domains and tasks. In: ICCV (2015)

Saliency Detection in 360° Videos

Ziheng Zhang, Yanyu Xu, Jingyi Yu, and Shenghua Gao(✉)

ShanghaiTech University, Shanghai, China
{zhangzh,xuyy2,yujingyi,gaoshh}@shanghaitech.edu.cn

Abstract. This paper presents a novel spherical convolutional neural network based scheme for saliency detection for 360° videos. Specifically, in our spherical convolution neural network definition, kernel is defined on a spherical crown, and the convolution involves the rotation of the kernel along the sphere. Considering that the 360° videos are usually stored with equirectangular panorama, we propose to implement the spherical convolution on panorama by stretching and rotating the kernel based on the location of patch to be convolved. Compared with existing spherical convolution, our definition has the parameter sharing property, which would greatly reduce the parameters to be learned. We further take the temporal coherence of the viewing process into consideration, and propose a sequential saliency detection by leveraging a spherical U-Net. To validate our approach, we construct a large-scale 360° videos saliency detection benchmark that consists of 104 360° videos viewed by 20+ human subjects. Comprehensive experiments validate the effectiveness of our spherical U-net for 360° video saliency detection.

Keywords: Spherical convolution · Video saliency detection
360° VR videos

1 Introduction

Visual attention prediction, commonly known as saliency detection, is the task of inferring the objects or regions that attract human's attention in a scene. It is an important way to mimic human's perception and has numerous applications in computer vision [1–3]. By far, almost all existing works focus on image or video saliency detection, where the participants are asked to look at images or videos with a limited field-of-view (FoV). And an eye tracker is adopted to record their eye fixations. The process, however, differs from the natural way human eyes perceive the 3D world: in real world, a participant actually **actively** explores the environment by rotating the head, seeking an omnidirectional understanding of the scene. In this paper, we propose to mimic this process by exploring the saliency detection problem on 360° videos.

Despite significant progresses in Convolutional Neural Networks (CNN) [4] for saliency detection in images/videos [5,6], there are very little, if few, studies on panoramic saliency detection. The brute-force approach of warping the

Z. Zhang and Y. Xu—equal contributions.

V. Ferrari et al. (Eds.): ECCV 2018, LNCS 11211, pp. 504–520, 2018.
https://doi.org/10.1007/978-3-030-01234-2_30

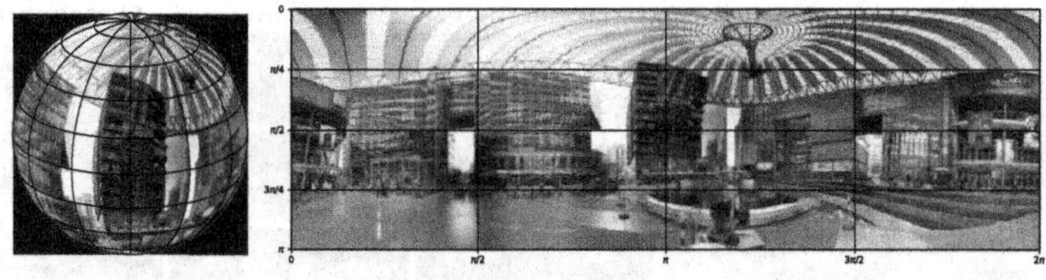

Fig. 1. Distortion introduced by equirectangular projection. **Left:** 360° image on sphere; **Right:** 360° image on equirectangular panorama

panoramic contents onto perspective views is neither efficient nor robust: partitioning the panoramas into smaller tiles and project the results using local perspective projection can lead to high computational overhead as saliency detection would need to be applied on each tile. Directly applying perspective based saliency detection onto the panorama images is also problematic: panoramic images exhibit geometric distortion where many useful saliency cues are not valid. Some latest approaches attempt to employ tailored convolutional networks for the spherical panoramic data. Yet, they either focus on coping with spherical data with radius components while ignoring distortions caused by equiangular cube-sphere representation [7], or dynamically stretching the kernels to fit the local content and therefore cannot achieve kernel parameter sharing [8]. Actually, when human explores the 360° contents, our brain uses the same mechanism to detect saliency when changing the view angle or FOV. In other words, if we leverage the CNN for 360° video saliency detection, the convolution operation corresponding to different view angle/FOV should maintain the same kernels.

To better cope the 360° video saliency detection task, we propose a new type of spherical convolutional neural networks. Specifically, we define the kernel on a spherical crown, and the convolution corresponds to the rotation of kernel on sphere. This definition has the parameter sharing property. Further, considering that the 360° videos are usually stored with equirectangular panorama, we propose to extend the spherical convolution to the panorama case by re-sampling the kernel based on the position of the patch to be convolved. We further propose a spherical mean square loss to compensate the distortion effect caused by equirectangular projection. In 360° videos, the participants search the environment continuously. This implies that the gaze in the previous frame affects the gaze in the subsequent frames. Then we propose to leverage such temporal coherence for efficient saliency detection by instantiating the spherical convolutional neural networks with a novel spherical U-Net [9]. Experiments validate the effectiveness of our scheme.

By far, nearly all saliency detection datasets are based on narrow FoV perspective images while only a few datasets on 360° images. To validate our approach, we construct a large-scale 360° videos saliency detection benchmark that consists of 104 360° videos viewed by 20+ human subjects. The duration of each video ranges from 20 s to 60 s. We use the a Glass eye tracker to track gaze. Figure 2 shows some example frames on several 360° videos in our dataset. We compare our spherical convolutional neural network with several state-of-the-

Fig. 2. The examples of five domains in our 360° video dataset

art techniques on this new data and show our technique significantly outperforms prior art in accuracy and robustness.

The contributions of this paper are summarized as follows: (i) A new type of spherical convolutional neural networks is defined, and the kernels are shared across all patches on the sphere. Thus our definition is more natural and useful for spherical saliency detection. We further extend it to panorama case; (ii) We propose a sequential saliency detection scheme and instantiate the spherical convolutional neural networks with a spherical U-net architecture for frame-wise saliency detection; (iii) We build a large-scale 360° video saliency detection dataset which would facilitate the evaluation of saliency detection in 360° videos. The dataset and code have been released to facilitate further research on 360° video saliency detection[1].

2 Related Work

2.1 Convolution Neural Networks for Spherical Data

Though CNN has demonstrated their effectiveness for many computer vision tasks [10,11], the data fed into traditional CNN are perspective images. To tackle the spherical data, methods in [12,13] firstly project a spherical image with equirectangular projection, then standard CNN is applied. However, such equirectangular projects introduce distortion in Fig. 1. The patches of the same size on sphere may correspond to regions of different shapes based on their coordinates (θ, ϕ). So the standard convolution with the shared kernels is no longer perceptually meaningful. To solve this problem, [8] propose to stretch kernels in standard CNN to fit the shape of the patch on the equirectangular plane in convolution. This can avoid the distortion problem to some extent. But the filters shape in their solution depends on the longitude of the patch on the sphere, consequently, the kernels in their method are not shared, which introduces the expensive computational and storage costs. Further, Boomsma et al. [7] propose to adopt the equiangular cubed-sphere representation for sphere data representation, then concentric cubed-sphere convolution is applied. But their solution is proposed for sphere data with radii components (like a solid ball), which differs from the data type of ours. Besides, equiangular cubed-sphere representation still

[1] GitHub: https://github.com/xuyanyu-shh/Saliency-detection-in-360-video.

introduce distortion in each facet, which damages to the accuracy of convolution. Different from these work, in [14,15], the spherical image is repeatedly projected to tangent planes at all locations, and the convolution is conducted on these planes. Although such solution improves accuracy, it also brings expensive computational costs. Further, the disjoint projection planes make the intermediate representation cannot be shared for higher layer convolution. Recently, Cohen et al.[16] propose a new type of Spherical CNN on SO(3) manifold, and their solution is expressive and rotation-equivariant. With Fast Fourier Transform, their solution can be greatly accelerated. However, the concept of SO(3) CNN is not so adhere to our intuition to process 2D spherical images and quite distincts from the concept of planner CNN.

Though many CNN models have been proposed for spherical data, none are customized for 360° videos. Actually, when we change the FOV in 360° videos, our brain actually uses the same mechanism for environment exploration. In other words, the kernels used for saliency detection should be shared across all views. This motivates us to design a new type of spherical CNN: we define kernels with the spherical crown shape, we rotate and convolve the kernel with patches on the sphere-polar coordinate system. [2] In this way, the kernel can be shared. So our solution is more natural and more interpretable for saliency detection in 360° videos.

2.2 Video Saliency Detection

Many efforts have been done to study the video saliency detection, either hand-crafted features based methods [17–20], or deep learning based methods [6,21–24], yet the study of video saliency detection in 360° videos is still at its primitive stage. [12,25] are two pioneer work along this direction, but the 360° data used in these work are static images. Actually, the videos with dynamic contents are more common in real applications. To understand the behavior of human in dynamic 360° videos, especially 360° sports videos, Hu et al.propose to predict the salient objects by feeding projected panorama images into CNN directly. However, the distortion of projection is not considered, which would reduce the accuracy. In addition, the salient objects are manually labeled, which does not necessarily reflect the real behavior of human visual attention. In order to better understand the users' behavior in VR scenes, we propose to study the eye fixation in 360° videos. To the best of our knowledge, this is the first work that works on eye fixation prediction in 360° videos. We also build a dataset to facilitate the evaluation of our work.

[2] Since the sphere image is usually stored with planar format, we actually project spherical image on the Euclidean plane with equirectangular projection, then we re-sample kernel based on the shape of the projected patch to be convolved, after that we convolved the target patch with the transformed kernel.

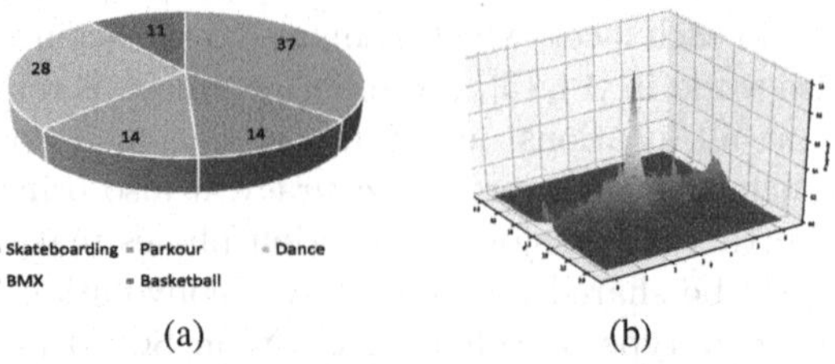

(a) (b)

Fig. 3. Dataset Analysis: (a) the distribution of the five sports domains based on the number of videos; (b) the distribution of eye fixations on equirectangular panorama. (Best viewed in color)

3 360° Dynamic Video Saliency Detection Dataset

3.1 Data Collection

We collect the 360° videos from Sports-360 dataset [13], and remove the video clips whose length is less than 20 s[3], and use the remaining 104 video clips as the data used for saliency detection in 360° videos. The video contents involve five sports (*i.e.* basketball, parkour, BMX, skateboarding, and dance), and the duration of each video is between 20 and 60 s. Figure 3(a) shows the distribution of five sports videos. Then we display the videos with an HTC VIVE HMD and a '*7invensun a-Glass*' eye tracker is embedded into the HMD to record the eye fixation points of the participants when they watching videos.

We recruit 27 volunteers (between 20 and 24 years) to participant in the experiments. All 104 videos are divided into 3 sessions and each session contains 35 360° videos. Volunteers are asked to watch 360° videos at a fixed starting location ($\theta = 90, \phi = 180$) in random orders. We set a shorter break (20 s) between 2 videos and a longer break (3 min) after watching 15 videos. We also calibrate the system after the long break. In the end, each video is watched by at least 20 volunteers. The total time used for data collection is about 2000 min.

Distribution of Gaze Points Figure 3 (b) shows the distribution of all eye fixation angle in θ, ϕ of all participants over all the videos on equirectangular panorama. The peak in the center of panorama ($\theta = 90, \phi = 180$) is because all participants explore the environment with the fixed starting location. Further, we can see that the eye fixation points mostly centered around the equator, which means the volunteers tend to explore the environment along the horizontal direction, and they seldom look down/up. There are almost no eye fixation points around north/south pole.

[3] We only use videos longer than 20 s rather than entire Sports-360 dataset because in [12] Sitzmann et al.evaluate the exploration time for a given still scene, and show that 'on average, users fully explored each scene after about 19 s'.

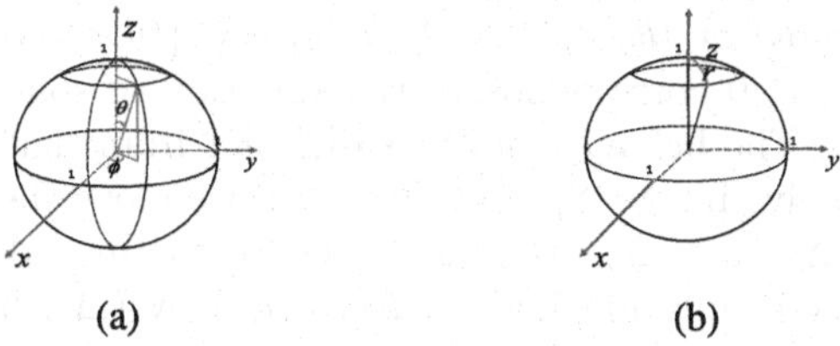

Fig. 4. (a) Spherical coordinate system: ϕ is the angle between X axis and the orthogonal projection of the line on the XOY plane, and θ is the angle between the Z axis and the line; (b) Spherical crown kernel: the red line represents the radius r. (Best viewed in color)

4 Spherical Convolutional Neural Networks

In this section, we introduce our spherical convolution on sphere and its extension on panorama. A new spherical mean square error (sphere MSE) loss is also introduced for spherical convolution on panorama. Note that the convolution operation in deep learning usually refers to correlation in math.

The spherical convolution. Spherical convolution is an operation on feature map f and kernel k on sphere manifold S^2. S^2 is defined as the set of points $x \in \mathbb{R}^3$ with norm 1, which can be parameterized by spherical coordinates $\theta \in [0, \pi]$ and $\phi \in [0, 2\pi]$ as shown in Fig. 4(a). To simplify the the notation, here we model spherical images and filters as continuous functions $f : S^2 \rightarrow \mathbb{R}^K$, where K is the number of channels. Then the spherical convolution is formulated as [26]:

$$[f * k](x) = \int_{S^2} f(Rn)k(R^{-1}x)dR \tag{1}$$

where n is the north pole and R is rotations on sphere represented by 3×3 matrices.

In this paper, filter k only have non-zero values in spherical crown centered at north pole, whose size is parameterized by r_k, which corresponds to orthodromic distance between north pole and borderline of the crown as shown in Fig. 4 (b). So the radius r_k controls the number of parameters in kernel k and the size of local receptive field. Larger r_k means there are more parameters in k and the local receptive field is larger.

Convolution on equirectangular panorama. The spherical images or videos are usually stored as 2-D panorama through equirectangular projection represented by (θ, ϕ) ($\theta \in [0, \pi]$ and $\phi \in [0, 2\pi]$). So we extend Eq. (1) to the convolution between feature map f and kernel k on projected panorama as

$$[f * k](\theta, \phi) = \iint f(\theta', \phi')k(\theta' - \theta, \phi' - \phi) \sin\theta' d\theta' d\phi' \tag{2}$$

There are several differences between spherical convolution on equirectangular and convolution on perspective image. Firstly, we denote the points set for the kernel centered at (θ_0, ϕ_0) as $\mathcal{D}_k(\theta_0, \phi_0) = \{(\theta, \phi) | g(\theta, \phi, \theta_0, \phi_0) \leq 0\}$, where $g(\theta, \phi, \theta_0, \phi_0) \leq 0$ corresponds to the equation of sphere crown (kernel) centered at (θ_0, ϕ_0). The behavior of $\mathcal{D}_k$ is different from that in standard convolution for perspective image. Specifically, when we move the kernel and when its center is $(\theta_0 + \Delta_\theta, \phi_0 + \Delta_\phi)$, the points set for the moved kernel cannot be directly obtained by simply moving the $\mathcal{D}_k(\theta_0, \phi_0)$ by $(\Delta_\theta, \Delta_\phi)$, which can be mathematically written as follows:

$$\begin{aligned} \mathcal{D}_k(\theta_0 + \Delta_\theta, \phi_0 + \Delta_\phi) &= \{(\theta, \phi) | g(\theta - \Delta_\theta, \phi - \Delta_\phi, \theta_0, \phi_0) \leq 0\} \\ &\neq \{(\theta + \Delta_\theta, \phi + \Delta_\phi) | g(\theta, \phi, \theta_0, \phi_0) \leq 0\} \end{aligned} \tag{3}$$

Secondly, there is a $\sin\theta'$ term in the integrand in spherical convolution in Eq. (2), which causes the different behavior of spherical convolution compared with the convolution for projective images. Thirdly, there does not exist padding in spherical convolution in Eq. (1) owing to the omnibearing view of 360° images. But, it indeed needs padding in convolution on equirectangular panorama in Eq. (2), owing to the storage format. The padding needed here is circle shift. For example, when kernel locates at the far left region, it needs to borrow some pixels from far right region for computing convolution. To simplify the notation, we also term the convolution on equirectangular panorama as spherical convolution. In this way, we can implement convolution on sphere by using convolution on equirectangular panorama.

We define sample rate on equirectangular panorama as the number of pixels per rad. So sample rate of panorama is $sr^\theta = H/\pi, sr^\phi = W/2\pi$ along θ and ϕ direction, respectively. Here H, W is the height and width of panorama. As a special case, for the kernel with radius equalling r_k, when the kernel is centered at north pole, its projection on equirectangular panorama would be a rectangular, whose size is denoted as $W_k \times H_k$, and the sample rate along θ and ϕ direction are given by $sr_k^\theta = H_k/r_k, sr_k^\phi = W_k/2\pi$.

Implement Details. For discrete spherical convolution on panorama, we set the kernel parameters to be learnt as the equirectangular projection of kernel centered at the north pole ($\theta \leq r_k$). So the kernel projected on equirectangular panorama corresponds to a rectangular of size $W_k \times H_k$. It is worth noting we can also set the kernels at other positions rather than north pole, yet sample grid of the kernel will change accordingly. The discrete spherical convolution on equirectangular panorama includes the following steps: determine non-zero region of kernel centered at (θ_i, ϕ_i) and obtain the set of points fallen into the kernel area $\mathcal{D}_k(\theta_i, \phi_i)$, rotate those points back to $\mathcal{D}_k(0, 0)$, re-sample the original kernel to find values for each sampling points in $\mathcal{D}_k(\theta_i, \phi_i)$.

Determine the points fallen into $\mathcal{D}_k(\theta_i, \phi_i)$. For the spherical crown kernel with radius r_k centered at (θ_i, ϕ_i), the points fallen into this kernel area with coordinates (θ, ϕ) satisfy the following equation:

$$\sin\theta_i \cos\phi_i \sin\theta \cos\phi + \sin\theta_i \sin\phi_i \sin\theta \sin\phi + \cos\theta_i \cos\theta = \cos\theta_k \tag{4}$$

which can be simplified as

$$\sin(\phi + \psi) = C \tag{5}$$

Algorithm 1. Obtain the set of grid points on the kernel area

Input: kernel radius r_k, kernel location θ_k, ϕ_k.
Output: The set of grid points on the kernel area S

$S \leftarrow \emptyset$
Calculate range of Θ:
$\Theta \in [\max(0, \theta_k - r_k), \min(\theta_k + r_k, \pi)]$
Calculate range of Φ for each $\theta \in \Theta$:
for Each $\theta \in \Theta$ **do**
    Find the solution of equation Eq. 5
    if There exists infinitely many solutions **then**
        $\phi \in [0, \pi]$
    else if There exists two solutions $\phi_1 < \phi_2$ **then**
        $\phi \in [\phi_1, \phi_2]$
    else if There exists no solutions **then**
        No grid points (θ, ϕ) on the kernel area
    end if
    Add (θ, ϕ) to S.
end for

where $\sin\psi = \frac{a}{\sqrt{a^2+b^2}}$, $\cos\psi = \frac{b}{\sqrt{a^2+b^2}}$, $C = \frac{d-c}{\sqrt{a^2+b^2}}$ and $a = \sin\theta_i \cos\phi_i \sin\theta$, $b = \sin\theta_i \sin\phi_i \sin\theta$, $c = \cos\theta_i \cos\theta$ and $d = \cos\theta_k$.

Once the kernel area on sphere is determined, we can sample the corresponding points on panorama to obtain the points needed for convolution. We list the main steps for such stage in Algorithm 1.

Rotate the set of Sampled Points Back to North Pole. Now that we have the sampled points of current kernel area, we also need to determine the correspondences between them to those kernel values centered at the north pole. To do this, we rotate these points back to original kernel region by leveraging matrix multiplication between their cartesian coordinate representations and rotation matrix along Y as well as Z axis. Note that after rotation, the sampled points might lie between original kernel points centered at the north pole.

Re-sample the Original Kernel. In order to obtain kernel values for sampled points that lie between original kernel points centered at the north pole, we use grid sampling technique as used in Spatial Transform Network [27], which is basically a general interpolation method for such re-sampling problem on 2D image. The third row in Fig. 5 shows the sampling grid corresponding to kernel located at $\theta = 0, \pi/4, \pi/2, 3\pi/4, \pi$ and $\phi = \pi$.

Finally, the result of spherical convolution is given by sum of element-wise multiplication between re-sampled kernel points and corresponding panorama points, divided by the total number of re-sampled kernel points.

Properties of spherical convolution. The sphere convolution has the following three properties: sparse interactions, parameter sharing, and equivariant representations.

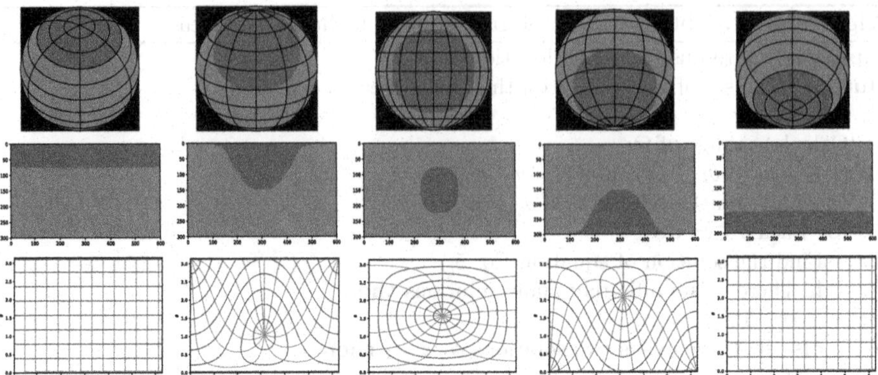

Fig. 5. Parameter sharing. This figure indicates how spherical crown kernel changes on sphere and projected panorama from north pole to south pole with angle interval equalling $\pi/4$. The first raw is the region of the spherical crown kernel in sphere. The second raw shows the region of spherical crown kernel in the projected panorama. The third row shows sampling grid corresponding to each kernel location. Red curve represents θ sampling grid and blue curve represents ϕ sampling grid

- **Sparse interactions.** Standard CNNs usually have sparse interactions, which is accomplished by making the kernel smaller than the input. Our proposed spherical CNN also have this important property. Such sparse connection greatly reduces the number of parameters to be learned. Further, the convolution in higher layers corresponds to gradually larger local receptive field, which allows the network to efficiently model the complicated interactions between input and output.
- **Parameter sharing.** Similar to the standard convolution for perspective image, the parameters of spherical crown kernel is the same everywhere on the sphere, which means the kernel is shared. This would greatly reduce the storage requirements of the model as well as the number of parameters to be learned. Kernel at different location is re-sampled as shown in Fig. 5.
- **Equivariant representations.** In both standard convolutions for perspective image and spherical convolution, the parameter sharing makes the layers with equivariance to translation property, which means if the input changes, the output changes in the same way.

4.1 Spherical Mean Squared Error (MSE) Loss

Mean Squared Error (MSE) loss function is widely used in perspective image based CNN. However, the standard MSE is designed for perspective image. For perspective image, discretization is performed homogeneously in space, which differs from the case of panorama. To adopt MSE loss to panorama, we weight the square error for each pixel on panorama with it's solid angle on sphere before average them.

We define the solid angle in steradian equals the area of a segment of a unit sphere in the same way a planar angle in radians equals the length of an arc of

Table 1. The architecture of the CNN

Layer	Operation	Input size	Input source	Output size	Kernel radius	Kernel size
0	Input	-	-	3 × 150 × 300	-	-
1	Spherical Conv	3 × 150 × 300	Layer 0	64 × 150 × 300	$\pi/32$	(8,16)
2	Max pooling	64 × 150 × 300	Layer 1	64 × 75 × 150	$\pi/32$	(8,16)
3	Spherical conv	64 × 75 × 150	Layer 2	128 × 75 × 150	$\pi/16$	(4,8)
4	Max pooling	128 × 75 × 150	Layer 3	128 × 38 × 75	$\pi/16$	(4,8)
5	Spherical conv	128 × 38 × 75	Layer 4	256 × 38 × 75	$\pi/4$	(4,8)
6	Max pooling	256 × 38 × 75	Layer 5	256 × 19 × 38	$\pi/4$	(4,8)
7	Spherical conv	256 × 19 × 38	Layer 6	256 × 19 × 38	π	(8,16)
8	Up-sampling	256 × 19 × 38	Layer 7	256 × 38 × 75	$\pi/4$	(4,8)
9	Spherical conv	(256 + 256) × 38 × 75	Layer 8 & 6	128 × 38 × 75	$\pi/4$	(4,8)
10	Up-sampling	128 × 38 × 75	Layer 9	128 × 75 × 150	$\pi/16$	(4,8)
11	Spherical conv	(128 + 128) × 75 × 150	Layer 10 & 5	64 × 75 × 150	$\pi/16$	(4,8)
12	Up-sampling	64 × 75 × 150	Layer 11	64 × 150 × 300	$\pi/32$	(4,8)
13	Spherical conv	(64 + 64) × 150 × 300	Layer 12 & 3	1 × 150 × 300	$\pi/32$	(4,8)

a unit circle, which is the following ratio: $\Omega = A/r^2$, where A is the spherical surface area and r is the radius of the considered sphere. Thus, for a unit sphere, the solid angle of the spherical crown with radius r and centered at the north pole is given as: $\Omega = 2\pi(1 - \cos r)$. It is desirable that the image patch corresponding to the same solid angle would have the same weight for sphere MSE, thus we arrive at the following objective function:

$$\mathcal{L} = \frac{1}{n}\sum_{k=1}^{n}\sum_{\theta=0,\phi=0}^{\Theta,\Phi} w_{\theta,\phi}(S_{\theta,\phi}^{(k)} - \hat{S}_{\theta,\phi}^{(k)})^2 \tag{6}$$

where $\hat{S}^{(k)}$ and $S^{(k)}$ are the ground truth saliency map and predicted saliency map for the kth image, and $w_{\theta,\phi}$ is weights for each points which is proportional to its solid angle and $w_{i,j} \propto \Omega(\theta, \phi)$. $\Omega(\theta, \phi)$ is solid angle corresponding to the sampled area on saliency map located at (θ, ϕ). In our implementation, we just set $w_{\theta,\phi} = \Omega(\theta, \phi)/4\pi$ (4π is the solid angle of the unit ball).

5 Spherical U-Net Based 360° Video Saliency Detection

5.1 Problem Formulation

Given a sequence of frames $V = \{v_1, v_2, \ldots, v_T\}$, our goal is to predict the saliency map corresponding to this video $S = \{s_2, s_2, s_3, \ldots, s_T\}$. So deep learning based 360° video saliency detection aims at learning a mapping G that maps input V to S. However, different from perspective videos whose saliency merely depends on the video contents, where a participant look at in 360° videos also depends on the starting position of the participant. We define s_0 as the eye fixation map at the starting position, which is the saliency map corresponding to the starting point, then the video saliency detection can be formulated as

$$G^* = \arg\min_F \|S - G(V, s_0)\|_F^2 \tag{7}$$

In practice, we can initialize s_0 with a Gaussian kernel centered at the staring position. Further, the participants actually watch the 360° video in a frame-by-frame manner, and the eye fixation in previous frame helps the prediction of that in next frame. So we can encode such prior into the objective and arrive at the following objective :

$$F^* = \arg\min_F \sum_{t=1}^{T} \|s_t - F(v_t, s_{t-1})\|^2 \quad (8)$$

Here F is the prediction function which takes the saliency map of previous frame and video frame at current moment as input for saliency prediction of current moment. Inspired by the success of U-Net [9] we propose to adapted it with a Spherical U-Net as F for the frame-wise saliency detection.

5.2 Spherical U-Net

The network architecture of Spherical U-Net is listed in Table 1. The input to the network is projected spherical images v_t at time t and project spherical saliency map s_{t-1} at time $t-1$. Similar to U-net [9], our spherical U-net also consists of a contracting path (left side) and an expansive path (right side). In the contracting path, there are three spherical convolutional layers followed by rectified linear unit (ReLU) and a 2×2 spherical max pooling is adopted to down-sample the data. The expansive path consists of three spherical convolutional layers followed by ReLU and up-sampling. For the last three spherical convolutional layer, their inputs are concatenation of the outputs of their previous layer and the corresponding layer with the same output size from the contracting path. A spherical convolution ins final layer is used to map each feature vector to a saliency map. In total the network has 7 spherical convolutional layers.

6 Experiments

6.1 Experimental Setup

We implement our spherical U-Net with the PyTorch framework. We train our network with the following hyper-parameters setting: mini-batch size (32), learning rate (3e-1), momentum (0.9), weight decay (0.00005), and number of iterations (4000).

Datasets. We evaluate our proposed spherical CNN model on both Salient360! dtaset and our video saliency dataset. Salient360! [28] is comprised of 98 different 360° images viewed by 63 observers. Our video saliency dataset consists of 104 360° videos viewed by 20 observers. For Salient360, we follow the standard training/testing split provided in [28]. For the experiments on our dataset, 80 videos are randomly selected as training data, and the remaining 24 videos are used for testing. All baseline methods are compared based on the same training/testing split. For image saliency, we regress the saliency maps directly from the RGB 360° images.

Metrics. We create the ground truth saliency maps through a way similar to spherical convolution using a crown Gaussian kernel with sigma equaling to 3.34°. Owing to the distortion during projection, it does not make sense to directly compare two panorama saliency maps like typical 2D saliency maps. Therefore, we utilize the metrics including CC, AUC-judd, and NSS introduced in [28] to measure the errors between the predicted saliency maps and the ground truth.

Baselines. We compare our proposed spherical U-Net with the following state-of-the-art: image saliency detection methods, including LDS [29], Sal-Net [5] and SALICON [30], video saliency detection methods, including GBVS [31] and a more recent dynamic saliency [32] and the 360° image saliency models [33]. Of all these methods, Sal-Net and SALICON are deep learning based methods, and we retrain the models with panorama images on the datasets used in our paper for performance comparison. We also design the following baselines to validate the effectiveness of our spherical model.

- *Standard U-Net.* Compared with our spherical U-Net method, the CNN and MSE loss in such baseline is conventional CNN and standard MSE loss.
- *Spherical U-Net w.o. sal.* Compared with our spherical U-Net method, the only difference is that the saliency of previous frame is not considered for the saliency prediction of current frame.

In addition, we measure human performance by following the strategies in [34]:

- *Baseline-one human*: It measures the difference between the saliency map viewed by one observer and the average saliency map viewed by the rest observers.
- *Baseline-infinite humans*: It measures the difference between the average saliency map viewed by a subset of viewers and the average saliency map viewed by the remaining observers.

Recent work has employed several top-down cues for saliency detection. Previous work [35] shows that human face boosts saliency detection. Therefore, we also design a baseline *Top-down cue (face)* to use human face as cue, and post-process saliency map following [35].

6.2 Performance Evaluation

We compare our method with all baselines in Table 2. It shows that our method outperforms all baseline methods on our video saliency dataset, which validates the effectiveness of our scheme for 360° video saliency detection.

In order to show the rotation equivariant in θ and ϕ direction, we rotate 60°, 120° along ϕ direction and 30°, 60° along θ direction on test data, and do data augmentation by rotating random degree on both direction on training set. The results are shown in Fig. 7. We can see that compared to rotation in ϕ direction,

Table 2. The performance comparison of state-of-the-art methods with our spherical U-Net on our video saliency dataset

	LDS [29]	Sal-Net [5]	SALICON [30]	GBVS [31]	Wang *et al.* [32]	SaltiNet [33]	Spherical U-Net w.o. sal	Standard U-Net	Top-down cue (face)	Ours	Baseline-one Human	Baseline-infinite Humans
CC	0.2727	0.2404	0.2171	0.1254	0.2929	0.2582	0.3716	0.2457	0.6250	0.6246	0.7641	0.7035
NSS	1.6589	1.3958	1.3178	0.8003	1.5869	1.4470	2.2050	1.3034	3.5339	3.5340	5.4339	5.6504
AUC-judd	0.8169	0.8266	0.8074	0.7799	0.7906	0.8579	0.8464	0.8300	0.8985	0.8977	0.7585	0.8634

that in θ direction slightly changes because of the change of sample grid when rotating along θ direction.

To evaluate the performance of our method on the Salient360! dataset, we have modified our model to directly predict the saliency map for a static 360° image. In Fig. 6, we can see that our method outperforms all baselines, which validates the effectiveness of our method for static 360° image.

6.3 Evaluation of Different Components in Spherical U-Net

We conduct ablation study by replacing the spherical CNN with standard CNN (*Ours w. standard conv*) and replacing spherical MSE with standard MSE (*Ours w. standard MSE*), respectively. The performance of these baselines is listed in table in Fig. 6. We can see that both spherical CNN and Spherical MSE contributes the performance.

Methods	CC	AUC-judd	NSS
LDS [29]	0.3134	0.6186	0.6703
Sal-Net [5]	0.2998	0.6397	0.6792
SALICON [30]	0.3233	0.6511	0.6918
Ours	0.4087	0.6594	0.6989

Baselines	CC	AUC-judd	NSS
Ours w. standard MSE	0.6189	3.1620	0.8685
Ours w. standard conv	0.2877	1.6145	0.8520
Ours w. smaller kernel	0.6023	3.219	0.8593
Spherical pooling	0.6253	3.5333	0.8980
Our Spherical U-Net	0.6246	3.5340	0.8977

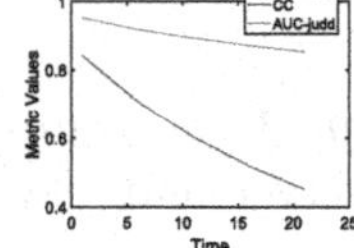

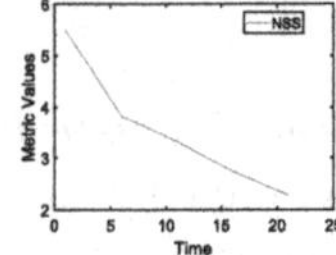

Fig. 6. The First: The performance comparison of state-of-the-art methods with our spherical CNN on Salient360 [36] dataset. **The Second:** The performance comparison of different components on our method on our video saliency dataset. **The Third** and **The Forth:** the performance of saliency map prediction for a longer time based on CC, AUC-judd, and NSS metrics respectively

We also evaluate spherical U-Net with different spherical kernel sizes and the comparison with spherical U-Net with smaller kernel sizes than our spherical U-Net (*Ours w. smaller kernel*) is shown in table in Fig. 6. We can see that larger kernel leads to better performance. One possible reason is that a larger spherical kernel could involve more parameters, which could increase the capability of our network. Another reason is that larger kernel increases kernel sample rate, which might improve the accuracy when re-sample the kernel.

6.4 Spherical Pooling

We do comparison between planner pooling and spherical pooling in the table in Fig. 6. In this paper, spherical pooling could be regarded as a special spherical convolution, similar to the relationship between planner ones. The spherical pooling outperforms planner pooling, responsible for consistency between receptive field of kernel with spherical feature maps. To note that, [16] also uses planner (3D) pooling to downsample feature maps. Since planner pooling achieves similar performance as spherical pooling and has lower computational cost, following [16], currently we use planner pooling.

6.5 Saliency Prediction for a Longer Time

Middle and right figures in Fig. 6 show the results when our model predicts saliency maps for a longer time based on CC, NSS, and AUC-judd metric. We can see that the performance of saliency prediction degenerates for as time elapse. One possible reason is that as time goes longer, the prediction of previous frame becomes less accurate, which consequently would affect the saliency detection of current frame.

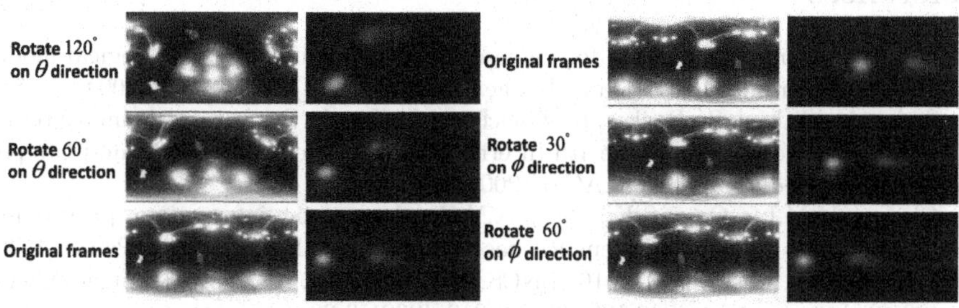

Fig. 7. The rotation equivariant in θ and ϕ direction: The first and third columns are rotated frames and the second and forth columns are our predictions

6.6 Time and Memory Costs

Our model is trained on four NVIDIA Tesla P40 GPUs. We calculate the average running time for each image batch. The average running time of our model is 5.1 s/iter. The spherical U-Net listed in Table 1 has about 6.07 M parameters, and it consumes 21×4 GB of memory when batch size is 32 when training. It takes about 36 h to train the model on the our video saliency dataset (the total number of iterations is 4000.).

7 Conclusion and Discussions

Our work attempts to exploit the saliency detection in dynamic 360° videos. To this end, we introduce a new type of spherical CNN where the kernels are shared across all image patches on the sphere. Considering that the 360° videos are stored with panorama, we extent spherical CNN to the panorama case, and we propose to re-sample kernel based on its location for spherical convolution on panorama. Then we propose a spherical U-Net for 360° video saliency detection. We also build a large-scale 360° video saliency dataset for performance evaluation. Extensive experiments validate the effectiveness of our proposed method. It is worth noting our spherical CNN is a general framework, it can also be applied to other tasks involving 360° video/image.

There still exists some space to improve our method for video saliency prediction. Currently, to simplify the problem, we only consider the saliency map of the previous frame for the prediction of current frame. Considering the saliency map over a longer time range may boost the performance, for example, we can also combine our spherical U-Net with LSTM. The combination of spherical CNN with other types of deep neural network is beyond the study scope of this paper, and we will leave them for future work.

Acknowledgement. This project is supported by the NSFC (No. 61502304).

References

1. Itti, L.: Automatic foveation for video compression using a neurobiological model of visual attention. IEEE Trans. Image Process. **13**(10), 1304–1318 (2004)
2. Setlur, V., Takagi, S., Raskar, R., Gleicher, M., Gooch, B.: Automatic image retargeting. In: Proceedings of the 4th International Conference on Mobile and Ubiquitous Multimedia, pp. 59–68. ACM (2005)
3. Chang, M.M.L., Ong, S.K., Nee, A.Y.C.: Automatic information positioning scheme in ar-assisted maintenance based on visual saliency. In: De Paolis, L.T., Mongelli, A. (eds.) AVR 2016. LNCS, vol. 9768, pp. 453–462. Springer, Cham (2016). https://doi.org/10.1007/978-3-319-40621-3_33
4. Krizhevsky, A., Sutskever, I., Hinton, G.E.: ImageNet classification with deep convolutional neural networks. In: Advances in Neural Information Processing Systems, pp. 1097–1105 (2012)
5. Pan, J., Sayrol, E., Giroinieto, X., Mcguinness, K., Oconnor, N.E.: Shallow and deep convolutional networks for saliency prediction, pp. 598–606 (2016)
6. Bazzani, L., Larochelle, H., Torresani, L.: Recurrent mixture density network for spatiotemporal visual attention. arXiv preprint arXiv:1603.08199 (2016)
7. Boomsma, W., Frellsen, J.: Spherical convolutions and their application in molecular modelling. In: Advances in Neural Information Processing Systems, pp. 3436–3446 (2017)
8. Su, Y.C., Grauman, K.: Learning spherical convolution for fast features from 360 imagery. In: Advances in Neural Information Processing Systems, pp. 529–539 (2017)
9. Ronneberger, O., Fischer, P., Brox, T.: U-Net: convolutional networks for biomedical image segmentation. In: Navab, N., Hornegger, J., Wells, W.M., Frangi, A.F. (eds.) MICCAI 2015. LNCS, vol. 9351, pp. 234–241. Springer, Cham (2015). https://doi.org/10.1007/978-3-319-24574-4_28
10. Schroff, F., Kalenichenko, D., Philbin, J.: FaceNet: a unified embedding for face recognition and clustering. In: Proceedings of the IEEE Conference on Computer Vision And Pattern Recognition, pp. 815–823 (2015)
11. Ren, S., He, K., Girshick, R., Sun, J.: Faster R-CNN: towards real-time object detection with region proposal networks. In: Advances in Neural Information Processing Systems, pp. 91–99 (2015)

12. Sitzmann, V., Serrano, A., Pavel, A., Agrawala, M., Gutierrez, D., Wetzstein, G.: Saliency in VR: how do people explore virtual environments? (2016)
13. Hu, H.N., Lin, Y.C., Liu, M.Y., Cheng, H.T., Chang, Y.J., Sun, M.: Deep 360 pilot: learning a deep agent for piloting through 360deg sports video (2017)
14. Su, Y.C., Grauman, K.: Making 360 video watchable in 2D: learning videography for click free viewing. arXiv preprint (2017)
15. Su, Y.C., Jayaraman, D., Grauman, K.: Pano2vid: automatic cinematography for watching 360° videos. In: Asian Conference on Computer Vision, pp. 154–171 (2016)
16. Cohen, T.S., Geiger, M., Koehler, J., Welling, M.: Spherical CNNs. arXiv preprint arXiv:1801.10130 (2018)
17. Zhong, S.h., Liu, Y., Ren, F., Zhang, J., Ren, T.: Video saliency detection via dynamic consistent spatio-temporal attention modelling. In: AAAI, pp. 1063–1069 (2013)
18. Zhou, F., Bing Kang, S., Cohen, M.F.: Time-mapping using space-time saliency. In: Proceedings of the IEEE Conference on Computer Vision and Pattern Recognition, pp. 3358–3365 (2014)
19. Itti, L., Dhavale, N., Pighin, F.: Realistic avatar eye and head animation using a neurobiological model of visual attention. In: Applications and Science of Neural Networks, Fuzzy Systems, and Evolutionary Computation VI, vol. 5200, pp. pp. 64–79. International Society for Optics and Photonics (2003)
20. Ren, Z., Gao, S., Chia, L.T., Rajan, D.: Regularized feature reconstruction for spatio-temporal saliency detection. IEEE Trans. Image Process. **22**(8), 3120–3132 (2013)
21. Bak, Ç., Erdem, A., Erdem, E.: Two-stream convolutional networks for dynamic saliency prediction. arXiv preprint arXiv:1607.04730 (2016)
22. Wang, W., Shen, J., Shao, L.: Video salient object detection via fully convolutional networks. IEEE Trans. Image Process. **27**(1), 38–49 (2018)
23. Chaabouni, S., Benois-Pineau, J., Hadar, O., Amar, C.B.: Deep learning for saliency prediction in natural video (2016)
24. Liu, Y., Zhang, S., Xu, M., He, X.: Predicting salient face in multipleface videos. In: Proceedings of the IEEE Conference on Computer Vision and Pattern Recognition, pp. 4420–4428 (2017)
25. Ruhland, K., et al.: A review of eye gaze in virtual agents, social robotics and HCI: Behaviour generation, user interaction and perception. Comput. Graph. Forum **34**(6), 299–326 (2015)
26. Driscoll, J.R., Healy, D.M.: Computing fourier transforms and convolutions on the 2-sphere. Adv. Appl. Math. **15**(2), 202–250 (1994)
27. Jaderberg, M., Simonyan, K., Zisserman, A., et al.: Spatial transformer networks. In: Advances in Neural Information Processing Systems, pp. 2017–2025 (2015)
28. Rai, Y., Gutiérrez, J., Le Callet, P.: A dataset of head and eye movements for 360 degree images. In: Proceedings of the 8th ACM on Multimedia Systems Conference, pp. 205–210. ACM (2017)
29. Fang, S., Li, J., Tian, Y., Huang, T., Chen, X.: Learning discriminative subspaces on random contrasts for image saliency analysis. IEEE Trans. Neural Netw. Learn. Syst. **28**(5), 1095–1108 (2017)
30. Huang, X., Shen, C., Boix, X., Zhao, Q.: SALICON: reducing the semantic gap in saliency prediction by adapting deep neural networks. In: IEEE International Conference on Computer Vision, pp. 262–270 (2015)
31. Harel, J., Koch, C., Perona, P.: Graph-based visual saliency. In: Advances in Neural Information Processing Systems, pp. 545–552 (2007)

32. Wang, W., Shen, J., Guo, F., Cheng, M.M., Borji, A.: Revisiting video saliency: a large-scale benchmark and a new model (2018)
33. Assens, M., Mcguinness, K., Giroinieto, X., O'Connor, N.E.: SaltiNet: scan-path prediction on 360 degree images using saliency volumes (2017)
34. Judd, T., Durand, F., Torralba, A.: A benchmark of computational models of saliency to predict human fixations. In: MIT Technical report (2012)
35. Goferman, S., Zelnikmanor, L., Tal, A.: Context-aware saliency detection. IEEE Trans. Pattern Anal. Mach. Intell. **34**(10), 1915 (2012)
36. Rai, Y., Callet, P.L.: A dataset of head and eye movements for 360 degree images. In: ACM on Multimedia Systems Conference, pp. 205–210 (2017)

Localization Recall Precision (LRP): A New Performance Metric for Object Detection

Kemal Oksuz, Baris Can Cam(✉), Emre Akbas, and Sinan Kalkan

Department of Computer Engineering,
Middle East Technical University, Ankara, Turkey
{kemal.oksuz,can.cam,eakbas,skalkan}@metu.edu.tr
http://image.ceng.metu.edu.tr

Abstract. Average precision (AP), the area under the recall-precision (RP) curve, is the standard performance measure for object detection. Despite its wide acceptance, it has a number of shortcomings, the most important of which are (i) the inability to distinguish very different RP curves, and (ii) the lack of directly measuring bounding box localization accuracy. In this paper, we propose "Localization Recall Precision (LRP) Error", a new metric specifically designed for object detection. LRP Error is composed of three components related to localization, false negative (FN) rate and false positive (FP) rate. Based on LRP, we introduce the "Optimal LRP" (oLRP), the minimum achievable LRP error representing the best achievable configuration of the detector in terms of recall-precision and the tightness of the boxes. In contrast to AP, which considers precisions over the entire recall domain, oLRP determines the "best" confidence score threshold for a class, which balances the trade-off between localization and recall-precision. In our experiments, we show that oLRP provides richer and more discriminative information than AP. We also demonstrate that the best confidence score thresholds vary significantly among classes and detectors. Moreover, we present LRP results of a simple online video object detector and show that the class-specific optimized thresholds increase the accuracy against the common approach of using a general threshold for all classes. Our experiments demonstrate that LRP is more competent than AP in capturing the performance of detectors. Our source code for PASCAL VOC AND MSCOCO datasets are provided at https://github.com/cancam/LRP.

Keywords: Average precision · Object detection
Performance metric · Optimal threshold · Recall-precision

Electronic supplementary material The online version of this chapter (https://doi.org/10.1007/978-3-030-01234-2_31) contains supplementary material, which is available to authorized users.

V. Ferrari et al. (Eds.): ECCV 2018, LNCS 11211, pp. 521–537, 2018.
https://doi.org/10.1007/978-3-030-01234-2_31

1 Introduction

Today "average precision" (AP) is the de facto standard for performance evaluation in object detection competitions [8,14,28], and in the studies on still-image object detection [6,13,16,24], video object detection [9,12,36] and online video object detection [17,34]. AP not only enjoys such vast acceptance but it also appears to be unchallenged. Except for a small number of papers which do ablation studies [13,24], AP appears to be the sole criterion used to compare object detection methods.

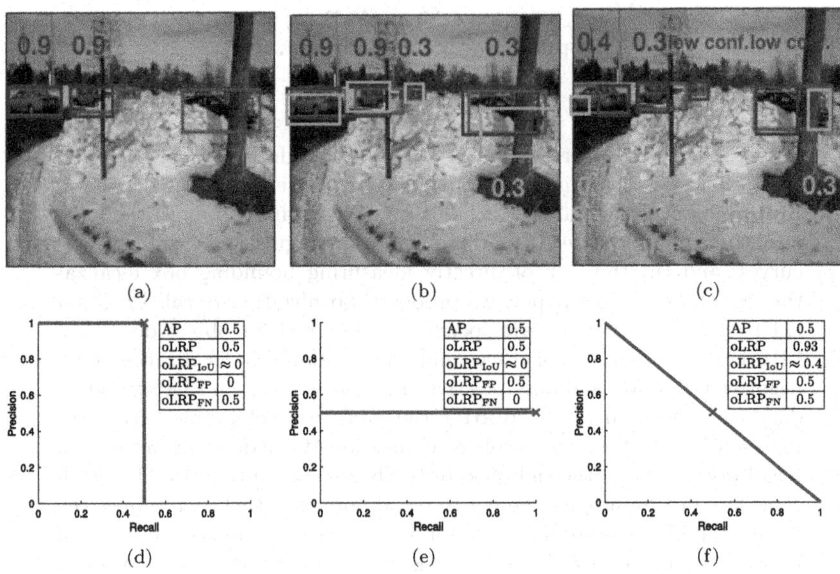

Fig. 1. Three different object detection results (for an image from ILSVRC [28]) with very different RP curves but the same AP. AP is unable to identify the difference between these curves. **(a, b, c)** Red, blue and green colors denote ground-truth, true positives; false positives respectively. Numbers are detection confidence scores. **(d, e, f)** RP curves, AP and LRP results for the corresponding detections in (a, b, c). Red crosses indicate Optimal LRP points. (Color figure online)

Despite its popularity, AP has certain deficiencies. First, **AP cannot distinguish between very different RP curves**: In Fig. 1, we present detection results of three hypothetical object detectors. The detector in (a) detects only half of the objects but with full precision; this is a low-recall-high-precision detector. In contrast, the detector in (b) detects all objects; however, for each correct detection it also produces a close-to-duplicate detection which escapes non-maxima suppression. Hence, detector (b) is a high-recall-low-precision detector. And the detector in (c) is in between; it represents a detector with higher precision at lower recall and vice versa. Despite their very different characteristics, the APs of these detectors are exactly the same (AP $=$ 0.5). One needs to inspect the RP curves in order to understand the differences in behavior, which can be time-consuming and impractical with large number of classes such as in the ImageNet object detection challenge [28] with 200 classes.

Another deficiency of AP is that **it does not explicitly include localization accuracy**: One cannot infer from AP the tightness level of the bounding box detections. Nevertheless, since extracting tighter bounding boxes is a desired property, nearly every paper on the topic discusses the issue mostly qualitatively [6,9,16,17,24] and some quantitatively by computing AP scores for different intersection-over-union (IoU) thresholds [13,16,24]. However, this quantitative approach does not directly measure the localization accuracy either and for the qualitative approach, it is very likely for the sample boxes to be very limited and biased. We discuss other less severe deficiencies of AP in Sect. 3.

A desirable performance metric is expected to include all of the factors related with performance. In object detection, the most important three factors are (i) the localization accuracy of the true positives (TP), (ii) the false positives (FP) rate and (iii) the false negative (FN) rate. Being able to evaluate a detector based on these factors is another desirable property for a performance measure since it can reveal improvement directions. Furthermore, a performance metric should reveal the RP characteristics of a detector (as LRP achieves in Fig. 1). This ability would benefit certain applications. For instance, using a high-precision detector is common in visual tracking methods [3,4,31,32,37], while initializing the tracker, known as *tracking by detection* as faster response times are required. Also, in online video object detection, the current approach is to use a still-image object detector with a general threshold (e.g., Association-LSTM [17] uses SSD [16] detections with confidence score above 0.8). A desirable performance measure should help in setting an optimal confidence score threshold per class.

In this paper, we propose a new metric called the "Localization-Recall-Precision Error" (LRP, for short). LRP involves appropriate components closely related to the precision, recall, and IoU and each parametrization of LRP corresponds to a point on the RP curve. We propose the "Optimal LRP", the minimum achievable LRP error, as the alternative performance metric to AP. Optimal LRP alleviates the drawbacks of AP, represents the tightness of the bounding-boxes and the shape of the RP curve via its components and is more suitable for ablation studies. Finally, based on Optimal LRP, a confidence score thresholding method is proposed to decrease the number of detections in an optimal manner. Our extensive experiments confirm that LRP is a highly capable metric for comparing object detectors thoroughly.

2 Related Work

Information Theoretic Performance Measures: Several performance measures have been derived on the confusion matrix. Among them, the most relevant one is the F-measure [25] defined as the harmonic mean of precision and recall. However, F-measure violates the triangle inequality, and therefore, it is not suitable as a metric [20] and it is not symmetric in the positive and negative classes.

These violations and its incapacity to measure bounding box tightness prevent its use for comparison among detectors in a consistent manner. Moreover, [5] points out that, except for accuracy, all information theoretic measures have undefined intervals. For example, F-measure is undefined when the number of TP is 0 even if there are detections. AP is an information theoretic measure, too, with deficiencies discussed in Sects. 1 and 3.

Point Multi-target Tracking Performance Metrics: Object detection is very similar to the multi-target tracking problem. In both problems, there are multiple instances to detect, and the localization, FN and FP rates are common criteria for success. Currently, component-based performance metrics are the accepted way of evaluating point multi-target tracking filters. The first metric to combine the localization and cardinality (including both FP and FN) errors is the Optimal Subpattern Assignment (OSPA) [29]. Following OSPA, several measures and metrics have been proposed as its variants [19,23,26,27,29,30,35]. Similarly, CLEAR multi-object tracking metrics [1] considers only FP and mismatch rate while ignoring the localization error. However, similar measures and metrics are lacking in the object detection literature, though similar performance evaluation problems are observed.

Setting the Thresholds of the Classifiers: The research on the optimization of a precision-recall balanced performance measure is mostly concentrated around the F-measure. [7] considers maximizing F-measure at the inference time using plug-in rules, while [18,33] offer maximization during training for support vector machines and conditional random fields. Similarly, [15] aims to find optimal thresholds for a probabilistic classifier based on maximizing the F-measure. Finally, [21] presents a theoretical analysis of optimization of the F-measure, which also confirms the threshold-F-measure relationship depicted in [15,22].

In summary, we see that existing methods mostly focus on the F-measure for optimizing the thresholds for classifiers, which, however, has the aforementioned drawbacks. Moreover, F-measure is shown to be concave with respect to its inputs, number of TPs and FPs [15], which makes the analytical optimization impossible. In addition, none of these studies have considered the object detection problem in particular, thus no localization error is directly included for these measures. Therefore, different from the previous work, we specifically are interested in performance evaluation and optimal thresholding of the deep object detectors. Moreover, we directly optimize a well-behaving function which has a smaller domain in practice in order to identify the class-specific thresholds.

3 Average Precision: An Analysis and Its Deficiencies

Due to space constraints, we omit the definition of AP and refer the reader to the accompanying supplementary material or [8]. There exist minor differences in AP's practical usage. For example, AP is computed by simply integrating over 11 points (that divide the entire recall domain in equal pieces) in the PASCAL VOC 2007 challenge [8] whereas in MSCOCO [14], 101 points are used. Precision values at intermediate points are simply interpolated to prevent wiggles in the curve, by setting it to the maximum precision obtained in the interval of higher recall than the current point. While a single intersection-over-union (IoU) threshold, which is 0.5, is used in PASCAL VOC [8]; a range of IoU thresholds (from 0.5 to 0.95) are used in MSCOCO; the average AP over this range of IoU thresholds is also called mAP.

AP aims to evaluate the precision of the detector over the entire recall domain. Thus, it favors the methods that have precision over the entire recall domain, instead of the detectors whose RP curves are nearer to the top-right corner. In other words, AP does not compare the maximum but the overall capability/performance of the detectors. The most important two deficiencies of AP are discussed in Sect. 1. In the following, we list other, more minor deficiencies.

AP is not Confidence-Score Sensitive. Since the sorted list of the detections is required to calculate AP, a detector generating results in a limited interval will lead to the same AP. As an example, consider only 2 detections with same confidence score in Fig. 1 out of 4 ground truths. Note that setting the confidence scores to any value (i.e. 0.01) leads to the same AP as long as the order is preserved.

AP does not suggest a confidence score threshold for the best setting of the object detector. However, in a practical application, detections are usually required to be filtered owing to time limitations. For example, the state-of-the-art online object detector [17] applies a confidence score threshold of 0.8 on the SSD method [16] and obtains $12fps$ in this fashion.

AP uses interpolation between neighboring recall values, which is especially problematic for classes with very small size. For example, "toaster" class of [14] has 9 instances in the validation 2017 set.

4 Localization-Recall-Precision (LRP) Error

Let X be the set of ground truth boxes and Y be the set of boxes returned by an object detector. To compute $\text{LRP}(X, Y_s)$, the LRP error of Y_s against X at a given score threshold s $(0 \leq s \leq 1)$ and IoU threshold τ $(0 \leq \tau < 1)$; first, Y_s, the set of detections with confidence score larger than s, is constructed and detections in Y_s are assigned to ground-truth boxes in X, as done for AP. Once the assignments are made, the following values are computed: (i) N_{TP}, the number of true positives; (ii) N_{FP}, the number of false positives; (iii) N_{FN}, the number of false negatives. Using these quantities, the LRP error is:

$$\text{LRP}(X, Y_s) := \frac{1}{Z} \left(w_{IoU} \text{LRP}_{IoU}(X, Y_s) + w_{FP} \text{LRP}_{FP}(X, Y_s) + w_{FN} \text{LRP}_{FN}(X, Y_s) \right), \quad (1)$$

where $Z = N_{TP} + N_{FP} + N_{FN}$ is the normalization constant; and the weights $w_{IoU} = \frac{N_{TP}}{1-\tau}$, $w_{FP} = |Y_s|$, and $w_{FP} = |X|$ control the contributions of the terms. The weights make each component easy to interpret, provide further information about the detector and prevent the total error from being undefined whenever the denominator of a single component is 0. LRP_{IoU} represents the IoU tightness of valid detections as follows:

$$\text{LRP}_{IoU}(X, Y_s) := \frac{1}{N_{TP}} \sum_{i=1}^{N_{TP}} (1 - IoU(x_i, y_{x_i})), \tag{2}$$

which measures the mean bounding box localization error resulting from correct detections. Another interpretation is that $1 - \text{LRP}_{IoU}(X, Y_s)$ is the average IoU of the valid detections.

The second component, LRP_{FP}, in Eq. 1 measures the false-positives:

$$\text{LRP}_{FP}(X, Y_s) := 1 - Precision = 1 - \frac{N_{TP}}{|Y_s|} = \frac{N_{FP}}{|Y_s|}, \tag{3}$$

and false negatives are measured by LRP_{FN}:

$$\text{LRP}_{FN}(X, Y_s) := 1 - Recall = 1 - \frac{N_{TP}}{|X|} = \frac{N_{FN}}{|X|}. \tag{4}$$

FP and FN components together represent precision-recall of the corresponding Y_s by $1 - \text{LRP}_{FP}(X, Y_s)$ and $1 - \text{LRP}_{FN}(X, Y_s)$ respectively. Denoting the IoU between $x_i \in X$ and its assigned detection $y_{x_i} \in Y_s$ by $IoU(x_i, y_{x_i})$, the LRP error can be equally defined in a more compact form as:

$$\text{LRP}(X, Y_s) := \frac{1}{N_{TP} + N_{FP} + N_{FN}} \left(\sum_{i=1}^{N_{TP}} \frac{1 - IoU(x_i, y_{x_i})}{1 - \tau} + N_{FP} + N_{FN} \right). \tag{5}$$

LRP penalizes each TP by its erroneous localization normalized by $1 - \tau$ to the [0,1] interval, each FP and FN by 1 that is the penalty upper bound. This sum of error is averaged by the total number of its contributors, i.e., $N_{TP} + N_{FP} + N_{FN}$. So, with this normalization, LRP yields a value representing the average error per bounding box in the [0,1] interval, where each component equally contributes to the error. When necessary, the individual importance of IoU, FP, FN can be changed for different applications. To this end, the prominent component can be multiplied by a factor (say C) both in the numerator and the denominator [19]. This implies having C artificial errors for each error of the prominent type.

Overall, the ranges of total error and the components are $[0, 1]$ and lower value implies better performance. At the extreme cases; 0 for LRP means that each ground truth item is detected with perfect localization, and if LRP is 1, then no valid detection matches the ground truth (i.e., $|Y_s| = N_{FP}$). LRP is undefined only when the ground truth and detection sets are both empty (i.e., $N_{TP} + N_{FP} + N_{FN} = 0$), i.e., there is nothing to evaluate.

As for the parameters, s is the confidence score threshold, and τ is the IoU threshold. Since the RP pair is directly identified by the FP&FN components, each different detection set Y_s corresponds to a specific point of the RP curve. For this reason, decreasing s corresponds to moving along the RP curve in the positive recall direction. τ defines minimum overlap for a detection to be validated as a TP. In other words, higher τ means we require tighter BBs. Overall, both parameters are related with the RP curve: A τ value sets the RP curve and an s value moves along the RP curve to evaluate the LRP error.

In the supplementary material, we prove that LRP is a metric.

5 Optimal LRP (oLRP) Error: The Performance Metric and Thresholder

Optimal LRP (oLRP) is defined as the minimum achievable LRP error with $\tau = 0.5$, which makes oLRP parameter independent:

$$\text{oLRP} := \min_{s} \text{LRP}(X, Y_s). \tag{6}$$

For ablation studies and practical requirements, different τ values can be adopted. In such cases, oLRP@τ can be used to denote the Optimal LRP error at τ.

oLRP searches among the confidence scores to find the best balance for competing precision-recall-IoU. The RP setting of the RP curve that oLRP has found corresponds to the top-right part of the curve, where the optimal balanced setting resides. We call a curve *sharper* than another RP curve, if its peak point at the top-right part is nearer to the $(1,1)$ RP pair. To illustrate, the RP curves in Fig. 1(d) and (e) are sharper than that in Fig. 1(f).

The components of oLRP are coined as optimal box localization (oLRP_{IoU}), optimal FP (oLRP_{FP}), and optimal FN (oLRP_{FN}) components. In this case, oLRP_{IoU} describes the mean average tightness for a class, and oLRP_{FP} and oLRP_{FN} together pertain to the sharpness of the curve since the corresponding RP pair is the maximum achievable performance value of the detector for this class. One can directly pinpoint the sharpness point by $1 - \text{oLRP}_{FP}$ and $1 - \text{oLRP}_{FN}$. Overall, different from AP, oLRP aims to find out the best class specific setting of the detector and it favors sharper ones that also represent better BB tightness.

Denoting oLRP error of class $c \in C$ by oLRP_c, Mean Optimal LRP (moLRP) is defined as follows:

$$\text{moLRP} := \frac{1}{|C|} \sum_{c \in C} \text{oLRP}_c. \tag{7}$$

As in mAP, moLRP is the performance metric for the entire detector. Mean optimal box localization, FP and FN components, denoted by moLRP_{IoU}, moLRP_{FP}, moLRP_{FN} respectively, are similarly defined as the mean of the class specific components. Different from the components in oLRP, the mean optimal FP and FN components are not necessarily on the average of the RP curves of all classes due to averaging moLRP_{FP} (i.e., precision) with different moLRP_{FN} (i.e., recall) values but still provides information on the sharpness of the RP curves as shown in the experiments.

Owing to its filtering capability, oLRP can be used for thresholding purposes. If a problem needs an image object detector as the backbone and processing is to be completed within limited time, then only a small subset of the detections should be selected. For such methods, using an overall confidence score for the object detector is a common approach [17]. For such a task, oLRP identifies the class-specific best confidence score thresholds. One possible drawback of this method is that validated detections can still be too large to be processed in the desired limited time. However, by accepting larger LRP errors, higher confidence scores can be set, but again in a class-specific manner. Second practical usage of oLRP is about the deployment of the devised object detector into a platform in which confidence scores are to be discarded for user-friendliness. In such a case, one needs to set the τ threshold considering the application requirements while optimizing for the best confidence score.

In essence, calculating oLRP is an optimization problem. However, thanks to the smaller search space, we propose to discretize the s domain into 0.01 spaced intervals and search exhaustively in this limited space.

6 Experimental Evaluation

In this section, we analyze the parameters of LRP, represent its discriminative power on common object detectors and finally show that the class specific thresholds increase the performance of a simple online video object detector.

Evaluated Object Detectors: We evaluate commonly used deep object detectors; namely, Faster R-CNN, RetinaNet, and SSD. For Faster R-CNN and RetinaNet variants, we use the models by [11] and for SSD variants, the models of [10] are utilized. For the variants, we use R50, R101 and X101 while referring to the ResNet-50, ResNet-101 and RexNeXt-101 backbones respectively and FPN for feature pyramid network. All models are tested on "MS COCO validation 2017" including 80 classes and 5000 images.

6.1 Analyzing Parameters s and τ

Using Faster R-CNN (X101+FPN) results of the first 10 classes and mean-error for clarity, the effects of the s and τ are analyzed in Fig. 2 and 3. We observe

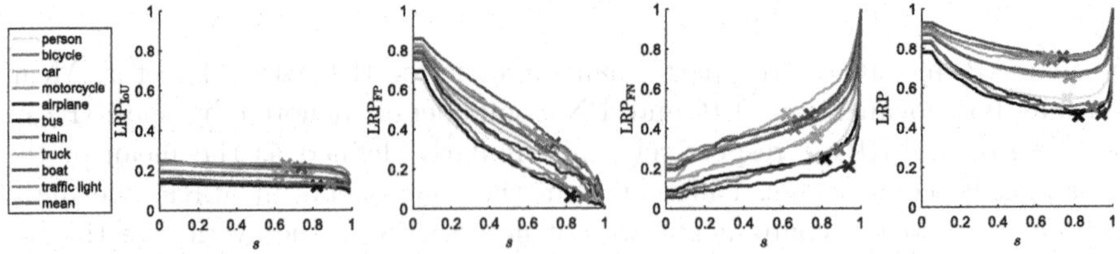

Fig. 2. For each class, LRP components & total error of Faster R-CNN (X101+FPN) are plotted against s. The optimal confidence scores are marked with crosses.

that box localization component is not significantly affected by increasing s, except for large s, where the error slightly decreases since the results tend to be more "confident". FP and FN components act in contrast to precision and recall respectively, as expected. Therefore, lower curves imply better performance for these components. Finally, the total error (oLRP) has a second-order shape. Since the localization error is not affected significantly by s, the behavior of the total error is mainly determined by FP and FN components, which result in the global minima of the total error to have a good precision and recall balance.

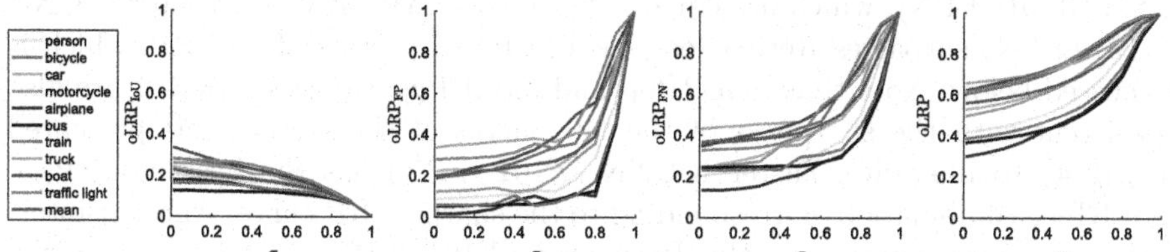

Fig. 3. For each class, oLRP and its components for Faster R-CNN (X101+FPN) are plotted against τ. The mean represents the mean of 80 classes.

In Fig. 3, oLRP and moLRP are plotted against different τ values. As expected, larger τ values imply lower the box localization component (oLRP_{IoU}). On the other hand, increase τ causes FP and FN components to increase rapidly, leading to higher total error (oLRP). This is intuitive since at the extreme case, i.e., when $\tau = 1$, there are hardly any valid detections and all the detections are false positives, which makes oLRP to be approximately 1. Therefore, oLRP allows measuring the performance of a detector designed for an application that requires a different τ by also providing additional information. In addition, investigating oLRP for different τ values represents a good extension for ablation studies.

Table 1. Performance comparison of common object detectors. R50, R101 and X101 represent the backbone networks used by ResNet-50, ResNet-101 and RexNeXt-101, respectively, and FPN refers to the feature pyramid network. s^*_{min} and s^*_{max} denote minimum and maximum class-specific thresholds respectively for oLRP. Note that unlike AP, lower scores are better for LRP.

	mAP	mAP@0.5	moLRP	$\text{moLRP}_{\text{IoU}}$	moLRP_{FP}	moLRP_{FN}	s^*_{min}	s^*_{max}
SSD-300	0.161	0.383	0.854	0.281	0.403	0.622	0.05	0.53
SSD-512	0.284	0.481	0.763	0.202	0.331	0.549	0.08	0.63
Faster R-CNN (R50)	0.348	0.557	0.714	0.183	0.292	0.484	0.18	0.93
RetinaNet (R50+FPN)	0.357	0.547	0.711	0.169	0.293	0.503	0.26	0.60
Faster R-CNN (R50+FPN)	0.379	0.593	0.689	0.175	0.259	0.454	0.41	0.94
RetinaNet (X101+FPN)	0.398	0.595	0.677	0.161	0.255	0.462	0.28	0.70
Faster R-CNN (R101+FPN)	0.398	0.613	0.673	0.168	0.255	0.436	0.37	0.94
Faster R-CNN (X101+FPN)	0.413	0.637	0.663	0.171	0.256	0.413	0.39	0.94

6.2 Evaluating Common Image Object Detectors

General Overview: Table 1 compares the detectors using mAP as the COCO's standard metric, mAP@0.50, moLRP and the class-specific threshold ranges. We observe that moLRP values are indicative of the known performances of the detectors. For any type of the detector, each new property (i.e., including FPN, increasing depth, using ResNext for Faster R-CNN and RetinaNet, increasing input size to 512 for SSD) decreases moLRP as expected. Moreover, the overall order is consistent with mAP except for RetinaNet (X101+FPN) and Faster R-CNN (R101+FPN), which are equal in terms of mAP; however, Faster R-CNN (R101+FPN) surpasses RetinaNet (X101+FPN) in terms of moLRP, which is discussed below. Note that moLRP_{FP} and moLRP_{FN} values in Table 1 are also consistent with the sharpness of the RP curves of the methods as presented in Fig. 4. To illustrate, Faster R-CNN (X101+FPN) has the best moLRP_{FP}, moLRP_{FN} combination, corresponding to the sharpest RP curve. Another interesting example pertains to the RetinaNet (X101+FPN) and Faster R-CNN (R50+FPN) curves. For these methods, moLRP_{FP} and moLRP_{FN} comparison slightly favors Faster R-CNN (R50+FPN), which is justified by their PR curves in Fig. 4.

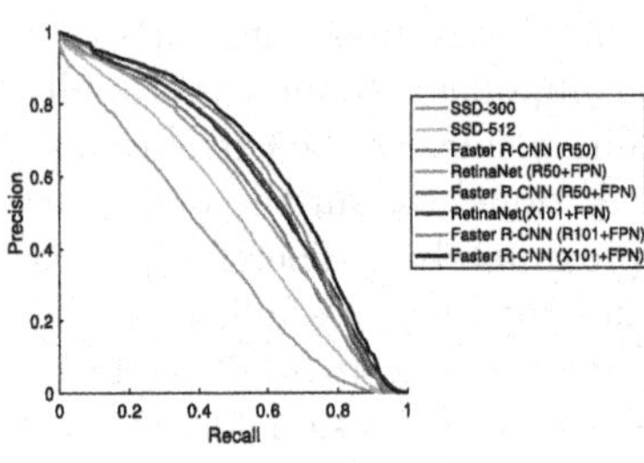

Fig. 4. Average RP curves of the common detectors.

Class-Based Comparison and Interpreting the Components: Now we analyze oLRP on a class-basis and look at the individual components to get a better feeling about the characteristics of methods – see Fig. 5. For all three classes, oLRP is determined at the RP pairs where there exists a sharp precision decrease on the top right part of the curve. Moreover, intuitively, these pairs provide a good balance between precision and recall. Considering the FP and FN components, one can infer the structure of the curve. For all methods, the "zebra" class has the sharpest RP curves which correspond to lower FP & FN error values. For example, Faster R-CNN has 0.069 and 0.188 FP and FN error values, respectively. Thus, without looking at the curve, one may consider that the peak of the curve resides at $1 - 0.069 = 0.931$ precision and $1 - 0.188 = 0.812$ recall. For the "broccoli" curve, a less sharp one, the optimal point is at $1 - 0.498 = 0.502$ and $1 - 0.484 = 0.516$ as precision and recall respectively. Similar to "zebra", these values suggest that the peak of the curve is around the center of the RP range. The localization component (oLRP_{IoU}) shows that the tightness of the boxes for the "bus" class is better than that of"zebra" for all detectors even though "zebra" has a sharper RP curve. For RetinaNet, average IoU is $1 - 0.106 = 0.894$ and $1 - 0.122 = 0.878$ for the "bus" and"zebra" classes respectively. With this analysis, we also see that it is easy to compare the tightness of the boxes among the methods and classes.

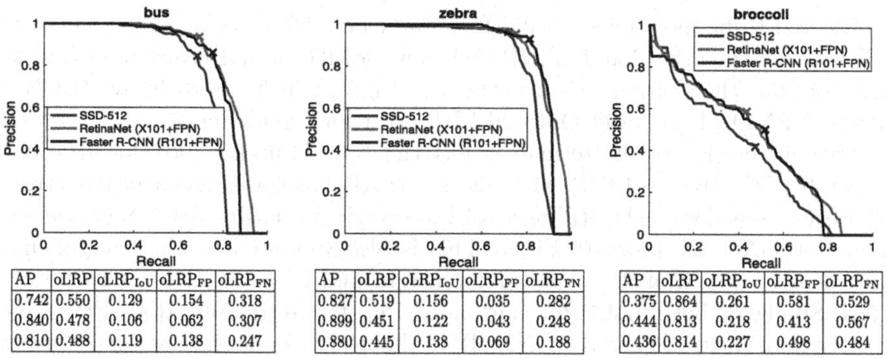

AP	oLRP	oLRP_{IoU}	oLRP_{FP}	oLRP_{FN}
0.742	0.550	0.129	0.154	0.318
0.840	0.478	0.106	0.062	0.307
0.810	0.488	0.119	0.138	0.247

AP	oLRP	oLRP_{IoU}	oLRP_{FP}	oLRP_{FN}
0.827	0.519	0.156	0.035	0.282
0.899	0.451	0.122	0.043	0.248
0.880	0.445	0.138	0.069	0.188

AP	oLRP	oLRP_{IoU}	oLRP_{FP}	oLRP_{FN}
0.375	0.864	0.261	0.581	0.529
0.444	0.813	0.218	0.413	0.567
0.436	0.814	0.227	0.498	0.484

Fig. 5. Example RP curves representing the optimal configurations marked with crosses. The curves are drawn for $\tau = 0.5$. The tables in the figures represent the performance of the methods with respect to AP and moLRP. The rows of the table correspond to SSD-512, RetinaNet (X101+FPN) and Faster R-CNN (R101+FPN) respectively. Note that unlike AP, lower scores are better for LRP.

Same mAP but Different Behaviors, Faster R-CNN vs. RetinaNet: Now we compare two detectors with equal AP in order to identify their characteristics using the components of moLRP; namely, RetinaNet (X101+FPN), a single shot detector and Faster R-CNN (R101+FPN), a two-step detector. Firstly, we use the box localization component ($\text{moLRP}_{\text{IoU}}$) in Table 1 to discriminate between these two detectors. The standard metric used in MS COCO aims to include the localization error by averaging over 10 mAP values. Since 1.8% difference for these two detectors is present in the mAP@0.5, one can infer that RetinaNet seems to produce more tight boxes. However, this inference is possible only by examining all 10 mAP results one by one and still it is not possible to quantize this tightness. In contrast, $\text{moLRP}_{\text{IoU}}$ directly suggests that, among all the detectors in Table 1, RetinaNet (X101+FPN) produces the tightest bounding boxes with an average tightness of $1 - 0.161 = 0.839$ in IoU terms.

Secondly, we compare the sharpness of the same two detectors, which are evidently different (Fig. 4). RetinaNet (X101+FPN) produces 486, 108 bounding boxes for 36, 781 annotations, whereas Faster R-CNN (R101+FPN) yields only 127, 039 thanks to its RPN method. For RetinaNet, confidence scores of 57% of the detections are under 0.1, and 87% of them are under 0.25 (these values are 29% and 56% for Faster R-CNN), which generally causes RetinaNet to have lower or equal precision than Faster R-CNN throughout the recall domain except for the tail of the RP curve. In the tail of RetinaNet, owing to its large number of results, it has some precision even though that of Faster R-CNN drops to 0. Figure 5 illustrates this phenomenon, which is best observed in the "zebra" curve. Even though RetinaNet has higher AP than Faster R-CNN with 0.899 to 0.880, this AP difference originates from the large number of RetinaNet detections, which causes the better RP curve tail. This shallow curve-longer tail phenomenon is observed to be more or less valid for more than 50 classes including the ones in Fig. 6. On the other hand, oLRP and thus moLRP do not favor these kind of detectors but the sharper ones as shown in Fig. 5, which causes Faster R-CNN (R101+FPN) to have lower Optimal LRP error for "zebra" class.

Overall, even though RetinaNet has the best bounding box localization, Faster R-CNN (R101+FPN) with the same AP has lower mean oLRP error. Moreover, considering the RP curve of these variants, Faster R-CNN is sharper than RetinaNet as shown in Fig. 4. This is also validated by the components with nearly equal moLRP_{FP} and difference in moLRP_{FN} in favor of Faster R-CNN. Similarly, both moLRP_{FP} and moLRP_{FN} for RetinaNet (R50+FPN) are greater than those of Faster R-CNN (R50) due to the same shallow curve-longer tail phenomenon, preventing its RP curves to be sharper. Again, what makes RetinaNet (R50+FPN) to have better performance regarding both mAP and moLRP is its strength to produce tight bounding boxes as shown in Table 1.

6.3 Better Threshold, Better Performance

In this experiment, we demonstrate a use-case where oLRP helps us to set class-specific optimal thresholds as an alternative to the naive approach of using a general threshold for all classes. To this end, we developed a simple, online video object detection framework where we use an off-the-shelf still-image object detector (RetinaNet-50 [13] trained on MS-COCO [14]) and built three different versions of the video object detector. The first version, denoted with B, uses the still-image object detector to process each frame of the video independently. The second and third versions, denoted with G and S, respectively, again use the still-image object detector to process each frame and in addition, they link bounding boxes across subsequent frames using the Hungarian matching algorithm [2] and update the scores of these linked boxes using a simple Bayesian rule (details of this simple online video object detector is given in the Supplementary Material). The only difference between G and S is that while G uses a validated threshold of 0.5 (see s^* of B in Table 2 and Fig. 1 in Supplementary Material for validation) as the confidence score threshold for all classes, S uses the optimal threshold per class which achieves the oLRP error. We test these three detectors on 346 videos of ImageNet VID validation set [28] for 15 object classes which also happen to be included in MS COCO.

AP vs. oLRP: We compare G with B in order to represent the evaluation perspectives of AP and oLRP – see Fig. 6 and Table 2. Since B is a conventional object detector, with conventional RP curves as illustrated in Fig. 6. On the other hand, in order to be faster, G ignores some of the detections causing its maximum recall to be less than that of B. Thus, these shorter ranges in the recall set a big problem in the AP evaluation. Quantitatively, B surpasses G by 7.5% AP. On the other hand, despite limited recall coverage, G obtains higher precision than B especially through the end of its RP curve. To illustrate, for the "boat" class in Fig. 6, G has significantly better precision after approximately between 0.5 and 0.9 recall even though its AP is lower by 6%. Since oLRP

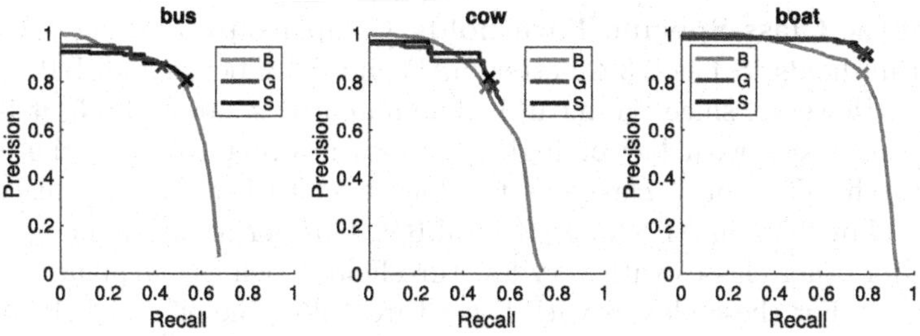

Fig. 6. Example RP curves of the methods. Optimal RP pairs are marked with crosses.

compares methods concerning their best configurations (i.e. the peak of their RP curves), this difference is clearly addressed comparing their oLRP error in which G surpasses S by 4.1%. Furthermore, the superiority of G is shown to be its higher precision since FN components of G and S are very close while FP component of G is 8.6% better, which is also the exact difference of precisions in their peaks of RP curves.

Therefore, while G seems to have very low performance in terms of AP, for 12 classes G reaches better peaks than B as illustrated by the oLRP values in Table 2. This suggests that oLRP is better than AP in capturing the performance details of the methods.

Table 2. Comparison among B, G, S with respect to AP & oLRP and their best class-specific configurations. The mean of class thresholds are assigned as N/A since the thresholds are set class-specific and the mean is not used. Note that unlike AP, lower scores are better for LRP.

	Method	airplane	bicycle	bird	bus	car	cow	dog	cat	elephant	horse	motorcycle	sheep	train	boat	zebra	mean
AP	B	**0.681**	**0.630**	**0.547**	**0.565**	**0.555**	**0.587**	**0.463**	**0.601**	**0.661**	**0.473**	**0.602**	**0.561**	**0.713**	**0.829**	**0.816**	**0.619**
	G	0.621	0.445	0.492	0.398	0.417	0.510	0.416	0.568	0.588	0.441	0.571	0.547	0.600	0.769	0.765	0.544
	S	0.645	0.535	0.500	0.485	0.419	0.492	0.434	0.569	0.589	0.444	0.573	0.545	0.609	0.792	0.782	0.561
oLRP	B	0.627	0.776	0.718	0.702	0.759	0.692	0.728	0.700	0.625	0.723	0.692	0.677	**0.583**	0.594	0.436	0.669
	G	0.606	0.783	0.691	0.727	**0.758**	0.679	0.714	**0.697**	0.614	**0.699**	**0.654**	**0.648**	0.586	0.553	0.432	0.656
	S	**0.603**	**0.762**	**0.687**	**0.688**	0.759	**0.678**	**0.712**	**0.697**	**0.613**	0.701	0.655	0.649	**0.583**	**0.551**	**0.425**	**0.651**
$oLRP_{IoU}$	B	0.182	0.271	0.169	0.177	0.207	0.145	0.166	0.203	0.170	0.155	0.192	0.154	0.159	0.199	0.128	0.179
	G	0.181	0.258	0.170	0.160	0.207	0.151	0.165	0.200	0.170	0.160	0.195	0.155	0.156	0.195	0.128	0.177
	S	0.186	0.270	0.170	0.173	0.207	0.148	0.170	0.200	0.170	0.160	0.194	0.155	0.159	0.197	0.131	0.179
$oLRP_{FP}$	B	0.080	0.228	0.300	0.203	0.303	0.224	0.242	0.248	0.095	0.246	0.158	0.141	0.099	0.163	0.034	0.184
	G	0.006	0.116	0.174	0.137	0.311	0.218	0.229	0.279	0.071	0.221	0.049	0.078	0.091	0.077	0.016	0.142
	S	0.087	0.226	0.184	0.193	0.320	0.182	0.269	0.283	0.075	0.231	0.084	0.078	0.110	0.089	0.030	0.163
$oLRP_{FN}$	B	0.383	0.427	0.478	0.477	0.499	0.504	0.533	0.394	0.395	0.540	0.448	0.494	0.344	0.224	0.220	0.424
	G	0.359	0.523	0.480	0.571	0.493	0.473	0.512	0.372	0.388	0.494	0.415	0.467	0.360	0.221	0.227	0.424
	S	0.326	0.389	0.489	0.461	0.488	0.490	0.480	0.369	0.385	0.493	0.406	0.468	0.339	0.203	0.202	0.398
s^*	B	0.38	0.31	0.44	0.27	0.49	0.61	0.42	0.49	0.49	0.52	0.45	0.51	0.41	0.45	0.31	N/A
	G	0.00	0.69	0.97	0.68	0.00	0.96	0.48	0.70	0.33	0.64	0.60	0.84	0.59	0.90	0.00	N/A
	S	0.00	0.54	0.98	0.45	0.00	0.91	0.49	0.64	0.39	0.58	0.63	0.85	0.55	0.89	0.54	N/A

Effect of the Class-Specific Thresholds: Compared to G, owing to the class-specific thresholds, S has 2.3% better mAP and 0.6% better moLRP as shown in Table 2. However, since the mean is dominated by s^* around 0.5, it is better to focus on classes with low or high s^* values in order to grasp the effect of the approach. The "bus" class has the lowest s^* with 0.27. For this class, S surpasses G by 8.7% in AP and 4.1% in oLRP. This performance increase is also observed for other classes with very low thresholds, such as "airplane", "bicycle" and "zebra". For these classes with lower thresholds, the effect of class-specific threshold on the RP curve is to stretch the curve in the recall domain (maybe by accepting some loss in precision) as shown in the "bus" example in Fig. 6. Not surprisingly, "cow" is one of the two classes for which AP of S is lower since its threshold is the highest and thereby causing recall to be more limited. On the other hand, regarding oLRP, the result is not worse since this time the RP curve is stretched through the positive precision, as shown in Fig. 6, allowing better FP errors. Thus, in any case, lower or higher, the threshold setting method aims to discover the best RP curve. There are four classes in total for which G is better than S in terms of oLRP. However, note that the maximum difference is 0.2% in oLRP and these are the classes with thresholds around 0.5. These suggest that choosing class-specific thresholds rather than the common general thresholding approach increases the performance of the detector especially for classes with low or high class-specific thresholds.

7 Conclusion

We introduced a novel performance metric, LRP, as an alternative to the dominantly used AP. LRP has a number of advantages over AP, which we demonstrated in the paper: (i) AP cannot distinguish between very different RP curves whereas LRP, through its error components, provides a richer evaluation in terms of TP, FN and localization. (ii) AP not does have a localization component and one needs to calculate AP@τ with different τ values. However, LRP explicitly includes a localization error component ($1 - \text{oLRP}_{\text{IoU}}$ gives the mean localization accuracy of a detector). (iii) There are many practical use cases where one needs to set a detection threshold in order to obtain detections to be used in a subsequent stage. Optimal LRP provides a practical solution to this problem, which we demonstrated for online video object detection.

Supplementary Material. Supplementary material contains a detailed definition of AP, a result on the distribution of confidence thresholds, a description of the online detector and the proof that LRP is a metric.

Acknowledgements. This work was supported by the Scientific and Technological Research Council of Turkey (TÜBİTAK) through project called "Object Detection in Videos with Deep Neural Networks" (project no 117E054). We also gratefully acknowledge (i) the support of NVIDIA Corporation with the donation of the Tesla K40 GPU and (ii) the computational resources kindly provided by Roketsan Missiles Inc. used for this research. Kemal Oksuz is supported by the TÜBİTAK 2211-A National Scholarship Programme for Ph.D. students.

References

1. Bernardin, K., Stiefelhagen, R.: Evaluating multiple object tracking performance: the clear mot metrics. EURASIP J. Image Video Process. **2008**(1), 246309 (2008). https://doi.org/10.1155/2008/246309
2. Bourgeois, F., Lassalle, J.C.: An extension of the munkres algorithm for the assignment problem to rectangular matrices. Commun. ACM **14**(12), 802–804 (1971)
3. Breitenstein, M.D., Reichlin, F., Leibe, B., Koller-Meier, E., Gool, L.V.: Robust tracking-by-detection using a detector confidence particle filter. In: IEEE International Conference on Computer Vision ICCV (2009)
4. Breitenstein, M.D., Reichlin, F., Leibe, B., Koller-Meier, E., Van Gool, L.: Online multiperson tracking-by-detection from a single, uncalibrated camera. IEEE Trans. Pattern Anal. Mach. Intell. **33**(9), 1820–1833 (2011)
5. Brzezinski, D., Stefanowski, J., Susmaga, R., Szczech, I.: Visual-based analysis of classification measures with applications to imbalanced data. arXiv: 1704.07122 (2017)
6. Dai, J., Li, Y., He, K., Sun, J.: R-FCN: object detection via region-based fully convolutional networks. In: Advances in Neural Information Processing Systems, NIPS (2016)
7. Dembczynski, K.J., Waegeman, W., Cheng, W., Hüllermeier, E.: An exact algorithm for F-measure maximization. In: Advances in Neural Information Processing, NIPS, pp. 1404–1412 (2011)
8. Everingham, M., Van Gool, L., Williams, C.K.I., Winn, J., Zisserman, A.: The pascal visual object classes (voc) challenge. Int. J. Comput. Vis. **88**(2), 303–338 (2010)
9. Feichtenhofer, C., Pinz, A., Zisserman, A.: Detect to track and track to detect. In: IEEE International Conference on Computer Vision, ICCV (2017)
10. Ferrari, P.: A keras port of single shot multibox detector. https://github.com/pierluigiferrari/ssd_keras. Accessed 13 Mar 2018
11. Girshick, R., Radosavovic, I., Gkioxari, G., Dollár, P., He, K.: Detectron. https://github.com/facebookresearch/detectron. Accessed 13 Mar 2018
12. Kang, K., et al.: T-CNN: tubelets with convolutional neural networks for object detection from videos. IEEE Trans. Circuits Syst. Video Technol. **PP**(99), 1 (2017)
13. Lin, T., Goyal, P., Girshick, R.B., He, K., Dollár, P.: Focal loss for dense object detection. In: IEEE International Conference on Computer Vision, ICCV (2017)
14. Lin, T.-Y., et al.: Microsoft COCO: common objects in context. In: Fleet, D., Pajdla, T., Schiele, B., Tuytelaars, T. (eds.) ECCV 2014. LNCS, vol. 8693, pp. 740–755. Springer, Cham (2014). https://doi.org/10.1007/978-3-319-10602-1_48
15. Lipton, Z.C., Elkan, C., Naryanaswamy, B.: Optimal thresholding of classifiers to maximize F1 measure. In: Calders, T., Esposito, F., Hüllermeier, E., Meo, R. (eds.) ECML PKDD 2014. LNCS (LNAI), vol. 8725, pp. 225–239. Springer, Heidelberg (2014). https://doi.org/10.1007/978-3-662-44851-9_15
16. Liu, W., et al.: SSD: single shot multibox detector. In: Leibe, B., Matas, J., Sebe, N., Welling, M. (eds.) ECCV 2016. LNCS, vol. 9905, pp. 21–37. Springer, Cham (2016). https://doi.org/10.1007/978-3-319-46448-0_2
17. Lu, Y., Lu, C., Tang, C.: Online video object detection using association LSTM. In: IEEE International Conference on Computer Vision, ICCV (2017)
18. Musicant, D.R., Kumar, V., Ozgur, A.: Optimizing F-measure with support vector machines. In: The Florida Artifical Intelligence Research Society Conference, FLAIRS Conference (2003)

19. Oksuz, K., Cemgil, A.T.: Multitarget tracking performance metric: deficiency aware subpattern assignment. IET Radar Sonar Navig. **12**(3), 373–381 (2018)
20. Powers, D.M.W.: What the F-measure doesn't measure: features, flaws, fallacies and fixes. arXiv: 1503.06410 (2015)
21. Puthiya Parambath, S., Usunier, N., Grandvalet, Y.: Optimizing F-measures by cost-sensitive classification. In: Advances in Neural Information Processing, NIPS (2014)
22. Quevedo, J.R., Luaces, O., Bahamonde, A.: Multilabel classifiers with a probabilistic thresholding strategy. Pattern Recogn. **45**(2), 876–883 (2012)
23. Rahmathullah, A.S., Garcia-Fernandez, A.F., Svensson, L.: Generalized optimal sub-pattern assignment metric. In: IEEE International Conference on Information Fusion, FUSION (2017)
24. Ren, S., He, K., Girshick, R., Sun, J.: Faster R-CNN: towards real-time object detection with region proposal networks. In: Advances in Neural Information Processing Systems, NIPS (2015)
25. Rijsbergen, C.J.V.: Information Retrieval. 2nd edn. Butterworth-Heinemann (1979)
26. Ristic, B., Vo, B.N., Clark, D.: Performance evaluation of multi-target tracking using the OSPA metric. In: IEEE International Conference on Information Fusion, FUSION (2010)
27. Ristic, B., Vo, B.N., Clark, D., Vo, B.T.: A metric for performance evaluation of multi-target tracking algorithms. IEEE Trans. Signal Process. **59**(7), 3452–3457 (2011)
28. Russakovsky, O., Deng, J., Su, H., Krause, J., Satheesh, S., Ma, S., Huang, Z., Karpathy, A., Khosla, A., Bernstein, M., Berg, A.C., Fei-Fei, L.: Imagenet large scale visual recognition challenge. Int. J. Comput. Vis. **115**(3), 211–252 (2015)
29. Schuhmacher, D., Vo, B.T., Vo, B.N.: A consistent metric for performance evaluation of multi-object filters. IEEE Trans. Signal Process. **56**(8), 3447–3457 (2008)
30. Shi, X., Yang, F., Tong, F., Lian, H.: A comprehensive performance metric for evaluation of multi-target tracking algorithms. In: International Conference on Information Management, ICIM (2017)
31. Shu, G., Dehghan, A., Shah, M.: Improving an object detector and extracting regions using superpixels. In: IEEE Conference on Computer Vision and Pattern Recognition, CVPR (2013)
32. Stalder, S., Grabner, H., Van Gool, L.: Cascaded confidence filtering for improved tracking-by-detection. In: Daniilidis, K., Maragos, P., Paragios, N. (eds.) ECCV 2010. LNCS, vol. 6311, pp. 369–382. Springer, Heidelberg (2010). https://doi.org/10.1007/978-3-642-15549-9_27
33. Suzuki, J., McDermott, E., Isozaki, H.: Training conditional random fields with multivariate evaluation measures. In: International Conference on Computational Linguistics and the Annual Meeting of the Association for Computational Linguistics, ACL-44 (2006)
34. Tripathi, S., Lipton, Z.C., Belongie, S.J., Nguyen, T.Q.: Context matters: refining object detection in video with recurrent neural networks. In: British Machine Vision Conference, BMVC (2016)

35. Vu, T., Evans, R.: A new performance metric for multiple target tracking based on optimal subpattern assignment. In: IEEE International Conference on Information Fusion, FUSION (2014)
36. Zhu, X., Dai, J., Yuan, L., Wei, Y.: Towards high performance video object detection. arXiv: 1711.11577 (2017)
37. Zou, X., Wen, J.: Detection of object security in crowed environment. In: IEEE International Conference on Communication Problem-Solving, ICCP (2015)

Lip Movements Generation at a Glance

Lele Chen(✉), Zhiheng Li, Ross K. Maddox, Zhiyao Duan, and Chenliang Xu

University of Rochester, Rochester, USA
lchen63@cs.rochester.edu

Abstract. In this paper, we consider the task: given an arbitrary audio speech and one lip image of arbitrary target identity, generate synthesized lip movements of the target identity saying the speech. To perform well, a model needs to not only consider the retention of target identity, photo-realistic of synthesized images, consistency and smoothness of lip images in a sequence, but more importantly, learn the correlations between audio speech and lip movements. To solve the collective problems, we devise a network to synthesize lip movements and propose a novel correlation loss to synchronize lip changes and speech changes. Our full model utilizes four losses for a comprehensive consideration; it is trained end-to-end and is robust to lip shapes, view angles and different facial characteristics. Thoughtful experiments on three datasets ranging from lab-recorded to lips in-the-wild show that our model significantly outperforms other state-of-the-art methods extended to this task.

Keywords: Lip movements generation · Audio visual correlation

1 Introduction

Cross-modality generation has become an important and emerging topic of computer vision and its broader AI communities, where examples are beyond the most prominent image/video-to-text [10,19] and can be found in video-to-sound [23], text-to-image [25], and even sound-to-image [4]. This paper considers a task: given an arbitrary audio speech and one lip image of arbitrary target identity, generate synthesized lip movements of the target identity saying the speech. Notice that the speech does not have to be spoken by the target identity, and neither the speech nor the image of target identity is required to be appeared in the training set (see Fig. 1). Solving this task is crucial to many applications, e.g., enhancing speech comprehension while preserving privacy or assistive devices for hearing impaired people.

Lip movements generation has been traditionally solved as a sub-problem in synthesizing a talking face from speech audio of a target identity [3,12,13,29]. For example, Bo et al. [12] restitch the lower half of the face via a bi-directional LSTM to re-dub a target video from a different audio source. Their model selects

L. Chen and Z. Li—Equal contribution.

V. Ferrari et al. (Eds.): ECCV 2018, LNCS 11211, pp. 538–553, 2018.
https://doi.org/10.1007/978-3-030-01234-2_32

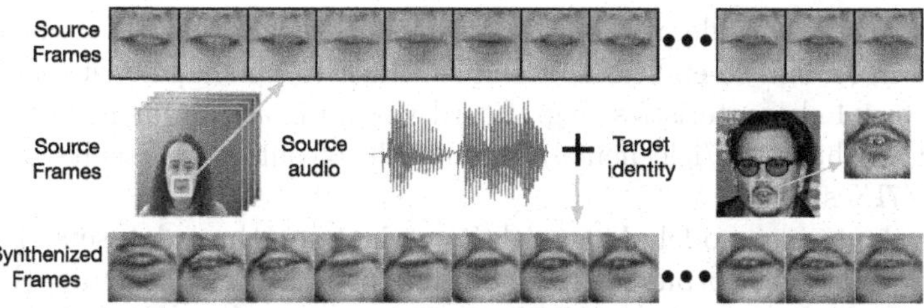

Fig. 1. The model takes an audio speech of the women and one lip image of the target identity, a male celebrity in this case, and synthesizes a video of the man's lip saying the same speech. The synthesized lip movements need to correspond to the speech audio and also maintain the target identity, video smoothness and sharpness

a target mouth region from a dictionary of saved target frames. More recently, Suwajanakorn et al. [29] generate synthesized taking face of President Obama with accurate lip synchronization, given his speech audio. They first use an LSTM model trained on many hours of his weekly address footage to generate mouth landmarks, then retrieve mapped texture and apply complicated post-processing to sharpen the generated video. However, one common problem for these many methods is that they retrieve rather than generating images and thus, require a sizable amount of video frames of the target identity to choose from, whereas our method generates lip movements from a single image of the target identity, i.e., at a glance.

The only work we are aware of that addresses the same task as ours is Chung et al. [6]. They propose an image generator network with skip-connections, and optimize the reconstruction loss between synthesized images and real images. Each time, their model generates one image from 0.35-second audio. Although their video generated image-by-image and enhanced by post-processing looks fine, they have essentially bypassed the harder questions concerning the consistency and smoothness of images in a sequence, as well as the temporal correlations of audio speech and lip movements in a video.

To overcome the above limitations, we propose a novel method that takes speech audio and a lip image of the target identity as input, and generates multiple lip images (16 frames) in a video depicting the corresponding lip movements (see Fig. 1). Observing that speech is highly correlated with lip movements even across identities, a concept grounds lip reading [1,7], the core of our paper is to explore the best modeling of such correlations in building and training a lip movement generator network. To achieve this goal, we devise a method to fuse time-series audio embedding and identity image embedding in generating multiple lip images, and propose a novel audio-visual correlation loss to synchronize lip changes and speech changes in a video. Our final model utilizes a combination of four losses including the proposed audio-visual correlation loss, a novel three-stream adversarial learning loss to guide a discriminator to judge both image quality and motion quality, a feature-space loss to minimize perceptual-level differences, and a reconstruction loss to minimize pixel-level differences, for a comprehensive consideration of lip movements generation. The whole system is trained in an end-to-end fashion and is robust to lip shapes, view angles, and different facial characteristics (e.g., beard v.s. no beard). Our code is available at https://github.com/lelechen63/3d_gan. Check out more results at https://youtu.be/7IX_sIL5v0c.

We evaluate our model along with its variants on three datasets: The GRID audiovisual sentence corpus (GRID) [8], Linguistic Data Consortium (LDC) [26] and Lip Reading in the Wild (LRW) [7]. To measure the quantitative accuracy of lip movements, we propose a novel metric that evaluates the detected landmark distance of synthesized lips to ground-truth lips. In addition, we use a cohort of three metrics, Peak Signal to Noise Ratio (PSNR), Structure Similarity Index Measure (SSIM) [32], and perceptual-based no-reference objective image sharpness metric (CPBD) [21], to measure the quality of synthesized lip images, e.g., image sharpness. We compare our model with Chung et al. [6] and an extended version of the state-of-the-art video Generative Adversarial Network (GAN) model [30] to our task. Experimental results show that our model outperforms them significantly on all three datasets (see "Full model" in Table 3). Furthermore, we also show real-world novel examples of synthesized lip movements of celebrities, who are not in our dataset.

Our paper marks three contributions. First, to the best of our knowledge, we are the first to consider the correlations among speech and lip movements in generating multiple lip images at a glance. Second, we explore various models and loss functions in building and training a lip movement generator network. Third, we quantify the evaluation metrics and our final model achieves significant improvement over state-of-the-art methods extended to this task on three datasets ranging from lab-recorded to lips in-the-wild.

2 Related Work

We have briefly surveyed work in lip movement generation in the Introduction section. Here, we discuss related work of each techniques used in our model.

A related but different task to ours is lip reading, where it also tackles the cross-modality generation problem. [1,7] use the correlation between lip movement and the sentences/words to interpret the audio information from the visual information. Rasiwasia et al. [24] use Canonical Correlation Analysis (CCA) [16] subspace learning to learn two intermediate feature spaces for two modalities where they do correlation on the projected features. Cutler and Davis [9] use Time Delay Neural Network [31] (TDNN) to extract temporal invariant audio features and visual features. These works have inspired us to model correlations between speech audio and lip movements in generating videos.

Audio variations and lip movements are not always synchronized in the production of human speech; lips often move before the audio signal is produced [2]. Such delay between audio and visual needs to be considered when designing a model. Suwajanakorn et al. [29] apply a time-delayed RNN without outputting value in the first few RNN cells. Therefore, the output is shifted accordingly to the delayed steps. However, such delay is empirically fixed by hand and thus, it is hard to determine the amount of delay for videos in-the-wild. We follow [31] to extract features with a large receptive field along temporal dimension, but use a convolutional network instead of TDNN that leads to a simpler design.

Adversarial training [14] is recently introduced as a novel and effective way to train generative models. Researchers find that by conditioning the model on additional information, it is possible to direct the data generation process [5,20,22]. Furthermore, GAN has shown its ability to bridge the gap between different modalities and produce useful joint representations. We also use GAN loss in our training but we show that combining it with other losses leads to better results.

3 Lip-Movement Generator Network

The overall data flow of our lip-movement generator network is depicted in Fig. 2. **In this paper, we omit channel dimension of all tensors for simple illustration**. Recall that the input to our network are a speech audio and one single image of the target identity, and the output of our network are synthesized lip images of the target identity saying that audio. The synthesized lip movements need to correspond to the speech audio, maintain the target identity, ensure the video smoothness, and be photo-realistic.

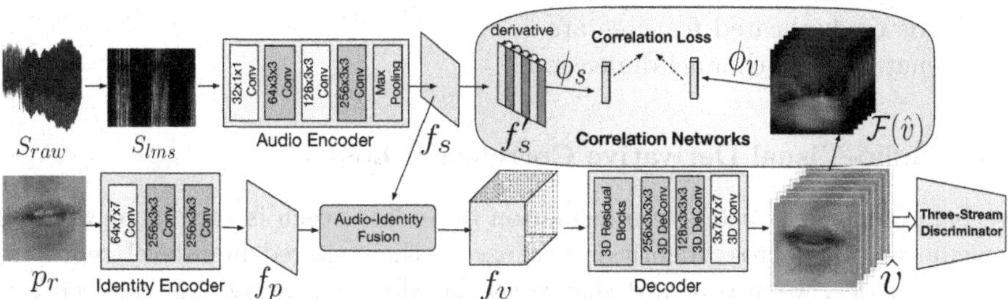

Fig. 2. Full model illustration. Audio encoder and identity encoder extracts and fuses audio and visual embeddings. Audio-Identity fusion network fuses features from two modalities. Decoder expands fused feature to synthesized video. Correlation Networks are in charge of strengthening the audio-visual mapping. Three-Stream discriminator is responsible for distinguishing generated video and real video

3.1 Audio-Identity Fusion and Generation

First, we encode the two-stream input information. For audio stream, the raw audio waveform, denoted as S_{raw}, is first transformed into log-mel spectrogram (see detail in Sect. 5.1), denoted as S_{lms}, then encoded by an audio encoder network into audio features $f_s \in \mathbb{R}^{T\times F}$, where T and F denote the number of time frames and frequency channels. For visual stream, an input identity image, denoted as p_r, is encoded by an identity encoder network. The network outputs image features $f_p \in \mathbb{R}^{H \times W}$, where H and W denote the height, width of the output image features.

We fuse audio features f_s and visual features f_p together, whose output, the synthesized video feature f_v, will be expanded by several residual blocks and 3D deconvolution operations to generate synthesized video $\hat{v}$. In order to make sure the synthesized clip is based on the target person and also captures the time-variation of speech, we investigate an effective way to fuse f_s and f_p to get f_v for generating a video. Here, the challenge is that the feature maps exist in different modalities, e.g., audio, visual, and audio-visual, and reside in different feature spaces, e.g., time-frequency, space, and space-time.

Our fusion method is based on duplication and concatenation. This process is depicted in Fig. 3. For each audio feature, we duplicate that feature along frequency dimension in each time step, i.e., from the size of $T \times F$ to the size of $T \times F \times F$. Image feature, which can be viewed as a template for video representation, is copied T times, i.e., from $H \times W$ to a new size $T \times H \times W$. We set $H = W = F$ in this method. Then, two kinds of duplicated features are concatenated along channel dimension.

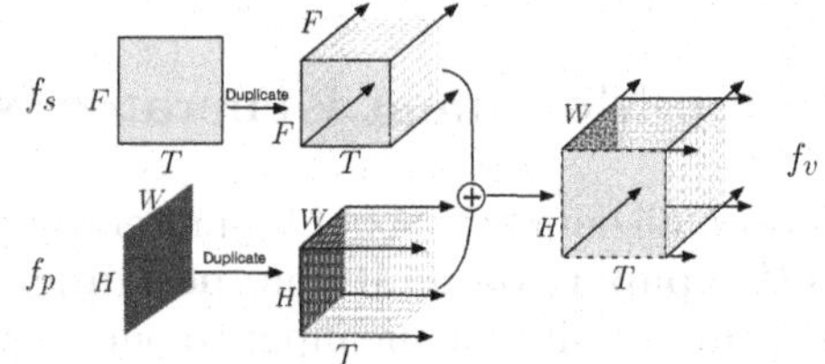

Fig. 3. Audio-Identity fusion. Transfer audio time-frequency features and image spatial features to video spatial-temporal features

3.2 Audio-Visual Derivative Correlation Loss

We believe that the acoustic information of audio speech is correlated with lip movements even across identities because of their shared high-level representation. Besides, we also regard that variation along temporal axis between two modalities are more likely to be correlated. In other words, compared with acoustic feature and visual feature of lip shape themselves, the variation of audio feature (e.g. the voice raising to a higher pitch) and variation of visual feature (e.g. mouth opening) have a higher likelihood to be correlated. Therefore, we propose a method to optimize the correlations of the two modalities in their feature spaces. We use f_s' in size of $(T-1) \times F$, the derivative of audio feature f_s (with size of $T \times F$) between consecutive frames in temporal dimension, to represent the changes in speech. It goes through an audio derivative encoder network ϕ_s, and thus, we have audio derivative feature $\phi_s(f_s')$. Similarly, we use $\mathcal{F}(v)$ to represent optical flows of each consecutive frames in a video v, where $\mathcal{F}$ is an optical flow estimation algorithm. It goes through an optical flow encoder network ϕ_v, and thus, we have $\phi_v(\mathcal{F}(v))$ to depict the visual variations of lip movements in the feature space. We use cosine similarity loss to maximize the correlation between audio derivative feature and visual derivative feature:

$$\ell_{corr} = 1 - \frac{\phi_s(f_s') \cdot \phi_v(\mathcal{F}(v))}{\|\phi_s(f_s')\|_2 \cdot \|\phi_v(\mathcal{F}(v))\|_2} \ . \tag{1}$$

Here, the optical flow algorithm applied to the synthesized frames needs to be differentiable for back-propagation [27]. In our implementation, we add a small number ($\epsilon = 10^{-8}$) to the denominator to avoid division by zero. In order to avoid trivial solution when ϕ_s and ϕ_v are learned to predict constant outputs $\phi_s(f_x')$ and $\phi_v(\mathcal{F}(v))$ which are perfectly correlated and the ℓ_{corr} will go to 0, we combine other losses during the training process (see Eq. 2).

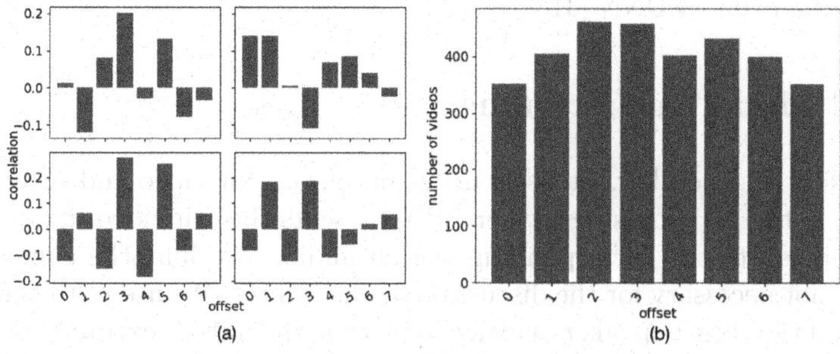

Fig. 4. (a): Correlation coefficients with different offsets of four example videos. (b): Number of videos of different offsets with which the video has the maximum correlation coefficient. X-axes of both (a) and (b) stands for time steps of flow field shifted forward

Correlation Networks. The audio and visual information are not perfectly aligned in time. Usually, lip shape forms earlier than sound. For instance, when we say word 'bed', upper and lower lips meet before speaking the word [2]. If such delay problem exists, aforementioned correlation loss, assuming audio-visual information are perfectly aligned, may not work. We verify the delayed correspondence problem between audio and visual information by designing a case study on 3260 videos randomly sampled from the GRID dataset. The solution for the delayed correspondence problem is given in the next paragraph. In the case study, for each 75-frame video v, we calculate the mean values of each 74 derivatives of audio s_{lms} and mean values of each 74 optical flow fields $\phi_v(\mathcal{F}_v)$. With respect to each video, we shift mean values of optical flows forward along time at different offsets (0 to 7 in our case study) and calculate Pearson correlation coefficients of those two parts. Results of four videos, calculated by aforementioned procedures, are shown in Fig. 4(a). Finally, we count the number of videos in different offsets at which the video has the largest correlation coefficient, as shown in Fig. 4(b). Figure 4 shows that different videos prefer different offsets to output the maximum correlation coefficient, which indicates that fixing a constant offset of all audio-visual inputs would not solve the problem of correlation with inconsistent delays among all videos in a dataset.

To mitigate such delayed correlation problem, we design correlation networks (as shown in Fig. 2) containing an audio derivative encoder ϕ_s and an optical flow encoder ϕ_v to extract features used for calculating the correlation loss in Eq. 1. These networks reduce the feature size but retain the temporal length simultaneously. The sizes of the two outputs are matched for calculating the correlation loss. We use 3D CNNs to implement these networks, which are also helpful to mitigate the fixed offset problem happens in previous works [29]. Both ϕ_s and ϕ_v output features with large receptive fields (9 for $\phi_s(f_s')$ and 13 for $\phi_v(\mathcal{F}_v)$), which consider the audio-visual correlation in large temporal dimension. Compared with time-delayed RNN proposed in [29], CNN can learn delay from the dataset rather than set it as a hyper-parameter. Besides, CNN architecture benefits from its weight sharing property leading to a simpler and smaller design than TDNN [31].

4 Full Model and Training

Without loss of generality, we use pairs of lip movement video and speech audio $\{(v^j, s^j)\}$ in the training stage, where v^j represents the jth video in our dataset and s^j represents the corresponding speech audio. We omit the superscript j when it is not necessary for the discussion of one sample. We use p_r to denote one lip image of the target speaker, which can provide the initial texture information. During training, we train over (v, s) in the training set and sample p_r to be one frame randomly selected from the raw video where v^j is sampled from to ensure that v and p_r contain the same identity. Therefore, the system is robust to the lip shape of the identity p_r. The objective of training is to generate a realistic video $\hat{v}$ that resembles v. For testing, the speech s and identity image p_r can be any speech and any lip image (even out of the dataset we used in training). Next, we present the full model in the context of training.

Our full model (see Fig. 2) is end-to-end trainable and is optimized according to the following objective function:

$$\mathcal{L} = \ell_{corr} + \lambda_1 \ell_{pix} + \lambda_2 \ell_{perc} + \lambda_3 \ell_{gen} \ , \tag{2}$$

where λ_1, λ_2 and λ_3 are coefficients of different loss terms. We set them as 0.5, 1.0, 1.0 respectively in this paper. The intuitions behind the four losses are as follows:

- ℓ_{corr}: Correlation loss, illustrated in Sect. 3.2, is introduced to ensure the correlation between audio and visual information.
- ℓ_{pix}: Pixel-level reconstruction loss, defined as $\ell_{pix}(\hat{v}, v) = \|v - \hat{v}\|$, which aims to make the model sensitive to speaker's appearance, i.e., retain the identity texture. However, we find that using it alone will reduce the sharpness of the synthesized video frames.
- ℓ_{perc}: Perceptual loss, which is originally proposed by [17] as a method used in image style transfer and super-resolution. It utilizes high-level features to compare generated images and ground-truth images, resulting in better

sharpness of the synthesized image. We adapt this perceptual loss and detail it in Sect. 4.1.

- ℓ_{gen}: Adversarial loss allows our model to generate overall realistic looking images and is defined as: $\ell_{gen} = -\log D([s^j, \hat{v}^j])$, where D is a discriminator network. We describe the detail of our proposed stream-stream GAN discriminator in Sect. 4.2.

4.1 Autoencoder and Perceptual Loss

In order to avoid over-smoothed phenomenon of synthesized video frames $\hat{v}$, we adapt perceptual loss proposed by Johnson et al. [17], which reflects perceptual-level similarity of images. The perceptual loss is defined as:

$$\ell_{perc}(\hat{v}, v) = \|\varphi(v) - \varphi(\hat{v})\|_2^2 \ , \tag{3}$$

where φ is a feature extraction network. We train an autoencoder to reconstruct video clips. To let the network be more sensitive to structure features, we apply six residual blocks after the convolution layers. We train the autoencoder from scratch, then fix the weights and use its encoder part as φ to calculate perceptual loss for training the full model.

4.2 Three-Stream GAN Discriminator

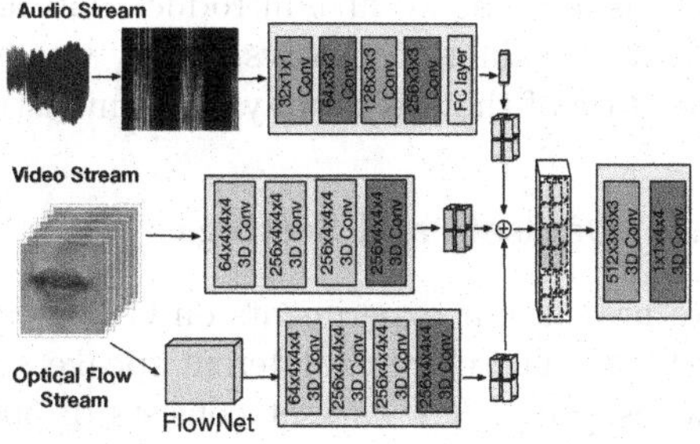

Fig. 5. Three-stream GAN discriminator illustration

The GAN discriminator in [30] for synthesizing video considers the motion changes implicitly by 3D convolution. In order to generate sharp and smooth changing video frames, we propose a three-stream discriminator network (see Fig. 5) to distinguish the synthesized video ($\hat{v}^j$) from real video (v^j) that not only considers motion explicitly and but also conditions on the input speech signal. The input to the discriminator is a video clip with the corresponding audio. We have the following three streams. For audio stream (also used in our generator), we first convert the raw audio to log-mel spectrogram, then use four convolutional layers followed by a fully-connected layer to get a 1D vector. We duplicate it to match features from other streams. For video stream, we use four 3D CNN layers to extract video features. In addition, we include an optical flow stream that attends to motion changes explicitly. We fine-tune the FlowNet [11], which is pre-trained on FlyingChairs dataset, to extract optical flows, then apply four 3D CNN layers to extract features.

Finally, we concatenate the three-stream features in channel dimension and let them go through two convolutional layers to output the discriminator probability. We adapt mismatch strategy [25] to make sure that our discriminator

Table 1. Dataset information. Validation set: known speakers but unseen sentences. Testing set: unseen speakers and unseen sentences

Dataset	GRID	LRW	LDC
Train	211k (37.5 h)	841k (159.8 h)	36k (6.4 h)
Val.	23 (4.2 h)	N/A	4k (0.7 h)
Test	7k (1.3 h)	40k (7.8 h)	6.6k (1.2 h)

is also sensitive to mismatched audio and visual information. Therefore, the discriminator loss is defined as:

$$\begin{aligned}\ell_{dis} = &- \log D([s^j, v^j]) \\ &- \lambda_p \log(1 - D([s^j, \hat{v}])) \\ &- \lambda_u \log(1 - D([s^j, v^k])), \quad k \neq j \ ,\end{aligned} \tag{4}$$

where v^k represents a mismatch real video. We set both λ_p and λ_u 0.5 in our experiment. The performance of the optical flow stream is discussed in Sect. 5.3.

5 Experiments

In this section, we first introduce datasets and experimental settings, and our adapted evaluation metrics. Then, we show ablation study and comparison to the state of the art. Finally, we demonstrate real-world novel examples.

5.1 Datasets and Settings

We present our experiments on GRID [8], LRW [7] and LDC [26] datasets (see Table 1). There are 33 different speakers in GRID. Each speaker has 1000 short videos. The LRW dataset consists of 500 different words spoken by hundreds of different speakers. There are 14 speakers in the LDC dataset in which each speaker reads 238 different words and 166 different sentences. Videos in GRID and LDC are lab-recorded while videos in LRW are collected from news. Our data is composed by two parts: audio and image frames. The network can output different numbers of frames. In this work, we only consider generating 16 frames of mouth region. As the videos are sampled at 25 fps, the time span of the synthesized image frames is 0.64 s. We use sliding window approach (window size: 16 frames, overlap: 8 frames) to obtain training and testing video samples over raw videos.

Audio: We extract audio from the video file with a sampling rate of 41.1 kHz. Each input audio is 0.64 s long (0.04×16). To encode audio, we first transform the raw audio waveform into the time-frequency domain by calculating the Log-amplitude Mel-frequency Spectrum (LMS). When we calculate the LMS, the number of samples between successive frames, the length of the FFT window, and the number of Mel bands are 512, 1024 and 128, respectively. This operation will convert a 0.64-s raw audio to a 64×128 time-frequency representation.

Images: First, we extract all image frames from videos. Then, we extract lip landmarks [18] and crop the image around the lip. Landmarks are only used for cropping and evaluation. We resize all of the cropped images to 64×64. So, each 0.64-s audio corresponds to a $16 \times 3 \times 64\times 64$ RGB image sequence.

We adopt Adam optimizer during training and fixed learning rates of 2×10^{-4} with weight decay of 4×10^{-4}, and coefficients β_1 and β_2 are 0.5 and 0.999, respectively. We initialize all network layers according to the method described in [15]. All models are trained and tested on a single NVIDIA GTX 1080Ti. During testing, generating one single frame costs 0.015 s.

5.2 Evaluation Metrics

To evaluate the quality of the synthesized video frames, we compute Peak Signal to Noise Ratio (PSNR) and Structure Similarity Index Measure (SSIM) [32]. To evaluate the sharpness of the generated image frames, we compute the perceptual-based no-reference objective image sharpness metric (CPBD) [21].

As far as we know, no quantitative metric has been used to evaluate the accuracy of generated lip movements video. Therefore, to evaluate whether the synthesized video $\hat{v}$ corresponds to accurate lip movements based on the input audio, a new metric is proposed by calculating the Landmark Distance (LMD). We use Dlib [18], a HOG-based facial landmarks detector, which is also widely used in lip-movement generation task and other related works [28,29], to detect lip landmarks on $\hat{v}$ and v, and mark them as LF and LR, respectively. To eliminate the geometric difference, we calibrate the two mean points of lip landmarks in LF and LR. Then, we calculate the Euclidean distance between each corresponding pairs of landmarks on LF and LR, and finally normalized them with temporal length and number of landmark points. LMD is defined as:

$$LMD = \frac{1}{T} \times \frac{1}{P} \sum_{t=1}^{T} \sum_{p=1}^{P} \|LR_{t,p} - LF_{t,p}\|_2 \ , \tag{5}$$

where T denotes the temporal length of video and P denotes the total number of landmark points on each image (20 points).

5.3 Ablation Study

We conduct ablation experiments to study the contributions of the three components in our full model separately: correlation loss, three-stream GAN discriminator and perceptual loss. The ablation study is conducted on GRID dataset. Results are shown in Table 2. Different implementations are discussed in below as well. The following ablation studies are trained and tested on the GRID dataset.

Perceptual Loss and Reconstruction Loss. Generally, we find that perceptual loss can help our model generate more accurate lip movements with higher

Table 2. Ablation results on GRID dataset. The full model (method (e)) uses all four losses as described in Sect. 4. For LMD, the lower the better. SSIM, PSNR and CPBD, the higher the better. We bold top-2 leading scores for each metric

Methods	(a)	(b)	(c)	(d)	(e)	(f)	(g)	(h)	(i)
ℓ_{pix}	✓		✓	✓	✓	✓	✓	✓	✓
ℓ_{perc}	✓	✓		✓	✓	✓	✓	✓	✓
ℓ_{corr}	✓	✓	✓		✓		✓		✓
ℓ_{corr} (Non-Derivative Corr.)						✓			
ℓ_{gen} (Three-Stream)		✓	✓	✓	✓	✓			
ℓ_{gen} (Two-Stream)							✓	✓	
ℓ_{gen} (Three-Str. Frame-Diff.)									✓
Metrics									
LMD	**1.24**	1.31	1.38	1.31	**1.18**	1.96	1.39	1.42	1.40
SSIM	**0.77**	0.71	0.72	0.70	**0.73**	0.52	0.68	0.59	0.66
PSNR	29.36	29.79	29.66	**29.80**	**29.98**	28.6	29.59	29.46	29.51
CPBD	0.01	0.18	0.17	**0.21**	0.18	**0.22**	0.19	0.18	0.21

image quality, and improve image sharpness at the same time (see method (c) v.s. method (e) in Table 2). If we compare method (b) with method (e), we can find that pixel-wise reconstruction loss can improve the LMD, SSIM and PSNR while decreasing the CPBD.

Correlation Models. When correlation loss is removed from final objective function Eq. 2, results are worse than final objective in LMD, SSIM and PSNR, demonstrating the importance of correlation loss in generating more accurate lip movement (see method (d) v.s. method (e) or method (g) v.s. method (h)).

Besides, we investigate a model variant, *Non-Derivative Correlation* (see method (f) in Table 2), for analyzing the necessity of applying derivative features to ϕ_s and ϕ_v. Instead of using the derivative of audio features and the optical flow, this variant just uses audio features f_s and video frames v directly as inputs. Neither the derivative nor the optical flow is calculated here. Other settings (e.g., network structure and loss functions) are identical with the full model (denoted as method (e) in Table 2). The comparison between method (e) and method (f) in Table 2 shows that derivative correlation model outperforms the *Non-Derivative Correlation* model in metrics such as SSIM, PSNR and LMD. With respect to *Non-Derivative Correlation* model, landmark distance is even worse than model without correlation loss (method (d)). The experimental result proves our assumption that it is the derivatives of audio and visual information rather than the direct features that are correlated. Furthermore, since *Non-Derivative Correlation* model fails to learn the derivative feature implicitly (i.e. convolutional layers fails to transform feature to their derivatives), using the derivatives of audio and visual features to do correlation as a strong expert prior knowledge is necessary.

GAN Discriminator. We find that ℓ_{gen} improves the CPBD result a lot (see method (a) and method (e) in Table 2), demonstrating that discriminator can improve the frame sharpness. Furthermore, we use two model variants to study the effectiveness of proposed three-stream GAN discriminator. ℓ_{gen} (Two-Stream) only contains audio stream and video stream. ℓ_{gen} (Three-Str. Frame-Diff.) replaces the optical flow with frame-wise difference, i.e., $L1$ distance between adjacent frames, as the third stream to capture motion changes. First, compared with the two-stream variant, our full model with proposed three-stream discriminator gives better result (see method (e) v.s. method (g)), which indicates the effectiveness of explicitly modeling motion changes among the frames. Second, compared with the three-stream frame-difference variant, the full model generates more realistic (higher CPBD) and accurate lip movements (lower LMD) (see method (e) and (i)), which indicates that optical flow is a better representation than frame-wise difference for modeling motion changes.

5.4 Comparison to State-of-the-Art

In this section, we compare our full model with two state-of-the-art methods [6, 30]. We extend [30] to a conditional GAN structure, which receives the same target image information and audio information as our models. There are a few changes made for ensuring a fair comparison with [6]: we did not pretrain the identity encoder; we changed two convolution layers to fit the image size (64×64); we omitted the De-blurring post-processing as we aim to compare directly the generative models themselves.

The quantitative results are shown in Table 3. We test our models on three different datasets. The results show that our proposed models outperform state-of-the-art models in most of the metrics. In terms of LMD and PSNR, our full model shows better performance than methods that use discriminator [30] or reconstruction loss [6]. Model proposed by Chung et al., based on reconstruction loss, generates blurred images, which makes them look unrealistic. We can see this phenomenon in the CPBD column. The LRW dataset consists of people talking in the wild so resolution is much smaller in terms of lip region. We need to scale up the ground truth to 64×64, which leads to a lower resolution and CPBD. We suspect this is the reason why we achieve a better CPBD than ground truth in LRW dataset.

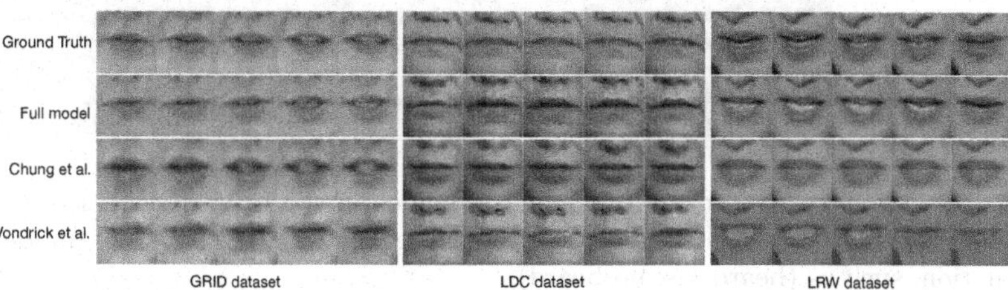

Fig. 6. Generated videos of our model on three testing datasets compared with state-of-the-art methods. In the testing set, none of the speakers were in the training set

Table 3. Results on three datasets. Models mentioned in this table are trained from scratch (no pre-training included) and be tested on each dataset a time. We bold each leading score

Method	GRID				LDC				LRW			
	LMD	SSIM	PSNR	CPBD	LMD	SSIM	PSNR	CPBD	LMD	SSIM	PSNR	CPBD
G. T.	0	N/A	N/A	0.141	0	N/A	N/A	0.211	0	N/A	N/A	0.068
Vondrick [30]	2.38	0.60	28.45	0.129	2.34	**0.75**	27.96	0.160	3.28	0.34	28.03	0.082
Chung [6]	1.35	**0.74**	29.36	0.016	2.13	0.50	28.22	0.010	2.25	0.46	28.06	**0.083**
Full model	**1.18**	0.73	**29.89**	**0.175**	**1.82**	0.57	**28.87**	**0.172**	**1.92**	**0.53**	**28.65**	0.075

The qualitative results compared with other methods are shown in Fig. 6. Our model generates sharper video frames on all three datasets, which has also been supported by the CPBD results, even if input identity images are in low resolution. We show additional results of our method in Fig. 7. Our model can generate realistic lip movement videos that are robust to view angles, lip shapes and facial characteristics in most of the times. However, sometimes our model fails to preserve the skin color (see the last two examples in Fig. 7), which, we suspect, is due to the imbalanced data distribution in LRW dataset. Furthermore, the model has difficulties in capturing the amount of lip deformations of each person, which is an intrinsic problem when learning from a single image.

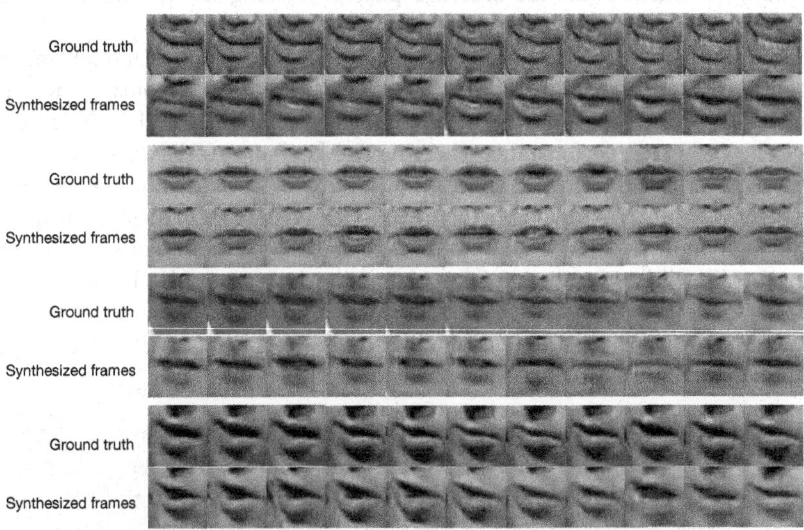

Fig. 7. Randomly selected outputs of the full model on the LRW testing set. The lip shape in videos not only synchronize well with the ground truth, but maintain identity information, such as (beard v.s. no beard)

5.5 Real-World Novel Examples

For generating videos given unpaired identity image and audio in the real-world, i.e., source identity of provided audio is different from the target identity and out of the datasets, our model can still perform well. Results are shown in Fig. 8, in which three identity images of celebrities are selected outside of the datasets the model trained on and the input audio is selected in GRID dataset. For our model trained on LRW, both identity images and audio are unseen. For our model trained on GRID, we leave the source identity out of the training.

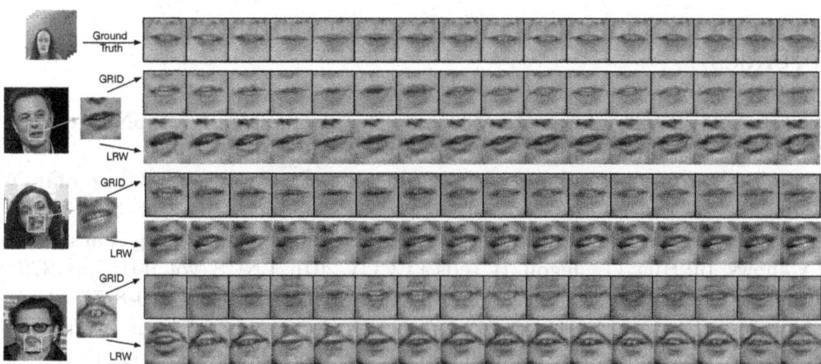

Fig. 8. The figure shows the generated images based on three identity images outside of dataset, which is also not paired with the input audio from GRID dataset. Two full models trained on GRID and LRW datasets are used here for a comparison

The videos generated by our model show promising qualitative performance. Both lip regions of Musk and Sandburg are rotated by some degrees. We can see that the rotation phenomenon in the generated video frames as well. Besides, our model can also retain beards in our generated clip when identity (target person) has beards as well. However, we observe that model trained on GRID dataset fails to reserve the identity information. Because of the fact that LRW dataset has much more identities than GRID dataset (hundreds v.s. 33), the model trained on LRW has better generalization ability.

6 Conclusion and Future Work

In this paper, we study the task: given an arbitrary audio speech and one lip image of arbitrary target identity, generate synthesized lip movements of the target identity saying the speech. To perform well in this task, it requires a model to not only consider the retention of the target identity, photo-realistic of synthesized images, consistency and smoothness of images in a video, but also learn the correlations between the speech audio and lip movements. We achieve this by proposing a new generator network, a novel audio-visual correlation loss and a full model that considers four complementary losses. We show significant improvements on three datasets compared to two state-of-the-art methods. There are several future directions. First, non-fixed length lip movements generation is needed for a more practical purpose. Second, it is valuable to extend our method to one generating full face in an end-to-end paradigm.

Acknowledgement. This work was supported in part by NSF BIGDATA 1741472, NIH grant R00 DC014288 and the University of Rochester AR/VR Pilot Award. We gratefully acknowledge the gift donations of Markable, Inc., Tencent and the support of NVIDIA with the donation of GPUs used for this research. This article solely reflects the opinions and conclusions of its authors and not the funding agents.

References

1. Assael, Y.M., Shillingford, B., Whiteson, S., de Freitas, N.: LipNet: end-to-end sentence-level lipreading. arXiv preprint arXiv:1611.01599 (2017)
2. Chandrasekaran, C., Trubanova, A., Stillittano, S., Caplier, A., Ghazanfar, A.A.: The natural statistics of audiovisual speech. PLOS Comput. Biol. **5**(7) (2009)
3. Charles, J., Magee, D., Hogg, D.: Virtual immortality: reanimating characters from TV shows. In: Hua, G., Jégou, H. (eds.) ECCV 2016. LNCS, vol. 9915, pp. 879–886. Springer, Cham (2016). https://doi.org/10.1007/978-3-319-49409-8_71
4. Chen, L., Srivastava, S., Duan, Z., Xu, C.: Deep cross-modal audio-visual generation. In: Proceedings of Multimedia Thematic Workshops. ACM (2017)
5. Chen, X., Duan, Y., Houthooft, R., Schulman, J., Sutskever, I., Abbeel, P.: InfoGAN: interpretable representation learning by information maximizing generative adversarial nets. In: Proceedings of NIPS. Curran Associates, Inc. (2016)
6. Chung, J.S., Jamaludin, A., Zisserman, A.: You said that? In: Proceedings of BMVC. Springer (2017)
7. Chung, J.S., Zisserman, A.: Lip reading in the wild. In: Lai, S.-H., Lepetit, V., Nishino, K., Sato, Y. (eds.) ACCV 2016. LNCS, vol. 10112, pp. 87–103. Springer, Cham (2017). https://doi.org/10.1007/978-3-319-54184-6_6
8. Cooke, M., Barker, J., Cunningham, S., Shao, X.: An audio-visual corpus for speech perception and automatic speech recognition. J. Acoust. Soc. Am. **120**(5), 2421–2424 (2006)
9. Cutler, R., Davis, L.S.: Look who's talking: speaker detection using video and audio correlation. In: Proceedings of ICME. IEEE (2000)
10. Das, P., Xu, C., Doell, R., Corso, J.J.: A thousand frames in just a few words: lingual description of videos through latent topics and sparse object stitching. In: Proceedings of CVPR. IEEE (2013)
11. Dosovitskiy, A., et al.: FlowNet: learning optical flow with convolutional networks. In: Proceedings of ICCV. IEEE (2015)
12. Fan, B., Wang, L., Soong, F.K., Xie, L.: Photo-real talking head with deep bidirectional LSTM. In: ICASSP. IEEE (2015)
13. Garrido, P., et al.: VDub: modifying face video of actors for plausible visual alignment to a dubbed audio track. Comput. Graph. Forum **34**(2), 193–204 (2015)
14. Goodfellow, I.J., et al.: Generative adversarial nets. In: Proceedings of NIPS. Curran Associates, Inc. (2014)
15. He, K., Zhang, X., Ren, S., Sun, J.: Delving deep into rectifiers: surpassing human-level performance on ImageNet classification. In: Proceedings of CVPR. IEEE (2015)

16. Hotelling, H.: Relations between two sets of variates. In: Kotz, S., Johnson, N.L. (eds.) Breakthroughs in Statistics, pp. 162–190. Springer, New York (1992). https://doi.org/10.1007/978-1-4612-4380-9_14
17. Johnson, J., Alahi, A., Fei-Fei, L.: Perceptual losses for real-time style transfer and super-resolution. In: Leibe, B., Matas, J., Sebe, N., Welling, M. (eds.) ECCV 2016. LNCS, vol. 9906, pp. 694–711. Springer, Cham (2016). https://doi.org/10.1007/978-3-319-46475-6_43
18. King, D.E.: Dlib-ml: a machine learning toolkit. JMLR **10**, 1755–1758 (2009)
19. Kulkarni, G., et al.: Baby talk: understanding and generating simple image descriptions. In: Proceedings of CVPR. IEEE (2011)
20. Mirza, M., Osindero, S.: Conditional generative adversarial nets. arXiv preprint arXiv:1411.1784 (2014)
21. Narvekar, N.D., Karam, L.J.: A no-reference image blur metric based on the cumulative probability of blur detection (CPBD). IEEE TIP **20**(9), 2678–2683 (2011)
22. Odena, A., Olah, C., Shlens, J.: Conditional image synthesis with auxiliary classifier GANs. In: Proceedings of ICML. PMLR (2017)
23. Owens, A., Isola, P., McDermott, J., Torralba, A., Adelson, E.H., Freeman, W.T.: Visually indicated sounds. In: Proceedings of CVPR. IEEE (2016)
24. Rasiwasia, N., et al.: A new approach to cross-modal multimedia retrieval. In: Proceedings of Multimedia. ACM (2010)
25. Reed, S.E., Akata, Z., Yan, X., Logeswaran, L., Schiele, B., Lee, H.: Generative adversarial text to image synthesis. In: ICML. PMLR (2016)
26. Richie, S., Warburton, C., Carter, M.: Audiovisual database of spoken American English. Linguistic Data Consortium (2009)
27. Rumelhart, D.E., Hinton, G.E., Williams, R.J.: Learning representations by back-propagating errors. Nature **323**(6088), 533–536 (1986)
28. Son Chung, J., Senior, A., Vinyals, O., Zisserman, A.: Lip reading sentences in the wild. In: Proceedings of CVPR. IEEE (2017)
29. Suwajanakorn, S., Seitz, S.M., Kemelmacher-Shlizerman, I.: Synthesizing Obama: learning lip sync from audio. ACM Trans. Graph. **36**(4), 95:1–95:13 (2017)
30. Vondrick, C., Pirsiavash, H., Torralba, A.: Generating videos with scene dynamics. In: Proceedings of NIPS. Curran Associates, Inc. (2016)
31. Waibel, A.H., Hanazawa, T., Hinton, G.E., Shikano, K., Lang, K.J.: Phoneme recognition using time-delay neural networks. IEEE Trans. Acoust. Speech Signal Process. **37**(3), 328–339 (1989)
32. Wang, Z., Bovik, A.C., Sheikh, H.R., Simoncelli, E.P.: Image quality assessment: from error visibility to structural similarity. IEEE TIP **13**(4), 600–612 (2004)

Small-Scale Pedestrian Detection Based on Topological Line Localization and Temporal Feature Aggregation

Tao Song, Leiyu Sun, Di Xie(✉), Haiming Sun, and Shiliang Pu

Hikvision Research Institute, Hangzhou, China
{songtao6,sunleiyu,xiedi,sunhaiming,pushiliang}@hikvision.com

Abstract. A critical issue in pedestrian detection is to detect small-scale objects that will introduce feeble contrast and motion blur in images and videos, which in our opinion should partially resort to deep-rooted annotation bias. Motivated by this, we propose a novel method integrated with somatic topological line localization (TLL) and temporal feature aggregation for detecting multi-scale pedestrians, which works particularly well with small-scale pedestrians that are relatively far from the camera. Moreover, a post-processing scheme based on Markov Random Field (MRF) is introduced to eliminate ambiguities in occlusion cases. Applying with these methodologies comprehensively, we achieve best detection performance on Caltech benchmark and improve performance of small-scale objects significantly (miss rate decreases from 74.53% to 60.79%). Beyond this, we also achieve competitive performance on CityPersons dataset and show the existence of annotation bias in KITTI dataset.

Keywords: Small-scale pedestrian detection · Multi-scale
Temporal feature aggregation · Markov random field · Deep learning

1 Introduction

Pedestrian detection is a critical problem in computer vision with significant impact on a number of applications, such as urban autonomous driving, surveillance and robotics. In recent years many works have been devoted to this detection task [1–3], however, there still leaves a critical bottleneck caused by various scales of pedestrians in an image [4,5]. Despite current detectors work reasonably well with large-scale pedestrians near the camera, their performance always sustains a significant deterioration in the presence of small-scale pedestrians that are relatively far from the camera.

Accurately detecting small-scale pedestrian instances is quite difficult due to the following inherent challenges: Firstly, most of the small-scale instances

Electronic supplementary material The online version of this chapter (https://doi.org/10.1007/978-3-030-01234-2_33) contains supplementary material, which is available to authorized users.

V. Ferrari et al. (Eds.): ECCV 2018, LNCS 11211, pp. 554–569, 2018.
https://doi.org/10.1007/978-3-030-01234-2_33

appear with blurred boundaries and obscure appearance, thus it is hard to distinguish them from the background clutters and other overlapped instances. Secondly and more insightfully, existing methods (e.g., Faster-RCNN [6], R-FCN [7]) heavily rely on bounding-box based annotations, which inevitably incorporates parts of false positives (e.g., background pixels that usually occupy more than half of the rectangular area), introducing ambiguities and uncertainties to confuse classifiers. This issue is more pronounced for small-scale pedestrian instances as they retain much less information compared with large-scale instances, thus the signal to noise ratio (SNR) is considerably decreased. In most related works [3–5] that aim to detect small-scale objects, one will *ONLY* resort to the perceptive fields of convolution. However, in our opinion, what impacts the performance of small-scale objects other than perceptive fields may reside in the very initial phase of machine learning pipeline, which is to say, the annotation phase.

On the other hand, according to the causal modeling idea proposed by [8], if one wonders whether there is a bias in bounding-box based annotations, he must figure out corresponding counterfactual: would the performance still be identical or even improved what if we had *NOT* applied bounding-box based annotations?

Fig. 1. Pedestrians over different scales could be modeled as a group of 2D Gaussian kernels, indicating that the top-bottom topological line possess high certainty. Our approach attempt to locate this topological line for pedestrian detection.

Motivated by above insight and counterfactual argument, we aim to address the scale variation problem with an alternative annotation, by simply locating the somatic topological line of each pedestrian as illustrated in Fig. 1. This top-bottom topology is proposed due to the following consideration factors: Firstly, human bodies of various scales could be modeled as a group of 2D Gaussian kernels with different scale variances [9,10]. It intuitionally supposes that pixels on the top-bottom topological centre line of a human body possess high certainty, while pixels close to pedestrian contour have relatively low confidence. This hypothesis especially aligns well with the fact that small-scale instances sustain blurred boundaries and obscure appearance. Secondly, body skeletons of large-size instances, which demonstrate the detailed topology of human bodies, can provide rich information for pedestrian detection [11–13]. However, (1) skeletons for small-scale instances cannot be recognized easily and (2) annotations of all the datasets are almost bounding-box, which is labor-intensive to transform them into skeletons. On the contrary, the proposed top-bottom topological line is a trade-off pivot to fuse the advantages of both automatic annotation generation and uncertainty elimination. Lastly, a simple but effective subjective test shows that compared with bounding-box based annotation, the proposed topological line demonstrates a much more consistency between annotators, especially for the small-scale instances as shown in Sect. 3.

On basis of the topological line annotation, we devise a fully convolutional network (FCN) that takes multi-scale feature representations and regresses the confidence of topological elements, i.e., top and bottom vertex, as well as the link edge between them. To eliminate ambiguous matching problem in crowded cases, a post-processing scheme based on Markov Random Field (MRF) is introduced to keep each predicted instance away from the other predicted instance with different designated objects, making the detection results less sensitive to occlusion. Moreover, we design a scheme to utilize temporal information by aggregating features of adjacent frames to further improve performance. Empirical evaluation reveals the novel TLL networks with or without temporal feature aggregation both lead to state-of-the-art performance on Caltech [14] and CityPersons [15] datasets.

In summary our key contributions are as follows:

- From the counterfactual view, we attempt to prove that topological annotation methodologies other than bounding box will introduce less ambiguity, which results in better performance and is especially effective for small-scale objects. Meanwhile, the deep-rooted bounding-box based annotation bias is challenged by our work, which is thought-provoking to rethink how to provide classifiers with discriminative information.
- We devise a unified FCN based network to locate the topological somatic line for detecting multi-scale pedestrian instances while introduce a post-processing scheme based on MRF to eliminate ambiguities in occlusion cases. A temporal feature aggregation scheme is integrated to propagate temporal cues across frames and further improves the detection performance.
- To the best of our knowledge, we achieve best detection performance on Caltech benchmark and improve performance of small-scale objects significantly (miss rate decreases from 74.53% to 60.79%). On CityPersons dataset, our proposed method obtains superior performance in occlusion cases without any bells and whistles. Beyond these, the existence of annotation bias in KITTI dataset is disclosed and analyzed.

2 Related Work

2.1 Multi-scale Object Detection

State-of-the-art methods for multi-scale object detection are mainly based on the pipeline of classifying region proposals and regressing the coordinates of bounding boxes, e.g., Faster-RCNN [6,7,16], YOLO [17,18] and SSD [19]. RPN+BF method [3] uses boosted forests classifiers on top of the region proposal network (RPN) and high-resolution convolutional features to effective bootstrapping for mining hard negatives. SA-FastRCNN [4] develops a divide-and-conquer strategy based on Fast-RCNN that uses multiple built-in subnetworks to adaptively detect pedestrians across scales. Similarly, [5] proposes a unified multi-scale convolutional neural network (MS-CNN), which performs detection at multiple intermediate layers to match objects of different scales, as well as an upsampling operation to prevent insufficient resolution of feature maps for handling small instances. Rather than using a single downstream classifier, the fused deep neural network (F-DNN+SS) method [20] uses a derivation of the Faster R-CNN framework fusing multiple parallel classifiers including Resnet [21] and Googlenet [22] using soft-rejection, and further incorporates pixel-wise semantic segmentation in a post-processing manner to suppress background proposals. Simultaneous Detection & Segmentation RCNN (SDS-RCNN) [23] improves object detection by using semantic segmentation as a strong cue, infusing the segmentation masks on top of shared feature maps as a reinforcement to the pedestrian detector. Recently, an active detection model (ADM) [24] based on multi-layer feature representations, executes sequences of coordinate transformation actions on a set of initial bounding-box proposals to deliver accurate prediction of pedestrian locations, and achieve a more balanced detection performance for different scale pedestrian instances on the Caltech benchmark. However, the above bounding-box based methods inevitably incorporates a large proportion of uncertain background pixels (false positive) to the human pattern, while impels the instances to be predicted as false negatives. In practice, it may lead to compromised results with particularly poor detections for small-scale instances. On the contrary, our approach relies on locating the somatic topology with high certainty, which is naturally flexible to object scale and aspect ratio variation.

2.2 Line Annotation

Line annotation is first proposed in [15,25] to produce high-quality bounding-box ground truths (GTs). The annotation procedure ensures the boxes align well with the center of the subjects, and these works show that better annotations on localisation accuracy lead to a stronger model than obtained when using original annotations. However, best results of these work are achieved on the validation/test set with a sanitised version of annotations, which is unfair when compared with other advanced methods evaluated on the original annotation set. What's more, the work in [25] shows that models trained on original/new and tested on original/new perform better than training and testing on different annotations. In contrast, our work utilizes the line annotation in a different way: the line annotation is not used to produce bounding-box GTs, but GTs themselves, and we design a FCN to regress the topological elements of the line. Meanwhile, tight bounding-boxes with a uniform aspect ratio could be automatically generated from each predicted topological lines and the detection results could be evaluated on the original annotation, which leads a fair comparison with the state-of-the-art methods.

2.3 Temporal Feature Aggregation

Temporal cues could be incorporated for feature reinforcement in object detection tasks. For example, TCNN [26] uses optical flow to map detections to neighboring frames and suppresses low-confidence predictions while incorporating tracking algorithms. FGFA [27] improves detection accuracy by warping and averaging features from nearby frames with adaptive weighting. However, its flow-subnet is trained on synthetic dataset [28], which obstructs itself from obtaining optical flow accurately in real scenes. A recent work, [29] creates a recurrent-convolutional detection architecture by combining SSD [19] with LSTM, and designs a bottleneck structure to reduce computational cost. Inspired by the above ideas, we unify the proposed TLL with recurrent network into a single temporally-aware architecture.

3 Annotation Comparison

To compare the line and bounding-box annotation methods, we design a simple subjective test. We extract 200 independent frames containing multi-scale pedestrians from Caltech training video-data, and hire 10 annotators to produced duplicate annotations via the two annotation methods separately. In each round, each annotator is shown the set of frames in random order and draws pedestrian instances by one annotation measure with a label tool. Annotators are asked to hallucinate head and feet if they are not visible. After that, pedestrian instances annotated by all 10 annotators are collected for evaluation. This procedure is indispensable since it's unreasonable to request each annotator exhaustedly outlines all, and the same instances from each image under the situation that many small-scales, defocus or blurred instances exist. Then we assess the two annotations using IoU (intersection over union) calculated between the overlap of 10 annotations and the union of them. Following [25], bounding-boxes with uniform aspect ratio could be automatically generated such that its centre coincides with the centre point of the manually-drawn axis. In Fig. 2, we compare the mean IoUs of two annotations for large-scale (pedestrian height ≥ 80 pixels) and small-scale (pedestrian height < 80 pixels) pedestrians. Note the bounding-box annotation instances are normalized to the same aspect ratio as line annotation ones for fair statistics.

The test result emphasizes that line annotation promotes more precise localisation on pedestrian than marking a bounding box, especially for small-scale instances. The reason lies in that annotators tend to align well with the center of subjects when drawing lines. While for the small-scale cases, even a few pixels mismatch on the bounding box annotation results in low IoUs, thus line annotation has a much lower variation compared with bounding-box. Besides, this test also tells us all the annotation methodologies are subjective and bounding-box

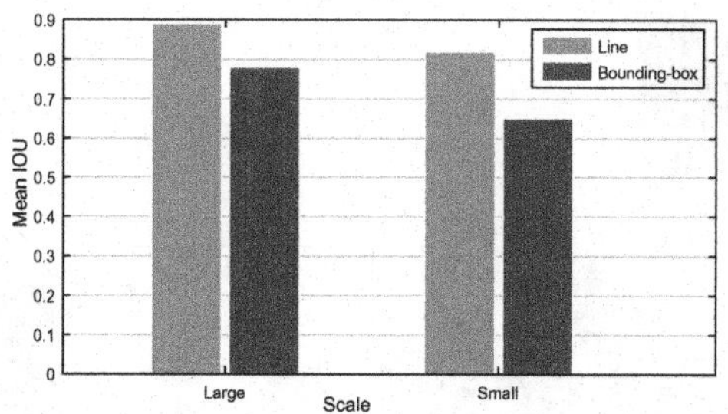

Fig. 2. Mean-IoUs comparison of two annotation for different scale pedestrians.

based ones are prone to produce bias as shown in Fig. 7(a), which confuses any classifiers to deteriorate performance.

4 TLL Detection Methodology

In this section, we describe the TLL detector for multi-scale pedestrians. As the core of our work, we firstly describe the single-shot network that regresses somatic topological elements. Then we discuss how to utilize the multi-scale representational features within the network, and employ the MRF scheme for dealing with crowd occlusion. Finally, the scheme of integrating TLL with temporal information for further detection improvement will be introduced.

4.1 Topological Line Localization Network

An overview of the single-shot TLL detection scheme is depicted in Fig. 3. The backbone of TLL is a Resnet-50 network, which is fast and accurate for object recognition [21]. We extend it to a fully convolutional version for an input image of arbitrary size, by using series of dilated-convolution, deconvolution, and skip connection methods. Specifically, as the default network has a feature stride of 32 pixels, which is too large to localize small-scale pedestrians, thus we remove the down-sampling in Conv5x and use dilated-convolution for keeping the receptive field, resulted in the final feature map as 1/16 of input size. Following the representation theory, higher layer features tend to encode more global and semantic information of objects that is robust against appearance variations, while outputs of lower layers provide more precise localization. We extract features from the last layer of each res-block started from Conv3 (i.e., Resnet50-Conv3d, Conv4f, Conv5c, detailed in Sect. 4.2.) and recover their spatial resolutions to 1/4 of the input size using deconvolution. These multi-layer representations are skip connected for regressing the top and bottom vertex confidence maps, as well as the map of link edge between them.

Every top and bottom vertex locations are modeled as a Gaussian peak. Let p_k be the ground-truth (GT) top/bottom vertex positions of i-th pedestrian in

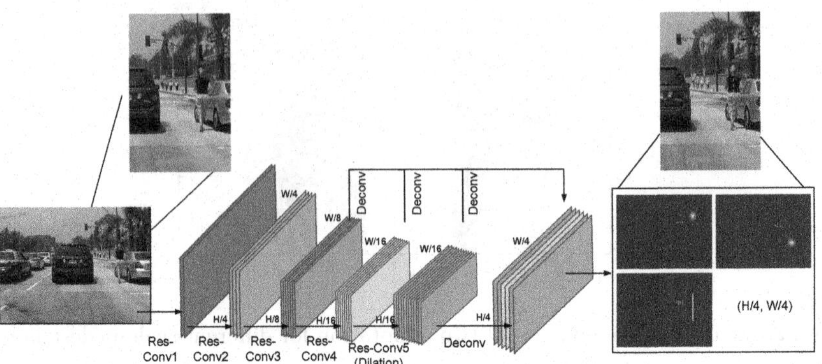

Fig. 3. An overview of single-shot TLL detection network.

the image, then the GT vertex confidence map $D(x)$, is formed by max aggregation of all N_k pedestrian peaks in the image.

$$D(x) = \max_{k \in N_k} d(x; p_k, \sigma) \tag{1}$$

where $x \in R^2$ stands for one pixel location in the confidence map, and $d(x; p, \sigma)$ is a two dimension Gaussian distribution with empirically chosen variance σ.

Link edge of a pedestrian $l(\mathbf{x})$ is modeled as a connecting line between the two vertexes, with a width scaled by the height of pedestrian. Pixel values of the line are given as a unit vector $\mathbf{v}$ in the direction from the top vertex pointing to the bottom vertex. Thus the GT link value map $L(x)$ is an average of all N_k pedestrian links in the image.

$$L(x) = \frac{1}{N_k} \sum_{k \in N_k} l_k(x) \tag{2}$$

where N_j is the total number of pedestrians within an image, and $l(x)$ is defined as:

$$l(x) = \begin{cases} \mathbf{v} \text{ if } x \text{ on link edge of a pedestrian} \\ 0 \text{ otherwise} \end{cases} \tag{3}$$

During training, mean squared error (MSE) is used to measure the difference between the predicted confidence maps and GT. The loss function f is defined as follows:

$$f = \|\tilde{D_t} - D_t\|_2^2 + \|\tilde{D_b} - D_b\|_2^2 + \lambda \|\tilde{L} - L\|_2^2 \tag{4}$$

where $\tilde{D_t}$ and $\tilde{D_b}$ stand for the predicted vertex confidence maps, $\tilde{L}$ stands for the predicted link map, and λ is a weighting factor that balances the vertex confidence error and link confidence error.

During inference, given an image I, candidate top and bottom vertex locations, $\tilde{t}_i$ and $\tilde{b}_j$, could be located by performing non-maximum suppression

(NMS) on the predicted vertex confidence maps $\tilde{D}_t$ and $\tilde{D}_b$. Then link score of each edge candidate (i.e., each pair of possible connections between candidate top and bottom vertexes) is calculated by measuring the alignment of the predicted link $\tilde{L}$ with the candidate edge that formed by connecting the candidate top and bottom vertexes.

$$E_{i,j} = \int_{u=0}^{u=1} \tilde{L}(p(u)) \cdot \frac{\tilde{b}_j - \tilde{t}_i}{\|\tilde{b}_j - \tilde{t}_i\|_2} du \tag{5}$$

where $p(u)$ indicates the sampling points along the edge candidate. Then based on the maximum confidence scores of each edge candidates, finding the top-bottom vertex pairs becomes a bipartite graph matching (BGM) [30] problem which could be easily solved by the Hungary algorithm [31]. Thus the predicted link of one vertex pair is determined as the topological line location of a pedestrian, with a detection score calculated by multiplication of vertex and link confidences.

4.2 Multi-scale Representation

It has been revealed in [4,24] that large-scale pedestrian instances typically exhibit dramatically different visual characteristics and internal features from the small-scale ones. For the network, pedestrian instances of different scales should have different responses at distinct feature representation layers. To investigate the optimal start of res-block features for skip connection in our network, we regress the confidence maps directly from different intermediate feature maps to visualize the responses at different convolutional layers for detecting pedestrians of various scales. Figure 4 illustrates the regressed link confidence maps from three intermediate convolutional layers, i.e., Resnet50-Conv2, Conv3 and Conv4.

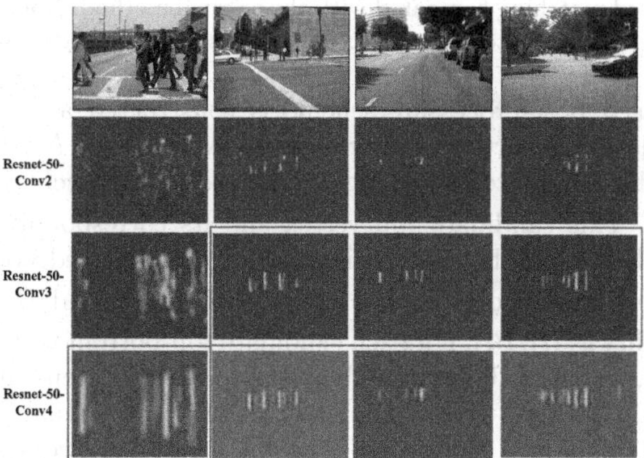

Fig. 4. Visualization of the predicted link maps from different intermediate layers. Red bounding boxes indicate the optimal activations across multiple representation. (Color figure online)

In general, convolutional features are effective only at a proper scale where optimal activation is obtained. Lower representation layers have a strong response for small-scale pedestrians, while large-scale pedestrian instances are usually detected by higher layers. Specifically, small-scale pedestrians are most comfortably picked up at Conv3, and large-scale ones are largely detected at Conv4. Interestingly, the much lower layer Conv2, does not have strong responses for each scale instances, the reason may due to its primitive and limited semantic characteristics. In practice, we choose Conv3 as a satisfactory starting layer for effective multi-scale representation.

4.3 MRF Based Matching

As presented above, BGM produces detection results depending on the maximum link scores of candidate top and bottom vertex pairs. Whereas, in crowd scenes, pedestrians often gather together and occlude each other. This may cause the TLL network to output very close vertices, and high link scores between each candidate pairs, leading to confused detection results. Thus, the crowd occlusion severely increases the difficulty in pedestrian localization. In order to robustly localize each individual pedestrian in crowd scenes, locations of its surrounding objects need to be taken into account.

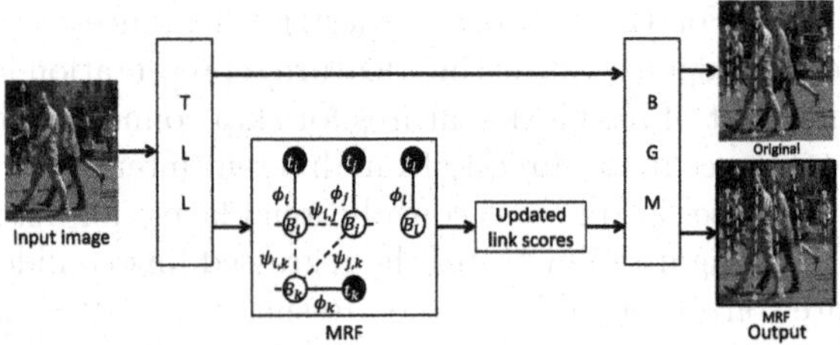

Fig. 5. MRF based matching compared with the original method. Note the dotted lines in red represents the mismatches under occlusion cases. (Color figure online)

A MRF based post-processing scheme is constructed as shown in Fig. 5. For one candidate top vertex t_i, there exists several (e.g., N_i) candidate bottom vertices whose link scores are high and close due to occlusion, denoted as $B_i = \left\{b_n^i\right\}_{n=1}^{N_i}$. This candidate top vertex and its corresponding bottom vertices form a subset, and they are designated as the observed node and hidden node respectively. Link scores $E_i = \left\{e_n^i\right\}_{n=1}^{N_i}$ between t_i and B_i are set as the joint compatibility $\phi_i\left(t_i, B_i\right)$. For each candidate top-bottom vertex pair $\left\{t_i, b_n^i\right\}$ within a subset, one virtual bounding-box is automatically generated with a uniform aspect ratio, forming VB_i. Then IoUs of every two virtual boxes from two different subsets could be calculated. The IoUs between two subsets reflect a neighboring relationship between them. The extent of two neighboring subset i and j away from each other is set as the neighboring compatibility:

$$\psi_{i,j}(B_i, B_j) = \exp\left(-IoU\left(VB_i, VB_j\right)/\alpha\right) \tag{6}$$

where α is a normalization parameter. Max-product algorithm is utilized to optimize the objective function:

$$\min_{B} \mathrm{p}(\{B\}) = \frac{1}{Z} \prod_{(i,j)} \psi_{i,j}(B_i, B_j) \prod_{i} \phi_i(t_i, B_i) \tag{7}$$

where Z is a normalization constant. After several iterations, MRF converges and optimized confidences $C_i = \left\{c_n^i\right\}_{n=1}^{N_i}$ of hidden node B_i could be obtained. Then link scores of the candidate vertex pairs $\left\{t_i, b_n^i\right\}$ are updated:

$$s_n^i = c_n^i * \sum\nolimits_{n}^{N_i} e_n^i \tag{8}$$

Finally, BGM is utilized to generate detection results on the basis of updated link scores. The MRF adds an extra constraint that pushes top-bottom vertex pairs away from each other, leading to less mismatches under occlusion cases.

4.4 Multi-frame Temporal Feature Aggregation

We seek to improve the detection quality by exploiting temporal information when videos are available. RNN has been verified as an effective way to make use of motion information [32,33]. Thus we try to unify the proposed TLL and recurrent network into a single temporally-aware architecture. Conv-LSTM [34] is incorporated as a means of propagating frame-level information across time. Specifically, for a video sequence, convolutional layers for representation are shared by each frame to extract spatial features, then multi-layer features of each frame are taken as input to the Conv-LSTM layer. At each time step, it refines output features on the basis of the state and input, extracts additional temporal cues from the input, and updates the state. Then outputs of Conv-LSTM are utilized for further regression. An illustration of our joint TLL+Conv-LSTM model can be seen in Fig. 6. Comparing with FGFA [27], Conv-LSTM implicitly aggregates feature maps in a more comprehensive way, which overcomes the feature scatter disadvantage of pixel-wise aggregation.

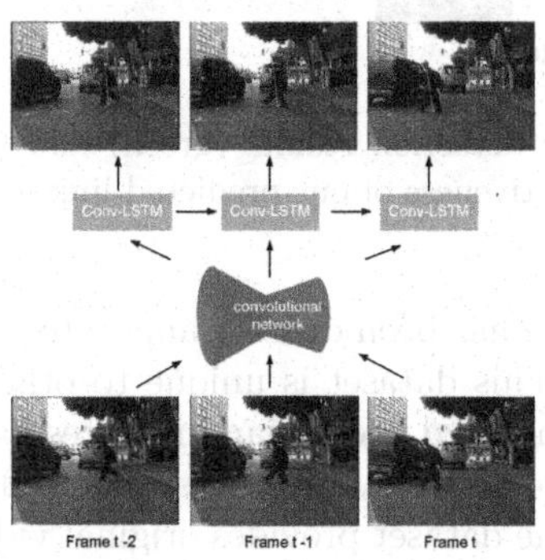

Fig. 6. Illustration of our joint TLL+Conv-LSTM model.

5 Experiments

5.1 Experiment Settings

We examine the proposed approach on widely used benchmarks including Caltech [14] and Citypersons [15]. We follow the standard evaluation metric: log miss rate is averaged over the false positive per image (FPPI) in $[10^{-2}, 10^{0}]$, denoted as MR. These datasets provide different evaluation protocols on the basis of annotation sizes and occlusion levels. One reason for choosing the two datasets is that they provide tight annotation boxes with normalized aspect ratio, thus the TLL detection results could be fairly evaluated on the original annotation, and compared with other state-of-the-art methods. Specifically, the top-down centre axis of each annotated bounding-box is used as the approximate GT topological line for training, which leads to no burden of additional human annotation on these datasets. From each predicted topological line, a tight bounding-box with uniform aspect ratio (0.41) could be automatically generated such that its centroid coincides with the centre point of the topological line. Then IoUs between this bounding-box and GT boxes could be calculated for the evaluation process. Tight and normalized annotation is important for the quantitative results during evaluation, as one correct detection may suffer a low IoU with its GT box with irregular aspect ratio (such as walking persons have varying width, as shown in Fig. 7(a)), resulted in a false positive to pull down *Precision*, while a false negative to pull down *Recall*, which results in only 38.72% average precision for the moderate test set on KITTI dataset [35] and in a sense reveals the annotation bias introduced by subjective judgement.

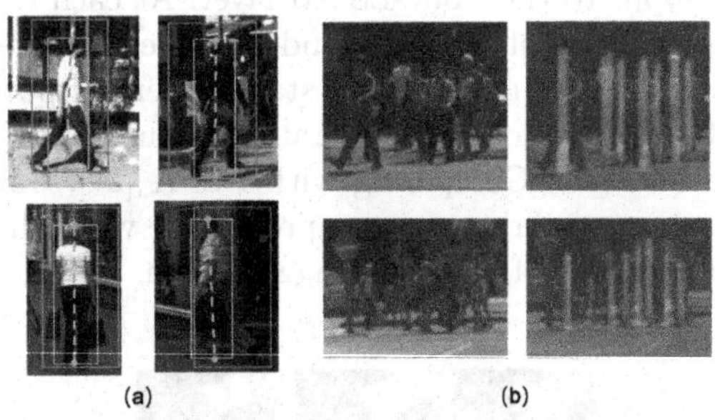

Fig. 7. (a) Samples of our detection results (green) and GT boxes (red) in KITTI validation set. (b) The effectiveness of our predicted link map in crowd scenes. (Color figure online)

Every frame in Caltech has been densely annotated with the bounding boxes of pedestrian instances. This dataset is unique to others for following reasons: First, over 70% of the annotated pedestrian instances have a height smaller than 100 pixels, including extremely tiny instances under 50 pixels, which is rare for other datasets. Second, the dataset provides original videos, on which our multi-frame aggregation methods could be evaluated. The standard test set of 4024 images is used for evaluation under different protocols.

CityPersons is a new pedestrian detection dataset on top of the semantic segmentation dataset CityScapes [36] and consists more crowded scenes compared with Caltech, and over 20% of pedestrian annotations overlap with another annotated pedestrian whose IoU is above 0.3. As CityPersons provides image samples only, its validation set with 500 images is used for the evaluation of our single-shot network.

5.2 Single-Shot Network

For the Caltech benchmark, following the typical protocol in literatures [3–5], we use dense sampling of the training data (every 3th frame, resulted in 42782 images). We compare a set of recently proposed state-of-the-art methods and quantitative results are listed in Table 1.

The proposed TLL demonstrates constantly competitive results with the state-of-the-arts, and achieves leading performance for small-scale objects (i.e., the Far and Middle protocols). Among them, performance on far-distance instances is improved most significantly, achieving a MR of 68.03%/67.69%

Table 1. Comparison results of TLL with recent state-of-the-art methods on standard test set of Caltech (lower is better).

Methods/MR (%)	Reasonable	All	Near	Middle	Far
RPN+BF [3]	9.58	64.66	2.26	53.93	100
SA-FastRCNN [4]	9.68	62.59	0.00	51.83	100
MS-CNN [5]	9.95	60.65	2.60	49.13	97.23
F-DNN+SS [20]	8.18	50.29	2.82	33.15	77.37
UDN+SS [37]	11.52	64.81	2.08	53.75	100
SDS-RCNN [23]	7.36	61.50	2.15	50.88	100
ADM [24]	8.64	42.27	0.41	30.82	74.53
TLL	8.45	39.99	0.67	26.25	68.03
TLL(MRF)	8.01	39.12	0.67	25.55	67.69
TLL(MRF)+FGFA [27]	7.92	38.58	0.99	24.39	63.28
TLL(MRF)+LSTM	7.40	37.62	0.72	22.92	60.79

Table 2. Comparison results of single-shot TLL with recent state-of-the-art methods on validation set of Citypersons (lower is better).

Methods/MR (%)	Reasonable	Heavy	Partial	Bare
Citypersons [15]	15.4	–	–	–
Repulsion Loss [38]	13.2	56.9	16.8	7.6
TLL	15.5	53.6	17.2	10.0
TLL(MRF)	14.4	52.0	15.9	9.2

with/without MRF, which clearly exceeds the best existing results, 74.53% of ADM, to the best of our knowledge. Middle-distance instances get an obvious gain from 30.82% to 26.25%/25.55% with/without MRF as well. For the near-distance ones, as the line annotation includes more background pixels on large-scale instances, TLL does not perform better than others but a similar MR close to 0% is achieved. Our approach outperforms the rest methods under the ALL protocol, in which significant occlusion exists. This is reasonable as the predicted link aligns well with the centre location of human body, as shown in Fig. 7(b), which naturally avoids the adverse factors faced by bounding-box based methods, since crowd occlusion makes these detectors sensitive to NMS. Moreover, the MRF adjusts the matching scores in an appropriate way, resulting in an even better performance. Our proposed method can achieve improved performance based on the *old* annotations, in an unprejudiced sense, without any human intervention, while [38] just reports performance evaluated on the *new* annotations [25], which is obviously unfair to compare it with other listed methods.

For the Citypersons, we take all 3000 images in train set for training, and use the annotated bounding-boxes in a similar way as Caltech. Quantitative results are listed in Table 2. Since the dataset consists more crowded scenes, it can be seen that MRF acts as a more important role, and the best result is achieved in the heavy occlusion case. Interestingly, TLL alone surpasses [38] when people are occluded from each other heavily, which is the case [38] proposed to solve with. Results in Table 2 demonstrate that it is better to provide less ambiguous information to classifiers instead of improving classifiers themselves.

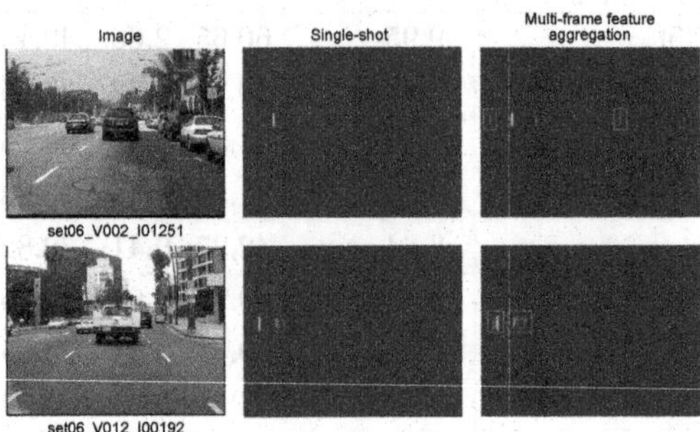

Fig. 8. Visualization examples of the multi-frame feature aggregation effect. Red bounding boxes indicate the enhanced high-activated feature locations. (Color figure online)

5.3 Multi-frame Feature Aggregation

Large feature channels in FCN will greatly increase the feature dimensions, bringing issues of computational overhead and memory consumption. To address this issue, we convert the multi-layer features before Conv-LSTM, down to 256 channels by using a 1×1 convolutional transform. This operation is similar as the bottleneck structure in [29], but more efficient. After that, Conv-LSTM layers with 256 channels are inserted into the single-shot TLL network. We try to incrementally stack Conv-LSTM layers to the network, however, due to difficulties in training multiple RNNs, experiments show that stacking two or more Conv-LSTMs is not beneficial. We unroll the Conv-LSTM to 5 time steps in consideration of the memory limitation and train the network with GT of each sampled frames.

Figure 8 illustrates the effect of multi-frame feature aggregation. Columns from left to right are the original image in Caltech test set, the prediction map of topological link edge confidence by single-shot network, and the one by Conv-LSTM based feature aggregation from adjacent frames. It can be seen that for some instances with defocus, blurred boundary and extremely tiny scale, the output feature activations from single-shot network are feeble, or even disappeared. In contrast, Conv-LSTM effectively aggregates the adjacent frame information to the reference frame, resulted in more high-activated features, which benefits the detection of small-scale objects. Quantitative result of the RNN based TLL is listed in Table 1. Figure 9 illustrates MR–FPPI curves for different scales objects together with best performance benchmarks on the Caltech standard image test set. We also list the result of our TLL combined with FGFA [27]. Compared with FGFA, RNN based aggregation propagates temporal information in a hidden strategy, which allows the network to transfer feature from nearby frames in a more self-driven way, and improves the comprehensive performance more significantly.

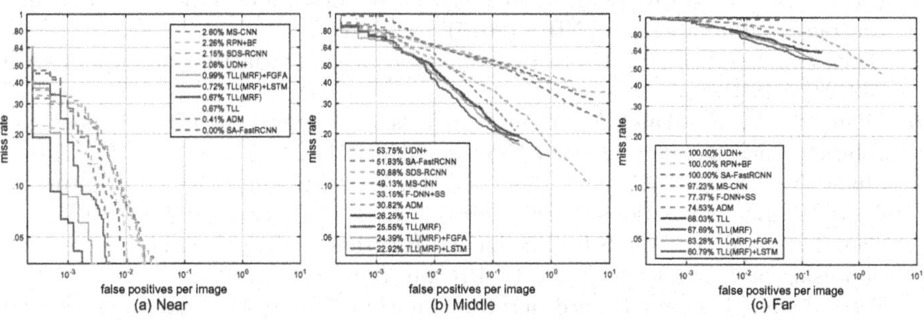

Fig. 9. Comparison of our proposed TLL approach with some state-of-the-art methods on the Caltech dataset under Near, Middle, and Far evaluation protocols.

6 Conclusions

In this work, we design a FCN based network to locate the somatic topological line for detecting multi-scale pedestrian instances while introduce a post-processing scheme based on MRF to eliminate ambiguities in occlusion cases. A temporal feature aggregation scheme is integrated to propagate temporal cues across frames and further improves the detection performance. From this work we conclude that: (1) problem itself may reside in the very origin of learning pipeline and it is more appropriate to provide more discriminative and less ambiguous information other than to just feed more information for achieving a better classifier. (2) One should abstract annotations with a more representative methodology. We hope it can inspire more works that focus on intrinsically solving with generic small-scale objects and heavily occlusion scenes.

References

1. Dollar, P., Wojek, C., Schiele, B., Perona, P.: Pedestrian detection: an evaluation of the state of the art. In: PAMI, pp. 743–761 (2012)
2. Dollar, P., Appel, R., Belongie, S., Perona, P.: Fast feature pyramids for object detection. In: PAMI (2014)
3. Zhang, L., Lin, L., Liang, X., He, K.: Is faster R-CNN doing well for pedestrian detection? In: Leibe, B., Matas, J., Sebe, N., Welling, M. (eds.) ECCV 2016. LNCS, vol. 9906, pp. 443–457. Springer, Cham (2016). https://doi.org/10.1007/978-3-319-46475-6_28
4. Li, J., Liang, X., Shen, S.M., Xu, T., Feng, J., Yan, S.: Scale-aware fast R-CNN for pedestrian detection. In: Multimedia (2015)
5. Cai, Z., Fan, Q., Feris, R.S., Vasconcelos, N.: A unified multi-scale deep convolutional neural network for fast object detection. In: Leibe, B., Matas, J., Sebe, N., Welling, M. (eds.) ECCV 2016. LNCS, vol. 9908, pp. 354–370. Springer, Cham (2016). https://doi.org/10.1007/978-3-319-46493-0_22
6. Ren, S., He, K., Girshick, R., Sun, J.: Faster R-CNN: towards real-time object detection with region proposal networks. In: NIPS (2015)
7. Dai, J., Li, Y., He, K., Sun, J.: R-FCN: object detection via region-based fully convolutional networks. In: NIPS (2016)
8. Balke, A., Pearl, J.: Probabilistic evaluation of counterfactual queries. AAA **I**, 230–237 (1994)
9. Zhang, C., Li, H., Wang, X., Yang, X.: Cross-scene crowd counting via deep convolutional neural networks. In: CVPR, pp. 833–841 (2015)
10. Zhang, Y., Zhou, D., Chen, S., Gao, S., Ma, Y.: Single-image crowd counting via multi-column convolutional neural network. In: CVPR, pp. 589–597 (2016)
11. Cao, Z., Simon, T., Wei, S.E., Sheikh, Y.: Realtime multi-person 2D pose estimation using part affinity fields. In: CVPR, pp. 7291–7299 (2017)
12. Papandreou, G., et al.: Towards accurate multi-person pose estimation in the wild. In: CVPR, pp. 4903–4911 (2017)
13. Li, C., Zhong, Q., Xie, D., Pu, S.: Skeleton-based action recognition with convolutional neural networks. In: ICMEW (2017)
14. Dollar, P., Wojek, C., Schiele, B., Perona, P.: Pedestrian detection: a benchmark. In: CVPR, pp. 304–311 (2009)
15. Zhang, S., Benenson, R., Schiele, B.: CityPersons: a diverse dataset for pedestrian detection. In: CVPR, pp. 3213–3221 (2017)
16. Girshick, R., Donahue, J., Darrell, T., Malik, J.: Rich feature hierarchies for accurate object detection and semantic segmentation. In: CVPR, pp. 580–587 (2014)
17. Redmon, J., Divvala, S., Girshick, R., Farhadi, A.: You only look once: unified, real-time object detection. In: CVPR, pp. 779–788 (2016)
18. Redmon, J., Farhadi, A.: Yolo9000: better, faster, stronger. In: CVPR, pp. 7263–7271 (2017)

19. Liu, W., et al.: SSD: single shot multibox detector. In: Leibe, B., Matas, J., Sebe, N., Welling, M. (eds.) ECCV 2016. LNCS, vol. 9905, pp. 21–37. Springer, Cham (2016). https://doi.org/10.1007/978-3-319-46448-0_2
20. Du, X., El-Khamy, M., Lee, J., Davis, L.: Fused DNN: a deep neural network fusion approach to fast and robust pedestrian detection. In: WACV (2017)
21. He, K., Zhang, X., Ren, S., Sun, J.: Deep residual learning for image recognition. In: CVPR, pp. 770–778 (2016)
22. Szegedy, C., Liu, W., Jia, Y., Sermanet, P., et al.: Going deeper with convolutions. In: CVPR, pp. 1–9 (2015)
23. Brazil, G., Yin, X., Liu, X.: Illuminating pedestrians via simultaneous detection & segmentation. In: ICCV, pp. 4950–4959 (2017)
24. Zhang, X., Cheng, L., Li, B., Hu, H.M.: Too far to see? Not really!—pedestrian detection with scale-aware localization policy. arXiv preprint (2017). arXiv: 1709.00235
25. Zhang, S., Benenson, R., Omran, M., Hosang, J., Schiele, B.: How far are we from solving pedestrian detection? In: CVPR, pp. 1259–1267 (2016)
26. Kang, K., Ouyang, W., Li, H., Wang, X.: Object detection from video tubelets with convolutional neural networks. In: CVPR, pp. 817–825 (2016)
27. Zhu, X., Wang, Y., Dai, J., Yuan, L., Wei, Y.: Flow-guided feature aggregation for video object detection. In: ICCV, pp. 408–417 (2017)
28. Dosovitskiy, A., Fischery, P., Ilg, E., et al.: FlowNet: learning optical flow with convolutional networks. In: ICCV, pp. 2758–2766 (2015)
29. Liu, M., Zhu, M.: Mobile video object detection with temporally-aware feature maps. arXiv preprint (2017). arXiv: 1711.06368
30. Hopcroft, J.E., Karp, R.M.: An $n^{5/2}$ algorithm for maximum matching in bipartite graphs. SIAM J. Comput. **2**(4), 225–231 (1973)
31. Kuhn, H.W.: The hungarian method for the assignment problem. 50 Years of Integer Programming 1958–2008 29–47
32. Ng, J.Y.H., Hausknecht, M., Vijayanarasimhan, S., Vinyals, O., Monga, R., Toderici, G.: Beyond short snippets: deep networks for video classification. In: CVPR, pp. 4694–4702 (2015)
33. Grushin, A., Monner, D.D., Reggia, J.A., Mishra, A.: Robust human action recognition via long short-term memory. In: IJCNN (2013)
34. Shi, X., Chen, Z., Wang, H., Yeung, D.Y., Wang, W., WOO, W.: Convolutional LSTM network: a machine learning approach for precipitation nowcasting. In: NIPS, pp. 802–810 (2015)
35. Geiger, A., Lenz, P., Urtasun, R.: Are we ready for autonomous driving? The Kitti vision benchmark suite. In: CVPR (2012)
36. Cordts, M., Omran, M., Ramos, S., et al.: The cityscapes dataset for semantic urban scene understanding. In: CVPR (2016)
37. Ouyang, W., Zhou, H., Li, H., et al.: Jointly learning deep features, deformable parts, occlusion and classification for pedestrian detection. In: PAMI (2017)
38. Wang, X., Xiao, T., Jiang, Y., Shao, S., Sun, J., Shen, C.: Repulsion loss: detecting pedestrians in a crowd. arXiv preprint (2017). arXiv: 1711.07752

VQA-E: Explaining, Elaborating, and Enhancing Your Answers for Visual Questions

Qing Li[1(✉)], Qingyi Tao[2,3], Shafiq Joty[2], Jianfei Cai[2], and Jiebo Luo[4]

[1] University of Science and Technology of China, Hefei, China
dylan.liqing@gmail.com
[2] Nanyang Technological University, Singapore, Singapore
[3] NVIDIA AI Technology Center, Westford, USA
[4] University of Rochester, Rochester, USA

Abstract. Most existing works in visual question answering (VQA) are dedicated to improving the accuracy of predicted answers, while disregarding the explanations. We argue that the explanation for an answer is of the same or even more importance compared with the answer itself, since it makes the question answering process more understandable and traceable. To this end, we propose a new task of VQA-E (VQA with Explanation), where the models are required to generate an explanation with the predicted answer. We first construct a new dataset, and then frame the VQA-E problem in a multi-task learning architecture. Our VQA-E dataset is automatically derived from the VQA v2 dataset by intelligently exploiting the available captions. We also conduct a user study to validate the quality of the synthesized explanations. We quantitatively show that the additional supervision from explanations can not only produce insightful textual sentences to justify the answers, but also improve the performance of answer prediction. Our model outperforms the state-of-the-art methods by a clear margin on the VQA v2 dataset.

Keywords: Visual question answering · Model with Explanation

1 Introduction

In recent years, visual question answering (VQA) has been widely studied by researchers in both computer vision and natural language processing communities [2,8,11,27,31,34]. Most existing works perform VQA by utilizing attention mechanism and combining features from two modalities for predicting answers.

Although promising performance has been reported, there is still a huge gap for humans to truly understand the model decisions without any explanation for them. A popular way to explain the predicted answers is to visualize attention maps to indicate *'where to look'*. The attended regions are pointed to trace the predicted answer back to the image content. However, the visual justification through attention visualization is implicit and it cannot entirely reveal what the

V. Ferrari et al. (Eds.): ECCV 2018, LNCS 11211, pp. 570–586, 2018.
https://doi.org/10.1007/978-3-030-01234-2_34

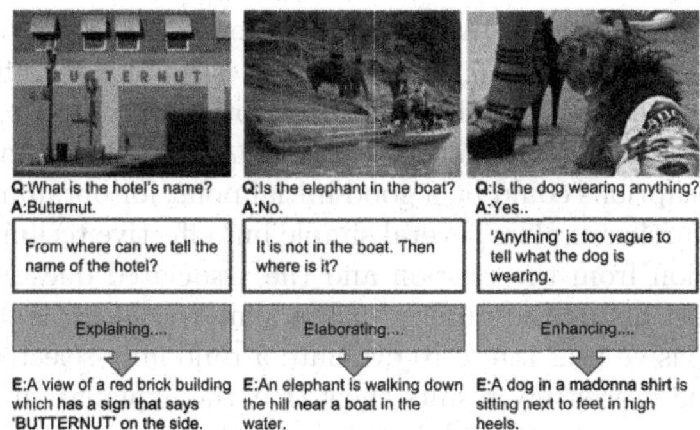

Fig. 1. VQA-E provides insightful information that can explain, elaborate or enhance predicted answers compared with the traditional VQA task. Q = Question, A = Answer, E = Explanation. (Left) From the answer, there is no way to trace the corresponding visual content to tell the name of the hotel. The explanation clearly points out where to look for the answer. (Middle) The explanation provides a real answer to the aspect asked. (Right) The word "anything" in the question refers to a vague concept without specific indication. The answer is enhanced by the "madonna shirt" in the explanation.

model captures from the attended regions for answering the questions. There could be many cases where the model attends to right regions but predicts wrong answers. What's worse, the visual justification is not accessible to visually impaired people who are the potential users of the VQA techniques. Therefore, in this paper we intend to explore textual explanations to compensate for these weaknesses of visual attention in VQA.

Another crucial advantage of textual explanation is that it elaborates and enhances the predicted answer with more relevant information. As shown in Fig. 1, a textual explanation can be a clue to justify the answer, or a complementary delineation that elaborates on the context of the question and answer, or a detailed specification about abstract concepts mentioned in the QA to enhance the short answer. Such textual explanations are important for effective communication since they provide feedbacks that enable the questioners to extend the conversation. Unfortunately, although textual explanations are desired for both model interpretation and effective communication in natural contexts, little progress has been made in this direction, partly because almost all the public datasets, such as VQA [2,8], COCO-QA [22], and Visual7W [34], do not provide explanations for the annotated answers.

In this work, we aim to address the above limitations of existing VQA systems by introducing a new task called VQA-E (VQA with Explanations). In VQA-E, the models are required to provide a textual explanation for the predicted answer. We conduct our research in two steps. First, to foster research in this area, we construct a new dataset with textual explanations for the answers. The VQA-E dataset is automatically derived from the popular VQA v2 dataset [8] by synthesizing an explanation for each image-question-answer triple. The VQA v2 dataset is one of the largest VQA datasets with over 650k question-answer pairs, and more importantly, each image in the dataset is coupled with five descriptions from MSCOCO captions [4]. Although these captions were written without considering the questions, they do include some QA-related information and thus exploiting these captions could be a good initial point for obtaining explanations free of cost. We further explore several simple but effective techniques to synthesize an explanation from the caption and the associated question-answer pair. To relieve concern about the quality of the synthesized explanations, we conduct a comprehensive user study to evaluate a randomly-selected subset of the explanations. The user study results show that the explanation quality is good for most question-answer pairs while being a little inadequate for the questions asking for a subjective response or requiring common sense (pragmatic knowledge). Overall, we believe the newly created dataset is good enough to serve as a benchmark for the proposed VQA-E task.

To show the advantages of learning with textual explanations, we also propose a novel VQA-E model, which addresses both the answer prediction and the explanation generation in a multi-task learning architecture. Our dataset enables us to train and evaluate the VQA-E model, which goes beyond a short answer by producing a textual explanation to justify and elaborate on it. Through extensive experiments, we find that the additional supervisions from explanations can help the model better localize the important image regions and lead to an improvement in the accuracy of answer prediction. Our VQA-E model outperforms the state-of-the-art methods in the VQA v2 dataset.

2 Related Work

Attention in Visual Question Answering. Attention mechanism is firstly used in machine translation [3] and then is brought into the vision-to-language tasks [9,10,15,18,19,28–33]. The visual attention in the vision-to-language tasks is used to address the problem of "where to look" [25]. In VQA, the question is used as a query to search for the relevant regions in the image. [31] proposes a stacked attention model which queries the image for multiple times to infer the answer progressively. Beyond the visual attention, Lu *et al.* [18] exploit a hierarchical question-image co-attention strategy to attend to both related regions in the image and crucial words in the question. [19] proposes the dual attention network, which refines the visual and textual attention via multiple reasoning steps. Attention mechanism can find the question-related regions in the image, which can account for the answer to some extent. [6] has studied how well the visual attention is aligned with the human gaze. The results show that when answering a question, current attention-based models do not seem to be "looking" at the same regions of the image as humans do. Although attention is a good visual explanation for the answer, it is not accessible for visually impaired people and is somehow limited in real-world applications.

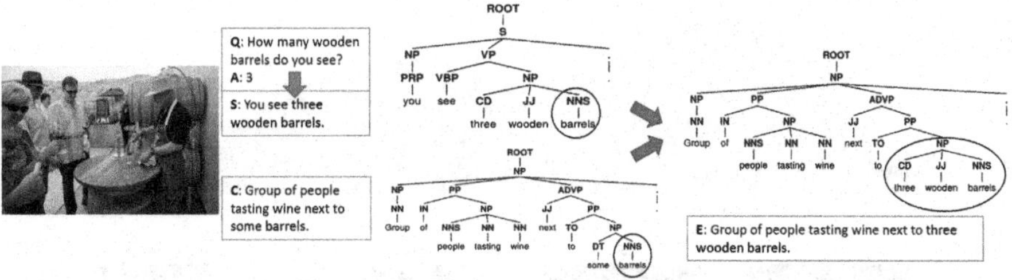

Fig. 2. An example of the pipeline to fuse the question (Q), the answer (A) and the relevant caption (C) into an explanation (E). Each question-answer pair is converted into a statement (S). The statement and the most relevant caption are both parsed into constituency trees. These two trees are then aligned by the common node. The subtree including the common node in the statement is merged into the caption tree to obtain the explanation.

Model with Explanations. Recently, a number of works [14,17,20] have been done for explaining the decisions from deep learning models, which are typically black boxes due to the end-to-end training procedure. [14] proposes a novel explanation model for bird classification. However, their class relevance metrics are not applicable to VQA since there is no pre-defined semantic category for the questions and answers. Therefore, we build a reference dataset to directly train and evaluate models for VQA with explanations. The most similar work to ours is *Multimodal Explanations* [20] that proposes a multimodal explanation dataset for VQA, which is human-annotated and of high quality. In contrast, our dataset focuses on textual explanations and is built free of cost and over six times bigger (269,786 v.s. 41,817) than theirs.

3 VQA-E Dataset

We now introduce our VQA-E dataset. We begin by describing the process of synthesizing explanations from image descriptions for question-answer pairs, followed by dataset analysis and a user study to assess the quality of our dataset.

3.1 Explanation Synthesis

Approach. The first step is to find the caption most relevant to the question and answer. Given an image caption $\mathcal{C}$, a question $\mathcal{Q}$ and an answer $\mathcal{A}$, we tokenize and encode them into GloVe word embeddings [21]: $W_c = \{\boldsymbol{w}_1, ..., \boldsymbol{w}_{T_c}\}, W_q = \{\boldsymbol{w}_1, ..., \boldsymbol{w}_{T_q}\}, W_a = \{\boldsymbol{w}_1, ..., \boldsymbol{w}_{T_a}\}$, where T_c, T_q, T_a are the number of words in the caption, question, and answer, respectively. We compute the similarity

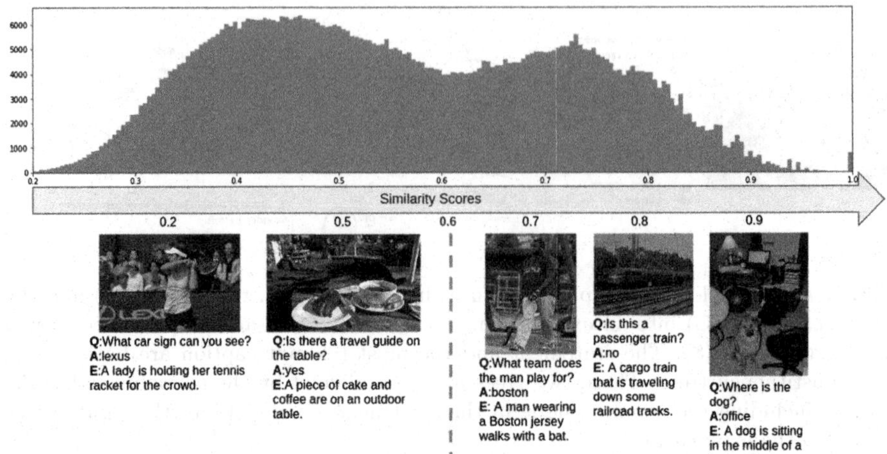

Fig. 3. Top: similarity score distribution. Bottom: illustration of VQA-E examples at different similarity levels.

between the caption and question-answer pair as follows:

$$s(\boldsymbol{w}_i, \boldsymbol{w}_j) = \frac{1}{2}(1 + \frac{\boldsymbol{w}_i^T \boldsymbol{w}_j}{||\boldsymbol{w}_i|| \cdot ||\boldsymbol{w}_j||}) \tag{1a}$$

$$S(\mathcal{Q}, \mathcal{C}) = \frac{1}{T_q} \sum_{\boldsymbol{w}_i \in W_q} \max_{\boldsymbol{w}_j \in W_c} s(\boldsymbol{w}_i, \boldsymbol{w}_j) \tag{1b}$$

$$S(\mathcal{A}, \mathcal{C}) = \frac{1}{T_a} \sum_{\boldsymbol{w}_i \in W_a} \max_{\boldsymbol{w}_j \in W_c} s(\boldsymbol{w}_i, \boldsymbol{w}_j) \tag{1c}$$

$$S(<\mathcal{Q}, \mathcal{A}>, \mathcal{C}) = \frac{1}{2}(S(\mathcal{Q}, \mathcal{C}) + S(\mathcal{A}, \mathcal{C})) \tag{1d}$$

For each question-answer pair, we find the most relevant caption, coupled with a similarity score. We have tried other more complex techniques like using Term Frequency and Inverse Document Frequency to adjust the weights of different words, but we find this simple mean-max formula in Eq. (1) works better.

To generate a good explanation, we intend to fuse the information from both the question-answer pair and the most relevant caption. Firstly the question and answer are merged into a declarative statement. We achieve this by designing simple merging rules based on the question types and the answer types. Similar rule-based methods have been explored in NLP to generate questions from declarative statements [13] (i.e., opposite direction). We then fuse this QA statement with the caption via aligning and merging their constituency parse trees. We further refine the combined sentence by a grammar check and correction tool to obtain the final explanation, and compute its similarity to the question-answer pair with Eq. 1. An example of our pipeline is shown in Fig. 2.

Similarity Distribution. Due to the large size and diversity of questions, and the limited sources of captions for each image, it is not guaranteed that a good explanation could be generated for each Q&A. The explanations with low similarity scores are removed from the dataset to reduce noise. We present some examples in Fig. 3. It shows a gradual improvement in explanation quality when the similarity scores increase. With some empirical investigation, we select a similarity threshold of 0.6 to filter out those noisy explanations. We also plot the similarity score histogram in Fig. 3. Interestingly, we observe a clear trough at 0.6 that makes the explanations well separated by this threshold.

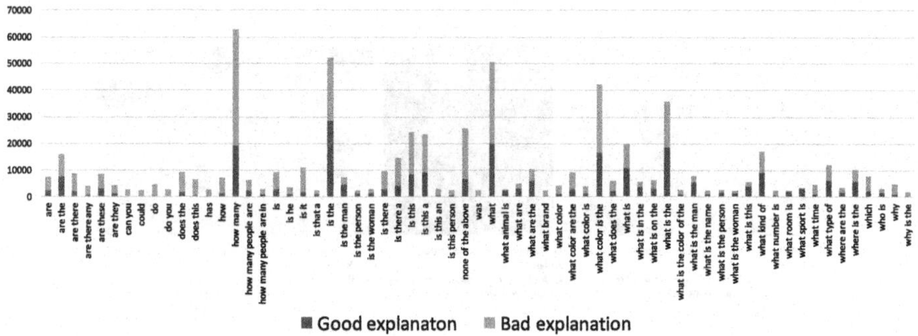

Fig. 4. Distribution of synthesized explanations by different question types.

Table 1. Statistics for our VQA-E dataset.

Dataset	Split	#Images	#Q&A	#E	#Unique Q	#Unique A	#Unique E
VQA-E	Train	72,680	181,298	181,298	77,418	9,491	115,560
	Val	35,645	88,488	88,488	42,055	6,247	56,916
	Total	108,325	269,786	269,786	108,872	12,450	171,659
VQA-v2	Train	82,783	443,757	0	151,693	22,531	0
	Val	40,504	214,354	0	81,436	14,008	0
	Total	123,287	658,111	0	215,076	29,332	0

3.2 Dataset Analysis

In this section, we analyze our VQA-E dataset, particularly the automatically synthesized explanations. Out of 658,111 existing question-answer pairs in original VQA v2 dataset, our approach generates relevant explanations with high similarity scores for 269,786 QA pairs (41%). More statistics about the dataset are given in Table 1.

We plot the distribution of the number of synthesized explanations for each question type in Fig. 4. While looking into different question types, the percentage of relevant explanations varies from type to type.

Abstract Questions v.s. Specific Questions. It is observed that the percentage of relevant explanations is generally higher for 'is/are' and 'what' questions than 'how', 'why' and 'do' questions. This is because 'is/are' and 'what' questions tend to be related to specific visual contents which are more likely being described by image captions. In addition, a more specific question type could further help in the explanation generation. For example, for 'what sport is' and for 'what room is' questions, our approach successfully generates explanations for 90% and 87% question and answer pairs, respectively. The rates of having good explanations for these types of questions are much higher than the general 'what' questions (40%).

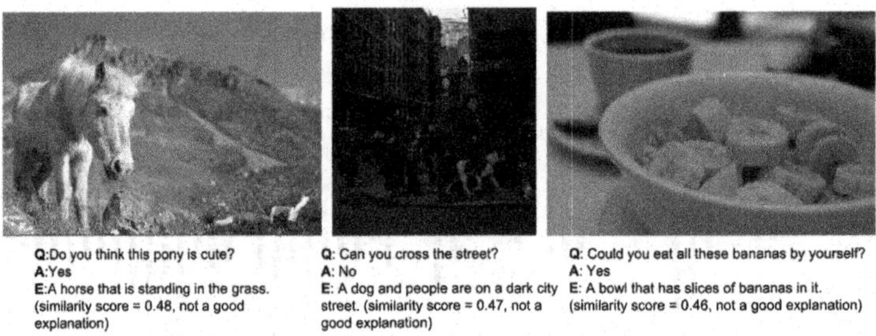

Q:Do you think this pony is cute?
A:Yes
E:A horse that is standing in the grass. (similarity score = 0.48, not a good explanation)
Q: Can you cross the street?
A: No
E: A dog and people are on a dark city street. (similarity score = 0.47, not a good explanation)
Q: Could you eat all these bananas by yourself?
A: Yes
E: A bowl that has slices of bananas in it. (similarity score = 0.46, not a good explanation)

Fig. 5. Subjective examples: our method cannot handle the questions involving emotional feeling (left), commonsense knowledge (middle) or behavioral reasoning (right).

Subjective Questions: Do You/Can You/Do/Could? The existing VQA datasets involve some questions that require subjective feeling, logical thinking or behavioral reasoning. These questions often fall in the question types starting with 'do you', 'can you', 'do', 'could', and etc. For these questions, there may be underlying clues from the image contents but the evidence is usually opaque and indirect and thus it is hard to synthesize a good explanation. We illustrate examples of such questions in Fig. 5 and the generated explanations are generally inadequate to provide relevant details regarding the questions and answers.

Due to the inadequacy in handling the above mentioned cases, we only achieve small percentages of good explanations for these question types. The percentages of 'do you', 'can you', 'do' and 'could' questions are 4%, 5%, 13% and 6% respectively which are far below the average 41%.

3.3 Dataset Assessment – User Study

It is not easy to use quantitative metrics to evaluate whether the synthesized explanations can provide valid, relevant and complementary information to the answers of the visual questions. Therefore, we conduct a user study to assess our VQA-E dataset from human perspective. Particularly, we measure the explanation quality from four aspects: *fluent*, *correct*, *relevant*, *complementary*.

Fluent measures the fluency of the explanation. A fluent explanation should be correct in grammar and idiomatic in wording. The *correct* metric indicates whether the explanation is correct according to the image content. The *relevant* metric assesses the relevance of an explanation to the question and answer pair. If an explanation is relevant, users should be able to infer the answer from the explanation. This metric is important to measure whether the proposed word embedding similarity can effectively select and filter the explanations. Through the user study, we evaluate the relevance of explanations from human understanding to verify whether the synthesized explanations are closely tied to their corresponding QA pairs. Last but not least, we evaluate whether an explanation is *complementary* to the answer. It is essential that the explanation can provide complementary details to the abbreviate answers so that visual accordance between the answer and the image could be enhanced.

Table 2. User assessment results for the synthesized explanation, the most similar caption, the random caption, and the generated explanation. To avoid bias, they are evaluated jointly and in each sample, their order is shuffled and unknown to users. They are assessed by the human evaluators in 1–5 grades: 1-very poor, 2-poor, 3-barely acceptable, 4-good, 5-very good. Here we show the average scores of 2,000 questions.

	Fluent	Correct	Relevant	Complementary
Synthesized explanation	4.89	4.78	**4.23**	**4.14**
Most similar caption	**4.97**	4.91	2.72	2.87
Random caption	4.93	**4.92**	1.91	2.12
Generated explanation (QI-AE)	3.89	3.67	3.24	3.11

Evaluation Results Summary. We show the human evaluation results in Table 2. Since the synthesized explanations are derived from existing human annotated captions, their average fluency and correctness scores are both close to 5. More importantly, their relevance and complementariness scores are both above 4, which indicates that the overall quality of the explanations is good from human perspective. These two metrics differentiate a general caption of an image and our specific explanation dedicated for a visual question-answer pair.

4 Multi-task VQA-E Model

Based on the well-constructed VQA-E dataset, in this section, we introduce the proposed multi-task VQA-E model. Figure 6 gives an overview of our model. Given an image $\mathcal{I}$ and a question $\mathcal{Q}$, our model can simultaneously predict an answer $\mathcal{A}$ and generate a textual explanation $\mathcal{E}$.

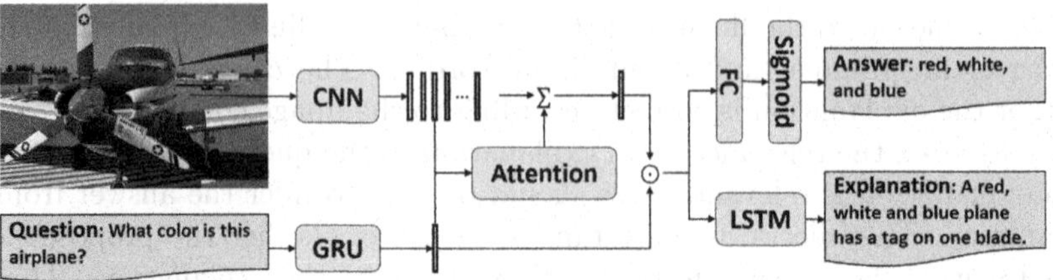

Fig. 6. An overview of the multi-task VQA-E network. Firstly, an image is represented by a pre-trained CNN, while the question is encoded via a single-layer GRU. Then the image features and question features are input to the Attention module to obtain image features for question-guided regions. Finally, the question features and attended image features are used to simultaneously predict an answer and generate an explanation.

4.1 Image Features

We adopt a pre-trained convolutional neural network (CNN) to extract a high-level representation ϕ of the input image $\mathcal{I}$:

$$\phi = \text{CNN}(\mathcal{I}) = \{\boldsymbol{v}_1, ..., \boldsymbol{v}_P\} \tag{2}$$

where $\boldsymbol{v}_i$ is the feature vector of the ith image patch and P is the total number of patches. We experiment with three types of image features:

- **Global.** We extract the outputs of the final pooling layer ('pool5') of the ResNet-152 [12] as global features of the image. For these image features, $P = 1$, and visual attention is not applicable.
- **Grid.** We extract the outputs of the final convolutional layer ('res5c') of ResNet-152 as the feature map of the image, which corresponds to a uniform grid of equally-sized image patches. In this case, $P = 7 \times 7 = 49$.
- **Bottom-up.** [1] proposes a new type of image features based on object detection techniques. They utilize Faster R-CNN to propose salient regions, each with an associated feature vector from the ResNet-101. The bottom-up image features provide a more natural basis at the object level for attention to be considered. We choose $P = 36$ in this case.

4.2 Question Embedding

The question $\mathcal{Q}$ is tokenized and encoded into word embeddings $W_q = \{\boldsymbol{w}_1, ..., \boldsymbol{w}_{T_q}\}$. Then the word embeddings are fed into a gated recurrent unit [5]: $\boldsymbol{q} = \text{GRU}(W_q)$. We use the final state of the GRU as the representation of the question.

4.3 Visual Attention

We use the classical question-guided soft attention mechanism similar to most modern VQA models. For each patch in the image, the feature vector $\boldsymbol{v}_i$ and the question embedding $\boldsymbol{q}$ are firstly projected by non-linear layers to the same dimension. Next we use the Hadamard product (i.e., element-wise multiplication) to combine the projected representations and input to a linear layer to obtain a scalar attention weight associated with that image patch. The attention weights $\boldsymbol{\tau}$ are normalized over all patches with softmax function. Finally, the image features from all patches are weighted by the normalized attention weights and summed into a single vector $\boldsymbol{v}$ as the representation of the attended image. The formulas are as follow and we omit the bias terms for simplicity:

$$\begin{aligned} \tau_i &= \boldsymbol{w}^T \left(\text{Relu}(W_v \boldsymbol{v}_i) \odot \text{Relu}(W_q \boldsymbol{q})\right) \\ \boldsymbol{\alpha} &= \text{softmax}(\boldsymbol{\tau}) \\ \boldsymbol{v} &= \sum_{i=1}^{P} \alpha_i \boldsymbol{v}_i \end{aligned} \tag{3}$$

Note that we adopt a simple one-glimpse, one-way attention, as opposed to complex schemes proposed by recent works [16,18,31].

Next, the representations of the question $\boldsymbol{q}$ and the image $\boldsymbol{v}$ are projected to the same dimension by non-linear layers and then fused by a Hadamard product:

$$\boldsymbol{h} = \text{Relu}(W_{qh} \boldsymbol{q}) \odot \text{Relu}(W_{vh} \boldsymbol{v}) \tag{4}$$

where $\boldsymbol{h}$ is a joint representation of the question and the image, and then fed to the subsequent modules for answer prediction and explanation generation.

4.4 Answer Prediction

We formulate the answer prediction task as a multi-label regression problem, instead of a single-label classification problem in many other works. A set of candidate answers is pre-determined from all the correct answers in the training set that appear more than 8 times. This leads to $N = 3129$ candidate answers. Each question in the dataset has $K = 10$ human-annotated answers, which are sometimes not same, especially when the question is ambiguous or subjective and has multiple correct or synonymous answers. To fully exploit the disagreement between annotators, we adopt soft accuracies as the regression targets. The accuracy for each answer is computed as:

$$\text{Accuracy}(a) = \frac{1}{K} \sum_{k=1}^{K} \min\left(\frac{\sum_{1 \le j \le K, j \ne k} \mathbb{1}(a = a_j)}{3}, 1\right) \tag{5}$$

Such soft target provides more information for training and is also in line with the evaluation metric.

The joint representation $\boldsymbol{h}$ is input into a non-linear layer and then through a linear mapping to predict a score for each answer candidate:

$$\hat{s} = \text{sigmoid}\left(W_o \ \text{Relu}\left(W_f \ \boldsymbol{h}\right)\right) \tag{6}$$

The sigmoid function squeezes the scores into $(0, 1)$ as the probability of the answer candidate. Our loss function is similar to the binary cross-entropy loss while using soft targets:

$$L_{\text{vqa}} = -\sum_{i=1}^{M}\sum_{j=1}^{N} s_{ij} \log \hat{s}_{ij} + (1 - s_{ij}) \log(1 - \hat{s}_{ij}) \tag{7}$$

where M are the number of training samples and $\mathbf{s}$ is the soft targets computed in Eq. 5. This final step can be seen as a regression layer that predicts the correctness of each answer candidate.

4.5 Explanation Generation

To generate an explanation, we adopt an LSTM-based language model that takes the joint representation $\boldsymbol{h}$ as input. Given the ground-truth explanation $\mathcal{E} = \{w_1, w_2, ..., w_{T_e}\}$, the loss function is:

$$\begin{aligned} L_{\text{vqe}} &= -\log(p(\mathcal{E}|\boldsymbol{h})) \\ &= -\sum_{t=0}^{T_e} \log(p(w_t|\boldsymbol{h}, w_1, ..., w_{t-1})) \end{aligned} \tag{8}$$

The final loss of multi-task learning is the sum of the VQA and VQE loss:

$$L = L_{\text{vqa}} + L_{\text{vqe}} \tag{9}$$

5 Experiments and Results

5.1 Experiment Setup

Model Setting. We use 300 dimension word embeddings, initialized with pre-trained GloVe vectors [21]. For the question embedding, we use a single-layer GRU with 1024 hidden units. For explanation generation, we use a single-layer forward LSTM with 1024 hidden units. The question embedding and the explanation generation share the word embedding matrix to reduce the number of parameters. We use Adam solver with a fixed learning rate 0.01 and the batch size is 512. We use weight normalization [24] to accelerate the training. Dropout and early stop (15 epochs) are used to reduce overfitting.

Model Variants. We experiment with the following model variants:

- **Q-E**: generating explanation from question only.
- **I-E**: generating explanation from image only.
- **QI-E**: generating explanation from question and image and only training the branch of explanation generation.

- **QI-A**: predicting answer from question and image and only training the branch of answer prediction.
- **QI-AE**: predicting answer and generating explanations, training both branches.
- **QI-AE(relevant)**: predicting answer and generating explanation and training both branches. The explanation used in this variant is the relevant caption obtained in the process of explanation synthesis in Sect. 3.1.
- **QI-AE(random)**: predicting answer and generating explanation and training both branches. The explanation is randomly selected from the ground-truth captions for the same image except the relevant caption.

5.2 Evaluation of Explanation Generation

In this section, we evaluate the task of explanation generation. Table 3 shows the performance of all model variants on the validation split of the VQA-E dataset. First, the I-E model outperforms Q-E. This implies that it is easier to generate an explanation from only the image than from only the question, and this *image bias* is contrary to the well-known *language bias* in the VQA where it is easier to predict an answer from only the question than from only the image. Second, the QI-E models outperform both the I-E and Q-E by a large margin, which means that both the question and the image are critical for generating good explanations. Attention mechanism is helpful for the performance and bottom-up image features are consistently better than grid image features. Finally, the QI-AE using bottom-up image features improves the performance further and achieves the best performance across all evaluation metrics. This shows that the supervision on the answer side is helpful for the explanation generation task, thus proving the effectiveness of our multi-task learning scheme.

Table 3. Performance of explanation generation task on the validation split of the proposed VQA-E dataset, where B-N, M, R, and C are short for BLEU-N, METEOR, ROUGE-L, and CIDEr-D. All scores are reported in percentage (%).

Model	Image Features	B-1	B-2	B-3	B-4	M	C	R
Q-E	-	26.80	10.90	4.20	1.80	7.98	13.42	24.90
I-E	Global	32.50	17.20	9.30	5.20	12.38	48.58	29.79
QI-E	Global	34.70	19.30	11.00	6.50	14.07	61.55	31.87
	Grid	36.30	21.10	12.50	7.60	15.50	73.70	34.00
	Bottom-up	38.00	22.60	13.80	8.60	16.57	84.07	34.92
QI-AE	Global	35.10	19.70	11.30	6.70	14.40	64.62	32.39
	Grid	38.30	22.90	14.00	8.80	16.85	87.04	35.16
	Bottom-up	**39.30**	**23.90**	**14.80**	**9.40**	**17.37**	**93.08**	**36.33**

5.3 Evaluation of Answer Prediction

In this section, we evaluate the task of answer prediction, as shown in Table 4. Overall, the QI-AE models consistently outperform QI-A models across all question types. This indicates that forcing the model to explain can help it predict a more accurate answer. We argue that the supervision on explanation in QI-AE models can alleviate the headache of language bias in the QI-A models, because in order to generate a good explanation, the model has to fully exploit the image content, learn to attend to important regions, and explicitly interpret the attended regions in the context of questions. In contrast, during the training of QI-A models without explanations, when an answer can be guessed from the question itself, the model can easily get the loss down to zero by understanding the question only regardless of the image content. In this case, the training sample is not fully exploited to help the model learn how to attend to the important regions. Another observation from Table 4 can further support our argument. The additional supervision on explanation produces a much bigger improvement on the attention-based models (Grid and Bottom-up) than the models without attention (Global).

QI-AE(random)-Bottom-up produces a much lower accuracy than QI-AE-Bottom-up, even lower than QI-A-Bottom-up. This implies that low-quality or irrelevant explanations might confuse the model, thus leading to a big drop in the performance. It also relieves the concern that the improvement is brought by learning to describe the image, rather than explaining the answer. This further substantiates the effectiveness of the additional supervision on explanation.

Table 5 presents the performance of our method and the state-of-the-art approaches on the test-standard split of VQA v2 dataset. Our method outperforms the state-of-the-art methods over the answer types 'Yes/No' and 'Other' as well as in the overall accuracy, while producing a slightly lower accuracy over the answer type 'Number' than BUTD [1,26].

Table 4. Performance of the answer prediction task on the validation split of VQA v2 dataset. Accuracies in percentage (%) are reported.

Model	Image features	All	Yes/No	Number	Other
QI-A	Global	57.26	77.19	39.73	46.74
	Grid	59.25	76.31	39.99	51.38
	Bottom-up	61.78	78.63	41.30	52.54
QI-AE	Global	57.92	78.01	40.46	47.25
	Grid	60.57	78.35	39.36	52.66
	Bottom-up	**63.51**	**80.85**	**43.02**	**54.16**
QI-AE (random)	Bottom-up	58.74	78.75	40.79	48.26
QI-AE (relevant)	Bottom-up	62.18	79.02	41.07	53.26

Table 5. Performance comparison with the state-of-the-art VQA methods on the test-standard split of VQA v2 dataset. BUTD-ensemble is an ensemble of 30 models and it will not participate in ranking. Accuracies in percentage (%) are reported.

Method	All	Yes/No	Number	Other
Prior [8]	25.98	61.20	0.36	1.17
Language-only [8]	44.26	67.01	31.55	27.37
d-LSTM+n-I [8]	54.22	73.46	35.18	41.83
MCB [7,8]	62.27	78.82	38.28	53.36
BUTD [26,1]	65.67	82.20	**43.90**	56.26
BUTD-ensemble [26,1]	70.34	86.60	48.64	61.15
Ours: QI-AE-Bottom-up	**66.31**	**83.22**	43.58	**56.79**

5.4 Qualitative Analysis

In this section, we show qualitative examples to demonstrate the strength of our multi-task VQA-E model, as shown in Fig. 7. Overall, the QI-AE model can generate relevant and complementary explanations for the predicted answers. For example, in the (a) of Fig. 7, the QI-AE model not only predicts the correct answer 'Yes', but also provides more details in the 'kitchen', i.e., 'fridge', 'sink', and 'cabinets'. Besides, the QI-AE model can better localize the important regions than the QI-A model. As shown in the (b) of Fig. 7, the QI-AE model gives the biggest attention weight on the person's hand and thus predicts the right answer 'Feeding giraffe', while the QI-A model focuses more on the giraffe, leading to a wrong answer 'Standing'. In the (c), both QI-AE and QI-E models attend to the right region, but these two models predict the opposite answers. This interesting contrast implies that the QI-AE model, which has to

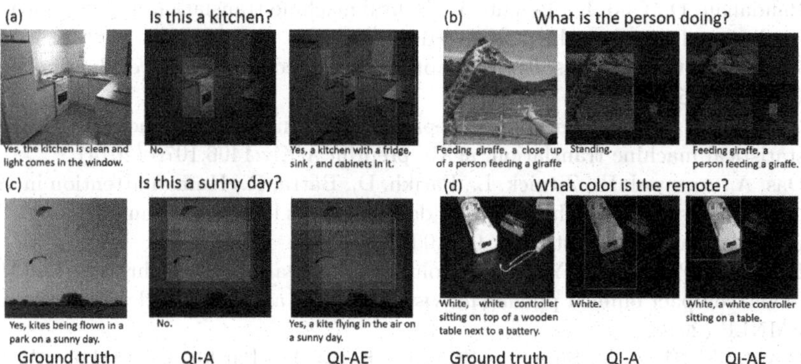

Fig. 7. Qualitative comparison between the QI-A and QI-AE models (both using bottom-up image features). We visualize the attention by rendering a red box over the region that has the biggest attention weight.

fully exploit the image content to generate an explanation, can better understand the attended region than the QI-A model that only needs to predict a short answer.

6 Conclusions and Future Work

In this work, we have constructed a new dataset and proposed a task of VQA-E to promote research on justifying answers for visual questions. Explanations in our dataset are of high quality for those visually-specific questions, while being inadequate for subjective ones whose evidences are indirect. For subjective questions, we will need extra knowledge bases to find good explanations for them.

We have also proposed a novel multi-task learning architecture for the VQA-E task. The additional supervision from explanations not only enables our model to generate reasons to justify predicted answers, but also brings a big improvement in the accuracy of answer prediction. Our VQA-E model is able to better localize and understand the important regions in images than the original VQA model. In the future, we will adopt more advanced approaches to train our model, like the reinforcement learning in image captioning [23].

Acknowledgements. We thank Qianyi Wu etc. for helpful feedback on the user study. This research is partially supported by NTU-CoE Grant and Data Science & Artificial Intelligence Research Centre@NTU (DSAIR). Jiebo Luo would like to thank the support of Adobe and NSF Award #1704309.

References

1. Anderson, P., et al.: Bottom-up and top-down attention for image captioning and visual question answering. In: CVPR (2018)
2. Antol, S., et al.: VQA: visual question answering. In: ICCV (2015)
3. Bahdanau, D., Cho, K., Bengio, Y.: Neural machine translation by jointly learning to align and translate. In: ICLR (2014)
4. Chen, X., et al.: Microsoft coco captions: Data collection and evaluation server. CoRR (2015)
5. Cho, K., et al.: Learning phrase representations using RNN encoder-decoder for statistical machine translation. arXiv preprint arXiv:1406.1078 (2014)
6. Das, A., Agrawal, H., Zitnick, L., Parikh, D., Batra, D.: Human attention in visual question answering: do humans and deep networks look at the same regions? Comput. Vis. Image Underst. **163**, 90–100 (2017)
7. Fukui, A., Park, D.H., Yang, D., Rohrbach, A., Darrell, T., Rohrbach, M.: Multimodal compact bilinear pooling for visual question answering and visual grounding. EMNLP (2016)
8. Goyal, Y., Khot, T., Summers-Stay, D., Batra, D., Parikh, D.: Making the V in VQA matter: Elevating the role of image understanding in visual question answering. In: CVPR (2017)
9. Gu, J., Cai, J., Wang, G., Chen, T.: Stack-captioning: coarse-to-fine learning for image captioning. In: AAAI (2018)

10. Gu, J., Wang, G., Cai, J., Chen, T.: An empirical study of language CNN for image captioning. In: ICCV (2017)
11. Gurari, D., et al.: VizWiz grand challenge: answering visual questions from blind people. In: CVPR (2018)
12. He, K., Zhang, X., Ren, S., Sun, J.: Deep residual learning for image recognition. In: CVPR (2016)
13. Heilman, M., Smith, N.A.: Good question! statistical ranking for question generation. In: Human Language Technologies: The 2010 Annual Conference of the North American Chapter of the Association for Computational Linguistics, HLT 2010, pp. pp. 609–617. Association for Computational Linguistics, Stroudsburg (2010). http://dl.acm.org/citation.cfm?id=1857999.1858085
14. Hendricks, L.A., Akata, Z., Rohrbach, M., Donahue, J., Schiele, B., Darrell, T.: Generating visual explanations. In: Leibe, B., Matas, J., Sebe, N., Welling, M. (eds.) ECCV 2016. LNCS, vol. 9908, pp. 3–19. Springer, Cham (2016). https://doi.org/10.1007/978-3-319-46493-0_1
15. Ilievski, I., Yan, S., Feng, J.: A focused dynamic attention model for visual question answering. In: ECCV (2016)
16. Kazemi, V., Elqursh, A.: Show, ask, attend, and answer: a strong baseline for visual question answering. arXiv preprint arXiv:1704.03162 (2017)
17. Li, Q., Fu, J., Yu, D., Mei, T., Luo, J.: Tell-and-answer: towards explainable visual question answering using attributes and captions. arXiv preprint arXiv:1801.09041 (2018)
18. Lu, J., Yang, J., Batra, D., Parikh, D.: Hierarchical question-image co-attention for visual question answering. In: NIPS, pp. 289–297 (2016)
19. Nam, H., Ha, J.W., Kim, J.: Dual attention networks for multimodal reasoning and matching. In: CVPR (2017)
20. Park, D.H., Hendricks, L.A., Akata, Z., Rohrbach, A., Schiele, B., Darrell, T., Rohrbach, M.: Multimodal explanations: justifying decisions and pointing to the evidence. In: CVPR (2018)
21. Pennington, J., Socher, R., Manning, C.: GloVe: global vectors for word representation. In: EMNLP, pp. 1532–1543 (2014)
22. Ren, M., Kiros, R., Zemel, R.: Image question answering: a visual semantic embedding model and a new dataset. NIPS **1**(2), 5 (2015)
23. Rennie, S.J., Marcheret, E., Mroueh, Y., Ross, J., Goel, V.: Self-critical sequence training for image captioning. In: CVPR (2017)
24. Salimans, T., Kingma, D.P.: Weight normalization: A simple reparameterization to accelerate training of deep neural networks. In: NIPS, pp. 901–909 (2016)
25. Shih, K.J., Singh, S., Hoiem, D.: Where to look: Focus regions for visual question answering. In: ICCV, pp. 4613–4621 (2016)
26. Teney, D., Anderson, P., He, X., Hengel, A.v.d.: Tips and tricks for visual question answering: learnings from the 2017 challenge. In: CVPR (2018)
27. Wu, Q., Shen, C., Liu, L., Dick, A., van den Hengel, A.: What value do explicit high level concepts have in vision to language problems? In: CVPR (2016)
28. Xu, H., Saenko, K.: Ask, attend and answer: exploring question-guided spatial attention for visual question answering. In: Leibe, B., Matas, J., Sebe, N., Welling, M. (eds.) ECCV 2016. LNCS, vol. 9911, pp. 451–466. Springer, Cham (2016). https://doi.org/10.1007/978-3-319-46478-7_28
29. Xu, K., et al.: Show, attend and tell: Neural image caption generation with visual attention. ICML **14**, 77–81 (2015)

30. Yang, X., Zhang, H., Cai, J.: Shuffe-then-assemble: learning object-agnostic visual relationship features. In: Ferrari, V., Hebert, M., Sminchisescu, C., Weiss, Y. (eds.) ECCV 2018, Part XII. LNCS, vol. 11216, pp. 38–54. Springer, Cham (2018)
31. Yang, Z., He, X., Gao, J., Deng, L., Smola, A.: Stacked attention networks for image question answering. In: CVPR, pp. 21–29 (2016)
32. You, Q., Jin, H., Wang, Z., Fang, C., Luo, J.: Image captioning with semantic attention. In: CVPR (2016)
33. Yu, D., Fu, J., Mei, T., Rui, Y.: Multi-level attention networks for visual question answering. In: CVPR (2017)
34. Zhu, Y., Groth, O., Bernstein, M., Fei-Fei, L.: Visual7W: Grounded question answering in images. In: CVPR, pp. 4995–5004 (2016)

Penalizing Top Performers: Conservative Loss for Semantic Segmentation Adaptation

Xinge Zhu[1(✉)], Hui Zhou[2], Ceyuan Yang[1], Jianping Shi[2], and Dahua Lin[1]

[1] CUHK-SenseTime Joint Lab, CUHK, Hong Kong, Hong Kong S.A.R.
zhuxinge123@gmail.com
[2] SenseTime Research, Beijing, China

Abstract. Due to the expensive and time-consuming annotations (e.g., segmentation) for real-world images, recent works in computer vision resort to synthetic data. However, the performance on the real image often drops significantly because of the domain shift between the synthetic data and the real images. In this setting, domain adaptation brings an appealing option. The effective approaches of domain adaptation shape the representations that (1) are discriminative for the main task and (2) have good generalization capability for domain shift. To this end, we propose a novel loss function, i.e., Conservative Loss, which penalizes the extreme good and bad cases while encouraging the moderate examples. More specifically, it enables the network to learn features that are discriminative by gradient descent and are invariant to the change of domains via gradient ascend method. Extensive experiments on synthetic to real segmentation adaptation show our proposed method achieves state of the art results. Ablation studies give more insights into properties of the Conservative Loss. Exploratory experiments and discussion demonstrate that our Conservative Loss has good flexibility rather than restricting an exact form.

1 Introduction

Deep convolutional neural networks have brought impressive advances to the state of the art across a multitude of tasks in computer vision [1–3]. At the same time, these significant leaps require a large amount of labeled data. For some pixel-level tasks, e.g., semantic segmentation, obtaining a fine-grained label is expensive and time-consuming. In [4], they report that it takes more than 90 min for manually labeling a single image. Recent advances in Computer Graphics [5] offer an alternative solution to address the data issue. In [5], they automatically capture both images and fine-grained labels from GTAV game with the speed faster than human in several orders of magnitude.

Electronic supplementary material The online version of this chapter (https://doi.org/10.1007/978-3-030-01234-2_35) contains supplementary material, which is available to authorized users.

V. Ferrari et al. (Eds.): ECCV 2018, LNCS 11211, pp. 587–603, 2018.
https://doi.org/10.1007/978-3-030-01234-2_35

However, models trained on the synthetic data fail to perform well on the real-world images. The main reason is the shift between training and test domains [6]. In the presence of the domain shift, the model trained on the synthetic data often tends to be biased towards the source domain (synthetic images), making them incapable to generalize to the target domain (real images).

Traditional approaches for domain adaptation mainly focus on the image classification task, which can be summarized as two lines: (1) minimizing the distance between the source and target distributions [7–9]; (2) explicitly ensuring that two distributions close to each other by adversarial learning [10,11]. Existing works [12,13] used the similar idea, i.e., gradient reversal layer, to our proposed loss in the domain adaptation for image classification, which was achieved by multiplying a negative scalar during the backpropagation. However, since there exist large category discrepancies between pixels in one image, the manner of uniformly reversing the gradients for all pixels with same scalar is not suitable for the structured prediction in the segmentation. Those drawbacks limit the gradient reversal layer to generalize to the segmentation adaptation.

Semantic segmentation provides pixel-level label for input image, which carries more dense and structured information than image classification, and thus making its domain adaptation difficult. Hence, the domain adaptation techniques in the classification task which focus on sparsely high-level features do not translate well to the segmentation adaptation [14]. Few works have explored the domain adaptation for segmentation [14–16]. Orthogonal to those works focusing on manipulating the data statistics [15] or applying the curriculum learning [14] to adaptation, we propose the novel Conservative Loss to realize it without introducing extra computational overhead.

We observe that with training step goes by, the performance on the target domain *first rises and then falls.* We show the trends of mIoU on the experiment of synthetic (GTAV data [5]) to real (Cityscapes data [4]) segmentation adaptation in Fig. 1. It can be observed that the performance on source domain and target domain would not reach the best at the same time because of the domain shift. Since there is no ground truth for target domain during training,

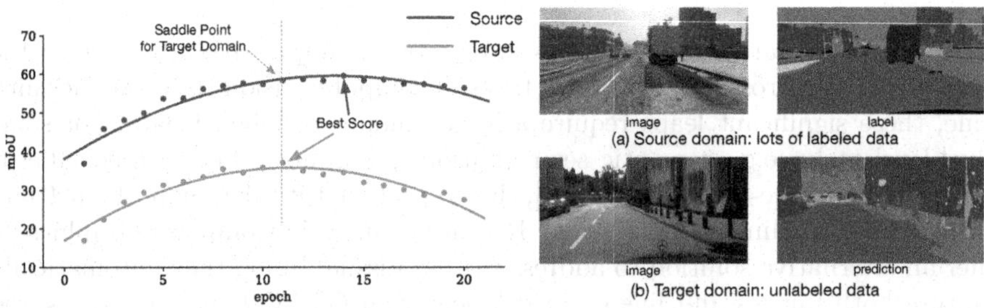

Fig. 1. We show the tendency of mIoU on the source domain and target domain. The curves indicate the trends and points denote the actual mIoU. Besides, we display the samples from source domain (GTAV) and target domain (Cityscapes)

it is required to find the saddle point of target domain on the source domain. It is note-worthy that the saddle point for target domain does bias to the best score on the source domain but not reach, which delivers a balance between the discriminativeness and domain-invariant. This phenomenon is consistent with many domain adaptation theories [17–19]. Therefore, we focus on learning representations with two following characteristics which are: (i) discriminative for semantic segmentation on the source domain (corresponding to the '*first rises*') and (ii) invariant to the change of domains.

In this paper, this is achieved by training with the Conservative Loss in an adversarial framework. The Conservative Loss is extremely simple. It holds two attributes corresponding to the properties of desired representations. First, when the probability of ground truth label on the source domain is low, the Conservative Loss enforces the network to learn more discriminative features via gradient descent, which corresponds to the first property of discriminativeness. Second, when the probability of ground truth label is much high, our loss penalizes this case by giving a negative value, which prevents the model from biasing to source domain training data further increasing the generalization capability. This corresponds to the second property of domain-invariant. Our loss function can be seen to seek the optimal parameters that deliver a saddle point of those two objectives. Furthermore, the generative adversarial network (GAN) [20] is also introduced to our model. Unlike some works [10,15] where they apply the feature-level discriminator, we utilize the GAN to further supplement the domain alignment by enforcing reconstructed images to be indistinguishable for the discriminator.

We conduct extensive experiments on synthetic to real segmentation adaptation. The proposed method considerably improves over previous state-of-the-art and achieves **9.3** points of mIoU gain on Synthia [21] to Cityscapes [4] experiment without introducing any extra computational overhead during evaluation. Ablation studies verify the effect of different components to our performance and give more insights into properties of our Conservative Loss. More discussions and visualization demonstrate the Conservative Loss has good flexibility rather than limiting to a fixed instantiation.

2 Related Work

Semantic Segmentation. Semantic segmentation is a highly active field, which is a task of assigning object label to each pixel of image. With the surge of deep segmentation model [3], most recent top-performing methods are built on the CNNs [1,22,23].

Huge amount of human effort is required to annotate the fined-grained semantic segmentation ground truth. According to [5], it did take about 60 min to manually segment each image. On the contrary, collecting data from video games such as GTAV [5] is much faster and cheaper compared with the human annotator. For example, [5] extracted 24,966 GTAV images with annotations within 49 hrs by using a GPU parallel method. However, it is hard to apply the model trained on the synthetic image to the real-world image because of their discrepant data distributions.

Domain Adaptation. Many machine learning methods rely on the assumption that the training and test data are in the same distribution. However, it is often the case that there exists some discrepancies [17,19], which leads to significant performance drop on the test data. Domain adaptation aims to alleviate the impact of the discrepancy between training and test data.

Domain Adaptation for Image Classification. Existing works on domain adaptation mostly focus on image classification problem. Conventional methods include Maximum Mean Discrepancy (MMD) [7–9], geodesic flow kernel [8], sub-space alignment [24], asymmetric metric learning [25], *etc.* Recently, domain adaptation approaches aim to improve the adaptability of deep neural networks [7,13,26–31].

Domain Adaptation for Semantic Segmentation. Much less attention has been given to domain adaptation for semantic segmentation task. The pioneering work in this task is [15], which combines the global and local alignment methods with a domain adversarial training. Another work [14] applies the curriculum learning to solve the domain adaptation from easy to hard. In [16], they propose an unsupervised learning to adapt road scene segmenters across different cities. In [32], they perform output space adaptation at feature level by an adversarial module. Unlike them constraining the distribution [15] or the output of the network [32], we propose the Conservative Loss to naturally seek the discriminative and domain-invariant representations.

Adversarial Learning. Recently, Generative Adversarial Network (GAN) [20] has raised great attention. Some works extend this framework for domain adaptation. CoGAN [11] achieves the domain adaptation by generating cross-domain instances. Domain adversarial neural networks [12] consider adversarial training for suppressing domain biases. In [10], they incorporate adversarial discriminative setting to help mitigate performance degradation. In our work, we also incorporate the GAN into our model, whose discriminator drives the source image towards the target one for promoting domain alignment.

3 Methodology

As presented above, the key to realize unsupervised domain adaptation is the discriminative and domain-invariant representations. The Conservative Loss is proposed to penalize the extreme cases and its goal is to deliver a balance between the discriminative and the domain-invariant representations. Furthermore, we introduce the generative adversarial networks to align the source and target embedding. Below, we first describe the framework of our model and its network blocks. Then, the Conservative Loss and its background are presented in details. Finally, the alternative optimization is provided.

3.1 Framework Overview

Our framework is illustrated in Fig. 2. In our setting, there are two domains: source domain (image and label) and target domain (image only). Our framework

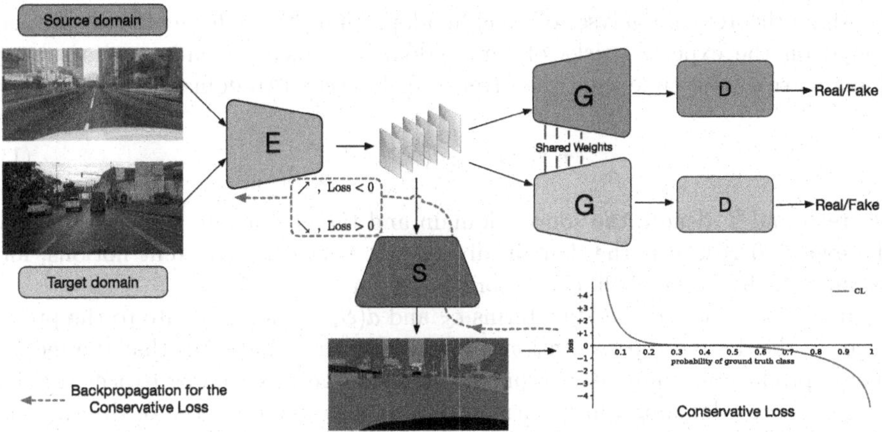

Fig. 2. The pipeline of our framework. E denotes the encoder, G denotes the generator, and D is the discriminator. S is the pixel-wise classifier for semantic segmentation. The red color represents the network blocks for the source domain, and the blue for the target domain. We also display the Conservative Loss and its backpropagation. ↗ represents the gradient ascend and ↘ denotes the gradient descend (Color figure online)

aims to achieve good performance on the target domain by applying the model trained on the source domain.

Our model consists of two major parts, i.e., GAN and Segmentation part. The GAN aims to align the source and target embedding. More specifically, the generator and discriminator are playing a minimax game [20], in which the generator takes source embedding as input and generates the target-like image to fool the discriminator, while the discriminator tries to classify the reconstructed image [10,11]. The segmentation part can be seen as a regular segmentation model. For each part, the detailed components are shown in the following:

- The encoder(E) performs the feature embedding given source or target image, whose architecture is a fully convolutional network. The generator(G) reconstructs the image based on the embedding. The discriminator(D) does classify the reconstructed images as real or fake. S is the pixel-wise classifier.
- The GAN consists of encoder, generator and discriminator.
- The segmentation part consists of encoder and pixel-level classifier. Note that the encoder does work in both GAN and Segmentation.

The detailed architecture of generators and discriminators is described in the supplementary material because of the limited page space.

3.2 Background

In this section, we briefly introduce the theory of domain adaptation and present its relation to our proposed loss.

Many theoretical analyses of domain adaptation [17–19] have offered a upper bound on the expected risks of target domain, which depends on its source domain error (test-time) and the divergence between two domains. Formally,

$$\epsilon_{\mathcal{T}} \leq \epsilon_{\mathcal{S}} + \frac{1}{2}d(\mathcal{S},\mathcal{T}) + \mathcal{C}, \tag{1}$$

where $\mathcal{S}$ and $\mathcal{T}$ denote the source domain and target domain, respectively. ϵ is the expected risk. d is the domain divergence, which has different notions, for example $\mathcal{H}$-divergence [19]. $\mathcal{C}$ is a constant term.

It can be observed that two terms $\epsilon_{\mathcal{S}}$ and $d(\mathcal{S},\mathcal{T})$ closely relate to the properties in the desired representations. The first term $\epsilon_{\mathcal{S}}$ indicates that the model should produce discriminative representations for getting smaller expected risks on the source domain, which corresponds to the first property of discriminativeness. The second term $d(\mathcal{S},\mathcal{T})$ defines the discrepancy distance between two distributions, in which the more similar the representations of both domains are, the smaller it is. This correlates with the second property of domain-invariant. More theoretical analyses are shown in the supplementary material.

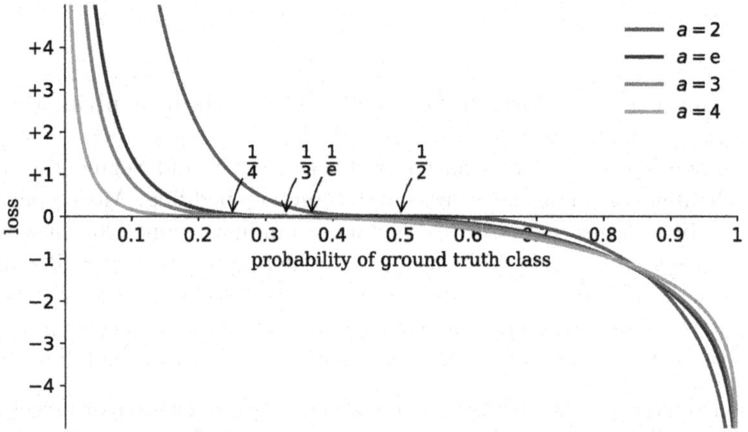

Fig. 3. The proposed Conservative Loss with different a. It can be observed that the Conservative Loss keeps low values in the middle level and punishes the extremely good or bad cases

3.3 Conservative Loss

As explained above, the desired representations should be discriminative for the main task on source domain and possess good generalization ability rather than getting into the overfitting. We thus propose the Conservative Loss for the semantic segmentation on the source domain, which carries the two following properties:

- When the probability of ground truth class is low, the loss function gives a positive value, which enables the network to learn a more discriminative feature by using gradient descent method.
- When the probability is high, the loss function delivers the negative value, which makes the network avoid the bias towards the source domain via the gradient ascend further learning the better generalization.

The Conservative Loss is formulated as:

$$\mathrm{CL}(p_t) = (1 + \log_a(p_t))^2 * \log_a(-\log_a(p_t)), \tag{2}$$

where p_t is the probability of our prediction towards ground truth. a is the base of logarithmic function, which also indicates the intersection point with x-axis, that is $\frac{1}{a}$. The Conservative Loss is visualized for several values of $a \in [2, \mathrm{e}, 3, 4]$ in Fig. 3, in which e is Euler's number and $\mathrm{e} \approx 2.718$. Specifically, $(1+\log_a(p_t))^2$ acts as a modulating factor, which delivers the large values when p_t is much low or high. $\log_a(-\log_a(p_t))$ is designed as the switch of gradient direction, in which when $p_t > \frac{1}{a}$ it is negative, otherwise it is positive.

In the following, we have raised two lemmas to analysis the appealing property of our Conservative Loss.

Lemma 1. *The objective function of domain adaptation system contains a saddle point, which relates to the zero point of Conservative Loss.*

As the pipeline in Fig. 2 shown, the full objective consists of two parts, including the loss $\mathcal{L}^s_{seg,p_t}$ for Segmentation and the loss $\mathcal{L}_{GAN}$ for GAN. The sign of $\mathcal{L}^s_{seg,p_t}$ dynamically depends on p_t. When p_t is much high, the negative value leads to the gradient ascend for escaping the bias to source domain. Otherwise, the positive value makes the features discriminative. It can be seen that our loss balances the two objectives (discriminativeness and domain-invariant) that shape the representations during learning, and its zero point acts as the saddle point. More details are shown in the supplementary material.

Lemma 2. *Our loss encourages the moderate examples in large range, which makes the overall optimization more stable.*

From the loss form, it can be observed that the loss focuses on the hard negatives and positives, and tends to give the low value for the probability in the middle level. For instance, with $a = \mathrm{e}$, the loss values of $p_t = 0.9$ and $p_t = 0.1$ are -1.8 and 1.4, respectively, while the loss values of $p_t = 0.5$ and $p_t = 0.6$ are -0.03 and -0.06. In such setting, the loss extends the range in which an example receives low loss, which brings a stable optimization even in the case of the gradient descend and ascend frequently alternate due to the joint optimization of $\mathcal{L}^s_{seg,p_t}$ and $\mathcal{L}_{GAN}$.

In practice we use a λ-balanced variant of the Conservative Loss:

$$\mathrm{CL}(p_t) = \lambda(1 + \log_a(p_t))^2 * \log_a(-\log_a(p_t)). \quad (3)$$

As our experiments will show, different balanced factors λ yield slightly different performance. While in our main experiments we use the Conservative Loss defined above, its exact form is not crucial. In Sect. 4.5 we offer other forms of our loss which also maintain the two properties, and experimental results demonstrate that they can also be effective.

3.4 Model Objective

Our full objective is to alternatively update the three network blocks, i.e., discriminators(D), generators(G) and encoder(E). Note that S is a pixel-level classifier which has no learnable parameters in our model. Hence, the objective contains three terms: $\mathcal{L}_D$, $\mathcal{L}_G$ and $\mathcal{L}_E$. We then explain the various losses used in our method and describe the alternative optimization scheme.

Adversarial Loss. Inheriting from GAN [20], we apply the adversarial losses which are derived from the discriminator to all three blocks. We term them as $\mathcal{L}_{\mathrm{GAN,D}}, \mathcal{L}_{\mathrm{GAN,G}}$ and $\mathcal{L}_{\mathrm{GAN,E}}$. For each adversarial loss it consists of two parts, i.e., $\mathcal{L}^s_{GAN}$ for the source image and $\mathcal{L}^t_{GAN}$ for the target image. Thus we can obtain the adversarial loss by $\mathcal{L}_{GAN} = \mathcal{L}^s_{GAN} + \mathcal{L}^t_{GAN}$. It is noted that for the encoder, the adversarial loss does a cross-domain update (i.e., classifying the image as real or fake from source domain to target domain and vice versa), which enforces the network to generate similar embeddings for two domains.

Reconstructed Loss. The generator performs the image reconstruction. We use L1 distance as $\mathcal{L}_{rec}$ because L1 encourages less blurring.

Segmentation Loss. As Sect. 3.3 introduced, the Conservative Loss is applied to the semantic segmentation in the domain adaptation setting.

During training, we iteratively optimize all three learnable parts (Encoder, Generator and Discriminator). During inference, only the encoder and segmentation classifier are used to produce the results on target domain. The alternating update scheme is described as following:

(1) Update discriminators: the overall loss is $\mathcal{L}_D = \mathcal{L}_{GAN,D}$.
(2) Update generators: the loss involves the adversarial loss and reconstructed loss. The overall loss is $\mathcal{L}_G = \mathcal{L}_{GAN,G} + \mathcal{L}_{rec}$.
(3) Update encoder: since the encoder does work in both two components, i.e., GAN and Segmentation, the overall loss is a combination of several losses, including adversarial loss and segmentation loss on source domain; $\mathcal{L}_E = \mathcal{L}_{GAN,E} + \mathcal{L}^s_{seg}$.

4 Experiments

4.1 Dataset

Following previous works [14,15], we use GTAV [5] or Synthia [21] dataset as the source domain with pixel-level labels, and we use Cityscapes [4] dataset as the target domain. We briefly introduce the datasets as following:

GTAV has 24,966 urban scene images rendered by the gaming engine GTAV. The semantic categories are compatible with the Cityscapes dataset. We take the whole GTAV dataset with labels as the source domain data.

Synthia is a large dataset which contains different video sequences rendered from a virtual city. We take SYNTHIA-RAND-CITYSCAPES [21] as the source domain data which provides 9,400 images from all the sequences with Cityscape-compatible annotations. Inheriting from existing methods [14], we take 16 common object categories for the evaluation.

Cityscapes is a real-world image dataset focused on the urban scene, which consists of 2,975 images in training set and 500 images for validation. The resolution of images is 2048×1024 and 19 semantic categories are provided with pixel-level labels. We take the **unlabeled training set** as the target domain data. The adaptation results are reported on the validation set.

4.2 Training Setup

In our experiments, we use the FCN8s [3] as the semantic segmentation model. The backbone is VGG16 [2] which is pretrained on the ImageNet dataset [33]. We apply the PatchGAN [34] as the discriminator, in which the discriminator tries to classify whether overlapping image patches are real or fake. Similar to EBGAN [35], we add the Gaussian noise to the generator. During training, Adam [36] optimization is applied with $\beta_1 = 0.9$ and $\beta_2 = 0.999$. For the Conservative Loss, we apply $a = \mathrm{e}$ and the balanced weight $\lambda = 5$. The ablation study will give more detailed explanations. Due to the GPU memory limitation, the images used in our experiments are resized and cropped to 1024×512 and the batch size is 1. More experimental settings will be available in the supplementary material.

Warm Start. In our experiments, two different training strategies are employed, which are cold start and warm start. The cold start is that the whole model is trained by using the Conservative Loss from scratch. The warm start indicates the model is trained by first using cross entropy loss and then using our Conservative Loss. Many works [37–39] demonstrate that the warm start strategy to gradient update provides a more stable training compared with cold start. As the ablation study will show, the warm start performs better than the cold start. In the next domain adaptation experiments, the model is trained using warm start strategy for fairness.

4.3 Results

In this section, we provide a quantitative evaluation by performing two adaptation experiments, i.e., from GTAV to Cityscapes and from Synthia to Cityscapes.

We compare our method with several existing models, including FCNWild [15], CDA [14] and [32]. FCNWild [15] applies the dilated network [40] as the backbone and the base model of [14] is the FCN8s-VGG19 [3]. Tsai *et al.* [32] adopts adversarial learning in the output space to perform feature adaptation. The detailed results of each category are available in the supplementary material.

Table 1. Results of domain adaptation from GTAV → Cityscapes. The bold values denote the best scores in the column.

Methods	Base	mIoU	mIoU gain
NoAdapt [15]	DilatedNet [40]	21.1	
FCNWild [15]	DilatedNet [40]	27.1	6.0
NoAdapt [14]	FCN8s [3]	22.3	
CDA [14]	FCN8s [3]	28.9	6.6
Tsai *et al.* [32]	FCN8s [3]	35.0	–
Ours-NoAdapt	FCN8s [3]	30.0	
Ours	FCN8s [3]	**38.1**	**8.1**

Table 2. Results of domain adaptation from Synthia → Cityscapes.

Methods	Base	mIoU	mIoU gain	mIoU-2
NoAdapt [15]	DilatedNet [40]	17.4		
FCNWild [15]	DilatedNet [40]	20.2	2.8	
NoAdapt [14]	FCN8s [3]	22.0		
CDA [14]	FCN8s [3]	29.0	7.0	
Tsai *et al.* [32]	FCN8s [3]	–	–	37.6
Ours-NoAdapt	FCN8s [3]	24.9		
Ours	FCN8s [3]	**34.2**	**9.3**	**40.3**

GTAV → Cityscapes. For a fairness, the result is evaluated over the 19 common classes. From Table 1 shown, our proposed method achieves the best performance (mIoU = **38.1**), which has **9.2** points higher than [14] and **11** points higher than [15]. Due to the different experimental settings and backbone network (baseline method [14] also mentions the difference), our own baseline performance is higher than other methods. However, the highlight is the **performance gain**. We can find that the proposed method yields an improvement of **8.1** points higher than 6.0 in [15] and 6.6 in [14].

Synthia → Cityscapes. We report the results of mIoU in Table 2. It is noted that [32] reported the results on Synthia [21] to Cityscapes adaptation with only 13 object categories (excluding wall, fense and pole). We also report this results as the mIoU-2. Our proposed model achieves a mIoU of **34.2**, and more importantly our model obtains a **9.3** points of performance gain which is higher than the performance gain of [14] (7.0) and [15] (2.8). Compared with [32] on 13 categories, our method also achieves the better performance. In particular, our model does not use any additional scene parsing data except the source domain and target domain data, while the [14] uses another dataset, i.e., PASCAL CONTEXT dataset, to obtain the superpixel label.

Table 3. Results of ablation study for different components in the proposed model. CL means the Conservative Loss. CE means the cross entropy loss

Model	FCN8s+CE	FCN8s+GAN+CE	FCN8s+GAN+CL
mIoU	30.0	34.4	38.1

Table 4. Results of ablation experiments for a and λ in the Conservative Loss

a (with fixed $\lambda = 5$)	2	e	3	4
mIoU	37.5	38.1	37.3	36.8
λ (with fixed $a = \mathrm{e}$)	1	5	10	20
mIoU	37.2	38.1	37.9	37.8

4.4 Ablation Study

In this section, we perform the thorough ablation experiments, including experiments with different components, different factors in the Conservative Loss and different training strategies. Those experiments demonstrate different contributions of components and provide more insights of our method.

Effect of Different Components. In this experiment, we show how each component in our model affects the final performance. We consider several cases as following: (1): the baseline model, which contains only the base segmentation model (FCN8s in our model) and is trained using source data only. (2) the FCN8s and GAN component, which consists of base model and GAN and is trained using both source data and target data with the cross entropy loss. (3) the full model, which involves three parts, i.e., base model, GAN and Conservative Loss. We perform the ablation experiments on GTAV → Cityscapes setting.

The results of ablation study are shown in Table 3. It can be observed that each component plays an important role in performance improvement. More specifically, our full model achieves the best results and obtains **8.1** points performance gain. The GAN part also gets 4.4 performance gain compared with

FCN8s+CE. Note that the GAN component could introduce the unlabeled target domain data into the whole model, so the Conservative Loss is applied based on the GAN and there is no variant of FCN8s+CL.

Effect of a and λ in the Conservative Loss. In this part, we design the ablation experiments for a and λ in the Conservative Loss. As shown in Eq. 2, a is the base of logarithm and denotes the intersection point with x-axis. λ is a balanced factor. We show the impacts of different a and λ in Table 4.

Since there are two variables, we perform the ablation study for one variable with another fixed. For the ablation of a (with fixed $\lambda = 5$), it can be observed that $a = \mathrm{e}$ achieves the best result. Furthermore, we can find that all different a obtain much better performance compared with the cross entropy loss (34.4 in Table 3), which demonstrates that our loss performs consistently better and has high robustness. For the ablation of λ (with fixed $a = \mathrm{e}$), different λ show slightly different results and $\lambda = 5$ obtains the best performance.

Warm Start and Cold Start. As described in Sect. 4.2, we use a warm start strategy to train the proposed model. In this experiment, we compare the two training strategies. For the cold start strategy, we clamp the Conservative Loss with $[\min = -10, \max = 10]$, while this constraint is not exist in the warm start. We use the λ-balanced Conservative Loss with $\lambda = 5$ and $a = \mathrm{e}$.

Table 5. Results of two training strategies, i.e., cold start and warm start. CL means the Conservative Loss

Loss function	[14]	CL with cold start	CL with warm start
mIoU	28.9	35.2	38.1

In Table 5, it can be observed that the Conservative Loss with cold start outperforms [14] with a large margin (6.3 points). The warm start performs better than the cold start because it enables the network to train stably.

4.5 Discussion

In this section, we design several experiments to verify the capability of the proposed method. We show the effect of adaptation on distribution to measure how domain gap is reduced in the feature level. We compared with several classification losses and homogeneous losses to show its superiority and flexibility.

Visualizations. To verify the effect of adaptation on the distribution, we use t-SNE [41] to visualize feature distributions in Fig. 4. 100 images are randomly selected from each domain and for each image the features from last convolutional layer (the channel size equals to class categories.) are extracted. We compare the distributions of our model with FCN8s (No adaptation). Four categories are sampled to display for a clearly visual effect. We observe that with the

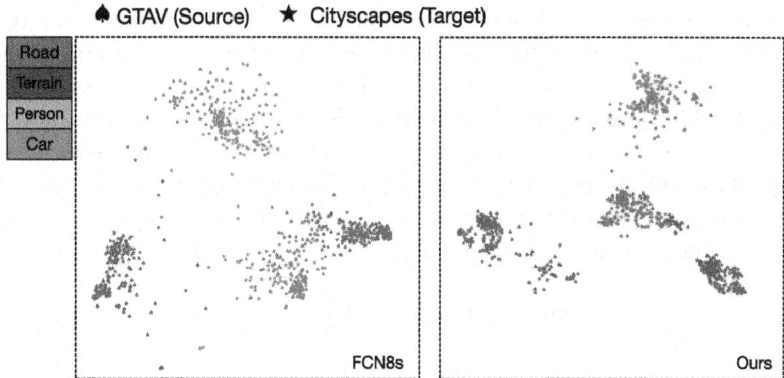

Fig. 4. We show the effect of adaptation on the distribution of the extracted features. ♠ denotes the point from source domain and ★ is from target domain

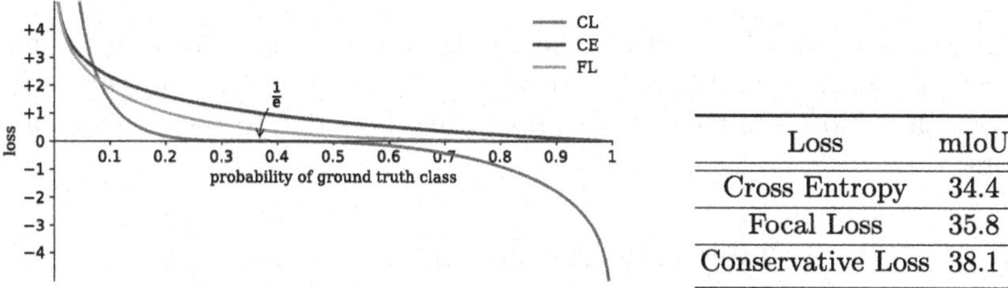

Loss	mIoU
Cross Entropy	34.4
Focal Loss	35.8
Conservative Loss	38.1

Fig. 5. The left figure shows three classification losses, including Cross Entropy loss (CE) in blue, Focal Loss (FL) in green and Conservative Loss (CL) in red. The right table shows the results of all three losses on GTAV → Cityscapes adaptation experiment (Color figure online)

adaptation applying, the distance between two domains with same class becomes closer and the discrepancy between different classes also gets clear.

Comparison with Other Classification Losses. In this experiment, we compare the Conservative Loss to Cross Entropy Loss and Focal Loss [42]. The Cross Entropy Loss is given by $\mathrm{CE}(p_t) = -\log(p_t)$, which is plotted in Fig. 5 with green line. To ensure fairness, we utilize the α-balanced Focal Loss $\mathrm{FL}(p_t) = -\alpha_t(1 - p_t)^2 \log(p_t)$ and warm start in the experiment of Focal Loss, and apply $\alpha_t = 5$ by using a cross-validation.

From the right table in Fig. 5, it can be observed that the Focal Loss obtains a better performance compared with the cross entropy loss because it focuses learning on hard negative examples. However, in the domain adaptation, the domain-invariant representations are crucial to achieve good adaptation performance. The Conservative Loss does enable the network to be insensitive to domain changes by punishing the extreme cases. It can be seen that the Conservative Loss yields higher result (**38.1**), and obtains more performance gain (**3.7**) than the Focal Loss (1.4) based on the cross entropy loss.

Effect of Homogeneous Losses. As shown in Sect. 3.3, the Conservative Loss has two properties: (1) when the p_t is low, the Conservative Loss enforces the network to learn discriminative features. (2) when the p_t is high, the loss enables the network to learn domain invariant features by gradient ascend method, which aims to penalize the extremely good cases. There are several losses that also maintain these two properties, for example the cubic equation. In this experiment, we propose several homogeneous losses to verify the effect of these two properties, which are given by:

$$\mathrm{Loss}_1 = -\lambda_1 (p_t - 0.5)^3, \tag{4}$$

$$\mathrm{Loss}_2 = -\lambda_2 (p_t - \frac{1}{\mathrm{e}})^3, \tag{5}$$

$$\mathrm{Loss}_3 = \begin{cases} -\alpha * (p_t - \frac{1}{\mathrm{e}})^3, \; p_t < \frac{1}{\mathrm{e}}, \\ -\beta * (p_t - \frac{1}{\mathrm{e}})^3, \; p_t \geq \frac{1}{\mathrm{e}}. \end{cases} \tag{6}$$

Equations 4 and 5 demonstrate the λ-balanced cubic equations with different intersection points, i.e., 0.5 and $\frac{1}{\mathrm{e}}$, respectively. Equation 6 is a piecewise function, which is more similar to the Conservative Loss due to these two balanced factors.

Table 6. Results of homogeneous losses

Loss function	CE	FL	Loss_1	Loss_2	Loss_3	CL
mIoU	34.4	35.8	36.5	36.7	37.8	38.1

We apply the adaptation experiment on GTAV → Cityscapes to verify their capabilities. The results are reported in Table 6. In order to ensure fairness, all experiments are performed based on the warm start and those hyper-parameters ($\lambda_1, \lambda_2, \alpha, \beta$) are chosen by using the cross-validation. We can observe that all homogeneous losses perform better than the cross entropy loss (34.4) and Focal Loss (35.8). Therefore, we can find that the exact form of the Conservative Loss is not crucial, and several homogeneous losses also yield comparable results and perform better than cross entropy loss and Focal Loss. Generally, we expect any loss function with similar properties as Conservative Loss to be equally effective.

5 Conclusion

In this paper, we have proposed a novel loss, the Conservative Loss, for the semantic segmentation adaptation. To enforce the network to learn the discriminative and domain-invariant representations, our loss combines the gradient descend and gradient ascend method together, in which it penalizes the extreme cases and encourages moderate cases. We further introduce the adversarial networks to our full model for supplementing the domain alignment. Extensive experiments demonstrate our model achieves state-of-the-art. Exploratory experiments show that the Conservative Loss has high flexibility without limiting to exact form.

Acknowledgments. This work is partially supported by the Big Data Collaboration Research grant from SenseTime Group (CUHK Agreement No. TS1610626).

References

1. Zhao, H., Shi, J., Qi, X., Wang, X., Jia, J.: Pyramid scene parsing network. In: CVPR, pp. 2881–2890 (2017)
2. Simonyan, K., Zisserman, A.: Very deep convolutional networks for large-scale image recognition. arXiv preprint arXiv:1409.1556 (2014)
3. Long, J., Shelhamer, E., Darrell, T.: Fully convolutional networks for semantic segmentation. In: CVPR, pp. 3431–3440 (2015)
4. Cordts, M., et al.: The Cityscapes dataset for semantic urban scene understanding. In: CVPR, pp. 3213–3223 (2016)
5. Richter, S.R., Vineet, V., Roth, S., Koltun, V.: Playing for data: ground truth from computer games. In: Leibe, B., Matas, J., Sebe, N., Welling, M. (eds.) ECCV 2016. LNCS, vol. 9906, pp. 102–118. Springer, Cham (2016). https://doi.org/10.1007/978-3-319-46475-6_7
6. Quionero-Candela, J., Sugiyama, M., Schwaighofer, A., Lawrence, N.D.: Dataset Shift in Machine Learning. The MIT Press, Cambridge (2009)
7. Geng, B., Tao, D., Xu, C.: DAML: domain adaptation metric learning. IEEE Trans. Image Process. **20**(10), 2980–2989 (2011)
8. Gong, B., Shi, Y., Sha, F., Grauman, K.: Geodesic flow kernel for unsupervised domain adaptation. In: CVPR, pp. 2066–2073. IEEE (2012)
9. Long, M., Cao, Y., Wang, J., Jordan, M.: Learning transferable features with deep adaptation networks. In: ICML, pp. 97–105 (2015)
10. Tzeng, E., Hoffman, J., Saenko, K., Darrell, T.: Adversarial discriminative domain adaptation. In: CVPR, vol. 1, p. 4 (2017)
11. Liu, M.Y., Tuzel, O.: Coupled generative adversarial networks. In: NIPS, pp. 469–477 (2016)
12. Ajakan, H., Germain, P., Larochelle, H., Laviolette, F., Marchand, M.: Domain-adversarial neural networks. arXiv preprint arXiv:1412.4446 (2014)
13. Ganin, Y., Lempitsky, V.: Unsupervised domain adaptation by backpropagation. In: ICML, pp. 1180–1189 (2015)
14. Zhang, Y., David, P., Gong, B.: Curriculum domain adaptation for semantic segmentation of urban scenes. In: ICCV, vol. 2, p. 6 (2017)
15. Hoffman, J., Wang, D., Yu, F., Darrell, T.: FCNs in the wild: pixel-level adversarial and constraint-based adaptation. arXiv preprint arXiv:1612.02649 (2016)
16. Chen, Y.H., Chen, W.Y., Chen, Y.T., Tsai, B.C., Wang, Y.C.F., Sun, M.: No more discrimination: cross city adaptation of road scene segmenters. In: ICCV, pp. 2011–2020. IEEE (2017)
17. Mansour, Y., Mohri, M., Rostamizadeh, A.: Domain adaptation: learning bounds and algorithms. arXiv preprint arXiv:0902.3430 (2009)
18. Ben-David, S., Blitzer, J., Crammer, K., Pereira, F.: Analysis of representations for domain adaptation. In: NIPS, pp. 137–144 (2007)

19. Ben-David, S., Blitzer, J., Crammer, K., Kulesza, A., Pereira, F., Vaughan, J.W.: A theory of learning from different domains. Mach. Learn. **79**(1–2), 151–175 (2010)
20. Goodfellow, I., et al.: Generative adversarial nets. In: NIPS, pp. 2672–2680 (2014)
21. Ros, G., Sellart, L., Materzynska, J., Vazquez, D., Lopez, A.M.: The SYNTHIA dataset: a large collection of synthetic images for semantic segmentation of urban scenes. In: CVPR, pp. 3234–3243 (2016)
22. Wu, Z., Shen, C., van den Hengel, A.: Wider or deeper: revisiting the ResNet model for visual recognition. arXiv preprint arXiv:1611.10080 (2016)
23. Noh, H., Hong, S., Han, B.: Learning deconvolution network for semantic segmentation. In: ICCV, pp. 1520–1528 (2015)
24. Fernando, B., Habrard, A., Sebban, M., Tuytelaars, T.: Unsupervised visual domain adaptation using subspace alignment. In: ICCV, pp. 2960–2967 (2013)
25. Kulis, B., Saenko, K., Darrell, T.: What you saw is not what you get: domain adaptation using asymmetric kernel transforms. In: CVPR, pp. 1785–1792 (2011)
26. Carlucci, F.M., Porzi, L., Caputo, B., Ricci, E., Bulò, S.R.: Autodial: automatic domain alignment layers. In: ICCV (2017)
27. Lu, H., et al.: When unsupervised domain adaptation meets tensor representations. In: ICCV, vol. 2 (2017)
28. Li, D., Yang, Y., Song, Y.Z., Hospedales, T.M.: Deeper, broader and artier domain generalization. In: ICCV, pp. 5543–5551. IEEE (2017)
29. Ghifary, M., Kleijn, W.B., Zhang, M., Balduzzi, D., Li, W.: Deep reconstruction-classification networks for unsupervised domain adaptation. In: Leibe, B., Matas, J., Sebe, N., Welling, M. (eds.) ECCV 2016. LNCS, vol. 9908, pp. 597–613. Springer, Cham (2016). https://doi.org/10.1007/978-3-319-46493-0_36
30. Busto, P.P., Gall, J.: Open set domain adaptation. In: ICCV, vol. 1 (2017)
31. Motiian, S., Piccirilli, M., Adjeroh, D.A., Doretto, G.: Unified deep supervised domain adaptation and generalization. In: ICCV, vol. 2 (2017)
32. Tsai, Y.H., Hung, W.C., Schulter, S., Sohn, K., Yang, M.H., Chandraker, M.: Learning to adapt structured output space for semantic segmentation. In: CVPR (2018)
33. Deng, J., Dong, W., Socher, R., Li, L.J., Li, K., Fei-Fei, L.: ImageNet: a large-scale hierarchical image database. In: CVPR, pp. 248–255. IEEE (2009)
34. Li, C., Wand, M.: Precomputed real-time texture synthesis with Markovian generative adversarial networks. In: Leibe, B., Matas, J., Sebe, N., Welling, M. (eds.) ECCV 2016. LNCS, vol. 9907, pp. 702–716. Springer, Cham (2016). https://doi.org/10.1007/978-3-319-46487-9_43
35. Zhao, J., Mathieu, M., LeCun, Y.: Energy-based generative adversarial network. arXiv preprint arXiv:1609.03126 (2016)
36. Kingma, D., Ba, J.: Adam: a method for stochastic optimization. arXiv preprint arXiv:1412.6980 (2014)
37. Loshchilov, I., Hutter, F.: SGDR: stochastic gradient descent with warm restarts. arXiv preprint arXiv:1608.03983 (2016)
38. Tirumala, S.S., Ali, S., Ramesh, C.P.: Evolving deep neural networks: a new prospect. In: 2016 12th International Conference on Natural Computation, Fuzzy Systems and Knowledge Discovery (ICNC-FSKD), pp. 69–74. IEEE (2016)
39. Zinkevich, M.: Theoretical analysis of a warm start technique. In: NIPS 2011 Workshop on BigLearn. Citeseer (2011)

40. Yu, F., Koltun, V.: Multi-scale context aggregation by dilated convolutions. arXiv preprint arXiv:1511.07122 (2015)
41. van der Maaten, L., Hinton, G.: Visualizing data using t-SNE. J. Mach. Learn. Res. **9**, 2579–2605 (2008)
42. Lin, T.Y., Goyal, P., Girshick, R., He, K., Dollár, P.: Focal loss for dense object detection. In: ICCV (2017)

CIRL: Controllable Imitative Reinforcement Learning for Vision-Based Self-driving

Xiaodan Liang[1,2(✉)], Tairui Wang[1], Luona Yang[2], and Eric Xing[1,2]

[1] Petuum Inc., Pittsburgh, USA
tairui.wang@petuum.com
[2] Carnegie Mellon University, Pittsburgh, USA
{xiaodan1,luonay1,epxing}@cs.cmu.edu

Abstract. Autonomous urban driving navigation with complex multi-agent dynamics is under-explored due to the difficulty of learning an optimal driving policy. The traditional modular pipeline heavily relies on hand-designed rules and the pre-processing perception system while the supervised learning-based models are limited by the accessibility of extensive human experience. We present a general and principled Controllable Imitative Reinforcement Learning (CIRL) approach which successfully makes the driving agent achieve higher success rates based on only vision inputs in a high-fidelity car simulator. To alleviate the low exploration efficiency for large continuous action space that often prohibits the use of classical RL on challenging real tasks, our CIRL explores over a reasonably constrained action space guided by encoded experiences that imitate human demonstrations, building upon Deep Deterministic Policy Gradient (DDPG). Moreover, we propose to specialize adaptive policies and steering-angle reward designs for different control signals (i.e. follow, straight, turn right, turn left) based on the shared representations to improve the model capability in tackling with diverse cases. Extensive experiments on CARLA driving benchmark demonstrate that CIRL substantially outperforms all previous methods in terms of the percentage of successfully completed episodes on a variety of goal-directed driving tasks. We also show its superior generalization capability in unseen environments. To our knowledge, this is the first successful case of the learned driving policy by reinforcement learning in the high-fidelity simulator, which performs better than supervised imitation learning.

Keywords: Imitative reinforcement learning · Autonomous driving

1 Introduction

Autonomous urban driving is a long-studied and still under-explored task [27,31] particularly in the crowded urban environments [25]. A desirable system is required to be capable of solving all visual perception tasks (e.g. object and

V. Ferrari et al. (Eds.): ECCV 2018, LNCS 11211, pp. 604–620, 2018.
https://doi.org/10.1007/978-3-030-01234-2_36

lane localization, drivable paths) and determining long-term driving strategies, referred as "driving policy". Although visual perception tasks have been well studied by resorting to supervised learning on large-scale datasets [20,39], simplistic driving policies by manually designed rules in the modular pipeline is far from sufficient for handling diverse real-world cases as discussed in [28,30]. Learning a optimal driving policy that mimics human drivers is less explored but key to navigate in complex environments that requires understanding of multi-agent dynamics, prescriptive traffic rule, negotiation skills for taking left and right turns, and unstructured roadways. These challenges naturally lead people to machine learning approaches for discovering rich and robust planning strategies automatically.

A line of researches [2,4,13,15,24,35] for learning policies follow the end-to-end imitation learning that directly maps sensor inputs to vehicle control commands via supervised training on large amounts of human driving data. However, these systems cannot be generalized to unseen scenarios and their performances are severely limited by the coverage of human driving data. For example, the model of Bojarski et al. [2] trained for road following fails for turning right/left. Moreover, it is difficult to pose autonomous driving with long-term goal-oriented navigation as a supervised learning problem as the autonomous vehicle needs to heavily interact with the environment including other vehicles, pedestrians and roadways.

It is thus desirable to have a richer control policy which considers a large amount of feedbacks from the environment including self-states, collisions and off-road conditions for autonomous driving. Deep reinforcement Learning (RL) offers, in principle, a reasonable system to learn such policies from exploration [33]. However, the amount of exploration required for large action space (such as a sequence of continuous steer angles, brakes and speeds) has prohibited its use in real applications, leading to unsatisfactory results by recent efforts on RL-based driving policy learning [6,30] in complex real-world tasks.

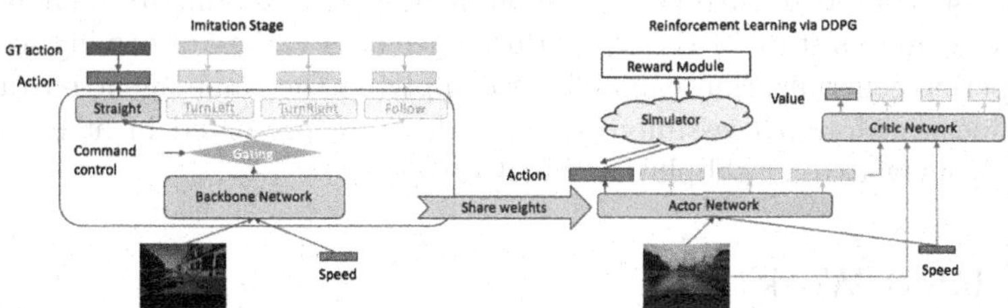

Fig. 1. An overview of our Controllable Imitative Reinforcement Learning (CIRL), including a controllable imitation stage and a reinforcement learning stage optimized via Deep Deterministic Policy Gradient (DDPG). The imitation stage first train the network by supervised learning with groundtruth actions from recorded human driving videos. Then we share the learned weights into the actor network and optimize both actor and critic with feedbacks from reward module by interacting with the simulator.

In this paper, we resolve this challenging planning task with our novel Controllable Imitative Reinforcement Learning (CIRL) that facilitates the continuous controllable deep-RL by exploiting the knowledge learned from demonstrations of human experts. The whole architecture is illustrated in Fig. 1. Our CIRL is based on the Deep Deterministic Policy Gradient (DDPG) [21] that is an off-policy replay-memory-based actor-critic algorithm. The conventional DDPG often falls into local optimal due to too much failed explorations for large action space. Our CIRL solves this issue by providing better exploration seeds for the search over the action space of the actor networks. Specifically, the actor networks are first warmed up by learned knowledge via imitation learning using human demonstrations in order to initialize the action exploration in a reasonable space. Then our CIRL incorporates DDPG to gradually boost the generalization capability of the learned driving policy guided by continuous reward signals sent back from the environment. Furthermore, to support the goal-oriented navigation, we introduce a controllable gating mechanism to selectively activate different branches for four distinct control signals (i.e. follow, straight, turn right, turn left). Such gating mechanism not only allows the model to be controllable by a central planner or the drivers' intent, but also enhances the model's capability by providing tailored policy functions and reward designs for each command case. In addition, distinct abnormal steer angle rewards are further proposed to better guide policies of each control signal as auxiliary aggregated rewards.

Our key **contributions** can be summarized as: (1) we present the first successful deep-RL pipeline for vision-based autonomous driving that outperforms previous modular pipeline and other imitation learning on diverse driving tasks on the high-fidelity CARLA benchmark; (2) we propose a novel controllable imitative reinforcement learning approach that effectively alleviates the inefficient exploration of large-scale continuous action space; (3) a controllable gating mechanism is introduced to allow models be controllable and learn specialized policies for each control signal with the guidance of distinct abnormal steer-angle rewards; (4) comprehensive results on public CARLA benchmark demonstrates our CIRL achieves state-of-the-art performance on a variety of driving scenarios and superior generalization capability by applying the same agent into unseen environments. More successfully driving videos are presented in https://www.youtube.com/watch?v=zhbpl8U_UW8&t=10s.

2 Related Work

Autonomous driving has recently attracted extensive research interests [25]. In general, prior approaches can be categorized into two different pipelines based on the modularity level. The first type is the highly tuned system that assembles a bunch of visual perception algorithms and then uses model-based planning and control [8]. Recently, more efforts have been devoted to the second type, that is, end-to-end approaches that learn to map sensory input to control commands [2, 4, 27, 35, 36, 38]. Our method belongs to the second spectrum.

End-to-End Supervised Learning. The key to autonomous driving is the ability of learn driving policy that automatically outputs control signals for steering wheel, throttle, brake, etc., based on observations. As a straight-forward idea, imitation learning that learns policies via supervised training on human driving data has been applied to a variety of tasks, including modeling navigational behavior [41], off-road driving [24,31], and road following [2,4,27,35,38]. These works differ in several aspects: the input representation (raw sensory input or pre-processed signals), predicting distinct control signals, experimenting on simulated or real data. Among them, [2,4,24,27] also investigated training networks for directly mapping vision inputs into control signals. The very recent work [4] relates to our CIRL in incorporating control signals into networks. However, supervised approaches usually require a large amount of data to train a model that can generalize to different environments. Obtaining massive data for all cities, scenarios and dynamical requires significant human involvement and is impractical since we cannot cover all possible situations that may happen. From the technical aspect, different from these works, our CIRL aims to learn advanced policies by interacting with the simulator guided by the imitation learning towards more and general complex urban driving scenarios. In addition, distinct abnormal steer-angle rewards are defined for each control signal, enabling the model to learn coherent specialized policies with human commonsense.

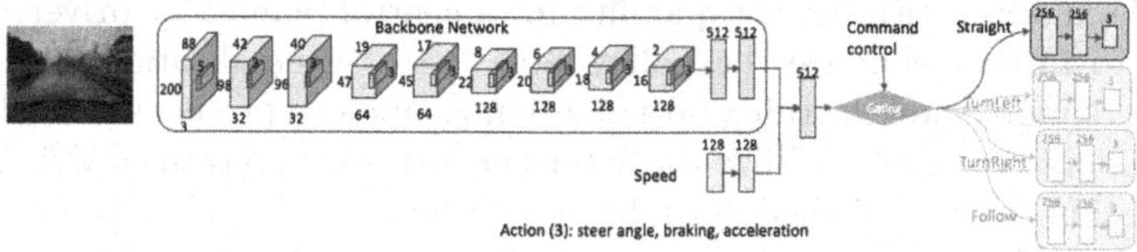

Fig. 2. Actor Network Architecture of CIRL. The gating function selectively activates different branches to predict three actions for "Straight", "TurnLeft", "TurnRight" and "Follow" commands.

Reinforcement Learning for Autonomous Driving. Reinforcement learning learns by a trial-and-error fashion, and does not require explicit supervision from human. Deep-RL or RL algorithm has been applied to a wide variety of tasks, such as object recognition [3,9,14,18,19], computer games [23], robot locomotion [7], scene navigation [40] and autonomous driving in the simulators [1,30,37]. The most critical challenges in real-world applications are the high-dimensional large-scale continuous action space. Learning an optimal policy using such exhaustive exploration is prone to be very time-consuming and easy to fall into local optimum after many episodes. It is thus desirable to find a feasible action space that can help speed up the exploration. Our CIRL addresses this issue by leveraging learned experiences by imitation learning to guide the reinforcement driving agent.

There exists some prior works also investigated the power of imitation learning. Generative Adversarial Imitation Learning (GAIL [12]) builds a generative model, which is a stochastic policy that produces similar behaviors to the expert demonstrations. InfoGAIL [17] extends GAIL into a policy where low-level actions can be controlled through more abstract, high-level latent variables. The most similar work to ours are DQfD [11], [16] and DDPGfD [34], which combines Deep Q Networks (DQN) with learning from demonstrations. However, DQfD is restricted to domains with discrete action spaces, DQfD, [16] and DDPGfD are not applicable for autonomous driving with significant different actor-critics, action spaces and reward definitions. Moreover, different with DDPGfD that loads the demonstration transitions into the replay buffer, we directly use the knowledge from demonstrations to guide the reinforcement explorations by initializing actor networks with pretrained model parameters via imitation learning. Our experiments show our strategy is particular better and more efficient than DDPGfD when applied to the autonomous driving simulator.

3 Controllable Imitative Reinforcement Learning

We illustrate the whole architecture of our CIRL method. To resolve the sample inefficiency issue in applying RL to complex tasks, our CIRL adopts an imitation stage and a reinforcement learning stage. First, given a set of human driving videos, we first use the supervised ground truth deterministic actions to pretrain the network. The command gating mechanism is incorporated to endow the model controllable capability for a central planner or drivers' intent. Second, to further enhance the policy with better generalization and robustness, the reinforcement learning optimization is employed to boost the ability of actor network. We first initialize the actor network with pretrained weights from the imitation stage, and then optimize it via the reward module by interacting with the simulator. Due to its superior performance on exploring continuous action space, we use the Deep Deterministic Policy Gradient (DDPG) as the RL optimization. Benefiting from the use of human driving demonstrations for initializing the actor network, the sample complexity can be significantly reduced to enable the learning within the equivalent of hours of exploration and interaction with the environment.

3.1 Controllable Imitation Learning

Given N human driving video sequences $v_i, i \in (1, \ldots, N)$ with the observation frame $I_{i,t}$, control command $c_{i,t}$, speed $s_{i,t}$, action $\mathbf{a}_{i,t}$ at each time step t, we can learn a deterministic policy network F via the basic imitation learning to mimic the human experts. Detailed network architecture of F is presented in Fig. 2. The control command $c_{i,t}$ is introduced to handle the complex scenarios where the subsequent actions also depend on the driver's intent in addition to the observation [4]. The action space $\mathbf{a}_{i,t}$ contains three continuous actions, that is steering angle $a^s_{i,t}$, acceleration $a^a_{i,t}$, and braking action $a^b_{i,t}$. The command $c_{i,t}$ is a categorical variable that control the selective branch activation via the gating function $G(c_{i,t})$, where $c_{i,t}$ can be one of four different commands, i.e. follow the lane (Follow), drive straight at the next intersection (Straight), turn left at the next intersection (TurnLeft), and turn right at the next intersection (TurnRight). Four policy branches are specifically learned to encode the distinct hidden knowledge for each case and thus selectively used for action prediction. The gating function G is an internal direction indicator from the system. The controllable imitation learning objective is to minimize the parameters θ^I of the policy network F^I, defined as:

$$\min_{\theta^I} \sum_{i}^{N} \sum_{t}^{T_i} \mathcal{L}(F(I_{i,t}, G(c_{i,t}), s_{i,t}), \mathbf{a}_{i,t}), \tag{1}$$

where the loss function L is defined as the weighted summations of L2 losses for three predicted actions $\hat{\mathbf{a}}_{i,t}$:

$$\mathcal{L}(\hat{\mathbf{a}}_{i,t}, \mathbf{a}_{\mathbf{i},\mathbf{t}}) = ||\hat{a}^s_{i,t} - a^s_{i,t}||^2 + ||\hat{a}^a_{i,t} - a^a_{i,t}||^2 + ||\hat{a}^b_{i,t} - a^b_{i,t}||^2, \tag{2}$$

For fair comparison between our CIRL and imitation learning, we use the same experiment setting as [6] to verify the effectiveness of boosting driving policies by our imitative reinforcement learning. The sensory inputs are images from a forward-facing camera, speed measurements from the simulator and control commands generated by the navigation planner.

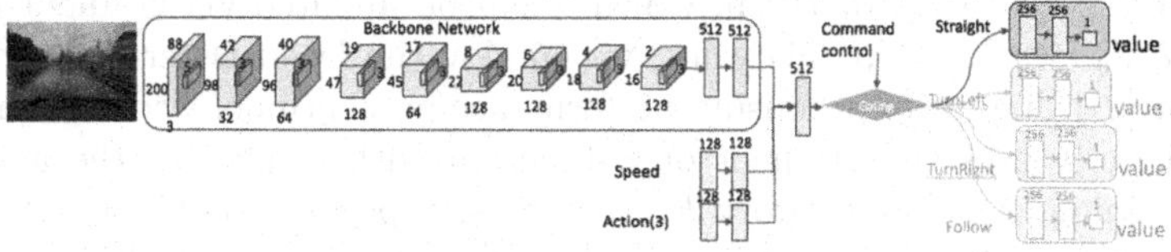

Fig. 3. Critic Network Architecture of CIRL. The action outputs from actor network are fed into critic network to obtained the estimated value.

3.2 Imitative Reinforcement Learning

Our CIRL uses the policy network F pretrained from conditional imitation learning to boost the sample efficiency of reinforcement learning to obtain more general and robust policies. We first present the underlying optimization techniques and then the reward designs.

Markov Decision Process. By interacting with the car simulator, the driving agent can be optimized based on a reward signal provided by the environment, with no human driving intervention, which can be defined as a Markov Decision Processes (MDPs) [32]. In the autonomous driving scenario, the MDP is defined by a tuple of $<I, C, S, A, R, P, \lambda>$, which consists of a set of states O defined with observed frames I, speeds S, control command C, a set of actions A, a reward function $R(o, \mathbf{a})$, a transition function $P(o'|o, \mathbf{a})$, and a discount factor γ. In each state $o = <I, c, s> \in O$, the agent takes an action $\mathbf{a} \in A$. After taking this action and interacting with the environment, the agent receives a reward

$R(o, \mathbf{a})$ and reaches a new state o' depending on the probability distribution $P(o'|o, \mathbf{a})$. To make the driving policies more realistic, we focus on the goal-directed navigation, that is, the vehicle has to reach a predetermined goal along the path generated by the topological planner. The new observation o' is thus updated by the simulator observation and a sequence of commands towards the goal. The episode is terminated when the vehicle reaches the goal, when the vehicle collides with an obstacle, or when a time budget is exhausted.

A deterministic and stationary policy π specifies which action the agent will take given each state. The goal of the driving agent is to find the policy π that maps states to actions that maximizes the expected discounted total reward. It can be thus learned by using a action value function: $Q^{\pi}(o, \mathbf{a}) = \mathbf{E}^{\pi}[\sum_{t=0}^{+\infty} \gamma^t R(o_t, \mathbf{a}_t)]$, where $\mathbf{E}^{\pi}$ is the expectation over the distribution of the admissible trajectories $(o_0, \mathbf{a}_0, \ldots, o_t, \mathbf{a}_t)$ by executing the policy π sequentially over the time episodes.

Imitative Deep Deterministic Policy Gradient. Since the autonomous driving system needs to predict continuous actions (steer angles, braking, and acceleration), we resort to the actor-critic approach for continuous control problem, and both actor and critic are parametrized by deep networks. Denoting the parameters of the policy network as θ, and μ as the initial state distribution, the actor-critic approach aims to maximize a mean value $J(\theta) = \mathbf{E}_{o \sim \mu}[Q^{(\pi|\theta)}(o, \pi(o|\theta))]$ in which θ can be updated via gradient descent as: $\theta + \alpha \nabla_{\theta} J(\theta) \rightarrow \theta$. In this work, we employ the Deep Deterministic Policy Gradient [21] due to its promising performance on continuous control problem, which directly uses the gradient of Q-function with respect to the action for policy training. A policy network F^{π} (actor) with parameters θ^{π} and an action-value function network F^{Q} (critic) with parameters θ^{Q} are jointly optimized. The detailed network architectures of F^{π} and F^{Q} are presented in Figs. 2 and 3.

Different from the conventional DDPG that randomly initializes the θ^{π}, our imitative DDPG proposes to load the pretrained θ^{I} in Eq. (1) via the imitation learning into θ^{π}, obtaining a new $\bar{\theta^{\pi}}$ as the parameter initialization. It thus enables to produce reliable new transitions $e = (o, \mathbf{a}, r = R(o, \mathbf{a}), o' \sim P(|o, \mathbf{a}))$ by acting based on $\mathbf{a} = \pi(o|\bar{\theta^{\pi}}) + \mathcal{N}$ where $\mathcal{N} \sim \mathrm{OU}(\mu, \sigma^2)$ is a random process allowing action exploration. $\mathrm{OU}(\cdot)$ denotes the Ornstein-Uhlenbeck process. Such further noisy exploration ensure that the agent's behavior does not converge prematurely to a local optimum. The key advantage of our imitative DDPG lies in better initialized exploration starting points by learning from human expects, which can help significantly reduce the exhaustive exploration in the early stage of DDPG that may cost a few days, as discussed in previous works [26]. Starting from a better state, the random action exploration allows RL to further refine actions according to the feedbacks from the simulator and results in more general and robust driving policies. The critic network is optimized by the one-step off-policy evaluation:

$$\mathcal{L}(\theta^{Q}) = \mathbf{E}_{(o, \mathbf{a}, r, o') \sim D}[R - Q(o, \mathbf{a}|\theta^{Q})]^2, \tag{3}$$

Fig. 4. Example observations of different environment settings. Training condition is used for training while the rest settings are used for testing. Besides the settings (first row) evaluated in [6], this work further validates the generalization capability of the model on four new settings (second row).

where D is a distribution over transitions e in the replay buffer and the one-step return $R = r + \gamma Q'((o', \pi'(o')|\bar{\theta^{\pi}}')|\theta^{Q'})$. $\bar{\theta^{\pi}}'$ and $\theta^{Q'}$ are parameters of corresponding target networks of F^{π} and F^{Q}, which are used to stabilize the learning. On the other hand, the actor network is further updated from the starting state from the controllable imitative learning:

$$\nabla_{\bar{\theta^{\pi}}} J(\bar{\theta^{\pi}}) \approx \mathbf{E}_{o,\mathbf{a}\sim D}[\nabla_{\mathbf{a}} Q(o, \mathbf{a}|\theta^{Q})_{|\mathbf{a}=\pi(o,\theta^{Q})} \nabla_{\theta_{\pi}} \pi(o|\bar{\theta^{\pi}})]. \tag{4}$$

Reward Module. Another contribution of our CIRL is our reward module tailored for the autonomous driving scenario. The reward is a sum of five terms according to the measurements from simulator: negatively weighted abnormal steer angles r_s, positively weighted speed r_v in km/h, and negatively weighted collision damage r_d, overlap with the sidewalk r_r, and overlap with the opposite lane r_o. The rewards are computed according to the simulator measurements after taking actions over the agent. First, the reward r_s for abnormal steer-angles w.r.t each command control is defined as:

$$r_s(c) = \begin{cases} -15 & \text{if } s \text{ is in opposite direction with c for TurnLeft and TurnRight} \\ -20 & \text{if } |s| > 0.2, \text{ c for Straight.} \end{cases} \tag{5}$$

Second, the reward r_v for speed measurements after performing actions on the simulator with respect to each common control is defined as:

$$r_v(c) = \begin{cases} \min(25, v) & \text{if c for Follow} \\ \min(35, v) & \text{if c for Straight} \\ v & \text{if } v \leq 20, \text{ c for TurnLeft and TurnRight} \\ 40 - v & \text{if } v > 20, \text{ c for TurnLeft and TurnRight} \end{cases} \tag{6}$$

Finally, the r_r and r_o are both set as -100 for having overlapping with the sidewalk and opposite lane, respectively. The collision damage r_d is as -100 for collision with other vehicles and pedestrians and as -50 for other things (e.g. trees and poles). The final reward r conditioning on different command controls is computed as:

$$r = R(o, \mathbf{a}) = r_s(c) + r_v(c) + r_r + r_o + r_d. \tag{7}$$

Note that exact penalty values are applied for all experiments in our benchmark according to their specific limitations, such as speeds and angles [6].

4 Experiments

4.1 Experiment Settings

Evaluation Benchmark. We conduct extensive experiments on the recently release CARLA car simulator benchmark [6] because of its superior high-fidelity simulated environment and open-source accessibility, compared to other simulators. A large variety of assets were produced for CARLA, including cars and pedestrians. CARLA provides two towns: Town 1 and Town 2. For fair comparison with other state-of-the-art policy learning methods [4,6], Town 1 is used for training and Town 2 exclusively for testing, as illustrated in Fig. 4. The weather conditions are organized in three groups, including Training Weather set, New Weather set and New Weather2 set. Training Weather set is used for training, containing clear day, clear sunset, daytime rain, and daytime after rain. New Weather set and New Weather2 set are never used during training and for testing the generalization. New Weather set includes cloudy daytime and soft rain at sunset, and New Weather2 set includes cloudy noon, midrainy noon, cloudy sunset, hardrain sunset. Besides three test settings evaluated in [6], we further evaluate four new settings for more paths in Town 2, New weather2 set as shown in the first row in Fig. 4.

State-of-the-Art Pipelines. We compare our CIRL model with three state-of-the-art pipelines in CARLA benchmark, that is modular pipeline (MP) [6], imitation learning (IL) [6], and reinforcement learning (RL) [6], and fairly compete with them on four increasingly difficult driving tasks, i.e. Straight, One turn, Navigation and Navigation with dynamic obstacles, illustrated in Fig. 5. Particularly, the baseline MP [6] decomposes the driving task into the following subsystems including perception, planning and continuous control, and its local planning resorts to completely rule-based predefined policies that are completely dependent on the scene layout estimated by the perception module. The baseline IL [6] takes the images from a forward-facing camera and command controls as inputs, and directly trains the model via supervised learning using human driving videos. Note that for fair comparison, we adopt the same network architecture and settings with their model during the controllable imitation stage. RL [6] is also a deep reinforcement learning pipeline that uses the asynchronous advantage actor-critic (A3C) algorithm [22]. Different from their used five reward terms, we empirically remove the distance rewards traveled towards the goal since the way-points used for estimating distances are too sparse to give valid feedbacks during exploration. In addition, we propose to use controllable abnormal steer-angle rewards to penalize the unexpected angle predictions.

Note that for all methods, one same agent is used on all four tasks and cannot be fine-tuned separately for each scenario. The tasks are set up as goal-directed navigation: an agent is randomly initialized somewhere in town and has to reach

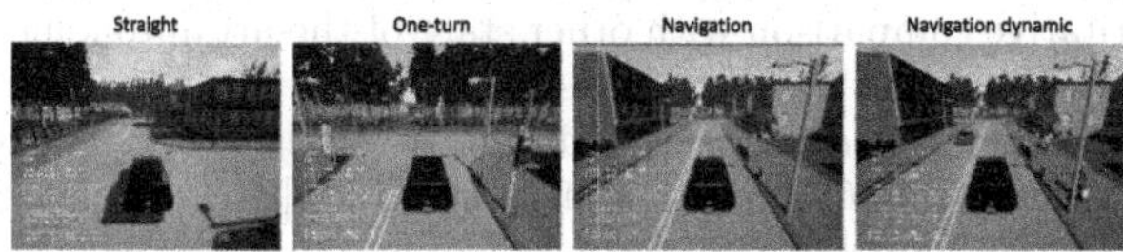

Fig. 5. Illustrated observations of four different tasks in the bird view.

a destination point. For each combination of a task, a town, and a weather set, the paths are carried out over 25 episodes. In each episode, the target of driving agent is to reach a given goal location. An episode is considered successful if the agent reaches the goal within a time budget, which is set to reach the goal along the optimal path at a speed of 10 km/h.

Implementation Settings. During the controllable imitation stage, to fairly demonstrate the effectiveness of our imitative reinforcement learning, we use the exact same experiment settings in [4] for pre-training actor network. 14 h of driving data collected from CARLA are used for training and the network was trained using the Adam optimizer. Further details are referred in [4].

During the imitative reinforcement learning stage, in terms of OU exploration parameters, we empirically set μ as 0, 0.15, and 0.5 and σ as 0.02, 0.05, 0 for steer-angle, speed and braking actions, respectively. The discount factor γ is set as 0.9. The initial learning rate of actor network is set as 0.00001 since it uses the shared weights from controllable imitation learning and the learning rate of critic network is set as 0.001. Learning and exploration rate are linearly decreased to zero over the course of training. The actor-critic networks are trained with 0.3 millions of simulation steps for roughly 12 h of non-stop driving at 10 frames per second. In contrast, existing reinforcement learning approach provided in [6] requires 10 millions of simulation steps corresponding to roughly 12 days of non-stop driving with 10 parallel actor threads. Our CIRL can obtain high percentage of successfully completed episodes after several hours with good sample efficiency, benefiting from a good exploration start boosted by the controllable imitation stage. The proposed method is implemented on TensorFlow framework. All models are trained on four NVIDIA GeForce GTX1080 GPUs.

4.2 Comparisons with State-of-the-Arts

Table 1 reports the comparisons with the state-of-the-art pipelines on CARLA benchmarks in terms of the percentage of successfully completed episodes under four different conditions. All results of MP, IL and RL were reported from [6]. For "Training conditions" task, the models are tested on the combination of Town 1, Training Weather setting which has different starting and target locations under the same general environment and conditions with the training stage. The rest test settings are conducted for evaluating more aggressive generalization, that is, adaption to the previously unseen Town 2 and to previously unencountered weather from the New Weather and New Weather2.

Table 1. Quantitative comparison with other state-of-the-art autonomous driving systems on four goal-directed navigation tasks. The table reports the percentage (%) of successfully completed episodes in each condition. Higher is better. The tested methods are: modular pipeline (MP) [6], imitation learning (IL) [6], and reinforcement learning (RL) [6] and our CIRL model.

Task	Training conditions				New town				New weather				New town/weather			
	MP	IL	RL	CIRL	MP	IL	RL	CIRL	MP	IL	RL	CIRL	MP	IL	RL	CIRL
Straight	98	95	89	**98**	92	97	74	**100**	100	98	86	**100**	50	80	68	**98**
One turn	82	89	34	**97**	61	59	12	**71**	**95**	90	16	94	50	48	20	**82**
Navigation	80	86	14	**93**	24	40	3	**53**	**94**	84	2	86	47	44	6	**68**
Nav. dynamic	77	**83**	7	82	24	38	2	**41**	**89**	82	2	80	44	42	4	**62**

We can observe that our CIRL substantially outperforms all baseline methods under all conditions, especially better than their RL baseline. Furthermore, our CIRL shows superior generalization capabilities in the rest three unseen setting (e.g. unseen new town), which obtains not perfect results but considerably better performance over other methods, e.g. 71% of our CIRL vs. 59% and 12% of IL and RL, respectively. More qualitative results are shown in Fig. 7, which provides some infraction examples that the IL model suffers from and our CIRL successfully avoids.

It is also interesting that both learning-based methods (IL and our CIRL) achieve comparable and better performances than the modular pipeline, although MP adopted the sophisticated perception steps (segmentation and classification) to identify key cues in the environment and used manually rule-based policies. One exception is that the modular pipeline performs better under the "New weather" condition than that of the training conditions, and both IL and CIRL are slightly inferior to it. But MP's results perform bad on navigation task and considerably decrease on all tasks in unseen "New town" and "New town/weather" conditions. The reason is that MP heavily depends on the perception stage that fails systematically under complex weather conditions in the context of a new environment, and rule-based policies that may fail for long-range goal-driven navigation. We can conclude that MP is more fragile to unseen environments than the end-to-end learning based models since the perception part itself is difficult and hard to adapt across diverse unknown scenes.

Table 2. The percentage (%) of successfully completed episodes of our CIRL on four new settings for further evaluating generalization.

Task	New town/path2	New town/weather2	New path	New weather2
Navigation	50	58	95	87
Nav. dynamic	38	47	87	86

Table 3. The percentage (%) of successfully completed episodes of our CIRL under different weather conditions for the navigation tasks in training town and new town.

Navigation task	CloudyNoon	MidRainyNoon	CloudySunset	WetCloudySunset	HardRainSunset
CIRL (Town 1)	92	96	96	64	56
CIRL (New town)	95	52	85	90	5

On the other hand, the conventional reinforcement learning [6] performs significantly worse than all other methods, even with considerably more training time: 12 days of driving in the simulator. The reason is that RL itself is well known to be brittle [10] and needs very time-consuming exploration to get reasonable results. Rather than video games in Atari [23] and maze navigation [5], the real-world tasks like self-driving require complex decision making to exploit visual cues, leading to severe sample inefficiency and unfeasible parameter search.

In contrast, the proposed CIRL effectively benefits from both merits of imitation learning (i.e. fast convergence) and traditional reinforcement learning (i.e. robust long-term decision making). Our CIRL that enhances the policies by only rough 12 h of driving explorations in car simulator can achieve significant better performances on all tasks than the best MP and IL methods. Different from previous RL models that conduct too much random and meaningless explorations in the beginning, the actor network in our CIRL can start the exploration in a good and reasonable point by transferring knowledge from the first controllable imitation stage. The reward feedbacks by driving and interacting with complex dynamics in the simulator can further facilitate the policy learning with better robustness and generalization capability.

4.3 Generalization Capability

The exact driving trajectories during training cannot be repeated during testing. Therefore performing perfectly on CARLA benchmark requires robust generalization, which is challenging for existing deep learning methods. As reported in Table 1, it is obvious that all methods perform closely to those in "Training conditions" under the "New weather" setting. However, their performances dramatically drop on the "New town" settings. For example, on the most challenging navigation task "Nav.dynamic" in the New town/weather setting, previous best MP and IL methods obtain only 44% and 42% complete success episodes compared to 62% of our CIRL. In general, our CIRL shows much better generalization capabilities over other methods, but still needs further improvements.

Besides the previous two types of generalization (i.e. unseen weather conditions and unseen new town), we further conduct more experiments on two another new conditions (i.e. more path trajectories and the New weather2 set) on two most difficult tasks to further evaluate more general cases, resulting in four new settings in Table 2. We can see that our model shows reasonably robust and good performance on different navigation paths and weather set. Adapting our CIRL to navigate in unseen towns can be improved by training in wider

Table 4. Ablation studies on one-turn task on four different settings.

Method (one-turn)	Training conditions	New town	New weather	New town/weather
CIRL w/o steer reward	91	65	96	76
CIRL w/ add replay	96	71	94	82
CIRL more simulation steps	95	68	98	80
Our CIRL	97	71	94	82

Table 5. Results on comma.ai dataset in terms of mean absolute error (MAE).

Model	PilotNet [2]	CIRL (CARLA)	CIRL from scrach	CIRL finetuning
Steer-angle MAE	1.208	2.939	1.186	**1.168**

Fig. 6. Example observations under distinct weather conditions. Better viewed in zoom.

range of different scenes. This further demonstrates well the advantages of integrating together the controllable imitation learning and DDPG algorithm into boosting driving policies towards more challenging tasks.

We also extensively dive into the affects of different weather conditions on driving generalization capability, as reported in Table 3. Driving behaviors under five weather conditions with distinct levels of difficulties are evaluated on both seen town and unseen town. We can observe promising results obtained under weathers with good visibility, such as CloudyNoon, CloudySunset. But regarding to more challenging rainy weathers, the model obtains very low successfully completed rates. One of main reasons is that the road and surrounding dynamics are extremely hard to be perceived as a result of heavy rains, as shown in Fig. 6.

4.4 Comparisons on Real Scenes

We report results of applying our CIRL trained on CARLA into real scenes in Table 5 on Comma.ai [29] dataset. To finetune on Comma.ai, we use pretrained network parameters before direction branches on CARLA and initialize 3 stacked fc-layers $(256, 256, 1)$ to predict one steer angle. The learning rate is set to 1e-3. We train 18 epochs and batch size is 256. "CIRL (CARLA)" denotes directly applying model trained on CARLA into prediction in real scenes. We can see that finetuning pretrained CIRL model on comma.ai ("CIRL finetuning") outperforms the baseline PilotNet and "CIRL from scratch" that is trained from scratch on Comma.ai. It verifies well that our CIRL model learned from the

Table 6. Success rates on *One Turn* task in New Town (i.e. validation town)

Reward	our_reward	our_reward×10	our_reward/10	w/o speed	w/o offroad & coll
Old weather	**71%**	70%	52%	20%	31%
New weather	**82%**	82%	68%	14%	28%

high-quality CARLA simulator can be easily transferred into real scenes to enhance driving policy learning for real autonomous vehicles.

4.5 Ablation Studies

We also conduct comprehensive experiments to verify the effects of each key component of our model, as reported in Table 4. Experiments are conducted on the challenging one-turn task on four different environments.

Different Strategies of Using Demonstrations. To validate the effectiveness of our imitative reinforcement learning, we compare our CIRL with DDPGfD [34] that performs learning from demonstrations for robotic manipulation problems. In contrast to our strategy of providing a better exploration start, DDPGfD instead loads the demonstration transitions into the replay buffer and keeps all transitions forever. We thus implement and incorporate the demonstrate replay buffer into our CIRL, and "CIRL w/add reply" denotes the results of this variant for running the same number of simulation steps with our CIRL. We can see there is no noticeable performance difference between "CIRL w/add reply" and our CIRL. It speaks well that the good starting point for exploration is already enough for learning reasonable policies in an efficient way. We also try the performance of pure DDPGfD on our task without using imitation learning to initialize the actor network, which is quite bad after several days of driving simulation due to the need of exhaustive exploration, we thus did not list their results. Note that for justifying the optimization step, we keep all experiments settings of all variants as same, e.g. reward design.

The Effect of Abnormal Steer-Angle Rewards. Different from the reward terms in [6], we propose to adopt specialized steer-angle rewards with respect to each command control. Our comparisons between "CIRL w/o steer reward" and "CIRL" further demonstrate the effectiveness of incorporating such rewards for stabilizing the action exploration by providing more explicit feedbacks.

The Effect of Simulation Step Number. One raised question for our CIRL is whether the performance can be further improved by performing RL policy learning with more simulation steps. "CIRL more simulation steps" reports results of running CIRL model for 0.5 million steps. We find that no significant improvement in terms of percentages of completely success episodes can be obtained in unseen driving scenarios. This verifies our model can achieve good policies by efficient sample exploration with the acceptable computation cost.

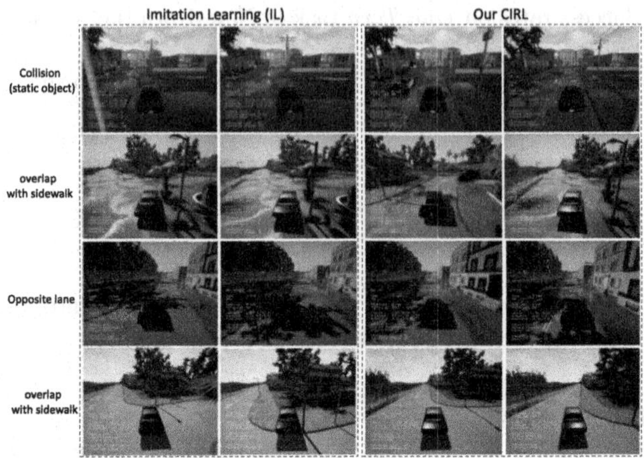

Fig. 7. Visualization comparisons between the imitation learning baseline [6] and our CIRL model. We illustrate some driving cases for straight and one-turn tasks, and show the IL baseline fails with some types of infractions (e.g. collision with static object, more than 30% overlap with Sidewalk, in opposite lane) while our CIRL successfully completes the goal-oriented tasks. For each case, two consecutive frames are shown.

On the other hand, this may motivate us to further improve model capability from other aspects, such as exploring more environments and video dynamics to improve the generalization ability.

Reward Function. Set scales of reward values following Coach RL framework[1] used in CARLA environment. Ablation studies on different reward scales for all rewards are reported in Table 6. We can observe that removing speed or offroad&collision reward significantly decreases the success rate. Moreover, using 10x larger reward values obtains minor performance difference while 10x smaller rewards lead to worse results.

5 Conclusion

In this paper, we propose a novel CIRL model to address the challenging problem of vision-based autonomous driving in the high-fidelity car simulator. Our CIRL incorporates controllable imitation learning with DDPG policy learning to resolve the sample inefficiency issue that is well known in reinforcement learning research. Moreover, specialized steer-angle rewards are also designed to enhance the optimization of our policy networks based on controllable imitation learning. Our CIRL achieves the state-of-the-art driving performance on CARLA benchmark and surpasses the previous modular pipeline, imitation learning and reinforcement learning pipelines. It further demonstrates superior generalization capabilities on a variety of different environments and conditions.

[1] https://nervanasystems.github.io/coach/.

References

1. Abbeel, P., Coates, A., Quigley, M., Ng, A.Y.: An application of reinforcement learning to aerobatic helicopter flight. In: Advances in Neural Information Processing Systems, pp. 1–8 (2007)
2. Bojarski, M., et al.: End to end learning for self-driving cars. arXiv preprint arXiv:1604.07316 (2016)
3. Cao, Q., Lin, L., Shi, Y., Liang, X., Li, G.: Attention-aware face hallucination via deep reinforcement learning. arXiv preprint arXiv:1708.03132 (2017)
4. Codevilla, F., Müller, M., Dosovitskiy, A., López, A., Koltun, V.: End-to-end driving via conditional imitation learning. arXiv preprint arXiv:1710.02410 (2017)
5. Dosovitskiy, A., Koltun, V.: Learning to act by predicting the future. arXiv preprint arXiv:1611.01779 (2016)
6. Dosovitskiy, A., Ros, G., Codevilla, F., López, A., Koltun, V.: CARLA: an open urban driving simulator. arXiv preprint arXiv:1711.03938 (2017)
7. Endo, G., Morimoto, J., Matsubara, T., Nakanishi, J., Cheng, G.: Learning CPG-based biped locomotion with a policy gradient method: application to a humanoid robot. Int. J. Robot. Res. **27**(2), 213–228 (2008)
8. Franke, U.: Autonomous driving. In: Computer Vision in Vehicle Technology (2017)
9. Han, J., Yang, L., Zhang, D., Chang, X., Liang, X.: Reinforcement cutting-agent learning for video object segmentation. In: Proceedings of the IEEE Conference on Computer Vision and Pattern Recognition, pp. 9080–9089 (2018)
10. Henderson, P., Islam, R., Bachman, P., Pineau, J., Precup, D., Meger, D.: Deep reinforcement learning that matters. arXiv preprint arXiv:1709.06560 (2017)
11. Hester, T., et al.: Learning from demonstrations for real world reinforcement learning. arXiv preprint arXiv:1704.03732 (2017)
12. Ho, J., Ermon, S.: Generative adversarial imitation learning. In: Advances in Neural Information Processing Systems, pp. 4565–4573 (2016)
13. Hou, Y., Hornauer, S., Zipser, K.: Fast recurrent fully convolutional networks for direct perception in autonomous driving. arXiv preprint arXiv:1711.06459 (2017)
14. Jie, Z., Liang, X., Feng, J., Jin, X., Lu, W., Yan, S.: Tree-structured reinforcement learning for sequential object localization. In: Advances in Neural Information Processing Systems, pp. 127–135 (2016)
15. Kim, J., Canny, J.: Interpretable learning for self-driving cars by visualizing causal attention. In: ICCV (2017)
16. Latzke, T., Behnke, S., Bennewitz, M.: Imitative reinforcement learning for soccer playing robots. In: Lakemeyer, G., Sklar, E., Sorrenti, D.G., Takahashi, T. (eds.) RoboCup 2006. LNCS (LNAI), vol. 4434, pp. 47–58. Springer, Heidelberg (2007). https://doi.org/10.1007/978-3-540-74024-7_5
17. Li, Y., Song, J., Ermon, S.: InfoGail: interpretable imitation learning from visual demonstrations. In: Advances in Neural Information Processing Systems, pp. 3815–3825 (2017)
18. Liang, X., Hu, Z., Zhang, H., Gan, C., Xing, E.P.: Recurrent topic-transition GAN for visual paragraph generation. In: ICCV (2017)
19. Liang, X., Lee, L., Xing, E.P.: Deep variation-structured reinforcement learning for visual relationship and attribute detection. In: 2017 IEEE Conference on Computer Vision and Pattern Recognition (CVPR), pp. 4408–4417. IEEE (2017)
20. Liang, X., Zhou, H., Xing, E.: Dynamic-structured semantic propagation network. In: Proceedings of the IEEE Conference on Computer Vision and Pattern Recognition, pp. 752–761 (2018)

21. Lillicrap, T.P., et al.: Continuous control with deep reinforcement learning. In: ICLR (2016)
22. Mnih, V., et al.: Asynchronous methods for deep reinforcement learning. In: International Conference on Machine Learning, pp. 1928–1937 (2016)
23. Mnih, V., et al.: Human-level control through deep reinforcement learning. Nature **518**(7540), 529 (2015)
24. Muller, U., Ben, J., Cosatto, E., Flepp, B., Cun, Y.L.: Off-road obstacle avoidance through end-to-end learning. In: Advances in Neural Information Processing Systems, pp. 739–746 (2006)
25. Paden, B., Čáp, M., Yong, S.Z., Yershov, D., Frazzoli, E.: A survey of motion planning and control techniques for self-driving urban vehicles. IEEE Trans. Intell. Veh. **1**(1), 33–55 (2016)
26. Plappert, M., et al.: Parameter space noise for exploration. arXiv preprint arXiv:1706.01905 (2017)
27. Pomerleau, D.A.: ALVINN: an autonomous land vehicle in a neural network. In: Advances in Neural Information Processing Systems, pp. 305–313 (1989)
28. Sallab, A.E., Abdou, M., Perot, E., Yogamani, S.: Deep reinforcement learning framework for autonomous driving. Electron. Imaging **2017**(19), 70–76 (2017)
29. Santana, E., Hotz, G.: Learning a driving simulator. arXiv preprint arXiv:1608.01230 (2016)
30. Shalev-Shwartz, S., Shammah, S., Shashua, A.: Safe, multi-agent, reinforcement learning for autonomous driving. arXiv preprint arXiv:1610.03295 (2016)
31. Silver, D., Bagnell, J.A., Stentz, A.: Learning from demonstration for autonomous navigation in complex unstructured terrain. Int. J. Robot. Res. **29**(12), 1565–1592 (2010)
32. Sutton, R.S., Barto, A.G.: Introduction to Reinforcement Learning, vol. 135. MIT Press, Cambridge (1998)
33. Sutton, R.S., Barto, A.G.: Reinforcement Learning: An Introduction, vol. 1. MIT Press, Cambridge (1998)
34. Večerík, M., et al.: Leveraging demonstrations for deep reinforcement learning on robotics problems with sparse rewards. arXiv preprint arXiv:1707.08817 (2017)
35. Xu, H., Gao, Y., Yu, F., Darrell, T.: End-to-end learning of driving models from large-scale video datasets. In: CVPR (2017)
36. Yang, L., Liang, X., Xing, E.: Unsupervised real-to-virtual domain unification for end-to-end highway driving. arXiv preprint arXiv:1801.03458 (2018)
37. You, Y., Pan, X., Wang, Z., Lu, C.: Virtual to real reinforcement learning for autonomous driving. arXiv preprint arXiv:1704.03952 (2017)
38. Zhang, J., Cho, K.: Query-efficient imitation learning for end-to-end simulated driving. In: AAAI, pp. 2891–2897 (2017)
39. Zhang, L., Lin, L., Liang, X., He, K.: Is faster R-CNN doing well for pedestrian detection? In: European Conference on Computer Vision, pp. 443–457 (2016)
40. Zhu, Y., et al.: Target-driven visual navigation in indoor scenes using deep reinforcement learning. In: 2017 IEEE International Conference on Robotics and Automation (ICRA), pp. 3357–3364 (2017)
41. Ziebart, B.D., Maas, A.L., Dey, A.K., Bagnell, J.A.: Navigate like a cabbie: probabilistic reasoning from observed context-aware behavior. In: Proceedings of the 10th International Conference on Ubiquitous Computing, pp. 322–331 (2008)

Statistically-Motivated Second-Order Pooling

Kaicheng Yu(✉) and Mathieu Salzmann

CVLab, EPFL, 1015 Lausanne, Switzerland
{kaicheng.yu,mathieu.salzmann}@epfl.ch

Abstract. Second-order pooling, a.k.a. bilinear pooling, has proven effective for deep learning based visual recognition. However, the resulting second-order networks yield a final representation that is orders of magnitude larger than that of standard, first-order ones, making them memory-intensive and cumbersome to deploy. Here, we introduce a general, parametric compression strategy that can produce more compact representations than existing compression techniques, yet outperform both compressed and uncompressed second-order models. Our approach is motivated by a statistical analysis of the network's activations, relying on operations that lead to a Gaussian-distributed final representation, as inherently used by first-order deep networks. As evidenced by our experiments, this lets us outperform the state-of-the-art first-order and second-order models on several benchmark recognition datasets.

Keywords: Second-order descriptors · Convolutional neural networks · Image classification

1 Introduction

Visual recognition is one of the fundamental goals of computer vision. Over the years, second-order representations, i.e., region covariance descriptors, have proven more effective than their first-order counterparts [2,11,31,38] for many tasks, such as pedestrian detection [46], material recognition [9] and semantic segmentation [6]. More recently, convolutional neural networks (CNNs) have achieved unprecedented performance in a wide range of image classification problems [20,22,30]. Inspired by the past developments in handcrafted features, several works have proposed to replace the fully-connected layers with second-order pooling strategies, essentially utilizing covariance descriptors within CNNs [24,29,32,34–36]. This has led to second-order or bilinear CNNs whose representation power surpasses that of standard, first-order ones.

This work was supported in part by the Swiss National Science Foundation.

Electronic supplementary material The online version of this chapter (https://doi.org/10.1007/978-3-030-01234-2_37) contains supplementary material, which is available to authorized users.

V. Ferrari et al. (Eds.): ECCV 2018, LNCS 11211, pp. 621–637, 2018.
https://doi.org/10.1007/978-3-030-01234-2_37

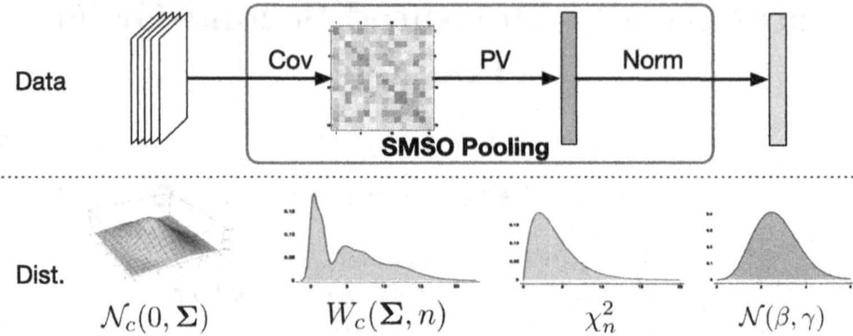

Fig. 1. Statistically-Motivated Second-Order (SMSO) pooling. Top: Our parametric compression strategy vectorizes a covariance matrix and normalizes the resulting vector. **Bottom:** Each of these operations yields a well-defined distribution of the data, thus resulting in a consistent framework, whose final representation follows a Gaussian distribution, as state-of-the-art first-order deep networks.

One drawback of these second-order CNNs is that vectorizing the covariance descriptor to pass it to the classification layer, as done in [24,32,34,36], yields a vector representation that is orders of magnitude larger than that of first-order CNNs, thus making these networks memory-intensive and subject to overfitting. While compression strategies have been proposed [13,27], they are either nonparametric [13], thus limiting the representation power of the network, or designed for a specific classification formalism [27], thus restricting their applicability.

In this paper, we introduce a general, parametric compression strategy for second-order CNNs. As evidenced by our results, our strategy can produce more compact representations than [13,27], with as little as 10% of their parameters, yet significantly outperforming these methods, as well as the state-of-the-art first-order [20,42] and uncompressed second-order pooling strategies [24,32,34,36].

Unlike most deep learning architectures, our approach is motivated by a statistical analysis of the network's activations. In particular, we build upon the observation that first-order networks inherently exploit Gaussian distributions for their feature representations. This is due to the fact that, as discussed in [15,23] and explained by the Central Limit Theorem, the outputs of *linear* layers, and thus of operations such as global average pooling, follow a multivariate Gaussian distribution. The empirical success of such Gaussian distributions of feature representations in first-order deep networks motivated us to design a compression strategy such that the final representation also satisfies this property.

To this end, as illustrated by Fig. 1, we exploit the fact that the covariance matrices resulting from second-order pooling follow a Wishart distribution [26]. We then introduce a parametric vectorization (PV) layer, which compresses the second-order information while increasing the model capacity by relying on trainable parameters. We show that our PV layer outputs a vector whose elements follow χ^2 distributions, which motivates the use of a square-root normalization that makes the distribution of the resulting representation converge to a Gaussian, as verified empirically in Sect. 3.4. These operations rely on basic algebraic transformations, and can thus be easily integrated into any deep architecture and optimized with standard backpropagation.

We demonstrate the benefits of our statistically-motivated second-order (SMSO) pooling strategy on standard benchmark datasets for second-order models, including the Describing Texture Dataset (DTD) [9], the Material in Context (MINC) dataset [5] and the scene recognition MIT-Indoor dataset [40]. Our approach consistently outperforms the state-of-the-art second-order pooling strategies, independently of the base network used (i.e., VGG-D [42] or ResNet-50 [20]), as well as these base networks themselves. Our code is publicly available at https://github.com/kcyu2014/smsop.

2 Related Work

Visual recognition has a long history in computer vision. Here, we focus on the methods that, like us, make use of representations based on second-order information to tackle this task. In this context, the region covariance descriptors (RCDs) of [46] constitute the first attempt at leveraging second-order information. Similarly, Fisher Vectors [2] also effectively exploit second-order statistics. Following this success, several metrics have been proposed to compare RCDs [3,37,39,43], and they have been used in various classification frameworks, such as boosting [12], kernel Support Vector Machines [47], sparse coding [7,16,49] and dictionary learning [18,19,33,44]. In all these works, however, while the classifier was trained, no learning was involved in the computation of the RCDs.

To the best of our knowledge, [17], and its extension to the log-Euclidean metric [21], can be thought of as the first attempts to learn RCDs. This, however, was achieved by reducing the dimensionality of input RCDs via a single transformation, which has limited learning capacity. In [22], the framework of [17] was extended to learning multiple transformations of input RCDs. Nevertheless, this approach still relied on RCDs as input. The idea of incorporating second-order descriptors in a deep, end-to-end learning paradigm was introduced concurrently in [24] and [36]. The former introduced the DeepO$_2$P operation, consisting of computing the covariance matrix of convolutional features. The latter proposed the slightly more general idea of bilinear pooling, which, in principle, can exploit inner products between the features of corresponding spatial locations from different layers in the network. In practice, however, the use of cross-layer bilinear features does not bring a significant boost in representation power [13,34], and bilinear pooling is therefore typically achieved by computing the inner products of the features within a single layer, thus becoming essentially equivalent to second-order pooling.

A key to the success of second-order pooling is the normalization, or transformation, of the second-order representation. In [24], the matrix logarithm was employed, motivated by the fact that covariance matrices lie on a Riemannian manifold, and that this operation maps a matrix to its tangent space, thus producing a Euclidean representation. By contrast, [36] was rather inspired by previous normalization strategies for handcrafted features [2,38], and proposed to perform an element-wise square-root and ℓ_2 normalization after vectorization of the matrix representation. More recently, [32,34] introduced a matrix square-root normalization strategy that was shown to outperform the other transformation techniques.

All the above-mentioned methods simply vectorize the second-order representation, i.e., covariance matrix. As such, they produce a final representation whose size scales quadratically with the number of channels in the last convolutional feature map, thus being typically orders of magnitude larger than the final representation of first-order CNNs. To reduce the resulting memory cost and parameter explosion, several approaches have been proposed to compress second-order representations while preserving their discriminative power. The first attempt at compression was achieved by [13], which introduced two strategies, based on the idea of random projection, to map the covariance matrices to vectors. These projections, however, were not learned, thus not increasing the capacity of the network and producing at best the same accuracy as the bilinear CNN of [36]. In [27], a parametric strategy was employed to reduce the dimensionality of the bilinear features. While effective, this strategy was specifically designed to be incorporated in a bilinear Support Vector Machine.

By contrast, here, we introduce a parametric compression approach that can be incorporated into any standard deep learning framework. Furthermore, our strategy is statistically motivated so as to yield a final representation whose distribution is of the same type as that inherently used by first-order deep networks. As evidenced by our experiments, our method can produce more compact representations than existing compression techniques, yet outperforms the state-of-the-art first-order and second-order models.

Note that higher-order information has also been exploited in the past [10, 28]. While promising, we believe that developing statistically-motivated pooling strategies for such higher-order information goes beyond the scope of this paper.

3 Methodology

In this section, we first introduce our second-order pooling strategy while explaining the statistical motivation behind it. We then provide an alternative interpretation of our approach yielding a lower complexity, study and display the empirical distributions of our network's representations, and finally discuss the relation of our model to the recent second-order pooling techniques.

3.1 SMSO Pooling

Our goal is to design a general, parametric compression strategy for second-order deep networks. Furthermore, inspired by the fact that first-order deep networks inherently make use of Gaussian distributions for their feature representations, we reason about the statistical distribution of the network's intermediate representations so as to produce a final representation that is also Gaussian. Note that, while we introduce our SMSO pooling strategy within a CNN formalism, it applies to any method relying on second-order representations.

Formally, let $\mathbf{X} \in \mathbb{R}^{n \times c}$ be a data matrix, consisting of n sample vectors of dimension c. For example, in the context of CNNs, $\mathbf{X}$ contains the activations of the last convolutional layer, with $n = w \times h$ corresponding to the spatial resolution of the corresponding feature map. Here, we assume $\mathbf{x}_i \in \mathbb{R}^c$ to follow a multivariate Gaussian distribution $\mathcal{N}_c(\boldsymbol{\mu}, \boldsymbol{\Sigma})$. In practice, as discussed in [15,23] and explained by the Central Limit Theorem, this can be achieved by using a *linear* activation after the last convolutional layer, potentially followed by batch normalization [23].

Covariance Computation. Given the data matrix $\mathbf{X}$, traditional second-order pooling consists of computing a covariance matrix $\mathbf{Y} \in \mathbb{R}^{c \times c}$ as

$$\mathbf{Y} = \frac{1}{n-1}\sum_{i=1}^{n}(\mathbf{x}_i - \boldsymbol{\mu})(\mathbf{x}_i - \boldsymbol{\mu})^T = \frac{1}{n-1}\tilde{\mathbf{X}}^T\tilde{\mathbf{X}}, \tag{1}$$

where $\tilde{\mathbf{X}}$ denotes the mean-subtracted data matrix.

The following definition, see, e.g., [26], determines the distribution of $\mathbf{Y}$.

Definition 1. *If the elements $\mathbf{x}_i \in \mathbb{R}^c$ of a data matrix $\mathbf{X} \in \mathbb{R}^{n \times c}$ follow a zero mean multivariate Gaussian distribution $\mathbf{x}_i \sim \mathcal{N}_c(0, \boldsymbol{\Sigma})$, then the covariance matrix $\mathbf{Y}$ of $\mathbf{X}$ is said to follow a Wishart distribution, denoted by*

$$\mathbf{Y} = \mathbf{X}^T\mathbf{X} \sim W_c(\boldsymbol{\Sigma}, n). \tag{2}$$

Note that, in the bilinear CNN [36], the mean is typically not subtracted from the data. As such, the corresponding bilinear matrix follows a form of non-central Wishart distribution [25].

Second-Order Feature Compression. The standard way to use a second-order representation is to simply vectorize it [24,36], potentially after some form of normalization [32,34]. This, however, can yield very high-dimensional vectors that are cumbersome to deal with in practice. To avoid this, motivated by [13,27], we propose to compress the second-order representation during vectorization. Here, we introduce a simple, yet effective, compression technique that, in contrast with [13], is parametric, and, as opposed to [27], amenable to general classifiers.

Specifically, we develop a parametric vectorization (PV) layer, which relies on trainable weights $\mathbf{W} \in \mathbb{R}^{c \times p}$, with p the dimension of the resulting vector. Each dimension j of the vector $\mathbf{z}$ output by this PV layer can be expressed as

$$z_j = \mathbf{w}_j^T \mathbf{Y} \mathbf{w}_j, \tag{3}$$

where $\mathbf{w}_j$ is a column of $\mathbf{W}$.

The distribution of each dimension $\mathbf{z}_j$ is defined by the following theorem.

Theorem 1 (Theorem 5.6 in [26]). *If* $\mathbf{Y} \in \mathbb{R}^{c \times c}$ *follows a Wishart distribution* $W_c(\mathbf{\Sigma}, n)$*, and* $\mathbf{w} \in \mathbb{R}^c$ *and* $\mathbf{w} \neq \mathbf{0}$*, then*

$$z = \frac{\mathbf{w}^T \mathbf{Y} \mathbf{w}}{\mathbf{w}^T \mathbf{\Sigma} \mathbf{w}} \tag{4}$$

follows a χ^2 *distribution with degree of freedom* n*, i.e.,* $z \sim \chi^2_n$.

From this theorem, we can see that each output dimension of our PV layer follows a scaled χ^2 distribution $\gamma \chi^2_n$, where $\gamma = \mathbf{w}_j^T \mathbf{\Sigma} \mathbf{w}_j$, with $\mathbf{\Sigma}$ the covariance matrix of the original multivariate Gaussian distribution.

Transformation and Normalization. As shown above, each dimension of our current vector representation follows a χ^2 distribution. However, as discussed above, first-order deep networks inherently exploit Gaussian distributions for their feature representations. To make our final representation also satisfy this property, we rely on the following theorem.

Theorem 2 ([50]). *If* $z \sim \chi^2_n$ *with degree freedom* n*, then*

$$z' = \sqrt{2z} \tag{5}$$

converges to a Gaussian distribution with mean $\sqrt{2n-1}$ *and standard deviation* $\sigma = 1$ *when* n *is large, i.e.,* $z' \sim \mathcal{N}(\sqrt{2n-1}, 1)$.

Following this theorem, we therefore define our normalization as the transformation

$$\mathbf{z}'_j = \sqrt{\alpha \mathbf{z}_j} - \sqrt{2n-1}, \tag{6}$$

for each dimension j, where we set $\alpha = 2/(\mathbf{w}_j^T \mathbf{\Sigma} \mathbf{w}_j)$ to correspond to Theorem 2, while accounting for the factor γ arising from our parametric vectorization above. Note that other transformations, such as $\log(z)$ and $(z/n)^{1/3}$, are known to also converge to Gaussian distributions as n increases [4,50]. We show that these operations yield similar results to the one above in Sect. 4.4.

Note that, according to Theorem 2, the mean and variance of the resulting Gaussian distribution are determined by the degree of freedom n, which, in our case, corresponds to the number of samples used to compute the covariance matrix in Eq. 1. Such pre-determined values, however, might limit the discriminative power of the resulting representation. To tackle this, we further rely on trainable scale and bias parameters, yielding a final representation

$$\mathbf{z}''_j = \beta_j + \gamma_j \mathbf{z}'_j, \tag{7}$$

where $\gamma_j > 0, \beta_j \in \mathbb{R}$. Note that this transformation is also exploited by batch normalization. However, here, we do not need to compute the batch statistics during training, since Theorem 2 tells us that the batches follow a consistent distribution.

Altogether, our SMSO pooling strategy, defined by the operations discussed above, yields a p-dimensional vector. This representation can then be passed to a classifier. It can easily be verified that the above-mentioned operations are differentiable, and the resulting deep network can thus be trained end-to-end.

3.2 Alternative Computation

Here, we derive an equivalent way to perform our SMSO pooling, with a lower complexity when p is small, as shown in the supplementary material. Note, however, that our statistical reasoning is much clearer for the derivation of Sect. 3.1 and was what motivated our approach.

To derive the alternative, we note that

$$\frac{1}{\sqrt{\alpha}}\mathbf{z}'_j = \sqrt{\mathbf{w}_j^T \mathbf{Y} \mathbf{w}_j} \tag{8}$$

$$= \sqrt{\mathbf{w}_j^T \left(\sum_{i=1}^{n} (\mathbf{x}_i - \mu)(\mathbf{x}_i - \mu)^T \right) \mathbf{w}_j} \tag{9}$$

$$= \sqrt{\sum_{i=1}^{n} \left(\mathbf{w}_j^T (\mathbf{x}_i - \mu)\right) \left((\mathbf{x}_i - \mu)^T \mathbf{w}_j\right)} \tag{10}$$

$$= \sqrt{\sum_{i=1}^{n} (\mathbf{w}_j^T \tilde{\mathbf{x}}_i)^2}, \tag{11}$$

where $\tilde{\mathbf{x}}_i = \mathbf{x}_i - \mu$.

So, in essence, given $\mathbf{X}$, $\mathbf{z}'$ can be computed by performing a 1×1 convolution, with weights shaped as $(1, 1, c, p)$ and without bias, followed by a global ℓ_2 pooling operation, and a scaling by the constant $\sqrt{\alpha}$. Note that ℓ_2 pooling was introduced several years ago [41], but has been mostly ignored in the recent deep learning advances. By contrast, feature reduction with 1×1 convolutions is widely utilized in first-order network designs [20,45]. In essence, this mathematically equivalent formulation shows that our second-order compression strategy can be achieved without explicitly computing covariance matrices. Yet, our statistical analysis based on these covariance matrices remains valid.

3.3 Relation to Other Methods

In this section, we discuss the connections between our method and the other recent second-order pooling strategies in CNNs. In the supplementary material, we compare the computational complexity of different second-order methods with that of ours.

Normalization. Bilinear pooling (BP) [36] also proposed to make use of a square-root as normalization operation. An important difference with our approach, however, is that BP directly vectorizes the matrix representation $\mathbf{Y}$. It is easy to see that the diagonal elements of $\mathbf{Y}$ follow a χ^2 distribution, e.g., by taking $\mathbf{w}$ in Theorem 1 to be a vector with a single value 1 and the other values 0. Therefore, after normalization, some of the dimensions of the BP representation also follow a Gaussian distribution. However, the off-diagonal elements follow a variance-gamma distribution, and, after square-root normalization, will not be

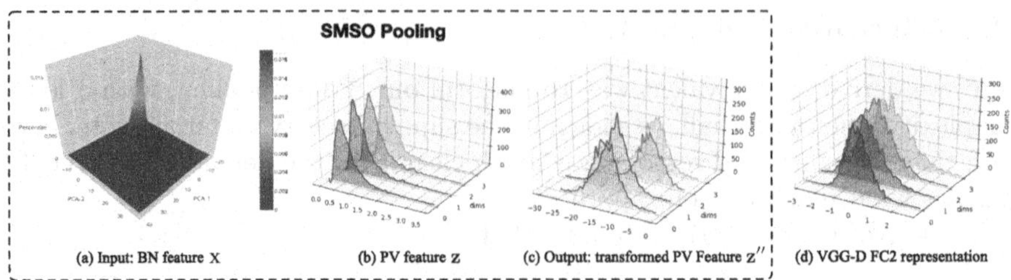

Fig. 2. Histograms of SMSO intermediate feature vectors. We plot the distribution of (a) the initial features $\mathbf{X}$, (b) the features after our PV layer $\mathbf{z}$, (c) the final representation $\mathbf{z}''$ and, for comparison, (d) first-order features after the last fully-connected layer in VGG-D [42]. Note that, as discussed in the text, these empirical distributions match the theoretical ones derived in Sect. 3.1, and our final representation does exploit the same type of distribution as first-order networks.

Gaussian, thus making the different dimensions of the final representation follow inconsistent distributions.

In [24] and [32], normalization was performed on the matrix $\mathbf{Y}$ directly, via a matrix logarithm and a matrix power normalization, respectively. As such, it is difficult to understand what distribution the elements of the final representation, obtained by standard vectorization, follow.

Compression. The compact bilinear pooling (CBP) of [13] exploits a compression scheme that has a form similar to ours in Eq. 3. However, in [13], the projection vectors $\mathbf{w}_j$ are random but fixed. Making them trainable, as in our PV layer, increases the capacity of our model, and, as shown in Sect. 4, allows us to significantly outperform CBP.

In [27], a model is developed specifically for a max-margin bilinear classifier. The parameter matrix of this classifier is approximated by a low-rank factorization, which translates to projecting the initial features to a lower-dimensional representation. As with our alternative formulation of Sect. 3.2, the resulting bilinear classifier can be obtained without having to explicitly compute $\mathbf{Y}$. This classifier is formulated in terms of quantities of the form $\|\mathbf{U}^T\mathbf{X}_i\|_F^2$, where $\mathbf{U}$ is a trainable low-rank weight matrix. In essence, this corresponds to removing the square-root operation from Eq. 11 and summing over all dimensions j. By contrast, our representation, ignoring the scale and bias of Eq. 7, is passed to a separate classification layer that computes a linear combination of the different dimensions with trainable weights, thus increasing the capacity of our model.

3.4 Empirical Distributions of SMSO Pooling

Our SMSO pooling strategy was motivated by considering the distribution of the representation at various stages in the network. Here, we study the empirical distributions of these features using the MINC dataset, discussed in Sect. 4, and with a model based on VGG-D. To this end, in Fig. 2, we provide a visualization of the distributions after the initial batch normalization (i.e., before computing the covariance matrix, see Sect. 4.1 for details), after our PV layer, and after square-root transformation with trainable scaling and bias. Specifically, for the initial features, because visualizing a Gaussian distribution in hundreds of dimensions is not feasible, we plot the distribution along the first 2 principal components. For our representations, where each dimension follows an independent Gaussian, we randomly select four dimensions and plot stacked histograms. As expected from the theory, the initial features are close to Gaussian, and the features after our PV layer therefore follow a long-tailed χ^2 distribution. The final features, after square-root normalization, scaling and bias, are much less skewed, and thus much closer to a Gaussian distribution, thus matching the type of distribution that the final representations of state-of-the-art deep networks follow, as shown in Fig. 2(d). To further verify this, we conducted a Shapiro-Wilk test on the final representation. This resulted in a p-value of $0.19 > 0.05$, which means that the Gaussian assumption is not rejected, sustaining our claim.

4 Experiments

Here, we first provide implementation details and introduce the baseline models. We then compare our approach to these baselines on four standard benchmark datasets, and provide an ablation study of our framework.

4.1 Implementation Details

We evaluate our method on two popular network architectures: the VGG-D network of [42] (a.k.a. VGG-16) and the ResNet-50 of [20]. For all second-order models discussed below, i.e., ours and the baselines, we remove all the fully-connected layers and the last max pooling layer from VGG-D, that is, we truncate the model after the ReLU activation following *conv5-3*. For ResNet-50, we remove the last global average pooling layer and take our initial features from the last residual block. As in [32], we add a 1×1 convolutional layer to project the initial features to $c = 256$ for all the experiments. Note that this is a linear layer, and thus makes the resulting features satisfy our Gaussian assumption.

Following common practice [13,27,32,36], we rely on weights pre-trained on ImageNet and use stochastic gradient descent with an initial learning rate 10 times smaller than the one used to learn from scratch, i.e., 0.001 for VGG-D and 0.01 for ResNet-50. We then divide this weight by 10 when the validation loss has stopped decreasing for 8 epochs. We initialize the weights of the new layers, i.e., the 1×1 convolution, the PV layer and the classifier, with the strategy of [14], i.e., random values drawn from a Gaussian distribution. We implemented our approach using Keras [8] with TensorFlow [1] as backend.

4.2 Baseline Models

We now describe the different baseline models that we compare our approach with. Note that the classifier is defined as a k-way softmax layer for all these models, as for ours, except for low-rank bilinear pooling, which was specifically designed to make use of a low-rank hinge loss.

Original Model: This refers to the original, first-order, models, i.e., either VGG-D or ResNet-50, pre-trained on ImageNet and fine-tuned on the new data. Other than replacing the 1000-way ImageNet classification layer with a k-way one, we keep the original model settings described in [42] and [20], respectively.

Bilinear Pooling (BP) [36]**:** This corresponds to the original, uncompressed bilinear pooling strategy, with signed square-root and ℓ_2 normalization after vanilla vectorization. In this case, we set $c = 512$, as in the original paper, as the feature dimension before computing the second-order representation. If the original feature dimension does not match this value, i.e., with ResNet-50, we make use of an additional 1×1 convolutional layer. Note that we observed that using either 512 or 256 as feature dimension made virtually no difference on the results. We therefore used $c = 512$, which matches the original paper.

DeepO$_2$P [24]**:** This refers to the original, uncompressed covariance-based model, with matrix logarithm and vanilla vectorization. Again, as in the original paper, we set $c = 512$ as the feature dimension before computing the covariance matrix, by using an additional 1×1 convolutional layer when necessary.

Matrix Power Normalization (MPN) [32]**:** This model relies on a matrix square-root operation acting on the second-order representation. Following the original paper, we set $c = 256$ by making use of an additional 1×1 convolutional layer before second-order pooling. Note that the improved bilinear pooling of [34] has the same structure as MPN, and we do not report it as a separate baseline.

Compact Bilinear Pooling (CBP) [13]**:** We report the results of both versions of CBP: the Random Maclaurin (RM) one and the Tensor Sketch (TS) one. For both versions, we set the projection dimension to $d = 8,192$, which was shown to achieve the same accuracy as BP, i.e., the best accuracy reported in [13]. As in the original paper, we apply the same normalization as BP [36].

Low Rank Bilinear Pooling (LRBP) [27]**:** This corresponds to the compression method dedicated to the bilinear SVM classifier. Following [27], we set the projection dimension to $m = 100$ and its rank to $r = 8$, and initialize the dimensionality reduction layer using the SVD of the Gram matrix computed from the entire validation set. Following the authors' implementation, we apply a scaled square-root with factor 2×10^5 after the *conv5-3* ReLU, which seems to prevent the model from diverging. Furthermore, we found that training LRBP from the weights of BP fine-tuned on each dataset also helped convergence.

4.3 Comparison to the Baselines

Let us now compare the results of our model with those of the baselines described in Sect. 4.2. To this end, we make use of four diverse benchmark image classification datasets, thus showing the versatility of our approach. These datasets are the Describing Texture Dataset (DTD) [9] for texture recognition, the challenging

Fig. 3. Sample images from DTD, MINC-2500, MIT-Indoor and CUB.

Material In Context (MINC-2500) dataset [5] for large-scale material recognition in the wild, the MIT-Indoor dataset [40] for indoor scene understanding and the Caltech-UCSD Bird (CUB) dataset [48] for fine-grained classification. DTD contains 47 classes for a total of 5,640 images, mostly capturing the texture itself, with limited surrounding background. By contrast, MINC-2500, consisting of 57,500 images of 23 classes, depicts materials in their real-world environment, thus containing strong background information and making it more challenging. MIT-Indoor contains 15,620 images of 67 different indoor scenes, and, with DTD, has often been used to demonstrate the discriminative power of second-order representations. The CUB dataset contains 11,788 images of 200 different bird species. In Fig. 3, we provide a few samples from each dataset. For our experiments, we make use of the standard train-test splits released with these datasets. For DTD, MIT-Indoor and CUB, we define the input size as 448×448 for all the experiments. For the large-scale MINC-2500 dataset, we use 224×224 images for all models to speed up training. Note that a larger input size could potentially result in higher accuracies [5]. For all datasets and all models, we use the same data augmentation strategy as in [34,36].

Experiments with VGG-D. We first discuss the results obtained with the VGG-D architecture as base model. These results are reported in Table 1 for all models and all datasets. In short, our SMSO framework with PV dimension $p = 2,048$ outperforms all the baselines by a significant margin on all three datasets. In particular, our accuracy is 7% to 19% higher than the original VGG-D, with *much* fewer parameters, thus showing the benefits of exploiting second-order features. MPN is the best-performing baseline, but, besides the fact that we consistently outperform it, has a much higher computational complexity and run time, as shown in the supplementary material. The second-order compression methods (CBP and LRBP) underperform the uncompressed models on average. By contrast, even with $p = 64$, we outperform most baselines, with a model that corresponds to 10% of the parameters of the most compact baseline.

In Fig. 4, we compare the training and validation loss curves of our approach with those of the best-performing baselines, BP and MPN, on DTD and MINC. Note that our model converges much faster than BP and tends to be more stable than MPN, particularly on DTD. This, we believe, is due to the fact that we rely on basic algebraic operations, instead of the eigenvalue decomposition involved

Table 1. Comparison of VGG-D based models. We report the top 1 classification accuracy (in %) of the original VGG-D model, uncompressed second-order models with different normalization strategies (BP, DeepO_2P, MPN), second-order compression methods (CBP-TS, CBP-RM, LRBP), and our approach (SMSO) with different PV dimensions. Note that our approach significantly outperforms all the baselines despite a more compact final representation (Feature dim.) and much fewer parameters (# param is the number of trainable parameters after the last convolutional layer).

Model name	Feature dim.	# param.	DTD [9]	MIT [40]	MINC [5]	CUB [48]
VGG-D [42]	4,096	119.64M	60.11	64.51	73.01	66.12
BP [36]	2.6×10^5	3.015M	67.50	77.55	74.50	81.02
MPN [32]	32,896	0.752M	68.01	76.49	76.24	84.10
DeepO_2P [24]	2.6×10^5	3.015M	66.07	72.35	69.29	-
CBP-TS [13]	8,192	0.189M	67.71	76.83	73.28	84.00
CBP-RM [13]	8,192	0.189M	63.24	73.89	73.54	83.86
LRBP [27]	100	0.068M	65.80	73.59	69.10	84.21
SMSO (*Ours*)	64	0.013M	68.18	75.37	74.18	82.66
SMSO (*Ours*)	2,048	0.057M	**69.26**	**79.45**	**78.00**	**85.01**

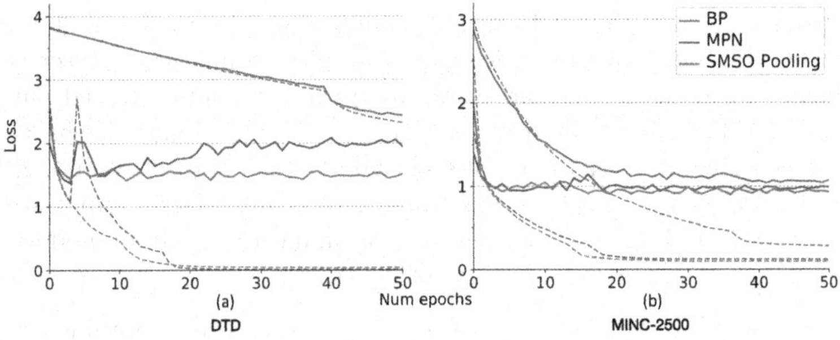

Fig. 4. Training and validation loss curves. We plot the training (dashed) and validation (solid) loss values as a function of the number of training epochs for our SMSO pooling strategy (orange), BP (green) and MPN (blue) on DTD (a) and MINC-2500 (b). Our models clearly converge faster than BP, and tend to be more stable than MPN, particularly on the smaller-scale DTD dataset. (Color figure online)

in MPN whose gradient can be difficult to compute, particularly in the presence of small or equal eigenvalues [24].

During these VGG-D based experiments, we have observed that, in practice, LRBP was difficult to train, being very sensitive to the learning rate, which we had to manually adapt throughout training. Because of this, and the fact that LRBP yields lower accuracy than uncompressed models, we do not include this baseline in the remaining experiments. We also exclude DeepO_2P from the next experiments, because of its consistently lower accuracy.

Table 2. Comparison of ResNet-50 based models. We report the top 1 classification accuracy (in %) of the original ResNet-50 model, uncompressed second-order models with different normalization strategies (BP, MPN), second-order compression methods (CBP-TS, CBP-RM), and our approach (SMSO). Note that, as in the VGG-D case, our model outperforms all the baselines, including the original ResNet-50, which is not the case of most second-order baselines. It also yields much more compact models than the second-order baselines. (# params. refers to the same quantity as in Table 1.)

Model name	Feature dim.	# param.	DTD [9]	MIT [40]	MINC [5]	CUB [48]
ResNet-50 [20]	2,048	4K	71.45	76.45	79.12	74.51
BP [36]	32, 896	752K	69.37	68.35	79.05	82.70
MPN [32]	32, 896	752K	71.10	72.12	79.83	85.43
CBP-TS [13]	8,192	189K	65.30	72.60	75.91	77.35
CBP-RM [13]	8,192	189K	62.35	67.81	74.15	-
SMSO (*Ours*)	64	13K	71.03	76.31	79.17	81.98
SMSO (*Ours*)	2,048	57K	**72.51**	**79.68**	**81.33**	**85.77**

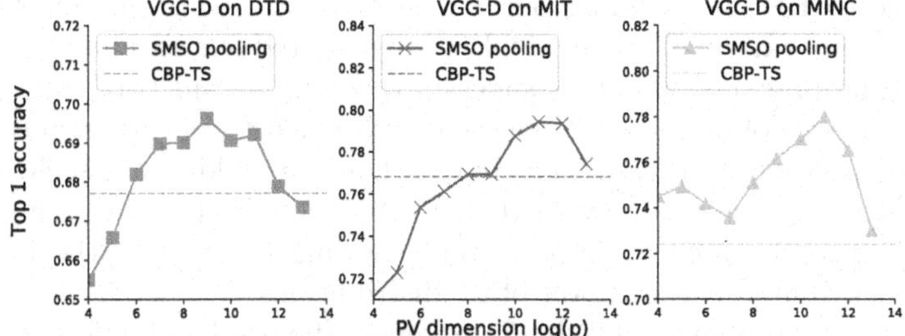

Fig. 5. Influence of the PV dimension p**.** We plot the top 1 accuracy as a function of the value p in logarithmic scale on MIT (left), MINC (middle) and DTD (right). Note that accuracy is quite stable over large ranges of p values, yielding as good results as the best-performing compression baseline (CBP-TS) with as few as $p = 64$ dimensions, corresponding to only 10% of the parameters of CBP-TS.

Experiments with ResNet-50. To further show the generality of our approach, we make use of the more recent, very deep ResNet-50 [20] architecture as base network. Table 2 provides the results of our SMSO framework with $p = 64$ and $p = 2,048$, and of the baselines. In essence, the conclusions remain unchanged; we outperform all the baselines for $p = 2,048$. Note that, here, however, the second-order baselines typically do not even outperform the original ResNet-50, whose results are significantly higher than the VGG-D ones. By contrast, our model is able to leverage this improvement of the base model and to further increase its accuracy by appropriately exploiting second-order features.

4.4 Ablation Study

We evaluate the influence of different components of our model on our results.

Influence of the PV Dimension. In our experiments, we proposed to set $p = 2,048$ or $p = 64$. We now investigate the influence of this parameter on our results. To this end, we vary p in the range $[2^4, 2^{13}]$ by steps corresponding to a factor 2. The curves for this experiment on the validation data of the three datasets with VGG-D based models are provided in Fig. 5. Note that our model is quite robust to the exact value of this parameter, with stable accuracies outperforming the best compression baseline for each dataset over large ranges. More importantly, even with $p = 64$, our model yields as good results as the best compression method, CBP-TS, with only 10% of its parameters.

Comparison of Different Distributions and Transformations. We conduct experiments to compare different final feature distributions on MINC-2500 with a VGG-D based model. The results are provided in Table 3. Without our PV compression and without transformation or normalization, the resulting features follow a Wishart distribution, yielding an accuracy of 75.97%, which is comparable to BP [36]. Adding our PV layer $p = 2,048$, but not using any transformation or normalization, yields χ^2-distributed features and an accuracy similar to the previous one. This suggests that our parametric compression is effective, since we obtain similar accuracy with much fewer parameters. Including the square-root transformation, but without the additional scale and bias of Eq. 7, increases the accuracy to 76.32%. Additionally learning the scale and bias boosts the accuracy to 78.00%, thus showing empirically the benefits of Gaussian-distributed features over other distributions.

In the last two columns of Table 3, we report the results of different transformations that bring the χ^2-distributed features to a Gaussian distribution, i.e., the cubic-root and the element-wise logarithm. Note that these two transformations yield accuracies similar to those obtained with the square-root. More importantly, all transformations yield higher accuracies than not using any (76.14%), which further evidences the benefits of Gaussian-distributed features.

Table 3. Comparison of different final feature distributions. We report the results of different combinations of vectorization (vec.), transformation (trans.) and normalization (norm.) strategies, yielding different final feature distributions. Here, $\mu = \sqrt{2n-1}$ from Theorem 2. Ultimately, these results show that bringing the data back to a Gaussian distribution with a trainable scale and bias yields higher accuracies.

Vec.	Flatten	PV					PV		
Trans.	-	-	Sqrt	Sqrt	Sqrt	-	Sqrt	Log	$\sqrt[3]{}$
Norm.	-	-	-	β	γ	β, γ	β, γ		
Dist.	$W_n(\Sigma)$	χ_n^2	$\mathcal{N}(\mu, 1)$	$\mathcal{N}(\beta, 1)$	$\mathcal{N}(\mu, \gamma^2)$	$\gamma\chi_n^2 + \beta$	$\mathcal{N}(\beta, \gamma^2)$		
Acc.	75.97	75.32	76.32	77.12	76.47	76.14	78.00	77.86	77.17

5 Conclusion

We have introduced a general and parametric compression strategy for second-order deep networks, motivated by a statistical analysis of the distribution of the network's intermediate representations. Our SMSO pooling strategy outperforms the state-of-the-art first-order and second-order models, with higher accuracies than other compression techniques for up to 90% parameter reduction. With a ResNet-50 base architecture, it is the only second-order model to consistently outperform the original one. While Gaussian distributions have proven effective here and for first-order models, there is no guarantee that they are truly optimal. In the future, we will study if other transformations yielding non-Gaussian distributions can help further improve second-order models.

References

1. Abadi, M., et al.: TensorFlow: large-scale machine learning on heterogeneous systems (2015). Software available from tensorflow.org. https://www.tensorflow.org/
2. Arandjelovic, R., Zisserman, A.: All about VLAD. In: CVPR, pp. 1578–1585 (2013)
3. Arsigny, V., Fillard, P., Pennec, X., Ayache, N.: Log-Euclidean metrics for fast and simple calculus on diffusion tensors. Magn. Reson. Med. **56**, 411–421 (2006)
4. Bartlett, M.S., Kendall, D.G.: The statistical analysis of variance-heterogeneity and the logarithmic transformation. Suppl. J. R. Stat. Soc. **8**(1), 128–138 (1946). http://www.jstor.org/stable/2983618
5. Bell, S., Upchurch, P., Snavely, N., Bala, K.: Material recognition in the wild with the materials in context database. In: CVPR (2015)
6. Carreira, J., Caseiro, R., Batista, J., Sminchisescu, C.: Semantic segmentation with second-order pooling. In: Fitzgibbon, A., Lazebnik, S., Perona, P., Sato, Y., Schmid, C. (eds.) ECCV 2012. LNCS, vol. 7578, pp. 430–443. Springer, Heidelberg (2012). https://doi.org/10.1007/978-3-642-33786-4_32
7. Cherian, A., Sra, S.: Riemannian sparse coding for positive definite matrices. In: Fleet, D., Pajdla, T., Schiele, B., Tuytelaars, T. (eds.) ECCV 2014. LNCS, vol. 8691, pp. 299–314. Springer, Cham (2014). https://doi.org/10.1007/978-3-319-10578-9_20
8. Chollet, F., et al.: Keras (2015). https://github.com/fchollet/keras
9. Cimpoi, M., Maji, S., Kokkinos, I., Mohamed, S., Vedaldi, A.: Describing textures in the wild. In: CVPR (2014)
10. Cui, Y., Zhou, F., Wang, J., Liu, X., Lin, Y., Belongie, S.: Kernel pooling for convolutional neural networks. In: CVPR (2017)
11. Dalal, N., Triggs, B.: Histograms of oriented gradients for human detection. In: CVPR, pp. 886–893 (2005)
12. Freund, Y., Schapire, R.E.: A decision-theoretic generalization of on-line learning and an application to boosting. Suppl. J. R. Stat. Soc. **55**, 119–139 (1997)
13. Gao, Y., Beijbom, O., Zhang, N., Darrell, T.: Compact bilinear pooling. In: CVPR, pp. 317–326 (2016)
14. Glorot, X., Bengio, Y.: Understanding the difficulty of training deep feedforward neural networks. In: AISTATS (2010)
15. Goodfellow, I., Bengio, Y., Courville, A.: Deep Learning. MIT Press, Cambridge (2016). http://www.deeplearningbook.org

16. Guo, K., Ishwar, P., Konrad, J.: Action recognition using sparse representation on covariance manifolds of optical flow. In: IEEE International Conference on Advanced Video and Signal Based Surveillance (AVSS) (2010)
17. Harandi, M.T., Salzmann, M., Hartley, R.: From manifold to manifold: geometry-aware dimensionality reduction for SPD matrices. In: Fleet, D., Pajdla, T., Schiele, B., Tuytelaars, T. (eds.) ECCV 2014. LNCS, vol. 8690, pp. 17–32. Springer, Cham (2014). https://doi.org/10.1007/978-3-319-10605-2_2
18. Harandi, M., Salzmann, M.: Riemannian coding and dictionary learning: Kernels to the rescue. In: CVPR (2015)
19. Harandi, M.T., Sanderson, C., Hartley, R., Lovell, B.C.: Sparse coding and dictionary learning for symmetric positive definite matrices: a kernel approach. In: Fitzgibbon, A., Lazebnik, S., Perona, P., Sato, Y., Schmid, C. (eds.) ECCV 2012. LNCS, pp. 216–229. Springer, Heidelberg (2012). https://doi.org/10.1007/978-3-642-33709-3_16
20. He, K., Zhang, X., Ren, S., Sun, J.: Deep Residual Learning for Image Recognition. In: CVPR, pp. 770–778 (2016)
21. Huang, C.H., Boyer, E., Angonese, B.D.C., Navab, N., Ilic, S.: Toward user-specific tracking by detection of human shapes in multi-cameras. In: CVPR (2015)
22. Huang, G., Liu, Z., Weinberger, K., van der Maaten, L.: Densely connected convolutional networks. In: CVPR (2017)
23. Ioffe, S., Szegedy, C.: Batch normalization: accelerating deep network training by reducing internal covariate shift. In: ICML (2015)
24. Ionescu, C., Vantzos, O., Sminchisescu, C.: Matrix backpropagation for deep networks with structured layers (2015)
25. James, A.T.: The non-central Wishart distribution. Proc. R. Soc. London. Ser. A Math. Phys. Sci. **229**(1178), 364–366 (1955). http://www.jstor.org/stable/99771
26. Johnson, R.A., Wichern, D.W., et al.: Applied Multivariate Statistical Analysis, vol. 4. Prentice-Hall, Englewood Cliffs (2014)
27. Kong, S., Fowlkes, C.: Low-rank bilinear pooling for fine-grained classification. In: CVPR (2017)
28. Koniusz, P., Tas, Y., Porikli, F.: Domain adaptation by mixture of alignments of second- or higher-order scatter tensors. In: CVPR (2017)
29. Koniusz, P., Zhang, H., Porikli, F.: A deeper look at power normalizations. In: CVPR, pp. 5774–5783 (2018)
30. Krizhevsky, A., Sutskever, I., Hinton, G.: ImageNet classification with deep convolutional neural networks. In: NIPS, pp. 1106–1114 (2012)
31. Lazebnik, S., Schmid, C., Ponce, J.: Beyond bags of features: spatial pyramid matching for recognizing natural scene categories. In: CVPR (2006)
32. Li, P., Xie, J., Wang, Q., Zuo, W.: Is second-order information helpful for large-scale visual recognition? In: ICCV (2017)
33. Li, P., Wang, Q., Zuo, W., Zhang, L.: Log-Euclidean kernels for sparse representation and dictionary learning. In: ICCV (2013)
34. Lin, T.Y., Maji, S.: Improved bilinear pooling with CNNs. In: BMVC (2017)
35. Lin, T.Y., Maji, S., Koniusz, P.: Second-order democratic aggregation. In: Ferrari, V., Hebert, M., Sminchisescu, C., Weiss, Y. (eds.) ECCV 2018, Part III. LNCS, vol. 11207, pp. 639–656. Springer, Cham (2018)
36. Lin, T., RoyChowdhury, A., Maji, S.: Bilinear CNN models for fine-grained visual recognition. In: ICCV, pp. 1449–1457 (2015)
37. Pennec, X., Fillard, P., Ayache, N.: A Riemannian framework for tensor computing. IJCV **66**, 41–66 (2006)

38. Perronnin, F., Sánchez, J., Mensink, T.: Improving the Fisher kernel for large-scale image classification. In: Daniilidis, K., Maragos, P., Paragios, N. (eds.) ECCV 2010. LNCS, vol. 6314, pp. 143–156. Springer, Heidelberg (2010). https://doi.org/10.1007/978-3-642-15561-1_11
39. Quang, M.H., San-Biagio, M., Murino, V.: Log-Hilbert-Schmidt metric between positive definite operators on Hilbert spaces. In: NIPS (2014)
40. Quattoni, A., Torralba, A.: Recognizing indoor scenes. In: CVPR, pp. 413–420 (2009)
41. Sermanet, P., Chintala, S., LeCun, Y.: Convolutional neural networks applied to house numbers digit classification. In: ICPR (2012)
42. Simonyan, K., Zisserman, A.: Very deep convolutional networks for large-scale image recognition. In: ICLR (2015)
43. Sra, S.: A new metric on the manifold of kernel matrices with application to matrix geometric means. In: NIPS (2012)
44. Sra, S., Cherian, A.: Generalized dictionary learning for symmetric positive definite matrices with application to nearest neighbor retrieval. In: Gunopulos, D., Hofmann, T., Malerba, D., Vazirgiannis, M. (eds.) ECML PKDD 2011. LNCS (LNAI), vol. 6913, pp. 318–332. Springer, Heidelberg (2011). https://doi.org/10.1007/978-3-642-23808-6_21
45. Szegedy, C., et al.: Going deeper with convolutions. In: CVPR, pp. 1–9, June 2015
46. Tuzel, O., Porikli, F., Meer, P.: Human detection via classification on Riemannian manifolds. In: CVPR, pp. 1–8 (2007)
47. Vapnik, V.: Statistical Learning Theory. Wiley-Interscience, New York (1998)
48. Wah, C., Branson, S., Welinder, P., Perona, P., Belongie, S.: The Caltech-UCSD birds-200-2011 dataset. Technical report (2011)
49. Wang, Q., Li, P., Zuo, W., Zhang, L.: RAID-G - robust estimation of approximate infinite dimensional Gaussian with application to material recognition. In: CVPR (2016)
50. Wilson, E.B., Hilferty, M.M.: The distribution of chi-square. Proc. Natl. Acad. Sci. **17**(12), 684–688 (1931)

Perturbation Robust Representations of Topological Persistence Diagrams

Anirudh Som[1(✉)], Kowshik Thopalli[1], Karthikeyan Natesan Ramamurthy[2], Vinay Venkataraman[1], Ankita Shukla[3], and Pavan Turaga[1]

[1] Geometric Media Lab, Arizona State University, Tempe, USA
{asom2,kthopall,vvenka18,pturaga}@asu.edu

[2] IBM Thomas J. Watson Research Center, Yorktown Heights, USA
knatesa@us.ibm.com

[3] Indraprastha Institute of Information Technology-Delhi, Delhi, India
ankitas@iiitd.ac.in

Abstract. Topological methods for data analysis present opportunities for enforcing certain invariances of broad interest in computer vision, including view-point in activity analysis, articulation in shape analysis, and measurement invariance in non-linear dynamical modeling. The increasing success of these methods is attributed to the complementary information that topology provides, as well as availability of tools for computing topological summaries such as persistence diagrams. However, persistence diagrams are multi-sets of points and hence it is not straightforward to fuse them with features used for contemporary machine learning tools like deep-nets. In this paper we present theoretically well-grounded approaches to develop novel perturbation robust topological representations, with the long-term view of making them amenable to fusion with contemporary learning architectures. We term the proposed representation as Perturbed Topological Signatures, which live on a Grassmann manifold and hence can be efficiently used in machine learning pipelines. We explore the use of the proposed descriptor on three applications: 3D shape analysis, view-invariant activity analysis, and non-linear dynamical modeling. We show favorable results in both high-level recognition performance and time-complexity when compared to other baseline methods.

Keywords: Invariance learning · Topological data analysis
Persistence diagrams · Grassmann manifold
Perturbed topological signature

A. Som and K. Thopalli—contributed equally.

Electronic supplementary material The online version of this chapter (https://doi.org/10.1007/978-3-030-01234-2_38) contains supplementary material, which is available to authorized users.

V. Ferrari et al. (Eds.): ECCV 2018, LNCS 11211, pp. 638–659, 2018.
https://doi.org/10.1007/978-3-030-01234-2_38

1 Introduction

Over the years, tools from topological data analysis (TDA) have been used to characterize the invariant structure of data obtained from a noisy sampling of an underlying metric space [24]. Invariance learning is a fundamental problem in computer vision, since common transformations can diminish the performance of algorithms significantly. Past work in invariance learning has fallen into one of two classes. The first approach involves ad-hoc choices of features or metrics between features that offer some invariance to specific factors [9]. However, this approach has suffered due to lack of generalizable solutions. The other approach is to increase the training size by collecting samples that capture all the variations of the data, so that the learning algorithm can implicitly marginalize out the variations. A similar effect can be achieved via simple data augmentation [50].

In this context, TDA has emerged as a surprisingly powerful tool to analyze underlying invariant properties of data before any contextual modeling assumptions or the need to extract actionable information kicks in. Generally speaking, TDA seeks to characterize the *shape* of high dimensional data by quantifying various topological invariants such as connected components, cycles, high-dimensional holes, level-sets and monotonic regions of functions defined on the data [24]. Topological invariants are those properties that do not change under smooth deformations like stretching, bending, and rotation, but without tearing or gluing surfaces. We illustrate the connections between topological invariants and learning invariant representations for vision via three applications:

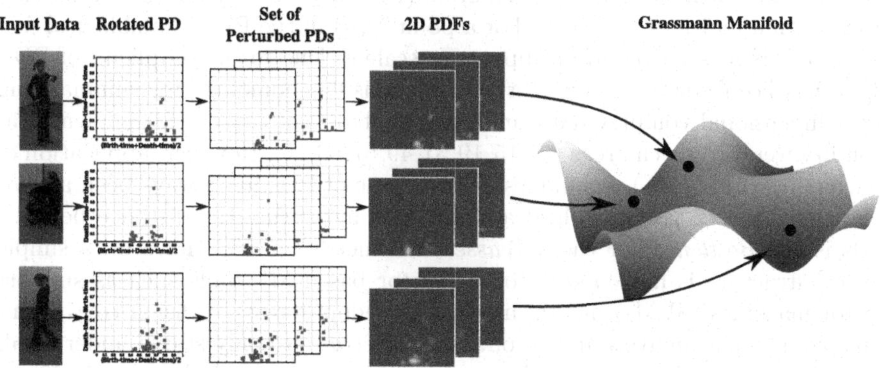

Fig. 1. Illustration of the sequence of steps leading to the proposed Perturbed Topological Signature (PTS) representation. For a given input dataset, the PDs are computed and transformed to maximally occupy the 2D space. A set of perturbed PDs is created, with each perturbed PD having its points displaced by a certain amount about its initial position. For each PD in the set, a 2D PDF is constructed using a Gaussian kernel function via kernel density estimation. The set of 2D PDFs capture a wide range of topological noise for the given input data and are summarized using a subspace structure, equivalent to a point on the Grassmann manifold.

(1) Point cloud shape analysis: Shape analysis of 3-dimensional (3D) point cloud data is a topic of major current interest due to emergence of Light Detection and Ranging (LIDAR) based vision systems in autonomous vehicles. It has been a difficult problem to solve with contemporary methods (*e.g.* deep learning) due to the non-vectorial nature of the representations. While there is interest in trying to extend deep-net architectures to point-cloud data [32,44, 46,53,72], the invariance one seeks is that of *shape articulation*, *i.e.* stretching, skewing, rotation of shape that does not alter the fundamental object class. These invariances are optimally defined in terms of topological invariants.

(2) Video analysis: One of the long-standing problems in video analysis, specific to human action recognition, is to deal with variation in *body type, execution style*, and *view-point* changes. Work in this area has shown that temporal self-similarity matrices (SSMs) are a robust feature and provide general invariance to the above factors [34]. Temporal self-similarities can be quantified by scalar field topological constructions defined over video features, leading to representations with encoded invariances not relying on brute-force training data.

(3) Non-linear dynamical modeling: Many time-series analysis problems have been studied under the lens of non-linear dynamical modeling: including motion-capture analysis, wearable-based activity analysis *etc.* Results from dynamical systems theory (Takens' embedding theorem [62]) suggest that the placement-invariant property may be related to the topological properties of reconstructed dynamical attractors via delay-embeddings.

One of the prominent TDA tools is persistent homology. It provides a multi-scale summary of different homological features [25]. This multi-scale information is represented using a persistence diagram (PD), a 2-dimensional (2D) Cartesian plane with a multi-set of points. For a point (b, d) in the PD, a homological feature appears at scale b and disappears at scale d. Due to the simplicity of PDs, there has been a surge of interest to use persistent homology for summarizing high-dimensional complex data and has resulted in its successful implementation in several research areas [14,15,19,31,49,57,63,66]. However, application of machine learning (ML) techniques on the space of PDs has always been a challenging task. The gold-standard approach for measuring the distance between PDs is the *Bottleneck* or the p-*Wasserstein* metric [45,65]. However, a simple metric structure is not enough to use vector based ML tools such as support vector machines (SVMs), neural networks, random forests, decision trees, principal component analysis and so on. These metrics are only stable under small perturbations of the data which the PDs summarize, and the complexity of computing distances between PDs grows in the order of $\mathcal{O}(n^3)$, where n is the number of points in the PD [11]. Efforts have been made to overcome these problems by attempting to map PDs to spaces that are more suitable for ML tools [3,5,12,48,51,52]. A comparison of some recent algorithms for machine learning over topological descriptors can be found in [54]. More recently, topological methods have also shown early promise in improving performance of image-based classification algorithms in conjunction with deep-learning [21].

Contributions: Using a novel perturbation framework, we propose a topological representation of PDs called *Perturbed Topological Signature* (PTS). To do this we first generate a set of perturbed PDs by randomly shifting the points in the original PD by a certain amount. A perturbed PD is analogous to extracting the PD from data that is subjected to topological noise. Next, we utilize a 2D probability density function (PDF) estimated by kernels on each of the perturbed PDs to generate a smooth functional representation. Finally, we simplify and summarize the end representation-space for the set of 2D PDFs to a point on the Grassmann manifold (a non-constantly curved manifold). The framework described above is illustrated in Fig. 1. We develop very efficient ML pipelines over these topological descriptors by leveraging the known metrics and statistical results on the Grassmann manifold. We also develop a stability proof of the Grassmannian representations w.r.t. the normalized geodesic distance over the Grassmannian and the *Wasserstein* metrics over PDs. Experiments show that our proposed framework recovers the lost performance due to functional methods, while still enjoying orders of magnitude faster processing times over the classical *p-Wasserstein* and *Bottleneck* approaches.

Outline of the Paper: Sect. 2 provides the necessary background on topological data analysis and the Grassmannian. Section 3 discusses related work, while Sect. 4 describes the proposed framework and end representation of the PD for statistical learning tasks. Section 5 describes the experiments and results. Section 6 concludes the paper.

2 Preliminaries

Persistent Topology: Consider a graph $\mathcal{G} = \{\mathcal{V}, \mathcal{E}\}$ on the high-dimensional point cloud, where $\mathcal{V}$ is the set of $|\mathcal{V}|$ nodes and $\mathcal{E}$ defines the neighborhood relations between the samples. To estimate the topological properties of the graph's shape, a simplicial complex $\mathcal{S}$ is constructed over $\mathcal{G}$. We denote $\mathcal{S} = (\mathcal{G}, \Sigma)$, where Σ is a family of non-empty level sets of $\mathcal{G}$, with each element $\sigma \in \Sigma$ is a simplex [25]. These simplices are constructed using the ϵ-neighborhood rule, ϵ being the scale parameter [25]. In TDA, Betti numbers β_i provide the rank of the homology group H_i. For instance, β_0 denotes the number of connected components, β_1 denotes the number of holes or loops, β_2 denotes the number of voids or trapped volumes, *etc.* They provide a good summary of a shape's topological features. However, two shapes with same Betti numbers can have very different PDs since PDs summarize the birth vs death time information of each topological feature in a homology group. Birth time (b) signifies the scale at which the group is formed and death time (d) is the scale at which it ceases to exist. The difference between the death and the birth times is the lifetime of the homology group $l = |d - b|$. Each PD is a multiset of points (b, d) in $\mathbb{R}^2$ and is hence represented graphically as a set of points in a 2D plane. The diagonal where $b = d$ is assumed to contain an infinite number of points since they correspond to groups of zero persistence.

We use the Vietoris-Rips (VR) construction denoted by VR($\mathcal{G}$, ϵ) to obtain simplicial complexes from $\mathcal{G}$ for a given scale ϵ [24]. An algorithm for computing homological persistence is provided in [25] and an efficient dual variant that uses co-homology is described in [20]. The VR construction obtains the topology of the distance function on the point cloud data. However, given a graph $\mathcal{G}$, and a function g defined on the vertices, it is also possible to quantify the topology induced by g on $\mathcal{G}$. For example, we may want to study the topology of the sub-level or super-level sets of g. This is referred to as *scalar field topology* since $g : \mathcal{V} \rightarrow \mathbb{R}$. A well-known application of this in vision is in 3D shape data, where the graph $\mathcal{G}$ corresponds to the shape mesh and g is a function, such as heat kernel signature (HKS) [60], defined on the mesh [40]. The PD of the H_0 homology group of the super-level sets now describes the evolving segments of regions in the shape. For instance, if we compute the PD of the super-level sets induced by HKS in an *octopus* shape, we can expect to see eight highly persistent segments corresponding to the eight legs. This is because the HKS values are high at regions of high curvature in the shape. In scalar field constructions, the PDs can be obtained efficiently using the Union-Find algorithm by first sorting the nodes of $\mathcal{G}$ as per their function magnitude and keeping a trail of the corresponding connected components [18].

Distance Metrics between PDs: PDs are invariant to rotations, translations and scaling of a given shape, and under continuous deformation conditions are invariant to slight permutations of the vertices [16,17]. The two classical metrics to measure distances between PDs X and Y are the *Bottleneck* distance and the *p-Wasserstein* metric [45,65]. They are appealing as they reflect any small changes such as perturbations of a measured phenomenon on the shape, which results in small shifts to the points in the persistence diagram. The *Bottleneck* distance is defined as $d_\infty(X,Y) = \inf_{\eta:X\rightarrow Y} \sup_{x\in X} \|x - \eta(x)\|_\infty$, with η ranging over all bijections and $\|.\|_\infty$ is the ∞-norm. Equivalently, the *p-Wasserstein* distance is defined as $d_p(X,Y) = (\inf_{\eta:X\rightarrow Y} \sum_{x\in X} \|x - \eta(x)\|_\infty^p)^{1/p}$. However, the complexity of computing distances between PDs with n points is $\mathcal{O}(n^3)$. These metrics also do not allow for easy computation of statistics and are unstable under large deformations [11].

Grassmann Manifold: Let n, p be two positive integers such that $n > p > 0$. The set of p-dimensional linear subspaces in $\mathbb{R}^n$ is called a Grassmann manifold, denoted by $\mathbb{G}_{p,n}$. Each point $\mathcal{Y}$ on $\mathbb{G}_{p,n}$ is represented as a basis, *i.e.* a linear combination of the set of p orthonormal vectors $Y_1, Y_2, \ldots, Y_p$. The geometric properties of the Grassmannian have been used for various computer vision applications, such as object recognition, shape analysis, human activity modeling and classification, face and video-based recognition, *etc.* [9,28,29,64]. We refer our readers to the following papers that provide a good introduction to the geometry, statistical analysis, and techniques for solving optimization problems on the Grassmann manifold [1,2,13,23,69].

Distance Metrics Between Grassmann Representations: The minimal geodesic distance ($d_\mathbb{G}$) between two points $\mathcal{Y}_1$ and $\mathcal{Y}_2$ on the Grassmann manifold is the length of the shortest constant speed curve that connects these points. To do this, the velocity matrix $A_{\mathcal{Y}_1,\mathcal{Y}_2}$ or the inverse exponential map needs to be calculated, with the geodesic path starting at $\mathcal{Y}_1$ and ending at $\mathcal{Y}_2$. $A_{\mathcal{Y}_1,\mathcal{Y}_2}$ can be computed using the numerical approximation method described in [42]. The geodesic distance between $\mathcal{Y}_1$ and $\mathcal{Y}_2$ is represented by the following equation: $d_{\mathbb{G}}(\mathcal{Y}_1, \mathcal{Y}_2) = trace(A_{\mathcal{Y}_1,\mathcal{Y}_2} {A_{\mathcal{Y}_1,\mathcal{Y}_2}}^{\mathrm{T}})$ or $d_{\mathbb{G}}(\mathcal{Y}_1, \mathcal{Y}_2) = \sqrt{trace(\theta^T\theta)}$. Here θ is the principal angle matrix between $\mathcal{Y}_1, \mathcal{Y}_2$ and can be computed as $\theta = \arccos(S)$, where $USV^T = \mathrm{svd}(\mathcal{Y}_1^T\mathcal{Y}_2)$. To show the stability of the proposed PTS representations in section 4, we use the normalized geodesic distance represented by $d_{\mathbb{NG}}(\mathcal{Y}_1, \mathcal{Y}_2) = \frac{1}{D} d_{\mathbb{G}}(\mathcal{Y}_1, \mathcal{Y}_2)$, where D is the maximum possible geodesic distance on $\mathbb{G}_{p,n}$ [33,39]. The symmetric directional distance (d_Δ) is another popular metric to compute distances between Grassmann representations with different p [61,67]. It is a widely used measure in areas like computer vision [7,8,43,56,70], communications [55], and applied mathematics [22]. It is equivalent to the chordal metric [71] and is defined as, $d_\Delta(\mathcal{Y}_1, \mathcal{Y}_2) = \left(\max(k,l) - \sum_{i,j=1}^{k,l} ({y_{1,i}}^{\mathrm{T}} y_{2,j})^2\right)^{\frac{1}{2}}$. Here, k and l are subspace dimensions for the orthonormal matrices $\mathcal{Y}_1$ and $\mathcal{Y}_2$ respectively. For all our experiments, we restrict ourselves to distance computations between same-dimension subspaces, *i.e.* $k = l$. The following papers propose methods to compute distances between subspaces of different dimensions [61,67,71].

3 Prior Art

PDs provide a compact multi-scale summary of the different topological features. The traditional metrics used to measure the distance between PDs are the *Bottleneck* and *p-Wasserstein* metrics [45,65]. These measures are stable with respect to small continuous deformations of the topology of the inputs [16,17]. However, they do poorly under large deformations. Further, a feature vector representation will be useful that is compatible with different ML tools that demand more than just a metric. To address this need, researchers have resorted to transforming PDs to other suitable representations [3,5,12,48,51,52]. Bubenik proposed persistence landscapes (PL) which are stable and invertible functional representations of PDs in a Banach space [12]. A PL is a sequence of envelope functions defined on the points in PDs that are ordered on the basis of their importance. Bubenik's main motivation for defining PLs was to derive a unique mean representation for a set of PDs which is not necessarily obtained using Fréchet means [45]. Their usefulness is however limited, as PLs can provide low importance to moderate size homological features that generally possess high discriminating power.

Rouse *et al.* create a simple vector representation by overlaying a grid on top of the PD and count the number of points that fall into each bin [52]. This method is unstable, since a small shift in the points can result in a different feature representation. This idea has also appeared in other forms, some of which are described below. Pachauri *et al.* transform PDs into smooth surfaces by fitting Gaussians centered at each point in the PD [48]. Reininghaus *et al.* create stable representations by taking a weighted sum of positive Gaussians at each point above the diagonal and mirror the same below the diagonal but with negative Gaussians [51]. Adams *et al.* design persistence images (PI) by defining a regular grid and obtaining the integral of the Gaussian-surface representation over the bins defined on each grid [3]. Both PIs and the multi-scale kernel defined by Reininghaus *et al.* show stability with respect to the Wasserstein metrics and do well under small perturbations of the input data. They also weight the points using a weighting function, and this can be chosen based on the problem. Prioritizing points with medium lifetimes was used by Bendich *et al.* to best identify the age of a human brain by studying its arterial geometry [10]. Cohen-Steiner *et al.* suggested prioritizing points near the death-axis and away from the diagonal [16].

In this paper, we propose a unique perturbation framework that overcomes the need for selecting a weighting function. We consider a range of topological noise realizations one could expect to see, by perturbing the points in the PD. We summarize the perturbed PDs by creating smooth surfaces from them and consider a subspace of these surfaces, which naturally becomes a point on the Grassmann manifold. We show the effectiveness of our features in Sect. 5 for different problems using data collected from different sensing devices. Compared to the *p-Wasserstein* and *Bottleneck* distances, the metrics defined on the Grassmannian are computationally less complex and the representations are independent of the number of points present in the PD. The proposed PTS representation is motivated from [28], where the authors create a subspace representation of blurred faces and perform face recognition on the Grassmannian. Our framework also bears some similarities to [5], where the authors use the square root representation of PDFs obtained from PDs.

4 Perturbed Topological Signatures

In this section we go through details of each step in our framework's pipeline, illustrated in Fig. 1. In our experiments we transform the axes of the PD from $(b, d) \rightarrow (\frac{b+d}{2}, d-b)$, with $b \leq d$.

Create a set of Perturbed PDs: We randomly perturb a given PD to create m PDs. Each of the perturbed PDs has its points randomly displaced by a certain amount compared to the original. The set of randomly perturbed PDs retain the same topological information of the input data as the original PD, but together capture all the probable variations of the input data when subjected to topological noise. We constrain the extent of perturbation of the individual points in the PD to ensure that the topological structure of the data being analyzed is not abruptly changed.

Convert Perturbed PDs to 2D PDFs: We transform the initial PD and its set of perturbed PDs to a set of 2D PDFs. We do this via kernel density estimation: by fitting a Gaussian kernel function with zero mean, standard deviation σ at each point in the PD, and then normalizing the 2D surface.

The obtained PDF surface is discretized over a $k \times k$ grid similar to the approach of Rouse *et al.* [52]. The standard deviation σ (also known as bandwidth parameter) of the Gaussian is not known a priori and is fine-tuned to get best results. A multi-scale approach can also be employed by generating multiple surfaces using a range of different bandwidth parameters for each of the PDs and still obtain favorable results. Unlike other topological descriptors that use a weighting function over their functional representations of PDs [3,51], we give equal importance to each point in the PD and do not resort to any weighting function. Adams *et al.* prove the stability of persistence surfaces obtained using general and Gaussian distributions (ϕ), together with a weighting function (f), with respect to the 1-*Wasserstein* distance between PDs in [3, Thm. 4, 9]. For Gaussian distributions, both L_1 and L_∞ distances between persistence surfaces $\rho_B, \rho_{B'}$ are stable with respect to 1-*Wasserstein* distance between PDs B, B', $\|\rho_B - \rho_{B'}\|_1 \leq \sqrt{\frac{10}{\pi}}\ \frac{1}{\sigma}\ d_1(B, B')$.

Projecting 2D PDFs to the Grassmannian: Let $\rho(x, y)$ be an unperturbed persistence surface, and let $\rho(x+u, y+v)$ be a randomly shifted perturbation. Under assumptions of small perturbations, we have using Taylor's theorem:

$$\rho(x+u, y+v) - \rho(x, y) \approx [\rho_x, \rho_y][u, v]^T \tag{1}$$

Now, in the following, we interpret $\approx$ as an equality, enabling us to stack together the same equation for all (x, y), to get a matrix-vector form $\overline{\rho}_{pert}^{u,v} - \overline{\rho} = [\overline{\rho}_x, \overline{\rho}_y]_{N\times 2}[u, v]^T_{2\times 1}$, where the overline indicates a discrete vectorization of the 2D functions. Here, N is the total number of discretized samples from the (x, y) plane. Now consider the set of all small perturbations of ρ, i.e. $span(\overline{\rho}_{pert}^{u,v} - \overline{\rho})$, over all $[u, v] \in \mathbb{R}^2$. It is easy to see that this set is just a 2D linear-subspace in $\mathbb{R}^N$ which coincides with the column-span of $[\overline{\rho}_x, \overline{\rho}_y]$. For a more general affine-perturbation model, we can show that the required subspace corresponds to a 6-dimensional (6D) linear subspace, corresponding to the column-span of the $N \times 6$ matrix $[\rho_x, \rho_y, x\rho_x, x\rho_y, y\rho_x, y\rho_y]$. More details on this can be found in the supplement. In implementation, we perturb a given PD several times using random offsets, compute their persistence surfaces, use singular value decomposition (SVD) on the stacked matrix of perturbations, then select the p largest left singular vectors, resulting in a $N \times p$ orthonormal matrix. Also, we vary the dimension of the subspace across a range of values. Since the linear span of our matrix can be further identified as a point on the Grassmann manifold, we adopt metrics defined over the Grassmannian to compare our perturbed topological signatures.

Stability of Grassmannian metrics w.r.t. Wasserstein: The next natural question to consider is whether the metrics over the Grassmannian for the perturbed stack are in any way related to the Wasserstein metric over the original PDs. Let the column span of $X = [\overline{\rho}_x, \overline{\rho}_y]$ be represented by $\mathcal{X}(\rho)$. Let ρ_1, ρ_2 be two persistence surfaces, then $\mathcal{X}(\rho_1), \mathcal{X}(\rho_2)$ are the subspaces spanned by $X_1 = [\overline{\rho}_{1,x}, \overline{\rho}_{1,y}]$ and $X_2 = [\overline{\rho}_{2,x}, \overline{\rho}_{2,y}]$ respectively. Following a result due to Ji-Guang [33], the normalized geodesic distance $d_{\mathbb{NG}}$ between $\mathcal{X}_1$ and $\mathcal{X}_2$ is upper bounded as follows: $d_{\mathbb{NG}}(\mathcal{X}_1, \mathcal{X}_2) \leq \|X_1\|_F . \|X_1^\dagger\|_2 . \frac{\|\Delta X\|_F}{\|X_1\|_F} = \|X_1^\dagger\|_2 . \|\Delta X\|_F$. Here, $\|X^\dagger\|_2$ is the spectral norm of the pseudo-inverse of X, $\|X\|_F$ is the Frobenius norm, and $\Delta X = X_1 - X_2$. In the supplement, a full derivation is given, showing $\|\Delta X\|_F^2 \leq \frac{10}{\pi} \frac{2}{\sigma^6} d_1^2(B_1, B_2) + 2\frac{\mathcal{K}^2}{\sigma^4} k_{max}^2 N$, where $d_1(B_1, B_2)$ is the 1-*Wasserstein* metric between the original unperturbed PDs, k_{max} is the maximum number of points in a given PD (a dataset dependent quantity), N refers to the total number of discrete samples from $[0,1]^2$ and $\mathcal{K} = \frac{1}{(\sqrt{2\pi}\sigma)^2}$. This is the critical part of the stability proof. The remaining part requires us to upper bound the spectral norm $\|X^\dagger\|_2$. The spectral-norm of the pseudo-inverse of X, i.e. $\|X^\dagger\|_2$, is simply the inverse of the smallest singular-value of X, which in turn corresponds to the square-root of the smallest eigenvalue of $X^T X$. i.e. $\|X^\dagger\|_2 = \sigma_{max}(X^\dagger) = \frac{1}{\sigma_{min}(X)} = \frac{1}{\sqrt{\lambda_{min}(X^T X)}}$.

Given that $X = [\overline{\rho}_x, \overline{\rho}_y]$, $X^T X$ becomes the 2D structure-tensor of a Gaussian mixture model (GMM). While we are not aware of any results that lower-bound the eigenvalues of a 2D GMMs structure-tensor, in the supplement we show an approach for 1D GMMs that indicates that the smallest eigenvalue can indeed be lower-bounded, if the standard-deviation σ is upper-bounded. For example, a non-trivial lower-bound is derived for $\sigma < 1$ in the supplement. It is inversely proportional to the number of components in the GMM. We used $\sigma = 0.0004$ for all our experiments. The approach in the supplement is shown for 1D GMMs, and we posit that a similar approach applies for the 2D case, but it is cumbersome. In empirical tests, we find that even for 2D GMMs defined over the grid $[0,1]^2$, with $0 < \sigma < 1$, the spectral-norms are always upper-bounded. In general, we find $\|X^\dagger\|_2 \leq k/\sqrt{g(\sigma)}$, where $g(\sigma)$ is a positive monotonically decreasing function of σ in the domain $[0,1]$, and k is the number of components in the GMM (points in a given PD). If we denote k_{max} and σ_{max} as the maximum allowable number of components in the GMM (max points in any PD in given database) and the maximum standard deviation respectively, an upper bound readily develops. Thus, we have

$$d_{\mathbb{NG}}(\mathcal{X}_1, \mathcal{X}_2) \leq \frac{k_{max}}{\sqrt{g(\sigma_{max})}} \sqrt{\frac{10}{\pi} \frac{2}{\sigma^6} d_1^2(B_1, B_2) + 2\frac{\mathcal{K}^2}{\sigma^4} k_{max}^2 N} \tag{2}$$

Please refer to the supplement for detailed derivation and explanation of the various constants in the above bound. We note that even though the above shows that the normalized Grassmannian geodesic distance over the perturbed topological signatures is stable w.r.t the 1-*Wasserstein* metric over PDs, it still relies on knowledge of the maximum number of points in any given PD across the entire dataset k_{max}, and also on the sampling of the 2D grid.

5 Experiments

In this section we first show the robustness of the PTS descriptor to different levels of topological noise using a sample of shapes from the SHREC 2010 dataset [41]. We then test the proposed framework on three publicly available datasets: SHREC 2010 shape retrieval dataset [41], IXMAS multi-view video action dataset [68] and motion capture dataset [4]. We briefly go over the details of each dataset, and describe the experimental objectives and procedures followed. Finally, we show the computational benefits of comparing different PTS representations using the $d_{\mathbb{G}}$ and d_{Δ} metrics, over the classical *p-Wasserstein* and *Bottleneck* metrics used between PDs.

5.1 Robustness to Topological Noise

We conduct this experiment on 10 randomly chosen shapes from the SHREC 2010 dataset [41]. The dataset consists of 200 near-isometric watertight 3D shapes with articulating parts, equally divided into 10 classes. Each 3D mesh is simplified to 2000 faces. The 10 shapes used in the experiment are denoted as S_i,

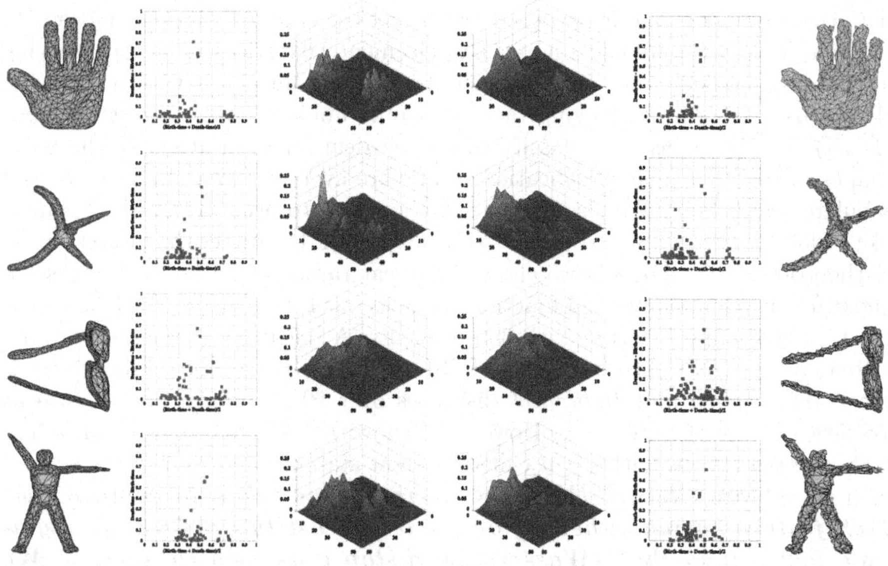

Fig. 2. Illustration of PD and PTS representations for 4 shapes and their noisy variants. Columns 1 and 6 represent the 3D shape with triangular mesh faces; columns 2 and 5 show the corresponding 9th dimension SIHKS function-based PDs. columns 3 and 4 depict the PTS feature of the PD for the original and noisy shapes respectively. A zero mean Gaussian noise with standard deviation 1.0 is applied on the original shapes in column 1 to get the corresponding noisy variant in column 6. The PTS representation shown is the largest left singular vector (reshaped to a 2D matrix) obtained after applying SVD on the set of 2D PDFs and lies on the $\mathbb{G}_{1,n}$ space.

$i = 1, 2, \ldots, 10$. The minimum bounding sphere for each of these shapes has a mean radius of 54.4 with standard deviation of 3.7 centered at (64.4, 63.4, 66.0) with coordinate-wise standard deviations of (3.9, 4.1, 4.9) respectively. Next, we generate 100 sets of shapes, infused with topological noise. Topological noise is applied by changing the position of the vertices of the triangular mesh face, which results in changing its normal. We do this by applying a zero-mean Gaussian noise to the vertices of the original shape, with the standard deviation σ varied from 0.1 to 1 in steps of 0.1. For each shape $\mathcal{S}_i$, its 10 noisy shapes with different levels of topological noise are denoted by $\mathcal{N}_{i,1}, \ldots, \mathcal{N}_{i,10}$.

Fig. 3. Sample SHREC 2010 shapes used to test robustness of PTS feature to topological noise.

A 17-dimensional scale-invariant heat kernel signature (SIHKS) spectral descriptor function is calculated on each shape [36], and PDs are extracted for each dimension of this function resulting in 17 PDs per shape. The PDs are passed through the proposed framework to get the respective PTS descriptors. The 3D mesh, PD and PTS representation for 4 of the 10 shapes (shown in Fig. 3) and their respective noisy-variants (Gaussian noise with standard deviation 1.0) is shown in Fig. 2. In this experiment, we evaluate the robustness of our proposed feature by correctly classifying shapes with different levels of topological noise. Displacement of vertices by adding varying levels of topological noise, interclass similarities and intraclass variations of the shapes make this a challenging task. A simple unbiased one nearest neighbor (1-NN) classifier is used to classify the topological representations of the noisy shapes in each set. The classification results are averaged over the 100 sets and tabulated in Table 1. We also compare our method to other TDA-ML methods like PI [3], PL [12], PSSK [51] and PWGK [38]. For PTS, we set the discretization of the grid $k = 50$. For PIs we chose the linear ramp weighting function, set k and σ for the Gaussian kernel function, same as our PTS feature. For PLs we use the first landscape function with 500 elements. A linear SVM classifier is used instead of the 1-NN classifier for the PSSK and PWGK methods. From Table 1, the 2-*Wasserstein* and *Bottleneck* distances over PDs perform poorly even at low levels of topological noise. However, PDs with 1-*Wasserstein* distance and PTS representations with $d_{\mathbb{G}}$, d_{Δ} metrics show stability and robustness to even high noise levels. ***Nevertheless, the average time taken to compare two PTS features using either $d_{\mathbb{G}}$ or d_{Δ} is at least two orders of magnitude faster than the 1-Wasserstein distance as seen in Table 1. We also observe that comparison of PIs, PLs and PWGK is an order of magnitude faster than comparing PTS features. However, these methods show significantly lower performance compared to the proposed feature, at correctly classifying noisy shapes as the noise level increases.***

Table 1. Comparison of 1-*Wasserstein*, 2-*Wasserstein*, *Bottleneck*, d_Δ and $d_\mathbb{G}$ methods for correctly classifying the topological representations of noisy shapes to their original shape.

Method	$\mathcal{N}_{i,1}$	$\mathcal{N}_{i,2}$	$\mathcal{N}_{i,3}$	$\mathcal{N}_{i,4}$	$\mathcal{N}_{i,5}$	$\mathcal{N}_{i,6}$	$\mathcal{N}_{i,7}$	$\mathcal{N}_{i,8}$	$\mathcal{N}_{i,9}$	$\mathcal{N}_{i,10}$	Average Accuracy (%)	Average Time Taken (10^{-4} sec)
PD (1-*Wasserstein*)	100.00	100.00	100.00	99.90	100.00	99.80	99.60	99.00	96.60	94.40	98.93	256.00
PD (2-*Wasserstein*)	97.50	98.00	98.10	97.20	97.20	96.00	94.40	92.80	90.30	88.50	95.00	450.00
PD (*Bottleneck*)	99.90	99.90	99.90	99.20	99.40	98.60	97.10	96.90	94.30	92.70	97.79	36.00
PI (L_1)	100.00	100.00	100.00	99.70	98.10	93.70	83.20	68.30	56.00	44.90	84.39	0.31
PI (L_2)	99.90	99.50	98.60	97.40	93.10	88.50	82.90	69.70	59.40	49.90	83.89	0.26
PI (L_∞)	89.10	83.00	80.20	78.90	78.40	69.90	68.60	64.00	61.90	56.80	73.08	0.12
PL (L_1)	99.20	99.70	99.00	98.50	98.50	97.30	95.90	92.30	89.10	84.50	95.40	0.74
PL (L_2)	99.10	99.70	98.90	98.50	98.30	96.90	95.60	92.10	89.00	84.30	95.24	0.76
PL (L_∞)	98.90	99.60	98.80	98.40	98.30	96.50	94.80	91.70	88.70	83.80	94.95	0.09
PSSK - SVM	100.00	100.00	100.00	100.00	100.00	100.00	91.60	90.00	89.80	89.00	96.04	4.55
PWGK - SVM	100.00	100.00	100.00	100.00	100.00	99.90	99.40	95.90	87.50	73.30	95.60	0.17
PTS ($d_\mathbb{G}$)	100.00	100.00	100.00	100.00	100.00	99.90	99.80	98.80	96.80	93.60	**98.89**	**2.30**
PTS (d_Δ)	100.00	100.00	100.00	100.00	100.00	99.90	99.90	99.30	97.10	94.10	**99.03**	**1.60**

5.2 3D Shape Retrieval

In this experiment, we consider all 10 classes consisting of 200 shapes from the SHREC 2010 dataset, and extract PDs using 3 different spectral descriptor functions defined on each shape, namely: heat kernel signature (HKS) [60], wave kernel signature (WKS) [6], and SIHKS [36]. HKS and WKS are used to capture the microscopic and macroscopic properties of the 3D mesh surface, while SIHKS descriptor is the scale-invariant version of HKS.

Using the PTS descriptor we attempt to encode invariances to shape articulations such as rotation, stretching, skewing. For the task of 3D shape retrieval we use a 1-NN classifier to evaluate the performance of the PTS representation against other methods [3,12,38,40,51]. A linear SVM classifier is used to report the classification accuracy of the PSSK and PWGK methods. Li *et al.* report best results after carefully selecting weights to normalize the distance combinations of their BoF+PD and ISPM+PD methods. As in [40], we also use the three spectral descriptors and combine our PTS representations for each descriptor. PIs, PLs and PTS features are also designed the same way as described before. The results reported in Table 2 show that the PTS feature (with subspace dimension $p = 1$) alone using the d_Δ metric achieves an accuracy of 99.50 %, outperforming other methods. The average classification result of the PTS feature on varying the subspace dimension $p = 1, 2, \dots, 25$ is 98.42±0.4 % and 98.72±0.25 % using d_Δ and $d_\mathbb{G}$ metrics respectively, thus displaying its stability with respect to the choice of p.

Table 2. Comparison of the classification performance of the proposed PTS descriptor with other baseline methods [40] on the SHREC 2010 dataset.

Method	BoF [40]	SSBoF [40]	ISPM [40]	PD (*Bottleneck*) [40]	PD (1-*Wasserstein*)	PD (2-*Wasserstein*)	BoF +PD [40]	ISPM +PD [40]	PI (L_1) [3]	PI (L_2) [3]	PI (L_∞) [3]	PL (L_1) [12]	PL (L_2) [12]	PL (L_∞) [12]	PSSK (SVM) [51]	PWGK (SVM) [38]	**PTS** (d_G)	PTS (d_Δ)
1-NN Accuracy (%)	97.00	97.50	97.50	98.50	98.50	98.50	98.50	99.00	88.50	87.50	89.50	95.00	95.00	95.00	98.50	99.00	**99.00**	**99.50**

5.3 View-Invariant Activity Analysis

The IXMAS dataset contains video and silhouette sequences of 11 action classes, performed 3 times by 10 subjects from five different camera views. The 11 classes are as follows - *check watch, cross arms, scratch head, sit down, get up, turn around, walk, wave, punch, kick, pick up.* Sample frames across 5 views for 2 actions are shown in Fig. 4. We consider only the silhouette information in the dataset for our PTS representations. For each frame in an action sequence we extract multi-scale shape distributions which are referred to as A3M, D1M, D2M and D3M, over the 2D silhouettes [58]. The multi-scale shape distribution feature captures the local to global changes in different geometric properties of a shape. For additional details about this feature, please see: [47,58,59].

For n frames in an action sequence and b bins in each shape distribution at a certain scale, an $n \times b$ matrix representing the action is obtained. Treating the n frames as nodes, scalar field topological PDs are calculated across each column, resulting in b PDs. PDs capture the structural changes along each bin in the distributions. We select 5 different scales for the multi-scale shape features, giving us $5b$ PDs per action which are passed through the proposed pipeline resulting in $5b$ PTS features. PTS features try to encode the possible changes with respect to view-point variation, body-type and execution style. To represent the entire action as a point on the Grassmannian, we select the first two largest singular vectors from each of the $5b$ PTS descriptors, apply SVD and choose 20 largest components.

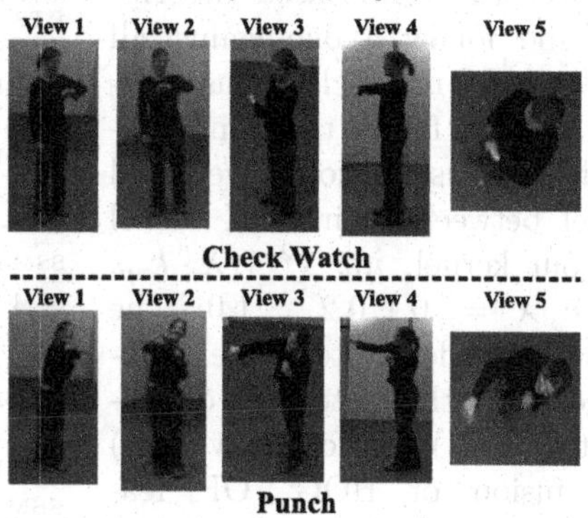

Fig. 4. Sample frames for "check watch" and "punch" action sequences from five views in the IXMAS dataset.

To perform multi-view action recognition, we train non-linear SVMs using the Grassmannian RBF kernel, $k_{rp}(\mathcal{X}_i, \mathcal{Y}_i) = \exp\Big(-\beta\|\mathcal{X}_i{}^{\mathrm{T}}\mathcal{Y}_i\|_F^2\Big)$, $\beta > 0$ [30]. Here, $\mathcal{X}_i$, $\mathcal{Y}_i$ are points on the Grassmannian and $\|.\|_F$ is the Frobenius norm. We set $\beta = 1$ in our implementations. Junejo *et al.* train non-linear SVMs using the χ^2 kernel over the SSM-based descriptors and follow a one-against-all approach for multi-class classification [34]. We follow the same approach and use a joint weighted kernel between their SSM kernel and our kernel, *i.e.* $\chi^2 + \lambda \cdot k_{rp}$, where $\lambda = 0.1, 0.2, \ldots 1.0$. The SSM-based descriptors are computed using the histogram of gradients (HOG), optical flow (OF) and fusion of HOG, OF features. The classification results are tabulated in Table 3. Apart from reporting results of PTS representations obtained using the multi-scale shape distributions, we also show recognition results of PTS feature computed over the HOG descriptor (PTS-HOG). We see significant improvement in the results by fusing different PTS features with the SSM-based descriptor. We also tabulate the mean and standard deviation values for all classification results obtained after varying λ from 0.1 to 1.0 and subspace dimension p from 1 to 10. These results demonstrate the flexibility and stability associated with the proposed PTS topological descriptor.

Table 3. Comparison of the recognition results on the IXMAS dataset. Results are presented for two combinations of train camera X and test camera Y. "Same Camera" denotes $X{=}Y$; "Any-To-Any" implies any combination of X, Y.

Method	Same Camera Accuracy (%)		Any-To-Any Accuracy (%)	
	Best	Mean±SD	Best	Mean±SD
SSM-HOG [34]	67.30	-	52.60	-
PTS-HOG	51.31	-	41.24	-
SSM-HOG + PTS-HOG	69.01	-	55.13	-
SSM-HOG + PTS-A3M	73.15	72.06±1.14	58.36	56.96±1.05
SSM-HOG + PTS-D1M	74.25	73.26±1.53	59.26	57.67±1.19
SSM-HOG + PTS-D2M	74.92	74.22±1.36	59.77	58.19±1.03
SSM-HOG + PTS-D3M	**76.18**	73.72±1.13	**60.33**	58.72±1.11
SSM-OF [34]	66.60	-	53.80	-
SSM-OF + PTS-A3M	72.02	70.25±1.06	58.85	57.48±0.93
SSM-OF + PTS-D1M	73.67	71.62±1.17	59.56	57.81±1.05
SSM-OF + PTS-D2M	73.45	72.53±1.12	60.60	59.05±1.11
SSM-OF + PTS-D3M	**74.41**	72.21±1.03	**61.51**	59.33±1.13
SSM-HOG-OF [34]	76.28	-	61.25	-
SSM-HOG-OF + PTS-A3M	79.30	78.05±0.71	64.93	63.58±0.65
SSM-HOG-OF + PTS-D1M	79.61	79.03±0.96	65.39	64.27±0.65
SSM-HOG-OF + PTS-D2M	79.86	79.35±0.76	65.70	64.62±0.83
SSM-HOG-OF + PTS-D3M	**81.12**	79.49±0.99	**66.16**	64.99±0.79

5.4 Dynamical Analysis on Motion Capture Data

This dataset consists of human body joint motion capture sequences in 3D, where each sequence contains 57 trajectories (19 joint trajectories along 3 axes). There are 5 action classes - *dance, jump, run, sit and walk*, with each class containing 31, 14, 30, 35 and 48 sequences respectively. H_1 homology group PDs are computed over the reconstructed attractor for each trajectory, resulting in 57 PDs per action [5] and the corresponding PTS feature is also extracted. We report the average classification performance over 100 random splits, with each split having 25 random test samples (5 samples from each class) and remaining 133 training samples. For SVM classification, we train non-linear SVMs using the projection kernel, $k_p(\mathcal{X}_i, \mathcal{Y}_i) = \|\mathcal{X}_i{}^{\mathrm{T}}\mathcal{Y}_i\|_F^2$ [29].

Table 4. Comparison of classification performance and the average time taken to compare two feature representations on the motion capture dataset.

Method	Accuracy (%)	Average Time Taken (10^{-4} sec)
PD (1-Wasserstein) NN [73]	93.68	22.00
Hilbert Sphere NN [5]	89.87	590.00
Hilbert Sphere PGA+SVM [5]	91.68	-
PTS (d_Δ) - NN	85.96	0.19
PTS - SVM	91.92	-

The results are tabulated in Table 4. PTS features have a classification accuracy of 85.96 % and 91.92 % using the 1-NN and SVM classifier respectively. While these results are slightly lower than the 1-*Wasserstein* metric, the proposed descriptor with the d_Δ metric is more than 2 orders of magnitude faster. Topological properties of dynamic attractors for analysis of time-series data has been studied and applied to tasks such as wheeze detection [27], pulse pressure wave analysis [26] and such applications are surveyed in [37]. We ask our readers to refer to these papers for further exploration.

Table 5. Comparison of the average time taken to measure distance between two PDs using the 1-Wasserstein, 2-Wasserstein and Bottleneck metrics, and between two PTS features using $d_{\mathbb{G}}$ and d_Δ metrics. The time reported is averaged over 3000 distance calculations between the respective topological representations for all three datasets used in Sect. 5.

Dataset	Average Number of Points in PD	Average Time Taken (10^{-4} sec)					Subspace Dimension (p) of PTS Feature
		1-Wasserstein	2-Wasserstein	Bottleneck	$d_{\mathbb{G}}$	d_Δ	
SHREC 2010 [41]	71	256.00 (Kerber *et al.* [35]: 219.00)	450.00 (Kerber *et al.* [35]: 237.00)	36.00 (Kerber *et al.* [35]: 295.00)	**2.30**	**1.60**	10
IXMAS [68]	23	16.00	16.00	3.43	**2.21**	**0.68**	20
Motion Capture [4]	27	22.00	22.00	2.72	**0.24**	**0.19**	1

5.5 Time-Complexity of Comparing Topological Representations

All experiments are carried out on a standard Intel i7 CPU using Matlab 2016b with a working memory of 32 GB. We used the Hungarian algorithm to compute the *Bottleneck* and *p-Wasserstein* distances between PDs. Kerber *et al.* take advantage of the geometric structure of the input graph and propose geometric variants of the above metrics, thereby showing significant improvements in runtime performance when comparing PDs having several thousand points [35]. However, extracting PDs for most real datasets of interest in this paper does not result in more than a few hundred points. For example, on average we observe 71, 23, 27 points in each PD for the SHREC 2010, IXMAS and motion capture datasets respectively. The Hungarian algorithm incurs similar computations in this setting as shown in Table 5. The $d_{\mathbb{G}}$ and d_{Δ} metrics used to compare different PTS representations (grid size $k = 50$) are fast and computationally less complex compared to the *Bottleneck* and *p-Wasserstein* distance measures. The average time taken to compare two topological signatures (PD or PTS) for each of the datasets is tabulated in Table 5. The table also shows the average number of points seen per PD and the subspace dimension p used for the PTS representation.

Table 6 shows the variation of the average time taken to compare PTS features on varying the grid size (k) of the 2D PDF. Here too the average time is reported after averaging over 3000 distance calculations between PTS features computed from PDs of the SHREC 2010 dataset. We observe that the time taken to compare two PTS features with a grid size $k = 500$ is two orders of magnitude greater than the time obtained for PTS features using $k = 5$. However, these times are still smaller than or on par with the times reported using *p-Wasserstein* and *Bottleneck* distances between PDs as seen in Table 5. For all our experiments we set $k = 50$ for our PTS representations and as shown in Table 5, the times reported for d_{Δ} and $d_{\mathbb{G}}$ are at least an order of magnitude faster than *Bottleneck* distance and two orders of magnitude faster than the *p-Wasserstein* metrics.

Table 6. Comparison of the average time taken to measure distance between two PTS features using $d_{\mathbb{G}}$ and d_{Δ} metrics w.r.t. variation in grid size k. The time reported is averaged over 3000 distance calculations between the topological representations for the SHREC 2010 dataset.

Grid size (k)	Average Time Taken (10^{-4} sec)										
	5	10	20	40	60	80	100	200	300	400	500
PTS ($d_{\mathbb{G}}$)	0.72	0.73	0.89	1.31	1.48	2.28	5.53	8.35	18.40	32.88	47.07
PTS (d_{Δ})	0.20	0.33	0.84	0.72	1.00	1.85	4.32	7.70	17.69	31.56	46.68

6 Conclusion and Discussion

We believe that a perturbed realization of a PD computed over a high-dimensional shape/graph is robust to topological noise affecting the original shape. Based on the type of data and application, topological noise can imply different types of variations, such as: articulation in 3D shape point cloud data; diversity in body structure, execution style and view-point pertaining to human actions in video analysis, *etc.* In this paper, we propose a novel topological representations called PTS that is obtained using a perturbation approach, taking first steps towards robust invariant learning with topological features. We obtained perturbed persistence surfaces and summarized them as a point on the Grassmann manifold, in order to utilize the different distance metrics and Mercer kernels defined for the Grassmannian. The $d_{\mathbb{G}}$ and d_{Δ} metrics used to compare different Grassmann representations are computationally cheap as they do not depend on the number of points present in the PD, in contrast to *Bottleneck* and *p-Wasserstein* metrics, which do. The PTS feature offers flexibility in choosing the weighting function, kernel function and perturbation level. This makes it easily adaptable to different types of real-world data. It can also be easily integrated with various ML tools, which is not easily achievable with PDs. Future directions include fusion with contemporary deep-learning architectures to exploit the complementarity of both paradigms. We expect that topological methods will push the state-of-the-art in invariant representations, where the requisite invariance is incorporated using a topological property of an appropriately redefined metric space. Additionally, the proposed methods may help open new feature-pooling options in deep-nets.

Acknowledgments. This work was supported in part by ARO grant number W911NF-17-1-0293 and NSF CAREER award 1452163.

References

1. Absil, P.A., Mahony, R., Sepulchre, R.: Riemannian geometry of grassmann manifolds with a view on algorithmic computation. Acta Applicandae Mathematica **80**(2), 199–220 (2004)
2. Absil, P.A., Mahony, R., Sepulchre, R.: Optimization Algorithms on Matrix Manifolds. Princeton University Press, Princeton (2009)
3. Adams, H., et al.: Persistence images: a stable vector representation of persistent homology. J. Mach. Learn. Res. **18**(8), 1–35 (2017)
4. Ali, S., Basharat, A., Shah, M.: Chaotic invariants for human action recognition. In: IEEE 11th International Conference on Computer Vision (ICCV), pp. 1–8 (2007)
5. Anirudh, R., Venkataraman, V., Natesan Ramamurthy, K., Turaga, P.: A Riemannian framework for statistical analysis of topological persistence diagrams. In: The IEEE Conference on Computer Vision and Pattern Recognition Workshops, pp. 68–76 (2016)
6. Aubry, M., Schlickewei, U., Cremers, D.: The wave kernel signature: a quantum mechanical approach to shape analysis. In: IEEE International Conference on Computer Vision Workshops (ICCV Workshops), pp. 1626–1633 (2011)
7. Bagherinia, H., Manduchi, R.: A theory of color barcodes. In: IEEE International Conference on Computer Vision Workshops (ICCV Workshops), pp. 806–813 (2011)
8. Basri, R., Hassner, T., Zelnik-Manor, L.: Approximate nearest subspace search. IEEE Trans. Pattern Anal. Mach. Intell. **33**(2), 266–278 (2011)
9. Begelfor, E., Werman, M.: Affine invariance revisited. In: IEEE Conference on Computer Vision and Pattern Recognition (CVPR), vol. 2, pp. 2087–2094. IEEE (2006)

10. Bendich, P., Marron, J.S., Miller, E., Pieloch, A., Skwerer, S.: Persistent homology analysis of brain artery trees. Ann. Appl. Stat. **10**(1), 198–218 (2016)
11. Bertsekas, D.P.: A new algorithm for the assignment problem. Math. Program. **21**(1), 152–171 (1981)
12. Bubenik, P.: Statistical topological data analysis using persistence landscapes. J. Mach. Learn. Res. **16**(1), 77–102 (2015)
13. Chikuse, Y.: Statistics on Special Manifolds, vol. 174. Springer Science & Business, New York (2012)
14. Chintakunta, H., Gentimis, T., Gonzalez-Diaz, R., Jimenez, M.J., Krim, H.: An entropy-based persistence barcode. Pattern Recogn. **48**(2), 391–401 (2015)
15. Chung, M.K., Bubenik, P., Kim, P.T.: Persistence diagrams of cortical surface data. In: Prince, J.L., Pham, D.L., Myers, K.J. (eds.) IPMI 2009. LNCS, vol. 5636, pp. 386–397. Springer, Heidelberg (2009). https://doi.org/10.1007/978-3-642-02498-6_32
16. Cohen-Steiner, D., Edelsbrunner, H., Harer, J.: Stability of persistence diagrams. Discret. Comput. Geom. **37**(1), 103–120 (2007)
17. Cohen-Steiner, D., Edelsbrunner, H., Harer, J., Mileyko, Y.: Lipschitz functions have Lp-stable persistence. Found. Comput. Math. **10**(2), 127–139 (2010)
18. Cormen, T.H., Leiserson, C.E., Rivest, R.L., Stein, C.: Introduction to Algorithms, 2nd edn. The MIT Press (2001)
19. Dabaghian, Y., Mémoli, F., Frank, L., Carlsson, G.: A topological paradigm for hippocampal spatial map formation using persistent homology. PLoS Computa. Biol. **8**(8), 1–14 (2012)
20. De Silva, V., Morozov, D., Vejdemo-Johansson, M.: Dualities in persistent (co) homology. Inverse Probl. **27**(12), 124003 (2011)
21. Dey, T.K., Mandal, S., Varcho, W.: Improved image classification using topological persistence. In: Hullin, M., Klein, R., Schultz, T., Yao, A. (eds.) Vision, Modeling & Visualization. The Eurographics Association (2017). https://doi.org/10.2312/vmv.20171272
22. Draper, B., Kirby, M., Marks, J., Marrinan, T., Peterson, C.: A flag representation for finite collections of subspaces of mixed dimensions. Linear Algebr. Appl. **451**, 15–32 (2014)
23. Edelman, A., Arias, T.A., Smith, S.T.: The geometry of algorithms with orthogonality constraints. SIAM J. Matrix Anal. Appl. **20**(2), 303–353 (1998)
24. Edelsbrunner, H., Harer, J.: Computational Topology: An Introduction. American Mathematical Society (2010)
25. Edelsbrunner, H., Letscher, D., Zomorodian, A.: Topological persistence and simplification. Discret. Comput. Geom. **28**(4), 511–533 (2002)
26. Emrani, S., Gentimis, T., Krim, H.: Persistent homology of delay embeddings and its application to wheeze detection. IEEE Signal Process. Lett. **21**(4), 459–463 (2014). https://doi.org/10.1109/LSP.2014.2305700
27. Emrani, S., Saponas, T.S., Morris, D., Krim, H.: A novel framework for pulse pressure wave analysis using persistent homology. IEEE Signal Process. Lett. **22**(11), 1879–1883 (2015). https://doi.org/10.1109/LSP.2015.2441068
28. Gopalan, R., Taheri, S., Turaga, P., Chellappa, R.: A blur-robust descriptor with applications to face recognition. IEEE Trans. Pattern Anal. Mach. Intell. **34**(6), 1220–1226 (2012)
29. Hamm, J., Lee, D.D.: Grassmann discriminant analysis: a unifying view on subspace-based learning. In: Proceedings of the International Conference on Machine Learning (ICML), pp. 376–383. ACM (2008)

30. Harandi, M.T., Salzmann, M., Jayasumana, S., Hartley, R., Li, H.: Expanding the family of Grassmannian kernels: an embedding perspective. In: Fleet, D., Pajdla, T., Schiele, B., Tuytelaars, T. (eds.) ECCV 2014. LNCS, vol. 8695, pp. 408–423. Springer, Cham (2014). https://doi.org/10.1007/978-3-319-10584-0_27
31. Heath, K., Gelfand, N., Ovsjanikov, M., Aanjaneya, M., Guibas, L.J.: Image webs: computing and exploiting connectivity in image collections. In: IEEE Conference on Computer Vision and Pattern Recognition (CVPR) (2010)
32. Hofer, C., Kwitt, R., Niethammer, M., Uhl, A.: Deep learning with topological signatures. arXiv preprint arXiv:1707.04041 (2017)
33. Ji-guang, S.: Perturbation of angles between linear subspaces. J. Comput. Math., 58–61 (1987)
34. Junejo, I.N., Dexter, E., Laptev, I., Perez, P.: View-independent action recognition from temporal self-similarities. IEEE Trans. Pattern Anal. Mach. Intell. **33**(1), 172–185 (2011)
35. Kerber, M., Morozov, D., Nigmetov, A.: Geometry helps to compare persistence diagrams. J. Exp. Algorithmics (JEA) **22**(1), 1–4 (2017)
36. Kokkinos, I., Bronstein, M., Yuille, A.: Dense scale invariant descriptors for images and surfaces. Ph.D. thesis, INRIA (2012)
37. Krim, H., Gentimis, T., Chintakunta, H.: Discovering the whole by the coarse: a topological paradigm for data analysis. IEEE Signal Process. Mag. **33**(2), 95–104 (2016). https://doi.org/10.1109/MSP.2015.2510703
38. Kusano, G., Hiraoka, Y., Fukumizu, K.: Persistence weighted Gaussian kernel for topological data analysis. In: International Conference on Machine Learning (ICML), pp. 2004–2013 (2016)
39. Li, C., Shi, Z., Liu, Y., Xu, B.: Grassmann manifold based shape matching and retrieval under partial occlusions. In: International Symposium on Optoelectronic Technology and Application: Image Processing and Pattern Recognition (2014)
40. Li, C., Ovsjanikov, M., Chazal, F.: Persistence-based structural recognition. In: IEEE Conference on Computer Vision and Pattern Recognition (CVPR), pp. 1995–2002 (2014)
41. Lian, Z., et al.: Shrec'10 track: non-rigid 3D shape retrieval. In: Eurographics Workshop on 3D Object Retrieval (3DOR), vol. 10, pp. 101–108 (2010)
42. Liu, X., Srivastava, A., Gallivan, K.: Optimal linear representations of images for object recognition. In: IEEE Computer Society Conference on Computer Vision and Pattern Recognition (CVPR) (2003)
43. Luo, D., Huang, H.: Video motion segmentation using new adaptive manifold denoising model. In: IEEE Conference on Computer Vision and Pattern Recognition (CVPR) (2014)
44. Masci, J., Boscaini, D., Bronstein, M., Vandergheynst, P.: Geodesic convolutional neural networks on Riemannian manifolds. In: IEEE International Conference on Computer Vision Workshops (ICCVW), pp. 37–45 (2015)
45. Mileyko, Y., Mukherjee, S., Harer, J.: Probability measures on the space of persistence diagrams. Inverse Probl. **27**(12), 124007 (2011)
46. Monti, F., Boscaini, D., Masci, J., Rodolà, E., Svoboda, J., Bronstein, M.M.: Geometric deep learning on graphs and manifolds using mixture model CNNs. IEEE International Conference on Computer Vision and Pattern Recognition (CVPR) (2017)
47. Osada, R., Funkhouser, T., Chazelle, B., Dobkin, D.: Shape distributions. ACM Trans. Graph. (TOG) **21**(4), 807–832 (2002)

48. Pachauri, D., Hinrichs, C., Chung, M.K., Johnson, S.C., Singh, V.: Topology-based kernels with application to inference problems in Alzheimer's disease. IEEE Trans. Med. Imaging **30**(10), 1760–1770 (2011)
49. Perea, J.A., Harer, J.: Sliding windows and persistence: an application of topological methods to signal analysis. Found. Comput. Math. **15**(3), 799–838 (2015)
50. Rahmani, H., Mian, A., Shah, M.: Learning a deep model for human action recognition from novel viewpoints. IEEE Trans. Pattern Anal. Mach. Intell. **40**(3), 667–681 (2017)
51. Reininghaus, J., Huber, S., Bauer, U., Kwitt, R.: A stable multi-scale kernel for topological machine learning. In: IEEE Conference on Computer Vision and Pattern Recognition (CVPR) (2015)
52. Rouse, D., et al.: Feature-aided multiple hypothesis tracking using topological and statistical behavior classifiers. In: SPIE Defense+Security (2015)
53. Scarselli, F., Gori, M., Tsoi, A.C., Hagenbuchner, M., Monfardini, G.: The graph neural network model. IEEE Trans. Neural Netw. **20**(1), 61–80 (2009)
54. Seversky, L.M., Davis, S., Berger, M.: On time-series topological data analysis: new data and opportunities. In: DiffCVML 2016, held in Conjunction with IEEE Conference on Computer Vision and Pattern Recognition Workshops, CVPR Workshops 2016, Las Vegas, NV, USA, 26 June–1 July 2016, pp. 1014–1022 (2016)
55. Sharafuddin, E., Jiang, N., Jin, Y., Zhang, Z.L.: Know your enemy, know yourself: block-level network behavior profiling and tracking. In: IEEE Global Telecommunications Conference (GLOBECOM 2010), pp. 1–6 (2010)
56. da Silva, N.P., Costeira, J.P.: The normalized subspace inclusion: robust clustering of motion subspaces. In: IEEE International Conference on Computer Vision (ICCV), pp. 1444–1450. IEEE (2009)
57. Singh, G., Memoli, F., Ishkhanov, T., Sapiro, G., Carlsson, G., Ringach, D.L.: Topological analysis of population activity in visual cortex. J. Vis. **8**(8), 11 (2008)
58. Som, A., Krishnamurthi, N., Venkataraman, V., Ramamurthy, K.N., Turaga, P.: Multiscale evolution of attractor-shape descriptors for assessing Parkinson's disease severity. In: IEEE Global Conference on Signal and Information Processing (GlobalSIP) (2017)
59. Som, A., Krishnamurthi, N., Venkataraman, V., Turaga, P.: Attractor-shape descriptors for balance impairment assessment in Parkinson's disease. In: IEEE Conference on Engineering in Medicine and Biology Society (EMBC), pp. 3096–3100 (2016)
60. Sun, J., Ovsjanikov, M., Guibas, L.: A concise and provably informative multi-scale signature based on heat diffusion. In: Computer Graphics Forum, vol. 28, pp. 1383–1392. Wiley Online Library (2009)
61. Sun, X., Wang, L., Feng, J.: Further results on the subspace distance. Pattern Recogn. **40**(1), 328–329 (2007)
62. Takens, F.: Detecting strange attractors in turbulence. In: Rand, D., Young, L.-S. (eds.) Dynamical Systems and Turbulence, Warwick 1980. LNM, vol. 898, pp. 366–381. Springer, Heidelberg (1981). https://doi.org/10.1007/BFb0091924
63. Tralie, C.J., Perea, J.A.: (quasi) periodicity quantification in video data, using topology. SIAM J. Imaging Sci. **11**(2), 1049–1077 (2018)
64. Turaga, P., Veeraraghavan, A., Srivastava, A., Chellappa, R.: Statistical computations on Grassmann and Stiefel manifolds for image and video-based recognition. IEEE Trans. Pattern Anal. Mach. Intell. **33**(11), 2273–2286 (2011)
65. Turner, K., Mileyko, Y., Mukherjee, S., Harer, J.: Fréchet means for distributions of persistence diagrams. Discret. Comput. Geom. **52**(1), 44–70 (2014)

66. Venkataraman, V., Ramamurthy, K.N., Turaga, P.: Persistent homology of attractors for action recognition. In: IEEE International Conference on Image Processing (ICIP), pp. 4150–4154. IEEE (2016)
67. Wang, L., Wang, X., Feng, J.: Subspace distance analysis with application to adaptive Bayesian algorithm for face recognition. Pattern Recogn. **39**(3), 456–464 (2006)
68. Weinland, D., Boyer, E., Ronfard, R.: Action recognition from arbitrary views using 3D exemplars. In: IEEE International Conference on Computer Vision (ICCV), pp. 1–7. IEEE (2007)
69. Wong, Y.C.: Differential geometry of grassmann manifolds. Proc. Natl. Acad. Sci. **57**(3), 589–594 (1967)
70. Yan, J., Pollefeys, M.: A general framework for motion segmentation: independent, articulated, rigid, non-rigid, degenerate and non-degenerate. In: Leonardis, A., Bischof, H., Pinz, A. (eds.) ECCV 2006. LNCS, vol. 3954, pp. 94–106. Springer, Heidelberg (2006). https://doi.org/10.1007/11744085_8
71. Ye, K., Lim, L.H.: Schubert varieties and distances between subspaces of different dimensions. SIAM J. Matrix Anal. Appl. **37**(3), 1176–1197 (2016)
72. Yi, L., Su, H., Guo, X., Guibas, L.: SyncSpecCNN: synchronized spectral CNN for 3D shape segmentation. IEEE International Conference on Computer Vision and Pattern Recognition (CVPR) (2017)
73. Zomorodian, A.: Fast construction of the vietoris-rips complex. Comput. Graph. **34**(3), 263–271 (2010)

SegStereo: Exploiting Semantic Information for Disparity Estimation

Guorun Yang[1], Hengshuang Zhao[2], Jianping Shi[3], Zhidong Deng[1(✉)], and Jiaya Jia[2,4]

[1] Department of Computer Science, State Key Laboratory of Intelligent Technology and Systems, Beijing National Research Center for Information Science and Technology, Tsinghua University, Beijing, China
ygr13@mails.tsinghua.edu.cn, michael@mail.tsinghua.edu.cn

[2] The Chinese University of Hong Kong, Shatin, Hong Kong
hszhao@cse.cuhk.edu.hk, leojia@cse.cuhk.edu.hk

[3] SenseTime Research, Beijing, China
shijianping@sensetime.com

[4] Tencent YouTu Lab, Shenzhen, China

Abstract. Disparity estimation for binocular stereo images finds a wide range of applications. Traditional algorithms may fail on featureless regions, which could be handled by high-level clues such as semantic segments. In this paper, we suggest that appropriate incorporation of semantic cues can greatly rectify prediction in commonly-used disparity estimation frameworks. Our method conducts semantic feature embedding and regularizes semantic cues as the loss term to improve learning disparity. Our unified model SegStereo employs semantic features from segmentation and introduces semantic softmax loss, which helps improve the prediction accuracy of disparity maps. The semantic cues work well in both unsupervised and supervised manners. SegStereo achieves state-of-the-art results on KITTI Stereo benchmark and produces decent prediction on both CityScapes and FlyingThings3D datasets.

Keywords: Disparity estimation · Semantic cues
Semantic feature embedding · Softmax loss regularization

1 Introduction

Disparity estimation is a fundamental problem in computer vision. It is important in depth prediction, scene understanding, autonomous driving, to name a few. The main goal of disparity estimation is to find corresponding pixels from

G. Yang and H. Zhao—Equal contribution.

Electronic supplementary material The online version of this chapter (https://doi.org/10.1007/978-3-030-01234-2_39) contains supplementary material, which is available to authorized users.

V. Ferrari et al. (Eds.): ECCV 2018, LNCS 11211, pp. 660–676, 2018.
https://doi.org/10.1007/978-3-030-01234-2_39

stereo images for inferring object distance according to the displacement between matching pixels.

Most previous methods [5,7,15,36] used hand-crafted reliable features to represent image patches and then selected matching pairs. They either formulate the task as supervised learning [22,26] based on current labeled dataset [14,41], or resort to unsupervised learning to form photometric loss for disparity prediction [13,17]. Recently, with the development of deep neural networks, the performance of disparity estimation is significantly improved [43]. The deep feature extracted from networks can exploit inherent global information in paired input compared to traditional methods, therefore benefits from a large number of training data either in supervised or unsupervised manner.

Although deep learning based methods produce impressive feature representation given its large receptive field, it is still difficult to overcome local ambiguity, which is a common problem in disparity estimation. For example, in Fig. 1, the disparity prediction in the center of road and vehicle area is not correct. It is because the matching clues for disparity estimation on those ambiguous areas are not enough to guide the model to seek correct direction for convergence, which is however the central objective for both supervised and unsupervised stereo learners.

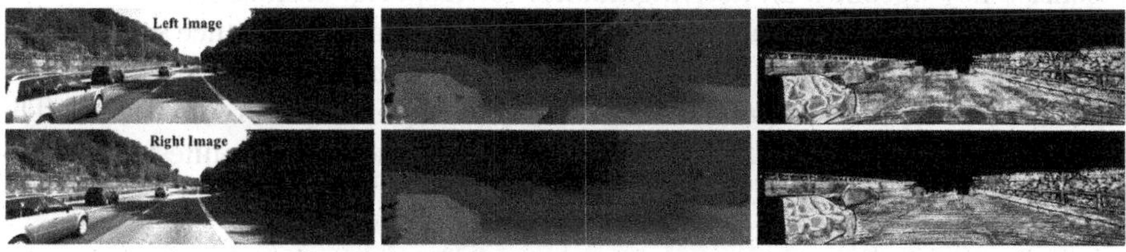

Fig. 1. Examples of prediction of unsupervised models on KITTI Stereo dataset. Left: input stereo images. Top-middle and top-right: colorized disparity and error maps predicted without semantic clues. Bottom-middle and bottom-right: colorized disparity and error maps predicted by *SegStereo*. With the guidance of semantic cues, disparity estimation of *SegStereo* is more accurate especially on the local ambiguous areas.

Human can perform binocular alignment well at ambiguous areas by exploiting more cues such as global perception of foreground and background, scaling relative to the known size of familiar objects, and semantic consistency for individuals. Such ambiguous areas in disparity estimation always locate in the central region given a big target. They are easy to deal with by semantic classification.

Based on the above-mentioned observation, we design an unified model called *SegStereo* that incorporates semantic cues into backbone disparity estimation network. Basically, we use the ResNet [19] with correlation operation [11] as the encoder and several deconvolutional blocks as decoder to regress a full-size disparity map. The correlation operation is designed in [11] to compute matching cost volumes based on pairs of feature maps. A segmentation sub-network is employed in our model to extract semantic features that are connected to the disparity branch as the *semantic feature embedding*. Moreover, we propose the warped semantic consistency via *semantic loss regularization*, which further enhances robustness of disparity estimation. Both semantic and disparity evaluation is fully-convolutional so that the proposed *SegStereo* enables end-to-end training.

Our *SegStereo* model with semantic clues embedded benefits both unsupervised and supervised training. In the unsupervised training, both photometric consistency loss and semantic softmax loss are computed and propagated backward. Both the semantic feature embedding and semantic softmax loss can introduce beneficial constraints of semantic consistency. The results evaluated on KITTI Stereo dataset [33] demonstrate the effectiveness of our strategies. We also apply the unsupervised model to CityScapes dataset [10]. It yields better performance than classical SGM method [21]. For the supervised training scheme, we adopt the supervised regression loss instead of unsupervised photometric consistency loss to train the model, which achieves state-of-the-art results on KITTI Stereo benchmark. We further apply the *SegStereo* model to FlyingThings3D dataset [31]. It reaches high accuracy with normal fine-tuning.

Our main contribution and achievement are summarized below.

- We propose a unified framework called *SegStereo* that incorporates semantic segmentation information into disparity estimation pipeline, where semantic consistency becomes an active guidance for disparity estimation.
- The semantic feature embedding strategy and semantic guidance softmax loss help train the system in both unsupervised and supervised manner.
- Our method achieves state-of-the-art results on KITTI Stereo datasets. The results on CityScapes and FlyingThings3D dataset also manifest the effectiveness of our method.

2 Related Work

Supervised Stereo Matching. Traditional methods design local descriptors to compute local matching cost [15,20], followed by some global optimization steps [21]. Zbontar and LeCun [43] are the first to use CNN for matching cost computation. Luo *et al.* [30] designed a siamese network that extracts marginal distributions over all possible disparities for each pixel. Chen *et al.* [8] presented a multi-scale deep embedding model that fuses feature vectors learned within different scale-spaces. Shaked and Wolf [38] proposed a highway network architecture with a hybrid loss that conducts multi-level comparison of image patches.

Inspired by other pixel-wise labeling tasks, the fully-convolution network (FCN) [29] was used to enable end-to-end learning of disparity maps. Mayer *et al.* [31] raised DispNet with a correlation module to encode matching cues instead of picking corresponding pairs from stereo images. Kendall *et al.* [25] proposed the GC-Net framework that combines contextual information by means of 3D convolutions over a cost volume. A three-stage network of Gidaris and Komodakis [16] implements a pipeline to detect, replace, and refine disparity errors respectively. Pang *et al.* [34] presented a cascade network where the second stage learned the residual between initial result and ground-truth values.

Yu *et al.* [42] designed a two-stream network for generation and selection of cost aggregation proposals respectively. Liang *et al.* [28] integrated disparity estimation and refinement into one network. It reaches state-of-the-art performance on KITTI benchmark [33]. Chang and Chen [6] exploited context information for finding correspondence by a pyramid stereo matching network. In contrast, our method concentrates on combining semantic information to improve disparity estimation by semantic feature embedding.

Unsupervised Stereo Matching. In recent years, a number of unsupervised learning methods based on spatial transformation were proposed for view synthesis, depth prediction, optical flow and disparity estimation. Unsupervised methods get rid of the dependence of ground-truth labels, which are always expensive to access. Flynn *et al.* [12] presented an image synthesis network called DeepStereo that learns a cost volume combined with a separate conditional color model. Xie *et al.* [40] designed a Deep3D network that minimizes pixel-wise reconstruction loss to generate right-view images.

Garg *et al.* [13] proposed an end-to-end framework to learn single-view depth by optimizing the projection errors in a calibrated stereo environment. The improved method [17] introduces a fully-differentiable structure and an extra left-right consistency check that leads to better results. A semi-supervised approach was proposed by Kuznietsov *et al.* [27] where supervised and unsupervised alignment loss are used to train the network for depth estimation. Yu *et al.* [23] focused on unsupervised learning of optical flow via photometric constancy and motion smoothness. Meister *et al.* [32] defined a bidirectional census loss to train optical flow. An iterative unsupervised learning network presented by Zhou *et al.* [45] adopts left-right checking to pick suitable matching pairs. Compared with these unsupervised methods, our model applies warping reconstruction to both photometric image and semantic maps, along with additional semantic feature embedding, to reliably estimate disparity.

Semantic-Guided Algorithms. Compared to disparity estimation, semantic segmentation is a high-level classification task where each pixel in the image is assigned to a class [7,29,39,44]. Several methods apply scene parsing information to other tasks. Guney and Geiger [18] leveraged object knowledge in MRF formulation to resolve stereo ambiguity. Bai *et al.* [2] tackled instance-level segmentation and epipolar constraints to reduce the uncertainty of optical flow estimation. A cascaded classification framework of Ren *et al.* [35] iteratively refines semantic masks, stereo correspondence and optical flow fields. Behl *et al.* [4] integrated the instance recognition cues into a CRF-based model for scene flow estimation.

With similar motivation to ours, Cheng *et al.* [9] designed an end-to-end trainable network called SegFlow, which enables joint learning for video object segmentation and optical flow. This model contains a segmentation branch and a flow branch whose feature maps concatenate. We differently focus on disparity estimation, where objects in the scene are captured at the same time so that stable structural information can be exploited. In addition, our *SegStereo* model also propagates softmax loss back to disparity branch by warping, which makes semantic information effective in the whole training process. In addition, our model enables unsupervised learning of disparity with photometric loss and semantic-aware constraints.

3 Our Method

In this section, we describe our *SegStereo* disparity estimation architecture, suitable for both unsupervised and supervised learning. We first present the basic network for disparity regression. Then we detail our incorporation strategies of semantic cues, including semantic feature embedding and semantic loss regularization. Both of them are effective to rectify disparity prediction. Finally, we show how disparity estimation is achieved under unsupervised and supervised conditions.

3.1 Basic Network Architecture

Our overall *SegStereo* network is shown in Fig. 2. The backbone network is ResNet-50 [19]. Instead of directly computing disparity on raw pixels, we adopt

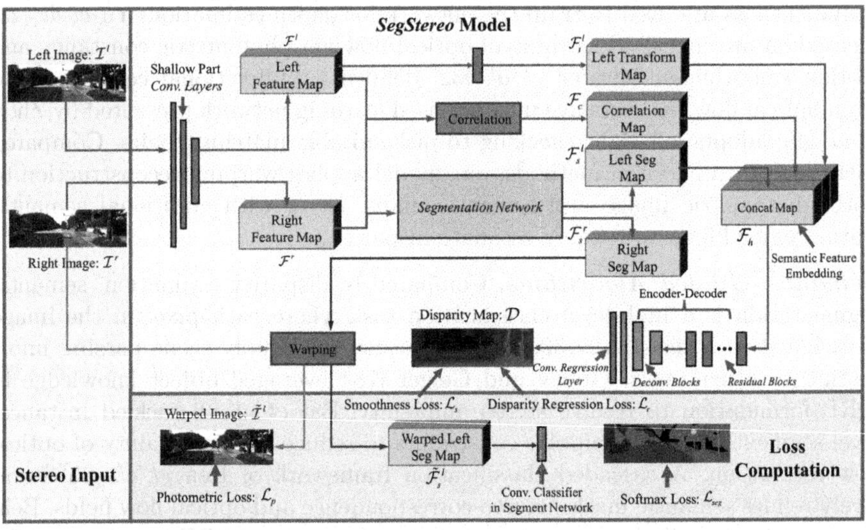

Fig. 2. Our *SegStereo* framework. We extract intermediate features $\mathcal{F}_l$ and $\mathcal{F}_r$ from stereo input. We calculate the cost volume $\mathcal{F}_c$ via the correlation operator. The left segmentation feature map ${\mathcal{F}_s}^l$ is aggregated into disparity branch as *semantic feature embedding*. The right segmentation feature map ${\mathcal{F}_s}^r$ is warped to left view for per-pixel semantic prediction with *softmax loss regularization*. Both steps incorporate semantic information to improve disparity estimation. The *SegStereo* framework enables both unsupervised and supervised learning, using photometric loss $\mathcal{L}_p$ or disparity regression loss $\mathcal{L}_r$.

the shallow part of ResNet-50 model to extract image features $\mathcal{F}^l$ and $\mathcal{F}^r$ on the paired input $\mathcal{I}^l$ and $\mathcal{I}^r$, which is known as robust to local context information encoding.

The cost volume features for stereo matching $\mathcal{F}_c$ are computed by correlation layer between $\mathcal{F}^l$ and $\mathcal{F}^r$, similar to that of DispNetC [31]. To preserve detail information on left stereo feature, we apply a convolution block on $\mathcal{F}^l$ and obtain transformed feature ${\mathcal{F}_t}^l$. Meanwhile, a segmentation network is utilized to compute semantic features ${\mathcal{F}_s}^l$ and ${\mathcal{F}_s}^r$ for left and right images respectively, sharing shallow layer representation with disparity network. The left transformed disparity features ${\mathcal{F}_t}^l$, the correlated features $\mathcal{F}_c$ and the left semantic features ${\mathcal{F}_s}^l$ are concatenated as hybrid feature representation $\mathcal{F}_h$. Here, semantic cues are preliminarily introduced to the disparity network as *Semantic Feature Embedding.*

After feature embedding, we feed $\mathcal{F}_h$ into the disparity encoder-decoder to get full-size disparity map $\mathcal{D}$. The disparity map is further used to warp right semantic feature ${\mathcal{F}_s}^r$ to left under *Semantic Loss Regularization*, detailed in Sect. 3.3. They constitute the key components of our framework. We describe more setting details in Sect. 4.1 and in supplementary material.

3.2 Semantic Feature Embedding

The basic disparity estimation frameworks work well on image patches with edges and corners where clear matching cues are located. It can be optimized with photometric loss in an unsupervised system or guided by supervised ℓ_1 norm regularization otherwise. The remaining major issue is on flat regions, as shown in the first row of Fig. 1. We use semantic cues to help prediction and rectify the final disparity map. As a result, we first incorporate the cues by embedding of semantic feature.

Our semantic feature embedding combines information from left disparity features ${\mathcal{F}_t}^l$, the correlated features $\mathcal{F}_c$ and the left semantic features ${\mathcal{F}_s}^l$. It contains the following advantages. (1) The employed segmentation branch shares the shallow computation with backbone disparity network for efficient computation and effective representation. (2) The semantic feature ${\mathcal{F}_s}^l$ gives more consistent representations on those flat regions compared to the disparity feature ${\mathcal{F}_t}^l$, which introduce object-level prior knowledge. (3) The low-level features and high-level recognition information are fused explicitly via the aggregation of ${\mathcal{F}_t}^l$, $\mathcal{F}_c$ and ${\mathcal{F}_s}^l$. The experiments in Sects. 4.5 and 4.6 further manifest that our semantic embedding helps disparity branch predict more convincing results in both unsupervised and supervised learning. In addition, the right semantic features ${\mathcal{F}_s}^r$ are reserved for the following semantic feature warping and loss regularization.

3.3 Semantic Loss Regularization

The semantic information cues can also guide learning of disparity as a loss term. As shown in Fig. 2, based on the predictive disparity map $\mathcal{D}$, we employ feature warping on the right segmentation map ${\mathcal{F}_s}^r$ to get the reconstructed left segmentation map $\tilde{\mathcal{F}_s}^l$, and use left segmentation ground truth labels as guidance to learn a per-pixel classifier. Finally, the semantic cues guidance loss $\mathcal{L}_{seg}$ is measured between classified warped maps and ground-truth labels.

When training the disparity network, the semantic loss $\mathcal{L}_{seg}$ is propagated back to disparity branch through semantic convolutional classifier and feature warping layer. Along with basic photometric loss $\mathcal{L}_p$ or regression loss $\mathcal{L}_r$, semantic loss $\mathcal{L}_{seg}$ imposes extra object-aware constraints to guide disparity training. The experiments prove that semantic loss regularization can effectively resolve the local disparity ambiguities, especially in the unsupervised learning period.

3.4 Objective Function

The semantic information detailed above can be used in both unsupervised and supervised systems. Here we detail the loss functions in these two conditions.

Unsupervised Manner. One image in a stereo pair can be reconstructed from the other with estimated disparity, which should be close to the original raw input. We utilize this property as photometric consistency to help learn the disparity in an unsupervised manner. Given estimated disparity $\mathcal{D}$, we apply image warping Φ on the right image $\mathcal{I}^r$ and get the warped left image reconstruction as $\tilde{\mathcal{I}}^l$. Then we adopt ℓ_1 norm to regularize the photometric consistency with photometric loss $\mathcal{L}_p$ expressed as

$$\mathcal{L}_p = \frac{1}{N}\sum_{i,j} \delta^p_{i,j} \|\tilde{\mathcal{I}}^l_{i,j} - \mathcal{I}^l_{i,j}\|_1, \tag{1}$$

where N is the number of pixels. $\delta^p_{i,j}$ is a mask indicator to avoid outlier as image boarder or occluded regions, where no pixel correspondence exists. If the resulting photometric difference on position (i, j) is greater than a threshold ϵ, $\delta^p_{i,j}$ is 0, otherwise, it is 1.

The photometric consistency enables disparity learning in an unsupervised manner. If there is no regularization term in $\mathcal{L}_p$ to enforce local smoothness of the estimated disparity, local disparity may be incoherent. To remedy this issue, we apply ℓ_1 penalty to disparity gradients $\partial\mathcal{D}$ with the smoothness loss $\mathcal{L}_s$ defined as

$$\mathcal{L}_s = \frac{1}{N}\sum_{i,j}[\rho_s(\mathcal{D}_{i,j} - \mathcal{D}_{i+1,j}) + \rho_s(\mathcal{D}_{i,j} - \mathcal{D}_{i,j+1})], \tag{2}$$

where $\rho_s(\cdot)$ is the spatial smoothness penalty implemented as generalized Charbonnier function [3].

With the semantic feature embedding and semantic loss, the overall loss in our unsupervised system is $\mathcal{L}_{unsup}$, containing the photometric loss $\mathcal{L}_p$, smoothness loss $\mathcal{L}_s$, and the semantic cues loss $\mathcal{L}_{seg}$. We note that disparity labels are not involved in loss computation so that disparity estimation is considered as an unsupervised learning process here. To balance learning of different loss branches, we introduce loss weights λ_p for $\mathcal{L}_p$, λ_s for $\mathcal{L}_s$, and λ_{seg} for $\mathcal{L}_{seg}$. Thus the total loss $\mathcal{L}_{unsup}$ is expressed as

$$\mathcal{L}_{unsup} = \lambda_p \mathcal{L}_p + \lambda_s \mathcal{L}_s + \lambda_{seg} \mathcal{L}_{seg}. \tag{3}$$

Supervised Manner. The proposed semantic cues for disparity prediction also works in supervised training, where the ground truth disparity map $\hat{D}$ is provided. We directly adopt the ℓ_1 norm to regularize prediction where the disparity regression loss $\mathcal{L}_r$ is

$$\mathcal{L}_r = \frac{1}{N_{\mathcal{V}}} \sum_{i,j \in \mathcal{V}} \|\mathcal{D}_{i,j} - \hat{\mathcal{D}}_{i,j}\|_1, \tag{4}$$

where $\mathcal{V}$ is the set of valid disparity pixels in $\hat{\mathcal{D}}$ and $N_{\mathcal{V}}$ is the number of valid pixels. For utilizing the semantic cues, both feature embedding and semantic softmax loss are adopted as described in Sects. 3.2 and 3.3. Loss weight λ_r is used for regression term $\mathcal{L}_r$. The overall loss function $\mathcal{L}_{sup}$ becomes

$$\mathcal{L}_{sup} = \lambda_r \mathcal{L}_r + \lambda_s \mathcal{L}_s + \lambda_{seg} \mathcal{L}_{seg}. \tag{5}$$

4 Experimental Results

In this section, we evaluate key components in the *SegStereo* model. We mainly pretrain the model on CityScapes dataset [10] and evaluate it on KITTI Stereo 2015 dataset [33]. We also compare the performance of our method with other disparity estimation methods on KITTI benchmark [33]. Further, we apply our *SegStereo* model to FlyingThings3D dataset [31] to assess performance on different scenes.

4.1 Model Specification

PSPNet-50 [44] is employed as a segmentation network due to its high performance. The layers (from "conv1_1" to "conv3_1") of PSPNet-50 are used as the shallow part. The extracted features $\mathcal{F}_l$ and $\mathcal{F}_r$ have a 1/8 spatial size to raw images. We select the output of "conv5_4" layer of PSPNet-50 as semantic features. The weights in the shallow part and segmentation network are fixed when training *SegStereo*.

For cost volume computation, we perform 1D-correlation [31] between $\mathcal{F}^l$ and $\mathcal{F}^r$ according to epipolar constraints. Both max displacement and padding size are set to 24 so that the channel number of correlated features $\mathcal{F}_c$ is 25. For left feature transformation, the kernel size of transformed convolutional layer is $1 \times 1 \times 256$. All of $\mathcal{F}_c$, $\mathcal{F}_t{}^l$ and $\mathcal{F}_s{}^l$ have the same spatial size. We directly concatenate them to form the hybrid feature map $\mathcal{F}_h$.

Disparity encoder behind hybrid features $\mathcal{F}_h$ contains 12 residual blocks. Several common convolutional operations in residual blocks are replaced with dilation patterns [44] to integrate wider context information. Disparity decoder consists of 3 deconvolutional blocks and 1 convolutional regression layer to output full-size disparity map. We provide more details in supplementary material.

The right segmentation map ${\mathcal{F}_s}^r$ is of 1/8 size to the raw image, while the estimated disparity map D is of full size. To perform feature warping, we first upsample ${\mathcal{F}_s}^r$ to the full size. We afterwards downsample warped feature map to 1/8 size and get the final reconstructed left segmentation feature map as $\tilde{\mathcal{F}_s}^l$.

4.2 Baseline Model Excluding Semantic Information

To validate the effect of incorporating semantic cues, we design a baseline model called *ResNetCorr* without any semantic information. The hybrid features $\mathcal{F}_h$ in *ResNetCorr* is concatenated with the correlated features $\mathcal{F}_c$ and left transformed features ${\mathcal{F}_t}^l$. The rest encoder-decoders are attached behind $\mathcal{F}_h$, as that of *SegStereo*. The softmax L_{seg} term is excluded in loss computation. We provide the structural definition of *ResNetCorr* model in supplementary material.

4.3 Datasets and Evaluation Metrics

The CityScapes dataset [10] is released for urban scene understanding. It provides rectified stereo image pairs and corresponding disparity maps precomputed by SGM algorithm [21]. It contains 5,000 high quality pixel-level finely annotated maps for left-view. These images are split into sets with numbers $2,975$, 500 and $1,525$ for training, validation and testing. In addition, this dataset provides $19,997$ stereo images and their SGM labels in extra training set. We will use these extra data for model pretraining.

The KITTI Stereo 2015 dataset [33] contains 200 training and 200 testing image pairs. The 200 training images also has semantic labels [1]. We mainly use the dataset for fine tuning and evaluation. The KITTI Stereo 2012 dataset [14] also provides disparity maps, which contain 194 training and 195 testing image pairs.

The FlyingThings3D dataset [31] is a virtual dataset for scene matching including optical flow estimation and disparity prediction. This dataset is rendered by computer graphics techniques with background objects and 3D models. It provides 22,390 images for training and 4,370 images for testing.

To evaluate the results, we apply the end-point-error (EPE), which measures the average pixel deviation and the bad pixel error (D1). The latter calculates the percentage of disparity errors below a threshold. Both the errors in non-occluded region (Noc) and all pixels (All) are evaluated.

4.4 Implementation Details

Our implementation of the *SegStereo* model is based on a customized Caffe [24]. We use the "poly" learning rate policy where current learning rate equals to the base one multiplying $(1 - \frac{iter}{max\_iter})^{power}$. Such learning policy is also adopted in [5,44] for better performance. When training on CityScapes dataset, we set base learning rate to 0.01, power to 0.9. Momentum and weight decay are set to 0.9 and 0.0001, respectively. These parameters of learning policy are kept on supervised fine-tuning process.

For data augmentation, we adopt random resizing, color shift and contrast brightness adjustment. The random factor is between 0.5 to 2.0. The maximum color shift along RGB axes is set to 10 and the maximum brightness shift is set to 5. The contrast multiplier is between 0.8 and 1.2. The "cropsize" is set to 513×513 and batch size is set to 16.

In unsupervised training, the loss weights λ_p, λ_s and λ_{seg} for photometric, softmax and smoothness terms are set to 1.0, 10.0, 0.1, respectively. The threshold ϵ in photometric loss is set to 10. When switching to supervised training, if providing semantic labels, the loss weights for λ_r, λ_s and λ_{seg} for regression, softmax and smoothness term are set to 1.0, 1.0, 0.1. If no semantic labels are provided, the loss weight of softmax term is set to 0. The Charbonnier parameters α, β and ϵ in smoothness loss term are 0.21, 5.0 and 0.001 as described in [23].

Table 1. Results of unsupervised training models on KITTI Stereo 2015 [33].

Model	Noc pixels		All pixels	
	EPE	D1 error	EPE	D1 error
1. Evaluation of semantic feature embedding				
ResCorr (photometric loss)	2.46	12.78	3.36	14.08
SegStereo (photometric loss)	**1.98**	**10.76**	**2.72**	**12.08**
ResCorr (photometric loss + smooth loss)	2.13	11.05	2.43	12.16
SegStereo (photometric loss + smooth loss)	**1.87**	**9.39**	**2.17**	**10.53**
2. Evaluation of softmax loss regularization				
SegStereo (photometric)	1.98	10.76	2.72	12.08
SegStereo (photometric + smooth)	1.87	9.39	2.17	10.53
SegStereo (photometric + smooth + softmax)	**1.61**	**8.95**	**1.89**	**10.03**
3. Comparison to other unsupervised methods				
Zhou [45]	–	8.61	–	9.91
Godard [17]	–	–	–	9.19
SegStereo (pretrain on Cityscapes dataset)	1.61	8.95	1.89	10.03
SegStereo (ft on KITTI Stereo dataset)	**1.46**	**7.70**	**1.84**	**8.79**

4.5 Unsupervised Learning

Semantic Feature Embedding. The first experiment in Table 1 compares the errors between *ResNetCorr* and *SegStereo* models. We observe that with semantic features from PSPNet-50, *EPE* is improved by 20% and the *D1 error* is reduced by 15% when only adopting photometric loss. When combining the photometric and smoothness losses to train the models, *EPE* is improved by 12% and the *D1 error* is reduced by 13%. It shows that semantic feature embedding significantly reduces the disparity errors.

Softmax Loss Regularization. The second experiment in Table 1 is to validate the effect of softmax loss regularization. Based on photometric loss, we use smoothness loss to penalize discontinuity on disparity maps, which reduces *EPE* from 2.72 to 2.17 and the D1 error from 12.08 to 10.53 on all pixels. With additional softmax loss to constrain semantic consistency, *EPE* decreases from 2.17 to 1.89 and the *D1 error* decreases from 10.53 to 10.03. Thus, the regularization of softmax loss reduces *EPE* by 13% and the *D1 error* by 5%, respectively.

Figure 3 shows results of different loss combinations (with or without softmax loss). We observe that the gain of softmax loss mainly arises on big objects, such as road and car, which directly help enhance disparity prediction on local ambiguous regions.

Finetune on KITTI Stereo Dataset. We compare our approach with other unsupervised methods in the third experiment as listed in Table 1. To adapt our model to KITTI dataset, we finely tune *SegStereo* on the 200 images of KITTI 2015 training set. We set the maximum iteration number to 500 and batch size to 16, so that 40 epochs are conducted. All photometric loss, smoothness loss

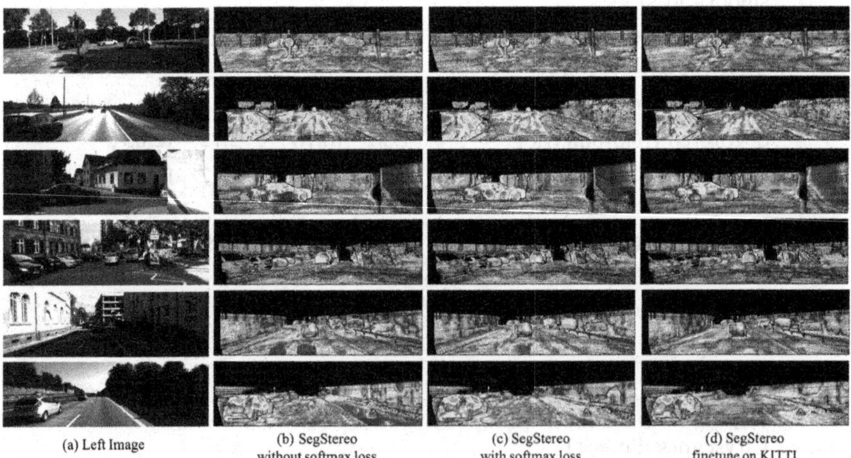

Fig. 3. Qualitative examples of unsupervised *SegStereo* models on KITTI Stereo 2015 dataset [33]. With the guidance of softmax regularization and additional fine-tune process, the accuracy of disparity is improved.

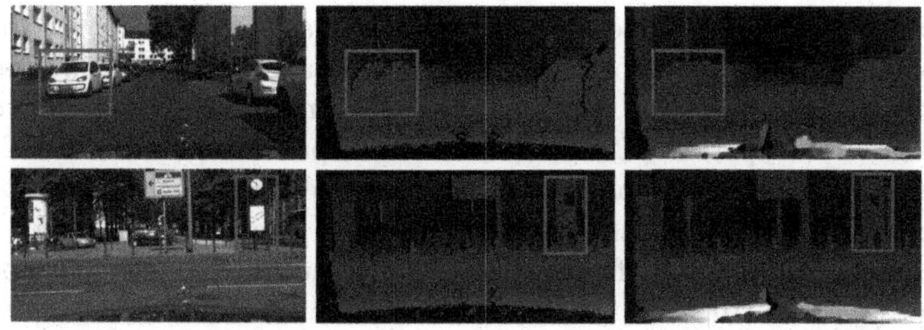

Fig. 4. Qualitative examples of unsupervised-learning version of the *SegStereo* model on CityScapes validation set [10]. From left to right: left input images, disparity maps predicted by SGM algorithm [21], and our disparity maps.

and softmax loss are used in this process. Qualitative results in Fig. 3 show that prediction errors are further reduced by fine-tuning. Our model outperforms the other two unsupervised methods [17,45] on KITTI 2015 benchmark.

CityScapes Results. We adapt the unsupervised *SegStereo* model to CityScapes dataset [10]. In Fig. 4, we give several examples to visualize quality on the validation set. Compared to the results of SGM algorithm [21], our method yields better structures in term of global scene information and details of objects.

4.6 Supervised Learning

KITTI Results. In supervised learning, the ground-truth disparity maps are directly applied to train our *SegStereo* model. As KITTI stereo dataset is too

Table 2. Results of supervised-training models evaluated on KITTI Stereo 2015 [33]

Model	Train				Test			
	EPE		D1		EPE		D1	
	Noc	All	Noc	All	Noc	All	Noc	All
1. Pretrained on Cityscapes dataset								
ResNetCorr	–	–	–	–	1.43	1.46	7.33	7.64
SegStereo	–	–	–	–	**1.39**	**1.41**	**7.01**	**7.34**
2. Pretrained on Cityscapes extra set and FlyingThings3D dataset								
ResNetCorr	–	–	–	–	1.19	1.21	5.46	5.64
SegStereo	–	–	–	–	**1.15**	**1.17**	**5.20**	**5.38**
3. Finetune on KITTI stereo 2012 and 2015 dataset								
ResNetCorr	0.40	0.41	0.68	0.76	0.73	0.76	2.13	2.40
SegStereo	0.40	0.41	0.65	0.70	0.73	0.75	2.11	2.30
SegStereo (corr13)	0.39	0.40	0.65	0.70	**0.66**	**0.70**	**1.96**	**2.25**

small, we pre-train our model on CityScapes dataset. Although the disparity maps computed by SGM algorithm contain errors and holes, they are useful for our model to get reasonable accuracy. The maximum iteration is set to $90K$. Different from unsupervised training, here the disparity regression loss $\mathcal{L}_r$ plays the major role. We also compare the performance between *ResNetCorr* and *SegStereo*. The first experiment in Table 2 shows that disparity error rate is slightly reduced by semantic feature embedding when we pretrain the models on CityScapes dataset [10].

In the second experiment, we fuse the extra training set in CityScapes and training set in FlyingThings3D dataset to pretrain *ResNetCorr* and *SegStereo*. Since there is no semantic labels in such two datasets, we do not compute softmax loss. The weights in segmentation branch of *SegStereo* is pretrained on CityScapes training set and fixed. We extend the maximum iterations to $500K$. Compared to the first experiment, with more training data, both *ResNetCorr* and *SegStereo* achieve higher accuracy. And the performance of *SegStereo* is still better than *ResNetCorr*.

Table 3. Comparison with other disparity estimation methods on the test set of KITTI 2015 [33]. Our method achieves state-of-the-art results on this benchmark.

Methods	Noc			All			Runtime (s)
	D1-bg	D1-fg	D1-all	D1-bg	D1-fg	D1-all	
SPS-st [41]	3.50	11.61	4.84	3.84	12.67	5.31	2
Content-CNN [30]	3.32	7.44	4.00	3.73	8.58	4.54	1
DispNetC [31]	4.11	3.72	4.05	4.32	4.41	4.34	**0.06**
MC-CNN [43]	2.48	7.64	3.33	2.89	8.88	3.89	67
PBCP [37]	2.27	7.71	3.17	2.58	8.74	3.61	68
Displets v2 [18]	2.73	4.95	3.09	3.00	5.56	3.43	265
L-ResMatch [38]	2.35	5.74	2.91	2.72	6.95	3.42	48
DRR [16]	2.34	4.87	2.76	2.58	6.04	3.16	0.4
GC-NET [25]	2.02	5.58	2.61	2.21	6.16	2.87	0.9
CRL [34]	2.32	3.12	2.45	2.48	3.59	2.67	0.47
DeepStereo [42]	2.06	5.32	2.32	2.17	5.46	2.79	1.13
iResNet [28]	2.07	**2.76**	2.19	2.25	**3.40**	2.44	0.12
PSMNet [6]	**1.71**	4.31	2.14	**1.86**	4.62	2.32	0.41
SegStereo (Ours)	1.76	3.70	**2.08**	1.88	4.07	**2.25**	0.6

In the third experiment, we use KITTI Stereo 2012 and 2015 datasets to finely tune our pretrained models from the second experiment. We set the maximum iteration to 90K and base learning rate to 0.01. To facilitate performance comparison, we split Stereo 2015 training set [30] so that 40 images are randomly selected for validation and the remaining 160 images are used for training. Table 2 lists errors on both training and validation sets. Compared to the *ResNetCorr* model, semantic feature embedding prevents overfitting and brings a certain improvement on disparity estimates.

To exploit more detailed matching cues on fine scales, we redesign *SegStereo*, where the shallow part is end with the "conv1_3" layer of PSPNet-50. To adapt to the increased feature map size, the maximum displacement and padding size of the correlation layer are both set to 96. We also up-sample the semantic feature maps from "conv5_4" layer for semantic feature embedding. This redesigned model is also pretrained on the fusion set of CityScapes and FlyingThings3D, followed by fine-tuning on KITTI Stereo dataset. The new *SegStereo* model (with remark "corr13" in Table 2) outperforms general *SegStereo* by leveraging more detail information.

Table 3 compares our model to other approaches on KITTI 2015 benchmark [33]. Our method achieves state-of-the-art results. Figure 5 gives several visual examples on KITTI 2015 test set. By incorporating semantic information, our *SegStereo* model is able to handle challenging scenarios. In supplementary material, we also provide results on KITTI 2012 benchmark [14] and segmentation results.

Fig. 5. Supervised-learning results on KITTI Stereo 2015 test sets [33]. By incorporating semantic information, our method is able to estimate accurate disparity. From left to right, we show left input images, disparity predictions of *SegStereo*, and error maps

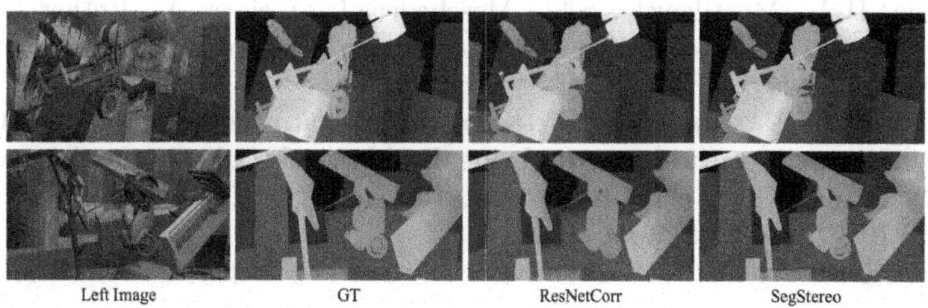

Fig. 6. Qualitative examples of *ResNetCorr* and *SegStereo* model on FlyingThings3D validation set [31]. From left to right, left images, ground-truth, *ResNetCorr* results and *SegStereo* results

Table 4. Comparison with other disparity estimation methods on the test set of FlyingThings3D [31].

Model	SGM [21]	DispNetC [31]	GC-Net [25]	CRL [34]	iResNet [28]	**ResNetCorr**	**SegStereo**
EPE	7.29	2.33	1.84	1.67	**1.27**	3.50	1.45
D1	16.18	10.04	9.67	6.70	4.90	8.45	**3.50**

FlyingThings3D Results. To illustrate that our *SegStereo* model can adapt to other datasets, we test the supervised-training *ResNetCorr* and *SegStereo* on FlyingThings3D dataset [31]. Here, we directly select the pretrained models from the second experiments of Table 2. The two models are compared with other methods on the validation set of FlyingThings3D in Table 4. With the guidance of semantic information, the *SegStereo* model outperforms *ResNetCorr* and becomes state-of-the-art, which indicates that segmentation modules is effective and general for disparity estimation across various datasets. Figure 6 shows several visual examples on validation set.

5 Conclusion

In this paper, we have proposed a unified model *SegStereo*, which integrates semantic feature maps into disparity prediction pipeline. A softmax loss is combined with common photometric loss or disparity regression loss to enable training in both unsupervised and supervised manners. Our *SegStereo* leads to more reliable results, especially on ambiguous areas. Experiments on KITTI Stereo datasets demonstrate the effectiveness of the semantic-guided strategy. Our method achieves state-of-the-art performance on this benchmark. Results on CityScapes and FlyingThings3D datasets further manifest its adaptability.

Acknowledgment. This work was supported in part by the National Key R&D Program of China under Grant No. 2017YFB1302200 and by Joint Fund of NORINCO Group of China for Advanced Research under Grant No. 6141B010318.

References

1. Alhaija, H.A., Mustikovela, S.K., Mescheder, L., Geiger, A., Rother, C.: Augmented reality meets deep learning for car instance segmentation in urban scenes. In: BMVC (2017)
2. Bai, M., Luo, W., Kundu, K., Urtasun, R.: Exploiting semantic information and deep matching for optical flow. In: Leibe, B., Matas, J., Sebe, N., Welling, M. (eds.) ECCV 2016. LNCS, vol. 9910, pp. 154–170. Springer, Cham (2016). https://doi.org/10.1007/978-3-319-46466-4_10
3. Barron, J.T.: A more general robust loss function. arXiv preprint arXiv:1701.03077 (2017)
4. Behl, A., Jafari, O.H., Mustikovela, S.K., Alhaija, H.A., Rother, C., Geiger, A.: Bounding boxes, segmentations and object coordinates: how important is recognition for 3D scene flow estimation in autonomous driving scenarios? In: ICCV (2017)

5. Brown, M., Hua, G., Winder, S.: Discriminative learning of local image descriptors. TPAMI **33**(1), 43–57 (2011)
6. Chang, J., Chen, Y.: Pyramid stereo matching network. In: CVPR (2018)
7. Chen, L., Papandreou, G., Kokkinos, I., Murphy, K., Yuille, A.L.: Semantic image segmentation with deep convolutional nets and fully connected CRFs (2015)
8. Chen, Z., Sun, X., Wang, L., Yu, Y., Huang, C.: A deep visual correspondence embedding model for stereo matching costs. In: ICCV (2015)
9. Cheng, J., Tsai, Y.H., Wang, S., Yang, M.H.: SegFlow: joint learning for video object segmentation and optical flow. In: ICCV (2017)
10. Cordts, M., et al.: The cityscapes dataset for semantic urban scene understanding. In: CVPR (2016)
11. Dosovitskiy, A., et al.: FlowNet: learning optical flow with convolutional networks. In: ICCV (2015)
12. Flynn, J., Neulander, I., Philbin, J., Snavely, N.: DeepStereo: learning to predict new views from the world's imagery. In: CVPR (2016)
13. Garg, R., Vijay Kumar, B.G., Carneiro, G., Reid, I.: Unsupervised CNN for single view depth estimation: geometry to the rescue. In: Leibe, B., Matas, J., Sebe, N., Welling, M. (eds.) ECCV 2016. LNCS, vol. 9912, pp. 740–756. Springer, Cham (2016). https://doi.org/10.1007/978-3-319-46484-8_45
14. Geiger, A., Lenz, P., Urtasun, R.: Are we ready for autonomous driving? The kitti vision benchmark suite. In: CVPR (2012)
15. Geiger, A., Roser, M., Urtasun, R.: Efficient large-scale stereo matching. In: Kimmel, R., Klette, R., Sugimoto, A. (eds.) ACCV 2010. LNCS, vol. 6492, pp. 25–38. Springer, Heidelberg (2011). https://doi.org/10.1007/978-3-642-19315-6_3
16. Gidaris, S., Komodakis, N.: Detect, replace, refine: deep structured prediction for pixel wise labeling. In: CVPR (2017)
17. Godard, C., Mac Aodha, O., Brostow, G.J.: Unsupervised monocular depth estimation with left-right consistency. In: CVPR (2017)
18. Guney, F., Geiger, A.: Displets: resolving stereo ambiguities using object knowledge. In: CVPR (2015)
19. He, K., Zhang, X., Ren, S., Sun, J.: Deep residual learning for image recognition. In: CVPR (2016)
20. Heise, P., Jensen, B., Klose, S., Knoll, A.: Fast dense stereo correspondences by binary locality sensitive hashing. In: ICRA (2015)
21. Hirschmuller, H.: Stereo processing by semiglobal matching and mutual information. TPAMI **30**(2), 328–341 (2008)
22. Hirschmuller, H., Scharstein, D.: Evaluation of stereo matching costs on images with radiometric differences. TPAMI **31**(9), 1582–1599 (2009)
23. Yu, J.J., Harley, A.W., Derpanis, K.G.: Back to basics: unsupervised learning of optical flow via brightness constancy and motion smoothness. In: Hua, G., Jégou, H. (eds.) ECCV 2016. LNCS, vol. 9915, pp. 3–10. Springer, Cham (2016). https://doi.org/10.1007/978-3-319-49409-8_1
24. Jia, Y., et al.: Caffe: convolutional architecture for fast feature embedding. In: ACM MM (2014)
25. Kendall, A., et al.: End-to-end learning of geometry and context for deep stereo regression. In: ICCV (2017)
26. Kong, D., Tao, H.: A method for learning matching errors for stereo computation. In: BMVC (2004)
27. Kuznietsov, Y., Stückler, J., Leibe, B.: Semi-supervised deep learning for monocular depth map prediction. In: CVPR (2017)

28. Liang, Z., et al.: Learning for disparity estimation through feature constancy. In: CVPR (2018)
29. Long, J., Shelhamer, E., Darrell, T.: Fully convolutional networks for semantic segmentation. In: CVPR (2015)
30. Luo, W., Schwing, A.G., Urtasun, R.: Efficient deep learning for stereo matching. In: CVPR (2016)
31. Mayer, N., et al.: A large dataset to train convolutional networks for disparity, optical flow, and scene flow estimation. In: CVPR (2016)
32. Meister, S., Hur, J., Roth, S.: UnFlow: unsupervised learning of optical flow with a bidirectional census loss. In: AAAI (2018)
33. Menze, M., Geiger, A.: Object scene flow for autonomous vehicles. In: CVPR (2015)
34. Pang, J., Sun, W., Ren, J., Yang, C., Yan, Q.: Cascade residual learning: a two-stage convolutional neural network for stereo matching. In: ICCV Workshop (2017)
35. Ren, Z., Sun, D., Kautz, J., Sudderth, E.B.: Cascaded scene flow prediction using semantic segmentation. In: ICCV Workshop (2017)
36. Revaud, J., Weinzaepfel, P., Harchaoui, Z., Schmid, C.: DeepMatching: hierarchical deformable dense matching. IJCV **120**(3), 300–323 (2016)
37. Seki, A., Pollefeys, M.: Patch based confidence prediction for dense disparity map. In: BMVC (2016)
38. Shaked, A., Wolf, L.: Improved stereo matching with constant highway networks and reflective confidence learning. In: CVPR (2017)
39. Vijay, B., Alex, K., Cipolla, R.: SegNet: a deep convolutional encoder-decoder architecture for image segmentation. TPAMI **39**(12), 2481–2495 (2017)
40. Xie, J., Girshick, R., Farhadi, A.: Deep3D: fully automatic 2D-to-3D video conversion with deep convolutional neural networks. In: Leibe, B., Matas, J., Sebe, N., Welling, M. (eds.) ECCV 2016. LNCS, vol. 9908, pp. 842–857. Springer, Cham (2016). https://doi.org/10.1007/978-3-319-46493-0_51
41. Yamaguchi, K., McAllester, D., Urtasun, R.: Efficient joint segmentation, occlusion labeling, stereo and flow estimation. In: Fleet, D., Pajdla, T., Schiele, B., Tuytelaars, T. (eds.) ECCV 2014. LNCS, vol. 8693, pp. 756–771. Springer, Cham (2014). https://doi.org/10.1007/978-3-319-10602-1_49
42. Yu, L., Wang, Y., Wu, Y., Jia, Y.: Deep stereo matching with explicit cost aggregation sub-architecture. In: AAAI (2018)
43. Zbontar, J., LeCun, Y.: Stereo matching by training a convolutional neural network to compare image patches. JMLR **17**(1), 2287–2318 (2016)
44. Zhao, H., Shi, J., Qi, X., Wang, X., Jia, J.: Pyramid scene parsing network. In: CVPR (2017)
45. Zhou, C., Zhang, H., Shen, X., Jia, J.: Unsupervised learning of stereo matching. In: ICCV (2017)

Uncertainty Estimates and Multi-hypotheses Networks for Optical Flow

Eddy Ilg(✉), Özgün Çiçek, Silvio Galesso, Aaron Klein, Osama Makansi, Frank Hutter, and Thomas Brox

University of Freiburg, Freiburg, Germany
{ilg,cicek,galessos,kleinaa,makansio,fh,brox}@cs.uni-freiburg.de

Abstract. Optical flow estimation can be formulated as an end-to-end supervised learning problem, which yields estimates with a superior accuracy-runtime tradeoff compared to alternative methodology. In this paper, we make such networks estimate their local uncertainty about the correctness of their prediction, which is vital information when building decisions on top of the estimations. For the first time we compare several strategies and techniques to estimate uncertainty in a large-scale computer vision task like optical flow estimation. Moreover, we introduce a new network architecture and loss function that enforce complementary hypotheses and provide uncertainty estimates efficiently with a single forward pass and without the need for sampling or ensembles. We demonstrate the quality of the uncertainty estimates, which is clearly above previous confidence measures on optical flow and allows for interactive frame rates.

Keywords: Convolutional neural networks · Optical flow estimation Uncertainty estimation

1 Introduction

Recent research has shown that deep networks typically outperform handcrafted approaches in computer vision in terms of accuracy and speed. Optical flow estimation is one example: FlowNet [6,12] yields high accuracy optical flow at interactive frame rates, which is relevant for many applications in the automotive domain or for activity understanding.

A valid critique of learning-based approaches is their black-box nature: since all parts of the problem are learned from data, there is no strict understanding

E. Ilg, Ö. Çiçek and S. Galesso—Equal contribution.

Electronic supplementary material The online version of this chapter (https://doi.org/10.1007/978-3-030-01234-2_40) contains supplementary material, which is available to authorized users.

V. Ferrari et al. (Eds.): ECCV 2018, LNCS 11211, pp. 677–693, 2018.
https://doi.org/10.1007/978-3-030-01234-2_40

on how the problem is solved by the network. Although FlowNet 2.0 [12] was shown to generalize well across various datasets, there is no guarantee that it will also work in different scenarios that contain unknown challenges. In real-world scenarios, such as control of an autonomously driving car, an erroneous decision can be fatal; thus it is not possible to deploy such a system without information about how reliable the underlying estimates are. We should expect an additional estimate of the network's own uncertainty, such that the network can highlight hard cases where it cannot reliably estimate the optical flow or where it must decide among multiple probable hypotheses; see Fig. 1. However, deep networks in computer vision typically yield only their single preferred prediction rather than the parameters of a distribution.

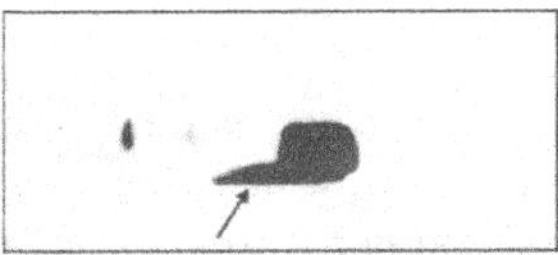

Fig. 1. Joint estimation of optical flow and its uncertainty. **Left:** Image from a KITTI 2015 sequence. **Middle:** Estimated optical flow. **Right:** The estimated uncertainty (visualized as heatmap) marks the optical flow in the shadow of the car as unreliable (pointed by the red arrow), contrary to the car itself, which is estimated with higher certainty. Marked as most reliable is the optical flow for the static background. (Color figure online)

The first contribution of this paper is an answer to the open question which of the many approaches for uncertainty estimation, most of which have been applied only to small problems so far, are most efficient for high-resolution encoder-decoder regression networks. We provide a comprehensive study of empirical ensembles, predictive models, and predictive ensembles. The first category comprises frequentist methods, the second one relies on the estimation of a parametric output distribution, and the third one combines the properties of the previous two. We implemented these approaches for FlowNet using the common MC dropout technique [7], the less common Bootstrapped Ensembles [19] and snapshot ensembles [11]. We find that in general all these approaches yield surprisingly good uncertainty estimates, where the best performance is achieved with uncertainty estimates derived from Bootstrapped Ensembles of predictive networks.

While such ensembles are a good way to obtain uncertainty estimates, they must run multiple networks to create sufficiently many samples. This drawback increases the computational load and memory footprint at training and test time linearly with the number of samples, such that these approaches are not applicable in real-time.

As a second contribution, we present a multi-headed network architecture that yields multiple hypotheses in a single network without the need of sampling. We use a loss that only penalizes the best hypothesis. This pushes the network to make multiple different predictions in case of doubt. We train a second network to optimally combine the hypotheses and to estimate the final uncertainty. This network yields the same good uncertainty estimates as Bootstrapped Ensembles, but allows for interactive frame rates. Thus, in this paper, we address all three important aspects for deployment of optical flow estimation in automotive systems: high accuracy inherited from the base network, a measure of reliability, and a fast runtime.

2 Related Work

Confidence Measures for Optical Flow. While there is a large number of optical flow estimation methods, only few of them provide uncertainty estimates.

Post-hoc methods apply post-processing to already estimated flow fields. Kondermann et al. [16] used a learned linear subspace of typical displacement neighborhoods to test the reliability of a model. In their follow-up work [17], they proposed a hypothesis testing method based on probabilistic motion models learned from ground-truth data. Aodha et al. [1] trained a binary classifier to predict whether the endpoint error of each pixel is bigger or smaller than a certain threshold and used the predicted classifier's probability as an uncertainty measure. All post-hoc methods ignore information given by the model structure.

Model-inherent methods, in contrast, produce their uncertainty estimates using the internal estimation model, i.e., energy minimization models. Bruhn and Weickert [3] used the inverse of the energy functional as a measure of the deviation from the model assumptions. Kybic and Nieuwenhuis [18] performed bootstrap sampling on the data term of an energy-based method in order to obtain meaningful statistics of the flow prediction. The most recent work by Wannenwetsch et al. [29] derived a probabilistic approximation of the posterior of the flow field from the energy functional and computed flow mean and covariance via Bayesian optimization. Ummenhofer et al. [28] presented a depth estimation CNN that internally uses a predictor for the deviation of the estimated optical flow from the ground-truth. This yields a confidence map for the intermediate optical flow that is used internally within the network. However, this approach treats flow and confidence separately and there was no evaluation for the reliability of the confidence measure.

Uncertainty Estimation with CNNs. Bayesian neural networks (BNNs) have been shown to obtain well-calibrated uncertainty estimates while maintaining the properties of standard neural networks [22,24]. Early work [24] mostly used Markov Chain Monte Carlo (MCMC) methods to sample networks from the distribution of the weights, where some, for instance Hamiltonian Monte Carlo, can make use of the gradient information provided by the backpropagation algorithm. More recent methods generalize traditional gradient based MCMC methods to the stochastic mini-batch setting, where only noisy estimates of the true gradient are available [5,30]. However, even these recent MCMC methods do not scale well to high-dimensional spaces, and since contemporary encoder-decoder networks like FlowNet have millions of weights, they do not apply in this setting.

Instead of sampling, variational inference methods try to approximate the distribution of the weights by a more tractable distribution [2,8]. Even though they usually scale much better with the number of datapoints and the number of weights than their MCMC counterparts, they have been applied only to much smaller networks [2,10] than in the present paper.

Gal and Ghahramani [7] sampled the weights by using dropout after each layer and estimated the *epistemic* uncertainty of neural networks. In a follow-up work by Kendall and Gal [15], this idea was applied to vision tasks, and the *aleatoric* uncertainty (which explains the noise in the observations) and the epistemic uncertainty (which explains model uncertainty) were studied in a joint framework. We show in this paper, that the dropout strategy used in all previous computer vision applications [15,26] is not the best one per-se, and other strategies yield better results.

In contrast to Bayesian approaches, such as MCMC sampling, bootstrapping is a frequentist method that is easy to implement and scales nicely to high-dimensional spaces, since it only requires point estimates of the weights. The idea is to train M neural networks independently on M different bootstrapped subsets of the training data and to treat them as independent samples from the weight distribution. While bootstrapping does not ensure diversity of the models and in the worst case could lead to M identical models, Lakshminarayanan et al. [19] argued that ensemble model averaging can be seen as dropout averaging. They trained individual networks with random initialization and random data shuffling, where each network predicts a mean and a variance. During test time, they combined the individual model predictions to account for the epistemic uncertainty of the network. We also consider so-called *snapshot ensembles* [11] in our experiments. These are obtained rather efficiently via Stochastic Gradient Descent with warm Restarts (SGDR) [21].

Multi-hypotheses Estimation. The loss function for the proposed multi-hypotheses network is related to Guzman-Rivera et al. [9], who proposed a similar loss function for SSVMs. Lee et al. [20] applied the loss to network ensembles and Chen and Koltun [4] to a single CNN.

3 Uncertainty Estimation with Deep Networks

Assume we have a dataset $\mathcal{D} = \{(\mathbf{x}_0, \mathbf{y}_0^{\text{gt}}), \ldots, (\mathbf{x}_N, \mathbf{y}_N^{\text{gt}})\}$, which is generated by sampling from a joint distribution $p(\mathbf{x}, \mathbf{y})$. In CNNs, it is assumed that there is a unique mapping from $\mathbf{x}$ to $\mathbf{y}$ by a function $f_{\mathbf{w}}(\mathbf{x})$, which is parametrized by weights $\mathbf{w}$ that are optimized according to a given loss function on $\mathcal{D}$.

For optical flow, we denote the trained network as a mapping from the input images $\mathbf{x} = (\mathbf{I}_1, \mathbf{I}_2)$ to the output optical flow $\mathbf{y} = (\mathbf{u}, \mathbf{v})$ as $\mathbf{y} = f_{\mathbf{w}}(\mathbf{I}_1, \mathbf{I}_2)$, where $\mathbf{u}, \mathbf{v}$ are the x- and y-components of the optical flow. The FlowNet by Dosovitskiy et al. [6] minimizes the per-pixel endpoint error

$$\text{EPE} = \sqrt{(u - u^{\text{gt}})^2 + (v - v^{\text{gt}})^2}, \tag{1}$$

where the pixel coordinates are omitted for brevity. This network, as depicted in Fig. 2a, is fully deterministic and yields only the network's preferred output $\mathbf{y} = f_{\mathbf{w}}(\mathbf{x})$. Depending on the loss function, this typically corresponds to the mean of the distribution $p(\mathbf{y}|\mathbf{x}, \mathcal{D})$. In this paper, we investigate three major approaches to estimate also the variance σ^2. These are based on the empirical variance of the distribution of an ensemble, a parametric model of the distribution, and a combination of both. The variance in all these approaches serves as an estimate of the uncertainty.

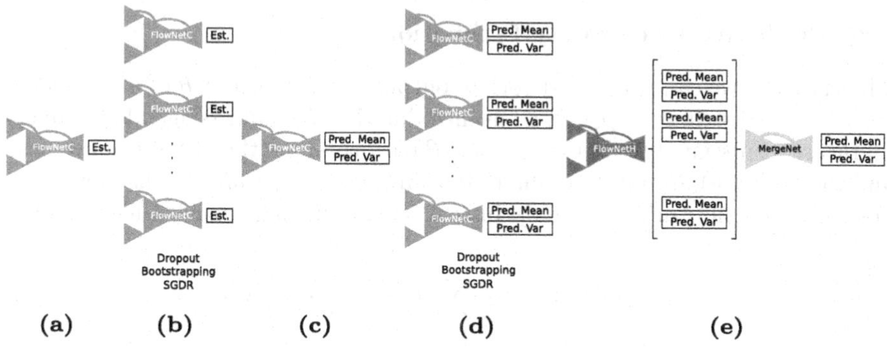

Fig. 2. Overview of the networks considered in this paper. **(a)** FlowNetC trained with EPE. **(b)** Same network as (a), where an ensemble is built using dropout, bootstrapping or SGDR. **(c)** FlowNetC trained with -log-likelihood to predict mean and variance. **(d)** Same network as (c), where an ensemble is built using dropout, bootstrapping or SGDR. **(e)** FlowNetH trained to predict multiple hypotheses with variances, which are merged to a single distributional output. Only **(a)** exists in this form for optical flow.

3.1 Empirical Uncertainty Estimation

A straightforward approach to get variance estimates is to train M different models independently, such that the mean and the variance of the distribution $p(\mathbf{y}|\mathbf{x}, \mathcal{D})$ can be approximated with the empirical mean and variance of the individual model's predictions. Let $f_{\mathbf{w}_i}(\mathbf{x})$ denote model i of an ensemble of M models with outputs $\mathbf{u}_{\mathbf{w}_i}$ and $\mathbf{v}_{\mathbf{w}_i}$. We can compute the empirical mean and variance for the $\mathbf{u}$-component by:

$$\boldsymbol{\mu}_{\mathbf{u}} = \frac{1}{M} \sum_{i=1}^{M} \mathbf{u}_{\mathbf{w}_i}(\mathbf{x}) \tag{2}$$

$$\boldsymbol{\sigma}_{\mathbf{u}}^2 = \frac{1}{M} \sum_{i=1}^{M} (\mathbf{u}_{\mathbf{w}_i}(\mathbf{x}) - \boldsymbol{\mu}_{\mathbf{u}})^2 \tag{3}$$

and accordingly for the $\mathbf{v}$-component of the optical flow. Such an ensemble of M networks, as depicted in Fig. 2b, can be built in multiple ways. The most common way is via Monte Carlo Dropout [7]. Using dropout also at test time, it is possible to randomly sample from network weights M times to build an ensemble. Alternatively, ensembles of individual networks can be trained with random weight initialization, data shuffling, and bootstrapping as proposed by Lakshminarayanan et al. [19]. A more efficient way of building an ensemble is to use M pre-converged snapshots of a single network trained with the SGDR [21] learning scheme, as proposed by Huang et al. [11]. We investigate these three ways of building ensembles for flow estimation and refer to them as Dropout, Bootstrapped Ensembles and SGDR Ensembles, respectively.

3.2 Predictive Uncertainty Estimation

Alternatively, we can train a network to output the parameters $\boldsymbol{\theta}$ of a parametric model of the distribution $p(\mathbf{y}|\mathbf{x}, \mathcal{D})$ as introduced by Nix and Weigend [25]. In the literature, Gaussian distributions (where $\boldsymbol{\theta}$ parameterizes the distribution's mean and the variance) are most common, but any type of parametric distribution is possible. Such networks can be optimized by maximizing their log-likelihood:

$$\log p(\mathcal{D} \mid \mathbf{w}) = \frac{1}{N} \sum_{i=1}^{N} \log p(\mathbf{y}_i \mid \boldsymbol{\theta}(\mathbf{x}_i, \mathbf{w})) \tag{4}$$

w.r.t. $\mathbf{w}$. The predictive distribution for an input $\mathbf{x}$ is then defined as:

$$p(\mathbf{y} \mid \mathbf{x}, \mathbf{w}) \equiv p(\mathbf{y} \mid \boldsymbol{\theta}(\mathbf{x}, \mathbf{w})). \tag{5}$$

While negative log-likelihood of a Gaussian corresponds to L_2 loss, FlowNet is trained with an EPE loss, which has more robustness to outliers. Thus, we model the predictive distribution by a Laplacian, which corresponds to an L_1 loss. The univariate Laplace distribution has two parameters a and b and is defined as:

$$\mathcal{L}(u|a, b) = \frac{1}{2b} e^{-\frac{|u-a|}{b}}. \tag{6}$$

As Wannewetsch et al. [29], we model the u and v components of the optical flow to be independent. The approximation yields:

$$\mathcal{L}(u, v|a_u, a_v, b_u, b_v) \approx \mathcal{L}(u|a_u, b_u) \cdot \mathcal{L}(v|a_v, b_v). \tag{7}$$

We obtain a probabilistic version of FlowNet with outputs a_u, a_v, b_u, b_v by minimizing the negative log-likelihood of Eq. 7:

$$-\log(\mathcal{L}(u|a_u, b_u) \cdot \mathcal{L}(v|a_v, b_v)) = \frac{|u - a_u|}{b_u} + \log b_u + \frac{|v - a_v|}{b_v} + \log b_v. \tag{8}$$

As an uncertainty estimate we use the variance of the predictive distribution, which is $\sigma^2 = 2b^2$ in this case. This case corresponds to a single FlowNetC predicting flow and uncertainty as illustrated in Fig. 2c.

3.3 Bayesian Uncertainty Estimation

From a Bayesian perspective, to obtain an estimate of model uncertainty, rather than choosing a point estimate for $\mathbf{w}$, we would marginalize over all possible values:

$$p(\mathbf{y} \mid \mathbf{x}, \mathcal{D}) = \int p(\mathbf{y} \mid \mathbf{x}, \mathbf{w}) p(\mathbf{w} \mid \mathcal{D}) d\mathbf{w} \tag{9}$$

$$= \int p(\mathbf{y} \mid \boldsymbol{\theta}(\mathbf{x}, \mathbf{w})) p(\mathbf{w} \mid \mathcal{D}) d\mathbf{w}. \tag{10}$$

This integral cannot be computed in closed form, but by sampling M networks $\mathbf{w}_i \sim p(\mathbf{w}|\mathcal{D})$ from the posterior distribution and using a Monte-Carlo approximation [24], we can approximate its mean and variance as:

$$p(\mathbf{y} \mid \mathbf{x}, \mathcal{D}) \approx \sum_{i=1}^{M} p(\mathbf{y} \mid \boldsymbol{\theta}(\mathbf{x}, \mathbf{w}_i)). \tag{11}$$

Since every parametric distribution has a mean and a variance, also the distributions predicted by each individual network with weights $\mathbf{w}_i$ yield a mean $\boldsymbol{\mu}_i$ and a variance $\boldsymbol{\sigma}_i^2$. The mean and variance of the mixture distribution in Eq. 11 can then be computed by the law of total variance for the $\mathbf{u}$-component (as well as for the $\mathbf{v}$-component) as:

$$\boldsymbol{\mu}_{\mathbf{u}} = \frac{1}{M} \sum_{i=1}^{M} \boldsymbol{\mu}_{\mathbf{u},i} \tag{12}$$

$$\boldsymbol{\sigma}_{\mathbf{u}}^2 = \frac{1}{M} \sum_{i=1}^{M} \left((\boldsymbol{\mu}_{\mathbf{u},i} - \boldsymbol{\mu}_{\mathbf{u}})^2 + \boldsymbol{\sigma}^2{}_{\mathbf{u},i} \right). \tag{13}$$

This again can be implemented as ensembles obtained by predictive variants of dropout [7], bootstrapping [19] or SGDR [11], where the ideas from Sects. 3.1 and 3.2 are combined as shown in Fig. 2d.

4 Predicting Multiple Hypotheses Within a Single Network

The methods presented in the Sects. 3.1 and 3.3 require multiple forward passes to obtain multiple samples with the drawback of a much increased computational cost at runtime. In this section, we propose a loss function to make multiple predictions within a single network. We call these predictions *hypotheses*. For the predicted hypotheses, we encourage multimodality by the design of the loss function [4,9,20]. This makes the predictions more diverse and leads to capturing more different solutions, but does not allow for merging by simply computing the mean as for the ensembles presented in the last section. Therefore, we also propose to use a second network that merges the hypotheses to a single prediction and variance, as depicted in Fig. 2e.

Since a ground-truth is available only for the single true solution, the question arises of how to train a network to predict multiple hypotheses and how to ensure that each hypothesis comprises meaningful information. To this end, we use a loss that punishes only the best among the network output hypotheses $\boldsymbol{y}_1, \ldots, \boldsymbol{y}_M$ [9]. Let the loss between a predicted flow vector $\mathbf{y}(i,j)$ and its ground-truth $\mathbf{y}^{\text{gt}}(i,j)$ at pixel i,j be defined by a loss functon l. We minimize:

$$L_{hyp} = \sum_{i,j} l(\boldsymbol{y}_{\text{best\_idx}(i,j)}, \boldsymbol{y}^{\text{gt}}(i,j)) + \Delta(i,j), \tag{14}$$

where best_idx(i,j) selects the best hypothesis per pixel according to the ground-truth:

$$\text{best\_idx}(i,j) = \underset{k}{\operatorname{argmin}} \left[\text{EPE}(\boldsymbol{y}_k(i,j), \boldsymbol{y}^{\text{gt}}(i,j)) \right]. \tag{15}$$

$\Delta = \Delta_u + \Delta_v$ encourages similar solutions to be from the same hypothesis k via one-sided differences, e.g. for the $\mathbf{u}$ component:

$$\begin{aligned} \Delta_u(i,j) = &\sum_{k;i>1;j} |y_{k,u}(i,j) - y_{k,u}(i-1,j)| \\ &+ \sum_{k;i;j>1} |y_{k,u}(i,j) - y_{k,u}(i,j-1)| \end{aligned} \tag{16}$$

For l, we either use the endpoint error from Eq. 1 or the negative log-likelihood from Eq. 8. In the latter case, each hypothesis is combined with an uncertainty estimation and l also operates on a variance $\boldsymbol{\sigma}$. Equations 15 and 16 remain unaffected. For the best index selection we stick to the EPE since it is the main optimization goal.

To minimize L_{hyp}, the network must make a prediction close to the ground-truth in at least one of the hypotheses. In locations where multiple solutions exist and the network cannot decide for one of them, the network will predict several different likely solutions to increase the chance that the true solution is among these predictions. Consequently, the network will favor making diverse hypotheses in cases of uncertainty. In Tables 3 and 4 of the supplemental material we provide visualizations of such hypotheses.

In principle, L_{hyp} could collapse to use only one of the hypotheses' outputs. In this case the other hypotheses would have very high error and would never be selected for back-propagation. However, due to the variability in the data and the stochasticity in training, such collapse is very unlikely. We never observed that one of the hypotheses was not used by the network, and for the oracle merging we observed that all hypotheses contribute more or less equally. We show this diversity in our experiments.

5 Experiments

To evaluate the different strategies for uncertainty estimation while keeping the computational cost tractable, we chose as a base model the FlowNetC architecture from Dosovitsky et al. [6] with improved training settings by Ilg et al. [12] and by us. A single FlowNetC shows a larger endpoint error (EPE) than the full, stacked FlowNet 2.0 [12], but trains much faster. Note that this work aims for uncertainty estimation and not for improving the optical flow over the base model. The use of ensembles may lead to minor improvements of the optical flow estimates due to the averaging effect, but these improvements are not of major concern here. In the end, we will also show results for a large stacked network to demonstrate that the uncertainty estimation as such is not limited to small, simple networks.

5.1 Training Details

In contrast to Ilg et al. [12], we use Batch Normalization [13] and a continuously dropping cosine learning rate schedule [21]. This yields shorter training times and improves the results a little; see Table 1. We train on FlyingChairs [6] and start with a learning rate of $2e-4$. For all networks, we fix a training budget of 600k iterations per network, with an exception for SGDR, where we also evaluate performing some pre-cycles. For SGDR Ensembles, we perform restarts every 75k iterations. We fix the T_{mult} to 1, so that each annealing takes the same number of iterations. We experiment with different variants of building ensembles using snapshots at the end of each annealing. We always take the latest M snapshots when building an ensemble. For dropout experiments, we use a dropout ratio of 0.2 as suggested by Kendall et al. [15]. For Bootstrapped Ensembles, we train M FlowNetC in parallel with bootstrapping, such that each network sees different 67% of the training data. For the final version of our method, we perform an additional training of 250k iterations on FlyingThings3D [23] per network, starting with a learning rate of $2e-5$ that is decaying with cosine annealing. We use the Caffe [14] framework for network training and evaluate all runtimes on an Nvidia GTX 1080Ti. We will make the source code and the final models publicly available.

Table 1. Optical flow quality on Sintel train clean with the original FlowNetC [12] and our implementation.

	Iter.	EPE
FlowNetC [12]	600k	3.77
FlowNetC [12]	1.2m	3.58
FlowNetC ours	600k	3.40

For the ensembles, we must choose the size M of the ensemble. The sampling error for the mean and the variance decreases with increasing M. However, since networks for optical flow estimation are quite large, we are limited in the tractable sample size and restrict it to $M = 8$. We also use $M = 8$ for FlowNetH.

For SGDR there is an additional pre-cycle parameter: snapshots in the beginning have usually not yet converged and the number of pre-cycles is the number of snapshots we discard before building the ensemble. In the supplemental material we show that the later the snapshots are taken, the better the results are in terms of EPE and AUSE. We use 8 pre-cycles in the following experiments.

5.2 Evaluation Metrics

Sparsification Plots. To assess the quality of the uncertainty measures, we use so-called sparsification plots, which are commonly used for this purpose [1,17, 18,29]. Such plots reveal on how much the estimated uncertainty coincides with the true errors. If the estimated variance is a good representation of the model uncertainty, and the pixels with the highest variance are removed gradually, the error should monotonically decrease. Such a plot of our method is shown in Fig. 3. The best possible ranking of uncertainties is ranking by the true error to the ground-truth. We refer to this curve as *Oracle Sparsification.* Figure 3 reveals that our uncertainty estimate is very close to this oracle.

Sparsification Error. For each approach the oracle is different, hence a comparison among approaches using a single sparsification plot is not possible. To this end, we introduce a measure, which we call *Sparsification Error.* It is defined as the difference between the sparsification and its oracle. Since this measure normalizes the oracle out, a fair comparison of different methods is possible. In Fig. 4a, we show sparsification errors for all methods we present in this paper. To quantify the sparsification error with a single number, we use the Area Under the Sparsification Error curve ($AUSE$).

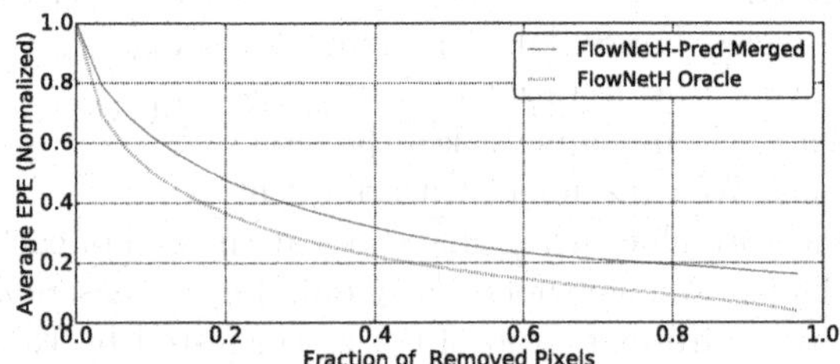

Fig. 3. Sparsification plot of FlowNetH-Pred-Merged for the Sintel train clean dataset. The plot shows the average endpoint error (AEPE) for each fraction of pixels having the highest uncertainties removed. The oracle sparsification shows the lower bound by removing each fraction of pixels ranked by the ground-truth endpoint error. Removing 20 percent of the pixels results in halving the average endpoint error.

Oracle EPE. For each ensemble, we also compute the hypothetical endpoint error by considering the pixel-wise best selection from each member (decided by the ground-truth). We report this error together with the empirical variances among the members in Table 2.

5.3 Comparison Among Uncertainties from CNNs

Nomenclature. When a single network is trained against the endpoint error, we refer to this single network and the resulting ensemble as empirical (abbreviated as *Emp*; Figs. 2a and b), while when the single network is trained against the negative log-likelihood, we refer to the single network and the ensemble as predictive (*Pred*; Figs. 2c and d). When multiple samples or solutions are merged with

Table 2. Comparison of flow and uncertainty predictions of all proposed methods with $M = 8$ on the Sintel train clean dataset. Oracle-EPE is the EPE of the pixel-wise best selection from the samples or hypotheses determined by the ground-truth. Var. is the average empirical variance over the 8 samples or hypotheses. Predictive versions (Pred) generally outperform empirical versions (Emp). Including a merging network increases the performance. FlowNetH-Pred-Merged performs best for predicting uncertainties and has a comparatively low runtime.

	Empirical (Emp)				Predictive (Pred)				Runtime
	AUSE	EPE	Oracle EPE	Var.	AUSE	EPE	Oracle EPE	Var.	
FlowNetC	-	3.40	-	-	0.133	3.62	-	-	**38** ms
Dropout	0.212	3.67	2.56	5.05	0.158	3.99	2.96	3.80	320 ms
SGDREnsemble	**0.191**	3.25	2.56	3.50	0.134	3.40	2.87	1.52	304 ms
BootstrappedEnsemble	0.209	3.41	2.17	9.52	0.127	3.46	2.49	6.15	304 ms
BootstrappedEnsemble-Merged					0.102	3.20	2.49	6.15	332 ms
FlowNetH-Merged	-	3.50	1.73	**83.32**	**0.095**	3.36	1.89	**52.85**	60 ms

a network, we add *Merged* to the name. E.g. FlowNetH-Pred-Merged refers to a FlowNetH that predicts multiple hypotheses and merges them with a network, using the loss for a predictive distribution for both, hypotheses and merging, respectively (Fig. 2e). Table 2 and Figs. 4a, b show results for all models evaluated in this paper.

Empirical Uncertainty Estimation. The results show that uncertainty estimation with empirical ensembles is good, but worse than the other methods presented in this paper. However, in comparison to predictive counterparts,

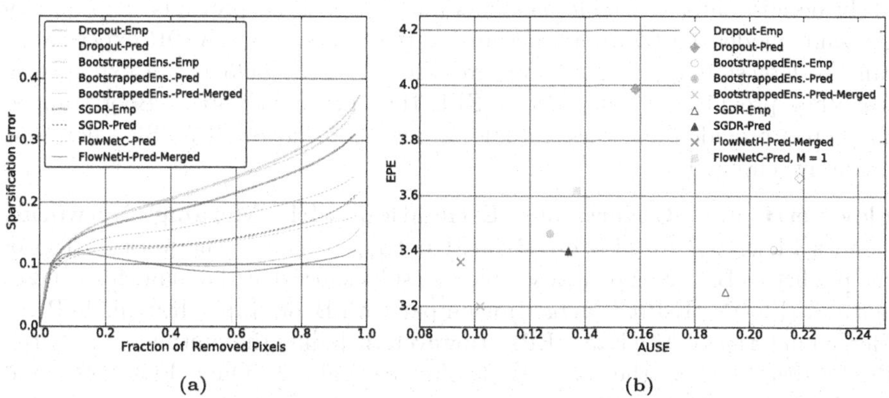

Fig. 4. **(a)** Sparsification error on the Sintel train clean dataset. The sparsification error (smaller is better) is the proposed measure for comparing the uncertainty estimates among different methods. FlowNetH-Pred-Merged and BootstrappedEnsemble-Pred-Merged perform best in almost all sections of the plot. **(b)** Scatter plot of AEPE vs. AUSE for the tested approaches visualizing some content of Table 2.

empirical ensembles tend to yield slightly better EPEs, as will be discussed in the following.

Predictive Uncertainty Estimation. The estimated uncertainty is better with predictive models than with the empirical ones. Even a single FlowNetC with predictive uncertainty yields much better uncertainty estimates than any empirical ensemble in terms of AUSE. This is because when training against a predictive loss function, the network has the possibility to explain outliers with the uncertainty. This is known as *loss attenuation* [15]. While the EPE loss tries to enforce correct solutions also for outliers, the log-likelihood loss attenuates them. The experiments confirm this effect and show that it is advantageous to let a network estimate its own uncertainty.

Predictive Ensembles. Comparing ensembles of predictive networks to a single predictive network shows that a single network is already very close to the predictive ensembles and that the benefit of an ensemble is limited. We attribute this also to loss attenuation: different ensemble members appear to attenuate outliers in a similar manner and induce less diversity, as can be seen by the variance among the members of the ensemble (column 'Var.' in Table 2).

When comparing empirical to predictive ensembles, we can draw the following conclusions: **(a)** empirical estimation provides more diversity within the ensemble (variance column in Table 2), **(b)** empirical estimation provides lower EPEs and Oracle EPEs, **(c)** all empirical setups provide worse uncertainty estimates than predictive setups.

Ensemble Types. We see that the commonly used dropout [7] technique performs worst in terms of EPE and AUSE, although the differences between the predictive ensemble types are not very large. SGDR Ensembles provide better uncertainties, yet the variance among the samples is the smallest. This is likely because later ensemble members are derived from previous snapshots of the same model. Furthermore, because of the 8 pre-cycles, SGDR experiments ran the largest number of training iterations, which could be an explanation why they provide a slightly better EPE than other ensembles. Bootstrapped Ensembles provide the highest sample variance and the lowest AUSE among the predictive ensembles.

FlowNetH and Uncertainty Estimation with Merging Networks. Besides FlowNetH we also investigated putting a merging network on top of the predictive Bootstrapped Ensembles. Results show that the multi-hypotheses network (FlowNetH-Pred-Merged) is on-par with BootstrappedEnsemble-Pred-Merged in terms of AUSE and EPE. However, including the runtime, FlowNetH-Pred-Merged yields the best trade-off; see Table 2. Only FlowNetC and FlowNetH-Pred-Merged allow a deployment at interactive frame rates. Table 2 also shows that FlowNetH has a much higher sample variance and the lowest oracle EPE. This indicates that it internally has very diverse and potentially useful hypotheses that could be exploited better in the future. For some visual examples, we refer to Tables 3 and 4 in the supplemental material.

5.4 Comparison to Energy-Based Uncertainty Estimation

We compare the favored approach from the previous section (FlowNetH-Pred-Merged) to ProbFlow [29], which is an energy minimization approach and currently the state-of-the-art for estimating the uncertainty of optical flow. Figure 5 shows the sparsification plots for the Sintel train final. ProbFlow has almost the same oracle as FlowNetH-Pred-Merged, i.e. the flow field from ProbFlow can equally benefit from sparsification, but the actual sparsification error due to its estimated uncertainty is higher. This shows that FlowNetH-Pred-Merged has superior uncertainty estimates. In Table 3 we show that this also holds for the KITTI dataset. FlowNetH outperforms ProbFlow also in terms of EPE in this case. This shows that the superior uncertainty estimates are not due to a weaker optical flow model, i.e. from obvious mistakes that are easy to predict.

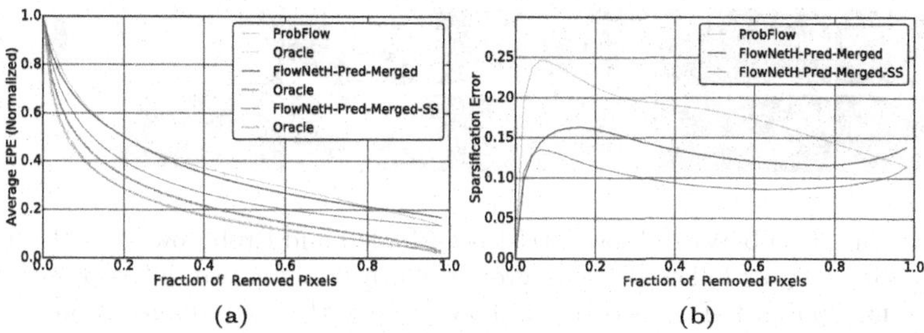

Fig. 5. Plots of the sparsification curves with their respective oracles **(a)** and of the sparsification errors **(b)** for ProbFlow, FlowNetH-Pred-Merged and FlowNetH-Pred-Merged-SS (version with 2 refinement networks stacked on top) on the Sintel train final dataset. KITTI versions are similar and provided in the supplemental material.

Table 3. Comparison of FlowNetH to the state-of-the-art uncertainty estimation method ProbFlow [29] on the Sintel train clean, Sintel train final and our KITTI 2012+2015 validation split datasets. The '-FT-KITTI' version is trained on FlyingChairs [6] first and then on FlyingThings3D [23], as described in Sect. 5.1 and subsequently fine-tuned on our KITTI 2012+2015 training split. FlowNetH-Pred-Merged, -S and -SS are all trained with the FlowNet2 [12] schedule described in supplemental material Fig. 6. Our method outperforms ProbFlow in AUSE by a large margin and also in terms of EPE for the KITTI dataset. †runtime taken from [29], please see the supplemental material for details on the computation of the ProbFlow outputs.

	Sintel clean		Sintel final		KITTI		Runtime
	AUSE	EPE	AUSE	EPE	AUSE	EPE	
ProbFlow [29]	0.162	1.87	0.173	3.34	0.466	8.95	38.1s†
FlowNetH-Pred-Merged-FT-KITTI	-	-	-	-	**0.086**	3.12	**60** ms
FlowNetH-Pred-Merged	0.117	2.58	0.128	3.78	0.151	7.84	**60** ms
FlowNetH-Pred-Merged-S	0.091	2.29	0.098	3.51	0.102	6.86	86 ms
FlowNetH-Pred-Merged-SS	**0.089**	2.19	**0.096**	3.40	0.091	6.50	99 ms

Table 3 further shows that the uncertainty estimation is not limited to simple encoder-decoder networks, but can also be applied successfully to state-of-the-art stacked networks [12]. To this end, we follow Ilg et al. [12] and stack refinement networks on top of FlowNetH-Pred-Merged. Different from [12], each refinement network yields the residual of the flow field and the uncertainty, as recently proposed by [27]. We refer to the network with the 1st refinement network as FlowNetH-Pred-Merged-S and with the second refinement network as FlowNetH-Pred-Merged-SS, since each refinement network is a FlowNetS [12].

The uncertainty estimation is not negatively influenced by the stacking, despite the improving flow fields. This shows again that the uncertainty estimation works reliably notwithstanding if the predicted optical flow is good or bad.

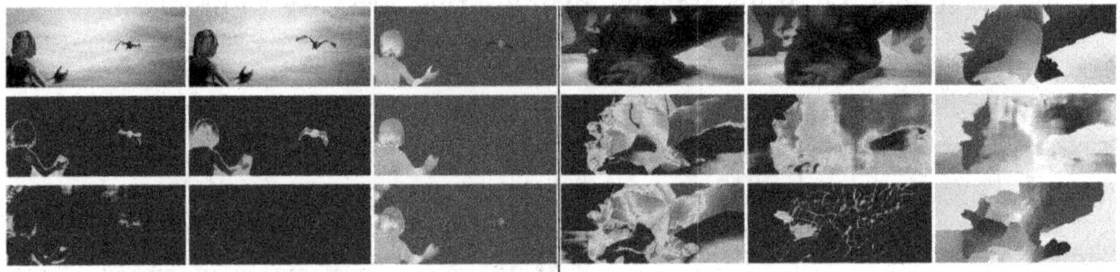

Fig. 6. Comparison between FlowNetH-Pred-Merged and ProbFlow [29]. The first row shows the image pair followed by its ground-truth flow for two different scenes from the Sintel final dataset. The second row shows FlowNetH-Pred-Merged results: entropy from a Laplace distribution with ground-truth error (we refer to this as *Oracle Entropy* to represent the optimal uncertainty as explained in the supplemental material), predicted entropy and predicted flow. Similar to the second row, the third row shows the results for ProbFlow. Although both methods fail at estimating the motion of the dragon on the left scene and the motion of the arm and the leg in the right scene, our method is better at predicting the uncertainties in these regions.

Figure 6 shows a qualitative comparison to ProbFlow. Clearly, the uncertainty estimate of FlowNet-Pred-Merged also performs well outside motion boundaries and covers many other causes for brittle optical flow estimates. More results on challenging real-world data are shown in the supplemental video which can also be found on https://youtu.be/HvyovWSo8uE.

6 Conclusion

We presented and evaluated several methods to estimate the uncertainty of deep regression networks for optical flow estimation. We showed that SGDR and Bootstrapped Ensembles perform better than the commonly used dropout technique. Furthermore, we found that a single network can estimate its own uncertainty surprisingly well and that this estimate outperforms every empirical ensemble. We believe that these results will apply to many other computer vision tasks, too. Moreover, we presented a multi-hypotheses network that shows very good performance and is faster than sampling-based approaches and ensembles. The fact that networks can estimate their own uncertainty reliably and in real-time is of high practical relevance. Humans tend to trust an engineered method much more than a trained network, of which nobody knows exactly how it solves the task. However, if networks say when they are confident and when they are not, we can trust them a bit more than we do today.

Acknowledgements. We gratefully acknowledge funding by the German Research Foundation (SPP 1527 grants BR 3815/8-1 and HU 1900/3-1, CRC-1140 KIDGEM Z02) and by the Horizon 2020 program of the EU via the ERC Starting Grant 716721 and the project Trimbot2020.

References

1. Aodha, O.M., Humayun, A., Pollefeys, M., Brostow, G.J.: Learning a confidence measure for optical flow. IEEE Trans. Pattern Anal. Mach. Intell. **35**(5), 1107–1120 (2013). https://doi.org/10.1109/TPAMI.2012.171
2. Blundell, C., Cornebise, J., Kavukcuoglu, K., Wierstra, D.: Weight uncertainty in neural network. In: Proceedings of the 32nd International Conference on Machine Learning (ICML 2015), pp. 1613–1622 (2015)
3. Bruhn, A., Weickert, J.: A confidence measure for variational optic flow methods. In: Klette, R., Kozera, R., Noakes, L., Weickert, J. (eds.) Geometric Properties for Incomplete data, pp. 283–298. Springer, Dordrecht (2006). https://doi.org/10.1007/1-4020-3858-8_15
4. Chen, Q., Koltun, V.: Photographic image synthesis with cascaded refinement networks. In: IEEE International Conference on Computer Vision (ICCV) (2017)
5. Chen, T., Fox, E., Guestrin, C.: Stochastic gradient Hamiltonian Monte Carlo. In: Proceedings of the 31st International Conference on Machine Learning (ICML 2014) (2014)
6. Dosovitskiy, A., et al.: FlowNet: learning optical flow with convolutional networks. In: IEEE International Conference on Computer Vision (ICCV) (2015)
7. Gal, Y., Ghahramani, Z.: Dropout as a Bayesian approximation: representing model uncertainty in deep learning. In: International Conference on Machine Learning (ICML) (2016)
8. Graves, A.: Practical variational inference for neural networks. In: Advances in Neural Information Processing Systems (NIPS), pp. 2348–2356 (2011)
9. Guzman-Rivera, A., Batra, D., Kohli, P.: Multiple choice learning: learning to produce multiple structured outputs. In: International Conference on Neural Information Processing Systems (NIPS) (2012)
10. Hernández-Lobato, J., Adams, R.: Probabilistic backpropagation for scalable learning of Bayesian neural networks. In: Proceedings of the 32nd International Conference on Machine Learning (ICML 2015) (2015)
11. Huang, G., Li, Y., Pleiss, G.: Snapshot ensembles: Train 1, get M for free. In: International Conference on Learning Representations (ICLR) (2017)
12. Ilg, E., Mayer, N., Saikia, T., Keuper, M., Dosovitskiy, A., Brox, T.: FlowNet 2.0: evolution of optical flow estimation with deep networks. In: IEEE Conference on Computer Vision and Pattern Recognition (CVPR) (2017)

13. Ioffe, S., Szegedy, C.: Batch normalization: Accelerating deep network training by reducing internal covariate shift. In: Bach, F., Blei, D. (eds.) Proceedings of the 32nd International Conference on Machine Learning. Proceedings of Machine Learning Research, vol. 37, pp. 448–456. PMLR, Lille, 07–09 July 2015. http://proceedings.mlr.press/v37/ioffe15.html
14. Jia, Y., et al.: Caffe: convolutional architecture for fast feature embedding. In: Proceedings of ACMMM, pp. 675–678 (2014)
15. Kendall, A., Gal, Y.: What uncertainties do we need in Bayesian deep learning for computer vision? In: International Conference on Neural Information Processing Systems (NIPS) (2017)
16. Kondermann, C., Kondermann, D., Jähne, B., Garbe, C.: An adaptive confidence measure for optical flows based on linear subspace projections. In: Hamprecht, F.A., Schnörr, C., Jähne, B. (eds.) DAGM 2007. LNCS, vol. 4713, pp. 132–141. Springer, Heidelberg (2007). https://doi.org/10.1007/978-3-540-74936-3_14
17. Kondermann, C., Mester, R., Garbe, C.: A statistical confidence measure for optical flows. In: Forsyth, D., Torr, P., Zisserman, A. (eds.) ECCV 2008. LNCS, vol. 5304, pp. 290–301. Springer, Heidelberg (2008). https://doi.org/10.1007/978-3-540-88690-7_22
18. Kybic, J., Nieuwenhuis, C.: Bootstrap optical flow confidence and uncertainty measure. Comput. Vis. Image Underst. **115**(10), 1449–1462 (2011). https://doi.org/10.1016/j.cviu.2011.06.008. http://www.sciencedirect.com/science/article/pii/S1077314211001536
19. Lakshminarayanan, B., Pritzel, A., Blundell, C.: Simple and scalable predictive uncertainty estimation using deep ensembles. In: NIPS Workshop (2016)
20. Lee, S., Purushwalkam, S., Cogswell, M., Ranjan, V., Crandall, D., Batra, D.: Stochastic multiple choice learning for training diverse deep ensembles. In: International Conference on Neural Information Processing Systems (NIPS) (2016)
21. Loshchilov, I., Hutter, F.: SGDR: stochastic gradient descent with warm restarts. In: International Conference on Learning Representations (ICLR) (2017)
22. MacKay, D.J.C.: A practical Bayesian framework for backpropagation networks. Neural Comput. **4**(3), 448–472 (1992)
23. Mayer, N., et al.: A large dataset to train convolutional networks for disparity, optical flow, and scene flow estimation. In: 2016 IEEE Conference on Computer Vision and Pattern Recognition (CVPR), pp. 4040–4048, June 2016. https://doi.org/10.1109/CVPR.2016.438
24. Neal, R.: Bayesian learning for neural networks. Ph.D. thesis, University of Toronto (1996)
25. Nix, D.A., Weigend, A.S.: Estimating the mean and variance of the target probability distribution. In: Neural Networks: IEEE World Congress on Computational Intelligence, vol. 1, pp. 55–60, June 1994. https://doi.org/10.1109/ICNN.1994.374138
26. Novotny, D., Larlus, D., Vedaldi, A.: Learning 3D object categories by looking around them. In: IEEE International Conference on Computer Vision (ICCV) (2017)
27. Pang, J., Sun, W., Ren, J.S.J., Yang, C., Yan, Q.: Cascade residual learning: a two-stage convolutional neural network for stereo matching. In: IEEE International Conference on Computer Vision (ICCV) Workshop (2017)
28. Ummenhofer, B., et al.: Demon: Depth and motion network for learning monocular stereo. In: IEEE Conference on Computer Vision and Pattern Recognition (CVPR) (2017). http://lmb.informatik.uni-freiburg.de//Publications/2017/UZUMIDB17

29. Wannenwetsch, A.S., Keuper, M., Roth, S.: ProbFlow: joint optical flow and uncertainty estimation. In: IEEE International Conference on Computer Vision (ICCV), October 2017
30. Welling, M., Teh, Y.: Bayesian learning via stochastic gradient Langevin dynamics. In: Proceedings of the 28th International Conference on Machine Learning (ICML 2011) (2011)

Normalized Blind Deconvolution

Meiguang Jin[1(✉)], Stefan Roth[2(✉)], and Paolo Favaro[1(✉)]

[1] University of Bern, Bern, Switzerland
{jin,paolo.favaro}@inf.unibe.ch
[2] TU Darmstadt, Darmstadt, Germany
stefan.roth@visinf.tu-darmstadt.de

Abstract. We introduce a family of novel approaches to single-image blind deconvolution, *i.e.*, the problem of recovering a sharp image and a blur kernel from a single blurry input. This problem is highly ill-posed, because infinite (image, blur) pairs produce the same blurry image. Most research effort has been devoted to the design of priors for natural images and blur kernels, which can drastically prune the set of possible solutions. Unfortunately, these priors are usually not sufficient to favor the sharp solution. In this paper we address this issue by looking at a much less studied aspect: the relative scale ambiguity between the sharp image and the blur. Most prior work eliminates this ambiguity by fixing the L^1 norm of the blur kernel. In principle, however, this choice is arbitrary. We show that a careful design of the blur normalization yields a blind deconvolution formulation with remarkable accuracy and robustness to noise. Specifically, we show that using the Frobenius norm to fix the scale ambiguity enables convex image priors, such as the total variation, to achieve state-of-the-art results on both synthetic and real datasets.

1 Introduction

The removal of blur in images has seen substantial progress in the past few decades with a wealth of efficient algorithms available today [7,24,36]. Advances have been made by exploring different energy formulations [5,24,44] as well as image priors [28,39,43,45,52] in both Bayesian [2,9,23,47] and deterministic frameworks [7,30,31]. Advanced image formation models [14,40,48] allow going beyond stationary blur, and, recently, a variety of deep learning approaches [4,15,16,25,26,35,38,41] have been proposed.

In its simplest form, blind deconvolution describes a blurry image y as the convolution between a latent blur k and a latent sharp image x. Because of the convolutional image formation model, there is an inherent scale ambiguity between these two unknowns. That is, one could multiply the blur k by a scale factor $s > 0$ and the image x by the reciprocal factor $1/s$ to obtain the same

V. Ferrari et al. (Eds.): ECCV 2018, LNCS 11211, pp. 694–711, 2018.
https://doi.org/10.1007/978-3-030-01234-2_41

blurry image y. To remove this ambiguity, it is common to impose that $|k|_1 = 1$. However, since the scale is arbitrary, so is this choice of normalization.[1]

Indeed, we could use any other norm in principle, such as the L^2 or Frobenius norm, and require $|k|_2 = 1$. More generally, we could apply an arbitrary p-norm and constrain $|k|_p = 1$, where $|\cdot|_p$ denotes the L^p norm. To the best of our knowledge, very little attention has been paid to the scale ambiguity between blur and image. We show that this choice matters much more than has been apparent, as it can significantly affect the performance of blind deconvolution algorithms. As we demonstrate later on, a more appropriate normalization can enable simple, convex image priors, such as total variation, reach state-of-the-art (SotA) image quality, which was previously possible only with more complex, non-convex priors [29,46]. Moreover, our scheme provably allows avoiding many difficulties that have hampered the practical implementation of SotA methods. This includes hand-tuned schedules for varying the amount of regularization across the iterations, approximating operators [29], or gradient steps.

Contributions: We would like to emphasize that we neither propose a novel image prior nor a novel blur prior. Rather, we *(1)* introduce a formulation of blind deconvolution with a novel, general **constraint** to fix the **scale ambiguity**; *(2)* provide a mathematical proof that shows for the first time a condition under which the sharp image is preferred over the blurry input image **even with classic convex image priors**;[2] *(3)* show that the proposed scale constraint **automatically** changes the amount of image regularization **across iterations**, avoiding custom-designed tuning typically used in most algorithms; *(4)* introduce two new algorithms that achieve **SotA** in terms of both accuracy and robustness.

2 Prior Work

Although blind deconvolution has been studied for more than two decades, it still remains a challenging task due to its ill-posed nature. Therefore, most methods for solving this problem differ in their regularization technique.

A common practice is to employ a regularization term for the sharp image x that encourages the sparsity of its gradients. This follows from the study of natural image statistics [37]. As a convex sparsity-inducing prior, the total variation

[1] Blind deconvolution is a mathematical problem with a corresponding physical problem (image deblurring). From the mathematical point of view, there is an ambiguous scale between the blur kernel and the sharp image, and L^1 normalization, as with any other arbitrary norm, is one possible choice to fix the scale of the blur kernel. However, as a model of a physical system, the blur kernel corresponds to the point spread function (PSF) of the camera lens(es), and in this case physics indicates that normalization is through the L^1 norm [3]. Therefore, we first solve the mathematical problem with an arbitrary norm, and then we map the final solution to a physically valid PSF by normalizing it in terms of L^1. This way we benefit from the mathematical freedom while ensuring physical validity in the end.

[2] Please note that prior work showed how convex image priors together with an L^1 constraint on the kernel *do not favor* the sharp image as a solution [22,30].

(TV), introduced by Rudin, Osher, and Fatemi [32] for denoising, has emerged as an effective choice also in blind deconvolution [5]. Despite the success of the TV prior in practice, Levin *et al.* [22] show that it favors blurry solutions. Perrone and Favaro [30] find that post normalization in the alternating minimization algorithm is responsible for the empirical success. Cho and Lee [8] show that under certain conditions, the MAP energy function can favor the correct solution. Beyond convex image priors, a wide variety of effective, non-convex methods has been proposed [7,36,44]. Wipf and Zhang [42] re-examine the common belief that the regularization term should encourage natural image statistics. They argue, instead, that the image prior should simply focus on discriminating between sharp and blurry images. Ideally this would be achieved with an L^0 regularizer, but the resulting objective is NP-hard. As a substitute, they suggest a logarithmic prior, which Babacan *et al.* [2] adopt with success. Different L^0 norm approximations have also been proposed [20,28,45]. Patch-based methods [24,39] sidestep classical regularizers and have shown impressive performance. However, they are usually computationally demanding due to searching for similar patches across scales [24] or finding sharp patches in an external dictionary [39].

Recently, due to the astounding success of deep learning, neural network-based motion deblurring approaches have been proposed [4,35]. [4] estimates Fourier coefficients of a deconvolutional filter to be applied to an input patch and shows remarkable reconstruction quality and speed. The main limitation of current learning-based approaches is that they do not generalize well to large blurs. Conventional approaches have remained superior in this regard. In this paper we also provide a theoretical result, hence focus on the simplest formulation of blind deblurring, where a blurry image is the result of a convolution. While already allowing practical applications, real blur can be much more complex. Great progress has been made on handling real blur, such as for camera shake [9,13,38,40], dynamic scenes [16–18,25,26], or object motion [11,27,34].

So far most approaches have focused on the design of image priors. Still, a variety of methods have also considered blur priors based on an L^1 or L^2 penalty [4,6,7,20,24,39,44,45] to either encourage the estimated blur kernel to be sparse or to discourage the trivial solution (*i.e.*, the estimated sharp image equals the blurry input). The recent work of Zhang *et al.* [49] is most closely related to ours. They also impose a unit Frobenius norm constraint on the blur kernel. Their analysis requires an explicit solution of the latent image given the blur kernel, which is challenging to obtain and requires approximations (*e.g.*, blur sparsity). In contrast, our analysis does not require an explicit solution; we present a novel proof for the TV prior that considers a family of normalizations, and we include a positivity constraint on the blur. Finally, we show that the scale ambiguity can be fixed so that even simple and efficient convex image priors yield SotA results outperforming [49], while provably avoiding the trivial solution.

3 Blind Deconvolution

A classic way to cast blind deconvolution [5] is to optimize

$$\min_{k,x} |y - k * x|_2^2 + \lambda |\nabla x|_2 \qquad \text{subject to } |k|_1 = 1, \quad k \geq 0, \tag{1}$$

where $\lambda > 0$ is a regularization parameter, $k \geq 0$ enforces element-wise non-negativity, and $|\nabla x|_2 \triangleq \sum_{i,j} |\nabla x_{ij}|_2$ denotes the discretized TV [32]. This formulation appeared with different modifications in several works [5,30,44]. One of its favorable properties is that the problem is convex in the blur k when the sharp image x is fixed and, vice versa, it is convex in x when fixing k. To see this, note that the constraints $|k|_1 = 1$ and $k \geq 0$ are equivalent to $\sum_i k_i = 1$ and $k \geq 0$. Thus, convergence analysis and several computationally efficient algorithms, such as alternating minimization, are available for this family of problems [12]. Unfortunately, solving the above formulation **globally** is known not to work [22,30], *i.e.*, it fails at recovering a sharp image. Specifically, the degenerate solution ($k = \delta$, $x = y$) yields a smaller energy than the true solution.

We now show that introducing a different scale normalization constraint allows transforming such a formulation into one that succeeds in recovering a sharp latent image. We then introduce two algorithms: one is used to study different scale normalizations, while the other is computationally efficient. Both achieve SotA results on standard synthetic and real datasets.

3.1 L^p Scale Normalization Constraint

As noted above, fixing the scale constraint via $|k|_1 = 1$ is an arbitrary choice due to the inherent scale ambiguity of the blind deblurring problem. Thus, let us consider the more general scale normalization $|k|_p = 1$, where $|\cdot|_p$ denotes the L^p norm. Our formulation with the L^p constraint then becomes

$$\min_{w,z} |y - w * z|_2^2 + \lambda |\nabla z|_2 \qquad \text{subject to } |w|_p = 1, \quad w \geq 0, \tag{2}$$

where for notational distinction from Problem (1), we have used w and z to denote the blur kernel and latent image, respectively. This formulation is not desirable as is, because it is not convex when solving for the blur kernel w due to the L^p constraint. However, we now show how to transform this formulation so that all alternating minimization steps involve convex optimization. First, let us relate the pair (k, x) to (w, z) via $k \triangleq {}^{w}/_{|w|_1}$ and $x \triangleq |w|_1 z$. Thus, $w*z = k*x$ and $|k|_p = {}^{|w|_p}/_{|w|_1}$. With the constraints on w in Problem (2) we have $|k|_p = {}^{1}/_{|w|_1}$. The above definitions plus constraints on w in Problem (2) are then equivalent to the new constraints $k \geq 0$, $|k|_1 = 1$, $w = {}^{k}/_{|k|_p}$, $z = |k|_p x$. Since the relations between k and w and between x and z are 1-to-1, we obtain

$$\min_{k,x} |y - k * x|_2^2 + \lambda |k|_p |\nabla x|_2 \qquad \text{subject to } |k|_1 = 1, \quad k \geq 0, \tag{3}$$

which is now convex in k for $p \geq 1$ and a fixed x.

Remark 1. Problem (3) is almost identical to the classic formulation of Problem (1), except for the **modified regularization term** $\lambda|k|_p|\nabla x|_2$. The weight λ is now scaled by the L^p norm of the blur k. When the blur k is close to a Dirac δ, the regularization will be the highest, and when the blur k is close to uniform, the regularization will be the lowest. It is thus clear that the proposed normalization is not equivalent to the classic L^1 case when $p > 1$.

Remark 2. We have transformed Problem (2) with the mappings $|k|_p = |w|_p/|w|_1$ and $x \triangleq |w|_1 z$ into Problem (3). Thus, the latent blur k in Problem (3) is always estimated as a valid PSF as in Problem (1).

The first question is then whether a choice of $p > 1$ brings any improvements to the set of solutions in the blind deconvolution formulation above. In the following proposition we show that this is indeed the case for $p \geq 2$.

Proposition 1. *Assume the gradients of the true sharp image x to be i.i.d. zero-mean Gaussian and the true blur kernel k to have finite support. Given a blurry image $y = k*x$ with the true blur k, Problem* (3) *then favors with high probability the true blur/image pair (k, x) over the trivial no-blur pair (δ, y) for $p \geq 2$.*

Proof. Both solutions make the data term $|y - k * x|_2^2 = 0$ and satisfy the constraints. The only term left in the objective function is therefore the joint prior $|k|_p|\nabla x|_2$ (note that the regularization parameter $\lambda > 0$ can be ignored). Therefore, we need to show that $|\delta|_p|\nabla y|_2 \geq |k|_p|\nabla x|_2$. **Blur term** $|k|_p$**:** This term can be left as is. **Blur term** $|\delta|_p$**:** We have that $|\delta|_p = 1, \forall p \in Z$. **Sharp image prior** $|\nabla x|_2$**:** Let us define $\nabla x_{ij} \doteq [\mathbf{u}_{ij}\ \mathbf{v}_{ij}]^\top$. Because of the assumptions on the gradient of a sharp image, we have that $\mathbf{u}_{ij}, \mathbf{v}_{ij} \sim \mathcal{N}(0, \sigma^2)$. Then, we obtain $|\nabla x_{ij}|_2 = \sqrt{\mathbf{u}_{ij}^2 + \mathbf{v}_{ij}^2} \sim \mathcal{X}_2$, where $\mathcal{X}_2$ denotes the Chi-squared distribution with two degrees of freedom. Its mean is $\mu_{\mathcal{X}} = \sqrt{\pi/2}\sigma$ and its variance $\sigma_{\mathcal{X}}^2 = (2 - \pi/2)\sigma^2$. Note that, because there are only two degrees of freedom and the Gaussian variables have zero mean, this is also equivalent to the Rayleigh distribution. Since we need to evaluate $|\nabla x|_2 \doteq \sum_{i=1}^N \sum_{j=1}^M |\nabla x_{ij}|_2$, we then need to compute the sum of MN independent Chi-squared (or Rayleigh) random variables. By using Chebyshev's inequality, we can write for any $\xi > 0$ $P\left(|^1/_{MN}|\nabla x|_2 - \mu_{\mathcal{X}}| < \xi\right) \geq 1 - \sigma_{\mathcal{X}}^2/MN\xi^2$. Therefore, for a sufficiently large MN the approximation

$$|\nabla x|_2 \simeq MN\sqrt{\tfrac{\pi}{2}}\sigma \tag{4}$$

will hold with very high probability.

Blurry Image Prior $|\nabla y|_2$**:** Let us define $|\nabla y_{ij}|_2 \doteq \sqrt{(k * \mathbf{u})_{i,j}^2 + (k * \mathbf{v})_{i,j}^2}$ so that $|\nabla y|_2 = \sum_{i,j} |\nabla y_{ij}|_2$. One can see that each $(k * \mathbf{u})_{i,j} \doteq \sum_{m,n} k_{m,n}\mathbf{u}_{i-m,j-n}$ is a zero-mean Gaussian with variance $\sigma^2|k|_2^2$. Thus, we also obtain that $|\nabla y_{ij}|_2$ is a Chi-squared distributed random variable, but with mean $\hat{\mu} = \sqrt{\pi/2}\sigma|k|_2$ and variance $\hat{\sigma}^2 = (2 - \pi/2)\sigma^2|k|_2^2$. The sum over the pixels (i, j) now needs additional care, because neighboring terms may not be independent. We use the assumption of a finite $W \times H$ support of k. Thus, we know that $|\nabla y_{ij}|_2$ is independent from $|\nabla y_{i+|\Omega|,j}|_2$. This suggests that we split the sum so that $\sum_{i,j} |\nabla y_{ij}|_2 = \sum_{p=1}^{W} \sum_{q=1}^{H} \sum_{i,j} |\nabla y_{p+Wi,q+Hj}|_2$. Then, by using the approximation of Eq. (4) we have $\sum_{i,j} |\nabla y_{p+Wi,q+Hj}|_2 \simeq \frac{MN}{WH}\sqrt{\frac{\pi}{2}}\sigma|k|_2$ and finally $|\nabla y|_2 \simeq \sum_{p=1}^{W} \sum_{q=1}^{H} \frac{MN}{WH}\sqrt{\frac{\pi}{2}}\sigma|k|_2 = MN\sqrt{\frac{\pi}{2}}\sigma|k|_2$. By putting all together, we have that $|\delta|_p|\nabla y|_2 \simeq MN\sqrt{\frac{\pi}{2}}\sigma|k|_2 \geq MN\sqrt{\frac{\pi}{2}}\sigma|k|_p \simeq |k|_p|\nabla x|_2$. This boils down to $|k|_2 \geq |k|_p$, which is true for $p \geq 2$. We can therefore conclude that $|\nabla y|_2 \geq |k|_2|\nabla x|_2 \geq |k|_p|\nabla x|_2$ for any $p \geq 2$ with high probability when MN is large enough. □

This result shows that by changing the scale normalization constraint, we have transformed Problem (1) with a trivial global solution into Problem (3), where the trivial solution is no longer preferred over the true one. Note that the optimal solution will be given as a trade-off between data term and image prior. To fully assess the impact of our scale normalization constraint, we propose two algorithms to minimize Problem (3) and test them on standard datasets.

3.2 Frank-Wolfe (FW) algorithm

Because of Proposition 1, we can now attempt to solve Problem (3) **globally**. We propose to use an alternating minimization method and run each alternating step until convergence. By denoting the iteration index as $t \geq 0$, we first update the latent image via

$$x^t = \arg\min_x |y - k^t * x|_2^2 + \lambda|k^t|_p|\nabla x|_2 \tag{5}$$

with the L-BFGS-B algorithm [50] with box constraints (imposing $x \geq 0$ and $x \leq 1$ at every pixel). Then, we solve

$$k^{t+1} = \arg\min_k |y - k * x^t|_2^2 + \lambda|k|_p|\nabla x^t|_2 \qquad \text{subject to } |k|_1 = 1, \quad k \geq 0 \tag{6}$$

with the Frank-Wolfe algorithm (FW) [10]. The algorithm is initialized with $k^0 = \delta$. We are not aware of any prior blind deconvolution method that solves each step of the alternating minimization problem above, particularly Eq. (6), **without approximations**. Note that in the FW algorithm we do not adapt the regularization weight λ with the iteration index t. We have not found prior methods capable of converging to the correct kernel when the latent blur is initialized with the Dirac δ and the regularization parameter is fixed. This is indeed not possible if the global minimum of the objective is the degenerate solution $(k = \delta, x = y)$. Note that changing the regularization during the iterations in a heuristic way means changing the original cost function that one intends to minimize.

3.3 Post-normalization (PN) algorithm

As we will see in the experiments, the FW algorithm tends to converge slowly (although still faster than many other SotA methods). As a more efficient implementation, we consider the method of Chan and Wong [5,30]. We thus derive an alternating gradient descent method. We minimize

$$E[x,k] \triangleq |y - k * x|_2^2 + \lambda |k|_p |\nabla x|_2 \tag{7}$$

with respect to x and k by alternating between

$$x^t = x^{t-1} - \epsilon_x \nabla_x E[x^{t-1}, k^{t-1}] \tag{8}$$

and

$$\hat{k}^t = k^{t-1} - \epsilon_k \nabla_k E[x^t, k^{t-1}], \quad \tilde{k}^t = \max\{0, \hat{k}^t\} \quad \text{and} \quad k^t = \tilde{k}^t / |\tilde{k}^t|_1 \tag{9}$$

with step sizes $\epsilon_x, \epsilon_k > 0$. This method, termed PN, is an approximate solver since the sequential updates of the blur do not correspond to an alternating minimization [30]. Nonetheless, when applied to Problem (1), it has been shown to perform well (albeit not with SotA results). In our experiments we show that the new L^2 blur normalization of Problem (3) can boost its performance dramatically. As with the FW algorithm, we initialize the blur with $k^0 = \delta$.

Remark 3. The prior $\lambda |k|_p |\nabla x|_2$ in Problem (3) has a very important role during sharp image estimation. Since the blur is fixed during the estimation of x, we can consider $\lambda |k|_p$ as a regularization weight. This weight changes as k is updated, in turn affecting the amount of regularization of the sharp image. Because we initialize the blur with a Dirac δ, the initial regularization is the highest possible. Then, as the blur gradually moves away from the Dirac δ, the amount of regularization decreases. This annealing of the regularization weight is similar to the heuristic schedule used in other methods [2,23,30,31]. However, note that in our case we obtain this desirable effect in a rigorous fashion from the objective (and by defining the blur initialization). Also note that **our scale constraint is different from adding an L^2 penalty on the blur as used in prior work** [6,7,24,39,44]. In our case the blur update is affected by the TV regularizer, thus adjusting the amount of blur regularization across iterations.

Remark 4. FW vs PN. FW and PN are both blind deconvolution algorithms. FW is an exact optimization in the sense that it optimizes exactly the original objective. PN instead uses an approximate algorithm to minimize the original objective. Hence, in the following section we use FW to demonstrate the theory and the accuracy. In the experimental section, we mainly use PN as it converges about 3 times faster than FW without losing much accuracy.

4 Scale Normalization Analysis

Our first experiment is to validate Proposition 1 empirically when gradient statistics are non-Gaussian. We use the whole BSDS dataset [1] (500 images) and randomly generate 100 different blurs as in [4] to yield triplets (blurry image y, sharp image x, blur kernel k). We do not add any noise such that every triplet satisfies exactly the convolutional model. We then compute the prior ratio $\frac{|\delta|_p |\nabla y|_2}{|k|_p |\nabla x|_2}$

to analyze how often the prior favors the true sharp image (*i.e.*, the ratio is above 1). Figure 1a shows the mean and standard deviation of the prior ratio as well as its minimum value (*i.e.*, the worst case) over the whole BSDS dataset for different values of p. We observe that for $p \geq 2$ the prior always favors the estimation of the sharp image (on all samples, and in particular, also in the worst case) as indicated by Proposition 1 for Gaussian image statistics.

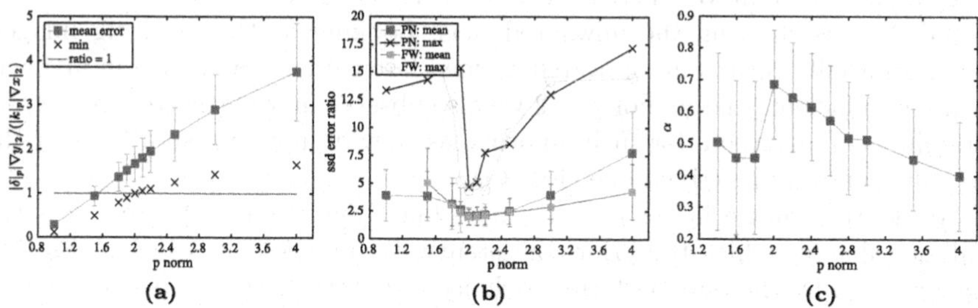

Fig. 1. **(a)** Evaluation of image prior ratios $|\delta|_p|\nabla y|_2/|k|_p|\nabla x|_2$ over triplets (blurry image y, sharp image x, blur kernel k) on the BSDS dataset [1]. The plot shows the mean, standard deviation, and the minimum value of the prior ratio for different values of p. The image prior favors sharp images when the computed prior ratio is above 1. This is always the case with $p \geq 2$. **(b)** Evaluation of different scale normalizations on 12 BSDS images [1] for 6 blurs [33]. We plot the mean and standard deviation of the SSD error ratio of the FW and PN methods for different values of p. The smallest SSD error ratio is achieved by $p = 2$. **(c)** Evaluation of the blur bias due to the p-norm. For different values of p, we plot the weight $\alpha \in [0, 1]$ (*i.e.*, the coefficient of the convex combination $k_\alpha = \alpha k^* + (1 - \alpha)k_{\text{unif}}$, see text) for which k_α has minimal MSE. As p increases beyond 2, α decreases and the estimated blur moves towards being uniform. This shows a clear bias that tends to smooth the blur kernel and therefore results in oversharpened image reconstructions.

Next, we explore different choices of p (between 1 and 4) for both the FW and PN algorithms. We randomly pick 12 images from the BSDS dataset [1], and combine them with 6 blurs from [33] to generate synthetic blurry images. We compute the Sum of Squared Difference (SSD) ratio on the estimated latent sharp image as proposed by [23]. We set $\epsilon_x = 0.005$ and $\epsilon_k = 0.001$. λ is tuned for each p-norm to obtain the best performance; the blur is initialized as a Dirac δ. We omit the results for the FW method with $p = 1$, since it gets stuck at the trivial solution. Note that the FW method converges more slowly than PN. The results of both algorithms are shown in Fig. 1b. We observe that $p = 2$ performs best among the different L^p norms.

Our last evaluation is to show that large p values tend to introduce a bias towards uniform blur. To that end, we combine an image from the BSDS dataset with a blur k^*, and then solve the blind deconvolution problem to estimate a blur kernel k for different p values. After obtaining results for different p values, we first spatially align the estimated blurs to the ground truth k^*, and then find the best match within a set of example kernels. To measure the bias, we generate the example set from convex combinations of the true blur k^* and the uniform blur k_{unif}, *i.e.*, $k_\alpha = \alpha k^* + (1-\alpha)k_{\text{unif}}$ for a few $\alpha \in [0,1]$ values. We then search for the optimal α for each p, such that k_α has the minimum mean square error (MSE) compared to the corresponding estimated blur. We repeat this experiment on 56 different image/blur pairs and plot the mean and standard deviation of different α weights for different p values in Fig. 1c. We observe that the estimated blur moves increasingly towards the uniform blur as p increases beyond 2, thus showing the unwanted bias. Looking at the resulting images, this bias initially results in an oversharpened latent image and then in artifacts when p is sufficiently large. For $p < 2$ we also observe more bias, stemming from instabilities of algorithm for such p-norms, as they do not consistently favor the true solution over the trivial one (Fig. 1a).

Considering that a larger p yields more bias (Fig. 1c) and that $p = 2$ is the smallest value for which the prior consistently favors the true solution (Fig. 1a) may explain why the best performing choice in practice is $p = 2$ (see Fig. 1b).

5 Experiments

We test our algorithms on the standard SUN deblurring dataset [39], containing 80 images of average size 1024×768 pixels, which have been synthetically blurred with the 8 blurs from [22] with 1% white Gaussian noise added. The evaluation uses the Sum of Squared Difference (SSD) ratio of [23]. We estimate kernels with various approaches, including ours, and use EPLL [51] to obtain final latent sharp images. Michaeli and Irani [24] pointed out that results with an error ratio below 5 can be considered visually pleasing. We follow this principle, consider an error ratio above 5 as a failure case, and count the number of failure cases for each method to quantify its robustness. In all our evaluations we achieve SotA performance in terms of accuracy, worst case errors, and robustness to noise, except for one case where we achieve second place. This highlights the importance of normalization in blind deconvolution.

Figure 2 shows some visual comparisons between our proposed `PN` method and other top-performing algorithms on the SUN dataset [39]. Results for other methods are collected from the corresponding authors' web page. We pick the worst input image for each algorithm and show the corresponding result obtained with our `PN` algorithm. It can be seen that the proposed algorithm succeeds in most cases. The worst input image for our algorithm is the same as for [31] (Fig. 2f). While the SSD ratio is above 5 in this case, our result is still visually pleasant.

Robustness. To better understand the robustness properties of our algorithm, we show the cumulative distribution of SSD error ratios across the whole SUN dataset [39] in Fig. 4 (left). We observe that our algorithm is on par with other SotA methods. More importantly, we see that our algorithm saturates to 100% faster than the other methods, since our algorithm's worst SSD error ratio is smaller than the others'. Moreover, most of our failure cases have an SSD error

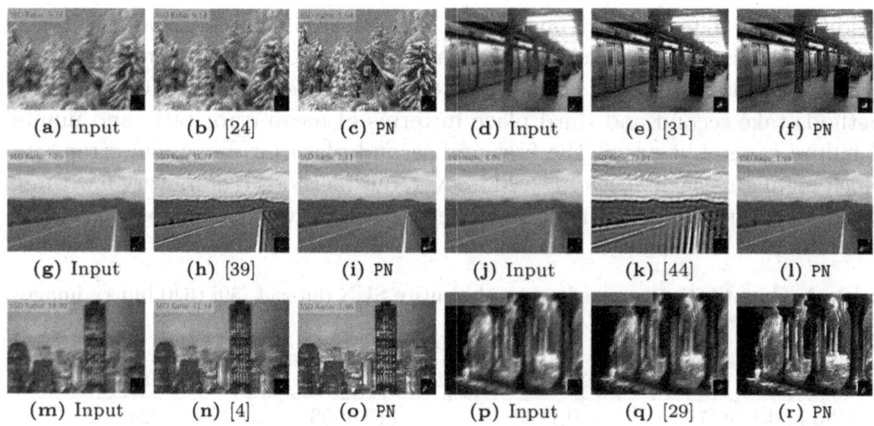

Fig. 2. Visual comparison of the results obtained from the top performers on the SUN dataset [39]. We pick the worst-case result for each top performer and show the corresponding output of our PN method. Our worst-case result is shown in (f).

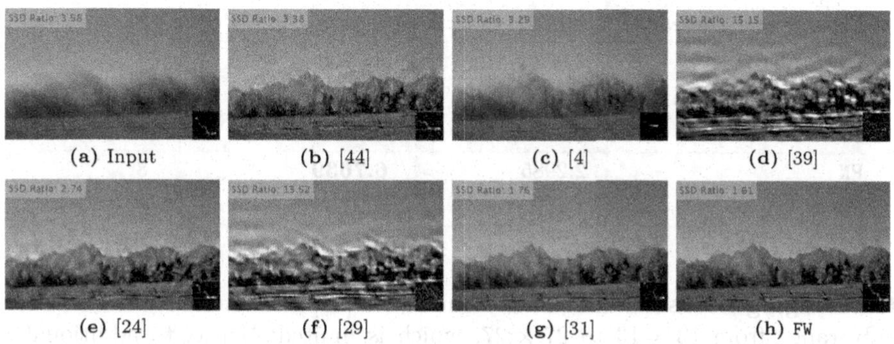

Fig. 3. One example image from the BSDS dataset [1] tested on different methods.

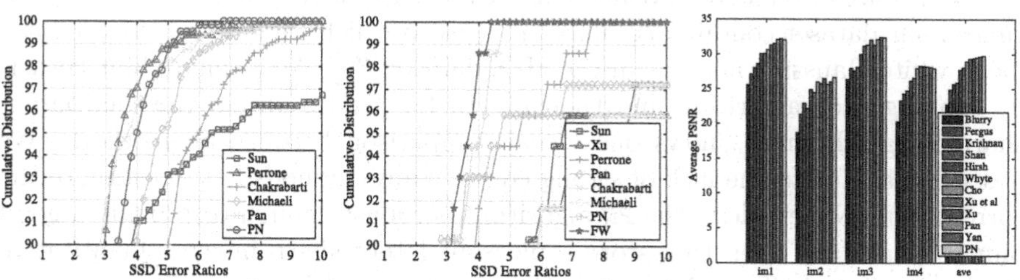

Fig. 4. Left: Cumulative distribution of the SSD error ratios on the whole SUN dataset [39]. Middle: Cumulative distribution of the SSD error ratios on the small BSDS dataset [1]. Right: Quantitative results on the Köhler *et al.* [19] dataset.

ratio below 6. There is only one failure case above 6, shown visually in Fig. 2f. Additionally, in Table 1 we show the mean error ratio, maximum error ratio, and number of failure cases for all methods on the SUN dataset [39]. Our proposed methods take second and third place in terms of mean error ratio and number of failure cases, but are at the first and second place for maximum error ratio, which highlights their *robustness*. Moreover, our methods require very few tuning parameters (and no adjustment of the regularization weight λ across iterations).

Table 1. Quantitative comparison on the entire SUN dataset [39] (640 blurry images).

Method	Mean error ratio	Maximum error ratio	Failure cases
Cho and Lee [7]	9.1983	113.4908	224
Krishnan *et al.* [20]	12.0150	142.6680	475
Levin *et al.* [23]	6.6948	44.1706	357
Sun *et al.* [39]	2.5813	35.7653	44
Xu and Jia [44]	3.8172	75.0363	98
Perrone and Favaro [31]	2.1140	8.5173	**7**
Chakrabarti [4]	3.0623	11.5760	64
Michaeli and Irani [24]	2.6171	9.1847	30
Pan *et al.* [29]	**1.9144**	23.2785	11
`PN`	2.2985	**6.7639**	8
`FW`	2.195	**6.213**	8

Challenging Blurs. Although the 8 blurs from [22] look realistic, the blur sizes only range from 13×13 to 27×27, which is limited. Hence, to additionally evaluate the robustness for all algorithms, we create a small dataset composed of 12 images randomly picked from the BSDS dataset [1]. We collect 6 blurs from [33], which are also recorded realistically. Blur sizes range from 21×21 to 41×41. Hence, our dataset contains 72 blurry images to which we have added 1% zero-mean white Gaussian noise as in the SUN dataset [39]. We estimate blur kernels by running each algorithm and then use EPLL [51] to obtain the final latent sharp image. Figure 3 shows one visual comparison between all methods. We observe that due to the lack of strong edges, many methods fail to estimate the correct blur. Nonetheless, the `PN` algorithm is robust enough to provide a good blur estimate and then to restore a pleasant latent sharp image. Quantitative results are given in Table 2 and show that our approach *consistently outperforms* all previous methods in all three metrics (mean error ratio, maximum error ratio, and the number of failure cases). Our `FW` and `PN` algorithms succeed on all 72 images. Figure 4 (middle) shows the cumulative distributions of the SSD error ratio for all competitors. We observe that the `FW` and `PN` algorithms perform very well. In 90% of all cases, our `FW` and `PN` algorithms obtain an error ratio below 3. We also evaluated only the `PN` method and the SotA method [29] on the full BSDS dataset (3000 blurry images from 500 sharp images with 6 blur kernels). Table 2 shows that the benefit of our approach on the full BSDS is even more pronounced than on the smaller subset. For both datasets, we consistently use the same parameter $\lambda = 0.016$ and apply a multi-scale pyramid scheme [24,29,31,39,46] to speed up convergence of both our PN and FW algorithms. We run 500 and 80 iterations at each scale for the PN and the FW algorithms, respectively.

Table 2. Quantitative comparison on the small BSDS dataset [1] (72 blurry images).

Method	Mean error ratio	Maximum error ratio	Failure cases
Sun *et al.* [39]	2.6482	15.1516	12
Xu and Jia [44]	3.6447	22.2717	13
Perrone and Favaro [31]	2.0930	7.4934	4
Chakrabarti [4]	3.7683	11.8088	9
Michaeli and Irani [24]	3.4577	23.0012	14
Pan *et al.* [29]	2.0583	13.5157	3
Yan *et al.* [46]	2.0224	12.2365	3
L^1 normalization	2.2106	7.8214	3
Weight decay (heuristic)	2.5911	8.7622	2
L^2 blur prior (classic)	2.4867	7.9534	4
PN	2.0113	4.6760	**0**
FW	**1.9826**	**4.3868**	**0**
Quantitative comparison on the full BSDS dataset [1] (3000 blurry images)			
Pan *et al.* [29]	2.956	68.976	325
PN	**2.0670**	**24.091**	**94**

L^2 vs L^1 Blur Normalization. To see the effectiveness of L^2 normalization, we compare the proposed Problem (3) with the classic Problem (1) on the BSDS test set. For Problem (1) we employ the same regularization weight scheme used in prior work [29,31,46]. By starting with a strong regularization, these methods avoid the trivial solution ($k = \delta$). Nonetheless, we observe that Problem (1) has an SSD ratio of 2.21 (0.2 worse than our PN) and three failure examples, which are shown in the second block of Table 2. Therefore, our L^2 blur normalization scheme outperforms the standard L^1 normalization.

Principled vs Heuristic Weight Decay. As an additional test, we modify the L^1 model to more closely mimic the regularization of Problem (2). Specifically, we artificially scale the regularization weight λ with the L^2 norm of the blur kernel. However, in this modification the blur estimation is carried as usual with Problem (1) (with post normalization). The SSD ratio of this modified algorithm on the BSDS dataset is 2.59, which is almost 0.6 worse than that of Problem (2).

Additionally, it has 2 failure cases as shown in the second block of Table 2. This demonstrates empirically that our exact formulation in Problem (2) is better than a heuristic weight decay rule.

Comparison to Additive L^2 Norm Blur Prior. We add an explicit L^2 blur regularization term to the objective function in Problem (1) as in SotA approaches [24,29,39,44,46]. This modification has an SSD error ratio of 2.48 and 4 failure examples, which we report in the second block of Table 2.

Köhler's Dataset (Real Data). We also evaluate our methods on the full dataset of Köhler *et al.* [19]. Quantitative results and one visual example are shown in Figs. 4 (right) and 6. Although this dataset contains blur from camera shake, the `FW` and `PN` algorithms yield visually pleasant estimates. Note that both algorithms were not explicitly designed for such non-uniform blur.

Table 3. Quantitative comparison (normalized L^2 error) of SotA approaches on Levin's dataset [22] (32 blurry images) with additive noise (*original* means no noise is added).

Method	Original	1%	2%	3%	4%	5%
Xu and Jia [44]	3.959	4.132	4.920	5.232	5.623	5.785
Pan *et al.* [29]	3.795	4.008	4.658	4.958	5.325	5.368
Yan *et al.* [46]	3.790	3.901	4.562	4.946	5.278	5.342
`PN`	**3.788**	**3.815**	**3.911**	**4.098**	**4.188**	**4.202**

Table 4. Quantitative comparison (PSNR) of SotA approaches on Köhler's dataset [19] (48 blurry images) under additive noise (*original* means no noise is added).

Method	Original	1%	2%	3%	4%	5%
Xu and Jia [44]	29.475	26.602	25.202	21.523	18.785	17.239
Pan *et al.* [29]	29.551	27.883	26.812	22.116	19.152	18.021
Yan *et al.* [46]	29.595	27.921	26.855	22.143	19.166	18.100
`PN`	**29.613**	**29.113**	**27.89**	**25.156**	**22.892**	**21.544**

Noise Sensitivity. Our numerical analysis in Sect. 4 is based on noise-free images as in [29]. It is important to note that all experiments shown in Sect. 5 are conducted on datasets (SUN and BSDS) in which 1% zero-mean Gaussian noise was added (Tables 1 and 2). To quantitatively evaluate the noise sensitivity of our method, we modify Levin's [22] and Köhler's [19] datasets by adding 1%, 2%, 3%, 4%, and 5% white Gaussian noise. Quantitative comparisons are shown in Tables 3 and 4. Blur kernel estimation errors are measured as the average of the normalized L^2 error $|\hat{k} - k|_2/|k|_2$, where $\hat{k}$ is the estimate and k is the ground truth. Notice that a quantitative comparison on the original dataset (no added noise) is also shown in Fig. 4 (right). Additionally, two visual comparisons on the original and 1% noise level images are shown in the 1st and 2nd rows of Fig. 5. One visual comparison on a real noisy image is shown on the third row of Fig. 5. We observe that our approach performs better than the SotA methods [29,44,46] and is overall also less sensitive to noise.

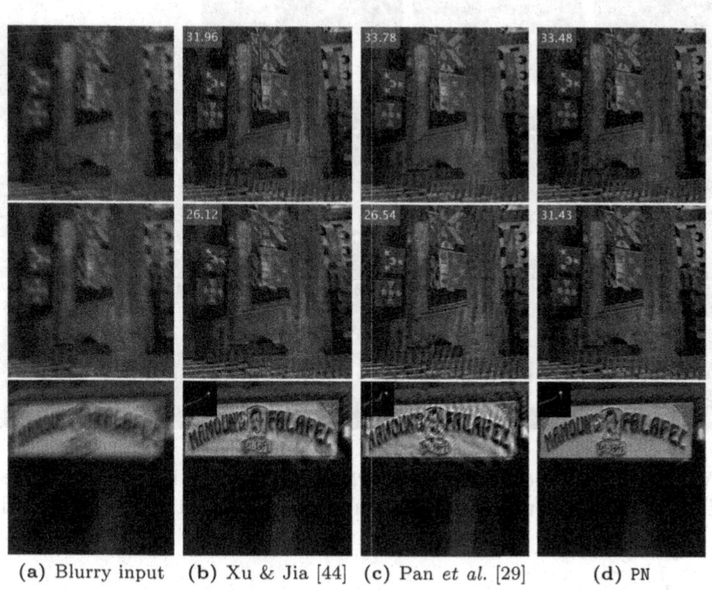

(a) Blurry input (b) Xu & Jia [44] (c) Pan *et al.* [29] (d) PN

Fig. 5. Visual comparison of results from [29,44] compared to the PN method on two real images from [19] and [21]. The first two rows show the deblurred results of an original image from [19] and its version with 2% added noise, respectively.

Comparison to [49]**.** Finally, we compare to the recent L^2 blur normalization approach of Zhang *et al.* [49]. Specifically, we compare on the dataset of Levin *et al.* [22], containing 32 real blurry images, for which the authors of [49] have supplied results. We find that the average of the normalized L^2 error of our kernel estimates is significantly better than in [49] (3.788 vs 5.452). In fact, our results consistently outperform [49] on each of the 32 estimates.

Limitations. One current limitation of the proposed approach is speed. To process a 400×400 blurry image with kernel size 41×41, our unoptimized Matlab code on our setup (Intel Core i7-3635QM, 16G RAM) for the PN and FW algorithms estimates the blur kernels in around 2 minutes and 6 min, respectively, whereas C++ implemented methods [44] only take less than 10 s. Still, ours are approximately 3× and 10× faster than other recent competitive methods [29,31]. Moreover, due to the convexity of each alternating iteration, we believe that the computational performance can be further improved. In Fig. 6 we show some of our worst failure cases on real images and compare our results with those of the

SotA approach from [29]. The first two rows show results in the case of large blur and saturation. In these cases, our results are not as accurate as those of [29]. Nonetheless, the reconstruction artifacts of our PN algorithm are still acceptable, which demonstrates its robustness to noise and saturation.

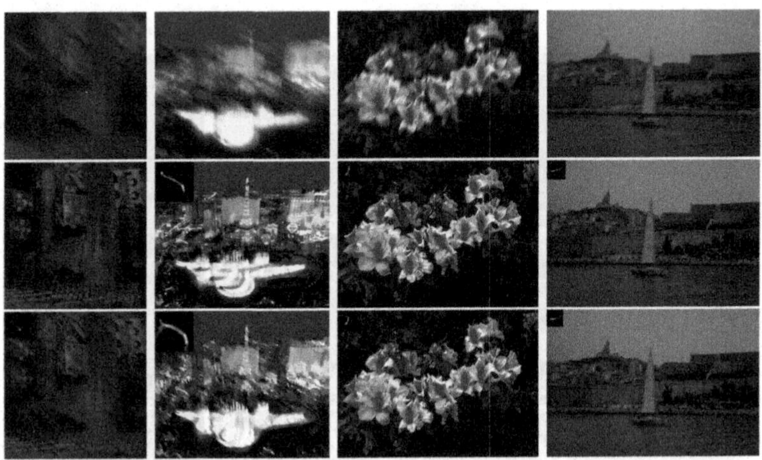

Fig. 6. Worst-case failure examples of our PN method on real images with camera shake from [19]. Top: blurry inputs. Middle: Results from [29]. Bottom: Results with PN.

6 Conclusion

We have introduced a novel scale normalization technique for blind deblurring based on L^p norms and shown both analytically and numerically that the choice $p = 2$ avoids trivial solutions that have challenged prior work. We demonstrated that our scale normalization can be interpreted as a rescaled classical objective in which the regularizer is adaptively weighted by the norm of the blur kernel. The resulting method is conceptually simple, obviates common heuristic adaptations of the regularization, and experiments on different datasets show SotA image reconstruction accuracy and a very high degree of robustness.

Acknowledgements. MJ and PF acknowledge support from the Swiss National Science Foundation on project 200021_153324.

References

1. Arbelaez, P., Maire, M., Fowlkes, C.C., Malik, J.: Contour detection and hierarchical image segmentation. IEEE TPAMI **33**(5), 898–916 (2011)
2. Babacan, S.D., Molina, R., Do, M.N., Katsaggelos, A.K.: Bayesian blind deconvolution with general sparse image priors. In: Fitzgibbon, A., Lazebnik, S., Perona, P., Sato, Y., Schmid, C. (eds.) ECCV 2012. LNCS, vol. 7577, pp. 341–355. Springer, Heidelberg (2012). https://doi.org/10.1007/978-3-642-33783-3_25

3. Born, M.: Principles of Optics - Electromagnetic Theory of Propagation, Interference and Diffraction of Light, 7th edn. Cambridge University Press, Cambridge (1999)
4. Chakrabarti, A.: A neural approach to blind motion deblurring. In: Leibe, B., Matas, J., Sebe, N., Welling, M. (eds.) ECCV 2016. LNCS, vol. 9907, pp. 221–235. Springer, Cham (2016). https://doi.org/10.1007/978-3-319-46487-9_14
5. Chan, T.F., Wong, C.: Total variation blind deconvolution. IEEE TIP **7**, 370–375 (1998)
6. Chaudhuri, S., Velmurugan, R., Rameshan, R.M.: Blind Image Deconvolution - Methods and Convergence. Springer, Heidelberg (2014). https://doi.org/10.1007/978-3-319-10485-0
7. Cho, S., Lee, S.: Fast motion deblurring. ACM Trans. Graph. **28**, 145:1–145:8 (2009)
8. Cho, S., Lee, S.: Convergence analysis of map based blur kernel estimation. In: ICCV (2017)
9. Fergus, R., Singh, B., Hertzmann, A., Roweis, S.T., Freeman, W.T.: Removing camera shake from a single photograph. ACM Trans. Graph. **25**(3), 787–794 (2006)
10. Frank, M., Wolfe, P.: An algorithm for quadratic programming. Naval Res. Logistics Q. **3**, 95–110 (1956)
11. Gast, J., Sellent, A., Roth, S.: Parametric object motion from blur. In: CVPR (2016)
12. Gorski, J., Pfeuffer, F., Klamroth, K.: Biconvex sets and optimization with biconvex functions: a survey and extensions. Math. Methods Oper. Res. **66**, 373–407 (2007)
13. Hirsch, M., Schuler, C.J., Harmeling, S., Schölkopf, B.: Fast removal of non-uniform camera shake. In: ICCV (2011)
14. Hirsch, M., Sra, S., Schölkopf, B., Harmeling, S.: Efficient filter flow for space-variant multiframe blind deconvolution. In: CVPR (2010)
15. Jin, M., Hirsch, M., Favaro, P.: Learning face deblurring fast and wide. In: CVPR Workshops (2018)
16. Jin, M., Meishvili, G., Favaro, P.: Learning to extract a video sequence from a single motion-blurred image. In: CVPR (2018)
17. Kim, T.H., Ahn, B., Lee, K.M.: Dynamic scene deblurring. In: ICCV (2013)
18. Kim, T.H., Lee, K.M.: Segmentation-free dynamic scene deblurring. In: CVPR (2014)
19. Köhler, R., Hirsch, M., Mohler, B., Schölkopf, B., Harmeling, S.: Recording and playback of camera shake: benchmarking blind deconvolution with a real-world database. In: Fitzgibbon, A., Lazebnik, S., Perona, P., Sato, Y., Schmid, C. (eds.) ECCV 2012. LNCS, vol. 7578, pp. 27–40. Springer, Heidelberg (2012). https://doi.org/10.1007/978-3-642-33786-4_3
20. Krishnan, D., Tay, T., Fergus, R.: Blind deconvolution using a normalized sparsity measure. In: CVPR (2011)
21. Lai, W., Huang, J., Hu, Z., Ahuja, N., Yang, M.: A comparative study for single image blind deblurring. In: CVPR (2016)
22. Levin, A., Weiss, Y., Durand, F., Freeman, W.T.: Understanding and evaluating blind deconvolution algorithms. In: CVPR (2009)
23. Levin, A., Weiss, Y., Durand, F., Freeman, W.T.: Efficient marginal likelihood optimization in blind deconvolution. In: CVPR (2011)
24. Michaeli, T., Irani, M.: Blind deblurring using internal patch recurrence. In: Fleet, D., Pajdla, T., Schiele, B., Tuytelaars, T. (eds.) ECCV 2014. LNCS, vol. 8691, pp. 783–798. Springer, Cham (2014). https://doi.org/10.1007/978-3-319-10578-9_51

25. Nah, S., Kim, T.H., Lee, K.M.: Deep multi-scale convolutional neural network for dynamic scene deblurring. In: CVPR (2017)
26. Noroozi, M., Chandramouli, P., Favaro, P.: Motion deblurring in the wild. In: Roth, V., Vetter, T. (eds.) GCPR 2017. LNCS, vol. 10496, pp. 65–77. Springer, Cham (2017). https://doi.org/10.1007/978-3-319-66709-6_6
27. Pan, J., Hu, Z., Su, Z., Lee, H., Yang, M.: Soft-segmentation guided object motion deblurring. In: CVPR (2016)
28. Pan, J., Hu, Z., Su, Z., Yang, M.: Deblurring text images via L0-regularized intensity and gradient prior. In: CVPR (2014)
29. Pan, J., Sun, D., Pfister, H., Yang, M.H.: Blind image deblurring using dark channel prior. In: CVPR (2016)
30. Perrone, D., Favaro, P.: Total variation blind deconvolution: The devil is in the details. In: CVPR (2014)
31. Perrone, D., Favaro, P.: A logarithmic image prior for blind deconvolution. IJCV (2016)
32. Rudin, L.I., Osher, S., Fatemi, E.: Nonlinear total variation based noise removal algorithms. Phys. D **60**, 259–268 (1992)
33. Schelten, K., Nowozin, S., Jancsary, J., Rother, C., Roth, S.: Interleaved regression tree field cascades for blind image deconvolution. In: WACV (2015)
34. Schelten, K., Roth, S.: Localized image blur removal through non-parametric kernel estimation. In: ICPR (2014)
35. Schuler, C.J., Hirsch, M., Harmeling, S., Schölkopf, B.: Learning to deblur. IEEE TPAMI **38**(7), 1439–1451 (2016)
36. Shan, Q., Jia, J., Agarwala, A.: High-quality motion deblurring from a single image. ACM Trans. Graph. **27**(3), 73 (2008)
37. Srivastava, A., Lee, A.B., Simoncelli, E.P., Zhu, S.: On advances in statistical modeling of natural images. J. Math. Imaging Vis. **18**, 17–33 (2003)
38. Sun, J., Cao, W., Xu, Z., Ponce, J.: Learning a convolutional neural network for non-uniform motion blur removal. In: CVPR (2015)
39. Sun, L., Cho, S., Wang, J., Hays, J.: Edge-based blur kernel estimation using patch priors. In: ICCP (2013)
40. Whyte, O., Sivic, J., Zisserman, A., Ponce, J.: Non-uniform deblurring for shaken images. IJCV **98**, 168–186 (2012)
41. Wieschollek, P., Schölkopf, B., Lensch, H.P.A., Hirsch, M.: End-to-end learning for image burst deblurring. In: Lai, S.-H., Lepetit, V., Nishino, K., Sato, Y. (eds.) ACCV 2016. LNCS, vol. 10114, pp. 35–51. Springer, Cham (2017). https://doi.org/10.1007/978-3-319-54190-7_3
42. Wipf, D., Zhang, H.: Revisiting Bayesian blind deconvolution. J. Mach. Learn. Res. **15**, 3595–3634 (2014)
43. Xiao, L., Wang, J., Heidrich, W., Hirsch, M.: Learning high-order filters for efficient blind deconvolution of document photographs. In: Leibe, B., Matas, J., Sebe, N., Welling, M. (eds.) ECCV 2016. LNCS, vol. 9907, pp. 734–749. Springer, Cham (2016). https://doi.org/10.1007/978-3-319-46487-9_45
44. Xu, L., Jia, J.: Two-phase kernel estimation for robust motion deblurring. In: Daniilidis, K., Maragos, P., Paragios, N. (eds.) ECCV 2010. LNCS, vol. 6311, pp. 157–170. Springer, Heidelberg (2010). https://doi.org/10.1007/978-3-642-15549-9_12
45. Xu, L., Zheng, S., Jia, J.: Unnatural L0 sparse representation for natural image deblurring. In: CVPR (2013)
46. Yan, Y., Ren, W., Guo, Y., Wang, R., Cao, X.: Image deblurring via extreme channels prior. In: CVPR (2017)

47. Zhang, H., Wipf, D.P., Zhang, Y.: Multi-image blind deblurring using a coupled adaptive sparse prior. In: CVPR (2013)
48. Zhang, H., Yang, J.: Intra-frame deblurring by leveraging inter-frame camera motion. In: CVPR (2015)
49. Zhang, Y., Lau, Y., Kuo, H.W., Cheung, S., Pasupathy, A., Wright, J.: On the global geometry of sphere-constrained sparse blind deconvolution. In: CVPR (2017)
50. Zhu, C., Byrd, R.H., Lu, P., Nocedal, J.: L-BFGS-B: fortran subroutines for large-scale bound constrained optimization. ACM Trans. Math. Softw. (1994)
51. Zoran, D., Weiss, Y.: From learning models of natural image patches to whole image restoration. In: ICCV (2011)
52. Zuo, W., Ren, D., Gu, S., Lin, L., Zhang, L.: Discriminative learning of iteration-wise priors for blind deconvolution. In: CVPR (2015)

Improving Generalization via Scalable Neighborhood Component Analysis

Zhirong Wu[1,2(✉)], Alexei A. Efros[1], and Stella X. Yu[1]

[1] UC Berkeley/ICSI, Berkeley, USA
xavibrowu@gmail.com
[2] Microsoft Research Asia, Beijing, China

Abstract. Current major approaches to visual recognition follow an end-to-end formulation that classifies an input image into one of the pre-determined set of semantic categories. Parametric softmax classifiers are a common choice for such a closed world with fixed categories, especially when big labeled data is available during training. However, this becomes problematic for open-set scenarios where new categories are encountered with very few examples for learning a generalizable parametric classifier. We adopt a non-parametric approach for visual recognition by optimizing feature embeddings instead of parametric classifiers. We use a deep neural network to learn the visual feature that preserves the neighborhood structure in the semantic space, based on the Neighborhood Component Analysis (NCA) criterion. Limited by its computational bottlenecks, we devise a mechanism to use augmented memory to scale NCA for large datasets and very deep networks. Our experiments deliver not only remarkable performance on ImageNet classification for such a simple non-parametric method, but most importantly a more generalizable feature representation for sub-category discovery and few-shot recognition.

Keywords: k-nearest neighbors · Large-scale object recognition
Neighborhood component analysis · Transfer learning
Few-shot learning

1 Introduction

Deep learning with end-to-end problem formulations has reshaped visual recognition methods over the past few years. The core problems of high-level vision, e.g. recognition, detection and segmentation, are commonly formulated as classification tasks. Classifiers are applied image-wise for recognition [19], region-wise for detection [30], and pixel-wise for segmentation [22]. Classification in deep neural network is usually implemented as multi-way parametric softmax and assumes that the categories are fixed between learning and evaluation.

Code & models available: https://github.com/zhirongw/snca.pytorch.

V. Ferrari et al. (Eds.): ECCV 2018, LNCS 11211, pp. 712–728, 2018.
https://doi.org/10.1007/978-3-030-01234-2_42

However, such a "closed-world" assumption does not hold for the open world, where new categories could appear, often with very few training examples. For example, for face recognition [40,41], new identities should be recognized after just one-time occurrence. Due to the open-set nature, one may want to generalize the feature embedding instead of learning another parametric classifier. A common practice for embedding is to simply chop off the softmax classification layer from a pretrained network and take the last layer features. However, such a transfer learning scheme is not optimal because these features only make sense for a linear classification boundary in the training space, most likely not for the new testing space. Instead of learning parametric classifiers, we can learn an embedding to directly optimize a feature representation which preserves distance metrics in a non-parametric fashion. Numerous works have investigated various loss functions (e.g. contrastive loss [10], triplet loss [14,26]) and data sampling strategies [47] for improving the embedding performance.

Non-parametric embedding approaches have also been applied to computer vision tasks other than face recognition. Exemplar-based models have shown to be effective for learning object classes [2] and object detection [25]. These non-parametric approaches build associations between data instances [23], and turn out to be useful for meta-knowledge transfer [25] which would not be readily possible for parametric models. So far, none of these non-parametric methods have become competitive in the state-of-the-art image recognition benchmarks such as ImageNet classification [31] and MSCOCO object detection [21]. However, we argue that time might be right to revisit non-parametric methods to see if they could provide the generalization capabilities lacking in current approaches.

We investigate a neighborhood approach for image classification by learning a feature embedding through deep neural networks. The core of our approach is a metric learning model based on Neighborhood Component Analysis (NCA) [8]. For each training image, NCA computes its distance to all the other images in the embedding space. The distances can then be used to define a classification distribution according to the class labels. Batch training with all the images is computationally expensive, thereby making the original NCA algorithm difficult to scale to large datasets. Inspired by prior works [48,49], we propose to store the embedding of images in the entire dataset in an augmented non-parametric memory.

The non-parametric memory is not learned by stochastic gradient descent, but simply updated after each training image is visited. During testing, we build a k-nearest-neighbor (kNN) classifier based on the learned metrics.

Our work makes three main contributions. (1) We scale up NCA to handle large-scale datasets and deep neural networks by using an augmented memory to store non-parametric embeddings. (2) We demonstrate that a nearest neighbor classifier can achieve remarkable performance on the challenging ImageNet classification benchmark, nearly on par with parametric methods. (3) Our learned feature, trained with the same embedding method, delivers improved generalization ability for new categories, which is desirable for sub-category discovery and few-shot recognition.

2 Related Works

Object Recognition. Object recognition is one of the holy grail problems in computer vision. Most prior works cast recognition either as a category naming problem [3,4] or as a data association problem [23]. Category naming assumes that all instances belonging to the same category are similar and that category membership is binary (either all-in, or all-out). Most of the research in this area is focused on designing better invariant category representations (e.g. bag-of-words [45], pictorial models [5]). On the other hand, data association approaches [2,23,24,50] regard categories as data-driven entities emergent from connections between individual instances. Such non-parametric paradigms are informative and powerful for transferring knowledge which may not be explicitly present in the labels. In the era of deep learning, however, the performance of exemplar-based approaches hardly reaches the state-of-the-art for standard benchmarks on classification. Our work revisits the direction of data association models, learning an embedding representation that is tailored for nearest neighbor classifiers.

Learning with Augmented Memory. Since the formulation of LSTM [13], the idea of using memory for neural networks has been widely adopted for various tasks [12]. Recent approaches on augmented memory fall into two camps. One camp incorporates memory into neural networks as an end-to-end differentiable module [9,46], with automatic attention mechanism [33,43] for reading and writing. These models are usually applied in knowledge-based reasoning [9,43] and sequential prediction tasks [38]. The other camp treats memory as a non-parametric representation [42,48,49], where the memory size grows with the data set size. Matching networks [42] explore few-shot recognition using augmented memory, but their memory only holds the representations in current mini-batches of 5–25 images. Our memory is also non-parametric, in a similar manner as storing instances for unsupervised learning [48]. The key distinction is that our approach learns the memory representation with millions of entries for supervised large-scale recognition.

Metric Learning. There are many metric learning approaches [8,17], some achieving the state-of-the-art performance in image retrieval [47], face recognition [35,40,44], and person re-identification [49]. In such problems, since the classes during testing are disjoint from those encountered during training, one can only make inference based on its feature representation, not on the subsequent linear classifier. Metric learning learning encourages the minimization of intra-class variations and the maximization inter-class variations, such as contrastive loss [1,37], triplet loss [14]. Recent works on few-shot learning [36,42] also show the utility of metric learning, since it is difficult to optimize a parametric classifier with very few examples.

NCA. Our work is built upon the original proposal of Neighborhood Component Analysis (NCA) [8] and its non-linear extension [32]. In the original version [32], the features for the entire dataset needs to be computed at every step of the optimization, making it computationally expensive and not scalable for large datasets. Consequently, it has been mainly applied to small datasets such as MNIST or for dimensionality reduction [32]. Our work is the first to demonstrate that NCA can be applied successfully to large-scale datasets.

3 Approach

We adopt a feature embedding framework for image recognition. Given a query image x, we embed it into the feature space by $v = f_\theta(x)$. The function $f_\theta(\cdot)$ here is formulated as a deep neural network parameterized by parameter θ learned from data D. The embedding v is then queried against a set of images in the search database D', according to a similarity metric. Images with the highest similarity scores are retrieved and information from these retrieved images can be transferred to the image x.

Since the classification process does not rely on extra model parameters, the non-parametric framework can naturally extend to images in novel categories without any model fine-tuning. Consider three settings of D'.

1. When $D' = D$, i.e., the search database is the same as the training set, we have closed-set recognition such as the ImageNet challenge.
2. When D' is annotated with labels different from D, we have open-set recognition such as sub-category discovery and few-shot recognition.
3. Even when D' is completely unannotated, the metric can be useful for general content-based image retrieval.

The key is how to learn such an embedding function $f_\theta(\cdot)$. Our approach builds upon NCA [8] with some of our modifications.

3.1 Neighborhood Component Analysis

Non-parametric Formulation of Classification. Suppose we are given a labeled dataset of n examples $x_1, x_2, ..., x_n$ with corresponding labels $y_1, y_2, ..., y_n$. Each example x_i is embedded into a feature vector $v_i = f_\theta(x_i)$. We first define similarity s_{ij} between instances i and j in the embedded space as cosine similarity. We further assume that the feature v_i is ℓ_2 normalized. Then,

$$s_{ij} = \cos(\phi) = \frac{v_i^T}{\|v_i\|\|v_j\|} = v_i^T v_j, \tag{1}$$

where ϕ is the angle between vector v_i, v_j. Each example x_i selects example x_j as its neighbor with probability p_{ij} defined as,

$$p_{ij} = \frac{\exp(s_{ij}/\sigma)}{\sum_{k\neq i} \exp(s_{ik}/\sigma)}, \quad p_{ii} = 0. \tag{2}$$

Note that each example cannot select itself as neighbors, i.e. $p_{ii} = 0$. The probability thus is called *leave-one-out* distribution on the training set. Since the range of the cosine similarity is in $[-1, 1]$, we add an extra parameter σ to control the scale of the neighborhood.

Let $\Omega_i = \{j | y_j = y_i\}$ denote the indices of training images which share the same label with example x_i. Then the probability of example x_i being correctly classified is,

$$p_i = \sum_{j \in \Omega_i} p_{ij}. \tag{3}$$

The overall objective is to minimize the expected negative log likelihood over the dataset,

$$J = \frac{1}{n} \sum_i J_i = -\frac{1}{n} \sum_i \log(p_i). \tag{4}$$

Learning proceeds by directly optimizing the embedding without introducing additional model parameters. It turns out that each training example depends on all the other exemplars in the dataset. The gradients of the objective J_i with respect to v_i is,

$$\frac{\partial J_i}{\partial v_i} = \frac{1}{\sigma} \sum_k p_{ik} v_k - \frac{1}{\sigma} \sum_{k \in \Omega_i} \tilde{p}_{ik} v_k, \tag{5}$$

and v_j where $j \neq i$ is,

$$\frac{\partial J_i}{\partial v_j} = \begin{cases} \frac{1}{\sigma}(p_{ij} - \tilde{p}_{ij}) v_i, & j \in \Omega_i \\ \frac{1}{\sigma} p_{ij} v_i, & j \notin \Omega_i \end{cases} \tag{6}$$

where $\tilde{p}_{ik} = p_{ik} / \sum_{j \in \Omega_i} p_{ij}$ is the normalized distribution within the groundtruth category.

Differences from Parametric Softmax. The traditional parametric softmax distribution is formulated as

$$p_c = \frac{\exp(w_c^T v_i)}{\sum_j \exp(w_j^T v_i)}, \tag{7}$$

where each category $c \in \{1, 2, ..., C\}$ has a parametrized prototype w_c to represent itself. The maximum likelihood learning is to align all examples in the same category with the category prototype. However, in the above NCA formulation, the optimal solution is reached when the probability p_{ik} of negative examples ($k \notin \Omega_i$) vanishes. The learning signal does not enforce all the examples in the same category to align with the current training example. The probability of some positive examples ($k \in \Omega_i$) can also vanish so long as some other positives align well enough to *i-th* example. In other words, the non-parametric formulation does not assume a single prototype for each category, and such a flexibility allows learning to discover inherent structures when there are significant intra-class variations in the data. Eq. 5 explains how each example contributes to the learning gradients (Fig. 1).

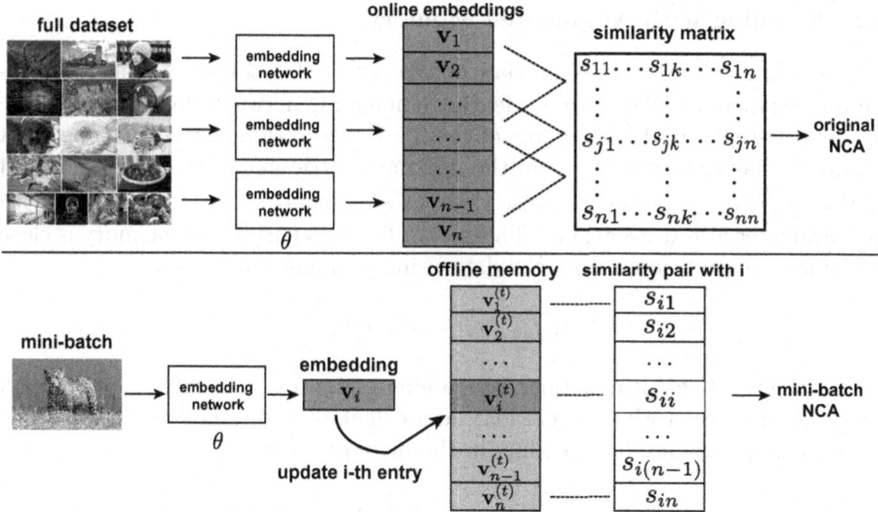

Fig. 1. The original NCA needs to compute the feature embeddings for the entire dataset for each optimization step. This is not scalable for large datasets and deep neural networks optimized with stochastic gradient descent. We overcome this issue by using an augmented memory to store offline embeddings forwarded from previous optimization steps. The online embedding is learned by back-propagation, while the offline memory is not.

Computational Challenges for Learning. Learning NCA even for a single objective term J_i would require obtaining the embedding as well as gradients (Eqs. 5 and 6) in the entire dataset. This computational demand quickly becomes impossible to meet for large-scale dataset, with a deep neural network learned via stochastic gradient descent. Sampling-based methods such as triplet loss [40] can drastically reduce the computation by selecting a few neighbors. However, hard-negative mining turns out to be crucial and typical batch size with 1800 examples [40] could still be impractical.

We take an alternative approach to reduce the amount of computation. We introduce two crude approximations.

1. We only perform gradient descent on $\partial J_i/\partial v_i$ as in Eq. 5, but not on $\partial J_i/\partial v_j$, $j \neq i$ as in Eq. 6. This simplification disentangles learning a single instance from learning among all the training instances, making mini-batch stochastic gradient descent possible.
2. Computing the gradient for $\partial J_i/\partial v_i$ still requires the embedding of the entire dataset, which would be prohibitively expensive for each mini-batch update. We introduce augmented memory to store the embeddings for approximation. More details follow.

3.2 Learning with Augmented Memory

We store the feature representation of the entire dataset as augmented non-parametric memory. We learn our feature embedding network through stochastic gradient descent. At the beginning of the $t+1$-*th* iteration, suppose the network parameter has the state $\theta^{(t)}$, and the non-parametric memory is in the form of $M^{(t)} = \{v_1^{(t)}, v_2^{(t)}, ..., v_n^{(t)}\}$. Suppose that the memory is roughly up-to-date with the parameter $\theta^{(t)}$ at iteration t. This means the non-parametric memory is close to the features extracted from the data using parameter $\theta^{(t)}$,

$$v_i^{(t)} \approx f_{\theta^{(t)}}(x_i), \quad i = 1, 2, ..., n. \tag{8}$$

During the $t+1$-*th* optimization, for training instance x_i, we forward it through the embedding network $v_i = f_{\theta^{(t)}}(x_i)$, and calculate its gradient as in Eq. 5 but using the approximated embedding in the memory as,

$$\frac{\partial J_i}{\partial v_i} = \frac{1}{\sigma}\sum_k p_{ik} v_k^{(t)} - \frac{1}{\sigma}\sum_{k \in \Omega_i} \tilde{p}_{ik} v_k^{(t)}. \tag{9}$$

Then the gradients of the parameter can be back-propagated,

$$\frac{\partial J_i}{\partial \theta} = \frac{\partial J_i}{\partial v_i} \cdot \frac{\partial v_i}{\partial \theta}. \tag{10}$$

Since we have forwarded the x_i to get the feature v_i, we update the memory for the training instance x_i by the empirical weighted average [49],

$$v_i^{(t+1)} \leftarrow m \cdot v_i^{(t)} + (1 - m) \cdot v_i. \tag{11}$$

Finally, network parameter θ is updated and learned through stochastic gradient descent. If the learning rate is small enough, the memory can always be up-to-date with the change of parameters. The non-parametric memory slot for each training image is only updated once per learning epoch. Though the embedding is approximately estimated, we have found it to work well in practice.

3.3 Discussion on Complexity

In our model, the non-parametric memory $M^{(t)}$, similarity metric s_{ij}, and probability density p_{ij} may potentially require a large storage and pose computation bottlenecks. We give an analysis of model complexity below.

Suppose our final embedding is of size $d = 128$, and we train our model on a typical large-scale dataset using $n = 10^6$ images with a batch size of $b = 256$. Non-parametric memory M requires 0.5 GB ($O(dn)$) of memory. Similarity metric and probability density each requires 2 GB ($O(bn)$) of memory for storing the value and the gradient. In our current implementation, other intermediate variables used for computing the intra-class distribution require another 2 GB ($O(bn)$). In total, we would need 6.5 GB for the NCA module.

In terms of time complexity, the summation in Eqs. 2 and 3 across the whole dataset becomes the bottleneck in NCA. However, in practice with a GPU implementation, the NCA module takes a reasonable 30% amount of extra time with respect to the backbone network. During testing, exhaustive nearest neighbor search with one million entries is also reasonably fast. The time it takes is negligible with respect to the forward passing through the backbone network.

The complexity of our model scales linearly with the training size set. Our current implementation can deal with datasets at the ImageNet scale, but cannot scale up to 10 times more data based on the above calculations. A possible strategy to handle bigger data is to subsample a few neighbors instead of the entire training set. Sampling would help reduce the linear time complexity to a constant. For nearest neighbor search at the run time, computation complexity can be mitigated with proper data structures such as ball-trees [7] and quantization methods [16].

4 Experiments

We conduct experiments to investigate whether our non-parametric feature embedding can perform well in the closed-world setting, and more importantly whether it can improve generalization in the open-world setting.

First, we evaluate the learned metric on the large-scale ImageNet ILSVRC challenge [31]. Our embedding achieves competitive recognition accuracy with k-nearest neighbor classifiers using the same ResNet architecture. Secondly, we study an important property of our representation for sub-category discovery, when the model trained with only coarse annotations is transferred for fine-grained label prediction. Lastly, we study how our learned metric can be transferred and applied to unseen object categories for few-shot recognition.

4.1 Image Classification

We study the effectiveness of our non-parametric representation for visual recognition on ImageNet ILSVRC dataset. We use the parametric softmax classification networks as our baselines.

Network Configuration. We use the ConvNet architecture ResNet [11] as the backbone for the feature embedding network. We remove the last linear classification layer of the original ResNet and append another linear layer which projects the feature to a low dimensional 128 space. The 128 feature vector is then ℓ_2 normalized and fed to NCA learning. Our approach does not induce extra parameters for the embedding network.

Learning Details. During training, we use an initial learning rate of 0.1 and drops 10 times smaller every 40 epochs for a total of 130 epochs. Our network converges a bit slower than the baseline network, in part due to the approximated updates for the non-parametric memory. We set the momentum for updating the memory with $m = 0.5$ at the start of learning, and gradually increase to

$m = 0.9$ at the end of learning. We use a temperature parameter $\sigma = 0.05$ in the main results. All the other optimization details and hyper-parameters remain the same with the baseline approach. We refer the reader to the PyTorch implementation [28] of ResNet for details. During testing, we use a weighted k nearest neighbor classifier for classification. Our results are insensitive to parameter k; generally any k in the range of 5–50 gives very similar results. We report the accuracy with $k = 1$ and $k = 30$ using single center crops.

Table 1. Top-1 classification rate on ImageNet validation set using k-nearest neighbor classifiers.

ResNet18				ResNet34				ResNet50			
Feature	d	$k = 1$	$k = 30$	Feature	d	$k = 1$	$k = 30$	Feature	d	$k = 1$	$k = 30$
Baseline	512	62.91	68.41	Baseline	512	67.73	72.32	Baseline	2048	71.35	75.09
+PCA	128	60.43	66.26	+PCA	128	65.58	70.67	+PCA	128	69.72	73.69
Ours	128	67.39	**70.58**	Ours	128	71.81	**74.43**	Ours	128	74.34	**76.67**

Table 2. Performance comparison of our method with parametric softmax.

Feature	Baseline		Ours	
	top-1	top-5	top-1	top-5
ResNet18	69.64	88.98	**70.58**	**89.38**
ResNet34	73.27	**91.43**	**74.43**	91.35
ResNet50	76.01	**92.93**	**76.67**	92.84

Table 3. Ablation study on the feature size and the temperature parameter.

d	k=1	k=30
256	67.54	70.71
128	67.39	70.59
64	65.32	69.54
32	64.83	68.01

σ	k=1	k=30
0.1	63.87	67.93
0.05	67.39	70.59
0.03	66.98	70.33
0.02	N/A	N/A

Main Results. Tables 1 and 2 summarize our results in comparison with the features learned by parametric softmax. For baseline networks, we extract the last layer feature and evaluate it with the same k nearest neighbor classifiers. The similarity between features is measured by cosine similarity. Classification evaluated with nearest neighbors leads to a decrease of 6% – 7% accuracy with $k = 1$, and 1% – 2% accuracy with $k = 30$. We also project the baseline feature to 128 dimension with PCA for evaluation. This reduction leads to a further 2% decrease in performance, suggesting that the features learned by parametric classifiers do not work equally well with nearest neighbor classifiers. With our model, we achieve a 3% improvement over the baseline using $k = 1$. At $k = 30$, we have even slightly better results than the parametric classifier: Ours are 1.1% higher on ResNet34, and 0.7% higher on ResNet50. We also find that predictions from our model disagree with the baseline on 15% of the validation set, indicating a significantly different representation has been learned.

Figure 2 shows nearest neighbor retrieval comparisons. The upper four examples are our successful retrievals and the lower four are failure retrievals. For the failure cases, our model has trouble either when there are multiple objects in the same scene, or when the task becomes too difficult with fine-grained categorization. For the four failure cases, our model predictions are "paddle boat", "tennis ball", "angora rabbit", "appenzeller" respectively.

Ablation study on model parameters. We investigate the effect of the feature size and the temperature parameter in Table 3. For the feature size, 128 features and 256 features produce very similar results. We start to see performance degradation as the size is dropped lower than 64. For the temperature parameter, a lower temperature which induces smaller neighborhoods generally produces better results. However, the network does not converge if the temperature is too low, e.g., $\sigma = 0.02$.

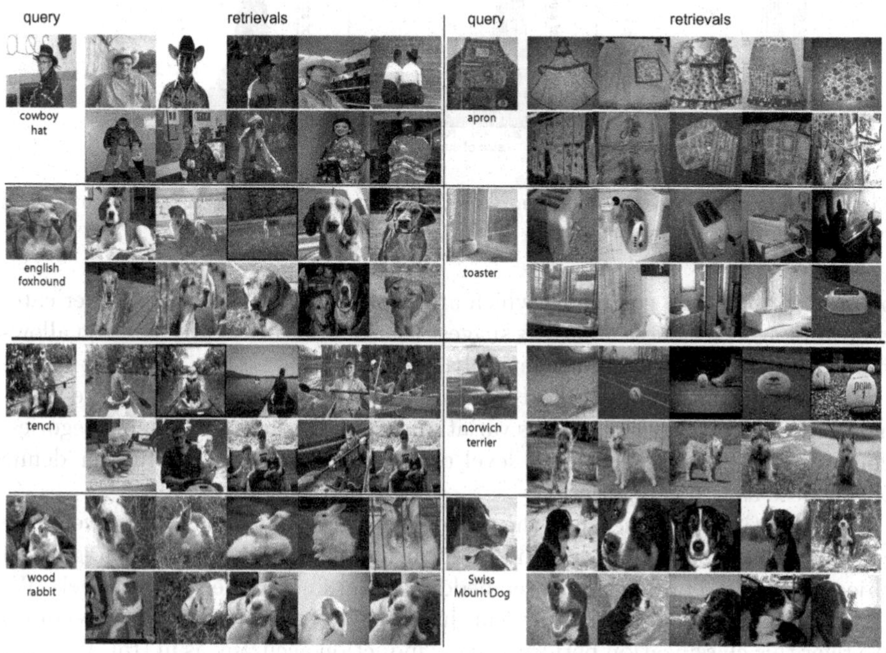

Fig. 2. Given a query, the figure shows 5 nearest neighbors from our model (1st row) and from the baseline model (2nd row). Top four examples show the successful cases and bottom four show the failure cases.

4.2 Discovering Sub-categories

Our non-parametric formulation of classification does not assume a single prototype for each category. Each training image i only has to look for a few supporting neighbors [34] to embed the features. We refer nearest neighbors whose probability density $\sum_j p_{ij}$ sum over a given threshold as a support set for i. In Fig. 3, we plot the histograms over the size of the support set for support density thresholds 0.5, 0.7 and 0.9. We can see most of the images only depend

Table 4. Top-1 induction accuracy on CIFAR100 and ImageNet1000 using model pre-trained on CIFAR20 and ImageNet127. Numbers are reported with k nearest neighbor classifiers.

CIFAR			ImageNet		
Task	20 classes	100 classes	Task	127 classes	1000 classes
Baseline	81.53	54.17	Baseline	81.48	48.07
Ours	81.42	**62.32**	Ours	81.62	**52.75**

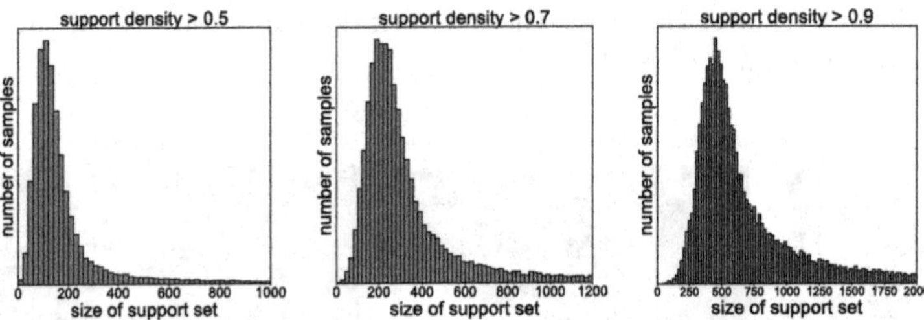

Fig. 3. Histogram of the size of support set in the ImageNet validation set given various support density thresholds.

on around 100 – 500 neighbors, which are a lot less than 1,000 images per category in ImageNet. These statistics suggest that our learned representation allows sub-categories to develop automatically.

The ability to discover sub-categories is of great importance for feature learning, as there are always intra-class variations no matter how we define categories. For example, even for the finest level of object species, we can further define object pose as sub-categories.

To quantitatively measure the performance of sub-category discovery, we consider the experiment of learning the feature embedding using coarse-grained object labels, and evaluating the embedding using fine-grained object labels. We can then measure how well feature learning discovers variations within categories. We refer this classification performance as induction accuracy as in [15]. We train the network with the baseline parametric softmax and with our non-parametric NCA using the same network architecture. To be fair with the baseline, we evaluate the feature from the penultimate layer from both networks. We conduct the experiments on CIFAR and ImageNet, and their results are summarized in Table 4.

CIFAR Results. CIFAR100 [18] images have both fine-grained annotations in 100 categories and coarse-grained annotations in 20 categories. It is a proper testing scenario for evaluating sub-category discovery. We study sub-category discovery by transferring representations learned from 20 categories to 100 categories. The two approaches exhibit similar classification performances on the 20 category setting. However, when transferred to CIFAR100 using k nearest neighbors, baseline features suffer a big loss, with 54.17% top-1 accuracy on 100 classes. Fitting a linear classifier for the baseline features gives an improved

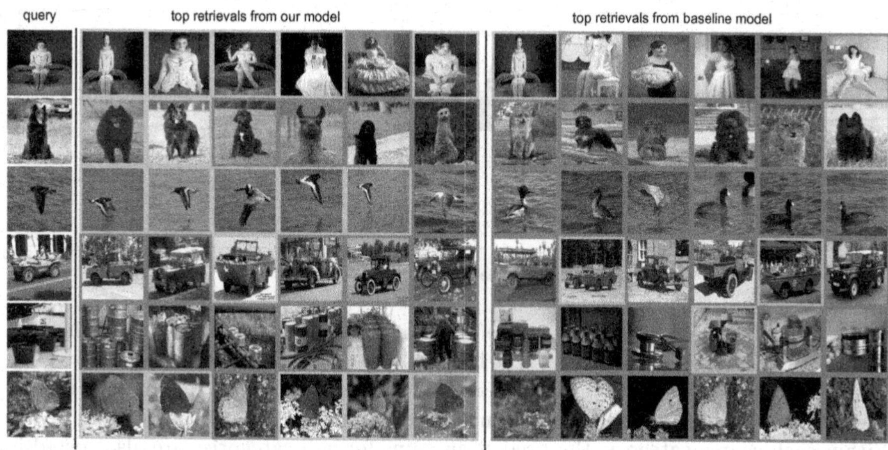

Fig. 4. Nearest neighbors from the models trained with ImageNet 127 classes and evaluated on the fine-grained 1000 classes. Correct retrievals are boxed with green outlines and wrong retrievals are with orange. (Color figure online)

58.66% top-1 accuracy. Using k nearest neighbor classifiers, our features are 8% better than the baselines, achieving a 62.32% recognition accuracy.

ImageNet Results. As in [15], we use 127 coarse categories by clustering the 1000 categories in a top-down fashion by fixing the distances of the nodes from the root node in the WordNet tree. There are 65 of the 127 classes present in the original 1000 classes. The other 62 classes are parental nodes in the ImageNet hierarchical word tree. The two models achieve similar classification performance (81% – 82%) on the original 127 categories. When evaluated with 1000 class annotations, our representation is about 5% better than the baseline features. The baseline performance can be improved to 52.0% by fitting another linear classifier on the 1000 classes.

Discussions. Our approach is able to preserve visual structures which are not explicitly presented in the supervisory signal. In Fig. 4, we show nearest neighbor examples compared with the baseline features. For all the examples shown here, the ground-truth fine-grained category does not exist in the training categories. Thus the model has to discover sub-categories in order to recognize the objects. We can see our representation preserves apparent visual similarity (such as color and pose information) better, and is able to associate the query with correct exemplars for accurate recognition. For example, our model finds similar birds hovering above water in the third row, and finds butterflies of the same color in the last row. In Fig. 5 we further show the prediction gains for each class. Our model is particularly stronger for main sub-categories with rich intra-class variations.

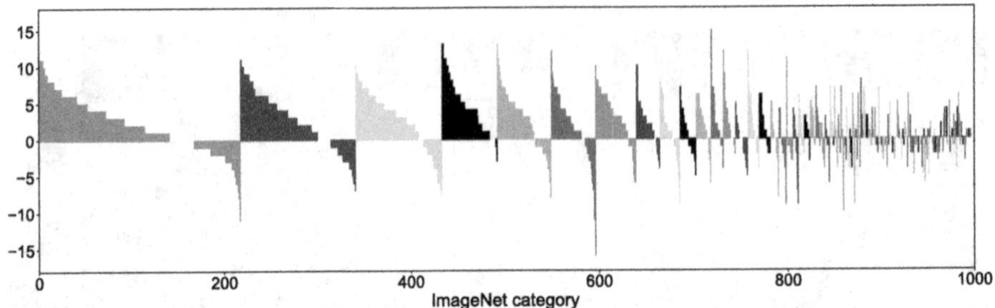

Fig. 5. Results for sub-category discovery on ImageNet. x axis scans through the fine-grained 1000 ImageNet categories. Each recycled color represents a coarse category. All coarse categories are sorted with decreasing order in terms of the number of sub-categories. y axis indicates the prediction gains of our model against the baseline model. Within each coarse category, the prediction gains for sub-categories are also sorted in a decreasing order.

Table 5. Few-shot recognition on Mini-ImageNet dataset.

Method	Network	FineTune	5-way setting		20-way setting	
			1-shot	5-shot	1-shot	5-shot
NN Baseline [42]	Small	No	41.1 ± 0.7	51.0 ± 0.7	-	-
Meta-LSTM [29]	Small	No	43.4 ± 0.8	60.1 ± 0.7	16.7 ± 0.2	26.1 ± 0.3
MAML [6]	Small	Yes	48.7 ± 0.7	63.2 ± 0.9	16.5 ± 0.6	19.3 ± 0.3
Meta-SGD [20]	Small	No	50.5 ± 1.9	64.0 ± 0.9	17.6 ± 0.6	28.9 ± 0.4
Matching Net [42]	Small	Yes	46.6 ± 0.8	60.0 ± 0.7	-	-
Prototypical [36]	Small	No	49.4 ± 0.8	$\mathbf{68.2} \pm 0.7$	-	-
RelationNet [39]	Small	No	$\mathbf{51.4} \pm 0.8$	61.1 ± 0.7	-	-
Ours	Small	No	50.3 ± 0.7	64.1 ± 0.8	$\mathbf{23.7} \pm 0.4$	$\mathbf{36.0} \pm 0.5$
SNAIL [27]	Large	No	55.7 ± 1.0	68.9 ± 0.9	-	-
RelationNet [39]	Large	No	57.0 ± 0.9	71.1 ± 0.7	-	-
Ours	Large	No	$\mathbf{57.8} \pm 0.8$	$\mathbf{72.8} \pm 0.7$	$\mathbf{30.5} \pm 0.5$	$\mathbf{44.8} \pm 0.5$

4.3 Few-Shot Recognition

Our feature embedding method learns a meaningful metric among images. Such a metric can be directly applied to new image categories which have not been seen during training. We study the generalization ability of our method for few-shot object recognition.

Evaluation Protocol. We use the mini-Imagenet dataset [42], which consists of 60,000 colour images and 100 classes (600 examples per class). We follow the split introduced previously [29], with 64, 16, and 20 classes for training, validation and testing. We only use the validation set for tuning model parameters. During testing, we create the testing episodes by randomly sampling a set of observation and query pairs. The observation consists of c classes (c-way) and s images (s-shot) per class. The query is an image from one of the$c$ classes. Each testing episode provides the task to predict the class of query image given $c \times s$ few shot observations. We create 3,000 episodes for testing and report the average results.

Network Architecture. We conduct experiments on two network architectures. One is a shallow network which receives small 84×84 input images. It has 4 convolutional blocks, each with a $3 \times 3 \times 64$ convolutional layer, a batch normalization layer, a ReLU layer, and a max pooling layer. A final fully connected layer maps the feature for classification. This architecture is widely used in previous works [6,42] for evaluating few-shot recognition. The other is a deeper version with ResNet18 and larger 224×224 image inputs. Two previous works [27,39] have reported their performance with similar ResNet18 architectures.

Fig. 6. Few shot learning examples in mini-Imagenet test set. Given one shot for each five categories, the model predicts the category for the new query image. Our prediction is boxed with green and the baseline prediction is with orange.

Results. We summarize our results in Table 5. We train our embedding on the training set, and apply the representation from the penultimate layer for evaluation. Our current experiment does not fine-tune a local metric per episode, though such adaptation would potentially bring additional improvement. As with the previous experiments, we use k nearest neighbors for classification. We use $k = 1$ neighbor for the 1-shot scenario, and $k = 5$ for the 5-shot scenario.

For the shallow network setting, while our model is on par with the prototypical network [36], and RelationNet [39], our method is far more generic.

For the deeper network setting, we achieve the state-of-the-art results for this task. MAML [6] suggests going deeper does not necessarily bring better results for meta learning. Our approach provides a counter-example: Deeper network architectures can in fact bring significant gains with proper metric learning.

Figure 6 shows visual examples of our predictions compared with the baseline trained with softmax classifiers.

5 Summary

We present a non-parametric neighborhood approach for visual recognition. We learn a CNN to embed images into a low-dimensional feature space, where the distance metric between images preserves the semantic structure of categorical labels according to the NCA criterion. We address NCA's computation demand by learning with an external augmented memory, thereby making NCA scalable for large datasets and deep neural networks. Our experiments deliver not only remarkable performance on ImageNet classification for such a simple non-parametric method, but most importantly a more generalizable feature representation for sub-category discovery and few-shot recognition. In the future, it's worthwhile to re-investigate non-parametric methods for other visual recognition problems such as detection and segmentation.

Acknowledgements. This work was supported in part by Berkeley DeepDrive. ZW would like to thank Yuanjun Xiong for helpful discussions.

References

1. Bromley, J., Guyon, I., LeCun, Y., Säckinger, E., Shah, R.: Signature verification using a "Siamese" time delay neural network. In: NIPS (1994)
2. Chum, O., Zisserman, A.: An exemplar model for learning object classes. In: CVPR. IEEE (2007)
3. Deng, J., Dong, W., Socher, R., Li, L.J., Li, K., Fei-Fei, L.: ImageNet: a large-scale hierarchical image database. In: CVPR. IEEE (2009)
4. Everingham, M., Van Gool, L., Williams, C.K., Winn, J., Zisserman, A.: The pascal visual object classes (VOC) challenge. IJCV **88**(2), 303–338 (2010)
5. Felzenszwalb, P.F., Huttenlocher, D.P.: Pictorial structures for object recognition. IJCV (2005)
6. Finn, C., Abbeel, P., Levine, S.: Model-agnostic meta-learning for fast adaptation of deep networks. arXiv preprint arXiv:1703.03400 (2017)
7. Friedman, J.H., Bentley, J.L., Finkel, R.A.: An algorithm for finding best matches in logarithmic expected time. ACM Trans. Math. Software (TOMS) **3**(3), 209–226 (1977)
8. Goldberger, J., Hinton, G.E., Roweis, S.T., Salakhutdinov, R.R.: Neighbourhood components analysis. In: NIPS (2005)
9. Graves, A., Wayne, G., Danihelka, I.: Neural turing machines. arXiv preprint arXiv:1410.5401 (2014)
10. Hadsell, R., Chopra, S., LeCun, Y.: Dimensionality reduction by learning an invariant mapping. In: CVPR. IEEE (2006)
11. He, K., Zhang, X., Ren, S., Sun, J.: Deep residual learning for image recognition. In: CVPR (2016)
12. Hinton, G.: Deep neural networks for acoustic modeling in speech recognition: the shared views of four research groups. Signal Process. Mag. **29**(6), 82–97 (2012)
13. Hochreiter, S., Schmidhuber, J.: Long short-term memory. Neural Comput. **9**(8), 1735–1780 (1997)
14. Hoffer, E., Ailon, N.: Deep metric learning using triplet network. In: Feragen, A., Pelillo, M., Loog, M. (eds.) SIMBAD 2015. LNCS, vol. 9370, pp. 84–92. Springer, Cham (2015). https://doi.org/10.1007/978-3-319-24261-3_7
15. Huh, M., Agrawal, P., Efros, A.A.: What makes imagenet good for transfer learning? arXiv preprint arXiv:1608.08614 (2016)
16. Jegou, H., Douze, M., Schmid, C.: Product quantization for nearest neighbor search. PAMI **33**(1), 117–128 (2011)

17. Koestinger, M., Hirzer, M., Wohlhart, P., Roth, P.M., Bischof, H.: Large scale metric learning from equivalence constraints. In: CVPR. IEEE (2012)
18. Krizhevsky, A., Hinton, G.: Learning multiple layers of features from tiny images (2009)
19. Krizhevsky, A., Sutskever, I., Hinton, G.E.: ImageNet classification with deep convolutional neural networks. In: NIPS (2012)
20. Li, Z., Zhou, F., Chen, F., Li, H.: Meta-SGD: Learning to learn quickly for few shot learning. arXiv preprint arXiv:1707.09835 (2017)
21. Lin, T.-Y., et al.: Microsoft COCO: common objects in context. In: Fleet, D., Pajdla, T., Schiele, B., Tuytelaars, T. (eds.) ECCV 2014. LNCS, vol. 8693, pp. 740–755. Springer, Cham (2014). https://doi.org/10.1007/978-3-319-10602-1_48
22. Long, J., Shelhamer, E., Darrell, T.: Fully convolutional networks for semantic segmentation. In: CVPR (2015)
23. Malisiewicz, T., Efros, A.A.: Recognition by association via learning per-exemplar distances. In: CVPR. IEEE (2008)
24. Malisiewicz, T., Efros, A.: Beyond categories: The visual memex model for reasoning about object relationships. In: NIPS (2009)
25. Malisiewicz, T., Gupta, A., Efros, A.A.: Ensemble of exemplar-SVMs for object detection and beyond. In: ICCV. IEEE (2011)
26. Mensink, T., Verbeek, J., Perronnin, F., Csurka, G.: Distance-based image classification: generalizing to new classes at near-zero cost. PAMI **35**(11), 2624–2637 (2013)
27. Mishra, N., Rohaninejad, M., Chen, X., Abbeel, P.: Meta-learning with temporal convolutions. arXiv preprint arXiv:1707.03141 (2017)
28. Paszke, A., et al.: PyTorch: tensors and dynamic neural networks in python with strong GPU acceleration, May 2017
29. Ravi, S., Larochelle, H.: Optimization as a model for few-shot learning (2016)
30. Ren, S., He, K., Girshick, R., Sun, J.: Faster R-CNN: towards real-time object detection with region proposal networks. In: NIPS (2015)
31. Russakovsky, O., et al.: ImageNet large scale visual recognition challenge. IJCV, **115**(3), 211–252 (2015)
32. Salakhutdinov, R., Hinton, G.: Learning a nonlinear embedding by preserving class neighbourhood structure. In: Artificial Intelligence and Statistics (2007)
33. Santoro, A., Bartunov, S., Botvinick, M., Wierstra, D., Lillicrap, T.: Meta-learning with memory-augmented neural networks. In: International Conference on Machine Learning (2016)
34. Schölkopf, B., Platt, J.C., Shawe-Taylor, J., Smola, A.J., Williamson, R.C.: Estimating the support of a high-dimensional distribution. Neural Comput. **13**(7), 1443–1471 (2001)
35. Schroff, F., Kalenichenko, D., Philbin, J.: FaceNet: a unified embedding for face recognition and clustering. In: CVPR (2015)
36. Snell, J., Swersky, K., Zemel, R.: Prototypical networks for few-shot learning. In: NIPS (2017)
37. Sohn, K.: Improved deep metric learning with multi-class n-pair loss objective. In: NIPS (2016)
38. Sukhbaatar, S., Weston, J., Fergus, R., et al.: End-to-end memory networks. In: NIPS (2015)
39. Sung, F., Yang, Y., Zhang, L., Xiang, T., Torr, P.H., Hospedales, T.M.: Learning to compare: Relation network for few-shot learning. arXiv preprint arXiv:1711.06025 (2017)

40. Taigman, Y., Yang, M., Ranzato, M., Wolf, L.: DeepFace: closing the gap to human-level performance in face verification. In: CVPR (2014)
41. Turk, M.A., Pentland, A.P.: Face recognition using eigenfaces. In: CVPR. IEEE (1991)
42. Vinyals, O., Blundell, C., Lillicrap, T., Wierstra, D., et al.: Matching networks for one shot learning. In: NIPS (2016)
43. Vinyals, O., Fortunato, M., Jaitly, N.: Pointer networks. In: NIPS (2015)
44. Wang, H., et al.: CosFace: large margin cosine loss for deep face recognition. arXiv preprint arXiv:1801.09414 (2018)
45. Weber, M., Welling, M., Perona, P.: Unsupervised learning of models for recognition. In: Vernon, D. (ed.) ECCV 2000. LNCS, vol. 1842, pp. 18–32. Springer, Heidelberg (2000). https://doi.org/10.1007/3-540-45054-8_2
46. Weston, J., Chopra, S., Bordes, A.: Memory networks. arXiv preprint arXiv:1410.3916 (2014)
47. Wu, C.Y., Manmatha, R., Smola, A.J., Krähenbühl, P.: Sampling matters in deep embedding learning. arXiv preprint arXiv:1706.07567 (2017)
48. Wu, Z., Xiong, Y., Stella, X.Y., Lin, D.: Unsupervised feature learning via non-parametric instance discrimination. In: CVPR (2018)
49. Xiao, T., Li, S., Wang, B., Lin, L., Wang, X.: Joint detection and identification feature learning for person search. In: CVPR (2017)
50. Zhang, H., Berg, A.C., Maire, M., Malik, J.: SVM-KNN: discriminative nearest neighbor classification for visual category recognition. In: CVPR. IEEE (2006)

Proximal Dehaze-Net: A Prior Learning-Based Deep Network for Single Image Dehazing

Dong Yang and Jian Sun(✉)

Xi'an Jiaotong University, Xi'an 710049, China
yangdong2010@stu.xjtu.edu.cn, jiansun@xjtu.edu.cn

Abstract. Photos taken in hazy weather are usually covered with white masks and often lose important details. In this paper, we propose a novel deep learning approach for single image dehazing by learning dark channel and transmission priors. First, we build an energy model for dehazing using dark channel and transmission priors and design an iterative optimization algorithm using proximal operators for these two priors. Second, we unfold the iterative algorithm to be a deep network, dubbed as *proximal dehaze-net*, by learning the proximal operators using convolutional neural networks. Our network combines the advantages of traditional prior-based dehazing methods and deep learning methods by incorporating haze-related prior learning into deep network. Experiments show that our method achieves state-of-the-art performance for single image dehazing.

Keywords: Single image dehazing · Prior learning
Deep neural network

1 Introduction

Haze is an atmospheric phenomenon that dust, smoke, or dry particles obscure the clarity of a scene. With hazes, only a portion of reflected lights reach the observer as a result of absorption in the atmosphere. Based on this observation, the captured image I of a hazy scene can be modeled as a linear combination of direct attenuation and airlight contributions [7,11,27,28]:

$$I(\mathrm{x}) = J(\mathrm{x})T(\mathrm{x}) + A(1 - T(\mathrm{x})), \tag{1}$$

where I is the image degraded by hazes, J is the scene radiance or haze-free image, A is the global atmospheric light and $T(\mathrm{x}) = \exp(-\eta d(\mathrm{x}))$ is the media transmission along the cone of vision which depends on scattering coefficient

Electronic supplementary material The online version of this chapter (https://doi.org/10.1007/978-3-030-01234-2_43) contains supplementary material, which is available to authorized users.

V. Ferrari et al. (Eds.): ECCV 2018, LNCS 11211, pp. 729–746, 2018.
https://doi.org/10.1007/978-3-030-01234-2_43

η and scene depth $d(\mathrm{x})$. Single image dehazing is an ill-posed inverse problem that requires to recover the unknown haze-free image J, atmospheric light A and transmission T from a single input image I. Therefore, it is essential to investigate effective haze-related priors to regularize this inverse problem.

Fig. 1. Single image dehazing results. (a) Input hazy image. (b) Recovered haze-free image using DCP. (c) Dark channel of input image. (d) Transmission map by DCP. (f)∼(h) Recovered haze-free image, dark channel and transmission by our network. (e) Comparisons on image blocks.

The traditional single image dehazing methods [2,5,7,11,18,27,28,30,31,38] have investigated various image priors. Tan et al. [28] assume that the contrast of hazy images is lower than haze-free images and propose to maximize the contrast of hazy images under the MRF framework. Fattal [7] uses independent component analysis for estimating the transmission in hazy scenes assuming that the transmission and surface shading are locally uncorrelated. He et al. [11] propose dark channel prior to estimate transmission based on the observation that the local minimum of color channels of haze-free images is close to zero. These prior-based methods are effective in single image dehazing due to the investigations of prior knowledge and understandings of the physical mechanism for hazes. However, these priors are mainly based on human observations and would not always hold for diverse real world images. For example, dark channel prior [11] is effective for most outdoor images but usually fails for those containing white scenery such as white walls or clouds in sky region, as shown in Fig. 1(b).

Recently, learning-based methods [4,14,15,20,21,29,34] have been introduced to image dehazing. Ren et al. [20] propose a multi-scale convolutional neural network (MSCNN) for learning the transmission map of the hazy image. It consists of a coarse-scale network predicting a holistic transmission map and a fine-scale network for refining the map. Inspired by haze-relevant features, Cai et al. [4] propose a trainable end-to-end system called DehazeNet for transmission estimation, with specially designed feature extraction layers. Instead of estimating transmission map and atmospheric light separately, Li et al. [14] propose AOD-Net by embedding the estimation of T and A into learning a new K-module. It directly generates the clean image through a light-weight CNN. The learning-based methods have shown promising results for single image hehazing. However, these methods usually take CNNs to learn a mapping from input hazy images to the transmissions or haze-free images, without considering haze-related priors to constrain the mapping space compared with the traditional methods.

In this paper, we propose a novel deep learning-based method that integrates haze imaging model constraints and image prior learning into a single network architecture. *First*, based on the haze imaging model, we formulate the inverse problem of single image dehazing as an energy model with haze imaging constraints in color and dark channel spaces, regularized by dark channel and transmission priors. *Second*, we design an iterative optimization algorithm using half-quadratic splitting, jointly estimating the transmission map and latent haze-free image. *Third*, we unfold this iterative algorithm to be a deep architecture, dubbed as *proximal dehaze-net*, to implicitly learn the transmission and dark channel priors by learning their corresponding proximal operators using convolutional neural networks. We justify the effectiveness of learned dark channel and transmission priors by ablation study and the learned proximal dehaze-net leads to state-of-the-art results on real and synthetic datasets.

To the best of our knowledge, this is the first work that uses CNNs to learn both dark channel and transmission priors for single image dehazing. Compared with traditional prior-based methods, our approach can discriminatively learn haze-related priors from training data instead of using hand-crafted priors. Compared with deep learning-based dehazing methods, our approach incorporates both haze imaging constraint and haze-related priors learning into the network architecture, which may provide a promising learning-based approach for solving the challenging inverse problem of dehazing.

2 Related Work

2.1 Dark Channel

The most related work to ours is the dark channel prior [11] (DCP) method. The dark channel of an image is defined as:

$$I^{dk}(\mathrm{x}) = \min_{c\in\{r,g,b\}} \Big(\min_{\mathrm{y}\in\Omega(\mathrm{x})} \big(I^c(\mathrm{y})\big)\Big), \tag{2}$$

where I^c is a color channel of I and $\Omega(\mathrm{x})$ is a local patch centered at x. The dark channel prior assumes that, in most non-sky patches, at least one color channel of a haze-free outdoor image has very low intensity at some pixels. According to dark channel prior, the transmission can be estimated as:

$$T = 1 - \omega \min_{c\in\{r,g,b\}} \Big(\min_{\mathrm{y}\in\Omega(\mathrm{x})} \big(\frac{I^c(\mathrm{y})}{A^c}\big)\Big). \tag{3}$$

DCP is effective for dehazing but may fail when the scene color is close to atmospheric light. Instead of constraining dark channel to be close to zero as in DCP, we learn dark channel prior by learning its corresponding proximal mapping from training data using a convolutional neural network, potentially being able to well approximate dark channels of haze-free images as shown in Fig. 1.

2.2 Learning CNNs for Image Inverse Problems

Recently, there have been several works to solve image inverse problems in deep learning frameworks [17,22,33,35,36]. Zhang et al. [36] train a set of effective denoisers and plug them in the scheme of half-quadratic splitting algorithm as a modular. Meinhardt et al. [17] solve the inverse problem in image processing using primal-dual hybrid gradient method and replace the proximal operator by a denoising neural network. In [22,33,35], the linear inverse problems are solved by learning proximal operators in the scheme of iterative optimization algorithms. These methods can well solve the linear inverse problems such as denoising, super-resolution, inpainting, non-blind deconvolution, compressive sensing MRI, etc.

Compared with these works, we focus on single image dehazing which is a challenging inverse problem with more unknown variables in imaging model. Instead of using common linear inverse models in these works, we specify single image dehazing as a non-linear inverse problem with dark channel and transmission priors (will be discussed in Sect. 3). We then propose an iterative solver and build a deep architecture incorporating the prior learning for single image dehazing. This proposed energy model and dehazing network are novel and the learned network achieves state-of-the-art results in single image dehazing.

3 Dehazing as an Inverse Problem

In this section, we first build an energy function with dark channel and transmission priors and then propose an iterative solver for energy minimization based on half-quadratic splitting (HQS) algorithm. This proposed energy model and its iterative optimization algorithm are the basis for building our proximal dehaze-net as discussed in Sect. 4.

3.1 Dehazing Energy Model

Considering the haze imaging model in Eq. (1), given a hazy image $I \in \mathbb{R}^{M \times N \times 3}$, we assume a known global atmospheric light $A \in \mathbb{R}^3$ and divide both sides of Eq. (1) by A in each color channel:

$$\frac{I^c(\mathrm{x})}{A^c} = \frac{J^c(\mathrm{x})}{A^c} T(\mathrm{x}) + (1 - T(\mathrm{x})), c \in \{r, g, b\}. \tag{4}$$

For simplicity, we denote I^c/A^c by P^c and J^c/A^c by Q^c. Then P, Q represent the scaled hazy image and latent haze-free image respectively. Thus Eq. (4) can be rewritten in a concise form as:

$$P^c = Q^c \circ T + (1 - T), \tag{5}$$

where $\circ$ is the element-wise product for matrices. We further assume that, within a local patch, the transmission map T is constant as in [11], then it holds that

$$P^{dk} = Q^{dk} \circ T + 1 - T, \tag{6}$$

where P^{dk}, Q^{dk} are dark channels of P, Q.

By enforcing Eq. (5) in color space and Eq. (6) in dark channel space as loss terms, we design a dehazing energy function:

$$\begin{aligned} E(Q,T) = \frac{\alpha}{2} \sum_{c\in\{r,g,b\}} \left\|Q^c \circ T + 1 - T - P^c\right\|_F^2 \\ + \frac{\beta}{2}\left\|Q^{dk} \circ T + 1 - T - P^{dk}\right\|_F^2 + f(T) + g(Q^{dk}), \end{aligned} \tag{7}$$

where α and β are coefficients for data terms. $f(T)$ and $g(Q^{dk})$ are regularization terms modeling the priors on transmission map T and dark channel Q^{dk}. The optimized haze-free image Q^* and transmission map T^* can be obtained by solving the following optimization problem:

$$\{Q^*, T^*\} = \arg\min_{Q,T} \; E(Q,T). \tag{8}$$

Regularization Terms of f and g. These two terms respectively model the transmission prior and dark channel prior. Multiple image priors can be taken for them, e.g., g for dark channel can be taken as L_0 or L_1 regularizer enforcing the dark channel close to zero. The transmission map is closely related to depth which is piecewise linear, and its regularizer f can be modeled by MRF [8,19] or TGV [5], etc. However, instead of using these hand-designed regularizations, we set them as uncertainties and aim to learn them from data using a deep learning approach.

Relationship to DCP Method. We find that DCP method is a special case of our model. When $\alpha = 0$, $f(T) = 0$ and $g(Q^{dk})$ strictly enforces that $Q^{dk} = 0$, then Eq. (7) has the solution of transmission $T^* = 1 - P^{dk}$, which is same as DCP in Eq. (3) when $\omega = 1$. The post-processing procedure of soft matting in DCP acts as an implicit transmission regularization.

Given this energy model, we next introduce how to design its optimization algorithm and deduce a deep architecture in Sects. 3.2 and 4 respectively.

3.2 Model Optimization

We now solve the optimization problem of Eq. (8) using half-quadratic splitting (HQS) algorithm. The HQS algorithm has been widely used in solving image inverse problems [9,10,13,32,35]. By introducing an auxiliary variable U to substitute the dark channel Q^{dk} of latent haze-free image, we derive the augmented energy function:

$$
\begin{aligned}
E(Q,T,U) = & \frac{\alpha}{2} \sum_{c\in\{r,g,b\}} \|Q^c \circ T + 1 - T - P^c\|_F^2 \\
& + \frac{\beta}{2}\|U \circ T + 1 - T - P^{dk}\|_F^2 + \frac{\gamma}{2}\|U - Q^{dk}\|_F^2 + f(T) + g(U),
\end{aligned} \tag{9}
$$

in which γ is a penalty weight, and when $\gamma \to \infty$, the solution of minimizing Eq. (9) converges to that of minimizing Eq. (7). We initialize $Q_0 = P$ and all elements of T_0 are ones, then for an iteration n of HQS algorithm, minimizing Eq. (9) can be achieved by solving three sub-problems for alternately updating U, T and Q.

Update U. Given the estimated haze-free image Q_{n-1} and transmission map T_{n-1} at iteration $n-1$, the auxiliary variable U can be updated as:

$$
U_n = \arg\min_U \frac{\beta}{2}\|U \circ T_{n-1} + 1 - T_{n-1} - P^{dk}\|_F^2 + \frac{\gamma}{2}\|U - Q^{dk}_{n-1}\|_F^2 + g(U), \tag{10}
$$

from which we can derive

$$
U_n = \text{prox}_{\frac{1}{b_n}g}\left(\hat{U}_n\right), \tag{11}
$$

where

$$
\hat{U}_n = \frac{1}{b_n}\left[\beta T_{n-1} \circ (P^{dk} + T_{n-1} - 1) + \gamma Q^{dk}_{n-1}\right], \tag{12}
$$

and $b_n = \beta T_{n-1} \circ T_{n-1} + \gamma$. The proximal operator is defined as:

$$
\text{prox}_{\lambda g}(V) = \arg\min_X \frac{1}{2}\|X - V\|_F^2 + \lambda g(X), \tag{13}
$$

assuming that $g(X)$ is separable for different elements in matrix X.

Update T. We next update the transmission map T. Given Q_{n-1} and U_n,

$$
\begin{aligned}
T_n = & \arg\min_T \frac{\alpha}{2}\sum_c \|Q^c_{n-1} \circ T + 1 - T - P^c\|_F^2 \\
& + \frac{\beta}{2}\|U_n \circ T + 1 - T - P^{dk}\|_F^2 + f(T).
\end{aligned} \tag{14}
$$

Then we derive

$$
T_n = \text{prox}_{\frac{1}{c_n}f}\left(\hat{T}_n\right), \tag{15}
$$

where

$$
\hat{T}_n = \frac{1}{c_n}\left[\textstyle\sum_c \alpha (Q^c_{n-1} - 1) \circ (P^c - 1) + \beta (U_n - 1) \circ (P^{dk} - 1)\right], \tag{16}
$$

and $c_n = \sum_c \alpha (Q^c_{n-1} - 1) \circ (Q^c_{n-1} - 1) + \beta (U_n - 1) \circ (U_n - 1)$.

Update Q. Given T_n and U_n, the haze-free image Q is updated as:

$$Q_n = \arg\min_{Q} \frac{\alpha}{2}\sum_c \|Q^c \circ T_n + 1 - T_n - P^c\|_F^2 + \frac{\gamma}{2}\|Q^{dk} - U_n\|_F^2. \tag{17}$$

Computing dark channel is to extract the smallest value from local color patch around each pixel. This operation can be implemented by a matrix D with value of one indicating the position of extracted minimal value, i.e., $\overrightarrow{Q^{dk}} = D\overrightarrow{Q}$, where $\overrightarrow{Q}$ is the vectorized Q. We further denote $\mathcal{T}_n \in \mathbb{R}^{M\times N\times 3}$ as a matrix with each color channel as T_n. Then Eq. (17) can be rewritten as:

$$\overrightarrow{Q}_n = \arg\min_{\overrightarrow{Q}} \frac{\alpha}{2}\|\overrightarrow{Q}\circ\overrightarrow{\mathcal{T}_n} + 1 - \overrightarrow{\mathcal{T}_n} - \overrightarrow{P}\|_2^2 + \frac{\gamma}{2}\|D\overrightarrow{Q} - \overrightarrow{U_n}\|_2^2, \tag{18}$$

which has the solution:

$$\overrightarrow{Q}_n = \frac{\alpha(\overrightarrow{P} + \overrightarrow{\mathcal{T}_n} - 1)\circ\overrightarrow{\mathcal{T}_n} + \gamma D^\top \overrightarrow{U_n}}{\alpha\overrightarrow{\mathcal{T}_n}\circ\overrightarrow{\mathcal{T}_n} + \gamma \mathrm{diag}(D^\top D)}. \tag{19}$$

The updated haze-free image Q_n can be derived by reshaping $\overrightarrow{Q_n}$ back to a matrix with the same size of input image. Note that the divisions in the Eqs. (12), (16), (19) are all element-wise operations. The detailed conduction of above equations can be found in supplementary material.

Special Case. If we discard transmission regularization term by setting $f(T) = 0$ and set the dark channel regularization term as L_1-norm, i.e., $g(Q^{dk}) = \sum_{\mathrm{x}\in\Omega}|Q^{dk}(\mathrm{x})|$ enforcing the dark channel sparse and close to zero, then the corresponding proximal operators in Eqs. (11) and (15) are defined as:

$$\mathrm{prox}_{\frac{1}{b_n}g}(\hat{U}_n) = \mathrm{softThresh}(\hat{U}_n, \frac{1}{b_n}), \tag{20}$$

$$\mathrm{prox}_{\frac{1}{c_n}f}(\hat{T}_n) = \hat{T}_n, \tag{21}$$

respectively, where softThresh$(\cdot, 1/b_n)$ is a soft thresholding function [6] with threshold $1/b_n$. We take this as the baseline of our method, denoted as *Ener-L_1*. An example of Ener-L_1 is shown in Fig. 2(c). Ener-L_1 is indeed effective for haze removal which is comparable to DCP. Through prior learning as will be discussed in next section, our proximal dehaze-net can better recover haze-free image as shown in Fig. 2(d).

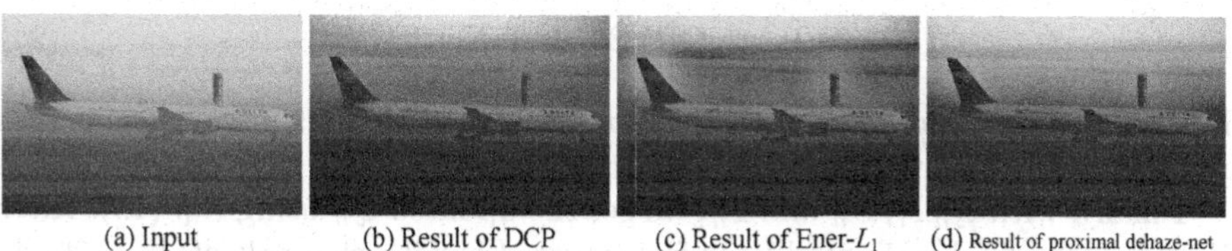

(a) Input (b) Result of DCP (c) Result of Ener-L_1 (d) Result of proximal dehaze-net

Fig. 2. An example of real image dehazing.

4 Proximal Dehaze-Net

Based on the above iterative optimization algorithm, we build a deep neural network for single image dehazing as illustrated in Fig. 3(a). The network is a structure with N stages implementing N iterations in the iterative optimization algorithm for solving Eq. (8). Each stage takes outputs of the previous stage U_{n-1}, T_{n-1} and Q_{n-1} (representing dark channel, transmission map and haze-free image respectively) as inputs and computes updated U_n, T_n and Q_n.

Instead of setting by hand the regularization terms of $g(\cdot)$ and $f(\cdot)$ (modeling dark channel and transmission priors) in the energy function of Eq. (7), we use deep CNNs to learn their corresponding proximal operators $\text{prox}_{\frac{1}{b_n}g}$ and $\text{prox}_{\frac{1}{c_n}f}$ for updating U_n and T_n in each stage n:

$$\begin{aligned} U_n &= \text{prox}_{\frac{1}{b_n}g}(\hat{U}_n) \triangleq \mathcal{G}(\hat{U}_n), \\ T_n &= \text{prox}_{\frac{1}{c_n}f}(\hat{T}_n) \triangleq \mathcal{F}(\hat{T}_n), \end{aligned} \tag{22}$$

where $\mathcal{G}$ and $\mathcal{F}$ are deep CNNs to be learned for representing the corresponding proximal operators. In this way, we design an end-to-end training architecture, dubbed as *proximal dehaze-net*. We will next introduce the network structure.

4.1 Network Design

As shown in Fig. 3(a), each stage of the proximal dehaze-net implements one iteration of model optimization discussed in Sect. 3.2, and the proximal operators are substituted by convolutional neural networks as in Eq. (22).

We now introduce the network structure for each stage. Please refer to Fig. 3(b) for better understanding. For the n-th stage, $\hat{U}_n$ is first computed by Eq. (12), then sent into a convolutional neural network, i.e., *D-Net*, to perform proximal mapping $\text{prox}_{\frac{1}{b_n}g}$. The updated dark channel is:

$$U_n = \mathcal{G}(\hat{U}_n) \triangleq \text{D-Net}(\hat{U}_n, P), \tag{23}$$

in which we concatenate $\hat{U}_n$ with hazy image P as input.

Similarly, $\hat{T}_n$ is first computed using Eq. (16), then concatenated with P and sent into another convolutional neural networks, *T-Net* and a *GIF-Block*, to perform proximal mapping $\text{prox}_{\frac{1}{c_n}f}$. The updated transmission map is:

$$T_n = \mathcal{F}(\hat{T}_n) \triangleq \text{GIF-Block}\big(\text{T-Net}(\hat{T}_n, P)\big), \tag{24}$$

T-Net and GIF-Block are respectively responsible for transmission estimation and guided image filtering (GIF) for better edge alignment with image edges.

Finally, with Q_{n-1}, U_n and T_n, we get the updated Q_n using Eq. (19). After N stages, the final estimated haze-free image J is with channels of $J^c = Q_N^c A^c$ for $c \in \{r, g, b\}$. We estimate the atmospheric light A according to [11]. We next introduce the structures of D-Net, T-Net and GIF-Block.

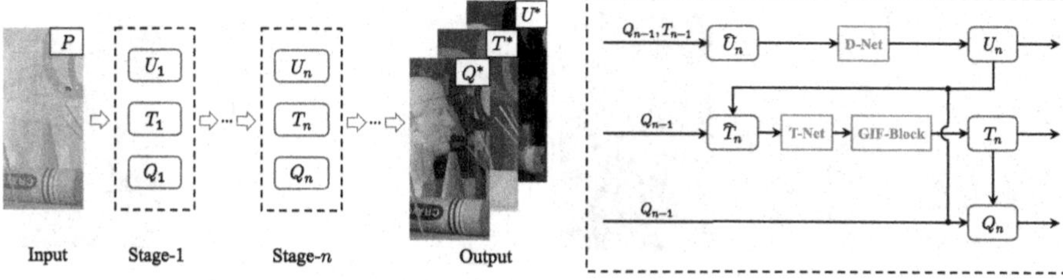

(a) Multi-stage network for image dehazing (b) Network structure for the n–th stage

Fig. 3. Architecture of proximal dehaze-net. (a) The network consists of multiple stages. The outputs U^*, T^*, Q^* are estimated dark channel, transmission map and dehazed image. (b) The detailed architecture for the n-th stage, in which the variables U_n, T_n and Q_n are successively updated by the algorithm described in Sect. 3.2. D-Net is to learn proximal mapping $\mathcal{G}$ for dark channel prior. T-Net and GIF-Block are to learn the proximal mapping $\mathcal{F}$ for transmission prior.

D-Net and T-Net. D-Net and T-Net have similar structures. They both include three cascaded convolutional blocks. Each block consists of a convolutional layer, a ReLU layer, a pooling layer and an upsampling layer. The convolutional layers in these blocks have nine 7×7 filters, nine 5×5 filters and nine 3×3 filters respectively. The last block is followed by another convolutional layer with one 1×1 filter. Then the output map is finally sent to a ReLU layer for D-Net or a sigmoid layer for T-Net. The ReLU layer aims to keep the output dark channel U non-negative, while the sigmoid layer is to keep the output transmission map T within $[0, 1]$.

GIF-Block. GIF-Block performs standard guided image filtering [12]. This block enforces the transmission map to be well aligned with image along edges. As shown in Fig. 3(b), GIF-Block takes the input image P as guidance and performs guided image filtering on the output of T-Net:

$$\text{GIF-Block}\left(\text{T-Net}(\hat{T}_n, P)\right) \triangleq \text{GIF}_P\left(\text{T-Net}(\hat{T}_n, P)\right), \tag{25}$$

using the guided filtering operator GIF_P with guidance of P. The GIF-block is a differentiable block implementing guided filtering represented by a computation graph. It is included as a part of our end-to-end trainable system more than just a post-processing step. More details on the algorithm and computation graph of GIF-Block can be found in the supplementary material.

To illustrate what were learned for these proximal mappings, in Fig. 4, we show an example of our learned proximal mappings for dark channel and transmission using the learned proximal dehaze-net (we will introduce network training in Sect. 4.2). Figure 4(b), (c) respectively show the dark channels and transmission maps before and after the proximal mappings of $\mathcal{G}$ and $\mathcal{F}$. We can observe that the learned proximal mapping $\mathcal{G}$ produces reasonable dark channel with low values but retaining the high values for white windows. The learned

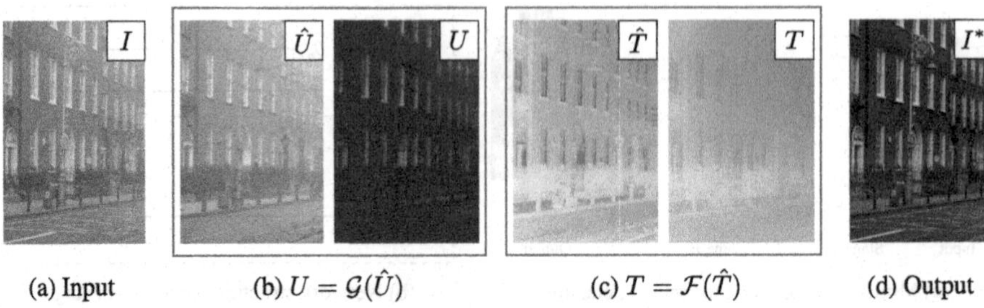

(a) Input (b) $U = \mathcal{G}(\hat{U})$ (c) $T = \mathcal{F}(\hat{T})$ (d) Output

Fig. 4. Effectiveness of using CNNs to learn proximal mappings for dark channel and transmission priors. The left and right images in (b) (c) respectively represent the inputs and outputs of proximal mappings $\mathcal{G}$ and $\mathcal{F}$ for dark channel and transmission. (d) Our final dehazing result.

proximal mapping $\mathcal{F}$ produces a smooth transmission map consistent with the underlying scenery depth.

4.2 Network Training

The training loss for each training image is defined as the sum of pixel-wise L_1 distances between the outputs of proximal dehaze-net $\{Q^*, T^*, U^*\}$ and the ground truths $\{Q^{\text{gt}}, T^{\text{gt}}, U^{\text{gt}}\}$:

$$\ell = \sum_{O \in \{Q,T,U\}} \sum_{\text{x}} \|O^*(\text{x}) - O^{\text{gt}}(\text{x})\|_1. \tag{26}$$

When training the proximal dehaze-net, we compute the gradients of loss w.r.t. the inputs of Eqs. (11), (15), (19) for back-propagation. Due to space limit, please refer to supplementary material for these gradients. In our implementation, the parameters of nets (including D-Net and T-Net) in different stages are not shared. Parameters of α and β in energy function are set to 1 and 5 respectively. We implement and train our network using MatConvNet[1] framework. We choose Adam solver with a learning rate of 0.001. We use a batch size of 10 and it usually takes 13.6 h to train a single stage network for 50 epochs on a Titan X GPU with 12 GB memory.

5 Experiments

In this section, we evaluate our method on both synthetic and real datasets and compare with the other state-of-the-art dehazing methods proposed in recent years.

[1] http://www.vlfeat.org/matconvnet/.

5.1 Datasets

Training Dataset. Our training dataset consists of three RGB-D datasets including NYU-Depth [26], Middlebury-Stereo [23–25] and MPI-Sintel [3]. We sampled 9000 pairs of RGB-D image patches in size of 240×240 from the training dataset. According to haze imaging model Eq. (1), given A and η, the hazy image and transmission are generated by the clean image and its corresponding depth map. For each pair of RGB-D image patches, we randomly select $A \in [0.7, 1]$ and $\eta \in [0.5, 1.5]$ to generate the ground truth transmission map and hazy image, then compute the dark channel from the clean image. Therefore we construct a set of 9000 training samples including hazy images, ground truth haze-free images, transmission maps and dark channels.

Test Datasets. To quantitatively evaluate the dehazing methods, we established two benchmark datasets – TestA and TestB for evaluating dehazing performance. For TestA, we use the RGB-D images from NYU, Middlebury and Sintel datasets (without overlapping with training images) to generate 548 full sized hazy images. We also establish a more realistic dataset TestB including 128 images by applying different hazes on HazeRD [37] dataset. In TestA, images are either taken indoors or computer generated, thus are different from the real-world outdoor hazy images. HazeRD provides real outdoor images with high-quality depth information, therefore enables us to better simulate real outdoor images taken under hazy condition.

5.2 Results on Synthetic Datasets

We first compare our network with recent methods for single image dehazing on both synthetic datasets – TestA and TestB. The compared methods include dark channel prior (DCP) [11], fast visibility restoration (FVR) [30], boundary constraint and contextual regularization (BCCR) [18], gradient residual minimization (GRM) [5], color attenuation prior (CAP) [38], non-local dehazing (NLD) [2], multi-scale CNN (MSCNN) [20], DehazeNet [4] and AOD-Net [14]. Among these methods, MSCNN, DehazeNet and AOD-Net are learning-based methods. For quantitative evaluation, we show the average peak signal-to-noise ratio (PSNR) and structural similarity (SSIM) index between the recovered images and ground truths.

As shown in Table 1, our proximal dehaze-net achieves best results in both PSNR and SSIM values on TestA and significantly improves the DCP [11] method by nearly 1 dB in PSNR. Since all learning-based methods do not include images in TestB as training data, it is fair to compare them on TestB. As shown in Table 1, our method achieves highest PNSR and SSIM on TestB and exceeds the second best learning-based method DehazeNet [4] by 0.61 dB in PSNR.

In Fig. 5, we show two examples of dehazing results and corresponding transmission maps from TestA and TestB. Compared with other methods, our proximal dehaze-net can better estimate transmission maps and produce more visually pleasant haze-free images with highest PSNR and SSIM values. Though DehazeNet [4] achieves relatively high PSNR as shown in Table 1, its results still

Table 1. Dehazing results on synthetic datasets TestA and TestB. We show the average PSNR and SSIM of the recovered images by the compared methods.

Methods		DCP [11]	FVR [30]	BCCR [18]	CAP [38]	NLD [2]	GRM [5]	MSCNN [20]	DehazeNet [4]	AOD-Net [14]	Ours
TestA	PSNR	18.32	15.18	16.00	16.63	17.87	18.45	17.37	19.17	18.00	**19.31**
	SSIM	0.8244	0.7599	0.7556	0.7050	0.7978	0.8043	0.7564	0.7888	0.7928	**0.8388**
TestB	PSNR	17.66	16.17	16.31	18.56	18.82	17.47	19.10	19.53	18.13	**20.14**
	SSIM	0.8430	0.8472	0.8337	0.8256	0.8355	0.7921	0.8540	0.8498	0.8266	**0.8932**

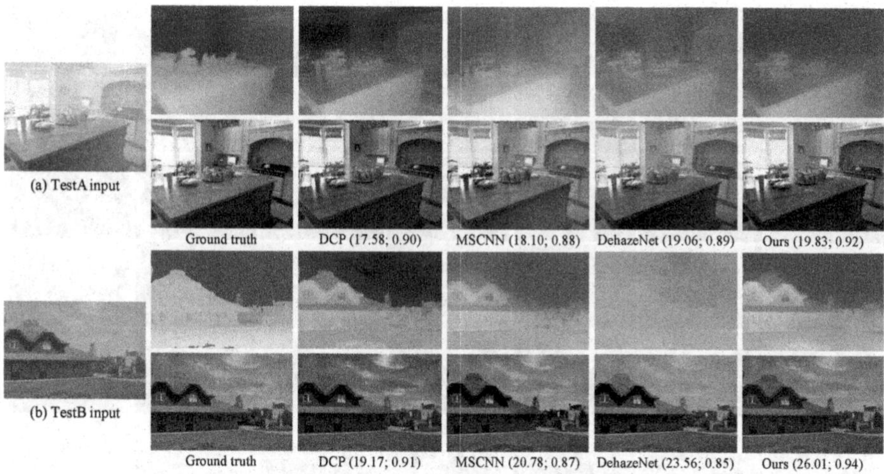

Fig. 5. Dehazing results on two examples from TestA and TestB. We show the recovered images and corresponding transmission maps by different methods. PSNR and SSIM values of dehazed images are shown in brackets.

contain hazes as shown in Fig. 5. On the other hand, DCP [11] can effectively remove the hazes, but sometimes may over-enhance the color contrast in these results. As a comparison, our method can well control the amount of removed hazes and produces visually natural results.

5.3 Results on Real Datasets

In Fig. 6, we also evaluate and compare our network with recent state-of-the-art methods [4,11,14,20,38] on real-world hazy images. The real-world example images are collected from Internet and previous works. For traditional methods, such as DCP [11] and CAP [38], the hazes are significantly removed and the results are with high color contrast. However, CAP sometimes blurs image textures and causes over-saturation in color, as observed in the 2nd and 4th images of Fig. 6. DCP can not properly deal with sky regions and is likely to introduce artifacts as shown in the 4th, 5th and 7th images of Fig. 6. It is interesting that the learning-based methods [4,14,20] trained on synthetic dataset generalize well to produce visually pleasant results for real image dehazing. However, as shown in the 4th and 6th images of Fig. 6, MSCNN [20] sometimes cause color distortion, which makes the recovered images seem unnatural. DehazeNet [4], although achieves high PSNR values on synthetic datasets, does not remove hazes as effectively as other methods, such as the 1st, 3rd and 7th images of Fig. 6. AOD-Net [14] usually slightly reduces image brightness and sometimes causes faded scene of foreground as shown in the 3rd and 6th images of Fig. 6. Our proximal dehaze-net, integrating haze imaging model with deep learning, can effectively remove hazes in different amounts while still keeping the results visually natural and pleasant.

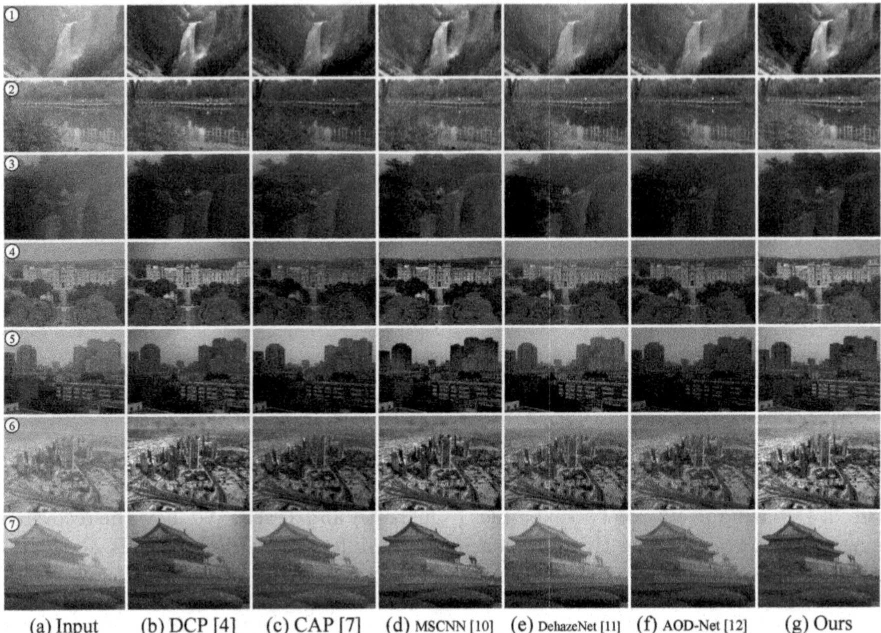

Fig. 6. Dehazing results on real images. Please zoom in for better illustration.

5.4 Ablation Study

To investigate the effect of learning dark channel and transmission priors for our network, we respectively discard dark channel regularization $g(U)$ and transmission regularization $f(T)$ in Eq. (9). We then denote our proximal dehaze-net without learning dark channel prior as *Net-ND* and without learning transmission prior as *Net-NT*. We train Net-ND and Net-NT with one stage from scratch and compare with Ener-L_1 (see Sect. 3.2) and Net-S1 (our proximal dehaze-net with one stage) on TestB. We show the PSNR and SSIM in Fig. 7(a). Compared with Net-S1, Net-NT without learning transmission prior decreases the PSNR by 0.64 dB, and Net-ND without learning dark channel prior decreases the PSNR by 4.72 dB, even lower than Ener-L_1. Therefore learning both priors, especially the dark channel prior, is essential for our approach.

To evaluate the effect of model complexity on performance, we trained proximal dehaze-nets with different filter sizes, filter numbers and number of stages. For *Net-L*, we use larger filter sizes by setting all convolutional kernels to be 7×7. For *Net-M*, we use 64 rather than only 9 filters in each convolution layer. We also trained our proximal dehaze-net with 2 stages, denoted as *Net-S2*. We show the PSNR and SSIM on TestB in Fig. 7(b), from which we can see that increasing network complexity promotes the PSNR by over 0.88 dB. However, we did not observe significant qualitative improvements visually using these more complex networks. Moreover, increasing network complexity increases the running time.

To be specific, the running times on a single GPU for these networks on an image of 480×640 are 0.058 s for Net-S1, 0.096 s for Net-S2, 0.077 s for Net-L and 0.143 s for Net-M respectively. For the sake of efficiency, we adopt Net-S1 as our final model and all reported results are based on Net-S1.

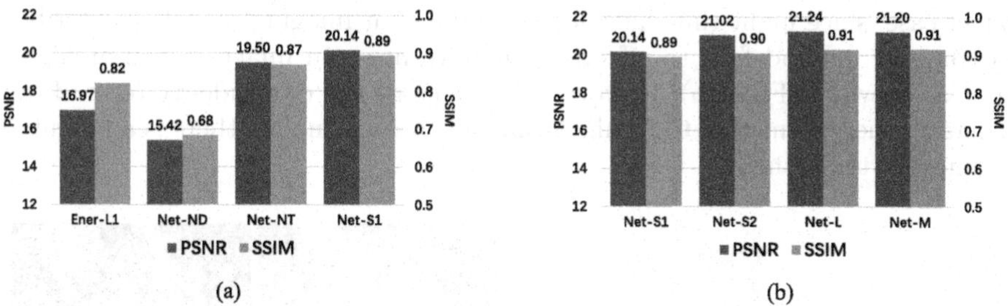

Fig. 7. Comparison of different network architectures on TestB dataset. (a) Results of our proximal dehaze-net and nets without prior learning. (b) Results of our nets in different complexities.

5.5 Extension to More Applications

Although our network is trained for image dehazing, we can also extend it to other tasks that are similar to dehazing. In Fig. 8(a), we show an example of underwater image enhancement. Ignoring the forward scattering component, the simplified underwater optical model [1] has similar formulation with haze imaging model. Our network can effectively remove haze-like effect in this underwater image. Although halation has a different imaging model, it brings haze-like effect to image. Our proximal dehaze-net can be directly applied to anti-halation image enhancement without need of re-training, as shown in Fig. 8(b). In Fig. 8(c), we also show an example of our network applied to a haze-free image to test the robustness. Our network does not change the image much and the result still looks natural and clear.

(a) Underwater image enhancement (b) Anti-halation enhancement (c) Haze-free image

Fig. 8. Extension to other applications.

5.6 Limitations

While our method behaves well on most natural images, it has limitations towards certain situations in which the photo is taken in heavy fog or at night-time. For the first case as shown in Fig. 9(a), image information is seriously lost due to heavy fog and it is hard for us to recover satisfactory result. For the latter case, since night-time haze follows a different imaging model as described in [16], our method fails to effectively remove hazes in images taken at night-time as shown in Fig. 9(b). However, if we change the data fidelity term of our dehazing energy function to fit night-time image haze model, there is a potential to improve the result.

(a) Heavy haze image dehazing (b) Night-time image dehazing

Fig. 9. Failure cases of our method.

6 Conclusion

In this paper, we proposed a novel proximal dehaze-net for single image dehazing. This network integrates haze imaging model, dark channel and transmission priors into a deep architecture. This is achieved by building an energy function using dark channel and transmission priors for single image dehazing, and learning these priors using their corresponding proximal operators in an optimization-inspired deep network. This energy function and proximal dehaze-net are novel for dehazing, and the learned network achieves promising results on both synthetic and real-world hazy images. In the future, we are interested in building realistic outdoor training dataset for dehazing or using outdoor clear images as supervision in a generative adversarial training framework.

Acknowledgement. This work is supported by National Natural Science Foundation of China under Grants 11622106, 61472313, 11690011, 61721002.

References

1. Ancuti, C.O., Ancuti, C., De Vleeschouwer, C., Bekaert, P.: Color balance and fusion for underwater image enhancement. IEEE Trans. Image Process. **27**(1), 379–393 (2018)
2. Berman, D., Treibitz, T., Avidan, S.: Non-local image dehazing. In: IEEE Conference on Computer Vision and Pattern Recognition (2016)

3. Butler, D.J., Wulff, J., Stanley, G.B., Black, M.J.: A naturalistic open source movie for optical flow evaluation. In: Fitzgibbon, A., Lazebnik, S., Perona, P., Sato, Y., Schmid, C. (eds.) ECCV 2012. LNCS, vol. 7577, pp. 611–625. Springer, Heidelberg (2012). https://doi.org/10.1007/978-3-642-33783-3_44
4. Cai, B., Xu, X., Jia, K., Qing, C., Tao, D.: DehazeNet: an end-to-end system for single image haze removal. IEEE Trans. Image Process. **25**(11), 5187–5198 (2016)
5. Chen, C., Do, M.N., Wang, J.: Robust image and video dehazing with visual artifact suppression via gradient residual minimization. In: Leibe, B., Matas, J., Sebe, N., Welling, M. (eds.) ECCV 2016. LNCS, vol. 9906, pp. 576–591. Springer, Cham (2016). https://doi.org/10.1007/978-3-319-46475-6_36
6. Donoho, D.L.: De-noising by soft-thresholding. IEEE Trans. Inf. Theory **41**(3), 613–627 (1995)
7. Fattal, R.: Single image dehazing. ACM Trans. Graph. (TOG) **27**(3), 72 (2008)
8. Fattal, R.: Dehazing using color-lines. ACM Trans. Graph. (TOG) **34**(1), 13 (2014)
9. Geman, D., Reynolds, G.: Constrained restoration and the recovery of discontinuities. IEEE Trans. Pattern Anal. Mach. Intell. **14**(3), 367–383 (1992)
10. Geman, D., Yang, C.: Nonlinear image recovery with half-quadratic regularization. IEEE Trans. Image Process. **4**(7), 932–946 (1995)
11. He, K., Sun, J., Tang, X.: Single image haze removal using dark channel prior. In: IEEE Conference on Computer Vision and Pattern Recognition (2009)
12. He, K., Sun, J., Tang, X.: Guided image filtering. In: Daniilidis, K., Maragos, P., Paragios, N. (eds.) ECCV 2010. LNCS, vol. 6311, pp. 1–14. Springer, Heidelberg (2010). https://doi.org/10.1007/978-3-642-15549-9_1
13. Krishnan, D., Fergus, R.: Fast image deconvolution using hyper-Laplacian priors. In: Advances in Neural Information Processing Systems (2009)
14. Li, B., Peng, X., Wang, Z., Xu, J., Feng, D.: AOD-Net: all-in-one dehazing network. In: IEEE International Conference on Computer Vision (2017)
15. Li, R., Pan, J., Li, Z., Tang, J.: Single image dehazing via conditional generative adversarial network. In: IEEE Conference on Computer Vision and Pattern Recognition (2018)
16. Li, Y., Tan, R.T., Brown, M.S.: Nighttime haze removal with glow and multiple light colors. In: Proceedings of the IEEE International Conference on Computer Vision, pp. 226–234 (2015)
17. Meinhardt, T., Moller, M., Hazirbas, C., Cremers, D.: Learning proximal operators: using denoising networks for regularizing inverse imaging problems. In: IEEE International Conference on Computer Vision (2017)
18. Meng, G., Wang, Y., Duan, J., Xiang, S., Pan, C.: Efficient image dehazing with boundary constraint and contextual regularization. In: IEEE International Conference on Computer Vision (2013)
19. Nishino, K., Kratz, L., Lombardi, S.: Bayesian defogging. Int. J. Comput. Vis. **98**(3), 263–278 (2012)
20. Ren, W., Liu, S., Zhang, H., Pan, J., Cao, X., Yang, M.-H.: Single image dehazing via multi-scale convolutional neural networks. In: Leibe, B., Matas, J., Sebe, N., Welling, M. (eds.) ECCV 2016. LNCS, vol. 9906, pp. 154–169. Springer, Cham (2016). https://doi.org/10.1007/978-3-319-46475-6_10
21. Ren, W., et al.: Gated fusion network for single image dehazing. In: IEEE Conference on Computer Vision and Pattern Recognition (2018)
22. Rick Chang, J.H., Li, C.L., Poczos, B., Vijaya Kumar, B.V.K., Sankaranarayanan, A.C.: One network to solve them all - solving linear inverse problems using deep projection models. In: IEEE International Conference on Computer Vision (2017)

23. Scharstein, D., Szeliski, R.: High-accuracy stereo depth maps using structured light. In: IEEE Conference on Computer Vision and Pattern Recognition (2003)
24. Scharstein, D., et al.: High-resolution stereo datasets with subpixel-accurate ground truth. In: Jiang, X., Hornegger, J., Koch, R. (eds.) GCPR 2014. LNCS, vol. 8753, pp. 31–42. Springer, Cham (2014). https://doi.org/10.1007/978-3-319-11752-2_3
25. Scharstein, D., Pal, C.: Learning conditional random fields for stereo. In: IEEE Conference on Computer Vision and Pattern Recognition (2007)
26. Silberman, N., Hoiem, D., Kohli, P., Fergus, R.: Indoor segmentation and support inference from RGBD images. In: Fitzgibbon, A., Lazebnik, S., Perona, P., Sato, Y., Schmid, C. (eds.) ECCV 2012. LNCS, vol. 7576, pp. 746–760. Springer, Heidelberg (2012). https://doi.org/10.1007/978-3-642-33715-4_54
27. Tan, R.T.: Visibility in bad weather from a single image. In: IEEE Conference on Computer Vision and Pattern Recognition (2008)
28. Tan, R.T., Pettersson, N., Petersson, L.: Visibility enhancement for roads with foggy or hazy scenes. In: IEEE Intelligent Vehicles Symposium (2007)
29. Tang, K., Yang, J., Wang, J.: Investigating haze-relevant features in a learning framework for image dehazing. In: IEEE Conference on Computer Vision and Pattern Recognition (2014)
30. Tarel, J.P., Hautiere, N.: Fast visibility restoration from a single color or gray level image. In: IEEE International Conference on Computer Vision (2009)
31. Tripathi, A., Mukhopadhyay, S.: Single image fog removal using anisotropic diffusion. IET Image Process. **6**(7), 966–975 (2012)
32. Wang, Y., Yang, J., Yin, W., Zhang, Y.: A new alternating minimization algorithm for total variation image reconstruction. SIAM J. Imaging Sci. **1**(3), 248–272 (2008)
33. Yang, Y., Sun, J., Li, H., Xu, Z.: Deep ADMM-Net for compressive sensing MRI. In: Advances in Neural Information Processing Systems (2016)
34. Zhang, H., Patel, V.M.: Densely connected pyramid dehazing network. In: IEEE Conference on Computer Vision and Pattern Recognition (2018)
35. Zhang, J., Pan, J., Lai, W.S., Lau, R.W.H., Yang, M.H.: Learning fully convolutional networks for iterative non-blind deconvolution. In: IEEE Conference on Computer Vision and Pattern Recognition (2017)
36. Zhang, K., Zuo, W., Gu, S., Zhang, L.: Learning deep CNN denoiser prior for image restoration. In: IEEE Conference on Computer Vision and Pattern Recognition (2017)
37. Zhang, Y., Ding, L., Sharma, G.: HazeRD: an outdoor scene dataset and benchmark for single image dehazing. In: IEEE International Conference on Image Processing (2017)
38. Zhu, Q., Mai, J., Shao, L.: A fast single image haze removal algorithm using color attenuation prior. IEEE Trans. Image Process. **24**(11), 3522–3533 (2015)

SDC-Net: Video Prediction Using Spatially-Displaced Convolution

Fitsum A. Reda(✉), Guilin Liu, Kevin J. Shih, Robert Kirby, Jon Barker, David Tarjan, Andrew Tao, and Bryan Catanzaro

Nvidia Corporation, Santa Clara, CA 95051, USA
{freda,guilinl,kshih,rkirby,dtarjan,jbarker,atao,bcatanzaro}@nvidia.com

Abstract. We present an approach for high-resolution video frame prediction by conditioning on both past frames and past optical flows. Previous approaches rely on resampling past frames, guided by a learned future optical flow, or on direct generation of pixels. Resampling based on flow is insufficient because it cannot deal with disocclusions. Generative models currently lead to blurry results. Recent approaches synthesis a pixel by convolving input patches with a predicted kernel. However, their memory requirement increases with kernel size. Here, we present *spatially-displaced convolution* (SDC) module for video frame prediction. We learn a motion vector and a kernel for each pixel and synthesize a pixel by applying the kernel at a displaced location in the source image, defined by the predicted motion vector. Our approach inherits the merits of both vector-based and kernel-based approaches, while ameliorating their respective disadvantages. We train our model on 428K unlabelled 1080p video game frames. Our approach produces state-of-the-art results, achieving an SSIM score of 0.904 on high-definition YouTube-8M videos, 0.918 on Caltech Pedestrian videos. Our model handles large motion effectively and synthesizes crisp frames with consistent motion.

Keywords: 3D CNN · Sampling kernel · Optical flow
Frame prediction

1 Introduction

Video prediction is the task of inferring future frames from a sequence of past frames. The ability to predict future frames could find applications in various domains – ranging from future state estimation for self-driving vehicles to video analysis. For a video prediction model to perform well, it must accurately capture not only how objects move, but also how their displacement affects the visibility and appearance of surrounding structures. Our work focuses on predicting one or more immediate next frames that are sharp, realistic and at high resolution (Fig. 1).

Electronic supplementary material The online version of this chapter (https://doi.org/10.1007/978-3-030-01234-2_44) contains supplementary material, which is available to authorized users.

V. Ferrari et al. (Eds.): ECCV 2018, LNCS 11211, pp. 747–763, 2018.
https://doi.org/10.1007/978-3-030-01234-2_44

Fig. 1. Frame prediction on a YouTube video frame featuring a panning camera. Left to right: Ground-truth, MCNet [34] result, and our SDC-Net result. The SDC-Net predicted frame is sharper and preserves fine image details, while color distortion and blurriness is seen in the tree and text in MCNet's predicted frame. (Color figure online)

Another attribute of the video prediction task is that models can be trained on raw unlabeled video frames. We train our models on large amounts of high resolution footage from video game sequences, which we find improves accuracy because video game sequences contain a large range of motion. We demonstrate that the resulting models perform well not only on video game footage, but also on real-life footage.

Video prediction is an active research area and our work builds on the literature [2–4,13,18–20,26,33,35,37]. Previous approaches for video prediction often focus on direct synthesis of pixels using generative models. For instance, convolutional neural networks were used to predict pixel RGB values, while recurrent mechanisms were used to model temporal changes. Ranzato et al. [28] proposed to partition input sequences into a dictionary of image patch centroids and trained recurrent neural networks (RNN) to generate target images by indexing the dictionaries. Srivastava et al. [31] and Villegas et al. [34] used a convolutional Long-Short-Term-Memory (LSTM) encoder-decoder architecture conditioned on previous frame data. Similarly, Lotter et al. [17] presented a predictive coding RNN architecture to model the motion dynamics of objects in the image for frame prediction. Mathieu et al. [21] proposed a multi-scale conditional generative adversarial network (GAN) architecture to alleviate the short range dependency of single-scale architectures. These approaches, however, suffer from blurriness and do not model large object motions well. This is likely due to the difficulty in directly regressing to pixel values, as well as the low resolution and lack of large motion in their training data.

Another popular approach for frame synthesis is learning to transform input frames. Liang et al. [14] proposed a generative adversarial network (GAN) approach with a joint future optical-flow and future frame discriminator. However, ground truth optical flows are not trivial to collect at large scale. Training with estimated optical flows could also lead to erroneous supervision signals. Jiang et al. [10] presented a model to learn offset vectors for sampling for frame interpolation, and perform frame synthesis using bilinear interpolation guided by the learned sampling vectors. These approaches are desirable in modeling large motion. However, in our experiments, we found sampling vector-based synthesis results are often affected by speckled noise.

One particular approach proposed by Niklaus et al. [23,24] and Vondrick et al. [36] for frame synthesis is to learn to predict sampling kernels that adapt to each output pixel. A pixel is then synthesized as the weighted sampling of a source patch centered at the pixel location. Niklaus et al. [23,24] employed this for the related task of video frame interpolation, applying predicted sampling kernels to consecutive frames to synthesize the intermediate frame. In our experiments, we found the kernel-based approaches to be effective in keeping objects intact as they are transformed. However, this approach cannot model large motion, since its displacement is limited by the kernel size. Increasing kernel size can be prohibitively expensive.

Inspired by these approaches, we present a spatially-displaced convolutional (SDC) module for video frame prediction. We learn a motion vector and a kernel for each pixel and synthesize a pixel by applying the kernel at a displaced location in a source image, defined by the predicted motion vector. Our approach inherits the merits of both sampling vector-based and kernel-based approaches, while ameliorating their respective disadvantages. We take the large-motion advantage of sampling vector-based approach, while reducing the speckled noise patterns. We take the clean object boundary prediction advantages of the kernel-based approaches, while significantly reducing kernel sizes, hence reducing the memory demand.

The contributions of our work are:

- We propose a deep model for high-resolution frame prediction from a sequence of past frames.
- We propose a spatially-displaced convolutional (SDC) module for effective frame synthesis via transformation learning.
- We compare our SDC module with kernel-based, vector-based and state-of-the-art approaches.

2 Methods

Given a sequence of frames $\mathbf{I}_{1:t}$ (the immediate past t frames), our work aims to predict the next future frame $\mathbf{I}_{t+1}$. We formulate the problem as a transformation learning problem

$$\mathbf{I}_{t+1} = \mathcal{T}\Big(\mathcal{G}\big(\mathbf{I}_{1:t}\big), \mathbf{I}_{1:t}\Big), \tag{1}$$

where $\mathcal{G}$ is a learned function that predicts transformation parameters, and $\mathcal{T}$ is a transformation function. In prior work, $\mathcal{T}$ can be a bilinear sampling operation guided by a motion vector [10,15]:

$$\mathbf{I}_{t+1}(x, y) = f\big(\mathbf{I}_t(x + u, y + v)\big), \tag{2}$$

where f is a bilinear interpolator [15], (u, v) is a motion vector predicted by $\mathcal{G}$, and $\mathbf{I}_t(x, y)$ is a pixel value at (x, y) in the immediate past frame $\mathbf{I}_t$. We refer this approach as a vector-based resampling. Figure 2a illustrates this approach.

An alternative approach is to define $\mathcal{T}$ as a convolution module that combines motion or displacement learning and resampling into a single operation [23,24,36]:

$$\mathbf{I}_{t+1}(x, y) = \mathrm{K}(x, y) * \mathbf{P}_t(x, y), \tag{3}$$

where $\mathrm{K}(x, y) \in \mathrm{R}^{\mathrm{N}\times\mathrm{N}}$ is an $\mathrm{N} \times \mathrm{N}$ 2D kernel predicted by $\mathcal{G}$ at (x, y) and $\mathbf{P}_t(x, y)$ is an $\mathrm{N} \times \mathrm{N}$ patch centered at (x, y) in $\mathbf{I}_t$. We refer this approach as adaptive kernel-based resampling [23,24]. Figure 2b illustrates this approach.

Since Eq. (2) considers few pixels in synthesis, its results often appear degraded by speckled noise patterns. It can, however, model large displacements without a significant increase in parameter count. On the other hand, Eq. (3) produces visually pleasing results for small displacements, but requires large kernels to be predicted at each location to capture large motions. As such, the kernel-based approach can easily become not only costly at inference, but also difficult to train.

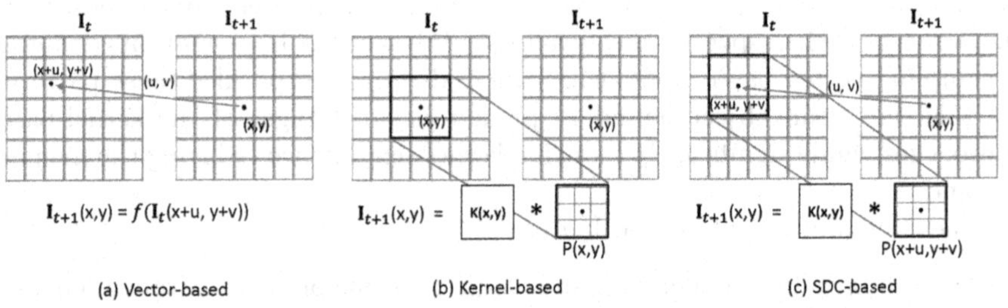

Fig. 2. Illustration of sampling-based pixel synthesis. (a) Vector-based with a bilinear interpolation. (b) Kernel-based, a convolution with a centered patch. (c) our SDC-based method, a convolution with a displaced patch.

2.1 Spatially Displaced Convolution

To achieve the best of both worlds, we propose a hybrid solution – the *Spatially Displaced Convolution* (SDC). The SDC uses predictions of both a motion vector (u, v) and an adaptive kernel $\mathrm{K}(x, y)$, but convolves the predicted kernel with a patch at the displaced location $(x + u, y + v)$ in $\mathbf{I}_t$. Pixel synthesis using SDC is computed as:

$$\mathbf{I}_{t+1}(x, y) = \mathrm{K}(x, y) * \mathbf{P}_t(x + u, y + v). \tag{4}$$

The predicted pixel $\mathbf{I}_{t+1}(x, y)$ is thus the weighted sampling of pixels in an $\mathrm{N} \times \mathrm{N}$ region centered at $(x + u, y + v)$ in $\mathbf{I}_t$. The patch $\mathbf{P}_t(x + u, y + v)$ is bilinearly sampled at non-integral coordinates. Figure 2c illustrates our SDC-based approach.

Setting $K(x, y)$ to a kernel of all-zeros except for a one at the center reduce the SDC to Eq. (2), whereas setting u and v to zero reduces it to Eq. (3). However, it is important to note that the SDC is not the same as applying Eqs. (2) and

(3) in succession. If applied in succession, the $\mathrm{N} \times \mathrm{N}$ patch sampled by $K(x, y)$ would be subject to the resampling effect of Eq. (2) as opposed to being the original patch from $\mathbf{I}_t$.

Our SDC effectively decouples displacement and kernel learning, allowing us to achieve the visually pleasing results of kernel-based approaches while keeping the kernel sizes small. We also adopt separable kernels [24] for $\mathrm{K}(x, y)$ to further reduce computational cost. At each location, we predict a pair of 1D kernels and calculate the outer-product of them to form a 2D kernel. This reduces our kernel parameter count from N^2 to 2N. In total, our model predicts $2\mathrm{N}+2$ parameters for each pixel, including the motion vector. We empirically set $N = 11$. Inference at 1080p resolution uses 174 MB of VRAM, which easily fits in GPU memory.

We develop deep neural networks to learn motion vectors and kernels adapted to each output pixel. The SDC is fully differentiable and thus allows our model to train end-to-end. Losses for training are applied to the SDC-predicted frame. We also condition our model on both past frames and past optical flows. This allows our network to easily capture motion dynamics and evolution of pixels needed to learn the transformation parameters. We formulate our model as:

$$\mathbf{I}_{t+1} = \mathcal{T}\Big(\mathcal{G}\big(\mathbf{I}_{1:t}, \mathbf{F}_{2:t}\big), \mathbf{I}_t\Big), \tag{5}$$

where transformation $\mathcal{T}$ is realized with SDC and operates on the most recent input $\mathbf{I}_t$, and $\mathbf{F}_i$ is the backwards optical flow (see Sect. 2.3) between $\mathbf{I}_i$ and $\mathbf{I}_{i-1}$. We calculate $\mathbf{F}$ using state-of-the-art neural network-based optical flow models [7,9,32].

Our approach naturally extends to multiple frame prediction $\mathbf{I}_{t+1:t+D}$ by recursively re-circulating SDC predicted frames back as inputs. For instance, to predict a frame two steps ahead, we re-circulate the SDC predicted frame $\mathbf{I}_{t+1}$ as input to our model to predict $\mathbf{I}_{t+2}$.

2.2 Network Architecture

We realize $\mathcal{G}$ using a fully convolutional network. Our model takes in a sequence of past frames $\mathbf{I}_{1:t}$ and past optical flows $\mathbf{F}_{2:t}$ and outputs pixel-wise separable kernels $\{\mathrm{K}_u, \mathrm{K}_v\}$ and a motion vector (u, v). We use 3D convolutions to convolve across width, height, and time. We concatenate RGB channels from our input images to the two optical flow channels to create 5 channels per frame. The topology of our architecture gets inspiration from various V-net type typologies [7,22,29], with an encoder and a decoder. Each layer of the encoder applies 3D convolutions followed by a Leaky Rectified Unit (LeakyRELU) [8] and a convolution with a stride $(1, 2, 2)$ to downsample features to capture long-range spatial dependencies. Following [7], we use $3 \times 3 \times 3$ convolution kernels, except for the first and second layers where we use $3 \times 7 \times 7$ and $3 \times 5 \times 5$ for capturing large displacements. Each decoder sub-part applies deconvolutions [16] followed by LeakyRELU, and a convolution after corresponding features from the contracting part have been concatenated. The decoding part also has several heads, one head for (u, v) and one each for K_u and K_v. The last two decoding layers of K_u and K_v use upsampling with a trilinear mode, instead of normal deconvolution, to minimize the checkerboard effect [25]. Finally, we apply repeated convolutions in each decoding head to reduce the time dimension to 1 (Fig. 3).

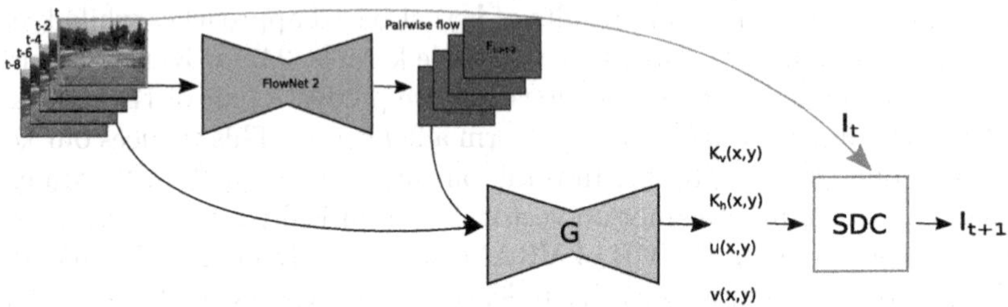

Fig. 3. Our model $\mathcal{G}$ takes in a frame sequence and pairwise flow estimates as input, and returns parameters for the SDC module to transform $\mathbf{I}_t$ to $\mathbf{I}_{t+1}$.

2.3 Optical Flow

We calculate the inter-frame optical flow we input to our model $\mathcal{G}$ using FlowNet2 [9], a state-of-the-art optical flow model. This allows us to extrapolate motion conditioned on past flow information. We calculate backwards optical flows because we model our transformation learning problem with backwards resampling, i.e. predict a sampling location in $\mathbf{I}_t$ for each location in $\mathbf{I}_{t+1}$.

It is important to note that the motion vectors (u, v) predicted by our model $\mathcal{G}$ at each pixel are not equivalent to optical flow vectors $\mathbf{F}_{t+1}$, as pure backwards optical flow is undefined (or zero valued) for dis-occluded pixels (pixels not visible in the previous frame due to occlusion). A schematic explanation of the disocclusion problem is shown in Fig. 4, where a 2×2 square is moving horizontally to the right at a speed of 1 pixel per step. The ground-truth backward optical flow at $t = 1$ is shown in Fig. 4b. As shown in Fig. 4c, resampling the square at $t = 0$ using the perfect optical flow will duplicate the left border of the square because the optical flow is zero at the second column. To achieve a perfect synthesis via resampling at $t = 1$, as shown in Fig. 4e, adaptive sampling vectors must be used. Figure 4d shows an example of such sampling vectors, in which a -1 is used to fill-in dis-occluded region. A learned approach is necessary here as it not only allows the disocclusion sampling to adapt for various degrees of motion, but also allows for a learned solution for which background pixels from the previous frame would look best in the filled gap.

2.4 Loss Functions

Our primary loss function is the L1 loss over the predicted image: $\mathcal{L}_1 = \left\|\mathbf{I}_{t+1} - \mathbf{I}_{t+1}^g\right\|_1$, where $\mathbf{I}_i^g$ is a target and $\mathbf{I}_i$ is a predicted frame. We found the L1 loss to be better at capturing small changes compared to L2, and generally produces sharper images.

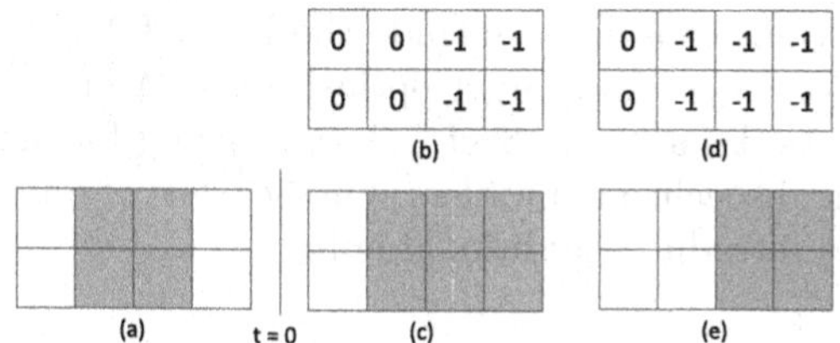

Fig. 4. Disocclusion illustration using backwards optical-flow. Values in top-row indicate vector magnitude in the horizontal axis. (a) frame at $t = 0$; (b) optical flow at $t = 1$; (c) output of resampling (a) using (b); (d) correct sampling vectors; and (e) resampling of (a) using (d). A direct use of optical-flow for frame prediction leads to undesirable foreground stretching in dis-occluded pixels.

We also incorporated the L1 norm on high-level VGG-16 feature representations [30]. Specifically, we used the perceptual and style loss [11], defined as:

$$\mathcal{L}_{perceptual} = \sum_{l=1}^{\mathrm{L}} \kappa_l \left\| \Psi_l(\mathbf{I}_{t+1}) - \Psi_l(\mathbf{I}^g_{t+1}) \right\|_1, \tag{6}$$

and

$$\mathcal{L}_{style} = \sum_{l=1}^{\mathrm{L}} \kappa_l \left\| \left(\Psi_l(\mathbf{I}_{t+1})\right)^{\intercal} \left(\Psi_l(\mathbf{I}_{t+1})\right) - \left(\Psi_l(\mathbf{I}^g_{t+1})\right)^{\intercal} \left(\Psi_l(\mathbf{I}^g_{t+1})\right) \right\|_1. \tag{7}$$

Here, $\Psi_l(\mathbf{I}_i)$ is the feature map from the lth selected layer of a pre-trained Imagenet VGG-16 for $\mathbf{I}_i$, L is the number of layers considered, and κ_l is a normalization factor $1/C_l H_l K_l$ (channel, height, width) for the lth selected layer. We use the perceptual and style loss terms in conjunction with the L1 over RGB as follows:

$$\mathcal{L}_{finetune} = w_l \mathcal{L}_1 + w_s \mathcal{L}_{style} + w_p \mathcal{L}_{perceptual}. \tag{8}$$

We found the finetune loss to be robust in eliminating the checkerboard artifacts and generates a much sharper prediction than L1 alone.

Finally, we introduce a loss to initialize the adaptive kernels, which we found to significantly speed up training. We use the L2 norm to initialize kernels K_u and K_v as a middle-one-hot vector each. That is, all elements in each kernel are set very close to zero, except for the middle element which is initialized close to one. When K_u and K_v elements are initialized as middle-hot vectors, the output of our displaced convolution described in Eq. (4) will be the same as our vector-based approach described in Eq. (2). The kernel loss is expressed as:

$$\mathcal{L}_{kernel} = \sum_{x=1}^{\mathrm{W}} \sum_{y=1}^{\mathrm{H}} \left(\left\| \mathrm{K}_u(x,y) - \mathbf{1}^{<\frac{\mathrm{N}}{2}>} \right\|_2^2 + \left\| \mathrm{K}_v(x,y) - \mathbf{1}^{<\frac{\mathrm{N}}{2}>} \right\|_2^2 \right), \tag{9}$$

where $\mathbf{1}^{<\frac{\mathrm{N}}{2}>}$ is a middle-one-hot vector, and W and H are the width and height of images.

Other loss functions considered include the L1 or L2 distance between predicted motion vectors (u, v) and target optical flows. We found this loss to lead to inferior results. As discussed in Sect. 2.3, optimizing for optical flow will not properly handle the disocclusion problem. Further, use of estimated optical flow as a training target introduces additional noise.

2.5 Training

We trained our SDC model using frames extracted from many short sequence videos. To allow our model to learn robust invariances, we selected frames in high-definition video game plays with realistic, diverse content, and a wide range of motion. We collected 428K 1080p frames from GTA-V and Battlefield-1 game plays. Each example consists of five $(t = 5)$ consecutive 256×256 frames randomly cropped from the full-HD sequence. We use a batch size of 128 over 8 V100 GPUs.

We optimize with Adam [12] using $\beta_1 = 0.9$, and $\beta_2 = 0.999$ with no weight decay. First, we optimize our model to learn (u, v) using $\mathcal{L}_1$ loss with a learning rate of $1e^{-4}$ for 400 epochs. Optimizing for (u, v) alone allows our network to capture large and coarse motions faster. Next, we fix all weights of the network except for the decoding heads of K_u and K_v and train them using our $\mathcal{L}_{kernel}$ loss defined in Eq. (9) to initialize kernels at each output pixel as middle-one-hot vectors. Then, we optimize all weights in our deep model using $\mathcal{L}_1$ loss and a learning rate of $1e^{-5}$ for 300 epochs to jointly fine-tune the (u, v) and (K_u, K_v) at each pixel. Since we optimize for both kernels and motion vectors in this step, our network learns to pick up small and subtle motions and corrects disocclusion related artifacts. Finally, we further fine-tune all weights in our model using $\mathcal{L}_{finetune}$ at a learning rate of $1e^{-5}$. The weights we use to combine losses are 0.2, 0.06, 36.0 for w_l, w_p, and w_s respectively. We used the activations from VGG-16 layers `relu1_2`, `relu2_2` and `relu3_3` for the perceptual and style loss terms. The last fine-tuning step of our training makes predictions sharper and produces visually appealing frames in our video prediction task. We initialized the FlowNet2 model with pre-trained weights[1] and fix them during training.

3 Experiments

We implemented all our Vector, Kernel, and SDC-based models using PyTorch [27]. To efficiently train our model, we wrote a CUDA custom layer for our SDC module. We set kernel size to 51×51 for the Kernel-based model as suggested in [24]. The kernel size for our SDC-based model is 11×11. Inference using our SDC-based model at 1080p takes 1.66 s, of which 1.03 s is spent on FlowNet2.

[1] https://github.com/lmb-freiburg/flownet2.

3.1 Datasets and Metrics

We considered two classes of video datasets that contain complex real world scenes: Caltech Pedestrian [5,6] (CaltechPed) car-mounted camera videos and 26 high definition videos collected from YouTube-8M [1].

We used metrics L1, Mean-Squared-Error (MSE/L2) [17], Peak-Signal-To-Noise (PSNR), and Structural-Similarity-Image-Metric (SSIM) [38] to evaluate quality of prediction. Higher values of SSIM and PSNR indicate better quality.

3.2 Comparison on Low-Quality Videos

Table 1 presents next frame prediction comparisions with BeyondMSE [21], PredNet [17], MCNet [34], and DualGAN [14] on CaltechPed test partition. We also compare with CopyLast, which is the trivial baseline that uses the most recent past frame as the prediction. For PredNet and DualGAN, we directly report results presented in [17] and [15], respectively. For BeyondMSE[2] and MCNet[3], we evaluated using released pre-trained models.

Table 1. Next frame prediction accuracy on Caltech Pedestrian [5, 6]. L2 results are in 1e−3.

Methods	L2	SSIM
BeyondMSE [21]	3.42	0.847
PredNet [17]	3.13	0.884
MCNet [34]	2.50	0.879
DualGAN [14]	2.41	0.899
CopyLast	5.84	0.811
Our Vector-based	2.47	0.902
Our Kernel-based	2.19	0.896
Our SDC-based	**1.62**	**0.918**

Our SDC-based model outperforms all other models, achieving an L2 score of 1.62×10^{-3} and SSIM of 0.918, compared to the state-of-the-art DualGAN model which has an L2 score of 2.41×10^{-3} and SSIM of 0.899. The MCNet which was trained on dataset that is equally as large as ours shows inferior results with L2 of 2.50×10^{-3} and SSIM of 0.879. CopyLast method has significantly worse L2 of 5.84×10^{-3} and SSIM of 0.811, making it a significantly less viable approach for next frame prediction. Our Vector-based approach has higher accuracy than our Kernel-based approach. Since the CaltechPed videos contain slightly larger motion, the Vector-based approach, which is advantageous in large motion sequences, is expected to perform better.

In Fig. 5, we present qualitative comparisons on CaltechPed. SDC-Net predicted frames are crisp, sharp and show minimal un-natural deformation of the highlighted car (framed in red). All predictions were able in picking up the right motion as shown with their good alignment with the ground-truth frame. However, both BeyondMSE and MCNet create generally blurrier predictions and unnatural deformations on the highlighted car.

3.3 Comparison on High-Definition Videos

Table 2 presents next frame prediction comparisons with BeyondMSE, MCNet and CopyLast on 26 full-HD YouTube vidoes. Our SDC-Net model outperforms

[2] https://github.com/coupriec/VideoPredictionICLR2016.

[3] https://github.com/rubenvillegas/iclr2017mcnet.

Fig. 5. Qualitative comparison for Caltech (set006-v001/506th frame). Left to right: Ground-truth, BeyondMSE, MCNet, and SDC-Net predicted frames. (Color figure online)

Table 2. Next frame prediction accuracy on YouTube-8M [1].

YouTube8M	L1	L2	PSNR	SSIM
BeyondMSE [21]	0.0271	0.00328	33.33	0.858
MCNet [34]	0.0216	0.00255	35.64	0.895
CopyLast	0.0260	0.00506	36.63	0.854
Our Vector	0.0177	0.00270	37.24	0.905
Our Kernel	0.0186	0.00303	**37.33**	0.904
Our SDC	**0.0174**	**0.00240**	37.15	**0.911**

all other models, achieving an L2 of 2.4×10^{-3} and SSIM of 0.911, compared to the state-of-the-art MCNet model which has an L2 of 2.55×10^{-3} and SSIM of 0.895.

In Fig. 6, SDCNet is shown to provide crisp and sharp frames, with motion mostly in good alignment with the ground-truth frame. Since our models do not hallucinate pixels, they produce visually good results by exploiting the image content of the last input frame. For instance, instead of duplicating the borders of foreground objects, our models displace to appropriate locations in the previous frame and synthesize pixels by convolving the learned kernel for that pixel with an image patch centered at the displaced location.

Since our approach takes FlowNet2 [9] predicted flows as part of its input, the transformation parameters predicted by our deep model are affected by inaccurate optical flows. For instance, optical flow for the ski in Fig. 6 (bottom right) is challenging, and so the ski movement was not predicted by our model as well as the movement of the skiing person.

In Fig. 7, we qualitatively show comparisons for MCNet, our Kernel-, Vector-, and SDC-based methods for a large camera motion. MCNet shows significantly blurry results and ineffectiveness in capturing large motions. MCNet also significantly alters the color distribution in the predicted frames. Our Kernel-based method has difficulty predicting large motion, but preserves the color

Fig. 6. Comparison of frame prediction methods. Shown from top to bottom are Ground-truth image, MCNet and SDC-Net results. SDCNet is shown to provide crisp and sharp frames, with motion mostly in good alignment with the ground-truth frame. MCNet results on the other hand appear blurry, with artifacts surrounding the persons (framed in red and orange). MCNet results also show checkerboard artifacts near the skis and on the snow background. (Color figure online)

distribution. However, the Kernel-based approach often moves components disjointly, leading to visually inferior results. Our Vector-based approach better captures large displacement, such as the motion present in this sequence. However, its predictions suffer from pixel noise. Our SDC-based method, which combines merits of both our Kernel- and Vector-based approaches, combines the ability of our Vector-based method to predict large motions, along with the visually pleasing results of our Kernel-based approach.

3.4 Comparison in Multi-step Prediction

Previous experiments showed SDCNet's performance in next frame prediction. In practice, models are used to predict multiple future frames. Here, we condition each approach on five original frames and predict five future frames on CaltechPed. Figure 8 shows that SDCNet predicted multiple frames are consistently favourable when compared to previous approaches, as quantified by L1,

Fig. 7. Comparison of frame prediction for large motion. Expected transformation is an upwards displacement with a slight zoom-in. While the Kernel-based, Vector-based, and SDC-based models were all trained with L1 and fine-tuned with style-loss to promote sharpness, note that the Vector-based result still loses coherence when predicting large displacement. On the other hand, the SDCNet is able to displace as much as the Vector-based model while maintaining sharpness. While the Kernel-based result is relatively sharp, it is conservative about predicting the upwards translation (note the relative distance of tiles to the bottom of the frame compared to the vector and SDC approaches). Further, there is a slight ghosting effect in the right-most tile of the Kernel-based result, which is not present in the SDC result.

L2, SSIM and PSNR over 120,725 unique Caltech Pedestrian frames. Figure 9 presents an example five-step prediction that show SDCNet predicted frames preserving color distribution, object shapes and their fine details.

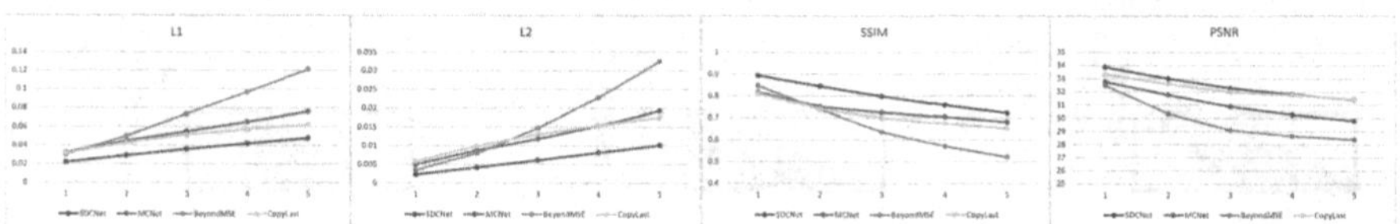

Fig. 8. Quantitative *five-step* prediction results for SDC-Net (blue), MCNet (orange), BeyondMSE (gray) and CopyLast (yellow). SDCNet shows consistently better results as quantified by L1, L2, PSNR and SSIM over 120,725 unique CaltechPed frames. (Color figure online)

Fig. 9. Qualitative *five-step* prediction results for MCNet (top row), SDCNet (middle row), and Ground Truth (bottom row). Both MCNet and SDCNet were conditioned on the same set of five frames (not seen in the figure).

3.5 Ablation Results

We compare our Vector-based with our SDC-based approach in Fig. 10. Our Vector-based approach struggles with disocclusions (orange box), as described in Sect. 2.3. In Fig. 10, the Vector-based model avoids completely stretching the glove borders, but still leaves some residual glove pixels behind. The Vector-based approach also may produce speckled noise patterns due to large motion (red box). Disocclusion and speckled noise are significantly reduced in the SDC-Net results shown in Fig. 10.

In Fig. 11, we present qualitative results for our SDC-based model trained using $\mathcal{L}_1$ loss alone vs $\mathcal{L}_1$ followed by our $\mathcal{L}_{finetune}$ given by Eq. (8). We note that using $\mathcal{L}_1$ loss alone leads to slightly blurry results, e.g. the glove (red box), and the fence (orange box) in Fig. 11. Figure 11 (center column) shows the same

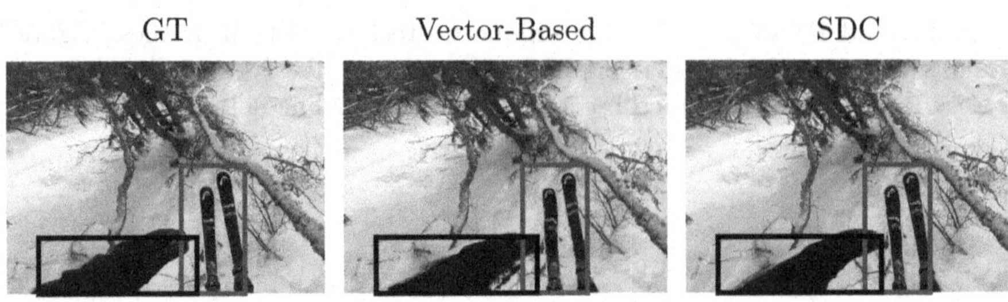

Fig. 10. Comparison of frame synthesis operations. Ground-truth frame (left), Vector-based sampling (middle), and SDC (right). Some foreground duplication (orange box) and inconsistent pixel synthesis (red box, may require zooming in) are present in the Vector-based approach but resolved in the SDC results. (Color figure online)

result after fine-tuning, with finer details preserved – demonstrating that the perceptual and style losses reduce blurriness. We also observed that the $\mathcal{L}_1$ loss helps capture large motions that are otherwise challenging to capture.

Figure 11 represents a challenging example due to fast motion. Since our model depends on optical flow, situations that are challenging for optical flow are also difficult for our model. The prediction errors can be seen with the relatively larger misalignment on the fence compared to the ground truth (orange box). Our approach also fails during scene transitions, where past frames are not relevant to future frames. Currently, we automatically detect scene transitions by analyzing optical flow statistics, and skip frame prediction until enough (five) valid frames to condition our models are available.

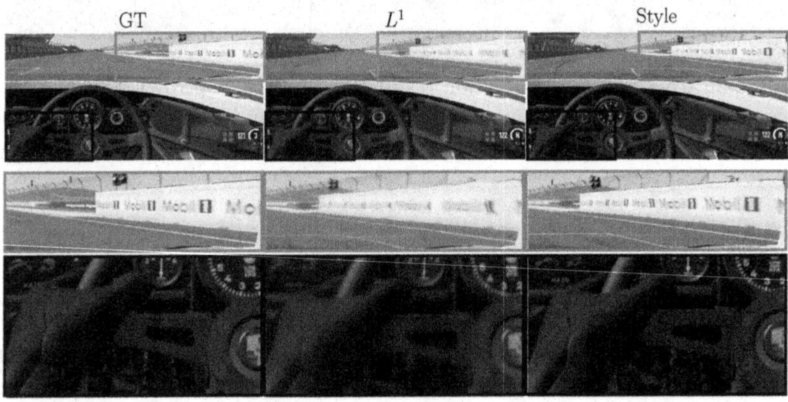

Fig. 11. Comparison of loss functions. Ground-truth (left), L1 loss (middle), and Fine-tuned result with style loss (right). Fine-tuning with style loss can improve the sharpness of results, as seen in the rendered text on the barriers and fence (orange crop) as well as the glove (red crop). (Color figure online)

4 Conclusions

We present a 3D CNN and a novel spatially-displaced convolution (SDC) module that achieves state-of-the-art video frame prediction. Our SDC module effectively handles large motion and allows our model to predict crisp future frames with motion closely matching that of ground-truth sequences. We trained our model on 428K high-resolution video frames collected from gameplay footage. To the best of our knowledge, this is the first attempt in transfer learning from synthetic to real life for video frame prediction. Our model's accuracy is dependent on the accuracy of the input estimated flows, thus leading to failures in fast motion sequences. Future work will include a study on the effect of multi-scale architectures for fast motion.

Acknowledgements. We would like to thank Jonah Alben, Paulius Micikevicius, Nikolai Yakovenko, Ming-Yu Liu, Xiaodong Yang, Atila Orhon, Haque Ishfaq and NVIDIA Applied Research staff for suggestions and discussions, and Robert Pottorff for capturing the game datasets used for training.

References

1. Abu-El-Haija, S., et al.: YouTube-8M: a large-scale video classification benchmark. arXiv preprint arXiv:1609.08675 (2016)
2. Babaeizadeh, M., Finn, C., Erhan, D., Campbell, R.H., Levine, S.: Stochastic variational video prediction. arXiv preprint arXiv:1710.11252 (2017)
3. Byeon, W., Wang, Q., Srivastava, R.K., Koumoutsakos, P.: Fully context-aware video prediction. arXiv preprint arXiv:1710.08518 (2017)
4. Denton, E., Fergus, R.: Stochastic video generation with a learned prior. arXiv preprint arXiv:1802.07687 (2018)
5. Dollár, P., Wojek, C., Schiele, B., Perona, P.: Pedestrian detection: a benchmark. In: CVPR, June 2009
6. Dollár, P., Wojek, C., Schiele, B., Perona, P.: Pedestrian detection: an evaluation of the state of the art. PAMI **34** (2012)
7. Dosovitskiy, A., et al.: FlowNet: learning optical flow with convolutional networks. In: Proceedings of the IEEE International Conference on Computer Vision, pp. 2758–2766 (2015)
8. He, K., Zhang, X., Ren, S., Sun, J.: Delving deep into rectifiers: surpassing human-level performance on ImageNet classification. In: Proceedings of the IEEE International Conference on Computer Vision, pp. 1026–1034 (2015)
9. Ilg, E., Mayer, N., Saikia, T., Keuper, M., Dosovitskiy, A., Brox, T.: FlowNet 2.0: evolution of optical flow estimation with deep networks. In: IEEE Conference on Computer Vision and Pattern Recognition (CVPR), vol. 2 (2017)
10. Jiang, H., Sun, D., Jampani, V., Yang, M.H., Learned-Miller, E., Kautz, J.: Super SloMo: high quality estimation of multiple intermediate frames for video interpolation. arXiv preprint arXiv:1712.00080 (2017)
11. Johnson, J., Alahi, A., Fei-Fei, L.: Perceptual losses for real-time style transfer and super-resolution. In: Leibe, B., Matas, J., Sebe, N., Welling, M. (eds.) ECCV 2016. LNCS, vol. 9906, pp. 694–711. Springer, Cham (2016). https://doi.org/10.1007/978-3-319-46475-6_43

12. Kingma, D.P., Ba, J.: Adam: a method for stochastic optimization. arXiv preprint arXiv:1412.6980 (2014)
13. Leibfried, F., Kushman, N., Hofmann, K.: A deep learning approach for joint video frame and reward prediction in Atari games. arXiv preprint arXiv:1611.07078 (2016)
14. Liang, X., Lee, L., Dai, W., Xing, E.P.: Dual motion gan for future-flow embedded video prediction. In: ICCV (2017)
15. Liu, Z., Yeh, R., Tang, X., Liu, Y., Agarwala, A.: Video frame synthesis using deep voxel flow. In: International Conference on Computer Vision (ICCV), vol. 2 (2017)
16. Long, J., Shelhamer, E., Darrell, T.: Fully convolutional networks for semantic segmentation. In: Proceedings of the IEEE Conference on Computer Vision and Pattern Recognition, pp. 3431–3440 (2015)
17. Lotter, W., Kreiman, G., Cox, D.: Deep predictive coding networks for video prediction and unsupervised learning. In: ICLR (2014)
18. Lu, C., Hirsch, M., Schölkopf, B.: Flexible spatio-temporal networks for video prediction. In: Proceedings of the IEEE Conference on Computer Vision and Pattern Recognition, pp. 6523–6531 (2017)
19. Luc, P., Neverova, N., Couprie, C., Verbeek, J., LeCun, Y.: Predicting deeper into the future of semantic segmentation. In: Proceedings of International Conference on Computer Vision, ICCV 2017, p. 10 (2017)
20. Mahjourian, R., Wicke, M., Angelova, A.: Geometry-based next frame prediction from monocular video. In: 2017 IEEE Intelligent Vehicles Symposium (IV), pp. 1700–1707. IEEE (2017)
21. Mathieu, M., Couprie, C., LeCun, Y.: Deep multi-scale video prediction beyond mean square error. In: International Conference on Learning Representations (2016)
22. Milletari, F., Navab, N., Ahmadi, S.A.: V-Net: fully convolutional neural networks for volumetric medical image segmentation. In: 2016 Fourth International Conference on 3D Vision (3DV), pp. 565–571. IEEE (2016)
23. Niklaus, S., Mai, L., Liu, F.: Video frame interpolation via adaptive convolution. In: IEEE Conference on Computer Vision and Pattern Recognition (2017)
24. Niklaus, S., Mai, L., Liu, F.: Video frame interpolation via adaptive separable convolution. In: IEEE International Conference on Computer Vision (2017)
25. Odena, A., Dumoulin, V., Olah, C.: Deconvolution and checkerboard artifacts. Distill (2016). https://doi.org/10.23915/distill.00003. http://distill.pub/2016/deconv-checkerboard
26. Oliu, M., Selva, J., Escalera, S.: Folded recurrent neural networks for future video prediction. arXiv preprint arXiv:1712.00311 (2017)
27. Paszke, A., et al.: Automatic differentiation in PyTorch (2017)
28. Ranzato, M., Szlam, A., Bruna, J., Mathieu, M., Collobert, R., Chopra, S.: Video (language) modeling: a baseline for generative models of natural videos. arXiv preprint arXiv:1412.6604 (2014)
29. Ronneberger, O., Fischer, P., Brox, T.: U-Net: convolutional networks for biomedical image segmentation. In: Navab, N., Hornegger, J., Wells, W.M., Frangi, A.F. (eds.) MICCAI 2015. LNCS, vol. 9351, pp. 234–241. Springer, Cham (2015). https://doi.org/10.1007/978-3-319-24574-4_28
30. Simonyan, K., Zisserman, A.: Very deep convolutional networks for large-scale image recognition. CoRR abs/1409.1556 (2014)
31. Srivastava, N., Mansimov, E., Salakhutdinov, R.: Unsupervised learning of video representations using LSTMs. In: ICML (2015)

32. Sun, D., Yang, X., Liu, M.Y., Kautz, J.: PWC-Net: CNNs for optical flow using pyramid, warping, and cost volume. arXiv preprint arXiv:1709.02371 (2017)
33. Van Amersfoort, J., Kannan, A., Ranzato, M., Szlam, A., Tran, D., Chintala, S.: Transformation-based models of video sequences. arXiv preprint arXiv:1701.08435 (2017)
34. Villegas, R., Yang, J., Hong, S., Lin, X., Lee, H.: Decomposing motion and content for natural video sequence prediction. In: ICLR (2017)
35. Vondrick, C., Pirsiavash, H., Torralba, A.: Generating videos with scene dynamics. In: Advances in Neural Information Processing Systems, pp. 613–621 (2016)
36. Vondrick, C., Torralba, A.: Generating the future with adversarial transformers. In: 2017 IEEE Conference on Computer Vision and Pattern Recognition (CVPR), pp. 2992–3000 (2017)
37. Vukotić, V., Pintea, S.-L., Raymond, C., Gravier, G., van Gemert, J.C.: One-step time-dependent future video frame prediction with a convolutional encoder-decoder neural network. In: Battiato, S., Gallo, G., Schettini, R., Stanco, F. (eds.) ICIAP 2017. LNCS, vol. 10484, pp. 140–151. Springer, Cham (2017). https://doi.org/10.1007/978-3-319-68560-1_13
38. Wang, Z., Bovik, A.C., Sheikh, H.R., Simoncelli, E.P.: Image quality assessment: from error visibility to structural similarity. IEEE Trans. Image Process. **13**(4), 600–612 (2004)

Person Search via a Mask-Guided Two-Stream CNN Model

Di Chen[1], Shanshan Zhang[1(✉)], Wanli Ouyang[2], Jian Yang[1(✉)], and Ying Tai[3]

[1] PCA Lab, Key Lab of Intelligent Perception and Systems for High-Dimensional Information of Ministry of Education, and Jiangsu Key Lab of Image and Video Understanding for Social Security, School of Computer Science and Engineering, Nanjing University of Science and Technology, Nanjing, China
{dichen,shanshan.zhang,csjyang}@njust.edu.cn

[2] SenseTime Computer Vision Research Group, The University of Sydney, Sydney, NSW, Australia
wanli.ouyang@sydney.edu.au

[3] Youtu Lab, Tencent, Shanghai, China
yingtai@tencent.com

Abstract. In this work, we tackle the problem of person search, which is a challenging task consisted of pedestrian detection and person re-identification (re-ID). Instead of sharing representations in a single joint model, we find that separating detector and re-ID feature extraction yields better performance. In order to extract more representative features for each identity, we propose a simple yet effective re-ID method, which models foreground person and original image patches individually, and obtains enriched representations from two separate CNN streams. On the standard person search benchmark datasets, we achieve mAP of 83.0% and 32.6% respectively for CUHK-SYSU and PRW, surpassing the state of the art by a large margin (more than 5 pp).

Keywords: Person search · Pedestrian detection
Person re-identification · Foreground

1 Introduction

The task of person search is first introduced by [1], which unifies the pedestrian detection and person re-identification in a coherent system. A typical person re-identification method aims to find matchings between the query probe and the cropped person image patches from the gallery, thus requiring perfect person detection results, which are hard to obtain in practice. In contrast, person search, which searches the queried person over the whole image instead of comparing with manually cropped person image locally, is closer to the real world applications. However, considering the tasks of detection and re-ID together brings domain-specific difficulties: large appearance variance across cameras, low resolution, occlusion, *etc.* In addition, sharing features between detection and re-ID

V. Ferrari et al. (Eds.): ECCV 2018, LNCS 11211, pp. 764–781, 2018.
https://doi.org/10.1007/978-3-030-01234-2_45

also accumulates errors from each of them, *e.g.* false alarms, misalignments and inexpressive person descriptors, which further jeopardizes the final person search performance.

Following [1], a few other works [2–5] have also been proposed for person search. Most of them [3–5] focus on an end-to-end solution based on Faster R-CNN [6]. Specifically, an axillary fully-connected (FC) layer is added upon the top convolutional layer of Faster R-CNN to extract discriminative features for re-identification. During training, they optimize a joint loss which is composed of the Faster R-CNN losses and a person categorization loss. However, we argue that it is not appropriate to share representations between the detection and re-ID tasks, as their goals contradict with each other. For the detection task, all people are treated as one class, and the goal is to distinguish them from the background, thus the representations focus on the commonness of different people, *e.g.* the body shape; while for the re-ID task, different people are deemed as different categories, and the goal is to maximize the differences in between, thus the representations focus on the characteristics of each identity, *e.g.* clothing, hairstyle, *etc.* In other words, the detection and re-ID tasks aim to model the inter-class and intra-class difference for people respectively. Therefore, it makes more sense to separate the two tasks rather than solving them jointly.

In the community of person re-ID, it is widely believed that discriminative information lies in foreground, while background is one of the detrimental factors and ought to be neglected or removed during feature extraction [7,8]. An intuitive idea would be to extract features on the foreground person patch only while ignoring the background area. However, simply abandoning all background information may harm the re-ID performance from two aspects. Firstly, the feature extraction procedure may gather errors from imperfect or noisy segmentation masks, *i.e.* identification information loss caused by fractional body shape. Secondly, background information sometimes acts as useful context, *e.g.* attendant suitcases, handbags or companions. Casting out all background area would neglect some informative cues for the re-ID problem. Therefore, we argue that it is more suitable to consider a compromised strategy of paying extra attention on the foreground person while also using the background as a complementary cue.

Inspired by the above discussions, we propose a new approach for person search. It consists of two stages: pedestrian detection and person re-identification. We solve them separately, without sharing any representations. Furthermore, we propose a Two-stream CNN to model foreground person and original image independently, which aims to extract more informative features for each identity and still consider the complementarity of the background. The whole framework is demonstrated in Fig. 1, and we will talk about more details in Sect. 3.

In summary, our contributions are three-folds:

- To the best of our knowledge, this paper is the first work showing that for the person search problem, better performance can be achieved by solving the pedestrian detection and person re-identification tasks separately rather than jointly.

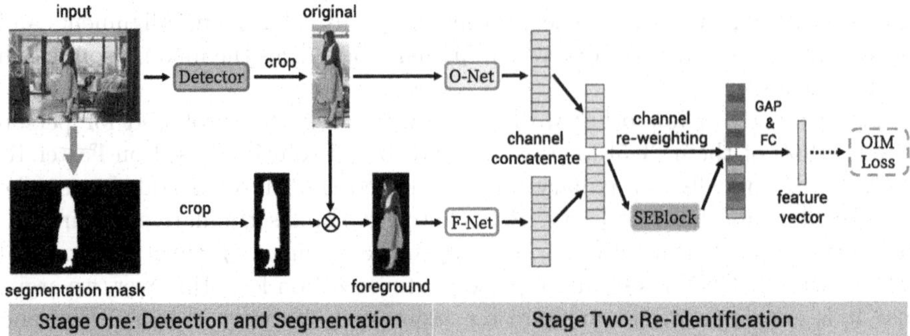

Fig. 1. The proposed framework for person search. It is composed of two stages: (1) Detection and segmentation. We use an adapted Faster R-CNN [9] as our pedestrian detector; the segmentation mask is generated by a MS COCO pre-trained FCIS model [10] without any fine-tuning; (2) Re-identification. The feature extractor is supervised by an Online Instance Matching (OIM) loss [3]. Please note that the detector and re-ID feature extractor are trained independently.

- We propose a Mask-Guided Two-Stream CNN Model (MGTS) for person re-id, which explicitly makes use of one stream from the foreground as the emphasized information and enriches the representation by incorporating another separate stream from the original image.
- Our proposed method achieves mAP of 83.0% and 32.6% on CUHK-SYSU [3] and PRW [2] benchmarks respectively, which improves over the state-of-the-arts by a large margin (more than 5 pp).

2 Related Work

We first review existing works on person search, which is a recently proposed topic. Since our person search method is composed of two stages: pedestrian detection and person re-identification, we also review some recent works in both fields.

Person Search. Person search has drawn much research interest since the publication of two large scale datasets: CUHK-SYSU [3] and PRW [2]. Zheng *et al.* [2] conduct a detailed survey on various *separated models* and propose to solve the person search problem in two separate models, one for detection and another for re-ID. Other works propose to solve the problem in an *end-to-end fashion* by employing the Faster R-CNN detector [6] for pedestrian detection and share the base network between detection and re-identification [3]. In [4], feature discriminative power is increased by introducing center loss [11] during training. Liu *et al.* [5] improve the localization policy of Faster R-CNN by recursively shrink the search area from the whole image till achieving precise location of the target person. In this paper, we first make a systematic comparison between *separated* *models* and *joint models*, and show that a separated solution improves both the detection and re-identification results.

Pedestrian Detection. Pedestrian detection is canonical object detection, especially when hand-crafted features are widely used. The classic HOG descriptor [12] is based on local image differences, and successfully represents the special head-shoulder shape of pedestrians. A deformable part model (DPM) [13] is proposed to handle deformations and still uses HOG as basic features. More recently, the integral channel feature (ICF) detectors [14–16] become popular, as they achieve remarkable improvements while running fast. In recent years, convnets are also employed in pedestrian detection and further push forward the progress [17–20]. Some works use the R-CNN architecture, which relies on ICF for proposal generation [17,18]. Aiming for an end-to-end procedure, Faster R-CNN [6] is adopted and it achieves top results by applying proper adaptations [9,21]. Therefore, we use the adapted Faster R-CNN detector in this paper.

Person Re-ID. Early person re-identification methods focus on manually designing discriminative features [22–26], using salient regions [27], and learning distance metrics [28–32]. For instance, Zhao *et al.* [25] propose to densely combine color histogram and SIFT features as the final multi-dimensional descriptor vector. Kostinger *et al.* [28] present KISS method to learn a distance metric from equivalence constraints. CNN-based models have attracted extensive attentions since the successful applications by two pioneer works [33,34]. Most of those CNN models can be categorized into two groups. The first group uses the siamese model with image pairs [33–38] or triplets [39,40] as inputs. The main idea of these works is to minimize the feature distance between the same person and maximize the distance between different people. The second group of works formulate the re-identification task as a classification problem [2,41,42]. The main drawback of classification models is that they require more training data. Xiao *et al.* [41] propose to combine multiple datasets for training and improve feature learning by domain guided dropout. Zheng *et al.* [2,42] point out that classification models are able to reach higher accuracy than siamese model, even without careful sample choosing.

Recently, attention mechanism [37,43–46] has been adopted to learn better features for person re-ID. For instance, HydraPlus-Net [43] aggregates multiple feature layers within the spatial attentive regions extracted from multiple layers in the network. PDC model [46] enriches the person representation with pose-normalized images and re-weights the features by channel-wise attention. In this paper, we also formulate person re-identification as a classification problem, and we propose to emphasize foreground information in the aggregated representation by adding an axillary stream with spatial attention (instance mask) and channel-wise re-weighting (SEBlock), which is similar to HydraPlus-Net and PDC model. However, our work differs from them in that the attention mechanism in our work is introduced with a different motivation, which is to consider the foreground-background relationship instead of local-global or part-whole relationship. In addition, the architecture of our model is more clear and concise, along with more practical training strategy without multi-staged fine-tuning.

3 Method

As shown in Fig. 1, our proposed person search method consists of two stages: pedestrian detection and re-identification. In this section, we first give an overview of our framework, and then describe more details for both stages individually.

3.1 Overview

A panoramic image is first fed into a pedestrian detector, which outputs several bounding boxes along with their confidence scores. We remove the bounding boxes whose confidence scores are lower than a given threshold. Only the remaining ones are used by the re-ID network.

A post-processing is implemented on the detected persons before they are sent to the re-ID stage. Specifically, we expand each RoI (Region of Interest) with a ratio of $\gamma(\gamma > 1)$ to include more context and crop out the person from the whole image. In order to separate the foreground person from background, we apply an off-the-shelf instance segmentation method FCIS [10] on the whole image, and then designate the person to the right mask via majority vote. After that, for each person, we obtain a pair of images, one containing only the foreground person, and the other containing both the foreground and the background. An illustration is shown in Fig. 2.

Next up, in the re-ID model, the pair images go through two different paths, namely *F-Net* and *O-Net*, for individual modeling. Feature maps from the two paths are then concatenated and re-weighted by an SEBlock [47]. After channel re-weighting, we pool the two dimensional feature maps into feature vectors using Global Average Pooling (GAP). Finally, the feature vectors are projected to an L2-normalized d-dimensional subspace as the final identity descriptor.

The pedestrian detector and re-ID model are trained independently. In order to avoid the mistakes resulting from the detector, we use the ground truth annotations instead of detections to train the re-ID model.

3.2 Pedestrian Detection

We use a Faster R-CNN [6] detector for pedestrian detection. The Faster R-CNN architecture is composed of a base network for feature extraction, a region proposal network (RPN) for proposal generation and a classification network for final predictions.

In this paper, we use VGG16 [48] as our base network. The top convolutional layer 'conv5_3' produces 512 channels of feature maps, where the image resolution is reduced by a factor of 16. According to [9], up-sampling the input image is a reasonable way for compensation.

RPN is built upon 'conv5_3' to predict pedestrian candidate boxes. We follow the anchor settings in [6] and set uniform scales ranging from the smallest and biggest persons we want to detect. The RPN produces a large number of proposals, so we apply a humble Non-Maximum Suppression (NMS) with an

Intersection over Union (IoU) threshold of 0.7 to remove repeating ones and also cut off low-scoring ones by a given threshold.

The remaining proposals are then sent to the classification network, where an RoI pooling layer ($512 \times 7 \times 7$) is used to generate the same length of features for each proposal. The final detection confidence and corresponding bounding box regression parameters are regressed by fully connected layers. After bounding box regression, another NMS with IoU threshold of 0.45 is applied and low-scoring detections are cut off.

The base net, RPN and classification network are jointly trained using Stochastic Gradient Descent (SGD).

3.3 Person Re-ID via a Mask-Guided Two-Stream CNN Model

After RoIs for each person are obtained (either from a detector or ground truth), we aim to extract discriminative features. First of all, we expand each RoI by a ratio of γ to include more context. Then, we propose a two-stream structure to extract features for foreground person and whole image individually. The features from both streams are concatenated as enriched representations for the RoIs and a re-weighting operation is applied to highlight more informative features while suppressing less useful ones.

Foreground Separation. The key step is to separate foreground and background for each RoI. We first apply an instance segmentation method FCIS [10] on the whole image to obtain segmentation masks for persons. After that, we associate each RoI with its corresponding mask by majority vote. Those pixels inside and outside the mask boundary are considered as foreground and background respectively. We describe the detailed separation procedure in Algorithm 1 and show an example in Fig. 2.

Two-Stream Modeling. After foreground separation, image pairs of each person are fed into the MGTS model. Specifically, foreground images go through F-Net and original images go through O-Net. Both F-Net and O-Net share the same architecture, but their network parameters are not shared. The corresponding feature maps, denoted as $\mathbf{F_F}, \mathbf{F_O} \in \mathbb{R}^{c \times h'' \times w''}$, are produced individually. Here c denotes the number of channels, h'', w'' are the height and width of $\mathbf{F_F}$ and $\mathbf{F_O}$. The feature maps are then concatenated along the channel axis as $\mathbf{F} \in \mathbb{R}^{2c \times h'' \times w''}$.

Feature Re-weighting. We further re-weight all the feature maps with an SEBlock [47], which models the interdependencies between channels of convolutional features. The architecture of an SEBlock is illustrated in Fig. 3. It is defined as a transformation from $\mathbf{F}$ to $\mathbf{F}'$:

$$
\begin{aligned}
\mathbf{F}' &= \mathbf{F} \cdot \mathbf{w}, \quad \text{where} \\
\mathbf{w} &= [w_1, w_2, \ldots, w_{2c}], \quad w_i \in [0, 1] \\
&= \sigma(\mathbf{W}_2 \delta(\mathbf{W}_1 f_{GAP}(\mathbf{F}))),
\end{aligned}
\tag{1}
$$

Algorithm 1. Foreground Separation

Input: RoI $\mathbf{b} \in \mathbb{N}^4$, expand ratio $\gamma \in \mathbb{R}$, image $\mathbf{I} \in \mathbb{R}^{h \times w \times 3}$, instance mask $\mathbf{M} \in \mathbb{N}^{h \times w}$
Output: Masked image for an instance $\mathbf{I}'_{\mathrm{M}} \in \mathbb{R}^{h' \times w' \times 3}$

1: $\mathbf{b}^\gamma \leftarrow$ expand $\mathbf{b}$ by γ
2: Crop out image patch $\mathbf{I}'$ from image $\mathbf{I}$ according to $\mathbf{b}^\gamma$
3: Crop out mask patch $\mathbf{M}'$ from mask $\mathbf{M}$ according to $\mathbf{b}^\gamma$
4: Find the dominant instance k inside $\mathbf{M}'$ by majority vote
5: Binarize $\mathbf{M}'$ by $\mathbf{M}'_b \leftarrow (\mathbf{M}' == k\ )$
6: Cast mask onto image by element-wise production: $\mathbf{I}'_{\mathrm{M}} \leftarrow (\mathbf{M}'_b \odot \mathbf{I}')$

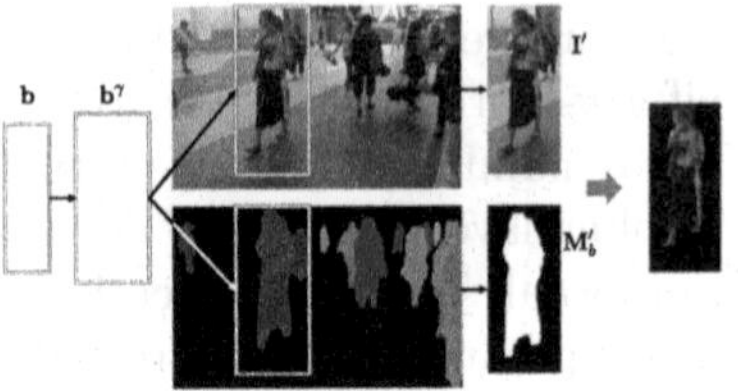

Fig. 2. Illustration of foreground separation

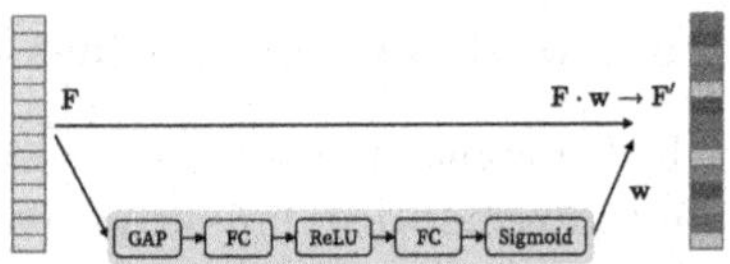

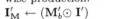

Fig. 3. Demonstration of an SEBlock [47]

σ and δ refer to the Sigmoid activation and the ReLU [49] function respectively. $\mathbf{W}_1$ and $\mathbf{W}_2$ are the weight matrix of two FC layers. f_{GAP} is the operation of GAP and $\cdot$ denotes channel-wise multiplication. SEBlock learns to selectively emphasis informative features and suppress less useful ones by re-weighting channel features using the weighting vector $\mathbf{w}$. In this way, foreground and background information are fully explored and re-calibrated, and hence help to optimize the final feature descriptor for person re-identification.

The re-weighted feature maps $\mathbf{F}'$ are then pooled to feature vectors $\mathbf{f} \in \mathbb{R}^{2c}$ by GAP, and further projected to a L2-normalized d-dimensional subspace by an FC layer:

$$\mathbf{x}^T = \frac{\mathbf{W}^T \mathbf{f}^T}{\|\mathbf{W}^T \mathbf{f}^T\|_2}, \mathbf{W} \in \mathbb{R}^{2c \times d}. \tag{2}$$

The whole MGTS model is trained with ground truth RoIs and supervised by an Online Instance Matching loss (OIM) [3]. The OIM objective is to maximize the expected log-likelihood:

$$\mathcal{L} = \mathbb{E}_{\mathbf{x}}[\log p_t], \quad \text{where} \tag{3}$$
$$p_t = \frac{\exp(\mathbf{v}_t^T \mathbf{x}/\tau)}{\sum_{j=1}^{L} \exp(\mathbf{v}_j^T \mathbf{x}/\tau) + \sum_{k=1}^{Q} \exp(\mathbf{u}_k^T \mathbf{x}/\tau)},$$

p_t denotes the probability of $\mathbf{x}$ belonging to class t. τ is a temperature factor similar to the one in Softmax function. $\mathbf{v}_t$ is the class central feature vector of the t-th class. It is stored in a lookup table with size L and incrementally updated

Fig. 4. Instance segmentation results on CUHK-SYSU (the first row) and PRW (the second row) generated by the open sourced version of FCIS [10]

during training with a momentum of η:

$$\mathbf{v}_t \leftarrow \eta \mathbf{v}_t + (1 - \eta)\mathbf{x}, \tag{4}$$

where $\mathbf{u}_k$ is a feature vector for an unlabeled person. A circular queue of size Q is used to store $\mathbf{u}_k$ vectors. It pops out old features and pushes in new features during training.

4 Experiments

In this section, we first introduce the datasets and evaluation protocols we use in our experiments, followed by some implementation details. After that, we show experimental results with comparison to state-of-the-art methods, followed by an ablation study to verify the design of our approach.

4.1 Datasets

CUHK-SYSU. CUHK-SYSU [3] is a large-scale person search database consisted of street/urban scene images captured by a hand-held camera or selected from movie snapshots. It contains 18, 184 images and 96, 143 pedestrian bounding boxes. There are a total of 8, 432 labeled identities, and the rest of the pedestrians are served as negative samples for identification. We adopt the standard train/test split provided by the dataset, where the training set includes 11, 206 images and 5, 532 identities, while the testing set contains 2, 900 probe persons and 6, 978 gallery images. Moreover, each probe person corresponds to several gallery subsets with different sizes, which are defined in the dataset.

PRW. The PRW dataset [2] is extracted from video frames captured with six cameras in a university campus. There are 11, 816 frames annotated with 34, 304 bounding boxes. Among all the pedestrians, 932 identities are tagged and the rest of them are marked as unknown persons similar to CUHK-SYSU. The training set includes 5, 134 images with 482 different persons. The testing set contains 2, 057 probe persons and 6, 112 gallery images. Different from CUHK-SYSU, the whole gallery set serves as the search space for each probe person.

4.2 Evaluation Protocol

Pedestrian Detection. Average Precision (AP) and recall are used to measure the performance of pedestrian detection. A detection bounding box is considered as a true positive if and only if its overlap ratio with any ground truth annotation is above 0.5.

Person Search. We adopt the mean Average Precision (mAP) and Cumulative Matching Characteristics (CMC top-K) as performance metrics for re-identification and person search. The mAP metric reflects the accuracy and matching rate of searching a probe person from gallery images. CMC top-K is widely used for person re-identification task, where a matching is counted if there is at least one of the top-K predicted bounding boxes overlapping with the ground truth with an IoU larger than or equal to a threshold. The threshold is set to 0.5 throughout the paper.

4.3 Implementation Details

We implement our system with Pytorch. The VGG-based pedestrian detector is initialized with an ImageNet-pretrained model. It is trained using SGD with a batch size of 1. Input images are resized to have at least 900 pixels on the short side and at most 1,500 pixels on the long side. The initial learning rate is 0.001, decayed by a factor of 0.1 at 60K and 80K iterations respectively and kept unchanged until the model converges at 100K iterations. The first two convolutional blocks ('conv1' and 'conv2') are frozen during training, while other layers are updated.

The RoI expand ratio γ is set to 1.3. Both F-Net and O-Net of our MGTS model are based on ResNet50 [50] and truncated at the last convolutional layer ('conv5_3'). The input image patches are re-scaled to an arbitrary size of 256×128 and the batch size is set to 128. The model is trained with an initial learning rate of 0.001, decayed to 0.0001 after 11 epochs and kept identical until early cutting after epoch 15. The temperature scalar τ, circular queue size Q and momentum η in OIM loss are set to 1/30, 5000 and 0.5 respectively. The feature dimension d is set to 128 through out the paper if not specified.

As of foreground extraction, we use the off-the-shelf instance segmentation method FCIS trained on COCO trainval35k [51] without any fine-tuning[1]. Sample results of instance masks from CUHK-SYSU and PRW are shown in Fig. 4, where we can see FCIS generalizes well to both datasets.

4.4 Comparison with State-of-the-Art Methods

In this subsection, we report our person search results on the CUHK-SYSU and PRW datasets, with a comparison to several state-of-the-art methods, including OIM [3], IAN [4], NPSM [5] and IDE [2]. Other than the above joint methods, we also compare with some methods which also solve the person search problem

[1] https://github.com/msracver/FCIS.

Table 1. Comparison of results on CUHK-SYSU with gallery size of 100

Method	mAP (%)	top-1 (%)
CNN + DSIFT + Euclidean	34.5	39.4
CNN + DSIFT + KISSME	47.8	53.6
CNN + BoW + Cosine	56.9	62.3
CNN + LOMO + XQDA	68.9	74.1
CNN + IDNet	68.6	74.8
OIM [3]	75.5	78.7
IAN [4]	76.3	80.1
NPSM [5]	77.9	81.2
Ours (CNN_v + IDNetOIM)	75.8	79.5
Ours (CNN_v + MGTS)	**83.0**	**83.7**

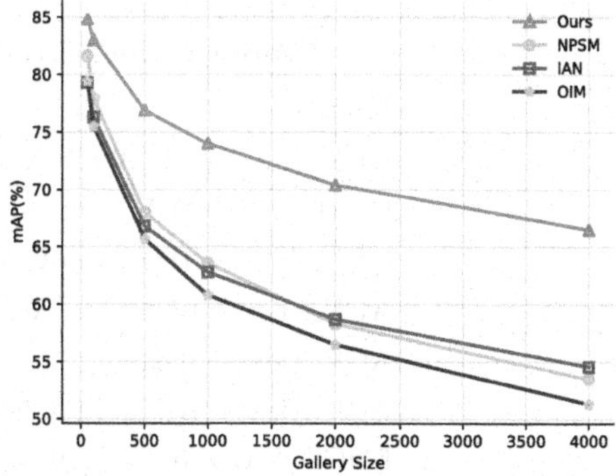

Fig. 5. Performance comparison on CUHK-SYSU with varying gallery sizes

in two steps of pedestrian detection and person re-identification, similar to our method. These methods use different pedestrian detectors (DPM [13], ACF [52], CCF [53], LDCF [54]), person descriptors (BoW [55], LOMO [26], DSIFT [25]) and distance metrics (KISSME [28], XQDA [26]).

Results on CUHK-SYSU. Table 1 shows the person search results on CUHK-SYSU with a gallery size of 100. We follow the notations defined in [3], where "CNN" denotes the Faster R-CNN detector based on ResNet50 and "IDNet" represents a re-identification net defined in [3]. Our VGG-based detector is marked as "CNN_v". IDNetOIM is a re-identification net trained with ground truth RoIs and supervised by an OIM loss. Compared with OIM, CNN_v + IDNetOIM slightly improves the performance by solving detection and re-identification tasks in two independent models. By further employing our proposed MGTS model, we achieve 83.0% mAP. Our final model outperforms the state-of-the-art method by more than 5 pp w.r.t. mAP, and 2.5 pp w.r.t. CMC top-1.

Moreover, we evaluate the proposed method (CNN_v + MGTS) under different gallery sizes along with other competitive methods. Figure 5 shows how the mAP changes with a varying gallery size of [50, 100, 500, 1000, 2000, 4000]. We can see that all methods suffer from a performance degeneration as the gallery size increases. However, our method outperforms others under different settings, which indicates the robustness of our method. Besides, we notice that the gap between our method and others become even larger as gallery size increases.

We also show some qualitative results of our method and the competitive baseline OIM in Fig. 7. As can be seen in the figure, our method performs better on hard cases where gallery persons wear similar clothes with the probe person, possibly with the help of context information in the expanded RoI, *e.g.* accompanied person (Fig. 7(a) and (d)), handrail (Fig. 7(d)), baby carriage (Fig. 7(e)) *etc.* It is also more robust on hard cases where gallery entries share both similar foreground and background to the probe person (Fig. 7(b) and (c)), where more subtle differences like hairstyle and gender shall be excavated from the emphasized foreground person. Figure 7(f) shows a failure case where both OIM and

Table 2. Comparison of results on PRW

Method	mAP (%)	top-1 (%)
DPM-Alex + LOMO + XQDA	13.0	34.1
DPM-Alex + IDE_{det}	20.3	47.4
DPM-Alex + IDE_{det} + CWS	20.5	48.3
ACF-Alex + LOMO + XQDA	10.3	30.6
ACF-Alex + IDE_{det}	17.5	43.6
ACF-Alex + IDE_{det} + CWS	17.8	45.2
LDCF + LOMO + XQDA	11.0	31.1
LDCF + IDE_{det}	18.3	44.6
LDCF + IDE_{det} + CWS	18.3	45.5
OIM [3]	21.3	49.9
IAN [4]	23.0	61.9
NPSM [5]	24.2	53.1
Ours (CNN_v + IDNetOIM)	28.2	66.7
Ours (CNN_v + MGTS)	**32.6**	**72.1**

MGTS suffer from bad illumination condition, which is rather challenging and needs more efforts in future works.

Results on PRW. In Table 2 we report the evaluation results on the PRW dataset. A number of combinations of detection methods and re-identification models are explored in [2]. Among them, DPM [13] + AlexNet [56]-based R-CNN with ID-discriminative Embedding (IDE_{det}) and Confidence Weighted Similarity (CWS) achieves the best performance. In contrast, joint methods including OIM, IAN and NPSM, all achieve better results. But it is unclear whether the improvement comes from a joint solution or the usage of deeper networks (ResNet50/ResNet101) and a better performed detector (Faster R-CNN).

For fair comparison, we also employ ResNet50 and Faster R-CNN in our framework, and achieve significant improvements compared to joint methods. Specifically, we outperform the state of the art by 8.4 pp and 10.2 pp w.r.t. mAP and top-1 accuracy. These results again demonstrate the effectiveness of our proposed method.

4.5 Ablation Study

From the experimental results in Sect. 4.4, we obtain significant improvement to our baseline method OIM [3] on both standard benchmarks. The major differences between our method and OIM are as follows: (1) We solve the pedestrian detection and person re-identification tasks separately rather than jointly, i.e. we do not share features between them. (2) In the re-identification net, we model the foreground and original image in two parallel streams so as to obtain enriched representations.

In order to understand the impact of the above two changes, we conduct analytical experiments on CUHK-SYSU at a gallery size of 100, and provide discussions in the following.

Integration vs. Separation. We investigate the impact of sharing features between detection and re-identification task on both performance.

Table 3. Integration/Separation study on CUHK-SYSU with gallery size of 100. (a): Detector performance comparison between a jointly trained model and a vanilla detector; OIM-ours is our re-implementation of OIM. (b): Re-ID performance comparison for an integrated person search model and a naïve re-ID model

(a)

Method	Joint	**AP(%)**	**Recall(%)**
OIM-ours	✓	69.5	75.6
CNN [3]	✗	78.0	75.7

(b)

Method	Joint	**mAP(%)**	**top-1(%)**
GT + OIM [3]	✓	77.9	80.5
GT + IDNetOIM	✗	78.5	81.7

In Table 3(a), we compare the detection performance of a jointly trained model and a vanilla detector. We can see that the jointly trained detector underperforms the vanilla one by 8.5 pp w.r.t. AP while reaching the same recall.

Similarly, we make a comparison on re-ID performance between a jointly trained model and a vanilla re-ID net in Table 3(b). The person search performance of a jointly trained OIM method is 0.6 pp and 1.2 pp lower in mAP and top-1 accuracy than a vanilla re-ID net (IDNetOIM).

From the above comparisons, we conclude that joint training harms both the detection and re-ID performance, thus it is a better solution to solve them separately.

Visual Component Study. In this part, we study the contributions of foreground and original image information to a re-ID system. To exclude the influence of detectors, all the following models are trained and tested using ground truth RoIs on CUHK-SYSU with a gallery size of 100. They are based on ResNet50 and supervised by an OIM loss.

Four variants to the input RoI patch and their combinations are considered: (1) Original RoI (**O**); (2) Masked foreground (**F**); (3) Masked background (**B**); (4) Expanded RoI (**E**) with a ratio of γ.

Comparison results are shown in Table 4, from which we make the following observations:

1. Background is an important cue for re-ID. The mAP drops by 2.8 pp when only the foreground is used, while discarding all background. More interestingly, using only background information yields an mAP of 34.2%, which can be further pushed to 38.7% if RoI is expanded.

Table 4. Visual component study. Legend: **O**: Original image; **F**: Masked image with foreground people only; **B**: Masked image with background only; **E**: Expand RoI with a ratio of γ

O	F	B	E	mAP (%)	top-1 (%)
✓				78.5	81.7
	✓			75.3	78.7
		✓		34.2	35.9
✓			✓	77.7	81.1
		✓	✓	38.7	40.0
✓	✓		✓	89.1	90.0

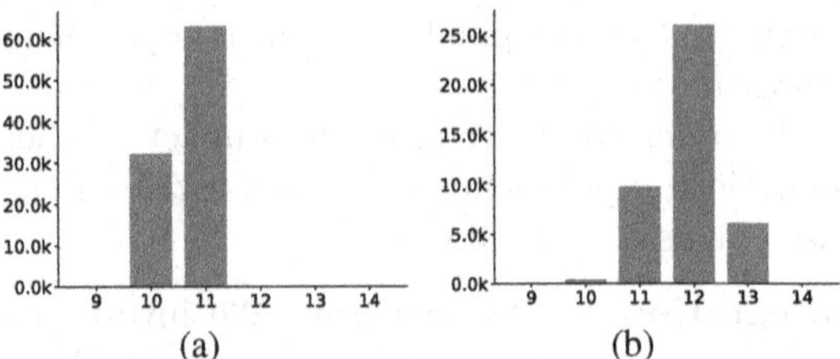

Fig. 6. SEBlock weights statistics for CUHK-SYSU (a) and PRW (b). x-axis denotes $N^{20}(F)$: the number of foreground-related weights among the top 20 largest ones. y-axis denotes the number of training instances

2. Modeling foreground and original image in two streams improves the results significantly. The two-stream model **O+F+E** reaches 89.1% mAP, surpassing the one-stream model **O+E** by 11.4 pp.

4.6 Model Inspection

To further understand the respective impact of the two streams, we provide an analysis on the SEBlock weights of foreground vs. original image representations. The analysis is implemented based on the trained models in Sect. 4.4, to which we feed all training samples in CUHK-SYSU (96, 143 proposals) and PRW (42, 871 proposals) respectively. For sample i, we compute three metrics: (1) average weight of F-Net channels, $Avg_i(F)$; (2) average weight of O-Net channels, $Avg_i(O)$; (3) number of channels that among top 20 of the whole network while come from F-Net, $N^{20}(F)$, the histograms of $N^{20}(F)$ for all training samples from two datasets are shown in Fig. 6.

Based on analyzing the above statistics, we have the following findings:

1. The inequation $Avg_i(F) > Avg_i(O)$ holds for all samples. It demonstrates that in general the foreground patch contributes more than the original patch to the final feature vector, as it involves more informative cues for each identity.
2. From Fig. 6, the majority of the top 20 channels come from the foreground stream for most samples. This observation indicates that the most informative cues are from the foreground patch.
3. Although the majority of the top 20 channels are represented by the foreground patch, we still observe that quite a few top channels are from the original patch. This is a good evidence showing the context information contained in the original image patch is helpful for the re-identification task.

Table 5. Re-ID performance of MGTS on CUHK-SYSU with different γ

Value of γ	1.0	1.1	1.2	1.3	1.4	1.5
mAP (%)	85.6	85.4	88.9	**89.1**	87.8	87.1
top-1 (%)	86.6	86.2	89.8	**90.0**	88.2	87.8

Table 6. Comparison results on CUHK-SYSU with gallery size of 100. The three models are all trained and tested with ground truth bounding boxes. Overall runtime includes pedestrian detection, mask generation (if used) and person feature extraction

Mask	mAP (%)	top-1 (%)	Overall runtime (s)
-	78.5	81.7	0.65
FCIS	**89.1**	**90.0**	1.27
Bounding box	85.1	86.0	0.69

Moreover, the impact of the amount of context information is inspected by changing the RoI expansion value γ. We conduct a set of experiments on CUHK-SYSU with a gallery size of 100 and list the results in Table 5, from which we can draw the intuitive conclusion that **(1)** the γ is relatively stable when $\gamma \in [1.2\ 1.5]$; and **(2)** a proper amount of context information is better than no context, while too much background could be harmful.

4.7 Runtime Analysis and Acceleration

We implement our runtime analysis on a Tesla K80 GPU. For testing a 1500×900 input image, our proposed approach takes around 1.3 s on average, including 626 ms for pedestrian detection, 579 ms for segmentation mask generation and another 64 ms for person re-identification.

We notice half of the computational time is used to generate the segmentation mask. In order to accelerate, we propose an alternative option to use the tight ground truth bounding boxes as 'weak' masks instead of the 'accurate' FCIS masks. The results are presented in Table 6, from which we can see that using 'accurate' FCIS masks yields better performance than using bounding box masks. However, using bounding boxes as weak masks still achieves promising results, which outperforms the single stream model without using any masks by a large margin ($\sim$7 pp mAP) at comparable time cost. Therefore, our proposed method can be accelerated by a factor of $\sim$2x with an acceptable performance drop, while still surpassing the state-of-the-art results.

Fig. 7. Qualitative search results from OIM [3] (upper row in each sub-figure) and our method (bottom row). The ranking and similarity score are shown under each image patch; "✓" denotes the correct matching. OIM would mistakenly assign high similarity to a wrong person wearing similar clothes to the probe, while our model successfully ranks it down. When faced with similar background, our method could emphasize the subtle difference on foreground people and return the correct ranking. (f) is a failure case with low visibility.

5 Conclusion

In this paper, we propose a novel deep learning based approach for person search. The task is accomplished in two steps: we first apply a Faster R-CNN detector for pedestrian detection on gallery images; and then make matchings between the probe image and output detections via a re-identification network. We obtain better results by training the detector and re-identification network separately, without sharing representations. We further enhance the re-identification accuracy by modeling the foreground and original image patches in two subnets to obtain enriched representations. Experimental results show that our proposed method significantly outperforms state-of-the-art methods on two standard benchmarks.

Inspired by the success of utilizing the segmented foreground patch for additional feature extraction, for future work, we will explore to optimize the segmentation masks and identification accuracy in a joint framework, so as to obtain finer masks.

Acknowledgments. This work was supported by the National Science Fund of China under Grant Nos. U1713208, 61472187 and 61702262, the 973 Program No. 2014CB349303, Program for Changjiang Scholars, and "the Fundamental Research Funds for the Central Universities" No. 30918011322.

References

1. Xu, Y., Ma, B., Huang, R., Lin, L.: Person search in a scene by jointly modeling people commonness and person uniqueness. In: ACM'MM (2014)
2. Zheng, L., Zhang, H., Sun, S., Chandraker, M., Yang, Y., Tian, Q.: Person re-identification in the wild. In: CVPR (2017)
3. Xiao, T., Li, S., Wang, B., Lin, L., Wang, X.: Joint detection and identification feature learning for person search. In: CVPR (2017)
4. Xiao, J., Xie, Y., Tillo, T., Huang, K., Wei, Y., Feng, J.: Ian: The individual aggregation network for person search. arXiv preprint arXiv:1705.05552 (2017)
5. Liu, H., Feng, J., Jie, Z., Jayashree, K., Zhao, B., Qi, M., Jiang, J., Yan, S.: Neural person search machines. In: ICCV (2017)
6. Ren, S., He, K., Girshick, R., Sun, J.: Faster R-CNN: towards real-time object detection with region proposal networks. TPAMI **39**(6), 1137–1149 (2017)
7. Le, C.V., Hong, Q.N., Quang, T.T., Trung, N.D.: Superpixel-based background removal for accuracy salience person re-identification. In: ICCE-Asia (2017)
8. Nguyen, T.B., Pham, V.P., Le, T.L., Le, C.V.: Background removal for improving saliency-based person re-identification. In: KSE (2016)
9. Zhang, S., Benenson, R., Schiele, B.: CityPersons: a diverse dataset for pedestrian detection. In: CVPR (2017)
10. Li, Y., Qi, H., Dai, J., Ji, X., Wei, Y.: Fully convolutional instance-aware semantic segmentation. In: CVPR (2017)
11. Wen, Y., Zhang, K., Li, Z., Qiao, Y.: A discriminative feature learning approach for deep face recognition. In: Leibe, B., Matas, J., Sebe, N., Welling, M. (eds.) ECCV 2016. LNCS, vol. 9911, pp. 499–515. Springer, Cham (2016). https://doi.org/10.1007/978-3-319-46478-7_31
12. Dalal, N., Triggs, B.: Histograms of oriented gradients for human detection. In: CVPR (2005)
13. Felzenszwalb, P.F., Girshick, R.B., McAllester, D., Ramanan, D.: Object detection with discriminatively trained part-based models. TPAMI **32**, 1627–1645 (2010)
14. Dollar, P., Tu, Z., Perona, P., Belongie, S.: Integral channel features. In: BMVC (2009)
15. Zhang, S., Bauckhage, C., Cremers, A.B.: Informed haar-like features improve pedestrian detection. In: CVPR (2014)
16. Zhang, S., Benenson, R., Schiele, B.: Filtered channel features for pedestrian detection. In: CVPR (2015)
17. Zhang, S., Benenson, R., Omran, M., Hosang, J., Schiele, B.: How far are we from solving pedestrian detection? In: CVPR (2016)
18. Zhang, S., Benenson, R., Omran, M., Hosang, J., Schiele, B.: Towards reaching human performance in pedestrian detection. TPAMI **40**(4), 973–986 (2018). https://ieeexplore.ieee.org/document/7917260/

19. Ouyang, W., Wang, X.: Joint deep learning for pedestrian detection. In: ICCV (2013)
20. Ouyang, W., Wang, X.: A discriminative deep model for pedestrian detection with occlusion handling. In: CVPR (2012)
21. Zhang, S., Yang, J., Schiele, B.: Occluded pedestrian detection through guided attention in CNNs. In: CVPR (2018)
22. Wang, X., Doretto, G., Sebastian, T., Rittscher, J., Tu, P.: Shape and appearance context modeling. In: ICCV (2007)
23. Gray, D., Tao, H.: Viewpoint invariant pedestrian recognition with an ensemble of localized features. In: Forsyth, D., Torr, P., Zisserman, A. (eds.) ECCV 2008. LNCS, vol. 5302, pp. 262–275. Springer, Heidelberg (2008). https://doi.org/10.1007/978-3-540-88682-2_21
24. Farenzena, M., Bazzani, L., Perina, A., Murino, V., Cristani, M.: Person re-identification by symmetry-driven accumulation of local features. In: CVPR (2010)
25. Zhao, R., Ouyang, W., Wang, X.: Unsupervised salience learning for person re-identification. In: CVPR (2013)
26. Liao, S., Hu, Y., Zhu, X., Li, S.Z.: Person re-identification by local maximal occurrence representation and metric learning. In: CVPR (2015)
27. Zhao, R., Oyang, W., Wang, X.: Person re-identification by saliency learning. IEEE Trans. Pattern Anal. Mach. Intell. **39**(2), 356–370 (2017)
28. Kostinger, M., Hirzer, M., Wohlhart, P., Roth, P.M., Bischof, H.: Large scale metric learning from equivalence constraints. In: CVPR (2012)
29. Li, X., Zheng, W.S., Wang, X., Xiang, T., Gong, S.: Multi-scale learning for low-resolution person re-identification. In: ICCV (2015)
30. Liao, S., Li, S.Z.: Efficient PSD constrained asymmetric metric learning for person re-identification. In: ICCV (2015)
31. Paisitkriangkrai, S., Shen, C., Van Den Hengel, A.: Learning to rank in person re-identification with metric ensembles. In: CVPR (2015)
32. Zhang, L., Xiang, T., Gong, S.: Learning a discriminative null space for person re-identification. In: CVPR (2016)
33. Yi, D., Lei, Z., Liao, S., Li, S.Z.: Deep metric learning for person re-identification. In: ICPR (2014)
34. Li, W., Zhao, R., Xiao, T., Wang, X.: DeepReID: Deep filter pairing neural network for person re-identification. In: CVPR (2014)
35. Ahmed, E., Jones, M., Marks, T.K.: An improved deep learning architecture for person re-identification. In: CVPR (2015)
36. Varior, R.R., Shuai, B., Lu, J., Xu, D., Wang, G.: A siamese long short-term memory architecture for human re-identification. In: Leibe, B., Matas, J., Sebe, N., Welling, M. (eds.) ECCV 2016. LNCS, vol. 9911, pp. 135–153. Springer, Cham (2016). https://doi.org/10.1007/978-3-319-46478-7_9
37. Liu, H., Feng, J., Qi, M., Jiang, J., Yan, S.: End-to-end comparative attention networks for person re-identification. IEEE Trans. Image Process. **26**(7), 3492–3506 (2017)
38. Xu, J., Zhao, R., Zhu, F., Wang, H., Ouyang, W.: Attention-aware compositional network for person re-identification. In: CVPR (2018)
39. Ding, S., Lin, L., Wang, G., Chao, H.: Deep feature learning with relative distance comparison for person re-identification. Pattern Recognit. **48**(10), 2993–3003 (2015)
40. Cheng, D., Gong, Y., Zhou, S., Wang, J., Zheng, N.: Person re-identification by multi-channel parts-based CNN with improved triplet loss function. In: CVPR (2016)

41. Xiao, T., Li, H., Ouyang, W., Wang, X.: Learning deep feature representations with domain guided dropout for person re-identification. In: CVPR (2016)
42. Zheng, L., Bie, Z., Sun, Y., Wang, J., Su, C., Wang, S., Tian, Q.: MARS: a video benchmark for large-scale person re-identification. In: Leibe, B., Matas, J., Sebe, N., Welling, M. (eds.) ECCV 2016. LNCS, vol. 9910, pp. 868–884. Springer, Cham (2016). https://doi.org/10.1007/978-3-319-46466-4_52
43. Liu, X., Zhao, H., Tian, M., Sheng, L., Shao, J., Yi, S., Yan, J., Wang, X.: HydraPlus-Net: attentive deep features for pedestrian analysis. In: ICCV (2017)
44. Li, W., Zhu, X., Gong, S.: Harmonious attention network for person re-identification. arXiv preprint arXiv:1802.08122 (2018)
45. Li, D., Chen, X., Zhang, Z., Huang, K.: Learning deep context-aware features over body and latent parts for person re-identification. In: CVPR (2017)
46. Su, C., Li, J., Zhang, S., Xing, J., Gao, W., Tian, Q.: Pose-driven deep convolutional model for person re-identification. In: ICCV (2017)
47. Hu, J., Shen, L., Sun, G.: Squeeze-and-excitation networks. arXiv preprint arXiv:1709.01507 (2017)
48. Simonyan, K., Zisserman, A.: Very deep convolutional networks for large-scale image recognition. In: ICLR (2015)
49. Nair, V., Hinton, G.E.: Rectified linear units improve restricted Boltzmann machines. In: ICML (2010)
50. He, K., Zhang, X., Ren, S., Sun, J.: Deep residual learning for image recognition. In: CVPR (2016)
51. Lin, T.-Y., et al.: Microsoft COCO: common objects in context. In: Fleet, D., Pajdla, T., Schiele, B., Tuytelaars, T. (eds.) ECCV 2014. LNCS, vol. 8693, pp. 740–755. Springer, Cham (2014). https://doi.org/10.1007/978-3-319-10602-1_48
52. Dollar, P., Appel, R., Belongie, S., Perona, P.: Fast feature pyramids for object detection. TPAMI **36**(8), 1532–1545 (2014)
53. Yang, B., Yan, J., Lei, Z., Li, S.Z.: Convolutional channel features. In: ICCV (2015)
54. Nam, W., Dollar, P., Han, J.H.: Local decorrelation for improved pedestrian detection. In: NIPS (2014)
55. Zheng, L., Shen, L., Tian, L., Wang, S., Wang, J., Tian, Q.: Scalable person re-identification: a benchmark. In: ICCV (2015)
56. Krizhevsky, A., Sutskever, I., Hinton, G.E.: Imagenet classification with deep convolutional neural networks. In: NIPS (2012)

Compound Memory Networks for Few-Shot Video Classification

Linchao Zhu[(✉)] and Yi Yang

CAI, University of Technology Sydney, Ultimo, NSW, Australia
Linchao.Zhu@student.uts.edu.au, Yi.Yang@uts.edu.au

Abstract. In this paper, we propose a new memory network structure for few-shot video classification by making the following contributions. First, we propose a compound memory network (CMN) structure under the key-value memory network paradigm, in which each key memory involves multiple constituent keys. These constituent keys work collaboratively for training, which enables the CMN to obtain an optimal video representation in a larger space. Second, we introduce a multi-saliency embedding algorithm which encodes a variable-length video sequence into a fixed-size matrix representation by discovering multiple saliencies of interest. For example, given a video of car auction, some people are interested in the car, while others are interested in the auction activities. Third, we design an abstract memory on top of the constituent keys. The abstract memory and constituent keys form a layered structure, which makes the CMN more efficient and capable of being scaled, while also retaining the representation capability of the multiple keys. We compare CMN with several state-of-the-art baselines on a new few-shot video classification dataset and show the effectiveness of our approach.

Keywords: Few-shot video learning · Video classification
Memory-augmented neural networks · Compound memory networks

1 Introduction

Deep learning models have been successfully applied to many tasks, e.g., image classification [8,16,25,29], image detection [22], video classification [12,24] and machine translation [28,36]. Convolutional Neural Networks (ConvNets) and Recurrent Neural Networks (RNNs) have become built-in modules in various fields. However, large amounts of labeled training data are required to train a deep neural network. To adapt an existing model to recognize a new category which was unseen during training, it may be necessary to manually collect hundreds of new training samples. Such a procedure is rather tedious and labor intensive, especially when there are many new categories. There is an increasing need to learn a classification model from a few examples in a life-long manner, which is also known as the few-shot learning task [23,32].

In a few-shot recognition setting, the network needs to effectively learn classifiers for novel concepts from only a few examples. Unlike traditional models

V. Ferrari et al. (Eds.): ECCV 2018, LNCS 11211, pp. 782–797, 2018.
https://doi.org/10.1007/978-3-030-01234-2_46

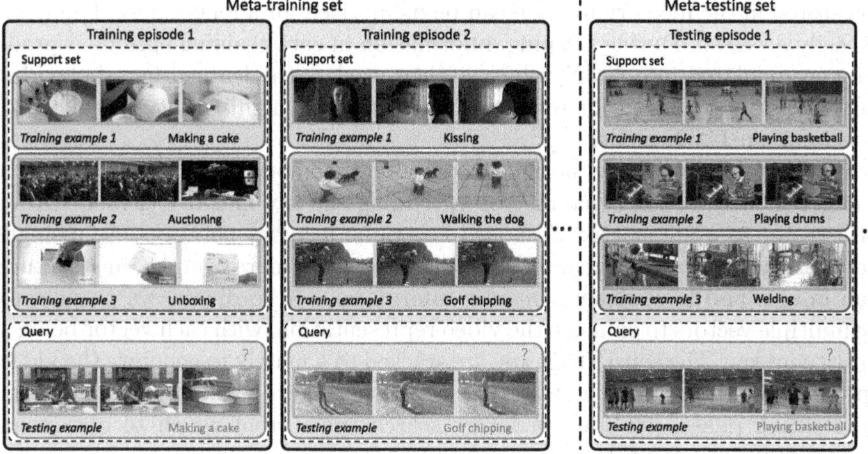

Fig. 1. The setting of the few-shot video classification. There are two non-overlapping datasets in this figure, i.e., meta-training and meta-testing. The meta-training set is for meta-learning and the meta-testing set is for evaluating the generalization performance on novel categories. The network is trained in an episodic way and each episode has a support set and a query example.

trained on many data samples, the model in a few-shot setting is trained to generalize across different episodes. In contrast to training new classifiers by fine-tuning, we propose a learning to learn approach under the meta learning paradigm [23]. We aim to enable a system to learn how to classify video data into a new category by exploiting a meta-training set. As shown in Fig. 1, the meta-training set consists of a number of episodes which mimic the few-shot learning task. In this example, there is only one positive exemplar per class in each episode, indicated by a red rectangle. There is no overlapping category between the training phase and testing phase. During the training phase, the system learns an optimal mechanism that best recognizes queries in all training episodes. When testing, the system directly adopts the learned optimal mechanism to classify each query in testing episodes.

In this paper, we focus on few-shot video representation learning. Videos have more complex structures than images, involving temporal information and more noise, e.g., camera motion, object scales, viewpoints. It is a more challenging task than few-shot image classification. Many videos usually contain hundreds of frames containing various scene dynamics. It could be difficult to understand the concept in a video when only few examples are provided.

We thus propose a compound memory network (CMN) structure for few-shot video classification. Our CMN structure is designed on top of the key-value memory networks [35] for the following two reasons. First, new information can be readily written to memory, which provides our model with better 'memorization' capability. In other words, MANNs are able to store and memorize an example long-term, even though the example has been seen only once. Second, information stored in the memory module can be memorized for a longer period and can be easily accessed. During training, information in each training episode is gradually accumulated into CMN, which is then used as the learned few-shot video classification mechanism for testing. It is worthwhile highlighting the following aspects of our CMN model.

First, we propose a new notion of compound memory networks with a much stronger representation capability by extending the key memory elements from a 1D vector to a 2D matrix. Standard key-value memory networks use a single vector as the key in each memory slot [19]. Videos are more complex in structure than images and have richer semantic information. Accordingly, we propose to use multiple vectors to enhance the video representation, with each vector being a constituent key. The constituent key are stacked to a matrix to generate the video representation in CMN. These stacked constituent keys work collaboratively in the training phase, providing a larger search space from which to obtain an optimal video representation.

Second, we introduce a series of hidden saliency descriptors as constituent keys in the memory slots of CMN. In many cases, user may be interested in different salient parts of a video. For example, given a video of a birthday party, some users may be more interested in the dancing scene, while others focus on the food and drinks. We propose a multi-saliency embedding algorithm which automatically detects multiple saliencies of interest in any given video. We extend the self-attention mechanism [18,31] by integrating a newly designed learnable variable to adaptively detect hidden salient genres within a video. The multi-saliency embedding algorithm learns a hidden saliency descriptor for each genre, which is then stacked as a video representation in CMN.

Third, we design a layered memory structure, which vastly improves efficiency while retaining the strong representation capability of CMN. The first layer stores the stacked constituent keys. We design an abstract memory on top of the first layer, which is equipped with reading and writing operations for retrieving and updating the constituent keys. The abstract memory compresses the stacked constituent keys into a vector and vastly improves training and testing efficiency. At the same time, the communication between the two layers ensures that abstract memory is able to retain the information from all constituent keys.

2 Related Work

Few-shot Classification. Early works from Miller et al. [20], Fei-Fei et al. [4] and Lake et al. [17] utilized generative models for one-shot learning. Koch [15] attempted to train a Siamese network in a supervised way. Santoro et al. [23] was the first work to successfully bridge memory-augmented neural works and one-shot learning. They took training examples in an episode as sequential inputs and trained the network to predict the label given previous examples. Vinyals et al. [32] used metric learning for few-shot recognition and utilized the attention kernel to measure the distance. Given a query, the network is trained to "point" to the nearest instance in the support set and the corresponding label is retrieved as the prediction. Ravi and Larochelle [21] trained a meta-learner based on Long Short-Term Memory (LSTM) [10] to generate updates for the classifier rather than using gradients. The meta-learner also learns a task-common weight initialization which captures shared knowledge across tasks. Finn et al. [5] used stochastic gradient descent as a meta-learner to update the parameters of the learner, which only learns the weight initialization. Snell et al. [26] applied a similar model to Vinyals [32], but they used Euclidean distance with their embedding function. Hariharan and Girshick [7] proposed the generation of images at testing time to improve few-shot recognition performance. Xu et al. [37] presented a key-value memory network to facilitate few-shot learning by extracting knowledge from external knowledge bases, e.g., noisy web images. However, their setting is not the meta-learning paradigm. These works focus on image few-shot recognition, whereas we aim to learn a few-shot video model, which requires modeling complex video data.

Video Classification. Video classification methods have evolved from using hand-crafted features, e.g., improved dense trajectories [33], to deep models, e.g., two-stream Convolutional Neural Networks (ConvNets) [24,34], 3D ConvNets [30], two-stream 3D ConvNets [3]. Recurrent Neural Networks have also been utilized to model video sequences [38,39]. Many efforts have been made to train a video classification model using large amounts of video data, however, it would be expensive to collect large datasets and retrain the classifier for all novel categories. The few-shot video classification task is more realistic in a real-world scenario, where the model will encounter novel categories that are never seen during training. The networks should be trained to adapt to new tasks.

Memory-Augmented Neural Networks. Memory-Augmented neural networks have gained increasing interest with the success of attention mechanism [2], Neural Turing Machine [6], and Memory Networks [35]. In RNNs, the states transferred between the steps can be interpreted as internal memory representations for the inputs. The state vector of the last step is usually used as the final representation for the whole input sequence. The fixed-size vector representation cannot encode long sequences in an effective way. Instead, the attention mechanism retains a sequence vectors as contexts for content-based addressing. The states in RNNs can change quickly over a few steps, while an external memory can retain information over the long term. Neural Turning Machine [6] is a computer-like network augmented with an external memory that can be addressed via content and location. The reading and writing operations are fully differentiable and weight updates through backpropagation are applied to every memory slot. Memory networks [35] and the improved end-to-end memory networks [27] have a large memory component for fact search and retrieval through content-based addressing. Key-value memory networks [19] decompose the memory into key and value parts, introducing a structural memory component to store question-answer pairs in a flexible way. Soft addressing is used in all these works, which is computationally expensive with growth of the memory size. Kaiser et al. [11] recently proposed a key-value memory module which performs hard updating to the memory, and a ranking loss is used to train the model to make accurate predictions. However, the memory stores only a fixed-size vector for an input, which is not suitable when the input is a long sequence, e.g., video data. We thus propose our compound memory network, in which each slot stores a series of vectors that are stacked as a matrix representation.

3 Few-Shot Video Classification Setup

In the few-shot video classification setting, we aim to train a network that can generalize to new episodes over novel classes. Each episode in a mini-batch mimics a few-shot classification task, which consists of a support set and a query set. The support set contains training videos and labels, while the query set is for evaluating the generalization performance. In an n-way, k-shot problem, the goal of each episode is to classify query videos into n classes with only a small number of support examples per class (k). Videos and labels in an episode are sampled from a meta set. The meta set has N classes ($N > n$), and each class has K examples ($K > k$). In our setup, there are three meta sets, i.e., meta-training set, meta-validation set and meta-testing set with $N_{training}$, $N_{validation}$ and $N_{testing}$ classes, respectively. The meta-training set is for meta-learning which minimizes the loss over training episodes. The meta-validation set is for hyper-parameter tuning. We report the accuracy on the meta-testing set. The three meta sets do not have overlapping categories. Following [23,32], we construct an episode by randomly choosing n classes from N categories in the meta set. For each class, k videos are selected from K examples. The label indices for n classes are randomly shuffled across different episodes, which prevents the model from memorizing the association between the input and the label.

In a standard video classification problem, there is a single training dataset D_{single} with fixed categories. Given an input/output pair ($\mathbf{x}$, y) sampled from D_{single}, the goal is to minimize the estimated loss over all training examples, i.e.,

$$\min_{\theta} \mathbb{E}_{(\mathbf{x},y)\sim D_{single}}[\mathcal{L}(\mathbf{x}, y)], \tag{1}$$

where θ represents the trainable parameters in a model.

In the few-shot video classification problem, training is conducted over a number of different episodes. An episode T_i sampled from meta-set $\mathcal{T}$ involves an episode length l, inputs $\mathbf{x}_t$, outputs y_t and a loss function $\mathcal{L}(x_t, y_t)$, where $t = \{1, 2, \dots, l\}$. During meta-training, the network is trained to predict the label of $\mathbf{x}_t$ at each step given previous input pairs $\{(\mathbf{x}_1, y_1), (\mathbf{x}_2, y_2), \dots, (\mathbf{x}_{t-1}, y_{t-1})\}$. The objective is to minimize the expected loss over mini-batches of episodes, i.e., $\min_\theta \mathbb{E}_{Ti\sim\mathcal{T}}[\sum_{t=1}^{l} \mathcal{L}_i(\mathbf{x}_t, y_t)]$.

4 Compound Memory Network

We first illustrate the multi-saliency embedding function that learns a fixed-size matrix representation for a variable-length video sequence. We then show

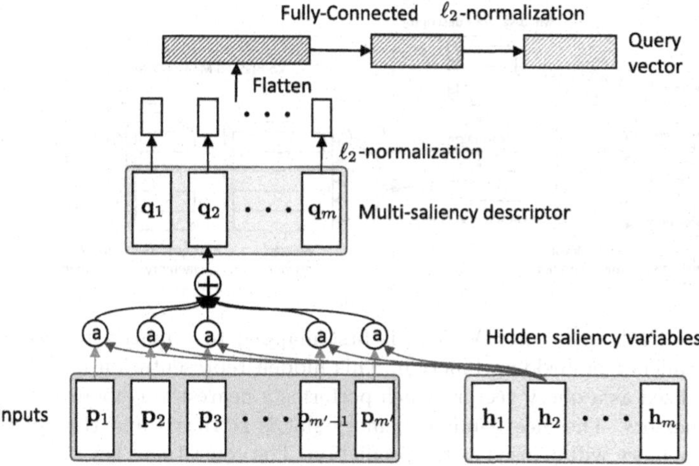

Fig. 2. Illustration of the input embedding model. The embedding function generates the multi-saliency descriptor $\mathbf{Q}$, which is flattened and normalized to a query vector.

the detailed structure of our Compound Memory Network, and introduce the novel components, i.e., the constituent keys, abstract memory, together with the accessing and updating operations.

4.1 Multi-saliency Embedding Function

Videos have variable lengths and should be encoded into a fixed-size matrix before being stored in memory. Given a query video $\mathbf{P} = \{\mathbf{p}_1, \mathbf{p}_2, \cdots, \mathbf{p}_{m'}\}$, where m' is the number of video frames and $\mathbf{p}_i$ is a frame-level representation extracted by a ConvNet, video $\mathbf{P}$ should be aggregated into a fixed-size matrix $\mathbf{Q}$. The representation $\mathbf{Q}$ consists of m stacked hidden descriptors $\{\mathbf{q}_1, \mathbf{q}_2, \cdots, \mathbf{q}_m\}$, and the size of each hidden descriptor is `hiden-size`. Note that the number of video frames m' varies across different videos, but m is a fixed number.

We design the multi-saliency embedding function (`MEF`) by introducing a hidden variable $\mathbf{H}$ with m components $\{\mathbf{h}_1, \mathbf{h}_2, \ldots, \mathbf{h}_m\}$. Each component $\mathbf{h}_j$ is used to detect one saliency in a video. For each input $\mathbf{p}_i$, a soft weight $\mathbf{a}_{ij}$ over $\mathbf{h}_j$ will be calculated which measures the relevance between the input and the component. The hidden descriptor $\mathbf{q}_j$ will be the weighted sum over the residual between $\mathbf{P}$ and $\mathbf{h}_j$. Thus, the `MEF` function can be formulated by

$$\mathbf{a}_i = \texttt{softmax}(\frac{\mathbf{p}_i \mathbf{H}^T}{\sqrt{d_{\texttt{hidden-size}}}}), \quad \mathbf{q}_j = \sum_{i=1}^{m} \mathbf{a}_{ij}(\mathbf{p}_i - \mathbf{h}_j), \tag{2}$$

where `softmax` is defined as, $\texttt{softmax}(\mathbf{e}) = \frac{\exp(e_i)}{\sum_i \exp(e_i)}$.

To calculate the relevance score between $\mathbf{p}_i$ and $\mathbf{h}_j$, we simply use dot-product but include a scaled factor $\frac{1}{\sqrt{d_{\texttt{hidden-size}}}}$ [31] followed by a `softmax`

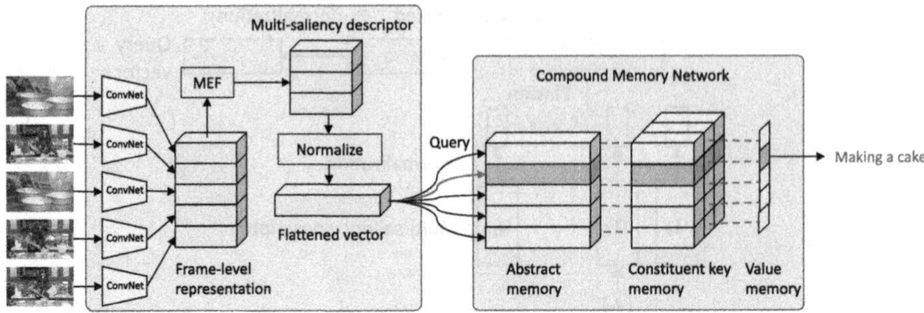

Fig. 3. Our CMN structure. A video is first mapped to a matrix representation via the multi-saliency embedding function. This hidden representation is then vectorized and normalized as a query vector, which performs a nearest neighbour search over the abstract memory. The most similar memory slot is retrieved and the label stored in the value memory will be used as the prediction. The constituent key memory contains the matrix representations of the inputs, while the abstract memory is constructed on top of the stacked constituent keys. (Color figure online)

function. The original sequence $\mathbf{P}$ is mapped to our multi-saliency descriptor $\mathbf{Q}$, *i.e.*, $\mathbf{Q} = \texttt{MEF}(\mathbf{P}, \mathbf{H})$. $\mathbf{Q}$ is then flattened and normalized to a vector, which will be discussed in Sect. 4.2 (Fig. 2). [18,31] introduced multi-hops attention to calculate multiple weighted sums over the inputs. In contrast, we introduce a hidden variable $\mathbf{H}$ to explicitly model the relation between the input and each hidden vector, which learns multiple descriptors for different salient parts in a video.

4.2 Compound Memory Structure

Our Compound Memory Network is a variant of the Key-Value Memory Networks, which has the key memory ($\mathcal{K}$) and the value memory ($\mathcal{V}$). Visual information is stored in the key part, while the label information is stored in the value part. Our key memory is a layered structure in which the first layer stores the constituent keys ($\mathcal{C}$) and the second layer is the abstract memory ($\mathcal{A}$). We also track the usage of each slot with an age memory ($\mathcal{U}$). Thus, the compound memory module ($\mathcal{M}$) can be represented by the following tuple,

$$\mathcal{M} = ((\mathcal{C}_{\texttt{ns}\times\texttt{nc}\times\texttt{cs}},\ \mathcal{A}_{\texttt{ns}\times\texttt{as}}), \mathcal{V}_{\texttt{ns}},\ \mathcal{U}_{\texttt{ns}}), \tag{3}$$

where $\texttt{ns}$ is the memory size, $\texttt{nc}$ is the number of constituent keys, $\texttt{cs}$ is the key size and $\texttt{as}$ is the abstract memory size (Fig. 3).

Two-Layer Key Memory. In the constituent key memory, we use multiple stacked constituent keys, which have stronger capability than a single vector, as the visual representation. In CMN, each constituent key is represented by a multi-saliency descriptor.

Note that $\mathbf{Q}$ is a matrix with shape (m, `hidden-size`) and there are `nc` keys in each slot of the constituent key memory. We let m be equal to `nc`, thus each descriptor in $\mathbf{Q}$ can be directly saved in the constituent key memory.

To enable fast nearest neighbour query, we introduce an abstract memory on top of the constituent key memory. The stacked keys are compressed to a vector and it is cached in the abstract memory. The abstract memory can be seen as a snapshot of the constituent key memory. The two sub-memory modules have the same number of slots, but they represent information at different levels.

We denote the stacked matrix representation in $\mathcal{C}$ as $\mathbf{C}$, and each constituent key is $\mathbf{c}_i$, $i \in \{1, \ldots, \mathtt{nc}\}$. We first normalize each constituent key with ℓ_2 normalization, *i.e.*, $\|\mathbf{c}_i\| = 1$. We then flatten the normalized $\mathbf{C}'$ to a vector followed by a Fully-Connected (`FC`) layer, which is then ℓ_2-normalized to a compressed representation. We denote the procedure as the `normalize` function,

$$\mathbf{c}_i{}' = \frac{\mathbf{c}_i}{\|\mathbf{c}_i\|}, \quad \mathbf{d}' = \mathtt{FC}(\mathtt{flatten}(\mathbf{C}')), \quad \mathbf{d} = \frac{\mathbf{d}'}{\|\mathbf{d}'\|}, \tag{4}$$

where a `FC` layer is simply a linear transformation layer, *i.e.*, $\mathtt{FC}(\mathbf{x}) = \mathbf{w}\mathbf{x}+b$. The compressed representation $\mathbf{d}$ is stored in the abstract memory, which will only be updated when the value in constituent key memory changes. The abstract memory keeps a one-to-one mapping to the constituent key memory, which will accelerate the query process.

Reading. Given a query vector $\mathbf{z} = \mathtt{normalize}(\mathbf{Q})$, nearest neighbour search is conducted over the abstract memory. We select the memory slot that is closest to the query $\mathbf{z}$ by, $\mathtt{NN}(\mathbf{z},\ \mathcal{A}) = \operatorname{argmax}_i\ \mathbf{z} \cdot \mathcal{A}[i]$. k-nearest slots (ordered by decreasing similarity) can be returned by,

$$(n_1, \ldots, n_k) = \mathtt{NN}_k(\mathbf{z},\ \mathcal{A}), \tag{5}$$

where n_1 is the memory slot that is most similar to the query. At the inference phase, $\mathcal{V}[n_1]$ will be our prediction for query $\mathbf{z}$.

Writing. The new information should be recorded in the memory to reflect the relation of new query $\mathbf{z}$ and the corresponding label y. The memory will not be updated via backpropagation which may catastrophically modify the information, but it will be refreshed with the following rule. Note that n_1 is the index of the nearest memory slot, and if the memory already returns the correct label, *i.e.*, $\mathcal{V}[n_1] = y$, we only update the n_1 memory slot. $\mathcal{A}[n_1]$, $\mathcal{U}[n_1]$ and $\mathcal{C}[n_1]$ will be updated, and leave $\mathcal{V}[n_1]$ unchanged.

$$\begin{aligned} \mathcal{C}[n_1][i] &\leftarrow \mathbf{q}_i + \mathcal{C}[n_1][i], \quad \text{for } i = 1, \ldots \mathtt{nc}, \\ \mathcal{A}[n_1] &\leftarrow \mathtt{normalize}(\mathcal{C}[n_1]), \quad \mathcal{U}[n_1] \leftarrow 0. \end{aligned} \tag{6}$$

The constituent key memory is updated by averaging the constituent keys $\mathcal{C}[n_1]$ and the multi-saliency descriptors $\mathbf{Q}$. The abstract memory $\mathcal{A}[n_1]$ is updated

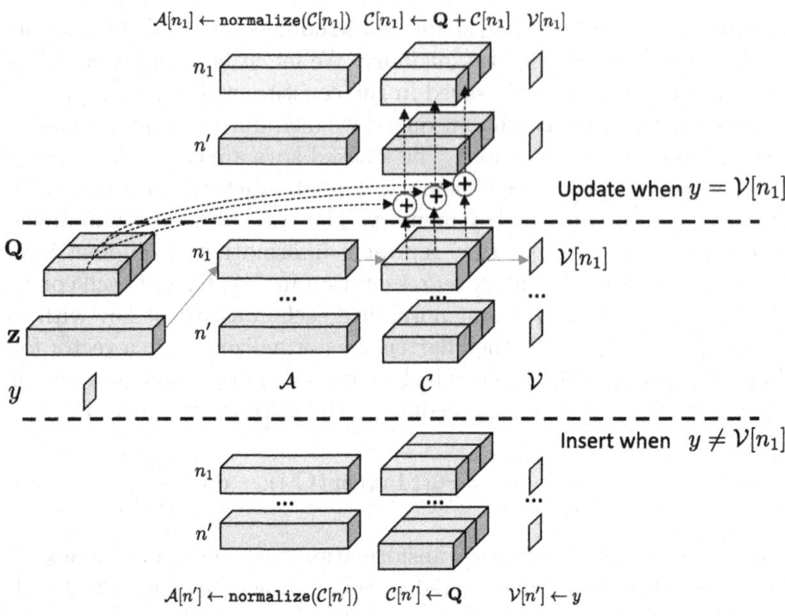

Fig. 4. Illustration of the update rule for CMN.

correspondingly. We also set $\mathcal{U}[n_1]$ to 0, which shows that slot n_1 has just been updated.

When $\mathcal{V}[n_1] \neq y$, the $(\mathbf{Q}, y)$ pair is stored in another memory slot to record the information. We choose the oldest memory slot n' that has not been updated for a long time,

$$n' = \arg\max_i (\mathcal{U}[i] + r_i), \tag{7}$$

where r_i is a random number to introduce randomness during slot selection. The memory will be updated by,

$$\begin{aligned} \mathcal{C}[n'][i] &\leftarrow \mathbf{q}_i, \quad \text{for } i = 1, \ldots, \texttt{nc}, \\ \mathcal{A}[n'] \leftarrow \texttt{normalize}(\mathcal{C}[n']), \quad \mathcal{V}[n'] &\leftarrow y, \quad \mathcal{U}[n'] \leftarrow 0. \end{aligned} \tag{8}$$

In this case, $\mathcal{V}[n']$ is also updated with the new label y. We illustrate the procedure in Fig. 4.

4.3 Training

Given a query $\mathbf{z}$ and a corresponding ground-truth label y, we retrieve top-k key-value pairs on memory indices $(n_1, \ldots, n_k)$ by Eq. 5. Let `i-pos` be the smallest index that $\mathcal{V}[n_{\texttt{i-pos}}] = y$ and `i-neg` be the smallest index that $\mathcal{V}[n_{\texttt{i-neg}}] \neq y$. We train the query vector $\mathbf{z}$ to be more similar to $\mathcal{A}[n_{\texttt{i-pos}}]$ than $\mathcal{A}[n_{\texttt{i-neg}}]$ with the following ranking loss,

$$\mathcal{L}(\mathbf{z}, y, \mathcal{A}) = \max(\alpha - \mathbf{z} \cdot \mathcal{A}[n_{\texttt{i-pos}}] + \mathbf{z} \cdot \mathcal{A}[n_{\texttt{i-neg}}], 0). \tag{9}$$

The similarity between the query and the positive key should be larger than the similarity between the query and the negative key by margin α. The loss will be 0 when the difference between the two similarities is beyond margin α.

The memory in each episode is cleared before operations are conducted. The clear operation simply initializes all memory variables to 0. During mini-batch training, information from multiple episodes are stored in the global memory. To avoid confliction in the label space, label ids across episodes should be different. The global label id can be calculated by,

$$\texttt{global-label-id} = \texttt{label-id} + \texttt{index} \times \texttt{k}, \tag{10}$$

where `k` is the number of classes, `label-id` is the shuffled label id in an episode and `index` is the index of the episode in the mini-batch. At the inference phase, the weights of the network are fixed except for the memory module, which will be updated with the support set examples.

5 Experiments

5.1 Datasets

There are no existing datasets for few-shot video classification, thus we collected the first dataset for few-shot video classification evaluation, which we will release for future research. We used videos from the recently released Kinetics dataset [13], which consists of 400 categories and 306,245 videos, covering videos from a wide range of actions and events, e.g., "dribbling basketball","robot dancing", "shaking hands","playing violin". We randomly selected 100 classes from the Kinetics dataset, each of which contains 100 examples. The 100 classes were split into 64, 12 and 24 non-overlapping classes for use as the meta-training set, meta-validation set and meta-testing set, respectively.

5.2 Implementation Details

In an n-way, k-shot problem, we randomly sampled n classes and each class has k examples, while an additional unlabeled example belonging to one of the n classes is used for testing. Thus each episode has $nk+1$ examples. We calculated the mean accuracy by randomly sampling 20,000 episodes in all experiments.

To obtain the frame-level feature representation, we forwarded each frame to a ResNet-50 [9] network that was pre-trained on ImageNet. We followed the basic image preprocessing procedure, whereby the image was first rescaled by resizing the short side to 256 and a 224×224 region was randomly cropped from the image. We cropped the central region during the inference phase.

We optimized our model with Adam [14] and fixed the learning rate to 1.0×10^{-4}. The margin α was set to 0.5 in all experiments. We tuned the hyperparameters on the meta-validation set, and stopped the training process when the accuracy on the meta-validation set began to decrease. The model was implemented with the TensorFlow framework [1].

Table 1. Results of 5-way few-shot video classification on the meta-testing set. The numbers are reported in percentages. Our CMN achieves state-of-the-art results.

Model	1-shot	2-shot	3-shot	4-shot	5-shot
RGB w/o mem	28.7	36.8	42.6	46.2	48.6
Flow w/o mem	24.4	27.3	29.8	32.0	33.1
LSTM(RGB) w/o mem	28.9	37.5	43.3	47.1	49.0
Nearest-finetune	48.2	55.5	59.1	61.0	62.6
Nearest-pretrain	51.1	60.4	64.8	67.1	68.9
MatchingNet [32]	53.3	64.3	69.2	71.8	74.6
MAML [5]	54.2	65.5	70.0	72.1	75.3
Plain CMN [11]	57.3	67.5	72.5	74.7	76.0
LSTM-emb	57.6	67.9	72.8	74.8	76.2
Ours	**60.5**	**70.0**	**75.6**	**77.3**	**78.9**

5.3 Evaluation

We compare our model with several baselines. We report 1-shot, 2-shot, 3-shot, 4-shot and 5-shot results on the 5-way classification task. In the first baseline, we utilize all the training data to pre-train the ResNet-50 network. At the testing stage, we fine-tune the network for each episode. The network is initialized with the pre-trained weights up to the last layer. The weights in the last layer is randomly initialized. We test the performance with different inputs. For "RGB w/o mem", we take RGB frames as inputs to train the network. For"Flow w/o mem", stack flows images are stacked as inputs to the network. To encode video with more sophisticated embedding function upon the frame-level features, we use an LSTM to aggregate temporal dynamics in a video. The LSTM takes the RGB features as inputs. It is fine-tuned for each episode. We denote this baseline as "LSTM (RGB) w/o mem". Another baseline is a nearest neighbour baseline ("Nearest-finetune"). We first finetune the ResNet-50 network to classify all classes in the meta-training set. We feed each frame as the input image and the video-level label is used as the label for each frame. Frames are first preprocessed with the procedure described above. We initialize the weights of the ResNet-50 network with the ImageNet pre-trained model. We train the network via stochastic gradient descent (SGD) with momentum 0.9. We set the initial learning rate to 0.01. We decrease the learning rate by 0.1 every 10 epochs. The batch size is 128. During inference, we feed the video frames to the finetuned ResNet-50 network and extract the activations from the last layer before final classification. We average the frame-level features and obtain a video-level representation of 2,048 dimension. We also apply ℓ_2 normalization before nearest neighbour search.

In the next baseline ("Nearest-pretrain"), we do not finetune the ResNet-50 network on the meta-training dataset, but directly utilize the pre-trained weights without modification. We embed the video with the same procedure in"Nearest-finetune", and then apply nearest neighbour search.

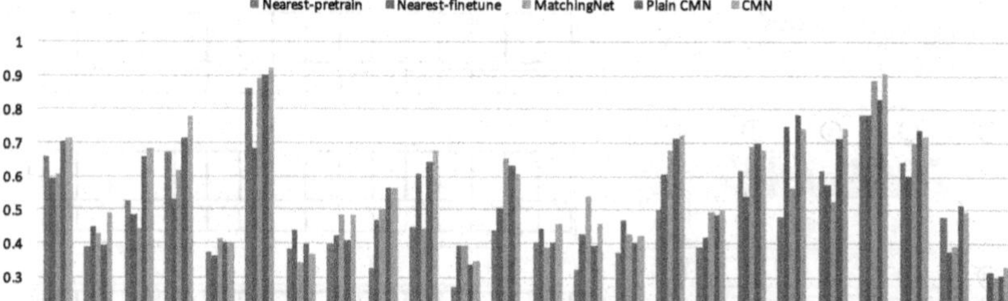

Fig. 5. Per class accuracy on the 5-way 1-shot setting. We show the accuracies of 24 classes on the meta-testing set.

We also show the result of the Matching Network [32] ("MatchingNet") on this dataset, which achieves state-of-the-art performance on the few-shot image classification task. We implement the Matching Network algorithms ourselves. We first feed the frames to a ResNet-50 network without fine-tuning. We average frame-level features to obtain a video-level feature. We then use the fully-conditional embedding (FCE) function proposed in [32] to embed the training examples. The FCE uses a bidirectional-LSTM and each training example is a function of all the other examples. To train MAML [5], we average the frame-level features and follow the default hyper-parameters in [5].

Another baseline is "Plain CMN" where we remove the constituent key memory from the model and use a video-level vector as video representation. We replace our embedding module with an LSTM function, while keeping the other settings the same. We denote this baseline as"LSTM-emb". We conduct this baseline to show the effectiveness of our compound memory network structure.

The results are shown in Table 1. We can see from Table 1 that our CMN improves the baselines in all shots. We observe that fine-tuning the ResNet-50 network on the meta-training set does not improve the few-shot video classification performance, but significantly harms performance. As there are no overlapping classes between the meta-training set and the meta-testing set, it is very likely that the model will overfit the meta-training set. Our CMN structure also outperforms the Matching Networks by more than 4% across all shots. Furthermore, our CMN structure outperforms the "Plain CMN", which demonstrates the strong representation capability of the constituent key memory. About 10% improvement is obtained between the 1-shot setting and the 2-shot setting, by only adding one example per class. The relative improvement decreases when more examples are added, e.g., the improvement from 3-shot to 4-shot is only

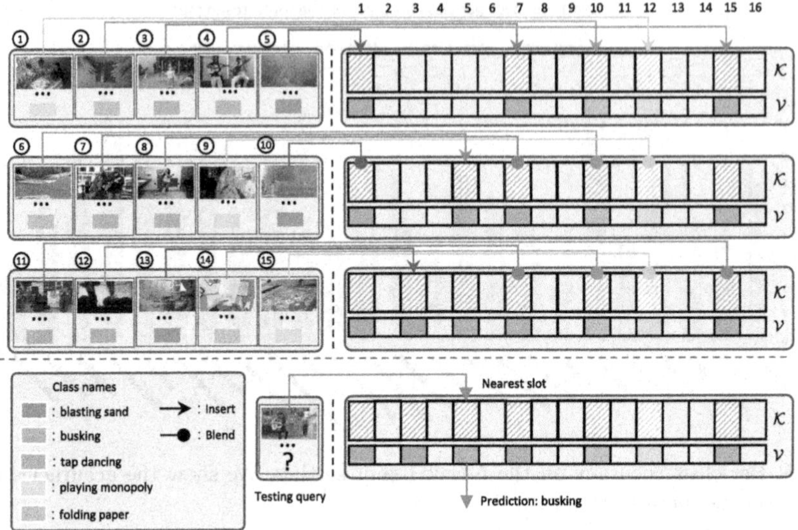

Fig. 6. We illustrate the inference procedure. There are 5 classes and the memory has 16 slots. Two different update rules will be used depending on the query results.

Table 2. Results of different memory sizes.

Model	1-shot	2-shot	3-shot	4-shot	5-shot
Mem-64	52.0	61.9	66.5	69.4	71.2
Mem-128	53.4	63.7	68.9	71.5	73.5
Mem-512	**55.1**	**65.3**	**70.1**	72.0	**74.2**
Mem-2048	55.0	65.0	69.7	**72.4**	74.1

1.7%. This shows that one-shot classification is still a difficult problem which can be further improved in the future.

The 1-shot accuracy for each class is shown in Fig. 5. We report the mean accuracy for class c over all episodes where the query label is c. The "hurling (sport)" category have the highest accuracy, while "hula hooping" and "stretching arms" achieve the worst performance with about 30% accuracy.

We illustrate the inference procedure in an episode in Fig. 6. In this 5-way 3-shot setting, the support set has 15 examples. Each example is sequentially fed to the network. This episode is divided into three groups, each of which has five examples with distinct labels. We arrange the episode in this way for better illustration. In row 1, all inputs are inserted into the memory. In row 2, the 7th example is inserted into a new slot in the memory, while other videos are blended into existing slots of the same category. In row 3, the 13th example is inserted. For the 11th example, the closest slot is the 15th slot and the two representations are averaged.

Table 3. Results of different numbers of multi-saliency descriptors.

Model	1-shot	2-shot	3-shot	4-shot	5-shot
Desc-1	53.7	63.5	68.3	70.9	73.3
Desc-5	**55.1**	**65.3**	**70.1**	**72.0**	**74.2**
Desc-10	53.2	62.9	68.2	70.0	72.3

Table 4. Results of different way few-shot video classification.

Model	1-shot	2-shot	3-shot	4-shot	5-shot
5-way	55.0	65.0	69.7	72.4	74.1
6-way	51.7	61.8	66.4	69.3	71.2
7-way	49.5	59.6	64.3	67.1	68.9
8-way	46.0	56.1	61.0	64.0	65.8

5.4 Ablation Study

We perform ablation experiments to explain our selections for the final model. The default setting is the 5-way few-shot classification. We show the performance of different memory sizes in Table 2, and the results of different numbers of constituent keys are shown in Table 3. We also report the results of other few-shot video classification tasks with different numbers of categories. We report the results on the meta-validation set, and choose only 10 frames during evaluation.

Memory Size. The results of different memory sizes are shown in Table 2. When the memory has a small number of slots, the performance is worse because some information has to be wiped out when new data arrives. Memory size of 512 achieves the best results. Increasing the memory size does not improve performance when the memory is large enough to record all the information.

The Number of Multi-saliency Descriptors. The result is shown in Table 3. It shows that multi-saliency descriptors with stronger representation capability obtain better performance than a single descriptor. The performance decreases when too many descriptors are used, because more parameters are introduced in the network.

N-way Classification. In all previous experiments, evaluations were conducted on the 5-way classification setting. n-way classification with larger n is a similar task to 5-way classification, but can be more difficult. As can be seen, the performance decreases when n increases (Table 4).

6 Conclusion

In this paper, we have proposed a compound memory network for few-shot video classification. This module stores matrix representations, which can be easily retrieved and updated in an efficient way. Our future work is to leverage multiple memory banks of different modality representations.

Acknowledgment. Our work is partially supported by the Data to Decisions CRC (D2D CRC) and the Cooperative Research Centres Programme. We gratefully acknowledge the support of NVIDIA Corporation with the donation of the TITAN X (Pascal) GPU. We thank AWS Cloud Credits for Research for supporting this research.

References

1. Abadi, M., et al.: TensorFlow: a system for large-scale machine learning. In: OSDI (2016)
2. Bahdanau, D., Cho, K., Bengio, Y.: Neural machine translation by jointly learning to align and translate. In: ICLR (2015)
3. Carreira, J., Zisserman, A.: Quo Vadis, action recognition? A new model and the kinetics dataset. In: CVPR (2017)
4. Fei-Fei, L., Fergus, R., Perona, P.: One-shot learning of object categories. TPAMI **28**(4), 594–611 (2006)
5. Finn, C., Abbeel, P., Levine, S.: Model-agnostic meta-learning for fast adaptation of deep networks. In: ICML (2017)
6. Graves, A., Wayne, G., Danihelka, I.: Neural Turing machines. arXiv preprint arXiv:1410.5401 (2014)
7. Hariharan, B., Girshick, R.: Low-shot visual recognition by shrinking and hallucinating features. In: ICCV (2017)
8. He, K., Zhang, X., Ren, S., Sun, J.: Deep residual learning for image recognition. In: CVPR (2016)
9. He, K., Zhang, X., Ren, S., Sun, J.: Identity mappings in deep residual networks. In: Leibe, B., Matas, J., Sebe, N., Welling, M. (eds.) ECCV 2016. LNCS, vol. 9908, pp. 630–645. Springer, Cham (2016). https://doi.org/10.1007/978-3-319-46493-0_38
10. Hochreiter, S., Schmidhuber, J.: Long short-term memory. Neural Comput. **9**(8), 1735–1780 (1997)
11. Kaiser, Ł., Nachum, O., Roy, A., Bengio, S.: Learning to remember rare events. In: ICLR (2017)
12. Karpathy, A., Toderici, G., Shetty, S., Leung, T., Sukthankar, R., Fei-Fei, L.: Large-scale video classification with convolutional neural networks. In: CVPR (2014)
13. Kay, W., et al.: The kinetics human action video dataset. arXiv preprint arXiv:1705.06950 (2017)
14. Kingma, D., Ba, J.: Adam: a method for stochastic optimization. In: ICLR (2015)
15. Koch, G.: Siamese neural networks for one-shot image recognition. Ph.D. thesis, University of Toronto (2015)
16. Krizhevsky, A., Sutskever, I., Hinton, G.E.: ImageNet classification with deep convolutional neural networks. In: NIPS (2012)
17. Lake, B., Salakhutdinov, R., Gross, J., Tenenbaum, J.: One shot learning of simple visual concepts. In: CogSci (2011)
18. Lin, Z., Feng, M., Santos, C.N.d., Yu, M., Xiang, B., Zhou, B., Bengio, Y.: A structured self-attentive sentence embedding. In: ICLR (2017)
19. Miller, A., Fisch, A., Dodge, J., Karimi, A.H., Bordes, A., Weston, J.: Key-value memory networks for directly reading documents. In: EMNLP (2016)
20. Miller, E.G., Matsakis, N.E., Viola, P.A.: Learning from one example through shared densities on transforms. In: CVPR (2000)
21. Ravi, S., Larochelle, H.: Optimization as a model for few-shot learning. In: ICLR (2017)
22. Ren, S., He, K., Girshick, R., Sun, J.: Faster R-CNN: towards real-time object detection with region proposal networks. In: NIPS (2015)
23. Santoro, A., Bartunov, S., Botvinick, M., Wierstra, D., Lillicrap, T.: Meta-learning with memory-augmented neural networks. In: ICML (2016)
24. Simonyan, K., Zisserman, A.: Two-stream convolutional networks for action recognition in videos. In: NIPS (2014)

25. Simonyan, K., Zisserman, A.: Very deep convolutional networks for large-scale image recognition. In: ICLR (2015)
26. Snell, J., Swersky, K., Zemel, R.S.: Prototypical networks for few-shot learning. In: NIPS (2017)
27. Sukhbaatar, S., Weston, J., Fergus, R., et al.: End-to-end memory networks. In: NIPS (2015)
28. Sutskever, I., Vinyals, O., Le, Q.V.: Sequence to sequence learning with neural networks. In: NIPS (2014)
29. Szegedy, C., Vanhoucke, V., Ioffe, S., Shlens, J., Wojna, Z.: Rethinking the inception architecture for computer vision. In: CVPR (2016)
30. Tran, D., Bourdev, L., Fergus, R., Torresani, L., Paluri, M.: Learning spatiotemporal features with 3D convolutional networks. In: ICCV (2015)
31. Vaswani, A., et al.: Attention is all you need. In: NIPS (2017)
32. Vinyals, O., Blundell, C., Lillicrap, T., Wierstra, D., et al.: Matching networks for one shot learning. In: NIPS (2016)
33. Wang, H., Schmid, C.: Action recognition with improved trajectories. In: ICCV (2013)
34. Wang, L., et al.: Temporal segment networks: towards good practices for deep action recognition. In: Leibe, B., Matas, J., Sebe, N., Welling, M. (eds.) ECCV 2016. LNCS, vol. 9912, pp. 20–36. Springer, Cham (2016). https://doi.org/10.1007/978-3-319-46484-8_2
35. Weston, J., Chopra, S., Bordes, A.: Memory networks. In: ICLR (2015)
36. Wu, Y., et al.: Google's neural machine translation system: bridging the gap between human and machine translation. arXiv preprint arXiv:1609.08144 (2016)
37. Xu, Z., Zhu, L., Yang, Y.: Few-shot object recognition from machine-labeled web images. In: CVPR (2017)
38. Ng, J.Y.-H., Hausknecht, M., Vijayanarasimhan, S., Vinyals, O., Monga, R., Toderici, G.: Beyond short snippets: Deep networks for video classification. In: CVPR (2015)
39. Zhu, L., Xu, Z., Yang, Y.: Bidirectional multirate reconstruction for temporal modeling in videos. In: CVPR (2017)

T^2Net: Synthetic-to-Realistic Translation for Solving Single-Image Depth Estimation Tasks

Chuanxia Zheng(✉), Tat-Jen Cham, and Jianfei Cai

School of Computer Science and Engineering,
Nanyang Technological University, Singapore, Singapore
chuanxia001@e.ntu.edu.sg, {astjcham,asjfcai}@ntu.edu.sg

Abstract. Current methods for single-image depth estimation use training datasets with real image-depth pairs or stereo pairs, which are not easy to acquire. We propose a framework, trained on synthetic image-depth pairs and unpaired real images, that comprises an image translation network for enhancing realism of input images, followed by a depth prediction network. A key idea is having the first network act as a wide-spectrum input translator, taking in either synthetic or real images, and ideally producing minimally modified realistic images. This is done via a reconstruction loss when the training input is real, and GAN loss when synthetic, removing the need for heuristic self-regularization. The second network is trained on a task loss for synthetic image-depth pairs, with extra GAN loss to unify real and synthetic feature distributions. Importantly, the framework can be trained end-to-end, leading to good results, even surpassing early deep-learning methods that use real paired data.

Keywords: Single-image depth estimation · Unpaired images
Synthetic data · Domain adaptation

1 Introduction

Single-image depth estimation is a challenging ill-posed problem for which good progress has been made in recent years, using supervised deep learning techniques [3,4,22,23] that learn the mapping between image features and depth maps from large training datasets comprising image-depth pairs. An obvious limitation, however, is the need for vast amounts of paired training data for each scene type. Building such extensive datasets for specific scene types is a high-effort, high-cost undertaking [9,32,34] due to the need for specialized depth-sensing equipment. The limitation is compounded by the difficulty that traditional supervised learning models face in generalizing to new datasets and environments [23].

To mitigate the cost of acquiring large paired datasets, a few unsupervised learning methods [7,10,20] have been proposed, focused on estimating accurate disparity maps from easier-to-obtain binocular stereo images. Nonetheless,

V. Ferrari et al. (Eds.): ECCV 2018, LNCS 11211, pp. 798–814, 2018.
https://doi.org/10.1007/978-3-030-01234-2_47

stereo imagery are still not as readily available as individual images, and systems trained on one dataset will find difficulty in generalizing well to other datasets (observed in [10]), unless camera parameters and rigs are identical in the datasets.

A recent trend that has emerged from the challenge of real data acquisition is the approach of training on synthetic data for use on real data [14,28,33], particularly for scenarios in which synthetic data can be easily generated. Inspired by these methods, we have researched a single-image depth estimation method that utilizes synthetic image-depth pairs instead of real paired data, but which also exploits the wide availability of unpaired real images. In short, our scenario is thus: we have a large set of real imagery, but these do not have corresponding ground-truth depth maps. We also have access to a large set of synthetic 3D scenes, from which we can render multiple synthetic images from different viewpoints and their corresponding depth maps. The main goal then is to learn a depth map estimator when presented with a real image. Consider two of the more obvious approaches:

1. Train an estimator using only synthetic image and depth maps, and hope that the estimator applies well to real imagery (**Naive** in Fig. 1).
2. Use a two-stage framework in which synthetic imagery is first translated into the real-image domain using a GAN, and then train the estimator as before (**Vanilla version** in Fig. 1).

The problem with (1) is that it is unlikely the estimator is oblivious to the differences between synthetic and real imagery. In (2), while a GAN may encourage synthetic images to map to the distribution of real images, it does not explicitly require the translated realistic image to have any physically-correct relationship to its corresponding depth map, meaning that the learned estimator will not apply well to actual real input. This may be somewhat mediated by introducing some regularization loss to try and keep the translated image "similar" in content to the original synthetic image (as in SimGAN [33]), but we cannot identify any principled regularization loss functions, only heuristic ones.

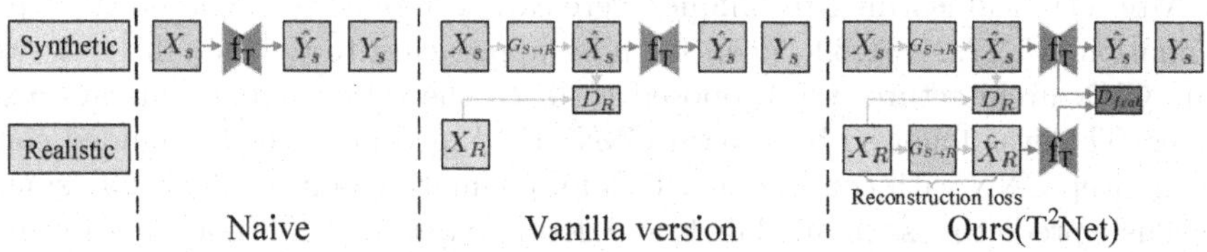

Fig. 1. Possible approaches to depth estimation using synthetic image-depth pairs (x_s, y_s) and unpaired real images x_r. See main text for details.

In this work, we introduce an interesting perspective on the approach of (2). We propose to have the entire inference pipeline be agnostic as to whether the input image is real or synthetic, *i.e.* it should work equally well regardless. To do so, we want the synthetic-to-realistic translation network to also behave as an identity transform when presented with real images, which is effected by including a reconstruction loss when training with real images.

The broad idea here is that, in a whole spectrum of synthetic images with differing levels of realism, *the network should modify a realistic image less than a more obviously synthetic image.* This is not true of original GANs, which may transform a realistic image into a different realistic image. In short, for the synthetic-to-real translation portion, real training images are challenged with a reconstruction loss, while synthetic images are challenged with a GAN-based adversarial loss [11]. This real-synthetic agnosticism is the principled formulation that allows us to dispense with an ad hoc regularization loss for synthetic imagery. When coupled with a task loss for the image-to-depth estimation portion, it leads to an end-to-end trainable pipeline that works well, and does not require the use of any real image-depth pairs nor stereo pairs (**Ours($\mathbf{T^2}$Net)** in Fig. 1).

In summary, the main contributions of this work are as follows:

1. A novel, end-to-end trainable architecture that jointly learns a synthetic-to-realistic translation network and a task network for single-image depth estimation, without real image-depth pairs or stereo pairs for training.
2. The concept of a wide-spectrum input translation network, trained by incorporating adversarial loss for synthetic training input and reconstruction loss for real training images, which is justified in a principled manner and leads to more robust translation.
3. The qualitative and quantitative results show that the proposed framework performs substantially better than approaches using only synthetic data, and can even outperform earlier deep learning techniques that were trained on real image-depth pairs or stereo pairs.

2 Related Work

For this paper, the two related sets of work are single image depth estimation methods, and unpaired image-to-image translation approaches.

After classical learning techniques were earlier applied to single-image depth estimation [15,17,21,31,32], deep learning approaches took hold. In [4] a two-scale CNN architecture was proposed to learn the depth map from raw pixel values. This was followed by several CNN-based methods, which included combining deep CNN with continuous CRFs for estimating depth values [23], simultaneously predicting semantic labels and depth maps [37], and treating the depth estimation as a classification task [1]. One common drawback of these methods is that they rely on large quantities of paired images and depths in various scenes for training. Unlike RGB images, real RGB-depth pairs are much scarcer.

To overcome the above-mentioned problems, some unsupervised and semi-supervised learning methods have recently been proposed that do not require image-depth pairs during training. In [7], the autoencoder network structure is translated to predict depths by minimizing the image reconstruction loss of image stereo pairs. More recently, this approach has been extended in [10,20], where left-right consistency was used to ensure both good quality image reconstruction and depth estimation. While the data availability for these cases was perhaps not as challenging since special capture devices were not needed, nevertheless they depend on the availability or collection of stereo pairs with highly accurate rigs for consistent camera baselines and relative poses. This dependency makes it particularly difficult to cross datasets (*i.e.* training on one dataset and testing on another), as evidenced by the results presented in [10]. To alleviate this problem, an unsupervised adaption method [36] was proposed to fine-tune a stereo network to a different dataset from which it was pre-trained on. This was achieved by running conventional stereo algorithms and confidence measures on the new dataset, but on much fewer images and at sparser locations.

Separately, several other works have explored image-to-image translation without using paired data. The earlier style-translation networks [8,16] would synthesize a new image by combining the "content" of one image with the "style" of another image. In [25], the weight-sharing strategy was introduced to learn a joint representation across domains. This framework was extended in [24] by integrating variational autoencoders and generative adversarial networks. Other concurrent works [18,38,40] utilized cycle consistency to encourage a more meaningful translation. However, these methods were focused on generating visually pleasing images, whereas for us image translation is an intermediate goal, with the primary objective being depth estimation, and thus the fidelity of 3D shape semantics in the translation has overriding importance.

In [33], a SimGAN was proposed to render realistic images from synthetic images for gaze estimation as well as human hand pose estimation. A self-regularization loss is used to force the generated target images to be similar to the original source images. However, we consider this loss to be somewhat ad hoc and runs counter to the translation effort; it may work well in small domain shifts, but is too limiting for our problem. As such, we use a more principled reconstruction loss as detailed in the next sections. More recently, a cycle-consistent adversarial domain adaption method was proposed [14] to generate target domain training images for digit classification and semantic segmentation. However this method is too complex for end-to-end training, which we consider to be an important requirement to achieve good results.

3 Method

Our main goal is to train an image-to-depth network f_T, such that when presented with a single RGB image, it predicts the corresponding depth map accurately.

In terms of data availability for training, we assume that we have access to a collection of individual real-world images x_r, *without* stereo pairing nor corresponding ground truth depth maps. Instead, we assume that we have access to a collection of synthetic 3D models, from which it is possible to render numerous synthetic images and corresponding depth maps, denoted in pairs of (x_s, y_s).

Instead of directly training f_T on the synthetic (x_s, y_s) data, we expect that the synthetic images are insufficiently similar to the real images, to require a prior image translation network $G_{S\to R}$ for domain adaptation to make the synthetic images more realistic. However, as discussed previously, existing image translation methods do not adequately preserve the geometric content for accurate depth prediction, or require heuristic regularization loss functions.

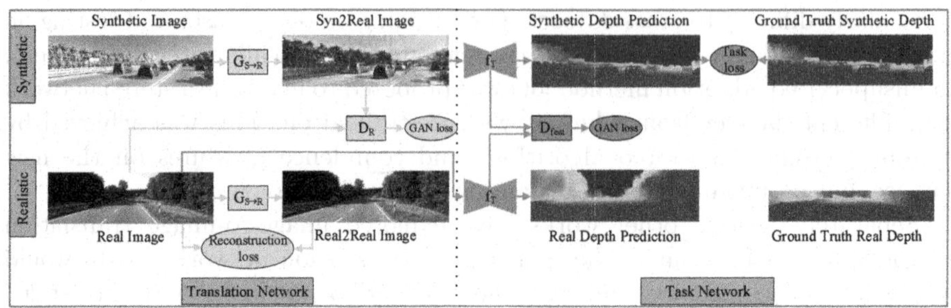

Fig. 2. The proposed T^2Net consists of the Translation part (left, orange) and Task prediction part (right, blue). See the main text for details. (Color figure online)

Our *key novel insight* is this: instead of training $G_{S\to R}$ to be a narrow-spectrum translation network that translates one specific domain to another, we will train it as a *wide-spectrum* translation network, to which we can feed a range of input domains, *i.e.* synthetic imagery as well as actual real images. The intention is to have $G_{S\to R}$ implicitly learn to apply the minimum change needed to make an image realistic, and consider this the most principled way to regularize a network for preserving shape semantics needed for depth prediction.

To achieve this, we propose the twin pipeline training framework shown in Fig. 2, which we call T^{2}Net to highlight the combination of an image ***t***ranslation network and a ***t***ask prediction network. The upper portion shows the training pipeline with synthetic (x_s, y_s) pairs, while the lower portion shows the training pipeline with real images x_r. Note that both pipelines share identical weights for the $G_{S\to R}$ network, and likewise for the f_T network. More specifically:

- For real images, we want $G_{S\to R}$ to behave as an autoencoder and apply minimal change to the images, and thus use a *reconstruction loss.*
- For synthetic data, we want $G_{S\to R}$ to translate synthetic images into the real-image domain, and use a *GAN loss* via discriminator D_R on the output. The translated images are next passed through f_T for depth prediction, and then compared to the synthetic ground truth depths y_s via a *task loss.*
- In addition, we also propose that the inner feature representations of f_T should share similar distributions for both real and translated images, which can be implemented through a feature-based GAN via D_{feat}.

Note that one key benefit of this framework is that it can and should be trained end-to-end, with the weights of $G_{S\to R}$ and f_T simultaneously optimized.

3.1 Adversarial Loss with Target-Domain Reconstruction

Intuitively, the gap between synthetic and realistic imagery comes from low-level differences such as color and texture (*e.g.* of trees, roads), rather than high-level geometric and semantic differences. To bridge this gap between the two domains, an ideal translator network, for use within an image-to-depth framework, needs to output images that are impossible to be distinguished from real images and yet retain the original scene geometry present in the synthetic input images. The distribution of real world images can be replicated using adversarial learning, where a generator $G_{S\to R}$ tries to transform a synthetic image x_s to be indistinguishable from real images of x_r, while a discriminator D_R aims to differentiate between the generated image $\hat{x}_s$ and real images x_r. Following the typical GAN approach [11], we model this minimax game using an *adversarial loss* given by

$$\mathcal{L}_{\text{GAN}}(G_{S\to R}, D_R) = \mathbb{E}_{x_r\sim X_R}[\log D_R(x_r)] + \mathbb{E}_{x_s\sim X_S}[\log(1 - D_R(G_{S\to R}(x_s)))] \tag{1}$$

where generator and discriminator parameters are updated alternately.

However, a vanilla GAN is insufficiently constrained to preserve scene geometry. To regularize this in a principled manner, we want generator $G_{S\to R}$ to behave as a *wide-spectrum* translator, able to take in both real and synthetic imagery, and in both cases produce real imagery. When the input is a real image, we would want the image to remain as much unchanged perceptually, and a *reconstruction loss*

$$\mathcal{L}_r(G_{S\to R}) = ||G_{S\to R}(x_r) - x_r||_1 \tag{2}$$

is applied when the input to $G_{S\to R}$ is a real image x_r. Note that while this may bear some resemblance to the use of reconstruction losses in CycleGAN [40] and α-GAN [30], ours is a unidirectional forward loss, and not a cyclical loss.

3.2 Task Loss

After a synthetic image x_s is translated, we obtain a generated realistic image $\hat{x}_s$, which can still be paired to the corresponding synthetic depth map y_s. This paired translated data $(\hat{x}_s, y_s)$ can be used to train the task network f_T. Following convention, we directly measure per-pixel difference between the predicted depth map and the synthetic (ground truth) depth map as a task loss:

$$\mathcal{L}_t(f_T) = ||f_T(\hat{x}_s) - y_s||_1 \tag{3}$$

We also regularize f_T for real training images. Since real ground truth depth maps are not available during training, a locally smooth loss is introduced to guide a more reasonable depth estimation, in keeping with [7,10,13,20]. As depth discontinuities often occur at object boundaries, we use a robust penalty with an edge-aware term to optimize the depths, similar to [10]:

$$\mathcal{L}_s(f_T) = |\partial_x f_T(x_r)|e^{-|\partial_x x_r|} + |\partial_y f_T(x_r)|e^{-|\partial_y x_r|} \tag{4}$$

where x_r is the real world image, and noting that f_T share identical weights in both real and synthetic input pipelines.

In addition, we also want the internal feature representations of real and translated-synthetic images in the encoder-decoder network of f_T to have similar distributions [6]. In theory, the decoder portion of f_T should generate similar prediction results from the two domains when their feature distributions are similar. Thus we further define a feature-level GAN loss as follows:

$$\mathcal{L}_{\mathrm{GAN}_f}(f_T, D_{\mathrm{feat}}) = \mathbb{E}_{f_{\hat{x}_s} \sim f_{\hat{X}_s}}[\log D_{\mathrm{feat}}(f_{\hat{x}_s})] + \mathbb{E}_{f_{x_r} \sim f_{X_r}}[\log(1 - D_{\mathrm{feat}}(f_{x_r}))] \quad (5)$$

where $f_{\hat{x}_s}$ and f_{x_r} are features obtained by the encoder portion of f_T for translated-synthetic images and real images respectively. As noted in [11], the optimal solution measures the Jensen-Shannon divergence between the two distributions.

3.3 Full Objective

Taken together, our full objective is:

$$\begin{aligned}\mathcal{L}_{\mathrm{T^2Net}}(G_{S\to R}, f_T, D_R, D_{\mathrm{feat}}) = & \mathcal{L}_{\mathrm{GAN}}(G_{S\to R}, D_R) + \alpha_f \mathcal{L}_{\mathrm{GAN}_f}(f_T, D_{\mathrm{feat}}) \\ & + \alpha_r \mathcal{L}_r(G_{S\to R}) + \alpha_t \mathcal{L}_t(f_T) + \alpha_s \mathcal{L}_s(f_T) \quad (6)\end{aligned}$$

where $\mathcal{L}_{\mathrm{GAN}}$ encourages translated synthetic images to appear realistic, $\mathcal{L}_r$ spurs translated real images to appear identical, $\mathcal{L}_{\mathrm{GAN}_f}$ enforces closer internal feature distributions, $\mathcal{L}_t$ promotes accurate depth prediction for synthetic pairs, and $\mathcal{L}_s$ prefers an appropriate local depth variation for real predictions. In our end-to-end training, this objective is used in solving for optimal f_T parameters:

$$f_T^* = \arg\min_{f_T} \min_{G_{S\to R}} \max_{D_R, D_{\mathrm{feat}}} \mathcal{L}_{\mathrm{T^2Net}}(G_{S\to R}, f_T, D_R, D_{\mathrm{feat}}) \quad (7)$$

3.4 Network Architecture

The transform network, $G_{S\to R}$, is a residual network (ResNet) [12] similar to SimGAN [33]. Limited by memory constraints and the large size of scene images, one down-sampling layer is used in our model and the output is only passed through 6 blocks. For the image discriminator networks, we use PatchGANs [33, 40], which have produced impressive results by discriminating locally whether image patches are real or fake.

The task prediction network is inspired by [10], which outputs four predicted depth maps of different scales. Instead of encoding input images into very small dimensions to extract global information, we instead use multiple dilation convolutions [39] with a large feature size to preserve fine-grained details. In addition, we employ different weights for the paths with skip connections [29], which can simultaneously process larger-scale semantic information in the scene and yet also predict detailed depth maps. The use of these techniques allows our task prediction network f_T to achieve state-of-the-art performance in our own real-supervised benchmark method (training f_T on pairs of real images and depth), even when the encoder portion of f_T is primarily based on VGG, as opposed to a more typical ResNet50-type network used in other methods [10,20].

4 Experimental Results

We evaluated our model on the outdoor KITTI dataset [9] and the indoor NYU Depth v2 dataset [34]. During the training process, we only used unpaired real images from these datasets in conjunction with synthetic image-depth pairs, obtained via SUNCG [35] and vKITTI [5] datasets, in our proposed framework.

4.1 Implementation Details

Training Details: In order to control the effect of GAN loss, we substituted the vanilla negative log likelihood objective with a least-squares loss [26], which has proven to be more stable during adversarial learning [40]. Hence, for GAN loss $\mathcal{L}_{\text{GAN}}(G_{S\to R}, D_R)$ in (1), we trained $G_{S\to R}$ by minimizing

$$\mathbb{E}_{x_s\sim X_s}[(D_R(G_{S\to R}(x_s))-1)^2]$$

and trained D_R by minimizing

$$\mathbb{E}_{x_r\sim X_r}[(D_R(x_r)-1)^2]+\mathbb{E}_{x_s\sim X_s}[D_R^2(G_{S\to R}(x_s))].$$

A similar procedure was also applied for the GAN loss in (5).

We trained our model using PyTorch. During optimization, the weights of different loss components were set to $\alpha_f = 0.1$, $\alpha_r = 40$, $\alpha_t = 20$, $\alpha_s = 0.01$ for indoor scenes and $\alpha_f = 0.1$, $\alpha_r = 100$, $\alpha_t = 100$, $\alpha_s = 0.01$ for outdoor scenes. For both indoor and outdoor datasets, we used the Adam solver [19], setting $\beta_1 = 0.5$, $\beta_2 = 0.9$ for the adversarial network and $\beta_1 = 0.95$, $\beta_2 = 0.999$ for the task network. All networks were trained from scratch, with a learning rate of 10^{-4} (task network) and 2×10^{-5} (translation network) for the first 10 epochs and a linearly decaying rate for the next 10 epochs. In addition, as the indoor synthetic images and real NYUDv2 images are visually quite different, they are easily distinguished by the discriminator. To balance the minimax game, we updated $G_{S\to R}$ five times for each update of D_R during the indoor experiments. Please see the supplementary material for more details.

Our f_T-only Benchmark Models: Besides our full T²Net model, we also tested our partial model which comprised solely the f_T task prediction network. We evaluated this in two scenarios: (1) an **"all-real"** scenario, in which we used real image and depth map pairs for training, for which we would expect to *upper bound* our full model performance, and (2) an **"all-synthetic"** scenario, in which we used only synthetic image-depth pairs and eschewed even unpaired real images, for which we would expect to *lower bound* our full model performance.

Evaluation Metrics: We evaluated the performance of our approach using the depth evaluation metrics reported in [4]:

RMSE(log) : $\sqrt{\frac{1}{|T|}\sum_{i=1}^{T}||\log\hat{y}_{r,i}-\log y_{r,i}||^2}$ **RMSE** : $\sqrt{\frac{1}{|T|}\sum_{i=1}^{T}||\hat{y}_{r,i}-y_{r,i}||^2}$

Sq. relative : $\frac{1}{|T|}\sum_{i=1}^{T}||\hat{y}_{r,i}-y_{r,i}||^2/y_{r,i}$ **Abs relative** : $\frac{1}{|T|}\sum_{i=1}^{T}|\hat{y}_{r,i}-y_{r,i}|/y_{r,i}$

Accuracy : % of $\mathbf{y_{r,i}}$ **s.t.** $max(\frac{\hat{y}_{r,i}}{y_{r,i}},\frac{y_{r,i}}{\hat{y}_{r,i}})=\delta<thr$

Fig. 3. Example output of our translation network for SUNCG [35] renderings. Top: synthetic images rendered from SUNCG. Middle: corresponding images after $G_{S\rightarrow R}$ translation. Bottom: real images from NYUDv2 [34] (no correspondence to above rows).

4.2 NYUDv2 Dataset

Synthetic Indoor Dataset: To generate the paired synthetic training data, we rendered RGB images and depth maps from the SUNCG dataset [35], which contains 45,622 3D houses with various room types. We chose the camera locations, poses and parameters based on the distribution of real NYUDv2 dataset [34] and retained valid depth maps using the criteria presented in [35]: (a) valid depth area (depth values in range of 1 m to 10 m) larger than 70% of image area, and (b) more than two object categories in the scene. In total we generated 130,190 valid views from 4,562 different houses, with samples shown in Fig. 3.

Translated Results: Figure 3 shows sample output from translation through $G_{S\rightarrow R}$. We observe that the visual differences between synthetic and real images are obvious: colors, textures, illumination and shadows in real scenes are more complex than in synthetic ones. Compared to synthetic images, the translated versions are visually more similar to real images in terms of low-level appearance.

Depth Estimation Results: In Table 1, we report the performance of our models (varying different application of the two GANs) as compared to latest state-of-the-art methods on the public NYUDv2 dataset. In the indoor dataset, these previous works were all based on supervised learning with real image-depth pairs. The gray rows highlight methods in which real image-depth pairs were *not* used in training. The **train-set-mean** baseline used the mean synthetic depth map in the training dataset as prediction, with the results providing an indication of the correlation between depth maps in the synthetic and real datasets. We also present results from our f_T-only benchmark models in the "all-real" and "all-synthetic" setups (see Sect. 4.1), which we expect to provide the upper bound and lower bound of our model respectively.

Our proposed models produced a clear gap to the train-set-mean baseline and the synthetic-only benchmark. While our models were unable to outperform the latest fully-supervised methods trained on real paired data, the full T^2Net model was even able to outperform the earlier supervised learning method of [21] on two of the three metrics, despite not using real paired data.

Table 1. Depth estimation results on NYUDv2 dataset [34]. *Gray rows indicate methods in which training is conducted* ***without*** *real image-depth pairs. Best supervised results are marked with *, while best unsupervised results are in bold.*

	lower is better				higher is better		
Method	Abs Rel	Sq Rel	RMSE	RMSE log	$\delta<1.25$	$\delta<1.25^2$	$\delta<1.25^3$
Ladicky et al. [21]	-	-	-	-	0.542	0.829	0.940
Eigen et al.[4] Fine	0.215	0.212	0.907	0.285	0.611	0.887	0.971
Liu et al. [23]	0.213	-	0.759	-	0.650	0.906	0.976
Eigen et al.[3] (VGG)	0.158	0.121*	0.641	0.214	0.769	0.950*	0.988*
Baseline, train set mean	0.439	0.641	1.148	0.415	0.412	0.692	0.856
Our f_T, all-real	0.157*	0.125	0.556*	0.199*	0.779*	0.943	0.983
Our f_T, all-synthetic	0.304	0.394	1.024	0.369	0.458	0.771	0.916
Our T²Net, D_{feat} only	0.320	0.405	0.991	0.343	0.480	0.792	0.933
Our T²Net, D_{image} only	0.274	0.336	1.001	0.325	0.496	0.814	0.938
Our full T²Net	**0.257**	**0.281**	**0.915**	**0.305**	**0.540**	**0.832**	**0.948**

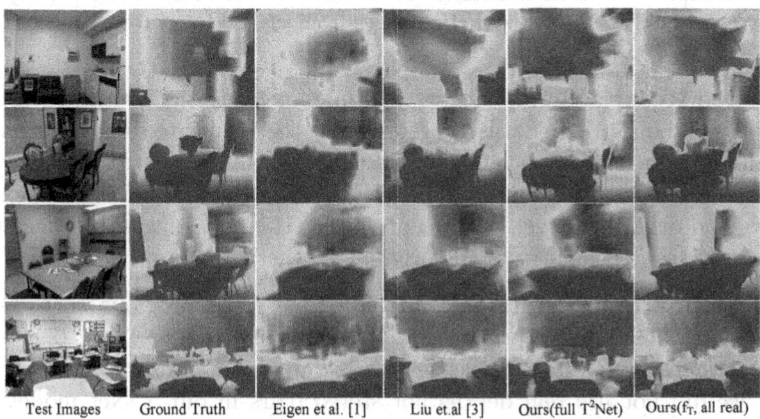

Fig. 4. Qualitative results on NYUDv2. All results are shown as relative depth maps (red = far, blue = close). See text for details. (Color figure online)

We also show qualitative results in Fig. 4. Although the absolute values of our predicted depths were not as accurate as the latest supervised learning methods, we observe that our T²Net model generates reasonably good relative depths with distinct furniture shapes, even without using real paired training data.

4.3 KITTI Dataset

Data Preprocessing: We used Virtual KITTI (vKITTI) [5], a photo-realistic synthetic dataset that contains 21,260 image-depth paired frames generated from different virtual urban worlds. The scenes and camera viewpoints are similar to the real KITTI dataset [27]; see samples in Fig. 5. However, the ground truth depths in vKITTI and KITTI are quite different. The maximum sensed depth in a real KITTI image is typically on the order of 80 m, whereas vKITTI has precise depths to a maximum of 655.3 m. To reduce the effect of ground truth differences, the vKITTI depth maps were clipped to 80 m.

Fig. 5. Example translated images for the outdoor vKITTI dataset [5]. (Right) the images in real KITTI. (Left) synthetic images from vKITTI and translated images.

Translated Results: Figure 5 shows examples of synthetic, translated, and real images from the outdoor datasets. As shown, the translated images have substantially greater resemblance to the real images than the synthetic images. Our translation network can visually replicate the distributions of colors, textures, shadows and other low-level features present in the real images, and meanwhile preserve the scene geometry of the original synthetic images.

Depth Estimation Results: In order to compare with previous work, we used the test split of 697 images proposed in [4]. Following [10], we chose 22,600 RGB images from the remaining 32 scenes for training the translation network. As before, we did not use real depths nor stereo pairs in our T^2Net models. The ground truth depth maps in KITTI were obtained by aligning laser scans with color images, which produced less than 5% depth values and introduced sensor errors. For fair comparison with state-of-the-art single view depth estimation methods, we evaluated our results based on the cropping given in [7] and clamping the predicted depth values within the range of 1–50 m.

Table 2 shows quantitative results of testing with real images of the KITTI dataset. We can observe that the performance of T^2Net has a substantial 9.1% absolute improvement compared to our all-synthetic trained model. Unlike the indoor results, the best performance comes from without D_{feat}. This is likely due to the translated images much closer to real KITTI, which does not need to match the feature distribution using D_{feat} adversarial learning. We also observe that our model despite training without real paired data, is able to outperform the method of [4] trained on real paired image-depth data, as well as the method of [7] trained on real left-right stereo data.

We also qualitatively compared the performance of the proposed model with the state-of-the-art in Fig. 6. We only chose two representatives that either used real paired color-depth images [4], or real left-right stereo images [10]. Compared to [4], our model can generate full dense depth maps of input image size. Our method is also able to detect more detail at object boundaries than [10], with

Table 2. Results on KITTI 2015 [27] using the split of Eigen *et al.* [4]. For dataset, K is the real KITTI dataset [27], CS is Cityscapes [2] and vK is the synthetic KITTI dataset [5]. L, R are the left and right stereo images, and I, D are the images and depths. *The gray rows highlight methods that did not use real image-depth pairs nor stereo pairs for training. Best real-supervised or stereo-based results are marked with *, while best unsupervised results are in bold.*

			lower is better				higher is better		
Method	Dataset	cap	Abs Rel	Sq Rel	RMSE	RMSE log	$\delta<1.25$	$\delta<1.25^2$	$\delta<1.25^3$
Eigen et al.[4] Fine	K(I+D)	0-80m	0.190	1.515	7.156	0.270	0.692	0.899	0.967
Garg et al.[7] L12 Aug.8x	K(L+R)	1-50m	0.169	1.080	5.104	0.273	0.740	0.904	0.962
Godard et al. [10]	CS+K(L+R)	1-50m	0.117	0.762	3.972	0.206	0.860	0.948	0.976
Kuznietsov et al. [20]	K(D+L+R)	1-50m	0.108*	0.595*	3.518*	0.179	0.875*	0.964*	0.988*
Baseline, train set mean	vK(I+D)	1-50m	0.521	11.024	10.598	0.473	0.638	0.755	0.835
Our f_T, all-real	K(I+D)	1-50m	0.114	0.627	3.549	0.178*	0.867	0.960	0.986
Our f_T, all-synthetic	vK(I+D)	1-50m	0.278	3.216	6.268	0.322	0.681	0.854	0.929
Our T²Net, D_{feat} only	vK(I+D) + K(I)	1-50m	0.233	2.902	6.285	0.300	0.743	0.880	0.938
Our T²Net, D_{image} only	vK(I+D) + K(I)	1-50m	**0.168**	**1.199**	**4.674**	**0.243**	**0.772**	**0.912**	**0.966**
Our full T²Net	vK(I+D) + K(I)	1-50m	0.169	1.230	4.717	0.245	0.769	**0.912**	0.965

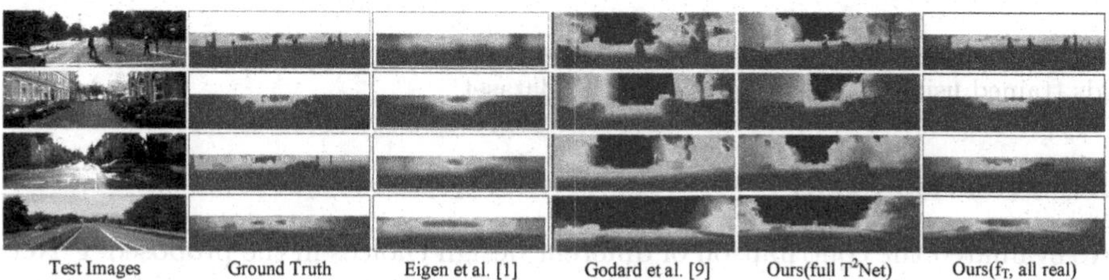

Fig. 6. Qualitative results on KITTI, Eigen split [4]. The ground truth depths in the original dataset were very sparse and have been interpolated for visualization.We converted the disparity maps provided in [10] to depth maps.

a likely reason being that the synthetic training depth maps preserved object details better. Another interesting observation is the predicted depth maps were treating glass windows as permeable based on synthetic data, while they were mostly sensed as opaque in the laser-based ground truth.

Performance on Make3D: To compare the generalization ability of our T²Net to a different test dataset, we used our full T²Net model, trained only on vKITTI paired data and (unpaired) real KITTI images, for testing on the Make3D dataset [32]. We evaluated our model quantitatively on Make3D using the standard C1 metric. The RMSE(m) accuracy is 8.935, Log-10 is 0.574, Abs Rel is 0.508 and Sqr Rel is 6.589. The qualitative results presented in Fig. 7 show that our model can generate reasonable depth map in most situations. The right part of Fig. 7 displays some failure cases, likely due to large building windows not being widely observed in the vKITTI datasets.

Fig. 7. Qualitative results on Make3D. For most cases the model generated reasonable depths except scenes with new object types not present in the synthetic data.

Fig. 8. The qualitative results of different unpaired image-to-image translation methods trained using vKITTI and real KITTI dataset.

4.4 Ablation Study

We evaluated the contribution of different design choices in the proposed T^2Net. Table 3 shows the quantitative results and Fig. 8 shows some example outputs of different methods for unpaired image translation.

End-to-End vs Separated: We began by evaluating the effect of end-to-end learning. We found that end-to-end training outperformed separated training of the translation network and task prediction network. One reasonable explanation is that task loss is a form of supervised loss for synthetic-to-realistic translation. This incentivizes the translation network to preserve geometric content present in a synthetic image.

We also experimented with the unpaired image translation network CycleGAN [40]. This model has two encoder-decoder translation networks and two discriminators, but we were limited by machine memory and trained the CycleGAN and task network separately. From Fig. 8, we found that while this model generated very visually realistic images, it also created some realistic-looking details that significantly distorted scene geometry. The quantitative performance is close to our separated training results.

No Image Reconstruction: We studied what happens when training without real-image reconstruction loss. In Fig. 8, we may surmise that the task loss in the depth domain is able to encourage reasonable depiction of scene geometry in the translation network. However the lack of a real image reconstruction loss appears to make it harder to generate high resolution images. In addition, we noticed that while the removal of reconstruction loss still led to relatively good results as seen in Table 3, this was only true in early training with best results in epoch 3, with accuracy dropping after more training epochs.

Table 3. Quantitative results of different variants of our T^{2}Net on KITTI using the split of [4]. All methods are trained without the real world ground truth.

	lower is better				higher is better		
Method	Abs Rel	Sq Rel	RMSE	RMSE log	$\delta<1.25$	$\delta<1.25^2$	$\delta<1.25^3$
baseline, synthetic only	0.278	3.216	6.268	0.322	0.681	0.854	0.929
vanilla task network, synthetic only	0.295	3.793	8.403	0.363	0.600	0.817	0.912
vanilla task network, full approach	0.259	2.891	6.380	0.324	0.694	0.853	0.927
separated training	0.234	2.706	6.068	0.293	0.747	0.882	0.942
separated training with CycleGAN	0.212	1.973	5.340	0.269	0.750	0.895	0.952
self-domain reconstruction	0.199	1.517	5.349	0.298	0.695	0.866	0.9420
No reconstruction loss(epoch 3)	0.201	1.941	5.619	0.286	0.741	0.882	0.945
No feature loss	**0.168**	**1.199**	**4.674**	**0.243**	**0.772**	**0.912**	**0.966**
No image GAN loss	0.233	2.902	6.285	0.300	0.743	0.880	0.938
our full approach	0.169	1.230	4.717	0.245	0.769	0.912	0.965

Target Reconstruction vs Self-Regularization: Since the self-regularization component of SimGAN is closest to our target-domain reconstruction concept, we also trained our full model with L1 reconstruction loss for synthetic imagery, which forces the generated target images to be similar to original input images. From Fig. 8, we observe that this is unable to work well for large domain shifts for the GAN loss and self-domain reconstruction loss play opposite roles in the translation task.

5 Conclusion and Future Work

We presented our T^{2}Net deep neural network for single-image depth estimation, that requires only synthetic image-depth pairs and unpaired real images for training. The overall system comprises an image translation network and a depth prediction network. It is able to generate realistic images via a learning framework that combines adversarial loss for synthetic input and target-domain reconstruction loss for real input in the translation network, and a further combination of a task loss and feature GAN loss in the depth prediction network. The T^{2}Net can be trained end-to-end, and does not require real image-depth pairs nor stereo pairs for training. It is able to produce good results on the NYUDv2 and KITTI datasets despite the lack of access to real paired training data, and even outperformed early deep learning methods that were trained on real paired data. In future, we intend to explore mechanisms that provide greater generalization capability across different datasets.

Acknowledgements. This research is supported by the BeingTogether Centre, a collaboration between Nanyang Technological University (NTU) Singapore and University of North Carolina (UNC) at Chapel Hill. The BeingTogether Centre is supported by the National Research Foundation, Prime Ministers Office, Singapore under its International Research Centres in Singapore Funding Initiative.

References

1. Cao, Y., Wu, Z., Shen, C.: Estimating depth from monocular images as classification using deep fully convolutional residual networks. IEEE Trans. Circuits Syst. Video Technol. (2017)
2. Cordts, M., et al.: The cityscapes dataset for semantic urban scene understanding. In: Proceedings of the IEEE Conference on Computer Vision and Pattern Recognition (CVPR) (2016)
3. Eigen, D., Fergus, R.: Predicting depth, surface normals and semantic labels with a common multi-scale convolutional architecture. In: Proceedings of the IEEE International Conference on Computer Vision (ICCV), pp. 2650–2658 (2015)
4. Eigen, D., Puhrsch, C., Fergus, R.: Depth map prediction from a single image using a multi-scale deep network. In: Advances in Neural Information Processing Systems (NIPS), pp. 2366–2374 (2014)
5. Gaidon, A., Wang, Q., Cabon, Y., Vig, E.: Virtualworlds as proxy for multi-object tracking analysis. In: 2016 IEEE Conference on Computer Vision and Pattern Recognition (CVPR), pp. 4340–4349. IEEE (2016)
6. Ganin, Y., Lempitsky, V.: Unsupervised domain adaptation by backpropagation. In: International Conference on Machine Learning (ICML), pp. 1180–1189 (2015)
7. Garg, R., Vijay Kumar, B.G., Carneiro, G., Reid, I.: Unsupervised CNN for single view depth estimation: geometry to the rescue. In: Leibe, B., Matas, J., Sebe, N., Welling, M. (eds.) ECCV 2016. LNCS, vol. 9912, pp. 740–756. Springer, Cham (2016). https://doi.org/10.1007/978-3-319-46484-8_45
8. Gatys, L.A., Ecker, A.S., Bethge, M.: Image style transfer using convolutional neural networks. In: 2016 IEEE Conference on Computer Vision and Pattern Recognition (CVPR), pp. 2414–2423. IEEE (2016)
9. Geiger, A., Lenz, P., Urtasun, R.: Are we ready for autonomous driving? The KITTI vision benchmark suite. In: Conference on Computer Vision and Pattern Recognition (CVPR) (2012)
10. Godard, C., Mac Aodha, O., Brostow, G.J.: Unsupervised monocular depth estimation with left-right consistency. In: IEEE Conference on Computer Vision and Pattern Recongition (CVPR) (2017)
11. Goodfellow, I., et al.: Generative adversarial nets. In: Advances in Neural Information Processing Systems (NIPS), pp. 2672–2680 (2014)
12. He, K., Zhang, X., Ren, S., Sun, J.: Deep residual learning for image recognition. In: Proceedings of the IEEE Conference on Computer Vision and Pattern Recognition, pp. 770–778 (2016)
13. Heise, P., Klose, S., Jensen, B., Knoll, A.: PM-Huber: PatchMatch with Huber regularization for stereo matching. In: 2013 IEEE International Conference on Computer Vision (ICCV), pp. 2360–2367. IEEE (2013)
14. Hoffman, J., et al.: CYCADA: cycle-consistent adversarial domain adaptation. arXiv preprint arXiv:1711.03213 (2017)
15. Hoiem, D., Efros, A.A., Hebert, M.: Automatic photo pop-up. ACM Trans. Graph. **24**(3), 577–584 (2005)
16. Johnson, J., Alahi, A., Fei-Fei, L.: Perceptual losses for real-time style transfer and super-resolution. In: Leibe, B., Matas, J., Sebe, N., Welling, M. (eds.) ECCV 2016. LNCS, vol. 9906, pp. 694–711. Springer, Cham (2016). https://doi.org/10.1007/978-3-319-46475-6_43

17. Karsch, K., Liu, C., Kang, S.B.: Depth extraction from video using non-parametric sampling. In: Fitzgibbon, A., Lazebnik, S., Perona, P., Sato, Y., Schmid, C. (eds.) ECCV 2012. LNCS, vol. 7576, pp. 775–788. Springer, Heidelberg (2012). https://doi.org/10.1007/978-3-642-33715-4_56
18. Kim, T., Cha, M., Kim, H., Lee, J.K., Kim, J.: Learning to discover cross-domain relations with generative adversarial networks. In: International Conference on Machine Learning (ICML), pp. 1857–1865 (2017)
19. Kingma, D.P., Ba, J.: Adam: a method for stochastic optimization. arXiv preprint arXiv:1412.6980 (2014)
20. Kuznietsov, Y., Stückler, J., Leibe, B.: Semi-supervised deep learning for monocular depth map prediction. In: Proceedings of the IEEE Conference on Computer Vision and Pattern Recognition (CVPR), pp. 6647–6655 (2017)
21. Ladický, L., Shi, J., Pollefeys, M.: Pulling things out of perspective. In: Proceedings of the IEEE Conference on Computer Vision and Pattern Recognition (CVPR), pp. 89–96 (2014)
22. Laina, I., Rupprecht, C., Belagiannis, V., Tombari, F., Navab, N.: Deeper depth prediction with fully convolutional residual networks. In: 2016 Fourth International Conference on 3D Vision (3DV), pp. 239–248. IEEE (2016)
23. Liu, F., Shen, C., Lin, G., Reid, I.: Learning depth from single monocular images using deep convolutional neural fields. IEEE Trans. Pattern Anal. Mach. Intell. (TPAMI) **38**(10), 2024–2039 (2016)
24. Liu, M.Y., Breuel, T., Kautz, J.: Unsupervised image-to-image translation networks. In: Advances in Neural Information Processing Systems (NIPS), pp. 700–708 (2017)
25. Liu, M.Y., Tuzel, O.: Coupled generative adversarial networks. In: Advances in Neural Information Processing Systems (NIPS), pp. 469–477 (2016)
26. Mao, X., Li, Q., Xie, H., Lau, R.Y., Wang, Z.: Multi-class generative adversarial networks with the L2 loss function. CoRR, abs/1611.04076, vol. 2 (2016)
27. Menze, M., Geiger, A.: Object scene flow for autonomous vehicles. In: Conference on Computer Vision and Pattern Recognition (CVPR) (2015)
28. Qiu, W., Yuille, A.: UnrealCV: connecting computer vision to unreal engine. In: Hua, G., Jégou, H. (eds.) ECCV 2016. LNCS, vol. 9915, pp. 909–916. Springer, Cham (2016). https://doi.org/10.1007/978-3-319-49409-8_75
29. Ronneberger, O., Fischer, P., Brox, T.: U-Net: convolutional networks for biomedical image segmentation. In: Navab, N., Hornegger, J., Wells, W.M., Frangi, A.F. (eds.) MICCAI 2015. LNCS, vol. 9351, pp. 234–241. Springer, Cham (2015). https://doi.org/10.1007/978-3-319-24574-4_28
30. Rosca, M., Lakshminarayanan, B., Warde-Farley, D., Mohamed, S.: Variational approaches for auto-encoding generative adversarial networks. arXiv preprint arXiv:1706.04987 (2017)
31. Saxena, A., Chung, S.H., Ng, A.Y.: 3-D depth reconstruction from a single still image. Int. J. Comput. Vision **76**(1), 53–69 (2008)
32. Saxena, A., Sun, M., Ng, A.Y.: Make3D: learning 3D scene structure from a single still image. IEEE Trans. Pattern Anal. Mach. Intell. **31**(5), 824–840 (2009)
33. Shrivastava, A., Pfister, T., Tuzel, O., Susskind, J., Wang, W., Webb, R.: Learning from simulated and unsupervised images through adversarial training. In: The IEEE Conference on Computer Vision and Pattern Recognition (CVPR) (2017)
34. Silberman, N., Hoiem, D., Kohli, P., Fergus, R.: Indoor segmentation and support inference from RGBD images. In: Fitzgibbon, A., Lazebnik, S., Perona, P., Sato, Y., Schmid, C. (eds.) ECCV 2012. LNCS, vol. 7576, pp. 746–760. Springer, Heidelberg (2012). https://doi.org/10.1007/978-3-642-33715-4_54

35. Song, S., Yu, F., Zeng, A., Chang, A.X., Savva, M., Funkhouser, T.: Semantic scene completion from a single depth image. In: Proceedings of the IEEE Conference on Computer Vision and Pattern Recognition (CVPR), pp. 1746–1754 (2017)
36. Tonioni, A., Poggi, M., Mattoccia, S., Di Stefano, L.: Unsupervised adaptation for deep stereo. In: Proceedings of the IEEE International Conference on Computer Vision (ICCV), pp. 1605–1613 (2017)
37. Wang, P., Shen, X., Lin, Z., Cohen, S., Price, B., Yuille, A.L.: Towards unified depth and semantic prediction from a single image. In: Proceedings of the IEEE Conference on Computer Vision and Pattern Recognition, pp. 2800–2809 (2015)
38. Yi, Z., Zhang, H., Tan, P., Gong, M.: DualGAN: unsupervised dual learning for image-to-image translation. In: Proceedings of the IEEE International Conference on Computer Vision (ICCV), pp. 2849–2857 (2017)
39. Yu, F., Koltun, V.: Multi-scale context aggregation by dilated convolutions. In: International Conference on Learning Representations (ICLR) (2016)
40. Zhu, J.Y., Park, T., Isola, P., Efros, A.A.: Unpaired image-to-image translation using cycle-consistent adversarial networks. In: Proceedings of the IEEE International Conference on Computer Vision (ICCV), pp. 2223–2232 (2017)

AMC: AutoML for Model Compression and Acceleration on Mobile Devices

Yihui He[2], Ji Lin[1], Zhijian Liu[1], Hanrui Wang[1], Li-Jia Li[3], and Song Han[1(✉)]

[1] Massachusetts Institute of Technology, Cambridge, USA
{jilin,songhan}@mit.edu
[2] Carnegie Mellon University, Pittsburgh, USA
[3] Google, Mountain View, USA

Abstract. Model compression is an effective technique to efficiently deploy neural network models on mobile devices which have limited computation resources and tight power budgets. Conventional model compression techniques rely on *hand-crafted* features and require domain experts to explore the large design space trading off among model size, speed, and accuracy, which is usually sub-optimal and time-consuming. In this paper, we propose AutoML for Model Compression (AMC) which leverages reinforcement learning to efficiently sample the design space and can improve the model compression quality. We achieved state-of-the-art model compression results in a fully automated way *without any human efforts*. Under 4× FLOPs reduction, we achieved **2.7%** better accuracy than the hand-crafted model compression method for VGG-16 on ImageNet. We applied this automated, push-the-button compression pipeline to MobileNet-V1 and achieved a speedup of **1.53**× on the GPU (Titan Xp) and **1.95**× on an Android phone (Google Pixel 1), with negligible loss of accuracy.

Keywords: AutoML · Reinforcement learning · Model compression CNN acceleration · Mobile vision

1 Introduction

In many machine learning applications (*e.g.*, robotics, self-driving cars, and advertisement ranking), deep neural networks are constrained by latency, energy and model size budget. Many works have been proposed to improve the hardware efficiency of neural networks by model compression [19,22,26]. The core of model compression technique is to determine the compression policy for each layer as they have different redundancy, which conventionally requires hand-crafted heuristics and domain experts to explore the large design space trading

Y. He and J. Lin—Equal contributions.

Electronic supplementary material The online version of this chapter (https://doi.org/10.1007/978-3-030-01234-2_48) contains supplementary material, which is available to authorized users.

V. Ferrari et al. (Eds.): ECCV 2018, LNCS 11211, pp. 815–832, 2018.
https://doi.org/10.1007/978-3-030-01234-2_48

off among model size, speed, and accuracy. The design space is so large that human heuristic is usually sub-optimal, and manual model compression is time-consuming. To this end, we aim to automatically find the compression policy for an arbitrary network to achieve even better performance than human strategy.

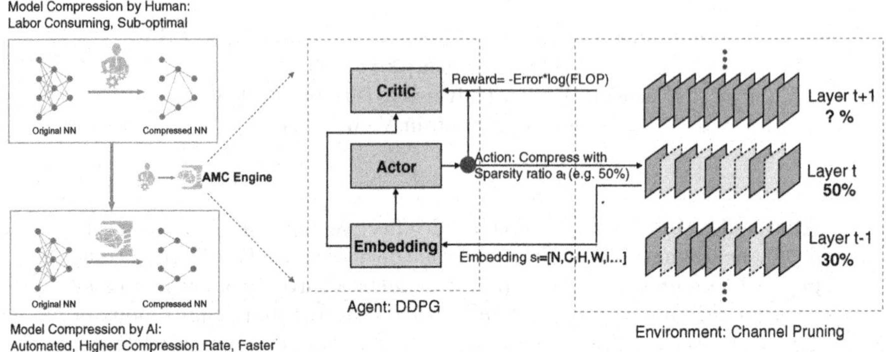

Fig. 1. Overview of AutoML for Model Compression (AMC) engine. Left: AMC replaces human and makes model compression fully automated while performing better than human. Right: Form AMC as a reinforcement learning problem. We process a pretrained network (*e.g.*, MobileNet-V1) in a layer-by-layer manner. Our reinforcement learning agent (DDPG) receives the embedding s_t from a layer t, and outputs a sparsity ratio a_t. After the layer is compressed with a_t, it moves to the next layer L_{t+1}. The accuracy of the pruned model with all layers compressed is evaluated. Finally, as a function of accuracy and FLOP, reward R is returned to the reinforcement learning agent.

As the layers in deep neural networks are correlated in an unknown way, determining the compression policy is highly non-trivial. The problem also has exponential complexity as the network goes deeper, which is infeasible to be solved by brute-force methods. Reinforcement learning methods have been widely approved to have better sample efficiency than random exploration and achieve better solution. Therefore, we propose AutoML for Model Compression (AMC) which leverages reinforcement learning to efficiently sample the design space and greatly improve the model compression quality. Figure 1 illustrates our AMC engine. When compressing a network, rather than relying on human experience or hand-crafted heuristics, our AMC engine automates this process and frees the compression pipeline from human labor.

We observe that the accuracy of the compressed model is very sensitive to the sparsity of each layer, requiring a fine-grained action space. Therefore, instead of searching over a discrete space, we come up with a continuous compression ratio control strategy with a DDPG [32] agent to learn through trials and errors: penalizing accuracy loss while encouraging model shrinking and speedup. The actor-critic structure also helps to reduce variance, facilitating stabler training. Specifically, our DDPG agent processes the network in a layer-wise manner. For each layer L_t, the agent receives a layer embedding s_t which encodes useful characteristics of this layer, and then it outputs a precise compression ratio a_t. After layer L_t is compressed with a_t, the agent moves to the next layer L_{t+1}. The validation accuracy of the pruned model with all layers compressed is evaluated without fine-tuning, which is an efficient delegate of the fine-tuned accuracy. This simple approximation can improve the search time not having to retrain the model, and provide high quality search result.

After the policy search is done, the best-explored model is fine-tuned to achieve the best performance.

We proposed two compression policy search protocols for different scenarios. For *latency-critical* AI applications (*e.g.*, mobile apps, self-driving cars, and advertisement rankings), we propose *resource-constrained* compression to achieve the best accuracy given the maximum amount of hardware resources (*e.g.*, FLOPs, latency, and model size), For *quality-critical* AI applications (*e.g.*, Google Photos) where latency is not a hard constraint, we propose *accuracy-guaranteed* compression to achieve the smallest model with no loss of accuracy.

We achieve *resource-constrained* compression by constraining the search space, in which the action space (pruning ratio) is constrained such that the model compressed by the agent is always below the resources budget. For *accuracy-guaranteed* compression, we define a reward that is a function of both accuracy and hardware resource. With this reward function, we are able to explore the limit of compression without harming the accuracy of models.

To demonstrate the wide and general applicability, we evaluate our AMC engine on multiple neural networks, including VGG [45], ResNet [21], and MobileNet-V1 [23], and we also test the generalization ability of the compressed model from classification to object detection. Extensive experiments suggest that AMC offers better performance than hand-crafted heuristic policies. For ResNet-50, we push the expert-tuned compression ratio [16] from 3.4× to **5**× with no loss of accuracy. Furthermore, we reduce the FLOPs of MobileNet-V1 [23] by 2×, achieving top one accuracy of 70.2%, which is on a better Pareto curve than 0.75 MobileNet-V1, and we achieve a speedup of **1.53**× on the Titan XP and **1.95**× on an Android phone.

2 Related Work

CNN Compression and Acceleration. Extensive works [12,17–20,34] have been done on accelerating neural networks by compression. Quantization [10, 41,55] and special convolution implementations [3,29,36,48] can also speed up the neural networks. Tensor factorization [15,27,30,35] decomposes weights into light-weight pieces, for example [11,14,51] proposed to accelerate the fully connected layers with truncated SVD; Jaderberg *et al.* [26] proposed to factorize layers into 1×3 and 3×1; and Zhang *et al.* [53] proposed to factorize layers into 3×3 and 1×1. Channel pruning [1,24,38,40] removes the redundant channels from feature maps. A common problem of these methods is how to determine the sparsity ratio for each layer.

Table 1. Comparisons of reinforcement learning approaches for models searching (NAS: Neural Architecture Search [57], NT: Network Transformation [6], N2N: Network to Network [2], and AMC: AutoML for Model Compression. AMC distinguishes from other works by getting reward without fine-tuning, continuous search space control, and can produce both accuracy-guaranteed and hardware resource-constrained models.

	NAS	NT	N2N	AMC
Optimize for accuracy	✓	✓	✓	✓
Optimize for latency				✓
Simple, non-RNN controller				✓
Fast exploration with few GPUs		✓	✓	✓
Continuous action space				✓

Neural Architecture Search and AutoML. Many works on searching models with reinforcement learning and genetic algorithms [5,37,42,46] greatly improve the performance of neural networks. NAS [57] aims to search the transferable network blocks, and its performance surpasses many *manually* designed architectures [9,21,47]. Cai *et al.* [6] proposed to speed up the exploration via network transformation [8]. Inspired by them, N2N [2] integrated reinforcement learning into channel selection. In Table 1, we demonstrate several merits of our AMC engine. Compared with previous work, AMC engine optimizes for both accuracy and latency, requires a simple non-RNN controller, can do fast exploration with fewer GPU hours, and also support continuous action space.

3 Methodology

We present an overview of our AutoML for Model Compression (AMC) engine in Fig. 1. We aim to automatically find the redundancy for each layer, characterized by sparsity. We train an reinforcement learning agent to predict the action and give the sparsity, then perform form the pruning. We quickly evaluate the accuracy after pruning but before fine-tuning as an effective delegate of final accuracy. Then we update the agent by encouraging smaller, faster and more accurate models.

3.1 Problem Definition

Model compression is achieved by reducing the number of parameters and computation of each layer in deep neural networks. There are two categories of pruning: fine-grained pruning and structured pruning. *Fine-grained pruning* [19] aims to prune individual unimportant elements in weight tensors, which is able to achieve very high compression rate with no loss of accuracy. However, such algorithms result in an irregular pattern of sparsity, and it requires specialized hardware such as EIE [18] for speed up. *Coarse-grained structured pruning* [31] aims to prune entire regular regions of weight tensors (*e.g.*, channel, row, column, block, *etc.*). The pruned weights are regular and can be accelerated directly with off-the-shelf hardware and libraries. Here we study structured pruning that shrink the input channel of each convolutional and fully connected layer.

Our goal is to precisely find out the effective *sparsity* for each layer, which used to be manually determined in previous studies [22,31,38]. Take convolutional layer as an example. The shape of a weight tensor is $n \times c \times k \times k$, where n, c are output and input channels, and k is the kernel size. For fine-grained pruning, the sparsity is defined as the number of zero elements divided by the number of total elements, *i.e.* $\#\text{zeros}/(n \times c \times k \times h)$. For channel pruning, we shrink the weight tensor to $n \times c' \times k \times k$ (where $c' < c$), hence the sparsity becomes c'/c.

3.2 Automated Compression with Reinforcement Learning

AMC leverages reinforcement learning for efficient search over action space. Here we introduce the detailed setting of reinforcement learning framework.

The State Space. For each layer t, we have 11 features that characterize the state s_t:

$$(t, n, c, h, w, stride, k, FLOPs[t], reduced, rest, a_{t-1}) \tag{1}$$

where t is the layer index, the dimension of the kernel is $n \times c \times k \times k$, and the input is $c \times h \times w$. $FLOPs[t]$ is the FLOPs of layer L_t. *Reduced* is the total number of reduced FLOPs in previous layers. *Rest* is the number of remaining FLOPs in the following layers. Before being passed to the agent, they are scaled within $[0, 1]$. Such features are essential for the agent to distinguish one convolutional layer from another.

The Action Space. Most of the existing works use discrete space as coarse-grained action space (*e.g.*, $\{64, 128, 256, 512\}$ for the number of channels). Coarse-grained action space might not be a problem for a high-accuracy model architecture search. However, we observed that model compression is very sensitive to sparsity ratio and requires fine-grained action space, leading to an explosion of the number of discrete actions (Sect. 4.2). Such large action spaces are difficult to explore efficiently [32]. Discretization also throws away the order: for example, 10% sparsity is more aggressive than 20% and far more aggressive than 30%.

As a result, we propose to use continuous action space $a \in (0, 1]$, which enables more fine-grained and accurate compression.

DDPG Agent. As illustrated in Fig. 1, the agent receives an embedding state s_t of layer L_t from the environment and then outputs a sparsity ratio as action a_t. The underlying layer is compressed with a_t (rounded to the nearest feasible fraction) using a specified compression algorithm (*e.g.*, channel pruning). Then the agent moves to the next layer L_{t+1}, and receives state s_{t+1}. After finishing the final layer L_T, the reward accuracy is evaluated on the validation set and returned to the agent. For fast exploration, we evaluate the reward accuracy without fine-tuning, which is a good approximation for fine-tuned accuracy (Sect. 4.1).

We use the deep deterministic policy gradient (DDPG) for continuous control of the compression ratio, which is an off-policy actor-critic algorithm. For the exploration noise process, we use truncated normal distribution:

$$\mu'(s_t) \sim \mathrm{TN}\left(\mu\left(s_t \mid \theta_t^{\mu}\right), \sigma^2, 0, 1\right) \tag{2}$$

During exploitation, noise σ is initialized as 0.5 and is decayed after each episode exponentially.

Following Block-QNN [54], which applies a variant form of Bellman's Equation [50], each transition in an episode is (s_t, a_t, R, s_{t+1}), where R is the reward after the network is compressed. During the update, the baseline reward b is subtracted to reduce the variance of gradient estimation, which is an exponential moving average of the previous rewards [6,56]:

$$\begin{aligned} Loss &= \frac{1}{N}\sum_i \left(y_i - Q\left(s_i, a_i \mid \theta^Q\right)\right)^2 \\ y_i &= r_i - b + \gamma Q(s_{i+1}, \mu(s_{i+1}) \mid \theta^Q) \end{aligned} \tag{3}$$

The discount factor γ is set to 1 to avoid over-prioritizing short-term rewards [4].

3.3 Search Protocols

Resource-Constrained Compression. By limiting the action space (the sparsity ratio for each layer), we can accurately arrive at the target compression ratio. Following [4,54,57], we use the following reward:

$$R_{err} = -Error \tag{4}$$

This reward offers no incentive for model size reduction, so we the achieve target compression ratio by an alternative way: limiting the action space. Take fine-grained pruning for model size reduction as an example: we allow arbitrary action a at the first few layers; we start to limit the action a when we find that the budget is insufficient even after compressing **all** the following layers with most aggressive strategy. Algorithm 1 illustrates the process. (For channel pruning, the code will be longer but similar, since removing input channels of layer L_t will also remove the corresponding output channels of L_{t-1}, reducing parameters/FLOPs of both layers). Note again that our algorithm is not limited to constraining *model size* and it can be replaced by other resources, such as FLOPs or the actual inference time on mobile device. Based on our experiments (Sect. 4.1), as the agent receives no incentive for going below the budget, it can precisely arrive at the target compression ratio.

Algorithm 1. Predict the sparsity ratio $\texttt{action}_t$ for layer L_t with constrained model size (number of parameters) using fine-grained pruning

```
▷ Initialize the reduced model size so far
if t is equal to 0 then
    W_reduced ← 0
end if

▷ Compute the agent's action and bound it with the maximum sparsity ratio
action_t ← μ'(s_t)
action_t ← min(action_t, action_max)

▷ Compute the model size of the whole model and all the later layers
W_all ← Σ_k W_k
W_rest ← Σ_{k=t+1} W_k

▷ Compute the number of parameters we have to reduce in the current layer if all
the later layers are pruned with the maximum sparsity ratio. α is the target sparsity
ratio of the whole model.
W_duty ← α · W_all − action_max · W_rest − W_reduced

▷ Bound action_t if it is too small to meet the target model size reduction
action_t ← max(action_t, W_duty/W_t)

▷ Update the accumulation of reduced model size
W_reduced ← W_reduced + action_t · W_t

return action_t
```

Accuracy-Guaranteed Compression. By tweaking the reward function, we can accurately find out the limit of compression that offers no loss of accuracy. We empirically observe that *Error* is inversely-proportional to $\log(FLOPs)$ or $\log(\#Param)$ [7]. Driven by this, we devise the following reward function:

$$R_{\text{FLOPs}} = -Error \cdot \log(\text{FLOPs}) \tag{5}$$

$$R_{\text{Param}} = -Error \cdot \log(\#\text{Param}) \tag{6}$$

This reward function is sensitive to *Error*; in the meantime, it provides a small incentive for reducing FLOPs or model size. Based on our experiments in Fig. 4, we note that our agent automatically finds the limit of compression.

4 Experimental Results

For fine-grained pruning [19], we prune the weights with least magnitude. The maximum sparsity ratio a_{max} for convolutional layers is set to 0.8, and a_{max} for fully connected layer is set to 0.98. For channel pruning, we use *max response* selection (pruning the weights according to the magnitude [20]), and preserve

Batch Normalization [25] layers during pruning instead of merging them into convolutional layers. The maximum sparsity ratios a_{max} for all layers are set to 0.8. Note that the manual upper bound a_{max} is only intended for faster search, one can simply use $a_{max} = 1$ which also produces similar results. Our actor network μ has two hidden layers, each with 300 units. The final output layer is a sigmoid layer to bound the actions within $(0, 1)$. Our critic network Q also had two hidden layers, both with 300 units. Actions arr included in the second hidden layer. We use $\tau = 0.01$ for the soft target updates and train the network with 64 as batch size and 2000 as replay buffer size. Our agent first explores 100 episodes with a constant noise $\sigma = 0.5$, and then exploits 300 episodes with exponentially decayed noise σ.

4.1 CIFAR-10 and Analysis

We conduct extensive experiments and fully analyze our AMC on CIFAR-10 [28]to verify the effectiveness of the 2 search protocols. CIFAR dataset consists of 50k training and 10k testing 32×32 tiny images in ten classes. We split the training images into 45k/5k train/validation. The accuracy reward is obtained on validation images. Our approach is computationally efficient: the RL can finish searching within **1 hour** on a single GeForce GTX TITAN Xp GPU.

FLOPs-Constrained Compression. We conducted FLOPs-constrained experiments on CIFAR-10 with channel pruning. We compare our approach with three empirical policies [22,31] illustrated in Fig. 2: *uniform* sets compression ratio uniformly, *shallow* and *deep* aggressively prune shallow and deep layers respectively. Based on sparsity distribution of different networks, a different strategy might be chosen.

In Table 2, we show us using reward R_{err} to accurately find the sparsity ratios for pruning 50% for Plain-20 and ResNet-56 [21] and compare it with empirical policies. We outperform empirical policies by a large margin. The best pruning setting found by AMC differs from hand-crafted heuristic (Fig. 2). It learns a bottleneck architecture [21].

Accuracy-Guaranteed Compression. By using the R_{Param} reward, our agent can automatically find the limit of compression, with smallest model size and little loss of performance. As shown in Table 2, we compress ResNet-50 with fine-grained pruning on CIFAR-10. The result we obtain has up to 60% compression ratio with even a little higher accuracy on both validation set and test set, which might be in light of the regularization effect of pruning.

Since our reward R_{Param} focuses on *Error* and offers very little incentive to compression in the meantime, it prefers the high-performance model with harmless compression. To shorten the search time, we obtain the reward using validation accuracy without fine-tuning. We believe if reward were fine-tuned accuracy, the agent should compress more aggressively, because the fine-tuned accuracy is much closer to the original accuracy.

Table 2. Pruning policy comparison of Plain-20, ResNets [21] on CIFAR-10 [28]. R_{Err} corresponds to FLOPs-constrained compression with channel pruning, while R_{Param} corresponds to accuracy guaranteed compression with fine-grained pruning. For both shallow network Plain-20 and deeper network ResNets, AMC outperforms *hand-crafted* policies by a large margin. This enables efficient exploration without fine-tuning. Although AMC makes many trials on model architecture, we have separate validation and test dataset. No over-fitting is observed.

Model	Policy	Ratio	Val Acc.	Test Acc.	Acc. after FT.
Plain-20 (90.5%)	Deep (handcraft)	50% FLOPs	79.6	79.2	88.3
	Shallow (handcraft)		83.2	82.9	89.2
	Uniform (handcraft)		84.0	83.9	89.7
	AMC (R_{Err})		**86.4**	**86.0**	**90.2**
ResNet-56 (92.8%)	Uniform (handcraft)	50% FLOPs	87.5	87.4	89.8
	Deep (handcraft)		88.4	88.4	91.5
	AMC (R_{Err})		**90.2**	**90.1**	**91.9**
ResNet-50 (93.53%)	**AMC (R_{Param})**	60% Params	**93.64**	**93.55**	-

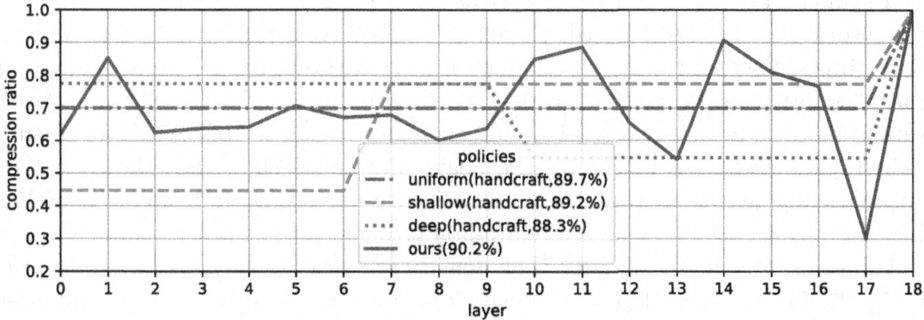

Fig. 2. Comparisons of pruning strategies for Plain-20 under 2×. *Uniform* policy sets the same compression ratio for each layer uniformly. *Shallow* and *deep* policies aggressively prune shallow and deep layers respectively. Policy given by AMC looks like sawtooth, which resembles the bottleneck architecture [21]. The accuracy given by AMC outperforms hand-crafted policies. (*better viewed in color*) (Color figure online)

Speedup Policy Exploration. Fine-tuning a pruned model usually takes a very long time. We observe a correlation between the pre-fine-tune accuracy and the post fine-tuning accuracy [20,22]. As shown in Table 2, policies that obtain higher validation accuracy correspondingly have higher fine-tuned accuracy. This enables us to predict final model accuracy without fine-tuning, which results in an efficient and faster policy exploration.

The validation set and test set are separated, and we only use the validation set to generate reward during reinforcement learning. In addition, the compressed models have fewer parameters. As shown in Table 2, the test accuracy and validation accuracy are very close, indicating no over-fitting.

4.2 ImageNet

On ImageNet, we use 3000 images from the **training set** to evaluate the reward function in order to prevent over-fitting. The latency is measured with 224×224 input throughout the experiments.

Push the Limit of Fine-Grained Pruning. Fine-grained pruning method prunes neural networks based on individual connections to achieve sparsity in both weights and activations, which is able to achieve higher compression ratio and can be accelerated with specialized hardware such as [17,18,39]. However, it requires iterative prune & fine-tune procedure to achieve decent performance [20], and single-shot pruning without retraining will greatly hurt the prediction accuracy with large compression rate (say $4\times$), which cannot provide useful supervision for reinforcement learning agent.

To tackle the problem, we follow the settings in [16] to conduct 4-iteration pruning & fine-tuning experiments, where the overall density of the full model is set to [50%, 35%, 25% and 20%] in each iteration. For each stage, we run AMC to determine the sparsity ratio of each layer given the overall sparsity. The model is then pruned and fine-tuned for 30 epochs following common protocol. With that framework, we are able to push the expert-tuned compression ratio of ResNet-50 on ImageNet from 3.4× to **5**× (see Fig. 4) without loss of performance on ImageNet (original ResNet50's [top-1, top-5] accuracy = [76.13%, 92.86%]; AMC pruned model's accuracy = [76.11%, 92.89%]). The density of each layer during each stage is displayed in Fig. 3. The peaks and crests show that the RL agent automatically learns to prune 3×3 convolutional layers with larger sparsity, since they generally have larger redundancy; while prunes more compact 1×1 convolutions with lower sparsity. The density statistics of each block is provided in Fig. 4. We can find that the density distribution of AMC is quite different

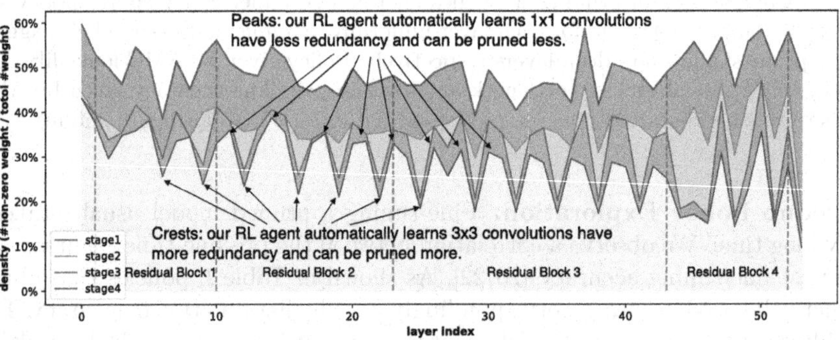

Fig. 3. The pruning policy (sparsity ratio) given by our reinforcement learning agent for ResNet-50. With 4 stages of iterative pruning, we find very salient sparsity pattern across layers: peaks are 1×1 convolution, crests are 3×3 convolution. **The reinforcement learning agent automatically learns that 3×3 convolution has more redundancy than 1×1 convolution and can be pruned more.**

from human expert's result shown in Table 3.8 of [16], suggesting that AMC can fully explore the design space and allocate sparsity in a better way.

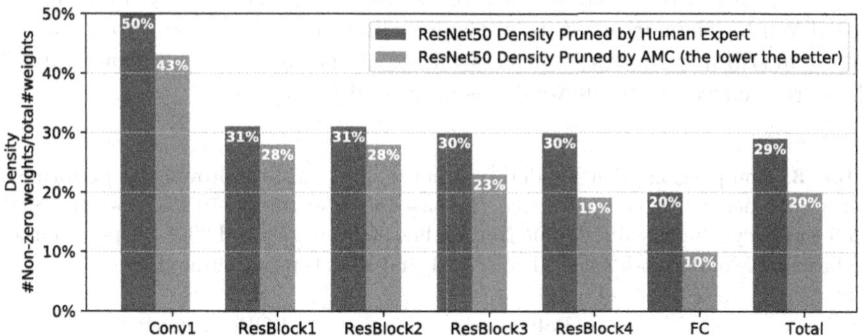

Fig. 4. Our reinforcement learning agent (AMC) can prune the model to a lower density compared with human experts without losing accuracy. (Human expert: 3.4× compression on ResNet50. AMC: 5× compression on ResNet50.)

Comparison with Heuristic Channel Reduction. Here we compare AMC with existing state-of-the-art channel reduction methods: FP [31], RNP [33] and SPP [49]. All the methods proposed a heuristic strategy to design the pruning ratio of each layer. FP [31] proposed a sensitive analysis scheme to estimate the sensitivity of each layer by evaluating the accuracy with single layer pruned. Layers with lower sensitivity are pruned more aggressively. Such method assumes that errors of different pruned layers can be summed up linearly, which does not stand according to our experiments. RNP [33] groups all convolutional channels into 4 sets and trains a RL agent to decide on the 4 sets according to input image. However, the action space is very rough (only 4 actions for each layer), and it cannot reduce the model size. SPP [49] applies PCA analysis to each layer and takes the reconstruction error as the sensitivity measure to determine the pruning ratios. Such analysis is conducted based on one single layer, failing to take the correlations between layers into consideration. We also compare our method to the original channel pruning paper (CP in Table 3), in which the sparsity ratios of pruned VGG-16 [45] are carefully tuned by human experts (`conv5` are skipped, sparsity ratio for `conv4` and remaining layers is 1 : 1.5). The results of pruned VGG-16 are presented in Table 3. Consistent with our CIFAR-10 experiments (Sect. 4.1), AMC outperforms all heuristic methods by more than **0.9%**, and beats human expert by **0.3%** without any human labor.

Apart from VGG-16, we also test AMC on modern efficient neural networks MobileNet-V1 [23] and MobileNet-V2 [44]. Since the networks have already been very compact, it is much harder to further compress them. The easiest way to reduce the channels of a model is to use uniform channel shrinkage, *i.e.* use a width multiplier to uniformly reduce the channels of each layer with a fixed ratio. Both MobileNet-V1 and MobileNet-V2 present the performance of different multiplier and input sizes, and we compare our pruned result with models of same computations. The format are denoted as *uniform (depth multiplier - input size)*. We can find that our method consistently outperforms the uniform baselines. Even for the current state-of-the-art efficient model design MobileNet-V2, AMC can still improve its accuracy by 1.0% at the same computation (Table 3). The pareto curve of MobileNet-V1 is presented in Fig. 5a.

Table 3. Comparison with handcrafted heuristics. AMC improves the performance over human heuristics. (For reference, the baseline VGG-16 has 70.5% top-1 and 89.9% top-5 accuracy; the baseline MobileNet-V1 has 70.9% top-1 and 89.9% top-5 accuracy; the baseline MobileNet-V2 has 71.8% top-1 and 91% top-5 accuracy).

	Policy	FLOPs	Δacc %
VGG-16	FP (handcraft) [31]	20%	−14.6
	RNP (handcraft) [33]		−3.58
	SPP (handcraft) [49]		−2.3
	CP (handcraft) [22]		−1.7
	AMC (ours)		**−1.4**
MobileNet V1	Uniform (0.75–224) [23]	56%	−2.5
	AMC (ours)	50%	**−0.4**
	Uniform (0.75–192) [23]	41%	−3.7
	AMC (ours)	40%	**−1.7**
MobileNet V2	Uniform (0.75–224) [44]	50%	−2.0
	AMC (ours)		**−1.0**

Speedup Mobile Inference. Mobile inference acceleration has drawn people's attention in recent years. Not only can AMC optimize FLOPs and model size, it can also optimize the inference latency, directly benefiting mobile developers. For all mobile inference experiments, we use TensorFlow Lite framework for timing evaluation.

We prune MobileNet-V1 [23], a highly compact network consisting of depth-wise convolution and point-wise convolution layers, and measure how much we can improve its inference speed. Previous attempts using *hand-crafted* policy to prune MobileNet-V1 led to significant accuracy degradation [31]: pruning MobileNet-V1 to 75.5% original parameters results in 67.2% top-1 accuracy[1], which is even worse than the original 0.75 MobileNet-V1 (61.9% parameters with 68.4% top-1 accuracy). However, our AMC pruning policy significantly improves pruning quality: on ImageNet, AMC-pruned MobileNet-V1 achieved 70.5% Top-1 accuracy with 285 MFLOPs, compared to the original 0.75 MobileNet-V1's 68.4% Top-1 accuracy with 325 MFLOPs. As illustrated in Fig. 5a, human

[1] http://machinethink.net/blog/compressing-deep-neural-nets/.

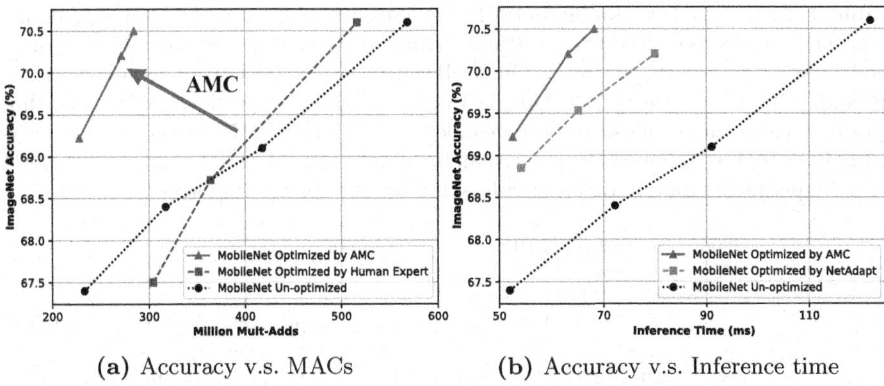

(a) Accuracy v.s. MACs (b) Accuracy v.s. Inference time

Fig. 5. (a) Comparing the accuracy and MAC trade-off among AMC, human expert, and unpruned MobileNet-v1. AMC strictly dominates human expert in the pareto optimal curve. (b) Comparing the accuracy and latency trade-off among AMC, NetAdapt, and unpruned MobileNet-V1. AMC significantly improves the pareto curve of MobileNet-V1. Reinforcement-learning based AMC surpasses heuristic-based NetAdapt on the pareto curve (inference time both measured on Google Pixel 1).

expert's hand-crafted policy achieves slightly worse performance than that of the original MobileNet-V1 under 2× FLOPs reduction. However, with AMC, we significantly raise the pareto curve, improving the accuracy-MACs trade-off of original MobileNet-V1.

By substituting FLOPs with latency, we can change from FLOPs-constrained search to latency-constrained search and directly optimize the inference time. Our experiment platform is Google Pixel 1 with Qualcomm Snapdragon 821 SoC. As shown in Fig. 5b, we greatly reduce the inference time of MobileNet-V1 under the same accuracy. We also compare our learning based policy with a heuristic-based policy [52], and AMC better trades off accuracy and latency. Furthermore, since AMC uses the validation accuracy before fine-tuning as the reward signal while [52] needs local fine-tuning after each step, AMC is more sampling-efficient, requiring fewer GPU hours for policy search.

We show the detailed statistics of our pruned model in Table 4. Model searched with 0.5× FLOPs and 0.5× inference time are profiled and displayed. For 0.5× FLOPs setting, we achieve **1.81**× speed up on a Google Pixel 1 phone, and for 0.5× FLOPs setting, we accurately achieve **1.95**× speed up, which is very close to actual 2× target, showing that AMC can directly optimize inference time and achieve accurate speed up ratio. We achieve 2.01× speed up for 1×1 convolution but less significant speed up for depth-wise convolution due to the small computation to communication ratio. AMC compressed models also consumes less memory. On GPUs, we also achieve up to 1.5× speedup, less than mobile phone, which is because a GPU has higher degree of parallelism than a mobile phone.

Table 4. AMC speeds up MobileNet-V1. Previous attempts using *hand-crafted* policy to prune MobileNet-V1 lead to significant accuracy degradation [31] while AMC pruned models well preserve the accuracy. On NVIDIA Titan XP GPU AMC achieves 1.53× speedup with batch size 50; On Google Pixel-1 CPU, AMC achieves 1.95× speedup with batch size one, while saving the memory by 34%. The AMC pruned MobileNet is not only faster but also more accurate than 0.75 MobileNet. The image size is 224 × 224 for all experiments and no quantization is applied for apple-to-apple comparison.

	Million MAC	Top-1 acc. (%)	Top-5 acc. (%)	GPU		Android				
				Lat. (ms)	Speed	Conv. (ms)	Depth. (ms)	Total (ms)	Speed	Memory
1.0 MobileNet-V1	569	70.9	89.5	0.46	2191 fps (1×)	110.4	12.8	123.3	8.1 fps (1×)	20.1 MB
0.75 MobileNet-V1	325	68.4	88.2	0.34	2944 fps (1.34×)	62.5	9.7	72.3	13.8 fps (1.71×)	14.8 MB
0.5× FLOPs **AMC (ours)**	285	70.5	89.3	0.32	**3127 fps (1.43×)**	58.8	9.5	68.3	**14.6 fps (1.81×)**	14.3 MB
0.5× Time **AMC (ours)**	272	70.2	89.2	0.30	**3350 fps (1.53×)**	55.0	8.3	63.3	**16.0 fps (1.95×)**	13.2 MB

Generalization Ability. We evaluate the generalization ability of AMC on PASCAL VOC object detection task [13]. We use the compressed VGG-16 (from Sect. 4.2) as the backbone for Faster R-CNN [43]. In Table 5, AMC achieves **0.7%** better mAP[0.5, 0.95]) than the best hand-crafted pruning methods under the same compression ratio. AMC even surpasses the baseline by **0.5%** mAP. We hypothesize this improvement as that the optimal compression policy found by the RL agent also serves as effective regularization.

Table 5. Compressing Faster R-CNN with VGG16 on PASCAL VOC 2007. Consistent with classification task, AMC also results in better performance under the same compression ratio on object detection task.

	mAP (%)	mAP [0.5, 0.95] (%)
Baseline	68.7	36.7
2× handcrafted [22]	68.3 (−0.4)	36.7 (−0.0)
4× handcrafted [22]	66.9 (−1.8)	35.1 (−1.6)
4× handcrafted [53]	67.8 (−0.9)	36.5 (−0.2)
4× AMC (ours)	**68.8 (+0.1)**	**37.2 (+0.5)**

5 Conclusion

Conventional model compression techniques use hand-crafted features and require domain experts to explore a large design space and trade off between model size, speed, and accuracy, which is usually suboptimal and labor-consuming. In this paper, we propose AutoML for Model Compression (AMC), which leverages reinforcement learning to automatically search the design space, greatly improving the model compression quality. We also design two novel reward schemes to perform both resource-constrained compression and accuracy-guaranteed compression. Compelling results have been demonstrated for MobileNet-V1, MobileNet-V2, ResNet and VGG on Cifar and ImageNet. The compressed model generalizes well from classification to detection tasks. On the Google Pixel 1 mobile phone, we push the inference speed of MobileNet-V1 from 8.1 fps to 16.0 fps. AMC facilitates efficient deep neural networks design on mobile devices.

Acknowledgements. We thank Quoc Le, Yu Wang and Bill Dally for the supportive feedback. We thank Jiacong Chen for drawing the cartoon on the left of Fig. 1.

References

1. Anwar, S., Sung, W.: Compact deep convolutional neural networks with coarse pruning. arXiv preprint arXiv:1610.09639 (2016)
2. Ashok, A., Rhinehart, N., Beainy, F., Kitani, K.M.: N2N learning: network to network compression via policy gradient reinforcement learning. arXiv preprint arXiv:1709.06030 (2017)
3. Bagherinezhad, H., Rastegari, M., Farhadi, A.: LCNN: lookup-based convolutional neural network. arXiv preprint arXiv:1611.06473 (2016)
4. Baker, B., Gupta, O., Naik, N., Raskar, R.: Designing neural network architectures using reinforcement learning. arXiv preprint arXiv:1611.02167 (2016)
5. Brock, A., Lim, T., Ritchie, J.M., Weston, N.: Smash: one-shot model architecture search through hypernetworks. arXiv preprint arXiv:1708.05344 (2017)
6. Cai, H., Chen, T., Zhang, W., Yu, Y., Wang, J.: Reinforcement learning for architecture search by network transformation. arXiv preprint arXiv:1707.04873 (2017)
7. Canziani, A., Paszke, A., Culurciello, E.: An analysis of deep neural network models for practical applications. arXiv preprint arXiv:1605.07678 (2016)
8. Chen, T., Goodfellow, I., Shlens, J.: Net2Net: accelerating learning via knowledge transfer. arXiv preprint arXiv:1511.05641 (2015)
9. Chollet, F.: Xception: deep learning with depthwise separable convolutions. arXiv preprint arXiv:1610.02357 (2016)
10. Courbariaux, M., Bengio, Y.: BinaryNet: training deep neural networks with weights and activations constrained to +1 or −1. arXiv preprint arXiv:1602.02830 (2016)
11. Denton, E.L., Zaremba, W., Bruna, J., LeCun, Y., Fergus, R.: Exploiting linear structure within convolutional networks for efficient evaluation. In: Advances in Neural Information Processing Systems, pp. 1269–1277 (2014)
12. Dong, X., Huang, J., Yang, Y., Yan, S.: More is less: a more complicated network with less inference complexity. arXiv preprint arXiv:1703.08651 (2017)

13. Everingham, M., Van Gool, L., Williams, C.K.I., Winn, J., Zisserman, A.: The PASCAL Visual Object Classes Challenge 2007 (VOC2007) Results. http://www.pascal-network.org/challenges/VOC/voc2007/workshop/index.html
14. Girshick, R.: Fast R-CNN. In: Proceedings of the IEEE International Conference on Computer Vision, pp. 1440–1448 (2015)
15. Gong, Y., Liu, L., Yang, M., Bourdev, L.: Compressing deep convolutional networks using vector quantization. arXiv preprint arXiv:1412.6115 (2014)
16. Han, S.: Efficient methods and hardware for deep learning. https://stacks.stanford.edu/file/druid:qf934gh3708/EFFICIENT%20METHODS%20AND%20HARDWARE%20FOR%20DEEP%20LEARNING-augmented.pdf
17. Han, S., et al.: ESE: efficient speech recognition engine with sparse LSTM on FPGA. In: Proceedings of the 2017 ACM/SIGDA International Symposium on Field-Programmable Gate Arrays, pp. 75–84. ACM (2017)
18. Han, S., Liu, X., Mao, H., Pu, J., Pedram, A., Horowitz, M.A., Dally, W.J.: EIE: efficient inference engine on compressed deep neural network. In: Proceedings of the 43rd International Symposium on Computer Architecture, pp. 243–254. IEEE Press (2016)
19. Han, S., Mao, H., Dally, W.J.: Deep compression: compressing deep neural networks with pruning, trained quantization and Huffman coding. arXiv preprint arXiv:1510.00149 (2015)
20. Han, S., Pool, J., Tran, J., Dally, W.: Learning both weights and connections for efficient neural network. In: Advances in Neural Information Processing Systems, pp. 1135–1143 (2015)
21. He, K., Zhang, X., Ren, S., Sun, J.: Deep residual learning for image recognition. In: Proceedings of the IEEE Conference on Computer Vision and Pattern Recognition, pp. 770–778 (2016)
22. He, Y., Zhang, X., Sun, J.: Channel pruning for accelerating very deep neural networks. In: Proceedings of the IEEE Conference on Computer Vision and Pattern Recognition, pp. 1389–1397 (2017)
23. Howard, A.G., et al.: MobileNets: efficient convolutional neural networks for mobile vision applications. arXiv preprint arXiv:1704.04861 (2017)
24. Hu, H., Peng, R., Tai, Y.W., Tang, C.K.: Network trimming: a data-driven neuron pruning approach towards efficient deep architectures. arXiv preprint arXiv:1607.03250 (2016)
25. Ioffe, S., Szegedy, C.: Batch normalization: accelerating deep network training by reducing internal covariate shift. arXiv preprint arXiv:1502.03167 (2015)
26. Jaderberg, M., Vedaldi, A., Zisserman, A.: Speeding up convolutional neural networks with low rank expansions. arXiv preprint arXiv:1405.3866 (2014)
27. Kim, Y.D., Park, E., Yoo, S., Choi, T., Yang, L., Shin, D.: Compression of deep convolutional neural networks for fast and low power mobile applications. arXiv preprint arXiv:1511.06530 (2015)
28. Krizhevsky, A., Hinton, G.: Learning multiple layers of features from tiny images (2009)
29. Lavin, A.: Fast algorithms for convolutional neural networks. arXiv preprint arXiv:1509.09308 (2015)
30. Lebedev, V., Ganin, Y., Rakhuba, M., Oseledets, I., Lempitsky, V.: Speeding-up convolutional neural networks using fine-tuned CP-decomposition. arXiv preprint arXiv:1412.6553 (2014)
31. Li, H., Kadav, A., Durdanovic, I., Samet, H., Graf, H.P.: Pruning filters for efficient convnets. arXiv preprint arXiv:1608.08710 (2016)

32. Lillicrap, T.P., et al.: Continuous control with deep reinforcement learning. arXiv preprint arXiv:1509.02971 (2015)
33. Lin, J., Rao, Y., Lu, J.: Runtime neural pruning. In: Advances in Neural Information Processing Systems, pp. 2178–2188 (2017)
34. Luo, J.H., Wu, J., Lin, W.: ThiNet: a filter level pruning method for deep neural network compression. arXiv preprint arXiv:1707.06342 (2017)
35. Masana, M., van de Weijer, J., Herranz, L., Bagdanov, A.D., Alvarez, J.M.: Domain-adaptive deep network compression. In: The IEEE International Conference on Computer Vision (ICCV), October 2017
36. Mathieu, M., Henaff, M., LeCun, Y.: Fast training of convolutional networks through FFTs. arXiv preprint arXiv:1312.5851 (2013)
37. Miikkulainen, R., et al.: Evolving deep neural networks. arXiv preprint arXiv:1703.00548 (2017)
38. Molchanov, P., Tyree, S., Karras, T., Aila, T., Kautz, J.: Pruning convolutional neural networks for resource efficient transfer learning. CoRR, abs/1611.06440 (2016)
39. Parashar, A., et al.: SCNN: an accelerator for compressed-sparse convolutional neural networks. In: 44th International Symposium on Computer Architecture (2017)
40. Polyak, A., Wolf, L.: Channel-level acceleration of deep face representations. IEEE Access **3**, 2163–2175 (2015)
41. Rastegari, M., Ordonez, V., Redmon, J., Farhadi, A.: XNOR-Net: ImageNet classification using binary convolutional neural networks. In: Leibe, B., Matas, J., Sebe, N., Welling, M. (eds.) ECCV 2016. LNCS, vol. 9908, pp. 525–542. Springer, Cham (2016). https://doi.org/10.1007/978-3-319-46493-0_32
42. Real, E., et al.: Large-scale evolution of image classifiers. arXiv preprint arXiv:1703.01041 (2017)
43. Ren, S., He, K., Girshick, R., Sun, J.: Faster R-CNN: towards real-time object detection with region proposal networks. In: Advances in Neural Information Processing Systems, pp. 91–99 (2015)
44. Sandler, M., Howard, A., Zhu, M., Zhmoginov, A., Chen, L.C.: Inverted residuals and linear bottlenecks: Mobile networks for classification, detection and segmentation. arXiv preprint arXiv:1801.04381 (2018)
45. Simonyan, K., Zisserman, A.: Very deep convolutional networks for large-scale image recognition. arXiv preprint arXiv:1409.1556 (2014)
46. Stanley, K.O., Miikkulainen, R.: Evolving neural networks through augmenting topologies. Evol. Comput. **10**(2), 99–127 (2002)
47. Szegedy, C., et al.: Going deeper with convolutions. In: Proceedings of the IEEE Conference on Computer Vision and Pattern Recognition, pp. 1–9 (2015)
48. Vasilache, N., Johnson, J., Mathieu, M., Chintala, S., Piantino, S., LeCun, Y.: Fast convolutional nets with FBFFT: a GPU performance evaluation. arXiv preprint arXiv:1412.7580 (2014)
49. Wang, H., Zhang, Q., Wang, Y., Hu, R.: Structured probabilistic pruning for deep convolutional neural network acceleration. arXiv preprint arXiv:1709.06994 (2017)
50. Watkins, C.J.C.H.: Learning from delayed rewards. Ph.D. thesis, King's College, Cambridge (1989)
51. Xue, J., Li, J., Gong, Y.: Restructuring of deep neural network acoustic models with singular value decomposition. In: INTERSPEECH, pp. 2365–2369 (2013)
52. Yang, T.J., et al.: NetAdapt: platform-aware neural network adaptation for mobile applications. arXiv preprint arXiv:1804.03230 (2018)

53. Zhang, X., Zou, J., He, K., Sun, J.: Accelerating very deep convolutional networks for classification and detection. IEEE Trans. Pattern Anal. Mach. Intell. **38**(10), 1943–1955 (2016)
54. Zhong, Z., Yan, J., Liu, C.L.: Practical network blocks design with q-learning. arXiv preprint arXiv:1708.05552 (2017)
55. Zhu, C., Han, S., Mao, H., Dally, W.J.: Trained ternary quantization. arXiv preprint arXiv:1612.01064 (2016)
56. Zoph, B., Le, Q.V.: Neural architecture search with reinforcement learning. arXiv preprint arXiv:1611.01578 (2016)
57. Zoph, B., Vasudevan, V., Shlens, J., Le, Q.V.: Learning transferable architectures for scalable image recognition. arXiv preprint arXiv:1707.07012 (2017)

Encoder-Decoder with Atrous Separable Convolution for Semantic Image Segmentation

Liang-Chieh Chen(✉), Yukun Zhu, George Papandreou, Florian Schroff, and Hartwig Adam

Google Inc., Mountain View, USA
{lcchen,yukun,gpapan,fschroff,hadam}@google.com

Abstract. Spatial pyramid pooling module or encode-decoder structure are used in deep neural networks for semantic segmentation task. The former networks are able to encode multi-scale contextual information by probing the incoming features with filters or pooling operations at multiple rates and multiple effective fields-of-view, while the latter networks can capture sharper object boundaries by gradually recovering the spatial information. In this work, we propose to combine the advantages from both methods. Specifically, our proposed model, DeepLabv3+, extends DeepLabv3 by adding a simple yet effective decoder module to refine the segmentation results especially along object boundaries. We further explore the Xception model and apply the depthwise separable convolution to both Atrous Spatial Pyramid Pooling and decoder modules, resulting in a faster and stronger encoder-decoder network. We demonstrate the effectiveness of the proposed model on PASCAL VOC 2012 and Cityscapes datasets, achieving the test set performance of 89% and 82.1% without any post-processing. Our paper is accompanied with a publicly available reference implementation of the proposed models in Tensorflow at https://github.com/tensorflow/models/tree/master/research/deeplab.

Keywords: Semantic image segmentation · Spatial pyramid pooling Encoder-decoder · Depthwise separable convolution

1 Introduction

Semantic segmentation with the goal to assign semantic labels to every pixel in an image [1–5] is one of the fundamental topics in computer vision. Deep convolutional neural networks [6–10] based on the Fully Convolutional Neural Network [8,11] show striking improvement over systems relying on hand-crafted features [12–17] on benchmark tasks. In this work, we consider two types of neural networks that use spatial pyramid pooling module [18–20] or encoder-decoder structure [21,22] for semantic segmentation, where the former one captures rich

V. Ferrari et al. (Eds.): ECCV 2018, LNCS 11211, pp. 833–851, 2018.
https://doi.org/10.1007/978-3-030-01234-2_49

contextual information by pooling features at different resolution while the latter one is able to obtain sharp object boundaries.

In order to capture the contextual information at multiple scales, DeepLabv3 [23] applies several parallel atrous convolution with different rates (called Atrous Spatial Pyramid Pooling, or ASPP), while PSPNet [24] performs pooling operations at different grid scales. Even though rich semantic information is encoded in the last feature map, detailed information related to object boundaries is missing due to the pooling or convolutions with striding operations within the network backbone. This could be alleviated by applying the atrous convolution to extract denser feature maps. However, given the design of state-of-art neural networks [7,9,10,25,26] and limited GPU memory, it is computationally prohibitive to extract output feature maps that are 8, or even 4 times smaller than the input resolution. Taking ResNet-101 [25] for example, when applying atrous convolution to extract output features that are 16 times smaller than input resolution, features within the last 3 residual blocks (9 layers) have to be dilated. Even worse, **26** residual blocks (**78** layers!) will be affected if output features that are 8 times smaller than input are desired. Thus, it is computationally intensive if denser output features are extracted for this type of models. On the other hand, encoder-decoder models [21,22] lend themselves to faster computation (since no features are dilated) in the encoder path and gradually recover sharp object boundaries in the decoder path. Attempting to combine the advantages from both methods, we propose to enrich the encoder module in the encoder-decoder networks by incorporating the multi-scale contextual information.

In particular, our proposed model, called DeepLabv3+, extends DeepLabv3 [23] by adding a simple yet effective decoder module to recover the object boundaries, as illustrated in Fig. 1. The rich semantic information is encoded in the

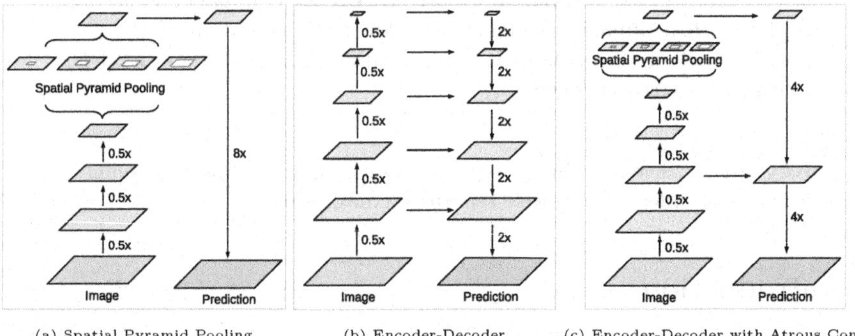

(a) Spatial Pyramid Pooling (b) Encoder-Decoder (c) Encoder-Decoder with Atrous Conv

Fig. 1. We improve DeepLabv3, which employs the spatial pyramid pooling module (a), with the encoder-decoder structure (b). The proposed model, DeepLabv3+, contains rich semantic information from the encoder module, while the detailed object boundaries are recovered by the simple yet effective decoder module. The encoder module allows us to extract features at an arbitrary resolution by applying atrous convolution.

output of DeepLabv3, with atrous convolution allowing one to control the density of the encoder features, depending on the budget of computation resources. Furthermore, the decoder module allows detailed object boundary recovery.

Motivated by the recent success of depthwise separable convolution [26–30], we also explore this operation and show improvement in terms of both speed and accuracy by adapting the Xception model [26], similar to [31], for the task of semantic segmentation, and applying the atrous separable convolution to both the ASPP and decoder modules. Finally, we demonstrate the effectiveness of the proposed model on PASCAL VOC 2012 and Cityscapes datasts and attain the test set performance of 89.0% and 82.1% without any post-processing, setting a new state-of-the-art.

In summary, our contributions are:

- We propose a novel encoder-decoder structure which employs DeepLabv3 as a powerful encoder module and a simple yet effective decoder module.
- In our structure, one can arbitrarily control the resolution of extracted encoder features by atrous convolution to trade-off precision and runtime, which is not possible with existing encoder-decoder models.
- We adapt the Xception model for the segmentation task and apply depthwise separable convolution to both ASPP module and decoder module, resulting in a faster and stronger encoder-decoder network.
- Our proposed model attains a new state-of-art performance on PASCAL VOC 2012 and Cityscapes datasets. We also provide detailed analysis of design choices and model variants.
- We make our Tensorflow-based implementation of the proposed model publicly available at https://github.com/tensorflow/models/tree/master/research/deeplab.

2 Related Work

Models based on Fully Convolutional Networks (FCNs) [8,11] have demonstrated significant improvement on several segmentation benchmarks [1–5]. There are several model variants proposed to exploit the contextual information for segmentation [12–17,32,33], including those that employ multi-scale inputs (*i.e.*, image pyramid) [34–39] or those that adopt probabilistic graphical models (such as DenseCRF [40] with efficient inference algorithm [41]) [37,39,42–51]. In this work, we mainly discuss about the models that use spatial pyramid pooling and encoder-decoder structure.

Spatial Pyramid Pooling: Models, such as PSPNet [24] or DeepLab [23,39], perform spatial pyramid pooling [18,19] at several grid scales (including image-level pooling [52]) or apply several parallel atrous convolution with different rates (called Atrous Spatial Pyramid Pooling, or ASPP). These models have shown promising results on several segmentation benchmarks by exploiting the multi-scale information.

Encoder-Decoder: The encoder-decoder networks have been successfully applied to many computer vision tasks, including human pose estimation [53], object detection [54–56], and semantic segmentation [11,21,22,57–64]. Typically, the encoder-decoder networks contain (1) an encoder module that gradually reduces the feature maps and captures higher semantic information, and (2) a decoder module that gradually recovers the spatial information. Building on top of this idea, we propose to use DeepLabv3 [23] as the encoder module and add a simple yet effective decoder module to obtain sharper segmentations.

Depthwise Separable Convolution: Depthwise separable convolution [27,28] or group convolution [7,65], a powerful operation to reduce the computation cost and number of parameters while maintaining similar (or slightly better) performance. This operation has been adopted in many recent neural network designs [26,29–31,66–68]. In particular, we explore the Xception model [26], similar to [31] for their COCO 2017 detection challenge submission, and show improvement in terms of both accuracy and speed for the task of semantic segmentation.

3 Methods

In this section, we briefly introduce atrous convolution [8,42,69–71] and depthwise separable convolution [26–29,67]. We then review DeepLabv3 [23] which is used as our encoder module before discussing the proposed decoder module appended to the encoder output. We also present a modified Xception model [26,31] which further improves the performance with faster computation.

3.1 Encoder-Decoder with Atrous Convolution

Atrous Convolution: Atrous convolution, a powerful tool that allows us to explicitly control the resolution of features computed by deep convolutional neural networks and adjust filter's field-of-view in order to capture multi-scale information, generalizes standard convolution operation. In the case of two-dimensional signals, for each location $\boldsymbol{i}$ on the output feature map $\boldsymbol{y}$ and a convolution filter $\boldsymbol{w}$, atrous convolution is applied over the input feature map $\boldsymbol{x}$ as follows:

$$\boldsymbol{y}[\boldsymbol{i}] = \sum_{\boldsymbol{k}} \boldsymbol{x}[\boldsymbol{i} + r \cdot \boldsymbol{k}]\boldsymbol{w}[\boldsymbol{k}] \quad (1)$$

where the atrous rate r determines the stride with which we sample the input signal. We refer interested readers to [39] for more details. Note that standard convolution is a special case in which rate $r = 1$. The filter's field-of-view is adaptively modified by changing the rate value.

Depthwise Separable Convolution: Depthwise separable convolution, factorizing a standard convolution into a *depthwise convolution* followed by a *pointwise convolution* (*i.e.*, 1×1 convolution), drastically reduces computation complexity. Specifically, the depthwise convolution performs a spatial convolution independently for each input channel, while the pointwise convolution is employed to combine the output from the depthwise convolution. In the TensorFlow [72] implementation of depthwise separable convolution, atrous convolution has been supported in the depthwise convolution (*i.e.*, the spatial convolution), as illustrated in Fig. 3. In this work, we refer the resulting convolution as *atrous separable convolution*, and found that atrous separable convolution significantly reduces the computation complexity of proposed model while maintaining similar (or better) performance.

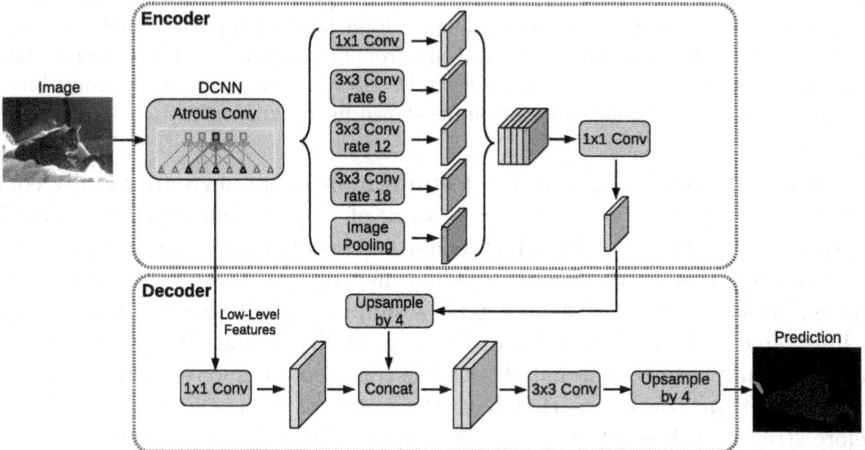

Fig. 2. Our proposed DeepLabv3+ extends DeepLabv3 by employing a encoder-decoder structure. The encoder module encodes multi-scale contextual information by applying atrous convolution at multiple scales, while the simple yet effective decoder module refines the segmentation results along object boundaries.

DeepLabv3 as Encoder: DeepLabv3 [23] employs atrous convolution [8,69–71] to extract the features computed by deep convolutional neural networks at an arbitrary resolution. Here, we denote *output stride* as the ratio of input image spatial resolution to the final output resolution (before global pooling or fully-connected layer). For the task of image classification, the spatial resolution of the final feature maps is usually 32 times smaller than the input image resolution and thus *output stride* = 32. For the task of semantic segmentation, one can adopt *output stride* = 16 (or 8) for denser feature extraction by removing the striding in the last one (or two) block(s) and applying the atrous convolution correspondingly (*e.g.*, we apply *rate* = 2 and *rate* = 4 to the last two blocks respectively for *output stride* = 8). Additionally, DeepLabv3 augments the Atrous Spatial Pyramid Pooling module, which probes convolutional features at multiple scales by applying atrous convolution with different rates, with the image-level features [52]. We use the last feature map before logits in the original DeepLabv3 as the encoder output in our proposed encoder-decoder structure. Note the encoder output feature map contains 256 channels and rich semantic information. Besides, one could extract features at an arbitrary resolution by applying the atrous convolution, depending on the computation budget.

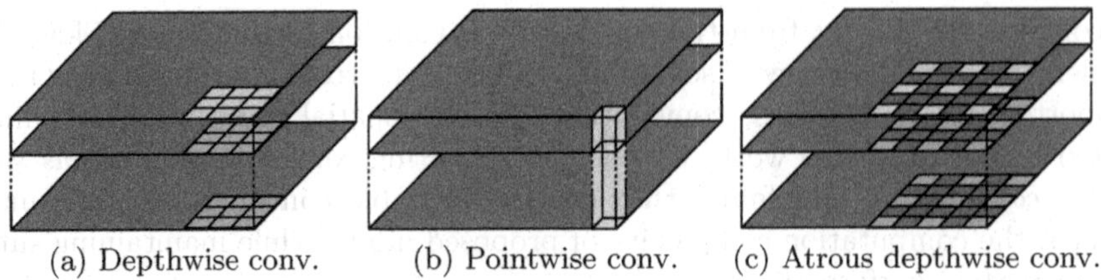

Fig. 3. 3×3 Depthwise separable convolution decomposes a standard convolution into (a) a depthwise convolution (applying a single filter for each input channel) and (b) a pointwise convolution (combining the outputs from depthwise convolution across channels). In this work, we explore *atrous separable convolution* where atrous convolution is adopted in the depthwise convolution, as shown in (c) with $rate = 2$.

Proposed Decoder: The encoder features from DeepLabv3 are usually computed with $output\ stride = 16$. In the work of [23], the features are bilinearly upsampled by a factor of 16, which could be considered a naive decoder module. However, this naive decoder module may not successfully recover object segmentation details. We thus propose a simple yet effective decoder module, as illustrated in Fig. 2. The encoder features are first bilinearly upsampled by a factor of 4 and then concatenated with the corresponding low-level features [73] from the network backbone that have the same spatial resolution (*e.g.*, Conv2 before striding in ResNet-101 [25]). We apply another 1×1 convolution on the low-level features to reduce the number of channels, since the corresponding low-level features usually contain a large number of channels (*e.g.*, 256 or 512) which may outweigh the importance of the rich encoder features (only 256 channels in our model) and make the training harder. After the concatenation, we apply a few 3×3 convolutions to refine the features followed by another simple bilinear upsampling by a factor of 4. We show in Sect. 4 that using $output\ stride = 16$ for the encoder module strikes the best trade-off between speed and accuracy. The performance is marginally improved when using $output\ stride = 8$ for the encoder module at the cost of extra computation complexity.

3.2 Modified Aligned Xception

The Xception model [26] has shown promising image classification results on ImageNet [74] with fast computation. More recently, the MSRA team [31] modifies the Xception model (called Aligned Xception) and further pushes the performance in the task of object detection. Motivated by these findings, we work in the same direction to adapt the Xception model for the task of semantic image segmentation. In particular, we make a few more changes on top of MSRA's modifications, namely (1) deeper Xception same as in [31] except that we do not modify the entry flow network structure for fast computation and memory efficiency, (2) all max pooling operations are replaced by depthwise separable convolution with striding, which enables us to apply *atrous separable convolution* to extract feature maps at an arbitrary resolution (another option is to extend the atrous algorithm to max pooling operations), and (3) extra batch normalization [75] and ReLU activation are added after each 3×3 depthwise convolution, similar to MobileNet design [29]. See Fig. 4 for details.

4 Experimental Evaluation

We employ ImageNet-1k [74] pretrained ResNet-101 [25] or modified aligned Xception [26,31] to extract dense feature maps by atrous convolution. Our implementation is built on TensorFlow [72] and is made publicly available.

The proposed models are evaluated on the PASCAL VOC 2012 semantic segmentation benchmark [1] which contains 20 foreground object classes and one background class. The original dataset contains 1,464 (*train*), 1,449 (*val*), and 1,456 (*test*) pixel-level annotated images. We augment the dataset by the extra annotations provided by [76], resulting in 10,582 (*trainaug*) training images. The performance is measured in terms of pixel intersection-over-union averaged across the 21 classes (mIOU).

We follow the same training protocol as in [23] and refer the interested readers to [23] for details. In short, we employ the same learning rate schedule (*i.e.*,

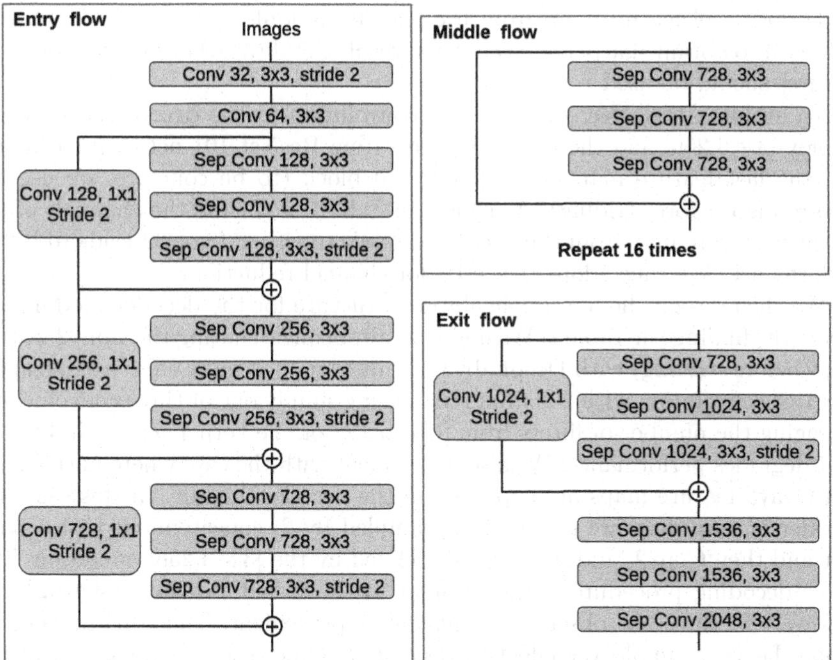

Fig. 4. We modify the Xception as follows: (1) more layers (same as MSRA's modification except the changes in Entry flow), (2) all the max pooling operations are replaced by depthwise separable convolutions with striding, and (3) extra batch normalization and ReLU are added after each 3×3 depthwise convolution, similar to MobileNet.

"poly" policy [52] and same initial learning rate 0.007), crop size 513 × 513, fine-tuning batch normalization parameters [75] when *output stride* = 16, and random scale data augmentation during training. Note that we also include batch normalization parameters in the proposed decoder module. Our proposed model is trained end-to-end without piecewise pretraining of each component.

4.1 Decoder Design Choices

We define "DeepLabv3 feature map" as the last feature map computed by DeepLabv3 (*i.e.*, the features containing ASPP features and image-level features), and $[k \times k, f]$ as a convolution operation with kernel $k \times k$ and f filters.

When employing *output stride* = 16, ResNet-101 based DeepLabv3 [23] bilinearly upsamples the logits by 16 during both training and evaluation. This simple bilinear upsampling could be considered as a naive decoder design, attaining the performance of 77.21% [23] on PASCAL VOC 2012 *val* set and is 1.2% better than not using this naive decoder during training (*i.e.*, downsampling groundtruth during training). To improve over this naive baseline, our proposed model "DeepLabv3+" adds the decoder module on top of the encoder output, as shown in Fig. 2. In the decoder module, we consider three places for different design choices, namely (1) the 1 × 1 convolution used to reduce the channels of the low-level feature map from the encoder module, (2) the 3 × 3 convolution used to obtain sharper segmentation results, and (3) what encoder low-level features should be used.

To evaluate the effect of the 1 × 1 convolution in the decoder module, we employ [3 × 3,256] and the Conv2 features from ResNet-101 network backbone, *i.e.*, the last feature map in res2x residual block (to be concrete, we use the feature map before striding). As shown in Table 1, reducing the channels of the low-level feature map from the encoder module to either 48 or 32 leads to better performance. We thus adopt [1 × 1,48] for channel reduction.

We then design the 3 × 3 convolution structure for the decoder module and report the findings in Table 2. We find that after concatenating the Conv2 feature map (before striding) with DeepLabv3 feature map, it is more effective to employ two 3×3 convolution with 256 filters than using simply one or three convolutions. Changing the number of filters from 256 to 128 or the kernel size from 3 × 3 to 1×1 degrades performance. We also experiment with the case where both Conv2 and Conv3 feature maps are exploited in the decoder module. In this case, the decoder feature map are gradually upsampled by 2, concatenated with Conv3 first and then Conv2, and each will be refined by the [3 × 3,256] operation. The whole decoding procedure is then similar to the U-Net/SegNet design [21,22]. However, we have not observed significant improvement. Thus, in the end, we adopt the very simple yet effective decoder module: the concatenation of the DeepLabv3 feature map and the channel-reduced Conv2 feature map are refined by two [3 × 3,256] operations. Note that our proposed DeepLabv3+ model has *output stride* = 4. We do not pursue further denser output feature map (*i.e.*, *output stride* < 4) given the limited GPU resources.

Table 1. PASCAL VOC 2012 *val* set. Effect of decoder 1×1 convolution used to reduce the channels of low-level feature map from the encoder module. We fix the other components in the decoder structure as using $[3 \times 3, 256]$ and Conv2.

Channels	8	16	32	48	64
mIOU	77.61%	77.92%	78.16%	**78.21%**	77.94%

Table 2. Effect of decoder structure when fixing $[1 \times 1, 48]$ to reduce the encoder feature channels. We found that it is most effective to use the Conv2 (before striding) feature map and two extra $[3 \times 3, 256]$ operations. Performance on VOC 2012 *val* set.

Features		3 × 3 Conv structure	mIOU
Conv2	Conv3		
✓		$[3 \times 3, 256]$	78.21%
✓		$[3 \times 3, 256] \times 2$	**78.85%**
✓		$[3 \times 3, 256] \times 3$	78.02%
✓		$[3 \times 3, 128]$	77.25%
✓		$[1 \times 1, 256]$	78.07%
✓	✓	$[3 \times 3, 256]$	78.61%

4.2 ResNet-101 as Network Backbone

To compare the model variants in terms of both accuracy and speed, we report mIOU and Multiply-Adds in Table 3 when using ResNet-101 [25] as network backbone in the proposed DeepLabv3+ model. Thanks to atrous convolution, we are able to obtain features at different resolutions during training and evaluation using a single model.

Baseline: The first row block in Table 3 contains the results from [23] showing that extracting denser feature maps during evaluation (*i.e.*, *eval output stride* = 8) and adopting multi-scale inputs increases performance. Besides, adding left-right flipped inputs doubles the computation complexity with only marginal performance improvement.

Adding Decoder: The second row block in Table 3 contains the results when adopting the proposed decoder structure. The performance is improved from 77.21% to 78.85% or 78.51% to 79.35% when using *eval output stride* = 16 or 8, respectively, at the cost of about 20B extra computation overhead. The performance is further improved when using multi-scale and left-right flipped inputs.

Coarser Feature Maps: We also experiment with the case when using *train output stride* = 32 (*i.e.*, no atrous convolution at all during training) for fast computation. As shown in the third row block in Table 3, adding the decoder brings about 2% improvement while only 74.20B Multiply-Adds are required. However, the performance is always about 1% to 1.5% below the case

Table 3. Inference strategy on the PASCAL VOC 2012 *val* set using *ResNet-101*. **train OS:** The *output stride* used during training. **eval OS:** The *output stride* used during evaluation. **Decoder:** Employing the proposed decoder structure. **MS**: Multi-scale inputs during evaluation. **Flip:** Adding left-right flipped inputs.

Encoder		Decoder	MS	Flip	mIOU	Multiply-Adds
train OS	eval OS					
16	16				77.21%	81.02B
16	8				78.51%	276.18B
16	8		✓		79.45%	2435.37B
16	8		✓	✓	79.77%	4870.59B
16	16	✓			78.85%	101.28B
16	16	✓	✓		80.09%	898.69B
16	16	✓	✓	✓	80.22%	1797.23B
16	8	✓			79.35%	297.92B
16	8	✓	✓		80.43%	2623.61B
16	8	✓	✓	✓	80.57%	5247.07B
32	32				75.43%	52.43B
32	32	✓			77.37%	74.20B
32	16	✓			77.80%	101.28B
32	8	✓			77.92%	297.92B

Table 4. *Single-model* error rates on ImageNet-1K validation set.

Model	Top-1 error	Top-5 error
Reproduced ResNet-101	22.40%	6.02%
Modified Xception	20.19%	5.17%

in which we employ *train output stride* = 16 and different *eval output stride* values. We thus prefer using *output stride* = 16 or 8 during training or evaluation depending on the complexity budget.

4.3 Xception as Network Backbone

We further employ the more powerful Xception [26] as network backbone. Following [31], we make a few more changes, as described in Sect. 3.2.

ImageNet Pretraining: The proposed Xception network is pretrained on ImageNet-1k dataset [74] with similar training protocol in [26]. Specifically, we adopt Nesterov momentum optimizer with momentum = 0.9, initial learning rate = 0.05, rate decay = 0.94 every 2 epochs, and weight decay $4e-5$. We use asynchronous training with 50 GPUs and each GPU has batch size 32 with image size 299×299. We did not tune the hyper-parameters very hard as the goal is to pretrain the model on ImageNet for semantic segmentation. We report the *single-model* error rates on the validation set in Table 4 along with the baseline reproduced ResNet-101 [25] under the same training protocol. We have observed 0.75% and 0.29% performance degradation for Top1 and Top5 accuracy when not adding the extra batch normalization and ReLU after each 3×3 depthwise convolution in the modified Xception.

The results of using the proposed Xception as network backbone for semantic segmentation are reported in Table 5.

Baseline: We first report the results without using the proposed decoder in the first row block in Table 5, which shows that employing Xception as network backbone improves the performance by about 2% when *train output stride* = *eval output stride* = 16 over the case where ResNet-101 is used. Further improvement can also be obtained by using *eval output stride* = 8, multi-scale inputs during inference and adding left-right flipped inputs. Note that we do not employ the multi-grid method [23,77,78], which we found does not improve the performance.

Adding Decoder: As shown in the second row block in Table 5, adding decoder brings about 0.8% improvement when using *eval output stride* = 16 for all the different inference strategies. The improvement becomes less when using *eval output stride* = 8.

Using Depthwise Separable Convolution: Motivated by the efficient computation of depthwise separable convolution, we further adopt it in the ASPP and the decoder modules. As shown in the third row block in Table 5, the computation complexity in terms of Multiply-Adds is significantly reduced by 33% to 41%, while similar mIOU performance is obtained.

Pretraining on COCO: For comparison with other state-of-art models, we further pretrain our proposed DeepLabv3+ model on MS-COCO dataset [79], which yields about extra 2% improvement for all different inference strategies.

Pretraining on JFT: Similar to [23], we also employ the proposed Xception model that has been pretrained on both ImageNet-1k [74] and JFT-300M dataset [26,80,81], which brings extra 0.8% to 1% improvement.

Test Set Results: Since the computation complexity is not considered in the benchmark evaluation, we thus opt for the best performance model and train it with *output stride* = 8 and frozen batch normalization parameters. In the end, our 'DeepLabv3+' achieves the performance of 87.8% and 89.0% without and with JFT dataset pretraining.

Qualitative Results: We provide visual results of our best model in Fig. 6. As shown in the figure, our model is able to segment objects very well without any post-processing.

Failure Mode: As shown in the last row of Fig. 6, our model has difficulty in segmenting (a) sofa *vs.* chair, (b) heavily occluded objects, and (c) objects with rare view.

Table 5. Inference strategy on the PASCAL VOC 2012 *val* set when using modified *Xception*. **train OS:** The *output stride* used during training. **eval OS:** The *output stride* used during evaluation. **Decoder:** Employing the proposed decoder structure. **MS:** Multi-scale inputs during evaluation. **Flip:** Adding left-right flipped inputs. **SC:** Adopting depthwise separable convolution for both ASPP and decoder modules. **COCO:** Models pretrained on MS-COCO. **JFT:** Models pretrained on JFT.

Encoder		Decoder	MS	Flip	SC	COCO	JFT	mIOU	Multiply-Adds
train OS	eval OS								
16	16							79.17%	68.00B
16	16		✓					80.57%	601.74B
16	16		✓	✓				80.79%	1203.34B
16	8							79.64%	240.85B
16	8		✓					81.15%	2149.91B
16	8		✓	✓				81.34%	4299.68B
16	16	✓						79.93%	89.76B
16	16	✓	✓					81.38%	790.12B
16	16	✓	✓	✓				81.44%	1580.10B
16	8	✓						80.22%	262.59B
16	8	✓	✓					81.60%	2338.15B
16	8	✓	✓	✓				81.63%	4676.16B
16	16	✓			✓			79.79%	54.17B
16	16	✓	✓	✓	✓			81.21%	928.81B
16	8	✓			✓			80.02%	177.10B
16	8	✓	✓	✓	✓			81.39%	3055.35B
16	16	✓			✓	✓		82.20%	54.17B
16	16	✓	✓	✓	✓	✓		83.34%	928.81B
16	8	✓			✓	✓		82.45%	177.10B
16	8	✓	✓	✓	✓	✓		83.58%	3055.35B
16	16	✓			✓	✓	✓	83.03%	54.17B
16	16	✓	✓	✓	✓	✓	✓	84.22%	928.81B
16	8	✓			✓	✓	✓	83.39%	177.10B
16	8	✓	✓	✓	✓	✓	✓	84.56%	3055.35B

4.4 Improvement Along Object Boundaries

In this subsection, we evaluate the segmentation accuracy with the trimap experiment [14,39,40] to quantify the accuracy of the proposed decoder module near object boundaries. Specifically, we apply the morphological dilation on 'void' label annotations on *val* set, which typically occurs around object boundaries. We then compute the mean IOU for those pixels that are within the dilated band (called trimap) of 'void' labels. As shown in Fig. 5(a), employing the proposed

Table 6. PASCAL VOC 2012 *test* set results with top-performing models.

Method	mIOU
Deep Layer Cascade (LC) [82]	82.7
TuSimple [77]	83.1
Large_Kernel_Matters [60]	83.6
Multipath-RefineNet [58]	84.2
ResNet-38_MS_COCO [83]	84.9
PSPNet [24]	85.4
IDW-CNN [84]	86.3
CASIA_IVA_SDN [63]	86.6
DIS [85]	86.8
DeepLabv3 [23]	85.7
DeepLabv3-JFT [23]	86.9
DeepLabv3+ (Xception) (http://host.robots.ox.ac.uk:8080/anonymous/NU9OS6.html)	87.8
DeepLabv3+ (Xception-JFT) (http://host.robots.ox.ac.uk:8080/anonymous/AF0NVP.html)	89.0

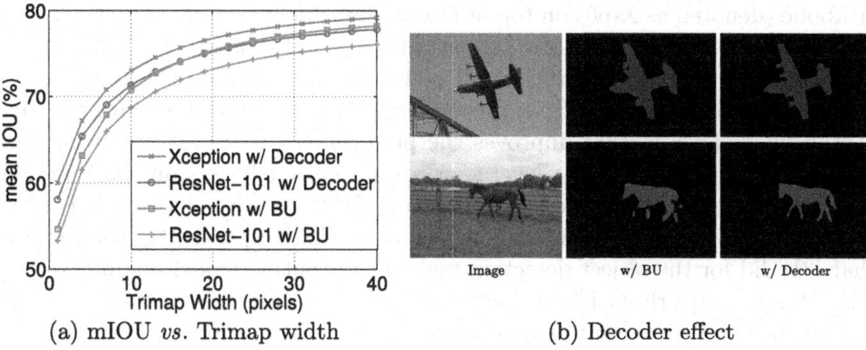

(a) mIOU *vs.* Trimap width (b) Decoder effect

Fig. 5. (a) mIOU as a function of trimap band width around the object boundaries when employing *train output stride* = *eval output stride* = 16. **BU:** Bilinear upsampling. (b) Qualitative effect of employing the proposed decoder module compared with the naive bilinear upsampling (denoted as **BU**). In the examples, we adopt Xception as feature extractor and *train output stride* = *eval output stride* = 16.

decoder for both ResNet-101 [25] and Xception [26] network backbones improves the performance compared to the naive bilinear upsampling. The improvement is more significant when the dilated band is narrow. We have observed 4.8% and 5.4% mIOU improvement for ResNet-101 and Xception respectively at the smallest trimap width as shown in the figure. We also visualize the effect of employing the proposed decoder in Fig. 5(b).

Fig. 6. Visualization results on *val* set. The last row shows a failure mode.

4.5 Experimental Results on Cityscapes

In this section, we experiment DeepLabv3+ on the Cityscapes dataset [3], a large-scale dataset containing high quality pixel-level annotations of 5000 images (2975, 500, and 1525 for the training, validation, and test sets respectively) and about 20000 coarsely annotated images.

As shown in Table 7(a), employing the proposed Xception model as network backbone (denoted as X-65) on top of DeepLabv3 [23], which includes the ASPP module and image-level features [52], attains the performance of 77.33% on the validation set. Adding the proposed decoder module significantly improves the performance to 78.79% (1.46% improvement). We notice that removing the augmented image-level feature improves the performance to 79.14%, showing that in DeepLab model, the image-level features are more effective on the PASCAL VOC 2012 dataset. We also discover that on the Cityscapes dataset, it is effective to increase more layers in the entry flow in the Xception [26], the same as what [31] did for the object detection task. The resulting model building on top of the deeper network backbone (denoted as X-71 in the table), attains the best performance of 79.55% on the validation set.

Table 7. (a) DeepLabv3+ on the Cityscapes *val* set when trained with *train_fine* set. (b) DeepLabv3+ on Cityscapes *test* set. **Coarse:** Use *train_extra* set (coarse annotations) as well. Only a few top models are listed in this table.

Backbone	Decoder	ASPP	Image-Level	mIOU
X-65		✓	✓	77.33
X-65	✓	✓	✓	78.79
X-65	✓	✓		79.14
X-71	✓	✓		79.55

(a) *val* set results

Method	**Coarse**	**mIOU**
ResNet-38 [83]	✓	80.6
PSPNet [24]	✓	81.2
Mapillary [86]	✓	82.0
DeepLabv3	✓	81.3
DeepLabv3+	✓	82.1

(b) *test* set results

After finding the best model variant on *val* set, we then further fine-tune the model on the coarse annotations in order to compete with other state-of-art models. As shown in Table 7(b), our proposed DeepLabv3+ attains a performance of 82.1% on the test set, setting a new state-of-art performance on Cityscapes.

5 Conclusion

Our proposed model "DeepLabv3+" employs the encoder-decoder structure where DeepLabv3 is used to encode the rich contextual information and a simple yet effective decoder module is adopted to recover the object boundaries. One could also apply the atrous convolution to extract the encoder features at an arbitrary resolution, depending on the available computation resources. We also explore the Xception model and atrous separable convolution to make the proposed model faster and stronger. Finally, our experimental results show that the proposed model sets a new state-of-the-art performance on PASCAL VOC 2012 and Cityscapes datasets.

Acknowledgments. We would like to acknowledge the valuable discussions with Haozhi Qi and Jifeng Dai about Aligned Xception, the feedback from Chen Sun, and the support from Google Mobile Vision team.

References

1. Everingham, M., Eslami, S.M.A., Gool, L.V., Williams, C.K.I., Winn, J., Zisserman, A.: The PASCAL visual object classes challenge - a retrospective. IJCV **111**, 98–136 (2014)
2. Mottaghi, R., Chen, X., Liu, X., Cho, N.G., Lee, S.W., Fidler, S., Urtasun, R., Yuille, A.: The role of context for object detection and semantic segmentation in the wild. In: CVPR (2014)
3. Cordts, M., Omran, M., Ramos, S., Rehfeld, T., Enzweiler, M., Benenson, R., Franke, U., Roth, S., Schiele, B.: The Cityscapes dataset for semantic urban scene understanding. In: CVPR (2016)
4. Zhou, B., Zhao, H., Puig, X., Fidler, S., Barriuso, A., Torralba, A.: Scene parsing through ADE20K dataset. In: CVPR (2017)
5. Caesar, H., Uijlings, J., Ferrari, V.: COCO-stuff: thing and stuff classes in context. In: CVPR (2018)
6. LeCun, Y., Bottou, L., Bengio, Y., Haffner, P.: Gradient-based learning applied to document recognition. In: Proceedings of the IEEE (1998)
7. Krizhevsky, A., Sutskever, I., Hinton, G.E.: ImageNet classification with deep convolutional neural networks. In: NIPS (2012)
8. Sermanet, P., Eigen, D., Zhang, X., Mathieu, M., Fergus, R., LeCun, Y.: OverFeat: integrated recognition, localization and detection using convolutional networks. In: ICLR (2014)
9. Simonyan, K., Zisserman, A.: Very deep convolutional networks for large-scale image recognition. In: ICLR (2015)
10. Szegedy, C., et al.: Going deeper with convolutions. In: CVPR (2015)

11. Long, J., Shelhamer, E., Darrell, T.: Fully convolutional networks for semantic segmentation. In: CVPR (2015)
12. He, X., Zemel, R.S., Carreira-Perpindn, M.: Multiscale conditional random fields for image labeling. In: CVPR (2004)
13. Shotton, J., Winn, J., Rother, C., Criminisi, A.: TextonBoost for image understanding: multi-class object recognition and segmentation by jointly modeling texture, layout, and context. IJCV **81**(2), 2–23 (2009)
14. Kohli, P., Torr, P.H., et al.: Robust higher order potentials for enforcing label consistency. IJCV **82**(3), 302–324 (2009)
15. Ladicky, L., Russell, C., Kohli, P., Torr, P.H.: Associative hierarchical CRFs for object class image segmentation. In: ICCV (2009)
16. Gould, S., Fulton, R., Koller, D.: Decomposing a scene into geometric and semantically consistent regions. In: ICCV (2009)
17. Yao, J., Fidler, S., Urtasun, R.: Describing the scene as a whole: joint object detection, scene classification and semantic segmentation. In: CVPR (2012)
18. Grauman, K., Darrell, T.: The pyramid match kernel: discriminative classification with sets of image features. In: ICCV (2005)
19. Lazebnik, S., Schmid, C., Ponce, J.: Beyond bags of features: spatial pyramid matching for recognizing natural scene categories. In: CVPR (2006)
20. He, K., Zhang, X., Ren, S., Sun, J.: Spatial pyramid pooling in deep convolutional networks for visual recognition. In: ECCV (2014)
21. Ronneberger, O., Fischer, P., Brox, T.: U-Net: convolutional networks for biomedical image segmentation. In: MICCAI (2015)
22. Badrinarayanan, V., Kendall, A., Cipolla, R.: SegNet: a deep convolutional encoder-decoder architecture for image segmentation. PAMI (2017)
23. Chen, L.C., Papandreou, G., Schroff, F., Adam, H.: Rethinking atrous convolution for semantic image segmentation. arXiv:1706.05587 (2017)
24. Zhao, H., Shi, J., Qi, X., Wang, X., Jia, J.: Pyramid scene parsing network. In: CVPR (2017)
25. He, K., Zhang, X., Ren, S., Sun, J.: Deep residual learning for image recognition. In: CVPR (2016)
26. Chollet, F.: Xception: deep learning with depthwise separable convolutions. In: CVPR (2017)
27. Sifre, L.: Rigid-motion scattering for image classification. Ph.D. thesis (2014)
28. Vanhoucke, V.: Learning visual representations at scale (invited talk). In: ICLR (2014)
29. Howard, A.G., et al.: MobileNets: efficient convolutional neural networks for mobile vision applications. arXiv:1704.04861 (2017)
30. Zhang, X., Zhou, X., Lin, M., Sun, J.: ShuffleNet: an extremely efficient convolutional neural network for mobile devices. In: CVPR (2018)
31. Qi, H., et al.: Deformable convolutional networks - COCO detection and segmentation challenge 2017 entry. In: ICCV COCO Challenge Workshop (2017)
32. Mostajabi, M., Yadollahpour, P., Shakhnarovich, G.: Feedforward semantic segmentation with zoom-out features. In: CVPR (2015)
33. Dai, J., He, K., Sun, J.: Convolutional feature masking for joint object and stuff segmentation. In: CVPR (2015)
34. Farabet, C., Couprie, C., Najman, L., LeCun, Y.: Learning hierarchical features for scene labeling. PAMI (2013)
35. Eigen, D., Fergus, R.: Predicting depth, surface normals and semantic labels with a common multi-scale convolutional architecture. In: ICCV (2015)

36. Pinheiro, P., Collobert, R.: Recurrent convolutional neural networks for scene labeling. In: ICML (2014)
37. Lin, G., Shen, C., van den Hengel, A., Reid, I.: Efficient piecewise training of deep structured models for semantic segmentation. In: CVPR (2016)
38. Chen, L.C., Yang, Y., Wang, J., Xu, W., Yuille, A.L.: Attention to scale: scale-aware semantic image segmentation. In: CVPR (2016)
39. Chen, L.C., Papandreou, G., Kokkinos, I., Murphy, K., Yuille, A.L.: DeepLab: semantic image segmentation with deep convolutional nets, atrous convolution, and fully connected CRFs. TPAMI **40**, 834–848 (2017)
40. Krähenbühl, P., Koltun, V.: Efficient inference in fully connected CRFs with Gaussian edge potentials. In: NIPS (2011)
41. Adams, A., Baek, J., Davis, M.A.: Fast high-dimensional filtering using the permutohedral lattice. In: Eurographics (2010)
42. Chen, L.C., Papandreou, G., Kokkinos, I., Murphy, K., Yuille, A.L.: Semantic image segmentation with deep convolutional nets and fully connected CRFs. In: ICLR (2015)
43. Bell, S., Upchurch, P., Snavely, N., Bala, K.: Material recognition in the wild with the materials in context database. In: CVPR (2015)
44. Zheng, S., et al.: Conditional random fields as recurrent neural networks. In: ICCV (2015)
45. Liu, Z., Li, X., Luo, P., Loy, C.C., Tang, X.: Semantic image segmentation via deep parsing network. In: ICCV (2015)
46. Papandreou, G., Chen, L.C., Murphy, K., Yuille, A.L.: Weakly- and semi-supervised learning of a DCNN for semantic image segmentation. In: ICCV (2015)
47. Schwing, A.G., Urtasun, R.: Fully connected deep structured networks. arXiv:1503.02351 (2015)
48. Jampani, V., Kiefel, M., Gehler, P.V.: Learning sparse high dimensional filters: image filtering, dense CRFs and bilateral neural networks. In: CVPR (2016)
49. Vemulapalli, R., Tuzel, O., Liu, M.Y., Chellappa, R.: Gaussian conditional random field network for semantic segmentation. In: CVPR (2016)
50. Chandra, S., Kokkinos, I.: Fast, exact and multi-scale inference for semantic image segmentation with deep Gaussian CRFs. In: Leibe, B., Matas, J., Sebe, N., Welling, M. (eds.) ECCV 2016. LNCS, vol. 9911, pp. 402–418. Springer, Cham (2016). https://doi.org/10.1007/978-3-319-46478-7_25
51. Chandra, S., Usunier, N., Kokkinos, I.: Dense and low-rank Gaussian CRFs using deep embeddings. In: ICCV (2017)
52. Liu, W., Rabinovich, A., Berg, A.C.: ParseNet: looking wider to see better. arXiv:1506.04579 (2015)
53. Newell, A., Yang, K., Deng, J.: Stacked hourglass networks for human pose estimation. In: ECCV (2016)
54. Lin, T.Y., Dollár, P., Girshick, R., He, K., Hariharan, B., Belongie, S.: Feature pyramid networks for object detection. In: CVPR (2017)
55. Shrivastava, A., Sukthankar, R., Malik, J., Gupta, A.: Beyond skip connections: top-down modulation for object detection. arXiv:1612.06851 (2016)
56. Fu, C.Y., Liu, W., Ranga, A., Tyagi, A., Berg, A.C.: DSSD: deconvolutional single shot detector. arXiv:1701.06659 (2017)
57. Noh, H., Hong, S., Han, B.: Learning deconvolution network for semantic segmentation. In: ICCV (2015)
58. Lin, G., Milan, A., Shen, C., Reid, I.: RefineNet: multi-path refinement networks with identity mappings for high-resolution semantic segmentation. In: CVPR (2017)

59. Pohlen, T., Hermans, A., Mathias, M., Leibe, B.: Full-resolution residual networks for semantic segmentation in street scenes. In: CVPR (2017)
60. Peng, C., Zhang, X., Yu, G., Luo, G., Sun, J.: Large kernel matters-improve semantic segmentation by global convolutional network. In: CVPR (2017)
61. Islam, M.A., Rochan, M., Bruce, N.D., Wang, Y.: Gated feedback refinement network for dense image labeling. In: CVPR (2017)
62. Wojna, Z., et al.: The devil is in the decoder. In: BMVC (2017)
63. Fu, J., Liu, J., Wang, Y., Lu, H.: Stacked deconvolutional network for semantic segmentation. arXiv:1708.04943 (2017)
64. Zhang, Z., Zhang, X., Peng, C., Cheng, D., Sun, J.: ExFuse: enhancing feature fusion for semantic segmentation. arXiv:1804.03821 (2018)
65. Xie, S., Girshick, R., Dollár, P., Tu, Z., He, K.: Aggregated residual transformations for deep neural networks. In: CVPR (2017)
66. Jin, J., Dundar, A., Culurciello, E.: Flattened convolutional neural networks for feedforward acceleration. arXiv:1412.5474 (2014)
67. Wang, M., Liu, B., Foroosh, H.: Design of efficient convolutional layers using single intra-channel convolution, topological subdivisioning and spatial "bottleneck" structure. arXiv:1608.04337 (2016)
68. Zoph, B., Vasudevan, V., Shlens, J., Le, Q.V.: Learning transferable architectures for scalable image recognition. In: CVPR (2018)
69. Holschneider, M., Kronland-Martinet, R., Morlet, J., Tchamitchian, P.: A real-time algorithm for signal analysis with the help of the wavelet transform. In: Combes, J.M., Grossmann, A., Tchamitchian, P. (eds.) Wavelets: Time-Frequency Methods and Phase Space, pp. 289–297. Springer, Heidelberg (1989). https://doi.org/10.1007/978-3-642-75988-8_28
70. Giusti, A., Ciresan, D., Masci, J., Gambardella, L., Schmidhuber, J.: Fast image scanning with deep max-pooling convolutional neural networks. In: ICIP (2013)
71. Papandreou, G., Kokkinos, I., Savalle, P.A.: Modeling local and global deformations in deep learning: epitomic convolution, multiple instance learning, and sliding window detection. In: CVPR (2015)
72. Abadi, M., Agarwal, A., et al.: TensorFlow: large-scale machine learning on heterogeneous distributed systems. arXiv:1603.04467 (2016)
73. Hariharan, B., Arbeláez, P., Girshick, R., Malik, J.: Hypercolumns for object segmentation and fine-grained localization. In: CVPR (2015)
74. Russakovsky, O., et al.: ImageNet large scale visual recognition challenge. IJCV **115**, 211–252 (2015)
75. Ioffe, S., Szegedy, C.: Batch normalization: accelerating deep network training by reducing internal covariate shift. In: ICML (2015)
76. Hariharan, B., Arbeláez, P., Bourdev, L., Maji, S., Malik, J.: Semantic contours from inverse detectors. In: ICCV (2011)
77. Wang, P., et al.: Understanding convolution for semantic segmentation. arXiv:1702.08502 (2017)
78. Dai, J., Qi, H., Xiong, Y., Li, Y., Zhang, G., Hu, H., Wei, Y.: Deformable convolutional networks. In: ICCV (2017)
79. Lin, T.-Y., et al.: Microsoft COCO: common objects in context. In: Fleet, D., Pajdla, T., Schiele, B., Tuytelaars, T. (eds.) ECCV 2014. LNCS, vol. 8693, pp. 740–755. Springer, Cham (2014). https://doi.org/10.1007/978-3-319-10602-1_48
80. Hinton, G., Vinyals, O., Dean, J.: Distilling the knowledge in a neural network. In: NIPS (2014)
81. Sun, C., Shrivastava, A., Singh, S., Gupta, A.: Revisiting unreasonable effectiveness of data in deep learning era. In: ICCV (2017)

82. Li, X., Liu, Z., Luo, P., Loy, C.C., Tang, X.: Not all pixels are equal: difficulty-aware semantic segmentation via deep layer cascade. In: CVPR (2017)
83. Wu, Z., Shen, C., van den Hengel, A.: Wider or deeper: revisiting the ResNet model for visual recognition. arXiv:1611.10080 (2016)
84. Wang, G., Luo, P., Lin, L., Wang, X.: Learning object interactions and descriptions for semantic image segmentation. In: CVPR (2017)
85. Luo, P., Wang, G., Lin, L., Wang, X.: Deep dual learning for semantic image segmentation. In: ICCV (2017)
86. Bulò, S.R., Porzi, L., Kontschieder, P.: In-place activated BatchNorm for memory-optimized training of DNNs. In: CVPR (2018)

Author Index

Printed in the United States
By Bookmasters